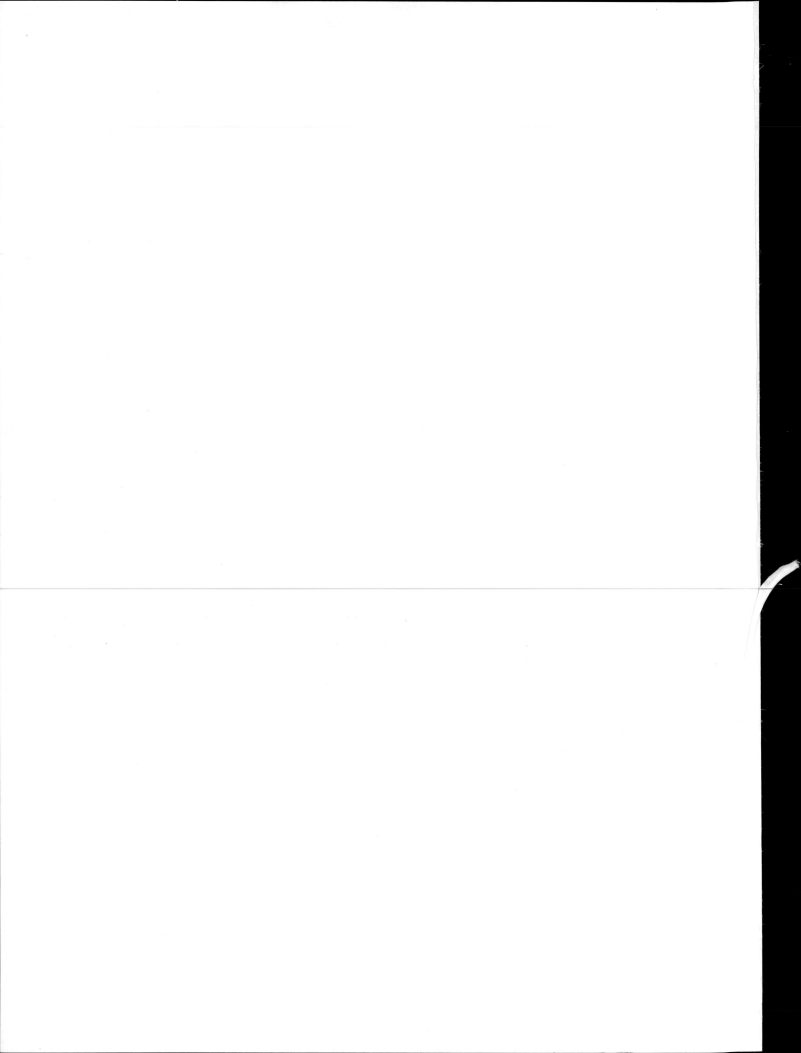

SOCIOLOGY
of EDUCATION

SOCIOLOGY
of EExDUCATION
An A-to-Z Guide

Volume 1

James Ainsworth, editor
Georgia State University

Los Angeles | London | New Delhi
Singapore | Washington DC

Los Angeles | London | New Delhi
Singapore | Washington DC

FOR INFORMATION:

SAGE Publications, Inc.
2455 Teller Road
Thousand Oaks, California 91320
E-mail: order@sagepub.com

SAGE Publications India Pvt. Ltd.
B 1/I 1 Mohan Cooperative Industrial Area
Mathura Road, New Delhi 110 044
India

SAGE Publications Ltd.
1 Oliver's Yard
55 City Road
London EC1Y 1SP
United Kingdom

SAGE Publications Asia-Pacific Pte. Ltd.
3 Church Street
#10-04 Samsung Hub
Singapore 049483

Senior Editor: Jim Brace-Thompson
Project Editor: Tracy Buyan
Cover Designer: Karine Hovsepian
Reference Systems Manager: Leticia Gutierrez
Reference Systems Coordinator: Anna Villasenor
Marketing Manager: Carmel Schrire

Golson Media
President and Editor: J. Geoffrey Golson
Director, Author Management: Susan Moskowitz
Production Director: Mary Jo Scibetta
Layout Editors: Kenneth W. Heller, Lois Rainwater
Copy Editors: Mary Le Rouge, Barbara Paris
Proofreader: Susan McRae
Indexer: J S Editorial

Library of Congress Cataloging-in-Publication Data

Sociology of education : an A-to-Z guide / James Ainsworth, Georgia State University, editor.
    pages cm
 Includes bibliographical references and index.
 ISBN 978-1-4522-0505-2 (cloth)
  1. Educational sociology--Encyclopedias. I. Ainsworth, James, editor of compilation.
 LC191.S63 2013
 306.43'2--dc23

                            2012046291

13 14 15 16 17 10 9 8 7 6 5 4 3 2 1

Contents

Volume 1

List of Articles   *vii*
Reader's Guide   *xiii*
About the Editor   *xix*
List of Contributors   *xxi*
Introduction   *xxix*
Chronology   *xxxiii*

Articles

A	*1*	H	*343*
B	*59*	I	*371*
C	*93*	J	*405*
D	*177*	K	*413*
E	*213*	L	*421*
F	*267*	M	*443*
G	*299*		

Volume 2

List of Articles   *vii*

Articles

N	*503*	T	*765*
O	*541*	U	*815*
P	*559*	V	*831*
Q	*615*	W	*843*
R	*623*	Y	*861*
S	*667*		

Glossary   *869*
Resource Guide   *877*
Appendix A: World Education Statistics   *883*
Appendix B: U.S. Education Statistics   *901*
Index   *935*

List of Articles

A

Ability Grouping
Abstract/Concrete Attitudes
Administration of Education
Adolescence
Adolescent Sexual Behavior
Adult Education
Adult Literacy
Advanced and Honors Classes
Advanced Degrees
Affirmative Action.
   See Race-Sensitive Admission Policies/
   Affirmative Action
Affluent Children
Afghanistan
After-School Programs
Age Grouping of Students
Aggressive Behaviors in Classrooms
Agricultural Education
Alabama
Alaska
Algeria
Alternative and Second Chance Education
American Samoa
Angola
Argentina
Arizona
Arkansas
Asian Americans
Assimilation Without Acculturation
At-Risk Students

Attitude/Achievement Paradox
Australia
Austria

B

Baccalaureate Education,
   Pre-International
Bahamas
Bangladesh
Banking Concept of Education
Barbados
Belgium
Bell Curve, The
Bernstein, Basil
Bidwell, Charles
Bilingual Education
Black Colleges and Universities,
   Historically
Black Cultural Capital
Blind Students
Bloom, Allen
Boarding Schools
Bourdieu, Pierre
Bowles, Samuel and
   Herbert Gintis
Brazil
Brookover, Wilbur B.
Brown v. Board of Education
Bulgaria
Burden of Acting White
Busing

C

California
Cambodia
Cameroon
Canada
Career and Technical Education
Catholic Schools
Charter Schools
Cheerleading Equity Policy
Child Care
Childhood
Chile
China
Class Inequality: Achievement
Class Inequality: College Enrollment and
    Completion
Class Inequality: High School Dropout Rates
Classroom Dynamics
Classroom Interactions: Teachers and Students
Classroom Interactions Between Students
Classroom Language
Cognitive Skill/Intellectual Skill
Coleman, James S.
Coleman Report, The
College Advising
College Proximity
College Transferring
Colombia
Colorado
Community Colleges
Complexity Theory
Concerted Cultivation/Natural Growth
Conflict Theory of Education
Congo, Democratic Republic of the
Connecticut
Constructivism
Content and Text Analysis
Cooled Out
Corporal Punishment
Costa Rica
Credit for Work Experience, College Students
Credit for Work Experience, High School Students
Critical Discourse Analysis
Critical Race Theory in Education
Critical Theory of Education
Cuba
Cultural Capital
Cultural Capital and Gender
Curriculum Standardization
Czech Republic and Slovakia

D

De Facto Tracking
Deaf Students
Delaware
Denmark
Deskilling of the Teaching Profession
De-Tracking
Dewey, John
Digital Divide/Digital Capital
Disabled Students
Discipline in Education
Diseases and Education
District of Columbia
Dominican Republic
Drinking and Education, Adolescent
Dropouts
Drug Use and Education
Durkheim, Émile

E

Early Childhood
Early Graduates
Earning Potential and Education
Ebonics (African American English) and Education
Ecuador
Educational Aspirations/Expectations
Educational Policymakers
Educationalization
Egypt
El Salvador
Elementary Education
English as a Second Language
English Proficiency/Fluent English Proficient
    Students
Epistemological Issues in Educational Research
Ethics in Education
Ethiopia
Ethnography
European Union
Expansion of Education
Extended Kinship and Education
Extracurricular Activities

F

Failing Schools
Family Structure and Education
Feeder Patterns/Catchment Zones
Feminist Critiques of Educational Practices
Feminist Critiques of Educational Research
Feminist Research Methodology

Field Trips
Finland
Florida
For-Profit Education
France
Freire, Paulo
Functionalist Theory of Education
Funding of Schools

G
Gender and School Sports
Gender Inequality: College Enrollment and
    Completion
Gender Inequality: College Major
Gender Inequality: High School Dropout Rates
Gender Inequality: Mathematics
Gender Inequality: Occupational Segregation
    of Teachers
Gender Inequality: Returns to Educational
    Investments
Gender Theories in Education
General Educational Development
Georgia
Germany
Ghana
Gifted Education
Gintis, Herbert.
    See Bowles, Samuel and Herbert Gintis
Globalization
Governmental Influences on Education
Grade Inflation
Grading
Grandparents' Role in Education
Greece
Guam, U.S. Virgin Islands
Guatemala
Guidance Counselors, Role of
Guyana

H
Haiti
Hallinan, Maureen
Hauser, Robert
Hawai'i
Head Start
Hermeneutics
Hidden Curriculum
High School Exit Exams
Higher Education
Home Schooling

Homeless Children
Homework
Honduras
Hong Kong
Household Educational Resources
Human Capital Theory
Hungary

I
Idaho
Illinois
Immersion
Immigrant Adaptation
Immigrants, Children of
Incarcerated Students
India
Indiana
Indonesia
Informal Fundraising in Schools
Intergenerational Closure
International Baccalaureate Education
International College Partnerships (Sister Colleges)
International Data
Iowa
IQ
Iran
Iraq
Ireland
Israel
Italy

J
Jamaica
Japan
Jencks, Christopher
Jordan

K
Kansas
Kentucky
Kenya
Kerckhoff, Alan C.

L
Labor Education
Labor Market Effects on Education
Laos
Lareau, Annette
Leadership in Schools
Lebanon

Lesbian, Gay, Bisexual, and Transgender Issues
    and Schooling
Liberal Arts Education
Libraries, School
Libya
Life Course Perspective and Education
Longitudinal Studies of Education
Louisiana

M
MacLeod, Jay
Madagascar
Magnet Schools
Maine
Malaysia
Marx, Karl (Marxism and Education)
Maryland
Massachusetts
Maternal Education
Maximally Maintained Inequality
Mentoring
Meritocracy
Mexican American Students
Mexico
Meyer, John
Michigan
Migrant Students
Military Involvement/Military Service
Minnesota
Mississippi
Missouri
Mobility, Contest Versus Sponsored
Montana
Montessori
Morale in Schools
Morocco
Multicultural Navigators
Multiculturalism/Multicultural Education
Multiracial Students
Museums
Music Education
Myanmar (Burma)

N
Nation at Risk, A
Native American Students
Nebraska
Neighborhood Effects
Nepal
Netherlands

Nevada
New Hampshire
New Jersey
New Mexico
New York
New Zealand
Nicaragua
Nigeria
No Child Left Behind
Noncompliant Believers, Cultural Mainstreamers,
    and Cultural Straddlers
North Carolina
North Dakota
North Korea
Norway

O
Oakes, Jeannie
Occupational Aspirations/Expectations
Ohio
Oklahoma
Online Education
Opportunity to Learn Standards
Oppositional Culture
Oregon
Overeducation

P
Pakistan
Palestinian Territories
Panama
Paraguay
Parent Education
Parental Cultural Capital
Parental Educational Expectations
Parental Involvement
Parent-Teacher Associations
Pennsylvania
Peru
Phenomenology, Existentialism, and Education
Philippines
Physical Education
Poland
Policy-Oriented Research
Political Activism (Student) and Student Movements
Popularity in School
Portugal
Positivism, Antipositivism, and Empiricism
Postmodernism and Education
Poverty and Education

List of Articles   **xi**

Preschool Programs
Prior Learning Assessment
Private Schools
Professional Socialization of Teachers
Puerto Rico

Q

Qualitative Research on Education
Quantitative Research on Education

R

Race and Cultural Capital
Race Sensitive Admission Policies/Affirmative Action
Race to the Top
Racial Climate on Campus
Racial Inequality: Achievement
Racial Inequality: College Enrollment and
  Completion
Racial Inequality: High School Dropout Rates
Racial Inequality: Returns to Educational
  Investments
Racism in Education
Reading to Children
Reggio Emilia Approach
Religious Education
Research Paradigms in Educational Studies
Reserve Officers' Training Corps (ROTC)
Residential Mobility and Education
Resistance Theory
Resource Allocation in Schools
Rhode Island
Romania
Rousseau, Jean-Jacques
Rural Schooling
Russia
Rwanda

S

Saudi Arabia
Savings for College/Education
School Catchment Zones, Politically Defined
  School Boundaries
School Choice
School Counseling
School Effects
School Mobility and Education
School Organization
School Reentry
School Size/Class Size
School-Parent Relationships

Schools as Bureaucracies
School-to-Work Transitions
Secondary Education
Self-Esteem
Service Learning
Sewell, William
Sex Education
Sexism in Education
Sibling Effects in Education
Singapore
Single-Parent Household Structure and Education
Single-Sex Education
Skipping Grades
Social Capital
Social Promotion and Grade Retention
Social Psychological Theories of Teaching
Social Role of the Teacher
Social Status of Teachers
Sociocultural Approaches to Learning and
  Development
South Africa
South Carolina
South Dakota
South Korea
Spain
Special Education
Sports and Schools
Standardized Testing
Status Attainment
Stepparent Household Structure and Education
Student Attachment to School
Student Roles in the Classroom
Student Work and Educational Effects
Student-Teacher Racial Mismatch
Student/Teacher Ratio
Study Abroad
Sudan
Summer School
Summer Setback
Suspensions
Sweden
Switzerland
Syria

T

Taiwan
Tanzania
Tardiness
Teacher Attrition
Teacher Decision-Making Power

Teacher Expectations
Teacher Placement and Staffing
Teacher Recruitment, Induction,
    and Retention
Technology Education
Technology in the Classroom
Teen Pregnancy and Education
Television and Education
Tennessee
Texas
Textbooks
Thailand
Theater Education
Title IX
Tournament Track Mobility
Tracking
Training of Teachers
Transitions, School
Trinidad and Tobago
Truancy
Turkey

U
Uganda
Ukraine
Underqualified Teachers
Unions of Teachers
United Kingdom
Urban Schooling
Utah
Uzbekistan

V
Venezuela
Vermont
Vietnam
Violence in Schools
Virgin Islands, U.S.
    See Guam, U.S. Virgin Islands
Virginia
Vocational Education.
    See Career and Technical Education
Voucher Programs

W
Waldorf
Washington
Wealth and Education
Weber, Max
West Virginia
Wisconsin
Women in Math/Science
Working Parents
Worldwide Education Revolution
Wyoming

Y
Year-Round School
Yemen
Youth Cultures and Subcultures
Youth Friendship and Conflict in Schools

Reader's Guide

Concepts in Sociology of Education

Abstract/Concrete Attitudes
Assimilation Without Acculturation
Attitude/Achievement Paradox
Banking Concept of Education
Concerted Cultivation/Natural Growth
Cooled Out
Cultural Capital
Hidden Curriculum
Household Educational Resources
Intergenerational Closure
Maximally Maintained Inequality
Meritocracy
Mobility, Contest Versus Sponsored
Social Capital
Summer Setback
Tournament Track Mobility

Education and Social Inequality:
Gender and Sexuality

Adolescent Sexual Behavior
Cheerleading Equity Policy
Cultural Capital and Gender
Gender And School Sports
Gender Inequality: College Enrollment and
   Completion
Gender Inequality: College Major
Gender Inequality: High School Dropout Rates
Gender Inequality: Mathematics
Gender Inequality: Occupational Segregation
   of Teachers

Gender Inequality: Returns to Educational
   Investments
Lesbian, Gay, Bisexual, and Transgender Issues
   and Schooling
Sex Education
Sexism in Education
Single-Sex Education
Teen Pregnancy and Education
Title IX
Women in Math/Science

Education and Social Inequality:
Race and Ethnicity

Asian Americans
Black Cultural Capital
Burden of Acting White
Ebonics (African American English) and Education
Immigrant Adaptation
Immigrants, Children of
Mexican American Students
Migrant Students
Multicultural Navigators
Multiculturalism/Multicultural Education
Multiracial Students
Native American Students
Noncompliant Believers, Cultural Mainstreamers,
   and Cultural Straddlers
Oppositional Culture
Race and Cultural Capital
Racial Climate on Campus
Racial Inequality: Achievement

Racial Inequality: College Enrollment
   and Completion
Racial Inequality: High School Dropout Rates
Racial Inequality: Returns to Educational
   Investments
Racism in Education

Education and Social Inequality: Social Class
Affluent Children
Class Inequality: Achievement
Class Inequality: College Enrollment
   and Completion
Class Inequality: High School Dropout Rates
Digital Divide/Digital Capital
Poverty and Education
Savings for College/Education
Wealth and Education

Education Beyond Schools
Cognitive Skill/Intellectual Skill
Credit for Work Experience, College Students
Credit for Work Experience, High School Students
Earning Potential and Education
Educational Aspirations/Expectations
Home Schooling
Incarcerated Students
IQ
Labor Market Effects on Education
Military Involvement/Military Service
Neighborhood Effects
Occupational Aspirations/Expectations
Online Education
Residential Mobility and Education
School Catchment Zones, Politically Defined
   School Boundaries
School Mobility and Education
School-to-Work Transitions
Student Work and Educational Effects

Education in the United States
Alabama
Alaska
American Samoa
Arizona
Arkansas
California
Colorado
Connecticut
Delaware
District of Columbia

Florida
Georgia
Guam, U.S. Virgin Islands
Hawai'i
Idaho
Illinois
Indiana
Iowa
Kansas
Kentucky
Louisiana
Maine
Maryland
Massachusetts
Michigan
Minnesota
Mississippi
Missouri
Montana
Nebraska
Nevada
New Hampshire
New Jersey
New Mexico
New York
North Carolina
North Dakota
Ohio
Oklahoma
Oregon
Pennsylvania
Puerto Rico
Rhode Island
South Carolina
South Dakota
Tennessee
Texas
Utah
Vermont
Virginia
Washington
West Virginia
Wisconsin
Wyoming

Educational Policies
Brown v. Board of Education
Busing
Curriculum Standardization
Educational Policymakers

Expansion of Education
Feeder Patterns/Catchment Zones
Funding of Schools
Governmental Influences on Education
Informal Fundraising in Schools
Leadership in Schools
Magnet Schools
No Child Left Behind
Opportunity to Learn Standards
Race Sensitive Admission Policies/Affirmative
    Action
Race to the Top
School Reentry

Educational Research Related Topics

Content and Text Analysis
Ethnography
Feminist Critiques of Educational Research
Feminist Research Methodology
International Data
Longitudinal Studies of Education
Policy-Oriented Research
Positivism, Antipositivism, and Empiricism
Qualitative Research on Education
Quantitative Research on Education
Research Paradigms in Educational Studies

Educational Theories and Philosophies

Conflict Theory of Education
Constructivism
Critical Discourse Analysis
Critical Race Theory in Education
Critical Theory of Education
Epistemological Issues in Educational Research
Feminist Critiques of Educational Practices
Functionalist Theory of Education
Gender Theories in Education
Hermeneutics
Human Capital Theory
Life Course Perspective and Education
Montessori
Phenomenology, Existentialism, and
    Education
Postmodernism and Education
Reggio Emilia Approach
Resistance Theory
Sociocultural Approaches to Learning
    and Development
Status Attainment
Waldorf

Family Influences and Involvement

Child Care
Extended Kinship and Education
Family Structure and Education
Grandparents' Role in Education
Homeless Children
Maternal Education
Parent Education
Parental Cultural Capital
Parental Educational Expectations
Parental Involvement
Parent-Teacher Associations
Reading to Children
School-Parent Relationships
Sibling Effects in Education
Single-Parent Household Structure and Education
Stepparent Household Structure and Education
Working Parents

Globalization and Educational Issues Around the World

Afghanistan
Algeria
Angola
Argentina
Australia
Austria
Bahamas
Bangladesh
Barbados
Belgium
Brazil
Bulgaria
Cambodia
Cameroon
Canada
Chile
China
Colombia
Congo, Democratic Republic of the
Costa Rica
Cuba
Czech Republic and Slovakia
Denmark
Dominican Republic
Ecuador
Egypt
El Salvador
Ethiopia

European Union
Finland
France
Germany
Ghana
Globalization
Greece
Guatemala
Guyana
Haiti
Honduras
Hong Kong
Hungary
India
Indonesia
International College Partnerships
   (Sister Colleges)
Iran
Iraq
Ireland
Israel
Italy
Jamaica
Japan
Jordan
Kenya
Laos
Lebanon
Libya
Madagascar
Malaysia
Mexico
Morocco
Myanmar (Burma)
Nepal
Netherlands
New Zealand
Nicaragua
Nigeria
North Korea
Norway
Pakistan
Palestinian Territories
Panama
Paraguay
Peru
Philippines
Poland
Portugal
Romania

Russia
Rwanda
Saudi Arabia
Singapore
South Africa
South Korea
Spain
Sudan
Sweden
Switzerland
Syria
Taiwan
Tanzania
Thailand
Trinidad and Tobago
Turkey
Uganda
Ukraine
United Kingdom
Uzbekistan
Venezuela
Vietnam
Yemen

Peer and Social Influences

Adolescence
Age Grouping of Students
Childhood
Classroom Dynamics
Classroom Interactions Between Students
Early Childhood
Intergenerational Closure
Morale in Schools
Political Activism (Student) and Student Movements
Popularity in School
Self-Esteem
Student Attachment to School
Student Roles in the Classroom
Youth Cultures and Subcultures
Youth Friendship and Conflict in Schools

Postsecondary Education

Adult Education
Adult Literacy
Advanced Degrees
Black Colleges and Universities, Historically
College Advising
College Proximity
College Transferring
Community Colleges

International College Partnerships
  (Sister Colleges)
Liberal Arts Education
Overeducation
Service Learning

School as an Organization and Workplace

Administration of Education
Alternative and Second Chance Education
Catholic Schools
Private Schools
Religious Education
Resource Allocation in Schools
School Organization
School Size/Class Size
Schools as Bureaucracies

School Discipline

Aggressive Behaviors in Classrooms
Corporal Punishment
Discipline in Education
Drinking and Education, Adolescent
Drug Use and Education
Suspensions
Tardiness
Truancy
Violence in Schools

School Systems, Structures, and Processes

Ability Grouping
Advanced and Honors Classes
After-School Programs
Agricultural Education
At-Risk Students
Baccalaureate Education, Pre-International
Bilingual Education
Blind Students
Boarding Schools
Charter Schools
Classroom Language
De Facto Tracking
Deaf Students
De-Tracking
Disabled Students
Dropouts
Early Graduates
Elementary Education
English as a Second Language
English Proficiency/Fluent English
  Proficient Students

Extracurricular Activities
Failing Schools
Field Trips
For-Profit Education
Grade Inflation
Grading
Head Start
High School Exit Exams
Homework
Immersion
International Baccalaureate Education
Libraries, School
Magnet Schools
Museums
Music Education
Physical Education
Preschool Programs
Reserve Officers' Training Corps (ROTC)
Rural Schooling
School Choice
School Effects
Secondary Education
Skipping Grades
Social Promotion and Grade Retention
Special Education
Sports and Schools
Standardized Testing
Study Abroad
Summer School
Technology Education
Technology in the Classroom
Television and Education
Textbooks
Theater Education
Tracking
Transitions, School
Urban Schooling
Voucher Programs
Year-Round School

Teachers/Counselors in Society

Classroom Interactions: Teachers and Students
Deskilling of the Teaching Profession
Ethics in Education
Guidance Counselors, Role of
Professional Socialization of Teachers
School Counseling
Social Psychological Theories of Teaching
Social Role of the Teacher
Social Status of Teachers

Student-Teacher Racial Mismatch
Student/Teacher Ratio
Teacher Attrition
Teacher Decision-Making Power
Teacher Expectations
Teacher Placement and Staffing
Teacher Recruitment, Induction,
  and Retention
Training of Teachers
Underqualified Teachers
Unions of Teachers

Theorists in Sociology of Education
Bell Curve, The
Bernstein, Basil
Bidwell, Charles
Bloom, Allen
Bowles, Samuel and Herbert Gintis

Brookover, Wilbur B.
Coleman Report, The
Dewey, John
Durkheim, Émile
Freire, Paulo
Hallinan, Maureen
Hauser, Robert
Jencks, Christopher
Kerckhoff, Alan C.
Lareau, Annette
MacLeod, Jay
Marx, Karl (Marxism and Education)
Meyer, John
Nation at Risk, A
Oakes, Jeannie
Rousseau, Jean-Jacques
Sewell, William
Weber, Max

About the Editor

James Ainsworth, Ph.D., received his bachelor's degree from the University of Southern California in 1989, a master's in sociology in 1993 from San Diego State University, and he joined the sociology faculty at Georgia State University in the fall of 1999, after receiving his Ph.D. in sociology from The Ohio State University.

His research addresses issues related to sociology of education, social stratification, race and ethnic relations, and the family. He has published his research in some of the leading sociology journals including multiple manuscripts in the *American Sociological Review*, *Social Forces*, *Sociology of Education*, and *The Journal of Marriage and the Family*. His work addresses issues such as (1) the oppositional culture explanation for racial disparities in educational performance; (2) the mediation of neighborhood effects on educational outcomes; (3) the differential returns to cultural capital across racial groups; (4) the effectiveness of bilingual education; (5) child well-being in single-parent households; (6) the relationship between labor market structure, participation in vocational education, and occupational trajectories; and (7) racial, class, and gender disparities in study abroad participation.

At Georgia State he teaches various undergraduate classes including Educational Sociology; Wealth, Power, and Inequality; Race and Ethnic Relations; and Social Research Methods. At the graduate level he teaches Social Inequality; Race and Ethnic Relations; Sociology of Education; and Ph.D.-level Statistics. The work he is most proud of is that which takes place at home, as he is the father of three: Maggie, Sienna, and Vince.

List of Contributors

Razak Abedalla
University of Pittsburgh

Susan Adams
Indiana University and Butler University

Charlotte Alice Agger
University of North Carolina at Chapel Hill

Matiul Alam
University of British Columbia

Ursula S. Aldana
University of California, Los Angeles

Nathan N. Alexander
Columbia University

Patrick Alexander
University of Oxford

Steven Alvarado
University of Notre Dame

Leanna Ampola
Loyola University Maryland

Karen E. Andreasen
Aalborg University

Lesley Andres
University of British Columbia

Gina M. Arnone
University of Pennsylvania

Shannon R. Audley-Piotrowski
University of Memphis

Janice Aurini
University of Waterloo

Efrat Avramovich
University of Pittsburgh

Marta Cristina Azaola
University of Southampton

David Baker
Pennsylvania State University

Christine Baker Mitton
Cleveland State University

Bianca J. Baldridge
Columbia University

Kara Balemian
College Board

Pamela R. Bennett
Johns Hopkins University

Nadia Benyamin
University of Northern Colorado

Nalini Asha Biggs
University of Oxford

David Bills
University of Iowa

William A. Bird
University of Nebraska, Lincoln

Katerina Bodovski
Pennsylvania State University

Helen Bond
Howard University

Kristen Brodie
Walden University

Derrick R. Brooms
University of Louisville

Rachelle J. Brunn
Virginia Polytechnic Institute and State University

Sarah Bryant
University of British Columbia, Okanagan

Edelina Burciaga
University of California, Irvine

Kri Burkander
Michigan State University

Jamie N. Burke
University of New Hampshire

W. Carson Byrd
Virginia Tech

Jessie Montana Cain
University of North Carolina at Chapel Hill

Rebecca M Callahan
University of Texas at Austin

Belinda M. Cambre
University of New Orleans

Carleen S. Carey
Michigan State University

Prudence L. Carter
Stanford University

Kay Castaneda
Ivy Tech Community College

Mark Causapin
Columbia University

Sarbani Chakraborty
University of Wisconsin, Madison

Aurora Chang
University of Wyoming

Jennifer Chen
Kean University

Hua-Yu Sebastian Cherng
University of Pennsylvania

Carolyn Chernoff
University of Pennsylvania

Laura Chinchilla
Rutgers University

Ming Ming Chiu
State University of New York, University at Buffalo

Evelyn Christian Ronning
Temple University

Kristin N. Cipollone
State University of New York, University at Buffalo

Jesus Cisneros
Arizona State University

Jamie Clearfield
University of Pittsburgh

Jessica S. Cobb
University of California, Berkeley

Nicole D. Collier
University of South Florida, St. Petersburg

Steven M. Collins
Indiana University

Jason C. Colombino
Boston College

Edward Comstock
American University

Dennis J. Condron
Oakland University

Thomas R. Conway
Saint Joseph's University

Dawan Coombs
University of Georgia

Siobhan M. Cooney
College Board

Kathleen Corley
Arizona State University

Rena Cornell Zito
Westminster College

Serafin M. Coronel-Molina
Indiana University Bloomington

Elizabeth Covay
Michigan State University

Mengtian Dang
University of Pittsburgh

Scott Davies
McMaster University

Bradley W. Davis
University of Texas at Austin

Aaron Davis
Independent Scholar

Laila De Klaver
University of Pittsburgh

Lori Delale-O'Connor
Child Trends

Omobolade (Bola) O. Delano-Oriaran
St. Norbert College

Karen DeMoss
The New School

Christina DeRoche
McMaster University

Kristi Lynn Donaldson
University of Notre Dame

Erica K. Dotson
Clayton State University

Ty-Ron M. O. Douglas
University of North Carolina at Greensboro

Douglas Downey
Ohio State University

Susan A. Dumais
Louisiana State University

Joel Dumba
University of Pittsburgh

Alyssa H. (Hadley) Dunn
Georgia State University

Catherine Dunn Shiffman
Shenandoah University

Ritam Dutta
Pennsylvania State University

Donna Eder
Indiana University

Aisha El-Amin
University of Illinois at Chicago

Manuel Espinoza
University of Colorado, Denver

Judson Everitt
Loyola University Chicago

Ryan Flessner
Butler University

Jillian C. Ford
Kennesaw State University

Sandra L. Foster
Regis University

John Mark Froiland
University of Northern Colorado

Landis Fryer
Loyola University Chicago

Brett Fugate
University of Colorado, Colorado Springs

Rachael Gabriel
University of Connecticut

Susan Galford
Indiana University

Melanie Jones Gast
DePaul University

Uttam Gaulee
University of Florida

Peter Ghazarian
Keimyung University

Yaron Girsh
Hebrew University of Jerusalem

Veysel Gokbel
University of Pittsburgh

Keith Goldstein
Hebrew University, Jerusalem

Laura M. Gomez
Arizona State University

Richard M. Gonzales
University of Texas at Austin

Gregory Gross
College of St. Rose

Alem Hailu
Howard University

Maureen T. Hallinan
University of Notre Dame

Christopher Hamilton
Washington University in St. Louis

Jason R. Harshman
Ohio State University

Nicholas D. (Daniel) Hartlep
Illinois State University

Judy Hartley
Early Care & Learning Council

Anna Henry
University of Missouri

Everett Herman
University of Pittsburgh

Dorothy Elizabeth Hines
Michigan State University

Jennifer Lee Hoffman
University of Washington

Patricia Hoffman-Miller
Prairie-View A&M University

Megan Holland
Harvard University

Jessica Holloway-Libell
Arizona State University

Rosalind Horowitz
University of Texas, San Antonio

Stephanie Howells
McMaster University

Jo-Anne Hurlston
Howard University

Nashaat Hussein
Misr International University, Cairo

Tozun Issa
London Metropolitan University

Marian Nell Jackson
University of New Orleans

W. James Jacob
University of Pittsburgh

D'Andrea L. Jacobs
Michigan State University

Lakshmi Jayaram
Virginia Tech

Chanel H. Jefferson
Independent Scholar

Jamie Patrice Joanou
Arizona State University

Willa Jones
Elsie Whitlow Stokes PCS

Justina Judy
Michigan State University

Tavis D. Jules
Loyola University Chicago, CEPS

Saltanat Kaliyeva
University of Pittsburgh

Somkiat Kamolpun
University of Pittsburgh

Grace Kao
University of Pennsylvania

Brian Kapitulik
Greenfield Community College

Emi Kataoka
Komazawa University

Alem Kebede
California State University, Bakersfield

Sean P. Kelly
Michigan State University

Jessica Kenty-Drane
Southern Connecticut State University

Caitlin Killian
Drew University

Soojin Kim
Rutgers University

Aaron Korora
Kent State University

Wendy L. Kraglund-Gauthier
Saint Francis Xavier University

Jonathan M. Kremser
Kutztown University of Pennsylvania

Kristiina Kruuse
University of Tartu

Amy G. Langenkamp
University of Notre Dame

Rachael Leavitt
University of Northern Colorado

Che-Wei Lee
University of Pittsburgh

Yin Lam Lee
St John's University, New York

Mare Leino
Tallinn University

Jessica Nina Lester
Washington State University

Rachel Leventhal-Weiner
University of Connecticut

Ashlee Lewis
University of South Carolina

Beth Lewis Samuelson
Indiana University Bloomington

Constance A. Lindsay
CNA Education

Jing Liu
Nagoya University

Christy Lleras
University of Illinois at Urbana-Champaign

Tim London
Queen's University, Belfast

Xiaolin Lu
University of Pittsburgh

Marguerite Lukes
City University of New York

Junhan Ma
University of Pittsburgh

Yingyi Ma
Syracuse University

Patricia Maloney
Yale University

Vida Maralani
Yale University

Michael J. Martin
University of Missouri

Sylvia L. M. Martinez
University of Colorado Colorado Springs

Ervin Matthew
Ohio State University

Janice McCabe
Florida State University

Jessica McCrory Calarco
University of Pennsylvania

Lila McDowell
University of Oxford

Heather Killelea McEntarfer
State University of New York, University at Buffalo

Mary E. M. McKillip
College Board

Patrick J. McQuillan
Boston College

Jal Mehta
Harvard University

David Mellor
University of Bristol

Analía Inés Meo
National Council of Scientific and Technological Research, Argentina

Donna Micheaux
University of Texas at Austin

Roslyn Mickelson
University of North Carolina, Charlotte

Marci Middleton
Shorter University
Piotr Mikiewicz
University of Lower Silesia
Lawrence J. Miller
Rutgers University
Caitlin Montague-Winebarger
University of Alaska, Fairbanks
Amy L. Moore
Capella University
Christopher B. Mugimu
Makerere University
Chandra Muller
University of Texas at Austin
Simon Pierre Munyaneza
Lycee de Ruhengeri Apicur
Yoruba T. Mutakabbir
Clemson University
Steve Myran
Old Dominion University
Molly Nackley Schott
Cleveland State University
Whitney Naman
Independent Scholar
Daniel C. Narey
University of Pittsburgh
Jennifer Ng
University of Kansas
Bethsaida Nieves
University of Wisconsin, Madison
Kiluba L. Nkulu
University of Kentucky
Keiichi Ogawa
Kobe University
Brandie M. Oliver
Butler University
Mariam Orkodashvili
Vanderbilt University
Emily Oros
University of Northern Colorado
Sarah M. Ovink
Virginia Polytechnic Institute and State University
Asil Ali Özdogru
Early Care & Learning Council
Mich Page
Independent Scholar
Maria T. Paino
University of Georgia
Maura Rosa Parazzoli
National University of Ireland, Maynooth

Toby L. Parcel
North Carolina State University
Lyn Parker
University of Western Australia
Noelle Paufler
Arizona State University
Hans Pechar
University of Klagenfurt
Lara C. Perez-Felkner
University of Chicago
Naomi Jeffrey Petersen
Central Washington University
Rachel Sutz Pienta
Valdosta State University
Eric John Plum
Shenandoah University
Brian Powell
Indiana University
Jeanne M. Powers
Arizona State University
Heather Price
University of Notre Dame
Jamilah Prince-Stewart
*Connecticut Coaliation for Achievement
Now (ConnCAN)*
Cassidy Puckett
Northwestern University
Elizabeth Rholetter Purdy
Independent Scholar
Lynn Purvis-Yund
University of Pittsburgh
Linda Quirke
Wilfrid Laurier University
Matthew H. Rafalow
University of California, Irvine
Karen Ragoonaden
*University of British Columbia,
Okanagan*
Louai Rahal
University of British Columbia
Fatema Rahman
Indiana University
Diana Carolina Ramos
University of Texas, San Antonio
Annette Rasmussen
Aalborg University
Robert K. Ream
University of California, Riverside
Linda Renzulli
University of Georgia

William Joshua Rew
Florida State University
Meredith Paige Richards
University of Texas at Austin
Isaias R. Rivera
Tecnologico de Monterrey (ITESM)
Sarah A. Robert
State University of New York, University at Buffalo
Mari Ann Roberts
Clayton State University
Sophia Rodriguez
Loyola University Chicago
M. Felicity Rogers-Chapman
Claremont Graduate University
Sharlonne Rollin
University of Georgia
Carrie Roseamelia
*State University of New York,
Upstate Medical University*
Susan Rakosi Rosenbloom
Drew University
Clara Ruebner Joergensen
University of Warwick
Dana Ruggiero
Purdue University
John Rury
University of Kansas
Cambria Dodd Russell
Columbia University
Sarah M. Ryan
Carnegie Mellon University
Dena Samuels
*University of Colorado
Colorado Springs*
Andrew Saultz
Michigan State University
Gokhan Savas
Syracuse University
Maryellen Schaub
Pennsylvania State University
Kate Makely Schechter
University of Pittsburgh
Cornelia Schneider
Mount Saint-Vincent University
Jonathan Schwarz
University of Notre Dame
Selim Selvi
University of Pittsburgh
Victor J. Sensenig
Pennsylvania State University

Ena Shelley
Butler University
Dara Shifrer
University of Texas at Austin
M Mahruf C Shohel
The Open University
Megan Shoji
University of Wisconsin, Madison
Alexia Shonteff
Arizona State University
Janelle M. Silva
University of Washington, Bothell
Jennifer Simon
Georgia State University
Elisabeth Julia Simon Thomas
University of California, Los Angeles
Jahni M. A. Smith
Teachers College, Columbia University
Jill M. Smith
Brandeis University
Christi Smith
Ohio State University
Massimiliano Spotti
Tilburg University
Andresse St. Rose
American Association of University Women
Amy M. Stalzer
Georgia State University
Christina R. Steidl
Emory University
Edward Geoffrey Jedediah Stevenson
Emory University
Meghan Stidd
National University
Mia J. W. Stokmans
Tilburg University
Kori James Stroub
University of Texas at Austin
Kathleen Sullivan Brown
University of Missouri St. Louis
Katy Swalwell
George Mason University
Sylvia Symonds
Arizona State University
Antonia Szymanski
Kirkwood Community College
Wei Tang
University of Pittsburgh
Beth Tarasawa
Washington State University, Vancouver

Carol A. Taylor
Sheffield Hallam University
Shelley Kathleen Taylor
University of Western Ontario
Barbara Thelamour
Michigan State University
Mara Casey Tieken
Bates College
J. Estrella Torrez
Michigan State University
Mitzi P. Trahan
University of Louisiana at Lafayette
Nan L. Travers
State University of New York, Empire State College
Marcella Bush Trevino
Barry University
Jonathan Tummons
Teesside University
Evan Underwood
University of Pittsburgh
Jennifer A. Vadeboncoeur
University of British Columbia
Liza Valle
University of Pittsburgh
Renira E. Vellos
University of British Columbia
Kristi Vinter
Tallinn University
Linda R. Vogel
University of Northern Colorado
Anne J Waliaula
University of Wisconsin, Madison
Haiyan Wang
Cornell University
Xiao Wang
University of Pittsburgh
Larisa Warhol
Arizona State University
Amber Warren
Indiana University
Nancy Wehrheim
University of Pittsburgh
John Weidman
University of Pittsburgh

Lois Weis
State University of New York, University at Buffalo
Eugenia L. Weiss
University of Southern California
Felix Weiss
University of Cologne
Greg Wetterstrand
University of British Columbia
Casey Megan White
University of North Carolina,
Chapel Hill
Robert Whiteley
University of British Columbia, Okanagan
Clemens Wieser
University of Vienna
Sarah Winkler Reid
Brunel Univeristy
Helena Worthen
University of Illinois, Champaign
Beth Wright
Loyola University Chicago
Christian Ydesen
Aalborg University
Huiyuan Ye
University of Pittsburgh
Vivian Yenika-Agbaw
Pennsylvania State University
Melda N. Yildiz
Kean University
Shengjun Yin
University of Pittsburgh
David Young
St. Francis Xavier University
Alma Zaragoza-Petty
University of California, Irvine
David Zarifa
Nipissing University
Xin Zhang
University of Pittsburgh
Yi Zhou
University of Pittsburgh
Lynn W. Zimmerman
Purdue University Calumet

Introduction

Sociology of education is one of the oldest, most vibrant, and increasingly popular subdisciplines in sociology. Dating back to 1925, the "Section on Educational Sociology" (now the Sociology of Education section) was one of only seven sections in the American Sociological Association (ASA). It has endured and is currently among the 10 largest sections in the ASA (out of 51 sections), with over 850 members; a nearly 300 member increase from 2001 to 2011. It is also one of the few subdisciplines with its own journal, *Sociology of Education*, sponsored by the ASA.

This work takes on the daunting challenge of reflecting the broad range of issues covered within this sub-discipline, and the results are impressive. With a total of 454 entries on the widest variety of topics, this work represents an unprecedented overview of the sociology of education. This is a worthy effort because the sociological study of education speaks to the core of sociology in general. It is through education that youth are socialized, norms are reinforced, and inequalities are perpetuated.

Formal education starts at the youngest of ages, and course education is a part of the entirety of Americans' lives. Education is a process of interaction and the staging ground of conflict and competition. Schools are complex organizations and are embedded in broad institutions. The topics covered in this work range from discussions of critical race theory to available quantitative longitudinal data sets, from policy oriented research to postmodernism, from preschoolers to graduate students, and from teachers to educational policymakers. In short, this work attempts to address the broadest range of educational topics.

What makes sociology of education such an exciting subdiscipline is that it so often acts as an intellectual bridge to other disciplines and subdisciplines. I think of the intellectual discourse in academic literatures as conversations, and sociologists of education tend to talk with wide audiences. For example, within sociology, these researchers and theorists often engage criminologists on topics of school delinquency or violence in schools, or sociologists on work when examining the school-to-work transition or vocational education.

Sociologists of education also dialogue with nonsociologists through interdisciplinary work. For example, psychological studies of students' self-esteem or locus of control have a longstanding influence on this field, as do the study of political influence on educational policy and the role economics plays in shaping the value of educational investments. In this introduction, I review some of the conversations that are represented in the entries of this work. These conversations have taken place over decades and reflect the evolution of thinking on major topics in sociology. They have shaped the most general of sociological theory, and influenced cutting-edge methodological developments in the field. While this brief introduction cannot do justice to the sheer breadth of these entries, perhaps reviewing a few of these conversations can provide a glimpse into what this work has to offer.

At the turn of the 20th century, W. E. B. Du Bois referred to the problem of race as "the problem of the century," and sociologists of education spent almost the entire last century trying to explain racial disparities in educational performance. Early on, such disparities were explained as a result of innate biological differences (later to be thought of as genetic differences.) This now debunked eugenics perspective fell out of favor after World War II when Hitler used the work of American researchers to justify his Aryan supremacy ideology. In the 1950s, the culture of poverty theory came into vogue as immutable biological causes of racial disparities were replaced with cultural causes that were assumed to be nearly immutable. It was not until the 1970s that broad structural inequities entered this conversation.

Oppositional culture theory was one of the first to highlight widespread discrimination against racial minorities and the relative lack of returns from educational investments for particular racial minorities. While this theory made the valuable contribution of pushing sociologists of education to think structurally about the educational race gap, unfortunately its policy implications were quite similar to the previous culture of poverty theory. That is, minority students, the theory argued, ought to reject pressure to resist school-related values and simply conform to the dominant norms of schools. Minority students continued to be blamed for their relative poor performance, as the theory targeted the assumed negative cultural response to schooling instead of what I believe is the true cause of racial inequality: structural inequities.

Responses to oppositional culture theory proved to be quite polarizing, and critics charged that broad monolithic theories could not reasonably be applied to whole racial groups such as African Americans. They pointed out that there were many high-achieving blacks who did not adopt an "oppositional culture," and a central question of the 1980s was how to explain their strong academic performance. Supporters of oppositional culture theory responded to these critics in the late 1980s by introducing the "burden of 'acting white' hypothesis." Essentially, this hypothesis suggests that when minority students do perform well in school, they run the risk of being negatively sanctioned by their same-race peers as "acting white." This negative peer pressure results, the theory suggests, in a pre-emptive low-effort syndrome in which some racial minority students reduce their school efforts in order to shield themselves from the taunts of their classmates. This point of view remains widely held in the public discourse as evidenced by Barack Obama's famous quote in his 2004 keynote address to the Democratic National Convention: "children can't achieve unless we … eradicate the slander that says a black youth with a book is acting white." However, over the past 15 years, both quantitative and qualitative research challenged this theory, and this recent research is well represented in this work.

Both quantitative and qualitative research has questioned the underlying assumptions of this theory. This recent research has found that minority children do not perceive more limited returns to their educational investments, that they are more likely to have positive school-related attitudes, and that they are rewarded by their peers for educational success rather than being subject to accusations of "acting white." Research is also coming around to taking seriously the pro-school attitudes of black students (i.e., the positive educational expectations that researchers have known about since *The Coleman Report* of the 1960s), rather than dismissing them as "wishful thinking" or "abstract attitudes" that do not predict school performance. In sum, the explanations for racial disparities in educational performance have changed significantly and this work reflects that evolution well.

This is far from the only theoretically driven intellectual dialogue represented in this work. The theories covered within these pages range from Jean Jacques Rousseau's classic masterpiece *Emile, or on Education* to modern feminist critiques of educational practices. Another example of a thread that links several entries flows from Karl Marx's influence in sociology of education. In the 1970s, two highly influential books with Marxist foundations came into prominence: Paulo Freire's *The Pedagogy of the Oppressed* and Samual Bowles and Herbert Gintis's *Schooling in Capitalist America*. Freire's work sparked the development of a major branch of sociology of education: critical theory of education. Since the early 1970s, theorists and researchers in this field have questioned the utility of the "banking concept of education" that treats students as empty receptacles that are to be filled with knowledge, and have challenged the duality of the student-teacher relationship. Instead of the culture of silence, so prevalent in contemporary education, Freire insisted that students ought to enter into a dialogue in which both become a learner and a teacher. Bowles and Gintis, also heavily influenced by Marx, take a more macro approach to critiquing the educational system. They claim that the social organization of schooling reflects the capitalist structure found in exploitive and alienating workplace environments.

As a result, the type of education a student receives reflects the class position of their parents, and thus unmeritocratically reproduces inequality in education and beyond. Others have also been influenced by Marx and have refined resulting concepts such as cultural capital, the hidden curriculum, and the digital divide. These concepts are all examined within these pages.

Another source of inequality that is examined in this work is the process through which socioeconomic status and wealth influence the educational success. Socioeconomic advantage in general, and wealth in particular, increase the opportunity for parents and grandparents to provide alternative forms of education to their children or grandchildren. The forms these advantages may take are many and varied. Within this work, you will find detailed treatments of privileged educational opportunities such as boarding schools, elite private schools (that may adopt educational philosophies such as Montessori, Reggio Emilia, or Waldorf), or homeschooling. Alternatively, parents may work within the public school system to gain advantage for their children by pushing for inclusion of advanced tracks (such as honors classes or international baccalaureate) or by forming charter schools. From the ability to send their children on study abroad or exposing them to engaging in extracurricular activities, to using their political influence to draw catchment zone boundaries, families with higher socioeconomic means provide advantages to their children in a process that has driven sociology of education research for decades.

On the other end of the socioeconomic spectrum is the plight of children in poverty. This work points out the research findings that show that much of the existing class disparities emerge in the summer months when students are not in school; the so-called summer setback. It is in the nonschool environment that advantaged children are exposed to "concerted cultivation," a strategy of exposing them to a wide range of age-specific, adult-supervised activities. These activities foster critically important noncognitive skills such as self-confidence, persistence, teamwork, and creative problem solving that further advantage high socioeconomic children. Poor children, on the other hand, are socialized through a process of "natural growth" in which they are permitted to determine their own activities. This natural growth approach, while it has its advantages, is yet another way poor children are disadvantaged overall. Some sociologists of education have argued for greater funding of preschool, after-school and summer school programs targeted to lower socioeconomic status students, and these policy recommendations could go a long way toward ameliorating educational disparities.

Another academic conversation reflected in this work is related to family influences on education. Profound demographic changes have taken place in the United States when it comes to family structure, and sociologists of education have studied these trends in detail. The consistent increase in nonmother/father household family structures has had profound effects on educational processes. As a result, sociologists have examined the impact of children living in single-parent households, stepparent households, grandparents' involvement in education, and the effect of sibship size on educational outcomes. The role of the parent has also garnered more attention. Parental involvement in schools has increasingly been sited as an important contributor to student success, and therefore parents are encouraged to read to their children, hold high educational expectations for them, and get involved in parent/teacher associations. These processes reflect a clear overlap between sociology of education and family sociology.

Teachers and the process of teaching is also prominently represented in this work, and rightfully so. Historically, there has been a deskilling of the teaching profession, and many are now highly critical of teacher-training programs, suggesting that they create too many underqualified teachers. That coupled with the problems of teacher attrition, burnout, and the retention of teachers needs to be increasingly focused upon. Beyond the state of the teaching profession, the process of teaching is also an important topic of study. This work takes on related issues by examining classroom interactions between teachers and students, student/teacher mismatch (in terms of race, gender, and class), the impact of student/teacher ratios, and teachers' educational expectations for their students. These topics, while not an exhaustive list, go a long way in describing the state of teachers and teaching in contemporary America.

Finally, while many of the entries focus on sociology of education within the United States (and there are even essays covering every state and many U.S. territories), a concerted effort was made to include contributions that focus on our evermore global world. This took the form of entries on topics such as children of immigrants and their linguistic assimilation in the United States. But there are dozens of entries that examine the sociology of education-related topics that are unique from various countries around the world. This represents a unique overview of the world from a sociology of education perspective, and I am pleased with the collective results.

In closing, I would like to state that I am proud and humbled to be a part of such an exhaustive effort to represent the field of sociology of education. I am struck by the scope of this work, and even more impressed by the leaders of the subdiscipline that are included among its authors. Finally, I would like to acknowledge the hard work of Geoff Golson, Sue Moskowitz, and everyone else at Golson Media and SAGE Reference for their dedication that has made this project a reality.

James Ainsworth
Editor

Chronology

1st and 2nd millennia B.C.E.: Early alphabets are difficult to master, and literacy, rather than being a universal aspiration, is a specialist skill primarily limited to scribes. The literacy rate in ancient Egypt, for instance, is believed to be less than 1 percent. It is somewhat higher in Mesopotamian kingdoms and Greece, where alphabets are simpler and writing itself is a less laborious process.

1st and 2nd millennia B.C.E.: In Vedic India (1500–600 B.C.E.), education is public at first and based around the Veda scriptures. As the caste system develops, access to education is restricted.

1st and 2nd millennia B.C.E.: In China under the Zhou Dynasty (1045–256 B.C.E.), the five national schools and four schools for the nobility teach the Six Arts: rites, music, archery, charioteering, calligraphy, and mathematics. Girls are taught rites, deportment, weaving, and silk production.

64 C.E.: The Jewish high priest Joshua ben Gamla institutes formal compulsory education for Jewish children. Although tradition has it that parents were required to teach their children in the household 1,000 years earlier, it is unclear how extensive or formal that instruction was. Textbooks in these early Jewish schools are all handwritten.

6th century: A Chinese poem called "The Thousand Character Classic" is devised as a primer for teaching Chinese characters to children; it remains in use for over a millennium.

605: Because the Chinese state is so heavily bureaucratic, it requires educated officials, leading to an imperial examination system, similar to a modern-day civil service exam. The exam system in turn leads to a system of schools to prepare young men to take the exam, in a curriculum based on Chinese classical texts; remarkably it remains in use until 1911 (though new texts are added to the curriculum).

8th century: In the early Muslim states, boys are taught reading, writing, and the basics of their religion.

8th century: In western Europe, Catholic monasteries are the centers of education and literacy, copying and maintaining Latin texts. Charlemagne, king of the Franks and emperor of the Holy Roman Empire from 768–814, promotes the liberal arts among the royalty, nobility, and courtiers. The expansion of his empire brings the monastic schools into contact with a greater number of texts and cultures.

12th century: Medieval universities in England, France, and Italy develop out of the monastic schools, offering courses of serious study in law, medicine, the arts, and science, in addition to theology.

12th century: The Catholic Church's Third Lateran Council in 1179 requires priests to provide access to free education to their parishioners, boosting literacy and education for the next two centuries—though most Europeans remain illiterate for generations to come.

14th century: In the Aztec culture, boys under 16 are required to attend school.

16th century: The Protestant Reformation emphasizes the importance of the individual reading and interpreting the Bible, leading to an increase in literacy rates and schooling. The subsequent Catholic counter-reformation, while rejecting the Protestant notion of literacy as a way of transferring power from priestly authorities to the individual, nevertheless further encourages individual reading and literacy.

16th century: In the Muslim world, elementary schools called *maktabs* are included in mosques, with a curriculum centered around literacy and grammar and the Koran used as a teaching tool.

1603–1867: The Edo period of Japan, during most of which the government imposed an isolation policy that prohibited Japanese from traveling abroad and foreigners from entering the country (except in specific trade zones). Japanese culture thrived. Under the Tokugawa shogunate, the samurai class flourished, and schools called hanko were opened for the children of samurai families. Numerous private elementary schools opened throughout the country to meet the demand to educate the children of lower classes, leading to an unusual circumstance in which literacy was widespread in Japan long before modernization, rather than as a result thereof as in much of the world.

1635: The Boston Latin School opens as the first public school in the United States (and remains the oldest in operation), with a mandatory curriculum in Latin and the classics.

1636: Harvard University is founded in Cambridge, Massachusetts, by the Massachusetts legislature (though it is today a private university). Though it lacks formal church affiliation, it is principally a seminary for Unitarian and Congregationalist clergy until the following century, and its modern reputation as a center of academic culture does not develop until its third century of operation.

1647: In Massachusetts Bay Colony, the Old Deluder Satan Act requires every town to maintain a grammar school. Early New England schools, which many early American schools in the next two to three centuries will closely resemble, are one-room schools governed by a locally elected board and serving a local school district. In contrast, European schools are directly controlled by the government. Subjects typically include reading, writing, spelling, grammar, arithmetic, history, and health.

1701: Yale University is founded in New Haven, Connecticut, as a seminary.

1740: Schools in Philadelphia are among the only American schools to provide girls with a substantive education, with a focus on reasoning skills. While it is typical in most of the country for girls, if they are educated at all, to be taught only reading and not writing, the education of girls in Philadelphia is motivated by class, rather than gender, concerns. Only the daughters of the elite attend school, and becoming more educated and worldly enhances that elite status.

1750–1820: In the years leading up to and following the American Revolution, the expansion of education is motivated in part by the desire to move away from European influences and toward a distinctly American culture and identity. The Constitution, however, does not address education directly, and under the Tenth Amendment's reserved powers clause, responsibility and control of school systems falls to the state governments. (Congressional involvement is justified under the commerce and general welfare clauses of Article 1.) Private schools are a popular recipient for charitable donations by the wealthy.

1750–1820: In the same period, the American attitude toward women and motherhood shifts to an idea historians now call "republican motherhood." While not concerned with women's rights as such— not a precursor to feminism nor even suffragism— republican motherhood elevates the role and treatment of women to closer to that of men. Just as daughters of the Philadelphia elite were educated in order to underscore their elitism, the idea now caught on that daughters of all Americans should be educated in order to instill the values of the republic in them.

1763: Prussia introduces the modern compulsory education system of public schools, which was soon adopted by other countries to produce more disciplined and obedient soldiers. Under most such systems, education is compulsory only for boys and may or may not be available to girls.

1764: Brown University is founded in Providence, Rhode Island, and is the first American college to accept students regardless of religious affiliation.

1777–1937: One metric of the federal government's limited role in education until the 20th century: in this 160-year period, Congress passes only 23 laws pertaining to education in contrast to the 33 laws it will pass in the next 24 years.

1784: The Institute of the Young Blind, one of the first schools for blind children, is founded in Paris.

1790s: Noah Webster's *Speller* becomes the most common textbook in the United States. It breaks down problems into smaller components and arranges them according to the age of the student, so that it can be easily taught and used in one-room schoolhouses where multiple ages are taught (the idea of grouping students in grades has not yet caught on). Unlike many of the textbooks that came before it, it is secular, with no mention of God or religious history.

1794: The first "normal school" opens in Paris, France, to train professors for postsecondary institutions.

19th century: Throughout the 19th century, education steadily expands in the United States, interrupted only by the Civil War. Expansion is earliest and most rapid in the northern industrial cities, and despite the widespread use of child labor, many historians credit the Industrial Revolution with boosting American interest in education. High schools in particular tend to be introduced in areas where there is a demand for skilled workers; schooling is slower to catch on in parts of the rural south and frontier, where children are most likely to be engaged in agricultural work. After the Civil War, "native schools" are opened by ex-slaves to promote literacy among African Americans.

Early 1800s: Professionalization of school administration in the United States begins as local school systems begin to hire principals and superintendants, transferring authority from civic authorities and elected officials to increasingly specialized professional educators.

1810: A normal school opens in France for the training of elementary school teachers.

1813: Yale introduces the four-point scale for grading, though it does not become standard at other institutions until the 20th century.

1817: The Connecticut Asylum at Hartford for the Instruction of Deaf and Dumb Persons is the first American school for the deaf.

1819: The Troy Female Seminary opens in Troy, New York, to train elementary school teachers.

1821: Boston opens the country's first public secondary school. By the end of the century, public secondary schools outnumber private ones.

1821: The Braille system is introduced to assist with the education and enrichment of the blind.

1837: Oberlin College, founded four years earlier, becomes the first coeducational college.

1837: The new Massachusetts secretary of education, Horace Mann, works to professionalize the state's teachers and increase the number of public schools.

1840: According to the census, about 55 percent of children between the ages of 5 and 15 attend school. Private secondary schools for girls of means have become common in the north.

1848: The constitution of the Netherlands is one of the first to regard education as a fundamental right.

1848: Horace Mann introduces Prussian "age grading" to Massachusetts schools: for the first time, students are grouped together in grades according to age, with a curriculum of progressive subjects arranged by grade. Multi-age classrooms become increasingly uncommon.

1850: Brown University president Francis Wayland writes, "The various courses should be so arranged that, insofar as is practicable, every student might study what he chose, all that he chose, and nothing but what he chose," an idea that will not be implemented by Brown for over a century and will continue to seem radical even then.

1855: Margarethe Meyer-Schurz opens the first German-language kindergarten in Wisconsin.

1857: The National Education Association, a nationwide teacher's union, is formed.

1861: Yale's Graduate School of Arts and Sciences is the first American school to award a Ph.D.; it is awarded to Clarence Winthrop Bowen.

1861: The Massachusetts Institute of Technology is founded in Cambridge, Massachusetts, in response to the Industrial Revolution.

1862: The first Morrill Land Grant Act grants federal land to the states to create colleges; states without sufficient federal land in their borders were issued land elsewhere that they could sell to fund the colleges. One of the act's aims was to punish the Confederate states by exclusion; they were granted land after the end of the war.

1865: Cornell University is founded by Western Union founder Ezra Cornell and New York state senator Andrew Dickson White. The school's intellectual inclusiveness, unusual for the time, is summed up by its motto, a slogan of Ezra's: "I would found an institution where any person can find instruction in any study." It is a coeducational school from its founding.

1865: When the Civil War ends, southern states under Reconstruction governments establish public primary school systems for both whites and blacks; nearly all schools are segregated by race, and black schools are consistently underfunded, sometimes ridiculously so.

1867: The U.S. Department of Education is established.

1867: New Jersey is the first state to ban corporal punishment in schools.

1868–1912: The Meiji period in Japan is a time of rapid modernization, in which the traditional class system is abandoned and an integrated public education system based directly on Prussia's replaces the

older overlapping systems of private and public class-based schools. In 1907 the duration of compulsory education is increased to six years.

1880: England becomes one of the last European countries to introduce compulsory education.

1881: The Phoenix Indian School opens in Arizona, one of the boarding schools opened to fulfill the federal government's requirement to assimilate American Indian children by teaching them English, religion, and vocational training. It soon becomes the largest such school and remains open until 1990.

1885: California schools begin segregating Asian and American Indians from whites, and many districts open "Mexican schools" to assimilate Mexican American students.

1890: The second Morrill Land Grant Act required that if any land-grant college used race as an admissions criterion, that state must form a separate land-grant institution for nonwhites, leading to the creation of many of the historically black colleges. Most of the black land-grant colleges are devoted to training teachers, which helps increase the quality of education at predominantly black schools throughout the country.

1890–1920: Over the course of the Progressive Era, school attendance in the United States increases over 700 percent (compared to the population increase of 70 percent). Over the same period, universities offer the first courses and degree programs in educational administration. As the government takes on more and more responsibilities, the role of the state in education increases. This period of educational expansion encompasses a political dimension, as public schooling is the easiest way to disseminate American identity and English proficiency to the children of recent waves of immigrants.

1890–1920: Colleges in this era help young men make the transition from rural farm life to the complex urban occupations their fathers could not train them for, while the development of elite academic centers in the northeast consolidates intellectual culture in that region.

1890–1920: Even before compulsory education has been adopted nationwide, pedagogues begin to advocate changes to the approach to education, promoting the intertwined relationship between education and democracy, and the idea of primary and secondary school not as a place to acquire skills but to realize the student's potential and impart social consciousness. Chief among these theorists is John Dewey, professor at the University of Chicago (1894–1904) and Columbia University (1904–30).

1900: The Association of American Universities is founded to standardize doctoral programs; today it's a forum for developing academic policies and research programs.

1900: White high schools, and a small number of black high schools, become common in southern cities. High schools in general are transitioning from schools that prepare students for college—and considered of little use to students with no such intentions—to a core element of the nationwide school system.

1900: Only four southern states have compulsory education, in comparison to 30 in the rest of the country.

1904: Stuyvesant High School in New York City pilots the first honors curriculum, originally for exceptional mathematics and science students.

1904: The Binet-Simon scale, an IQ test to help identify special-needs children, is developed in France.

1904: The National Child Labor Committee is formed with the goal of abolishing child labor, and supports compulsory education as one solution.

1907: Maria Montessori, the first Italian woman to practice medicine, opens a school in an impoverished neighborhood in Rome for children ages 2 to 9. In the process of running the school, she develops an approach to education informed by the study of human development and a focus on movement and independence.

1910: The first nursery school opens in the United States. As the American family shrinks and living arrangements change—with fewer multigenerational households—nursery schools become an important source of both childcare and socialization, guided by the growing interest in childhood development.

1916: The Stanford revision of the Binet-Simon scale, sometimes called the Stanford-Binet test, is developed, with broader goals than the original French test. Despite a scale derived from the scores of middle-class white children, it becomes the most frequently relied-upon IQ test in the United States.

1916: Abraham Flexner's *A Modern School* calls for the de-emphasizing of the classics in school curricula.

1916: French becomes the foreign language of choice for most students, World War I decimating the popularity of German, which had previously been the most-studied language.

1917: Mississippi is the final U.S. state to pass a compulsory education law.

1920: 32 percent of high-school-age teenagers are enrolled in high school, compared to 7 percent in 1890. Even though the growth of high schools is unevenly distributed, favoring wealthy states and urban centers, it is far faster and further reaching in the United States than anywhere else in the world. Even the ambition of universal high school for all income classes is uniquely American.

1920s: The terms *gifted* and *giftedness* in their modern educational context are first introduced, originally in reference to students who performed exceptionally on IQ tests.

1920s: Swiss psychologist Jean Piaget develops his first theories of child development, which later inform the design of elementary and pre-kindergarten schools.

1925: In *Pierce v. Society of Sisters*, the U.S. Supreme Court rules that a 1922 Oregon law requiring public school attendance is a violation of personal liberty, and that state-accredited private schools or home-schooling must be viable options.

1929: Maria Montessori founds the Association Montessori Internationale, which becomes one of the organizations that certifies Montessori schools established according to her principles.

1929: The Great Depression does more to end child labor nationwide than legislative attempts did, as the number of adults seeking work is so much greater than the demand for labor. Adults are now willing to work cheaply enough that there is no longer any demand for child workers except on family farms.

1944: The Servicemen's Readjustment Act, better known as the G.I. Bill, funds college or vocational training for servicemen returning from World War II, and continues to make educational funding available to soldiers to the present day. The G.I. Bill is actually passed as a compromise; Republicans rejected Democrats' call for broad-based education spending, but aid to G.I.s had bipartisan support. Colleges quickly become overwhelmingly male, and remain so for the rest of the century.

1944: The General Educational Development (GED) credential, a high school diploma equivalence, is introduced to make it easier for returning veterans who did not complete high school to take advantage of the G.I. Bill; before long, civilians are made eligible for the GED, as well.

1944: During and after World War II, high school attendance becomes common in the rural south for the first time.

1947: After India gains independence, much of the country adopts Mahatma Gandhi's system of Nai Talim ("basic education"), in which children produce traditional handicrafts as part of the learning experience. By the 1960s this model is largely abandoned in favor of the curriculum advocated by Jawaharlal Nehru, the first Indian prime minister, which combines a technical education with a liberal arts curriculum as part of the country's drive for industrialization.

1948: San Diego city officials institute a district-wide screening process for honors students, the oldest honors program still in place today, with 16 schools devoted to gifted education and a class size limit of 15 students.

1954: *Brown v. Board of Education* ends de jure racial segregation in the United States when the Supreme Court rules that separate educational facilities for different races are inherently unequal. The decision helps boost the civil rights movement and also inspires bitter opposition on the part of stalwart segregationists. In 1957, President Dwight Eisenhower deploys part of the 101st Airborne Division to ensure

black students' entry into integrating Little Rock Central High School. Even 10 years after *Brown*, Alabama governor George Wallace's political currency consists principally of segregationist coin.

1958: The National Defense Education Act, precipitated by the Soviet launch of Sputnik the previous year and a recent increase in college attendance, provides funding to all levels of American education. The goal is to avoid falling behind the Soviets in scientific achievement; beneficiaries of the funding are required to sign an affidavit forswearing overthrow of the American government, a requirement removed in 1962 when McCarthyism fell out of favor.

1960s: The flurry of social changes and activist movements in this decade sometimes camouflage how significant it is for American public education, which becomes better funded and more professionalized while tailoring programs to the needs of a diverse student population. States begin to pass laws requiring state testing and licensing for teachers.

1960s: The experimental college movement advocates new approaches to education, including cost-free courses, community- and service-focused education, courses taught by nonprofessor specialists in a given field, discussion groups without professors, and other ideas. Most of these approaches are pursued in schools-within-schools based in traditional colleges like Tufts University and the University of Washington.

1960: New College of Florida is founded in Sarasota as one of the first private experimental colleges. Though not as radical in its experiment as schools like Hampshire or Evergreen that succeed it, its strong focus on academic inquiry leads to similar features, including narrative evaluations instead of grades and a strong commitment to writing and personalized education. Famed historian Arnold J. Toynbee interrupts his retirement to join the faculty.

1962: In Ypsilanti, Michigan, the HighScope Perry Preschool opens to serve impoverished African American children ages 3 and 4. Rather than a simple daycare program, the preschool is designed to bridge the achievement gap between low-income children and the rest of the population.

1963: IBM partners with Stanford's Institute for Mathematical Studies in the Social Sciences to develop educational software for elementary schools.

1965: The Higher Education Act funds low-interest loans and federal grant money for college students, as well as subsidizing a number of college libraries, community colleges, vocational schools, and other academic entities. Combined with the long-term effects of the G.I. Bill (for one thing, many more of 1965s' teenagers are the children of college graduates than would be the case without that bill), the growth of white-collar industries and the middle class, and the escalation of the Vietnam War (and the ability to avoid the draft by enrolling in college), the bill contributes to the gradual trend of college education's perception as an expectation rather than a luxury. College begins to become the rule rather than the exception; attitudes towards college change as a result, fueling student protest movements, demands for student rights (especially over self-determination and freedom from behavioral rules, such as the rule against opposite-sex guests in dormitories), and the growing experimental college movement.

1965: The then-controversial Elementary and Secondary Education Act (ESEA) involves the federal government in public school to the greatest extent yet seen, providing funds for school libraries, supplemental education centers, and education agencies providing for the educational needs of low-income children. The Republican Party opposes the bill en masse, on the grounds that it constitutes federal tampering with local matters.

1965: The Johnson administration also initiates Head Start, a preschool initiative designed to provide high-quality early childhood education to children of poverty, in the form of an eight-week summer program. Too many of the teachers hired are unqualified—adequate daycare providers but not educational professionals. The summer program is immediately followed by a year-round program that is somewhat more successful and that has continued to be funded with revised program standards and additional provisions for disabled, bilingual, and bicultural students.

1965: In Amherst, Massachusetts, Hampshire College is founded by other local schools in what will become the Five College Consortium: Amherst College, Smith College, Mount Holyoke College, and the University of Massachusetts Amherst. Rather than radically altering their own curriculums, the colleges, which share some resources and open their classes to one another's students, choose to found a new institution as an experiment in alternative education. The school combines many of the more radical possibilities for education, rather than compromising by introducing small changes to an existing program. Opening in 1970, Hampshire eschews grades and general education requirements and requires intensive writing work from its students, culminating in a thesis. Students are involved in policymaking decisions, and community service in the Third World is a graduation requirement.

1967: The computer programming language LOGO is created expressly for the purpose of being a simple language to teach to elementary school children.

1969: In *Tinker v. Des Moines*, the Supreme Court upholds students' right to free speech in a case dealing with a peaceful Vietnam War protest.

1969: Brown University adopts its New Curriculum, introducing new interdisciplinary courses, dropping general education requirements, and simplifying grades.

1969: College of the Atlantic, a private experimental college, opens in Bar Harbor, Maine, in order to stabilize the economy in the months of the year when tourism wanes. The curriculum is based on human ecology, the only bachelor's degree offered by the school, which has perhaps the strongest interdisciplinary focus of any bachelor's degree granting institution in the world. There are no separate departments; every faculty member is both a human ecologist and a specialist in another field, ranging from political science and peace studies to art and film.

1970: Oberlin College becomes one of the first colleges to convert some of its dormitories to mixed-sex dorms, and is the focus of several magazine and television "exposes" alleging sexual activity and immorality.

1971: In the *Swann v. Charlotte-Mecklenburg Board of Education* case, busing, magnet schools, and compensatory education are approved as means of overcoming the perpetuation of racially segregated schools by residential segregation.

1971: Massachusetts is only the second state to ban corporal punishment in schools.

1972: The Education Amendments Act includes a Title IX amendment forbidding gender bias in federally funded education programs, leading to an increase in funding for women's athletics.

1972: Giftedness is formally defined in a federal government report as "evidence of or potential for advanced academic achievement."

1973: In *San Antonio v. Rodriguez*, the Supreme Court rules that education is not a fundamentally protected constitutional right.

1974: The *Oregon Trail* computer game is introduced as an educational game about pioneer life.

1978: The ESEA is reauthorized and federal funds continued to be made available to local school programs. Eligibility for funding is broadened; funds may be used school-wide if 75 percent of the student body is low-income.

1979: The Department of Education Organization Act elevates the Secretary of Education to a cabinet-level position subject to appointment confirmation in congressional proceedings.

1983: Apple Computer introduces the Apple IIe. In contrast to the expensive Macintosh introduces the following year, the IIe has lower production costs than its predecessors while retaining backwards compatibility; it becomes a popular model for schools adding computers to their curriculum.

1986: China passes the Compulsory Education Law, raising teachers' salaries and making teachers' colleges tuition-free while instituting national standards for teacher qualifications, exams, textbooks, and curricula. Control of schools is decentralized, at the long-term expense of rural schools. For the first time since the advent of China's communist government, the pursuit of social equality is de-emphasized in educational policy, in favor of greater academic achievement.

1988: ESEA is reauthorized with the further caveat that standardized test schools will be used to assess school performance, reflecting the decade's concern with standards-based performance and the exaggerated threat of a prosperous, well-educated Japan.

1991: Minnesota enacts the first law permitting charter schools in the United States.

1996: The Oakland School district declares that the primary language of many of its African American students is *Ebonics*—a term coined in 1973 but unfamiliar to most of the American populace until this proclamation. The district sets aside funds to help African American students to become proficient in standard English in order to aid in their development and performance.

2001: The ESEA is reauthorized under the name No Child Left Behind.

2003: No Child Left Behind is amended to require that students be given the option of transferring out of schools that fail to perform to a certain level, to require certification qualifications for teachers, and to offer supplemental services to underperforming schools and school districts.

2004: A French law outlaws the ostentatious wearing of religious symbols in public schools, leading to a controversy over the wearing of the hijab by female Muslim students (who, many argue, were the intended target of the law).

2005: Immediately following Hurricane Katrina, the Orleans Parish School Board declared the New Orleans Public Schools (NOPS) school system indefinitely closed. The state legislature of Louisiana responded by transferring control of the schools to the Recovery School District, which is operated by the state's Department of Education and consists of the state's failing and jeopardized schools. Most of the schools of the NOPS were converted to charter schools, making New Orleans the only city in the country where the majority of public school students attend charter schools.

2009: As part of the American Recovery and Reinvestment Act, the Obama administration develops Race to the Top, a federally funded grant program. RTT grants are awarded to states that propose school reforms targeting the retention of effective teachers, improvements to low-achieving schools, the creation of student data systems, and the raising of standards and accountability systems.

2012: Since 2010, the total amount of student loan debt held by Americans has exceeded the total amount of credit card debt. In late 2011, it passed the $1 trillion mark, having grown by $200 billion in a single year. A combination of factors drives the student loan debt crisis, the criticality of which is overshadowed by the prevailing worldwide financial crisis: increases in college enrollment, rising tuition costs, a declining correlation between a college degree and increased lifetime earnings, and serious levels of unemployment among recent college graduates. Even that unemployment problem is only partly the result of the financial crisis; a separate component is that the supply of young college-educated workers drastically exceeds the demand for inexperienced workers.

2012: Enrollment in law school increases as college graduates seek to delay their entrance into the job market while attaining a degree perceived as prestigious; in actuality there are far more lawyers than jobs, and the refusal of law schools to curtail enrollment leads to some limited congressional and media discussions about their role in the growth of student loan debt.

Bill Kte'pi
Independent Scholar

Ability Grouping

Ability grouping is the common educational practice of separating students based on actual or purported ability in the same grade into different instructional groups with differing levels of aptitude or achievement. At the elementary school level, teachers often sort students into smaller groups within the classroom for reading or math instruction; this practice is often referred to as within-class or homogenous-ability grouping. Teachers may also practice within-class grouping by selecting out a few students to either receive more specialized help if they are performing below their peers, or to provide more challenging material to high-achieving students. In middle and high school, older students may be placed into different classrooms, classes, or course sequences based on either real or expected academic achievement and/or completion of prerequisite coursework. Research shows that low-income and racial minority students are disproportionately placed into lower-ability groups during elementary school. In addition, students in lower-ability groups learn less over time than students in higher-ability groups. There is also evidence that the practice of ability grouping may exacerbate educational inequality. Studies using national survey data indicate that lower grouped students learn much less and higher-grouped students perform better than similar students who are not grouped for instruction.

Ability Grouping and Social Stratification in Elementary Schools

The practice of grouping students for instruction within the classroom versus whole-class instruction where students are taught as a single group is widespread in American elementary schools. In theory, students who are grouped for instruction within the classroom are taught material with similar academic content, regardless of what group they are assigned, but at a pace and depth that reflects each group's ability level. The assumption is that ability grouping will reduce disparities among students with differing ability levels by enabling teachers to adjust their level of instruction to the ability of the group. For example, teachers can teach material at a higher level and faster pace for more academically advanced students, and at a slower pace for students who are struggling with the material, thereby improving overall student achievement. Another assumption is that students learn better when they are in homogenous, smaller groups, where instruction is tailored to their ability level, and when they are not given material that is too difficult or too easy for them. Based on these assumptions, the practice of within-class grouping during the early years of schooling should result in equal or greater performance among students in classrooms where ability grouping is utilized, compared to students who are in heterogeneous groups or classrooms.

The arguments against ability grouping are threefold. First, rather than improving overall student learning and achievement, ability grouping may actually foster educational inequality by providing fewer opportunities to learn for lower-grouped students. In theory, students in all ability group levels should receive material with similar academic content. However, studies have generally found that lower-grouped students are taught less demanding academic material, often experience greater repetition, receive less encouragement from teachers, and with respect to grouping for reading instruction specifically, are less likely to read phrases, sentences, and paragraphs that facilitate reading comprehension compared to students in higher-reading groups. Second, researchers are concerned about the process by which students are assigned to ability groups, particularly what kinds of students are assigned to lower-ability groups. Poor and racial minority students are disproportionately found in lower-ability groups in elementary school and in less demanding classes in middle school. Several studies have also shown that teachers often assign students to different instructional groups based on their perceived ability, rather than their actual test scores, and may use student behavior (for example, work effort and engagement) as a factor in their group assignment.

Finally, researchers worry about the impact of grouping on student's social and psychological wellbeing, particularly for children who are placed into lower-ability groups. Students are often aware of what group they are placed into and where in the status order this group falls, even during the earliest years of schooling. If there are opportunities for students to move out of lower groups and into higher groups, then the practice of grouping could actually motivate students to work harder and improve overall student achievement. However, mobility between groups is often limited, particularly for African American and Hispanic students. The result, critics argue, is that lower-grouped students have less contact with higher-achieving peers. This restriction, coupled with lower teacher expectations, may cause lower-grouped students to suffer losses in self-esteem and begin to think of themselves as less capable and less academic than students placed in the more advanced or higher-achieving instructional groups. The concern is that ability grouping may act as a self-fulfilling prophecy whereby students only work up to the level of the group.

Ability Grouping Effects on Student Outcomes

By in large, studies suggest that grouping has significant effects on learning, even after controlling for race and ethnicity, family socioeconomic status, and prior achievement. Among grouped students, those who are placed in lower groups learn less than if they were placed in higher groups over time. Longitudinal studies based on national survey data collected by the U.S. Department of Education also provide evidence that grouping practices do not result in increased or even similar achievement gains between grouped and nongrouped students. Rather, these studies have shown that students placed in lower groups in elementary school learn less over time and higher-grouped students learn more compared to similar students in nongrouped classrooms, even after taking into account differences in student test scores at the beginning of the school year and family background. A recent meta-analysis of 66 experimental and quasi-experimental studies found the effects of ability grouping varied depending on the level of student ability, with lower-ability students actually learning more if they were in heterogeneous-ability groups, medium-ability students learning slightly more in homogenous-ability groups, and higher-ability students learning equally well in both homogenous and heterogeneous groups or classrooms.

This suggests that ability grouping may have differential effects on learning depending on the ability level of the student. In addition, studies have found that African American and Hispanic students may be particularly harmed by the practice of ability grouping. Recent studies using data from a national sample of elementary students have also found that African American and Hispanic students are more likely to be placed in lower reading groups, and once there, they learn less than similar white students who are also lower grouped. In addition, at least one national study has shown grouping to be a net-loss practice whereby African American and Hispanic students who were lower grouped learned less over time than higher-grouped students gained compared to students in nongrouped classrooms.

Studies on the impact of grouping on social-psychological well-being during elementary school have been mixed. While some studies have shown that students placed in higher-ability groups have better self-esteem and more positive attitudes toward school than students placed in lower-ability groups, others found no difference in students' educational expectations or perceptions of themselves as cooperative and responsible. Fewer studies have examined how grouping may impact actual behavior in the classroom.

Utilizing data from a national sample of elementary students, studies have shown that students who were higher grouped for reading instruction were more likely to have better work habits and be more attentive and organized compared to students placed in lower-reading groups at the end of the school year, after taking into account prior differences on these measures at the beginning of the school year. Overall, research suggests that placing students into different groups based on actual or perceived ability may not only deprive students in the lower groups of better instruction and teacher attention, but may also limit their opportunities to learn the skills and behaviors needed for academic success.

Christy Lleras
University of Illinois at Urbana-Champaign

See Also: Oakes, Jeanie; School Organization; Tracking.

Further Readings

Condron, Dennis. "An Early Start: Skill Grouping and Unequal Reading Gains in the Elementary Years." *Social Problems,* v.54/1 (2008).

Hallinan, Maureen T. and Aage B. Sørensen. "Ability Grouping and Student Friendships." *American Educational Research Journal,* v.22 (1985).

Lleras, Christy and Claudia Rangel. "Ability Grouping Practices in Elementary School and African American/Hispanic Achievement." *American Journal of Education,* v.115/2 (2009).

Rosenbaum, James E. "Social Implications of Educational Grouping." *Review of Research in Education,* v.8 (1980).

Slavin, Robert E. "Ability Grouping and Student Achievement in Elementary Schools." *Review of Educational Research,* v.57 (1987).

Tach, Laura and George Farkas. "Learning-Related Behaviors, Cognitive Skills, and Ability Grouping When Schooling Begins." *Social Science Research,* v.35 (2006).

Abstract/Concrete Attitudes

Race, ethnic, and social class differences in adolescents' educational performance persist, despite decades of efforts to reform school practices. In the United States, students from black, Latin American, and Native American backgrounds are less likely to do well in school compared to their white or Asian American peers of comparable socioeconomic backgrounds. Similarly, poor and working-class youth tend to perform worse and leave school earlier than those from more prosperous families. Even though educational outcomes generally reflect a society's patterns of stratification, racial and class differences in outcomes are somewhat perplexing given disadvantaged youths' almost universal endorsement of education for individual and group advancement. The concept of dual educational attitudes, composed of abstract and concrete dimensions, offers insights for understanding both the phenomenon of poorer educational performance and the apparent inconsistency between the stated positive attitudes toward education and the modest performance of many youths from lower income and/or disadvantaged minority backgrounds.

The concept of dual educational attitudes approaches the disjuncture between attitudes and behavior by conceptualizing people's beliefs about education as multidimensional. Mickelson introduced the concepts of abstract and concrete educational attitudes by demonstrating that adolescents' attitudes toward education take two forms. The first, abstract attitudes, is based on the dominant American ideology about education and opportunity that education unlocks doors to social mobility and remedies poverty, inequality, and other societal ills. According to this perspective, a person's educational credentials are evaluated by merit. Abstract attitudes toward education do not vary by race or social class because there is a broadly shared belief in the American Dream, in which opportunity through education exists for everyone.

People simultaneously adhere to a second belief system, concrete attitudes, which treat the relationship between education and opportunity with greater skepticism, especially among people from less privileged socioeconomic and racial backgrounds. Concrete attitudes are influenced by the social class, race, and ethnic forces that shape individual and group experiences in the opportunity structure. The beliefs about education and opportunity that undergird concrete attitudes are grounded in the varying material realities that people experience. Concrete attitudes differ from abstract attitudes in that they reflect an individual's perception of the essential material realities of his or her family's experiences in which education may or may not lead to status maintenance or upward mobility. Because concrete attitudes reflect the material world in which adolescents live, students' educational performance is informed much more by this set of beliefs than by their abstract attitudes.

Concrete attitudes reveal students' perceptions of their probable returns on education from the opportunity structure. Importantly, if family members' educational credentials are rewarded fairly in the opportunity structure, as is the case with many highly educated whites and Asians, adolescents' concrete attitudes are likely to be very similar to their abstract attitudes. But if family members' educational credentials are not rewarded fairly in the opportunity structure because of racial, ethnic, or class bias, as is the case with many low-income, black, and Latin American youth, adolescents' concrete attitudes are likely to contrast sharply with their abstract attitudes.

Empirical Evidence

Mickelson's 1983 research with Los Angeles-area adolescents first demonstrated the existence of abstract and concrete attitudes and their relationships to educational performance. She surveyed roughly 1,800 high school seniors in nine high schools located across two southern California counties. She found that students simultaneously held abstract and concrete attitudes, and their abstract attitudes were uniformly positive, but concrete attitudes varied with students' social class background and race. Only concrete attitudes predicted cumulative grade point averages. Significant social class differences existed in concrete attitudes within each racial group. Across white, black, and Asian American samples, middle-class students' concrete attitudes were more positive and their scholastic performance was better than those of their co-ethnic, working-class peers. While blacks and Asian American youth held significantly more pessimistic concrete attitudes than white students, the achievement patterns of Asian American students were more similar to those of whites than blacks.

Ogbu surveyed 2,245 black, Chinese, and Latin American youth in Oakland, California, about educational strategies and community forces. Triangulating survey data with ethnographies of the families, Ogbu found dual educational attitudes widespread among adults and children. He reported that students and parents from all three groups espoused favorable abstract attitudes toward education and opportunity, as well as more cautious or cynical concrete attitudes

and educational strategies that often diverged from their universally positive abstract attitudes.

Mickelson later replicated her original findings with black and white high school and middle school students in Charlotte, North Carolina. She found that middle and high school students held both abstract and concrete attitudes, but only concrete attitudes predicted achievement. In 2005, Mickelson and Kathryn Borman fielded the Charlotte survey among seniors in six Hillsboro County, Florida, high schools. They found that black, white, and Latin American students held both concrete and abstract attitudes, but only concrete attitudes predicted achievement.

Three scholars used Mickelson's original scales in different areas of the country. Carter conducted a mixed-method study of 68 low-income black and Latin American adolescents living in Yonkers, New York in 2005. She found that concrete attitudes were positively correlated with individuals' grades. Herman investigated racial differences in academic attitudes and performance among mono-racial and multiracial high school students from northern California and the midwest. Her results revealed that the grades of multiracial students were related to their concrete beliefs. Harris used the Maryland Adolescent Development in Context Study (MADICS) to examine adolescents' educational values and beliefs. The MADICS data include 14 of Mickelson's original abstract and concrete attitude items. Harris's approach to race differences in achievement differentiates between "perceived barriers to opportunity (despite education)" and "perceived value of schooling for mobility."

Conclusion

Two decades of empirical research using multidimensional attitude scales developed by Mickelson and other scholars confirm the existence of dual educational attitudes among racially, socioeconomically, and geographically diverse secondary school students. This corpus of research suggests the utility of multidimensional constructs for understanding class and ethnic differences in school performance. Abstract and concrete educational attitudes contribute to understanding how social forces, such as the dominant ideology, family background, and the structure of opportunity shapes academic outcomes. Additionally, the multidimensional attitude approach accounts for the paradox of virtually universal positive attitudes toward education, even among those who either underachieve or fail in school. Most research on attitudes toward education measures idealistic notions of the connections between education and opportunity. Because everyone agrees at this level of abstraction, there is little variation. An attitude that does not vary cannot predict a behavior that varies. People's concrete attitudes vary by socioeconomic status, race, and ethnicity. Because performance also varies along these dimensions, concrete attitudes predict achievement. The paradox disappears when achievement is examined in relationship to concrete attitudes.

Abstract and concrete attitudes have important implications for educational policy. Many reformers approach school improvement as if educational processes and institutions exist in a social vacuum. They assume that if standards are raised, tests and measurements are refined and linked to improved curricula, and teacher quality is enhanced, students will ipso facto learn more, stay in school, and attain higher levels of education. The key policy implication suggested by the relationship of concrete attitudes to academic achievement is that without a fundamental transformation of the larger opportunity structure, the underachievement of many youth is likely to persist, even in the face of the best-designed and most lavishly funded educational reforms. This is because adolescents read reality more closely than books. As concrete attitudes show, adolescents are aware that hard work and persistence in school only make sense if there is a fairly close match between the promise and reality of opportunity through education.

Roslyn Mickelson
University of North Carolina at Charlotte

See Also: Attitude/Achievement Paradox; Morale in Schools; Racial Inequality: Achievement.

Further Readings

Carter, P. *Keepin' It Real.* New York: Oxford University Press, 2005.

Harris, A. *Kids Don't Want to Fail. Oppositional Culture and the Black-White Achievement Gap.* Cambridge, MA: Harvard University Press, 2011.

Herman, M. "The Black-White-Other Achievement Gap: Testing Theories of Academic Performance Among Multiracial and Monoracial Adolescents." *Sociology of Education,* v.82 (2009).

Mickelson, R. A. "The Attitude-Achievement Paradox Among Black Adolescents." *Sociology of Education,* v.63 (1990).

Mickelson, R. A. "Subverting Swann: First- and Second Generation Segregation in the Charlotte-Mecklenburg Schools." *American Educational Research Journal,* v.38 (2001).

Mickelson, R. A., S. Okazaki, and D. Zheng. "Reading Reality More Closely Than Books: The Opportunity Structure and Adolescent Achievement." In *Transforming Schools.* Peter Cookson Jr. and Barbara Schneider, eds. New York: Garland, 1995.

Ogbu, J. U. "Community Forces and Minority Educational Strategies: A Comparative Study." *Final Report to Russell Sage Foundation* (1995).

Administration of Education

The administration of education is a relatively young, applied, and academic field of study, having its roots in the American Industrial Revolution. Current conceptions of school administration are deeply seated in its past and understanding the topic requires a historic accounting that looks at its changing views. Within more contemporary views, the terms *administration* and *leadership* are often used interchangeably, in large measure because it is difficult to differentiate them conceptually. In the late 1800s, a superintendent from Providence, Rhode Island, was quoted as saying "The right management of schools is one of the largest social problems with which this generation is struggling." More than 100 years later, there continues to be a drive to identify and refine appropriate and effective models of educational administration. In today's climate of standards, accountability, and evidence-based practice, school administrators are in the hot seat to help transform schools to meet contemporary expectations of education. While earlier conceptions of the administration of education were shaped more by the values and beliefs of politics and business seeking uniformity and efficiency, today's conceptions increasingly recognize the complexities of school organizations and the multifaceted and integrated skills, knowledge, and dispositions that educational administrators need.

History of Educational Administration

While education has been an important part of human history, school administration is a relatively new concept. It has only been since the establishment of massive public education at the time of the Industrial Revolution that the far more complex infrastructures required to manage schools and school systems necessitated the systematic oversight of education. The history and development of educational administration was a progression from practical and applied skills, to specialized professional knowledge, to academic and research-based knowledge. Each of these periods was greatly impacted by their political, social, economic, and scientific climates. Initially, public schools in the United States were administered as an extension of the local authorities, with no training or specific educational theoretical base. These early school leaders utilized practical and applied administrative skills taken from leadership concepts found in politics, business, and industry. In the late 1700s, the first examples of the legal recognition of school administration were seen; and some years later, superintendents and school principals were widely hired by local school systems, creating tensions around the transition of power from local authorities to professional educators. By the mid-1800s, more specific school administration skills were identified, and the transition from control by local authorities to a separate school administration began to take place. As the United States shifted from a largely agrarian to an increasingly urban and industrial society, educational systems became larger and more complex and required specialized professional knowledge. Between 1890 and 1920, school attendance increased by more than 700 percent, compared to an overall population increase of nearly 70 percent in the same time period. Child labor and compulsory schooling laws helped create a massive school system in a relatively short time.

These transitions of power and the theoretical basis for the administration of schools were greatly shaped by the massive changes occurring in business and manufacturing as a result of the American Industrial Revolution. Nathan Bishop, the first superintendent of schools in Boston, emphasized that the same principles of efficiency and productivity found in manufacturing and business could be directly utilized in administering schools. Similarly, other noted educators of the time emphasized military precision, punctuality, and silence as student habits needed to be shaped by schools in preparation for life in an industrial society. Greatly influenced by changes in the nature of work in urban industrial centers, educators believed efficiency was very important; if mechanization and strict time schedules worked well on the factory floor, then these practices could be transformed for use in schools and classrooms. This was largely influenced by a belief in universality, that concepts could be readily adopted from one domain and be applicable in another. School administrators in this time period thought of themselves as managers of efficiency. As the theories and knowledge of educational administration grew, university-based training programs began to emerge, the first at the University of Michigan in the late 1800s. In the early 1900s, Columbia University offered the first doctorate with an emphasis in educational administration. This shift in the field emphasized the academic, research-based knowledge of school administration and put pressure on programs of preparation to change from a focus on applied knowledge to academic knowledge, marking the beginning of the long-held tension between theory and practice in the field of educational administration.

Theories and Changing Views of Educational Administration

Over the course of the relatively brief history of educational administration, a number of theories have shaped the field. Initially, the administration of schools was largely atheoretical, adopting the assumptions and administrative practices of local authorities, business, and industry. Many of the early school administrators were actually teachers tasked with the additional responsibility of managing the school. Over time, the beliefs and practices became more theoretically driven and more technically specific and varied. The earliest conceptions of school administration were hierarchical and autocratic and viewed the role of school leaders as managerial, what one superintendent called a "conductor on the educational railroad." This conductor on the educational railroad metaphor was rooted in positivist assumptions and heavily influenced by a belief in universality, that a successful administrative structure in one domain would be effective in another. These educational administrators believed that human behavior could be reduced to a set of universal truths—the gap between perception and reality could be closed, one could find predictability in the external world, and that this was the single best administrative structure for schools. Educational leaders of the time set out to find universal truth and to emulate the modern corporate structure. The bureaucracies that grew out of this time period became well entrenched in the administration of schools and would influence practice well into the present.

During the Progressive Era (1890–1940), there was an effort to minimize or eliminate politics from schooling, giving professional educators greater authority and seeking to make fundamental changes in how schools treated and educated children, with the emphasis of uniformity and efficiency called into question and replaced by greater individual agency and democratic emphasis. The Progressive movement was a reaction to the increasingly scientific emphasis of schooling and beliefs in uniformity and universality. While the theories of teaching and learning of the Progressive Era were influential in the field of education in general, they were never able to penetrate the highly autocratic bureaucracies that had become so well established during the American Industrial Revolution. The instability of the Great Depression, the success of the military-industrial complex during World War II, and the conservatism of the 1950s allowed administrative theories of uniformity and efficiency to go largely unchanged during this period.

In many respects, the administrative theories and bureaucracies that grew out of the Industrial Revolution were taken from business and manufacturing, without critical examination of the differences between producing goods and educating children. While educators during the Progressive Era called into question the treatment of students as the "products" of schooling and undermining their efficacy as learners, the science of management and beliefs in uniformity gave the greatest shape to the theories of administration of schools. In many respects, the field of education did not have its own science of education. Beginning in the 1940s, the Theory Movement, influenced by logical positivism, deductive reasoning, a faith in the social sciences, and a belief that administration is a generic, generalizable concept that is applicable to all organizations, sought to study educational administration. For the next several decades, the Theory Movement attempted to legitimize and professionalize educational administration as a field of scholarship within the academic community.

By the 1960s, many scholars of school administration began questioning the positivist and science of management premises of the Theory Movement, arguing that the beliefs in single and universal best practices allowed school administrators to be shortsighted and obsessed with efficiency. These critics argued that theory could provide frameworks for understanding

school organizations, but that they were too complex to be explained with a single theory, that they eluded a positivist solution. Scholars contended that organizations could not be understood without understanding the various stakeholders: teachers, students, and their communities. These arguments led to calls to understand schools as more complex organizations, contextualized culturally, historically, and socially, which rejected the command and control orientation of established administrative bureaucracies. In addition, these scholars turned away from a technical and procedural approach to educational administration, instead emphasizing a balance of values and artful practice. In addition, growing interests in protecting the rights of historically underserved students helped give new shape to how educational administration was conceptualized and practiced. The Elementary and Secondary Education Act of 1965, the Education for all Handicapped Children (Public Law 94-142), *Brown v. Board of Education,* the Civil Rights Act of 1960, and the Voting Rights Act of 1965, among other landmark legislation, marked a significant turning point in educational administration. Schools could no longer be administered in uniform and systematic ways because policy and legislation required the diversity of students' needs to be served and protected. These changing values and beliefs about the nature of school organizations, along with the social and political emphasis on civil rights, led to several decades of school reform efforts.

Educational Administration Today: Accountability, Research on Effective Practice, and Challenges for the Future

Today, the administration of schools is in yet another period of change influenced by the social, economic, and political climate. The end of the period of school reform that grew out of the reaction to the Theory Movement was marked by growing dissatisfaction with the state of education and the perception of a failure to meet the needs of a changing workforce. The publication of *A Nation at Risk: The Imperative for Educational Reform,* in 1983, captured this dissatisfaction and marked another turning point in education in general. It had a significant impact on the administration of education. The No Child Left Behind legislation that grew out of this dissatisfaction set into motion state accountability systems nationwide that required schools to meet minimum performance standards. Contemporary school administration is in a period of flux, with significant tensions between theory and practice. On the one hand, research in effective educational administration is increasingly focused on instructional leadership, which emphasizes building organizational capacity around research-based instructional principles, while the political and practical realities of accountability has created enormous pressures on school administrators to meet state and national accountability standards. In many respects, the historically rooted beliefs and practices of the administration of schools, with its emphasis on uniformity and efficiency, can be seen at work in this period of accountability.

Schools administrators across the country have required the alignment of curriculum with state and national standards, the teaching of these subjects into clear linear sequences of discrete content, frequent assessment, and the strict supervision of these systems to ensure the intended output in the improvement of test scores. Unfortunately, these efforts tend to treat students as the product of schooling, something the general field of education and educational psychology has shown to undermine student performance. There is little evidence at this time that the administrative structures that have emphasized uniformity in meeting learning standards have had any impact on increasing student performance. Learning mathematics, for example, cannot be conceptualized as an assembly line of math content. Instead, learning mathematics requires a developmental view, where math concepts are understood as interrelated and build on each other in complex ways that defy a linear–sequential method of teaching and learning. The pressures that current school administrators have experienced to meet accountability standards may cause them to be shortsighted and narrowly focused on efficiency, actually undermining student learning.

In recent years, there has been increasing agreement among scholars regarding the key features of effective school leadership. These include: the importance of setting coherent directions for the organization, which includes promoting inclusion and high expectations, engaging stakeholders, promoting group efficacy, and developing and communicating a shared vision; developing the skills and knowledge of teachers and other staff; refining and stretching the organizational structure to promote greater collaboration and better connections to families and other stakeholders, as well as assuring a safe and efficient learning environment; and last, to be the instructional leader that assures the use of effective instructional practices, assessment and monitoring of student learning, and aligning instructional resources. These findings are at odds with the enormous pressures on school administrators to turn their schools into test-taking factories and represent a number of significant theory-to-practice gaps. What we know as a field about effective teaching, learning, and organizational improvement is difficult to keep in balance with the political and social pressures that manifest themselves in the current accountability legislation, policy, and practices. The future of the quality of education rests in large measure with educational administrators' ability to better capitalize on the fields' tremendous knowledge base and avoid the historic tendency to replicate the bureaucracies that grew out of the push to be built on product and efficiency-oriented assumptions about the administration of education.

Steve Myran
Old Dominion University

See Also: Governmental Influences on Education; Leadership in Schools; No Child Left Behind; School Organization; Schools as Bureaucracies.

Further Readings

Boyan, N. J., ed. *Handbook of Research on Educational Administration.* New York: Longman, 1988.

Cuban, L. "Reforming Again, Again, and Again." *Educational Researcher,* v.21/1 (1990).

Cubberly, E. P. *State School Administration.* Boston: Houghton-Mifflin, 1927.

Darling-Hammond, L., M. LaPointe, D. Meyerson, M. T. Orr, and C. Cohen. *Preparing Leaders for a Changing World: Lessons From Exemplary Leadership Development Programs.* Palo Alto, CA: Stanford Educational Leadership Institute, Stanford University, 2007.

Leithwood, K., K. S. Louis, S. Anderson, and K. Wahlstrom. *How Leadership Influences Student Learning.* Ontario: Center for Applied Research and Educational Improvement & Ontario Institute for Studies in Education, 2004.

Orr, M. T. and M. E. Barber. "Collaborative Leadership Preparation: A Comparative Study of Partnerships and Conventional Programs and Practices." *Journal of School Leadership,* v.16/6 (2006).

Richmon, Malcolm J. "Values in Educational Administration: Them's Fighting Words!" *International Journal of Leadership in Education,* v.7/4 (2004).

Tyack, D. *The One Best System.* Cambridge, MA: Harvard University Press, 1974.

Wahlstrom, K., K. Seashore, K. Leithwood, and S. Anderson. *Learning From Leadership: Investigating the Links to Improved Student Learning Research Report Executive Summary.* Center for Applied Research and Educational Improvement, University of Minnesota, 2010.

Waters, T., R. J. Marzano, and B. McNulty. *Balanced Leadership: What 30 Years of Research Tells Us About the Effects of Leadership on Student Achievement.* Aurora, CO: Mid-Continent Research for Education and Learning, 2003.

Adolescence

When young children become adolescents, they mature sexually and begin acquiring adult duties and responsibilities. Adolescents' brains mature to aid their adaptation to adulthood as they explore evolving social relationships with family, peers, and sexual partners, and develop their identities. Social changes in the early 1900s gave birth to a period of adolescence between childhood and adulthood, typically marked by puberty and ranging from ages 13 to 19, though this period varies across societies, cultures, and generations. Universal education and child labor laws moved children into schools and out of the work force, thereby extending the period of dependence on their parents (or guardians). As young children's access to adequate nutrition and health care increases, they grow up healthier and enter puberty earlier. As adolescents undergo puberty, they become sexually mature, and eventually acquire adult roles, duties, and legal responsibilities (for example, voting, working, marrying, accountability for criminal actions, and military service).

Adolescent Brain

Puberty and continuing maturation substantially changes adolescents' brains to increase both their emotional intensity and thinking skills, resulting in greater competence to address social issues. Up until about age 15, adolescents' brains increase neurotransmitter activity, accelerate nerve signals, and multiply connections among nerve cells, resulting in higher brain speed. Changes in adolescents' brains enable them to react faster, feel emotions more intensely, and

respond more readily to rewards (especially social rewards) compared to both younger children and adults. As a result, unexpected events provoke greater stress, faster responses, and more intense emotional responses, especially hormone-driven aggressiveness among boys. Changes in adolescent brains also improve working memory, control over their attention, abstract thinking, and meta-cognitive skills. With more space in adolescents' working memory, their brains can process more information in parallel, resulting in greater processing power. Adolescents' greater working memory aids their attention by allowing them to focus on essential information and to ignore irrelevant information.

Their working memory and attention focus also helps adolescents simultaneously consider multiple concrete examples (such as self-perceptions and perceptions of others) to highlight and isolate their common abstract core concepts. Furthermore, their abstract skills allow them to imagine other possibilities outside of their current reality. These changes allow adolescents to develop their meta-cognitive skills, including self-awareness, awareness of others, planning, and evaluation. Together, these brain changes enable more advanced thinking to address complex problems such as emotional control, autonomy, and interpersonal relationships. For example, adolescents can use their meta-cognitive skills during a stressful situation to pause, recognize their emotions, and then control them, resulting in greater self-discipline. Adolescents' greater working memory, planning, and evaluation skills enable them to imagine and consider multiple options along multiple criteria, which they increasingly use to question others' assertions. Applying their meta-cognitive skills, they begin to differentiate between evidence-based rules (e.g., wearing more clothes to stay warm) and tradition-based rules (e.g., curfew).

Social Interactions

Because of adolescents' greater awareness of themselves and of others, their social interactions with parents and peers change, along with their identities. As they become aware of different views (e.g., those of parents and peers), they may start questioning them, which can result in conflicts with parents who had become accustomed to their children's earlier, simpler responses. For example, adolescents often challenge what they perceive as unnecessary restrictions on their autonomy (e.g., privacy). As meta-cognitive skills continue developing past age 30, adolescents' meta-cognitive skills are not yet mature. As a result, adolescents may readily evaluate ideas critically from their perspective, but they often have more difficulty integrating multiple views to satisfy the needs of all parties. As adolescents approach adulthood and articulate more compelling arguments, their parents often acquire greater respect for their views, allowing them greater independence and less supervision. Negotiating exactly how much independence an adolescent should have is often a point of contention between adolescents and their parents.

Peers

As peers typically allow an adolescent more autonomy than family members, adolescents often spend much more time with peers and much less time under adult supervision. Adolescents tend to identify with peers based on common interests (e.g., band, football, and the school newspaper) and form exclusive groups of peers with whom they are particularly close (cliques). Cliques can help socialize adolescents into its group norms, acquire and practice social and collaboration skills (e.g., sharing, empathy, and leadership) to achieve shared goals and develop their identity. Because of adolescents' greater awareness of themselves and of others, they become more sensitive to their social ranking among peers (peer social status) and how public success (or failure) enhances (or reduces) their social status (social comparison). During this time, adolescents are especially susceptible to peer pressure, and may view their peers as more important and influential than their parents.

As adolescents are often concerned about the approval of their peers, they may engage in high-risk behaviors (including unlawful behaviors) to obtain it, especially from sexually attractive peers. As adolescents reach sexual maturity, they seek sexual partners. However, their sexual socialization varies widely depending on their society, ranging from highly restrictive societies that disprove of all forms of sexual contact to sexually permissive societies that encourage adolescents to openly explore their sexuality. In more sexually permissive societies, adolescents engage in romantic relationships. As adolescents mature and develop the emotional and cognitive skills (e.g., emotional control and empathy) to aid maintenance of romantic relationships, the prevalence and duration of these relationships tend to increase. During these romantic relationships, they typically experience strife that can end these relationships and cause intense emotional distress. Without sufficient social support and development of meta-cognitive skills to address such emotional distress, adolescents can become depressed and suicidal.

Identities

As adolescents develop better understandings of themselves, others, and their relationships, they imagine many possible identities of who they want to become. Often, they present different public self images (faces) that may vary across audiences, settings, and time. For example, they may experiment with family, classroom, peer, and work identities. Exploring these possibilities may result in sudden changes as the adolescent chooses or rejects attitudes, behaviors, or identities in various contexts. With greater experience, they may integrate some of these identities or leave them relatively compartmentalized for relevant audiences and situations.

Puberty marks the beginning of adolescence, greater sexual maturity, advanced thinking skills, and appropriation of adult responsibilities. As adolescents develop sexual characteristics that reflect their physical transition to adulthood, their brains also develop faster processing speed, faster reactions, and more intense emotional responses. Cognitively, adolescent brains show improved working memory, attention control, imaginative abstract thinking, planning skills, evaluation skills, and awareness of oneself and others. As a result of their greater social awareness, they challenge their current family and peer relationships while exploring and developing new ones. Through these social explorations, adolescents acquire and practice social skills, achieve shared goals, develop their identity, and enhance their opportunities for social, economic, and political success in broader society.

Ming Ming Chiu
State University of New York, Buffalo

See Also: Adolescent Sexual Behavior; Drinking and Education, Adolescent; Teen Pregnancy and Education.

Further Readings

Chiu, Ming Ming. "Learning Strategies." In *Encyclopedia of Adolescence*, Roger Levesque, ed. New York: Springer (2011).

Collins, Andrew, Deborah Welsh, and Wyndol Furman. "Adolescent Romantic Relationships." *Annual Review of Psychology*, v.60 (2009).

Steinberg, Lawrence. *Adolescence.* New York: McGraw-Hill, 2010.

Adolescent Sexual Behavior

Adolescent sexual behavior encompasses the variety of sexual activities that youth engage in, from abstinence to intercourse. Much of adolescent sexual behavior falls into the categories of foreplay, or "outercourse," which refers to activities that do not carry the risk of acquiring sexually transmitted infections (STIs). These activities include anything other than sexual intercourse, such as deep kissing, caressing, mutual masturbation, and heavy petting. According to studies by the Kaiser Family Foundation, a majority of adolescents in the United States and Canada experience intercourse by the age of 18. Rates of sexual activity increase with the age of adolescents, and there is a continued trend toward earlier ages of first intercourse. In 2009, 46 percent of all high school students in the United States reported having sexual intercourse in the previous year.

School curriculum can be one of the best sources for information about sex and sexual health. Health and physical education curricula usually include a component of sexual health education, such as personal skill building, values inventories, and sexual decision-making strategies. Many state education systems include contraception knowledge and social acceptance of birth control. This information contributes to sexual safety and the use of protection against unwanted pregnancy and sexually transmitted infections. Sexual health curriculum in the United States and Canada is influenced by social, religious, and cultural contexts. Teaching about sex can be uncomfortable for regular classroom teachers. Teacher education programs are generally silent on sexual health curriculum, methodologies, and strategies. Frequently, specialists are trained or contracted to teach sex education components of state curriculum. Sexual health educators must be well trained, trustworthy, and comfortable with the subject matter. The numbers of adolescents participating in sexual activity; the rates of unintended pregnancy; and the prevalence of STIs, teen abortion, and adolescent child birth rates have steadily declined over the past two decades. Sexuality, marriage, and childbearing have become less closely linked. Schools contribute to the regulation of sexual activity through curricula addressing birth control, safe sex, STI prevention, and healthy decision making.

In 2010, 20 percent of boys and girls 13 to 14 years old reported to the Kaiser Family Foundation having had sexual intercourse in the previous year, while 30 percent of 15- to 17-year-olds and 65 percent of 18- and 19-year-olds, regardless of gender, reported having had sexual intercourse the previous year. Boys consistently report more sexual activity than girls. By the age of 20, four out of five girls have had sexual intercourse. Girls who have not had sex by this age cite not having met the right partner, concern with the perceived social stigma surrounding sex, or fear of STIs and pregnancy as reasons for not engaging in sex. Black high school students are more likely to have had sex (65 percent) than white (42 percent) and Hispanic students (49 percent). Before the age of 13, 15 percent of black, 7 percent of Hispanic, and 4 percent of white students report initiating sex. Initiation of sexual behavior is associated with peer group norms. Education on safe sexual practices and healthy decision making can help adolescents make wise decisions related to sex. Twenty-six percent of sexually active high school boys and 17 percent of sexually active high school girls reported drug use during their most recent sexual encounter. Approximately 1 in 10 high school students have experienced "dating violence," with 7 percent of those students reporting that sexual intercourse was forced on them.

Adolescents rely on the Internet and television to identify social norms and to acquire information about sexuality. Some Web sites on the internet can be an reliable sources for information about sex; however, information regarding sex acquired from the Internet must be carefully screened. In the 1980s, abstention was the most common form of birth control. Today, the birth control pill or latex condoms are preferred methods of contraception for adolescents. Non-use of condoms may explain the prevalence of the STI Chlamydia among adolescents. In the United States in 2009, teenage pregnancy rates were 39.1/1,000 females, with African American, Hispanic, and Native American teens twice as likely to get pregnant as white and Asian adolescents. Abstinence is the forgoing of indulgence in sexual activity, while virginity refers to no sexual intercourse. Adolescents who have taken a virginity pledge are less likely to use condoms or birth control. Virginity pledgers are just as likely to have premarital sex as those who did not take a pledge.

Robert F. Whiteley
Sarah Bryant
University of British Columbia, Okanagan

See Also: Adolescence; Sex Education; Teen Pregnancy and Education.

Further Readings

Boston Women's Health Collective and J. Norsigian, eds. *Our Bodies Ourselves.* 2011 ed. New York: Touchstone Paperback/Simon & Schuster, 2011.

Brooks-Gunn, J. and F. F. Furstenberg Jr. "Adolescent Sexual Behavior." *American Psychologist,* v.44/2 (1989).

Crockett, L. J., M. Raffaelli, and K. L. Moilanen. "Adolescent Sexuality: Behavior and Meaning." In *Blackwell Handbook of Adolescence,* Gerald R. Adams and Michael D. Berzonsky, eds. Malden, MA: Blackwell Publishing, 2003.

Health Reference Center. "Virginity Study." *Pediatrics for Parents,* v.25/1 (2009).

Kaiser Family Foundation. "Sexual Health of Adolescents and Young Adults in the United States." (January 2011).

Rathus, S. A., J. S. Nevid, L. Fichner-Rathus, and E. S. Herold. *Human Sexuality in a World of Diversity.* 3rd ed. Toronto: Pearson Education Canada, 2010.

Statistics Canada. "Trends in Teen Sexual Behavior and Condom Use." *Health Reports,* v.19/3 (2008).

Adult Education

Over the last 70 years, interest in adult education has increased. In 1948, the United States began providing educational benefits to veterans. The United Nations Educational, Scientific, and Cultural Organization (UNESCO) and the Organisation for Economic Co-operation and Development (OECD) have worked with governments worldwide to increase adult learning opportunities. Focus on adult basic and post-secondary education has gained increased attention as education and economic vitality are linked. Malcolm Knowles (considered the grandfather of adult education) introduced the concept of andragogy in the 1970s to capture emerging educational theories and practices designed for adult learners. Andragogy means "man leading" (as contrasted to pedagogy, which means "child leading") and puts the adult learner in the center of an interactive learning process, rather than as a passive recipient of information. The basic tenet of andragogy is that the adult learner is self-directed and brings past experiences and knowledge to the learning process. In addition, the adult learner has developed a self-identity and self-referential characteristics, including motivational and goal-setting drivers, which are used to self-regulate the learning.

Adults are ready to learn, based on their developmental stage and life tasks, which trigger motivating factors to learn. Adults want to understand "why" something is learned, along with the "what" and "how," and want to understand that learning within the context of their life, community, and culture. While adult education historically seeks to reframe learning, challenge traditional educational structures, and aid social reform, it can also reinforce the status quo and existing inequalities and marginalize non-dominant groups. Critiques of andragogy point out that its concepts do not take into account cultural or social contexts, or how those contexts define expected learning content and delivery. Educational settings are political and value-laden, and cultural and social beliefs and structures bias the ways in which individuals frame and interpret their experiences. These critiques have helped expand adult learning theories over the past four decades.

Adult Education Settings

Adult education can be categorized into formal, non-formal, and informal learning experiences. Formal learning is purposed and focused and takes place within formalized organizational structures, such as educational systems or mandatory workplace training. In formal learning settings, there is a facilitator using pre-established curriculum with specified learning goals and expected outcomes. Often, adult education within higher education takes place through continuing education programs, but over the last few decades, there are a growing number of institutions that focus mostly on adults. In addition, online learning has provided greater opportunities for adults to engage in formal postsecondary education around their busy lives with work and family. Nonformal learning includes organized learning experiences that take place outside of the formal learning setting. These are usually voluntary, short-term (such as workshops or personal lessons offered through local organizations or individuals), and rarely have prerequisites.

Often, adults engage in nonformal learning experiences because of personal interest or need to learn new skills or improve existing skills. Nonformal learning experiences still utilize facilitators and have a set agenda for the learning experience. Nonformal learning experiences can complement formal learning by working on similar skills, but outside the formal setting (e.g., adult basic educational programs preparing adults for a high school equivalency exam). Some nonformal learning opportunities supplement formal education by providing learning experiences not taught in formal settings to address community, societal, and civic issues such as health care, drug addiction, or immigration. Yet other nonformal learning opportunities provide alternate learning to formal settings, such as religious training, whereby individuals learn about their history, culture, and society within an indigenous context.

Informal learning occurs through a variety of experiences not associated directly with formal or nonformal settings. It occurs through everyday interactions and self-directed inquiry. The informal learning route is situational and circuitous. Self-directed inquiry takes place when an individual is trying to solve a problem or is curious about a topic. The person may go to the library, ask experts, or search the Internet to find answers to an issue or question. Much of the informal learning that takes place for individuals, however, is incidental, resulting from various life experiences. For example, knowing how to parent comes from the experience of parenting; the experience gives rise to the knowledge. Knowing how to parent a child with a disability may rise from the experiences, but coupled with learning from the Internet, reading, or talking with an expert, that knowledge becomes enhanced. Much of work-based learning takes place informally, rather than through formal training. Continuously, an individual is negotiating workplace experiences, whether to solve immediate problems or issues, to remain an effective employee, or to fit into the social milieu. The work environment can be contested, full of biases, restrictions, and cultures; it can be changing, requiring constant monitoring, feedback, and modifications based on conditions and issues; it can be transformational, providing new perspectives and resulting in changes of behavior and knowledge. For example, leaders in organizations often develop more skills through experiencing difficult situations, coaching employees, and correcting error than from any formal course or workshop on leadership.

Theories, research, and practices from many fields, such as sociology, psychology, critical social theory, neuroscience, education, and philosophy, have been brought together to explain one of the most complex phenomena—how adults learn. Adult learning is not explained by one theory, but by many different frameworks or models that have been integrated or juxtaposed. Adult learning research and theories tend to fall within one of two general areas: the personal learning experience or contextual learning experience, regardless of the formal, nonformal, or informal nature of the learning.

Personal Learning Experiences

Research and theories that focus on the personal aspects of the adult learner explore individual attributes, such as self-concepts, preferences, motivation, and self-development. For example, self-regulated learning theories explore how the individual's self-concepts, self-scripts, and motivations interact with choices and feedback, seeking to adjust cognitive structures to learn best from the given experience. Life span theories explore how the adult changes over time as they move through stages of life (e.g., from young adulthood to parenthood and to retirement), and how these changes impact the ways in which adults learn. Experiential learning theories examine how the individual engages in experiences and how introspection and critical reflection makes meaning of these experiences. Transformative learning theories seek to explain significant shifts in perspectives or behaviors based on experience.

Neuroscience has made significant advances in recent years on the ways that adults learn and develop from experiences. Previously, neuroscientists thought that brain cells were restricted to a set number, which became more limited with age. More recently, neuroscience has begun to understand brain plasticity, the ways in which neural networks interconnect and chemically change based on the types and intensity of experiences. The latest work has revealed that the brain reproduces new neurons daily, which only survive if used immediately in complex cognitive tasks. In addition, scientists surmise that the new neurons aid in the learning process, enhancing the mind's capacity to learn even more. The adage that "you can't teach an old dog new tricks" is no longer valid; in fact, the old dog might increase its capability to learn new tricks the more it tries.

The brain's capacity to learn is dependent on the types of experiences and the complexity of problems solved. As the brain encounters experiences, the sensory input stimulates the neural pathways through chemicals that are released from one neuron to the next neuron at the neural synapse. The intensity of the experience and the value of the experience impact the levels of chemicals being released and can permanently change future chemical releases based on similar experiences. The neural chemicals impact neighboring neurons, forming networks of neurons, which continually respond together; neurons that fire together, wire together. Each new experience is assessed by neural structures previously formed by past experiences and in turn adds to the interpretation of the next experience. Experiences, therefore, are central to the adult learner, and these experiences shape consciousness, emotions, personal attributes, memory, motivation, self-regulation, responses to new experiences, and how a person learns.

Contextual Learning Experiences

Critiques of personal learning experience theories are quick to point out that the individual is not functioning in isolation from context. The struggle of the human experience is to balance the need for individualization and for belonging within the social and cultural structures that the individual lives and experiences. The degree to which an individual views him or herself as an individual, or part of a community, is dependent on how culture defines the individual and the community. Critical social theories stress the relationship of cultural and social norms on an individual's development. Social and cultural constructs of power (who is in power, who is not, and the relationship between the two) are critical in a person's understanding of his or her place in the world and the ways in which an individual learns. Theories emerging from oppression, such as feminist, gay/lesbian, and Africentric perspectives have provided important viewpoints on how different groups of people interpret experiences and form structures of learning.

Community learning is also an important construct in some cultures. Western approaches typically focus on the individual as the entity of learning, while other parts of the world perceive learning through a community lens. For example, in Kyrgyzstan, yurt felt making can only be done with others; the techniques require at least one other person to accomplish. In contrast, house building in the United States usually requires more than one person, but the skills are inherently individual. Adult education in community-focused versus individually focused environments is necessarily different. Life experiences also play a role in the context within which the individual learns. Memory is encoded with value and intensity. When a person has experienced discriminatory or

detrimental treatments, memory encodes the intensity and emotional value, which in turn can impact future learning experiences. Formal learning contexts can either support or be detrimental to learning. For example, a child who feels ridiculed for mistakes in public settings may resist future learning experiences as an adult that require public presentation.

Research has indicated that the role of other individuals within the learning context can either enhance or deter learning. Key individuals in a person's life (e.g., family members, teachers, colleagues, or religious leaders) can provide guidance, encouragement, feedback, and model learning processes; however, the position of these key individuals can impose an adverse power relationship that impacts learning. Mentors play a specific role that is more purposeful and directed toward constructive feedback and encouragement in relationship to specific and broader aspects of what is being learned. Research has also indicated that peer-to-peer relationships (e.g., study groups, mentoring, and tutoring) can also augment learning. Learning from someone else who is also engaged in the learning process reduces the differential between positions, providing camaraderie within the learning process.

Directions in Adult Education

Economic concerns worldwide have increased the awareness of and directions in adult education. Linking higher education and workplace learning is becoming a vital agenda across many nations. The Internet and mobile communications have opened up learning opportunities to people who didn't have access previously. Online learning has increased over the last decade and more adults are participating in educational opportunities. Increasingly, educational institutions accept credits recommended through the assessment of prior learning sources (such as standardized examinations, military experiences, formal training, and nonformal and informal learning experiences). Open education resources are becoming more widely available, providing higher education at greatly decreased or no cost. Community learning has also started changing with mobile and Internet connections. During emergencies, expert advice and assessment of situations can occur and information can get to groups to learn how to cope with elements of the crisis through mobile communications. Worldwide learning is available through mobile devices as long as connectivity is possible. Increasingly, concepts of adult education are being applied in formal, nonformal, and informal learning opportunities, increasing the knowledge capability globally. As learning becomes less restricted, even more caution needs to be in place to understand how learning occurs and the cultural and social influences that impact that learning.

Nan L. Travers
Empire State College

See Also: Community Colleges; Mentoring; Prior Learning Assessment.

Further Readings

Brookfield, S. D. *The Power of Critical Theory: Liberating Adult Learning and Teaching.* San Francisco, CA: Jossey-Bass, 2005.

Edelman, G. *Wider Than the Sky: The Phenomenal Gift of Consciousness.* New Haven, CT: Yale University Press, 2004.

Jarvis, P. *Adult Education and Lifelong Learning: Theory and Practice. 4th ed.* New York: Routledge, 2010.

Merriam, S. B., R. S. Caffarella, and L. M. Baumgartner, eds. *Learning in Adulthood: A Comprehensive Guide.* 3rd ed. San Francisco, CA: Jossey-Bass, 2007.

Shors, T. J. "Saving New Brain Cells." *Scientific American* (March 2009).

Adult Literacy

Adult literacy is defined as a person's reading and writing competencies. Simple arithmetic skills are sometimes included in the definition. Illiteracy refers to a person's inability to read or write for basic daily functioning. Within the field of sociology of education, adult literacy is well referenced in literacy studies, especially those that are designed and intended for improving the literacy skills of adult immigrants and native English-speaking adults who do not possess reading and writing skills for daily functioning. With reference to the National Assessment of Adult Literacy (NAAL) published in 2003, an estimate of 30 million adults who are age 16 and older in the United States are below basic (prose) literacy level, that is, their reading and writing competencies are insufficient for everyday literacy activities. Among this group of people, 44 percent were immigrants from countries where English was not their native language. When comparing the two major groups within the "below basic literacy skills" category, adult immigrants from other countries face bigger challenges than their native English-speaking counterparts because of a lack of social connections, as well as a lack of shared cultural practices with other Americans.

Many of them seek help from local government agencies and nongovernmental organizations for free-of-charge or low-cost English as a second language (ESL) instruction. In view of this social need, the U.S. government has been providing funding for adult education programs since the 1960s. The first adult education legislation bill was endorsed by President Johnson in 1964, which initiated federally funded adult education programs for persons 18 years or older. In 1981, ESL programs were supported by the act. The Adult Education Act brought hope to adult immigrants who needed ESL classes, but could not afford them. However, according to ProLiteracy America, the resources are still very limited, with an average wait period of 1.5 months for ESL instruction.

Adult Learners as an Underprivileged Social Group

School-age students who are receiving formal instruction have secured much more resources than adults with insufficient literacy skills. According to ProLiteracy America, the total annual government expenditure for adults in literacy education programs (including ESL) is approximately $310 per enrollee, when compared to $7,500 per enrollee in K–12 education, and $16,000 per enrollee in higher education. Adults who are in need of literacy instruction have been recognized as an underprivileged social group within society. The reasons are threefold: (1) adult immigrants have passed the critical period (before the age of 13 years old), according to developmental psychologists and applied linguistics, who hypothesize that learning is better begun at an early age, thus funding for them is supposed to yield a less desirable learning outcome; (2) adult education is often viewed as a service of secondary importance because it is for people who failed in the educational system; and (3) adult immigrants who are in need of literacy instruction include people from other countries who are not U.S. citizens, typically people with low income and socioeconomic status, and some of them are undocumented immigrants, who are viewed as an extra burden to the already heavily laden educational system. Therefore, adult learners are not only facing challenges at the linguistic and cultural levels, but also challenges for gaining social recognition and resources.

Reconceptualization of Adult Literacy

Many researchers defended the rights of adult learners because they saw social injustice in the status quo. They believed that in order to bring social change to this social group, the definition of literacy had to be changed. They criticized the original definition as monolithic, skill-based, and insensitive to contextual changes at the societal level. They referred to new literacy studies, led by scholars such as Brain Street and James Gee in the 1990s, and urged for an ideological definition that portrayed literacy as a historically, culturally, and socially situated practice. In spite of notions such as "schema" and "mental models" developed by psycholinguists, Brian Street's "literacy events and practices" foreground the "shared" cultural contextual assumptions that are subliminal, yet critical for daily functioning with other people in society. As such, adult literacy is no longer limited to reading, writing, and math skills. Rather, it has been reconceptualized as socially constructed, culturally situated, shared, and learned. For example, in an ESL class, adult learners are not merely decoding information given by the teacher; they are also learning the way of "doing" an ESL class in an American context, that is, they are also learning the "literacy practice" of an ESL class in an American context. An adult immigrant's sharing of his or her home culture would also be considered learning for others, because literacy is no longer limited to the reading and writing skill-sets for task completion. It is broadened to include the everyday sharing of culturally specific information with other people inside and outside of the classroom.

Sociocultural Turn and Social Change

In the recent decade, many researchers referred to sociocultural theories such as Bakhtin's dialogism and heteroglossia; Bourdieu's concepts of cultural, capital, and symbolic capitals; Moll's funds of knowledge; and Lave and Wenger's communities of practice, and they redefined learning as a social construction. The sociocultural turn brought about subversive changes to the negative assumptions of adult learners, who were traditionally perceived to be high school dropouts. With the new conceptualization of adult literacy, adult learners are no longer perceived and positioned at the receiving end of the teaching and learning processes. The adult learner's first language and culture, their

literacy practices in their home countries, and their life histories have become invaluable social assets, which contribute to the diversity and multiculturalism of classes, as well as to society. Though federal funding is still limited, demand for adult literacy instruction is on the rise. There is a shared hope that more researchers' findings may influence policymakers to provide high-quality education services to adults in need of literacy instruction in the 21st century.

Yin Lam Lee
St John's University, New York

See Also: Adult Education; Immersion; Immigrant Adaptation; Immigrants, Children of; Multiculturalism/Multicultural Education; Multiracial Students; Sociocultural Approaches to Learning and Development.

Further Readings
Askov, Eunice. "Adult Literacy." In *Handbook of Adult and Continuing Education,* Arthur L. Wilson and Elisabeth R. Hayes, eds. San Francisco: Jossey-Bass, 2000.
National Adult Education Professional Development Consortium. "History of the Adult Education Act." http://www.naepdc.org/issues/AEAHistort.htm (Accessed April 2010).
National Assessment of Adult Literacy (NAAL). "National Adult Literacy Survey." http://www.nces.ed.gov/naal/kf_demographics.asp#1 (Accessed March 2010).
ProLiteracy America. *U.S. Adult Literacy Programs: Making a Difference.* New York: ProLiteracy Worldwide, 2003.
Street, Brian, ed. *Cross-Cultural Approaches to Literacy.* Cambridge, MA: Cambridge University Press, 1993.

Advanced and Honors Classes

For students who either excel in certain subjects or who might benefit from an additional challenge or enrichment, advanced or honors classes were created in the educational system. These classes not only offer curricular enhancements, but also the chance to prepare for advanced placement exams. The honors programs of today do not resemble those of the early 20th century, however. Early honors programs were not a conglomeration of specific classes. Rather, entire schools were devoted to provide advanced education. New York City, Chicago, and San Diego were among the first to address the need for providing such advanced programs. With the advent of the Industrial Age, science, math, and engineering were considered the most sought-after skills and careers. In the early 20th century, the concept of advanced or honors education focused on the areas of science and math, and did not typically include students younger than high school age. Developers of advanced and honors programs did not focus on social issues as part of the curriculum until much later. In 1926, using the examples set forth by the New York schools, the first elementary school implemented an honors program. This school made a set of changes, however, extending its honors and advanced instruction to include content other than just math and science. The methods of instruction were also altered and a list of instructional goals, geared toward students enrolled in the honors program, was established. This list of goals became a template for other emerging honors programs across the country and included the following: develop selected themes, issues, concepts, and real-world problems; develop critical and creative thinking skills; develop problem-solving skills; develop meta-cognitive skills that foster independent and self-directed learning; develop high-level advanced communication skill in oral, written, viewing, and technological modes; and develop self-understandings and social skills that promote healthy relationships and coping mechanisms.

From Selection to Open Enrollment

As time passed and the tide of educational thought began to change, honors and advanced classes also began to change. Programs that were once highly selective and governed by intelligence quotient scores slowly began to allow teachers and parents to place students in accelerated and advanced courses. Many of the same goals pertaining to critical and applied thinking still existed, but the depth at which instructors were allowed to venture depended upon the intellectual composition of each group. In subjects pertaining to liberal arts, or the "soft" sciences, more instruction and related discussions were focused on social issues, political climates, and their effects upon society as a whole. Instructors responsible for math- or science-related courses, however, found that more students would question the necessity of the skills taught. These instructors reported feeling frustrated that the enrichment and extension of instruction they

had once enjoyed had all but vanished. Additionally, the increase in the number of advanced placement courses (which allow students to receive college credit while still in high school) left these same instructors with less room for enriching activities that could benefit collegiate performance in the long run. Teachers of elementary age students also felt that open enrollment served as a detriment to the honors and advanced classes that had traditionally been in place. Teachers had once been able to determine which students would be placed and in which subjects. Under the newer open enrollment rules, however, students were often placed in all advanced classes or none at all. Many reported a general level of frustration because their teaching techniques had to be altered in ways that negated the purpose of the advanced classes. Likewise, students reported an increase in frustration with courses they were not as strong in and a general lowering of self-esteem as a result. Many teachers and administrators in all levels of public education advocate a return to the original system of selection, allowing students to participate in the advanced classes that would provide the most benefit with a reasonable amount of challenge.

Advanced and Honors Classes Today

Advanced and honors classes today serve as the gateway to college for many high school students. These classes offer the best opportunity for the development of critical thinking skills necessary for success in the college environment. However, student initiative and parental support are often necessary in the enrollment process. In other words, students must seek enrollment to take advantage of the opportunities that advanced and honors classes offer. With this information in mind, it is not difficult to see that a certain socioeconomic disparity exists in the demographics of students enrolled in advanced and honors classes. In Chicago's schools, teachers and administrators often encourage higher achieving students to enroll, but only those students with a high degree of self motivation and/or an abundance of familial support tend to follow through. For this reason, many students in lower socioeconomic groups do not take advantage of the classes that are available. By the same token, some school districts overlook students in lower socioeconomic groups, assuming that they do not have the necessary aptitude to succeed in either college or the advanced and honors classes. Disparities with regard to class, race, and other social factors can be attributed to these factors.

Just as the lack of enrollment can be viewed as problematic, so can the enrollment of students who may be less qualified to participate. With open enrollment still a commonality within many public school districts, advanced and honors classes have become more limited in their ability to focus on the creative, critical, and problem-solving thought processes that were once envisioned. Depending on the particular class composition, teaching and applying these critical thought skills is somewhat limited. With the advent of advanced technologies, a disproportionate number of honors and advanced students are granted access in comparison to their nonadvanced counterparts. While administrators discuss ways to improve the system, students are forced to endure, grabbing as many advanced opportunities as possible and benefitting from the instruction provided across grade levels and content areas.

Kristen Brodie
Walden University

See Also: Ability Grouping; Gifted Education; IQ.

Further Readings

Bandura, A., and E. A. Locke. "Negative Self-Efficacy and Goal Effects Revisited." *Journal of Applied Psychology,* v.88/1 (2003).

Gentry, M. and S. V. Owen. "Secondary Student Perceptions of Classroom Quality: Instrumentation and Differences Between Advanced/Honors and Nonhonors Classes." *Journal of Secondary Gifted Education,* v.16/1 (2004).

Schulz, S. "The Gifted: Identity Construction Through the Practice of Gifted Education." *International Education Journal,* v.5/5 (2005).

Swartz, R. "Affirming the 'S' in HBSE Through the Socio-Cultural Discourses of Lev Vygotsky, Barbara Myerhoff, Jerome Bruner, and Ken Gergen." *Journal of Human Behavior in the Social Environment,* v.19/7 (2009).

Advanced Degrees

Advanced degrees refer to university degrees beyond a bachelor's degree, including master's, doctor's, and first-professional degrees. The number of people who earn advanced degrees is growing, especially among women. Just 40 years ago, women earned relatively few advanced degrees, but today, women earn more than half of all advanced degrees. Advanced degree holders are more likely to have higher earnings and lower levels of unemployment than people with less education. However, long completion times and high attrition rates, especially for doctoral students, are a concern. In the United States, the master's degree is the first graduate degree.

Master's degrees typically require one to two years of full-time study beyond the bachelor's degree, and are awarded in academic and professional fields. The Master of Arts (M.A.) and Master of Science (M.S.) are awarded in the liberal arts and sciences for advanced scholarship and research. Master's degrees in professional fields include the: Master of Business Administration (M.B.A), Master of Education (M.Ed.), Master of Fine Arts (M.F.A.), Master of Music (M.M.), Master of Public Administration (M.P.A.), Master of Public Policy (M.P.P.), and Master of Social Work (M.S.W.). A few professional master's programs, the Master of Laws (LL.M.), and the Master of Science in certain medical fields, require completion of a first-professional degree. Also, the Master of Divinity degree is usually considered a first-professional degree, rather than a master's degree. Doctor's degrees (also referred to as doctorates or doctoral degrees) are awarded in the liberal arts, sciences, and professional fields. In some fields, completion of a master's degree is a prerequisite. The Doctor of Philosophy (Ph.D.) is the highest academic degree and requires completion of coursework that leads to mastery in a specific field, comprehensive exams to test knowledge, and demonstrated ability to do original academic research. The last requirement is met by completing and defending a doctoral dissertation in an oral examination by a committee of scholars. Doctor's degrees are also awarded in business (D.B.A.), education (Ed.D.), engineering (D.Eng. or D.E.S.), and musical arts (D.M.A.).

First-Professional Degrees

In the United States, first-professional degrees are awarded in 10 fields that are not offered at the undergraduate level. Several first-professional degrees include the term *doctor*, but are not equivalent to doctoral degrees. In many cases, master's and doctor's degrees are available in these fields, but can only be completed after earning the first-professional degree. First-professional degrees are awarded in the following fields: chiropractic, Doctor of Chiropractic (D.C. or D.C.M.); dentistry, Doctor of Dental Science

(D.D.S.) or Doctor of Medical Dentistry (D.M.D.); law, Juris Doctor (J.D.) or Bachelor's of Law (LL.B.); medicine, Doctor of Medicine (M.D.); osteopathic medicine, Doctor of Osteopathy or Osteopathic Medicine (D.O.); optometry, Doctor of Optometry (O.D.); pharmacy, Doctor of Pharmacy (Pharm. D.); podiatry, Doctor of Podiatry (D.P. or Pod.D) or Podiatric Medicine (D.P.M.); theology, the Master of Divinity (M. Div.), Master of Hebrew Letters (M.H.L.), or Bachelor of Divinity (B.D.); and veterinary medicine, Doctor of Veterinary Medicine (D.V.M.). First-professional degrees require completion of the academic requirements to practice the profession, at least two years of college work before enrolling in the degree program, and a total of at least six years of college work to complete the degree program, including previously required college work. The requirements for first-professional degrees are regulated by the relevant professional associations, state boards, and religious authorities for degrees in theology.

Number of Advanced Degrees Earned

A growing number of people are enrolling in graduate programs and earning advanced degrees. Over the last 40 years, the number of master's, doctor's, and first-professional degrees awarded in the United States increased dramatically. The number of master's degrees swelled from 230,509 in 1970 to 656,800 in 2009. The number of doctoral degrees awarded more than doubled from 32,107 in 1970 to 67,716 in 2009, and in 1970, 37,946 first-professional degrees were awarded compared to 92,004 in 2009. The majority of master's degrees were earned in two fields: business and education. More than half of master's degrees (52.8 percent) awarded in 2009 were in those two fields. Another 9 percent of master's degrees were awarded in health professions and 6 percent were awarded in engineering and engineering technologies. Law is the most popular field for first-professional degree holders. In 2009, almost half of all first-professional degrees (47.9 percent) were awarded in law. The next most popular fields were medicine and pharmacy, where 17.4 and 12.3 percent of degrees were awarded, respectively. The remaining degrees were in theology (5.8 percent), dentistry (5.3 percent), osteopathic (4.0 percent), chiropractic (2.7 percent), veterinary medicine (2.6 percent), optometry (1.5 percent), and podiatry (0.5 percent). In 2009, over 12,000 doctor's degrees were awarded in health professions and related clinical sciences, more than any

other field. This is a major change. In 1970, only 518 doctoral degrees were awarded in health professions, less than 2 percent of all doctor's degrees awarded. Other popular fields for doctor's degrees in 2009 were education (13.3percent), engineering and engineering technologies (11.8 percent), and biological and biomedical sciences (10.3 percent).

Diversity Among Advanced Degree Holders

Historically, women earned fewer advanced degrees than men, but by 2008, women earned at least half of all advanced degrees. In 1970, 40 percent of master's degrees went to women, compared to 60 percent in 2009. During the same time period, women went from earning 14.3 percent of doctor's degrees to earning more than half (52.3 percent). Similarly, women earned 6.3 percent of first-professional degrees in 1970, but today earn almost half (49 percent). Overall, the number of advanced degrees earned by both men and women has increased steadily over the last few decades. The pool of advanced degree holders has also become more diverse by race and ethnicity over time. In 1990, African Americans, Hispanics, Asian Americans, and American Indians earned 10.6 percent of master's, 8.5 percent of doctor's, and 13.3 percent of first-professional degrees. By 2009, racial and ethnic minorities earned nearly a quarter (23.4 percent) of master's degrees, 16.5 percent of doctor's, and 26.5 percent of first-professional degrees. Additionally, in 2009, foreign nationals earned 12.1 percent of master's degrees, 24.9 percent of doctor's degrees, and 2.2 percent of first-professional degrees.

Advanced Degrees in the Labor Market

According to the most recent census data, 10.5 percent of the U.S. population 25 years and older hold an advanced degree. Advanced degrees prepare people for more specialized kinds of occupations that often offer higher pay. Census data also show that in general, as educational attainment increases, earnings also increase. Therefore, advanced degree holders typically earn more than workers with a bachelor's degree or less education. Among advanced degree holders, those with doctoral degrees earn more than master's degree holders. However, workers with first-professional degrees have higher median earnings than those with doctoral degrees. Additionally, people with advanced degrees are more likely to work full-time and year-round and experience lower levels of unemployment compared to people with lower levels of education. For example, in 2008, 55 percent of all U.S. workers worked full-time, year round compared to 60 percent of workers with master's degrees, 67 percent of workers with first-professional degrees, and 68 percent of workers with doctorate degrees.

Current Issues

High attrition rates and long completion times are concerns primarily for doctoral students. In engineering and many sciences, students take four to five years, on average, to complete their doctoral degrees, but in the humanities and social sciences a significant number of students can take 10 years or more to earn their degree. Furthermore, some students fail to complete their degrees even after 10 or more years, resulting in a waste of student and faculty time and effort and financial resources. The Council of Graduate Schools, which represents over 500 graduate schools in the United States and Canada, studies this issue as part of the Ph.D. Completion Project to help improve completion rates among doctoral degree students. The low representation of women (and minorities) in some fields is also a concern. Although women earn the majority of master's and doctoral degrees overall, they earn a majority of those degrees in education, health, and psychology, and earn a much smaller share of degrees in Science, Technology, Engineering, and Mathematics (STEM fields). Science and engineering fields are major forces in innovation and economic growth and the demand for highly educated workers in these fields is expected to grow. Many see increasing women's participation in these fields as a way to meet those workforce demands.

Andresse St. Rose
American Association of University Women

See Also: Gender Inequality: College Enrollment and Completion; Higher Education; Women in Math/Science.

Further Readings

Aud, S., et al. "The Condition of Education 2011." U.S. Department of Education, National Center for Education Statistics. Washington, DC: U.S. Government Printing Office, 2011.

Council of Graduate Schools. "Ph.D. Completion and Attrition: Policies and Practices to Promote Student Success." Washington, DC: U.S. Department of Education, 2010.

Snyder, T. D. and S. A. Dillow. "Digest of Education Statistics 2010." National Center for Education Statistics, Institute of Education Sciences. Washington, DC: U.S. Department of Education, 2011.

Affirmative Action

See Race-Sensitive Admission Policies/ Affirmative Action

Affluent Children

Affluent children have always garnered significant advantages in terms of exposure to educational opportunities and access to extracurricular activities. Social science research typically focuses on the relationship between poverty and individual student outcomes, overlooking the school life experiences of affluent children. Family affluence grants children access to high-quality schools in safe neighborhoods or private schooling, and affords the ability to buy academic support in the form of tutors, special lessons, and travel. Taken together, attendance in a resource-rich school, involvement in specialized activities, and exposure to diverse life experiences provide affluent children with important capital resources, developing a worldview beyond the local community.

This expanded worldview builds confidence in dealing with authority and cultivates skills in negotiating aspects of school life. Affluent children often understand formal rules as fluid, rather than rigid, negotiating boundaries more than their less affluent peers. Through this exposure to authority and as a result of their accumulated advantages, affluent children are also able to comply with and negotiate an unwritten system of rules more easily than their less affluent peers. These unwritten rules go beyond simple expectations of decorum in the classroom, to include a sense of entitlement about their grades and other accolades. Like their parents, these children expect that many aspects of schooling, from grades to leadership positions in extracurricular activities to space in gifted and talented programs, are available through negotiation, rather than through meritocratic achievement.

Structural Benefits

Affluence benefits students both structurally and socially. At the structural level, schools sort students using labels or tracking. Tracking at the high school level works in favor of affluent children, but even earlier, students coming from affluent families may be granted preferential treatment. In her research, Annette Lareau exposes how affluent parents see themselves as partners with the school in cultivating their children's intellect and talents. In their family context, these children have already learned proper behavior that appeases authority figures. Transferring this skill to the classroom early on garners positive attention and support, avoiding any potentially damaging labels. In adolescence, high schools are more likely to track affluent children into college preparatory courses. Affluent parents unhappy with their children's placement in school will challenge authority, pushing schools to reconsider their assignments. Children, in turn, learn that certain facets of school life are negotiable.

Social Benefits

At the social level, when grouped with similarly advantaged peers, affluent children develop something akin to class-consciousness about their position in the school and their future life paths. Caroline Hodges Persell and Peter Cookson, in their study of elite private school students, show that affluent children with ambitious postsecondary plans hold one another to a higher standard while developing a sense of entitlement about their future opportunities. When all students believe that they are on a path to college, this becomes a group aspiration, reinforcing individual performance and aspirations. Additionally, Maureen Hallinan's work on tracking provides support for the notion that when grouped together, the consciousness around future possibilities is internalized to such an extent that those in higher tracks become even more dedicated to their postsecondary aspirations.

Affluence implies that there is a singular class dimension related to opportunity for individual students. There is some disagreement as to whether affluence provides the same or different kinds of opportunities to students when considering race and gender more closely. Annette Lareau shows that affluent families of different race/ethnic groups cultivate opportunities for their children similarly. Mary Patillo contends that while family wealth provides better opportunities, especially at the neighborhood level, white students will maintain advantages when compared to their black middle-class counterparts. Because affluence is so strongly associated with race/ethnicity and place, less attention has been paid to stratification along gender lines. Advances in gender equity at all levels of education have created opportunities for women, regardless of affluence. While historically, family affluence is closely linked to postsecondary attendance regardless of individual achievement, students may also accumulate social and cultural capital in school. Because affluence has a legacy from generation to generation, it is difficult for poverty-stricken children to match the accomplishments and aspirations of their affluent peers.

Rachel Leventhal-Weiner
University of Connecticut

See Also: Class Inequality: Achievement; Household Educational Resources; Meritocracy; Poverty and Education; Private Schools; Wealth and Education.

Further Readings

Cookson, Peter and Caroline Persell. *Preparing for Power: America's Elite Boarding Schools.* New York: Basic Books, 1985.

Hallinan, Maureen T. "School Differences in Tracking Effects on Achievement." *Social Forces,* v.72/3 (1994).

Lareau, A. *Home Advantage: Social Class and Parental Intervention in Elementary Education.* Lanham, MD: Rowman & Littlefield, 2000.

Lareau, A. *Unequal Childhoods: Class, Race, and Family Life.* Berkeley: University of California Press, 2003.

Pattillo, Mary. "Black Middle-Class Neighborhoods." *Annual Review of Sociology,* v.31/1 (2005).

Sewell, William, Archibald Haller, and Alejandro Portes. "The Educational and Early Occupational Attainment Process." *American Sociological Review,* v.34/1 (1969).

Afghanistan

The Islamic Republic of Afghanistan is home to more than 30 million people. It is a mountainous country with a diverse population of many ethnic groups. The largest of these, Pahstuns, make up just over 40 percent of the population, followed by 27 percent Tajiks and smaller numbers of Hazara, Uzbek, Aimak, Turkmen, Baloch and others. It is equally diverse in languages with two official languages–Afghan Persian or Dari, the mother tongue of 50 percent of the population, and Pashto, the native language of 35 percent of the population. Another 11 percent of the population speaks Turkic languages and another 30 languages can be found in wide use.

History and Social Structure

In 1747, Ahmad Shah Durrani unified Pahtun tribes to create Afghanistan. During the 19th century, Afghanistan fought two wars against the British. Following the Second Afghan War, the British were forced to recognize Abdur Rahman, who had been living in exile under Russian protection, as amir in 1880. Abdur Rahman is largely recognized as the creator of the modern Afghan state and he and his grandson, King Amanullah, instituted a strong military system. The British withdrew entirely in 1919. Military spending and development continued through the end of World War II. By the 1960s, the United States also began investing in Afghanistan, particularly in transportation infrastructure, while Soviet investment focused on more visible interventions in urban areas. Following a 1973 coup d'etat, Mohammad Daoud instituted an ambitious seven year plan to propel industrial development. In 1978 the Soviet-supported People's Democratic Party of Afghanistan gained power. By 1989, the Russians withdrew and the country entered a period of civil war that led to increased power for the Taliban. Since 2001, Afghanistan has been the site of a United States and Allied Forces war.

Educational Structure

In the early 20th century, education was organized through the Madrasa, which was centered in Islamic tradition but provided an opportunity for study in writing, poetry and literature, history, and science. In 1909, the government established the first board of education to establish primary schools and a teacher-training course. Traditional education also offered vocational training in crafts, farming, and commerce. By the 1920s, Kabul boasted a number of primary and secondary schools, including a school for girls and adult education. The 1931 constitution made primary education compulsory and placed all education under the control of the state. Between 1932 and 1970, girls' enrollment in primary schools increased from 900 to 92,500 students. In 1947, resources and authority were extended to provincial education offices. By the late 1950s, primary education educated girls and boys

together. By the late 1960s, women had made substantial gains at the university level when the women's faculty at the University of Kabul were integrated into the extant facilities and departments; women also made strides in politics. International collaboration with European universities, including the University of Paris, the University of Bonn, and the University of Cologne, expanded opportunities for Afghani intellectuals in the 1970s. U.S. universities, including Columbia University and the University of Nebraska, provided assistance to the nation in developing higher education. During the 1980s, Soviet advisors encouraged the expansion of education. These gains were hindered by the rise of the Mujahadeen government in the early 1990s. In 1995 the Taliban closed all avenues to education for girls in their realm. By 1999, a United Nations Educational, Scientific and Cultural Organization (UNESCO) study found that only 4.5 percent of girls and 53 percent of boys were enrolled in school. Military conflict over the past decade has further eroded educational facilities and human capital. The oldest institution, Kabul University, founded in 1932, currently offers 14 fields of study and has a variety of international partnerships.

Current Challenges

Afghanistan's challenges in providing formal education are severe. For decades, Afghanistan has lost its most educated members to out-migration following periods of war. In the decade following the communist takeover, 6 million of a total population of 16 million Afghanis fled the country. Given the continuing military conflicts of the 21st century, access to education remains limited. In rural areas, basic school facilities are still lacking. Nongovernmental agencies and Allied military forces currently work with local leaders to prioritize educational goals. Some estimates suggest that primary enrollment rose to about 7 million students by 2010, with 37 percent female students. As of 2012, there are no reports of efforts to provide mixed-gender classrooms. The challenge is to create a national education policy and rebuild the educational system, while attending to issues of gender and access. Education is currently organized by the Ministry of Education, with substantial assistance being provided from international aid groups, including European nongovernmental organizations and the U.S. Agency for International Development (USAID).

Christi Smith
Ohio State University

See Also: Gender Ineqaulity: College Enrollment and Completion; Iran; Iraq.

Further Readings
Barfield, Thomas J. *Afghanistan: A Cultural and Political History.* Princeton, NJ: Princeton University Press, 2012.

Dupree, Nancy. "Cultural Heritage and National Identity in Afghanistan." *Third World Quarterly,* v.23/5 (2002).

Emadi, Hafizulla. "State, Modernization and Rebellion: U.S.-Soviet Politics of Domination of Afghanistan." *Economic and Political Weekly,* v.26/4 (1991).

Moghadam, Valentine. "Building Human Resources and Women's Capabilities in Afghanistan: A Retrospect and Prospects." *World Development,* v. 22/6 (1994).

Samady, Saif. "Modern Education in Afghanistan." *Prospects,* v.31/4 (December 2001).

Spink, Jeaniene. "Education and Politics in Afghanistan: the Importance of an Education System in Peacebuilding and Reconstruction." *Journal of Peace Education,* v. 2/2 (2005).

After-School Programs

After-school programs provide organized and supervised activities for school-age children. The need for after-school programs in the United States emerged because of historical changes in American education and the workforce. Evaluations of programs show that high-quality programs foster positive outcomes in participating students. Current issues with implications for the future include: funding, staff professionalism, and advocacy. After-school programs are commonly defined as structured or unstructured, supervised programs for school-age children conducted before or after school hours. Programs may extend services to other out-of-school times such as evenings, weekends, days when school is closed, school vacations, summer break, teacher institute days, or parent-teacher conference days. Programs may be located in school buildings or in other community facilities that lend themselves to the space requirements necessary for after-school programming.

Program content varies widely and may include: academic support, educational experiences, recreation and sports, life-skills development, and visual and performing arts and crafts. By federal and state statute in the United States, enrollment in after-school programs has to include all children and youth who are eligible to attend public or private schools. Reasonable accommodation must be provided for children and youth in need of special developmental and linguistic services. In other countries, after-school care might be provided through extracurricular activities, test-preparation "cram" schools, or other less-structured activities. After-school programs offer a third space to students, in addition to public spaces of schools and private spaces of homes. These programs take place in a shared social domain between families and schools and could provide different types of care, such as instruction, protection, and containment. While some programs focus on academic enrichment outcomes, others are designed to protect children and youth from harm or to contain their delinquent behaviors.

History

The emergence and growth of after-school programs in the United States was influenced by changes in the American workforce, education, and family structure. Decreasing rates of children's participation in labor, along with increasing educational expectations in the form of compulsory education reform in the late 19th century, shifted children from factories to schools. Rising rates of maternal employment in the 20th century created the need for children to be supervised during after-school hours. Risks associated with children caring for themselves, as in the "latchkey children" who wore their house keys around their necks, and unsafe environments of urban neighborhoods, fueled the demand for supervised and structured after-school programs. Research also pointed out the need for after-school programs in comparison to self-care, which was found to lead to less desirable outcomes in children's academic and social competence.

Federal policies on after-school care facilitated quality program development and implementation throughout the United States. President Nixon vetoed the Comprehensive Child Development Act of 1971, but the Child Care and Development Block Grant, now called the Child Care Development Fund (CCDF), was passed by Congress in 1990. States may choose to use funding from CCDF and Elementary and Secondary Education Act (ESEA) Title I funding for after-school care. During the Clinton administration, 21st-Century Community Learning Centers (21CCLCs) legislation was passed to support the development of after-school programs for students from high-poverty and low-performing schools. Even though funding for 21CCLCs was reduced between 2002 and 2007, the annual funding has remained around $1 billion since 2008. The overall annual funding that can be used for after-school programs, including CCDF, ESEA, and 21CCLCs, reaches over $13 billion. Furthermore, the American Recovery and Reinvestment Act of 2009 provided $4.35 billion for the Race to the Top grant over the four years for states to implement educational improvement strategies, including after-school programming.

In addition to federal funding, state and local governments appropriated funds for the development and evaluation of after-school programs. States like California and cities such as New York, Boston, and Chicago established innovative initiatives to support after-school programs in their regions. Developments in after-school program areas are also made possible by contributions from national research centers, grant-making agencies, and advocacy and training organizations such as the Harvard Family Research Project, Yale Child Study Center, Charles Stewart Mott Foundation, William T. Grant Foundation, Afterschool Alliance, and Fight Crime: Invest in Kids.

Program Evaluations

After-school programs present many advantages by providing alternative activities that can stimulate higher levels of student and family engagement and by creating opportunities for innovative approaches to learning and teaching. Outcomes of after-school programs are evaluated through academic, social, and behavioral competencies of students participating in those programs. Many studies report favorable outcomes for after-school programs as contexts of complementary learning and positive development. After-school programs and other educational enrichment experiences, such as early care and learning programs and school-community clinics, are cited for their instrumental role in increasing student retention and closing the achievement gap between students from different racial and ethnic backgrounds. Some other large-scale, meta-analytic studies found little to no effect. These seemingly contrasting findings point to the fact that quality of programming in after-school settings plays a major role in the success of the programs.

High-quality after-school programs with a strong focus on character development, academics, safety, and general well-being of the child tend to lead to the most desired outcomes. Structured programming and adult supervision were key elements of program quality. Program purpose, content, and personnel are other components of high-quality after-school programs. High-performing after-school programs offer three or more daily activity options and focus on health, wellness, and the well-being of children and youth. Programs that have clear goals and objectives, well-planned content, and qualified professional staff are essential in creating a quality after-school experience that facilitates student participation and engagement. Evaluations of various after-school programs point out the importance of program staff members in creating and sustaining a high-quality after-school program. Qualified staff provides activities and environments that are stimulating and engaging for students' learning and development.

Socioeconomic status and social class of children's parents play an important role in the use and management of children's after-school time. In her book, *Unequal Childhoods*, Annette Lareau presents different cases of children, where middle- and upper-class families engage in "concerted cultivation" through organized activities, including after-school programs, and working-class and poor families engage in "accomplishment of natural growth" through unstructured leisure activities like free play and hanging out with friends. The number of children participating in after-school programs is on the rise, from 11 percent of all K–12 students in 2004 to 15 percent in 2009. There is also an increasing trend of racial gap in the utilization of after-school programs. African American children are twice as likely as white children to participate in after-school programs. This racial difference has increased over the last decade. African American families are more likely to have single-parent households, live in poor neighborhoods, and receive subsidies for center-based care, including after-school care. Racial differences in after-school program participation may have implications for differences in students' experiences and program outcomes.

Program Funding

Funding for after-school programs continues to be a central issue for program participants, administrators, and communities. State and local investments in after-school programs face as many setbacks and challenges as they do expansions in funding. Successful funding efforts require innovation, collaboration, flexibility, and persistence. Local funding first involves relationship building, then maximizing available resources with the city or town, the county, school districts, local colleges, community foundations, organizations, and local businesses and corporations. On the other hand, funding success is usually partnered with frequent and severe federal and state budget reduction to program funding. Federal and state funding for after-school programs continue to shrink, as do foundation grants and local funds. Reduced funding support not only influences availability and quality, but also accessibility of existing programs. Lower-class and underprivileged families face the challenge of additional tuition fees and program costs.

Among the many challenges that after-school programs face, recruitment and professional development of qualified staff members rise to the top. A high level of staff turnover is often an issue for many programs. Closely tied to after-school regulation and funding, staff professional development and training should not be ignored for a high quality, high-functioning after-school program. Adequate professional development funding is essential for a program to meet licensing standards. Most states indicate a specific number of professional development hours per year required for an individual to work in an after-school program. Required training must first meet any state standard, and then prepare the staff member in particular areas of knowledge. A core body of knowledge identified by national professionals is adopted and recognized as a standard for training content. Beyond the learning aspect, professional preparation promotes professionalism and leadership in the field.

Public Policy

Informed and involved parents seek and expect to find the best available care for their children. A more informed consumer group influences the demand and supply for high-quality programs that are licensed and inspected by state agencies. Family involvement and engagement in after-school programs is an essential component of program quality. Effective communication and working relationships between parents and program staff greatly contribute to program success. After-school programs with a family-centered approach are more likely to create complementary learning environments and community partnerships. In addition to parents, advocates work to inform and educate decision makers regarding the critical components of a high-quality after-school program. Advocacy activities to promote stable, safe, and structured after-school programs focus on necessary funding. To ensure high quality in after-school programs and personnel, advocates deliver a consistent message to policymakers and legislators while building a relationship of trust. Often, the first task of advocates is to develop the awareness of the value of time spent by children and youth in high-quality after-school programs, which cultivate characteristics that promote school success, teach important life skills, and have a positive influence in society.

Likewise, an informed legislative body or regulatory council is more apt to promulgate legislation and develop regulations that raise the quality bar to meet consumer demand. Research-based evidence demonstrates that children and youth who participate in a quality after-school program are more likely to experience school success and continue in their schooling. Funders follow evidence of research-based quality programming that contributes to school success, child well-being, and productive citizenry. For example, Fight Crime: Invest in Kids has advocated and promoted child and youth involvement in organized activities between 3 P.M and 6 P.M., the after-school hours when juvenile crime and substance use is at its peak. Significant public policy issues include funding, regulations, and recruiting and retaining qualified staff members. After-school programs compete annually, often monthly, with other nonprofit organizations for funding support. Without adequate funding, it is unlikely that high-quality and affordable after-school programs can continue. Education, information, and public awareness play a pivotal role in funding success. State licensing regulation requirements for after-school programs also impact program costs. Program administration and staff must be vigilant to perpetually remain in compliance with state licensing regulations. Without sufficient funds for basic operational costs such as rent, salaries and benefits, professional development, supplies, transportation, and insurance, recruiting and retaining professional staff who are equipped to work with multiple age groups presents an ongoing challenge.

Asil Ali Özdogru
Judy Hartley
Early Care & Learning Council

See Also: Child Care; Race to the Top; Summer School; Year-Round School; Youth Friendship and Conflict in Schools.

Further Readings

Afterschool Alliance. "America After 3pm: The Most In-Depth Study of How America's Children Spend Their Afternoons." http://www.afterschoolalliance.org/AA3_Full_Report.pdf (Accessed December 2011).

Garey, Anita Ilta. "Social Domains and Concepts of Care: Protection, Instruction, and Containment in After-School Programs." *Journal of Family Issues,* v.23/6 (2002).

Hynes, Kathryn and Felicia Sanders. "Diverging Experiences During Out-of-School Time: The Race Gap in Exposure to After-School Programs." Pennsylvania State University Working Paper No. 09–06 (September 2009).

Lareau, Annette. *Unequal Childhoods: Class, Race, and Family Life.* 2nd ed. Berkeley: University of California Press, 2011.

Age Grouping of Students

The age grouping of students, that is the homogeneous grouping of students based on the single factor of age, has been a standard feature of public schools since the establishment of massive public education during the American Industrial Revolution. Prior to this period the mixed-age, or multigrade grouping of students was the de facto standard in small rural schools. However, this was not so much theoretically or empirically derived but a practical issue because of a smaller numbers of students. While many educators have advocated for other approaches to the grouping of students, the state of evidence to date provides little consensus on what is most effective and age grouping remains the norm.

The Influence of the Industrial Revolution on the Age Grouping of Students

The age grouping of students in public schools was greatly influenced by the industrial revolution and the population shifts to the urban industrial centers, the changes in the nature of work, and the interests in the science of management and the associated focus on uniformity and efficiency. Educators of this time period were influenced by the philosophy of universality; that concepts could be readily adopted from one discipline and be applicable in another. As such educators believed that the mechanization and uniformity that was used to great effect on the factory floor could be transformed for use in schools and classrooms. Nathan Bishop, the first superintendent of schools in Boston in the mid-1800s, emphasized that the same principles of efficiency and productivity found in manufacturing and business could be directly utilized in administering schools. Similarly, in the late 1800s the National Education Association emphasized the importance of, punctuality, regularity, attention, and silence as skills children should acquire for life in an industrial and commercial society.

During this time period, educators believed that a single best system was possible; a uniform educational structure that would serve the needs of all students in the community. Strict time tables with ringing bells, separate facilities for different subgroupings of students, subject matters taught largely in isolation from each other, and age grouping of students all develop from the influence of a single uniform approach to education. In this way, the age grouping of students was a natural extension of these beliefs in uniformity and a single best system. Many credit Horace Mann, the secretary of education for the state of Massachusetts in the mid-1800s with the widespread implementation of the age-grouping of students into grade levels. This system assumed a great deal of uniformity in the developmental needs of children; that children could be taught the same material uniformly and sequentially.

Within this factory model of education are assumptions about teaching and learning; where students are the passive recipients of knowledge and teachers are responsible for delivering this content. Today educators increasingly understand that this conceptualization of teaching and learning is out of step with the learning and cognitive sciences which demonstrate the importance of active engagement in learning, positive self-concept and self-efficacy, motivation, metacognition, and a host of other factors that point to a notably different conceptualization of teaching and learning than what Nathan Bishop imagined.

Trends in Non-Age Grouping of Students

While the age grouping of students has continued to be the standard by which most schools are organized, there have been a number of challenges to this approach, which have included heterogeneous, vertical, and family grouping, ungraded and nongraded classes, multigrade and looping. However it wasn't until the late 1950s when educators began criticizing the convention. Since that time, the mixed age grouping of students has been advocated by many educators who have argued that this approach is more consistent with family and neighborhood groupings. Some have argued that the mixed age grouping of students resulted in both improved academic and social outcomes.

Despite this evidence, there remains little consensus among scholars if in fact non-age grouping improves learning or social emotional outcomes and if so, specifically how and why. One related area of research does suggest that accelerating high ability learners into higher grades did have a positive impact on both students learning and social emotional development. Other scholars have questioned the likelihood of implementing such changes given the many practice and policy challenges which include, age group structured facilities, curriculum, teacher licensing and hiring policies, and textbooks, among others. Given these and other challenges, to date there has been no lasting changes to the structure and organization of schools related to the age grouping of students, and the practice remains the standard, leaving other approaches to grouping students on the periphery.

Steve Myran
Old Dominion University

See Also: Ability Grouping; Advanced and Honors Classes; Classroom Dynamics; Discipline in Education; Montessori; School Choice; School Size/Class Size.

Further Readings

Doty, Duane and William Torrey Harris. "Statement of the Theory of Education in the United States as Approved by Many Leading Educators." Washington, DC: Government Printing Office, 1874.

Gutierrez, R. and R. E. Slavin. "Achievement Effects of the Nongraded Elementary School: A Retrospective Review." http://www.search.proquest.com/docview/629 22335?accountid=12967 (Accessed September 2012).

Pratt, D. "On the Merits of Multiage Classrooms. Their Work Life." *Research in Rural Education*, v.3/3 (1986).

Sims, D. "A Strategic Response to Class Size Reduction: Combination Classes and Student Achievement in California." *Journal of Policy Analysis and Management*, v.27/3 (2008).

Steenbergen-Hu, S. and S. M. Moon. "The Effects of Acceleration on High-Ability Learners: A Meta-Analysis." *Gifted Child Quarterly*, v.55/1 (2011).

Tyack, D. *The One Best System*. Cambridge, MA: Harvard University Press, 1974.

Aggressive Behaviors in Classrooms

Aggressive behaviors in the classroom present a problem for both teaching and learning in the school context. Although less studied in comparison to issues of school-level violence, research about aggressive behaviors in the classroom describes types and patterns of aggression, characteristics of students involved in such behaviors and teacher responses, as well as long-term effects of exposure to aggression in the classroom. Scholars also note the importance of the classroom environment on aggressive behaviors and suggest ways to manage and improve such behaviors. Although aggression is defined and measured in various ways according to (multi)disciplinary perspectives, aggressive behavior in the classroom is most often grouped into two broad categories: physical and relational. Physical aggression primarily involves an assault against another student or teacher. Relational aggression refers to behaviors that threaten or damage relationships, to include friendships, group inclusion, and feelings of acceptance. Relational aggression often occurs through manipulative behaviors that result in alienation, isolation, and exclusion. With both forms of aggression, both aggressor and victim are most often of the same sex. Aggression in the classroom is more physical in the younger grades and becomes more relational as children become older.

Patterns of Aggression

The literature documents differences in patterns of aggression based on gender, race, geography, and psychological well-being. In middle and high school, boys are more likely to be both physical aggressors and victims. In contrast, female students are more commonly involved in relational aggression. The gendered nature of aggression in the classroom is thought to be connected to broader socialization processes—that is, gendered social norms control the physicality of girls' bodies and hence they engage in relational forms of aggression instead, while physical aggression signals a powerful expression of masculinity for adolescent boys and such behaviors are more prevalent among this group as a result. Also, African American students and those in urban classrooms are more likely to have been exposed to aggression in the classroom in comparison to their white peers, and those attending rural schools. In addition, racial/ethnic minority male students are most often sanctioned for aggressive behavior in the classroom. These racial/spatial trends are connected to biased sociocultural expectations that focus attention on aggressive behaviors by racial/ethnic minority students, leading to higher rates of identification. In contrast, predominantly young white girls engaged in the relational aggression "mean girls" phenomenon are not as commonly identified or sanctioned for such behaviors in the classroom. Finally, low self-esteem is a predictor of both physical and relational aggression in the classroom, for students of both sexes, and across race and geography.

Long-Term Effects

Research notes that exposure to aggressive classroom behavior usually does not cause long-term effects when the duration of the exposure is less than one year. However, even relatively less exposure may still lead to serious effects when students are also exposed to violence and aggression in other social spheres, such as in their neighborhoods and families. Long-term effects of experiencing aggression in the classroom include depression, peer rejection, social isolation, and low self-esteem for victims and aggressors alike. The primary way scholars suggest improving aggressive behaviors in the classroom is through improving the environment. The literature suggests that positive classroom environments promote positive behavior. In particular, safer and more peaceful classroom environments predict less aggressive behaviors. Classroom environments are also more predictive of positive behavior than the overall school environment. Experts suggest targeted intervention plans that focus on specific classrooms, where physical and/or relational aggression has been observed, and explicitly address problems in the environment, rather than blaming aggressive behaviors in the classroom on "problem kids."

Suggestions for effective management of classroom aggression include training teachers on identifying aggression (physical and relational) and relevant intervention techniques, promoting positive peer relationships, and involving parents. Teachers are integral in addressing aggressive behaviors in the classroom. The literature emphasizes the importance of teacher firmness, restructuring classroom management with incentive and reward systems, rather than punishment, as well as choosing curriculums that teach self-control, self-defense, and respect for others.

In terms of peer relations, research finds that when nonaggressive students help victims of aggression, it helps lower the classroom aggression levels overall. Additionally, peer observation of aggression, without attempted intervention, actually perpetuates the behaviors and emboldens the aggressor. Parents and other care-giving adults could be involved in reducing aggressive behaviors through creation and participation in mentorship programs.

Lakshmi Jayaram
Virginia Tech

See Also: At-Risk Students; Classroom Interactions Between Students; Discipline in Education; School Counseling; Violence in Schools.

Further Readings

Kuppens, S., et al. "Individual and Classroom Variables Associated With Relational Aggression in Elementary-School Aged Children: A Multilevel Analysis." *Journal of School Psychology,* v.46/6 (2008).

Mercer, Sterett H., et al. "Predicting Change in Children's Aggression and Victimization Using Classroom-Level Descriptive Norms of Aggression and Pro-Social Behavior." *Journal of School Psychology,* v.47 (2009).

Thomas, Duane E., et al. "The Impact of Classroom Aggression on the Development of Aggressive Behavior Problems in Children." *Development and Psychopathology,* v.18/2 (2009).

Thomas, Duane E., et al. "The Influence of Classroom Aggression and Classroom Climate on Aggressive–Disruptive Behavior." *Child Development,* v.82/3 (2011).

Young, Ellie L., et al. "Relational Aggression Among Students." *Education Digest,* v.76/7 (2011).

Agricultural Education

Agricultural education was primarily a rural phenomenon in America. Since the formation of the Land Grant University System in 1862, agricultural education has served to increase the agricultural output of farmers while improving the lives of rural people and building rural communities. Agricultural education broadly includes education in (for purpose of career preparation) and education about (for the purpose of agricultural awareness or literacy) agriculture, food, and natural resources, as well as a multitude of subtopics related to families and communities. Agricultural education typically occurs within three different settings: postsecondary institutions, the Cooperative Extension Service, and schools. Formal, organized agricultural education in the United States was federally funded with the passage of the Morrill Land-Grant Act of 1862. Each state was endowed 30,000 acres to provide education for the common person that focused on agricultural, engineering, and military sciences. The purpose of the Land-Grant Institutions was later expanded with the implementation of the Hatch Act of 1887, which established agricultural experimental stations; and the Smith-Lever Extension Act of 1914, which established a service component with the Cooperative Extension Service. The number of Land-Grant Institutions was later expanded in 1890 to include historically black colleges and universities in the segregated south, and again in 1994 for 31 tribal colleges. Agriculture is also taught at many four-year and two-year institutions outside of the Land-Grant Institutions. The mission of Land-Grant Institutions has evolved over the last 150 years. Agricultural research is arguably the centerpiece of Land-Grant Institutions, while the goal of diffusing agricultural knowledge and providing accessible agricultural education to the public has shifted to extension and other postsecondary agricultural institutions. The philosophy of agricultural practices within Land-Grant Institutions has also transformed over the century. Environmentalism and sustainability have emerged as important ideas that either guide or conflict with the original purpose to increase the agricultural output of farmers.

Cooperative Extension Service

The Cooperative Extension Service is the outreach component for the Land-Grant System. The Cooperative Extension Service is controlled by the U.S. Department of Agriculture and National Institute of Food and Agriculture, managed by the Land-Grant Institution of each state, and facilitated at a local level such as a county. The Cooperative Extension Service was formalized with the passage of the Smith-Lever Extension Act of 1914, with the intent to disseminate the latest research. The initial focus of the Cooperative Extension Service was to improve rural lives, agricultural practices, and rural communities. The subsequent decline of rural population and farmers after World War II has meant that the Cooperative

Extension Service has increasingly worked in urban and suburban counties. The purpose of the Cooperative Extension Service's programs is to improve local communities through educational programs that reach out to youth and adults. The programs vary from county to county, based on the local context. The programs of extension can be broadly conceptualized in the following categories: agriculture and environmental education, 4-H organization, community and economic development, and family services. The 4-H organization is the largest youth development group in America with over six million youth members.

The number of school-based agricultural education programs grew dramatically during the early 1900s. The movement to include agriculture in schools was spurred first by the Country Life Movement, and was later formalized with the passage of the Smith-Hughes Vocational Education Act of 1917. The Country Life Movement advocated for agriculture as a course of instruction that would improve labor and livelihood, and by 1917, there were over 3,000 school-based agriculture programs. The Smith-Hughes Act formalized federal funding for school-based agricultural education, but limited instruction to vocational topics. Subsequent legislation and social movements have attempted to shift school-based agricultural education away from the vocational agriculture focus, yet the legacy of vocational agriculture remains today.

A majority of school-based agricultural education programs are currently considered part of a larger umbrella of career and technical education programs. Agricultural education programs that operate without federal support are rare. Most school-based programs are for high school students, but the number of middle school (5th–8th graders) programs has been growing steadily. School-based agriculture programs have three components: classroom instruction, supervised agricultural experiences (SAEs), and the National FFA Organization (FFA). Classroom instruction includes all instructional activities during the normal school day. SAEs are individualized student projects based on agricultural careers that occur primarily outside the class. The projects can be a student owning an entrepreneurial enterprise (i.e., production of livestock or crops), a student working as a regular business employee, or a student conducting an agri-science research project. Students are encouraged to start SAE projects during their freshman year and continue the projects through graduation and into their careers. The FFA is the student organization for agricultural education. The FFA is not extracurricular, but rather intracurricular, and teachers apply what is taught in the classroom with activities that build students, schools, and communities through conferences, conventions, and award programs. FFA membership has been steady, at 500,000 members for the past decade.

Michael J. Martin
University of Missouri

See Also: Career and Technical Education; Occupational Aspirations/Expectations; Rural Schooling.

Further Readings
Association of Public and Land-Grant Universities. http://www.aplu.org (Accessed August 2012).

McDowell, G. R. *Land-Grant Universities and Extension into the 21st Century.* Ames: Iowa University Press, 2001.

Phipps, L. J., E. W. Osborne, J. E. Dyer, and A. Ball. *Handbook on Agricultural Education in Public Schools.* Clifton Park, NY: Thomson Delmar Learning, 2008.

Alabama

Alabama is a southern state in the United States, bordered on the north by Tennessee, on the east by Georgia, on the west by Mississippi, and to the south by Florida. Part of Alabama also touches the Gulf of Mexico to form the Gulf Coast. Its capital city is Montgomery, its largest city is Birmingham, and its oldest city is Mobile, which was founded by French colonists. Although states to the west were more directly impacted, Alabama received damage from the 2005 landfall of Hurricane Katrina, particularly in the Mobile Bay area. Dauphin Island received the majority of the damage. Following the explosion of the British Petroleum (BP) Deepwater Horizon oil well, the subsequent spill impacted the Gulf Coast beaches of Alabama. The state is also prone to tornados. The most recent outbreak, over the course of three days in April 2011, left especially catastrophic damage across the state. More than 230 people were killed in Alabama alone over the course of the three-day outbreak. The damage was particularly devastating in Tuscaloosa, home of the University of Alabama. Although predominantly agricultural in its economic activity, Alabama has become one of the nation's top

automotive manufacturers and steel producers. The state also houses the George C. Marshall Space Flight Center, the space shuttle propulsion center for the National Aeronautics Space Association (NASA), and Space Camp in Huntsville.

History of Public Education
Prior to statehood, there was little movement to establish schools. When the state joined the Union in 1819 as the 22nd state, Alabama was required to adhere to the Southwest Ordinance of 1790, which mandated the provision of public education throughout the state. Like other states, Alabama's earliest paths to education were available only to those who could afford private tuition. Male children of the elite were provided private schools and tutoring. Because Alabama relied on a primarily agricultural-based economy, the need for an educated populace was limited. The Reconstruction period brought a brief emphasis on progressive education, but was quickly replaced by a period of low support and funding.

In 1881, the state established the Tuskegee Institute to train black teachers. The first superintendent of the school was Booker T. Washington, and today, the school remains one of the most celebrated historically black colleges in the United States. Alabama's history

Table 1 Elementary and secondary education characteristics

	Alabama	U.S. (average)
Total number of schools	1,615	1,988
Total students	755,552	970,278
Total teachers	49,363.24	60,766.56
Pupil/teacher ratio	15.31	15.97

Source: U.S. Department of Education, National Center for Education Statistics, Common Core of Data (CCD), 2010–11.

Table 2 Elementary and secondary education finance

	Alabama	U.S. (average)
Total revenues	$7,693,742,227	$11,464,385,994
Total expenditures for education	$7,908,315,848	$11,712,033,839
Total current expenditures	$6,832,439,210	$9,938,906,259

Source: U.S. Department of Education, National Center for Education Statistics, Common Core of Data (CCD), "National Public Education Financial Survey," FY08 (2007–08).

is very similar to that of the surrounding southern states. Education can be characterized by a lack of funding and attendance, and a complete disregard for ensuring equitable opportunities for both black and white students. The state passed a state sales tax to help fund education in 1937, one of the first state initiatives toward the establishment of a system of public education. Inequity in school facilities ensued, largely by racial and economic lines.

Desegregation

Alabama was often at the center of the struggle for civil rights. Perhaps most famous was the December 1, 1955, event when Rosa Parks refused to comply with an order to give up her seat on a Montgomery, Alabama, bus to a white man. This action resulted in her arrest and led to the 381-day boycott of Montgomery city buses. The boycott was organized by the newly formed Montgomery Improvement Association (MIA), led by a young pastor named Dr. Martin Luther King Jr. In 1965, hundreds of demonstrators marched from Selma to Montgomery, but were attacked as they crossed the Edmund Pettus Bridge, which was broadcast nationally. Two weeks later, King led 3,200 marchers successfully to the capital. Months later, President Lyndon Johnson signed into law the Voting Rights Act. While much of the events surrounding the boycott were peaceful, violence characterized much of the struggle for civil rights.

Resistance proposed by state leaders often led to riots and bombings of black churches, killing young children. Alabama state leaders, including Governor George Wallace, vehemently opposed the desegregation of schools and universities within the state. He blocked the entrance to the schools until he was forced aside by the Alabama National Guard and intervention by federal courts. Wallace did, however, initiate a junior college system throughout the state. While Wallace strongly opposed desegregation, nearly a decade after the blockades, a failed assassination attempt on his life led Wallace to reevaluate his position on race relations. He later repudiated racism and led the effort to heal his state's wounds.

Statistics

Alabama has 67 countywide and 65 citywide school districts, containing 1,523 public schools, servicing 749,084 students in the 2010–11 school year. A total of 58 percent of the student population are white, while 34.5 percent are African American, and 4.5 percent are Hispanic. The chief state school officer is the state superintendent of education, appointed by the nine-member State Board of Education. All members are elected by the populace. The governor of Alabama, by virtue of the elected position, serves as a voting member and president of the board. Alabama is one of three states that holds elections for local countywide school district superintendents. Alabama is home to 14 two- and four-year public universities, and 17 private universities. In 2011, the state of Alabama passed a strict immigration bill, causing many Hispanic residents to flee the state. The bill originally contained language preventing illegal immigrants from attending school, but that component was removed from the legislation. Today, the state still struggles with racial equality and opportunity for its students. Student achievement and accountability remain at the forefront of discussions. Similar to the challenges in other states, Alabama students perform with high levels of proficiency on state-mandated exams, but achieve at much lower levels on national exams.

Belinda M. Cambre
University of New Orleans

See Also: *Brown v. Board of Education;* No Child Left Behind; Racial Inequality: Achievement; Racism in Education.

Further Readings

Culpepper Clark, E. *The Schoolhouse Door: Segregation's Last Stand at the University of Alabama.* New York: Oxford University Press, 1995.

Jackson, Harvey. *Inside Alabama: A Personal History of My State.* Tuscaloosa: University of Alabama Press, 2004.

Sheckler Finch, Jackie. *It Happened in Alabama.* Guilford, CT: Globe Pequot Press, 2011.

Alaska

Alaska is the largest state in the United States, with an area of 663,268 square miles (1,717,854 square kilometers), located in the northwest extremity of the North American continent, with Canada to the east, the Arctic Ocean to the north, and the Pacific Ocean to the west and south. The state nickname is "The Last Frontier" and the state motto is "North to the Future." The capital of Alaska is Juneau, and the largest city is Anchorage. The highest point in Alaska is Mount McKinley in Denali National Park, at 20,320 feet (6194 meters). According to the 2010 U.S. Census, Alaska has a population of 710,231, of whom approximately half live within the Anchorage metropolitan area. Alaska is the 47th state by population and is the least densely populated state of the United States. Between 2000 and 2010, the population of Alaska increased by 13.3 percent, according to the U.S. Census. Alaska has an unemployment rate of 8.5 percent and is the sixth-wealthiest state in per capita income. Purchased from Russia in 1867, Alaska has been shaped by its native population, Russian settlers, and the American government.

History and Social Structure

Numerous indigenous people occupied Alaska for thousands of years prior to the arrival of Europeans. While these native societies still exist today, they were greatly affected by Russian colonization, starting in the 17th century. Prior to the arrival of the Russians, it is believed that education among the native population was centered around survival, with storytelling acting as a way to pass on historical lessons. In 1741, Vitus Bering led an expedition for the Russian Navy into Alaska and returned to Russia with sea otter pelts. This began the influx of Russian settlers and fur traders into Alaska, beginning with the Aleutian Islands. Under the Russians, Russian America, as Alaska was called, became a fur-trading mecca. Prior to being purchased by the United States, formal education efforts came primarily from the Russian Orthodox Church and Russian American Company. These institutions provided schools for Alaska native people in Kodiak, Southeast Alaska, and the Aleutian Islands. Literacy programs thrived, especially in the Aleutians, where many people became proficient readers and writers in both the Russian and Aleut languages. Alaska was purchased by the United States from Russia in 1867 for $7.2 million.

Alaska was loosely governed by the military initially, and starting in 1884, was administered as a district with a governor and district court. That same year, the first official federal legislations impacting Alaska, the Organic Act, was passed. This act established civil government in Alaska and provided the legal basis for the federal provision of education. The act delegated responsibility for providing education for children of all races to the government, and

Table 1 Elementary and secondary education characteristics

	Alaska	U.S. (average)
Total number of schools	518	1,988
Total students	132,104	970,278
Total teachers	8,170.64	60,766.56
Pupil/teacher ratio	16.17	15.97

Source: U.S. Department of Education, National Center for Education Statistics, Common Core of Data (CCD), 2010–11.

Table 2 Elementary and secondary education finance

	Alaska	U.S. (average)
Total revenues	$2,289,218,808	$11,464,385,994
Total expenditures for education	$2,274,715,347	$11,712,033,839
Total current expenditures	$1,918,374,844	$9,938,906,259

Source: U.S. Department of Education, National Center for Education Statistics, Common Core of Data (CCD), "National Public Education Financial Survey," FY08 (2007–08).

four years later, specifically to the Bureau of Education. The federal government established day schools in villages and a limited number of vocational state boarding schools in the late 1800s. Instruction consisted of reading, writing, math, industrial skills, and patriotic citizenship, with an English-only policy governing all language and curriculum decisions. By the early 1900s, the number of non-native people coming into Alaska territory had increased steadily because of the discovery of gold and commercial fishing and timber industries. The Bureau of Education was not able to provide adequate schooling for all the new students, and the U.S. Congress granted authority to individual communities in Alaska to incorporate and establish schools, allowing them to maintain the schools through taxation.

In 1905, Congress passed the Nelson Act that provided for establishment of schools, with the governor of the Alaska territory acting as the ex-officio superintendent, but only white children and children of mixed blood were allowed to attend. The Nelson Act ushered in the dual system of education in Alaska, where schools for Alaska native students were run by the Bureau of Education, and schools for white students and a limited number of civilized native students were operated by the Alaska territory and towns. By 1931, the Bureau of Education had assumed responsibility for not only the education, but also the social welfare of most rural native people. Its services included education, as well medical services, the Reindeer Service (an effort to bolster the economy for Alaska natives by introducing reindeer herding), cooperative stores, an orphanage, and three industrial schools. The belief behind the Bureau of Education was that it was important to transform Alaska natives into civilized and Christian Americans, using education as the mechanism for achieving this assimilation.

In 1936, Congress passed the Alaska Reorganization Act, which authorized the creation of village governments and constitutions. Today, there are 227 federally recognized tribal governments in Alaska, but it was not until 2000 that the governor of Alaska signed an order directing state agencies and officials to recognize and respect these entities. From 1936 to 1954, 46 federally operated rural schools were transferred to the territory, but by 1954, the momentum for bringing the two school systems together had ceased. Throughout the 1950s, the majority of Alaska native students attended elementary school in rural villages where there was only one school and the only options open to students who wished to attend high school were the distant Bureau of Indian Affairs high schools or church-affiliated boarding schools. During the 1960s and 1970s, government efforts were aimed at providing equal opportunities to fight the war on poverty. Education was identified as both the cause and cure for inequality, and Headstart and Community Action Programs were instituted in villages across Alaska. During this time, oil was discovered in Alaska, which led to the passage of the Alaska Native Claims Settlement Act, providing the native population title to over 40 million acres of land and $962.5 million in compensation for lands ceded to the federal government.

Changing Education in Alaska

In 1976, the state of Alaska settled the Molly Hootch case by establishing high schools in every community where there was an elementary school, ensuring that students who graduated the eighth grade could continue their high school education while remaining in their homes. Finally, in the 1980s, the dual system of education was closed, with the state of Alaska controlling all of the schools. Since then, the focus of education in rural Alaska has shifted from equal education for all to ensuring that while Alaska native students have the same life opportunities as other students,

they are also taught in their native languages, incorporating traditional knowledge in the school curriculum. Today, the Alaska Department of Education and Early Development administers 53 school districts containing 508 public schools, 27 charter schools, and 27 correspondence schools, with a total student population of 129,999. Challenges to education in Alaska today revolve around a highly decentralized system of schools and districts, as well as severe teacher shortages and decreasing numbers of Alaska native teachers in rural areas. Native sponsored initiatives, such as a comprehensive set of cultural standards and relevant and tested curriculum resources that build upon Alaska native ways of knowing, can help define education for the coming years.

Dana Ruggiero
Purdue University

See Also: Elementary Education; Hawai'i; Native American Students.

Further Readings

Alaskool.org. "History of Alaska Native Education and Education Today." http://www.alaskool.org/native_ed/native_ed_intro.htm (Accessed December 2011).

Barnhardt, C. "A History of Schooling for Alaska Native People." *Journal of American Indian Education,* v.40/1 (2001).

State of Alaska. "State of Alaska Report Card to the Public 2010." http://www.eed.state.ak.us/report card/2009-2010/reportcard2009-10.pdf (Accessed December 2011).

Algeria

Algeria is the largest country in Africa, covering an area of 926,645 square miles (2,400,000 square kilometers) and is bordered on land by Tunisia, Libya, Niger, Mali, Mauritania, western Sahara, and Morocco. Its northern coastline on the Mediterranean Sea stretches 620 miles (998 kilometers) and it is protected from the expanding Sahara Desert in the south by the Atlas Mountains. The World Bank estimates the population at 35,468,208, and 99 percent of the population is of Arab-Berber descent (the remaining percent is European in origin). From its oil and natural gas revenues, its primary exports, Algeria has been able to build significant foreign exchange reserve, about $173 billion. In early 2011, inflation was 5.7 percent, and roughly 20 percent of its population lived below the poverty line. A former colony of France, Algeria achieved independence in 1962. Although French is still used widely throughout Algeria, the official national language is Arabic, and almost all business is conducted in Arabic. The Berber dialects are also recognized by the government and are used by various populations within the nation.

History and Social Structure

The foundations of the current education system in Algeria come from the French system during the French colonization from 1862 to 1962. Originally designed to educate Europeans and to continue the French cultural pattern, the great majority of students in school during colonization were the children of the colonists. For Algerian students who did make it to school, French was the language of instruction, and Arabic, if taught, was optional. In 1949, school segregation ended, and to increase Algerian enrollments in school, the 1954 Constantine Plan was implemented. However, the Eurocentric curriculum remained taught exclusively in French, and less than a third of Algerian children were enrolled in primary school, while only 30 percent and 10 percent of the students at the secondary and university levels, respectively, were Algerian. After independence, the first changes to be implemented were to make the Arabic language as the medium of instruction and to include the addition of religion to the curriculum. In 1992, English was introduced as a foreign language alongside French, and in 2003, Berber-language instruction began.

Educational Structure

The efficacy of the French colonial government is still pervasive. In 1971, a compulsory period of nine years of primary education was introduced. In 1976, all private schools were abolished; they were reinstated in 2004. The majority of schools in Algeria remain public, however, the educational system is operated jointly under the Ministry of Education and the Ministry of Religious Affairs. Islam is a required part of the curriculum. In 2011, 4.3 percent of gross domestic product (GDP) was allotted to education. Secondary education is compulsory, and lasts for three years. There are three branches of secondary education: general, specialized, and technical/vocational.

Students in general secondary and specialized secondary education study for three years and sit for the baccalaureate exam. Successful students are awarded the Baccalauréat de l'Enseignement secondaire, which grants access to higher education. Students must take a general exam in every subject studied, and earn a combined average of at least 50 percent to pass.

While failure is high, about one in three students succeeds, the rest go on to a second examination round, where only 5 to 10 percent succeed. In total, less than half of those completing secondary school manage to obtain their baccalaureate. The technical and vocational secondary branch prepares students for industry and other technical occupations. Technical/vocational studies average between one and four years, and give students the mobility to access to higher education. Universities, specialized institutes, national institutes of higher education, and teacher training institutes, which fall under the responsibility of the Ministry of Higher Education and Scientific Research, as well as by institutes run by other ministries, provide higher education opportunities. There are upwards of 140 such institutions of higher education in Algeria, including 47 universities and university centers. These numbers continue to grow as higher education expands. Universities in Algeria have been reformed to reflect more American and European academic standards: three- to four-year bachelor's degree programs and two years for a master's degree.

Current Issues

The literacy rate in Algeria is 69.9 percent, with the literacy rate among women 20 percent lower than that of men. The high rate of illiteracy is one of the many difficulties facing education in Algeria; one in three Algerian adults cannot read or write. As such the government actively promotes adult literacy classes. This rate is high because of the dropout and truancy rates among children. Despite the fact that schooling is free and compulsory, roughly 9 percent of school-age girls and 3 percent of school-age boys do not attend primary school. More than half of the secondary school population drop out before graduation. The Algerian government has stressed teacher education, but the lack of qualified teachers, coupled with growth in the number of school children, has stifled educational developmental goals. Additionally, the gender equity gap remains in Algerian educational structures. In the face of the Arab Spring, the Algerian government responded with political action, and lifted state of emergency restrictions and the state's monopoly on the media. Many smaller protests continue, built mainly on socioeconomic disparities. It remains to be seen if future actions will occur to pressure the government to continue to reform and develop education within the country.

Landis Fryer
Loyola University Chicago

See Also: Libya; Morocco; Nigeria.

Further Readings
Evans, M., and J. Phillips. *Algeria: Anger of the Dispossessed.* New Haven, CT: Yale University Press, 2007.

McDougall, J., ed. *Nation, Society and Culture in North Africa.* London: Frank Cass Publishers, 2003.

Metz, H. C., ed. *Algeria: A Country Study.* Washington, DC: GPO for the Library of Congress, 1994.

Roberts, H. *Battlefield Algeria 1988–2002: Studies in a Broken Polity.* London: Verso, 2002.

Stora, B. *Algeria, 1830–2000: A Short History.* Ithaca, NY: Cornell University Press, 2001.

Alternative and Second Chance Education

Although alternative education and second chance education are frequently collapsed into one category, they are different in a number of significant ways and could rightly be separated into two distinct categories. Alternative education is defined by nontraditional approaches to learning and teaching that are seen to enrich the experiences of students. It is frequently based on philosophical, political, and psychological theories and/or practices about the role of education in society, the development of democratic citizens, and/or the creation of rich and developmentally appropriate contexts for learning. Second chance education is typically defined by the type of participant: usually young people who have been pushed out of mainstream schooling or who have otherwise disengaged from schools. It is offered as a pathway for completing a high school equivalency program or diploma and is becoming increasingly common in the current neoliberal climate of accountability and testing. While alternative and second chance education frequently share at least two common characteristics—smaller classroom and school size in relation to mainstream schools, and flexibility with respect to how each student moves through curricular pathways—the contrast between them is instructive. For example, they often differ in relation to the purpose of education, student and teacher demographics, curricula and assessment, preparation for postsecondary school, funding and governance structure, and history.

The lack of clear definitions, documentation, and variability across types of schools makes research difficult. Differences in school systems in the United States, England, Canada, and Australia also compound research dilemmas. Regardless of these difficulties, research is urgently needed to examine issues including: the way "school choice" plays out when limited options, transportation, and referral are taken into account; the reasons why students stay enrolled or leave and where they go; the nature of student-teacher relationships; effectiveness in learning and teaching and accountability measures; the effects of potential privilege or stigma resulting from attendance; and innovative practices that may be informative for mainstream schools. In the best situation, alternative education has functioned as an educational laboratory that produces unique, pioneering, and groundbreaking approaches to education. In the worst situation, alternative and second chance education contributes to social tracking and inequity.

Rationale for Alternatives to Mainstream Schooling
A commonly accepted rationale for alternative education is that it enables educators to adapt an educational approach—including curricula, pedagogy, and assessment—to meet the needs of individual students in ways that typically cannot be met in mainstream schooling. Usually, there are philosophical, political, and psychological theories and practices that provide a comprehensive foundation for alternative educational approaches. The history of providing alternatives to mainstream schooling began alongside the development of schooling as an institution. As mainstream schooling increased its mass and compulsory reach, alternative and second chance schools evolved. The rapid growth of alternative education in the United States was in the 1950s–1980s, while the growth of schools for second chance education has been increasing more recently in relation to the neoliberal policy context.

At the turn of the 20th century, with the pressures of industrialization and urbanization, alternative philosophies of education surfaced in many countries as mass and compulsory education was increasingly seen as a method for addressing immigration and developing the labor force in England, the United States, Canada, and European countries. By the second decade, Summerhill School was established in England by Alexander S. Neill, Waldorf education was established in Germany by Rudolf Steiner, and Maria Montessori's methods were already being imported from Italy to the United States. The Reggio Emilia approach was also established after World War II in Italy. Though each of these educational approaches differs, they have in common a commitment to addressing the needs and interests of each child while providing rich and engaging learning environments. In addition, the appeal of alternatives to mainstream schooling was fueled, in part, by the Progressive education movement in the United States, with its focus on engaging students in democratic practices during schooling, rather than delaying participation in a democratic environment until after school and by building diverse curricula from students' current interests while maintaining a commitment to educative experiences, or meaningful and authentic experiences with long-term effects.

During the 1960s and 1970s, in the United States, two movements with different philosophical and political roots led to the development of many nontraditional schools. The Freedom Schools Movement, a nationwide effort, was aimed at expanding access to education and working toward desegregation after the Supreme Court ruled against "separate but equal" segregation in the 1954 case of *Brown v. Board of Education.* Educators in these schools were committed to increasing access to education and reducing the effects of oppression and discrimination on the basis of race. A second movement, called the Free Schools Movement, was aimed at reducing the institutional effects of socialization through the process of schooling and enabling children and youth to develop in less structured and restrictive environments. Educators and students in Free Schools worked together to design learning contexts, curricula, and experiences quite divergent from the structured, age-grouped classrooms in mainstream schools.

Global View

By the 1980s, alternative education was touted as a strategy for school reform at the same time that neoliberal reforms in England, the United States, Canada, and Australia were moving toward marketizing education by increasing privatization, competition, accountability for teachers, and standardized testing for students. Under the Thatcher administration, neoliberal policies gave rise to a national curriculum and increased parent choice while reducing the power of the local education authorities and teachers. These policies also opened the door for increased competition for spaces in schools and threatened undersubscribed schools with closure. In the United States, policies developed in response to *A Nation at Risk* (1983) had similar effects that have been exacerbated by the threat of reduced funding in the No Child Left Behind Act (2001). In Canada, the Progressive Conservative Party led a Common Sense Revolution (1995–2003) to reduce government spending on social welfare initiatives like education and health and increase accountability. In education, this led to the public ranking of schools and, ultimately, to a type of social class streaming between schools. In Australia, where the school leaving age is 16, there has been a decline in a social service view of education since the 1990s. In addition, the creation of Technical and Further Education (TAFE) colleges, originally designed to provide an alternative to mainstream schooling, shifted to providing industry-related skills in response to industry-defined needs and purposes for education.

Often, these "standards based" reforms are linked with educational policies with little, if any, additional funding. Holding teachers accountable through student testing has limited the scope of teaching and reduced perspectives of learning and education. Federal policies that link testing outcomes to job stability and funding, or high stakes testing, have increased the number of student push outs and dropouts, rather than increasing graduation rates. Though the stated intention of neoliberal policies in education is supplying efficient and skilled workers for the workforce, policies that do not consider the social, economic, and material conditions of students and their parents often fail to meet this aim.

The current neoliberal policy context—with its reductionist approach to learning, teaching, and the purposes of education—appears to necessitate second chance education in order to ensure that citizens have minimum education credentials. School completion credentials are associated with successful participation in a knowledge-based economy, and dropping out of school has been associated with high costs at both the individual and social levels. At an individual level, dropping out of school has been associated with low literacy and skills, as well as difficulty in finding a job and/or a high quality job, tendency to earn lower incomes, and increased likelihood of short-term and part-time employment that is less secure. At a societal level, the costs of early school leaving have been linked to higher incidence of alcohol abuse, illegal drug abuse, negative health outcomes, higher health care budget expenditure, higher death rates, criminal behavior, and more people on social assistance. In addition, however, dropping out and school failure, especially in the United States, are often decontextualized, without an examination of the social conditions associated with school leaving.

Characteristics of Effective Alternative and Second Chance Schools

Often, alternative education looks different in different places because it reflects the interests of the students in a particular site, student-teacher relationships, and financial and community resources, as well as grounding philosophical, political, and psychological theories and practices. The most common characteristics of alternative schools include: small class sizes, an emphasis on student-teacher relationships, diverse and personalized curricula and assessment, and flexible scheduling, including blocked classes, extended-day programs, and weekend and year-round learning. In addition, effective alternative schools that maintained student engagement through to high school completion and in many cases provided students with the skills to continue their education beyond their compulsory school years in Canada, Australia, and the United States include some of the following characteristics: cultural sensitivity, especially in dealing with race/ethnicity issues and issues around Aboriginality; extensive use of computers and related technology; career oriented goals and opportunities for employment; clear codes of conduct; intensive support services, including health care and childcare; and multiple options for earning credentials, like portfolios and work-life experience credits. These are also frequent characteristics of second chance schools.

Criteria for Admission: Choice, Access, or Requirement

Many alternative educational programs in both the United States and Canada, even those identified as schools of choice, specify admission criteria for students accessing these programs. Although enrollment is open, such that students can attend school across catchment boundaries, some schools use previous grades, the availability of transportation, parental knowledge, and parental income as factors in determining who has access and is enrolled. Some schools also use waiting lists and lotteries, in particular when the numbers of students who wish to attend far exceeds the total number of new students who can be admitted. While second chance education emphasizes dropout prevention and the re-engagement of students in the process of schooling, participation may or may not be voluntary for students. While some students who leave school early return to schooling of their own accord, others may be required to attend school in alternative settings. In this situation, their participation cannot be considered a choice. The most common criteria for required admission is the labeling of a student as at risk of dropping out of school for a variety of reasons, such as: truancy, physical abuse, substance abuse or possession, poverty, minority status, homelessness, pregnant or parenting, and academic failure. Admission as a consequence of suspension or expulsion may also be a reason for referral to second chance programs.

General Typology: Alternative Schools and Programs

There are five general types of schools or programs that are alternatives to mainstream schools. Magnet and Charter Schools and Alternative Programs tend to be part of the public school system. Independent and Private Schools tend to exist outside of the public school system. The location of schools inside the public school system tends to limit how different an alternative school can be. Outside of the public school system, alternative schools typically have fewer restrictions. Magnet schools are public schools and are administered through the public school system. Students attend magnet schools by choice because they offer specialized curricula—for example, with a math and science or performing arts focus—and enrollment is open to attract students across catchment boundaries. In the United States, magnet schools were, in part, a response to desegregation in the late 1960s and early 1970s, although busing and transportation issues have complicated attendance in practice. Charter schools are also public schools and are typically administered through the public school system, but have a charter that releases them from some of the rules, regulations, and policies that apply to other public schools. Charter approval requires an alternative form of accountability; as an autonomous public school, charter schools are still accountable for student achievement. Students attend charter schools by choice, often because of a specialized philosophical, pedagogical, or curricular approach.

Some public schools offer alternative programs as alternatives to dropping out, for example programs for pregnant or parenting teens, while others require enrollment in alternative programs as an alternative to disciplinary measures or suspension. In the first situation, student choice may or may not accurately describe the enrollment of students; and in the second, enrollment is not a choice. Independent schools are independent from the public school system in terms of finances and governance: They rely on funding from tuition fees and donations, and are governed by a board of directors. Independent school status enables the board to make decisions about curricula, pedagogy, and assessment. Private schools with religious affiliation are sometimes collapsed with independent schools, although their funding and governance may be linked with a larger religious organization. In this case, the larger religious organization maintains some, if not all, of the control over funding and governance.

Gathering information on the number of alternative and second chance schools and students served is complicated by the diversity of definitions and inconsistent style of reporting. In general, in 2009–10, there were approximately 98,800 public elementary and secondary schools in operation, of which approximately 11,000 to 19,000 were public alternatives. At the same time, approximately 28,000 private schools were in operation. Participation in alternative education in the United States is increasing in both public alternative schools and private schools. From 1993 to 2007, the percentage of children attending a public school that was not their assigned school, and hence a school of choice, increased from 11 to 16 percent. The percentage of children attending a private school also increased from 8 to 9 percent for a private religious school and 2 to 3 percent for a private secular school, according to the U.S. Department of Education.

Critiques

There are a number of critiques of alternative and second chance education. First, the ideal of offering alternatives to mainstream schooling as a strategy for school reform has not materialized. The financial resources required for tuition and fees often limit access to independent and private alternatives and access to public alternatives is reduced by transportation and oversubscription. Second, some programs are specifically designed as punitive for students who exhibit disciplinary or social challenges. Oftentimes, students that are referred to alternative programs as a consequence for their disruptive behaviors face widely differing definitions of failure to comply with rules. As a result, students in second chance schools disproportionately represent students who are male, members of minority groups, and students who live in poverty. Third, some programs are cited as providing inferior education, poor academic preparation, and not allowing students to meet the skill levels required for advanced educational institutions. Fourth, questions around the assessment and evaluation of programs often return to the discussion of how to assess learning. Alternative schools attached to the public school system, where funding is regulated through prescribed student assessments, may be evaluated in ways that do not reflect their objectives. As alternative schools try to comply with standards of evaluation, they face pressures to modify their programs in ways that are more rigid and less beneficial to their students. Finally, participation in alternative and second chance education, when it is voluntary, is sometimes seen as a way to segregate students who are different and, therefore, a way to misdirect and ignore problems created by public schooling, rather than reforming public school education in ways that make it socially just and equitable.

Renira E. Vellos
Jennifer A. Vadeboncoeur
University of British Columbia

See Also: At-Risk Students; Charter Schools; Class Inequality: High School Dropout Rates; Dropouts; Magnet Schools; Montessori; Private Schools; Racial Inequality: High School Dropout Rates; Reggio Emilia Approach.

Further Readings

Farrell, Joseph P. "Education in the Years to Come: What We Can Learn From Alternative Education." In *Changing Education: Leadership, Innovation and Development in a Globalizing Asia Pacific*, P. D. Hershock, M. Mason, and J. N. Hawkins, eds. Hong Kong: Springer, 2008.
Kelly, Deirdre. *Last Chance High: How Girls and Boys Drop In and Out of Alternative Schools.* New Haven, CT: Yale University Press, 1993.

Lehr, Camilla A., E. J. Lanners, and Cheryl M. Lange. "Alternative Schools: Policy and Legislation Across the United States." Alternative Schools Research Project, Institute on Community Integration (UCEDD). University of Minnesota, 2003.

National Center for Education Statistics. "Digest of Education Statistics: 2010." http://www.nces.ed.gov/programs/digest/d10 (Accessed December 2011).

Raywid, Mary Anne. "Alternative Schools: The State of the Art." *Educational Leadership,* v.52/1 (1994).

U.S. Department of Education. "The Condition of Education, 2009: Indicator 32, Parental Choice of School." Washington, DC: National Center for Education Statistics, Institute of Education Sciences, 2009.

American Samoa

Samoan socialization practices continue to be fertile ground for social scientific theorizing about the role of schooling in society. American Samoan schools are in a unique position between the goals of American educational systems and traditional cultural knowledge. American Samoa comprises a group of seven islands located in the South Pacific. These islands were settled about 3,500 years ago; Samoans are part of a pan-Pacific ethnic group known as Polynesians, with similar genetic, linguistic, and cultural characteristics. Europeans first discovered the Samoan Islands in 1722; the first missionaries arrived in the 1820s. Some Samoan leaders were eager to learn from Europeans, because the new knowledge these visitors brought (e.g., religion and guns) often meant more power. America became interested in the Samoan Islands in the 1830s in order to protect American interests and its resident citizens. American Samoa has been an unorganized, unincorporated territory of the United States since 1900.

Prior to contact with Europeans, Samoan education was informal, consisting primarily of adults or older siblings teaching children the skills and responsibilities that were necessary for food and material cultural production and social role fulfillment. For girls, their primary responsibility was childcare and household maintenance; they were also required to learn weaving, medicinal plant identification, and cloth making/design, usually from an older female relative. Depending on her social position, a girl may also learn certain ceremonial dances, language, and drink preparation. Boys learned from an older male relative how to: plant and cultivate foodstuffs, cook, fish/hunt, and fight. Boys also entered into more formal craft apprenticeships with skilled artisans to learn canoe or house building, or tattooing, for example. Margaret Mead, the first anthropologist to study Samoan culture, noted the critical differences between the schooling of boys and the schooling of girls in the 1920s. Whereas a boy's success in learning could mean greater status for him and his family, girls' learning was less comprehensive and greater proficiency in their tasks meant that they would be more likely to have an early marriage or be confined to the household when they wanted more freedom.

First Formal Schools

The first formal schools were the faifeau schools set up by the London Missionary Society and Catholic, Mormon, and Methodist institutions, where young boys and girls would primarily learn theology and Bible scripture, as well as some math, history, and geography, all taught in Samoan. By 1902, there were 57 such church schools, and many of them continue to instruct young people in Bible scripture, writing, and math. The first public school opened in 1904, with 46 students between 6 and 12 years old, and was administered by the U.S. Naval Administration. By the early 1920s, there were 20 such schools, evidencing the interest and importance that Samoans placed on formal schooling as a means to manage the interactions with foreigners (in Samoan, palagi). Over the years, the U.S. Naval Administration attempted to "modernize" formal education through English language instruction up to an eighth-grade level, using American curricular materials.

With the transfer of administration of American Samoa to the U.S. Department of the Interior in 1951, there were renewed attempts to reform the public educational system, most notably through the implementation of Educational Television, from 1963 to the early 1970s. Teachers from the United States, primarily, were hired to create English-only programs in all subjects that were broadcast to K–12 classrooms across the territory; Samoan teachers provided classroom-based clarification and assessment. The impact of this project brought many aspects of Westernization to American Samoa, including English language immersion, electricity, walled building structures (as opposed to the traditional Samoan open architecture), and access to the American way of life as seen on television programs. Many Samoan leaders and scholars point to this period as a pivotal move toward Americanization at the expense of traditional Samoan culture and language.

At present, the educational system in American Samoa (AS) comprises 29 public schools, 15 private schools, and numerous faifeau schools. The ethnic breakdown of the six public high schools is roughly 97 percent Samoan, 2 percent Asian/Pacific Islander, and 1 percent other; out of a total of 4,653 students, all are designated eligible for Free Reduced Lunch. With over half of the world population of Samoans living abroad, American Samoans are increasingly concerned about the educational preparation of young people for higher education and career opportunities overseas. Over the last five years, there has been increasing pressure on the AS Department of Education (ASDOE) to standardize curricula, assess student achievement, and ensure teacher professional preparation, as part of an attempt to conform to No Child Left Behind (NCLB). Many of these efforts have been localized to provide the best chance for success of Samoan students, including Samoan language instruction. There are several challenges to implementing the mandates of NCLB, including persistent low proficiency in English, an increasing school population without parallel growth in qualified teachers and adequate classroom space and curricular materials, and adequate measures of the effectiveness of reform programs.

Evelyn Christian Ronning
Temple University

See Also: English as a Second Language; English Proficiency/Fluent English Proficient Students; Globalization; No Child Left Behind; Television and Education.

Further Readings
Mead, Margaret. *Coming of Age in Samoa.* New York: Penguin Books, 1943.

Schramm, W., et al. *Bold Experiment: The Story of Educational Television in American Samoa.* Palo Alto, CA: Stanford University Press, 1981.

Thomas, R. "Evaluation Consequences of Unreasonable Goals. The Plight of Education in American Samoa." *Educational Evaluation and Policy Analysis,* v.3/2 (1981).

Angola

Angola is located in southern Africa and bordered on land by the Republic of Congo, Democratic Republic of the Congo, Zambia, and Namibia; Angola's western border is the Atlantic Ocean, and its coastline is approximately 994 meters (1,600 kilometers) long. Angola occupies roughly 481,321 square miles (1,246,620 square kilometers), with the World Bank placing the 2011 total population at 19,081,912. Approximately 37 percent of the population is ethnic Ovimbund, and the remaining groups include: Kimbundu (25 percent), Bakongo (13 percent), Estico (mixed native African and European, 2 percent), European (1 percent), and those who identify as other (22 percent). Although Angola gained independence from Portugal in 1975, Portuguese remains the official language, while Bantu and other African languages are commonplace throughout the nation. For close to 30 years, civil war ravaged Angola, and it was not until 2002 that the nation found relative economic and political stability. The oil and diamond industries have spurred recent economic growth. In 2006, Angola became a member of the Organization of the Petroleum Exporting Countries (OPEC), and oil production and processing comprise 85 percent of gross domestic product (GDP). Although agriculture is the largest domestic employer, close to 50 percent of the country's food supply is imported. Recently, a reconstruction boom has led to growth in the construction sector. Still, some international estimates place 40.5 percent of the population living below the poverty line.

Educational Attainment and the Impact of War
Before Angola received independence in 1975, it was embroiled in what became two-and-a-half decade-long civil war involving three groups—the National Front for the Liberation of Angola (FNLA), the Popular Movement for the Liberation of Angola (MPLA), and the National Union for the Total Independence of Angola (UNITA)—that were formed during the 1950s and 1960s to fight against colonial rule. The three groups were never united, because each had different political philosophies and goals. Each group had support from separate ethnic groups and fought against each other and the Portuguese. Political unrest in Portugal in early 1975 led to the new Portuguese government granting Angola its independence, but the three factions could not reconcile their differences and move the nascent nation forward. The MPLA,

which controlled the capital and much of the coast, received backing from the Soviet Union and Cuba, while South Africa and the United States backed the FNLA and UNITA.

The effect is that from the late 1970s through the late 1980s, Angola became a proxy arena for the Cold War to play out in Southern Africa. The *CIA World Factbook* suggests that upward of 1.5 million people were killed and 4 million people were displaced during the decades-long civil war. According to the United Nations, Angola ranks 148th out of 187 countries in the Human Development Indicators, and up to 75 percent of the population are considered extremely poor. Despite vast mineral and oil reserves and an annual two-digit economic growth rate, the government only allocates 2.6 percent of GDP toward education. As a result, the level of human development and educational attainment within Angola remains low, and more than 30 percent of the adult population is illiterate.

Educational Structure

The educational structure in Angola is divided into three tiers: general basic (eight years), secondary education (up to four years) and higher education (five to six years). General basic education in Angola is free and compulsory and is broken into a 4–2–2 cycle. Most children start general basic at the age of 6 or 7. Around the age of 14, students can go into two tracks for secondary education: pre-university or technical (which includes teacher training). The pre-university track lasts for three years, while the technical track lasts for four. The first university in Angola, University Agostinho Neto (formerly the University of Angola) was established in Luanda in 1963 by the Portuguese and has a faculty for science, engineering, law, medicine, economics, and agriculture. The Angolan university system has developed considerably, and at present there are 23 operating higher education institutions in the nation. Despite the mandate that children attend school, both primary and secondary enrollments remain low, because millions of children do not attend school for reasons ranging from poor access, lack of teachers, and lack of schools.

The impact of the civil war continues to have repercussions for Angola. The infrastructure has been devastated, the loss of human life is high, and underdevelopment of human capital is entrenched. Landmines still permeate the interior of the nation, one of the most significant dangers that keep away humanitarian aid and agricultural development within the interior.

Further, millions of returned refugees, primarily women and children, add pressure to already low levels of resources. Despite this, there is now a movement by the government to improve Angola's educational system. The Education Ministry is now experimenting with a Cuban-style teaching method in its most populous states and, if successful, plans to implement it in other areas of the nation. The Angolan government seeks to eliminate or significantly reduce illiteracy by 2014. With revenues from exports, Angola should use a significant portion to improve its education system. With ratification and adoption of the Convention on the Rights of the Child, the Angolan government has committed to the Education for All (EFA) goals of free education and elimination of gender disparities.

Landis Fryer
Loyola University Chicago

See Also: Brazil; Cuba; Uganda.

Further Readings

Chabal, P., and N. Vidal. *Angola: The Weight of History.* New York: Columbia University Press, 2007.

Ciment, J. *Angola and Mozambique: Postcolonial Wars in Southern Africa.* New York: Facts on File, 1997.

Miller, F. P., A. F. Vandome, and J. McBrewster. *Education in Angola.* Saarbrücken, Germany: VDM Publishing House, 2010.

Rotberg, R. I. *Ending Autocracy, Enabling Democracy: The Tribulations of Southern Africa, 1960–2000.* Cambridge, MA: World Peace Foundation, 2002.

Argentina

Argentina is one of the largest countries in Latin America, located in southern South America. In 2010, its population was 40,117,096. It has rich natural resources, an export-oriented agricultural sector and a differentiated industrial production. In 2010, the annual growth of the gross domestic product (GDP) was 9.2 percent. GDP per capita (calculated in current U.S. dollars) was $9,124. Official estimates (whose methodological rigor has recently been challenged by different academic and nonacademic organizations) indicate that, for the first semester of 2011, 8.3 percent of the population living in urban areas was below the poverty line. According to the Central Intelligence Agency, private estimates indicate that around 30 percent of the population lives below the poverty line. From 1975 onward, poverty and social inequalities increased, although the situation improved after 2003. The Gini index grew from 0.36 in 1975 to 0.46 in 2009.

History and Social Structure

At the beginning of the 19th century, Argentina obtained its independence from the Spanish Empire. Following the configuration of an oligarchic and liberal national state, free, secular, compulsory primary education was introduced in 1884 in order to foster social integration, national identity, and consensus. Secondary and university education was mainly aimed at the formation of social and political elites. At the turn of the 19th century, the oligarchic political system was challenged and the beginning of a more inclusive political era began. Argentina encompassed a very diverse sociocultural population. In 1914, European immigrants represented more than a quarter of the population, and border country immigrants represented 2.6 percent, while there are no official estimates for indigenous communities.

From the mid-1940s to the early 1950s, the consolidation of a populist state was characterized by the introduction of social rights and the political participation of previously excluded social groups in a context of high levels of employment. In the 1950s, immigrants from neighboring countries became more visible (only surpassing Europeans in 1991 and representing 2.6 percent of the 2001 population). Primary education enrollment rates expanded rapidly, while secondary and university education also grew (albeit at slower pace) and diversified. During the 1960s and 1970s, various local versions of the welfare state grew out of the political conflict between alternating civil and military governments. The quality of state education worsened at a time when social demand for it was growing. By the mid-1970s, what would be a long-term crisis of the welfare state had begun, breaking a period of sustained economic growth.

Democracy returned in 1983, at which point access, participation, and diversity became pivotal notions in educational debates. The number of secondary school and university students significantly increased. The 1990s began with macro-economic prosperity and culminated in the economic and political crisis of 2001, resulting in a dramatic increase in poverty and unemployment. A national educational law altered the governance and the academic structure of the education system in 1993. Deconcentration of central aspects of secondary and tertiary education policymaking, together with the establishment of a core national curriculum and greater curricular leverage for provinces and schools, was introduced.

During the 1990s, state expenditure increased, and was mainly oriented toward the implementation of reform and the introduction of educational policies targeted at poor groups. At the end of the 1990s, the expansion of elementary and secondary education (whose lower level became compulsory in 1993) was accompanied by high levels of social exclusion. Since 2003, Argentina has experienced a period of economic recovery. State funding for education, science and technology has increased and, in 2010, represented 6.4 percent of GDP. In 2006, a National Educational Law, among other changes, established: the legal obligation of expanding educational services for all 4 year olds; compulsory upper secondary schooling; the obligation of extending school time for primary education; an increase (to four) in the number of years required for teacher training; and the bilingual and intercultural education modality, targeting indigenous communities, who represented 1.7 percent of the population in 2004.

Educational Structure

Compulsory education includes a reception year (for 5-year-olds) and 12 years of primary and secondary education. Pupils may not (formally) be allocated to different types of schools or tracks based on their record of educational achievement. Underachievement may lead to repeating a school year during primary or secondary school. Upon completion of secondary education, students may enroll at higher education institutions. Argentina has one of the highest graduation rates in Latin America for basic education. Primary schooling became almost universal in the 1990s (with a net school rate of 95.7 percent in 1991), and secondary schooling has rapidly grown from a net school rate of 32.8 percent in 1970 to an estimated 71.5 percent in 2001. In 2001, 90.8 percent of children (net school rate) attended compulsory elementary schooling. However, access varies considerably across provinces, socioeconomic groups, and types of schools (public and private), particularly with respect to elementary and secondary schooling.

Together with Brazil, Colombia, and Peru, Argentina belongs to the group of Latin American countries with medium educational achievement in language and mathematics at the primary school level. In 2006, 6.1 percent of pupils repeated at least one year in primary school and the corresponding figure was 11 percent at secondary level. These percentages are similar to the average for Latin America, but higher than that of Chile. The inter-annual dropout rate in 2009–10 was 1.44 percent (over six school years) at primary school, and 9.3 and 15.5 percent at lower and secondary school, respectively (over six school years).

Current Challenges

The need to guarantee equal opportunities to learn across provinces and types of schools, together with the improvement of the quality of state education, is a key challenge. Quantitative and qualitative studies evidence the existence of social and educational inequalities across and within provinces and types of schools (public and private). Different national educational policies are addressing these issues. For example, the National Education Law 26206 has introduced two ways to organize the academic structure of basic education, and these should replace the heterogeneous provincial ones by 2012.

The promotion of inclusive secondary schooling is a top priority of the current educational agenda. The redefinition of traditional pedagogy (which includes access to and use of new technology) and the recognition of social and educational diversity among pupils are pillars of this transformation. One of the most ambitious initiatives in this direction is the national program Conectar Igualdad (Connect Equality), which will distribute 3 million netbooks to pupils, teachers, and head teachers by 2012.

Analía Inés Meo
National Council of Scientific and Technological Research

See Also: Bilingual Education; Chile; Poverty and Education.

Further Readings

Central Intelligence Agency. "The World Factbook. South America: Argentina." http://www.cia.gov/library/publications/the-world-factbook/geos/ar.html (Accessed December 2011)

Filmus, Daniel. *Estado, Sociedad y Educación en la Argentina de fin de Siglo. Proceso y Desafíos ("State, Society and Education in Argentina at the End of the Century: Process and Challenges")*. Buenos Aires, Argentina: Troquel, 1999.

Instituto Nacional de Estadísticas y Censos de la República Argentina. "Censo Nacional de Población y Vivienda 2010." ("National Population Census 2010"). http://www.indec.gov.ar (Accessed December 2011).

Rivas, Axel, Alejandro Vera, and Pablo Bezem. *Radiografía de la Educación Argentina ("Argentinean Education X-Ray")*. Buenos Aires: Fundación CIPPEC; Fundación Arcor; Fundación Roberto Noble, 2010.

Sistema de Información de Tendencias Educativas en América Latina, "Argentina. Perfiles de Países." ("Argentina. Country Profiles"). http://www.siteal.iipe-oei.org/sites/default/files/perfil_argentina.pdf (Accessed December 2011).

World Bank. "Argentina." http://www.data.worldbank.org/country/argentina (Accessed December 2011).

Arizona

Bordering California to the west and Mexico to the south, Arizona was one of the fastest growing states between 2000 and 2010. According to the U.S. census, in 2010, Arizona was home to 6.4 million residents, a 25 percent increase since 2000. Approximately 60 percent of the state's population resides in Maricopa County, the state's largest metropolitan area, which includes the state's capital, Phoenix.

The majority (59 percent) of the state's population growth over the past decade occurred within Maricopa County, one of the most populous counties in the United States. Arizona is also among the most racially diverse states in the United States. In the 2010 census, 58 percent of the residents were white, 30 percent were of Hispanic or Latino origin, 4 percent were black, approximately 5 percent were American Indian and Alaska Natives, 3 percent were Asian/Pacific Islander and the remaining 3 percent reported two or more races. The U.S. Congress created the Territory of Arizona in 1863, out of portions of the Gadsden Purchase and the territories ceded to the United States from Mexico after its defeat in the U.S.–Mexican War. Arizona was admitted as the 48th state in the union in 1912. The first territorial legislature allocated $1,500 in 1864 to support mission schools. In 1867, the state legislature gave towns the authority to collect taxes to support public schools; the Tucson School District 1 opened the first public school in the territory in 1868, with an enrollment of 55 boys. In the 1870s, the legislature required communities to collect property taxes to support schools. By 1900, the territory had 428 public schools that taught 16,500 students.

Racial Diversity

In 1909, the Arizona territorial legislature passed a law requiring the segregation of African American students that was subsequently incorporated into state law. Black parents unsuccessfully challenged the state's segregation laws in 1912 and 1927. Segregation was legal in Arizona until 1953 and 1954, when the Arizona Superior Court declared segregation unconstitutional in two separate cases; the latter was announced four days before the Supreme Court announced its historic decision in *Brown v. Board of Education*. While Mexican American students were not subject to legalized segregation, many school districts established separate Mexican schools and classrooms. While districts claimed that the separate schools and classrooms were necessary because of Mexican American students' inability to speak English, many districts placed students without testing their language skills. Moreover, Mexican Americans

Table 1 Elementary and secondary education characteristics

	Arizona	U.S. (average)
Total number of schools	2,380	1,988
Total students	1,071,751	970,278
Total teachers	50,030.62	60,766.56
Pupil/teacher ratio	21.42	15.97

Source: U.S. Department of Education, National Center for Education Statistics, Common Core of Data (CCD), 2010–11.

Table 2 Elementary and secondary education finance

	Arizona	U.S. (average)
Total revenues	$10,283,842,005	$11,464,385,994
Total expenditures for education	$10,538,885,516	$11,712,033,839
Total current expenditures	$8,403,220,614	$9,938,906,259

Source: U.S. Department of Education, National Center for Education Statistics, Common Core of Data (CCD), "National Public Education Financial Survey," FY08 (2007–08).

were the targets of de facto segregation in other public facilities, including swimming pools, churches, and movie houses. The experience of Native American students differed because of their status under federal law. Currently, there are 21 federally recognized tribes in Arizona; one quarter of state lands are reservation and tribal communities. After the Civil War, the federal government attempted to force American Indians to assimilate to American society by requiring American Indian children to attend boarding schools located outside of their reservations, where they were forced to learn and speak English and attend church, received vocational training, and were taught that the "white man's ways" were superior to their religious and cultural traditions. One of these was the Phoenix Indian School in central Phoenix, which opened in 1881, and by 1899, was the largest school of its type; Phoenix Indian School remained open until 1990.

In 1885, the territorial legislature authorized the institutions that evolved into two of its public universities: the Territorial Normal School at Tempe, and the University at Tucson. The Territorial Normal School opened its doors a year later to its first class of 33 students; its mission was to train teachers to work in the state' public schools. Classes began at the University of Tucson in 1891. In 1893, the legislature approved the founding of the Northern Territorial Normal School in Flagstaff, which began offering classes in 1893. In 1927, the state legislature passed a law creating and providing state funds to support junior colleges. Almost 150 years after it was founded, the Tempe Territorial Normal School has evolved into Arizona State University, a research-intensive university and one of the largest public universities in the United States. In addition to its other public universities, the University of Arizona and Northern Arizona University, Arizona has 10 community college districts governed by locally elected boards. The Maricopa Community College District is the largest in the state, and includes 10 community colleges, two skills centers, and satellite campuses serving the communities surrounding Phoenix. Arizona's public schools serve a growing population of English language learners (ELLs).

In 2009, 31 percent of children ages 5 to 17 spoke a language other than English at home; the vast majority of these were Spanish speakers. In November 2000, Arizona voters passed Proposition 203, which mandated English immersion for ELL students. In English immersion classes, all instruction and instructional materials are in English and the use of students' native language in the classroom is minimized. In 2006, the state legislature mandated the revision of the structure of English immersion classes; ELL students are placed in a daily four-hour English Language Development block until they exit the ELL program. Arizona also consistently ranks among the lowest states in per-pupil educational expenditures.

Jeanne M. Powers, Jesus Cisneros
Kathleen Corley, Alexia Shonteff
Arizona State University

See Also: Bilingual Education; Mexican American Students; Native American Students.

Further Readings
Kids Count Data Center, Annie E. Casey Foundation. "Data Across States." http://www.datacenter.kidscount .org/data/acrossstates/Map.aspx?loct=2&ind=5199&dt m=11678&tf=867 (Accessed January 2012).

Mackun, P. and S. Wilson. "Population Distribution and Change (C2010BR-01)." Washington D.C.: U.S. Census, 2011.

National Center for Education Statistics. "The Condition of Education 2011 (NCES 2011-033)." Washington, DC: U.S. Government Printing Office, 2011.

Nielson, Aileen Pace, ed. *Dust in Our Desks: Territory Days to the Present in Arizona Schools.* Tempe: Arizona State University College of Education, 1985.

Powers, Jeanne M. "Forgotten History: Mexican American School Segregation in Arizona From 1900–1951. *Equity & Excellence in Education,* v.41/4 (2008).

U.S. Census Bureau. "2010 State and County QuickFacts: Arizona." http://www.quickfacts.census.gov/qfd/ states/04000.html (Accessed January 2012).

Arkansas

The state of Arkansas covers 52,000 square miles in the southern United States. In the center of the state is the capital, Little Rock; the Ouachita and Ozarks mountains lie to the northwest, while the Delta floodplains line the eastern part of the state. Arkansas's economy relies on agriculture and the service industry; headquarters of the discount chain Wal-Mart are located in Bentonville. Currently, about 2.9 million people live in the state, 77 percent of them white, 15

percent black, 6 percent Latino, and 1 percent Asian. Arkansas's history as a slave state still shapes its educational system today. Caddo, Tunica, Quapaw, and Osage Indian tribes first occupied the Arkansas area. In 1686, the French established the first permanent European settlement, and a small frontier economy of hunting and trading developed. The United States acquired the land as a part of the Louisiana Purchase in 1803. During the early 1800s, the cotton industry rapidly expanded; this expansion was fueled by slave labor, and, as cotton plantations grew in the Delta region, the state's African American population also grew. Arkansas joined the Union in 1836 as a slave state. Education during the colonial period and early statehood was typically informal. Some communities had schools, though teaching quality and session length varied according to the desires and resources of the communities. A few private academies existed, as did a handful of missionary-run Indian schools. Slaves were usually prevented from organizing formal schools. After Arkansas joined the Confederacy in 1861, the Civil War occupied the state's attention and resources. Reconstruction provided political office and voting rights to black residents, though these rights and representation diminished in the latter 1800s under Democratic control and the influence of the Ku Klux Klan. Share-cropping sustained the cotton industry and also preserved economic and social inequities between white and black residents.

Educational Growth
Educational gains after the war were noteworthy, but small. The University of Arkansas, a land-grant institution then known as Arkansas Industrial University, opened in Fayetteville in 1872. The new state constitution called for public education for both black and white children, and school enrollment grew. Yet, opposition to taxes—and white opposition to the education of African American children—limited this growth and kept quality minimal. Communities struggled to find and pay qualified teachers, and schools were highly subject to local control and resources. Northern missionaries and philanthropists funded some schools, and black communities often supported their community schools, but widespread public education continued to be limited, especially for black and rural students.

The Great Depression hit the state's agricultural base hard, further reducing educational funds, and state officials, in an effort to cut expenses, offered

Table 1 Elementary and secondary education characteristics

	Arkansas	U.S. (average)
Total number of schools	1,128	1,988
Total students	482,114	970,278
Total teachers	34,272.80	60,766.56
Pupil/teacher ratio	14.07	15.97

Source: U.S. Department of Education, National Center for Education Statistics, Common Core of Data (CCD), 2010–11.

Table 2 Elementary and secondary education finance

	Arkansas	U.S. (average)
Total revenues	$4,674,052,684	$11,464,385,994
Total expenditures for education	$4,800,319,951	$11,712,033,839
Total current expenditures	$4,156,367,988	$9,938,906,259

Source: U.S. Department of Education, National Center for Education Statistics, Common Core of Data (CCD), "National Public Education Financial Survey," FY08 (2007–08).

little assistance. School desegregation did not have much support among Arkansas's white communities, and after the 1954 *Brown v. Board of Education* decision, anti-integrationists sought to delay integration. In 1957, Governor Orval Faubus, in direct defiance of the federal government, ordered Arkansas's National Guard to prevent the desegregation of Little Rock's Central High School. His anti-integration stance was largely supported within the state, and his actions became a national symbol of white resistance to integration. President Eisenhower sent federal troops to escort nine black students to Central High and protect them from the surrounding riots, yet desegregation, which typically meant the closure of black schools, gained little traction until the early 1970s. In many Delta communities, private education thrived as white students avoided the newly desegregated public schools.

Quality of Education

Toward the end of the 20th century, the quality of Arkansas' public education system garnered more attention. Governor Bill Clinton addressed teacher quality through a number of reforms, and in 2002, the Arkansas Supreme Court ruled in *Lake View v. Huckabee* that the state, in relying upon local property

taxes to fund its schools, had failed to provide an equitable and adequate education to all children. The decision sparked a number of reforms, including the controversial Act 60, which mandated consolidation of districts with less than 350 children and led to the closure of many districts across the state. During the 2009–10 school year, Arkansas enrolled about 467,000 public school students, most in traditional public schools, though some in the state's 29 charter schools. Arkansas also has a number of private school or home-school students. By 2010, the state's higher education system had 33 two- or four-year public institutions and 11 private institutions, together enrolling 172,000 full- and part-time students.

A commissioner of education heads the public education system, and the nine-member State Board of Education writes educational policy; all of these positions are appointed by the governor. Business leaders and philanthropies such as the Wal-Mart Foundation and the Walton Family Foundation also play a role in shaping the state's schools through their funding and reform efforts. Though recent governors have maintained their interest in the state's schools, Arkansas continues to wrestle with a number of educational issues. The overall quality of public schooling lags behind other states. In 2009, 27 percent of the state's eighth graders achieved proficiency or above on the National Assessment of Educational Progress math test; the same proportion reached that level on the reading test. Large gaps in educational opportunity and achievement also exist between the state's white and minority students, with students of color often attending poorer schools and lagging behind their white counterparts on standardized tests. Education leaders and policymakers continue to confront funding inequities and consolidation issues.

Mara Casey Tieken
Bates College

See Also: *Brown v. Board of Education;* Racial Inequality: Achievement; Racism in Education.

Further Readings
Arkansas Department of Education. http://www .arkansased.org/index.html (Accessed December 2011).
Central Arkansas Library System. "The Encyclopedia of Arkansas History and Culture." http://www .encyclopediaofarkansas.net (Accessed December 2011).

Moneyhon, Carl. *Arkansas and the New South 1874–1929.* Fayetteville: University of Arkansas Press, 1997.

Stockley, Gary. *Ruled by Race: Black/White Relations in Arkansas From Slavery to the Present.* Fayetteville: University of Arkansas Press, 2009.

U.S. Department of Education. "United States Education Dashboard." http://www.dashboard.ed.gov/dashboard.aspx?i=d8&id=5&wt=0 (Accessed December 2011).

Asian Americans

Discourse of Asian Americans and education primarily focuses on the high educational and labor force outcomes of Asian Americans relative to blacks and Hispanics (and often whites). While these patterns support the stereotype of Asian Americans as "model minorities," these images ignore the issue of selection of Asian American immigrants. Explanations of the higher educational attainment of Asian Americans include the following:

1. Selection of immigrants by socioeconomic status
2. Higher levels of achievement and attainment because of differences in cultural orientation toward education
3. Focus of Asian Americans on educational performance because of perceptions that some avenues toward socioeconomic achievement may be closed to them

In the 2010 census, approximately 17.3 million individuals, or 5.6 percent of the U.S. population, reported an Asian ancestry. Among individuals who selected only one race (approximately 97 percent of the U.S. population), 14.7 million or 4.8 percent of the population identified as Asian. About one-quarter of Asian Americans are of Chinese or Taiwanese descent, with Filipinos, South Asians, Koreans, and Vietnamese making up other large proportions of Asians in the United States. Asians made up the fastest-growing population between 2000 and 2010, with a 43.3 percent increase over this decade. Among school-aged children in the 2008 and 2009 school year, Asian/Pacific Islander students accounted for 5 percent of the total primary and secondary student population. A majority of Asian American students are children of immigrants, as 67 percent of Asian Americans were foreign born, according to the 2007 American Community Survey. Children of immigrants of all races and ethnicities account for approximately 25 percent of children under the age of 18. Of these students, Asians comprise 18 percent of children of immigrants and 24 percent of foreign-born children (also commonly referred to as first-generation immigrants), which is a high proportion when compared to the 5 percent that Asians comprise in the United States.

The population of Asian Americans has been affected by highly restrictive immigration policies since the late 19th century. In 1882, the Chinese Exclusion Act ended all immigration from China and barred Chinese people already residing in the United States from obtaining citizenship. A similar immigration law in 1907 targeted the Japanese, and the Asiatic Barred Zone Act 10 years later ended immigration for all other Asian groups. The population of Asian Americans today comprises almost entirely immigrants and their descendents who arrived after 1965, the year that the Hart-Cellar Act was enacted. This allowed immigrants from Asia (and elsewhere) to again migrate to the United States. In addition, the Hart-Cellar Act invoked a preference system that specifically targeted well-educated individuals from other countries to be able to enter the United States.

Academic and Labor Outcomes

Asian Americans, overall, have had very high educational achievement and attainment since the 1980s. In 2008, according to the American Community Survey, among individuals 25 years or older, half of all Asian Americans reported having a bachelor's degree or higher (versus 28 percent among the total U.S. population age 25 and older), and 20 percent reported having a graduate or professional degree (versus 10 percent of the total U.S. population age 25 and older). Although the overall educational attainment of Asian Americans is high, there is also substantial variation among Asian ethnic groups. For example, 68.3 percent of Asian Indians have at least a bachelor's degree, while only 11.8 percent of Laotians report having the same level of attainment. Asians Americans are also highly represented in science, technology, engineering, and mathematics majors in higher education, which some scholars argue is a strategy among Asian Americans to avoid potential discrimination in the workplace and garner marketable credentials.

Asian Americans also outperform other racial/ethnic groups in terms of test scores. According to the 2011 National Assessment of Educational Progress (NAEP), only 2 percent of fourth graders who scored below the 25th percentile were Asian, compared to 31 percent who were white, 28 percent who were black, and 34 percent who were Hispanic. Among those who scored at the 75th percentile or greater, 10 percent were Asian, compared to 72 percent who were white, 5 percent who were black, and 10 percent who were Hispanic. Among eighth graders in 2011, Asians earned an average score of 303, compared to 293 for whites, 270 for Hispanics, and 262 for blacks. Research that examines the primary and secondary education of Asian Americans finds that Asian Americans do better in most academic subjects than other racial/ethnic groups at almost all stages of education. Similar to arguments that scholars make about Asian Americans in the workforce, some researchers argue that Asian American students and parents place more emphasis on academic achievement because they may perceive other avenues of success as closed to them. For example, according to a 1995 study by Kao, Asian Americans eighth graders did have higher grades than whites. However, mathematics and readings test scores for Asian American eighth graders as a whole and separated by large ethnic groups were no different from whites after factoring in socioeconomic characteristics. The population of Asians in the United States is unique because of immigration laws, and therefore background characteristics should be considered. Moreover, there is a wide spectrum of achievement among Asian ethnicities.

Another body of literature focuses on nonacademic experiences of Asian Americans, including extracurricular participation and friendship networks. Inside and outside of schools, Asian immigrants are more likely to not participate in school sports than their native-born counterparts or native whites after controlling for a host of background factors. However, both native-born and immigrant Asian American students report fewer friends and less informal interaction compared to native whites. Studies also show that Asian American youth, particularly new arrivals, report lack of social support, general feelings of invisibility, and explicit confrontations with instances of racism. According to the American Community Survey, in 2010, the household income among single-race Asian Americans was $67,000, compared to $52,500 for white households. However, there is considerable variation among Asian ethnic groups. For example,

Asian Indians have a median household income of $90,700, while Hmong report a median household income of $45,200. Only 3.5 percent of Japanese households live in poverty, compared to 27.8 percent of Hmong households.

Pressure to Succeed

Given Asian Americans' comparatively high educational and labor outcomes and the pressure many youth face to succeed, portrayals of Asians as "model minorities" are still salient in contemporary discussions. Some ethnographic work explores the high expectations that many Asian American students face. This body of literature argues that the pressure to succeed is inextricably linked to the immigrant experience for almost all Asian students in the United States. While stereotypes of academic excellence may appear flattering at first, they also have highly negative consequences on Asian Americans, as well as other minority groups. If Asians are seen as having a superior cultural orientation toward educational achievement, then other minority groups may be seen as having deficient cultural values. Moreover, model minority stereotypes and popular explanations of why Asian Americans are successful ignore Asian groups with lower attainment and socioeconomic factors that explain high academic and labor outcomes.

Overall, many prominent scholars of Asian Americans have questioned the usefulness of using one pan-ethnic as a category to represent the experiences of such a wide spectrum of groups. Using "Asian" as a racial category assumes a pre-existing relationship among new immigrants from Asian countries that may not exist. Also, averages using this category often hide great disadvantages that many smaller groups face, such as the Laotian, Hmong, and Cambodian. This is of particular relevance when racial categories are used in policies designed to address racial and ethnic inequalities.

Hua-Yu Sebastian Cherng
Grace Kao
University of Pennsylvania

See Also: Cultural Capital; Immigrants, Children of; Multiracial Students.

Further Readings

Barringer, H. R., D. T. Takeuchi, and P. Xenos. "Education, Occupational Prestige, and Income of Asian Americans." *Sociology of Education,* v.63 (1990).

Kao, G. "Asian Americans as Model Minorities? A Look at Their Academic Performance." *American Journal of Education,* v.103 (1995).

Kao, G. and Marta Tienda. "Educational Aspirations of Minority Youth." *American Journal of Education,* v.106 (1998).

Lee, J. and M. Zhou, eds. *Asian American Youth: Culture, Identity, and Ethnicity.* New York: Routledge, 2004.

Louie, Vivian S. *Compelled to Excel: Immigration, Education, and Opportunity Among Chinese Americans.* Palo Alto, CA: Stanford University Press, 2004.

Sakamoto, Arthur, Kim Goyette, and ChangHwan Kim. "Socioeconomic Attainments of Asian Americans." *Annual Review of Sociology,* v.35 (2009).

Xie, Yu and Kim Goyette. "Social Mobility and the Educational Choices of Asian Americans." *Social Science Research,* v.32 (2003).

Assimilation Without Acculturation

In the process of becoming Americanized, immigrants face linguistic, cultural, social, and ethnic identity challenges. Research on assimilation and acculturation has recurrently addressed the question of why some immigrant groups seem to become Americanized quickly, while others do so more slowly. Studies have therefore examined whether the delay or acceleration of these assimilative/acculturative processes influences the mobility of individual immigrants and groups of immigrants. As a result, assimilation and acculturation have come to be viewed through a lens of "mobility." Using a lens of mobility, immigrants are seen to assimilate downward or upward.

Second Generation

The substantial increase in population of non-European immigrants, especially Asian and Caribbean peoples after 1965, has encouraged the development of alternative paradigms in which to study immigrants' accession into mainstream society or declension into a permanent underclass. This phenomenon of upward and downward mobility has led some sociologists to coin terms such as *second generation decline* and *second generation revolt*, referring to the immigrants' patterns of mobility as a direct function of their generational status in the United States. As a part of the theory of segmented assimilation, Herbert Gans proposed that acculturation and assimilation are processes by which immigrants become more like nonimmigrants culturally and socially. Gans uses the label *second generation decline* to describe when second generation immigrants are unable to improve their social position. Joel Perlmann and Roger Waldinger describe "second generation revolt" as happening when second generation immigrants acquire an oppositional frame of reference, instead of maintaining a structural-functionalist paradigm (the sentiment that because of blocked opportunities, they will continue to work and study extremely hard in order to overcome these structural obstacles).

Still others insist that delayed acculturation, a process whereby immigrants attempt to not become like nonimmigrants in cultural or social terms, yields the best outcomes. Margaret Gibson calls this latter strategy accommodation and acculturation without assimilation. Gibson's theory is important since co-ethnic communities help maintain and extend moral and material resources, allowing for "selective acculturation" and the maintenance of cultural and ethnic identity. As Gibson's work on "accommodation without assimilation" states, immigrants who are embedded in co-ethnic communities stand a greater chance of not assimilating downward since dissonant and/or generational gaps are prevented from forming.

Becoming Americanized

Accommodation without assimilation is the idea that immigrants do not necessarily have to become one with the culture by adopting mainstream and dominant cultural ways of life and/or knowing in order to be successful. Historically, it was a widely held belief that assimilation was the best route for an immigrant to become upwardly mobile. In traditional times, immigrants who shed their previous ethno-cultural ways of being were believed to have better outcomes, namely, outcomes that were occupational, social, and educational in nature. Prior to the conceptualization of segmented assimilation, the traditional view of acculturation was "straight line" assimilation. The term *straight line* foreshadows this classical theory's thought that there was a predictable and linear trajectory for immigrants who became Americanized. The idea that out of many, one, or *e pluribus unum*, is a historical relic of this rationalization. The reality, though, is that the need for new concepts of assimilation and acculturation is because of a global phenomenon: the movement of people around the world. Classical assimilative theories were the mainstream and dominant thought in sociological circles, until a countervailing theory known as "segmented assimilation" gained sociological currency. Segmented assimilation, a newer sociological paradigm created by Alejandro Portes and Rubén Rumbaut, was necessary for two main reasons. The first reason was because of the upsurge in non-European immigrants that came to the shores of the United States after 1965. The second reason was caused by the fact that the U.S. economy was rapidly changing after 1965.

Straight line assimilation accounted for the mobility trajectories of Europeans in an industrializing context. The need for alternative assimilative explanations for non-European immigrants came after 1965, when many U.S. immigrants came from countries outside of Europe. The 1965 Immigration Act changed the landscape of the immigrants who came to America. The economy in 1965 was also different than in earlier years, which affected what kinds of immigrants wished to come to the United States. These two changes, coupled with the inadequacy of straight line assimilation theories, led to the formation of segmented assimilation. Segmented assimilation puts forth the idea that retention of language and cultural habits enables certain immigrant children to perform well in schools, despite tremendous disadvantages.

Paramount to this theory is that it provides an explanatory framework that can be used to account for educational, social, or occupational success amid disadvantages and diverse structural environments (i.e., modes of incorporation or reception, or economic changes). Many still contend that integration by modeling mainstream culture and values will lead to the best outcomes, and many early studies document this line of reasoning. These early studies have a common explanatory framework that prioritizes adaptation of the mainstream and dominant culture. However, segmented assimilation, or the promotion of assimilation (accommodation) that values preservation of ethnicity, is useful for sociology of education as a field, especially given that demographers indicate that the large racial shift taking place now will continue, and this shift will occur in the United States as a postindustrial economy and society.

Nicholas D. Hartlep
Illinois State University

See Also: Cultural Capital; Immigrant Adaptation; Immigrants, Children of; Noncompliant Believers, Cultural Mainstreamers, and Cultural Straddlers.

Further Readings

Bowskill, M., E. Lyons, and A. Coyle. "The Rhetoric of Acculturation: When Integration Means Assimilation." *British Journal of Social Psychology,* v.46/1 (2007).

Gans, H. "Acculturation, Assimilation, and Mobility." *Ethnic and Racial Studies,* v.30/1 (2007).

Portes, A. and R. G. Rumbaut. *Immigrant America: A Portrait.* Berkeley: University of California Press, 2006.

Sarroub, L. K. *All American Yemeni Girls: Being Muslim in a Public School.* Philadelphia: University of Pennsylvania Press, 2005.

Telles, E. E. and V. Ortiz. *Generations of Exclusion: Mexican Americans, Assimilation, and Race.* New York: Russell Sage Foundation, 2008.

At-Risk Students

Students who are likely to fail or drop out of school are defined as at-risk. They are vulnerable to becoming academically ill-equipped and disengaged (withdrawing from classes and through suspension and/or expulsion), thus increasing school failure. According to Robert Slavin, though some students graduate, they do not have the competency to succeed in life, as many have insufficient school experience. African American, low-income, and immigrant children were placed in schools that offered basic education, tracking them for factory, field, and domestic jobs. The insufficient or lower quality of education provided to these students placed them in at-risk positions of failing or dropping out. The 1966 *Coleman Report* highlights research that shows schools' failure in meeting the needs of students at risk. In recent years, major national initiatives (including the 1983 A Nation At Risk report, 2002 No Child Left Behind Act, and the 2010 Race to the Top) have propelled discussions on the academic status of these students. The "at-risk student" terminology historically referred to students with identifiable physical and cognitive disabilities; it now includes social factors. Students were labeled as disadvantaged; then in the 1980s, "at-risk students" emerged. In the 1990s, many scholars recoined the terminology *students at risk* or *students in at-risk*

Table 1 Percentage of children under age 18 living in poverty, by living arrangements and race/ethnicity

Race/ethnicity and subgroup	All children related to householder	LIVING ARRANGEMENT		
		Married parents	Female parent, no spouse present	Male parent, no spouse present
Total[1]	17.5	8.1	41.4	19.7
White	10.1	5.0	31.4	14.5
Black	34.1	11.2	48.6	28.4
Hispanic	27.1	17.7	48.7	24.3
Mexican	28.6	20.4	50.5	25.1
Puerto Rican	31.6	10.4	52.1	27.1
Cuban	12.7	7.0	28.6	13.4
Dominican	34.1	13.6	50.9	23.0
Salvadoran	19.8	10.9	41.8	17.3
Other Central American	25.1	14.9	45.6	24.3
South American	14.3	9.1	29.8	17.6
Other Hispanic or Latino	20.9	9.4	43.0	23.8
Asian	11.1	8.1	30.6	15.8
Asian Indian	7.5	6.4	21.3	20.1
Chinese[2]	10.5	8.4	26.1	17.8
Filipino	5.0	2.7	16.3	7.9
Japanese	9.9	7.3	25.4	41.7
Korean	10.8	7.4	36.1	9.0
Vietnamese	15.2	10.6	35.7	15.4
Other Asian	19.9	14.8	45.0	19.3
Native Hawai'ian/Pacific Islander	25.6	18.6	37.7	35.6
American Indian/Alaska Native	32.7	17.9	51.5	30.5
Two or more races	17.9	5.2	38.5	19.8

[1] Total includes other race/ethnicity categories not separately shown.
[2] Excludes Taiwanese. Taiwanese is included in the "Other Asian" category.

Children are classified by either their parent's marital status or, if no parents are present in the household, by the marital status of the related householder. Poverty information was available for children who were related to the householder. Therefore, this table excludes any children who were not related to the householder or who are recorded as the householder or spouse of the householder. To define poverty, the U.S. Census Bureau utilizes a set of money income thresholds that vary by family size and composition. A family, along with each individual in it, is considered poor if the family's total income is less than that family's threshold. The poverty thresholds do not vary geographically and are adjusted annually for inflation using the Consumer Price Index. The official poverty definition counts money income before taxes and does not include capital gains and noncash benefits (such as public housing, Medicaid, and food stamps). Race categories exclude persons of Hispanic ethnicity.

Source: National Center for Education Statistics, U.S. Department of Commerce, Census Bureau, American Community Survey, 2007.

situations. The present label places students first, as compared to the former that emphasizes risk factors. Studies project that by 2020, most of U.S. public school students will be at risk.

There are multiple variables that place students at risk, including race, language, poverty, family structure, sexuality, teenage pregnancy, substance abuse, bullying, and gender. These factors are so wide and diverse that they have the potential to affect all students. Authors such as Karen Irsmsher suggest that by 2020, most of U.S. public school students will be in conditions that place them at risk.

Many students of color and language minorities are experiencing failure in the nation's public schools. They are disengaged in classrooms, dropping out of school early and at high rates, limited in exposure to rigorous curriculum, experiencing low teacher quality and expectations, and are disproportionately placed in special education.

The school structures used (teaching styles, school culture, curricula approaches, and assessment methods) are not in sync with their individual needs—resulting in school failure or high dropout rates. The Children's Defense Fund (CDF) reports that African American students are three times as likely as Caucasian and Asian/Pacific Islander students, and more than twice as likely as Latin American students, to be suspended. Students from all socioeconomic backgrounds are at risk of failure from school; however, those who come from single-parent households are more likely to experience failure in school. The CDF reported that in 2008, about 14.1 million children were poor. These children have higher probabilities of doing poorly in school or dropping out as compared to children from higher socioeconomic backgrounds. Furthermore, children living in single-parent households are more likely to be low-achievers, or suspended or expelled from school. Many of the children who come from low-income families, with no financial stability, are displaced, move from home to home, and/or are in foster care, and lack adequate health insurance and nutritious food. The economic downturn has resulted in many parents working out of the house while children go to unsupervised homes where they are more likely to consume alcohol, use drugs, and engage in inappropriate behavior.

The National School Climate 2009 survey of middle and high school students revealed that about two-thirds of students felt unsafe as a result of their sexuality. Many had experienced physical and verbal harassment and assault. All these factors caused one-third of students to miss at least a day of school, placing them at risk of dropping out. There are additional factors including teenage pregnancy, substance abuse, homelessness, and obesity that affect student success. The intersection of risk factors places some students in higher probabilities of being in at-risk situations. Many students become disengaged because of teaching styles, school culture, curricula approaches, and assessment methods that are not in sync with their needs, affecting school performance. School structures have failed African American students, as they are more likely to be held back, suspended, and expelled from school. In 2009, records reflect higher percentages of African American and Latin American students missing more than three days of school more often than white students.

Implications

Various programs have been developed to address the needs of students in at-risk situations. Robert Rossi and Samuel C. Stringfield posit the shift from a single focus on crisis intervention to more preventive programs that address multiple issues, thus impacting multiple risk factors. George Morrison suggests four approaches. Compensation programs help overcome low academic performance, including: Head Start, Title I, Upward Bound, and after-school or summer programs. Intervention programs support students and their families in removing the risk factors or their influences, including parenting classes for teenagers. Transition services include helping students who move from high school to the employment sector; they attend morning classes that connect core content areas with occupational fields and in the afternoon students apply these skills to a job. Prevention programs, such as sex and drug education programs, hinder the risk factors and were created to prevent specific behaviors. Many students are exposed to some of these variables that put them in a position to consider dropping out. Full-service schools must be created that are comprehensive and family and community centered. In addition, they must meet the social, intellectual, and emotional developmental needs of children.

Omobolade (Bola) O. Delano-Oriaran
St. Norbert College

See Also: After-School Programs; Dropouts; Head Start; School-to-Work Transitions; Suspensions.

Further Readings

California Research Dropout Research Project. "Why Students Drop Out of School: A Review of 25 Years of Research." http://www.cdrp.ucsb.edu/pubs_reports.htm (Accessed December 2011).

Children's Defense Fund. "State of America's Children 2010." http://www.childrensdefense.org/child-research-data-publications/data/state-of-americas-children-child-poverty-2010.html (Accessed December 2011).

Education Resources Information Center. http://www.eric.ed.gov (Accessed December 2011).

Morrison, George S. *Teaching in America*. Boston: Allyn and Bacon, 1997.

National Center for Education Statistics. "Status and Trends in the Education of Racial and Ethnic Minorities." http://www.nces.ed.gov/pubs2010/2010015/indicator4_16.asp (Accessed December 2011).

Slavin, Robert et al. *Effective Programs for Students at Risk*. Boston: Allyn and Bacon, 1989.

Attitude/Achievement Paradox

One of the more puzzling patterns in the sociology of education is the combination of blacks' generally pro-school attitudes, yet poor school performance—what Mickelson called the "attitude/achievement paradox." This puzzle was evident as far back as the 1966 *Coleman Report*, where the authors concluded that blacks "give a picture of students who report high interest in academic achievement, but whose reported interest is not translated through effective action into achievement." More modern scholars, such as George Farkas et al., have noted the paradox in contemporary data. Explanations for the paradox can be roughly divided into two camps. The first questions the legitimacy of blacks' attitudes. In contrast, the second accepts blacks' pro-school attitudes as legitimate, but notes how blacks may face special challenges converting attitudes into achievement. Although the debate is difficult to resolve definitively, the weight of evidence is more consist with the latter view.

Blacks' Pro-School Attitudes Lack Credibility

A straightforward way of explaining the attitude/achievement paradox is to discount black's positive attitudes. Some scholars view blacks' optimism as too good to be true. Given their disadvantaged socioeconomic position, continued residential segregation, and unfair treatment in the labor market, the fact that blacks express more pro-school attitudes than whites strikes some as implausible. Farkas et al. express this concern regarding blacks' pro-school attitudes:

African American students tend to give surprisingly optimistic answers to these questions, answers that are typically inconsistent with the students'

objective circumstances. Thus these survey items may be an inadequate indicator of these students' complex social psychology.

Blacks also disclose negative information about their school attitudes and behaviors, making it awkward to push this explanation too far. In Shaker Heights, Ohio, John U. Ogbu found plenty of black youths willing to admit that they were uninterested in schooling and that they thought that blacks did not try as hard as whites in school. When researchers explicitly ask blacks about race-based barriers to success, blacks freely acknowledge them. Given their willingness to disclose information that does not necessarily present their racial/ethnic group positively, the notion that blacks are eager to project a psychologically protective pro-school image is limited.

Rather than discounting all attitudes, a variation suggests that some attitudes matter, while others do not. For example, Roslyn Arlin Mickelson distinguished between abstract attitudes as reflecting "dominant American ideology that holds that education is the solution to most social problems," versus concrete attitudes that reflect "the material realities in which education may or may not lead to social mobility." Her solution to the paradox depends on empirical support for a key proposition—blacks' pro-school attitudes are restricted to the kinds that do not matter for achievement. Mickelson reported support for this position by studying 1,193 high school seniors surveyed in the spring of 1983 in eight Los Angeles high schools. She found that blacks tended to be more pro-school than whites on abstract attitudes such as "Education is the key to success in the future," but that these kinds of attitudes failed to predict grades. In contrast, blacks reported more negative concrete attitudes for items such as "Based on their experiences, my parents say people like us are not always paid or promoted according to our education," and these kinds of attitudes predicted grade point average. This argument represented a compelling solution to the attitude/achievement paradox because it acknowledged that blacks express pro-school attitudes, but explained why these can be combined with such low achievement—the attitudes for which blacks are so positive are also the ones that are of no consequence.

Other scholarship questions this position, however. For example, blacks' educational expectations are unusually high, according to Daniel Solorzano, but the relationship between educational expectations and achievement appears comparable between blacks and whites. Using the nationally representative NELS data, Douglas Downey, James Ainsworth, and Zhenchao Qian first identified several indicators of school attitudes for which blacks were more pro-school than whites. They then tested which attitudes predicted educational outcomes and found little support for the position that blacks' pro-school attitudes are restricted to the kinds that do not affect achievement. The authors also considered a related question: Is blacks' attitude/achievement relationship unusual relative to other minority groups? They found that attitude/achievement correlations are similar among blacks, Asian Americans, and Hispanics, but slightly stronger among whites. Notably, there was no evidence that blacks were an anomalous group.

Challenges Changing Attitudes

Given these patterns, some scholars are viewing blacks' pro-school attitudes with greater credibility. Because achievement depends on much more than attitudes, it is possible that blacks' pro-school attitudes are legitimate (or at least as legitimate as those of other minority groups), but their school achievement lags behind that of whites because blacks face other challenges. Blacks' well-documented disadvantages in terms of socioeconomic standing (i.e., parents' education, occupation, and income), family structure, neighborhood resources, school resources, and wealth may combine to countervail the advantages accrued by good attitudes toward school. Models demonstrating the attitude/achievement paradox typically statistically control for some of these disadvantages, but it is unlikely that they fully account for the many disadvantages that blacks experience. In most statistical models in which many observables (e.g., socioeconomic status and family structure) are used to equalize racial/ethnic groups, blacks are likely still disadvantaged in ways that are difficult to measure.

One example of a disadvantage that is rarely included in statistical models, discriminatory processes, may undermine blacks' efforts to convert attitudes into achievement. When it comes to buying a home or applying for a job, gatekeepers continue to think less of blacks. These same prejudices may persist in schools in a way that makes it more difficult for blacks to convert expectations into achievement. For example, white and high-socioeconomic teachers tend to evaluate the classroom behavior of black students less favorably than black teachers. While this

may explain why blacks' attitude/achievement correlations are not as strong as whites, why blacks have such pro-school attitudes in the first place requires explanation. Most scholars have assumed that both historical and current disadvantages should lead to discouragement among blacks, but blacks have made important improvements in the last century. Other scholars note how blacks acknowledge the social barriers that exist, but that they also maintain optimism about the future. These positive attitudes may be a function of witnessing continued improvement over generations. Black youths are more likely than whites to agree that their children will be better off than they are.

On its surface, the combination of blacks' pro-school attitudes and poor school performance presents a puzzle. One explanation for this paradox is that blacks' pro-school attitudes should not really be believed. This explanation is not fully convincing, however, because attitude/achievement correlations for blacks are only modestly weaker than for whites, and are comparable to those of other minority groups (e.g., Asian Americans and Hispanics). Rather than discount blacks' pro-school attitudes, an alternative explanation views them as credible, acknowledging how blacks face greater barriers converting attitudes into achievement.

Douglas Downey
Ohio State University

See Also: Classroom Interactions: Teachers and Students; Morale in Schools; Racial Inequality: Achievement; Racism in Education; Self Esteem.

Further Readings

Ainsworth, James W. "Why Does It Take a Village? The Mediation of Neighborhood Effects on Educational Achievement." *Social Forces,* v.81/1 (2002).

Ainsworth-Darnell, James W. and Douglas B. Downey. "Assessing the Oppositional Culture Explanation for Racial/Ethnic Differences in School Performance." *American Sociological Review,* v.63/4 (1998).

Coleman, James Samuel. "Equality of Educational Opportunity." Washington, DC: U.S. Government Printing Office, 1966.

Conley, Dalton. *Being Black, Living in the Red: Race, Wealth, and Social Policy in America.* Berkeley: University of California Press, 1999.

Downey, Douglas B., James W. Ainsworth, and Zhenchao Qian. "Rethinking the Attitude-Achievement Paradox Among Blacks." *Sociology of Education,* v.82/1 (2009).

Farkas, George, et al. "Does Oppositional Culture Exist in Minority and Poverty Peer Groups?" *American Sociological Review*, v.67/1 (2002).

Hochschild, Jennifer L. *Facing Up to the American Dream: Race, Class, and the Soul of the Nation.* Princeton, NJ: Princeton University Press, 1995.

Mickelson, Roslyn Arlin. "The Attitude-Achievement Paradox Among Black Adolescents." *Sociology of Education*, v.63/1 (1990).

Ogbu, John U. *Black American Students in an Affluent Suburb: A Study of Academic Disengagement.* Mahwah, NJ: L. Erlbaum Associates, 2003.

Australia

The Commonwealth of Australia is the world's sixth-largest country, with a total area of 2,941,299 square miles (7,617,930 square kilometers). The population was estimated at 22.6 million in June 2011. With a 2.7 percent annual growth rate in 2010, Australia's economy had $39,699 per capita and $882.4 billion total gross domestic product (GDP). Australia is among the most developed countries in the Southern Hemisphere. As a major exporter of agriculture products and natural resources, its economic sector includes agriculture, the service industry (such as tourism, banking, education), and mining. The inflation rate of Australia was 3.1 percent in December 2011 and the unemployment rate was at 5.1 percent in January 2012. Among members of the G20 and many other international economic organizations, the rapid development of the Australian economy can be largely attributed to open-market policies that favor global trade and investment.

History and Social Structure

The first inhabitants of Australia, or indigenous Aborigines, preserve one of the world's oldest cultures and spoke hundreds of distinct languages. Isolated for millennia before James Cook first claimed the continent for Great Britain in 1770, Aborigines inhabited much of the continent and many of the neighboring islands (including Tasmania and the Torres Strait Islands). Cook's discoveries paved the way for the establishment of a new colony. Many of the first European migrants in Australia included convicts from Britain, gold rush settlers, political refugee families

from Germany, and various others from Greece, Russia, and Turkey. It is made up of six states and two territories: Queensland, New South Wales, Tasmania, Victoria, South Australia, West Australia, Australian Capital Territory, and Northern Territory. Education of all states and territories is under the control of the federal government, which provides equal access to all citizens. Two influential declarations were endorsed to ensure the pursuit of excellence and mass education, namely the Adelaide Declaration on National Goals for Schooling in the Twenty-first Century (1999) and the Melbourne Declaration on Educational Goals for Young Australians (2001). The former reflected the national goals of promoting academic attainment for all students, while the latter addresses the significant influence of education on an Australian core value of building a democratic society with diverse cultures.

Basic education became compulsory during the late 19th century, and each state government has its own education acts. Australian education had significant setbacks during the Great Depression and World Wars I and II. Afterward, it made tremendous achievements nationwide. Some important federal legislation in the last 40 years include the Racial Discrimination Act (1975), Sex Discrimination Act (1984), Affirmative Action Act (1986), Human Rights and Equal Opportunity Act (1986), Disability Discrimination Act (1992), Higher Education Support Act (2003), Schools Assistance Act (2004), and Skills Australia Act (2008). In 2006, government education leaders agreed to encourage greater collaboration, student and faculty mobility, exchange opportunities, and quality assurance in higher education in what later became known as the Brisbane Communiqué (as of 2008, 52 countries were signatories of this agreement). More recent higher education reforms include a focus on quality assurance to establish the Tertiary Education Quality and Standards Agency (TEQSA) in January 2012. In the Australian economy, education is among the largest industries and plays an integral role in public policy and political debates. Public spending on education was reported at 4.4 percent of the total GDP in 2008.

Educational Structure

Preschool education (also called kindergarten) is not mandatory, but is available in a variety of settings. Primary and secondary education is compulsory for Australian citizens and permanent residents. Primary education comprises either six or seven years of education (years 1–6/7), depending on the state or territory. All government and most private primary schools are coeducational. Secondary education is divided into secondary/high school (years 7/8–10) and senior secondary school/college (years 11–12). Secondary education also overlaps with vocational education and training (VET) opportunities that span higher education at the most advanced levels. Most government secondary schools are coeducational; there are many single-sex private schools. In addition to government school offerings, Australia has well-developed private sector involvement in the education system. The traditional school year includes between 200 and 209 days. The Department of Education, Employment and Workplace Relations oversees all areas of education at the federal level and is responsible for leadership and employment training. Each state and territory also has a department of education, which works directly with local level schools and communities.

Of the approximately 1.99 million students enrolled in primary school in 2009, 49 percent were females and 31 percent were enrolled in private schools. Also in the same year, secondary education included roughly 2.26 million students, of which 48 percent were female and 33 percent were enrolled in private schools. The higher education system is divided into advanced training in VET areas and universities. Higher education degrees available to student graduates include two-year associate degrees, three to five year bachelor's degrees, one to two year master's degrees, and doctoral degrees (usually between four and five years in length). Approximately 1.08 million students enrolled in tertiary education in 2007 (55 percent female).

Current Issues

There are growing demands from both internal and external forces that shape Australia's current education reform initiatives. Expanding higher education outreach and programs is a central policy issue for the government through 2020. It is a primary source of revenue, where thousands of students from countries in Asia, Oceania, and other global regions come to study in Australia and enjoy one of the world's top higher education systems (international students comprise 26 percent of all Australian higher education enrollments). In the light of emerging world trends in a knowledge-based economy, there are three strategic goals in alignment with national policies and strategic directions. First, there is a need to increase emphasis on high-quality and cost-effective programs at all education levels. Second, there is a need to continue to build a sustainable learning environment within Australian communities, including investing in life-long learning programs and improving the distribution of instructional materials through optimal mediums. Third, the government is striving to overcome inequalities in education nationwide, including social justice issues like the conflicts between oversized classrooms and a shortage of teachers in Aboriginal education.

The Australian Agency for International Development (AusAID) works with partner governments overseas on education reforms by addressing the importance of financial sustainability, governance, and strengthening monitoring and evaluation systems. AusAID is active in helping enhance bilateral relationships by supporting school-funding initiatives (e.g., fee-free policies), provide assistance to strengthen school governance and planning systems, and ameliorate the delivery systems for provision of instructional materials. In terms of current education racial inequalities, the Aboriginal and Torres Strait Islander Education Action Plan (2010–14) offers a guideline to help bridge the gap between indigenous and nonindigenous students within Australian schools and educational departments. This plan addresses six key areas: improve the readiness for attending school, engagement and connections, attendance, enhancing literacy and numeracy skills, leadership, quality teaching and workforce development, and pathways to real post-school options, including finding meaningful employment.

W. James Jacob
Junhan Ma
University of Pittsburgh

See Also: Canada; Indonesia; New Zealand; Singapore; United Kingdom.

Further Readings

AusAID. "Current Issues in Education: Working Through Partner Government Systems in the Education Sector." Canberra, Australia: AusAID Education Resource Facility, 2011.

Jones, Phillip E. *Education in Australia.* Hamden, CT: Archon Books, 1974.

Marginson, Simon. "The Global Position of Australian Higher Education 2020: Summary Paper." Melbourne, Australia: Centre for the Study of Higher Education, University of Melbourne, 2008.

Marks, Gary N. and Julie McMillan. "Declining Inequality? The Changing Impact of Socio-Economic Background and Ability on Education in Australia." *British Journal of Sociology,* v.54/4 (2003).

Partridge, Percy H. *Society, Schools, and Progress in Australia.* New York: Pergamon Press, 1968.

Austria

Austria is a landlocked country in the center of Europe. It has an area of 83,858 square kilometers and a population of 8.4 million. Immigration has risen in recent years; in 2010, around 10 percent of the population was non-Austrian citizens. The population is aging; in 2009, 23 percent were 60 years and over. In 2010, gross domestic product (GDP) per capita was 30,700 euros based on purchase power parity, and unemployment was 4.4 percent. Since 1995, Austria has been a member of the European Union. It has a federal political structure comprising nine provinces and a federal government. General legislation for all educational matters rests with the federal parliament. The organization of the schools, the curriculum, and the arrangements of school life are much the same throughout the country. In 2009, 18 percent of the 25- to 64-year-old population had not completed more than compulsory school at age 15, 63 percent had a qualification at the upper secondary level, and 19 percent had tertiary education. Among the 25- to 34-year-old population, 88 percent had a qualification above compulsory school and 21 percent had tertiary qualification.

In early modern times, education in Europe was strongly affected by the clash between Catholicism and Protestantism. When the Habsburg dynasty opted for counter reformation, Austrian universities and gymnasia (schools for the elite) were handed over to the religious order of the Jesuits who were in charge of Austrian education until the late 18th century. Because the Catholic Church placed little emphasis on lay Bible reading, literacy rates up to the 18th century were low compared to the Protestant countries of Germany. However, emperors of enlightened absolutism were pioneers in introducing compulsory schooling for children. After 1848, Austria reshaped its elite segment according to the neohumanist principles of higher learning. Gymnasia and universities became secular institutions. During the second half of

the 19th century, universities quickly caught up to the standards of German research universities, and at the turn of the century, some Austrian universities were among the top tier of that era. As in Germany, the educated middle classes enjoyed an exceptional high social standing. In 1869, the Catholic Church lost control over the compulsory nonelite segment of education.

However, a contract with the Vatican continued to grant the Catholic Church significant privileges, such that the state paid teacher salaries in private Catholic schools. After 1918, the transformation from a huge multinational empire to a small nation created serious problems. Severe and long-lasting damage to schools and higher education institutions was inflicted by the successive Austro-fascist and Nazi regimes. As a result, the country lost most of its productive intellectual elite. Expansion of higher learning, starting in the 1960s, eroded the hegemony of the educated middle classes over cultural affairs. Yet, they were still powerful enough to prevent structural reforms of the education system. At a time when most European countries moved toward comprehensive schooling at the lower secondary level, Austria—like other German-speaking countries—maintained the practice of early selection into various academic streams at age 10.

Educational Structure

Pre-primary education is called kindergarten; it is a responsibility of the municipalities and is not regarded as part of the formal school structure. Education is compulsory between the ages of 6 and 15 years. About 6 percent of the pupils attend private schools which are mostly run by the Roman Catholic Church or affiliated institutions. Most private schools conform to state laws and can issue certificates equivalent to state schools. Primary school consists of grades 1 through 4, and is the only comprehensive school. Streaming starts when students transfer to secondary schools. Lower secondary education consists of grades 5 through 8, and is divided into the "main school," called the Hauptschule, that used to provide education for the masses, and the gymnasium that used to be the school for the elite. Educational expansion starting in the 1960s blurred this distinction, but institutional differentiation still exists. Upper secondary education that consists of grades 9 through 12 is divided into the academically oriented gymnasium and different types of vocational education. Students who graduate from the gymnasium, called Matura, are entitled to enroll at universities.

Full-time vocational schools are divided into middle and higher branches. Students who graduate from the latter are also entitled to enroll at universities. Students who leave the system by the end of compulsory schooling usually start an apprenticeship in the dual system that combines practical training at a firm with formal instruction at a vocational school. The well-developed vocational training at the secondary level is one reason for lower participation at the tertiary level. In 2009, entry rates into tertiary education of students below the age of 25 were 51 percent in Austria, compared with an Organisation for Economic Co-operation and Development (OECD) average of 60 percent. Tertiary education in Austria is characterized by weak differentiation.

Until 1993, when a nonuniversity sector called Fachhochschulen was introduced, research universities had a monopoly in higher education. Because of the late development of non-university alternatives, enrollment in higher education is still dominated by research universities. In 2010, 81 percent of the students were enrolled at universities, 15 percent were enrolled at the non-university sector of higher education, and 4 percent were enrolled at other postsecondary institutions. In 2008, total expenditure for education was 5.4 percent of GDP, of which 0.2 percent was private. Expenditure for pre-primary education was 0.5 percent, for primary and secondary schools 3.6 percent, and for tertiary education 1.3 percent of GDP.

Current Issues

Although all aspects of Austrian education are strongly affected by the significant expansion of gymnasia and universities that commenced in the 1960s, the structure of the system is still shaped by the legacy of the former elite system that was characterized by a sharp division between the education of the ordinary people and the cultivated elite. The notion of a separate track for elite education is reflected in the binary structure of teacher training. Only teachers for the gymnasium and vocational equivalents are educated at universities; teachers for compulsory schools are trained at nonuniversity institutions.

In the course of educational expansion, the consequences of early tracking at age 10 have changed significantly. The nonelite track of compulsory schooling, which until the 1960s enrolled the vast majority of the age cohort, is becoming very unpopular. Today, talented students who would have taken up highly skilled vocational apprenticeships are sent to the gymnasium. As a result, only the disadvantaged remain at the Hauptschule. The perseverance of the elite concept can also be observed at the transition to higher education. Universities do not have the right to admit students because graduates of gymnasia are "entitled" to enroll at any university and any subject. The concept of "sponsored mobility" explains the pattern of early selection of academically talented students who are relieved of competitive pressure when they enter postsecondary education.

Hans Pechar
University of Klagenfurt

See Also: Germany; Mobility, Contest Versus Sponsored; Tracking.

Further Readings

Cohen, Gary B. *Education and Middle-Class Society in Imperial Austria, 1848–1918.* West Lafayette, IN: Purdue University Press, 1996.

Melton, James Van Horn. *Absolutism and the Eighteenth-Century Origins of Compulsory Schooling in Prussia and Austria.* Cambridge: Cambridge University Press, 1988.

Pechar, Hans. "Austrian Higher Education Meets the Knowledge Society." *Canadian Journal of Higher Education,* v.34/3 (2004).

B

Baccalaureate Education, Pre-International

The Pre-International Baccalaureate is an educational program developed by the International Baccalaureate (IB) for students 3 to 16 years old. The Pre-International Baccalaureate is a precursor to the IB Diploma Programme that is offered during the last two years of school for students 16 to 18 years old. The Pre-International Baccalaureate was developed to meet the needs of educational institutions requesting preliminary studies in order to enrich and support the scholastic endeavors of prospective IB Diploma students.

Founded in 1968, the IB is an international educational organization located in Geneva, Switzerland. Its purpose is to facilitate the international mobility of students preparing for university by providing schools with a common pre-university curriculum, a common set of external examinations, and a diploma recognized by universities around the world. The IB is present in 3,324 schools in 141 countries. IB North America was established in 1977, and works with schools in the United States, Canada, and the Caribbean. The greatest concentration of IB programs is in the United States, where 90 percent of the programs are integrated into public schools. The Pre-International IB comprises two programs of education. The Primary Years Programme (PYP) for students ages 3 to 12 and the Middle Years Programme (MYP) for students ages 11 to 16. The PYP and MYP can be offered individually, or as a continuum in preparation for the diploma program.

The PYP, with the goal of raising primary students' skills and knowledge and to prepare them for entrance into the MYP, was piloted in 1996, and authorized in 1997. Within five years, as many as 87 PYP were implemented in schools in 43 countries worldwide. While the PYP prepares students for the IB Middle Years Program, it is not a prerequisite for it. The PYP focuses on the development of the whole child as an inquirer, both locally and globally. The subject areas taught in the PYP are language, social studies, mathematics, science and technology, arts, and personal, social, and physical education. In accordance with the mandates of a globalized curriculum, students are required to learn a second language during the course of the program. Assessment is carried out by teachers according to strategies provided by the IB and according to local curricular guidelines.

Middle Years Program

The International Baccalaureate (IB) Middle Years Program (MYP) is an educational program intended for students ages 11 to 16. The MYP adheres to the study of eight subject areas: mother tongue, a second language, humanities, sciences, mathematics, arts, physical education, and technology. Like the PYP, the MYP was developed and piloted in the mid-1990s. Similarly to the PYP, within five years, 51 countries had adopted this program. The MYP provides a framework of academic challenge by encouraging students to pursue a critical understanding of the connections between traditional subjects and the real world. An important component of this program is the development of critical skills within a diverse, inclusive, and international context. In the final year of the program, students also engage in a personal project, which allows them to demonstrate the understandings and skills that they have developed throughout the program. The program is often taught throughout the middle-school years and the first two years of high school. Typically, middle schools and high schools work in coordination with each other when the program cannot be entirely hosted within one combined school. Even though the full MYP program lasts five years, more limited programs can be adopted with permission from the International Baccalaureate Organization (IB).

Educating the Whole Person

In both the PYP and MYP, teachers integrate local and global curricula through the lens of the IB framework of inquiry. Framed within international worldviews, students are challenged by rigorous, thought-provoking comprehensive courses. Research skills and sophistication in writing and presenting are significant outcomes of the program. The Pre-International IB program promotes the education of the whole person, emphasizing intellectual, personal, emotional, and social growth through all areas of knowledge. To this end, the Pre-International Baccalaureate prepares students for the rigors of the International Baccalaureate Diploma program by providing them with foundational skills in the areas of literacy, numeracy, and technology and by focusing on the development of independent critical and creative skills within a global perspective. By working with schools, governments, and international organizations to develop programs of international education, the Pre-International Baccalaureate Program encourages students to become lifelong learners and engaged and dynamic citizens who understand and practice intercultural awareness and global citizenship.

Karen Ragoonaden
University of British Columbia, Okanagan

See Also: Globalization; International Baccalaureate Education; School Mobility and Education; Standardized Testing; Student Roles in the Classroom.

Further Readings

Hill, I. "International Education as Developed by the International Baccalaureate Organization." In *The SAGE Handbook of Research in International Education,* M. Hayden, et al., eds. London: Sage, 2007.
International Baccalaureate (IB). *IB Learner Profile Booklet.* Geneva: International Baccalaureate Organization, 2008.
Peterson, A. D. C. *Schools Across Frontiers: The Story of the International Baccalaureate and the United World Colleges.* 2nd ed. La Salle, IL: Open Court, 2003.
Wells, J. "International Education, Values and Attitudes: A Critical Analysis of the International Baccalaureate (IB) Learner's Profile." *Journal of Research in International Education,* v.10/2 (2011).

Bahamas

The Commonwealth of the Bahamas, consisting of 29 islands, 661 cays, and 2,987 islets, covers 5,382 square miles (13,939 square kilometers) and is located in the Atlantic Ocean north of Cuba and southeast of the United States, less than 60 miles (100 kilometers) from Florida. The Bahamas gained independence from the British in 1973, but still retains its membership in the Commonwealth Nations, which means that Queen Elizabeth II of the United Kingdom—represented by a governor—is the head of state, but the Bahamian prime minister holds executive powers. The World Bank estimated its population at 313,312 in 2011 and the 2011 Human Development Index ranked the Bahamans 53 out of 187 countries surveyed, giving it a high developed country index.

Most Bahamians are the descendants of African slaves, and prior to independence, whites, then just 10 percent of the population, controlled both the government and the economy. The highest level of employment was the civil service, teaching, nursing, or the church. The Bahamas, now with a service-based economy, has been a member of the Caribbean Community (CARICOM) since 1983 and its major exports are pharmaceuticals, cement, rum, crawfish, and refined petroleum products. Situated in the turbulent Atlantic Ocean hurricane zone, the Bahamas is frequently plagued by poor weather during hurricane season. In September 2004, for example, the Bahamas suffered from the devastating effects of Hurricane Frances, and then Hurricane Jean just three weeks later.

Challenges of Education

The Houghton Report of 1958 pointed out the challenges of education on the island and made recommendations to rectify these, including the 1962 Education Act and the establishment of the Ministry of Education in 1964, which became a contributing member of the University of the West Indies that same year. The foundation for education reform was laid out in the Focus on the Future White Paper of 1972 that details the plans for education in an independent Bahamas. After independence, education received a large share of the national budget, and the abolition of the Common Entrance examination (grade nine) in 1974 was meant to ensure access, inclusion, and equity in education. The Maraj Report of 1974, which provided a blueprint for education expansion of the 1970s and 1980s, recommended sweeping changes for systemwide planning, decentralization, preschool education, and the development of technical and vocational education (TVET). In the early1980s, TVET became a priority, along with human resource development (HRD) and World Bank–funded Bahamian efforts.

The 1980s were also marked by the expansion of the school system in response to recommendations of two task forces that were commissioned to analyze teacher education and student examination. First, in 1982, curriculum reform encouraged the consolidation and standardization of educational provision across the islands. Second, in 1985, standardized assessments for third, sixth, and eighth grades were implemented. Third, in 1987, junior and senior high schools were replaced by single phased secondary schools with grades 7 through 12. Finally, in 1993, the Task Force on Education recommended the implementation of the following:

- Locally designed national secondary school certificate examinations
- Curriculum restructuring
- Increased access to education
- Enhancements in human resource development, administration, management, and partnerships in education

In 1995, the Inter-Development Bank (IDB) provided a $33 million loan for the improvement of primary and secondary education, as well as the construction of two senior high schools.

For all children ages 5 to 17, education is mandatory and free for attendance to government schools. After the primary level (grades 1–6) students can transfer into junior high (grades 7–9), and then senior high (grades 10–12). In some Bahamian districts, grades 1–9 are combined in all-age schools. Net enrollment at both the primary and secondary school levels is estimated at 92 percent and the national literacy rate is 99 percent. Around 24 percent of the national budget is allocated to education.

The 2004 Strategic Plan lists its goals as the achievement of the seamless path to postsecondary or tertiary education or to the world of work for Bahamian citizens. The College of the Bahamas, a two-year institution established in 1974, is now converting to a four-year institution. In 2005, the IDB provided $18 million for training focused on improving overall education management and strengthening early education. Current educational reforms are focused on the following:

1. Preschool—developing preschool programs for the vulnerable, national standards in preschool centers, staff training, and upgrading
2. TVET—the alignment of TVET with secondary and postsecondary activities through the establishment of a National Training Agency and the development of competency-based courses
3. Technology—better technology integration to enhance teacher capacity and delivery of quality technical support and training to staff via distance technology.

Tavis D. Jules
Loyola University Chicago, CEPS

See Also: Barbados, Cuba, Guyana, Trinidad and Tobago.

Further Readings
Bahamas Ministry of Education. "Ten Year Education Plan" (2009). UNESCO. http://www.planipolis.iiep .unesco.org/upload/Bahamas/Bahamas_Aug_2009_20 _year_Education_Plan.pdf (Accessed August 2012).
CARICOM. *The Future of Education in the Caribbean.* Georgetown, Guyana: CARICOM, 1993.
Craton, Michael and Gail Saunders. *Islanders in the Stream: A History of the Bahamian People: Volume Two: From the Ending of Slavery to the Twenty First Century.* Athens: University of Georgia Press, 2000.
Saunders, Gail. *Bahamian Society After Emancipation.* Kingston, Jamaica: Ian Randle Publishing, 1990.

Bangladesh

Bangladesh is located above the Bay of Bengal, surrounded by Myanmar on the southeast and India on the north, northeast, and west. This fertile and lush country comprises an area of 55,211 square miles (143,998 square kilometers), with an estimated population of 158,570,535 million, the seventh most populated country in the world. Its economy depends on agriculture and forestry, fishing, mining and quarrying, and manufacturing. Bangladesh's gross domestic product (GDP) increased 6.7 percent during 2011 because of strong manufacturing, a bumper harvest, and a healthy service sector. In 2010, the poverty level declined to 31.5 percent because of growth and development, which propelled and strengthened the education and health sectors in comparison to its population. In 2010, Bangladesh's external debt stocks declined to 22.8 percent of gross national income. In 2011, the International Development Association (IDA) approved $1.2 billion for the Padma Multipurpose Bridge Project that will connect the secluded southwest region to the mainland.

Two-Nation Theory

In 1947, India separated from Britain and divided into two countries on the basis of religion, Pakistan and India. Since east Bengal, present-day Bangladesh, was inhabited predominantly by Muslims, this region became a part of Pakistan and was renamed East Pakistan. West Pakistan, present-day Pakistan, and East Pakistan were unified under one government on the basis of religious faith, known as the Two-Nation Theory. During this period, the educational system branched into segments: English-medium, Bengali-medium, and Urdu-medium schools. Arabic continued to be taught during religious studies. In 1952, Dhaka University students protested against central government in West Pakistan, after West Pakistan declared Urdu as the official language. Since most East Pakistanis spoke in the Bengali language, they saw this as an insult. In 1971, The Pakistan Army waged a nine-month war against East Pakistan that ended in defeat. On December 16, 1971, East Pakistan becomes a sovereign state named Bangladesh in honor of the Bengali language. Bangladesh's independence from Pakistan transformed its educational structure. The educational system eliminated Urdu from the school and students were offered to attend either Bengali-medium or English-medium schools.

The educational structure of Bangladesh falls under three categories: general, madrasa (Islamic school), and technical-vocational. General education in Bangladesh includes free primary education (grades 1–5); secondary education divided into three parts: junior secondary (grades 6–8), secondary (grades 9–10), and higher secondary (grades 11–12); and tertiary education, including colleges and universities. Approximately 47 percent of primary schools are Government Primary Schools (GPS). The educational structure is headed by two ministries, the Ministry of Education (MoE) and the Ministry of Primary and Mass Education Division (MoPME). From the late 1990s to 2003, primary enrollment increased from 90 to 98 percent, with a 44 percent increase at the secondary level, marking Bangladesh's education system excellence compared to similar countries of per-capita income. During the 2010–11 school year, the Ministry of Education noted that 4.22 percent of GDP was allocated to their department. In 2005, Grade 10 examination pass scores increased 50 percent within two years. Approximately 1,962 schools receive financial awards because of successful Grade 10 examination scores. The University Grants Commission (UGC) of Bangladesh oversees, organizes, assesses, and aids established public, private, and international universities. The Educational Commission of 2003 initiated many large initiatives from teacher training, providing a single-track curriculum for secondary level education, creating 10 foreign language centers, privatization of textbooks, recruiting qualified teachers, and establishing an accreditation council. Bangladesh successfully achieved gender parity in education, with increased enrollment from girls of all socioeconomic backgrounds, accomplishing one of the Millennium Development Goals. The Bangladesh government provides free textbooks to all schools and stipends to low-income students.

Although Bangladesh's educational structure improved after independence, it is attempting to provide universal primary enrollment by 2015. Bangladesh lacks a standard achievement test to assess primary school students and check the quality of education. Although the poverty level is decreasing, there is a need for low-income students to attend school in densely populated areas. School facilities and locations needs improvement and repairs to accommodate the large student population. There is a strong emphasis on teachers' training and decreasing the teacher-student ratio, since it stands at 1:54 at the primary level. Bangladesh's National Curriculum and Textbook

Board (NCTB) needs professional and permanent staff, equipment, and resources to develop curriculum and high-quality textbooks. There is a pressing need to create textbooks in the Bangla language.

Fatema Rahman
Indiana University

See Also: India; Pakistan; Poverty and Education.

Further Readings

Ahmed, Salahuddin. *Bangladesh: Past and Present.* Delhi, India: Aph Publishing Corporation, 2004.

Bangladesh Bureau of Statistics. "GCP of Bangladesh at 2007–08 to 2010–11." http://www.bbs.gov.bd/WebTestApplication/userfiles/Image/BBS/GDP_2011.pdf (Accessed December 2011).

Bangladesh Ministry of Education. http://www.moedu.gov.bd (Accessed December 2011).

Bangladesh Ministry of Primary and Mass Education. http://www.mopme.gov.bd (Accessed December 2011).

Heitzman, James and Robert L. Worden, eds. *Bangladesh: A Country Study.* Washington, DC: U.S. Government Printing Office, 1989.

Hossain, Akhand Akhtar. "Macroeconomic Policies and Agricultural Terms of Trade, Bangladesh, 1952–2005." *Journal of Contemporary Asia,* v.39/2 (2009).

Imam, Syeda Rumnaz. "English as a Global Language and the Question of Nation-Building Education in Bangladesh." *Comparative Education,* v.41/4 (2005).

Musa, Monsur. "Politics of Language Planning in Pakistan and the Birth of a New State." *International Journal of the Sociology of Language,* v.118 (1996).

Banking Concept of Education

Paulo Freire (1921–97), a Brazilian educator, philosopher, and critical theorist, coined the phrase *banking concept of education* in an essay of the same name published in his book *Pedagogy of the Oppressed.* Freire proposed that the traditional form of education is like banking: the teacher makes deposits into the students (the accounts). Freire contended that because education reflects the political reality of a society, it plays out the power relationships within society, and this teacher-centered style of education serves to maintain the status quo and to oppress the less powerful and the powerless. He contrasted this type of education to problem posing, which is student centered. He proposed that in order for the power differential to be equalized, problem-posing education should be implemented. This type of student-centered education would be liberatory because it would teach students, therefore the citizenry, how to think critically and have an active voice in society. He proposed that only in this way can the citizenry develop the necessary awareness to avoid becoming victims of oppression, and avoid victimizing or oppressing others.

The banking concept of education refers to various aspects of the educational experience. The foundational notion is that the teacher is the expert authority figure who imparts knowledge to students. The students are meek, compliant listeners, which also implies that the teacher teaches primarily through lecturing. As the expert, the teacher makes all decisions about what is going to be taught, with no input from the students. The teacher also has the responsibility, right, and power to discipline students. The teacher's authority is central to the educational experience, so that it becomes more of a "teacher's experience" than a "student's experience." This submission to authority then plays itself out in the lives of the citizens who do know or understand that they can have a voice in society at all levels. Those in power continue to wield their authority, dictating their decisions and mandates in much the same way as the authoritarian teacher.

Freire believed that education and literacy were the keys to social change and that an educated citizenry could overcome oppressive conditions. He proposed that in order to achieve this level of awareness, education should be problem posing. In this student-centered type of education, teaching and learning are processes in which students actively engage in inquiry and dialog among themselves and with the teacher. Shared activity is learned, in which one student or the teacher does not have power over the others. Each participant has a voice and learns how to express themselves. Freire's work has influenced proponents of social reconstructionism and critical pedagogy.

Lynn W. Zimmerman
Purdue University Calumet

See Also: Critical Theory of Education; Freire, Paulo; Teacher Decision-Making Power.

Further Readings

Freire, P. *Pedagogy of the Oppressed*. New York: Continuum Books, 1970.

Giroux, H. *Teachers as Intellectuals: Toward a Critical Pedagogy of Learning*. South Hadley, MA: Bergin & Garvey, 1988.

Hooks, B. *Teaching to Transgress: Education as the Practice of Freedom*. New York: Routledge, 1994.

Kincheloe, J. L. *Knowledge and Critical Pedagogy: An Introduction*. London: Springer, 2008.

McLaren, P. *Life in Schools: An Introduction to Critical Pedagogy in the Foundations of Education*. 5th ed. New York: Merrill, 2007.

Shapiro, H. Svi and David E. Purpel, eds. *Critical Social Issues in American Education: Democracy and Meaning in a Globalizing World*. 3rd ed. Mahwah, NJ: Lawrence Erlbaum, 2005.

Barbados

Barbados, a colony of Britain until 1966, is a 166-square-mile (430-square-kilometer) island located in the Atlantic Ocean about 200 miles (320 kilometers) northeast of Trinidad and Tobago and about 450 miles (720 kilometers) northwest of Guyana in South America. The World Bank estimates its 2011 population to be 286,705. Most Barbadians are the descendants of African slaves brought to the island during the 17th century to work the sugar cane plantations. Barbados, now a center for financial services and tourism, is economically and politically stable, making it one of the more populated and affluent Caribbean nations. According the 2011 Human Development Index, Barbados ranked 47 out of 187 countries surveyed, giving it a very high developed country rating and placing it above the regional average.

Barbados was a member of the Caribbean Free Trade Association (CARIFTA) in 1968, its post cursor the Caribbean Community (CARICOM) in 1973, and the Caribbean Single Market in 2006. Barbados is estimated to be a high-income country and its major exports are sugar and molasses, rum, other foods and beverages, chemicals, electrical components, and clothing. Barbados is a Commonwealth Nation, which means that Queen Elizabeth II of the United Kingdom—represented by a governor—is the head of state, but its prime minister holds executive powers.

Education grants awarded through the state in the early 1900s allowed for the expansion and achievement of mass primary education. However, beyond the primary level, educational opportunities in Barbados were reserved for the fortunate elite (mainly whites and non-blacks) and a few privileged blacks. By 1952, with suffrage obtained by the black majority, Barbadians began to vote for educational reforms. Such reforms included the following:

- Introduction of Secondary Modern Schools (comprehensive schools)
- Establishment of the Common Entrance Examination (for grade 9) in 1959
- Abolition of fees for government grammar schools in 1962
- Financial assistance for private secondary school.

The University of the West Indies (UWI), established in 1948, opened a third campus in Cave Hill, Barbados, in 1963. In 1972, Barbados joined the Caribbean Examination Council (CXC), which provides secondary school exit examinations in the form of the Caribbean Secondary School Certification Examination (CSEC) and the Caribbean Advanced Proficiency Examinations (CAPE) and in 1983, a national advisory commission on education was created.

Post-colonial education reform under the Democratic Labour Party was premised upon modernization and expansion of mass schooling, universal and free primary education, and secondary schooling for all. During this period, the education budget was reduced from 20.2 percent in 1979–80 to 17 percent in 1986–87. By 1997, the basic education provision had been achieved at the primary and secondary level, and near the end of the 1990s, more primary and secondary students were enrolled in private schools than in government schools. In 1998, Barbados received a Caribbean Development Bank loan ($31.5 million) and an Inter-American Development Bank loan ($85 million) to establish EduTech, aimed at reforming the national curriculum and associated teaching methodologies.

Educational Requirements

Starting from age 3, children have two years of pre-primary education, followed by seven years of primary education (grades K–6), then they write the Barbados Secondary School Entrance Examination (BSSEE). Students then have five years of secondary school (grades 7–12), after which they will write the CSEC. If they wish to pursue further studies, some students will spend two additional years (grades 13–14) in secondary school and write CAPE to be awarded the CXC Associate Degree, or go directly to university or work. Students seeking admission to UWI need a minimum of five passes (of either grades A, B, or C) at CXC, including passes in both mathematics and English. To date, Barbados boasts the highest enrollment rate for tertiary education within CARICOM. The Barbadian literacy rate is 99 percent. The education budget in Barbados averages between 14 and 20 percent. In 2001, Barbados received an EU grant for 1.32 million euros toward development of a skill-intensive and multilingual program to prepare Barbadians for the international labor market. This grant went toward improving physical facilities and training capabilities, and developing infrastructure. Today, the challenges facing education in Barbados center on: the provision of access, the lack of the utilization of community management in schools, the movement from teacher-based education to student-based education, and the underutilization of partnerships in education.

Tavis D. Jules
Loyola University Chicago, CEPS

See Also: Bahamas; Cuba; Guyana; Trinidad and Tobago.

Further Readings

CARICOM. *The Future of Education in the Caribbean.* Georgetown, Guyana: CARICOM, 1993.
Ministry of Education Youth Affairs and Culture. "Education in Barbados: Information Handbook" (2000). http://www.mes.gov.bb/UserFiles/File/Education_in_Barbados.pdf (Accessed August 2012).
Ministry of Education Youth Affairs and Culture. "Historic Developments of Education in Barbados" (2000). http://www.mes.gov.bb/UserFiles/File/Historical_Developments.pdf (Accessed August 2012).

Belgium

Belgium is a northwestern European nation with a 2009 population of 10,661,000. It houses the headquarters of the European Union. Belgians are largely urban residents and enjoy both low poverty rates and high life-expectancy rates. The Belgian population has represented a blend of cultures, languages, and religions throughout the country's history, which resulted in the development of separate schools to serve the main language communities of Dutch, French, and German speakers. Other educational options include private schools and home schooling. Different types of schools and instructional methodologies are common, and freedom of school choice remains a hallmark of Belgian education. Education is compulsory for ages 6 through 18 and literacy is almost universal. The rapid aging of the Belgian population has resulted in recent declines in educational enrollments at lower levels. Belgium has placed a strong cultural value on education throughout its history. The area that became Belgium has been under Roman, Carolingian, Austrian, Spanish, French, and Dutch rule during the course of its history, prior to its emergence as an independent nation in the early 19th century. An early educational system began to emerge under ancient Roman rule, and again under the Carolingian empire. Belgium became part of the Netherlands under the 1814–15 Congress of Vienna, but declared its independence in 1830. Belgium has enjoyed a long history of economic development, from early commerce to later industrialization, which has influenced educational funding and development.

Funding and Regulation

Belgian state funding and regulation of public education dates back to Article 17 of the 1831 Belgian Constitution, which was carried over as Article 24 under Belgium's current constitution. The national government mandated eight years of compulsory education in 1914, extending the requirement to 12 years in 1983. A system of free private schools developed alongside the official state school system. The Catholic Church runs most of Belgium's private schools. Social and political tensions between the systems were in part resolved through a 1958 political agreement and subsequent national legislation extending official government recognition and funding to both systems, ensuring sufficient schools of each type, and offering parents freedom of choice. Another result of this agreement has been a rapid rise in government education expenditures. The national government has also recently begun to oversee the growing practice of home schooling.

The development of the Belgian educational system was also heavily influenced by the tensions between the country's various cultural and linguistic groups. The establishment of French as the national language led to a Flemish movement to receive equal treatment and educational instruction in their native language. Legislation passed in 1932 and 1962 to 1963 mandated that primary and secondary education was to be delivered in the dominant language of each region, whether French, Dutch, or German. Regional ministries of education locally implement national educational policy: the Department for Educational Development within the Dutch language communities in Flanders and Brussels, the Department for Educational Development within the French language communities in Wallonia and Brussels, and the Department of Education within the German language communities in the eastern region. Schools are similarly structured across the three regions, although differences in curriculum and methodology occur. Preschools are free and widely available for children beginning at 2.5 years of age. Preschool is a popular alternative to daycare, with over 90 percent enrollment of eligible children. There is also a well-developed private school system, with the majority of schools Roman Catholic. Other alternatives include international schools and home schooling. Freedom of parental choice of schools has a strong tradition in Belgian education and parental involvement in their children's education is strongly encouraged.

Educational Structure

Belgium provides six years of free, universal, and compulsory primary education, covering ages 6 to 12, and is divided into three two-year cycles. The overall primary school attendance rate in 2009 was 99 percent and the overall primary completion rate was 90 percent. Compulsory secondary education lasts six years, covering ages 12 to 18, and is similarly divided. Primary education covers a broad range of subjects, including reading, writing, mathematics, biology, history, language, and religion. Education has a strong language component, with most students learning two or more languages. Repeating (doubling) of grades is common, and does not carry much social stigma. Secondary students may follow one of four different educational tracks: general, technical, vocational, or artistic. Special secondary educational programs are available for students with physical or mental disabilities. Higher education is widely available at state and private institutions within Flemish and French communities. Enrollment is open to all students possessing a qualifying diploma, although certain fields of study may have additional entrance requirements. There is

also a government-mandated registration fee. Bachelor's, master's, and doctoral degrees are offered. Belgian students had a 2009 overall school life expectancy of 16.4 years, with many remaining in school until their 20s, and overall literacy rates are almost universal.

Marcella Bush Trevino
Barry University

See Also: Catholic Schools; European Union; Germany.

Further Readings

Brusselman-Dehairs, C. and M. Valcke. "Belgium." In *The Education Systems of Europe,* Wolfgang Horner, ed. Dordrecht: Springer, 2007.

Cammaerts, Emile. *Belgium: From the Roman Invasion to the Present Day.* Toronto: FQ Books, 2010.

Ibanez-Martin, Jose Antonio and Gonzalo Jover. *Education in Europe: Policies and Politics.* Boston: Kluwer Academic, 2002.

Bell Curve, The

Eugenics is the exploration of links connecting heredity with physical and mental outcomes in the pursuit of a more desirable species. Many eugenicists in the early 20th century openly endorsed selective breeding and forced sterilization of humans as a means to weed out undesirable behavioral problems like alcoholism and criminality, as well as physical traits such as deafness and mental retardation. The term *eugenics* was coined by British statistician Francis Galton in 1883. Galton's early work expanded the discipline of psychometrics and explored the idea of hereditary intelligence. The eugenics movement's chief proponent in America was Charles B. Davenport (1866–1944). Initially constructed through private financing, the Eugenics Record Office (ERO) was founded by Davenport in 1910, and remained the chief eugenics research organization in the United States until its doors closed in 1944.

Early functions of the ERO included building indexes of American families' traits, garnering support for the eugenics movement, and advising potential marriage partners about the eugenical "fitness" of their marriage. Largely as a result of the backlash against Nazi racial abuses and human experimentation, support for eugenics in the United States faded quickly at the onset of World War II. Funding and support for eugenics research began to dry up, resulting in lessened interest in the subject over subsequent decades. A renewed interest in exploring the connections among heredity, race, class structure, and intelligence was sparked by Charles Murray, a political scientist, and Harvard psychology professor Richard Herrnstein in their controversial text, *The Bell Curve: Intelligence and Class Structure in American Life.* Originally published in 1994, the controversial text ignited a national debate about race relations and drew an instant firestorm of critical response.

Heredity Versus Socioeconomic Status

In *The Bell Curve*, Murray and Herrnstein present several major arguments. The authors claim that an intelligence quotient (IQ) is influenced by heredity and environmental factors and is a better predictor of achievement, behavior, criminality, and success than socioeconomic status or education level. Further, they purport that because IQ is hereditary and largely immutable, increased spending on social programs, particularly welfare reforms, will not have a significant impact and may in fact perpetuate the divide and worsen conditions for those less fortunate. Murray and Herrnstein warned against the creation of an intellectually stratified society, with a "cognitive elite" becoming separated from those of average and below average intelligence, a dangerous social trend. Downplaying the role of race, and emphasizing the role of intellectual advancement and cognition, Murray continues to explore this phenomenon in his latest text, *Coming Apart*. The most controversial claim in *The Bell Curve* was that blacks have lower IQs than whites because of heredity, thus making blacks genetically inferior. This particular claim created a huge outcry and ongoing debate both in support of and against the claim that IQ is largely hereditary, immutable, and race-specific.

A number of critiques of *The Bell Curve* and its claims regarding intelligence, race, and class structure have been cited, including attacks on the methodology. The source of data considered "most satisfactory" by Herrnstein and Murray in *The Bell Curve* were the results of over 12,000 administrations of the Armed Forces Qualification Test (AFQT). Critics of *The Bell Curve* have pointed out that AFQT is not an IQ test, and the sample of Americans to which it has been administered may not be reliable for generalization upon the larger, national population. Some argue that applying a mathematical model to genetics and race, without consideration for the interaction between genetics and environment, is flawed. According to the American Psychological Association, there are differences in average IQ between racial groups, but no consensus among researchers as to the cause. Critics claim that using biology and genetics in particular as predictor of life success, with no control for systematic racism, discrimination, and other environmental factors, is faulty. In their discussion of race and intelligence, Herrnstein and Murray are prone to self-contradiction.

For example, the authors assert that intelligence is largely hereditary and remains static over time at the individual level. Some of the data and research referenced in the book contradicts this assertion; specifically those that find positive changes in intelligence for African Americans who have migrated north or are adopted into higher socioeconomic status households. Critics admit that the "bell curve of intelligence" is arguable, but contend that even if there is some merit to the issue of genetics and inherited IQ, it is not permanent. Intelligence is not immutable; rather, intelligence is malleable and can improve over time. Proponents of the incremental theory of intelligence contend that with the right kind of targeted effort and supports, individuals can become "smarter," that is, aptitude and one's propensity to learn is increased and individuals become more intelligent. Researchers and educational reformers continue to explore the role of intelligence when considering strategies to eliminate the achievement gap among various racial groups and to address issues related to class structure and socioeconomic status in American life.

Bradley W. Davis
Donna Micheaux
University of Texas at Austin

See Also: Class Inequality: Achievement; Cognitive Skill/Intellectual Skill; IQ; Meritocracy; Poverty and Education; Racial Inequality: Achievement.

Further Readings

Jacoby, Russel and Naomi Glauberman, eds. *The Bell Curve Debate: History, Documents, Opinions.* New York: Times Books, 1995.

Murray, Charles A. *Coming Apart: The State of White America, 1960–2010.* New York: Crown, 2012.

Resnick, Lauren. B. "From Aptitude to Effort: A New Foundation for Our Schools." *Daedalus*, v.124/4 (1995).

Bernstein, Basil

Basil Bernstein (1924–2000) was a world-recognized sociologist who examined language styles within the context of family and social class. He is most known for his theory of codes, which showed how mother–child and school language influenced the achievement of students and sustained a social class. His work gained attention in the early 1970s during a period dominated by a "deficit model" of low-income populations. Bernstein's theoretical perspectives continue to be addressed in educational research, but also inform a range of social science research.

Background and Achievements

Bernstein attended the London School of Economics and earned a degree in sociology. He later completed a Ph.D. in Linguistics at University College, London. He received a number of honorary doctorates from Athens, Lund, and in Sweden. He was the Karl Mannheim chair of the Sociology of Education, Institute of Education, at the University of London. In 2001, he received the American Sociological Association, Sociology of Education Section, Willard Waller Award for Lifetime Contributions to the Sociology of Education. He is most known for his theory of the elaborated and restricted codes and authoring a four-volume set titled *Class, Codes and Control*. Bernstein argued that there were everyday speech communication patterns characteristic of social groups that reflected the life of the group and, ultimately, influenced success in school, achievement, and position in society. He argued that the restricted communicative style was used by low-income families, specifically in mother–child interaction, while the elaborated communication style was used by middle-class mothers and approached academic discourse. Bernstein's later work focused on the instructional discourse of education, the transmission of knowledge, and its influence on social groups.

The restricted code was characterized as a language style that was abbreviated because of a group's ability to hold information in common. Thus, subjects or objects of discussion, places and concepts, were left out of the talk as it was assumed that the listener had this knowledge already at hand. It might also be viewed as an informal, context-dependent, interpersonal language. In contrast, the elaborated code presented information with more detail, more words, and with such completeness that it might be understood by someone unfamiliar with the content. The elaborated code was viewed as a communication closer to that used in formal, institutional schooling. Although some viewed the codes as advancing a deficit model, Bernstein noted in his volumes on the codes that one style was not better than the other, but each represented family cultures and modes of meaning in the Michael A. K. Halliday-sense. Finally, the restricted code was part of a closed-role system, where the speaker and listener assumed defined roles that were known to each. In contrast, the elaborated code reflected a more open-ended role system, where roles were fluid. Each language system was viewed by Bernstein as influential in the socializing of children, school achievement, and advancement in society. The elaborate code user was able to navigate both restricted and elaborated codes and, thus, was considered at an advantage in school and life.

Bernstein's theory of codes increased attention to mother–child interaction, language as a vehicle of power and control in society, and language as a socializing factor and regulator of knowledge inside and outside schools. There has been important follow-up empirical and longitudinal research. Ruqaiya Hasan conducted a 10-year empirical examination of mother–child interaction. She confirmed Bernstein's theory, showing that middle-class families interacted significantly differently than low-income families and explained that these differences influenced educational achievement. Still more recently, Hart and Risely's longitudinal study of 43 families and 1,300 hours of parent-child talk showed that professional families of 3-year-olds had uttered 20 million more words than welfare families. They convey not only significant quantitative differences in communication, but also (as Bernstein proposed) cross-generational learning effects. Bernstein's work is worthy of attention from sociologists, curriculum and instruction evaluation experts, language and policy experts, and others seeking to increase the opportunities and life potential of low-income children. It is important that one consider Bernstein's theory of codes in the context of his times and today. They were said to be influenced by Emile Durkheim, but today are relevant for multiple disciplines. Bernstein's work has influenced the study of language as power, cultural meaning systems, privileges of some social groups, the evolution of culture and power over time and across generations, and knowledge acquired and used across contexts.

Rosalind Horowitz
University of Texas, San Antonio

See Also: Class Inequality: Achievement; Maternal Education; Wealth and Education.

Further Readings

Atkinson, P., S. Delamont, and B. Davies, eds. *Discourse and Reproduction: Essays in Honor of Basil Bernstein.* Creskill, NJ: Hampton Press, 1995.

Bernstein, Basil. *Class, Codes and Control.* 4 vols. London: Routledge & Kegan Paul, 1973, 1977, and 1990.

Bernstein, Basil. "Education Cannot Compensate for Society." *New Society* (London), v.15/387 (1970).

Hart, Betty and Todd R. Risely. *Meaningful Differences in the Everyday Experience of Young American Children.* Baltimore, MD: Paul H. Brookes, 1995.

Sadovnik, Alan R., ed. *Knowledge and Pedagogy: The Sociology of Basil Bernstein.* Norwood, NJ: Ablex, 1995.

Bidwell, Charles

Charles Bidwell is an American sociologist, noted for his contributions to sociology of education through his analyses of the formal and informal organizations of schools, social networks within the school system, and the intersection of each with social psychological processes and student outcomes. Bidwell began his career theoretically and empirically exploring the organizational nature of schools. Building off of Willard Waller's work, he looked at how schools serve students, the roles of students and faculty within the school, and the bureaucratic nature of the school system. Until this point, there was fragmented research in areas of school organization, but no one theory or call for research tying it together to look at schools and classrooms as social systems. Though there may be rules, policies, or ideas broadly governing what should occur in schools, Bidwell also described schools as loosely coupled social systems. Simply put, schools maintain autonomy within school districts. Within schools, principals and teachers are also granted large amounts of independence to determine what to do and how to do it, with little formal oversight. In this way, teachers are able to determine what happens in their classrooms in terms of instruction style and assessments.

However, Bidwell also pointed out the difficulty in this, because there is a complex interaction between rational and practical actions within the school. On one hand, teachers must uniformly serve and assess students to ensure consistent and fair progress. Conversely, this can prove problematic, because students differ on a number of characteristics (e.g., motivation, personality, and effort) that can affect how a teacher views and interacts with them. The latter, he claims, can lead to debureaucratization within schools. This early work linked the bureaucracy of the school system with what happens in the classrooms between students and teachers. It also described the complex nature of schools and highlighted areas for future research. The appeal and importance of organizational research on schools is clear for policy: these factors of the school system can be adjusted and changed as needed, whereas the clientele of the schools—namely, students and their parents—cannot. Bidwell continued his inquiry into school organization throughout his career, but later integrated links to student outcomes as a way of exploring both the inputs and outputs of the school system. Because of measurement and statistical limitations, much of the early school-effects literature did not make clear distinctions between the school (the organization) and schooling (the process by which students learn). He called for research to understand how organizational conditions—of the school, faculty networks, and individual classrooms—help shape learning opportunities in how resources are divided up, drawn upon, or even affect instructional styles or how students learn.

Teacher Networks

In his earlier work, Bidwell paid little attention to the informal collegial networks formed among teachers and their role in the schooling process. Later, he amended this and focused extensively on informal teacher networks and examined how they affect organizational functioning, effective instruction, and student outcomes in terms of achievement and socialization. He explored both theoretical and empirical questions related to how faculty networks form, how they are sustained and stabilize formal structures within the system, and their interactions with students and school and district administration. Bidwell viewed these networks as beneficial for the work of teaching, but also for the functioning of the school. He saw faculty networks as aiding teachers in problem solving, professional socialization, and adapting to (or resisting changes to) the school structure and bureaucracy in the system. He was interested in the interplay of stability and change within schools, particularly the role of faculty networks in maintaining consistent instruction and instructional practices as the clientele of the schools shifted over the years. Bidwell also called attention to the role of social psychology in the educational arena throughout his career. Here, he described how the structure of school organization affects how teachers and students define school and schooling (which shapes their interactions, roles, and behaviors within it), creates opportunities and constraints within the system, and reconstructs the school and the process of schooling through sustained interactions. His work has looked at how social psychological processes can help legitimate the school system, and he also introduced discussions of exchange to understand the creation of goodwill and social order in the classroom.

Kristi Lynn Donaldson
University of Notre Dame

See Also: Policy-Oriented Research; School Effects; School Organization; Schools as Bureaucracies; Social Role of the Teacher.

Further Readings

Bidwell, Charles E. "The Problem of Classroom Goodwill." In *Stability and Change in American Education: Structure, Processes, and Outcomes.* Maureen H. Hallinan, Adam Gamoran, Warren Kubitschek, and Tom Loveless, eds. New York: Eloit Werner, 2003.

Bidwell, Charles E. "The School as a Formal Organization." In *Handbook of Organizations*, James G. March, ed. Chicago: Rand-McNally, 1965.

Bidwell, Charles E. and John D. Kasarda. "Conceptualizing and Measuring the Effects of School and Schooling." *American Journal of Education*, v.88/4 (1980).

Bidwell, Charles E. and Jeffrey Y. Yasumoto. "The Collegial Focus: Teaching Fields, Collegial Relationships, and Instructional Practice in American High Schools." *Sociology of Education*, v.72/4 (1999).

Bilingual Education

Bilingual education refers to the instructional use of two languages in school. Although bilingual programs are implemented in education systems worldwide, the goals and pedagogical approaches vary widely. Therefore, much debate surrounds efforts to implement bilingual programs. Within the United States, recent educational policies have been generally unsupportive of bilingual education. There are three general models of bilingual education. They differ in terms of their goals concerning students' language skills, cultures, and positions in society. Within each model, educators employ a range of program types with the aim of meeting the respective model's goals. Program types vary in a number of respects, such as: the student populations they serve (e.g., only minority language students, or all students), the proportion of instructional time and the kinds of instructional activities allotted to each language, the characteristics of the teachers (e.g., trained, or untrained bilingual teachers), and the extent of school and community support. Typically, the languages utilized in any model of bilingual education include the dominant language and a minority language of a community. Here, the terms *dominant* and *minority* do not necessarily describe the number of speakers, but instead the relative power of a language in a given community.

Goals of the first model, transitional bilingual education, include minority language students' rapid acquisition of the dominant language, assimilation to the dominant culture, and successful participation in wider society. This model intends to support minority language students temporarily by utilizing native language supports during a period of transition to exclusive use of the dominant language. Transitional bilingual programs often serve relatively recent immigrants to a country. Programs vary in terms of the duration of the transition period and the particular kinds of native language supports provided to students. The second model is referred to as developmental or maintenance bilingual education. This model aims to maintain language minority students' native language skills, while also developing new skills in the dominant language. Importance is placed on fluency in both languages, as well as biliteracy. Programs under this model also seek to affirm the civil rights of language minority groups. The third model, enrichment bilingual education, is characterized by pluralism. This model celebrates linguistic and cultural diversity and seeks to promote the autonomy of ethnic and cultural groups. By providing space for students to develop skills in the minority language and utilize those skills to accomplish academic tasks, these enrichment bilingual programs seek to redefine the minority language as a valuable source of knowledge for all students. In order to achieve the goal of high levels of academic achievement in both languages, educators might implement two-way bilingual programs (also called dual-language, bilingual immersion, and two-way immersion) that serve both minority-language students and dominant-language students.

Advocates and Opponents

Advocates of bilingual education consistently espouse several principles of native language instruction. For instance, they point to research evidence for the notion that one's native language is the most effective medium for literacy instruction in that it taps into existing linguistic awareness, whereas second-language instruction does not. They assert that new readers can then transfer some native language literacy skills to texts written in another language. Advocates also argue that when teachers pay little or no attention to students' home languages and cultures, students may learn to disassociate their languages and cultures (and themselves) from any ideas of academic and career success. On the other hand, a bilingual setting is an opportunity to challenge the existing low status of minority languages and provide space for their speakers to develop positive self-images. Opponents, however, argue that bilingual education is expensive and that limited funds are better spent elsewhere, such as on the teaching of English to adult immigrants. They also dispute the benefits of bilingual programs, maintaining instead that such programs effectively segregate language minority children. From this perspective, bilingual programs reduce language minority students' opportunities to learn the dominant language and culture, thus limiting their ability to participate in broader society and reach their earning potential.

Bilingual Education Policies in the United States

A steady and significant increase in English language learner enrollment has brought languages to the forefront of U.S. educational research and policy. Despite some researchers' attempts to convince policymakers and the general public of the benefits of native language instruction, recent shifts in educational policies reflect an English-only movement. On a national level, considerable changes to the educational services provided to language minority students came with the passage of the No Child Left Behind Act (NCLB) in 2001. Previously, the Bilingual Education Act of 1968 (the Title VII amendment to the Elementary and Secondary Education Act of 1965) provided legislative support for bilingual education. School districts seeking to implement bilingual programs could receive federal funding by applying for competitive grants. The bill moved through various phases over the course of 34 years, with a number of reauthorizations. Influenced by *Lau v. Nichols*, the case that decided that the San Francisco school system had not adequately provided for its English language learners, the first reauthorization of the Bilingual Education Act in 1974 declared English as a second language (ESL) programs as insufficient in addressing the needs and rights of English language learners. The bill defined a bilingual program as one that provides instruction both in English and a student's native language.

As it moved forward, supporters of the bill were at odds with some citizens and policymakers. Those opposed to the bill worried that bilingual programs were too expensive, while proponents argued that the benefits, such as lower dropout and unemployment rates, would far outweigh the costs. Advocates fought to protect and improve the Bilingual Education Act throughout the debate. The final reauthorization, in 1994, was marked by a removal of the enrollment cap, which had limited the amount of time that a student may participate in Bilingual Education Act programs to three years. The bill called not only for the usage of a student's native language, but also for the development of native language skills. In 2001, NCLB replaced the Improving America's Schools Act of 1994. It is the most recent reauthorization of the Elementary and Secondary Education Act. Title III of NCLB, named the Language Instruction for Limited English Proficient and Immigrant Students Act, replaced the Bilingual Education Act. Title III calls on educators to focus on developing the English language skills of language minority students, with the goal of quickly transitioning them to English-only classrooms. Federal funding is now allocated based on the number of English language learners enrolled, without regard to the pedagogical approach and goals of a given program. Considering the high stakes associated with English assessments and the rapid reclassification of English language learners as English proficient under NCLB, schools are unlikely to spend their limited resources on bilingual education.

Gina M. Arnone
University of Pennsylvania

See Also: Classroom Language; Cultural Capital; English as a Second Language; Immigrants, Children of.

Further Readings

García, Ofelia, and Colin Baker, eds. *Bilingual Education: An Introductory Reader.* Clevedon, UK: Multilingual Matters, 2007.

Hornberger, Nancy H., ed. *Continua of Biliteracy: An Ecological Framework for Educational Policy, Research and Practice in Multilingual Settings.* Clevedon, UK: Multilingual Matters, 2003.

Ruiz, Richard. "Orientations in Language Planning." *NABE Journal,* v.8/2 (1984).

Black Colleges and Universities, Historically

Historically black colleges and universities (HBCUs) are institutions that were founded for the education of African Americans at a time when they were banned from enrolling in other educational institutions in the United States. However, they do not deny admission to others, and many HBCUs today are diverse and some are majority white institutions. The Higher Education Act of 1965 defines an HBCU as any historically black college or university that was created prior to 1964, with a sole mission based on the education and advancement of African Americans. The U.S. Department of Education also requires that the institution be fully accredited or making reasonable progress toward accreditation. According to the registry of HBCUs held by the U.S. Department of Education Historically Black Colleges and Universities Initiative, there are 105 functioning HBCUs in the United States. Cheney University was the first HBCU, founded in 1837 as the Institute for Colored Youth in Philadelphia, Pennsylvania, by Richard Humphreys, a Quaker philanthropist born on a West Indies plantation. Beginning as a meager institute for youth, Cheney University developed into a Normal School in 1913 with its principal aim to train teachers, then transformed into a state college, and then became an integral part of the University System of Higher Education in Pennsylvania. The late Edward Bradley, popular television anchor and host of the CBS program *60 Minutes*, was a distinguished alumnus of Cheney University.

This legacy of excellence has been recognized by the U.S. government which has given HBCUs its unwavering support. While HBCUs make up a mere 3 percent of the colleges and universities in the United States, they produce almost 20 percent of the undergraduate degrees earned by African Americans. According to the United Negro College Fund, which affiliates with many HBCUs, approximately 50 percent of HBCU graduates continue their education at the graduate level. Recognizing the potential of HBCUS as a source of intergenerational advancement, President Jimmy Carter signed Executive Order 12232 into law, creating federal programs to support, strengthen, and expand the role of HBCUs in American society in 1980.

Carter's order resulted in the establishment of the White House Initiative on HBCUs that oversees and guides the role of HBCUs in modern society. Every president since Carter has reaffirmed the order and their support to HBCUs, including Presidents Ronald Reagan, George Bush, Bill Clinton, and George W. Bush. The 44th president of the United States, Barack Obama, signed into law Executive Order 13532 that continued the promotion and advancement of HBCUs as an important source of educational opportunity in the United States.

History of HBCUs

The history of HBCUs mirrors the growth and development of the nation. Several laws or acts were passed after the Civil War that aided the development of HBCUs, even though they were punitive in nature. After the end of the Civil War, in 1865, Abraham Lincoln established the Freedmen's Bureau. The bureau was charged with helping freed men, women, and children adjust to freedom. The bureau later began efforts to educate and uplift the skills of the more than 4 million freed slaves, who were thirsty for education that had been denied to them under slavery. The bureau invested nearly $5 million in developing schools for former slaves. Most HBCUs were initially founded as schools or training institutes, and then took on the charge of educating teachers in Normal Schools, and gradually emerged as major institutions of higher learning. However, missionary societies like the American Missionary Association (AMA) and other religious aid organizations and philanthropists greatly aided the efforts of the bureau. They worked individually or in conjunction with the Freedmen's Bureau to provide educational opportunities to former slaves, until the bureau was dismantled in 1872. The AMA founded 11 HBCUs in the south for former slaves. However, The National Land-Grant Colleges Act of 1862, also referred to as the First Morrill Act, set the stage for the Freedmen's Bureau by making access to higher education more accessibility to everyone. In 1890, the Second Morrill Act was passed that resulted in the development of 19 HBCUs.

HBCUs and Educational Attainment

Although there are only 105 remaining HBCUs, they produce needed African American graduates in key areas for the nation. HBCUs graduate a significant portion of the bachelor's degrees to African American students in STEM fields, according to the National Science Foundation. STEM fields consist of degrees in science, technology, engineering, and mathematics. HBCUs are also major producers of African Americans with doctorates in the STEM fields. According to the National Center for Education Statistics, approximately 24 percent of African American students graduate from HBCUs with undergraduate, graduate, and professional degrees each year in the United States. HBCUs also play an important role in providing educational opportunities for women and girls of color. HBCUs enrolled approximately 14 percent of all African American college and university students as of 2008, and females accounted for more than 61 percent of the student population, according to the National Center for Education Statistics.

At Howard University, a leading HBCU in the Washington, D.C., area, female enrollment is consistently higher than male enrollment. However, this varies depending upon the discipline and degree, such as in the STEM fields. The gap between the male and female enrollment at Howard University has steadily increased each year. This is much the same on many coed HBCU campuses. Black male undergraduate enrollment decreased at Howard University by 3,070 from 1994 to 1995 to 2,499 in 2009 and 2010. Female enrollment stayed fairly steady, declining only about 52 students from 4,958 to 4,906. The National Center for Education Statistics found that for the last 40 years, the enrollment of women has consistently been higher than the enrollment of men in HBCUs, but this is also a trend in traditionally white universities. Not only are women enrolling in higher numbers, they are also earning 60 percent of the associate's, bachelor's, and master's degrees at HBCUs since 1990–91. The graduation rate of African American female students

from HBCUS is greater than that of African American males. The black females graduation rate was 43.1 percent compared with that of black males, at 28.5 percent. It is important to note that while black females have higher enrollment and graduation rates from HBCUs than black males, they are under-represented at other universities and in certain academic fields such as in the STEM fields in all universities.

HBCUs and the Role of Activism

In addition to leading the nation in producing African American graduates in important majors and disciplines, HBCUs have also been important sites for activism, both historically and in modern times. In 1960, four college students from North Carolina A&T University, in Greensboro, North Carolina, an HBCU, conducted a sit-in at a local segregated Woolworth store in Greensboro. Students from HBCUs largely made up the ranks of the Student Nonviolent Coordinating Committee (SNCC). The SNCC organized sit-ins, participated in the freedom rides, and played a leading role in the 1963 March on Washington, D.C. Dr. Martin Luther King, Jr. was a former Morehouse College student. Thurgood Marshall, a Howard University School of Law graduate, played an important role in the successful Supreme Court ruling of *Brown v. Board of Education.*

HBCUs and the Future

After the Freedmen's Bureau closed, the establishment of HBCUs was fueled by the passage of *Plessey v. Ferguson.* This act made it legal to segregate in public facilities, including the schoolhouse. HBCUs emerged from a tradition of separate but equal that was eventually struck down in 1954, when the Supreme Court handed down *Brown v. Board of Education of Topeka, Kansas.* Traditionally white colleges and universities that had barred African Americans from enrolling now were required to do so by law. This landmark victory resulted in competition for students, as African Americans could now attend primarily white institutions (PWIs) instead of just HBCUs. In recent times, HBCUs have seen mergers and some closures because of a number of factors, including financial difficulty, deteriorating architecture, mismanagement, and competition for students. Proposals suggesting that HBCUs merge with PWIs have raised questions about relevance and whether HBCUs, with their unique missions and histories, would stay intact under such structure. In 2011, Louisiana Governor Bobby Jindal put forth a proposal suggesting that Southern University at New Orleans (SUNO), an HBCU, be merged with the University of New Orleans, which is a PWI. The measure was defeated, but the question of relevancy is raised as HBCUs move into the 21st century.

Helen Bond
Howard University

See Also: Black Cultural Capital; *Brown v. Board of Education*; Racial Climate on Campus.

Further Readings

Fiore, D. J. and W. W. Hill. *Creating Personal Success on the Historically Black College and University Campus.* Belmont, CA: Wadsworth Publishing, 2011.

Palmer, R. T. and J. L. Wood, eds. *Black Men in College: Implications for HBCUs and Beyond.* New York: Routledge, 2011.

Stephen, P. and L. L. Shafer. "Historically Black Colleges and Universities, 1976–2001." Washington, DC: Government Printing Office: U.S. Department of Education, National Center for Education Statistics, 2004.

Black Cultural Capital

Black cultural capital encompasses multiple codes, styles, preferences, and tastes that assist black students in gaining entry into cultural spaces of affinity. Black cultural capital also denotes ethnic and cultural authenticity for status in social relationships. With regard to the process of schooling, black cultural capital is essential to the social and academic experiences of black youth in navigating racially and culturally complex school contexts. Further, black cultural capital shapes the status of social relationships within culturally and socially marginalized communities. In formal schooling contexts, teachers and schools often dismiss black students' cultural expressions, such as language, style of dress, response to teaching practices, and methods of learning as deficient. Employing black cultural capital within peer groups validates the cultural repertoires of black youth.

Dominant cultural capital often denotes high status tastes, preferences, and norms that are exclusionary. Nondominant cultural capital also encompasses norms, styles, and preferences; however, this form of capital is largely used to gain entry or to express in-group affiliation. In a study with high school aged black youth in Yonkers, New York, sociologist Prudence Carter refers to non-dominant cultural capital as "black" cultural capital. Through her work, she found that black cultural capital was vital in her participants' understanding of themselves, sense of belonging, and group affiliation. Cultural capital, defined by Pierre Bourdieu and Jean-Claude Passeron, suggests that there are particular sets of cultural codes, attitudes, tastes, and preferences that either prevent or support a person's entry into particular social spaces and institutions. Critics of traditional notions of cultural capital have argued that its ethnocentric bias serves the interests of those who are primarily white and affluent, as they compete for and negotiate avenues of power and status attainment. More contemporary iterations of the concept contend that cultural capital varies across multiple social spaces—and has both dominant and nondominant features. As a "nondominant" form, black cultural capital hinges on the idea that dominant and nondominant forms of cultural capital exist.

Nondominant forms of cultural capital are not often valued or appreciated in settings where dominant forms are respected and considered primary. Understanding the multiple dimensions of cultural capital is crucial to understanding the ways in which youth of color navigate complex social and academic circumstances within schools. Empirical studies have shown how students have found successful ways to make dominant and nondominant cultural capital coexist. Further, studies have also shown that utilizing nondominant forms of cultural capital does not negate the value of dominant forms with regard to economic and social progress, and educational achievement.

Cultural Styles

Cultural capital has a hand in sustaining and reproducing the structure of power within the education system. Some cultural theorists have discussed the ways in which black students reject school norms for fear of being labeled as "acting white" and being ridiculed by their peers. However, other scholars have discussed that black youth have always valued education and that succeeding in school does not connote acting white, rather they strive to maintain cultural ties to their peers and affinity groups. Their display of black cultural capital provides social and cultural meaning to their lives, but is oftentimes rejected by schools. Teachers and schools tend to consider the cultural styles and repertoires of black youth as deficient and in opposition to their cultural expectations. Because nondominant forms of cultural capital are not highly regarded outside of certain social spaces, they are often viewed in opposition to the cultural norms and expectations set by the traditional school context.

Schools are not neutral spaces, rather they acknowledge, value, and encourage the acquisition of dominant cultural capital employed by the dominant class. Students that possess dominant cultural codes, norms, and styles begin school at an advantage, understanding the sociocultural processes that inform schooling. However, lower-income students are forced to play catch up in order to acquire these codes in order to successfully navigate their learning. This knowledge changes the discussion regarding low achievement being attributed to ability, versus cultural knowledge, resources, and repertoires communicated by the family—which places students from low-income backgrounds at a disadvantage. Through a number of empirical works studying the experiences of black youth in schools, researchers have found that black youth feel as though teachers are evaluating them solely based on their cultural expressions in school settings. The navigation between black cultural capital and dominant forms of cultural capital is a skill that black youth struggle to master in effective ways that allows them the group affiliation needed to traverse racially hostile and culturally isolating educational experiences. Conflicts over style, language, taste, and expression shapes the relationships students have with adults in their schools. Many black students have found ways to balance the acquisition of both dominant and nondominant forms of cultural capital—as this balance and negotiation are essential for economic, social, and academic mobility.

Bianca J. Baldridge
Columbia University

See Also: Classroom Interactions: Teachers and Students; Cultural Capital; Ebonics (African American English) and Education; Racism in Education.

Further Readings

Bourdieu, P. and J. C. Passeron. *Reproduction in Education, Society, and Culture.* London: Sage, 1977.

Carter, P. "'Black' Cultural Capital, Status Positioning, and Schooling Conflicts for Low-Income African American Youth." *Social Problems,* v.50/1 (2003).

Roscingo, V. J. and J. W. Ainsworth-Darnell. "Race, Cultural Capital, and Educational Resources: Persistent Inequalities and Achievement Returns." *Sociology of Education,* v.72 (1999).

Blind Students

Blind and low-vision students' access to formal schooling has been a topic of significant importance for centuries, but still remains a great challenge. In 2010, the World Health Organization (WHO) estimated that over 285 million people of all ages were visually impaired, of whom about 39 million were totally blind. About 90 percent of them live in developing countries where disabled children, including the visually impaired and blind students, are often discriminated against, marginalized, overlooked, excluded, hidden away, abandoned, or used for begging, instead of integrating them into existing public education systems. Educational reforms, ensuring equal access and opportunities for the visual impaired and blind students in both developing and Western societies, have been long overdue. The issue of educating visual impaired and blind students has contributed to development of many approaches and action programs addressing their day-to-day and long-term needs through government-run and nonprofit institutional systems.

History

History of such institution-based housing for special needs children and adults goes back to ancient Egyptian civilization. During the Middle Kingdom (2040–1640 B.C.E.), rehabilitation programs were initiated to extend social care to the blind. Later, in the 4th and 5th centuries, some special needs care centers (hospices) were found in Israel and Syria, where blind students were given religious education. Similar programs ware founded on a small scale in Europe, and a hospice was established in the early 7th century in northwest France. In the 11th century, several of these schools were built in France, and around 1260, the king of France founded more of these hospices, some of which housed 300 to 1,350 blind students. Other European countries, including Belgium, Italy, and Germany, established similar hospices during this period. Teaching methods were also improved over time. Italian mathematician developed a way to teach the blind about the engraved shapes on metals by 1501, and others used similar ideas in producing literacy resources using curved wood. In about 1650, dot-based alphabets were introduced to represent letters in code-like format. In 1711, Nicholas Saunderson developed a technique to do mathematical calculations, and by 1784, maps were designed with raised lines. Valentin Hauy (1745–1821) was the first Frenchman to establish a school for the blind in Paris, incorporating literacy, numeracy, and music in the curriculum. This program became a model for others. Louis Braille (1809–52), who became blind from an accident, discovered the best possible method of communication and learning for the blind and visually impaired at the age of 15 years old. The Braille system that employs six punched dots was completed in 1834, and 20 years later, France adopted Braille as the official language of communication for the blind.

Specialized Settings

Schooling of the blind student in specialized settings has been in place since the early 18th century, and literature for blind people was introduced by the Romans with alternative formats and scripts, which were written using embossed letters. In the United States, the first school for the blind was founded in Watertown, Massachusetts, in 1829, called the New England Asylum for the Blind, which was changed to the Perkins School for the Blind. Later, in 1860, the Missouri School for the Blind was established to use Braille's method for reading and writing. In the 1880s, the United States made elementary education for the blind compulsory, and this initiative was followed by Great Britain in 1893, ensuring elementary education and vocational training among children and youths under the Elementary Education Act. In 1892, American Braille was introduced by a school teacher, Joel West Smith, in a more simplified manner. A Braille typewriter was also introduced at the Illinois School for the Blind. In 1941, David Abraham, another teacher at the Perkins School, invented a new Brailler to replace bulky typewriters. In 1951, 2,000 Brailler machines were produced to help teach blind and visually impaired students across North America. Such Brailler machines are still in use, and new generation computer-based adaptive technologies have added new dimensions to the teaching of blind and low-vision students.

Considering the social and economic inequality problems of blind people, early educational intervention can improve their status and help contribute to their real life situations with great success and accomplishment. Educators, immediate society, family members, and blind students must learn to view blindness as a physical characteristic. A high unemployment rate and lack of opportunities for the blind in both Western and developing societies is not because of blindness problems, it is because of prejudice, lack of integration, lack of skills and educational training, and most importantly, social and economic inequalities in society. Although about 15 percent of visually impaired and blind students are achieving their goals in Western societies, and about 5 percent are thriving in developing nations, it is imperative to educate the public in order to establish an environment for the positive and productive roles that blind people can have. With the invention of new technologies and globalized social realities, it is an opportune time to change the perception of blindness and promote a deeper understanding of what it means to be blind. Since only about 10 percent of blind children in the developing world have access to basic education, and a limited number of schools offer education to the blind and low-vision students in decontextualized settings in the modern world, it is practical to develop an integrated educational approach. Such an approach will help provide blind students with similar opportunities and educational experiences as for sighted children. If teachers are properly trained and resources are made available, the gap between sighted and nonsighted students in terms of their educational accomplishments, employment, and social integration will be significantly reduced.

Matiul Alam
University of British Columbia

See Also: Deaf Students; Disabled Students; Special Education.

Further Readings

Best, Harry. *The Blind: Their Condition and the Work Being Done for Them in the United States.* New York: Macmillan, 1919.

Gillespie, A., C. Best, and B. O'Neill. "Cognitive Function and Assistive Technology for Cognition: A Systematic Review." *Journal of the International Neuropsychological Society,* v.18 (2012).

Keller, Helen, with Anne Sullivan and John A. Macy. *The Story of My Life.* New York: Doubleday, Page & Co., 1903.

Pascolini D. and S. P. Mariotti. "Global Estimates of Visual Impairment: 2010." *British Journal Ophthalmology,* v.96/5 (2012).

Sacks, O. "The Mind's Eye: What the Blind See." *New Yorker Magazine* (July 28, 2003).

Shapiro, Arthur H. *Everybody Belongs.* London: Routledge, 2000.

Winzer, Margret A. *The History of Special Education.* Washington, DC: Gallaudet University Press, 1993.

Bloom, Allan

The main argument of Allan David Bloom's (1930–92) *The Closing of the American Mind: How Higher Education Has Failed Democracy and Impoverished the Souls of Today's Students* (1987), is that the declining popularity of the classic liberal arts in American colleges and universities since the 1960s has led to the diminishment of the soul (at the individual level) and democracy (at the societal level). A professor of social thought at the University of Chicago at the time of publication, Bloom wrote from the point of view of an academic insider. Bloom believed that American institutions of higher learning had moved away from their most important mission, which was to provide what he called a "liberal education" to its students. A liberal education, for Bloom, was an academic program consisting of classic Western literature, history, and philosophy, and centered upon the canonical "great books." He advocated a move away from currently popular historicist and critical theory approaches to the humanities that thought bred a kind of skepticism that thwarts the development of convictions and the ability to make value distinctions. He imagined that his ideal program would expose students to timeless questions and give them the means to answer them, thereby creating adults whose reasoning skills and solid understanding of the nature and man lead them to conduct "good" lives.

Restriction of Freedom

Bloom viewed many of the modern academic disciplines and fields of study that had gained traction in the academy as the result of various social movements of the 1960s as "propaganda" that exalted relativism. His idealistic vision of higher education was one that was removed from what he saw as transitory contemporary political concerns. Bloom did not like what he saw as the academy's new focus on individual development; he counter-intuitively saw it as tied to restriction of freedom resulting from an "impoverishment of alternatives" based on either majority opinion or the varied opinions of fragmented minority groups. He even went so far as to draw a parallel between the influence on the academy of 1960s mass movements and those of fascist 1930s Germany in the shunning of rationality by those who claimed moral superiority. Bloom had little confidence that the majority of academics would get behind his program. He believed that most social scientists and scholars of the humanities had fallen prey to faddish student protests and social movements, while natural scientists were too enamored of their methods of inquiry. Furthermore, he advocated for something that ran counter to two seemingly contradictory trends that he disapproved of: academic overspecialization and dilettantism, which were tied to a growing emphasis on pre-professionalism and the banishment of the "core curriculum" and course requirements, in favor of academic "breadth." Perhaps counterintuitively, he regarded the academy's new focus on individual development as tied to a restriction of academic freedom that he believed was the result of the influence of majority opinion on the academy, on one hand, and those of various minority factions on the other.

Bloom saw these academic trends as detrimental to the development of the "democratic personality" because he felt that they promoted a relativistic stance and a focus on equality and rights that made it hard for the educated public to rally around and make value judgments regarding shared public goals and ideals. He feared that institutions of higher learning had capitulated to public opinion and threatened democracy by failing to instill the essential value of reason (over emotion) in its students. He saw exposure to great books as a means both for compensating for capabilities that have been lost in the contemporary democratic individual and as a means of encouraging people to participate in the democratic process. Bloom had little confidence that American colleges and universities would heed his call for a return to an academic program that he believed would further what he deemed as its true vocation of engendering true liberation in its participants. However, he believed that the academy—as a democratic society's last true center for the life of the mind—still contained a kernel of the old philosophical vanguard that could shine as a beacon for world outside its walls.

Jill M. Smith
Brandeis University

See Also: Curriculum Standardization; Educational Policymakers; Phenemenology, Existentialism, and Education.

Further Readings

Bloom, Allan. *The Closing of the American Mind: How Higher Education Has Failed Democracy and Impoverished the Souls of Today's Students.* New York: Simon & Schuster, 1987.

Bloom, Allan. *Giants and Dwarfs.* New York: Touchstone Books, 1991.

Sleeper, Jim. "Allan Bloom and the Conservative Mind." *New York Times* (September 4, 2005).

Boarding Schools

Boarding schools, or residential schools, are learning institutions where students study and live either for part or the entire school year. In some instances, faculty and administration dwell in the same locale. Boarding schools were created out of practicality because of difficulties in student's transportation between home and school. These institutions draw upon two different frameworks: private schools (secular or religious), and government-funded schools. In the United States, boarding schools are closely associated with the history of the American Indian. However, in the United Kingdom, boarding schools have a longer history associated with the elite class. American Indian boarding schools emerged in the Americas in the late 19th century as a result of the U.S. government's hope of forced assimilation and an effective resolution to the "Indian Problem." Forcibly taken from their homes, American Indian children were placed in off-reservation boarding schools and were permitted only limited amounts of time with their families. As the first country to create and implement such boarding schools, the United States became the home of over 100 boarding schools spread across the nation. Over 100,000 indigenous children were placed in these residential schools.

The most well-known boarding school, the Carlisle Indian Industrial School (1879–1918) was established in Carlisle, Pennsylvania, by General Richard Henry Pratt and housed a total of 10,000 students throughout its existence. In a time when the Anglo American sentiment viewed Native Americans as individuals beyond civilization, Pratt aspired "to save the man, kill the Indian." He firmly believed that Native American children were capable of becoming citizens as long as they were cleansed of any language, culture, spirituality, or education related to their native life. After observing the effectiveness of the Hampton Institute (founded in 1868 in Hampton, Virginia) in educating and assimilating African American youth, Pratt determined that the same could be done for young American Indians. Serving as a "Friend to the Indian," Pratt enrolled 19 Native American men in the Hampton Institute in 1878 to prove that with assimilation through total immersion, American Indians could also become part of dominant U.S. society.

Native American Boarding Schools

In 1947, the U.S. government renamed the Office of Indian Affairs as the Bureau of Indian Affairs (BIA) and charged the agency to preside over 26 Indian Boarding Schools. Meanwhile, Christian missionaries of various denominations established religious residential schools. The ethos of both the BIA and Christian missionary schools was to immerse Native American children in Euro-American culture, supplanting the students' names, languages, food, and cultural practices with Anglo-American culture. American Indian Boarding Schools hit their peak enrollment of 60,000 students in 1973; however, because of public pressure, they saw a steady decline throughout the 1980s and 1990s. Public outcry resulted from studies such as the Kennedy Report and the National Study of American Indian Education, which highlighted boarding schools' inhumane conditions. In 2007, there were an estimated 10,000 Native American children attending tribally governed boarding schools. Similarly, other countries adopted Pratt's model of schooling as a resolution to their "Indian Problems." Canada (1840s–1996) and Australia (1869–1969) ceased operating indigenous boarding schools, and publicly apologized and/or gave reparations to their respective indigenous communities (Australia, 2007; Canada, 2008).

A more contemporary form of boarding schools, completely unrelated to the forced assimilation of Native American children, are private boarding schools meant for general students in seventh through 12th grades. Built upon the framework of British public schools (a term correlating with the American private school), U.S. private boarding schools may operate as single-sex, religious, or military boarding schools. Student population within private boarding schools ranges from smaller institutions of 100 students to larger institutions of 1,200 students. There are approximately 300 boarding schools in the United States and Canada. In some instances, private boarding schools may provide an additional post-graduation year to help students prepare for college. The most notable boarding school is Choate Rosemary Hall in Wallingford, Connecticut, whose alumni include John F. Kennedy, Terry O'Neill, and Paul Mellon.

Current Day

Globally, boarding schools still operate, sharing similarities with their earlier models. Boarding schools are born out of practicality and cost-effectiveness; pupils unable to travel long distances find it easier to live and study in the same location. While schools in the United States restrict student enrollment to secondary grades, other societies allow primary grade children to attend boarding schools. Present-day boarding schools are spaces for young children to gain industrial, linguistic, and cultural skills for employment. While this may appear similar to American Indian Boarding Schools, the difference lies in that children now voluntarily enter school doors. In countries such as India, Bangladesh, and China, children leave their rural villages for urban boarding schools in hopes of bettering their lives. Boarding schools also promote gender equality, such as in India. Indian girls are encouraged to attend residential schools as a means to improve the quality of education of all children, and to narrow gender and social gaps. In other instances, boarding schools are utilized as places for religious education, where young boys are sent for spiritual training.

J. Estrella Torrez
Michigan State University

See Also: Native American Students; Private Schools; Residential Mobility and Education.

Further Readings

Adams, D. W. *Education for Extinction: American Indians and the Boarding School Experience (1875–1928).* Lawrence: University of Kansas Press, 1995.

Child, B. J. *Boarding School Seasons: American Indian Families (1900–1940).* Lincoln: University of Nebraska Press, 1998.

Cookson, P. and C. H. Persell. *Preparing for Power: America's Elite Boarding Schools.* New York: Basic Books, 1987.

Kashit, Y. *Boarding Schools at the Crossroads: The Influence of Residential Education Institutions on National and Societal Development.* New York: Haworth Press, 1998.

Bourdieu, Pierre

Pierre Bourdieu (1930–2002), an internationally renowned French social scientist, is important in the history of social theory in general and the sociology of education in particular. First, he spelled out the principles of generative structuralism, a perspective that primarily aims at overcoming the dichotomy between social physics and social phenomenology. These paradigms one-sidedly focus either on extra-individual structural properties, or representations embedded in the symbolic world. Second, by integrating research and theory, Bourdieu was able to avoid "concept fetishism." In fact, his main concepts—such as habitus, capital, and field—had intellectual precursors, but were sharpened through researches that he conducted. Bourdieu never shied away from using multiple methodologies, ranging from correspondence analysis to ethnography. Third, Bourdieu broke the traditional barrier between multiple disciplines. Fourth, Bourdieu did not elude politics in the name of axiological neutrality. Instead, he was—especially later in his life—a public intellectual, who was mindful of the scientific ethos that research entails.

In Bourdieu's generative structuralism, there are three major concepts (habitus, field, and capital) that run through his oeuvre (37 books, plus 400 articles). He defines habitus as socially conditioned sensibilities through which individuals both perceive and generate social practices. Fields, which are closely knit to habitus, are "a network, or a configuration, of objective relations between positions." Each field has its own logic, although fields are not insulated social entities. The dynamics of fields cannot be understood without the critical role played by economic, social, cultural, and symbolic capitals. Capital is an "accumulated labor" appropriated in the form of "social energy" that acts both as a force and a principle, encompassing the social world. Mostly existing in the form of material goods, economic capital has the distinct characteristics of being acquiescent to numerical depiction and institutionalized in the form of legal rights. Social capital, in contrast, refers to the social funds that actors hold as a result of their place in the juncture of social connections. Cultural capital refers to symbolic goods existing in the mode of linguistic and cultural competence, largely institutionalized in the form of educational credentials utilized by agents to uphold their reputation. Of the four forms of capital, symbolic capital is distinct, since without being specifically related to a social field, it is used to legitimate the possession of other forms of capital.

Education and Society

Bourdieu developed his sociology of education in four major books connected by the same thread of a relational approach. In his first work, *The Inheritors*, Bourdieu (with J. Passeron) examined the gap between the democratic ideals of French society and the outcomes of its educational system. Far from neutralizing inequality, the latter acted as an instrument of selection and exclusion, wherein the underprivileged are denied access to higher education. For example, during the 1960s, only six percent of children with peasant background were placed in tertiary academic institutions. This was in large part because of the advantage of the children of the upper classes, who are able to perform well according to the "techniques and habits of thought" of academic institutions, for which the home environment acts as a springboard. This salient conclusion shatters the myth that the acquisition of cultural capital in schools is determined by natural presupposition.

The book *Reproduction in Education Society and Culture* takes this issue further (with Passeron). In addition to providing ample evidence on pedagogical processes in motion accompanied by a historicist approach, Reproduction provides a cogent theory of social reproduction, along with an implicit theory of transformation. Here, Bourdieu and Passeron contend that "pedagogic action," a form of resocialization taking place both at school and outside the academic setting, serves as an instrument of reproducing statuses. Pedagogic action is thus a form of symbolic violence in which a "cultural arbitrary" is imposed on society at large by an "arbitrary power." More exactly, the educational system, instead of serving as a mediating

institution through which the creed of ascription is buried, acts as a "classificatory machine" that imposes authorized modes of segregation and incorporation. From this perspective, the problem of inequality cannot be resolved by simultaneous processes of equal access to resources and a truly "rational pedagogy" that endows students with appropriate cultural capital throughout schooling.

In *The State Nobility,* based on data derived from the family backgrounds and inclinations of students who attended prestigious universities and later assumed important positions, Bourdieu addresses the problem of the connection between elite schools and professional practices. Here, Bourdieu concludes that in France, the relationship between the two is akin to the role that titles played in feudal societies. In these societies, educational titles serve both as an official certification of technical competence and "sign values" that certain individuals possess unique dispositions thereby misrecognized as natural endowments. Thus, the uneven distribution of titles, through which the state nobility are consecrated by the state, serves as a means of perpetuating hierarchies, since individuals disproportionately are able to convert, although not in a mechanical fashion, economic capital into cultural capital, which in turn allows them to amass political and administrative capitals. Consequently, education is an important aspect of the sociocultural dynamics through which the arbitrariness of the distribution of power is both disguised and legitimized. *State Nobility,* by addressing the homology—"resemblance within a difference"—between the field of higher education and fields of power, uniquely demonstrates the symbiosis between the sociologies of power and education.

Homo Academicus, the fourth important work of Bourdieu on education, is different than the aforementioned books, although the same assumptions are operative. In this book, Bourdieu accomplishes two objectives simultaneously: He carries out an academic self-analysis, while examining the features and the procedures involved in French university fields. In the latter case, he reveals "tribal secrets" of the academy that his colleagues are not comfortable putting under public transcript. Subsequently, *Homo Academicus* distinguishes itself as a work of reflexivity in which the structural composition and principles inherent in academic settings are examined, without sparing the investigator. However, reflexivity is intended to reinforce scientific inquiry, rather than indulging in the academic relativism characteristic of postmodernists.

Bourdieu's work thus hones the sociological imagination, both methodologically and substantively. Methodologically, scholars understand the relevance of correspondence analysis in revealing relational processes, especially when data collection and analysis are theoretically informed. Substantively, scholars recognize that the academic field is based on varied classifications and struggles reigning in transacademic orders. Although the logic of the academic field is inimitable, its systems of classification and operations can only be comprehended if the homology existing between it and society at large is recognized. This in turn allows an understanding of the origins of events like May 1968 which, according to Bourdieu, was precipitated by a "crisis of succession" caused by morphological changes in the composition of students and faculty.

Alem Kebede
California State University, Bakersfield

See Also: Class Inequality: Achievement; France; Social Capital.

Further Readings

Bourdieu, P. *Distinction: A Social Critique of the Judgment of Taste.* Cambridge, MA: Harvard University Press, 1984.

Bourdieu, P. *Homo Academicus.* Cambridge, MA: Polity Press, 1988.

Bourdieu, P. *The State Nobility.* Cambridge, MA: Polity Press, 1996

Bourdieu, P. and J. Passeron. *The Inheritors.* Chicago: University of Chicago Press, 1979.

Bourdieu, P. and J. Passeron. *Reproduction in Education Society and Culture.* Beverly Hills, CA: Sage, 1977.

Bowles, Samuel and Herbert Gintis

Since the 19th century movement toward mass education in the United States, Horace Mann's interest in fostering an education that was public has been a continual theme embedded in the public school system. Still, the purpose of schooling in America has been viewed as capitalistic, based on individualism and meritocracy, which counters the initial intention of a public education that should be premised on equitable educational standards. In *Schooling in Capitalist America* (1976), Bowles and Gintis contest the utility of schools in reproducing social stratification and socialized capitalism in society. The merits of this ideology have been contested as studies have argued that agency plays a role in whether individuals continue the class-based rationale.

The purposes of public education in the United States have long been debated. Horace Mann's 19th-century movement toward mass education was premised on the ideology that education was the great equalizer in promoting a more robust workforce and educated working class. Public schooling was additionally considered a method for reducing criminal activity, increasing employment productivity, and reducing the proportion of impoverished communities. Entering the 20th century, student progression toward high school and college resulted in increasingly high numbers of youth flooding into classrooms. The movement toward high school credentialism and attendance to Ivy League higher educational institutions resulted in a saturation of degrees. As public school students enrolled in the late 1960s, high school youth graduating with a diploma and attending college declined to under 50 percent. The movement toward compulsory schooling had minimal effect on the perceived value of a diploma as dropout rates of youth became more visible on a national scale.

Schools in a Capitalistic Society

The Coleman Report (1966), also called *Equality of Educational Opportunity,* and the *Brown* decision played a key role in highlighting educational inequality and inequities that had not been addressed. Schools were viewed as a measure for continuing discrimination and social exclusion of African Americans, Hispanics, immigrant populations, and the poor from the opportunities that the privileged class possessed. Egalitarianism in society and schools was not tied to marginalized populations, but was perceived as part of maintaining a capitalistic system. Embedded in capitalism was the concept of privilege, marginalization, and exploitation of workers to maximize profit. Bowles and Ginits's examination of the role of schools in a capitalistic society underscored how the class-based system was used to reproduce inequality and continue the status quo.

Bowles and Gintis introduced the concept of social reproduction to explore how schooling in capitalist

America has implications for how youth are educated. Social reproduction theory asserts that schools mirror the social class structure of society by creating a hierarchy of skills, knowledge, and ability based on the privileged class. The primary purpose of schools is to recreate the societal structure evident in society through discrimination and exclusion of the working class and poor. This conceptual framework is comparable to functionalism as individuals fill particular slots in society. However, the preparation and opportunities award to individuals varies and is based on a class system. In *Schooling in Capitalist America,* Bowles and Gintis argue that there is a hidden curriculum of schools. The hidden curriculum is geared toward the privileged class and is based on their cultural capital that society views as legitimized knowledge. In relation to schools, the hidden curriculum is manifested through particular mannerisms, ways of speaking, and epistemologies that are premised on a class system. Within this system, individual and collective identities are excluded that counter the standard created and valued by social institutions.

Confined by Environmental Conditions

Bowles and Gintis use these concepts to discuss intergenerational inequality and how society reproduces generations of people that are confined by the environmental conditions that they inhabit. These inequalities extend from society to schools and recreate a systematic outcome that is embedded within the structure of opportunity and inequity. In this way, Bowles and Gintis contend that schools act as socialization mechanisms through curriculum, policies, and teacher pedagogy that is deemed valid. This socialization is referred to as correspondence principle or theory and highlights the how the structure of schooling and intangibles of the educational process are structured to benefit the privileged class. The reward structure in schools is based on its structure in society. Yet, this is influenced by the latent value that is dictated by the class-based social system.

Theories proposed by Bowles and Gintis have been debated since their introduction in the 1960s by sociologists, psychologists, and educational professions. Researchers assert that Bowles and Gintis remove individual agency from the inequalities embedded in education and assume that students buy into the silent agendas of schools to benefit the privileged class. It is argued that without individual acceptance of the inequality, the extent expressed by Bowles and

Gintis is not unearthed. The working class is viewed as simply following orders, without recognition for how individuals may desire their positionality within a functionalist framework. Further discontent is evident in the application of Bowles and Gintis within the framework of egalitarianism by questioning whether equality can be achieved, and whose responsibility it is to sustain it in education in the long term.

Dorothy Hines
Michigan State University

See Also: Affluent Children; Social Promotion; Tracking; Wealth and Education.

Further Readings

Bowles, Samuel and Herbert Gintis. *A Cooperative Species: Human Reciprocity and Its Evolution.* Princeton, NJ: Princeton University Press, 2011.

Bowles, Samuel and Herbert Gintis. *Schooling in Capitalist America: Education Reform and the Contradictions of Economic Life.* Chicago: Haymarket Books, 2011.

Cole, Mike, ed. *Bowles and Gintis Revisited: Correspondence and Contradiction in Education Theory.* New York: Falmer Press, 1988.

Brazil

Brazil is among the largest of the South American countries, with an area of about 3,287,612 square miles (8,514,877 square kilometers), slightly smaller than the United States. It is the fifth-largest country in the world. It occupies nearly half of South America, sharing 9,777 miles (15,735 kilometers) of boundaries with 10 countries: Argentina, Bolivia, Colombia, French Guiana, Guyana, Paraguay, Peru, Suriname, Uruguay, and Venezuela, and 4,655 miles (7,491 kilometers) on the Atlantic Coast. About 60 percent of the Amazon rainforest stretches across northern Brazil, the world's biggest. In 2011, the World Bank estimated Brazil's population at 196,655,014.

Its economy is dependent on manufacturing transport equipment, steel, airplanes, paper, electric machinery, iron ore, soybeans, footwear, textile, lumber, chemicals, cement, coffee, autos, and automotive parts, as well as mining, agriculture, and energy. In the past, its economy relied heavily on agricultural activities, such as sugar production and cattle ranching. Exploitation of gold and precious stones were also part of traditional economic activities. Brazil experienced a high growth rate of about five percent, and its total gross domestic product (GDP) was estimated at over $3.1 trillion, making it world's fifth largest economy by the end of 2012. Currently, GDP per capita income is about $11,600. However, a fourth of the population still lives below the poverty line. Brazil is a former Portuguese colony and was ruled under a constitutional monarchy, and until 1985, a dictatorial administrative period shaped its language, culture, demographics, economics, and educational structure.

History and Social Structure

In the 15th century, Brazil was a tribal society with a heritage of thousands of years of community-based living in the woods by indegenous people. The name Brazil originated from the name of the country's popular trophical tree, brazilwood, which became a commercial interest when Portuguese navigator Pedro Álvares Cabral and his crew saw them during their first arrival in early 1500. After their arrival, the country became a colony of Portugal. Brazil became independent from Portugal on September 7, 1822, but remained a constitutional monarchy, which was ended in1889 through a military coup.

During 1930 to 1934, 1937 to 1945, and 1964 to 1985, the country saw military and dictatorial rules that influenced the structure of economic and social institutions. In 1985, the last phase of a 21-year-old military dictatorship ended through an election, and finally in 1989, Brazil saw a free presidential election involving the general public. Since then, Brazil has emarged a more democratic society. In 2002, Lula da Silva, a leader representing the working class majority, was elected. In 2010, Dilma Vana Rousseff, a female leader, became president. Transition in Brazil's sociopolitical system from dictatorial to socialist (1989–92), and more recently to open market, but people-centered collaborative systems have significantly impacted mass participation in its nation-building mission. Brazil is now a rapidly advancing a knowledge economy–based society.

The descendants of Portuguese migrants comprise the majority of the present population. The dominant religious culture came from Portugal, and other European traditions shaped their spiritual representation. According to a 2010 census, about 65 percent of the population are Roman Catholic, 22 percent are Protestant, 8 percent are nonreligious, and 5 percent comes from other religions and belief systems. Portuguese is spoken by almost 99 percent of the population. There are about 210 other languages, of which about 180 languages are spoken by indigenous people.

By the 1960s, internationally recognized Brazilian educational thinker Paulo Freire proposed education as a process of cultural action for freedom, justified universal rights to education for every citizen, called for curriculum reform, and revolutionized a literacy movement among the poor for social change. As a consequence, he was imprisoned in 1964, and exiled to Bolivia and then Chile by the military dictatorship. However, he was able to continue to influence education with projects in other countries, his new position at Harvard University as a professor and a consultant to the United Nations Educational, Scientific and Cultural Organization (UNESCO), and by writing some highly influential books, including Pedagogy of the Oppressed and Education for Critical Consciousness. Historically, the pre-colonial education system in Brazil was informal in nature. It emphasized oral traditions based local contextual knowledge of indigenous or tribal people. The colonial era resumed in 1540 with a mission to facilitate evangelization of youngsters under the auspices of the Society of Jesus (Jesuits) through missionary and public schools.

Groundwork for educational reform was first initiated in 1772, under the auspices of the Learned Societies of Brazil (the Sociedade Scientifica), and in the late 18th century, colonial authorities established higher education schools to teach the sciences and engineering, including the Instituto Militar de Engenharia and the Escola Politécnica, one of the world's oldest engineering schools. In 1816, the first Royal School of Sciences, Arts and Crafts was established. Presently it is known as Escola Nacional de Belas Artes. The early 19th century was also marked by establishment of music schools, medical schools, and naval academies. By the end of 19th century, about 20 percent people could read and write. Today, Brazil has progressed considerably with literacy initiatives. In 2010, it was estimated that about 91.1 percent of the population, with 90.4 percent of males and 91.4 percent of females aged 15 and over considered literate, and school enrollments for children aged 7 to 14 rose to about 98 percent. The literacy rate for ages 15 to 24 remains one of the highest among South American countries, with 97.9 percent for females, 95.78 for males, and 96.58 percent for the combined youth population.

Educational Structure

Formal education in Brazil includes Educação Infantil (preschool) for children ages 4 to 6 years, Ensino Fundamental (elementary school) for children of ages 6 to 15 years, grades 1 through 9, and Ensino Médio (high school or secondary school) for youths ages 16 to 18 years, grades 10 through 12. Infants from birth to 3 years of age are looked after by nurses prior to entering preschool programs. While preschool education is optional and funded by local or city governments, elementary education is mandatory and funded by city or state governments, and secondary education is solely funded by state governments. After completion of 2,200 hours of instructional time in the secondary schools system, and completion of a centrally conducted vestibular entrance examination, students can continue their postsecondary Ensino Superior program at universities and colleges. Public university education is fully funded by the state or federal governments.

There are about 200 national universities and institutions, offering undergraduate, graduate, and postgraduate programs similar to other European countries. In total, there are about 2,500 postsecondary institutions operating in the country. Many of these institutions offer four-year bachelor of arts (B.A.) or bachelor of science (B.S.) programs, and one to two year master's degrees similar to those offered in North America in terms of instructional or credit hours (up to 4,800 instructional hours or 120 credits for the bachelor's degrees, and about 30 credits for master's degrees). Doctoral degrees are also considered equivalent in time span and research. Education spending was estimated in 2009 at 12 percent of all government spending, and over 5 percent of national GDP.

Current Issues

Brazil has made considerable progress in educational and social indicators during the last two decades. However, it remains a difficult policy objective to ensure equal access and quality education to all. Gender and ethnicity related disparity continues to influence future human research development strategies of the country. Although gender difference is not an issue at the elementary level, it becomes evident gradually at higher levels. Male academic underperformance at the secondary level, especially among black, brown, tribal, and other minority youths, and a marked decrease in their enrollment at the postsecondary level is a concern. Over 60 percent of those who complete university programs are women.

This trend continues to grow, although quality academic programs are still dominated by men. While black and brown citizens represent about half of the national population, they complete about 6.5 years of education compared to their white counterparts, who receive about 8.5 years. About 75 percent of the underperforming poor students are either black or brown, and about 2 percent complete college programs, compared to about 10 percent of white students. On the other hand, about 20 percent of the black and brown adults lack literacy skills, compared to 6 percent of white adults. These inequalies are well-known factors affecting the socioeconomic integration of people of color, who represent 73 percent of the national poor population. Although elementary education is mandatory and Brazil is determined to achieve the Millennium Development goal of universal education by 2015, ensuring truly equal opportunities for all remains a challenge.

Despite the fact that school enrollment is slowing down, demand for futuristic continuing education among youth and adults is increasing. According to the World Bank in 2010, 23.54 million students entered a secondary education program, which is .45 percent fewer compared to the previous year. However, because of some emerging factors, including demand within the knowledge economy-based job market, globalization, technological innovations, and ongoing rapid industrialization, it is expected that by 2020, enrollment in postsecondary programs will reach nine million. Brazil's school curriculum and teacher education programs need a significant shift to incorporate inclusivity, sustainability, and improved technology-based instructional programs for its rapidly growing knowledge based economy and diverse society.

Matiul Alam
University of British Columbia

See Also: Argentina; Paraguay; Peru; Poverty and Education; Venezuela.

Further Readings

Brazilian Institute of Geography and Statistics. "A Economia Brasileira no 4º Trimestre de 2011: Visão Geral" ("The Brazilian Economy in the 4th Trimester of 2011: General Overview"). http://www.ibge.gov.br/english/default.php (Accessed April 2012).

Freire, Paulo. *Cultural Action for Freedom.* Cambridge, MA: Harvard University Press, 1972.

Freire, Paulo. *Pedagogy of the Oppressed*. New York: Continuum International Publishing, 2000.

Rodrigues, Aryon Dall'Igna. "Sobre as línguas indígenas e sua pesquisa no Brasil." *Ciência e Cultura*, v.57/2 (2005).

Spalding, E., C. L. Klecka, E. Lin, S. J. Odell, and J. Wang. "Social Justice and Teacher Education: A Hammer, a Bell, and a Song." *Journal of Teacher Education*, v.61 (2010).

Telles, Edward Eric. *Race in Another America: The Significance of Skin Color in Brazil*. Princeton, NJ: Princeton University Press, 2004.

Brookover, Wilbur B.

Wilbur Brookover (1911–2003) was born near Bippus, Indiana. He served in the U.S. Navy during World War II before becoming a professor at Indiana State Teachers College, and later at Michigan State University. His academic focus was in sociology. He also served as the mayor of East Lansing, Michigan, from 1971 to 1975. He died on April 6, 2003, at the age of 92. Brookover was one of many people who testified before the Supreme Court regarding the landmark case, *Brown v. Board of Education of Topeka*. His testimony focused on the sociological and psychological effects of school segregation upon African American students. Brookover asserted that students forced to attend racially segregated schools were not allowed to learn all they should about functioning in social situations because they were limited to only the behaviors and actions of people of the same race. In other words, segregated learners were not allowed to learn from the behaviors and actions of students from different racial groups. Brookover testified that this situation was unacceptable and contributed to a stunted social education for segregated students.

Child Development

Brookover spent much of his professional life studying various sociological elements related to the field of education. He studied the ways in which educator understanding of child development affected their ability to create successful school environments. Brookover's thought was that the more teachers knew and understood about child development, the better equipped they would be to handle the overall process of education. These teachers would be able to create learning environments that were appropriate for each stage throughout the elementary school years. Developmentally appropriate environments, Brookover believed, would lead the way toward developmentally appropriate instruction. Brookover became a leading proponent of these developmentally appropriate environments, touting the benefits to instruction as a whole. His belief was that when students were taught at the correct developmental level, they would learn most efficiently.

This concept of developmental appropriateness was later extended to include the social environment, as well as the learning aspect of the classroom. Brookover began studying the various attitudes and beliefs related to self-esteem and self-concept. Focusing on the elementary grades, he gathered information about how socialization affected the way a student viewed his self-worth, as well as his ability to adjust to new social situations within the school setting. Additionally, Brookover studied the concept of the school as a community. In other words, he looked to see if particular schools operated as individual communities within their larger city-communities. Further, he studied the ways in which the overall school program operated in the particular school community system. Not only did he determine that schools operated as small communities, he also discovered that teachers who believed in the community function of the school tended to approach instruction with a different set of methodologies than teachers who did not buy the community theory.

In addition to his work regarding developmental issues, Brookover studied other sociological topics. One of the areas he studied was the social environment of schools and how it related to the school's overall achievement. Focusing on elementary schools, Brookover sought to discover which environmental factors might affect how third, fourth, and fifth graders performed academically, regardless of their socioeconomic status. He was able to gather information through a series of questionnaires that asked about students' self-concept within the school setting. Additionally, the questionnaires approached these issues with regard to the present and the future. In other words, Brookover sought to learn about students' sense of futility. He was able to learn that students, to some degree, allow the expectations of others to determine how they will behave or respond in social settings.

Another study involved a set of U.S. history teachers and their relationship with their students. In this study, Brookover compared the knowledge of students with teachers who maintained open, friendly relationships with their students and those who had more authoritative teachers. In other words, some of the history teachers were characterized as trying to become a friend to students, while others kept their classroom interactions at a more businesslike, professional level. The goal was to see if the friendly teachers were able to teach as much information over a period of time as the teachers who were less friendly and more businesslike. In short, Brookover discovered that teachers who valued friendly relationships with their students tended to teach significantly less history than teachers who ran more orderly, autocratic classrooms. Creating a learning environment that was more casual and less professional was found to be detrimental to student learning and performance.

Kristen Brodie
Walden University

See Also: *Brown v. Board of Education*; Class Interactions: Teachers and Students; Training of Teachers.

Further Readings

Brookover, Wilbur B. "Learning and the School's Social System." *Psyccritiques,* v.26/8 (August 1981).

Brookover, Wilbur. "The Social Roles of Teachers and Pupil Achievement." *American Sociological Review,* v.8/4 (August 1943).

Brookover, Wilbur B. and John B. Holland. "An Inquiry Into the Meaning of Minority Group Attitude Expressions." *American Sociological Review,* v.17 (1952).

Brookover, Wilbur B. and Shailer Thomas. "Self-Concept of Ability and School Achievement." *Sociology of Education,* v.37/3 (Spring 1964).

Brown v. Board of Education

We come then to the question presented: Does segregation of children in public schools solely on the basis of race, even though the physical facilities and other 'tangible' factors may be equal, deprive the children of the minority group of equal educational opportunities? We believe that it does.

—*Brown v. Board of Education* (1954).

Brown stands as a pivotal case in judicial history, overturning the precedent of separate but equal facilities set by *Plessey v. Ferguson* in 1896, and highlighting the court's role in changing national policy. In 1950, the National Association for the Advancement of Colored People (NAACP) recruited African American parents in Topeka, Kansas, to attempt to enroll their children in white elementary schools; when the children were denied, the NAACP filed a class action suit on their behalf, named after plaintiff Oliver Brown.

It was the 12th case challenging segregation in Kansas public schools since 1879, when the state legalized racially segregated elementary schools in cities with populations over 15,000. Similar challenges to the standard of separate but equal were gaining momentum nationwide. In South Carolina, African American parents joined a class action lawsuit filed by the NAACP, challenging the inferior conditions faced by children in Clarendon County's racially segregated schools. In Delaware, two cases filed in 1951 by Louis Redding similarly challenged disparate facilities on behalf of African American parents. In Washington, D.C., a suit was filed on behalf of 11 African American junior high school students denied admittance to the city's brand new school for whites. In Virginia, the NAACP filed a case supporting the grassroots protest of African American students over inadequate classroom facilities. Although U.S. District Courts tended to rule in favor of equal facilities, the rulings applied only to the schools directly in question, African American students were not given access to white schools, and the rulings were seldom acted upon by the school boards.

In 1952, these five cases reached the docket of the U.S. Supreme Court, where they were consolidated under the name *Oliver Brown et al. v. the Board of Education of Topeka.* Thurgood Marshall argued the case for the NAACP, finishing the battle begun by Charles Hamilton Houston, who died in 1950. After the court failed to reach a decision in 1952, the case was resubmitted. In 1954, the U.S. Supreme Court ruled unanimously that segregation was unconstitutional on the grounds that it violated the Fourteenth Amendment, but requested another round of arguments in order to decide how to implement the decision. In 1955, the Supreme Court ordered lower courts to require desegregation in Brown II. Between 1955–60, federal judges heard more than 200 school desegregation cases.

The implementation of Brown triggered numerous racial confrontations and much white resistance. While thousands of young people gathered in Washington, D.C., to march in support of integration, southern white legislatures and school boards began a campaign of "Massive Resistance," including the signing by 101 congressmen of the "Southern Manifesto," arguing that the federal government had no power to force states to integrate schools. Virginia's Prince Edward County closed their schools for five years, rather than integrate. In several famous instances, federal agents were sent to control rioting and protect African American students.

For example, a U.S. Army division and a federalized Arkansas National Guard protected nine students integrating Central High School in Little Rock in 1957. Likewise, President Kennedy deployed Army and federalized National Guard forces to control rioting upon the arrival of James Meredith at the University of Mississippi and to escort Vivian Malone and James A. Hood as they crossed Governor George Wallace's personal blockade at the schoolhouse door to enroll at the University of Alabama.

Related Cases

- *Green v. County School Board of New Kent County.* 1968. Ordered states to dismantle segregated schools, gauging compliance on facilities, staff, faculty, transportation, and extracurricular activities.
- *Swann v. Charlotte-Mecklenburg Board of Education.* 1971. Approved a variety of means of overcoming residential segregation in the perpetuation of racially segregated schools—including busing, magnet schools, and compensatory education.
- *Keyes v. Denver School District No. 1.* 1973. Distinguished between segregation resulting from private choices (de facto), which is constitutional, and state-mandated segregation (de jure), which is unconstitutional.
- *Milliken v. Bradley.* 1974. Blocked metropolitan-wide desegregation plans, effectively reducing Brown's impact on racially isolated urban districts.
- *Riddick v. School Board of the City of Norfolk, Virginia.* 1986. Determined that districts

meeting the *Green* requirements can be returned to local control.

Although Brown set a new legal precedent for integration, court cases nationwide continued to challenge the longevity and implemenation of integrated schooling. Studies suggest that integration reached peak levels in 1988, but that by 2000, schools were more segregated than in 1970, when busing for desegregation began. Other studies link resegregation to racial achievement gaps and other educational inequalities.

Christina R. Steidl
Emory University

See Also: Busing; Governmental Influences on Education; Racism in Education; School Catchment Zones, Politically Defined School Boundaries.

Further Readings

Brown v. Board of Education, 347 U.S. 483 Supreme Court of the United States. 1954.

Kluger, Gary. *Simple Justice: The History of Brown v. Board of Education and Black America's Struggle for Equality.* New York: Random House, 1976.

Orfield, Gary, Susan E. Eaton, and the Harvard Project on School Desegregation. *Dismantling Desegregation: The Quiet Reversal of Brown v. Board of Education.* New York: New Press, 1996.

National Park Service. "*Brown v. Board of Education National Historical Site.*" http://www.nps.gov/brvb/index.htm (Accessed December 2011).

Bulgaria

Bulgaria is situated in the Balkan Peninsula in southeastern Europe with an area of 42,823 square miles (110,912 square kilometers), bordered on the east with the Black Sea, Romania to the north, Macedonia and Serbia to the west, Turkey to the southeast, and Greece to the south. The official language is Bulgarian. The World Bank estimates the population at 7,364,570. Sofia, the capital city, has a population of 1.27 million and is the 12th-largest city in the European Union (EU). Its economy depends on brown coal (lignite), iron ore, oil, and natural gas. Bulgaria experienced a slight downturn, but has weathered the global economic crisis well. It has a gross domestic product (GDP) of $96.8 billion, with 12.8 percent of the population living below the poverty line. Bulgaria was settled in the 6th century by Slavic tribes. In 679, Bulgar tribes subjugated the Slavs and then settled permanently in the territory of Bulgaria. The first Bulgarian empire was established from 681 to 1018, and the second Bulgarian empire from 1186 to 1396. Tsar Boris adopted Christianity in 865. Boris III was dictator from 1935 to 1944, when the Soviets assumed control 1944 through 1989. Bulgaria became a parliamentary republic in 1991, joining the North Atlantic Treaty Organization (NATO) in 2004 and the European Union (EU) in 2007. The population is represented by Bulgars (83.9 percent), Turks (9.4 percent), and Gypsies (Roma), Jews, and Tatars (6.7 percent). Minorities continue to experience discrimination in education and business. The population has declined since World War II. Issues affecting the decline include aging of the population, low birth rate, and depopulation of villages as cities continue to grow.

The government is based on a civil law system with the constitution of the Republic of Bulgaria as the supreme law. The Grand National Assembly passed the constitution in July 1991. Bulgaria's president, Georgi Parvanov, is head of state. Boyko Borissov is prime minister and head of government. The Council of Ministers, the executive body of the government, directs domestic and foreign policy. The country is predominantly Eastern Orthodox (85 percent), with Muslims (13 percent), and Catholics (1 percent). Bulgaria has an industrialized market economy. After World War II, the agricultural-based economy was replaced by industries in engineering, metallurgy, chemistry, and electronics. The Soviet-style economy, whereby the government controlled all land, resources, and industry, was predominant until 1989. Land was collectivized in 1958, and farmed according to the principles of an agricultural production cooperative in which labor, income, and resources were jointly pooled by members. A stagnant economy with food shortages during the Soviet era led to market-oriented reform in the 1990s. Most collectivized land has now been returned to the original owners. Inflation was at 3 percent, and unemployment was 11.4 percent in 2011. The labor force was engaged in services (56.1 percent), industry (36.4 percent), and agriculture (7.5 percent).

The first schools were established in 1835. Education is free to Bulgarian citizens at all levels, and an eight-year elementary education is mandatory. Most schools have computers and Internet access. Teaching styles are lecture-based and theoretical. Segregation because of geographic boundaries and cultural discrimination prevents many rural or ethnic students from receiving adequate education. Approximately 52 percent of Turkish and Roma children complete the eighth grade, and by ninth grade, only 9 percent continue. These groups make up nearly 20 percent of Bulgaria's population, yet 60 percent are not enrolled in school for even basic education. Roma children are especially likely to end up in schools for the mentally disabled because of the general population's negative cultural views. Parents of Roma girls may keep them at home to protect their virginity. Bulgarian high school students are some of the most illiterate in Europe. Approximately 41 percent of 15 year olds possess basic reading skills, the lowest percentage of the 25 countries of the EU.

The Modernization of Education (MES) has emphasized curriculum reform with vocational and technology education. The government spends 3.3 percent yearly on education, less than the EU average of 5 percent. Bulgaria has struggled to bring its educational standards up to market needs since accession and integration into the EU. Other proposals for reform include increased participation in upper secondary and higher education, decentralization of schools, and enhanced teacher training.

Kay Castaneda
Ivy Tech Community College

See Also: European Union; Multiculturalism/Multicultural Education; Romania.

Further Readings

Agee, Jim and Jacqueline Solis. "Sofia 2004 Conference Report." *Slavic and East European Information Resources,* v.6/4 (2005).

Bairaktarova, Diana, Monica F. Cox, and Demetra Evangelou. "Leadership Training in Science, Technology, Engineering and Mathematics Education in Bulgaria." *European Journal of Engineering Education,* v.36/6 (2011).

Ilieva, Mariana and Senia Terzieva. "The New State Policy for Teacher Education and Training in Bulgaria: An Overview of Provision for Vocational Education." *European Journal of Teacher Education,* v.23/3 (December 2000).

Burden of Acting White

The acting-white phenomenon is defined as a negative label placed on African American and other non-white students by their peers as a result of exhibiting what they consider traits that are antithetical to their cultural communities and unique histories. Traits that incite this labeling can include excelling in school, interracial dating, dressing and speaking in a certain way, and the perceived close association with white peers at the expense of their ethnic or racial peer groups. Researchers have observed this phenomenon and the consequences associated with it more in integrated school settings than in segregated school settings. Integrated school settings provide more opportunities for cross-cultural and interracial contact, and therefore more opportunities to demonstrate these behaviors. The consequences or associated burdens of being labeled as acting white include stigma, shame, and ostracism from one's racial or social group. In recent years, researchers have taken a second look at the acting-white hypothesis, suggesting that similar levels of peer pressure may exist across all groups. However, they still suggest that African American students reap fewer benefits from high academic achievement than their white counterparts.

Cultural-Ecological Foundations

The foundations for the acting-white phenomenon originated as one explanation for the black–white achievement gap. Nigerian-born educational anthropologist John Ogbu's research sought to shed light on the persistence of this gap, as well as compare the response to schooling among immigrants and racial minorities. Ogbu's research is frequently cited by the scholars and has helped further define the concept and popularize it among the academic community. Ogbu developed the cultural-ecological (CE) theory of minority student achievement to explain the acting-white hypothesis. CE is usually employed to explain why even high-achieving African American students, who have the potential for academic excellence, fail to persist. The CE theory is also used to better understand academic differences and persistence in achievement among immigrant groups and African Americans. One component of CE attempts to explain why high-achieving immigrants seem to thrive under the same or similar conditions where African Americans seem to fail. In particular, Ogbu sought to differentiate among African immigrants, which he described

as functional immigrants. He felt that African Americans who alienated themselves from the larger group in order to become academically successful were rendered dysfunctional.

Ogbu conducted several ethnographic studies to shed light on these questions. Ogbu's and Fordham qualitative research, such as the 1986 seminal study cited in the *Urban Review*, helped highlight the problem among African American high school students in a high school in Shaker Heights, Ohio. In addition to school factors, Ogbu concluded that community forces, which he argued needed more study, greatly impacted how African American students perceived and responded to educational opportunities. Ogbu's research often used a comparative approach. He compared the approaches to education and assimilation in general by voluntary minorities, involuntary minorities, and autonomous minorities. Voluntary minorities are immigrants that migrated to the United States by choice in search of a better way of life. In response, voluntary minorities embraced what Ogbu calls an instrumental approach to assimilation that encourages a greater degree of integration of the cultural norms and expectations of the larger society. Their success is partly a result of survival strategies that reward high academic achievement, in ways that were adverse to African Americans because of their caste-like place in American society.

Involuntary minorities, such as African Americans, were brought to the United States as slaves by force. As a result, Ogbu argues that they developed an oppositional approach to assimilation that discourages the adoption of cultural norms or expectations that were deemed the domain of white society. The oppositional approach is characterized by the rejection of white cultural norms as a way to maintain in-group solidarity. Autonomous minorities, like Jews, according to Ogbu's CE theory, have a more complicated position in American society. While they experience somewhat similar levels of discrimination and prejudice, they are not positioned as a caste-like racial minority. Their degrees of upward mobility are not as hindered by cultural prejudice. Therefore, autonomous minorities' adoption of larger societal values is typically rewarded, and is not seen as atypical for their group.

Competing Explanations

Other researchers have questioned Ogbu's claim about the acting-white hypothesis on several grounds. They suggest that how minority students respond to education is complicated by several interrelated factors. Some argue that Ogbu's analysis of acting white insufficiently considers structural factors, like poverty, and that it employs the deficit theory as a primary factor of explanation. The deficit theory in education places the blame for academic disparities on students, their families, and their deprived lives. This theory is often advanced in the context of another theory referred to as culture of poverty. This theory suggests that the deficiencies in academic achievement and other social indices of black people and other minorities are of their own making, and result from deficits in both their moral and cultural characters. Other questions have arisen regarding whether self-reported data are misleading because it focuses more on popularity indicators, rather than real structural inequalities. Other explanations focus on the relative worth of education among racial minorities. The benefits of education for African Americans are often not the same as for others because of racial discrimination and other inequalities in American society. A college degree may not have the same earning power for racial minorities when compared to that of some immigrants and whites. These researchers suggest that educational attainment may be viewed differently because it does not reward in an equitable manner.

Other competing explanations suggest that the acting-white phenomenon may be misunderstood and misidentified. In a focus group discussion in 1999, psychologist Angela Neal-Barnett asked students to define what acting white meant. They identified a range of behaviors, from speaking a certain way to the selection of friends to the kind of clothes worn to the location of one's neighborhood. Only a few responses focused on academic traits, suggesting that the phenomenon was more cultural than academic. More recent studies suggest that both African Americans and white students view education positively, citing that peer pressure exists across groups, resulting in rewarding ability in sports and the arts over academics. This explanation suggests that peer pressure impacts African Americans' response to schooling in negative ways, which is also shared by white students as an American cultural trait of anti-intellectualism and overall declining academic performance in American schooling.

Helen Bond
Howard University

See Also: Black Cultural Capital; Racial Inequality: Returns to Educational Investments; Racism in Education.

Further Readings

Berube, M. R. *Eminent Educators: Studies in Intellectual Influence.* Westport, CT: Greenwood Press, 2000.

Ogbu, J. U. "Variability in Minority School Performance: A Problem in Search of an Explanation." *Anthropology & Education Quarterly,* v.18/4 (1987).

Wildhagen, T. "Testing the 'Acting White' Hypothesis: A Popular Explanation Runs Out of Empirical Steam." *Journal of Negro Education,* v.80/4 (2011).

Busing

In the wake of equal opportunity pursuits, busing children away from their neighborhoods into racially homogenous schools was considered a valuable option in an attempt to create equal access to public elementary and secondary education. This strategy was used throughout northern and southern states as one method of school desegregation, beginning in the 1970s. Busing for racial balance meant that each school was to be a reflection of the larger community, with the goal of eradicating racially identifiable schools. Responses to busing differed greatly along racial lines, and the strategy received both support and criticism. As a result of the *Brown v. Board of Education* decision in 1954, the doctrine of "separate but equal" was deemed unconstitutional, and the Supreme Court set the path for desegregating public education. In *Brown II* in 1955, the Supreme Court ruled that states were responsible for creating and maintaining equal educational opportunities for all students.

In the years following *Brown II*, from 1955 until 1965, segregation in schools was still widespread. The Supreme Court's mandate of desegregating schools "at all deliberate speed" had shown rather small increments of improvement. In the Deep South, black students entered predominantly white schools in small numbers, and even fewer white students entered predominantly black schools. These same trends held true throughout northern states. In effect, segregated schooling had continued at all levels of education. The maintenance of segregated schools was primarily because of widespread segregated housing patterns, especially in urban cities. Residential patterns had developed along racial lines and had progressed from non-whites being denied access to inner-city living to white residents maintaining racial homogeny in selected city neighborhoods and in suburban cities. The residential patterns were mainly from local, state, and federal legislations that were complicit in establishing racially exclusive neighborhoods. In fact, residential segregation was intensified by zoning ordinances, racially restrictive covenants, construction programs, and urban renewal. Thus, students needed to cross neighborhood lines in order for desegregation to take form.

Racial Integration

In attempting to implement the *Brown II* decree, many school systems held that children should be bused in order to achieve racial integration. A series of court rulings affirmed the use of busing as a means of achieving school desegregation. In 1970, the court ordered the Pontiac, Michigan, board to revise boundary lines for attendance purposes and to use busing as a means to achieve maximum integration in the *Davis v. School District of the City of Pontiac, Inc.* case. In *Swann v. Charlotte-Mecklenburg School District*, in 1971, the Supreme Court upheld busing black and white students. Similar rulings were ordered in several states in an effort to overcome residential segregation patterns.

These rulings were necessary, since attempts at integration were futile in the wake of Brown. The courts recommended a number of remedies and recognized busing as just one way to achieve desegregation. In Swann, the Supreme Court approved cross-district busing as a public school integration plan. In arguing for the use of busing, many school officials, educators, and parents maintained that the benefits outweighed the costs. In general, court-ordered busing plans required busing students from inner-city neighborhoods to predominantly white areas; in some instances, whites were to be bused into black school communities. Additionally, the general goals of busing were to increase educational achievement of black students (not at the expense of white students) and eliminate racial prejudices. Most of these efforts were met with great resistance.

The mainline of support for busing was the need to circumvent racially segregated housing patterns. If students were left to attend their neighborhood schools, then schools would remain easily identifiable by race. Advocates argued that options such as "free choice" would not lend themselves to accomplishing integration because of widespread resistance. As a result, they insisted that desegregation needed intentional measures and maintained that busing was a necessary method. In arguing for busing, advocates challenged the integration decree through the court system and maintained that transporting students to school was already common in many school districts throughout the nation. Therefore, busing was a logical tool that could be used to remedy educational discrimination.

Opposition to busing was strong and fervent, especially at the local level. Many predominantly white school districts and their patrons actively resisted busing—and desegregation. They argued that busing naturally disrupted neighborhood schools, was too expensive, and it increased racial tensions. Opponents also charged that busing children for educational purposes lacked sufficient benefits. In resisting busing, white parents moved and enrolled their children in private schools, while some district lines were redrawn. Although it was upheld as a practical option to achieve integration, enforcement of busing was elusive and it continued well into the 1990s with varying degrees of success. In some districts, busing disproportionately burdened nonwhite students, primarily because of the length of time spent on buses, while other districts remained highly segregated. Since Brown, strong public support for integrated schools has been thwarted by an equally strong opposition to busing, the principal tool used to achieve that goal.

Derrick Brooms
University of Louisville

See Also: *Brown v. Board of Education*; Expansion of Education; Racism in Education; School Choice.

Further Readings

Armor, D. J. "The Evidence on Busing." *Public Interest*, v.28 (1972).

Foster, G. W. "Desegregating Urban Schools." *Harvard Educational Review*, v.18/31 (February 1973).

Hennessey, G. "The History of Busing." *Educational Forum*, v.43/1 (1978).

Orfield, G. *Must We Bus? Segregated Schools and National Policy.* Washington, DC: Brookings Institution, 1978.

California

California has the largest youth population of any state in the United States, thus it is home to a wide array of primary, secondary, and postsecondary schools. California students are racially diverse, and the schools have historically struggled to provide underrepresented minorities with equitable educational opportunities. With 6 million students, California public primary and secondary schools serve a larger population than any other state. California students are racially diverse—over half of the student population is Latino, and the schools also serve sizeable Asian American and black populations. About a quarter of public school students in California are white. The California public school system is also linguistically diverse. Approximately 40 percent of California students do not speak English as their primary language at home, and a quarter of California students are classified as English learners. A total of 50 languages are represented among those spoken by English learners, although over half of these students speak Spanish. The public school system serves a high percentage of low-income students. More than half of California students participate in the National School Lunch Program.

California has approximately 9,900 public schools, including 750 charter schools. The public schools are administered at the state and local levels. The State Board of Education is appointed by the governor and is responsible for curriculum and assessment, and the California Department of Education is responsible for administering laws pertaining to education. Locally elected school boards administer schools through districts and are responsible for fiscal expenditures. Approximately two-thirds of the funds received by districts are general purpose funds allocated on a per-pupil basis, and the remaining third are designated for specific purposes. School funding in California is below the national average. In part, this is because of constraints caused by the 1978 passage of Proposition 13, a ballot initiative that amended the California Constitution to place tight restrictions on property taxes. Proposition 13 was passed in response to rapidly increasing housing prices, but also as a backlash to the *Serrano v. Priest* case.

The complaint in *Serrano* argued that California's policy of using local property taxes to fund local schools led to great disparities between schools in rich and poor areas. In response to this case, the state of California altered its funding system to cap the amount of property tax revenue that could fund local public schools and redistribute any surplus to schools with less funding. However, the decrease in available revenue caused by the passage of Proposition 13 meant that the primary source of school funding switched to general state funds. Because general funds tend to be more variable than property taxes, voters passed Proposition 98 in 1988, which established a base level of funding that the state must provide to schools in the annual budget.

Segregation in Public Primary and Secondary Schools

California public schools are marked by a history of struggle over racial segregation. In the late 1800s, the school code reversed itself multiple times in terms of segregating certain racial groups from whites, but by 1885, the code prescribed the segregation of students of Indian and Asian descent, though it did not mention Mexican or black students. This did not effectively preclude schools from discriminating against Mexican and black students, however, and during the Progressive Era, a number of cities established "Mexican Schools" that focused on Americanization, rather than formal education. In a precursor to *Brown v. Board of Education,* five Mexican American fathers filed suit against their Orange County school districts to end this practice in the case of *Mendez v. Westminster.* In 1947, the Ninth Circuit Court ruled that the segregation of Mexican students was prohibited under the limited finding that California law only provided for the segregation of students with "Chinese, Japanese, or Mongolian parentage."

All de jure segregation was repealed later that year through a law enacted by Governor Earl Warren. Despite this victory, de facto segregation has continued in many school districts. In 1968, with the support of Chicano community organizers, high school students in East Los Angeles staged a series of walkouts, called "Blowouts," to protest the conditions in primarily Chicano/Latino schools. In 1970, under the suit of *Spangler v. Pasadena,* Pasadena Unified School District in L.A. County became the first district west of the Mississippi to be ordered by a court to desegregate its schools. Similar lawsuits were filed in other districts, including San Francisco. Despite protests and desegregation efforts, California public schools remain highly segregated. In 2008, over 40 percent of Latino students and over 30 percent of black students attended schools where 90 to 100 percent of the student body consisted of underrepresented minorities. These intensely segregated schools are far more likely than other schools to lack sufficient instructional materials, safe and decent school facilities, and experienced teachers.

In addition to this vast network of public schools, children in California are also educated in nonpublic and private schools. Approximately 15,000 California students attend nonpublic schools that are publicly funded, but privately operated to support students with exceptional needs. Over 500,000 California students are enrolled in private schools, and more than three-quarters of these attend schools with a religious affiliation. California private schools serve a variety of unique needs and interests, from Montessori schools to elite college preparatory schools.

Universities and Colleges

California's vast array of public universities, professional schools, and colleges are managed through three separate systems: the University of California (UC) system, the California State University system (CSU), and the California Community Colleges system. This tripartite division was established in 1960 with the passage of the Donahoe Higher Education Act, which approved large portions of the Master Plan for Higher Education in California, 1960–1975. The master plan was designed in response to a number of factors, including the increase in the population of college-age youth because of the baby boom, the increase in college attendance following the G.I. Bill, the proliferation of autonomous universities receiving public funding, and competition between these universities for awarding various types of degrees. The master plan was intended to meet these expanded needs while reducing costs.

Under the plan, each of the three systems serves a unique educational mission. The UC system is the state's primary institution of academic research and has sole authority to grant doctoral degrees and to provide instruction in law, dentistry, medicine, and veterinary medicine. UC has nine university campuses with both graduate and undergraduate programs, one campus with a graduate school alone, and one with a law school alone. UC is also responsible for administering the Lawrence Livermore National Laboratory. The system's flagship institution, UC Berkeley, is widely considered the top public university in the nation. The CSU system has 23 campuses that provide undergraduate, graduate, and professional education up to the master's degree, and may also offer doctoral degrees through joint programs with UC or private institutions. The primary mission of CSU is undergraduate education, though faculty research may also be encouraged. The CSU system historically began as a system of "normal schools" (schools that educate teachers); today, CSU still trains about 60 percent of California teachers. The California Community Colleges system provides vocational and lower-division academic instruction, as well as remedial instruction and courses in English as a second language.

Table 1 Elementary and secondary education characteristics

	California	U.S. (average)
Total number of schools	10,340	1,988
Total students	6,289,578	970,278
Total teachers	260,806.30	60,766.56
Pupil/teacher ratio	24.12	15.97

Source: U.S. Department of Education, National Center for Education Statistics, Common Core of Data (CCD), 2010–11.

Table 2 Elementary and secondary education finance

	California	U.S. (average)
Total revenues	$71,224,023,937	$11,464,385,994
Total expenditures for education	$73,868,615,768	$11,712,033,839
Total current expenditures	$61,570,554,977	$9,938,906,259

Source: U.S. Department of Education, National Center for Education Statistics, Common Core of Data (CCD), "National Public Education Financial Survey," FY08 (2007–08).

The highest degree available from the Community Colleges system is an associate's degree. Community college students may complete their training at the community college level or transfer to a four-year institution.

California public universities have twice received national attention in the debate over affirmative action in admissions. First, in the 1978 case of *Bakke v. California*, the Supreme Court ruled racial quotas unconstitutional in response to actions by UC Davis medical school, though the court upheld the ability of public schools to consider race or ethnicity as one aspect of the admissions process. In 1996, California again received national attention when voters passed Proposition 209, which prohibited public institutions from considering race or ethnicity in hiring and admissions. This effectively ended the practice of affirmative action at California public universities. Proposition 209 had devastating effects on the admission enrollment of black and Latino students; for example, at UCLA, 5.5 percent of all students admitted in 1996 were black; this proportion declined to 2 percent by 2006. African American and Latino students remain underrepresented in California universities, though to a far greater extent in the UC system than in the CSU system.

California is home to 146 private, nonprofit institutions of higher education and 160 private, for-profit institutions; both of these numbers are more than four times the national average. A number of California colleges and universities are considered highly prestigious, including Stanford University, the California Institute of Technology, the Claremont colleges, and the University of Southern California.

Jessica S. Cobb
University of California, Berkeley

See Also: Asian Americans; Community Colleges; Educational Policymakers; Funding of Schools; Government Influences on Education; Mexican American Students.

Further Readings

Schrag, Peter. *Paradise Lost: California's Experience and America's Future.* New York: New Press, 1998.

Taylor, Angus E. *The Academic Senate at the University of California: Its Role in the Shared Governance and Operation of the University.* Berkeley, CA: Institute of Governmental Studies, 1998.

Wollenberg, Charles. *All Deliberate Speed: Segregation and Exclusion in California Schools 1855–1975.* Berkeley: University of California Press, 1976.

Cambodia

Cambodia is a southeastern Asian nation with a 2009 population of 14.8 million, a growing percentage of which is of school age. Most of the population is rural and employed within the agricultural sector. The poverty rate remains high, despite economic development. Cambodia's Buddhist and French colonial heritage shaped its early educational system. Its modern system had to be rebuilt after the destruction of the Khmer Rouge in the 1970s. Most Cambodian children achieve some level of primary education, and the 2009 adult literacy rate approached 80 percent. The educational system is still plagued by many problems, however, including large educational divides along rural/urban, gender, and income groups. Cambodia's educational attainments remain low by global comparison.

Cambodia's early formal education system has been traced back to the 13th century, and was closely tied to Buddhism. Buddhist temples known as *wats* housed libraries and provided instruction to males. The French colonial government introduced a system of primary and secondary education based on that of France when Cambodia became a French colony. The system was established under the 1917 Law on Education, with an emphasis on civil service training. The native Khmer population had little access to education under French rule. After gaining independence, the new Cambodian government established a universal system of education. A number of public vocational institutes and universities were founded in the 1950s and 1960s.

Prince Sihanouk's overthrow led to the emergence of the Khmer Rouge regime under notorious dictator Pol Pot in 1975. The Khmer Rouge targeted the nation's educational system as a central component in its efforts to reshape Cambodian society. Manual labor and government loyalty were valued over learning and criticism. Educational materials were destroyed and school buildings were repurposed. Many teachers and educated persons fled the country, while those who remained faced persecution or forced labor. Estimates range from 75 to 90 percent of educators murdered or exiled by the regime's end in 1979. Cambodia's new PRK government had to almost entirely rebuild the educational system after 1979. Teacher recruitment and increased student enrollment was the main focus, as illiteracy rates rose over 40 percent, and many failed to obtain a basic education. Emphasis on enrollment resulted in lack of attention to the quality of services provided. Teachers were inadequately trained and classes were held in rundown buildings, or even outside. Ongoing civil conflicts and Vietnamese occupation shifted political attention and resources away from education in the 1980s.

Educational changes in the 1990s and early 2000s included increased governmental control, educational expenditures, and infrastructure; decentralization of government control; improved teacher training; the development of new curricula textbooks; and the introduction of more active learning methods. Increased educational availability, student enrollments, and basic literacy have been the primary goals of the modern Cambodian educational system. Cambodia's current constitution mandates six years of universal, free compulsory education. Cambodia had a 2009 primary education completion rate of 92 percent and school-life expectancy total of 7.3 years, according to United Nations Children's Fund (UNICEF) statistics. The Ministry of Education, Youth, and Sports is the national government agency responsible for oversight of the public education system. Cambodia also houses a growing number of private schools at all educational levels. Preschool for students aged 3 to 5 years is available on a limited basis. The primary level encompasses 1st through 6th grades, and is compulsory. Secondary level education is not mandatory. The lower secondary level encompasses seventh through ninth grades, and the upper secondary level encompasses 10th through 12th grades. Students must sit for exit examinations to graduate secondary school with a diploma (*bac dup*). Examination scores are also used to determine admittance to universities. Cambodia maintains a system of higher education, but participation is slight, at just over 2 percent of the population. Adult Cambodians also have access to nontraditional educational opportunities, such as adult literacy programs.

Cambodia's current formal education system faces numerous problems, including: high national poverty rates and parental educational expenses; and insufficient government funding, teacher training, educational attainment, pay levels, educational facilities, and supplies. Results include large class sizes and high grade-level repetition rates. Rural/urban, income, and gender divides in educational access, quality, and attainment levels are ongoing problems with deep social and cultural roots. Girls were traditionally expected to remain at home and provide domestic and childcare assistance. Sex trafficking and child labor prevent others from enrolling. Parents will still educate their sons first, if forced to choose, because of financial constraints.

Government programs include the Education Strategic Sector Plan (ESSP) and the National Education for All Plan 2003–15. International nongovernmental organizations such as UNICEF, World Education, and the World Bank have emerged as vital sources of educational funding, but attempts to introduce new curricula and teaching methods can meet resistance from administrators. Initiatives include expanding educational access within traditionally underserved regions and populations, scholarship programs, increased educational resources, improved funding allocation, and national and local level capacity building.

Marcella Bush Trevino
Barry University

See Also: France; Poverty and Education; Rural Schooling.

Further Readings

Ayres, David M. *Anatomy of a Crisis: Education, Development, and the State in Cambodia, 1953–1998.* Honolulu: University of Hawai'i Press, 2000.

Keng, Chan Sopheak and Thomas Clayton. "Schooling in Cambodia." In *Going to School in East Asia.* Gerald A. Postiglione and Jason Tan. Westport, CT: Greenwood Press, 2007.

World Bank. "Education in Cambodia" (2007). http://web .worldbank.org (Accessed February 2012).

Cameroon

Cameroon, often referred to as Africa in miniature for its rich and diverse topography and customs, has a complex educational system. Formal schooling at the primary level is mandatory for every child, although this does not necessarily mean that everyone takes advantage of the opportunity or that girls and boys access it equally. While tuition is waived, parents still have to purchase books, uniforms, and other school supplies, which can be costly, depending on the family's income level. The most recent World Bank estimate of the population of Cameroon is 19.6 million, with an annual population growth rate of 2.2 percent. Cameroon's economy is heavily dependent on agriculture, and has a 39.9 percent poverty rate. The country shares borders with the Central African Republic, Chad, Equatorial Guinea, Gabon, Nigeria, and the Democratic Republic of the Congo. It occupies an area of approximately 183,398 square miles (475,000 square kilometers). Cameroon is one of the few countries in Africa that boasts an adult literacy rate of 68 to 76 percent. There are approximately eight major ethnic groups and 24 major African language groups. However, English and French serve as the two official languages used for educational and administrative purposes.

Cameroon's history is unique. During the latter half of the 19th century through the early part of the 20th century, Cameroon was colonized by Germany (1884–1916). Later, it became a mandate of France (1914–60) and Britain (1916–61). During the postwar era, it was partitioned into two mandates; a third of the country (southern and northern) was designated as British Cameroon, and two-thirds as French. The British parts of the country were both attached to Nigeria. European colonial rule dominated this pre-independence phase. In 1960, French Cameroon gained its independence; and in 1961, through a plebiscite, southern British Cameroon opted to join French Cameroon to form a Federal Republic of Cameroon, while British northern Cameroon remained with Nigeria. In 1972, through a referendum, Cameroon became the United Republic of Cameroon. Today it has reverted to its pre-federated name, the Republic of Cameroon. In regard to education, in the 1800s, Baptist missionaries from Jamaica and Europe created the earliest schools; the Germans continued this practice to expand a local elite class to serve their administrative purposes. The British and the French built on this tradition, however, maintaining a paternalistic or assimilationist attitude. Today, there are several public and private schools across the country that serve Anglophone and Francophone communities.

The complex nature of the educational system in Cameroon is a product of its complicated colonial history. The curriculum and education reflect the country's colonial heritage, with Anglophone Cameroon modeling its education after the British system and Francophone Cameroon after the French. In the mid-1990s, there was an unsuccessful attempt to harmonize the dual system. Formal education for both Anglophone and Francophone Cameroonians is designed as a three-tier system, not counting nursery school/*l'ecole maternelle* (two years).

These tiers include the primary school/*l'ecole primaire* (six years), secondary grammar school/*l'ecole secondaire* (seven years in two cycles—lower and upper), and post secondary. At the secondary level, there is also a technical/vocational track. At the end of the second and third tiers, students must pass a national examination to move on to the next level. Three ministries that enforce educational reforms in Cameroon are the Ministries of Basic Education, Secondary Education, and Higher Education. There are seven public and four private universities across the country. Of the seven public universities, one is modeled after the Anglo-Saxon tradition. While the rest profess to be bilingual, for the most part, they are heavily French oriented. Attempts to harmonize the two systems continue to pose challenges to the government. Curricular reforms now include cyber education, and more attempts are being made to increase female and rural participation in education.

Vivian Yenika-Agbaw
Pennsylvania State University

See Also: Bilingual Education; Career and Technical Education; France; United Kingdom.

Further Readings

DeLancey, Mark W. *Cameroon: Dependence and Independence.* Boulder, CO: Westview Press, 1989.

Fonkeng, George Epah. *The History of Education in Cameroon.* Lewiston, NY: Edwin Mellen Press, 2007.

Mbaku, John Mukum. *Culture and Customs of Cameroon.* Westport, CT: Greenwood Press, 2005.

Canada

Canada is the second-largest country in the world, with an area of 3,854,085 square miles (9,984,670 square kilometers). It is situated in North America between the Pacific Ocean to the west, the Atlantic Ocean to the east, the Arctic Ocean to the north—along with Greenland to the northeast—and the United States to the south. Canada shares the world's longest international boundary with the United States, at 5,525 miles (8,891 kilometers). Statistics Canada estimated Canada's total population in 2011 at 34,349,200, of whom only about 17 percent fall under 15 years of age, 69 percent fall between the ages of 15 to 64 years old, and the remaining 13 percent are age 65 years and older. Canada is one of the wealthiest countries in the world.

According to the World Bank, its gross domestic product (GDP) was $1.758 trillion, and per capita income was $51,147 in 2011. The country had a moderate unemployment rate of 7.1 percent and life expectancy at birth was 81 years in 2011. Canada's heritage is rooted in indigenous traditions, a French and British colonial past, emerging multiculturalism, and a strong democratic system that have shaped its demographics, economics, society, and educational structure.

History and Social Structure

The Canadian confederation is comprised of 10 provinces: Alberta, British Columbia, Manitoba, New Brunswick, Newfoundland and Labrador, Nova Scotia, Ontario, Prince Edward Island, Quebec, and Saskatchewan; and three territories: Northwest Territories, Nunavut, and Yukon. In the late 15th century, British and French explorers entered and settled the Canadian Atlantic Coast. By 1763, British colonial power established full authority over the Atlantic region, including Quebec, New Brunswick, and Nova Scotia.

Canada came into existence as a new country on July 1, 1867, through a confederation of four leading provinces: Nova Scotia, New Brunswick, Ontario, and Quebec, and was later joined by nine other provinces and territories. Prior to the European explorer's settlement, Canadian land was inhabited by various groups of Aboriginal people comprised of the First Nations, Inuit, and other indigenous groups. Until European explorers came, the indigenous population was believed to be about 350,000. Presently, there are about 53 indigenous languages. The remaining 94 percent of the population comes from diverse cultural traditions representing over 200 ethnic origins and 200 home languages. Because of colonial legacies, Canada has two major linguistic groups and official languages, English and French. More than 57 percent of the population speak English and about 22 percent speak French.

Canada has a highly skilled knowledge-based economy. Almost all Canadian youths and adults have basic literacy and numeracy skills, about one-quarter of adults have university degrees, and an additional one-third have either college degrees or trade certificates. Historically, Canadian education was founded in informal settings involving family, community, and church in the 17th century. Children were encouraged to learn basic literacy skills, along with trades and life skills such as gardening and spinning, utilizing community resources. Gradually, this program evolved into a formal public schooling system throughout Canada in 1840. Although schools were funded by the government, religious bodies remained in control of the curriculum and management, and in 1870, boarding and residential schools were introduced. Native children were seriously marginalized through unequal, disrespectful, and decontextualized treatment of their culture in the curriculum. Schools were used as an instrument to domesticate, shape, and reform indigenous ways of living.

During the 19th century, 150,000 First Nations, Inuit, and Métis children were removed from their home and cultural communities in the name of education. In 1961, all 130 residential schools were closed. In 2007, the Canadian government paid $1.9 billion to the survivors of those residential schools, and on June 11, 2008, Prime Minister Stephen Harper delivered an official apology. Attempts are being made to improve the quality of education by incorporating contextually responsive curriculum and instructional systems at every level. Although schooling at the elementary and secondary level is mainly funded by the provinces and territories, university and college education is significantly funded by the federal government. For example, during the 2007 to 2008 academic year, universities were supported with 9.3 percent of the government's collective revenue, which was $36.7 billion. However, more strategic and program-specific funding is necessary to cope with required innovations and global challenges.

Educational Structure

Education in Canada is a provincial responsibility. Each province and territory maintains its educational structure. Formal education in Canada includes early childhood education, comprising junior kindergarten (ages 4–5) in Ontario and preschool or kindergarten (ages 5–6) in other provinces. Next, levels of formal schooling are offered through elementary (ages 6–14, grades 1–8), secondary (ages 14–18, grades 9–12 and up), and tertiary (postsecondary) education programs. In Quebec, Ontario, and the rest of the Canadian provinces, student's age groups corresponding to their grade levels vary slightly. Entry-level tertiary programs are designed to address these variations and to bridge the gap between the secondary and undergraduate level through pre-university courses, certificates, diplomas, and associate degrees. Mid-level tertiary programs are offered at undergraduate settings through advanced-level community colleges, technical institutes, trade and vocational training centers, and universities. Programs offered at this level are similar in all the provinces. Finally, advanced-level tertiary programs are offered through postgraduate institutes and universities. All the postgraduate level institutions have memberships with the Association of Universities and Colleges of Canada (AUCC). Also, membership with other associations, such as the Canadian Association for Graduate Studies (CAGS), the Association of Canadian Community Colleges (ACCC), the Association for Biblical Higher Education (ABHE), and the Association of Theological Schools (ATS) are encouraged for accreditation purposes, depending on the nature of their programs.

The AUCC and other professional accrediting agencies ensure that Canadian academic qualifications are competitive, recognized, and respected around the world. In 2012, AUCC had 97 member universities, CAGS had 63 member universities, ACCC had 131 member colleges, ABHE had 19 member colleges and universities, and ATS had over 50 church-based accredited member schools in Canada. According to Statistics Canada, about 5.1 million students were enrolled in publicly funded elementary and secondary schools, and there were 337,600 educators nationwide, making the student-teacher ratio a little over 14 percent during 2009–10. Enrollment of students has been declining: the student population was about 5.4 million from 1999 to 2000. From 2009 to 2010, about 351,000 students graduated from government-run secondary schools, with dropout rates of 6.6 percent for young women and 10.3 percent for young men. School participation among the First Nations students in some parts of Canada is significantly high. For example, in 2009–10, in British Columbia, there were 55,270 First Nations students attending schools among 649,952 students, of whom 580,486 attended public and 69,466 attended private school systems, making about 11 percent of students. However, a large percentage of First Nations students who attend schools experience poor success rates. According to a 2006 census, about 60 percent of First Nations students ages 20 to 24 who reside on reservations had still not completed secondary school or the equivalent.

Statistics Canada data suggest that there were over a million students enrolled in postsecondary studies in 2006–07. Records show that 460,962 full-time students attended regular postsecondary programs, of whom 45 percent were male and 55 percent female; 148,089 part-time students, with about 56.5 percent female, attended regular postsecondary courses; 428,805 participants attended full-time college certificate or diploma and other programs at the college level, of whom about 57 percent were female; 80,901 students, over 61 percent female, enrolled in similar part-time college certificate or diploma classes; and 22,014 students were enrolled in undergraduate certificate or diploma courses, with over 62 percent female, and 243 were enrolled in graduate certificate or diploma courses, with 48 percent female. Canada is leading the world with the highest rate of postsecondary education completion. Canadian schools are also attracting a large number of international students; in 2008, 8 percent of students were international.

Current Issues

Modernization of the Canadian education system, valuing the knowledge economy, sustainability, and innovation are under way to meet the challenges of 21st century society. In 2009, the Canada Foundation for Innovation initiated a $750 million project to facilitate cutting-edge research infrastructure, and over $2 billion was allocated for capacity building of postsecondary institutions. Further, $3 billion was allocated over a six-year period to facilitate job training for the unemployed. As a donor country, in response to the Millennium Development Goals, Canada is committed ensure that by 2015, children everywhere in the world, boys and girls alike, will be able to complete a full course of primary schooling. Accordingly, Canada will continue to lobby G8 countries to ensure that the proposed $16 billion is raised to boost the required investment in education, and that Canada's share of $5.6 billion over four years is paid. Both provincial and federal governments are becoming increasingly concerned about required educational innovations, technology integration, usefulness of education and training, environmental responsiveness, and student centeredness. Since Canada is one of the most diverse, multicultural countries in the world, curriculum contents are derived from a diverse perspective. It is widely believed in Canada that new education programs are vehicles for positive change toward a knowledge-based society, and they must be designed to reduce participants' social gaps, inequalities, and injustices.

Matiul Alam
University of British Columbia

See Also: Gender Inequality: College Enrollment and Completion; Multiculturalism/Multicultural Education; Native American Students; Technology Education.

Further Readings
Aman, C. and C. Ungerleider. "Aboriginal Students and K-12 School Change in British Columbia." *Horizons*, v.10/1 (2008).
Ghosh, R., A. Abdi, and A. Naseem. "Identity in Colonial and Postcolonial Contexts: Select Discussions and Analyses." In *Decolonizing Democratic Education: Trans-Disciplinary Dialogues,* A. Abdi and G. Richardson, eds. Rotterdam, Netherlands: Sense Publishers, 2008.
Rubenson, Kjell, et al. *Adult Learning in Canada: A Comparative Perspective.* Results From the Adult Literacy and Life Skills Survey, 2007.
Shaker, P. "Preserving Canadian Exceptionalism." *Education Canada*, v.49/1 (2009).

Statistics Canada. *Canada Year Book.* Federal Publications (Queen of Canada). Catalogue no 11-402-XPE, 2010.

Career and Technical Education

Career and technical education, historically referred to as vocational education, is a segment of the U.S. educational system intended to help individuals explore and plan for occupations, obtain knowledge and abilities necessary for success within specific occupational areas, and develop interpersonal skills necessary for success in the workplace. Career and technical education programs serve both youth and adults, and are commonly found throughout the United States within public and private schools, and career and technical centers separate from schools. Currently, seven commonly recognized career and technical education areas of study exist in the United States: agriculture, business, family and consumer sciences, marketing, health sciences, trade and industrial, and technology. Career and technical education programs may potentially provide courses in as few as one to as many as all seven areas of study, depending upon the size and scope of the career and technical education program. The number of areas of study provided within career and technical education programs are often determined by federal, state, and local funding; career preparation demands within a community, area, or region; and availability of career and technical education teachers, staff, and administrators.

The most common place for career and technical programs are within public comprehensive high schools. Currently, over 90 percent of all public high schools offer some form of career and technical course work; many high schools require one unit of introductory level career and technical education coursework for graduation, such as computer science or personal financial management. Another common venue for career and technical education programs is within career and technical centers. Career and technical centers typically serve two major groups of individuals. The first group of individuals consists of youth who spend part of their school day within a comprehensive high school and the other part of their day taking coursework within the career and technical center. The second group of people served by career and technical centers are adults enrolled part-time in career and technical education programs to enhance their current occupational skills.

Most career and technical education teachers typically hold a bachelors or higher degree and are often required to have experience or preparation in one or more of the following: content knowledge related to specific occupational areas, pedagogical knowledge necessary to facilitate effective educational settings, and/or related work experience within a specific occupational area. Career and technical education teachers are most often responsible for instructing only career and technical education courses. However, some educators may serve in a dual-purpose role as both a career and technical education teacher, while also teaching courses outside career and technical education.

Content Delivery Within Career and Technical Education Programs

Career and technical educators deliver content to students utilizing a combination of methods, including formal instruction, laboratory practice, and work-based learning experiences, allowing individuals to "learn by doing" through practice. Introductory-level career and technical education courses provide a broad overview of an entire industry, while more specialized courses involve advanced principles and skills utilized within a career area. In many career and technical education programs, individuals can choose to take courses in one specific area of study, or may choose to take courses in numerous areas of study. For example, a freshman agricultural education student may enroll in a general agriculture course, and later enroll in agriculture courses focusing on specific segments of the agricultural industry during subsequent high school years. Many career and technical education programs offer career technical student organizations to provide individuals with activities beyond the classroom to enhance what is learned during formal instruction as well as better develop leadership, interpersonal, and citizenship skills. An example would be a Business Professionals of America club associated with a business education program within a school.

Early Vocational Preparation in America

Career and technical education is largely a product of societal demands and federal legislation throughout the 20th century. However, vocational preparation has existed in some form throughout American history. In colonial America and through most of the 19th century, vocational preparation occurred outside schools primarily in two ways: duplication of career skills through observation, or apprenticeship training. Duplication of career skills often involved little formal instruction and was most often a product of observation and mimicking the skills used for particular trades or occupation; the skills were most often observed and mimicked from family members or other individuals with whom the youth had constant contact. An example of the duplication method would be an individual who acquires tailoring skills from observing and working with parents who owned a tailor shop. The apprenticeship approach was a more systematic method for career training, often involving structured instruction and preparation related to a specific vocational area. The apprenticeship approach required youth to spend extensive amounts of time, often spanning several years, learning specific occupational skills from individuals who possessed occupational skills outside the youth's family. An example would be an individual leaving his or her home to live and work with a blacksmith to become a skilled blacksmith.

The rise of the industrial era in the United States in the 18th and 19th centuries led to an increase in demand for a skilled workforce. Formalized education became increasingly accessible because of an increase in the number of public schools: The public education system in the United States during this time was intended to provide an opportunity for the "common man" to receive a formal education in basic subjects including reading, writing, and mathematics. However, few individuals saw the value of such an education and how it could benefit their lives. Youth would often leave formal education at an early age, often before adolescence, to enter increasingly available occupations with more attainable and desirable characteristics.

Entering the 20th century, laws requiring youth to attend public schools became predominant. A new challenge was faced: providing a balanced education of a general curriculum, while teaching skills necessary for successful career entry into an ever-growing American economy. State and local educational leaders began to develop a systematic means to merge vocational courses into public schools beginning in the first decade of the 20th century. Proponents of vocational education within schools argued that vocational education would serve both students and industry to provide trained workers who were ready for existing jobs. This was the beginning of formal vocational education programs in public schools throughout the United States. A downside to the locally based vocational skill preparation system was a lack of consistent and updated vocational curriculum, preparation of educators to teach vocational courses, and fair and consistent funding.

Key Career and Technical Education Events

To provide a higher level of quality and consistency across vocational programs nationally, federal legislation and funding was provided throughout the 20th century. Numerous key events and individuals have shaped how career and technical education programs have been and are currently offered in a variety of settings. Some of the most significant events to shape career and technical education in the United States include:

- *Early 1900s to 1916*: Several organized entities, including the Commission on Industrial and Technical Education, the Commission on National Aid for Vocational Education, and the National Society for the Promotion of Industrial Education, promoted the need for high systematic vocational training in the United States to meet the needs of American industry.
- *The Smith-Hughes Act of 1917*: The first federal legislation that provided continuous funding for integrating vocational education programs as a separate, but integrated component within U.S. public comprehensive secondary high schools. The funding established the beginning of a nationally recognized vocational education curriculum, salaries for vocational educators, and government entities to monitor and assess the quality of vocational education programs.
- *The Vocational Education Act of 1963*: The intent of this legislation was to improve the quality of current vocational education program facilities as well as extend vocational education programs to underserved groups, including: socioeconomically disadvantaged persons; mentally or physically disadvantaged persons; and individuals who had not completed high school, but were able to dedicate themselves to the study of a vocation full time. The legislation also provided advanced vocational training for employed individuals. The legislation provided funding for new

vocational facilities, staff, and initiatives to maintain the quality of vocational programs.

- *The Carl D. Perkins Act of 1984* (amended in 1990, 1998, and 2006): This legislation continued to expand initiatives providing vocational education programs to disadvantaged groups. The amendments to the Perkins Act have resulted in: increased accountability for vocational teachers; continued improvement of curriculum to match changing industry needs; linking academic and vocational curriculum standards; and most recently, implementing the term *career and technical education,* (rather than *vocational education*) to describe the area of education as a means for career readiness as well as transfer of knowledge to multiple contexts, such as advanced training and degrees.

Past and Future Objectives of Career and Technical Education

Vocational educational programs were originally intended to prepare individuals with specific skill sets to enter specific careers within industry immediately following school. Vocational education programs were designed to create a "finished product" by providing individuals with a specific skill set to go out into the industrial world and use those specific skills within an occupation they were trained to enter. For most of the 20th century, using vocational education to create individuals with specific skill sets was an acceptable means to fulfill the labor demands of American industry. At the end of the 20th century and beginning of the 21st century, society and industrial demands have required career and technical education programs to change the philosophy of preparing individuals for future occupations. If career and technical education programs are to prepare individuals to be successful in today's workforce, it is no longer acceptable to merely equip individuals with specific skills for specific careers. Instead, career and technical education must be used as a context to introduce and prepare individuals with career skills while developing critical thinking and personal skills necessary for success in the 21st century industry landscape.

William Bird
University of Nebraska, Lincoln
Anna Henry
University of Missouri

See Also: Agricultural Education; Community Colleges; Family Structure and Education; School-to-Work Transitions; Technology Education.

Further Readings
Gordon, H. R. D. *The History and Growth of Career and Technical Education in America.* 3rd ed. Long Grove, IL: Waveland Press, 2008.
Lynch, R. L. "High School Career and Technical Education for the First Decade of the 21st Century." *Journal of Vocational Education Research*, v.25/2 (2000).
Scott, J. L. and M. Sarkees-Wircenski. *Overview of Career and Technical Education.* Homewood, IL: American Technical Publishers, 2001.
Walter, D. H. "Social Efficiency Reexamine: The Dewey-Snedden Controversy." *Curriculum Inquiry*, v.7/1 (1977).
Wonacott, M. E. *History and Evolution of Vocational and Career-Technical Education: A Compilation.* Columbus, OH: ERIC Clearinghouse on Adult, Career, and Vocational Education, 2003.

Catholic Schools

The mission of Catholic schools is to teach students the Catholic faith with its beliefs and practices, to provide students with an outstanding academic education, and to socialize them for adulthood by preparing them to be responsible citizens with a concern for social justice. Catholic schools are countercultural in their emphasis on the sacred, while reflecting aspects of the secular culture of the society in which they are embedded. Catholic schools are found in virtually every country. In 2011, there were about 136,000 Catholic schools worldwide enrolling almost 50 million students. In the United States, Catholic schools enroll about 6 percent of the school-age population. Other nonpublic schools comprise about 4 percent of the population, with the remaining 90 percent attending public schools or being home schooled.

The number of U.S. Catholic schools and students has declined since its peak in the early1960s. Two factors account for this decline. The first is a response to changes in the Catholic Church dating from the Second Vatican Council in 1968. Prior to the council, Catholic schools were staffed primarily by religious sisters, brothers, and priests. Subsequent to the council's call for renewal, many of these teachers and administrators left religious life and continued working in Catholic schools as salaried lay Catholics. Since their work had been voluntary, their departure was and continues to be a heavy financial burden for these Catholic schools. They have tried to survive financially with support from parents, parishioners, and donors, but with changing economic conditions, funding Catholic schools is becoming increasingly more difficult, and many schools have become insolvent. As a result, Catholic schools throughout the country are being closed or consolidated, and the proportion of students in Catholic schools is shrinking. Vatican 2 also directed Catholic school personnel to exercise preferential treatment for the poor. In response, Catholic schools are reaching out to serve disadvantaged and at-risk students whose families can do little to help finance the schools. The Church no longer sees its instructional mission solely as serving Catholic students. In order to teach all students who want a Catholic education, especially those in greatest need, they are accepting more non-Catholic and socioeconomically deprived students. These changes have made the financial situation of Catholic schools ever more tenuous.

Funding Catholic Education Worldwide
The United States is among the countries with the strictest regulations governing public funding of religious schools. The separation of church and state required by the U.S. Constitution forbids public financing of religious schools. In sharp contrast, other countries, such as Australia and Ireland, provide government support for all schools, regardless of religious affiliation. Some countries superimpose a small restriction on this policy. For example, New Zealand covers all expenses for religious schools, except for the property on which the schools are built. The land belongs to the diocese and devoting state funds to it would violate New Zealand's separation of church and state. Similarly, Germany subsidizes religious schools by paying 90 percent of their expenses. In many countries, variation in school financing policies is found across and within provinces, districts, cities, and states. James Mulligan reports, for example, that Ontario, Canada, provides equal financial support for private and public schools, while other Canadian provinces offer only partial support, or none at all.

Similarly, Mexico funds Catholic schools in some districts, but not in others. France does not recognize any religion, but establishes special contracts with private schools that are given government salary support for teachers, on condition that the school adopts the national curriculum. Private schools are denied government funds if they want to follow a different curriculum. In England and Wales, Catholics must pay taxes to support their public school system, as well as an additional 10 percent to cover their Catholic school expenses. In the United States, some states are experimenting with student vouchers to help families pay private school tuition. In addition, many Catholic schools are establishing development boards to help raise funds for their schools. These and other approaches to school financing provide hope to Catholics as they search for ways to support their schools in a new fiscal environment.

Student Academic Achievement and the "Catholic School Advantage"

Over the past few decades, American sociologists of education have paid particular attention to two aspects of Catholic education: comparisons between Catholic and public schools on student academic achievement, and comparisons between the two sectors on adherence to the common school ideal. In empirical analyses of nationally representative longitudinal surveys, James Coleman and his colleagues looked at the achievement of Catholic high school students in the 1970s and 1980s. They found that students in Catholic high schools achieved higher standardized test scores than those in public high schools. This became known as the "Catholic school advantage." They also showed that the academic advantage of Catholic schools is greatest for disadvantaged and minority students. Subsequently, scholars replicated these findings in other national surveys.

The higher achievement of Catholic school students was attributed to rigorous course taking, strict discipline, high teacher expectations, a safe and orderly environment, closely monitored student attendance, regularly assigned homework, close student-teacher relationships, and a faith-based community of learners. Many studies of sector effects on student achievement were conducted under societal and institutional conditions different from the present. Recent studies show that the Catholic school advantage continues to hold at the high school level. However, neither public nor Catholic schools have consistently higher achievement gains at lower grade levels. Moreover, in all cases, poverty seems to be a stronger predictor of growth in achievement than school sector.

Another factor may have contributed to sector effects on student achievement over the past couple of decades. Toward the end of the 20th century, numerous educational reforms were implemented in both public and Catholic schools. For example, Anthony Bryk proposed a conceptual model of school improvement that was adopted in the Chicago public school system over a decade ago. The components of the model are leadership, parent-community ties, professional capacity of faculty and staff, a student-centered learning climate, and ambitious instruction. The implementation of the model fostered considerable growth in student achievement. During this same period, Catholic schools made fundamental changes in the structure and organization of their educational institutions. They replaced parish-based schools with regional schools and consortia, established a president-principal model of governance, introduced a technology-supported curriculum, and enriched professional development. These reforms affected student learning in both school sectors, but may have had a stronger impact on one than the other. This could have changed the Catholic school advantage, at least at the K–8 grade levels.

Catholic Schools, Public Schools, and the Common School Ideal

Both Catholic and public school systems in the United States were founded to provide all students with equal opportunities to learn. This goal became known as the common school ideal. Attaining this ideal depends on three factors: an open admissions policy, access to a common curriculum, and the insulation of students from the negative influence of background on achievement. Analyses show that neither Catholic nor public schools fully attain this goal. Theoretically, U.S. public schools have provided open admissions since the founding of the public school system. In practice, open access is becoming an established policy only over time. Milestones include school desegregation, mainstreaming, and school accountability for raising the achievement of all groups of students. An obstacle to open admissions is the differential access of students to charter or magnet schools caused by lack of transportation. Another obstacle is the difficulty that disabled students confront in obtaining instruction commensurate with their ability. Catholic schools set their admissions policies and academic standards. The Catholic school system was established in response to the Protestant orientation of public school curriculum. The church encouraged parents to send their children to Catholic schools in order for them to learn about both their religion and secular subjects. The schools had no formal admissions requirements, other than affiliation with the parish church.

In his broad overview of the history of U.S. Catholic schools, Harold Buetow emphasizes the rapid expansion of the Catholic school system, beginning in the early 20th century. In addition to expected population growth, the school-age population in the United States gained many immigrants from Catholic countries in Europe. The number of Catholic schools increased to accommodate this growth.

The economic, social, and cognitive diversity of the American population led to the establishment of selective Catholic schools noted for their academic excellence and less prestigious, but successful parish and independent schools. When the Second Vatican Council (1962–65) urged Catholics to renew their commitment to serving the poor and disadvantaged, Catholic educators channeled many of their resources to inner-city schools. As a result, the costs of supporting Catholic schools increased dramatically. White flight aggravated the situation, leaving many urban Catholic schools with low enrollment and insufficient funds to support themselves.

To increase enrollment and sustain the schools financially, Catholic schools granted admissions to non-Catholic students, non-English speaking students, students with weak academic backgrounds, and children with mild special needs. Accepting a more heterogeneous student body created a diverse, multicultural learning environment for all students in a school. As a result, the student composition of today's Catholic schools bears a stronger resemblance to that of public schools than in the past. Both school sectors have a higher proportion of minority, underprivileged, and at-risk students, and a smaller proportion of white students than the nation as a whole. In practice, neither school sector has what could be considered open admission to all students, although Catholic schools continue to be less open than public schools, partly because of the financial burden created by tuition costs.

The second indicator of adherence to the common school ideal is access to a high-quality curriculum. Public school curricula require students to take a certain number of academic courses and allow them to enroll in a limited number of elective courses. Unfortunately, low-achieving, socioeconomically disadvantaged and minority students are often assigned to unchallenging required classes with poor quality instruction. Catholic schools require that all their students enroll in a rigorous academic curriculum. Electives are usually scheduled before and after school. Differences in the curriculum offerings and requirements between the two sectors indicate that the academic requirements in Catholic schools provide their students with more opportunities to learn than public schools, with the possible exception of elite public and Catholic schools in the suburbs that tend to have similarly challenging academic programs.

A third indicator of adherence to the common school ideal is the extent to which a school reduces the influence of a student's ascribed characteristics on academic achievement. The stronger the relationship between student background and achievement, the greater the extent to which a school exacerbates educational inequalities. Analyses show that the association between background characteristics and achievement is weaker in Catholic schools than in public schools, and that the academic advantage of Catholic schools is greatest for disadvantaged and minority students.

A few studies of the association between background and achievement reveal mixed results. Differences between public and Catholic schools on student test scores, access to a quality curriculum, and the influence of student background on achievement reveal significant, serious equity issues in both school sectors. Extant research and policy ignores some of these issues, particularly for elementary and middle school students in contemporary schools. Further study will continue to elucidate the processes that reduce inequality of educational opportunity in public and nonpublic schools in the United States and in similar schools worldwide.

Maureen Hallinan
University of Notre Dame

See Also: Ethics in Education; Funding of Schools; Poverty and Education; Religious Education; School Choice.

Further Readings

Bryk, Anthony S., Penny Bender Sebring, Elaine Allensworth, Stuart Luppescu, and John Q. Easton. *Organizing Schools for Improvement: Lessons From Chicago.* Chicago: University of Chicago Press, 2010.

Bryk, Anthony S., Valerie E. Lee, and Peter B. Holland. *Catholic Schools and the Common Good.* Cambridge, MA: Harvard University Press, 1993.

Buetow, H. *A History of United States Catholic Schooling.* National Catholic Educational Association, 1985.

Carbonaro, William and Elizabeth Covay. "School Sector and Student Achievement in the Era of Standards Based Reforms." *Sociology of Education,* v.83 (2010).

Coleman, James, et al. *Equality of Educational Opportunity.* Washington, DC: U.S. Department of Health, Education and Welfare, 1966.

Coleman, James S. and Thomas Hoffer. *Public and Private Schools: The Impact of Communities.* New York: Basic Books, 1987.

Coleman, James S., Thomas Hoffer, and Sally B. Kilgore. *High School Achievement: Public, Catholic, and Private Schools Compared.* New York: Basic Books, 1982.

Coleman, James S., Thomas Hoffer, and Sally B. Kilgore. "Cognitive Outcomes in Public and Private Schools." *Sociology of Education,* v.55 (1982).

Grant, Mary and Thomas Hunt. *Catholic Education in the United States.* New York: Garland Publishing, 1992.

Gray, Mark and Mary Gautier. *Primary Trends, Challenges and Outlook: A Report on Catholic Elementary Schools 2000–2005.* Washington. DC: Georgetown University Press, 2006.

Hallinan, Maureen T. and Warren Kubitschek. "School Sector, School Poverty, and the Catholic School Advantage." *Catholic Education: A Journal of Inquiry and Practice,* v.14/2 (2010).

Mulligan, James T. *Catholic Education: Ensuring a Future.* Ottawa, Canada: Novalis, St. Paul University, 2006.

Charter Schools

Relative to traditional public schools, charter schools are a new organizational form of education. Charter schools educate over 1 million children in the United States, which account for a little over 1 percent of students. This number grows annually, as more charter schools continue to open their doors. The charter school movement officially began in 1991, when Minnesota became the first state to pass a law making charter schools legal. Charter schools are public schools that offer an alternative to the traditional public school by freeing the creators from oversight and many government regulations. Since 1991,

41 states, Washington, D.C., and Puerto Rico have embraced the charter school law (excluding Alabama, Kentucky, Montana, Nebraska, North Dakota, South Dakota, Vermont, Washington, and West Virginia), and in 2011 Mississippi revoked their charter school law, bringing that number back down to 40 states. The charter school movement created a shift in the school choice market. Private, parochial, and home schooling are no longer the only options for parents looking to move their children from their neighborhood school. The introduction of charter school laws across the country encouraged clients (i.e., parents, teachers, and students) to consider education as part of a market. The rhetoric surrounding the charter school movement focuses on the ability of charter schools to improve academic achievement and accountability in the public school realm.

School Choice

During the 1990s and the early 21st century, an increasing shift in the educational choice market occurred, with charter schools becoming a dominant presence in choice discussions. One of the more unique elements of charter school policy and law is that lay people and management groups (i.e., parents, teachers, community members, and educational management organizations) can apply for and start a charter school, pending approval from their state or district board. This is the only public organizational form of schooling that can be started and operated by people or groups, other than a local educational agency or state. Charter school administrators agree to federal standards and minimal oversight laws, while also adhering to their outlined mission statements; but, local and state school boards retain the right to close charter schools if they find that the charter school is not performing or operating adequately. The inception of charter schools is considered a "compromise" by many educational scholars, indicative of the overarching shift toward an educational system of "choice." With regard to "who" gets the choice, charter schools are aimed at parents who have the ability to vote with their children's feet and enroll students in a public school option other than their neighborhood school. Moreover, charter schools do not require vouchers or special permissions for families; the only tangible restriction for parents is a potential lottery system if the charter school is in high demand.

Media attention and bipartisan support for charter schools encourage the growth in popularity. There are several big-name charter schools creating a positive image across the nation, given their well-publicized academic success. These schools include the Knowledge is Power Program (KIPP), and the Promise Academy Charter Schools, associated with Geoffrey Canada's Harlem Children's Zone (HCZ). However, as successful as these big names have been in educating their students, not all charter schools are KIPP or HCZ schools. Films such as *Waiting for Superman* and *The Lottery* have also encouraged the charter school movement by underscoring academic achievements of the extremely successful charter schools. As a result, the media presence in the charter school debate has been largely positive for charter schools, despite a lack of consensus among educational scholars regarding their viability. Charter schools differ substantially by region, state, and even city, given laws, norms, and practices; and this makes it difficult to understand as a national trend in policy. Nevertheless, charter school law allows these public schools to imitate the private school sector with regard to organizational structure, such as hiring practices, management, and supervisory decisions, and relative autonomy. Although charter schools mimic the organizational structure of private schools, they do not enroll and serve the same demographic population as the private schools in the United States. Instead, charter schools enroll a much higher percentage of racial minorities and students eligible for free/reduced lunch than private schools. Similarly, charter schools do not boast academic successes across the board.

Segregation

Charter schools appear to defeat partisanship in political debates, garnering approval from both sides of the political fence. However, there is some opposition to charter schools garnered from civil rights activists. Civil rights activists argue that charter schools contribute to segregation within the public education sector, rather than reduce rates of segregation, and some social science research concludes similarly. Therefore, despite national pressure to further escalate the charter school movement, civil rights advocates urge policymakers to resist endorsing an effort that serves to further stratify the student population. Black students are not the only racial group experiencing these trends within charter schools; all racial minority groups tend to attend schools that are either predominantly minority (50–100 percent minority) or "racially isolated minority" schools (90–100 percent minority),

according to the Civil Rights Project. Recent research on charter school populations reveals that charter schools are more stratified than their traditional public school counterparts in the states that allow charter schools. Findings demonstrate specific cases of charter schools that do not contribute to further stratification and do a good job racially integrating students, but these cases do not accurately mirror the general population of charter schools. This finding points to a "return to school segregation." In fact, opponents of school choice argue that extant inequalities will only escalate and serve privileged populations of students.

Charter schools are touted as a potential solution to low scores in public education. However, scholars continue to disagree on whether or not charter schools are successful, and there is not enough evidence yet to settle the debate. Reports on charter school achievement and accountability demonstrate controversial evidence that charter schools are out-performing their traditional school counterparts.

Mixed evidence from research using the NAEP data shows that charter school students perform worse than traditional public school students in fourth grade; but the findings do not persist in eighth grade, and the scores are not statistically different from one another. Findings from a case study of Washington, D.C., reveal that parents of students in charter schools report greater levels of satisfaction with their children's teacher, principal, and services. Research on academic achievement in the state of North Carolina revealed that, compared to similar traditional public school students, charter school students are slightly more likely to perform at a higher level on state achievement tests. A Florida study found that charter school achievement improves as the school ages; and by the fifth year, the math scores are caught up, but reading scores surpass traditional public schools.

When charter schools are linked to a public school district, they do not differ from the public schools; when charter schools are not linked to a public school district, they perform significantly less well than traditional schools. Other research suggests that older charter schools produce students with higher academic outcomes in reading and math. However, many studies only focus on one city or case studies of only a few schools. This research does not lend itself to generalizable findings for the charter school market. Unlike traditional public schools, charter schools can close their doors if they do not meet federal, state, local, or self-imposed standards. The reasons for charter school closure range from financial and management failures to academic or facility shortcomings. Thus far, the most common reasons for closure are financial, academic, and enrollment problems, with special education the least cited reason for a charter school closure. Approximately 12 percent of charter schools across the United States have closed their doors, since the first charter school opened in 1991.

Linda Renzulli
Maria T. Paino
University of Georgia

See Also: School Catchment Zones, Politically Defined School Boundaries; School Choice; School Mobility and Education; School Organization; Schools as Bureaucracies.

Further Readings

Hoxby, Caroline M. "School Choice and School Productivity: Could School Choice Be a Tide That Lifts All Boats?" In *The Economics of School Choice*. Chicago: University of Chicago Press, 2003.

Lubienski, Sarah Theule and Christopher Lubienski. "School Sector and Academic Achievement: A Multilevel Analysis of NAEP Mathematics Data." *American Educational Research Journal*, v.43 (2006).

Renzulli, Linda A. and Lorraine Evans. "School Choice, Charter Schools, and White Flight." *Social Problems*, v.52 (2005).

Sass, Tim R. "Charter Schools and Student Achievement in Florida." *Education Finance and Policy*, v.1 (2006).

Schneider, Mark and Jack Buckley. "Making the Grade: Comparing DC Charter Schools to Other DC Public Schools." *Educational Evaluation and Policy Analysis*, v.25 (2003).

Cheerleading Equity Policy

Like many other aspects of school-based sports, cheerleading is a uniquely American sport phenomenon. The earliest cheerleading started with men who rallied students at college football games before the turn of the century. Women began to participate in the 1920s; however, it remained a largely male-dominated activity until World War II. Since then, cheerleading has evolved into a women-dominated activity, common in high school, college, and professional sports. Today, it includes sideline cheering at athletic events, competitive cheering competitions, and dance and drill teams. Despite the athletic ability needed in this activity, it is not yet defined as a sport.

Cheerleading in schools and colleges raises significant questions about the role of physical activity and sport under Title IX. In March 2009, Quinnipiac University cut the women's volleyball team and replaced it with competitive cheerleading. These changes were challenged under Title IX, and in July 2010, a court ruled that competitive cheerleading did not meet the requirements. To qualify as a sport under Title IX, the ruling suggested that competitive cheerleading in colleges and universities must be a fully developed and organized activity characterized by: competitions against other squads in a defined season, have coaches and practices, resemble all other varsity sports at an institution in structure and operation, and be organized by a governing organization. The primary goal of the activity must be competition. Although competitive cheerleading meets some of the requirements, it lacks sufficient development in others. For example, the number and quality of competitions is a concern. The availability of conference, state, regional, and national competition is limited. With no National Collegiate Athletic Asosciation (NCAA)-sanctioned emerging sport or championship status, meeting the quality of competition standard remains a challenge.

Before Title IX, cheerleading was the only school-sponsored physical-activity in which girls could participate and represent their high school or college. Sideline pom-pom squads that performed individual jumps and maneuvers to entertain and rally the crowd characterized this traditional form. Title IX did little to call into question the legitimacy of cheerleading, Even as sporting activities have grown for women, cheerleading continues to grow among women at a similar rate. The contemporary image and activity of cheerleading has evolved from a form of sideline rally and entertainment to one that now includes strenuous tumbling, jumps, and tossing maneuvers. These acrobatic performances still occupy a specific place for entertaining the crowd at athletic events during time outs, between periods, or at half time. However, these acrobatic skills and performances are also part of an organized activity where the primary goal is competition, complete with scoring, judges, and a national champion-type award structure. Like gymnastics, figure skating, or synchronized swimming, cheering teams are judged on elements that require strength, skill, and agility found only in highly athletic activities. Today, estimates for competitive cheerleading include 1.5 million participants and as many as 4 million participants when other youth, middle school, and professional sideline cheering activities are included.

Long considered a school-sponsored activity or part of the overall entertainment of professional athletic events, competitive cheer squads challenge deeply held assumptions about gender in school-sponsored sports. A contemporary view of cheerleading and Title IX illustrate the challenges of integrating competitive cheerleading into the traditional varsity sport offerings among high schools and colleges. Squads feature high numbers of women participants, making it an attractive alternative to football, which lacks a gender partner in calculating proportionality. Contemporary cheerleading is a space for the display of girls and women's physical empowerment. Yet, the gendering of cheerleading as a feminized domain and repositioning competition as its primary goal raises questions as to whether it is an extracurricular activity or a sport. Whether on the sideline or in competition, cheerleading does not disrupt traditionally held assumptions about gender and sport. The strenuous skills and athleticism typically associated with sports are mediated in the context of cheerleading's feminized characteristics. Girls who participate in cheerleading can possess the athletic characteristics typically associated with men's sports.

However, like other school-based sports that are gender-separated, a single-gender model of participants that conform to traditionally feminine characteristics dominates cheerleading. The gender separated form of school-based sport legislated under Title IX that perpetuates traditional gender roles further reinforces contemporary cheerleading as a marginalized, sideline activity.

Jennifer Lee Hoffman
University of Washington

See Also: Extracurricular Activities; Feminist Critiques of Educational Practices; Gender and School Sports; Sports and Schools; Title IX.

Further Readings

Adams, N. G. and P. J. Bettis. *Cheerleader! Cheerleader! An American Icon*. New York: Palgrave Macmillan, 2003.

Biedieger v. Quinnipiac University, 728 U.S. F. Supp. 2d 62 (2010) U.S. Dist.

Boyce, R. "Cheerleading in the Context of Title IX and Gendering in Sport." *Sport Journal*, v.11/3 (2008).

Brake, D. L. "Complicating Equal Participation: What Counts as a Sport, Which Sports Should Women Play, and Which Women Should Play Them?" In *Getting in the Game: Title IX and the Women's Sports Revolution*. New York: New York University Press, 2010.

Women's Sports Foundation. "Cheerleading, Drill Team, Danceline and Band As Varsity Sports: The Foundation Position." http://www.womenssportsfoundation.org/home/advocate/title-ix-and-issues/title-ix-positions/cheerleading_drill_team_danceline_and_band_as_varsity_sports (Accessed February 2012).

Child Care

Organized child care in the United States began in 1910 with a nursery school modeled after the open air nursery concept launched in Europe by the McMillan sisters. In the 1930s, the Works Progress Administration funded almost 2,000 nurseries during the Great Depression to support preschool children from struggling families. Congress later provided matching funds to open child care centers during World War II to enable women to work in factories and shipyards while their husbands served in the war. After the war ended, the federal government did not fund child care programs again until 1964, with the launch of Head Start, a school readiness program for preschool children from low-income families.

In 1972, sweeping new legislation was passed by both the House and the Senate to begin a long-term initiative of universal child care. However, the Comprehensive Child Development Act was vetoed by President Nixon, who feared that government involvement in child care was too communistic. Federal support re-emerged in the 1980s and 1990s, with low-income and welfare transition subsidies for child care; as well as the Child Care and Development Block Grant, which now authorizes the current Child Care and Development Fund (CCDF). In 2011, the CCDF distributed $5 billion in child care subsidies throughout the country for low-income families. Controversy surrounds the use of the funds, however, since the states are not required to limit the subsidy payments to only licensed child care programs.

There are three basic categories of child care options: child care centers; family child care homes; and care from family, friends, or neighbors. Child care centers are designed to provide services to groups of children under 5 years old. Center-based child care programs are typically licensed by a state regulating agency, and are required to meet at least the minimum standards for health and safety. Some states also regulate nutrition and food service; criminal history checks for staff members; financial and labor management practices; curriculum and classroom environments; and teacher performance. Center-based child care programs operate in a variety of business models, including government-funded nonprofits, corporate chains, proprietary franchises, privately owned for-profits, employer-sponsored on-site centers, and faith-based programs. About 24 percent of families in the United State choose center-based child care programs. Family child care (FCC) providers operate a child care program in their home. Some providers create a designated section of the house specifically for child care, such as the basement or a converted garage. Others integrate the child care elements throughout their home. Licensing rules for FCC homes vary from state to state, but many homes are not inspected by a regulating authority. States with stricter guidelines limit the number of children a provider may care for without a license. Even licensed FCC homes, however, are infrequently inspected.

Many states provide consumer access to the licensing database that enables families to review an FCC provider's inspection reports, complaints, and license status. About 20 percent of parents select family child care providers to care for their children. The most commonly selected child care option is care provided by family members, friends, or neighbors (FFN). This broad category refers to care provided by babysitters, nannies, grandparents, and other caregivers not required to obtain a license. An estimated 50–78 percent of parents select FFN care for their children under the age of 5. Research suggests that although FFN care providers are typically less educated than licensed providers, they exhibit higher quality interactions with children and have lower adult–child ratios.

The National Association for the Education of Young Children (NAEYC) is the principal organization for establishing and overseeing quality standards in early childhood center-based programs. NAEYC defines quality in child care programs by the presence of three critical elements: low teacher-child ratios; small group sizes; and experienced, educated teachers. These primary program characteristics serve as the foundation for meeting the remaining national early child care and education standards in the areas of relationships with children, families, and the community; curriculum and learning environments; teaching and child assessment; and program management. Child care centers that meet these standards can participate in the NAEYC accreditation process to indicate the high quality programming they offer. Family child care providers have a similar accreditation option through the National Association for Family Child Care. Despite the research-based standards in place to assist programs, there are barriers to achieving high quality.

High operating costs, frequent staff turnover, inadequately trained and inexperienced staff, and insufficient oversight by regulating agencies are all contributors to reduced program quality. Despite $10 billion in federal support last year, a report of state child care standards and oversight rankings revealed a national average score of 87 out of 150 possible points. The most common deficiencies were: not requiring criminal history checks for teachers, not requiring teachers to have a high school diploma or child care training, and not providing sufficient oversight of licensing and inspections. The diffusion of responsibility over standards oversight appears to be the largest contributor to the inconsistency in quality from program to program.

Amy L. Moore
Capella University

See Also: Childhood; Early Childhood; Reggio Emilia Approach; Student/Teacher Ratio.

Further Readings

Fiene, Richard. "We Can Do Better: NACCRRA's Ranking of State Child Care Center Standards and Oversight." http://www.naccrra.org/publications/naccrra -publications/we-can-do-better-2011.php (Accessed December 2011).

Gordon, Ann M. and Kathryn W. Browne. *Beginnings and Beyond: Foundations in Early Childhood Education.* 8th ed. Belmont, CA: Wadsworth-Cengage, 2011.

National Association for the Education of Young Children (NAEYC). "Overview of the NAEYC Early Childhood Program Standards." http://www.naeyc.org/files/academy/file/OverviewStandards.pdf (Accessed December 2011).

Susman-Stillman, Amy and Patti Banghart. *Quality in Family, Friend, and Neighbor Child Care Settings.* New York: Child Care and Early Education Research Connections, 2011.

Childhood

While definitions of childhood vary across cultural contexts and disciplines, generally childhood can be understood as the period in a human's life spanning from birth to adulthood. Adulthood, however, is assumed to begin at varying ages throughout the world, between the ages of 13 and 21. The ways in which childhood is understood and conceptualized, however, varies. In many parts of the world, children and childhood are viewed as socially passive and are not provided with the same capacity as adults and adulthood. In these contexts, children are seen as requiring the protection of both families and the state. Yet, in many other parts of the world, there remains a much less clear distinction between childhood and adulthood, and children often become self-sufficient at a very young age.

Similarly, in developmental psychology, childhood is understood as the time in a person's life from birth until adolescence. Within this period, a child experiences four developmental stages: infancy, toddlerhood, early childhood, and late childhood. For developmental psychologists, these developmental stages are individual, linear in their sequence, and typically universal in their application. For sociocultural theorists and cultural psychologists, however, childhood and development are context dependent and vary significantly across cultural contexts. Development is seen as something that occurs through relationships and a child's interactions with his or her environment.

This development may occur in a linear, cyclical, or nonlinear manner, and varies greatly between children. For social constructivists, childhood as a period of time inherent to a human being's life trajectory is a social construction, and the ways in which childhood is viewed and understood is dependent on cultural values and norms. Accordingly, contemporary thought is moving away from the notion of one universal childhood and toward an understanding that children throughout the world come in all shapes and sizes and may be different according to gender, race, ethnicity, ability, health, and age.

Despite these differing understandings of childhood, children, and development, there are some distinct ways that children differ from adults. Young people tend to be marginalized within most societies, like the elderly or the disabled, and therefore encounter difficulty in expressing agency over their lives. This marginalization plays out socially as children are often disenfranchised from decisions regarding their care and guardianship, education, health, and well-being, as well as geographically, as urban laws and practices tend toward the promotion and maintenance of adult-centered spaces. This marginalization has contributed significantly to an increase in the study of children and childhood, as well as the creation of laws to protect the rights of children.

Changing View of Childhood

Just as conceptualizations of childhood differ across cultural contexts and across theoretical disciplines, conceptualizations of children and childhood have varied throughout past centuries. Prior to the 17th century, children were in many cultures viewed and depicted as miniature adults, and it wasn't until industrialization and the mid-1800s that children in the Western world were perceived as requiring protection from exploitation, particularly child labor. This was in response to the demand for the inexpensive child labor that industry required, and the often-dangerous working climates that children experienced. As the need for child labor decreased, and after the advent of the common school, conceptualizations of childhood in the Western world moved away from work and toward a vision of childhood as a time of innocence and play, a perspective that still holds for the majority of Western cultures.

The marginalization experienced by children and the exploitation of children historically, socially, and economically, has led to the development of laws both nationally and internationally to protect the human rights of children. The Convention on the Rights of the Child (CRC), for example, is a legally binding human rights treaty developed by the United Nations to ensure basic human rights for all persons under the age of majority. The convention was drafted in 1989, and is overseen by the Committee on the Rights of the Child. The CRC asserts that because of children's physical and mental immaturity, specific parameters must be put in place to ensure their basic human rights across the globe. These human rights include civil, cultural, social, economic, and political rights. Some of the articles within the CRC specifically address identity rights, the right to life and survival, the right to development, and the right to a relationship with biological parents. The CRC classifies children as persons under the age of 18, unless legal age of majority is designated otherwise in their nation of residence. It asserts that nations must act in the best interest of children, and has been ratified by all member nations, except Somalia and the United States.

There is a growing movement to develop research practices that encourage involving children in all aspects of the research process. This movement embraces a move toward research with children instead of research on or about children. This rights-based approach to research incorporates children's perspectives into the conceptualization of research projects, as well as into the design and implementation of research studies. This involvement adheres to the perspective that no one can speak to the needs, wants, and concerns of children more than they can.

Jamie Patrice Joanou
Arizona State University

See Also: Adolescence; Early Childhood; Sociocultural Approaches to Learning and Development; Youth Cultures and Subcultures.

Further Readings

Archard, David. *Children: Rights and Childhood.* London: Routledge, 2004.

Aries, Phillipe. *Centuries of Childhood: A Social History of Family Life.* Robert Baldick, trans. New York: Random House, 1962.

Boas, George. *The Cult of Childhood.* London: Warburg Institute, 1966.

Chile

The Republic of Chile is the third-largest country in South America. It shares its northern border with Peru, and its eastern border with Argentina is the third-largest international border in the world (3,200 miles long). In July 2012, its population was estimated at 17.07 million. Chile is a country of enormous geographical diversity. Large copper and nitrate deposits are among the nation's most important minerals and constitute a significant proportion of the country's economy. Agriculture is predominantly located in the central region of the country. Roughly 35 percent of the total population lives in the nation's capital city of Santiago and 86 percent lives in urban settings. In 2010, the gross domestic product (GDP) of Chile was $212 billion, and the annual growth of GDP was 5.2 percent. Chile is a multinational society because of its long colonized period. Many people are descendants of the Europeans, mainly Spanish, but also Italian, German, Irish, and French; the majority of the population is considered *mestizo* (of European and indigenous descent).

History and Social Structure

The area now known as Chile is home to numerous indigenous peoples (or Amerindians) and was part of the great Inca empire prior its exposure to Europeans. In the 16th century, the first Spanish conquistadores arrived in Chile in pursuit of gold. Chile became a Spanish colony on February 12, 1541, and many indigenous peoples resisted colonization efforts until independence. As early as 1810, Bernardo O'Higgin helped organize a revolutionary military campaign against the Spanish colonial government and loyalists; independence was finally achieved on February 12, 1818, and O'Higgin became the nation's first head of state. While some changes were implemented under O'Higgin's leadership, education reforms were slow and in many ways the education system continued to resemble that which existed during the colonial period. In the early 20th century, Chile established its first presidential regime as part of a representative democratic government (this form of government continues today). Working-class and middle-class citizens could participate in the general election process.

Between 1973 and 1989, Chile had a military government led by General Augusto Pinochet. From 1990 to the present, Chile returned to its democratic government with an elected president who serves as the head of state. From then on, the country implemented a series of economic reforms, with the key objective of building a foreign investment–friendly environment. From 1990 to 2003, the government implemented a large education reform effort that focused on improving the equity and quality of education nationwide. The government increased its education budget four times from 1990 to 2004; in 2008, public spending on education was 3.99 percent of total GDP. The government expended 14.7 percent per student of GDP per capita on primary education in 2008 (an increase from 12.1 percent in 1998); for secondary education, the amount was 16 percent in 2008, compared to 13.8 percent in 1998. In 2009, the net enrollment ratio of students in primary education was 94 percent and 83 percent for secondary education students. The combined literacy rate of adults 15 years or older was 99 percent in 2008.

Educational System

The education system in Chile is diverse, with a more inclusive school choice system than other countries in the world. The education system can be divided into four levels: preschool (for children who are less than 6 years old), primary/elementary school (which consists of eight years of compulsory education for pupils from 6 to 13 years old), secondary/high school (which offers students a two-pronged approach of science-liberal and vocational-technical education), and higher education. Chile's secondary education science-liberal track is composed of regular subjects, such as literature, math, history; while the vocational-technical education focuses on developing practical and technical skills in trade-based career paths. Secondary education became compulsory for students aged 14 to 17 in 2003, consisting of four grades and a choice of two types of diplomas. The higher education system is comprised of universities, professional institutes, and technical centers. Public and private universities that were founded before 1980 have the right to receive state aid. Students have to pay for their higher education, while loans and scholarships for lower-income students are available.

Chile has had recent gains in higher education enrollments, with a gross enrollment ratio of 59 percent in 2009 (up from 38 percent in 1999). Since 1981, and based upon their administration and funding sources, schools can be categorized into four types: municipal, which are public schools funded by municipal governments; private subsidized, which are partially funded by the government; private paid, which are financed by parents; and corporation schools (vocational schools), which received government support and are managed by local businesses. The government oversees the evaluation, supervision, and standards of primary and secondary education; private schools must adhere to curriculum standards outlined by the government.

Current Issues

Despite the government's efforts to provide quality education for students, regardless of their economic condition and location, three noticeable types of inequalities have emerged. First, quality private education opportunities are not available to all students, especially those from low socioeconomic status backgrounds. Second, the quality of public education differs, depending on such issues as location (urban vs. rural settings) and the socioeconomic background of students. Finally, higher education inequalities persist, largely depending on the same factors as the primary and secondary levels. Higher education and secondary education student protests from May 2011 to January 2012 highlight the general public's discontent over unequal education opportunities.

Those who attend the lowest performing schools are often at a significant disadvantage when it comes to competing with their age-group counterparts on higher education entrance examinations. Also, financial aid reform is needed to help make quality higher education more accessible and affordable to all interested in pursuing a higher education degree. The government is faced with a delicate balancing act of striving to meet current student demands to provide equal education opportunities for all, regardless of their background and if they reside in remote or rural areas of the country.

Mengtian Dang
W. James Jacob
University of Pittsburgh

See Also: Argentina; Peru; Rural Schooling.

Further Readings

Arango, Adrea. *The Failings of Chile's Education System: Institutionalized Inequality and a Preference for the Affluent.* Washington, DC: Council on Hemispheric Affairs, 2008.

Cox, Cristian. *Innovation and Reform to Improve the Quality of Primary Education: Chile.* Paper commissioned for the EFA Global Monitoring Report 2005, the Quality Imperative. Paris: United Nations Educational, Scientific and Cultural Organization (UNESCO), 2005.

Elacqua, Gregory, Dante Contreras, and Felipe Salazar. "Scaling Up in Chile: Larger Networks of Schools Produce Higher Student Achievement." *Education Next*, v.8/3 (2008).

Organisation for Economic Co-operation and Development (OECD) and the United Nations Educational, Scientific and Cultural Organization (UNESCO). *Challenges of the Chilean Education System.* Santiago, Chile: OECD and UNESCO, in collaboration with Ministry of Education of Chile, 2010.

Republic of Chile. "The Education System." Embassy of Chile. http://www.chile-usa.org (Accessed February 2012).

China

The People's Republic of China's society and culture has long valued education, and it has expanded schooling in the last three decades. However, educational opportunities are increasingly unequal because of growing economic disparity. China's hierarchical school system also hinders underprivileged students' access to education. Government exams, economic rewards, and collectivist beliefs have encouraged Chinese parents to support children's education. The Keju civil service exam system from 606 to 1905 not only selected mainland China's government officials, but also gave financial rewards, prestige, power, and fame to their extended family, thereby encouraging collectivist beliefs, values, and norms. In this collectivist culture, extended family members often live nearby, encourage children to study hard and remind them that their success or failure affects their entire family's reputation. As many Chinese families only have one child, most parents strongly support their child's education, regardless of gender.

In the last three decades, China's economic reforms (e.g., privatization and free trade) sharply increased economic growth, raising real gross domestic product (GDP) per capita from $379 to $7,500 from 1978 to 2010, which increased children's learning both directly (e.g., more public schools) and indirectly (e.g., more health care) to yield healthier students with more learning opportunities. Moving away from social equality (emphasized during the Great Leap Forward, the Socialist Education Movement, and the Cultural Revolution), Deng Xiaoping reformed education to reward academic achievement and sharply increased education spending, especially in science, engineering, and technology. As enrollment for six-year primary school rose from 20 to 99 percent from 1949 to 2011, China's youth literacy rate likewise rose from 20 to 99 percent. While privatizing agriculture and removing food price controls both increased equality and economic growth, other economic reforms facilitated corruption and favored coastal areas (especially urban residents), all of which raised regional income inequality (Gini) between coastal and inland provinces from 57 to 71 percent from 1978 to 2000. Facing sharp economic inequality between inland rural areas and coastal cities, families moved to find higher paying jobs, which weakened family ties.

Accompanying economic reform, education reform yielded higher academic achievement, but greater inequality. China passed the Compulsory Education Law in 1986, which raised teacher salaries and made teachers' colleges tuition-free to pursue nine years of free, universal education. While this reform specified national standards for curricula, textbooks, examinations, and teacher qualifications, it abandoned the drive for social equality in favor of greater academic achievement and decentralized control of schools. Articles 8 and 12 of this law required local governments to provide free education only for their registered residents, not for children of internal migrants. Because many migrant parents could not pay the migrant children school fee (*Jiedufei*), 10 percent of primary-school age and 80 percent of middle-school age migrants did not attend school in 2006. China also decentralized school control in the provinces and counties, allowing them to modify school budgets and curricula. This decentralization facilitates corruption at each layer of government, so that far less than the national budget for education (13 percent in 2007) actually reaches students. Many school principals seek funding from local businesses or individuals to compensate for these inadequate school budgets. Hence, actual school budgets vary widely across regions. Richer schools (especially in coastal cities) are tuition-free and attract better teachers and staff. In poorer, rural regions, however, many families pay substantial tuition fees for poorly educated teachers and staff. As a result, less than 25 percent of children in rural areas completed nine years of schooling in 2008 (compared to 60 percent of children in cities). While most schools are public, education reform also encouraged private schools, and 14 million students enrolled in 70,000 private schools in 2004.

Preschool to University

Both student enrollment and teacher training generally form pyramids with fewer, highly talented ones at the top. While most children attended primary schools (99 percent) and middle school (98 percent), fewer matriculated in senior high schools (23 percent), vocational schools (20 percent), or universities (19 percent). Likewise, teachers at higher levels of schooling received more training. Children with special needs are often outcasts, and only 0.3 percent attended special education schools in 2008. China does not proscribe a national preschool curriculum, but some counties fund preschools to varying degrees. About 30 percent of 3–6 year old children enrolled in preschool programs. Preschool teachers are typically middle-school graduates who then attend a two- or three-year training program. Children who are 6 to 7 years old begin attending a six-year primary school five days a week (reduced from six days a week in 1997), and their teachers are typically middle-school graduates, some of whom received associate degrees from junior teacher colleges (40 percent in 2003). These teachers spend 60 percent of their class time teaching mathematics and Chinese (the national dialect Putonghua and often pinyin), the only two subjects on middle-school entrance exams. The rest of their curriculum includes science, social science, arts, physical education, morality, and politics. Foreign language education (often English) begins in third grade. Poorer rural schools often have a smaller curriculum focused on Chinese, mathematics, and morality.

Middle-school (or junior-secondary school) teachers are high school graduates who then enrolled in two- or three-year teacher training programs at a teacher training institute, teacher's college, or teacher-training university. The three-year middle-school curriculum devotes more time to English, physics, chemistry, politics, and physical education, which in addition to Chinese and mathematics are all on the high school entrance exam. These exam scores determine the high school that a student will attend. Students whose high school entrance-exam scores are too low to attend high school might attend vocational schools, which do not lead to higher education. Furthermore, vocational teacher training has no specific standards and varies widely across provinces, from independent institutes to universities. As most vocational schools offer narrow specializations that lack the flexible training needed for changing workforce needs, firms typically prefer to hire high school graduates and provide them with firm-specific training. As a result, higher-ability teachers and students prefer high schools over vocational schools.

High schools (or senior secondary schools) are sharply stratified by enrolling students' high school entrance exam scores, with the best teachers paid the highest salaries to teach at the most prestigious high schools. Although the 1986 law abolished elite, resource-rich secondary schools for the best students ("key schools"), they persist under other names and exacerbate education inequality. High school teachers are high school graduates with four additional years of teacher training at a teacher training institute, teacher's college or a teacher-training university. High school curricula typically include Chinese, English, mathematics, sciences, computer science, social science, arts, and physical education. High-school graduates with sufficiently high scores on the national entrance exam for universities (resumed in 1977) can attend a public university. Like high schools, universities are sharply stratified by students' university entrance-exam scores. Since 1998, China has been expanding university enrollment, but also concentrating educational resources to create 100 elite universities (especially those focused on science or engineering, through the 211 project). Still, only 30 percent of university faculty had postgraduate degrees in 2005. Unlike primary and secondary schools, universities create their curricula, hire their staff, and select their students.

School and Classroom Culture

China has a hierarchical culture, in which status inequities are more openly accepted than in most Western societies. Hence, province- and county-level officials often hire school staff and adjust the curricula to local needs. A teacher at a school is often selected to become its principal, typically with little or no leadership training (especially in primary schools and middle schools). Principals rarely share decision making with or delegate responsibilities to teachers, and parents and teachers rarely participate in school governance. China's curricula, textbooks, and classroom lessons emphasize breadth over depth.

As school budgets depend on their graduates' exam scores and acceptances to the best schools at the next level of study, teachers typically use exam-based textbooks and design suitable class lessons to cover all possible content on entrance exams. Furthermore, teachers often work together within and across schools. Groups of teachers often prepare lessons together, discuss curriculum standards, and share teaching methods (especially in urban schools). In addition, education administrative agencies direct good teachers ("first-class" teachers) to demonstrate their classroom teaching to other teachers at other schools and in other school districts, thereby enhancing teacher quality over time. Chinese classroom instruction focuses on refined lectures and repeated practice. The refined lectures are polished, coherent lessons that integrate foundational knowledge content and skills. Concerned about maintaining discipline, teachers often lecture to the entire class (especially with 40–60 students per class). The refined lectures unite teaching content and classroom discourse through coherent connections among concepts that guide students toward their learning goal for each lesson. To learn this content, students typically rely on rote memorization (written and oral repetition).

Ming Ming Chiu
State University of New York, Buffalo

See Also: Asian Americans; Globalization; Poverty and Education; Rural Schooling.

Further Readings

Chiu, Ming Ming. "Country Changes and Student Learning: China's Economy, Families and Cultural Values." *Journal of Education Research*, v.2 (2008).

Hsü, Immanuel Chung-yueh. *The Rise of Modern China.* New York: Oxford University, 2000.

Wang, Xiufang. *Education in China Since 1976.* Jefferson, NC: McFarland, 2003.

Class Inequality: Achievement

Families whose members are more educated, earn higher incomes, or have higher social status (socioeconomic status) can provide their children with more educational resources and learning opportunities. These children can then capitalize on these additional resources and opportunities to learn more. Furthermore, students in higher socioeconomic status families often attend schools with more resources and live in countries with more resources, all of which support higher academic achievement. Last, students in these families can often obtain a larger share of school or country resources to aid their learning, even though this inequality can hurt the overall achievement of the school or the country.

Family

Families differ with respect to their human capital (e.g., education), financial capital (wealth), social capital (social network resources), and cultural capital (knowledge of dominant culture and society). As a result, children in different families often do not have access to the same educational resources and enter school with different skills and competencies. Some families have adults who are more educated (human capital), and these highly educated adults can both supervise children more actively and teach them more information and skills. They can review the homework of their children (especially those in elementary school) and praise them for successfully completing it. By monitoring children's work and creating suitable reward structures, they encourage them to study diligently. They can also engage children through both education-specific activities and general activities to help them learn. For example, a parent might talk with a child about school matters such as their science projects, or recent elections. Family members can interact with children by chatting during dinner, telling one another stories, building towers of blocks together, or generally spending time together. Through these interactions, older family members can serve as role models, ask provoking questions, or give explicit instructions, all of which can help children learn.

Families with more human capital often have more cultural possessions and experiences (cultural capital) and can help their children understand the cultures of their family, school, and local community. Cultural possessions at home (e.g., paintings and poetry) can exemplify the importance of one's culture and facilitate family communication about cultural values and norms. During cultural conversations, family members can model appropriate societal behaviors and explain cultural norms to help their children better understand teachers' and classmates' expectations. Better understanding of their expectations can help these children behave appropriately and build better relationships at school. As a result of better relationships with their teachers and classmates, children with more cultural capital might receive more learning opportunities, be more motivated, learn more, and be more successful at school.

Elite families also often have greater wealth (financial capital) and can provide their children with more resources and activities. For example, richer families often give their children more physical resources (e.g., a quiet study room, computers, and books), thereby creating a richer learning environment. These families also tend to appreciate and buy higher quality resources, such as age-appropriate books and computer software for their children. Buying their children many educational resources also highlights stronger family commitment to their learning. Furthermore, noneducational resources, such as expensive clothes, serve as status symbols that can enhance children's status among their peers, which helps them make friends at school and have more positive attitudes about school. Richer families can also pay for stimulating activities, such as summer camps and travel to other countries, to enhance their children's learning experiences. Richer families often have larger and richer social networks of highly skilled or educated family, friends, and acquaintances (social capital). These families can enhance their children's social capital by connecting them to their social network. The members of their family's extensive social network can offer additional complementary material, human, social, and cultural capital to support these children's learning.

School

Students from privileged families often attend schools with high socioeconomic status schoolmates, high-quality physical resources, and effective teachers. Students can benefit from these privileged schoolmates' family capital, material resources, diverse experiences, and high academic expectations. The schools that privileged students attend often have better physical conditions and more educational materials than other schools, so students in these schools often capitalize on these greater learning opportunities to learn more. Higher socioeconomic status students also typically benefit from attending schools with higher teacher-to-student ratios and better-qualified teachers (e.g., with university degrees). Superior teachers also show more effective teaching processes, such as maintaining better student discipline and relationships with their students—both of which are linked to higher student achievement. Teachers also tend to give higher socioeconomic status students more attention compared to lower-income students (privilege bias), which tends to reduce overall school achievement.

Country

Students in countries with higher real gross domestic product (GDP) per capita (e.g., Japan) often capitalize on their countries' greater resources to learn more. Richer countries can raise student learning directly through education spending (e.g., on books and teacher training) or indirectly through higher nutritional standards or better health care. For example, children in poorer countries (e.g., Albania) often lack basic nutrition, are born prematurely, or face exposure to potentially harmful environments (e.g., lead poisoning)—all linked to lower student achievement. Students in countries with greater inequality with respect to distribution of family income often experience diminishing marginal returns or homophily bias, which tend to lower overall academic achievement. Consider a thirsty woman and two glasses of water. She greatly values the first glass of water and drinks it all. Her thirst quenched, she hardly values the second glass of water and does not finish it. This lower value of extra resources is diminishing marginal returns. Hence, a poor student likely learns more from an extra book than a rich student would. In more equal countries (e.g., Norway), poorer students often have more resources and benefit more from them compared to richer students, resulting in higher achievement overall.

Greater equality might also increase overall student achievement through people's preference to interact with others who are similar to themselves (homophily bias). As a result, more students in relatively equal countries have similar family socioeconomic status, cooperate more often, and share more resources more often, resulting in higher achievement overall. In countries with greater equality, students' extensive sharing also dilutes the links between family characteristics and student achievement. Likewise, these countries with greater equality often distribute resources across schools more equitably, which often reduces differences in students' achievement.

Class inequality can affect academic achievement within the family, at school, or within a country. Privileged families provide their children with more financial, human, social, or cultural capital. Using this capital, children are more likely to understand others' expectations, have better relationships with teachers and students, learn more in school, and complete more years of school. These children benefit from the greater educational resources of both high socioeconomic status schoolmates and elite schools. Meanwhile, students in richer countries benefit from more public educational and noneducational resources that aid learning. Lastly, less equal schools or countries show lower overall academic achievement.

Ming Ming Chiu
State University of New York, Buffalo

See Also: Class Inequality: College Enrollment and Completion; Class Inequality: High School Dropout Rates; Cultural Capital; Social Capital.

Further Readings

Chiu, M. M. "Inequality, Family, School, and Mathematics Achievement." *Social Forces*, v.88/4 (2010).

Chiu, M. M. and Wing Yin Bonnie Chow. "Classroom Discipline: School, Teacher, Economic, and Cultural Differences Across 41 Countries." *Journal of Cross-Cultural Psychology*, in press.

Chiu, M. M. and Wing Yin Bonnie Chow. "Culture, Motivation, and Reading Achievement." *Learning and Individual Differences*, v.20 (2010).

Class Inequality: College Enrollment and Completion

Students from lower socioeconomic classes—most typically defined as students whose parents have low education, income, and occupational status—are less likely than their counterparts to attend and complete college. This underrepresentation of low-income students in higher education has become an increasing concern as the United States continues to fall behind other nations in the percent of adults holding tertiary degrees. The gap in college access and completion, based on class, can be traced to social barriers, inadequate academic preparation, rising college costs, and the funneling of low-income students into community colleges. In the early 19th century, higher education mainly served sons from elite families.

Thomas Jefferson, however, argued that control of power by the wealthy was a threat to democracy and that public higher education was essential for ensuring civic participation. Access to higher education began

to open with the passing of the Morrill Act of 1862, which marked the beginning of federal involvement in education by providing states with federal land to promote public education. During the 20th century, access expanded further, first with the passing of the G.I. Bill in 1944, and then again during the civil rights era, when antidiscrimination laws were instituted and federal grant and loan programs were established for low-income students. Over the past 30 years, the number of students accessing college has increased for all socioeconomic groups, but inequality in access and degree attainment based on social class persists.

Student ability, in terms of high school achievement, is a strong predictor of college enrollment and persistence, yet students from lower socioeconomic families tend to have low academic performance. The status attainment model, theorized by Blau and Duncan and further developed by William Sewell, presents a primarily functionalist view of the path from social class beginnings to ability, to educational attainment, and ultimately to occupation and earnings. It suggests that the social structure in place is fair and offers the highest rewards to the most talented, despite the fact that it disproportionately rewards those from higher socioeconomic classes. Later sociologists of education took a closer look at the mechanisms that lead students from lower socioeconomic classes to have lower academic achievement.

Beginning with Alan Kerckhoff and rooted in Max Weber's notion of the competition between social groups for scarce rewards in an economically stratified society, sociologists of education have argued that students are often constrained by their environment in the choices they make and that schools act to stratify students. Pierre Bourdieu contended that, through their social group membership, students from high-status families possess the resources and attributes (cultural capital) that benefit them in education, because the values of the dominant culture are reflected in what is valued in the educational system. Bourdieu also argued that these students possess resources through social networks (social capital), which increase their ability to reach educational success (theories developed further by James Coleman).

The constraints that occur throughout a student's early life compound upon each other—termed cumulative disadvantage—and ultimately limit college access and success. Students from lower socioeconomic classes tend to be clustered with other lower socioeconomic students in low-quality schools that lack the resources to adequately prepare them for educational success, including parents who know how to navigate the educational system. Low-quality schools offer less rigorous curricula and especially lack in opportunities for advanced mathematics, honors, and advanced placement coursework. At the same time, when students from lower socioeconomic classes attend economically diverse schools, they are socialized to assume a particular place in the class structure through mechanisms such as tracking, and are less likely to have access to the information, guidance, and resources that their higher-socioeconomic peers do.

Since the 1980s, there has been a shift away from grants and need-based college scholarships—the types of aid that are most helpful to lower socioeconomic class students—toward loans and merit-based awards. Students from lower socioeconomic classes are more likely to pay for remedial courses, and the daily expenses of college living can present both financial and social hurdles. College costs not only affect those already in college, they also serve as barriers to the pool of qualified high school graduates by eroding motivation to apply. As access to college has expanded, concerns of "Access to what?" have grown. Lower socioeconomic class students are more likely to attend less-selective institutions that rely heavily on tuition for their funding, and are primarily tracked into two-year institutions where a student's chances of attaining a baccalaureate degree are lowered. They are also overrepresented among those who postpone college enrollment, making them more likely to transition to other roles such as parenthood, the military, or the workforce, and less likely to attend a four-year institution and complete a degree. These gaps in access and persistence are found even when considering high-ability students from lower socioeconomic class backgrounds, a rising concern termed *talent loss*.

Mary E. M. McKillip
Kara Balemian
College Board

See Also: Class Inequality: Achievement; Cooled Out; Dropouts; Racial Inequality: College Enrollment and Completion.

Further Readings

Alon, S. "The Evolution of Class Inequality in Higher Education: Competition, Exclusion, and Adaptation." *American Sociological Review*, v.74 (2009).

Deil-Amen, R. and R. L. Turley. "A Review of the Transition to College Literature in Sociology." *Teachers College Record*, v.109/10 (2007).

Mortenson, T. G. "Family Income and Educational Attainment, 1970–2009." *Postsecondary Opportunity: Public Policy Analysis of Opportunity for Postsecondary Education*, v.221 (2010).

Class Inequality: High School Dropout Rates

A consistent relationship exists between social class and pathways through K–12 schooling: success at school increases as a function of parental social class. The consequences of these effects influence the extent to which individuals engage and succeed in postsecondary schooling, if at all, as well as the kinds of postsecondary schooling: vocational, community college, or university. Documented by *The Coleman Report* (1966), the persistent relationship between social class and school success provides a significant challenge to the ideal of meritocracy: the assumption that success at school is a function of the merit of an individual's work. Though social class is a central concept in sociology, various competing definitions exist.

Current statistics from the United States, Australia, and Canada reveal the ongoing relationship between indicators of social class and school success. Marx's social theory emphasized capital and labor power, arguing that inequality exists because of class-based domination and exploitation. There is an explicit normative judgment in his work: a commitment to expose the ways that individuals' opportunities are a function of the structures within which they live, rather than their individual attributes or capacities. Weber emphasized both class and status, along with skills as resources, and their effects in determining advantages and disadvantages, including opportunities for improving life chances.

Social class may be defined as (1) attributes and conditions of individuals, for example, their education, occupation, and income; (2) the nature of the positions that individuals occupy in the distribution of material inequality, for example, working class and middle class; or (3) the nature of the social relations between these positions. Current studies tend to examine individual attributes and conditions with the assumption that changes made to these attributes and conditions will improve social class position. From this perspective, class is an objective location in a gradational distribution of material inequality: Classes exist like rungs in a ladder, lower class, working class, middle class, and upper class, according to Wright. A research question may be: What explains variations in the distribution of material inequality and life chances? An alternative, relational approach focuses on the nature of the positions, as well as the relationship between the positions, and the relationship of individuals to resources, assets, and income. From this perspective, mobility must balance across the system: Upward mobility for some entails the downward mobility for others. The relational approach foregrounds the role of class-based positions and processes as central to the generation of power relations. A research question may be: How does concerted cultivation by upper-class parents confer advantages to their children while disadvantaging children from lower-class families?

Current Statistics in the United States, Australia, and Canada

In the United States, Chapman, Laird, Ifill, and Kewal Ramani reported the "event dropout rate," defined as the percentage of 15 to 24 year olds who drop out of grades 10 through 12 from one October to the next, in this case, October 2008 to October 2009. In 2009, the event dropout rate of students from low-income families (7.4 percent) was just over five times the rate of students from high-income families (1.4 percent). Low income, in 2009, was defined as the bottom 20 percent of all family incomes, or with $17,997 or less family income; middle-income was defined between 20 percent and 80 percent of all family incomes; high-income was defined as the top 20 percent of all family incomes, or families with $86,820 or more in family income in 2009. Between 1995 and 2009, the event rates for students from low-income and middle-income families had a downward trend, and students from high-income families stayed relatively the same.

In Australia, Lyn Robinson, Mike Long, and Stephen Lamb reported that in 2009, social background, defined as the education of parents and the occupation of fathers, is highlighted as an identifying factor for subgroups of children and youth in need of the "most assistance" to complete a year 12 or vocational qualification. The lower the educational

background of parents, the higher the percentage of youth, between the ages of 20 and 24, without an initial qualification, who were also not studying and not in full-time work: "youth at risk." For example, youth whose mothers did not finish secondary school education were more likely to be at risk (13.4 percent females, 7.3 percent males); youth whose fathers did not finish secondary school were more likely to be at risk (14.4 percent females, 8.8 percent males); youth whose fathers attained year 12 were less likely to be at risk (3.1 percent females, 4.1 percent males). The rate was also higher among youth with fathers who were unemployed (15.8 percent females, 15.0 percent males) or in manual occupations, including machinery, drivers, and laborers, (10.8 percent females, 6.1 percent males). The lowest percentage of youth in this high risk subgroup had fathers in managerial or professional positions (2.9 percent females, 3.3 percent males).

In Canada, Bowlby and McMullen reported that social background, defined as family structure (single, two-parent, or mixed families), parental education, and parental occupation was correlated with dropping out. Both dropouts and graduates were most likely to have lived in two-parent families, with either two biological or adoptive parents, but graduates to a greater extent: Just over half of dropouts lived in two parent families, while three quarters of graduates did. The percentage of dropouts whose parents had not completed high school was three times that of graduates (26.9 percent dropouts, 8.7 percent graduates). Mothers of dropouts were more likely to be working in sales and service jobs than mothers of graduates (35.8 percent mothers of dropouts, 25.1 percent mothers of graduates). They were more than twice as likely to be in occupations in manufacturing, primary processing, utilities, trades, transport, and equipment operations (17 percent mothers of dropouts, mothers of 8.4 percent graduates). Two-thirds of fathers of dropouts (63.9 percent) were in occupations in manufacturing, primary processing, utilities, trades, transport, and equipment operations, while about 41.2 percent of graduates had fathers working in these occupations.

While the likelihood of dropping out of school increases for low-income students and students from backgrounds that include indicators of lower social class, being a member of the lower social classes also increases as a function of having dropped out: a vicious cycle. Dropping out of school has been associated with high individual and social costs, including: low literacy and skills, along with difficulty finding a job, lower income, and increased likelihood of less secure, short-term and part-time employment; higher death rates, incidence of alcohol abuse, illegal drug abuse, and negative health outcomes; and higher health care budget expenditure, criminal behavior, and need for social assistance.

Social Class and the Process of Schooling

Dropping out is a process that occurs over time, therefore, the statistics do not reflect children and youth who are beginning to disengage or becoming alienated. The process of dropping out, early school leaving, or being pushed out may begin by "tuning out" in class, and then lead to skipping classes. The mismatch between home and school culture, classroom speech genres, and social practices; a lack of good relationships with teachers; feeling incapable or like a failure; and the pressures associated with standards-based reforms, including teacher accountability and student testing all tend to exacerbate social class differences.

The relationship between social class and the process of schooling was theorized by Sameul Bowles and Herbert Gintis as one of economic reproduction through structural correspondence between social relations and relationships of production: social relations in education habituate students to the discipline of the workplace and foster the development of different types of demeanor, self-presentation, self-image, and social class identification. Extensions of this theory were made through empirical research conducted by Anyon, who highlighted the role of differences in curricula, pedagogy, and methods of assessment affecting students' thinking and behavioral skills and, ultimately, their relationships to capital, including the means and ownership of production, to authority, and to work practices. Bourdieu's theory provided a broad conceptualization for thinking through advantages and disadvantages related to social class through forms of capital that, in addition to financial capital, are linked to schooling as significant assets, including cultural capital, such as skills, knowledge, and credentials, and social capital, such as social networks and relationships.

Several mechanisms for maintaining class-based advantages and disadvantages work through the class-based character of schooling. First, opportunity hoarding occurs when a group of individuals collectively exclude another group of individuals from access to better conditions. An example, credentialing, both improves the skills and, potentially, the productivity of the labor force, while restricting the supply of credentialed laborers; the value of a graduate holding a specific kind or level of credential depends in part on the scarcity of it. Second, concentration of advantage occurs in schools, communities, and workplaces where members of a particular social class are concentrated. Concentrated class-based interests and needs are privileged and, along with resources, maintained, thereby sustaining advantages. Third, concerted cultivation, proposed by Lareau, highlights the systematic preparation of children for college by their parents, rather than relying on school personnel. This parental involvement provides children of upper-class families with additional advantages with long-term consequences. Areas in need of future research include studying the differential outcomes of siblings, for example, in relation to financial and time-related resource expenditures of parents, as well as maintaining the authenticity of social class analyses through intersections with race, ethnicity, and/or gender.

Jennifer Vadeboncoeur
Renira E. Vellos
University of British Columbia

See Also: Alternative and Second Chance Education: Bowles, Samuel and Herbert Gintis; *Coleman Report, The*; Gender Inequality: High School Drop Out Rates; Lareau, Annette; Marx, Karl (Marxism and Education); Racial Inequality: High School Drop Out Rates; Weber, Max.

Further Readings

Anyon, Jean. "Social Class and the Hidden Curriculum of Work." *Journal of Education*, v.162/1.

Bernstein, Basil. *Class, Codes, and Control.* Vol. 1. London: Routledge & Kegan Paul, 1970.

Bourdieu, Pierre. "The Forms of Capital." In *The Handbook of Theory and Research for the Sociology of Education*, J. Richardson, ed. Westport, CT: Greenwood Press, 1986.

Bowles, Samuel and Herbert Gintis. *Schooling in Capitalist America: Educational Reform and the Contradictions of Economic Life.* New York: Basic Books, 1976.

Chapman, Chris, J. Laird, N. Ifill, and A. Kewal Ramani. *Trends in High School Dropout and Completion Rates in the United States: 1972–2009* (NCES 2012-006). U.S. Department of Education. Washington, DC: National Center for Education Statistics, 2011.

Lareau, Annette. *Unequal Childhoods: Class, Race, and Family Life.* 2nd ed. Berkeley: University of California Press, 2011.

Marx, Karl. *A Contribution to the Critique of Political Economy,* M. Dobb, ed. New York: International Publishers, 1970.

Packer, Martin. *Changing Classes: School Reform and the New Economy.* New York: Cambridge University Press, 2000.

Robinson, Lyn, Mike Long, and Stephen Lamb. *How Young People Are Faring 2011: The National Report on the Learning and Work Situation of Young Australians.* Melbourne, Victoria: The Foundation for Young Australians, 2011.

Weber, Max. "Protestantism and the Rise of Modern Capitalism." In *Readings in Introductory Sociology,* D. H. Wrong and H. L. Gracey, eds. 2nd ed. New York: Macmillan, 1972.

Classroom Dynamics

Both teachers and students handle the dynamics of classroom interaction through interpreting actions and communicating perceived meaning. Characteristics of these dynamics are highlighted in the concept of contingency of interaction and through the relationship of technology and interaction. Classroom dynamics is an effect of interaction. Interaction is a sequence of individual actions that are modified subsequent to the actions of others. Interaction can be conceptualized as a complex system that is agent based, nonlinear, and path dependent. Individual agents have the capacity to act independently and based on their own choice. In the classroom context, interaction takes place between teacher and student. In this context, individual actions are delimited by the roles of the teacher and the student that create specific expectations and restrict independence and choice. Role dependency of student and teacher reflects in classroom communication, where a students' answer to a question of the teacher has to meet the expectations of both the teacher and the peer audience. Interaction between individuals is non-linear because it is based on interpretation. Teacher and students act on their interpretation of the action of others.

Every interpretation is contingent, meaning that it is not true or false, but merely plausible. Since interpretations of both individuals are contingent, Niklas Luhmann and Karl Schorr introduce the concept of double contingency in interaction to frame its dynamics. The quality of teaching relies on reducing contingency by developing plausible interpretations of student actions. When students struggle to accomplish a task in class, teachers have to interpret student actions in respect to the task in order to support their learning. Interaction is path dependent since interactions of students and teachers are not only affected by the current situation, but also by their history of interactions.

The knowledge constructed in previous interactions creates a cognitive horizon in relation to which interpretations of current interactions are developed. This horizon develops from both individual experience and collective cultural belief and might bias interpretations. Teachers who consider the math ability of their female students to be lower than that of their male students, even when test scores are comparable, are likely to act upon such a bias.

Technology and Classroom Dynamics

To reduce the complexity of classroom interaction, the student population has to be small and students should have more or less homogeneous performance. However, teachers often have to work with large classes and with students of different performance levels. This situation makes it difficult to address individual learning requirements. At the same time, teachers are requested to meet curricular requirements that demand teachers to take control of events. Such requirements facilitate technological teaching and learning. A technological view replaces complex relationships of interaction with causal relationship. Learning in school becomes a technology in terms of content, time, and in respect to its social function. Contents of learning in school are predetermined in curricula that disregard student interests. Time of learning in school is structured in lesson plans and leaves little time to respect individual learning requirements. The social function of teaching and learning is to produce individuals that society calls for, individuals that display socially desired character traits and are skilled in specific subject areas.

In contrast to the conceptual framing of teaching and learning as a complex system outlined above, this critical technological framing highlights one of the fundamental contradictions of classroom interaction: On the one hand, teachers have to manage classroom dynamics as if teaching and learning had a technological relation. On the other hand, teaching and learning interaction has been characterized as complex, contingent, and nonlinear. These characteristics point to fundamental problems of a technological framing of teaching and learning: The theorem of double contingency emphasizes the necessity of mutual interpretation of actions to reduce contingency. It equally underpins that intentions of teaching and intentions of learning have to be negotiated to arrive at interaction productive for learning. Ultimately, the theorem of double contingency renders the technological expectation that actions of teaching will cause actions of learning unrealistic.

Dynamics Among Teaching, Learning, and Education

Classroom interaction is dedicated to teaching and learning, which can be understood as impartment and acquisition of knowledge in the context of sociology of knowledge. In respect to impartment and acquisition of knowledge, the teacher operates as an agent between students and the topic and acts as a negotiator of knowledge. In class, the teacher elicits and negotiates concepts related to the topic with students. Teachers have to link their actions of imparting knowledge to student actions of acquiring knowledge to create dynamics in interaction that scaffold learning. Insufficient dynamic scaffolding is revealed through phenomena such as student boredom, a signifier of the individual's retreat from teaching and learning particularly prominent in compulsory education. To help students become engaged in working on a topic, learning about it, and acquiring knowledge, teacher actions reach beyond teaching the subject and imparting knowledge. As the social role of the teacher is to help students work on the topic, teachers have to educate students. Educative action can be identified by positive and negative moments. Negatively, educative action takes place as inhibiting students from actions other than those aligned with working on the topic. Positively, educative actions aim to guide students to a habitus productive for the acquisition of knowledge. Teachers have to rely on educative actions when interaction on the level of imparting and acquiring knowledge is disturbed, or a shared focus on collaborative work is not found.

Classroom interaction is framed by institutional and social demands, but nevertheless produces interactive order in respect to acquiring and imparting knowledge. The order of classroom interaction is not sustained by a normative consensus, but rather by individuals who cooperate to sustain a course of events and patterns of interaction. Classroom interaction cannot be used as a means to realize institutional demands, but depends on at least minimal commitment of students. To reach commitment, teachers and students communicate about learning in class. Interaction on the level of imparting and acquiring knowledge depends on coming to a situated understanding of students and teacher that something is learned. Learning is identified through mutual understanding that a state changes from not knowing to knowing. If this understanding is not reached in different stages of classroom interaction, teaching and learning cannot proceed. Without communication of learning in the classroom, attempts to have an effect on learning through teaching stand no chance. Situated interpretations of actions in the classroom and reactions that connect to these actions, are key to handling classroom dynamics and enabling students to acquire knowledge through interaction.

Clemens Wieser
University of Vienna

See Also: Classroom Interactions: Teachers and Students; Ethnography; Hermeneutics; Teacher Decision-Making Power; Technology in the Classroom.

Further Readings

Leander, Kevin M. "Silencing in Classroom Interaction: Producing and Relating Social Spaces." *Discourse Processes*, v.34/2 (2002).

Luhmann, Niklas and Karl Eberhard Schorr. *Problems of Reflection in the System of Education.* Münster, Austria: Waxmann, 2000.

Vanderstraeten, Raf. "The School Class as an Interaction Order." *British Journal of Sociology of Education*, v.22/2 (2001).

Classroom Interactions: Teachers and Students

The definition of teaching implies an interaction between teacher and student. Yet, such interactions are often ignored for macro-level educational concerns. When scholars do consider these interactions, the research that they produce is largely divided along disciplinary lines. Education psychologists focus on linking specific teacher behaviors to student outcomes, or on explaining variations in such interactions as a function of individual-level attributes. Sociologists of education instead view teacher-student interactions as a function of the social organization of the school environment, and use these structural relationships to explain why teacher-student interactions matter for learning and achievement.

Research on teacher-student interactions often examines how these exchanges matter for students' learning and achievement, and how they vary with the characteristics of students and teachers. While some scholars recognize students' active role in shaping teachers' responses to them, most research still focuses on teacher-initiated interactions. This is likely because such research is typically aimed at developing standards for effective teaching. Scholars find, for example, that teaching styles and the quality of teacher-student relationships both matter for student outcomes. Students tend to do better in school and to feel more attached to school when they have teachers who they perceive as friendly, caring, and supportive. Similarly, students who experience a stronger sense of connectedness to teachers and others at school tend to be more engaged in learning and more successful in school. Such findings align with research suggesting that positive relationships with adults have myriad benefits for children and youth.

Studies also highlight aspects of academic interactions between teachers and students that are beneficial for student outcomes. Research shows, for example, that students do better in school when they have teachers who actively engage them in learning, and when their teachers positively evaluate their performance or effort in front of their peers (which may influence not only the students' academic self-competence, but also their peers' treatment of them). Similarly, research on teacher expectations consistently shows that students are more successful with teachers who set high standards for students, and who couple these expectations with support and encouragement. Such expectations matter both directly and through their impact on students' educational expectations. Despite such evidence, however, some scholars also caution that the process of teaching is far more complicated (involving multiple, often competing goals, and countless strings of interaction with a classroom full of students) than these correlations imply. Thus, they stress that scholars have only a limited understanding of the full complexity of teacher-student interactions and their consequences for student outcomes.

Variation in Teacher-Student Interaction

Scholars have found that the nature and frequency of teacher-student interaction can also vary with the characteristics of those involved. For example, while male students interact more frequently with teachers, girls experience more positive teacher-student interactions. Boys, it seems, misbehave more frequently than girls, prompting teachers to more closely monitor their behavior. There is also some evidence that teachers interact more negatively with black students and with those from disadvantaged backgrounds, directing less praise and more criticism toward these students than to their white and more privileged peers. Such differential treatment is often linked to research showing that teachers often have lower expectations for poor, working-class, and minority students. While the evidence is somewhat mixed, studies also show that teachers unintentionally favor high-achieving students over lower-achieving ones, interacting with them in more positive and supportive ways, and also setting higher expectations for their performance. Similarly, despite some evidence that teachers use praise to motivate low-achieving students, most research finds instead that teacher accolades go mainly to highly successful students. Low-achieving students, in turn, are often aware of teachers' differential treatment of them.

Such awareness negatively impacts students' beliefs about their ability and potential, which in turn reduces their effort and achievement. While studies regularly find substantial variability in teacher-student interactions across teachers, they have been less successful in linking these variations to teacher characteristics like gender, training, and experience. Similarly, while scholars like Lisa Delpit have sparked debate about race and culture in teacher-student interactions, evidence is mixed as to whether teachers and students from similar racial backgrounds interact more positively than those from different racial backgrounds.

Structure of Teacher-Student Interactions

Considering variability in teacher-student relationships, other research focuses less on individual-level characteristics. Instead, ethnographers like Dan Lortie, Philip Jackson, and Robert Dreeben examine the organizational and structural factors (e.g., the teacher's position of authority in the classroom) that shape classroom interactions. They find that variability in teacher-student interaction is largely a function of the fact that teachers are largely autonomous, with very little oversight of their teaching methods, and very few agreed-upon standards of what constitutes good or effective teaching. Such research is also concerned with understanding how teacher-student interactions matter for student learning and achievement, though it focuses more on process than effect size. In this vein, scholars like Donna Eder, Jeannie Oakes, and Ray Rist highlight how tracking and ability grouping play a key role in generating unequal educational opportunities. They show that students from disadvantaged and minority backgrounds are more likely to be assigned to lower tracks and groups, and that teachers tend to devote less instructional time, support, and attention to students in lower-ability groups and academic tracks. Similarly, research on school structure demonstrates that teachers in more disadvantaged school settings interact less with students and are less supportive of them. Studies link such findings to the fact that teachers in such schools often have lower expectations for students and a lower sense of efficacy and personal responsibility for students' learning.

Other research instead looks at students' feelings about school as a critical mechanism by which teacher-student interactions influence learning outcomes. Scholars like Chandra Muller show that when teachers are caring and respectful of students, and when they listen to and praise them, students develop stronger feelings of attachment to school, which in turn lead to higher levels of educational achievement and attainment. While some studies find only a limited impact of teacher praise and caring on student outcomes, this is likely because teachers do not use these behaviors simply for academic ends. Rather, praise, caring, and other similar behaviors seems to serve a variety of other functions in the classroom, such as expressing an emotional connection with a particular student or responding to student behaviors that are aimed at eliciting attention from the teacher. Existing research, however, has paid relatively little attention to the non-academic consequences of teacher-student interactions. While a few studies explore teachers' impact on students' social and behavioral development, they say little about how teacher-student interactions might help students to learn these critical skills.

Jessica McCrory Calarco
University of Pennsylvania

See Also: Ability Grouping; Classroom Dynamics; Classroom Interactions Between Students; Teacher Expectations; Tracking.

Further Readings
Brophy, Jere E. *Teacher-Student Relationships*. Oxford, UK: Holt, Rinehart, & Winston, 1974.
Cohen, Elizabeth G. "Sociology and the Classroom: Setting the Conditions for Teacher–Student Interaction," *Review of Educational Research*, v.42/4 (1972).
Delpit, Lisa. *Other People's Children: Cultural Conflict in the Classroom*. New York: New Press, 1995.
Dreeben, Robert. *On What Is Learned in School*. Reading, MA: Addison-Wesley, 1968.
Eder, Donna "Ability Grouping as a Self-Fulfilling Prophecy: A Micro-Analysis of Teacher–Student Interaction." *Sociology of Education*, v.54/3 (1981).
Jackson, Philip W. *Life in Classrooms*. New York: Holt, Rinehart & Winston, 1968.
Lortie, Dan C. *Schoolteacher: A Sociological Study*. 2nd ed. Chicago: University of Chicago Press, 2002.
Oakes, Jeannie. *Keeping Track: How Schools Structure Inequality*. New Haven, CT: Yale University Press, 2005.
Rist, Ray C. "HER Classic: Student Social Class and Teacher Expectations: The Self-Fulfilling Prophecy in Ghetto Education." *Harvard Educational Review*, v.70/3 (2000).

Classroom Interactions Between Students

Students can interact during whole-class discussions (when students respond to one another, in cross-discussions), pair/small group work, student presentations' question and answer sessions. While student and teacher responsibilities differ across these activities, students typically address a complex problem, propose ideas, question them, evaluate them, implement them, and reflect on them. During these student interactions, they can improve their learning and social processes, as well as their outcomes. Still, students will face difficulties during these interactions, which teachers must address. To initiate these classroom interactions among students, a teacher asks a complex question/problem, often with many answers or solution methods. Ideally, a single student cannot solve the problem, but students can collaborate to solve it (a zone of proximal development problem).

Students can benefit from group work through greater efficiency, shared understanding, emotional support, motivation, and mutual help. By dividing responsibilities, they can work more efficiently (with distributed responsibilities). In more structured activities, each student has rotating roles (e.g., proposer of new ideas, supporter, critic, facilitator, or reporter). By distributing responsibilities, each student focuses on a subset of the problem. With more attention and cognitive resources to achieve a subgoal, a student is less likely to be distracted and make mistakes. Furthermore, students can work to their strengths, which further reduce errors and increase efficiency. Distributed responsibilities also increase the visibility of both cognitive processes (e.g., new ideas, elaborations, and repetitions) and higher order meta-cognitive processes (e.g., questions and evaluations) to help students build shared understanding. When students express new ideas and elaborate them, they explicitly communicate through words, actions, and facial expressions, thereby helping other students understand these ideas and expanding their shared knowledge base. In response, repetitions can indicate shared knowledge. Greater visibility also facilitates other students' questions and evaluations to recognize the limits of their shared understanding (e.g., knowledge gaps and flawed ideas).

Faced with the limits of their understanding, students can feel confused or frustrated. Distributing responsibilities among several students also distributes the risk of failure and its consequences. With less personal risk and lower failure costs, students might feel less anxious and more motivated to persevere. Other students can also provide emotional support; for example, humor, encouragement, or clarifying explanations can alleviate confusion or frustration. Emotional support and laughter can also help build friendships and shared group identity, thereby increasing students' motivation to learn together. When students help one another, both the helper and the recipient benefit. Helpers benefit cognitively by elaborating their ideas and socially by earning higher status and building friendships. Meanwhile, recipients see a different way to understand the situation that can help fill their knowledge gap.

Student interactions can yield many benefits, including improved understanding of the immediate content, higher subsequent achievement, improved meta-cognitive skills, positive beliefs about learning, and stronger communication and social skills. After successfully solving a problem together, each student can reflect on the solution, consolidate understandings, and then recall this experience when facing a similar problem alone (internalization). Students who engage in more classroom interactions also show higher achievement than other students. When students listen to, recognize, and challenge other students' views, they improve their meta-cognition. Students who engage in more classroom interactions are more likely than other students to view themselves as active thinkers. Last, students who participate in more classroom interactions often have better speaking and listening skills.

However, students can also face many difficulties during classroom interactions. When students misallocate resources, suffer status effects, or miscommunicate, teachers can help student re-allocate their resources, identify and act against status effects, and improve their communication skills. Although students collectively have more knowledge than a single student, they can access inappropriate resources (e.g., cognitive, social, or physical), choose inappropriate strategies, or mis-schedule their time. For example, a student might give unneeded advice, fail to offer emotional support, misuse feedback, recommend wrong procedures, or underestimate the time needed to solve a problem. As a result, students can hinder, rather than help one another. Teachers can anticipate these difficulties by modeling appropriate behaviors or addressing these difficulties by asking guiding questions to help students learn.

Conclusion

Status is an agreed-upon rank order, and status differences can hinder student interactions by distorting participation and evaluations. Students perceived to have higher competencies for an activity have higher status, through directly relevant characteristics such as past achievement (a primary status characteristic), or through less-related ones such as race (a diffuse status characteristic). Based on these expectations, students often selectively invite and inappropriately defer to high-status students' opinions while discouraging, undervaluing, or outright ignoring lower-status students' ideas. By doing so, members enact their expectations of high-status students dominating the interaction to the detriment of both lower-status students and the overall outcome.

To reduce status effects, teachers can encourage classroom conversation norms that ask for and expect input from all students. To counteract status effects, teachers can find opportunities to legitimately raise the status of low-status students, both by recognizing their accomplishments and by designing activities that create and publicize their expertise. Poor communication skills (potentially exacerbated by cultural differences) can hinder communication, reduce participation, and harm social relationships. Miscommunications can yield misunderstandings and lead students to work at cross-purposes. Furthermore, face attacks (e.g., "you're clearly wrong") and emotional conflicts can reduce participation from students who fear embarrassment or retribution. In extreme cases, such conflicts can end the conversation and even friendships. To enhance students' communication skills, teachers can model desirable behaviors (e.g., polite disagreements to save face) and give students sufficient time to think deeply before expressing their ideas.

Ming Ming Chiu
State University of New York, Buffalo

See Also: Classroom Dynamics; Classroom Interactions: Teachers and Students; Student Roles in the Classroom.

Further Readings

Chiu, Ming Ming. "Adapting Teacher Interventions to Student Needs During Cooperative Learning." *American Educational Research Journal*, v.41 (2004).

Chiu, Ming Ming. "Flowing Toward Correct Contributions During Groups' Mathematics Problem Solving: A Statistical Discourse Analysis." *Journal of the Learning Sciences*, v.17/3 (2008).

Johnson, David and Roger Johnson. "Cooperative Learning Methods: A Meta-Analysis." *Journal of Research in Education*, v.12/1 (2002).

Classroom Language

Classroom language represents the method of communication in school settings throughout the world. It defines the verbal application of language expectations acceptable to teachers, family members, other children, and the community. Within the norms of classroom language, additional considerations of dialect must be considered as a demonstration of various local, regional, national, and international differences. Classroom language, therefore, is valuable, despite local dialect or national origin. Recognition of the local language of children is an important component of the educational process, with implications for teaching and learning. The role of education in the United States was historically viewed as a foundation of American society, designed to develop and prepare citizens in the roles and responsibilities of citizenship. The provision of education established the immersion of English in the instructional process to ensure acceptable discourse. The application and use of English as a standard classroom language in school buildings codified the notion of "standard" English for the children of settlers, while simultaneously establishing modes of communication for immigrant children. While dialects from different regions were acceptable, English as a foundation of language was strictly enforced.

Throughout the 19th century and the first half of the 20th century, English remained the standard classroom language in the United States. Moreover, many countries throughout the world insisted that children learn their local languages, as well as English, to more effectively communicate with English-speaking countries. Children, therefore, were instructed in languages consistent with the norms and cultures of their region, without substantial interference in the acquisition of knowledge; transference of knowledge occurred seamlessly, without regard to language variations, dialect, or linguistic style.

The second half of the 20th century witnessed a dramatic change in the classroom language patterns of children attending schools in the United States and Europe. The influx of immigrants seeking economic or political stability resulted in a marked increase of students speaking in classroom languages other than English. While the majority of immigrant students in the United States often spoke Spanish, a multitude of languages and dialects from the international community existed, sometimes with multiple dialects in one classroom. Classroom language was no longer homogeneous; it immediately represented a series of challenges for teachers, administrators, and the community of educators. The resultant impact of English language learners on the instructional and learning capacity of students became the primary foci of national and international education experts, particularly in an atmosphere of accountability.

As a result, educators adopted an established curricular approach, incorporating acceptable classroom language as an essential component of teaching and learning. Immigrant students were instructed in English and their native languages as a foundation for transferring essential knowledge. English language learners in many states are now provided the opportunity to use their native language, in particular Spanish, where summative assessments are concerned. The provision of summative assessments in a language format consistent with the requirements of English language learners allows the measurement of student performance consistent with their classroom language ability, as opposed to their ability to understand and comprehend English. Effective communication is often associated with education and class in society. Children are judged by their ability to communicate in an acceptable style, consistent with local norms and school culture. Classroom language denotes the ability of the student to manage and demonstrate proper language use, dialect, and intellect, while maintaining cultural connections established through dialect, ethnicity, gender, and nationalism. Too often, the absence of cultural descriptors often used in classroom language prohibits the acquisition of knowledge in a meaningful and acceptable context. Additionally, teachers and other educators assume that the absence of acceptable language skills is reflective of the absence of intellect. Teachers may view students with poor classroom language skills as intellectually inept, lacking basic options and choices in education and in life.

As a social construct, classroom language embodies the scope of social and educational interactions observed by teachers in school settings on an international scale. The ability to communicate and understand instructions, methods, and abstract theories is bound by the ability of the student to understand the spoken word in terms and language understood by the learner. Classroom language that is inconsistent with native languages has the capacity to interfere with the transference of knowledge to the detriment of society and the community. If students cannot understand the spoken classroom language, they cannot internalize the process of reading, comprehension, mathematics, and other academic requirements. This loss of intellectual capital may be the result of classroom language barriers, as opposed to diminished intellectual capacity. Teachers, administrators, and educational institutions must systematically strive to interpret the classroom language of all students, irrespective of ethnicity or national origin. The complexity of classroom interactions requires that all students are provided with the opportunity to demonstrate intellectual capacity, despite perceived deficiencies by the social norms of schools and society.

Patricia Hoffman-Miller
Prairie View A&M University

See Also: Bilingual Education; Classroom Interactions: Teachers and Students; Ebonics (African American English) and Education; Immigrant Adaptation.

Further Readings

Ball, A. "Empowering Pedagogies That Enhance the Learning of Multicultural Students." *New York: Teachers College Record*, v.102 (2000).

Delpit, L. and J. K. Dowdy. *The Skin That We Speak: Thoughts on Language and Culture in the Classroom*. New York: The New Press, 2008.

Ogbu, J. "Beyond Language: Ebonics, Proper English, and Identity in a Black-American Speech Community." *American Educational Research Journal*, v.36 (1999).

Cognitive Skill/ Intellectual Skill

Cognitive skill refers to an individual's ability to gain meaning and knowledge from their experiences and information that is presented to them. Cognition is the capacity to learn and think about new information, the ability to process and articulate that acquired knowledge, and then relate and apply it to previously gained information. Through the course of a person's lifetime, they are typically able to increase their cognitive skills to process information more easily. In the past, there have been various theories indicating different highlighted areas of cognitive skill, as well as several noteworthy individuals with theories on how cognitive skill is acquired during an individual's life. Without having developed cognitive skills, children are more likely to fall behind in school because of not being able to integrate the new information that is taught to them with their previously learned knowledge.

Areas of Cognitive Skill

Cognitive skills can be broken down into categories and there are various theories that describe them. When comparing well known theories of cognitive skills, Cattell-Horn-Carroll (CHC) theory is the most comprehensive and research-supported theory from a psychometric approach. Within CHC theory, there are a total of 10 broad abilities. Crystallized intelligence/knowledge includes the depth and span of an individual's gained knowledge, as well as the ability to communicate knowledge and reason using previously learned experiences or exposures. Fluid intelligence/reasoning includes the ability to solve problems that are not automatically performed. General knowledge is the breadth and depth of acquired knowledge, not including the universal experiences of the person's culture. Quantitative knowledge is an individual's ability to understand concepts and relationships related to mathematics. Reading/writing is a person's capacity to perform basic reading and writing skills. Short-term memory includes being able to acquire and grasp information immediately and use that information within seconds. Long-term storage and retrieval involves an individual storing information and retrieving it at a later time. Visual spatial abilities include being able to perceive, analyze, synthesize, and think with visual components, including storing and recalling representations that are visual. Auditory processing is an individual's ability to analyze, synthesize, and discriminate auditory stimuli. The 10th broad ability is cognitive processing speed, and involves performing automatic cognitive tasks, including when attention and concentration is needed.

Another theorist, Robert J. Sternberg, who was a prominent figure in researching human intelligence, formulated the triarchic theory of intelligence. This theory was innovative because it was one of the first theories to take a cognitive approach and go against the psychometric approach. Sternberg's theory encompasses three parts: componential, experiential, and practical. The componential subtheory is related to analytical giftedness. This involves being able to take apart problems and find solutions. The second stage of Sternberg's theory includes the experiential subtheory, which encompasses how well a task can be performed, depending on the familiarity of the individual to the task. This includes novel situations, where an individual has never experienced the task before, and automated situations where the task has been performed multiple times and is now done with little or no extra thought.

The third subtheory is the practical or contextual subtheory, which includes the processes of adaptation, shaping, and selection. Through these three processes, a person is able to develop an ideal fit among themselves and their environment. Adaptation is where an individual makes a change within themselves to adjust better to their surroundings. Shaping is when a person changes their environment to better fit their needs, and selection occurs when a completely new environment replaces the previous one that was found unsatisfying to meet their goals. Sternberg indicates that the successfulness in how a person fits to their environment and interacts with daily situations reflects their degree of intelligence. He also concludes that an individual is not limited to excelling in just one of the three various intelligences. Instead, people may acquire a combination of all three and have elevated levels of intelligence in all three theories.

Theories of Cognitive Skill Acquirement

Throughout history, there have been numerous theorists who have devoted their lives in understanding the development of thinking and intelligence. One individual was Jean Piaget, whose work on children's intellectual development was enormously influential. Piaget theorized that children's thinking does not develop smoothly, but at certain periods of development their thinking goes into new areas and capabilities. He proposed that before specific ages of transition development, children do not have the capability of understanding things in certain ways and focus on discovery learning. His stages included the sensorimotor, which is from birth to 2 years old. During this phase, children are able to differentiate themselves from objects. The preoperational stage takes place from 2 years to 7 years, and is when the child learns to use language and represent objects through the use of words and images. Children's thinking during this phase is still self-involved and they have difficulty taking others' viewpoints.

During the concrete operational stage, when children are between the ages of 7 and 11, the child can think logically about objects and events, as well as classify objects according to several features. The final stage is defined as the formal operational stage, developed at age 11 and older, where a child can think logically about abstract problems, as well as test hypotheses.

There are also theorists known as Neo-Piagetian theorists, who believe in Piaget's idea of cognitive developmental stages, but advance it by building on his four stages, most often including problem-finding as a fifth stage of development. Within this stage, an individual can determine what problem they are facing and make a decision on how to solve that challenge.

Lev Vygotsky was another theorist who shared many of Piaget's views on child development, but put much more emphasis on the social aspects of learning. He believed that learning and development is a social, collaborative activity. Vygotsky perceived that development proceeds from the outside to internalization. Through this process, the person absorbs their knowledge from their environment. Vygotsky considered that child development after the age of 2 was partially determined by language. Vygotsky also proposed that all learning should be connected. He is well known for his Zone of Proximal Development, which is the observation that when children learn a particular task, they begin by not being able to do the specific task. Then, over time, the child is able to do the task with assistance, and then finally being able to do the task without assistance after scaffolding has taken place.

Susan Galford
Indiana University

See Also: Ability Grouping; *Bell Curve, The*; Disabled Students; IQ; Special Education.

Further Readings

Flanagan, D. P. and P. L. Harrison, eds. *Contemporary Intellectual Assessment: Theories, Tests, and Issues.* New York: Guilford Press, 2005.

Mooney, C. G. *Theories of Childhood: An Introduction to Dewey, Montessori, Erikson, Piaget, and Vygotsky.* St. Paul, MN: Redleaf Press, 2000.

Piaget, J. *The Child's Conception of the World.* New York: Littlefield Adams, 1990.

Coleman, James S.

James S. Coleman (1926–95) was a central figure in the sociology of education during the second half of the 20th century. His empirical research and theoretical contributions were often controversial and fundamentally shifted the field. An indicator of his influence is that he remained on the list of most highly cited sociologists more than 15 years after his death. Coleman is best known for his work in which he collected and analyzed large-scale databases to address policy questions about equality of educational opportunity. In the sociology of education, he also contributed major insights into the social organization of adolescent society. In sociology more broadly, he made important contributions in the area of mathematical sociology and social theory. Coleman's work is characterized by (1) a simultaneous attention to the individual and in the social context, arguing that individual actions are a function of their social and normative context, and those individual actions shape that context as well; and (2) the perspective that individual action is rooted in rationality.

Equality of Educational Opportunity (EEO), often called *The Coleman Report*, was published in 1966, after it was commissioned by the U.S. Department of Health, Education, and Welfare in response to the Civil Rights Act of 1964, which mandated a study of equality of educational opportunity. At the time, school resources were used to measure school quality, and the primary concern was that schools attended by African Americans had worse resources than those attended by whites. Coleman's findings created a major stir because they defied conventional wisdom, showing instead that enhancing schools' resources alone would not improve students' opportunities because students' achievement also depended on the family backgrounds of the other students in the school. African American students benefited from sitting next to white students in the classroom, and white students were not harmed when they shared schools with African Americans. These findings touched off a major controversy over school desegregation, accompanied by policy initiatives to attempt to desegregate schools.

Following his EEO study, from 1968 to 1973, Coleman conducted a study called "Recent Trends in School Segregation," of family responses to desegregation, in which he argued that city-wide policies to desegregate schools, for example through mandatory busing, produced "white flight," whereby white families moved to suburbs outside the boundaries of desegregation action to avoid desegregated schools. In the 1980s, Coleman conducted a study, "High School Achievement," comparing the effects of public, Catholic, and private schools on students' achievement. He found that Catholic schools improved students' achievement, particularly among students whose families had lower socioeconomic status. These findings were embraced by proponents of a movement to broaden school choices beyond the public arena, through vouchers and charter schools, and by those interested in public funding of religious schools. In contrast to how some incorrectly interpreted the findings from EEO, that there was little effect of schools on students' achievement, findings from "High School Achievement" showed important effects of schools on students' achievement.

With "High School Achievement," Coleman and his colleagues showed that the functional communities that existed in Catholic schools, communities in which association with a faith-based community formed the basis of relations, were communities where norms would be enforced, obligations met, and information shared, enhancing trust among members, thereby creating a foundation for social capital to emerge and be maintained. With this theoretical contribution, Coleman also elaborated on the roles of parents, schools, and communities in the education of children and adolescents. This was extended through his work from 1988 through the early 1990s on parental involvement in schools.

Another important strand of Coleman's contribution to sociology of education began with "The Adolescent Society," a 1961 study conducted early in his career. With this study, Coleman investigated the social world of adolescents within schools and the impact of the adolescent society on students' achievement. He argued that adolescent subcultures and the norms and values embedded in their relationships had a profound impact on youth's behaviors. In contrast to his more policy-driven research, "Adolescent Society" and its 1974 related study, "Youth in Transition," focused on the social systems within the high school, structures that were a function of students' relationships with one another and which Coleman argued were largely independent of adult influences. "Adolescent Society" was novel because it relied on survey data and emphasized the perspective of adolescents, and especially because it involved individuals nested in the social system in the school, a system that changed because of the behaviors of the adolescents.

Chandra Muller
University of Texas at Austin

See Also: Adolescence; Busing; Catholic Schools; *Coleman Report, The*; Social Capital.

Further Readings
Clark, Jon, ed. *James S. Coleman*. London: Falmer Press, 1996.
Coleman, James S. *The Adolescent Society: The Social Life of Teenagers and Its Impact on Education*. New York: Free Press of Glencoe, 1961.
Coleman, James S. *Foundations of Social Theory*. Cambridge, MA: Belknap Press of Harvard University Press, 1990.
Coleman, James S. *Introduction to Mathematical Sociology*. New York: Free Press, 1964.
Coleman, James S. "Social Capital in the Creation of Human Capital." *American Journal of Sociology*, v.94 (1988).
Coleman, James S. "Youth: Transition to Adulthood." *NASSP Bulletin*, v.58 (1974).
Coleman, James S., E. Q. Campbell, C. J. Hobson, J. McPartland, A. M. Mood, F. D. Weingeld, and R. L. York. *Equality of Educational Opportunity*. Washington DC: U.S. Government Printing Office, 1966.
Coleman, James S. and Thomas Hoffer. *Public and Private High Schools: The Impact of Communities*. New York: Basic Books, 1987.
Coleman, James S., Thomas Hoffer, and Sally Kilgore. *High School Achievement: Public, Catholic, and Private Schools Compared*. New York: Basic Books, 1982.

Coleman Report, The

The Coleman Report (formally named *Equality of Educational Opportunity*) is one of the most influential works in the sociology of education. The findings of this report informed public perception, changed educational policy, and continue to shape research on education. The U.S. Department of Education commissioned James Coleman (1914–91), a sociologist of education, and several other scholars to conduct this study to fulfill a provision of the 1964 Civil Rights Act. They were asked to determine whether children of different races, colors, religions, and national origins experience equal educational opportunity in America. The study, of unprecedented scale for the time, employed quantitative data on 645,000 students in 4,000 public schools.

One of the more controversial findings of the report was that differences in family background contribute much more to students' academic outcomes than differences in schools. Furthermore, the characteristics of the students at the school, or the peer environment, mattered more for academic achievement than school funding or teachers' characteristics. The findings of this report were used to support the racial desegregation of schools during the 1970s and 1980s. Sections 2 and 3 of *The Coleman Report* were the most relevant to school policy and the most controversial.

Section 2: Differences in School Quality

Section 2 of *The Coleman Report* compared the quality of students' schools to determine whether all students experienced equal educational opportunity. Coleman and colleagues examined differences in teachers' salaries, the number of books in each library, the age of buildings and textbooks, and principal and teacher attitudes about the school and students. They also measured teachers' vocabulary aptitudes and the characteristics of each school's student body. Their most controversial finding was that the differences between schools attended by racial minorities and by whites were small, especially in comparison to differences in students' out-of-school resources. As a result of racial (and thus socioeconomic) segregation, the biggest differences across schools were in the characteristics of the student bodies. Segregation describes how some schools serve mostly racial minority students (who are more likely to be poor) and other schools serve mostly white or middle-class students. Because of segregation, the peer environments at the schools of black and white students exhibited very different social and academic characteristics.

Section 3: Impacts on Achievement

Section 3 of *The Coleman Report* explored which inputs made the most difference for students' academic achievement. Coleman and colleagues measured achievement through students' verbal and math skills, and knowledge in the sciences and humanities. Their data grouped students into the racial categories of white, black, Mexican American, Puerto Rican, Oriental American, and American Indian, but they especially focused on whites and blacks because of the political issues of the time. They found that whites and Asian Americans had the highest levels of achievement, and blacks and Puerto Ricans had the lowest levels. Section 3 established that students' family backgrounds were much more closely associated with their academic outcomes than the characteristics of their school.

Among school characteristics, the characteristics of students' peers mattered more than teachers' characteristics, and teachers' characteristics mattered more than other school characteristics like per-pupil expenditure. The characteristics of peers vary across schools as a result of residential and school segregation in America. Coleman and colleagues emphasized that the academic disadvantages of students in high-minority schools are compounded because they are surrounded by peers who are also disadvantaged. Peers may be related to students' achievement in part because of differences in social psychological characteristics. Of all of the measures of family background, and student and school characteristics, Coleman and his colleagues found that the degree to which students felt control over their environment was most closely related to their level of academic achievement. Racial minorities felt less control over their environment than white students. Although the degree to which students feel control is more closely related to family than school characteristics, Coleman and colleagues showed that students of every race feel more control over their environment in schools with a higher proportion of white students.

Conclusion

The major policy implication that emerged from these findings was that schools needed to be desegregated if black students were ever to experience comparable levels of achievement. Coleman and colleagues argued that educational policy shouldn't focus exclusively on "nonpersonal resources" in schools, especially because their findings showed that family background and peers (youths' two main social environments) mattered the most for academic achievement. Coleman and colleagues believed that the in-school experience would have to match the intensity of the out-of-school experience for schools to really impact achievement. The characteristics of the students at the school were the biggest difference across schools, and peers mattered more than other school characteristics for achievement levels. Thus, for schools to be more "intense" than families, policy reform would need to focus on changing peer environments. *The Coleman Report* concluded that peer environments were inherently unequal within a racially segregated system, and that school desegregation was essential.

Throughout the 1970s, school segregation levels decreased, particularly in the southern United States. The proportion of black students in majority white schools peaked in the 1980s. Busing students to schools outside of their neighborhood was one means by which this was accomplished. Because of high levels of public resistance and a reluctance to enforce legislative mandates, racial segregation in schools returned to 1960s levels by the mid-1990s. In 1975, Coleman recanted his position somewhat, stating that school desegregation efforts might actually increase residential segregation because of "white flight." White flight is when white people move away from areas as black people move in. Coleman attributed the failure of desegregation efforts in part to white flight. White flight contributed to the development of suburbs, and resulted in whites and blacks having separate school districts, rather than just separate schools.

Coleman said that desegregation efforts would now have to be extended beyond central cities to the entire metropolitan area to be effective. He also stated that desegregation may not be as worthwhile as he had suggested in the 1960s because the logistics were so taxing, and because later studies found that the effects were not as sizeable. Nonetheless, *The Coleman Report* continues to inspire debate and research.

Dara Shifrer
University of Texas at Austin

See Also: *Brown v. Board of Education*; Busing; Funding of Schools; Household Educational Resources; Racial Inequality: Achievement.

Further Readings

Borman, Geoffrey and Maritza Dowling. "Schools and Inequality: A Multilevel Analysis of Coleman's Equality of Educational Opportunity Data." *Teachers College Record*, v.112/5 (2010).

Coleman, James S. "Racial Segregation in the Schools: New Research With New Policy Implications." *Phi Delta Kappan*, v.57/2 (1975).

Coleman, James S., et al. *Equality of Educational Opportunity.* Washington, DC: National Center for Educational Statistics, 1966.

Gamoran, Adam and Daniel A. Long. *Equality of Educational Opportunity: A 40-Year Retrospective.* WCER Working Paper No. 2006-9. Madison: Wisconsin Center for Education Research, 2006.

Mosteller, Frederick and Daniel P. Moynihan. *On Equality of Educational Opportunity.* New York: Random House, 1972.

Ravitch, Diane. "*The Coleman Report* and American Education." In *Social Theory and Social Policy: Essays in Honor of James S. Coleman*, Aage B. Sørensen and Seymour Spilerman, eds. Westport, CT: Praeger, 1993.

College Advising

Advising, like other educational activities, is concerned with student development and learning. Advisors promote these basic tenets by supporting students in creating and fulfilling educational and life goals. The construction of these goals is shaped by opportunity, potential, and environment. Advising has a short formal history in American higher education, but is now a complex profession with varied models and frameworks underpinning service delivery.

Today, college advisors must be attuned to academic needs, as well as social and environmental factors, to make college graduation a reality as they assist students in degree attainment. Formal academic advising began at Johns Hopkins University in 1889, and by the late 1930s, most colleges offered such services. The impetus for this change was the increased specialization of coursework, majors, and careers, as well as the growth in the size of college administration. These developments elevated the role of faculty in aiding students in their elective course selections, which allowed students to individualize their educational experience and pursue their interests. Before this time, students had few choices regarding their coursework, so college advising played a small part in their academic experience. Administrators, faculty, and students viewed academic advising as a simple process, with little thought to the quality of the process or its implications.

In the mid-1930s, with the birth of the field of student affairs, the notion arose that colleges needed professionals to serve as student advocates and help students develop their life purpose inside and outside the classroom. With this professional rise, formal advising became an integral college service. Starting in the l940s, the stimulus for improving academic advising came with the G.I. Bill, the civil rights movement, and the development of community colleges. These factors created a spike in college attendance and increased the proportion of diverse students. Student success was linked to the quality of academic advising, but at the same time, advising appeared to be one of the weakest components of students' college experience. Concerns were raised that college advisors, particularly at community colleges, engaged in the active "cooling out" process of discouraging underprepared and/or ethnically diverse students from rigorous coursework and major choices, but there is little evidence of its existence. Finally, in 1979, college advising became a legitimate student affairs professional field with the creation of the National Academic Advising Association, an academic community established to improve college advising.

Models of College Advising

Although advising is often a shared role in the college context, two distinct models of advising exist. A decentralized advising structure comprises advising activities provided by faculty and/or staff within individual academic departments. Within this model, academic departments may choose to have only faculty provide advising, or may have an advising office in each department. Advantages to the decentralized model include lower costs, increased faculty–student interaction, and greater access to faculty expertise. Disadvantages may include accessibility, timeliness of advising, faculty unfamiliarity with policies and requirements, and inconsistency of advising practices. Also, students unsure of their major or changing majors may find it difficult to determine where to turn for help. The centralized model of advising consists of a separate administrative department for professional advisors. Advantages to this model include consistency in the quality of advising, availability of advisors, and a one-stop shop for students needing information and resources. Undecided students and those changing majors may find a centralized model more efficient in serving their needs.

Disadvantages to the centralized approach include the additional costs of operating a separate department, the loss of faculty–student relationships, and the loss of faculty expertise. Centralized models may also feel the strain of increased enrollment, and without a continual college commitment to the centralized model, advisor caseloads can quickly become unmanageable. Many campuses use a hybrid of these models, where advising is shared between advising centers and academic departments, with centralized advising for special populations, such as undeclared or first-year students. The hybrid approach seeks to take advantage of the strengths of both the decentralized and centralized models while reducing the effects of each model's weaknesses. However, the hybrid model has its own weaknesses, especially when students transition from one model to the other. As with centralized advising, the hybrid model necessitates close coordination among academic departments and centralized offices.

Traditional Versus Developmental Advising

Traditional advising, also known as prescriptive advising, consists of an authoritative relationship between advisor and student. In this method, the advisor is viewed as an expert who provides solutions to specific problems, without consideration of the whole student. The student development movement changed this as students began to be recognized as physical, mental, emotional, and spiritual men and women who develop in varying degrees in college. Within advising, this movement popularized a developmental advising approach. Arthur Chickering's seven vectors, Alexander Astin's theory of involvement, and Vincent Tinto's retention work played pivotal roles in calling for advising to be an interaction process of helping students develop autonomy, purpose, and competency, as well as encouraging them to take ownership of their educational process. In the developmental model, advisors must consider the student as a whole, with complex social and environmental factors that can facilitate or impede the attainment of educational and life goals. In practice, this can prove difficult because students may expect an authoritative answer to their questions. It can be easier for advisors to prescribe answers or assume what students' needs are, rather than spending the time and resources necessary to advise developmentally.

Advising Today's Students

Today, college advisors are charged with innovating the technological format and delivery of advising services as student needs have shifted and as student types have changed. For example, nontraditional and commuter students require advising typically at after-hours times, seeking flexible advising hours either in person or online. Additionally, college advisors must understand what type of student benefits from group advising versus one-on-one advising. Group advising promotes camaraderie through the facilitation of a shared experience in an academic context, which appears more beneficial for first-generation and other underrepresented students. One-on-one advising appears more beneficial for men, athletes, transfers, and distance learners because these students desire fast and personal service. Given the myriad of backgrounds and experiences, it is important for college advisors to use a variety of methods to help students reach their academic goals, including social work techniques and cross-cultural effective communication skills. Quality academic advising for all students is more than setting a student's schedule for the next semester; it involves an awareness of student development theory and looking at a student's life goals from a holistic perspective.

Sylvia L. M. Martinez
Brett Fugate
University of Colorado Colorado Springs

See Also: Cooled Out; Educational Aspirations/ Expectations; Higher Education; Sociocultural Approaches to Learning and Development.

Further Readings

Bahr, Peter R. "Cooling Out in the Community College: What Is the Effect of Academic Advising on Students' Chances of Success?" *Research in Higher Education*, v.49 (2008).

Gordon, Virginia N. *The Undecided College Student: An Academic and Career Advising Challenge*. 3rd ed. Springfield, IL: Charles C. Thomas, 2011.

Gordon, Virginia N., Wesley R. Habley, and Thomas J. Grites. *Academic Advising: A Comprehensive Handbook*. 2nd ed. San Francisco, CA: Jossey-Bass, 2008.

College Proximity

College proximity refers to the distance between a particular college or university and a prospective student's home. Research on the importance of college proximity to college enrollment decisions suggests that, all else being equal, most students would like to attend a college close to their home. Choosing a college based on proximity may have both positive and negative effects for college attendance, attainment, and career trajectory. Researchers began examining the effects of college proximity on the college choice process in the 1920s. Early studies suggested that cities or counties with colleges had higher rates of college attendance.

These results influenced some educators to call for greater proliferation of colleges, particularly community colleges, in order to increase attendance rates.

However, other research found that individual student characteristics, such as test scores and socioeconomic status, mediate the association between college attendance and living near a college. Early studies of the effects of proximity tended to focus on single institutions or communities and the financial benefits of attending a college close to home. Newer research also considers non-financial aspects, such as homesickness and cultural preferences for adult children to live at home until marriage. Proximity studies typically employ a measure of the distance to the college nearest each surveyed respondent. Recent research by Ruth N. López Turley, an associate professor of sociology at the University of Wisconsin, instead captures the number of colleges within a reasonable commuting range, since students with access to multiple colleges may not simply pick the nearest one.

Research on the effects of college proximity has identified two mechanisms by which having colleges nearby may influence the college choice process. First, higher rates of college attendance may be encouraged by the convenience of having a college in close proximity. Having colleges nearby makes gathering information about college simpler; prospective students can easily visit the campus, learn about application procedures, and speak with current students and faculty. Attending a nearby college is convenient financially; students can pay in-state tuition, live at home, and reduce commuting costs. Finally, attending a college in close proximity reduces the emotional toll of college attendance by allowing students to maintain frequent contact with friends and family. Second, higher rates of college-going may result from a predisposition to college attendance encouraged by having colleges nearby. That is, having a college in a particular community may engender a college-going culture among youth in that community. This college-going culture may result from university partnerships with local schools, businesses, and organizations. A local college's involvement with the community may foster a belief in the importance of higher education, and increase awareness of attendance requirements and other types of college knowledge.

Research suggests that convenience is the more likely explanation for increased college attendance in communities with colleges nearby. While the direct effect of college proximity on likelihood of attendance is small, a net of other variables, such as test scores and high school grades studies, find that geographic context is important for the college choice process.

The effects of college proximity vary by student income, gender, and race/ethnicity. Having a college nearby encourages college attendance among low-income students who cannot afford to move away from home. Some studies find that women are more likely to attend college if they can continue to live at home. Students and families may prefer a nearby college because of traditional gender roles that value protection of girls and women by keeping them close to home. Finally, family encouragement to stay at home while attending college varies by race/ethnicity.

Some Latin American groups may adhere to cultural values and traditions that include a preference for adult children to reside with parents and contribute to the family economy. Thus, some groups are more likely to make college decisions based on proximity, and to be diverted to a two-year college if a nearby four-year college is not available. In sum, college proximity appears to be important for the decision to attend college, and for selecting what type of college to attend. The convenience, cost savings, and emotional benefits of attending college nearby may be counterbalanced by some drawbacks: continued responsibilities to care for younger siblings, perform household chores, or contribute to the family economy, which may distract students from timely college completion. Finally, if choosing a nearby college means attendance at a two-year rather than a four-year college, the likelihood of four-year degree attainment may be decreased.

Sarah M. Ovink
Virginia Polytechnic Institute and State University

See Also: Community Colleges; Residential Mobility and Education; Transitions, School.

Further Readings

Cooke, Thomas J. and Paul Boyle. "The Migration of High School Graduates to College." *Educational Evaluation and Policy Analysis*, v.33 (June 2011).

Tinto, Vincent. "College Proximity and Rates of College Attendance." *American Educational Research Journal*, v.10/4 (1973).

Turley, Ruth N. López. "College Proximity: Mapping Access to Opportunity." *Sociology of Education*, v.82 (2009).

College Transferring

Since the 1970s, there has been a rise in the number of women, low-income, minority, and nontraditional age students entering college for the first time. As the demographic composition of American undergraduates has changed, so has the typical college experience. Today, well over 50 percent of undergraduates attend more than one institution. Transferring between different schools and types of schools (two- and four-year) has become increasingly common, and these patterns have become representative of larger inequalities in higher education. The traditional college transfer is a student moving from a two-year college to a four-year college or university. However, in recent years, not only are more students transferring than ever before, they are also moving among more institutions and in different directions.

There are many variations in the pattern of student movement among institutions. Along with traditional transferring, students may also engage in reverse transferring, moving from a four-year to a two-year school and lateral transferring, moving from a four-year to a four-year or from a two-year to a two-year school. Scholars have coined the term *swirling* to describe students who transfer among multiple schools, and the term *double-dipping* to identify students who maintain concurrent enrollment in two or more institutions. Research has found that students who begin their postsecondary careers in two-year colleges are more likely to transfer than those who start off in four-year schools, and students who attend public four-year institutions are more likely to transfer than those who attend private, nonprofit institutions. Lower socioeconomic status students and minorities have lower rates of traditional transfers and are more likely to engage in reverse transfers compared to other students. Higher socioeconomic status students are more likely to engage in lateral transfers among four-year institutions compared to lower socioeconomic status students.

The main reason why students transfer from a two-year to a four-year institution is to obtain a bachelor's degree. However, students face a number of obstacles along this path. Scholars have argued that many community colleges "cool out" bachelor's degree aspirations and instead funnel students toward more vocational programs and degrees. Others have found that community colleges "warm up" aspirations, but fail to make clear that remedial courses do not count toward accumulating transfer credits, causing students to become frustrated and spend time and money they did anticipate fulfilling prerequisites. Although there is a great deal of research on traditional transferring, it is only more recently that sociologists have focused on the other types of transferring, and there is less research on why students may engage in reverse or lateral transferring or swirl among institutions.

Some research has found that low academic achievement, particularly among lower socioeconomic status students, may play a role in why these students engage in reverse transfers to two-year colleges. Students may not be academically prepared for college-level coursework because of less rigorous high school curriculums and may struggle with maintaining sufficient grades to continue their enrollment. Researchers have also hypothesized that some students may engage in double-dipping (enrolling simultaneously in two or more intuitions) to avoid difficult courses at one institution or to make up credit deficits. Students may engage in reverse or lateral transfers because of financial constraints. Transferring to a community college from a four-year public or private university usually brings a reduction in tuition expenses and room and board (as most community college students live at home with their parents). This may partly explain why disadvantaged students are more likely to reverse transfer.

Recent research has found that students who begin their postsecondary careers in four-year schools and enroll in multiple intuitions are less likely to graduate, and if they do graduate, they take longer to do so. Researchers have also found that students from different social backgrounds pursue pathways with very different implications. Many middle- and upper-income students who pursue nontraditional college enrollment and attend multiple institutions continue to be enrolled in school, so they do not face significant barriers to finishing their college degrees in a timely manner. Lower income students, however, are more likely to take time off inbetween enrollments, which presents many challenges.

Megan Holland
Harvard University

See Also: Class Inequality: College Enrollment and Completion; Community Colleges; Racial Inequality: College Enrollment and Completion; Transitions, School.

Further Readings

Goldrick-Rab, Sara. "Following Their Every Move: An Investigation of Social-Class Differences in College Pathways." *Sociology of Education*, v.79/1 (2006).

McCormick, Alexander. "Swirling and Double-Dipping: New Patterns of Student Attendance and Their Implications for Higher Education." *New Directions for Higher Education*, v.2003/121 (2003).

Rosenbaum, James E., Regina Deil-Amen, and Ann E. Person. *After Admission: From College Access to College Success.* New York: Russell Sage Foundation, 2006.

U.S. Department of Education. "The Road Less Traveled: Students Who Enroll in Multiple Institutions." http://nces.ed.gov/pubsearch/pubsinfo.asp?pubid=2005157 (Accessed June 2012).

Colombia

Colombia is the fifth-largest Latin American country, with an area of 439,733 square miles. It is located in the northwestern corner of South America and is bordered by Panama to the northwest, Venezuela and Brazil to the east, and Peru and Ecuador to the southwest. The population of Colombia has grown dramatically over the past four decades, according to the World Bank, from 11.5 million in 1951 to an estimated 46 million in 2010, with more than 60 percent of the population between the ages of 15 and 64. The economy is diverse, with main exports of petroleum, coffee, coal, minerals, bananas, and flowers. Despite decades of sustained economic growth, Colombia remains one of the most unequal countries in Latin America and the Caribbean, with over one-third of the population living in poverty. Despite improvements over the last two decades in children's access to health care and school attendance, according to the World Bank, Colombia continues to struggle to provide food, clean water, safety, and a quality education for its children.

Colombia is one of the oldest democracies in Latin America. However, the government has battled economic inequality, poverty, and violence stemming from political terrorism, paramilitary groups, drug cartels, and criminal gangs for the last 50 years. According to United Nations Educational, Scientific and Cultural Organization (UNESCO), the armed conflict has negatively affected education through the destruction and closing of schools, displacement of children and teachers fleeing the conflict, and the financial burden of funding the military, which has meant fewer resources available for public education.

The Colombian educational system has three levels: preschool, basic cycle, and middle secondary. Preschool includes one compulsory year at age 5, followed by five years of basic primary and four years of basic secondary. The last level of schooling is middle secondary, lasting two years. Students who have completed 10 years of compulsory schooling plus the middle secondary must pass an examination for entrance into postsecondary institutions. While the constitution guarantees its citizens 10 years of education, it has not necessarily been free. Until recently, laws made it possible for local governments to charge fees for students in public schools. Private schools play a prominent role in Colombia. An estimated 20 percent of students attend private schools during the primary years and 35 percent of students are enrolled in private schools during the secondary grades. In the capital city of Bogotá, over 70 percent of secondary schools are private. During the late 1990s, a series of educational policies were implemented that increased governmental funding to improve access to education. These efforts were successful, particularly with respect to primary enrollment, which is nearly universal. Secondary enrollment has increased considerably, from 50 percent in 1991 to 68 percent in 2009, but is still quite low compared to other developed countries. Like many Latin American and Caribbean countries, Colombia continues to face problems with retention and completion of secondary schooling. Approximately one in 10 children do not complete primary and one in four students drop out before completing secondary school. These numbers are considerably higher in rural regions and among students from poorer families.

Constitutional reform in 2007 mandated yearly increases in educational spending. However, Colombia continues to struggle with issues of school quality and equity in the distribution of educational resources across different regions. For example, many schools still lack basic equipment such as textbooks and desks and suffer from low teacher quality. The Bogotá Chamber of Commerce recently found that more than one-quarter of schools do not have access to water, and almost half of all schools have no library and inadequate bathrooms. According to recent data compiled on academic performance from international projects, including the Programme for International Student Assessment (PISA) and Trends in International Mathematics and Science Study (TIMSS), student achievement is relatively low, particularly in math and science, compared to Latin American and other middle-income countries and given its total gross domestic product. For example, nearly half of students scored below basic proficiency in mathematics on the PISA standardized test. Colombia has instituted a number of reforms in recent decades aimed at improving school quality, including the Rural Education Program (Programa de Educacion Rural, PER), a secondary school voucher program for private schools, and the creation of a national system of evaluation in 1998 to evaluate student performance, ensure that students learn established levels of competency, and monitor disparities among schools across the country.

Christy Lleras
University of Illinois at Urbana-Champaign

See Also: Ecuador; Panama; Peru; Poverty and Education; Venezuela.

Further Readings
Rangel, Claudia and Christy Lleras. "Educational Inequality in Colombia: Family, Background, School Quality and Student Achievement in Cartagena." *International Studies in Sociology of Education*, v.20/4 (2009).

United Nations Educational, Scientific and Cultural Organization (UNESCO). "School-Based Violence in Colombia: Links to State-Level Armed Conflict, Educational Effects and Challenges" (2010). http://unesdoc.unesco.org/images/0019/001912/191228e.pdf (Accessed August 2012).

World Bank. *The Quality of Education in Colombia: An Analysis and Options for Policy Agenda.* Washington, DC: World Bank, 2008.

Colorado

Diverse groups and ideas in Colorado have long generated progress and conflict. Admitted as the 38th state to the Union in 1876, the eastern portion of the state was purchased by the federal government as part of the Louisiana Purchase in 1803, and the western portions were purchased from Mexico in the Treaty of Guadalupe Hidalgo in 1848. Native Americans created cliff dwellings in the state prior to 1299 at Mesa Verde; however, the Ute Indians are the oldest continuous residents of the state.

In 1541, Spanish explorers gave the state its name, which means "red" in Spanish, because of the red color of the Colorado River. In 1851, the first non-native settlement was established and ushered in a period of conflict between new settlers and the numerous Indian tribes, including the Ute, Cheyenne, Arapahoe, Kiowa, Comanche, Plains, Pawnee, and Sioux tribes, peaking in 1865 and ending in 1868. The discovery of gold in 1858 near what is now Denver precipitated the gold rush and drew miners to the area, which became a territory in 1861. Colorado was the second state in the nation to give women the right to vote, in 1894, following Wyoming's lead. Steel and sheep processing were two early industries in the state, followed by the growth of sugar beet refineries in the early 1900s, which grew as the state became the leader in irrigated land in the nation and produced more and diverse produce. Ski resorts and tourism boomed in the 1950s and 1960s, as well as the oil and coal industries.

Higher education was an early priority in the state. In 1864, 13 years after settlement of the state began, the Colorado Seminary was chartered, which later became the University of Denver. The School of Mines was established in 1871, as the railroad extended to Denver. In 1874, the University of Colorado was established in Boulder through a $15,000 appropriation of the territorial legislature and opened in 1877, the same year that an agricultural college was established in Fort Collins, which would later become Colorado State University. In 1874, the Colorado College was also established in Colorado Springs, where the Air Force Academy was later established in 1948. By 2010, 105 institutions of higher education existed in the state. There were 200 public school districts, 1,734 public schools, and 154 charter schools in Colorado in 2010, serving over 843,000 students, and 50,209 students attended the 398 private schools in the state. The public schools serve a diverse student population, with 57 percent of students reported as white, 32 percent Hispanic, 5 percent black, 3 percent Asian or Pacific Islander, and 1 percent Native American or Alaskan Native. Close to 40 percent of the students served by Colorado public schools qualified for free or reduced lunches.

Drawn by the growing agricultural, industrial, and service industries, diversity grew dramatically in Colorado in the 1960s, particular in the Denver area.

Table 1 Elementary and secondary education characteristics

	Colorado	U.S. (average)
Total number of schools	1,835	1,988
Total students	843,316	970,278
Total teachers	48,542.99	60,766.56
Pupil/teacher ratio	17.37	15.97

Source: U.S. Department of Education, National Center for Education Statistics, Common Core of Data (CCD), 2010–11.

Table 2 Elementary and secondary education finance

	Colorado	U.S. (average)
Total revenues	$8,113,611,122	$11,464,385,994
Total expenditures for education	$8,927,548,451	$11,712,033,839
Total current expenditures	$7,338,766,443	$9,938,906,259

Source: U.S. Department of Education, National Center for Education Statistics, Common Core of Data (CCD), "National Public Education Financial Survey," FY08 (2007–08).

By 1970, Latin Americans comprised 13 to 15 percent of the metropolitan area served by the Denver Public School (DPS) system, with 9.1 percent black, 89 percent white, and less than 1 percent Native American and Asian residents. In 1974, DPS became one of the first northern city school systems to be ordered by the U.S. Supreme Court to desegregate what was determined to be an unconstitutional dual system of schooling. Although the minority population of the metropolitan area continued to grow through the 1990s, with 23 percent Latin American and 12 percent black populations in the 1990 census, the state-supervised busing plan implemented in 1974 was discontinued in 1995. Citing that the current mayor of Denver was black, his predecessor was Hispanic, and that a black woman had been the superintendent of DPS, as well as black and Hispanic representation in both city and state elected positions, the ruling judge declared that, "The new political power of Denver's black and Hispanic populations will guarantee that a fair share of public school money will be channeled to largely black and Hispanic schools." Resegregation quickly took hold as a 2003 Harvard University study reported that the number of Latin American students attending a majority white school slipped from 62 percent in 1991 to 1992 to 44 percent in 2001 to 2002, while the state's Latin

American population continued to increase. Colorado was still ranked in the top 10 states for black student integration, despite a 16 percent decrease in black students attending a majority white school.

Educational equity and adequacy remain persistent challenges to Colorado policymakers. Educational funding to support the learning needs of students in the state is an ongoing challenge. Colorado state support ranks 40th for K–12 public education and 48th for higher education, a situation that has been exacerbated by economic slumps and three constitutional amendments. The Gallagher Amendment was passed in 1982, setting a statewide cap on the taxable values of residences. The Taxpayer Bill of Rights (TABOR) was approved in 1992, limiting annual growth in state revenue to inflation plus the percentage of change in the state's population. Amendment 23, passed by the voters in 2000, requires the state to increase per pupil funding and total state funding for categorical K–12 programs by at least the rate of inflation, plus one percentage point through fiscal year 2010–11, and by the rate of inflation thereafter.

The Gallagher and TABOR amendments place the state in a precarious position to meet the fiscal responsibilities required by Amendment 23, as the state is required to balance its budget for each fiscal year, although Referendum C in 2005 allowed money collected over the TABOR limit to be spent on public education through 2010. Since the 2009 recession, public schools have had to cut millions from their budgets annually in terms of staff and programs, while public universities and colleges have implemented annual tuition increases in the double digits. How resources can be used to equitably meet the educational needs of an increasingly diverse student population remains the critical question in Colorado.

Linda R. Vogel
University of Northern Colorado

See Also: Native American Students; Neighborhood Effects; Racism in Education.

Further Readings

Colorado Department of Education. http://www.cde.state.co.us (Accessed August 2012).

Forrest, Kenton. *History of the Public Schools of Denver: A Brief History (1859–1989) and Complete Building Survey of the Denver Public Schools.* Denver, CO: Tramway Press, 1989.

Lee, Chungmei. "Denver Public Schools: Resegregation, Latino Style" (January 2006). http://sobek.colorado.edu/~preuhs/urban/denversegregation.pdf (Accessed December 2011).

Community Colleges

The community college originated in the United States in the early 20th century to answer the need for a more skilled workforce. Today, community colleges typically offer a terminal two-year associate's degree designed to prepare students either for the lower-to-mid-level skilled job market or for transfer to a bachelor's degree–granting institution. Community colleges typically have three main objectives: to expand educational opportunities to a greater portion of the population (especially under-represented minorities and older students); to provide training for the immediate job market (particularly in technical fields); and to serve the local community by promoting the development of an educated and skilled local workforce, offering noncredit courses in a wide range of academic and nonacademic subjects, and providing cultural and technical resources to the community.

At times, the wide range of goals of community colleges has made it difficult for them to fulfill their varied mandates. Today's community college is a combination of two forms of educational institution that arose at the turn of the last century: vocational training programs (often focusing on teacher education) that were tacked on to public high schools, and small private colleges that focused on meeting local needs. Early community colleges were notable for their accessibility to women, as teacher education was typically one of their primary missions. About half of early community colleges were publicly funded, while the other half were private. From the 1930s to the 1980s, the number of nonpublic community, junior, and technical colleges declined, however, while the number of public schools in these categories increased significantly. In the 1960s, the number of community colleges and attendees grew significantly as education was touted as an important means of ameliorating societal inequalities. From 1960 to 1990, as community colleges expanded their focus on occupational training and continuing education, they decreased their focus on facilitating the transfer of students to four-year colleges and universities.

From 1972 to 1996, the proportion of students beginning at a four-year college and transferring down to a community college nearly tripled, from 45 to 11 percent. The interest in community colleges' traditional "transfer mission" (to four-year institutions) has once again increased in the past decade; as costs at four-year colleges and universities rise, students find that beginning their college career at less expensive community colleges has financial pay-offs.

In January 2011, there were a total of 1,167 community colleges in the United States, out of which 993 were public, 143 private, and 31 under Native American tribal authority. In the fall of 2008, 12.4 million students in the United States were enrolled in community colleges, of which 7.4 million were enrolled for credit and 5 million on a noncredit basis. In the same year, 40 percent of community college students were enrolled full time, while 60 percent were enrolled part time. The majority (58 percent) was women and the minority (42 percent) was men. In the 2007 to 2008 academic year, the average (mean) age of a community college student was 28 years old, and the median age was 23.

Approximately 39 percent of students were 21 years old or younger; 45 percent were between the ages of 22 and 39; and 15 percent were age 40 or older. A total of 42 percent of students represented the first generation in their families to attend college. In the fall of 2008, community college students constituted 44 percent of all U.S. undergraduates and 43 percent of all first-time freshmen. Only about 10 percent of students who enter community colleges end up getting a bachelor's degree, even though studies show that between 50 and 80 percent of incoming community college students enter with that goal. Possible institutional explanations for low transfer rates include the inability of community colleges to prepare students and insufficient remedial programming. Other explanations focus on the individual student and may include poor prior academic preparation, low aspirations, or an inability to pay for school. Macrolevel explanations could involve social and political forces such as economic recession, political underrepresentation, and shifts in the labor market.

Although much of the support for community colleges is based on the assumption that they provide a bridge to four-year colleges and universities, it has been argued that they also play a large role in dissuading many students from transferring by "cooling-out" or managing their ambitions. According to one argument, many unprepared students are encouraged to attend community college and are then steered into vocational fields as it becomes apparent that they are not viable candidates for transfer to four-year institutions. The likelihood of transfer is strongly influenced by parental socioeconomic status. Also, blacks and Hispanics have lower transfer rates than whites and Asians (although this is not statistically significant if compared with whites of similar age, gender, and socioeconomic status). Since the 1990s, gender no longer has a powerful effect on transfer rates. The age of college entrance does, however, have a powerful impact on likelihood of transfer, with older entering students less likely to transfer than their younger peers—a situation that can largely be explained by differences in educational aspirations, choice of major, and external demand. Over the years, many community colleges have undergone a process of vocationalization, where their focus shifted from liberal arts preparation to training for the immediate job market. This vocationalization was a reaction to the mismatch between their students' aspirations and the occupational opportunities available to them, and served as a way for administrators to find their niche and market their institutions.

At present, there are three critical issues facing community colleges. First, there is the question of whether public community colleges should redefine their historic commitment to open access. Related to this is the question of whether remedial classes should continue to be offered by regular departments or transferred to a separate division. Second, there is the question of whether public community colleges should form mutually beneficial alliances or partnerships with for-profit "career" colleges. Third, there is the question of whether public community colleges should establish a separate national accrediting body. The present day also brings with it a call for community colleges to offer more distance learning opportunities and course offerings with an international focus, while enduring constraints in public funding.

Jill M. Smith
Brandeis University

See Also: Career and Technical Education; College Advising; College Transferring.

Further Readings
American Association of Community Colleges. "Fast Facts." http://www.aacc.nche.edu/AboutCC/Pages/fastfacts.aspx (Accessed December 2011).

Brint, Steven and Jerome Karabel. *The Diverted Dream: Community Colleges and the Promise of Educational Opportunity in America, 1900–1985*. New York: Oxford University Press, 1989.

Dougherty, Kevin J. and Gregory S Kienzl. "It's Not Enough to Get Through the Open Door: Inequalities by Social Background in Transfer From Community Colleges to Four-Year Colleges." *Teachers College Record*, v.108 (2006).

Complexity Theory

Complexity theory offers a means to conceptualize the workings of nonlinear systems as their multiple interacting and diverse elements adapt to constantly changing environments. Such nonlinear systems could include students, classrooms, schools, school districts, or national educational systems. To enact the analytic potential of complexity theory, theorists draw extensively on the notion of the complex adaptive system. This heuristic—derived from crossdisciplinary research in fields as varied as economics, physics, ecology, and math—can illuminate how a system's diverse elements interact to generate novel, emergent behavior for the system as a whole.

This conceptual structure helps one understand what a system does as it negotiates and adapts to ever-shifting contexts. Nothing stands alone; everything is interconnected and interdependent. In education, countless studies acknowledge that schools are systems made up of subsystems, embedded in still other systems. It is sensible, then, to understand schools and related educational processes systemically, to explore the dynamic interactions on and between multiple levels of the system. This discussion of complexity theory highlights its metaphorical potential. Mathematically inclined theorists also enact this analytic construct in compelling ways, while still drawing on a common conception of the complex adaptive system.

Ontologically, relationships are at the heart of complexity theory, and those that emerge in complex systems reveal a random-but-predictable nature. Because individual elements possess autonomy and can act to both shape and be shaped by the system, one cannot know how they will self-organize. Nonetheless, system dynamics consistently generate discernible patterns and fall within standard ranges. This random-but-predictable aspect of complex systems emerges because even though individual elements could act quite randomly, control parameters shape interactions so that distinct and somewhat consistent outcomes emerge, lending a measure of predictability to an ultimately unpredictable system. Even though complex systems reveal distinct patterns and trends, at differing levels, a complex system can look very different. Interactions on one level may generate macro-level patterns of a decidedly different nature. The disparate but interconnected elements, interacting in unpredictable ways, collectively accomplish what individual elements could not do independently, and in ways that cannot be preordained or predicted. A single brain cell can accomplish relatively little, but every brain holds amazing potential. Similar structures at different levels of a complex system produce radically different outcomes.

Moreover, as complex adaptive systems, including schools, comprise multiple elements that affect and are affected by each other in a continuous feedback loop, they cannot be fully understood by merely assessing their component parts. Such systems should be understood at their point of emergence, when system elements self-organize into discernible patterns—when the system is doing what the system does. In the complex adaptive system of schools and schooling, complexity theory tends to focus on relationships among students, teachers, and administrators. When most effective, complex adaptive systems are said to be on the "edge of chaos." That is, interactions among elements are not so random and unpredictable that the system seems overwhelmed. But neither are interactions so routine, predetermined, and predictable that the system stagnates, reproducing the status quo ad infinitum. A healthy complex system is a learning system in a state of constant disequilibrium, balanced between chaos and stagnation, while continuously responding to diverse circumstances based on information fed back into the system. When on the edge of chaos, a synergy can emerge among system elements. When interactions are complementary and mutually beneficial, the sum of the whole can exceed the sum of the individual parts.

Consider the failure of various educational reform initiatives. In brief, many have ignored the multiple, interrelated, and interacting elements of the educational system. Conceptualizing the educational system as composed of isolated and discrete structures, they assume that complex phenomena can be understood by analyzing their constituent parts, when in fact the sum of the whole is greater and more complex than the sum of the individual parts. Consequently, reforms often modify one or two system elements, apart from related elements, expecting to generate the intended outcome through a linear, cause-and-effect relationship. Those who promoted school integration, for instance, assumed that mixing African American and white students would lead to greater achievement by African American students.

Little attention was given to the processes of school integration. In similar fashion, many No Child Left Behind policies assume that implementing high-stakes, standardized exams will drive enhanced student achievement. From the perspective of complexity theory, both initiatives appear naïve. More factors, some indeterminable at the outset, ultimately shape student achievement. If reforms ignore the multiple, interacting, and shifting factors of a complex adaptive system, they will likely reproduce the status quo. The longstanding achievement gap between Anglo and Asian students and their African American and Latin American counterparts speaks to the power of the educational status quo to reproduce itself, despite well-intended efforts at school integration. Likewise, the performance of U.S. public school students on international exams and the National Assessment of Educational Process reveals that high-stakes exams have not transformed student learning in the United States. From a complexity perspective, these reforms ignored the systemic nature of educational reform, ultimately attending to too few of the many elements that comprise the educational system.

Patrick J. McQuillan
Boston College

See Also: Busing; No Child Left Behind; Resistance Theory; School Organization; Urban Schooling.

Further Readings

Bryk, A. S. and B. Schneider. *Trust in Schools: A Core Resource for Improvement*. New York: Russell Sage Foundation, 2002.

Buell, M. J. and D. J. Cassidy. "The Complex and Dynamic Nature of Quality in Early Care and Educational Programs: A Case for Chaos." *Journal of Research in Childhood Education*, v.15/2 (2001).

Davis, B., et al. *Engaging Minds: Learning and Teaching in a Complex World*. Mahwah, NJ: Erlbaum, 2000.

Fullan, M. *Leading in a Culture of Change*. San Francisco: Jossey-Bass, 2001.

Hoban, G. *Teacher Learning for Educational Change*. Philadelphia: Open University Press, 2002.

Wheatley, M. J. *Leadership and the New Science: Discovering Order in a Chaotic World*. San Francisco: Berrett-Koehler Publishers, 1999.

Concerted Cultivation/ Natural Growth

Annette Lareau drew the concepts of "concerted cultivation" and the "accomplishment of natural growth" from her qualitative research on 88 families in the midwestern and northeastern United States. She carried out intensive naturalistic observations of 12 of these families in the mid-1990s. In *Unequal Childhoods*, Annette Lareau concludes that middle-class families differ from working-class and poor families in key ways: organized leisure activities, language, boundaries between adults and children, interactions with kin, and interventions with institutions. Working-class and poor parents enact the accomplishment of natural growth. Their children participate in few, if any, organized leisure activities. Parents use directives in speaking to children, see a clear boundary between the activities of adults and children, families have extensive interactions with kin, and parents do not tend to intervene with institutions on their children's behalf. Middle-class parents enact concerted cultivation, attempting to develop children's talents and abilities through organized leisure activities and lessons, by eliciting children's thoughts and feelings, and actively intervening on their children's behalf in institutional settings.

Current professional standards encourage a pattern of what amounts to concerted cultivation, as parents are encouraged to deliberately foster children's cognitive and social skills. Annette Lareau asserts that childrearing coheres by social class, with social class more predictive than either gender or race.

Under the accomplishment of natural growth, working-class and poor parents believe that children will thrive with food, shelter, and love. Parents keep children safe, regulate behavior, enforce discipline, and allow children long stretches of leisure time, without the intervention of adults. These children enjoy a relatively autonomous world, where they spend time with siblings and cousins, with much informal, spontaneous play. These children take real pleasure in their play and generally do not complain about being "bored." In these families, adults do not emphasize children's performance, and do not seem obligated to cultivate children's displays of creativity. Language is a practical tool; parents offer short, clear directives, and expect children to be polite and respectfully obedient. For example, one mother in the study would instruct children to wash up by simply saying "bathroom," while handing the child a washcloth. Parents do not typically negotiate or offer explanations. Within institutional settings, parents depend on the expertise of professionals. Parents may distrust the judgment of teachers, but tend to not to openly challenge them.

Middle-class parents who undertake concerted cultivation try to actively develop their children's talents through organized activities, word play, and involvement in institutional settings. Concerted cultivation is characterized by a frenetic pace of daily life, as children tend to participate in a multitude of organized activities, such as sports, music, and other lessons. Spontaneous play is rare, as activities and play dates are organized by adults. Given scheduling demands of children's activities, time spent with extended family is rare. Parents emphasize reasoning, engaging in verbal jousting and word play; they rarely use directives, except in matters of health or safety, such as insisting that their children eat vegetables. Instead, parents deliberately and systematically use extensive verbal negotiation with children; Annette Lareau observed a general pattern of children bargaining with parents for small accommodations. Parents groom their children in advance of interactions with professionals. For instance, one middle-class mother coaxed her son prior to a doctor's appointment, prompting him to assertively ask questions; consequently, her son easily engages the doctor in conversation.

The logic of concerted cultivation holds that parents should closely monitor their children's progress in institutional settings, intervening early and often, if needed. For instance, after her daughter initially missed the admission cutoff for a gifted-and-talented program, one middle-class mother quickly and successfully appealed the school's decision, and was able to have her child admitted.

Constraint, Entitlement and the Transmission of Differential Advantages

Annette Lareau argues that working-class and poor children, raised with the accomplishment of natural growth, tend to develop an emerging sense of constraint. Like their parents, these children are cautious and at times distrustful of professionals. They are not coached to be assertive, and are unlikely to negotiate or tailor interactions to their advantage. With no experience making demands on professionals, when they confront institutions, families are unable to make rules work in their favor. In contrast, under the logic of concerted cultivation, middle-class children come to expect that institutional rules will be tailored to their needs. They see themselves as entitled to special attention from adults, with a right to pursue their preferences in institutional settings. They are at ease when interrupting a professional, or making demands, such as asking a teacher to lower the blinds in a classroom. These two logics of childrearing are not equally valued in social settings. Schools support concerted cultivation, as teachers selectively praise organized activities like tournaments over informal games played with cousins. Professionals advocate developing children's educational interests, eliciting their thoughts and opinions, and taking an active role in schooling. These principles are out of step with the tenets of the accomplishment of natural growth. For instance, when one working-class mother adopted a passive role—deferring to teachers, and seeing her daughter's education as the school's responsibility—teachers emphasized the importance of parental involvement, and reported being disappointed that the mother failed to take a more active, interventionist role.

Families who undertake concerted cultivation as a child rearing strategy transmit negotiation and other verbal skills. Children become skilled at reasoning, advocating for themselves, and customizing interactions with institutions to suit their needs. Annette Lareau maintains that interventions with teachers, coaches, and others yielded real social profits, as when one mother successfully lobbied for her daughter's entry into a gifted program. Yet, concerted cultivation does not guarantee advantage, as not all parents' interventions are successful. Annette Lareau argues that more attention should be paid to the drawbacks of middle-class parenting. For instance, middle-class children are prone to whining, and appear disoriented when they are not presented with an organized activity. Children raised according to the logic of the accomplishment of natural growth are very autonomous in filling their time and easily amuse themselves. Yet, this social competence is potentially less valuable than the verbal skills, confidence with authority, and feeling comfortable making demands on professionals that are characteristic of middle-class children Annette Lareau observed, who are raised through concerted cultivation.

Linda Quirke
Wilfrid Laurier University

See Also: Bernstein, Basil; Childhood; Class Inequality: Achievement; Ethnography; Extracurricular Activities; Lareau, Annette; Parental Cultural Capital; Parental Involvement; Qualitative Research on Education.

Further Readings

Bodovski, Katerina and George Farkas. "'Concerted Cultivation' and Unequal Achievement in Elementary School." *Social Science Research*, v.37 (2008).

Bourdieu, Pierre. "The Forms of Capital." In *Handbook of Theory and Research for the Sociology of Education*, J. G. Richardson, ed. Westport, CT: Greenwood Press, 1986.

Hofferth, Sandra. "Linking Social Class to Concerted Cultivation, Natural Growth and School Readiness." In *Disparities in School Readiness: How Families Contribute to Transitions Into School*, Alan Booth et al., eds. New York: Lawrence Erlbaum Associates, 2008.

Irwin, Sarah and Sharon Elley. "Concerted Cultivation? Parenting Values, Education and Class Diversity." *Sociology*, v.45/3 (2011).

Vincent, Carol and Stephen J. Ball. "'Making Up' the Middle-Class Child: Families, Activities and Class Dispositions." *Sociology*, v.41/6 (2007).

Conflict Theory of Education

Conflict theory posits that conflict is a fundamental part of the social order, and that schools are a critical site in the reproduction of social inequality, particularly class conflict and racial stratification. Schools are not meritocratic; individual talent and hard work do not necessarily guarantee success. Larger social forces produce unequal outcomes that favor the powerful and inequality within and among schools helps maintain reproduction of the status quo. Conflict theorists see education as maintaining existing power structures while creating a docile workforce or underclass. Karl Marx, Max Weber, and Émile Durkheim address the relationship of education and social conflict, albeit in different ways. Conflict theory in education remains a robust area of inquiry. Key contemporary works were authored in the late 1970s and early 1980s by Randall Collins et al. Durkheim did not envision long-term social conflict as inevitable or likely. Rather, Durkheim saw widespread education, alongside industrialization and specialization, as a way to reduce class conflict by creating new relationships and opportunities for workers and managers alike. Marx, on the other hand, argued that class conflict was inevitable and steadily increasing, ultimately leading to the overthrow of capitalism. Education could not reduce or transform class conflict; it could only reflect ongoing exploitations and struggle. Weber also focused on the importance of conflict in society, but did not see the overthrow of capitalism as an end to exploitation and domination. Rather, inequalities of power, prestige, and income would remain a source of conflict in capitalist and non-capitalist societies.

The social and political tumult of the late 1960s and 1970s was a crucial period for contemporary conflict theories of education. Conflict theorists advanced two main arguments regarding meritocracy and ideology. The first argument is that, contrary to conventional wisdom, schools are not meritocratic institutions. Rather than a system where intelligent and hard-working students from all class backgrounds can succeed, go on to further education, and then join the professional class through a high-status education requiring advanced educational credentials, modern conflict theorists see schools as places that reproduce social inequality. In a society where jobs are allotted based on credentials (credentials that more often than not reflect class status, not individual merit or achievement), the relationship of education to occupation is weak. Outside of families, schools are the major sorting mechanism in an unequal society. The extreme difference in outcomes of schooling students from different class backgrounds is not the result of differences in innate intelligence, but rather the result of the ways schools sort students in order to serve the interests of dominant status groups. The second argument is that, contrary to conventional wisdom, schools are not ideologically neutral places.

Schools teach a hidden curriculum of class status and power. Skills, knowledge, and values taught in school serve to reinforce the power of the middle and upper classes. Schools teach membership in a particular status group, from self-presentation, dress, and manners to tastes and interests. Students from high-status groups tend to attend high-status schools, where they fit into the class culture of the organization. High-status occupations then tend to hire graduates of high-status schools because those graduates share the same status culture. Students from low-status groups face substantial handicaps from their earliest moments in schools. These handicaps are exacerbated by sorting and tracking in and among schools. While students from low-status groups often believe that educational credentials may be the key to elite professions, this is the exception, rather than the rule.

Social Reproduction of Inequality

In most industrialized nations, more people have more access to more education than at any other time in history, but increased access to education and rising attainment in school credentials have failed to create the system of meritocracy and social mobility often ascribed to widespread education. Rather than creating social and economic opportunities, schools serve to maintain the interests of those in power by creating a docile workforce while rewarding students from economically powerful groups. For conflict theorists, schools are a primary and crucial site of social reproduction. Class conflict, racial stratification, and other social inequalities are maintained through various sorting and legitimizing mechanisms within and among schools. IQ testing, standardized testing, tracking, and magnet schools are all examples of processes that sort students to provide different access to curriculum, resources, and power.

School funding based on property taxes create a system of separate and unequal public schools based on geographic location, which is associated with race and class inequality. While schools and society promote a meritocratic ideal, where individual hard work leads to economic and social success, conflict theory holds that a meritocratic view is a sort of false consciousness, working to privilege those with power, by legitimizing their structural advantages as the result of individual effort. Conflict theory counters the notion of education as the key to social mobility, instead analyzing how schools treat individual students and demographic groups differently in order to maintain status quo.

The conflict model theorizes that education is most important as symbolic capitol, and is relatively unimportant in occupational attainment. For jobs where educational credentials are seen as important, it is actually education's symbolic function as a credential and as a representation of membership in an elite status group. For example, the Harvard University of the early 20th century was seen as two separate places: that of the eating clubs (elite status groups) and that of the scholarship boys (subordinate status groups). The two Harvards were not equivalent and rarely mixed socially, in school or after graduation. For students at the elite Harvard, social connections and family history largely determined their admission to the school and virtual guarantee of high social status after graduation. Academics rarely entered the picture, exemplified in the notion of "the gentleman's C." For the scholarship boys, many of whom were Jewish or ethnic whites from lower- to middle-class backgrounds, their presence at Harvard was based on academic performance. Some of these scholarship boys did rise in social and economic status based on their Harvard diplomas, but in many cases that was from the impact of the Harvard credential. Then and now, academic content mastery rarely connects directly to jobs.

The link between social class and occupational attainment has remained strong throughout the 20th century, although the increased presence of women and those from subordinate status groups (e.g., people of color, Jews, and first-generation immigrants) has changed school and work demographics to some extent. Conflict theory in general examines how schools, from kindergartens to universities, reproduce and legitimate this link between social class and occupation. Rather than technical skills, intellectual prowess, or academic achievement, education serves more as a mark of membership in a particular status group. As educational requirements for employment continue to rise, the relationship of educational content to job skills becomes increasingly divergent. Social status, based on class and race or ethnicity, remains a critical determinant not only for occupation, but also school experience and outcome. Educational requirements or credentials reflect the interests of the powerful, even as education is touted as the key to social mobility and economic success.

Sorting

Schools reproduce social inequality through sorting. Students are sorted into groups largely based on social class; these groups often attend separate schools, and within the same school they often have such different access to resources and opportunities that it is as if students attend physically separate schools. In a system where there is a semblance of school "choice" between public, private, parochial, and charter schools, family socioeconomic status often determines which school a student will attend. Wealthy families have the most "choice," in that they have the financial and social resources to choose a private or parochial school. In school systems where funding is dependent on property taxes, areas with wealthy homeowners have schools with more resources. Students from wealthy homes have social and cultural capital, or modes of talk, behavior, dress, experience, and entitlement that are aligned with the dominant class. Teachers and standardized tests often conflate middle- or upper-class culture with intelligence, intentionally or otherwise. Students from dominant status groups are multi-privileged, not only in their social standing and family resources, but also in the way their teachers treat them.

If a kindergarten teacher asks her students, "Should we take our seats now?" when it is time to sit on the floor in a circle, students who are familiar with that sort of indirect questioning as a command are likely to sit on the floor in a circle. The teacher may see those students as "school-read," "well-socialized," and "intelligent," but many argue that what is being rewarded is home class culture. Broadly speaking, middle-class white children are likely to speak the same language at school as at home—not just English (in the United States), but a particular kind of English. In contrast, students who hear "Should we take our seats now?" as an actual choice, may choose to continue playing, or stand in the corner. The teacher sees these students, often from working-class or subordinate status group homes, as disruptive or less intelligent. Had students been told, "It is time to sit in a circle on the floor," the outcome may have been different. This is just one example of the subtle ways that class status is translated into an identity as a successful or failing student within the classroom.

Outside of rewarding or penalizing individual students for class status, schools also sort students within the same school by tracking. In the United States, students of color and students from poor and working-class homes are overrepresented in special education and behaviors challenged classrooms, vocational (non-academic) tracks, and other low-level academic and basic skill classes. Students for whom English is not their first language are often separated from the rest of the school in English as a second language (ESL) classrooms, where material is covered more slowly and at a more basic level than in other classrooms. Students are less likely to be able to switch to more challenging classes because they do not have the background material. At the same time, white students and students from class-privileged homes are overrepresented in advanced placement and gifted classes that cover academically challenging material, prepare students for college entrance exams, and socialize students in the habits and language of the middle- and upper-middle classes.

Another way that students are sorted by "intelligence" or "ability" that actually rewards social class privilege is standardized testing. From IQ tests to the SATs, test questions not only ask students to reflect on material that may be familiar to those in privileged situations, the tests also use class-coded language. High school students in a well-resourced public school that offers AP calculus and other high-level math and science classes will likely have more exposure to the test material in their daily classes than students in a school where "business math" (basic arithmetic) is a core course offering. In the case of college entrance exams, students from privileged backgrounds are also more likely to have access to private test preparation coaching, practice tests, and even in-school support for optimum test results. Given the ways in which schools reproduce inequality, conflict theorists predict that most educational reform would need to be accompanied by broader social and economic changes in order to be effective

Carolyn Chernoff
University of Pennsylvania

See Also: Bowles, Samuel and Herbert Gintis; Class Inequality: Achievement; Cultural Capital; Durkheim, Emile; Functionalist Theory of Education; Labor Market Effects on Education; MacLeod, Jay; Marx, Karl; Meritocracy; Social Capital; Standardized Testing; Weber, Max.

Further Readings

Bourdieu, P. *Reproduction.* Beverley Hills, CA: Sage, 1977.

Bowles, Samuel and Herbert Gintis. *Schooling in Capitalist America.* New York: Basic Books, 1976.

Collins, Randall. *The Credential Society.* New York: Academic Press, 1979.

Congo, Democratic Republic of the

The Democratic Republic of the Congo (DRC) lies at the center of the African continent, bordering the Central African Republic and south Sudan in the north; Uganda, Rwanda, Burundi and Tanzania in the east; Zambia and Angola in the south; and the Republic of Congo in the west. It became an independent nation in 1960, following 23 years of being privately owned by King Leopold II, and 52 years under colonial Belgian rule. The DRC's size is estimated at around 905,000 square miles and the population at over 70 million. Since its inception at the Berlin Conference in 1885, the county's name has repeatedly changed: from the Congo Free State (1885), to Belgian Congo (1908), Republic of Congo–Kinshasa (1960), Democratic Republic of Congo (1964), Republic of Zaire (1971), and then the Democratic Republic of Congo in 1997. From 1885 to the present, the DRC's history is marked by many years of political instability linked to post-independence violence between 1960 and 1964, a military coup in 1965, armed rebellions in 1977 and 1978, invasion by foreign armies in 1996, and armed rebellions between 1998 and 2012. Political instability and lack of progressive educational policies are major obstacles to economic, political and social development.

The colonial power structure heavily influenced the Democratic Republic of the Congo by elevating educated natives into leadership roles. The colonial leadership model also left lasting impacts on the educational system in the country. Congolese natives practiced indigenous education before Belgian rule. Through separate rites of passage, boys and girls were initiated into adult life differently, but following a common role-play model. Boys were trained in productive skills, prepared to tend the land, then to become husbands, family providers, and community leaders. Girls were also trained to tend the land and were prepared to become wives, child bearers, and mothers. Colonial formal education replaced indigenous education, but it did not significantly alter the social structure of education. Formal education, part of the "civilizing mission" of the Belgians, was technically introduced to the Congo in 1906, when King Leopold II signed an agreement with the Vatican to establish elementary schools run by Catholic missions, but funded and supervised by the colonial government. Very few schools existed before then. Furthermore,

colonial education was male-dominated, creating a class of Westernized elite (*les évolués*). Members of the new elite were integrated into "civilized" high culture, and they enjoyed power and privileges over their less educated peers and women.

The colonial authority saw substantial economic capital, worthy of investment, in male education. Female education offered moral benefits to ensure family cohesion. Congolese natives likely foresaw opportunities for gaining access to material privileges by associating with white people. However, the colonizer feared that formal education might plant seeds of rebellion and political activism in the hearts of the new elite. In a sense, colonial educational policies reinforced and fostered arrogant and sexist attitudes in regard to the role of other members of Congolese society. After indigenous Congolese gained political sovereignty in 1960, their administration took steps toward equality of opportunity in educating the young. Nevertheless, the social and cultural past of the Congolese people virtually ensured that the gap would persist between boys and girls, and between the elite and the uneducated members of society.

The Democratic Republic of the Congo needs policies to ignite a spirit of creativity and innovation and to lift up the much-neglected educational system. Commitment to both the quality and the quantity of education will help resolve social and cultural ambivalence, setting the course for effective change. As long as educational disparities and social inequalities persist, it will be hard to rise above the social forces that have shaped and informed Congolese educational policies for over a century. Overcoming arrogance and patriarchal attitudes that both the colonial authority and indigenous customs upheld in defining the identities and roles of women, girls, and the uneducated masses remains a challenge. A reversal of such long-held beliefs has the potential to free the Congo from captivity to the past and allow orderly emergence as a nation that can tap into female energy, not only to give life, but also to nurture a sense of collective consciousness and care in order to address the Congo's most pressing cultural, economic, political, and social issues.

Kiluba L. Nkulu
University of Kentucky

See Also: Cultural Capital and Gender; Educational Policymakers; Feminist Critiques of Educational Practices.

Further Readings

Georis, Pol. *Essai d'Acculturation par l'Enseignement Primaire au Congo.* Brussels: Centre scientifique et médical de l'Université libre de Bruxelles (CEMUBAC), 1962.

Gingrich, L. Newt. *Belgian Education Policy in the Congo, 1945–1960.* Ph.D. dissertation. New Orleans, LA: Tulane University, 1971.

Nkulu, Kiluba L. *Serving the Common Good: A Postcolonial African Perspective on Higher Education.* New York: Peter Lang, 2005.

Connecticut

Though the third-smallest state geographically, Connecticut ranks 29th in population (3.5 million). A total of 23 percent of the population is less than 18 years old. An affluent state, Connecticut ranks third in U.S. income (median $67,000). Median home values are $279,000. Almost 90 percent of state residents earned a high school diploma and nearly 35 percent possessed a bachelor's degree or more. Over 9 percent of the state population lives below the federal poverty line, and unemployment was 8.4 percent as of November 2011. Connecticut has had the worst jobs rate in the United States for the last 20 years, with stagnant job creation and continued loss of high-skilled positions and simultaneous increase in low-skilled and low-wage positions. The loss of skilled labor positions is fueling, in part, Governor Malloy's 2012 education reform effort, which aims to eliminate the achievement gap and educate Connecticut workers for highly skilled positions, thereby attracting and retaining companies dependent upon this segment of the labor force.

Historically, Connecticut's public education system parallels the development of public education throughout New England. Colonial townships organized a local education system consisting of a teacher who instructed a multi-age class in a one-room school house or in their home. State oversight of public education commenced in the 19th century under the efforts of Henry Barnard, who fought to ensure universal access to schools. In 1899, compulsory education became law, ordering children ages 7 through 16 to attend school. State-supported higher education began in 1849 with the funding of a teacher-training

academy, the New Britain Normal School (later renamed Central Connecticut State University), followed by the creation of the University of Connecticut (1881). Several notable elite private institutions were founded in Connecticut, including the country's third oldest independent school, the Hopkins School (1660), Yale University (1701), and Wesleyan University (1831).

Education Statistics

Today, there are 1,165 publicly funded K–12 schools in Connecticut, with about 570,000 students. In terms of diversity, student demographics reveal a student body that is: 64 percent white (a figure that has fallen every year since 2005), nearly 18 percent Hispanic, 14 percent black, 4 percent Asian, and less than 1 percent Native American. In 2009, nearly a third of all public school students qualified for free- or reduced-price lunches, and almost one in five students did not complete high school within five years. The Connecticut Association of Independent Schools currently comprise 97 accredited 501(c)(3) nonprofit institutions that serve over 30,000 students. Independent schools like Choate Rosemary Hall, the Hotchkiss School, Taft School, and Brunswick School, considered among the best in the country, serve as direct feeders to Ivy

Table 1 Elementary and secondary education characteristics

	Connecticut	U.S. (average)
Total number of schools	1,184	1,988
Total students	560,546	970,278
Total teachers	42,951.39	60,766.56
Pupil/teacher ratio	13.05	15.97

Source: U.S. Department of Education, National Center for Education Statistics, Common Core of Data (CCD), 2010–11.

Table 2 Elementary and secondary education finance

	Connecticut	U.S. (average)
Total revenues	$9,464,064,950	$11,464,385,994
Total expenditures for education	$9,576,901,243	$11,712,033,839
Total current expenditures	$8,336,789,224	$9,938,906,259

Source: U.S. Department of Education, National Center for Education Statistics, Common Core of Data (CCD), "National Public Education Financial Survey," FY08 (2007–08).

League universities. Over 202,000 students attend Connecticut's 46 public and private colleges and universities.

Connecticut has the largest achievement gap of any state in the nation. Although ranked in the top 10 nationally, 2011 National Assessment of Educational Progress (NAEP) test scores for Connecticut public school students are flat, with almost no improvement from the previous year, and in some test areas NAEP scores have not increased in a decade. On nearly every NAEP comparison, Connecticut ranks first in the achievement gap for every racial/ethnic subgroup comparison. Racial isolation in schools has plagued Connecticut's public school system, prompting a state Supreme Court decision. *Sheff v. O'Neill* (1996) decided in favor of plaintiff parents who alleged that their children's racial isolation in Hartford's public schools ensured that they received a subpar education relative to white suburban peers in surrounding districts. The court majority opinion explained that regardless of de jure or de facto segregation, the state was obligated to provide equal educational access to all Connecticut school children. The aftermath of the decision included numerous settlement attempts and the 1997 legislation, An Act Concerning Educational Choices and Opportunities, all of which encouraged affirmative and voluntary action from the state and municipalities to racially integrate schools. This included an increase in magnet and regional charter schools and open choice programs that reserved spots for urban students in suburban schools.

Economic equity in funding the public school system has been an important policy area since 1988, when the state implemented the Education Cost Sharing Formula. The formula is Connecticut's mechanism for distribution of state dollars across its municipalities. The formula accounts for total number of students, learning needs of said students (e.g., English-language learners, impoverished, special education) and a given district's ability to generate funding via property taxes, providing an adequate education for each child as determined by state law. The formula has come under criticism since its implementation, undergoing at least 30 revisions to redress perceived inequities and underfunding of districts. In 2005, The Connecticut Coalition for Justice in Education Funding (CCJEF), a broad-based coalition of stakeholders from varying cities and towns across the state, filed suit against the state of Connecticut for inadequate funding of public schools. In *CCJEF v. Rell* (now

Malloy), the plaintiffs allege that because the state underfunds the Education Cost Sharing Formula, it inadequately prepares students for future education and employment endeavors and disproportionately affects students of color. CCJEF appealed the Hartford Superior Court's 2007 dismissal, and in March 2010, gained ground when the Connecticut State Supreme Court ruled that the case may proceed as the state is constitutionally obligated to provide all children an equal education. CCJEF is currently waiting to be heard before the Connecticut Supreme Court to address whether the state has provided adequate funding and standards to ensure that public school students were provided constitutionally adequate educational opportunities. The case is expected to proceed to trial in 2014.

Jessica Kenty-Drane
Southern Connecticut State University
Jamilah Prince-Stewart
Connecticut Coalition for Achievement Now (ConnCAN)

See Also: Racial Inequality: Achievement; Resource Allocation in Schools; School Choice.

Further Readings

Connecticut State Department of Education. "The Condition of Education in Connecticut, October 2011." http://www.sde.ct.gov/sde/lib/sde/pdf/publications/COE_2011.pdf (Accessed January 2012).

Ricklin, Leslie P. "Education in Connecticut." Connecticut's Heritage Gateway. http://www.ctheritage.org/encyclopedia/topicalsurveys/education.htm (Accessed January 2012).

Constructivism

Constructivism, as both an epistemology and pedagogy, covers a range of theories about the nature of knowledge and its acquisition. Constructivist theories have in common a manifestly structuralist epistemology, typical of 20th-century modernity, that challenges the dualistic Cartesian and empiricist conceptualizations of knowledge—as well as the positivistic behaviorist theories and pedagogies—and the presumption that internal knowledge represents or mirrors the external world.

To varying degrees and in different ways, constructivist scholars hold that, rather than being passive receivers of an objectively available external truth, individual subjects actively construct knowledge through the development of increasingly sophisticated mental structures and by building knowledge on top of previously acquired knowledge. Challenging the primacy of rote, memorization, and lecture in classical pedagogy, many constructivists agree that students should develop knowledge through experimentation and facilitated experience, rather than acquiring it through prepackaged forms from teachers, books, or other texts. However, constructivists do not preclude traditional teaching techniques as much as give them new context and purpose. Constructivists further argue that the naïve classical pedagogies ignore the highly individual and stage-dependent structures upon which children formulate knowledge.

Constructivist theory emerged from the work of two 20th century psychologists: Lev Vygotsky and Jean Piaget. While Piaget was interested in how individuals developed through their idiosyncratic interaction with the environment, Vygotsky analyzed development as the internalization of culturally mediated symbol systems. For Piaget, the child progressively builds knowledge structures—sensorimotor, preoperational, concrete operations, and formal operational—through their biological development and their corresponding experience in the world. New concepts form out of challenging experiences that cause the child to question old assumptions or to form new theories through processes of assimilation and accommodation. In assimilating, the child simplifies or stereotypes complex external phenomena, giving them meaning in accordance with existing schema. In accommodating, the child modifies existing schema to adapt to new or conflicting information or stimuli.

Vygotsky came to similar conclusions about human development, but emphasized the communal development of representational systems. For example, he argued that in "civilized" societies, humans replace concrete operations of memory with abstract logical systems that allow them to make more advanced use of memory. Through communal experience, "primitive" cultures move from photographic and other concrete uses of memory to a self-conscious reflection on the operation of memory, at which point they begin to use memory tools—sign systems ranging from writing to systems of knots, notches in feathers, number systems, and maps—in order to employ (dominate) memory in more sophisticated ways.

From these origins, contemporary constructivism can usefully be understood as having two main branches—social constructivism, which traces its origins more specifically to Vygotsky, and a more traditional Piagetian psychological constructivism. Focusing on the social dimensions of knowledge, social constructivism studies the political and social dimensions of knowledge discourses and disciplines, the political and social dimensions of knowledge acquisition, and the position of learners within structures of power and knowledge. More traditional forms of constructivism are more focused on the student-subject in processes of knowledge formation.

While education scholars vigorously debate the conclusiveness of the empirical evidence for the efficacy of constructivist pedagogy, constructivism remains increasingly popular in the classroom. Educators have embraced teaching techniques influenced by constructivist theories, ranging from group work to exercises that develop students' meta-knowledge of their learning processes. Despite widespread enthusiasm for these learning strategies, some argue that teachers without a sophisticated understanding of constructivism transmogrify constructivist ideals into oversimplified "hands-off" approaches.

While constructivist techniques are influential in many disciplines, they have been especially influential in science, math, and teacher education. In science and math, for example, constructivist approaches seek to inculcate durable mental models and problem-solving processes and dispositions, relying less on solution and answer-based lessons. In the constructivist classroom, the teacher becomes more of a facilitator who evaluates and guides, than a lecturer who provides answers. For example, following Vygotsky's idea of the zone of proximal development (ZPD), the teacher (and the classroom) serves as a resource for the student to solve problems out of their zone, and ultimately, development occurs when the student internalizes an understanding and no longer requires assistance to achieve the task.

Edward Comstock
American University

See Also: Classroom Interactions: Teachers and Students; Classroom Interactions Between Students; Dewey,

John; Epistemological Issues in Educational Research; Positivism, Antipositivism, and Empiricism; Sociocultural Approaches to Learning and Development.

Further Readings

Mayer, Richard. "Should There Be a Three-Strikes Rule Against Pure Discovery Learning? The Case for Guided Methods of Instruction." *American Psychologist*, v.59/1 (2004).

Piaget, Jean. *The Psychology of Intelligence*. New York: Routledge, 1950.

Vygotsky, Lev. *Mind in Society*: *The Development of Higher Psychological Processes*. Cambridge, MA: Harvard University Press, 1978.

Content and Text Analysis

The methods of content analysis and text analysis are used by social scientists and researchers when they gather data through different kinds of surveys, questionnaires, interviews, narratives, and formal or informal conversations. In each of these instances of research, various types of texts, both written and spoken, are produced. In many cases, the data accumulated are substantial and need systematic, rational, or consistent organization, processing, and analysis in order to produce meaningful research results, and draw viable and valid conclusions that would be used in further policymaking. Thus, both methods facilitate the transformation of voluminous and disorganized raw data into a meaningful analyzable material, but in different ways and using different techniques.

Content analysis is the longest established empirical method of social investigation. Content analysis is the process of classifying and quantifying the contents of the research material in a systematic way so that the basic structure of contents is identified. The term is usually applied to analyzing documentary or visual material, but the method can also be applied to the analysis of answers to open-ended questions in surveys and research. In other words, the technique is the construction of communication content in quantitative terms. The technique of content analysis produces the quantitative data that can be processed by computer. The data can also be analyzed statistically.

Content Analysis

In the process of content analysis, a set of categories is created by a researcher. These categories highlight the issues studied. The content is classified according to these predefined categories, also often referred to as *codes*. Thus, coding is an important step in content analysis. It facilitates the transformation of the raw data into analyzable form. The process of categorization and coding involves assigning each category a numerical value to facilitate computer processing or statistical analysis. The essential part of the method is to define the categories as precisely as possible in order to minimize the degrees of subjectivity, bias, and judgmental predisposition of the various researchers involved in the study. Another research method, often used for the analysis of interview narratives and texts produced in surveys, questionnaires, and interviews, is text analysis. Many scholars, especially in Europe, use the term *text analysis* for studying the linguistic and extralinguistic structures of different types of text. Text analysis is a predominantly qualitative research method. Text analysis offers a more interpretive approach to the analysis of any type of written or spoken piece of cohesively connected linguistic and extra-linguistic units that build up communicative discourse.

Text Analysis

Although text analysis might emphasize frequently used or semantically significant lexical units, its main aim is the interpretation of the words, phrases, syntactic structures, and concepts used by communicants and the understanding of meanings and attitudes that the communicants attach to the material of analysis. It is a process of situating any text within wider social, political, or cultural contexts for its understanding. Text analysis maintains that no single text exists in isolation from wider contexts in which it has been produced, processed, or deciphered.

The specialized communities who produce and interpret a text laden its constituent parts with contextualized meanings that make up the meaning of the whole text. During the text analysis process, the constituent parts and units of the text acquire communicative function. Text analysis is increasingly approaching and acquiring the features of the method of critical discourse analysis. Moreover, situated in a given communicative context, any text builds up discourse instance and acquires many of the features of the latter. Although some scholars support the rigid distinction between text analysis and critical discourse analysis, the method of critical discourse analysis is often used in parallel with text analysis, since increasing number of scholars realize the inseparability of these two qualitative research methods.

Content analysis can produce quantifiable data that may not be valid, owing to the subjective and biased attitude of the researchers involved. This is why the method is often criticized. For the same reason, content analysis is regarded as a predominantly quantitative research technique in order to avoid bias and subjectivity that is characteristic of qualitative research. Moreover, qualitative content analysis is increasingly regarded as a residual category involved in the procedures of coding or interpreting communicative content. Another issue concerns the fact that the category that occurs most frequently in the content is regarded as the most significant one in the process of analysis. This contingency of significance of any category upon the frequency of its usage is also regarded as one of its drawbacks, since the most frequently used category does not necessarily make it the most significant one.

While quantitative content analysis is mainly involved in frequency counts of categories, qualitative content analysis organizes categories by means of condensing substantially meaningful codes in a systematic or rational way, that is, from the most value-laden category to the least value-laden one. This paradoxical juxtaposition of quantitative and qualitative ways of content analysis often engenders discussions on the primacy of one technique over the other. But actually, the two techniques complement each other and, hence, researchers often use both techniques to fill in the gaps and shortcomings of each method. While quantitative content analysis measures the variables in numerical terms, qualitative content analysis looks into the significance and meaning that these variable bear for the society. Therefore, this quantitative–qualitative distinction of content analysis revives the long-running disputes between positivism and interpretivism. Regarding text analysis method, the major issue raised is its "dry," decontextualized character. Thus, conducting hyper-textual analysis, in which any given text is placed within another larger textual unit or context, is an increasingly used method by researchers. During content and text analysis, the distinction should be made between oral/written, individual/group questioning, and types of surveys and questionnaires. This will give direction to the research to be conducted and the results obtained.

Analysis in Education

Regarding the usage of content and text analysis methods in the field of education, researchers have widely utilized them while investigating such topics as: social class variations in educational attainment; the linkages between educational opportunities/aspirations and social class mobility; perceptions of education quality, access and equity among teachers, students, parents, and policymakers; and perceptions of students, academics, and educators of codes of conduct, ethics, and professional misconduct within academic institutions. The researches have textually analyzed and interpreted the data obtained through interviews and surveys conducted on these issues. Content analysis of surveys, policy documents, and Web site information has been used in studies that have produced categories such as equity, access, equality, education opportunities, and aspirations and has been used for formulating recommendations and strategies for further policymaking in education. Most studies on corruption in education have also been based either on the textual and conceptual analysis of the interpretations and perceptions that respondents offer in the interviews regarding corrupt and illegal practices in educational institutions, or on the content analysis of written and spoken media reports and debates on the issue.

Mariam Orkodashvili
Vanderbilt University

See Also: Bernstein, Basil; Critical Discourse Analysis; Qualitative Research on Education; Quantitative Research on Education.

Further Readings

Orkodashvili, M. "Corruption, Collusion and Nepotism in Higher Education and on the Labor Market in Georgia." *European Education: Issues and Studies*, v.43/2 (2011).

Orkodashvili, M. "Higher Education Reforms in the Fight Against Corruption in Georgia." *Demokratizatsiya. Journal of Post-Soviet Demokratization*, v.18/4 (2010).

Orkodashvili, M. "Leadership Challenges in the Fight Against Corruption in Higher Education in Georgia." *John Ben Sheppard Journal of Practical Leadership*, v.5/1 (2010).

Triventi, M. "Stratification in Higher Education and Its Relationship With Social Inequality: A Comparative Study of 11 European Countries." *European Education Review*, v.27/6 (2011).

Cooled Out

Cooled out is a term used to describe the inactivity or withdrawal of an individual from an educational environment or other unit of society in which specific ambitions and goals were diverted to lower expectations and outcomes. The removal of oneself from secondary or postsecondary studies occurs across a diverse array of dimensions, including geographic area, type of institution, socioeconomic background, gender, race, class, and a host of other categories. The cooled out function in the educational system may also reproduce social stratification if students eliminate themselves or are institutionally removed from the educational attainment pool compared to other groups. The social stratification function enables a sorting function to occur in higher education, such that economic class structures and societal roles remain intact and according to the view of dominant groups. The term *cooled out* has been used to describe students who lack the academic ability to succeed in college, especially at two-year colleges and community colleges.

The cooled out function was applied to higher education by Burton Clark, who proposed that institutions and students engage in practices to provide a less harsh denouncement of failure when individual aspirations collide adversely with academic achievement. Symptoms or resultant actions that indicate a cooled out state include academic disengagement, avoidance of the postsecondary environment, denial of failure, and substitute activities not related to academic outcomes.

As a result of being cooled out, students do not aspire to or obtain bachelor's degrees; rather, students pursue or are advised to pursue one to two years of college or alternatively, vocational training. Steps that institutions take to determine whether students have the academic aptitude for collegiate level work upon admission involve pretesting for remediation and course placement, tracking of introductory and foundational course outcomes, and counseling sessions with students based on accumulated records. In this context, the cooled out function socializes students into accepting educational outcomes that are different from their aspirations, and are often much lower. The cooled out function also absolves academic institutions that offer bachelor's and higher degrees from accepting students with academic aptitude deficiencies and/ or low socioeconomic backgrounds. The acceptance of students who need remedial support by community colleges serves to further insulate higher education institutions from accepting masses of students under access initiatives.

Individuals in society have a means of sharing disappointment and failure with others without causing harm or emotional anguish through the cooled out function. In a description of the roles that individuals and organizations play in adapting to failure, Ervin Goffman described the functions that various groups play in providing a muted response to deficiencies and ineffectiveness. Cooling out serves to manage individual and group ambitions within society through various means of showing and counseling to accept specific realities that serve as gatekeepers against the backdrop of democratic ideals. Cooled out is a consequence of idealistically encouraging achievement and acquisition in the face of the realism of limited opportunities at structural and individual levels. The covert aspects of being "cooled out" enable agents and institutions of society to encourage maximum effort, aspiration, and ambition, without incurring blame, protest, or malfeasance for unfulfilled expectations, assumptions, promises, and ideals. Germane to the process is the existence of alternatives that individuals and groups would accept when primary goals are declared unattainable by those in power.

Marci Middleton
Shorter University

See Also: College Advising; College Transferring; Community Colleges; Dropouts.

Further Readings

Cohen, A. M. and F. B. Brawer. *The American Community College.* 4th ed. San Francisco: Jossey-Bass, 2003.

Floyd, D. L., M. L. Skolnik, and K. Walker, eds. *The Community College Baccalaureate: Emerging Trends and Policy Issues.* Sterling, VA: Stylus Publishing, 2005.

Hagedorn, L. S. "The Role of Urban Community Colleges in Educating Diverse Populations." *New Directions for Community Colleges,* v.127 (2004).

Townsend, B. K. and S. B. Twombly, eds. "Community Colleges: Policy in the Future Context." *Educational Policy in the 21st Century.* Vol. 2, B. A. Jones, ed. Westport, CT: Ablex Publishing, 2001.

Corporal Punishment

For several decades, scholars from different disciplines have examined different parenting styles and their effects on children's wellbeing and school success. Among other things, different forms of discipline, including corporal punishment, were studied. Research has shown that authoritative parenting (characterized by firm boundaries, warm relationships between parents and children, and positive discipline) as opposed to authoritarian parenting (firm boundaries accompanied by punitive discipline) benefits children by leading to a wide range of positive outcomes. The children of parents who are responsive to their needs, who are warm and supportive, who permit them to be active participants in establishing rules, and who use reasoning as a main disciplinary practice, are more likely to demonstrate more positive social behaviors and better educational outcomes. For example, the Study of Early Child Care and Youth Development found that higher externalizing behavior at age 9 was predicted by maternal depression, harsh discipline, and low maternal sensitivity. Conversely, a study of African American Head Start children revealed that mothers who utilized more positive parenting practices and were more supportive of their children had children who exhibited higher pro-social skills and lower externalizing behavior.

Specific child and parental characteristics are associated with the use of corporal punishment. Preschool children and boys are more likely to be spanked than girls and older children. Single mothers, low-income parents, African Americans, and conservative Protestants are more likely to use physical punishment. The use of corporal punishment by poor parents, single mothers, and minority parents has been explained by stress theory. The coincidence of economic hardship, discrimination, and the stress of being a parent results in parental inability to use other forms of discipline. However, a prevalence of corporal punishment in the south and among conservative Protestants suggests that this form of discipline is deeply embedded in the cultural patterns of these groups, thus supporting the socialization theory. The literature lacks a clear consensus on the effects of corporal punishment on children. It has been argued that the link between physical discipline and children's outcomes is culturally specific, and that discipline strategies may operate in different ways across different family contexts. Specifically, the prevalence of this form of discipline and its cultural and social acceptance may mediate its

negative effects; thus, physical punishment should be studied in the context of other parenting factors, such as parental warmth, and should be distinguished from physical abuse. For example, some studies found that spanking was associated with aggressive behavior only for children of white mothers.

On the other hand, several studies reported that the use of corporal punishment is associated with higher incidences of externalizing behavior in children. In the short run, parents achieve desirable behavior and compliance, but in the long run, studies found a detrimental effect on children's self-control, aggressive and antisocial behavior, moral internalization, quality of parent-child relationship, and mental health. A

Table 1 Corporal punishment in U.S. public schools, 2005–06 school year: data released March 2008

State	Number of students hit	Percentage of total students
Alabama	33,716	4.5
Arkansas	22,314	4.7
Arizona	16	<0.0
Colorado	8	<0.0
Florida	7,185	0.3
Georgia	18,249	1.1
Idaho	111	0.04
Indiana	577	0.05
Kansas	50	0.01
Kentucky	2,209	0.3
Louisiana	11,080	1.7
Missouri	5,159	0.6
Mississippi	38,131	7.5
North Carolina	2,705	0.2
New Mexico	705	0.2
Ohio	672	0.04
Oklahoma	14,828	2.3
South Carolina	1,409	0.2
Tennessee	14,868	1.5
Texas	49,197	1.1
Wyoming	0	0

Almost 40 percent of all the cases of corporal punishment occur in just two states: Texas and Mississippi. If Arkansas, Alabama, and Georgia are added, these five states account for almost three-quarters of the nation's school paddlings.

Source: Center for Effective Discipline, July 1, 2010.

more recent study, employing a large nationally representative sample of the American elementary school students (the Early Childhood Longitudinal Study—Kindergarten Cohort) reported that parental use of corporal punishment during kindergarten was associated with lower fifth-grade math achievement. No significant racial differences were found in these effects, thus contradicting the notion that physical discipline is detrimental to only certain groups of students. This study also contradicted the findings that parental warmth buffers the negative effects of physical discipline. No study to date has reported positive effects of corporal punishment, and scholars continue to debate the negative consequences of corporal punishment.

The international lawmaking community largely views corporal punishment as a violation of international human rights law. The Convention on the Rights of the Child (1989) was the first international treaty to specifically focus on the physical, social, cultural, political, and civil rights of children. Although the United States played a crucial role in the drafting of the convention, it is one of two countries (with Somalia) that signed, but did not ratify the treaty. The Council of Europe explicitly stated in 2005 that "any corporal punishment of children is in breach of their fundamental right to human dignity and physical integrity," and called for a coordinated campaign to make Europe "a corporal punishment-free zone for children." To date, 31 countries have instituted universal bans on corporal punishment (both in school and at home), with Sweden being the first in 1979, followed by Finland, Norway, Austria, Croatia, Cyprus, Denmark, Latvia, Bulgaria, Germany, Israel, Iceland, Romania, Ukraine, Hungary, Greece, the Netherlands, New Zealand, Portugal, Spain, Uruguay, Venezuela, Togo, Costa Rica, Moldova, Luxembourg, Liechtenstein, Poland, Tunisia, Kenya, and south Sudan.

The United States has taken few steps in this direction. Corporal punishment by parents is permitted in 49 states (with the exception of Minnesota, where several statutes taken together can be interpreted as prohibiting corporal punishment, although there is no official state ban). A ban of corporal punishment at home has never been given serious debate at the national level, and the following 19 states still allow it in school: Alabama, Arizona, Arkansas, Colorado, Florida, Georgia, Idaho, Indiana, Kansas, Kentucky, Louisiana, Mississippi, Missouri, North Carolina, Oklahoma, South Carolina, Tennessee, Texas, and Wyoming. School districts can ban the use of corporal punishment at the local level, even if it is not banned at the state level, and many school districts around the country do so.

Katerina Bodovski
Pennsylvania State University

See Also: Discipline in Education; Parental Involvement; Poverty and Education.

Further Readings

Baumrind, D. "Parenting Styles and Adolescent Development." In *The Encyclopedia of Adolescence*. J. Brooks-Gunn, et al., eds. New York: Garland, 1991.

Bodovski, K. and M. J. Youn. "Love, Discipline and Elementary School Achievement: The Role of Family Emotional Climate,. *Social Science Research*, v.39/4 (2010).

Gershoff, E. and S. Bitensky. "The Case Against Corporal Punishment of Children." *Psychology, Public Policy, and Law*, v.13/4 (2007).

Global Initiative to End All Corporal Punishment of Children. http://www.endcorporalpunishment.org (Accessed August 2012).

Costa Rica

Costa Rica ("rich coast") is a small (19,961 square mile [51,700 square kilometer]), peaceful country in Central America. It is situated between Nicaragua and Panama, and covers only 0.03 percent of the surface of the globe. Nevertheless, it proudly shelters 6 percent of the existing biodiversity in the entire world; 25 percent of the country is composed of conservation and natural, protected territory. One-third of the 4,576,562 inhabitants (2011) of Costa Rica live in the higher-lying central valley, where the capital city of San Jose is situated. It is rich in wildlife, natural diversity, and pristine sandy beaches along its Pacific and Caribbean coasts. Cordillera Central is a volcanic chain of mountains with partly active volcanoes, passing through the country from north to south. Tourists are attracted by the huge variety of rain and fog forests and undisturbed beaches, which are on the 660 kilometers of coast on the Pacific and Atlantic seas. Colossal volcanoes are some of the unique attractions in Costa Rica's national parks. Costa Rica is bordered by Nicaragua to the north, Panama to the south and southeast, the Pacific Ocean to the west and south, and the Caribbean Sea to the east.

Costa Rica takes pride in having more than 100 years of democratic tradition, and more than half a century without an army, since 1948. The political system is represented by three powers: the executive, legislative, and judicial. The Supreme Court is considered the fourth power of the republic. Every four years, national elections take place. Among other positions of popular representation, the president of the republic is elected through direct representation by secret ballot. Since 1870, elementary schooling has been free and compulsory to all children between the ages of 6 and 13. According to the United Nations *Human Development Report 2007–2008*, Costa Rica's literacy rate is 96 percent. About 45 percent of total population lives in cities. The national language is Spanish, and the majority of the population is Roman Catholic. Approximately 32 percent of the population is under 15 years old, and the average number of children per woman is 3.2. Half of the children were born out of wedlock, and one-third of them have no official father. About 22 percent of people live in poverty or in extreme poverty, which means that their income lies below the minimum wage of $180 per month. Currently, 70 percent of the working population is in the areas of industry, crafts, and services; 15 percent in agriculture; and 15 percent in public services.

The Costa Rican educational system is ranked 32nd in the world, the highest in Latin America, according to the World Economic Forum *Global Competitiveness Report 2008–2009*. The public schooling system is universal, free, and compulsory for Costa Rican citizens. The school system is open to all, but there are big differences in the quality of education. Private, half-private, and some public schools offer good quality education and teach both English and computers. However, 92 percent of children attend public schools. The class size at public schools is on average 38 students, and the infrastructure is inadequate. Although the government is constitutionally required to allocate at least 6 percent of the country's gross domestic product (GDP) to the educational budget, 90 percent of this is spent on salaries.

School education is divided into three levels: one year in preschool, six years in primary school, and five years in high school, with the *Bachillerato* at the end. For the most part, this final exam is a prerequisite for further study. There are a few technical schools, in which the youth can do career training without a Bachillerato. It is an official obligation to attend school for nine years, however in practice this is very different; out of 100 students who start primary school, 67 finish 6th grade, 25 reach 11th grade, and 15 stay to the end of high school and do the Bachillerato. The highest dropout rate is 20 percent in the seventh and 10th grades. The main reasons are the financial burden for families, bad teaching quality, and child and youth labor. Costa Rica has 60 universities, five of which are public, and the rest are privately owned and managed. The Ministry of Education, through the National Council of Higher Education (CONESUP), supervises them. The most prominent is the University of Costa Rica. There is also a UN-mandated university called the University for Peace (UPEACE).

M. Mahruf C. Shohel
Open University

See Also: Class Inequality: High School Dropout Rates; Dropouts; High School Exit Exams; Labor Market Effects on Education.

Further Readings

Escalante, M. A. "A History of Education in Costa Rica." Paper presented at the V Congress of the Americas Popular Culture Association Meeting, Universidad de las Americas, Puebla, Mexico, October 18–20, 2001.

Funkhouser, E. "Cyclical Economic Conditions and School Attendance in Costa Rica." *Economics of Education Review*, v.14 (1999).

Seligson, M. A. and E. N. Muller. "Democratic Stability and Economic Crisis: Costa Rica, 1978–1983." *International Studies Quarterly*, v.31 (1987).

Credit for Work Experience, College Students

While the concept of awarding college credit for learning outside of the classroom has existed for decades, the idea has gained a new popularity in recent years. In addition to traditional programs, such as externships that encourage current students to seek extracurricular opportunities for credit, many schools are applying the same principal to enrolling students. Advocates believe that offering new students credit for work experience completed prior to enrollment has the potential to address some of the most pressing human capital and equity concerns in higher education today, namely increasing college attainment and the affordability of a college education in the United States. Awarding credit for work experience can encourage adults and other nontraditional students to enroll in or complete college degrees, which can create a more educated and internationally competitive workforce. According to the National Center for Education Statistics, only about 30 percent of adults 25 and older in the United States have a bachelor's or more advanced degree. Among these adults, significant disparities exist between races; for instance, only 20 percent of black adults and 14 percent of Hispanic adults have a bachelor's or higher degree. Such programs may diminish the achievement gap by making degree attainment more viable for students from these backgrounds.

For some potential students, particularly those who joined the workforce immediately after high school, the cost of college attendance is prohibitively high. From 2009 to 2010, the total cost of undergraduate tuition, room, and board was estimated at $15,014 at public four-year institutions and $7,703 at public two-year institutions. Costs have been rising steadily, increasing over 30 percent from 2000 to 2001 and 2009 to 2010. Awarding college credit for learning that occurs outside of the classroom prior to enrollment can make a college education more affordable by decreasing the number of classroom-based credits that a student must earn, which shortens the time to degree completion.

While students must still pay to have these credits assessed and counted, the costs are oftentimes significantly lower than the charges for an equivalent number of in-class credits. Credit for work experience has benefits for students beyond financial savings. Students in these programs are not forced to take classes on material that they have already mastered in order to satisfy degree requirements. They are able to immediately enroll in classes that offer new and more challenging material, which leads to increased student engagement. In some cases, students will be able to complete their degrees more quickly, allowing them to save money and return more quickly to the workforce. This may be particularly important for students motivated by professional goals or those trying to balance financial limitations with their desire to pursue a degree.

Assessing Student Knowledge

Colleges primarily use standardized exams or portfolio-based evaluations to assess the knowledge that students have gained through their learning experiences outside of the traditional classroom. Qualifying experiences could stem from working, volunteering, military service, or independent study. Individual schools set policies on whether or not credits earned through such programs reduce the total number of credits a student must earn, or if they can only be used to waive required core classes in lieu of advanced courses or electives. Two of the most popular exam-based demonstrations of a student's prior knowledge are the College-Level Examination Program (CLEP) and the DANTES Subject Standardized Tests (DSST). The CLEP includes 33 predominantly multiple choice exams, while the DSST includes 38 exams. The DSST was developed as part of a Department of Defense program that provides educational opportunities to military personnel and veterans. Today, DSST exams are open to both military personnel and civilians. The registration fee for each CLEP exam is approximately $77, and the DSST fee for civilians is $80.

Portfolio assessments to determine whether to award credit for work experience are conducted on a college-by-college basis. In most cases, student portfolios include a written reflection and a detailed description of their experience, which includes linking course objectives with specific aspects of their learning. The student may also submit supporting evidence, such as syllabi from corporate training courses, or letters of support from managers or other authorities.

Because of the time-consuming nature of portfolio evaluation, these assessments can be more expensive than exam-based prior learning assessments, and sometimes include a submission fee and a per-credit fee. Portfolios are often reviewed by designated faculty members who decide how many credits to award, if any. Recently, third-party services have emerged to streamline the credit-for-experience process for colleges and students in response to the growing market. These services offer resources and guidance to students, as well as help institutions to expedite decisions and standardize the requirements. Building a portfolio can empower students by encouraging them to reflect on their progress and by validating the knowledge they gained through experiences outside of the classroom. In addition to student empowerment, earning credit for work experience is associated with other positive academic outcomes. A study by Council for Adult and Experiential Learning (CAEL) followed over 60,000 adult students enrolled from 2001 to 2002 for seven years. They found that students who earned credit for prior work experience finished their degrees in less time and had higher graduation rates than other adult students. Overall, credit for work experience programs can take several forms, depending on the needs of the school and their expected student applicants. These programs can reduce the cost of a college education for adult and other nontraditional students while increasing student engagement and empowerment. Because this program promotes enrollment and completion for this group, it is of growing importance to policymakers and scholars.

Casey White
University of North Carolina at Chapel Hill

See Also: Adult Education; Class Inequality: College Enrollment and Completion; Community Colleges; Prior Learning Assessment; Racial Inequality: Achievement.

Further Readings

Council for Adult and Experiential Learning (CAEL). "Fueling the Race to Postsecondary Success: A 48-Institution Study of Prior Learning Assessment and Adult Student Outcomes" (March 2010). http://www .cael.org/pdfs/PLA_Fueling-the-Race (Accessed August 2012).

Fiddler, M., et al. *Assessing Learning: Standards, Principles and Procedures.* 2nd ed. Chicago: Council for Adult and Experiential Learning, 2006.

National Center for Education Statistics. "Findings From the Condition of Education: Nontraditional Undergraduates" (2002). http://nces.ed.gov/pubs2002 /2002012.pdf (Accessed August 2012).

Credit for Work Experience, High School Students

Learning occurs both inside and outside of the classroom. Credit for work experience is one approach to preparing students to move from school to career. It enables students who are 16 years of age or older and who are working to earn high school credit for their work experience. In order for credit to be awarded, the work experiences are connected to a career path. The work experience provides students with an opportunity to link secondary school concepts to a workplace and explore training in career paths after high school. Skills learned in credit for work experience that may be linked to student experiences involve time management, meeting deadlines, following directions, problem-solving, responsibility, and working in teams.

The work experiences enable students to make informed career choices. Credit for work experience is established in some school systems as a cooperative work experience during a school term for a specific number of hours. The hours are used to raise grade point averages and add to a student's resume for employability after high school. The credit for work experience is also a means to network with professionals across various industries. These individuals may be called upon for letters of referral. The credit for work experience may be beneficial for a career technical diploma upon graduation. The career and marketing skills gained through the program enable a student to have more knowledge.

Often, programs in which students are paid and gain credit are labeled as high school internships, cooperative education, or youth apprenticeships. According to the U.S. Department of Education, Office of Vocational and Adult Education's Career Resource Network (2012), the following are brief descriptions of work credit that can be used for high school purposes. High school internships provide structured, on-the-job work activities in which school credit is earned for participation. The program lasts a specified period of time, ranging from two to eight weeks, and can be classified as either paid or unpaid. Often, internships are offered during summer months. Cooperative Education programs provide job-related classroom instruction in combination with on-the-job instruction. Required courses are merged with part-time employment under the auspices of a work agreement between the employer, school, student, and the student's parent(s) or legal guardian(s). Youth apprenticeship programs also combine classroom instruction with on-the-job training. A training plan is developed and agreed upon between the employer and the student for a period from two to five years, with only one to two years occurring while a student is in high school. The student is paid for the on-the-job training portion of the apprenticeship.

High school work experience or work-based learning is beneficial because it allows students to explore and experience a workplace firsthand. This work credit is often linked to occupational education courses. Students have opportunities to see what skills are needed, to observe how knowledge from school applies to employment, and to learn further details about career pathways they are considering. School systems establish specific guidelines associated with such programs in terms of entrance into a credit for work experience program, parameters for continued matriculation, credit allocation based on time on the job, on-site contacts by school coordinators, interviews, work permits, portfolios, alignment with career paths, and transportation.

Marci Middleton
Shorter University

See Also: Credit for Work Experience, College Students; General Education Development; School-to-Work Transitions.

Further Readings

Blank, S. P., S. DeLuca, and A. Estacion. "High School Dropout and the Role of Career and Technical Education." *Sociology of Education*, v.81/4 (2008).

Bloom, D. "Programs and Policies to Assist High School Dropouts in the Transition to Adulthood." *Future of Children, Transition to Adulthood*, v.20/1 (2010).

Rothstein, D. S. "High School Employment and Youths' Academic Achievement." *Journal of Human Resources*, v.42/1 (2007).

Tyler, J. H. and M. Lofstrom. "Finishing High School." *Future of Children, Americas High Schools*, v.19/1 (2009).

Critical Discourse Analysis

Critical discourse analysis (CDA), a methodology of social research, examines the reproduction of power inequities through texts, including oral, written, visual, and/or multimodal texts. CDA is used in educational research to investigate the way that both linguistic and discourse practices contribute to the structuring of hierarchical social relations in educational institutions, along with the repercussions of these practices on material conditions in the social context. By analyzing the perspectives and ideologies that are naturalized and perpetuated through texts, as well as those that are excluded and silenced, CDA promotes an awareness of how language functions to produce and/or reproduce inequality. Ideally, CDA can be used as a semiotic resource, a resource for making meaning, by individuals and groups with less power in order to expose the assumptions and limitations of dominant discourses. The mastery and appropriation of semiotic resources is part of the purpose of education, from a critical pedagogical perspective.

Language, power, and domination are three central concepts in CDA. Critical discourse analysts conceptualize language as constitutive of social practices: Language can be used to both describe and construct reality. Power is the ability of a social group or an institution to set the material conditions through which individuals and members of different social groups live, learn, and think. Domination occurs when power is unequally distributed among social groups, leading to asymmetrical power relations. In CDA, explicit and implicit processes of domination are differentiated; the focus of analysis is on implicit processes. For example, domination may be reproduced explicitly through coercion, or implicitly through manipulation and the consent of the dominated.

Teun Van Dijk distinguishes between direct control and cognitive control; cognitive control is the product of manipulation through the production of public discourses. He applied CDA to analyze how public discourses promote preferred models of reading and interpreting social events and how these models function to legitimize and reproduce social inequities. Norman Fairclough also distinguishes between domination through acts of coercion and domination through manufactured consent, or hegemony. Using Antonio Gramsci's definition of hegemony, domination with consent is constructed through the diffusion and reproduction of a dominant notion of common sense: one that legitimizes the inequities in social structures. Legitimacy is gained when inequities are assumed to be outcomes of the natural order of things, rather than as outcomes of historical and humanly constructed social processes. Hegemonic ideologies that form common sense legitimize the asymmetrical power relations in a given social structure. Counterhegemonic ideologies challenge, question, and disrupt the reproduction of asymmetrical power relations.

CDA of Education and Popular Culture

Education and popular culture are institutions that, along with other institutions, contribute to social structures. Ideologies and dominant perspectives are reproduced through educational policies, through the linguistic and discourse practices that shape the interactions between the administration and the teachers, the teachers and students, and between students. CDA examines the ideological functioning of texts—including policy, classroom interaction, conversations, and popular culture—that emerge in educational contexts and about participants in education and society.

The ideological functioning of a text is the discrepancy between the explicit or stated function of the text and its actual ideological functioning. For example, a critical discourse analysis of the No Child Left Behind Act and Reading First legislation, by Haley Woodside-Jiron, examines the ways that policy defines action and rules for action with socializing effects on values and goals. Her work highlights the relationships between policy and teaching practices, and how reading as a social practice is defined through applications of policy. This analysis identifies how a constructed consensus advances a singular approach to literacy learning that denied groups of children full participation in reading programs and reproduces the inequities that it is purported to address.

Along with policies, CDA can also be used in the analysis of visual and multimodal texts, like movies about schooling and youth culture. An ideological analysis of the movies *Mean Girls*, *Thirteen*, and *Ghost World*, by Deirdre Kelly and Shauna Pomerantz, reveals discrepancies between the declared objectives of these movies and their implicit ideological functioning. Positioned as representing the "normal," "everyday" "school girl," these movies ideologically function to distance young women from active, constructive participation in social practices by associating power and rebellion with meanness (*Mean Girls*), risk behaviour (*Thirteen*), and disconnectedness (*Ghost World*). Constructions of power that operate through cruel, risky, and alienated behaviour deny the possibility of explorations of anger and rebellion through alliances and/or socially just actions and relationships, thus influencing the experiences of schooling for young women.

Appropriation of Critical Language Awareness

CDA promotes critical language awareness: an awareness of the ideological functioning of language that disrupts common sense understandings of language and redefines them. In this way, language used to advance dominant ideologies and perspectives on reality can be appropriated by individuals and social groups to articulate different perspectives on social events, and to disrupt the reproduction of inequality through counter discourses. This position, consistent with critical pedagogy, supports the purpose of education as the active involvement of students in the transformation of their reality through dialogic learning and naming their lived experience.

Deb Hill notes that education is an essential element in any counter-hegemonic struggle, and counter-hegemonic discourses cannot be historically effective without the process of education. To develop agency in the process of meaning making and in the production of public discourse, educators can engage students in the appropriation of various semiotic resources. Individuals participate in the process of meaning making by talking, walking, their choice of dress, and their use of the semiotic resources that are available.

CDA has been used to reveal the reproduction of inequities in terms of gender, race/ethnicity, sexual identity, and social class through oral, written, and multimodal texts. Jan Grue noted that inequities that affect the lives of individuals with disabilities are underexplored through critical discourse analysis. While CDA reveals how hegemony is perpetuated through texts and textual practices, many analyses do not suggest counter-hegemonic textual practices. In response, Jim Martin proposed Positive Discourse Analysis (PDA), a complement to CDA, which focuses on the creation of new texts, narratives, and multimodal genres that provide emancipatory alternatives to their hegemonic counterparts.

Louai Rahal
Jennifer A. Vadeboncoeur
University of British Columbia

See Also: Classroom Language; Critical Theory of Education; Ethics in Education; No Child Left Behind.

Further Readings

Caldas-Coulthard, et al. *Texts and Practices: Readings in Critical Discourse Analysis*. London: Routledge, 1996.

Grue, Jan. "Discourse Analysis and Disability: Some Topics and Issues." *Discourse and Society*, v.22/5 (2011).

Hill, Debbie J. "A Brief Commentary on the Hegelian-Marxist Origins of Gramsci's 'Philosophy of Praxis.'" *Educational Philosophy & Theory*, v.41/6 (2009).

Kelly, Deirdre M. and Shauna Pomerantz. "Mean, Wild, and Alienated: Girls and the State of Feminism in Popular Culture." *Girlhood Studies*, v.2/1 (2009).

Kress, Gunther, et al. *Multimodal Teaching and Learning: The Rhetorics of the Science Classroom.* London: Continuum, 2001.

Martin, J. "Positive Discourse Analysis: Power, Solidarity and Change." *Journal of English Studies*, v.4/14 (2006).

Van Dijk, Teun, ed., *Handbook of Discourse Analysis.* Vol. 4. New York: Academic Press, 1985.

Woodside-Jiron, Haley. "Language, Power, and Participation." In *An Introduction to Critical Discourse Analysis in Education*, R. Rogers, ed. Mahwah, NJ: Lawrence Erlbaum Associates, 2004.

Critical Race Theory in Education

Critical race theory (CRT) focuses on a critical examination and analysis of race, law and power. CRT's two main premises include (1) that white supremacy and whiteness as property are foundational to U.S. legal practices and the system itself and (2) that the notion of colorblindness is counterproductive to achieving racial emancipation. CRT contends that racism is engrained in the fabric of American society, emphasizing institutional racism rather than individual racism. White privilege, according to CRT, perpetuates the marginalization of people of color and must be recognized before any progress is made in the realm of racial equality.

CRT scholars, including Kimberle Crenshaw, Richard Delgado, Neil Gotanda, Mari Matsuda, Gary Peller, and Kendall Thomas, are committed to connecting their professional work to social struggle, specifically within the communities with which they interact. CRT scholars also emphasize what Crenshaw coined as "intersectionality," that is, the dependent and interactive ways in which various socially and culturally constructed categories (such as race, class, sexuality, religion, gender, and ability) interact on multiple levels to manifest themselves as inequality in society. CRT aims to advance a social justice framework and to challenge conventional accounts of educational and other institutions as well as the processes that shape them.

Social Construction of Race

Critical race theorists maintain that race is both socially constructed and a real lived experience. Social constructionism became prevalent in the 1970s when it became widely recognized that, while the biological concept of race was simply false, race was absolutely real and consequential as a sociopolitical notion. Michael Omi and Howard Winant's *Racial Formation in the United States* has become a crossdisciplinary classic, widely cited for its critical contributions to the study of race. Of its many contributions, its primary assertion is that race functions as "an autonomous field of social conflict, political organization, and cultural/ideological meaning." In contrast to the paradigms of ethnicity, class, and nation, racial formation, according to Omi and Winant, is "the sociohistorical process by which racial categories are created, inhabited, transformed, and destroyed."

The constructionist contribution to the understanding of race is crucial because it provides a foundational starting point and shared meaning from which to examine the significance and value of race in the context of the United States. Literature by scholars including Susan Cameron, Susan Wycoff, and Ronal Takaki supports that race is neither a biological or genetic reality but rather a socially constructed reality enacted and imposed by white supremacy Other scholars posit that race is a social, cultural, and political creation which itself continues to change in definition. Omi and Winant's theory of racial formation, emphasizes the social nature of race, the absence of any essential racial characteristics, the historical flexibility of racial meanings and categories, the conflictual character of race at both the "micro-" and "macro-social" levels, and the irreducible political aspect of racial dynamics.

Critical Race Within Education

CRT has spread to other disciplines including education and specifically, has extended into educational theory, research and practice. Critical race education scholars analyze and examine the dynamics, impact and consequences of power and privilege in the schooling process. Issues such as affirmative action, "acting white," bilingual decuation, tracking, high stakes testing, school financing, school discipline and academic inequities are among their focus. Specific methodological tools such as counter-storytelling and narrative analysis are utilized in an effort to understand the failure of schools. Counter-storytelling in this way integrates students' (and others') experiential knowledge as a form of legitimate knowledge. Daniel Solórzano and Tara Yosso define counter-storytelling as a method of telling the stories of those people whose experiences are not often told (i.e., those on the margins of society). The counterstory is also a tool for exposing, analyzing, and challenging the majoritarian stories of racial privilege. Counter-stories can shatter complacency, challenge the dominant discourse on race, and further the struggle for racial reform. Such story-telling also serves to help overcome ethnocentrism by introducing "new" worldviews.

Gloria Ladson-Billings and William Tate launched their critical, groundbreaking work, "Towards a Critical Race Theory in Education," where they argue that a critical race perspective in education can be analogous to that of critical race theory in legal scholarship. They propose that within education, race continues to be a salient yet largely untheorized notion in the United States, that the United States is based on property rights (rather than human rights) and that the intersection of race and property create a useful critical tool for understanding educational inequities. In other words, racism remains endemic and engrained within American life, and in this way, remains as such within the educational sphere.

CRT sees the school curriculum as a culturally specific artifact designed to maintain white supremacy. This means that non-white narratives are silenced, especially when they challenge this master narrative. The race-neutral or colorblind approach to curriculum conflates all people of color, presuming a homogenized all-inclusive group which can be simply explained. This approach leads to distortions, misconceptions, stereotypes, and outright omissions of curricular content. Such limited access to knowledge denies all students, and especially students of color, of a complete, multidimensional, and accurate education.

Critical race theorists suggest that African Americans are seen as intellectually and culturally deficient by educators, therefore instructional strategies that usually involve some sort of remediation rather than focusing on higher order cirtical thinking skills are promoted. New research efforts are rejecting deficit models and calling for educators to teach about racism explicitly so that students can recognize this particular form of oppression and engage in proactive measures to struggle against it. Intelligence testing and high-stakes testing, according to critical race theorists, has further exacerbated the idea that African Americans are deficient. These assessments tend to illustrate what students may not know on a specific test but fail to demonstrate the strengths and skills that students bring to the educational experience.

School funding particularly underscores inequity and racism in schooling. Critical race theorists argue that the inequality that exists in school funidng is a direct function of institutional racism. The inability of African Americans to access and qualify for educational opportunities, employment, and housing creates an ongoing cycle of low educational achievement. Thus, African Americans can conceivably not suffer from one act of racism, and, at the same time, suffer from the consequences of systemic racism. Critical race theorists further argue that funding inequities stem from racism and white self-interest. Schooling is administered differently by variou state legislatures. One of the most common practices of states is to fund schools based on propterty taxes. Typically, this translates to wealthier communities having better-funded schools. Critical race theorists reject the notion that per pupil spending does not matter when educational inequity is discussed. They challenge those reformers who claim that property is somehow irrelevant in predicting academic achievement.

Critical race theorists argue that desegregation has not served as a solution to schooling inequities but rather has only benefited whites. So, while African American students continued to be underserved and African American student achievement continued to suffer, whites were able to take advantage of opportunities such as magnet programs without having to leave the system altogether and without any inconvenience on their part. CRT is the fastest growing and most controversial movement in legal scholarship, inspiring debate in the same manner that critical legal studies did in the 1980s. While it is still a young movement, it is one that shows no sign of slowing down. The field of education's adoption of CRT has raised consciousness regarding equality within schooling processes. The challenge for critical race theorists in education is to continue to move from intellectual theory to mainstream practice.

Aurora Chang
University of Wyoming

See Also: Racial Climate on Campus; Racial Inequality: Achievement; Racial Inequality: College Enrollment and Completion; Racial Inequality: High School Dropout Rates; Racism in Education.

Further Readings

Crenshaw, K., et al. *Critical Race Theory: The Key Writings That Formed the Movement.* New York: New Press, 1995.

Delgado, R. and J. Stefancic. *Critical Race Theory: An Introduction.* New York: New York University Press, 2001.

Delgado, R. and J. Stefancic. *Critical Race Theory: The Cutting Edge.* 2nd ed. Philadelphia: Temple University Press, 2000.

Ladson-Billings, Gloria and William Tate. "Toward a Critical Race Theory in Education." *Teachers College Record*, v.97/1 (1995).

Matsuda, M., et al. *Words That Wound: Critical Race Theory, Assaultive Speech, and the First Amendment.* Boulder, CO: Westview Press, 1993.

Omi, M. and H. Winant. *Racial Formation in the United States: From the 1960s to the 1990s.* 2nd ed. New York: Routledge, 1994.

Parker, Laurence, et al. *Race Is—Race Isn't: Critical Race Theory and Qualitative Studies in Education.* Boulder, CO: Westview Press, 1999.

Solórzano, Daniel and Tara Yosso. "Critical Race Methodology." *Qualitative Inquiry*, v.8 (2002).

Valdes, Francisco, J. M. Culp, and A. P. Harris. *Crossroads, Directions, and a New Critical Race Theory.* Philadelphia: Temple University Press, 2002.

Yosso, T. J. *Critical Race Counterstories Along the Chicana/Chicano Educational Pipeline.* London: Routledge, 2006.

Critical Theory of Education

Critical theories of education are philosophical, political, and pedagogic responses to real world circumstances, which attempt to shift the purposes, scope, aims, and delivery of education to enable cultural and social transformation through the progressive growth of individuals. They pay particular attention to the situation of oppressed and marginalized groups and seek to contest the ideologies of dominant social relations and established needs, which proponents view as key to the reproduction and naturalization of current social and global inequalities. A critical theory of education is rooted in an understanding of the features of currently existing capitalist societies, their relations of subordination and domination, but also their contradictions and the openings these produce for progressive social change through transformative practices that proponents believe will generate a better society. Critical theorists argue for the reconstruction of education systems along what they see as more genuinely democratic and multicultural lines, while rejecting what they view as obsolete elitist, idealist, antidemocratic, and traditionalist concepts of education. Critical theories of education are therefore normative projects for social transformation that can even be viewed as having strong utopian dimensions. A critical theory of education and society denotes ways of viewing, conceptualizing, categorizing, and mapping connections that makes visible vested interests and power relations, with the aim of constructing more egalitarian alternatives.

The philosophical background for such critiques of education consists in the main part in the work of the Frankfurt School of critical theory that was developed in the mid-20th century by a group of German American scholars, such as Herbert Marcuse, who built on and adapted the theories of Karl Marx. Further developments have also seen the incorporation of the pragmatist philosophies of John Dewey, the critical pedagogy of Paulo Freire, and the critiques of poststructuralism, in order to adequately face and challenge the realities of societies today. Moreover, critical theorists provide radical critiques of existing systems of education while providing progressive alternative models that, they argue, are more democratically relevant within the contemporary world.

Greek and Marxist Theories

A foundational belief of all critical theory approaches is that education is a process that has transformational benefits for the individual, and that such benefits will culminate in an enriched, inclusive, and socially just society. A critical theory of education therefore has many common elements with the classical Greek philosophies of education. For the Greek philosophers, a proper education involved the search for the good life and the good society. Critical theorists of education do not, however, unreflectively employ ideas from this period because the Greek education system was highly elitist in its production of citizens, who were mainly male and upper class. Rather, their approach is one of "redemptive criticism," where (in a similar vein to the work of Walter Benjamin) ideas from the past are resurrected and reconstructed in order to build critical theories of the present and proposals for a better future. Through a radical historicism then, critical theorists argue that it is possible to reveal the work of discourses of power and domination in classical education systems while retaining some aspects of the idealist notion that education is central to shaping and forming fully realized human beings.

The Marxist critique of ideology is also central to critical theories of education. This approach situates the analysis of education within dominant social relations and the current system of political economy. From a Marxist perspective, the assumptions of the established system are systematically criticized so that an alternative model of educational theory and practice can be constructed that aims to overcome the oppression, inequalities, and limitations that existing institutions of schooling support. Because Marxist ideas are fundamentally Romantic—especially in Marx's early writings—there is a shared idealism with Greek philosophy concerning the fulfillment of human potential.

Unlike the classical Greeks, though, the Marxist critique contains a further necessary element: the radical examination and restructuring of the models and ideologies of education in order to free every person from the restraints of the capitalist system, meaning that everyone can contribute creatively to democratic human culture and society. Herbert Marcuse, a member of the Frankfurt School of scholars, presented a critique of education systems in Western countries developed from this position. Writing in the 1960s and 1970s, Marcuse saw the education system in the United States as an aspect of what he termed the "one dimensional society," meaning a social order that stifles negativity, critique, and transformative practice. He held this in contrast to the German concept of *Bildung*, where the purpose of education is to transcend the immediate conditions of human existence in order to enrich individuals and wider culture. Marcuse argued that the growing instrumentalism in schooling reduced learning to the economic and bureaucratic needs of the present, thereby subverting the mandate of education to realize a better future. From Marcuse's position, negativity is a positive concept because it is negation that allows for social contradictions to be overcome through the establishment of genuine freedom for all.

Modern Theory

Douglas Kellner and colleagues argue that Marcuse's educational project has lost none of its importance in the contemporary world, where they claim that a radical politics aimed at emancipation and a non-repressive society is urgently needed. They note that, similar to the period when Marcuse was writing, the spaces for negativity and political resistance continue to be eroded today. In line with thinkers like Marcuse and Kellner, critical theorists of education continue to argue for counter-institutions and pedagogies that foster democratic social transformation through the full growth of individuals. Critics such as Michael Apple argue that sustained efforts to impose a neoliberal agenda in schooling that follows the logics of business, capital, the market, and industry has had a deeply negative effect on education. Such critical theorists contend that dominant trends, such as the standardizing of the curriculum and teaching toward tests, have done nothing to cultivate learning, a sense of community, strengthen individuality, promote democratic participation, or improve social justice.

In place of what they describe as the neoliberal agenda, they seek to propose alternative concepts and practices for schooling, building on, for example, the pragmatist philosophies of John Dewey, the critical pedagogies of Paulo Freire and Ivan Illich, and the critiques of poststructuralism. At the center of any critical theory of education, therefore, there is an alternative model for educating that departs from the market-orientated model that dominates Western societies, but that equally claims to be constructed for and embedded in the realities of today's world. Instead of the logic of market capitalism, critical pedagogies engage in issues like overcoming differences between cultures while developing unsettled and open forms of democracy that (it is believed) will be more adept at incorporating marginalized groups and solving conflicts between cultures.

Critical theorists of education often employ the work of pragmatist philosopher John Dewey. Here, the term *pragmatist* is used to signify a philosophy that is grounded in its ability to be practically applied, meaning that theory should ideally emerge through and from actual practices while being applicable to their ongoing development. Dewey held that it was impossible to have a democratic society without a certain kind of education system. For a strong democracy to work, he argued that everyone must have access to education so that they are equipped with the skills to participate in social and political life. In order to understand democratic and political processes and to contribute as a good person and competent actor in democratic life, every person must be properly informed and educated. For Dewey, education should be practical and have the key objective of improving everyday life and society. Learning is an experimental, pragmatic, and evolving process where a person learns by doing. Mistakes are anticipated and accepted as a natural aspect of the method of trial and error, which is vital for the learning of life skills that will gradually and eventually improve democratic society.

The Brazilian writer Paulo Freire argued that oppressed and marginalized peoples comprise an underclass that has never been able to share in the benefits of education. For Freire, it was not that the ruling class should provide the education system for the underclass; rather, they should educate themselves by developing a "pedagogy of the oppressed." Central to such a strategy is the transformation of oppressed individuals from the "object" to the "subject" of education, where an object is seen as an empty vessel, a subject is viewed as an active and valued contributor and participant. Through becoming a subject, Freire argued, the marginalized individual is able to develop into a fully realized human being. He contended that object-oriented forms of education worked along the "banking" model, which involved forms of indoctrination and the enforcement of conformity to dominant values, where the marginalized are taught to accepted their subordinate and submissive status, and thus participate in the reproduction of social inequality. In contrast, Freire maintained that subject-oriented models of education required the creation of a dialogical pedagogy, a style of learning that would be empowering to the oppressed. He believed that such systems would allow the educated the right to generate their themes for study, to fully participate in their education, and to continually engage in a dialogue with their teachers.

In a similar vein to Freire, Ivan Illich argued strongly that dominant conceptions of education and schooling should be opposed, going so far as to argue for the "de-schooling" of society. Illich believed that schooling needed to be replaced with an entirely different system, which should be grounded in what he termed "tools for conviviality." Convivial tools—in contrast to dominant schooling—are modes of educating that promote different forms of knowledge in an environment of congeniality and community. These new modes of educating, he argued, should help cultivate "multiple literacies," so that the accepted ways of seeing, understanding, and interacting with the world were broader, and better reflected the realities of all people. For Illich, rather than schooling, which brought individuals into systems of dependency and control (in much the same way as Freire envisaged), de-schooling would help foster autonomy and self-realization through more equal forms of communication, debate, participation, and decision making in approaches to learning.

Poststructuralist Critiques

Critical theorists of education often attempt to temper the idealism of these philosophies of education by drawing on the poststructuralist critiques of modern theory. From a poststructuralist perspective, it has been argued that many dimensions of human life are neglected in the alternative modes of educating that were presented throughout the 20th century; their notions of subjectivity and democracy in particular are singled out as failing to address issues of difference such as gender, race, and sexuality. Poststructuralism emphasizes the vital significance of difference, with proponents stressing that the voices and experiences of myriad marginalized groups have not been accounted for by modernist theories. Feminists such as bell hooks, for example, have drawn on poststructuralist and multicultural research in order to illustrate how the oppressed underclass is not only comprised in social class terms. hooks stresses that women and people of color have also been traditionally marginalized within education and society, and it is therefore vital that any critical theory of education attends to their experiences when attempting to construct alternative modes of educating and learning. Although many modernist critical pedagogies neglect such issues of otherness and difference, many contemporary scholars continue to develop critical approaches that adapt and reconstruct the work of Marcuse, Freire, and others, in order to constantly challenge and change systems and modes of schooling, arguing that this task must be undertaken in the interest of social justice in an increasingly unequal global context.

David Mellor
University of Bristol

See Also: Banking Concept of Education; Conflict Theory of Education; Feminist Critiques of Educational Practices; Feminist Critiques of Educational Research; Freire, Paulo; Marx, Karl; Postmodernism and Education.

Further Readings
Freire, Paulo. *Pedagogy of the Oppressed*. New York: Continuum, 2001.

Giroux, H. *Theory and Resistance in Education*. Westport, CT: Bergin & Garvey, 2001.

Kellner, D., et al., eds. *Marcuse's Challenge to Education*. Lanham, MD: Rowman & Littlefield, 2009.

Cuba

The Republic of Cuba, a Spanish colony until 1898, is largest island in the Antilles Archipelago at 42,803 square miles (110,860 square kilometers). The island is located roughly 90 miles (145 kilometers) from Florida. The World Bank estimated its population to be 11,087,330 in 2011. African slaves were imported to work the coffee and sugar plantations, although the majority of the population of Cuba is descended from European Spaniards. According to the 2002 census, the population of Cuba is 65.1 percent white, 24.8 percent mulatto and mestizo, and 10.1 percent black. The 2011 Human Development Index ranked Cuba 51 out of 187 countries surveyed, giving it a high developed country rating. The Cuban economy is state-run, and its major economic exports are nickel, sugar, tobacco, shellfish, medical products, citrus, and coffee. Unofficial estimates place Cuba's economic growth rate at around 2.5 percent annually. Since 1961, a U.S. economic embargo has been in force.

Cuban education has undergone three periods: (1) mass education (1959–62), (2) education for economic development (1962–68), and (3) making the new citizen (1965–90). In pre-revolution Cuba, education was not accessible to the masses and it was estimated that the literacy rate was around 60 percent. The Cuban Literacy Campaign of 1961, or Year of Education, premised upon political and economic development, began after the Cuban Revolution under Fidel Castro and aimed at creating a unifying communist *conciencia* and eradicating widespread illiteracy. The Cuban Literacy Campaign focused on creating literacy brigades to build schools, train new educators, and teach reading and writing, while engendering a skilled labor force. During the late 1950s, several army barracks were transformed into schools, and by the mid-1960s, boarding schools emerged as a way to create revolutionary citizens and encourage greater participation for rural women in the emerging industrial society. The notion of collectivism within education was also expanded through the creation of polytechnic education, which emphasized learning scientific principles and the ability to handle tools and equipment. As far as higher education, universities—including the University of Havana (founded in 1728)—saw expanded enrollment in engineering, agriculture, and natural sciences, and decreases in the humanities and law.

While the reforms of the 1960s made great achievements in education, including illiteracy eradication and expansion of mass schooling, education during the 1970s saw a shift from quantitative gains to qualitative improvements as closer ties emerged with the Soviet Union. Educational overhauls began at the First National Congress on Education and Culture in 1971. There, delegates proposed changes and improvement in the structure of education since dropout rates were high (particularly in rural areas), the curriculum was outdated and textbooks were inappropriate, and teacher-training programs were inadequate. With a mixture of Marxism and Cuban historicism, the Second Congress for Young Communists of 1972 called for drastic measures against youths who had antisocial behavior, especially those who had not studied or worked, and the use of 10th graders to teach at the secondary level in the countryside. The 1976–81 five-year plan called for longer classroom hours and the reduction of the number of schooling years from 13 to 12. In the 1980s, education was again given prominence after the Mariel boatlift, when over 125,000 Cubans fled the nation. Teacher education became the central focus, and by 1981, over 3,500 Cuban schoolteachers, professors, and advisers were working in over 20 counties. The Cuban educational system is an amalgamation of study and work. Economic development in Cuba has been linked to education, with the hopes of creating an egalitarian society through a work-study program that marries manual labor in the countryside with school attendance.

Student education begins with three years of kindergarten, followed by six years of primary school (grades 1–6), and three years of basic secondary (grades 7–9). After basic secondary, students can choose between three years of pre-university/upper secondary education (grades 10–12), or three years of technical and professional education. The collapse of the Soviet Union and the disappearance of Soviet aid led to tight rationing of energy, food, and consumer goods. As secondary and higher educational enrollment boomed, the 1980s left an overeducated populace. With the end of the Cold War came great migration from the countryside to the cities, and Havana had to limit its population in 1997.

By the early 1990s, several internal austerity measures were instituted, the educational budget began to decrease to about 23 percent of the total budget, teachers and other trained professionals migrated, student stipends were redefined as student loans, and slight curriculum and pedagogical modifications occurred. At the beginning of the 2000s, investment in the form of human resources remained a prime priority and school systems were still expected to serve the economy. The renewal of popular education saw English replacing Russian as the foreign language of choice, and civic education was introduced at ninth grade to enforce an early attitude toward participation. About 10 percent of the annual budget is devoted to education, and the overall literacy rate is around 99 percent.

Tavis D. Jules
Loyola University Chicago, CEPS

See Also: Bahamas; Barbados; Trinidad and Tobago.

Further Readings

Blum, Denise F. *Cuban Youth and Revolutionary Values.* Austin: University of Texas Press, 2011.

Brenner, Philip, et al., eds. *A Contemporary Cuba Reader.* Lanham, MD: Rowman & Littlefield, 2008.

Carnoy, Martin. *Cuba's Academic Advantage: Why Students in Cuba Do Better in School.* Palo Alto, CA: Stanford University Press, 2007.

Gott, Richard. *Cuba: A New History.* New Haven, CT: Yale University Press, 2004.

Cultural Capital

Cultural capital is a term referring to unequally distributed cultural resources that can give students an advantage in the school setting. The idea is that culture, like financial capital, is a resource that distinguishes individuals and provides them with benefits. Thus, cultural capital enables students to relate better to teachers, attain better grades, and/or reach higher levels of education than students lacking cultural capital. Since the development of the concept, researchers have taken the term in multiple directions when applying it in research.

Although cultural capital is a popular concept in the sociology of education, questions remain regarding its true meaning and effects. Cultural capital is a concept developed by French sociologist Pierre Bourdieu. In studying schools in France in the 1960s and 1970s, he discovered that students from working-class backgrounds tended to drop out at higher rates than their middle-class peers. He came to the conclusion that the culture of schools favored students from middle-class backgrounds who had the cultural resources most representative of what he termed the "dominant culture." He argued that cultural capital has three forms: embodied, institutionalized, and objectified. Embodied cultural capital includes one's tastes, communication styles, and knowledge of the culture that is valued by society. Objectified cultural capital refers to concrete cultural objects, such as a symphony or a work of art. It requires embodied cultural capital to be truly appreciated. Institutionalized cultural capital refers to educational credentials, such as higher degrees. Institutionalized cultural capital is earned partially from the embodied cultural capital possessed by the student.

Pierre Bourdieu argued that most of the accumulation of cultural capital takes place in the home, as a child is socialized. In middle-class families, children are exposed to an appreciation of the arts, the preferred styles of speaking and writing, and a general disposition toward the dominant culture. In working-class and poor homes, this cultural capital is not developed. When students enter school, those from the middle class are at an advantage because of their previous accumulation of cultural capital. This allows these students a more seamless transition to the school environment, which operates within the dominant culture. Working-class students experience a disjuncture between their home environments and the school because the school demands a different set of cultural resources than those possessed by these children. Cultural capital can be taught in schools, but the most natural forms are those that are transmitted in the home. Because of their lack of cultural capital, working-class students struggle in the school setting and often self-select out of pursuing additional education.

A few students are able to succeed educationally, which helps perpetuate the belief that schools operate as meritocracies, rather than settings for the reproduction of social inequality. Middle-class students possess the cultural capital to master the course material and communicate well with teachers, who recognize their cultural capital and encourage them to continue with their schooling. In this way, the social class structure reproduces, so that those from the middle class remain in the middle class and those from the working class, for the most part, remain in the working class.

The concept of cultural capital has been studied extensively in the United States, Europe, and Asia. Cultural capital is measured differently, depending on whether the research conducted is quantitative or qualitative. In quantitative research, cultural capital is typically measured as attendance at museums, concerts, or theater; lessons in art, music, drama, or dance; and occasionally reading behavior. Some studies have focused on parents' educational attainment or parents' cultural practices and reading behavior. Various outcomes have been studied including grades, test scores, teachers' evaluations of students, and educational attainment.

Results of these studies have been mixed, with some finding no effects of cultural capital, some finding weak effects that illustrate cultural capital's ability to reproduce the social class structure, and some finding that cultural capital can work as a vehicle for mobility for working-class students. Qualitative cultural capital research, on the other hand, examines the interactions that students and parents have with teachers and school administrators, teachers' perceptions of students' behavior, and students' and teachers' general knowledge of how to navigate the educational system. Results from these studies have been less focused on finding a cultural capital effect on specific outcomes such as grades, and more focused on detailing how cultural processes differ by social class.

There are several criticisms of cultural capital research. One is that cultural capital research assumes that there is only one type of cultural capital—that of the upper class—and that poor and minority students do not have any cultural capital. Several researchers have investigated alternative forms of cultural capital, such as "black cultural capital," and have shown how they are advantageous in different contexts. A second criticism is that operationalizations of cultural capital are so diverse that some have very little to do with the initial definition given by Pierre Bourdieu. Related to this criticism is the argument that many researchers use the cultural capital concept outside of its theoretical context. Until recently, most sociologists of education examined cultural capital in isolation from Pierre Bourdieu's broader theory of social reproduction, which also includes the concepts of habitus and field.

Current research focuses on finding the best measurements for cultural capital, discerning the mechanisms through which cultural capital translates into educational outcomes, and incorporating other facets of Pierre Bourdieu's theory, including habitus and field.

Susan A. Dumais
Louisiana State University

See Also: Black Cultural Capital; Cultural Capital and Gender; Parental Cultural Capital; Race and Cultural Capital.

Further Readings

Bourdieu, Pierre. "The Forms of Capital." In *Education: Culture, Economy, and Society*, A. H. Halsey, Hugh Lauder, Phillip Brown, and Amy Stuart Wells, eds. Oxford: Oxford University Press, 1997.

Kingston, Paul W. "The Unfulfilled Promise of Cultural Capital Theory." *Sociology of Education*, extra issue (2001).

Swartz, David. *Culture and Power: The Sociology of Pierre Bourdieu*. Chicago: University of Chicago Press, 1997.

Cultural Capital and Gender

The concept of cultural capital is one of the central pillars of French sociologist Pierre Bourdieu's theoretical formulation of cultural and social reproduction. Cultural capital is a usable resource or form of power. Its possession or lack thereof influences whether an individual will be able to gain advantage in a given field such as education or the labor market.

The ability to possess cultural capital and to convert it eventually into economic and symbolic capital depends on the intersection of social class and gender. Bourdieu specified several forms of capital that contribute to the reproduction of the structure of power relationships and symbolic relationships by social class and gender. Of these forms of capital—which include economic, social, and symbolic—cultural capital has received considerable attention. In his theory of reproduction, Bourdieu posits that rather than being socially neutral, educational institutions are part of a larger universe of symbolic institutions that reproduce existing power relationships.

The Dominant Class

The culture that is transmitted and rewarded by the educational system reflects the culture of the dominant class. The dominant class is usually defined as those from higher social backgrounds; however, from his early writings onward, Bourdieu argued that gender—that is, being male—also defines dominance.

Families of higher social status transmit the culture that is the dominant culture. Children from higher social backgrounds acquire cultural resources such as habits, dispositions, and good taste at home, and enter the educational system already familiar with the dominant culture. Schools reinforce particular types of linguistic competence, authority patterns, and types of curricula that can be decoded by students who possess the cultural capital to do so. Students who possess the "correct" form of cultural capital excel in school; as such, cultural capital is transformed into legitimate academic qualifications. As a result, some children are more easily able to access academic rewards.

Over time, academic credentials are converted into economic capital and earning power. Differential academic achievement that is believed to be the result of differential ability is actually the result of the amount and nature of cultural capital transmitted by the family. As a result, transmission of cultural capital from parents to children is recognized as legitimate competence, and is not recognized as capital. Cultural capital is considered to be a key mechanism through which values, privileges, and status of the dominant culture is reproduced. That is, background inequalities are converted into differential academic attainments and rewards.

Relationship to Social Class

The relationship between cultural capital and gender is similar to that of social class. Cultural resources are differentially acquired by girls and boys, and are rewarded differentially by the school. Acquisition of the information and education offered by the school is dependent on the abilities of girls and boys—in conjunction with social class—to receive and decode it, which in turn depends on previously acquired cultural capital. These cultural resources have the potential to remain gendered throughout their school careers. Today, girls in almost all Western countries are more likely than boys to succeed

at all levels of education, and higher proportions of women than men earn bachelor's degrees. However, women continue to be underrepresented in academia and industry, and in particular, in most fields of science and technology. Cultural capital and its role in cultural reproduction can be used to explain this phenomenon. In educational systems, such as those existing in North America, curricular differentiation is an outcome of courses completed in high school. Students who do not possess the prerequisites, such as 11th grade algebra, are unable to enroll in 12th grade algebra.

Postsecondary Education

Students who graduate from high school without specific prerequisites may be disqualified from enrolling in postsecondary programs for which these courses are required. It is not unusual for girls to leave certain educational pathways, such as mathematics and science, early in their senior years of secondary school. Educated parents who possess adequate knowledge and dispositions are able to help their female and male children choose courses, shape expectations for further education, and stave off certain educational verdicts by teachers. However, girls and boys may acquire unequal levels of cultural capital via differential educational experiences. Examples include the following, both at home and in schools: encouragement of boys to manipulate equipment; lack of role models in certain fields for girls; and less exposure to and experiences with science and technology-related toys, games, and competitions. Differences in attitudes and achievement in certain subjects are often attributed to differential ability levels of girls and boys, rather than gendered cultural capital.

"Masculine" Disciplines

In academic disciplines exhibiting masculine tendencies, such as aggressive learning environments, girls and young women with the requisite cultural and academic capital and related dispositions to permit them to enroll in certain programs of study may simply exclude themselves. Even for those who escape initial exclusion from certain academic disciplines, persistence declines over time as they conclude that such programs are "not for me."

Conclusion

Overt barriers to education and employment, such as discriminatory admission and hiring policies, have been largely eliminated; however, sex segregation in many fields or disciplines persists. Specific covert practices in certain fields of study tend to reproduce the culture of the dominant group through processes that may well have begun early in a girl's or boy's educational career.

Also, as societies strive to adopt policies that support gender equity, disciplines and occupations dominated by men increasingly adopt other indirect mechanisms of reproduction, such as policies unfriendly to families that push women out of disciplines such as science or law.

Lesley Andres
University of British Columbia

See Also: Cultural Capital; Gender Inequality: College Enrollment and Completion; Social Capital.

Further Readings

Bourdieu, Pierre. *Masculine Domination.* R. Nice, trans. Palo Alto, CA: Stanford University Press, 2001.

Bourdieu, Pierre. *Pascalian Meditations.* R. Nice, trans. Palo Alto, CA: Stanford University Press, 2000.

Bourdieu, Pierre and Jean-Claude Passeron. *Reproduction in Education, Society, and Culture.* R. Nice, trans. London: Sage, 1977.

Curriculum Standardization

Contemporary educational climates and cultures are characterized by standardization practices. The need or requirement to ensure that different elements of curriculum are standardized—are measured against uniformly agreed upon benchmarks or performance indicators—occupies the position of a dominant discourse, according to J. Gee.

Within political cultures, there is a broad consensus that the overall goal of the standardization of curriculum is the correct one. There are three issues used to explore the issue of curriculum standardization in depth: how curriculum is defined, the justification for standardization, and how standardization is performed within educational institutions and workplaces.

Defining Curriculum

The term *curriculum* refers to a course or program of study (e.g., the sociology curriculum or the chemistry curriculum), or to a broader area of educational provision (e.g., the vocational curriculum, a term that encompasses all provision within vocational, technical, and craft-based subject areas; this term is frequently positioned opposite the academic curriculum). It can also be used to refer to areas of educational provision according to the normal age range of the students in question, definitions that do not take account of the subject matter undertaken (e.g., the early years curriculum or the higher education curriculum). These are all common uses of the term *curriculum* as used by educationalists, policymakers, employers, and other stakeholders within education and training systems, easily differentiated through their contexts. These definitions of *curriculum* are used in discussions about standardization practice.

Dominant discourses of curriculum can be understood as containing several interlocking elements. First, there is course content, the specified content of a unit of program of study that has been agreed, normally by an awarding or examining body, as describing the knowledge, ability, or skill that students will acquire or accomplish as a consequence of participation. Student accomplishment needs to be made publicly available, or otherwise capable of being communicated to society at large.

Therefore, the second key element is assessment and accreditation, processes by which the extent of the student's learning can be evaluated against predetermined criteria that are derived from the course content, and translated through a process of certification into a warrant that students carry with them when they leave the educational setting. The third key element is the teaching staff: If a curriculum is to be successfully acquired by a student, it needs to be delivered or facilitated by a suitably qualified professional educator or other professional who has a recognized training or teaching expertise.

Researchers and sociologists of education offer a number of other definitions of curriculum, however. Concepts such as the "planned curriculum" and the "received curriculum," which differentiate between the ways a curriculum is planned and specified and the ways in which it is delivered and experienced in the classroom, raise important questions about how standardization can be enacted, but do not in themselves impact dominant discourses of standardization.

Concepts such as the *total curriculum* define curriculum as including everything that is needed to allow a curriculum to be enacted: not only programs of study, but also people (teaching staff, academic support staff), infrastructure (systems, routines), admissions policies, artifacts (textbooks, virtual learning platforms), and even buildings, as related by A. Kelly. The impact of this broader conceptualization of curriculum is contestable. It is difficult to standardize buildings, although curricular authorities commonly audit the provision of sufficient and appropriate technical and vocational equipment for the delivery of the vocational curriculum in tertiary colleges and workplace or adult education settings. However, it is relatively straightforward to standardize people or, more properly, aspects of human performance, through practices such as a requirement for a mandatory teaching qualification or professional license to practice, or through other human resource management strategies, such as staff training or continuing professional development, according to J. Garrick.

Informal education and informal learning in the workplace pose particular problems for educationalists and sociologists of education when trying to understand curriculum and the different elements that define it. Research into forms of learning that occur outside formal institutional contexts (usually drawing on ethnographic and/or anthropological methodologies) provide accounts of learning based on apprenticeship models. These models describe apprentice learners' acquisition or immersion into recognized bodies of knowledge or practice that are discrete and identifiable, but which do not fit into dominant definitions of curriculum because they exist outside of formal educational structures, lacking documentation (such as a published syllabus) and accreditation (such as a formal qualification). Models of learning such as these center around models that distinguish between a learning curriculum, which consists of those afforded instances or circumstances where learning can happen irrespective of whether any formal instruction is intended, and a teaching curriculum, which is aligned to dominant definitions of curriculum.

Justifications for Curriculum Standardization

Justifications for standardization across curricula practices are varied, and are rooted in several different, and sometimes competing, ideological and/or philosophical perspectives pertaining to education and training more generally. These can be defined in terms of perceived pedagogical benefits (where pedagogy is taken to include any practice that contributes to learning, teaching and assessment). They can also be defined in terms of how professional groups (including school teachers, college teachers, and university lecturers) are rendered accountable for the work that they do, and the extent to which professional autonomy should be tempered by external inspection and audit.

An important principle of the standardization of curriculum provision is that the way in which the individual student experiences the curriculum should be broadly comparable to the experience of any other student who is engaged in the same program of study, but at a different institution. Within an education system, all of the students on a particular program will experience that program in a broadly comparable manner. In order for this uniformity of provision to be rendered publicly viewable, institutions, governments, and examining bodies use a variety of mechanisms and artifacts to standardize and thereby render accountable the different curricular practices that are occurring at any given time. These mechanisms need to be able to speak to a diverse group of stakeholders in the education process, who can be conveniently summarized as: students, employers, professions, industries, examining bodies, and funding agencies. Students need to be satisfied that they are not being disadvantaged academically or developmentally through having chosen to study at one institution as opposed to another.

Employers need to be satisfied that potential employees' certificates, or other forms of professional endorsement, are similarly devoid of any disparities in trustworthiness as a consequence of having been gained from study at any particular institution. Professions and industries need to be confident that entrants to those professions have all of the required threshold knowledge or competences that their qualifications purport to represent. Examining bodies need to be confident that their qualifications are delivered by suitably qualified staff in locations that are appropriately resourced. Funding agencies need to be satisfied that public money is being appropriately spent, according to current policy, as described by Jonathan Tummons.

Within contemporary post-industrial capitalist societies, neoliberal discourses of accountability have informed debates about professionalism to the extent that what are now seen as antiquated notions of professional autonomy have been replaced by a discourse of professional accountability. It is the expectation that the work of professional, or other chartered or accredited groups, is presented for public scrutiny in such a way that other professional groups and lay service users are able to access any information that they might require in order to make evaluative judgments about the professional service in question, as per I. Taylor. From this perspective, curriculum standardization can be seen as a mechanism through which these models of new professionalism can be enacted in the workplace.

Performance of Curriculum Standardization

The ways in which curricula are actually standardized, those processes and policies that are employed in order to ensure curriculum standardization, vary across different educational sectors, funding regimes, and both institutional and national boundaries. Nonetheless, a number of common themes can be observed. These rely on the use of both people (teachers, managers, school auditors, and inspectors) and technologies (quality assurance systems, reports, and user evaluations).

Different kinds of people are involved in standardization processes. Their engagement varies in level and intensity, and some of the people involved in standardization activities are more willing or knowing participants than others. The most conspicuous group of people involved are inspectors or auditors: distinct professional groups who, following a period of appropriate training, are licensed or otherwise warranted to carry out audits of particular forms of curricular provision. This might be through the sampling or moderation of test or examination papers and results by chief examiners, moderators, and verifiers. This might also be through the observation and evaluation of classroom or workshop-based teaching sessions that might be assessed as part of a broader portfolio of continuing professional development (CPD) or evaluated against externally imposed criteria as part of a quality assurance system. Such observations may also be performed by mentors or peers and may be co-opted to form part of a formal evaluation system. Local institutional systems and practices may also be subject to audit for the purposes of standardization. Such audits tend to draw on the documentation that is prepared within an organization for the purposes of establishing ways of working within curriculum schema. Audits such as these may also involve speaking with members of staff within

the organization who are responsible for the establishment and management of these systems. The final group that is involved in curriculum standardization is the students themselves. Across all phases of educational provision, different mechanisms have merged over recent years that are intended to authentically capture the "voice of the student." The promotion of the opinion of the service user within professional cultures more generally is characteristic of neoliberal discourses of professionalism, and is particularly prevalent within educational contexts, where a range of student-led and parent-led bodies meet with representatives from teaching, administrative, and policy groups at different times during the academic cycle.

Curriculum standardization is therefore a technically complex task that, if it is to be meaningful and legitimate, needs to be accomplished across institutional, temporal, and even spatial boundaries. These boundaries are made more fluid and more complex by the proliferation of e-learning. The work of the organization or other body of people who are tasked with curriculum standardization therefore needs to sample the work of curriculum design and delivery from across all of those institutions where the curriculum is delivered. This is usually done on a cyclical basis: Over the course of a cycle of years, institutions are audited. Audits may be carried out on a particular area of provision (e.g., the inspection of a specified curriculum by the examining body that endorses the qualifications offered at a particular school or college) or on the institution as a whole (e.g., by an inspectorate that has been given cross-sector authority, usually empowered by a governmental warrant or similar device). The scope of such institution-wide inspections might involve a combination of these modes of standardization.

Critical Perspectives on Curriculum Standardization

Criticisms of curriculum standardization center on two key themes. Some arguments suggest that the quality assurance discourse on which curriculum standardization rests is in some way distorting curriculum provision as a whole. Some arguments suggest that the ways in which professionals are enveloped within standardization practices serves to diminish, not strengthen the practices and ethics of the profession. The ways in which curriculum provision can be distorted by the requirements of standardization are akin to the ways in which assessment practices are responsible for "curriculum creep," a term used to describe the way in which curriculum delivery is focused on elements of the curriculum that are assessed ("teaching to the test"). Critics of standardization practices argue that the high-stakes inspections and evaluations that are characteristic of audit cultures (defined as high-stakes because they may be linked to formal staff probation, evaluation, and performance) discourage professional risk-taking because practitioners feel unable to deviate from patterns of practice that are reliable or trustworthy. Teachers or lecturers whose work is audited are more likely to rely on a relatively narrow repertoire of pedagogic strategies in their practice. Critics of standardization point to diminished concepts of creative teaching, which tend to narrowly focus on issues such as meeting diverse learning styles or encouraging creativity within arts education, in order to illustrate their argument.

The argument that audit cultures lead to a diminished professionalism is more controversial. This argument rests on the notion that professional educators are co-opted into performing audit or quality assurance roles, such as inspection or observation. These are portrayed as autonomous and empowering, with the professionals acting in their interests as individual practitioners, for example, through explaining the audit or standardization role through the language of continuing professional development. They are also portrayed as enacted for the benefit of the profession as a whole, for example through describing inspection processes as owned and enacted by practitioners for practitioners, based on criteria that are in some way negotiated by representative members of the profession (typically, a professional body or trade union), rather than externally imposed, according to M. Strathern.

This leads to the creation of a new professional class or group, the occupational definition of which is informed by its role within standardization and quality assurance processes, rather than within academic or pedagogic processes. The consequence of this is a fragmented professionalism, where members of that profession perform monitoring and surveillance roles on other members of the profession. In this way, conflicting discourses of professionalism that value accountability at the expense of autonomy are introduced into organizations and workplaces, with subsequent implications for the politics of these professional groups.

Conclusion

A critical understanding of curriculum standardization needs to take account of the multiple and sometimes conflicting definitions of curriculum. These definitions of curriculum foreground different aspects of educational provision, which in turn inform different elements of curriculum standardization processes. These processes encompass the activities of individual professionals, the working practices of professions, and the procedures of the institutions within which they work. There can be no serious or meaningful gainsaying of curriculum standardization: Curriculum provision should be as uniform as possible so that the curriculum, as an element of educational provision more generally, can be accessed or acquired without prejudice, bias, or privilege. However, more critically aware definitions of curriculum serve in turn to problematize standardization, and suggest that notwithstanding the ways in which curricula are specified, differences in delivery are a constant and unavoidable element of curriculum. According to this reading of curriculum, differences in, for example, the social or economic status of students or of the location of a school or college will impact curriculum. Dominant discourses of audit are seen as sustaining a form of curriculum standardization that suppresses debates about the social and economic factors that affect educational provision, suggesting that curriculum is enacted equally across different contexts, as noted by B. Bernstein.

Jonathan Tummons
Teesside University

See Also: Administration of Education; Educational Policymakers; Governmental Influences on Education; Hidden Curriculum; Schools as Bureaucracies.

Further Readings

Bernstein, B. *Class Codes and Control IV: The Structuring of Pedagogic Discourse.* London: Routledge, 1990.

Coffield, F., ed. *The Benefits of Informal Learning.* Bristol, UK: Policy Press, 2000.

Garrick, J. *Informal Learning in the Workplace: Unmasking Human Resource Development.* London: Routledge, 1998.

Gee, J. *Social Linguistics and Literacies: Ideology in Discourses.* 2nd ed. London: Routledge Falmer, 1996.

Kelly, A. V. *The Curriculum: Theory and Practice.* London: Sage, 2004.

Lave, J. and E. Wenger. *Situated Learning: Legitimate Peripheral Participation.* Cambridge: Cambridge University Press, 1991.

Strathern, M., ed. *Audit Cultures: Anthropological Studies in Accountability, Ethics and the Academy.* London: Routledge, 2000.

Taylor, I. *Developing Learning in Professional Education.* Buckingham, UK: Open University Press/Society for Research into Higher Education, 1997.

Tummons, J. *Curriculum Studies in the Lifelong Learning Sector.* Exeter, UK: Learning Matters, 2009.

Czech Republic and Slovakia

The Czech Republic and Slovakia are located in central Europe. Both countries have placed a high value on education throughout much of their histories because of its importance to economic development. The region also has a long history of cultural, religious, and ethnic diversity and conflict, which has shaped the educational system. The former Czechoslovakia emerged from Soviet rule in 1989, and became the independent nations of the Czech Republic and Slovakia in 1993. Despite their separation, the two nations continue to share similarly modeled school systems and similar problems transitioning to a democratic and decentralized system. Early regional populations included the Celts and Germanic and Slavonic tribes, with the Slavs among the earliest groups to establish schools in the area. Byzantine missionaries and invading Magyars also visited the area.

Early Influences

The crusades of the 12th and 13th centuries brought Christianity and a strong Roman Catholic influence to the region and its educational system, which continued under the Holy Roman Empire. Economic growth led to further educational development, including the beginning of higher education. Holy Roman Emperor Charles IV (1346–78) founded what became Charles University in Prague in 1348, the region's first university. General education was restricted to children from wealthy or noble families.

The Hussite revolution of the 15th century and the Protestant Reformation of the 16th century introduced religious diversity in both society and education. Germanic influences swept education during the reign of the Austro-Hungarian Empire beginning in 1526. Educational reformer Johann Amos Comenius introduced a more uniform and secular education system in the 17th century and is still remembered annually on Teacher's Day (March 28). The first legislation mandating compulsory education appeared in 1774 as part of Hapsburg ruler Marie Therese's economic development initiatives. The length of compulsory education was extended from six to eight years in 1869. The Germanic influence on culture and education resulted in the emergence of a movement to preserve the region's native language and culture. The Czechoslovak Republic emerged as an independent nation in 1918, upon the defeat of the Austro-Hungarian Empire after World War I. Industrialization and economic development accelerated both under the Hapsburg dynasty and in the years following independence, encouraging the growth and funding of education and the introduction of vocational schools.

Modern Era

Educational development in Czechoslovakia suffered severe setbacks during World War II and postwar Soviet governance. Germany occupied the country following Adolph Hitler's invasion of 1939, resulting in school and university closures, widespread destruction of the educational infrastructure, and the extermination of Czechoslovakian Jews and other minorities under the Holocaust. Educational rebuilding began in 1945, but was soon halted by Soviet takeover. The Soviet Union transformed the country to one of its Communist satellites in 1948, later reasserting control through the military suppression of the 1968 rebellion known as the Prague Spring. The educational system became state controlled and highly centralized under Soviet models and teaching methods. Czechoslovakia emerged from communist rule after the 1989 Velvet Revolution, ushering in a transitional period. In 1993, the former Czechoslovakia became two separate nations: the Czech Republic and Slovakia. Both countries have faced the challenges of decentralizing their educational systems in the wake of democratization and the introduction of a market economy and ongoing regional conflicts, such as the 1990s Balkan Wars. Education was an important component of the post-communist transition.

The Ministry of Education, Youth, and Sports oversees education through the university level.

Private schools have appeared and individual schools have had more authority over curriculum development after the end of Soviet rule. Private schools are both religious and nonparochial in nature, and may receive enrollment-based state funding. Czech and Slovak are the official state languages and primary languages of instruction for the Czech Republic and Slovakia, respectively, although instruction in additional languages, such as German and English, is common. Pre-primary school covers ages 3 to 6 and is not compulsory but is widely utilized. The compulsory primary level begins at age 6 for both countries and is broken into two components: primary and lower secondary schools.

The upper secondary level is not compulsory, and generally lasts through ages 15 to 19. Students may select either general education schools, known as *gymnasiums*, or vocational and technical schools. Teachers evaluate students on a scale of one to five, with report cards issued twice during the school year. Students complete final examinations (Maturita) upon completion of their secondary studies. Those students who wish to continue to higher education must successfully complete a second set of entrance examinations. Higher education can consist of university or professional studies at public, state, or private institutions. Public universities are free for qualified students. Common degree offerings include bachelor's, master's, engineering, and doctoral degrees. There are numerous fields of study and languages of instruction, including Czech, German, and English. Nontraditional higher education options include distance, adult, or lifelong learning, and private adult technical and vocational training programs.

Education was internationally targeted as a vital component in the successful transition from the state-controlled communist system to a democracy and private market economy. Transitional problems have included the fragmentation, inefficiency, and duplication of services, lack of clear delegation of authority, lack of administrative training, and lack of innovation in curriculum and teaching methods. International organizations, such as the European Union and the World Bank, have provided funding and assistance. Specialized vocational and instructional technology education has been emphasized because of the need for a skilled workforce.

Older problems balancing the needs of all culture groups also remain. Modern ethnic groups include Czech, Slovak, Moravian, Roma (Gypsy), Polish, German, Silesian, and Hungarian, all of which have a long tradition in the region. Socially and culturally disadvantaged groups continue to face prejudice, discrimination, and subsequent diminished educational opportunities, although improvements have been made in this area. The Roma (Gypsies) are among the most affected of these groups, with many Romani children educated in special schools for those with mental or physical disabilities.

Marcella Bush Trevino
Barry University

See Also: European Union; Labor Market Effects on Education; Russia.

Further Readings

Horner, Wolfgang, ed. *The Education Systems of Europe.* Dordrecht, Netherlands: Springer, 2007.

Ibanez-Martin, et al. *Education in Europe: Policies and Politics.* Boston: Kluwer Academic, 2002.

Ministry of Education, Youth, and Sports of the Czech Republic. http://www.msmt.cz/index.php?lang=2 (Accessed February 2012).

D

De Facto Tracking

In theory, de facto tracking differentiates teaching and learning based on the academic level and prior performance of a student under a fair and meritocratic educational system. De facto tracking, at its best, provides curricula and opportunities to learn in ways that correspond with students' abilities. Under this system, a students' academic success is the chief factor in his or her educational attainment and occupational rewards. Meritocratic ideology, however, is based on the assumption that all students begin their education on a level playing field, but in practice, it does not take into account pervasive systemic social inequalities that privilege some students at the expense of others.

Researchers have documented how the virtually universal pedagogical practice of tracking stratifies the educational process, overwhelmingly placing students with dominant social identities in higher-level courses, and placing lower-income students and students of color in lower-level courses. In fact, despite the ideological adherence to meritocracy beliefs in the educational system, little evidence of meritocratic matching of course placement has been found. There are concrete racial/ethnic and socioeconomic determinants that further serve to reproduce generational educational and occupational inequalities.

Programmatic tracking began as a consequence of integration efforts after the *Brown* decision, which magnified differences in academic performance between students of different racial/ethnic backgrounds. Under programmatic tracking, students were grouped by presumed ability into a mutually exclusive program that determined course choice across subjects, with rare mobility between tracks. For instance, programmatic tracks such as industrial training and home economics began as popular curricular tracks to train black, Latin American, and impoverished students for occupational and social roles that were deemed appropriate for their intellectual and moral capabilities. Placement was based on the perceived need to prepare students for careers similar to those of their parents, thus recreating and legitimizing inequality. Consequently, these programs established racially distinctive tracks in nominally integrated schools, essentially resegregating students by race/ethnicity and class and systematically excluding them from higher status curricula.

As a result of civil rights leaders, educators, and the public, who began to view these programmatic tracking structures as nonacademic, racist, and based on low teacher expectations and prejudice, widespread dismantling of tracking began. Urban schools in particular, comprised largely of low-income students and students of color, instituted vertically differentiated tracks, allowing students to enroll in disparate course levels for different subjects. Today, a de facto tracking system exists, where placements are flexible across subject areas and assignment can be in "advanced," "general," or "remedial." De facto tracking becomes exacerbated through the tendency of high-tracked and low-tracked students to choose different electives. For example, high-tracked students enroll more frequently in foreign language, arts, and music classes, whereas low-tracked students enroll more frequently in vocational education classes. These elective courses are intended to be heterogeneous in make-up, but become homogenous. It is argued that this is a natural outcome of a meritocratic system, whereas others contend that the system perpetuates racial/ethnic and socioeconomic segregation and inequality. Either way, the result of de facto tracking is a stratified system where students are clustered based on constricted views of students' merit and demographic background.

Despite inequities in the operation and outcomes of a de facto tracking system, there is a strong debate around its practice in schools. Proponents emphasize the many instructional benefits of achievement-based homogeneous classrooms. Tracking is touted as an efficient way to deliver curricula to ability-grouped students. Yet, track placement overwhelmingly benefits those in the higher tracks as they are more likely to experience quality teaching, higher expectations, and achievement-orientated classmates. These students have different academic socializing experiences, increased academic achievement, and higher rates of high school graduation and college attendance compared to students in lower tracks. Critics of tracking contend that, despite the theoretical ability to move vertically to higher-level tracks, this happens only on rare occasions. Thus, maturity in motivation and effort are not accounted for in de facto tracking environments, which disproportionately disadvantage students of color and impoverished students, who most likely begin in lower tracks. Additionally, de facto tracking influences students' educational abilities, identities, and attitudes. The low-level placement becomes magnified as students in those classes experience a less academically rigorous learning environment, limiting opportunities to learn, reinforcing stereotypes, and perpetuating inequalities. Additionally, low-track placement has been correlated with a self-fulfilling prophecy, where the low expectations students encounter regarding their academic abilities are realized through tracking practices.

De facto tracking persists because the system rewards students who demonstrate familiarity with dominant cultural capital, where well-educated parents are in a position to advocate for educational advantages for their children, and are aware that high-track placement is coveted in the competition for college admission. The system primarily inhibits the upward mobility of students of color and impoverished students through a complex interdependence of structural systems and cultural assumptions that work against their educational achievement. De facto tracking shapes learning opportunities and influences students' educational achievement and labor market outcomes. These consequences lead many in the educational system and the public alike to call for a second de-tracking movement. They call for a heterogeneous system, where everyone has equal access to the curriculum, with high expectations for all students, allowing all students the opportunity to develop in the classroom and beyond.

Sylvia L. M. Martinez
Dena Samuels
University of Colorado Colorado Springs

See Also: Ability Grouping; Class Inequality: Achievement; De-Tracking; Meritocracy; Racial Inequality: Achievement; Teacher Expectations; Tracking.

Further Readings

Lucas, Samuel. *Tracking Inequality: Stratification and Mobility in American High Schools*. New York: Teachers College Press, 1999.

Lucas, Samuel and Mark Berends. "Sociodemographic Diversity, Correlated Achievement and De Facto Tracking." *Sociology of Education*, v.75/4 (2002).

Oakes, Jeannie. *Keeping Track: How Schools Structure Inequality.* 2nd ed. New Haven, CT: Yale University Press, 2005.

Deaf Students

Because the disability of hearing impairment is intimately tied to language, education has played a much more significant role in shaping deafness than other disabilities. The history of Deaf and Hard of Hearing (DHH) education is marked by debates around sign language versus "oralism," and only in recent decades have sign languages been accepted as the natural and legitimate language of the deaf. Educational research focuses on DHH student achievement, noting consistent disparities. There are growing accounts of deaf cultures and DHH education and communities around the world. There have been accounts of DHH individuals receiving education in ancient Greece and Renaissance Spain, but formal schooling for DHH students was not established until the 18th century in Europe. In 1817, Thomas Hopkins Gallaudet and Laurent Clerc founded the American School for the Deaf in Hartford, Connecticut, borrowing what they had learned in France, and so American Sign Language (ASL) has its roots in both French and British Sign Languages (FSL and BSL). Though sign language was used as a mode of instruction for a time in these schools, the "oral" method was heavily promoted in the late 1800s, promoting speech and lip-reading. In the 1950s, William C. Stokoe, who is often referred to as the "father of ASL," joined Gallaudet University and in researching the linguistics of sign languages declared ASL to be a legitimate, independent language, leading to a change in educational policy in the 1970s and 1980s. Gallaudet University, established in 1864, is now considered the "Mecca" for DHH education and research, and has served to create a national deaf culture, fostering the National Association of the Deaf (NAD). The Americans with Disabilities Act (ADA) of 1990 protects people who are DHH by requiring, for example, that colleges and universities provide sign language interpreters.

Until recent decades, almost all DHH children who were included in formal education attended segregated boarding schools for the DHH. Because these are costly and rare, there has been a recent emphasis in inclusive deaf education, and now only 10 percent of DHH students attend segregated schools. Much of the research focus on DHH education explores why these students consistently achieve less well academically than hearing peers, and how to improve DHH education. Research has shown that DHH students are less likely to monitor their language comprehension as they read and that they tend to show shorter memory spans as compared to hearing peers of the same age. They are also stereotyped as "impulsive." Some argue that these beliefs and behaviors are in part because of "over-protective" parents and teachers. There is also criticism over the lack of sign language fluency of some teachers and generally lower standards. Children who are native signers and who have grown up with sign language from infancy show greater abilities in visuospatial memory than hearing peers. While both signing and "oral" DHH students frequently

begin schooling with less knowledge than their peers, research has established that they have the same intellectual potential. There has been an intense debate over the use of cochlear implants with young DHH children. While the technology results in improved academic achievement, deaf culture advocates fear the "genocide" of their community. Television in many countries is closed captioned and there have been major advances in mobile phone technology, computers with Web-cams, and voice-to-text programs. In high-income countries, the affordability and ubiquity of these technologies have increased quality of life.

When the word *Deaf* is capitalized, it denotes a cultural identity, rather than audiological ability. Deaf culture is the shared use of a sign language, and a Deaf community is a group of people with similar shared experiences. The term *attitudinal deafness* is a way of describing an identity not tied to audiological levels. For instance, a hearing child of a deaf parent might still identify as part of the Deaf community. The term *audism* describes the social stigma that positions being hearing above deafness, and oral languages as superior to sign languages. There are also different ways of being DHH, such as deafened adults, who became DHH at a later age, and have an established hearing identity. People who identify as hard-of-hearing often feel that they are "between worlds" because they interact with both Deaf communities and hearing ones.

There are growing accounts of DHH education in non-Western contexts. In developing countries, DHH education has traditionally been funded by religious institutions, though governments, with the assistance of international aid, are increasingly providing free schooling and even teacher training. These initiatives often borrow curriculum and pedagogy from the United States, resulting in the spread of ASL. There have also been accounts of "shared signing communities" where hereditary deafness in an isolated region (often an island) results in the use of sign language by most community members, regardless of auditory ability. The most famous of these is the Martha's Vineyard Deaf, though others have been documented in Japan, Bali, Ghana, Mexico, Thailand, Surinam, Jamaica, Israel, Brazil, and Papua New Guinea.

Nalini Asha Biggs
University of Oxford

See Also: Bilingual Education; Disabled Students; Special Education.

Further Readings

Groce, N. E. *Everyone Here Spoke Sign Language: Hereditary Deafness on Martha's Vineyard.* Cambridge, MA: Harvard University Press, 1985.

Humphries, T. L. and C. A. Padden. *Inside Deaf Culture.* Cambridge, MA: Harvard University Press, 2005.

Marschark, M. and P. E. Spencer. *Oxford Handbook of Deaf Studies, Language, and Education.* Vol. 2. New York: Oxford University Press, 2010.

Delaware

With a land area of only 2,489 square miles, Delaware is the second-smallest of the American states. It is the only state that was claimed at different points in its history by the Swedish, Dutch, and English. Delaware is known as the "First State" because it was the first state to ratify the U.S. Constitution, in 1787. Delaware shares a northern border with Pennsylvania, and Maryland is located to the south and west. Toward the east, New Jersey lies across the Delaware River and Delaware Bay, which empties into the Atlantic Ocean. Delaware has a population of 897,934, according to the 2010 census. Although Dover is the state capital, the largest city is Wilmington. Delaware has a long history of commitment to education and came in first place when federal education grants were awarded under President Obama's Race to the Top (RTT) program. This program provided $119 million over a four-year period for further improving education in Delaware.

The area that became Delaware was first inhabited by the Lenni Lenape of the Algonkian tribe, around 1400. Two centuries later, the area was discovered by Englishman Henry Hudson, who had mounted an exploration for the Dutch East India Company. The following year, the area was given the name of Delaware to honor Lord De La Warr, the governor of Virginia. By 1631, the first Dutch colonists had arrived, but that colony was destroyed by Native Americans. In 1638, Fort Christina was settled on the area that became Wilmington, making it the first permanent settlement in Delaware. In 1681, Delaware became part of William Penn's Pennsylvania colony. Ultimately becoming a separate colony, Delaware was the first American colony to call itself a state after independence from Britain was declared in 1776.

By the early 19th century, the need for public education was a nationwide issue. In 1829, the state legislature passed the Free School Act that established the public school system. Four years later, Newark College, which ultimately became the University of Delaware, was established. Delaware was a slave-owning state, but chose to remain in the Union during the Civil War. In 1875, the state funded two segregated school systems. In 1913, the first women's college was established in Newark. Delaware's segregated school system was abolished in the 1950s by the Supreme Court ruling in *Brown v. Board of Education*. The 1990s ushered in a period of major educational reform in Delaware. Educators worked with parents and business and community leaders to develop a comprehensive renovation plan. Performance standards were established in reading, writing, math, science, and social studies, and the Delaware Student-Testing Program was established in 1996 to evaluate progress in these fields. A package of laws dealing with accountability and school promotion was subsequently implemented.

In 2009, the Race to the Top (RTT) program, the cornerstone of President Barack Obama's educational program, was established. With millions of dollars at stake, states were invited to apply for grant money.

Table 1 Elementary and secondary education characteristics

	Delaware	U.S. (average)
Total number of schools	218	1,988
Total students	129,403	970,278
Total teachers	8,933	60,766.56
Pupil/teacher ratio	14.49	15.97

Source: U.S. Department of Education, National Center for Education Statistics, Common Core of Data (CCD), 2010–11.

Table 2 Elementary and secondary education finance

	Delaware	U.S. (average)
Total revenues	$1,690,557,129	$11,464,385,994
Total expenditures for education	$1,795,613,214	$11,712,033,839
Total current expenditures	$1,489,594,218	$9,938,906,259

Source: U.S. Department of Education, National Center for Education Statistics, Common Core of Data (CCD), "National Public Education Financial Survey," FY08 (2007–08).

Awards were based on the ability of individual states to follow through on implementing standards and assessments to determine readiness for colleges and jobs, building data systems that were capable of measuring growth and serving as information avenues for teachers and principals, recruiting and retaining effective teachers and principals, and targeting low-performing schools for special assistance. When grants were announced, Delaware had come in first, winning 456.4 points out of a possible 500, as a result of having demonstrated a history of commitment to education and having legislation already in place that improved the state's chances of meeting designated goals. At the K–12 level, specific goals focused on reducing racial and income achievement gaps that show up on National Assessment of Educational Progress tests and increasing reading and math scores for fourth and eighth graders by a minimum of 19 percent. Within the area of higher education, officials committed to increasing college enrollment from 59 to 70 percent by 2014. Delaware spends more than a billion dollars a year on educational programs for K–12, and the federal funds allotted through RTT have been an important element in improving education in the state. In order to meet the goals established by RTT, teachers closely monitor student progress in order to understand what kind of testing best demonstrates that students have learned the material. The state also established the "partnership zone" program to form alliances in which state and local communities work directly with the 10 lowest-performing schools to improve student test scores.

There are approximately 126,801 students enrolled in the public school systems of Delaware, and 81.1 percent of those are in Title I schools. There are 237 schools in 19 school districts, and the state has established 21 charter schools. Some 8,640 teachers work in the various school districts. The student/teacher ratio is 14.7 and Delaware spends $12,390 per pupil each year. The student population is predominately white (51.6 percent). A third of them are African American, and around 11 percent are Hispanic. Approximately 47 percent of students are eligible for free lunches. When taking national achievement tests, 4th and 8th grade students tend to rank somewhat higher than the public average. Teacher evaluations are considered important in Delaware. Teachers who rank "highly effective" are required to undergo one announced observation each year and a summative evaluation every two years. Each year, teachers are evaluated on

how much their students improve. Teachers who are not deemed effective may be dismissed.

Elizabeth Rholetter Purdy
Independent Scholar

See Also: Race to the Top; Standardized Testing; Teacher Recruitment, Induction, and Retention.

Further Readings

McNeil, Michele. "Delaware Pushes to Meet Race to Top Promises." *Education Week*, v.30/32 (2011).

National Center for Education Statistics. "State Profiles: Delaware." http://nces.ed.gov/nationsreportcard/states (Accessed February 2012).

Vision 2015. http://www.vision2015delaware.org (Accessed February 2012).

Denmark

The Kingdom of Denmark comprises Denmark proper and two autonomous provinces, the Faroe Islands and Greenland. Denmark proper is located between the Baltic Sea (to the west) and the North Sea (to the east), and is bordered by Germany in the south. The country is 16,621 square miles (43,098 square kilometers) and, along with Norway and Sweden, is part of the cultural region known as Scandinavia. Denmark's population is over 5.5 million people, with approximately 87 percent ethnic Scandinavians, in part because of its border regions, the homogenizing influence of the Lutheran State Church, its late industrialization, and restrictive immigration policy. However, the number of nonethnic Scandinavian immigrants has increased in recent years, causing tensions between the Danes and the immigrant community over social and cultural differences, the support of the welfare state for immigrant unemployment, and expected assimilation and integration into the Danish culture.

School History

Denmark, one of the oldest kingdoms in the world, was established around 900 as a Viking settlement. Christianity was introduced in 965, and with it came social stratification and rudimentary education. Initially, only Catholic dogma was taught in the Catholic monastery schools. This changed as Denmark began to flourish, and counting, trades, and crafts were introduced in the schools, helping shape a practical as well as dogmatic education. The Lutheran Reformation in 1532, however, abolished the Catholic Church in Denmark, and shuttered monastery schools. The cathedrals, land, and schools of the Catholic Church were given to the Crown, thus establishing the first rudimentary form of government-supported education. This new "public education," however, was more primitive than the Lutheran grammar schools that were established in 1539 to teach classical humanism to the upper classes. During this historical period, Denmark's reign as a world power was coming to an end; its loss of the Thirty Years War in 1648 contributed to its further decline on the world stage. In response, the absolute power of the monarchy was established in 1660, with strict Lutheranism enforced, including universal confirmation, to increase nationalism. This led to the creation of Calvary schools in 1721, in order to ensure some literacy in the lower classes prior to religious confirmation.

Although the Calvary schools provided some public education, it was not until the influence of the Enlightenment movement in the early 19th century that education was reorganized to fully include the masses. During this time, agrarian reforms and growing nationalism created a class of independent farmers who supported schooling the lower classes in Danish language and culture in *Folkeskoles* (people's schools). This movement influenced the Education Act of 1814, which required compulsory education for seven years in both municipal and rural regions. Initially, subjects included religion, reading, writing, and arithmetic, and each school uniquely reflected its location. However, as primary education served more people, education became more mechanized and unequal; higher education was still limited to the upper classes. The monarchy's staunch control of schools, as well as budding nationalism after the Napoleonic War, led to N. F. S. Grundtvig's founding of *Folkelighojskole* in 1844, where "ordinary" people were capable of enlightenment, and education should reflect a national identity. This movement grew to include residential and adult educational institutions that served to enlighten, instead of train, ordinary people. This new type of education helped ease the transition of Denmark into a democratic monarchy in 1849. Christen Kold further translated Grundtvig's ideas about a liberal education into the "free school" movement, which served as an alternative to state-funded education, and influenced the Primary School Act of 1855, allowing parents choice in their children's education.

As the 20th century approached, education in Denmark evolved to reflect egalitarian social reforms and rapid industrialization. The Education Act of 1894 improved teacher training, and the Education Act of 1903 established transition schools to allow all children, regardless of social class, access to secondary and higher education. Further educational decrees in 1937, 1958, and 1975 made education more egalitarian, gender equal, and informal. Educational reform in the early 1990s individualized student instruction to enhance students' desire to learn and prepare for active participation in a democracy. The Danish tax-funded welfare state, created in 1963, currently supports education at all levels, including university training and adult education, and heavily subsidizes private and religious schools to ensure parental choice.

Contemporary Schooling

In the 21st century, current educational issues include gender inequality in the sciences and the integration of immigrants into Danish society. Denmark's recent low scores on international achievement tests in science highlight the lack of student preparation for science careers, and may damper Denmark's future participation in the increasingly global economy. Furthermore, science is the only field of study that remains gendered; even science curriculum reform has not increased the number of females who study science. The recent increase in immigration has also led to a reexamination of the education system.

Traditionally, children of immigrants have underperformed in the Danish school system, and this has led to a high unemployment rate for non-Danes across subsequent generations. There is now target integration of immigrants into the labor market through adult education programs; immigrant adults can receive extensive education in language, culture, and social norms. However, the current teaching of Danish as a second language is not proficient for entrance into higher education, cementing immigrants' lack of social mobility. The pressure for immigrants to fully integrate into the Danish culture has further strained the relationship among immigrants, Danes, and public education, which serves a dual purpose of education and integration. Immigrants are turning to state-subsidized private schools for education, supported by the Danish welfare state, in order to retain their native culture. In order to be a productive society, Denmark will need to resolve the tension between the welfare state, parental choice for education, and the pressure for immigrant integration.

Basic compulsory education in Denmark is run by the Ministry of Education and begins at age 7 (first grade) with an option for preschool at age 6; it continues until age 16 (ninth grade) with an option for an additional year (10th grade). Special education students are streamlined into traditional classes, as every child, regardless of education level, receives an individuated lesson plan. Parents can choose to send their children to the public *Folkeskole* or to state-subsidized private or religious primary and continuation schools. After age 16, students can choose two paths: general upper secondary education, or vocationally oriented programs. There are also adult vocational programs for certification, as part of the Danish mission for life-long learning for all its citizens, as well as a path for adults who want to return to higher education. Only six percent of students do not continue some kind of education after the *Folkeskole*. There are two forms of general upper secondary education: the gymnasium and the higher preparatory examination (HF) courses. The gymnasium qualifies students for admission to the university or other higher education studies. The higher preparatory examination is for young people and adults who left the education system, but want to return to receive a university education. The two types of vocationally oriented programs focus on commercial vocations (HHX) and more technological subjects, including the natural sciences (HTX).

Shannon R. Audley-Piotrowski
University of Memphis

See Also: Class Inequality: Achievement; Denmark; Finland; Immigrant Adaptation; Sweden.

Further Readings

Allardt, Erik. *Nordic Democracy: Ideas, Issues, and Institutions in Politics, Economy, Education, Social and Cultural Affairs of Denmark, Finland, Iceland, Norway, and Sweden.* Cohenhagen, Denmark: Det Danske Selskab, 1981.
Egelund, Niels. "Country Briefing: Special Education in Denmark." *European Journal of Special Needs Education,* v.15/1 (2000).
Miller, Kenneth E. *Denmark.* Oxford: Clio Press, 1987.

Deskilling of the Teaching Profession

Deskilling of the teaching profession has been a recurring, contentious issue, especially since the 1970s, most prominently debated in the Anglo-American world. The issue has been primarily discussed from two perspectives: deskilling because of bureaucratic control in general, and the debilitating effect on the teaching profession because of the merging interests of an enhanced centralizing tendency of the state and private commercial interests. The first perspective was debated through the 1970s and until the mid-1980s. The next phase of the deskilling debate emerged out of the discernible tendencies of bureaucratic-managerial control on teaching since the early 1990s, and has seen a revival in the new millennium because of the global spread of the neoliberal agenda in education. The *Oxford English Dictionary* suggests a definition of *deskill* as the following:

- To convert an employment or a workplace from one that requires skilled workers, to one that does not.
- To reduce the number of skilled workers in an employment sector.
- To render a skilled worker into an unskilled one. Deskilling of the teaching profession could involve all three processes.

Deskilling of the teaching profession is often used to mean an imposed loss or degeneration of skills of teachers. The word *skill*, when used with its prefix, as in "de-skill," is used in a paradoxical sense, however, when referring to the teaching profession. That is, the word *deskilling* is used to pose a strong criticism against the technical, bureaucratic, or managerial control of pedagogy and curriculum that delimit the holistic craft and educational learning of teaching (as a skill) and reduce it to mechanistic, rule-bound, discreet skill-based modes of teaching and learning.

Concept of a Public Service Profession

There is a lack of a consensus on the concept of "profession," and whether teaching is a profession or not. Professionalism is a socially constructed, historically changing concept, with no inherent qualities attached to it. A professional is conceived as a qualified specialist, with competencies achieved through institutionalized formal education, training, and licensed credentials in a particular field. This acquired expert knowledge is not interchangeable. Professional membership is exclusionary in this sense, and often generates a distinct communal identity, commitment, and organizational associations. A continuing, conflicting, but interdependent relation between autonomy and interference, therefore, exists between professions like teaching and the modern nation-states, within which the concept of professionalization developed in the 19th century as a result of industrialization and liberal democratic movements. Each profession has rights and privileges that are not given to others. These rights especially refer to professional autonomy and self-regulation based on some professional codes of ethics; and the privileges of job security and other benefits derive from the recognition of professions like teaching as a public service. A public service professional enters into a contractual and bargaining relationship with the state, which is his/her employer. Autonomy of the professional (which is also a gated concept, as it ironically comes through enforced standards on entry, knowledge, skills, and performance) is granted by society because professions are expected to function for the public good, not private benefit. However, the boundary of what constitutes public service, and who is performing it and who is not, is not always clear.

The boundary between a profession and an occupation is also not beyond challenge, because it raises critical questions like whose knowledge and what kinds of knowledge forms should be considered to matter enough for an occupation to be considered as a profession that is exclusionary and commands social prestige, status, and power. Professionals have been criticized for their monopolistic claims to specialized knowledge and expertise, which are often enabled through centralized bureaucratic systems of the state.

One of the most radical criticisms of the official system of education, and an indirect attack on the monopoly of knowledge, marking teaching as a profession, came from Ivan Illich in 1970 in the United States, whose views are susceptible to being (mis)used by the neoliberal agenda. In *Deschooling Society*, Illich contends that public schools under the bureaucratic control of the state act as the domain of elite control. Public schoolteachers were seen as obstructions to learning because state sponsored credentialization of teachers blocked possibilities for any ground-up, spontaneous, organic, partnership-based learning.

One of the hidden curricula that Illich cites is the ritualization of university degrees and credentials that continue class distinctions, and public school teachers perpetuate such distinctions through their select privileged access to higher education and training. Thus, Illich eloquently described the deskilling mechanisms of the working-class children and communities, and not the teaching profession. His views, in part, were not entirely different from the prevalent bodies of work of the 1970s and 1980s, where teachers were seen as agents of capital and the state bureaucracy who were inadvertently deskilling (especially) working-class children who had resources, creative understanding, and knowledge that was made redundant by the school system. Theorists also noted the complexity of the situation pertaining to the social position of teachers, who were also seen somewhat as victims located within a hierarchically organized, bureaucratic school system, which was also leading to the deskilling of teachers. In this case, the plight of the teachers, albeit professionals, was conceived to be similar to that of industrial workers. The primary framework was drawn from Harry Braverman's work in 1974, *Labor and Monopoly Capital*, situated in the industrial context of the United States.

Deskilling of Teachers as Workers

Braverman noted that management, working in the interest of capital, controls and deskills the laboring class through its monopoly of knowledge of the whole labor process, using the principles of scientific management. The monopoly works through a division of labor between managers and workers, with the former in charge of the design and planning, and the latter merely responsible for its implementation. The worker gets deskilled in the process because of a lack of decision-making power, or lack of use of his/her embodied, situated knowledge. Deskilling also works through fragmentation of work into smallest units of tasks for managerial control and coordination. Rationalization reduces the complexity of work to routinized standardized units. Fragmented specialization permits recruitment of lesser-skilled individuals, who are cheaper to hire than higher-skilled workers. This depresses overall wages and intensifies workload, thereby enhancing productivity through mechanisms of efficiency. Although Braverman's analysis was conducted in a factory context, some scholars have argued for the comparability of conditions of deskilled factory workers and that of teachers as professionals.

It is within this broader framework that scholars have been examining proletarianization, deskilling, and disempowerment of teachers from the 1980s to the present. Within this perspective, deskilling can be conceived through two primary lenses—bureaucratization and privatization/commodification/corporatization of schooling. However, historical works suggest that there is continuity of some of the conditions of teachers' work. Loss of autonomy of teachers in exercising discretion began with their simultaneous induction into the large centralized, hierarchized bureaucratic structures as salaried professionals that replaced decentralized schooling because of multiple historical contingencies, including concern for order, organization, and efficiency in an era of massive migration and immigration in the 19th century. Detailed supervision-based bureaucratic structures emerged through a gendered division of labor, with male superintendents in higher education taking on the managerial power and conceiving the largely female teacher force with school-level education or undergraduate degrees as implementers of decisions.

Through strong progressive and civil rights movements, public schools emerged as one of the foundations of democratic civic culture in the Anglo-American context. This phase of bureaucratic control, described as bureau professionalism by some, retained the ethos of public service, cooperation, and commitment to social justice. Administration and management of schooling was firmly socialized within the parameters of the field of education. A significant shift has occurred since the 1990s, and the relationship between the professionals and the small but strong state has altered in the Anglo-American world, with effects elsewhere too. This shift away from bureau-professional identity to another phase of deskilling of teachers is attributed to the penetration of new managerialism in the education sector.

New managerialism is characterized by the following ethos and practices: competition, efficiency, consumer-orientation, marginalization of unions, and discouragement of dissent. School administration and leadership is shifting from individuals with educational degrees and experiences to those with generic management degrees, with little or no experience in education. Business-model based technical proficiency has replaced context-based, child-centered pedagogy. Centralizing policies on the other hand, like the No Child Left Behind Act in the United States and advocacy for assessment elsewhere, have intensified and expanded test-based accountability regimes. This has led to a flourishing market of powerful private enterprises. Not only does bureaucratic control through standardized testing come to determine how and what teachers should know, teach, do, and be able to demonstrate through their student tests achievements, the diverse private market surrounding the testing regime often tends to dictate teaching practices.

Public schools in the United States buy prepackaged modules from private entities that have meticulously detailed instructions for teachers on how to conduct instruction and what the appropriate student response should be. These lesson modules also contain achievement and diagnostic tests aligned with state standards. These modular packages assume that education and learning can be reduced to discreet skills, fulfilling the Bravermanian managerial control of teaching tasks. Instead of using their professional judgment, teachers are embroiled in a testing, target and benchmarking, and sorting system of education for demonstrable accountability.

On the other hand, school choice and various modes of privatization lead to fragmentation of state and university regulation of teacher education and credentials. When individual schools are allowed to decide who to recruit and with what qualification, it risks drastic alteration, or in many a cases lowering of teacher qualification that lowers wages and de-professionalizes teaching. In the global context, an indiscriminate trend of recruitment of untrained individuals with minimal qualifications is already prevalent.

In addition, alternate credential routes like Teach For America (TFA) programs have reignited the debate on professionalism because of the unpreparedness of many TFA graduates, who have gone through compressed training, instead of going through the long route of teacher education programs. Thus, the state in its neoliberal guise partners with private or commercial interests in a way that disempowers teachers because these current enhanced test-based and choice-based mechanisms of accountability reveal a loss of trust in the professional judgments of teachers that is then justified in calls for external regulations. However, according to some scholars, it is also the state that can restore the status of the teaching profession.

Sarbani Chakraborty
University of Wisconsin, Madison

See Also: Curriculum Standardization; Standardized Testing; Teacher Expectations; Teacher Placement and Staffing; Teacher Recruitment, Induction, and Retention.

Further Readings

Apple, Michael. "Creating Difference: Neo-Liberalism, Neo-Conservatism and the Politics of Educational Reform." *Educational Policy*, v.18/1 (2004).

Compton, Mary and Lois Weiner, eds. *The Global Assault on Teaching, Teachers, and Their Unions: Stories for Resistance.* New York: Palgrave Macmillan, 2008.

Darling-Hammond, Linda. *The Flat World and Education: How America's Commitment To Equity Will Determine Our Future.* New York: Teachers College Press, 2010.

Gewirtz, Sharon, Pat Mahony, Ian Hextall, and Allan Cribb, eds. *Changing Teacher Professionalism: International Trends, Challenges and Ways Forward.* New York: Routledge, 2009.

Kincheloe, Joe L. *Critical Pedagogy Primer.* New York: Peter Lang, 2008.

De-Tracking

De-tracking is a movement to end the grouping of students into separate courses based on perceived ability. Students are often tracked into various academic programs in both formal and informal ways. Those in favor of de-tracking believe that it both causes divisions and supports existing discord between students; these often happen along racial/ethnic and socioeconomic lines. Often, schools claim that they do not have official tracking practices, but nearly all schools categorize students in some way. These categorizations result in vastly differing school experiences for students in different tracks. Many educators and administrators are convinced that both teaching and learning will be easier if students are grouped homogeneously by perceived ability. De-tracking advocates, on the other hand, believe that while tracking may be a practice with positive intentions, it has terrible consequences that support inequality and work against principles of social justice.

The roots of tracking practices in the United States can be traced to the early 20th century, when large populations of immigrant children began to attend school. Many school officials at the time believed that in order to educate this diverse population, students must be sorted into groups. Regarding the advent of tracking practices, prominent school reformers advocated abandoning democratic ideals of equality in favor of specialized educational practices. In early 20th-century America, paranoia around the influence of immigrant students coincided with an increased confidence in standardized achievement and IQ tests; these kinds of measures made the process of sorting students seem more scientific. Early on, students were sorted into tracks such as academic, general, or vocational, with some students chosen to be prepared for college and others prepared for work as electricians or secretaries. During the mid-20th century, tracking practices were relatively extreme, and students in large, comprehensive high schools were placed in all-encompassing tracks that dictated precisely which courses they took.

Momentum around de-tracking began to build in the mid-1980s as the inequalities produced by tracking began to surface. Jeannie Oakes's landmark work, *Keeping Track,* chronicled tracking practices and provided empirical evidence of the negative impacts of tracking on students who are labeled "low ability." Typically, students were segregated into separate tracks within the school, with minority students often pushed into the lower tracks. Often, students in the lowest tracks were placed with the teachers who were the least qualified and skilled. In the early 1990s, both Massachusetts and California issued statewide mandates that tracking must be ended or drastically reduced in middle schools. Across these two states, schools exercised local autonomy and successfully implemented the policy in a variety of ways. During this period, courts even mandated de-tracking reforms as part of efforts to desegregate and promote equality in schools; in 1994, this happened in the San Jose Unified School District. When de-tracking was at its most popular, multiple prominent political and educational organizations, including the National Governors Association, the National Education Association, the National Council of Teachers of English, and the California Department of Education voiced their support of de-tracking.

While the movement was popular during the 1990s, response to de-tracking reform was not consistent. Many teachers favored de-tracking, but public figures and parents resisted the reform. Because of this mixed response, de-tracking was never ingrained as a school practice. Data from the National Educational Longitudinal Study of 1988 showed that in core subject areas, fewer than 20 percent of students were in heterogeneously grouped classrooms. A 1993 study similarly reported that, nationally, most students were enrolled in primarily homogeneously grouped classrooms. Finally, a 2000 survey of Maryland's public high schools showed that just 13 percent of high schools did not employ tracking in the core subject areas. Taken together, these surveys seem to suggest that despite the efforts of de-tracking advocates, American classrooms remain stratified by ability.

Despite the de-tracking movement, tracking practices have remained relatively stable. Contemporary tracking practices are less extreme than in the past, with students enrolling in courses in different tracks in each subject area. This is likely because many educators generally support the way that tracking is currently practiced. Often, educators feel that tracking simplifies classroom instruction. When creating lessons, teachers tend to feel that planning becomes more streamlined.

Teachers also often find themselves receiving pressure from the parents of students in higher ability groups as they feel tracking supports even greater learning for their child. Students who are assigned to low ability groups, however, do not enjoy the same benefits, in fact scoring lower on standardized tests than when placed in mixed or high ability groups. Even those in favor of de-tracking note that teaching in de-tracked schools and classrooms can present different challenges than teaching in a tracked school. Often, teachers feel that when they are teaching in de-tracked classes, they have to make a choice to either teach to the mid-range of ability in the classroom or leave some of the intended content out in order to serve the needs of all of the students in the class. In practice, de-tracking presents a set of challenges that can be financially and logistically challenging. Teachers often need some professional development around teaching in a de-tracked class, and schools need to implement curricular modifications for de-tracking to be successful. Although the de-tracking movement never took off on a large scale, it changed the way that the public and educational institutions approach tracking by raising awareness about the potential inequalities produced by tracking.

Ashlee Lewis
University of South Carolina

See Also: Ability Grouping; School Organization; Tracking.

Further Readings

Boaler, J. "How a Detracked Mathematics Approach Promoted Respect, Responsibility, and High Achievement." *Theory Into Practice*, v.45/1 (2006).

Burris, C. C. and D. T. Garrity. *Detracking for Excellence and Equity.* Alexandria, VA: Association for Supervision and Curriculum Development, 2008.

Loveless, T. *The Tracking Wars: State Reform Meets School Policy.* Washington, DC: Brookings Institution Press, 1999.

Oakes, J. *Keeping Track: How Schools Structure Inequality.* 2nd ed. New Haven, CT: Yale University Press, 2005.

Rubin, B. C. "Detracking in Context: How Local Constructions of Ability Complicate Equity-Geared Reform." *Teachers College Record*, v.110/3 (2008).

Dewey, John

John Dewey (1859–1952), an American psychologist, philosopher, educator, and social critic, was born in Burlington, Vermont, on October 20, 1859. In 1879, he graduated from the University of Vermont, where he was greatly influenced by the work of T. H. Huxley, the English evolutionist. After teaching high school for two years, Dewey decided to study philosophy. He completed his Ph.D. studies in 1884 at Johns Hopkins University in Baltimore, Maryland. During his studies, he was greatly influenced by Hegelian philosophy rooted in German idealism, and experimental psychology, which could be used to apply scientific methodology to the human sciences.

He taught at the University of Michigan from 1884 to 1894, with a one-year break at the University of Minnesota in 1888. He left the University of Michigan to accept a position as chair of the Department of Philosophy, Psychology, and Pedagogy at the University of Chicago. While at the University of Chicago, Dewey began moving away from idealism to pragmatism, a newly developing American school of thought based in empiricism. Pragmatism influenced his approach to pedagogy, and as founder and director of the laboratory school at the university, he was able to develop and implement his ideas, resulting in his first major work related to education, *The School and Society* (1899). He was elected president of the American Psychological Association in 1899, and in

1905, he became president of the American Philosophical Association.

In 1904, Dewey left Chicago, largely because of disagreements with administration about the laboratory school. From 1905 until his retirement in 1929, Dewey taught at Columbia University in New York. He continued to teach as professor emeritus until 1939. During his time at Columbia, Dewey wrote prolifically. He published two of his most influential volumes during that time. *How We Think,* published in 1910, applied his theory of knowledge to education, and *Democracy and Education* was published in 1916. In this work, he expounded on his notions about the interactive and social process of developing the mind and the intellect. Through the years, Dewey developed a philosophy that was influenced by evolutionary theories. He began to see thought as the product of interactions between a person and the environment and that knowledge was the "instrument" that guided and controlled the interactions, an approach he called "instrumentalism." Dewey saw a direct link between instrumentalism and social theory. He contended that humans are from the outset social beings and that the individual can only achieve success and satisfaction through existing in an environment that promotes these interactions. Within the social context, the achievement of socially defined ends produces a satisfying life for the individual. Moral and social problems are defined in relation to and guide humans to meet these ends.

These notions informed Dewey's approach to education. He strongly believed that a democratic form of life in which a community is made up of individuals who interact with and respond to society's need through cooperation and a sense of public spirit was the ideal social context. Education's role was to develop these democratic habits in children from an early age, so that they could effectively operate as active members of the community through self-directed learning guided by the teacher. Rather than supporting repressive institutions that prohibited exploration and growth, Dewey asserted that school reform should focus on the development of the whole student.

This could be accomplished through a curriculum that focused on problem-solving and the development of critical thinking skills. One role of the teacher is to develop approaches by which the student can make connections between the information being presented and prior knowledge, therefore creating new knowledge that is an amalgam of the two. This idea is a cornerstone of "constructivism."

Progressive education as influenced by Dewey was an attempt to democratize education in several ways. During the early 1900s, there was a strong push for creating vocational education for the masses and reserving academic education for the elite. The 1920s was also the time when efficiency and scientific techniques that relied on standardization and quantitative measurements were implemented by many school systems across the United States. Progressive educators advocated an education for everyone, which focused on developing the whole child, the emotional and creative as well as the intellect, and relied strongly on "learning by doing," so that children could develop the skills needed to be active members of a democratic community and society.

Dewey saw that his ideas were sometimes misinterpreted, so he cautioned that student-centered education does not mean that the student has no direction or guidance. There must be a balance provided through the expertise of the teacher that meets what the child wants to know and what they need to know. Dewey's reputation as a philosopher and educational theorist continued to grow, as did his reputation as a supporter of and activist on contemporary issues, such as women's suffrage, teachers' rights (including the right to unionize), domestic and international politics, and world peace. He was a long-term member of the American Federation of Teachers (a teachers' union), and was the founder of the American Association of University Professors. Dewey died in New York City on June 1, 1952.

Lynn W. Zimmerman
Purdue University Calumet

See Also: Concerted Cultivation/Natural Growth; Ethics in Education; Sociocultural Approaches to Learning and Development.

Further Readings

Dewey, John. *Democracy and Education.* New York: Macmillan, 1916 [Copyright renewed 1944].

Gouinlock, J., ed. *The Moral Writings of John Dewey.* Amherst, NY: Prometheus Books, 1994.

McDermott, J., ed. *The Philosophy of John Dewey.* Chicago: University of Chicago Press, 1989.

Morris, D. and I. Shapiro, eds. *The Political Writings of John Dewey.* Indianapolis, IN: Hackett, 1993.

Digital Divide/ Digital Capital

The *digital divide* is a term coined to refer to the gap between those who have access to computers, and those who do not. In the mid-1990s, the term sparked political concern, and President Bill Clinton formed incentives for large businesses and corporations to donate computers and other forms of technology to poorer communities and schools. From that point on, computers were increasingly acknowledged as valuable resources within a technologically burgeoning society. The introduction of technology within the last few decades accentuates social inequalities, and the continued disparity in access to computers and technology creates a deeper division between the social classes. Educational researchers who focus on computers and technology view the digital divide as a social problem. Most educational research on computers and technology supports human capital theory, because it indicates that an increase in computer access/use will improve academic outcomes. By the new millennium, however, researchers had noted a second divide. Though computer access has increased, closing the original digital divide, there is still a gap in the skill sets of computer users. Therefore, it is not enough to simply place computers within the walls of a classroom or the houses of the poor; they must also be accompanied by an individual who is savvy enough to use and teach others how to gain from such implements of technology.

Digital Divide

Educational researchers acknowledge both digital divides (i.e., in access and specific skill sets). The authors working within this literature mostly focus on how skill attainment contributes to students' achievements and academic outcomes via computers. However, researchers disagree on the benefits or shortcomings of computer use and academic use of computers. Empirical evidence is controversial, and some research finds that computers improve achievement in the classroom and at home, but other research suggests that computer use has a negative effect on academic achievement.

The research that demonstrates computers increasing or decreasing achievement tends to highlight human capital as the mechanism by which computers directly impact knowledge and proficiency. Research indicates that access to computers is increasing on the whole, implying a reduction in the first digital divide, but the benefits of the narrowing gap are less clear. Researchers have found that elementary-aged students who have access to and use computers consistently perform at higher rates than their non-using counterparts. Other research demonstrates that computer use may not be helping students achieve gains in all areas within the classroom, and thus only supports some skill sets. Thus, it is still unclear if computer use transfers into improved educational outcomes. The conflicting findings leave researchers unsure of how computers are important for students and educators.

Researchers turned to specific uses of computers in order to determine how academic or educational programs contribute to the claims that student's academic achievement is a result of computer use. Some of these studies find that how a student uses a computer is the most important aspect of computer use, regardless of quantity, emphasizing quality computer use over frequency. Moreover, the majority of the inequality exists in the sphere of computer/technology use, not access. For example, students in poor and urban or rural areas are significantly less likely to learn more sophisticated computer skills than their wealthier, suburban counterparts. These findings suggest that the second digital divide is a more significant barrier, given the uneven distribution of skills. Essentially, teaching students to learn intellectual tools on the computer is where time is best spent. Additionally, an overabundance of time on the computer may even detract from academic outcomes if students spend excessive amounts of time on the computer engaging in nonacademic activities, thus it is not just access to computers, but rather how students use the computers.

Digital Capital

The digital divide also manifests itself through another source of capital. Digital capital refers to the digital dimension of cultural capital, where technological knowledge, expertise, and competence can be used as exchange value within a technological/information-age society, conferring both power and status upon individuals who proficiently demonstrate their knowledge. The addition of the digital dimension updates the understanding of Pierre Bourdieu's cultural capital by incorporating modern technologies and innovations. Bourdieu intended to shed light upon differential educational outcomes, stating that accumulated cultural capital can be exchanged for gains in academic achievement. A gain in computer and technological knowledge will lead to other advantages, particularly within the educational sphere. Indicators of the digital dimension of cultural capital stem from what teachers or authority figures deem worthy, which makes the addition of technology/computers a logical next step in developing the theoretical dimensions of cultural capital. Research on the concept of digital capital contends that students who possess knowledge of computers and other digital devices may gain actual skills, but more importantly, they are presenting themselves as culturally competent members of the information-age society. The digital dimension to cultural capital has the same theoretical mechanisms as cultural capital. In other words, traditional measures of cultural capital in educational literature (i.e., high-brow arts) function to provide students with both knowledge/skills and esteem. Theoretically, in the digital information age, cultural capital is obtained from computer competency. Thus, when the advantages of cultural capital are considered, digital should be measured, as well as the ballet.

This updated theoretical foundation allows researchers to focus on the complex nature of the relationship between technology and academic achievement, helping understand the complicated social processes behind student achievement and the demonstration of computer competency. By doing so, issues of computer proficiency affecting academic achievement, the relationship between computer proficiency and teacher's evaluations of students, and how teachers affect the relationship between computer proficiency and academic achievement can be explored. Technology is increasing in ubiquity and the educational environments of children continuously change in order to accommodate the proliferation of computers and the digital age. Research suggests that simply providing computers, however, will not close the digital divide. Students must be proficient on the computer, and it must be visible to others, specifically their teachers. The digital divide acknowledges that individuals experience different levels of access and expertise of computers. The concept of digital capital takes into account both direct and indirect effects of computer skills/use on academic achievement. The disadvantages created by the two digital divides and discrepancies in the acquisition of digital capital contribute to the continued stratification within schools and educational outcomes.

Maria T. Paino
University of Georgia

See Also: Cultural Capital; Human Capital Theory; Technology Education; Technology in the Classroom.

Further Readings
Attewell, Paul, Belkis Suazo-Garcia, and Juan Battle. "Computers and Young Children: Social Benefit or Social Problem?" *Social Forces*, v.82 (2003).
Hargittai, Eszter. "Digital Na(t)ives? Variation in Internet Skills and Uses Among Members of the "Net Generation." *Sociological Inquiry*, v.80 (2010).
Mesch, Gustavo S. and Ilan Talmud. *Wired Youth: The Social World of Adolescence in the Information Age*. New York: Psychology Press. 2010.
Robinson, Laura. "A Taste for the Necessary: A Bourdieuian Approach to Digital Inequality." *Information, Communication, & Society*, v.12 (2009).
Zhang, Chan, Mario Callegaro, and Melanie Thomas. "More Than the Digital Divide?: Investigating the Differences Between Internet and Non-Internet Users." *Informing Science*, v.12 (2009).

Disabled Students

The term *disabled student* refers to a student who is considered to have an impairment (mental, physical, sensory, emotional, or cognitive), which impacts, limits, or restricts the student's learning processes and social participation to the extent that he or she needs particular additional support in order to acquire an education. The learning content offered to a student with disabilities can reach from basic life skills to academic content knowledge. Worldwide, students with disabilities have progressively acquired the right to education. However, especially in developing countries, access to education for children with disabilities is still lacking.

Often, it underscores general difficulties to provide education for all children in those countries, but the general lack of educational funding has the most far-reaching negative consequences for this population. According to the World Health Organization (WHO), for example, the difference between the percentage of disabled children and the percentage of nondisabled children attending primary school ranges from 10 percent in India to 60 percent in Indonesia. However, since the 19th century, students with disabilities have increasingly been present in the educational system at all levels, from preschool to university settings.

The history of the presence of students with disabilities in the educational system is one of many controversies involving changes in status, and terminology. The education of students with disabilities goes back to as early as the 17th century, with academics and doctors like Jean Marc Gaspard Itard or Edouard Séguin. However, representations of disability and impairment considered those students different from other children, and therefore created separate institutions, schools, and classrooms considered appropriate for those learners. Thus, segregated schooling dominated the major part of the history of education of students with disabilities, as specialists considered them unable to attend regular classes. It appeared that specialized support was delivered best in segregated settings, either in specialized institutions or in specialized classrooms.

This led to students with disabilities starting to attend school at all levels of the educational system, with the Columbia Institute for the Deaf, Dumb and Blind granting college degrees starting in 1864. In 1948, it was followed by the establishment of a program for students with disabilities at the University of Illinois at Urbana-Champaign, which was then a consequence of the presence of disabled veterans whose need for rehabilitation and reintegration into civil society had become a priority. The development of assistive technology has increasingly supported the education of students with disabilities, especially with the evolution of computers, adaptive software, and hardware. The big push toward the inclusion of students with disabilities into regular educational settings only began during the 1970s, and has led to an international movement to foster inclusive education for all students with disabilities.

From the Medical Model Toward the Social Model of Disability

The way that persons (and more specifically students) with disabilities have been labeled and categorized has changed over time. The label of *disability* is rather recent, and dates back to the 1980s, when a major shift in the paradigm occurred in how we see people with disabilities. Before, terms like *retardation*, *handicapped*, *idiocy*, and *crippled* were frequently used to categorize certain groups of students who were excluded from mainstream education and schooled in special educational settings (or for many, were not schooled at all). Those categorizations stemmed from an emerging science attempting to properly assess all kinds of impairments, and medicalized the perceptions of impairment to the point that the disabling conditions of the environment were not taken into account. Disability was only seen as being caused directly by disease, trauma, genetic disorders, or other health conditions.

This perception changed with the paradigm that shifted the emphasis from a purely medical model that only sought the reasons for disability inside the individual, toward the social model of disability. The analysis shifts from the simple analysis of an assumed deficiency in the individual, toward the conditions in which disability occurs. A normative context can disable individuals to participate in social life. For example, a person in a wheelchair is only disabled if he or she cannot access a building because there are no elevators or ramps. In this context, a person might have an impairment (being paraplegic), but the person is only disabled if the accessibility of a building (e.g., school or university) is limited, which is not the fault of the person in the wheelchair, but which is the responsibility of society. The WHO defines disability as the following:

The interaction between individuals with a health condition (e.g., cerebral palsy, Down syndrome, and depression) and personal and environmental factors (e.g., negative attitudes, inaccessible transportation and public buildings, and limited social supports).

Today, the most common phrase used in the field is *person/student/child with a disability*, as it recognizes the disability not as something inherent in the person, but something that originates in the interaction between the human being and his/her environment. It is considered the responsibility of the school to adapt the physical and social environment, as well as learning content, to the needs of the student with a disability. The development of inclusive education, the United Nations (UN) Convention on the Rights of the Child of 1989, as well as the UN Convention on the Rights of Persons with Disabilities of 2006 are pushing toward the notion of accessibility in the largest sense possible. This means that the regular classroom is commonly seen as the appropriate place for students with disabilities to learn, as this offers maximal access to participation in society. Segregated settings are increasingly seen as restricting life and learning opportunities, thus excluding students with disabilities from participation in society. The Centre for Studies on Inclusive Education (CSIE) has developed support materials and tools, such as the Index for Inclusion, in order to support the inclusion of students with disabilities into regular schools. Those materials also aim at giving the students a voice, to become involved in the process of their education.

Disability and the WHO

The WHO has elaborated the International Classification of Fucntioning, Disability and Health (ICF), which uses the term *disability* as an umbrella term for impairments, activity limitations, and participation restrictions. According to the WHO, in 2011, about 15 percent of the world's population lives with some form of disability, of whom 2 to 4 percent experience significant difficulties in functioning. This number is higher than previous WHO estimates, which date from the 1970s, and suggested a figure of around 10 percent. This global estimate for disability is on the rise because of population aging and the rapid spread of chronic diseases, as well as improvements in the methodologies used to measure disability. The WHO, in its 2011 World Report on Disability, recommends addressing the situation of students with disabilities on several levels. Its recommendations include the implementation of inclusive legislation, national plans and policies, the improvement of funding, the recognition of diversity and individual differences in school, the addition of specialized support where necessary, the building of teacher capacity, the removal of physical and attitudinal barriers, and the involvement of the disability community.

Disability Studies and Students With Disabilities

The field of disability studies, which has emerged over the last 30 years, acknowledges the person with a disability as an actor, and analyzes critically the contexts and environments that people with disabilities are facing on a daily basis. Disability studies have grown out of the field of sociology of disability, as well as out of the people first movements that empowered people with disabilities to get involved with political activism in order to change their life circumstances. It has shown how institutions and practices have contributed to the oppression of people with disabilities. Educational institutions, especially segregated special educational institutions, have been part of their analysis. As disability studies also has a clear activist focus, it has been pushing for the abolishment of specialized

Figure 1   Percentage of children ages 3 to 5 and ages 6 to 21 served under the Individuals with Disabilities Education Act by race/ethnicity: 2007

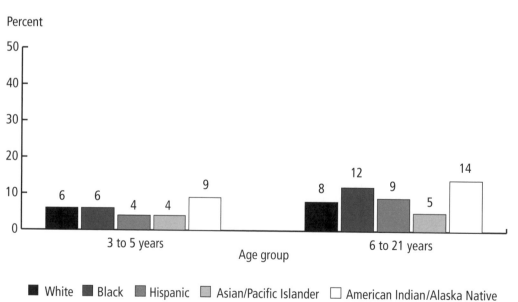

Note: Race categories exclude persons of Hispanic ethnicity.
Source: National Center for Education Statistics, U.S. Department of Education, Office of Special Education Programs (OSEP), 2007.

institutions in order to develop inclusive settings, which offer education for all children and students, regardless of their disability or impairment, ethnic or social background, or sexual orientation. Using the social model of disability, disability studies has moved the focus on individual impairment to an analysis of disability in a social and cultural context, which identifies and addresses the disabling conditions of the environment. Thus, disability has become part of the diversity and heterogeneity that educational systems need to learn to handle, side-by-side with issues of social class, sexual orientation, and ethnic, religious, and racial background.

Students With Disabilities and Inclusive Education

Since 1994, inclusive education has become the biggest worldwide call for educational reform. The Salamanca Conference of 1994 called for the inclusion of all students with disabilities. Since then, this movement has been increasing and culminated in the United Nations Convention on the Rights of Persons with Disabilities in 2006 (access to inclusive education is defined as a right in Article 24). The convention has been signed by over 150 states and ratified by more than 100 states, and has triggered many debates and conversations in countries like France and Germany, including how to reorganize the educational system in order to fulfill the mandate of inclusive education. Many countries still rely heavily on the use of special education settings, which are often considered counterproductive to the inclusion of students with disabilities.

The challenge of inclusive education is to ensure not only the physical presence of students with disabilities in the regular classroom, but also to develop a high-quality approach to inclusive education, which reorganizes learning and teaching in very heterogeneous groups. Furthermore, inclusive education only fulfills its mandate if it leads toward increased social participation opportunities, and the removal of barriers in employment and everyday life. From this perspective, the inclusion of students with disabilities is an ideal goal, and stakeholders have to work on the process of improving education.

Attitudes toward the disability and traditional representations of how school should look hinder the development of alternative pedagogies that support diverse learners in the regular classroom. Thus, the development of inclusive schooling is a long-term goal, as different countries are dealing with their distinct realities and traditions pertaining to the education of students with disabilities. Schools need to develop strategies of inclusive education, and staff, especially teachers, need to be trained to respond properly to this very complex challenge.

Students With Disabilities and Their Peer Group

Besides the study of educational institutions, there is also a growing concern in microsociological studies of the lived experience of students with disabilities in the classroom. Students in segregated and inclusive settings have moved in the lens of sociological researchers, especially as a consequence of the generalization of inclusive education. It is about assessing how past and current practices of inclusive education, mainstreaming, and special education have affected the experience of the student with disabilities and those of his or her peers. Behind those studies is once more the question of social participation and the search for elements that can facilitate this participation. Studies have shown that certain ways of facilitating inclusion in the regular classroom can have counterproductive effects. For example, the presence of educational assistants or the use of assistive technology, if not properly introduced and used, can have stigmatizing effects for the student with disabilities.

Also, students with disabilities have reported that the presence of adults can exclude them from interacting with their peer group. It has been shown that the more a school community and a teacher have explicit policies, strategies, and methods to foster inclusive education, the better the student with a disability will be included in the peer group. The importance of teacher education in this field is primordial, in three different ways: knowledge about the impairment; knowledge about possible adaptations; and knowledge about group dynamics, stigma, and labeling theory pertaining to students in the classroom.

Education and Training for Labor Market Participation

Educating students with disabilities attempts to achieve the goal to facilitate their access to social participation and, more specifically, to the labor market. Labor market participation remains a big challenge for people with disabilities. According to the World Health Organization, worldwide data show that employment rates are lower for disabled men (53 percent) and disabled women (20 percent) than for nondisabled men

(65 percent) and nondisabled women (30 percent). In Organisation for Economic Co-operation and Development (OECD) countries, the employment rate of people with disabilities (44 percent) was slightly over half that for people without disabilities (75 percent).

Many industrialized countries have established quota supposed to compel employers to hire more workers with disabilities, but this hiring goal is not even achieved for the public service. In order to enhance labor market participation, there is an increasing amount of postsecondary initiatives aiming at education and training people with disabilities. Those programs are aiming at enhancing skills, resources, and coaching for people with disabilities, simultaneously educating people with disabilities as future employees and potential employers about how to work together. Increasing labor market participation will become one of the essential challenges for the education and training of students with disabilities, as people with disabilities are generally more vulnerable to live in conditions of poverty because of extra costs, such as medical care, assistive devices, or personal support. Supporting their employment is a way to help people with disabilities to foster their independence and participation in society. It is the next logical step and the next challenge after developing inclusive education in elementary and secondary school, as well as in university settings.

Cornelia Schneider
Mount Saint-Vincent University

See Also: At-Risk Students; Blind Students; Deaf Students; IQ; Special Education; Training of Teachers; Youth Cultures and Subcultures; Youth Friendship and Conflict in Schools.

Further Readings

Albrecht, G. L. and Gale Group. *Encyclopedia of Disability.* Thousand Oaks, CA: Sage, 2006.

Barnes, C. and G. Mercer. *Exploring Disability: A Sociological Introduction.* 2nd ed. Malden, MA: Polity Press, 2010.

Obiakor, F. E., J. P. Bakken, and A. F. Rotatori, eds. *History of Special Education.* Bingley, UK: Emerald, 2011.

Schneider, C. "'Ready for Work': Feeling Rules, Emotion Work and Emotional Labour for People With Disabilities." *Interactions,* v.4 (2010).

Slee, R. *The Irregular School: Exclusion, Schooling and Inclusive Education.* Hoboken, NJ: Routledge, 2010.

Discipline in Education

Public schools within the United States use a variety of disciplinary practices, each with roots in a specific philosophy of learning, behavior, and control. For example, corporal punishment (while used far less than in years past) is on one end of the extreme, with mutually developed social contracts detailing acceptable behaviors and consequences with students on the other. Historically, school discipline has been positioned as the means of maintaining control and order while shaping future citizens. School disipline, and the related concept of classroom management, have been identified as some of the most challenging aspects found in the day-to-day life of schools. Public schools have been a site for the formation of citizens that display particular behaviors, with classroom and schoolwide disciplinary practices justified in reference to particular social expectations (e.g., walk in lines, wait patiently for a turn, and be quiet in hallways). A 2004 national Gallup poll focused on identifying the most pressing issues facing schools showed that concerns about school discipline ranked second only to financial problems.

Further, school disciplinary practices have often been linked to concerns regarding teacher retention. Lack of teacher preparation around disciplinary practices and frustrations linked to student behavior have been cited as top reasons for why teachers leave the classroom, according to R. Ingersoll. In studies examining teachers' beliefs about their readiness to address behavior challenges, middle and secondary school teachers reported being significantly less able and ready to manage challenging student behaviors than primary school teachers.

Varied Disciplinary Approaches

Approaches to school discipline have ranged from highly behavioral methods (e.g., corporal punishment) to humanistic approaches (e.g., focusing on meeting basic needs) to cognitive programs (e.g., identifying meaningful behavioral goals that students can work toward). Purely behavioral approaches often focus on token systems, in which students are tangibly rewarded (e.g., earn points or tickets) for good behavior, and are similarly punished by predetermined consequences for bad behavior. Humanistic approaches often incorporate a greater focus on meeting student needs, emphasizing the importance of addressing basic needs. In a school with a humanistic approach, teachers are encouraged to assure that their students' basic needs (e.g., food and safety) are met first and foremost, with misbehavior interpreted in relationship to the students' overall needs and desires. A cognitive approach might focus more on the ways in which students can develop intrinsic motivation to behave responsibly, involving students in the development of school policies, classroom rules, and even consequences for misbehavior. The cognitive approach assumes that students will monitor their behavior when they are motivated to comply with rules that they understand and believe in. Many school disciplinary practices are a blend across multiple perspectives.

Disciplinary approaches might take a preventative or an "after-the-act" orientation. The goal of a preventative orientation is to proactively create a learning environment that prevents disciplinary issues from arising. While this is the noted goal of many school systems, in reality, many of the disciplinary practices used in the service of this goal are punitive—punishing the actor (i.e., student) only after the "misbehavior" or "illegal" act has occurred. Punishments can range from loss of privileges, to out-of-school suspension, or even expulsion. School discipline practices, particularly suspensions and other exclusionary practices used to address behaviors deemed as "serious," are far less effective than expected. For instance, students who have been previously suspended are more likely to be suspended again. While purely punitive approaches may posit that an extreme punishment extinguishes unwanted behaviors, in the case of school discipline, the opposite is sometimes true.

Students are not the only actors who defy the expectations of behaviorism in the case of suspensions and explusion. While an initial explusion might be for an action deemed "extremely serious," research has shown that repeated suspensions are often given for less serious offenses, such as bad attitudes. Thus, adults seem to give extreme punishments for less and less serious offenses of repeat offenders. Such evidence highlights the ways in which disciplinary systems function as cycles, and how once caught in a disciplinary cycle, students are likely to remain in it, potentially dropping out or being pushed out of school. Research has also shown that students who experience less academic success and higher levels of family conflict are more likely to become caught up in a cycle of disciplinary exclusion. Even so, regardless

of previous behavioral histories, students who are given opportunities to develop social responsibility have been shown to break cycles of failure and display behaviors deemed conducive to learning. For example, students who actively participate in developing school policies and classroom practices that result in a sense of autonomy are more likely to move beyond this cycle of failure.

Commercialized Approaches to Discipline

Beyond the varied approaches (e.g., behavioral, humanistic, and cognitive) and perspectives (e.g., preventative) that shape many disciplinary approaches, at present, there are also commercialized programs that provide schools with specific tools and ways of dealing with disciplinary concerns.

For instance, positive behavior supports (PBS) is a schoolwide discipline approach grounded in applied behavioral analysis. In this approach, students who display desirable behaviors are rewarded through token systems or other measures, while those who display undesirable behaviors are punished. Within this approach, students are given opportunities to practice the expected behaviors, with such behaviors most often defined by school authorities (e.g., teachers and administrators). J. Warren et al. conducted a case study of the use of PBS in an inner-city middle school, reporting that after two years of implemeting the approach, there was a decrease in office referrals.

Nonetheless, others have argued that such a behaviorally oriented approach may undermine students' ability to understand what is fair and just. In contrast, there are other schoolwide approaches that seek to address the cognitive, affective, social, and ethical needs of students. Programs that are examples of this approach include Responsive Classroom. One such approach, the Child Development Project (CDP), has been designed to foster relationships between students and teachers, promote intrinsic motivation, and involve students in establishing school policies and engaging in conflict resolution. Research has shown that when students are involved in school disciplinary practices, they are more apt to follow expectations; thus, approaches such as CDP, while used far less often than more punitively oriented approaches, have a positive affect on school climate.

Inequitable Disciplinary Practices

School disciplinary practices have historically been applied in inequitable ways. Some researchers have noted that while schoolwide or district-wide discipline policies often aim to create equitable practices, disciplinary practices still result in more minority students, males, and students with disabilities being punished. For instance, in middle schools, males are more likely than females to be suspended, and in general, African American males are suspended three times more often than their peers. Recently, suspension and expulsion rates have dramatically increased.

While transitions from elementary to middle school have been linked to increases in misbehavior and suspension rates, other research links disciplinary concerns to students' home lives, years of academic failures, and/or school characteristics that cultivate unsafe learning environments (e.g., punitive disciplinary policies, teacher beliefs, and poor student-teacher relationships). Nonetheless, zero tolerance policies (policies that result in the suspension or expulsion of students who exhibit "severe" behaviors) are also linked to increases in suspension and expulsion rates. Such policies were initially developed within the criminal justice system and were introduced into public schools in the mid-1990s. The introduction of zero tolerance policies occurred along with the passage of the Gun Free Schools Act of 1994 (GFSA).

Initially, the GFSA mandated that students who brought a weapon to school had to be expelled for one year. Eventually, this policy was modified, and now includes a wide variety of "misbehaviors." While the GFSA legislation was purportedly designed to promote school safety, it has given discretionary freedom to school administrators to modify the legislation. This discretionary freedom has resulted in broad criteria for determining the student behaviors worthy of punishment with expulsion or suspension. Consequently, student behaviors (e.g., insubordination) that had previously been dealt with through in-school discipline practices were quickly criminalized.

There is growing concern with such disciplinary practices, because they often result in students' exclusion from learning opportunities for long periods of time. In the case of *Goss v. Lopez* in 1975, the U.S. Supreme Court decided that it was unjustifiable to deny a student an education because of behavioral challenges, therefore requiring students expelled for more than 10 days of school to be provided an education. Relatedly, research around zero tolerance disciplinary practices has continually highlighted their ineffectiveness, as well as the ways in which they contribute to student academic failure.

Furthermore, some researchers have reported that such disciplinary practices increase violence in schools, as teacher and student relationships suffer in such settings. With effective teaching and disciplinary practices linked to positive relationships with students, some schools, even with an official policy of zero tolerance, have aimed to move to more holistic and humanistically oriented models. From a historical perspective, school discipline practices have resulted in inequitable outcomes, resulting in research exploring how and why such practices are employed in schools. The entire range of approaches to school discipline, from behaviorist to cognitive to more blended approaches, all influence school climate, teachers, and student learning and behavior. Disciplinary approaches dramatically shape students' educational experiences and opportunities in terms of their relationships with teachers, the amount of time spent in or out of school, and the ways in which their behavior is positioned as a learning experience or criminal act.

Jessica Nina Lester
Washington State University
Rachael Gabriel
University of Connecticut

See Also: Aggressive Behaviors in Classrooms; At-Risk Students; Classroom Dynamics; Classroom Interactions: Teachers and Students; Teacher Decision-Making Power.

Further Readings
Christle, C., C. M. Nelson, and K. Jolivette. "School Characteristics Related to the Use of Suspension." *Education and Treatment of Children*, v.27/4 (2004).
Evans, K. and J. N. Lester. "Classroom Management and Discipline: Responding to the Needs of Young Adolescents." *Middle School Journal*, v.41/3 (2010).
Evans, K. R. and J. N. Lester. "Disturbing 'Distractions': Speaking Back to Racialized School Discipline Practices." *Cultural Studies/Critical Methodologies*, v.12/2 (2012).
Evans, K. and J. N. Lester. "Zero Tolerance: Moving the Conversation Forward." *Intervention in Schools and Clinics* (June 22, 2012).
Ingersoll, R. "Teacher Turnover and Teacher Shortages." *American Educational Research Journal*, v.38/3 (2001).
Morrison, G. M., S. Anthony, M. Storino, and C. Dillon. "An Examination of the Disciplinary Histories and the Individual and Educational Characteristics of Students

who Participate in an In-School Suspension Program." *Education and Treatment of Children*, v.24/3 (2001).

Skiba, R. J. *Zero Tolerance, Zero Evidence: An Analysis of School Disciplinary Practice*. Bloomington: Indiana Education Policy Center, 2000.

Warren, J., et al. "Urban Applications of School-Wide Positive Behavior Support." *Journal of Positive Behavior Interventions*, v.5/2 (2003).

Diseases and Education

Major public health challenges impact educational efforts worldwide, with human immunodeficiency virus and acquired immune deficiency syndrome (HIV/AIDS), malaria, and tuberculosis (TB) causing the most fatalities. They are daily threats for a large population of people concentrated in developing countries, creating additional barriers to educational development, as well as impacting what these regions require from their educational institutions. Education interacts with these diseases in multiple ways. First, education can be used to prevent or mitigate disease, by providing individuals with the information they need to make healthy choices.

Education can also be used as a force for social, cultural, economic, or political change. Major epidemics such as HIV/AIDS, malaria, and TB are in part a result of extreme poverty, lack of human rights, lack of access to education, and other contextual challenges. Education is also significantly impacted by these and similar diseases. Where epidemics are concentrated, orphans require special needs and teachers spend less time in the classroom because of illness, disability, and death. Schools also are sometimes the easiest venue for reaching a large proportion of the population, especially at an age when there is a "window of hope," and so schools take on extra responsibilities.

HIV/AIDS

In 2009, there were over 1.8 million AIDS-related deaths, the vast majority in developing countries, especially in sub-Saharan Africa. While people living with HIV in resource-rich countries can live long and healthy lives, the majority of people living with HIV do not have access to antiretroviral therapy (ART). For every one person who goes on ART, another two become infected with HIV. The most economically

sustainable prevention method is education. Around the world, educational institutions are integrating HIV/AIDS prevention into their curriculum, especially where the epidemic is generalized, meaning that there are high rates of HIV among the general population.

In generalized epidemics (such as in sub-Saharan Africa) the most common infection pathway is heterosexual sex, and so the prevention education mirrors this with campaigns promoting Abstinence, Being faithful to one's partner, and Condoms (ABC). In many countries, this has been integrated into the school-based curriculum. While many religious groups and some traditional beliefs cause resistance to the "B" and "C," rates of condom use are rising, and consequently rates of infection are slightly decreasing in most generalized epidemics. There are also community-based educational campaigns using edutainment, TV, radio, billboards, and pamphlets.

Where the epidemic is concentrated among populations, such as people who share needles or men who have sex with men, educational campaigns are implemented through public health programs outside the classroom. These higher risk groups are often already stigmatized, and such targeted programs can sometimes have negative side effects, causing additional stigma. In high- and middle-income countries, the HIV/AIDS epidemic is more concentrated in these higher risk groups. Educational efforts also aim to change the social, economic, and political conditions that allow for HIV/AIDS to be a pandemic. The human rights of women, gay men, and sex workers are particularly important in reducing rates of HIV. Women are more likely to become infected because of both biological and social/cultural/economic vulnerabilities. Sex work and same-sex relationships are criminalized, even resulting in the death penalty in some countries. Stigma is one of the biggest barriers for people engaging in voluntary counseling and testing, and seeking out ART. Because some of the biggest living costs for people in developing countries are school-related, providing free and accessible education to vulnerable populations can help mitigate HIV/AIDS. Stigma does not rest with the infected individual alone, and the millions of children made orphans or vulnerable because of AIDS carry this stigma within their communities and schools, often facing significant hardships.

Tuberculosis (TB)

Over 14 million people are infected with TB. Economically devastating because it affects primarily young adults in their most productive years, it is strongly linked with poverty. It is also linked with HIV/AIDS, with about one-quarter of all TB deaths also AIDS-related. Having HIV/AIDS makes one extremely susceptible to TB, with about 13 percent of new TB cases HIV-linked. The vast majority of these cases are in developing countries, but numbers have fallen by about 35 percent over the last 10 years. About 26 percent of people living with TB know their status. Public health campaigns use informal education to increase knowledge about symptoms and treatment, while indirectly formal education helps by increasing economic independence and personal agency.

Malaria and Other Diseases

With over half the world's population at risk of malaria, over 800,000 individuals, mostly children, die from this mosquito-borne disease each year. International aid efforts to increase access to anti-malarial interventions have improved numbers, with some African countries seeing reductions by more than 50 percent. These include insecticide-treated nets for prevention, and sprays and anti-malarial drugs for treatment. Educational efforts aim to increase the use of these nets and sprays, as well as to promote treatment for malaria. While HIV/AIDS, TB, and malaria are the biggest killers worldwide, they are often interrelated and linked to other health issues. Polio is still common in some parts of the world, alongside measles and other common, communicable diseases resulting in blindness, deafness, and physical disability or death. While these diseases are almost entirely preventable, they are common among the poorest populations. Diseases commonly considered medieval relics, such as leprosy, cholera, and even the plague still kill and disable people worldwide. Education serves to mitigate the contextual causes for these diseases, as well as spread knowledge about their biological causes and prevention tools.

Impact on Schools and Children

In areas where there is a high prevalence of these diseases and related health issues, schools must cope with heightened levels of psychological problems, abuse, stigma, and food insecurity. AIDS-orphans (children who have lost at least one caregiver to an AIDS-related illness) are especially susceptible to these issues, including clinical levels of depression, post-traumatic stress disorder, and anxiety. These problems are exacerbated and often rooted in local issues such as genocide, becoming or affected by refugees, and other forms of social marginalization. When health issues combine with these contextual problems, the result is increased alcohol and drug abuse, sex work, and additional forms of physical and emotional disability. Treatment for HIV/AIDS, TB, and malaria are relatively expensive for the large majority of the world, and are often difficult to procure because of limited supply or geographic isolation. Children, especially girls, are much more likely to be removed from school when a family member becomes ill because of financial strain, as well as the need for a home-based caregiver.

Schools often become providers of medical, psychological, and nutritional care, as well as educational institutions. This in turn puts pressure on already scarce resources. In these settings, the sociology of local education efforts is often framed by the impact of these diseases. In addition to nutritional supplements and mental health care, many schools in high-prevalence areas such as southern Africa lose teaching hours because of AIDS-related disability and death among teachers. Teachers, having a relatively higher socioeconomic status in their communities, frequently have higher rates of HIV, and in many southern African countries, loss of teaching hours because of these illnesses is a significant issue. There is the additional problem of teacher-student relationships.

In low-resource areas, it is not uncommon for students to exchange favors and goods with teachers. Adolescent girls are increasingly targeted in areas where sexually transmitted diseases have a high prevalence because they are perceived to be "clean." When schools increase fees or other educational needs are not otherwise met, children and adolescents living in poverty can be lured into unequal relationships. Educational efforts in these regions are attempting to address the increased gender gap made by these related health issues.

In order to avoid stigma-related issues, teachers and staff must work to ensure confidentiality of students with some diseases or health problems. In the United States, for instance, any student living with HIV can be protected by section 504 of the Rehabilitation Act of 1973. If an Individualized Education Plan (IEP) is required to ensure necessary modifications or adaptations to instruction, the Individuals with Disabilities Education Act (IDEA) supports special education needs. Other countries have similar legal provisions, but depending on available resources, these might or might not be enacted.

Nalini Biggs
University of Oxford

See Also: Adolescent Sexual Behavior; Disabled Students; Lesbian, Gay, Bisexual, and Transgender Issues and Schooling; Special Education.

Further Readings

Beck, E. J., N. Mays, and A. W. Whiteside, eds. *The HIV Pandemic: Local and Global Implications.* New York: Oxford University Press, 2008.

Biggs, N. A., ed. *Education and HIV/AIDS (Education as a Humanitarian Response).* London: Continuum Books, 2011.

Cluver, L. and M. Orkin. "Cumulative Risk and AIDS-Orphanhood: Interactions of Stigma, Bullying and Poverty on Child Mental Health in South Africa." *Social Science and Medicine,* v.69/8 (2009).

Epstein, H. *The Invisible Cure: Why We Are Losing the Fight Against AIDS in Africa.* New York: Picador, 2008.

Pisani, E. *The Wisdom of Whores.* London: Granta Books, 2008.

District of Columbia

Washington, D.C., is the capital of the United States. It enjoys a unique status as a city not located within a state. Governance is characterized by a complex system of federal and local regulations. The municipal government was established in 1802, and the school system was established in 1804. In 1864, the city opened public schools for black children, in a system separate from white students. The school system has functioned under various governing entities, including those instituted via congressional oversight, and in some cases locally elected.

In 1954, school segregation ended with the *Brown v. Board of Education* lawsuit. In the aftermath of that lawsuit, black student enrollment steadily increased over time, while white enrollment declined in most urban areas. This trend was especially pronounced in the District of Columbia. From 1965 through 1974 especially, the school system was characterized by inequities as enrollment of black students steadily

increased and white enrollment decreased because of a variety of factors, including white flight to the suburbs, segregated housing patterns, and open enrollment. From 1974 to 2007, various cycles of reform occurred as the District of Columbia gained home rule. The Home Rule Act moved the power of government from the congressional to the local level. This provided for an elected mayor and the Council of the District of Columbia.

As Home Rule took effect, a particular outlet for local activists looking to get involved in politics was the school board. The school board was the first set of elected offices available to local politicians. In 1995, because of financial malfeasance, Congress instituted a Control Board, an entity that was in charge of fiscal matters for the city. One of the major activities of the Control Board was stripping the school board of power, because the school board was viewed as a major detriment to city financial health and functioning. Following the Control Board, the city's education systems were marked by instability. From 1991 to 2007, there were seven superintendents.

Under then Mayor Adrian Fenty, the city council enacted the District of Columbia Public Education Reform Amendment Act of 2007. This reform included a variety of provisions, including turning the

Table 1 Elementary and secondary education characteristics

	District of Columbia	U.S. (average)
Total number of schools	235	1,988
Total students	71,284	970,278
Total teachers	5,925.33	60,766.56
Pupil/teacher ratio	12.03	15.97

Source: U.S. Department of Education, National Center for Education Statistics, Common Core of Data (CCD), 2010–11.

Table 2 Elementary and secondary education finance

	District of Columbia	U.S. (average)
Total revenues	$1,364,047,878	$11,464,385,994
Total expenditures for education	$1,589,567,803	$11,712,033,839
Total current expenditures	$1,282,436,803	$9,938,906,259

Source: U.S. Department of Education, National Center for Education Statistics, Common Core of Data (CCD), "National Public Education Financial Survey," FY08 (2007–08).

Board of Education into an advisory panel and the creating of a state department of education, named the Office of the State Superintendent of Education (OSSE). Title I Establishment of Mayoral Accountability for the District of Columbia Public Schools (DCPS) establishes DCPS as a subordinate agency under the mayor; the mayor appoints the chancellor, confirmed by the council, which establishes the Department of Education, headed by deputy mayor for education.

The act also amends the Home Rule Act to require the mayor to submit the DCPS budget to the City Council for approval, repeals the Home Rule Act provision creating a Board of Education, and delineates the Title III State Education Agency functions and responsibilities. Currently, all state-level education functions are assigned to the state education office, including federal grants, early childhood education, adult education, and standards. Finally, the act establishes a State Board of Education, which advises the chief state school officer on state education policy issues for all local education agencies in the district. The most important function of the State Board is determining state standards and implementing the No Child Left Behind state accountability plan.

Challenges

Special education has also emerged as a particularly challenging area in D.C. education. The system has been characterized by two class action lawsuits that require the district to engage in a variety of activities to ensure that special education services in the city meet the federal requirement for providing all students with a free and appropriate public education. Parents of students with disabilities brought two class action lawsuits against DCPS, claiming that DCPS violated the federal law known as the Individuals with Disabilities Education Act (IDEA). In the first lawsuit, known as *Blackman*, parents stated that after they requested due process hearings, hearings were not held, and hearing decisions were not issued on time. In the second lawsuit, known as *Jones*, parents stated that once they received hearing decisions or entered into a settlement agreement with DCPS, DCPS did not provide all the services that had been ordered or agreed to. The judge put the two cases together to make one case known as Blackman–Jones. In 1998, the judge agreed with the parents that DCPS violated IDEA when it did not hold timely hearings and did not provide all the services ordered or agreed to. The

only issue remaining was what the penalty should be for DCPS's violations. An additional case under which the city is still required to report to judicial authorities is the *Petties* case, which asserted that payments for students who were placed in a nonpublic setting or assigned to receive third-party services were not being paid in a timely fashion. The court sided with plaintiffs.

The district still has not been released fully from either of the class action lawsuits, although authorities are working to fulfill all requirements. Currently, education in the District of Columbia is characterized by a complex system of federal and local rules. Achievement has remained fairly stagnant over time. Charter schools now enroll 40 percent of the city's K–12 students. In addition to charters and DCPS, there exists a community college of the District of Columbia located within the University of the District Columbia system.

Constance A. Lindsay
CNA Education

See Also: Charter Schools; No Child Left Behind; Special Education; Urban Schooling.

Further Readings

District of Columbia Public Schools. http://dcps.dc.gov/portal/site/DCPS (Accessed August 2012).

Keating, Dan and V. Dion Haynes. "Can D.C. Schools Be Fixed?" *Washington Post* (June 10, 2007).

Dominican Republic

The Dominican Republic is the second-largest Caribbean nation, with an area of 18,704 square miles. The eastern two-thirds of the island of Hispaniola are occupied by the Dominican Republic, with Haiti occupying the western third. The Central Intelligence Agency (CIA) *Factbook* estimates the population at 9,956,648. The Dominican Republic, with the second-largest economy in Central America and the Caribbean, is classified as a middle-income, developing country by the World Bank. Natural resources and government services support the economy. Most Dominicans are employed in the agriculture or tourism industries. The Dominican Republic's gross domestic product (GDP) in terms of purchasing power parity is $9,922 per capita. Approximately 42 percent of the Dominican population lives below the poverty line, according to the *CIA World Factbook*. The Dominican Republic was originally colonized by Spain, and continues to exhibit Spanish cultural influences in its educational system.

Early Schools
The first Dominican school, started by Franciscan friars, opened in 1501, the same year that the first African slaves were brought to Hispaniola. The University of Santo Domingo opened in 1538 as the oldest university in the New World. In 1822, Haitian forces invaded and took control of Santo Domingo. Under Haitian rule, education declined in Santo Domingo. Lacking resources and students, the university closed. By 1844, the members of a secret society called La Trinitaria declared independence from Haiti. La Trinitarians made the establishment of an educational system a priority upon independence.

Primary schools were established in the Dominican Republic in 1845. Classes were separated by sex and attendance was voluntary. The new republic lacked resources to strengthen these schools, so the national government contributed little financially to the schools. Local city councils shouldered the burden of supporting primary schools. Private schools were more stable in the new country. By 1860, 31 out of 35 schools in Santo Domingo were private institutions. Nevertheless, private schools were not meeting the needs of the population. During the same period, approximately 29 out of 100 school-age children were receiving instruction; moreover, estimates place the illiteracy rate as high as 80 percent.

By 1879, normal schools were operating. The first classes of teachers graduated in 1887. Institutions, such as the Institute for Young Ladies, which graduated its first teachers in 1887, would produce a core of teachers to support Dominican education through the end of the 19th century. At the turn of the century, education continued to be limited in some localities, and illiteracy rates rose, despite an emphasis on public education. The government struggled to financially support education. Occupation by U.S. forces during 1918 brought significant changes to public education in the Dominican Republic. School attendance became mandatory and coeducational. The National Council on Education was created to oversee public instruction. By 1920, the military government opened more

than several thousand schools, enrolling more than 100,000 students. During implementation of mandatory schooling under the Trujillo regime, which began in 1930, the Dominican Republic experienced an unprecedented period of wealth. Though the education system benefited financially, it also suffered from President Trujillo's dictatorship and personality cult.

During the post-Trujillo era, the Dominican government struggles to meet the education needs of its populace. Contributions from organizations such as the World Bank have bolstered the number of schools and educational opportunities. Educational opportunities in urban areas continue to exceed those available in rural areas. Also, poor Dominicans are less likely than the middle or elite classes to complete secondary school and secure a job. The 2003 banking crisis in the Dominican Republic increased school dropout rates. The Dominican Republic Youth Development Project set out to train 28,000 young adults ages 16 to 29, many of whom were dropouts, for the workplace. The project, started in 2006, sought to strengthen the link between employer needs and secondary school curriculum.

Modern Education in the Dominican Republic
Education is free and compulsory from ages 5 to 14 in the Dominican Republic, and approximately 2.2 percent of the gross national product is invested in education. That percentage is lower than the percentage invested in other Latin American countries such as Panama, Chile, and Venezuela. Students in rural areas may have limited access to schools. Formal education begins with one year of preschool, though preschool is not mandatory. Approximately 38 percent of eligible children are enrolled in preschool. Primary school lasts six years.

According to the World Bank, 88.5 percent of students complete the primary level of schooling. However, a great discrepancy exists between male and female primary persistence rates. A total of 58 percent of boys starting first grade reach fifth grade, while 87 percent of girls starting first grade reach fifth grade. A total of 85 percent of primary teachers have earned the standard teaching credential. Middle school is two years beyond primary school. Secondary education comprises the final years of compulsory education. About 67 percent of youth are enrolled in secondary education. There are four different types of secondary education: teacher training, vocational training, polytechnics, and a six-year *liceo* program. After completing these final four years, a *bacheloritto* degree, which is similar to a high school diploma, is awarded. Low-income students struggle to complete secondary education. Wealthy families send their children to private and/or parochial schools. The University of Santo Domingo is the Dominican Republic's public university; tuition is free, and the university is funded by the national government.

Yoruba T. Mutakabbir
Clemson University

See Also: Haiti; Poverty and Education; Rural Schooling.

Further Readings

Alvarez, Benjamin. "Reforming Education in the Dominican Republic." USAID/Dominican Republic: Education Sector Assessment, 2000.

Chapman, Francisco. "Illiteracy and Educational Development in the Dominican Republic: An Historical Report." Ph.D diss., Department of Education, University of Massachusetts, Amherst, 1987.

Haylock, Arthur. "The Growth of Institutions of Higher Education in the Dominican Republic 1962–1984." Ph.D. diss., Department of Administration and Higher Education, University of Alabama, Tuscaloosa, 1987.

Sellew, Kathleen. *Dominican Republic: A Study of the Educational System of the Dominican Republic and a Guide to the Academic Placement of Students Institutions.* Washington, DC: American Association of College Registrars, 1987.

World Bank. "Dominican Republic." http://data .worldbank.org/country/dominican-republic (Accessed January 2012).

Drinking and Education, Adolescent

Alcohol is the most widely used drug in the world. While adults are not immune to its detrimental effects, adolescents are especially at risk. Excessive drinking interferes with educational development. In order to combat adolescent drinking, social scientists research its causes and effects, and educators invest in prevention programs. Historically, societies did not make the distinction of adolescence, a phase in the lifecycle prior to adulthood, but after childhood. Rather, adolescents were considered old enough to enter the workforce and drink alcohol.

In the late 19th century, a temperance movement began in the United States. In 1919, the U.S. government ratified the Eighteenth Amendment, which forbade the sale of alcohol. Following the repeal of the amendment in 1933, age restrictions were placed. The limits fluctuated slightly, until the National Minimum Drinking Age Act of 1984 forced all states to comply with the age of 21. Most countries, excepting some Muslim nations where alcohol is prohibited, are content with drinking limits of 16 and 18 years of age. In Europe, alcohol consumption is more tolerated, as adolescents are found to drink less than Americans for the sake of intoxication. Depending on the cultural history of drinking, underage alcohol consumption may be more tolerated in some countries, despite the legal limits.

Alcohol decreases inhibitions, allowing adolescents to fit in easier at parties and other social events. Furthermore, alcohol intoxication can make the individual forget about ongoing problems, providing a temporary refuge for troubled youth. However, alcohol is a dangerous and addictive drug. Besides physiological damage, drinking affects behaviors. Inebriated youth are prone to engage in risky sexual activity, conduct crimes, and hurt themselves and others. Most commonly, youth who engage in excessive drinking will become delinquent and irresponsible. Furthermore, the sheer amount of time spent drinking will impair school performance and career development. Studies of high-risk adolescents often explore alcoholism in the family.

However, there is a growing body of evidence that pinpoints diverse high-risk groups in specific contexts, including: males, dropouts, juvenile delinquents, subcultures, and college students. Vulnerability to the negative effects of drinking may vary. Certain youth have higher levels of resilience. In general, a combination of social, psychological, and emotional problems during adolescence and not alcohol alone lead to a downward spiral of drinking and educational failures, which may progress into adulthood.

Research and Theories

Studies most often rely on self-reported school-based surveys. A plethora of such studies have been conducted in the United States (e.g., Monitoring the Future, the National Longitudinal Study of Adolescent Health) and internationally (e.g., the European

School Survey on Alcohol and other Drugs, and the Health Behavior in School-Aged Children Survey).

Findings on the connection between alcohol consumption and education may differ as a result of methodology, such as the following:

- How alcohol intake and education are measured
- The causation process assumed
- Whether additional factors are included in the model

Research often examines types of drinking, such as binge drinking, or educational expectations, such as college aspirations. Researchers must grapple with the potentially spurious relationship between drinking and education: Drinking can cause school failure, and school failure can cause drinking. Social indicators are often included, such as friends' drinking and parental monitoring.

Sociologists of education often investigate how social contexts affect drinking and education. Deviance studies may focus on parent and peer influences. Drinking may relate to problems at home or elsewhere. For example, social bonding/control theory claims strong ties with others, such as parents and teachers, prevent individuals from becoming delinquent. Theories of peer influences often highlight hedonistic environments. Strain theory suggests that subcultures, such as punks, drink as a form of rebellion. Differential association theory highlights the importance of the type of peer group with whom adolescents associate: Adolescents who hang out with students who drink and fail academically will conform to the values of their deviant peers.

Cognitive theories explain adolescents' drinking motivations. Tension-reduction theory contends that youth use alcohol to cope with stress from other problems, such as failing in school or dysfunctional homes. Expectation theories associate drinking with preconceived notions of the inevitability of becoming a drinker. Labeling theory claims that certain subgroups perceive that outside society has branded them with stigma associated with low expectations. Economic theories may examine the availability of alcohol and marketing influences, or the perceived gains and losses of drinking. Young people can perceive positive social outcomes from drinking that counteract the negative effects, enabling them to rationally choose to drink.

Prevention Programs

Because legal regulations alone cannot redress the problem of adolescent drinking, most schools offer alcohol and drug education programs from elementary to high school age. Despite attempts to curb underage drinking, the problem persists, and the efficacy of in-school alcohol awareness programs has fallen into question. Alcohol prevention can take a variety of approaches. Many American programs promote abstinence. Frequently, students are warned about the physical dangers of drinking, such as drunk driving, synergistic reactions, and addiction. The premise of temperance education is that by making adolescents aware of the dangers of alcohol, they will be more reluctant to try it. Instructional methods include encounters with knowledgeable people from the community on alcohol risks. To keep students from succumbing to peer pressure, these programs attempt to counter peer norms that ostracize abstainers, for example, stigmatization of the "straight-edge movement."

Many European prevention programs teach that alcoholism is an endemic disease. Adolescents are instructed about stages of problematic drinking behaviors. Contrary to temperance-style education, these programs differentiate limited alcohol use from abuse. While assuming that adolescents will experiment with alcohol, these programs seek to ameliorate the potential danger by encouraging adolescents to wait until they reach a suitable age, and then to drink responsibly. Assessing the effectiveness of alcohol education requires an understanding of how intervention will impact not only the students' current alcohol and education status, but also their behavior as adults. It is believed that educational programs can prevent adolescents from abusing alcohol, stopping the problem before it starts.

Keith Goldstein
Hebrew University of Jerusalem

See Also: Adolescence; At-Risk Students; Drug Use and Education; Parental Involvement; Youth Cultures and Subcultures.

Further Readings

Bachman, J. G., P. M. O'Malley, J. E. Schulenberg, L. D. Johnston, P. Freedman-Doan, and E. Messersmith, E. *The Education-Drug Use Connection: How Successes and Failures in School Relate to Adolescent Smoking,*

Drinking, Drug Use, and Delinquency. Mahwah, NJ: Lawrence Erlbaum, 2008.

Chatterji, Pinka. "Does Alcohol Use During High School Affect Educational Attainment? Evidence From the National Education Longitudinal Study." *Economics of Education Review,* v.25 (2006).

Crosnoe, Robert. "The Connection Between Academic Failure and Adolescent: Drinking in Secondary School." *Sociology of Education,* v.79/1 (2006).

Mensch, Barbara S. and Denise B. Kandel. "Dropping Out of High School and Drug Involvement." *Sociology of Education,* v.61/2 (1988).

Staff, J., M. E. Patrick, E. Loken, and J. L. Maggs. "Teenage Alcohol Use and Educational Attainment." *Journal of Studies on Alcohol and Drugs,* v.69/6 (2008).

Dropouts

A dropout is a student who enrolls in a program of post-compulsory education for which they are academically suitable, but who then withdraws before completion of the course or gaining qualifications. It is therefore possible to distinguish a dropout as a person who deliberately withdraws from a course of study from one who has failed to achieve because of making inadequate academic progress: a push-out. Dropouts can be further subdivided into total or partial withdrawals. Total withdrawal is when a student completely withdraws from the institution. Partial withdrawal is characterized by students not attending some parts of their study program. Although dropout numbers are now widely collected all over the world, the reasons for students withdrawing are still an under-researched area. Statistically, noncompletion rates remain stubbornly high in many institutions, and have been for decades.

Monitoring student dropout rates varies between institutions, authorities, states, and countries; therefore, global comparisons are impossible. Estimates of how many people actually drop out of postcompulsory education varies from 2 percent to over 80 percent, depending on the way dropout has been defined and the data has been gathered. Analyzing dropouts' reasons for withdrawal is further complicated by the need to recognize significant variations such as ethnicity, gender, disability, and socioeconomic status, all of which can contribute to the underlying causes of an individual's decision to drop out.

Reasons for Dropping Out

The ethos of an education provider has a significant impact on student retention. The most prestigious organizations seem to have fewer dropouts. Most providers recognize their responsibility for retention and make strenuous efforts to keep students once they have been enrolled by providing pastoral support (e.g., health care, emotional support and counseling, and helping resolve social or family disputes). Students deemed "at risk" of dropping out are identified and targeted for supportive interventions, but such strategies have met with mixed success. One danger of this approach is labeling a student as being "at risk," since this can provoke withdrawal. Interventions will only succeed if the underlying reasons for students dropping out are understood and accepted.

There is a widespread belief among many teachers that dropouts are self-selecting failures: Recognizing their own lack of ability, they leave before it is proven. Alternatively, official statistics gathered by authorities show that personal financial problems are the major cause of student withdrawal. Both scenarios present the problem as the student's fault, and therefore outside the institution's control. Ethnographic research, challenges these viewpoints, particularly since it is often the most able (gifted) students, and many from socioeconomically advantaged families, who drop out, according to Renzulli and Park. Ethnography also sheds some light on the impact of ethnicity, gender, and other significant differences that are concealed within purely quantitative analyses, and overcomes the problem caused by people giving researchers socially acceptable responses to questions. It is far more socially acceptable, for example, for a pregnant teenager to say that she has money problems, rather than explain why unplanned motherhood prevents completion of her studies.

Two further categories of dropouts have been identified from the statistics: early and late. Early dropouts often cite "the wrong course" as their reason for leaving. Their pre-enrollment expectations fail to match their experience once they became a student. This mismatch between the expectations of the prospective student and what they actually encounter when in the course is a mixture of academic demands, cultural expectations, and the ethos prevailing within an institution. For the late category of dropout, manifest and latent functions of education in modern society play a role.

Few people would argue with the idea that education manifestly provides knowledge and skills for the workforce. However, there is some argument about the latent function of education; education programs keep large numbers of people busy, in a productive way, while simultaneously keeping them out of the workforce and unemployment statistics. For many people, continuing their education is perceived as irrelevant since personal experience shows that social mobility through educational achievement is inapplicable to their interests. However, in many countries, social-welfare payment rules, coupled with fewer employment opportunities for unqualified people, force these individuals into education because there is no suitable alternative. They drift into education programs because they have no real choice, but as soon as a better opportunity presents itself, they drop out.

Capitalism has also had a profound effect upon the way that education is viewed by society, and in the post-compulsory sector, there is a growing trend that positions education as a commodity. Alongside this viewpoint are the students who see themselves as consumers: they buy a course. Because these students are customers, they will leave a program when they are satisfied, irrespective of whether or not it has ended, or that they have achieved its qualification aims. The relationship with the education provider is simply a commercial transaction. These individuals do not view themselves as traditional students; they therefore do not perceive themselves as a dropout. The last category of dropout is the person caught up in a life crisis. Although statistically, this category accounts for very few dropouts, examining the social characteristics of students can help institutions identify those individuals most at risk. Poverty, persistent ill health (physical or mental), disrupted family life, and other dysfunctional social characteristics can at least alert an institution to the possibility that some individuals may require more help complete their studies. While life's misfortunes cannot be prevented by an education provider, systems of pastoral support and appropriate, timely interventions may go some way toward helping a student from dropping out altogether.

Intervention and Dropout Ramifications

When society explores the issue of student dropout, it usually does so in terms of negative consequences. The discourse is one of wastage and unfulfilled potential. In the United States, for example, it is estimated by the Alliance for Excellent Education that 7,000 students dropped out of high school every day in 2010. A great deal of pressure has therefore been placed on

institutions to improve student retention. Recently, monitoring procedures have been improved, and this has fuelled the recognition for much better pre-enrolment advice and guidance. With better information given to students before they embark upon a program of study, fewer will find themselves on the wrong course. In the case of drifters and life-crisis dropouts, many institutions now recognize the benefits of a meaningful, immediate intervention. It is problematic though, to question whether or not an intervention is appropriate for consumer dropouts. These individuals are quite clear about their motives, even though they conflict with the requirements of the education provider; but since they have made a deliberate choice and paid for it, intervention may be unwelcome and inappropriate.

It is not inevitable that all dropouts will turn to delinquency, crime, and antisocial or dysfunctional behaviors, as so much popular media coverage suggests. Considering dropout from an individuals' point of view can reveal positive befits both to them and society. For some people, dropping out enables them to pursue a "once-in-a-lifetime" opportunity or resolve a personal dilemma. There are some very famous dropouts, including Andrew Lloyd Weber (musician and composer), Bill Gates (founder of Microsoft) and Mark Zuckerberg (founder of Facebook). However, for the majority of dropouts, having fewer qualifications will make them less competitive in the jobs market and, therefore, may substantially lower their economic productivity. Finally, student dropout is a complex interaction between students' social backgrounds, their psychological makeup, and the way in which these connect with the prevailing culture and ideology of an education provider. Institutions must accept the significant role they play in this interaction; otherwise, dropouts will always be blamed for this waste.

Mich Page
Independent Scholar

See Also: Class Inequality: High School Dropout Rates; Educational Aspirations/Expectations; Ethnography; Functionalist Theory of Education; Gender Inequality: High School Dropout Rates; Racial Inequality: High School Dropout Rates; Teen Pregnancy and Education.

Further Readings

Alliance for Excellent Education. "Fact Sheet 2010." http://www.all4ed.org (Accessed July 2012).

American Youth Policy Forum. "Whatever It Takes: How Twelve Communities Are Reconnecting Out-of-School Youth" (2006). Education Resources Information Center. http://www.eric.ed.gov (Accessed October 2011).

Finn, J. "How to Make the Dropout Problem Go Away." *Educational Researcher*, v.20/1 (1991).

Kirsch, I., H. Braun, K. Yamamota, and A. Sam. *America's Perfect Storm: Three Forces Changing Our Nation's Future.* Princeton, NJ: Educational Testing Service, 2007.

Page, M. "Collecting Slices of College Dropouts' Lives." In *Biography and Education: A Reader*, M. Erben, ed. London: Falmer Press, 1998.

Renzulli, J. and S. Park. "Gifted Dropouts: The Who and the Why." *Gifted Child Quarterly*, v.44/4 (2000).

Swart, C. "Diminish Drop-Out Danger." *FE News* (November 12, 2010).

Drug Use and Education

The consumption of illicit substances and the impact on education has been the subject of national concern for decades. The intensity and importance of the topic has led to a significant amount of research, discussion, and various policy implementations to curb the use of drugs in American schools. The substances predominately consumed by adolescents are cigarettes, marijuana, and alcohol. Other illicit substances, such as cocaine, ecstasy, and prescription and nonprescription medications tend to make a much rarer appearance and do not present themselves with the consistency and severity of cigarettes, marijuana, and alcohol. No matter the substance, the use of illicit drugs are directly associated with poor educational outcomes, discipline problems, and legal dilemmas.

Drug use is associated with several interrelated risk factors and variables that can accumulate over time. Understanding the role of risk, resilience, and protective factors is important in developing effective interventions. Drug abuse education has been found to be an important intervention, because when youth understand the risks associated with illicit drug use and other risky behaviors, they are less likely to engage in them.

In 1969, President Richard Nixon called for a national federal and state anti-drug policy, identifying drug abuse as a serious threat to the nation when he publicly recognized the significant increase in drug-related criminal activity, including juvenile arrests. Two years later, President Nixon declared the infamous war on drugs, denouncing drug use as Public Enemy Number One. The national threat of drug abuse continued its reign at the forefront of this nation's attention in the 1980s, as it was highlighted by the Reagan administration's zero tolerance policy.

This led to President Ronald Reagan's signing of the Anti-Drug Abuse Act of 1986, which further allocated funding and support to Nixon's war on drugs. Also, in the 1980s, the heightened concern surrounding drug abuse in school-age adolescents led to the implementation of a program called Drug Abuse Resistant Education, or D.A.R.E. The focus of this program was and still is substance abuse prevention through the education of adolescents about drugs, gangs, and violence. The association of gangs and violence with the use of drugs is well documented. His program, which started in Los Angeles in 1983, has now developed into an international phenomenon as its implementation is seen in 75 percent of the school districts in the United States and in over 40 countries. In 1989, President George H. W. Bush created the Office of National Drug Control Policy (ONDCP), and in doing so, appointed the nation's first drug czar, who sought to coin drug abuse as socially unacceptable. Despite the federal government's efforts, the use of illicit substances, particularly by adolescents, steadily climbed throughout the 1990s.

As a result, over the last decade, policymakers have focused on and are trending toward stronger punitive measures to counteract student disciplinary problems. This movement has been coined "zero-tolerance" policies. Along with the zero-tolerance policies has come the utilization of metal detectors, random urinalysis testing, and the marked presence of school security and law enforcement officials in and around schools. This is a typical educational experience for urban schools in poor neighborhoods, and may subject black and Latino males to early contact with the juvenile justice system. Whether the zero-tolerance policy, along with the current substance abuse education efforts, are succeeding in decreasing substance abuse and its negative associates, has been the subject of much scrutiny and debate, possibly leading to the implementation of a different policy measure.

In more recent times, the Obama administration has revealed a plan through one of its school security administrators for the U.S. Department of Education to better schools and create a more secure school through an overall improvement of education. It is hoped that this will prompt a higher level of involvement by children in their academic studies, and foster a stronger school community. Such a change is predicted to lead to less spending on metal detectors, school security personnel, and an increase in student services such as counseling and extracurricular activities.

Impact of Illicit Drug Use on Educational Attainment and Achievement

Neuroscientists find that persistent drug abuse alters the chemistry of the teenage brain, particularly the pleasure circuitry, in ways that are more long-lasting than previously thought. Drugs create stronger addictive capacities in the adolescent brain at a time when the prefrontal cortex—the seat of rational judgment—is maturing. The adolescent who consumes an illicit substance, whether alcohol, cigarettes, or marijuana, on a regular basis, tends to demonstrate weaker academic performance than the adolescent who abstains. There are a variety of reasons that give credence to this phenomenon. The findings from a study by social scientist Dr. Ivory Toldson revealed stark racial differences in drug usage among school youth. African American males had much higher levels of engagement with drugs prior to the sixth grade than their white or Latino counterparts. They also live in more densely crowed urban areas in female-headed households and experienced higher levels of poverty than their white or Latino counterparts.

One impact of illicit drug use on education is the lack of persistence on the part of drug users to complete high school. The connections between illicit drug use and dropout rates are legendary. The National Institute on Drug Abuse has particularly noted that Hispanic youth show the highest rates of school dropout, followed by African American youth. The impact on school persistence and engagement is negatively affected by drugs that can be cumulative over time. Some studies indicate that poor school performance is a significant risk factor for drug use. Others suggest a more nuanced inverse relationship between drug and poor school performance. Students who perform poorly in school are more likely to abuse drugs, and vice versa. Another explanation of the relation is that poor school performance is stressful, and drugs are used as a coping mechanism. Whatever the

relationship, drug usage is correlated with poor school performance. Compared with 10 percent of students in high school with an "A" grade point average with 40 percent of students with a "C" grade point average, the "C" student was much more likely to use alcohol, marijuana, and cocaine, than the "A" student. Many studies confirm this finding, and suggest that helping students improve school performance can lower drug usage in schools.

Drug use is also thought to impact learning and concentration disorders such as attention-deficit hyperactivity disorder (ADHD) among school age and college youth. ADHD is a medical diagnosis of hyperactivity, the inability to focus and concentrate, and signs of impulsivity. The symptoms must exceed what is expected of a typical child in the same developmental age range. A study of 1,550 undergraduate students at Louisiana State University found a relationship between drug usage, ADHD, and a lower grade point average. The authors of the study, Claire Advokat, Devan Guidry, and Leslie Martino, could only speculate about the nature of the relationship. However, several studies have confirmed that hyperactive students who undergo stimulant treatment for ADHD with drugs like Ritalin were not under any increased risk for drug addiction in adulthood. A study conducted by the Clinical Research Program in Pediatric Psychopharmacology at Massachusetts General Hospital in Boston, Massachusetts, Harvard Medical School, discovered that children who were treated with stimulants like Ritalin in school actually demonstrated a decreased risk for drug use in adulthood. Other studies show mixed results as to whether ADHD and other hyperactivity disorders are associated with illegal drug usage.

Truancy or skipping school was examined in a study by Kimberley Henry at the Department of Psychology at Colorado State University. She anonymously surveyed approximately 1,000 11th graders at a school in the United States in 2006. She was interested in finding out if engaging in illicit drug use was a common activity when students skipped school. Other research questions focused on the seriousness of the truancy and what drugs students may have used while truant. Henry discovered that using drugs was a common activity while skipping school. More importantly, she moved beyond the already confirmed connection between truancy and drug use to truancy as a favored private space for high school students to experiment with drugs. Unsupervised settings with no adults are ideal environments for risky behavior. Reducing truancy may reduce illicit drug use. The study has limitations. The results may have limited generalizability to minority students or students in a different SES class because the sample was primarily composed of white middle-class students.

Risk and Resilience

Understanding the relationship between risk, resilience, and protective factors is important in assessing the impact of illicit drug use on students and designing appropriate interventions. A risk factor like poverty predisposes or increases the possibility of a negative outcome for individuals. However, when youth recognize the risks associated with certain behaviors, they are less likely to engage in them. This is strong rationale for drug abuse education for students, families, and communities. Since illicit drug use is also associated with other risky behaviors, such as unprotected sex and gang activity, the impact on academic achievement can be cumulative. This means that one risk factor can be the consequence of another, or even the complex interaction of a number of environmental variables. Consider how illegal drug use is also associated with risky environments, such as dangerous neighborhoods, lack of parental supervision, and poverty. This makes the impact on educational achievement a cumulative, interconnected process that is difficult to untangle. This is called cumulative risk, which suggests that as risk factors increase, so will the probability of negative outcomes. However, there is not a threshold or point at which intervention cannot be helpful in the reduction of risk. This is important as the threshold model of risk suggests that a point of no return is possible. Most social scientist disagree, arguing that intervention is helpful at any stage in children and youth's lives.

Interventions such as drug abuse education, a positive school climate, and loving and supportive parents can all serve as protective factors. Protective factors lower the accumulation of risk by acting as a buffer. Protective factors in schools include a feeling of belonging, acceptance of diversity, high academic achievement, and feeling safe. These positive conditions help thwart illicit drug use, which in turn lessens school disengagement. School disengagement is defined as a lack of interest fueled by a lack of belonging and acceptance in the school community. It is a strong indicator for disciplinary referrals, truancy, and dropout for all youth, but especially African American males. Feeling safe in school is a very strong protective factor for children and youth who use illicit drugs. It is closely connected with school persistence. Irrespective of race, gender, ethnicity, or socioeconomic status, a positive affect or a good feeling about school were associated with the reduced likelihood of drug activity. Risk, resilience, and protective factors work hand-in-hand. They help explain how the ability to withstand adversity plays out in the lives of children and youth who use drugs. Protective factors can be found in the individual, family, school, and community.

Intersection of Policy, Schools, and Law

In response to the problem of drug abuse in schools and its associated delinquent and even criminal activity, schools have moved toward the recent trend of zero-tolerance policies. These unforgiving polices set forth harsh penalties for criminal conduct on school grounds, including substance abuse. Schools were further prompted to adopt such a policy in response to legislative enactments of similar, but not as stringent policies, such as the Gun Free Schools Act, which sets minimum disciplinary standards in response to situations where a student brings a firearm to school. The judicial system has been generally supportive of schools' implementation and rigorous enforcement of zero-tolerance policies when appropriately administered. Schools have adopted highly aggressive drug enforcement policies in recent years that are directly related to sharp increases in the rates of juvenile crime.

Unfortunately, many of these policies result in a disproportionate number of minority children, especially black and Latino males, interfacing with the criminal or juvenile justice system. These policies include the implementation of highly visible school security personnel, whether private school security guards or actual police officers assigned to patrol a particular school for illegal activity. Generally, school security personnel are trained to be on high alert for illegal activity such as drug use, truancy, violence, and weapon possession. Furthermore, the known link between illicit substances like marijuana, cocaine, and prescription pills, and firearms, and the increase in violence in schools, has led to the utilization of metal detectors in many schools nationwide. These metal detectors are designed to detect any metal object on a student's person or in the student's belongings as he or she enters the school in an effort to prevent the introduction of contraband into the school. The ultimate goal is to curb or prevent any violent events from occurring, particularly where a weapon could be involved. Other policies schools are trending toward are random urinalysis testing for students participating in extracurricular activities and school-sponsored sports programs. Such random urinalysis is yet another policy that has been upheld or sanctioned by the judicial system as it balanced students' constitutional rights against the school's interest in discouraging and curbing drug abuse in its' students.

Substance Abuse Education and Prevention

Along with the basic adoption or even creation of zero-tolerance policies, schools have continually sought to implement comprehensive substance abuse education and prevention measures. Confronted with the rising tide of substance use in adolescents, schools began to address the problem with varied responses, including the implementation of various programs and community tools, including the following:

- Recognizing individual student risk factors, such as attitudes toward drug use, parental drug use, lack of commitment to school, poor academic performance, antisocial behavior, associating with drug abusers, and family problems
- Equipping students with the skills and tools to combat peer pressure and other environmental and social influences often associated with drug use
- Cooperation between schools, the community, and law enforcement agencies in combating school-related drug abuse
- Utilizing a community police model that allows trained law enforcement officers to visit schools to educate students on drug prevention.

The use of drugs by school-age adolescents can lead to other significant troubles, beyond educational success and failure. Oftentimes, drug use is associated with legal dilemmas that can arise as a result of substance abuse. The same peer pressure an adolescent experiences in regard to illicit substances applies to the involvement in gangs, violence, or other illegal activity. Possession of any illicit substance is illegal and subject to criminal penalty. Possession of any drug on school grounds can not only lead to an arrest and criminal prosecution, but also to suspension or expulsion from school. The possession of cigarettes and alcohol by any person underage (as determined on a state-by-state basis) is also considered illicit, and users are prohibited from entering school grounds, leading to the same consequences as possession of marijuana or cocaine.

Many schools employ local police departments to conduct sweeps throughout schools, using dogs trained in the detection of narcotics. Not only have schools implemented various processes to rid the adolescent community of drugs, but so has the judicial system. A student who enters school grounds automatically is not afforded the full panoply of Fourth Amendment rights as it relates to the suspicion of the use or possession of narcotics (or any criminal activity). Legally, school officials or police officers have to meet certain legal standards before searching a student for possession of an illicit substance. That legal standard is called "reasonable suspicion" and is often defined as a well-founded suspicion of criminal activity. It is what constitutes reasonable suspicion that separates the citizen on the outside of the school to the student inside of school grounds. This lower grade of reasonable suspicion, applicable to the student versus the nonstudent, provides school officials and police officers with the power or right to search the suspected student based on not necessarily a reasonable suspicion, but more so what the law has coined a "mere" or "bare" suspicion. This suspicion could arise from a school official observing certain signs of drug use, odors indicative of a certain substance, or even an anonymous or student tip.

Students who are subject to prosecution following an arrest on possession of a prohibited substance are then very likely to enter the juvenile justice system. Generally, the juvenile justice system, depending on the nature and severity of the charges, will likely offer juveniles a range of options. These options could include a diversionary program that would divert the juvenile's pending criminal charges from the court system and into a process or program that allows the juvenile the opportunity to have the charges dismissed. Typically, the juvenile would be required to perform community service hours, attend school regularly, complete substance abuse and psychological evaluations, and seek counseling. The counseling would include any substance abuse treatment deemed necessary. Other options could include a period of probation or placement into a residential facility, a stricter form of juvenile sanctions, either of which could include many of the same conditions, but with a more strict supervisionary process.

Chanel H. Jefferson
Independent Scholar

See Also: Adolescence; At-Risk Students; Drinking, and Education, Adolescent; Racism in Education; Urban Schooling.

Further Readings

Bachman, Jerald, et. al. *The Education-Drug Use Connection: How Successes and Failures in School Relate to Adolescent Smoking, Drinking, Drug Use, and Delinquency.* New York: Taylor & Francis, 2008.

Lane, K., M. J. Connelly, J. Mead, M. Gooden, and S. Eckes, eds. *The Principal's Legal Handbook.* 4th ed. Dayton, OH: Education Law Association, 2008.

Messersmith, E. *The Education-Drug Use Connection: How Successes and Failures in School Relate to Adolescent Smoking, Drinking, Drug Use, and Delinquency.* Mahwah, NJ: Lawrence Erlbaum, 2008.

Stader, David L. *Law and Ethics in Educational Leadership.* Saddle River, NJ: Pearson Education, 2007.

United Nations Office on Drugs and Crime. *Schools: School-Based Education for Drug Abuse Prevention.* New York: United Nations, 2004.

Durkheim, Émile

French sociologist Émile Durkheim (1858–1917) has played a fundamental part in the development of the sociology of education. Born in 1858, Durkheim is considered one of the fathers of the discipline of sociology, and his work has also had a profound impact within other fields in the social sciences, perhaps most notably in the field of British social anthropology. Along with Marcel Mauss (also his nephew), Paul Fauconnet, and other followers centered around the famous journal *L'Année Sociologique*, Durkheim was pivotal in the establishment of sociology as a discipline based on scientific method, the analysis of empirical data, and on the existence of "social facts"—inalienable social phenomena that exist objectively in society and that serve to shape the actions and beliefs of individuals in a way that preserves and prolongs the existence of that society. Durkheim applied this view

of society, and this approach to the study of society, to a wide range of social concerns. Principal among these was education, although Durkheim is often better remembered for his seminal work on sociological method (*Rules of the Sociological Method*), religion (*The Elementary Forms of Religious Life*), suicide (*Suicide*), and the division of labor (*The Division of Labour in Society*). Recently, through new English translations and retrospectives of Durkheim's life and work (by scholars such as Steven Lukes, W. S. F. Pickering and G. Walford, and Marcel Fournier), sociologists of education have been reminded of his dedication to the sociology of education and the profound impact that he had in this field. While Durkheim lectured frequently on pedagogy and education, he produced only a few publications on this topic during his career. Much of what remains of Durkheim's theories of education is derived from lecture notes compiled after his death. These lecture notes were reworked as books, but it would be several decades before sufficient demand led to their translation into English.

Function of Education

This is evidenced in the influence that Durkheim had on the establishment of functionalism as the dominant paradigm in the sociology of education during most of the 20th century, particularly in the United States, as seen in the work of such sociological heavyweights as Talcott Parsons and George Peter Murdock. For Durkheim, education played the key role in maintaining the healthy functioning of society. Education was for Durkheim the vehicle for transmitting norms, values, beliefs, and knowledge between generations.

Crucial to the success of education, in this sense, was its capacity to nurture homogeneity in the young—to equip them with the common ways of being that would allow them to function productively as part of a future adult collective. Education for Durkheim was ideological in the most unproblematic sense of the term: The role of teachers was to pursue the reproduction of ideal values, beliefs, and morals, alongside the kinds of knowledge necessary to suit the diverse economic and civic needs of society. This vision of education was also pragmatic and practical, rather than abstract: Framing these ideas within the rational secularism of France's Third Republic, Durkheim was intent on establishing a sociological view of education that would have practical and immediate implications for broader French society. As Steven Lukes suggests, Durkheim envisioned that this would be achieved, drawing on Rousseau, through an approach to pedagogy founded in scientific method and in learning from the empirical; in finding out about real "things" (including society) through experience. In Durkheim's ideal of education, each individual would in this way be taught to know his or her place in society, both in terms of morality and in terms of vocation. Education serves to replicate society, not to change it. The survival of a society lay in the ability of its system of education to achieve these aims.

Moral Education

At the heart of Durkheim's sociology of education is the idea that education is about establishing the basis for a shared morality within a given society. Durkheim viewed a system of morality as the lynchpin to society. Without a shared sense of morality, a society would crumble; and education was the principle means to secure this shared sense of norms and values. In *Moral Education* (1925), Durkheim sets out his idea of how children can be taught to adopt a set of shared moral values based on self-discipline, freedom, and order. In keeping with his rational, secular, scientific view of society, society, not God or some other higher power, provided the ultimate moral authority. This proved a point of concern for Durkheim, for society did not appear to represent the same kind of strong moral authority as may be found in religious belief. A partial (if somewhat problematic) solution to this issue emerges in the convergence of "society" with "the nation": The nation is a manifestation of society and provides a compelling set of ideological beliefs within which morality can be framed and maintained. Nationalism, or a firm belief in the moral code associated with a national identity, thus becomes part of the educational project as envisioned by Durkheim.

This view was influenced by his strong patriotism and belief in the ideals of France's Third Republic. But at the same time, Durkheim was a relativist: He recognized that moral codes varied between societies, and that there was no way of arguing that one moral code was superior to another. The survival of any particular society is predicated on the ability of its system of education—formal or informal—to maintain these morals, but there is no such thing, in theory, as a universal sense of morality shared by all societies across time.

Criticisms

Durkheim has been criticized for failing to reconcile this relativism with the role of national identity, or nationalism, as a framework for establishing shared moral values through education. Durkheim has also been criticized for presenting too static and homogeneous a picture of society, and for neglecting the inequalities and hierarchies that a Marxist interpretation of the social functions of education might bring to the surface. Crucially, as Walford and Pickering suggest, his theories of education have also been critiqued for their lack of empirical basis: Despite Durkheim's efforts to place science at the heart of sociology, there is little in his work that is based on empirical research beyond his anecdotal experience of education. Yet, despite these potential shortcomings, Durkheim remains a figure of fundamental importance, both in the history of sociology of education, and in its contemporary practice. Many of his ideas about education—especially those about morality and order—resonate particularly closely with some of the most pressing issues and concerns represented in popular, political, and educational discourse in Western society today.

Patrick Alexander
University of Oxford

See Also: France; Functionalist Theory of Education; Social Role of the Teacher; Sociocultural Approaches to Learning and Development.

Further Readings

Durkheim, É. *Education and Sociology,* S. D. Fox, trans. Chicago: Free Press, 1965.

Durkheim, É. *The Evolution of Educational Thought,* P. Collins, trans. London: Routledge and Kegan Paul, 1977.

Durkheim, É. *Moral Education: A Study in the Theory and Application of the Sociology of Education,* E. K. Wilson and H. Schurer, trans. New York: Free Press, 1961.

Lukes, S. *Emile Durkheim. His Life and Work: A Historical and Critical Study.* London: Routledge, 1973.

Pickering, W. S. F. *Durkheim: Essays on Morals and Education.* London: Penguin, 1979.

Walford, G. and W. S. F. Pickering. *Durkheim and Modern Education.* London: Routledge, 1998.

E

Early Childhood

The conception of childhood, which attaches special meaning to this stage and where children are at the center of family life, is a modern invention. In the feudal West, life was communal: The family served important functions such as giving life and name and passing on property, but important intimate elements of daily life were public for most of the population. Children joined adults in day-to-day life soon after weaning, and were viewed as small adults. The "modern family" emerged during the 17th century as the centerpiece of daily life and children were at the center of it. The role of family and school as institutions in modern, middle-class life took prominence, defining this distinct phase in life and thereby removing children from the day-to-day adult world.

Social historians attribute the enhancement of children's status to various causes. The most frequently occurring theme in the literature points to the influence of changing family demography. A few social historians also note that the dramatic changes in children's lives were brought about in part by the rise of mass schooling. Schooling, they argue, separated children from adult society so that by the second half of the 19th century, education dominated children's lives and led to heightening distinctions between age groups.

The American family changed dramatically over the course of the 20th century. Many important and interrelated changes took place, including changes in later timing of marriage, higher divorce rates, lower fertility, lower child mortality, increasing educational attainment, and more employment outside the home. More recently, time use studies have been used in describing trends in childhood. These studies generally find differences in the lives of children with stay-at-home mothers in comparison to women employed outside the home. For example, the rise in maternal employment has diminished the amount of time that women spend in childcare activities and has increased the amount of time that children spend in daycare. As a consequence, these children spend less time in activities like reading, sleeping, and eating, and employed mothers spend less time engaged in activities with their children. Other work finds some differences between mothers who work part time in comparison with mothers who work full time or stay at home. Finally, recent research suggests converging trends in time use for children of working and stay-at-home mothers.

The expansion of schooling to include all sectors of society largely occurred in the 20th century. School expansion, first in Europe and the United States, and now worldwide, has included a steady increase in the amount of time spent in formal education, as well as a growth of formally elite institutions. There is extensive research documenting the upward expansion of schooling to ever-older children; however, there is significantly less research on the expansion of schooling downward to younger children—kindergarten and preschool—and in many ways, its history lies in stark contrast to the upward expansion of schooling. Unlike upward expansion, there is little human capital logic in the expansion of schooling to younger children. Instead, widespread cultural ideas about the benefits of education and the enhancement of the individual draw parents and their young children into the realm of education at earlier and earlier ages as the power of education as an institution grows in the United States. For example, kindergarten was not part of the original school schedule; 19th-century reformers saw the kindergarten as a separate educational experience with distinct goals and philosophy. But the role of kindergarten transformed as enrollments grew and advocates crafted a movement to include 5-year-olds into the routine school schedule. Currently, there is near universal enrollment in kindergarten and preschool is expanding rapidly. There is evidence that these historical changes have significantly changed societal norms around both childhood and parenting over the latter half of the 20th century.

The last several decades have brought a heightened public awareness that early childhood experiences influence school performance. School readiness is not determined solely by individual abilities. Rather, it is encouraged and nurtured by people and environments. Research shows that the achievement gap appears before the onset of formal schooling, thus implying that some children have an advantage because their early experiences more successfully prepare them for the challenges of formal schooling. Research on the persistence of the achievement gap in childhood frequently looks at differences in family background and parenting styles for explanations. Emerging literature from the Early Childhood Longitudinal Study—Kindergarten shows that children who start kindergarten with greater cognitive knowledge and skills, who are read to frequently and who have more positive approaches to learning, have an academic advantage over children who do not start kindergarten with these resources.

Furthermore, the evidence suggests that school readiness activities are associated with family background. For example, household income is positively related to the quality of cognitive stimulation in the home environment of young children, resulting in economically disadvantaged children being less ready for school than their middle-income peers, and

black and Hispanic children being less ready for kindergarten than white children. In addition to family background, parenting style is also associated with school readiness. For example, maternal achievement expectations, quality of the mother-child interaction, maternal warmth, the availability of play materials in the home, and early language development are all associated with school readiness. There is also some evidence to suggest that family background characteristics impact parenting styles with regard to school readiness. Parent linguistic style is intimately connected to family socioeconomic status and has long-term implications for children's school success.

Maryellen Schaub
Pennsylvania State University

See Also: Childhood; Meyer, John; Parental Involvement; Preschool Programs.

Further Readings

Aries, P. *Centuries of Childhood: A Social History of Family Life.* New York: Vintage Books, 1962.

Hart, B. and T. Risley. *Meaningful Differences in the Everyday Experience of Young American Children.* Baltimore, MD: Paul Brookes, 1995.

Hofferth, S. L. and J. Sandberg. "How American Children Spend Their Time." *Journal of Marriage and the Family,* v.63 (2001).

Meyer, J. W. "The Effects of Education as an Institution." *American Journal of Sociology,* v.83 (1977).

Schaub, M. "Parenting for Cognitive Development From 1950–2000: The Institutionalization of Mass Education and the Social Construction of Parenting in the United States." *Sociology of Education,* v.83 (2010).

Early Graduates

An early high school graduate is a student who has completed all his or her high school graduation course requirements ahead of the regular June schedule for seniors in a four-year high school program. An early post-secondary graduate is a student who has completed all the necessary course credits of a degree or diploma in advance of the traditional four-year time frame. An increasing number of students are designing their learning programs to graduate early. Their motivations to graduate early are varied, and include reasons of finances, interest, and eagerness to enter the job market. Early graduation comes with both benefits and drawbacks for students and for the institutions from which they leave early. Early high school graduation programs are specifically designed to minimize financial barriers to postsecondary education, to ease the transition between the two models of education, and to increase high school completion rates. Some high school students graduate early because of their participation in alternative schooling, where the flow of course materials may be personalized to address their individual learning needs and motivations. Others are able to register in more than what is considered a regular course load. Many early high school graduates have been classified as "gifted," and take either an increased course load or transferrable postsecondary credits in order to be challenged intellectually. For others, motivation to graduate early from high school stems from the potential to earn specialized scholarships and other financial incentives.

To prepare students for the demands of postsecondary learning, in the United States, the National Center for Education and the Economy has partnered with eight states to pilot 10th grade standardized exams through the Board Examination Systems Program. If participants succeed in these exams, they are granted their high school diploma and are eligible to enroll in a community college program. Other districts are experimenting with dual high school–college enrollment where schools pay the student's college tuition, resulting in a reduction in state tax expenditures in education. Early graduation from high school has implications for students beyond the academic realm. It is seen as a positive motivator to students to remain focused on their studies, rather than lose interest in their senior year.

However, students who graduate early from high school may miss key adolescent rites of passage, including high school prom, athletics, volunteer and part-time work—all key elements thought to add to growing maturity and a sense of responsibility. Early graduates tend to be younger than many of their postsecondary peers, and they may experience challenges adjusting to their newfound locus of control for academics and to the social pressures of postsecondary campus life. Students considering early high school graduation are advised to seek both academic and career counseling as they explore their options. Proponents of early high school graduation feel that the time spent between early completion of high school and entrance to a postsecondary institution is time to be spent on remediation and academic preparation for the rigor of a higher level of academic expectations. There are mixed reviews as to whether a college application is strengthened by evidence of increased academic workload in a senior year, rather than taking the time to broaden educational and societal perspectives.

Early graduation rates among postsecondary institutions have been increasing steadily since the early 1980s, coinciding with sharp increases in tuition rates, and more recently, an increased recognition of advanced placement credits. Some reports link early high school graduation with early graduation from a postsecondary institution. More of a student-driven initiative, two of the most common reasons students give for graduating early include financial pressures and employment opportunities. Some early graduates find employment easier in January, a time when there is less competition in the job market than in the spring, when most students complete their degrees.

Other early graduates use their winter term to focus on graduate school applications. The Advanced Placement (AP) program involves standardized curriculum and coursework that is considered equivalent to postsecondary credit courses at participating institutions. If high school students achieve a minimum score as set by the institution, they can receive credit for an equivalent course, often at the introductory level of study. Some early graduates have completed credit coursework during the summer months, either face-to-face, or increasingly online. These credits are either transferred from their home university, or from another institution. Others are able to graduate early by enrolling in more than a regular course load each term. Key to graduating early is carefully planning course load schedules in terms of available enrolment options and required degree prerequisites.

Conclusion

Early graduation has a negative financial impact on postsecondary institutions because of lost revenue from tuition enrollment and student fees. In response, some institutions have set a maximum number of AP credits transferred into a degree or diploma program. Others have focused on admitting more transfer students from other institutions and limiting the number of credits that can be earned in the spring and summer terms. Administrators tend to dissuade students from early graduation, citing the value of the time spent in educative pursuits, the benefits of extracurricular activities, and the experiences gained from service learning, cooperative education, and international placements as reasons to delay degree completion and entry to the work force. Students are also encouraged to take additional special-interest courses during their final, eighth term to apply early to in-house master's programs.

Wendy L. Kraglund-Gauthier
Saint Francis Xavier University

See Also: College Advising; Gifted Education; High School Exit Exams; Skipping Grades; Summer School.

Further Readings

National Education Association (NEA). *And They're Off! How States Are Re-Examining Students' Early Graduation From High School.* Washington, DC: NEA Education Policy and Practice Department, 2010.

Wahlstrom, K. and E. Riedel. *College in the Schools Follow-Up Student Survey: A Survey of Alumni Five Years After Participation.* Centre for Applied Research and Educational Improvement, University of Minnesota, 2004.

Ward, Diane and Joel Vargas. *Incentives for Early Graduation: How Can State Policies Encourage Students to Complete High School in Less Than Four Years?* Boston: Jobs for the Future, 2011.

Earning Potential and Education

Earning potential in relation to a person's level of education is the focus of much discussion. While the cost of a college education continues to rise, many are stating that the cost is money well spent when the earning potential of particular professions is considered. Further, earning degrees beyond the bachelor's level is thought to increase that earning potential. Men and women see increases in their salaries with the acquisition of more advanced degrees, even though the ratios representing that growth are not equal. A gap exists between men and women with regard to salaries and overall earning potential.

Workers with a high school diploma only tend to see their earning potential remain flat, even with multiple years of experience at a particular job, and regardless of age. A high school education alone severely limits a worker's earning potential. Workers, who began college and did not earn a degree, fare better than those with a high school diploma alone, but still see their earnings over time remain somewhat flat. The completion of an associate's degree helps some, but not much with regard to earnings over time and considering experience.

A more significant increase in earnings in relation to age and experience is seen among workers who earn a bachelor's degree. Workers in this category see their salaries steadily increase, commensurate with their age and number of years of experience. An even larger increase in earnings in relation to age and experience is seen among workers who earn a master's degree. The most significant increase is seen in those workers who earn doctoral and professional degrees. These workers see the most growth, over time, as they age and acquire more years of experience in their fields. Over the course of a lifetime, the amount of possible earnings can be roughly calculated to include increases in both age and years of experience in a given field. A worker who does not finish high school can expect lifetime earnings of about $766,951. Workers with a high school diploma alone can expect to earn about $1 million. Those with a bachelor's degree can expect to earn $1.8 million, and those with advanced degrees can expect anywhere from $2.1 to $4 million.

Earning Gap Between Men and Women

Many studies have been conducted to examine the gap between the salaries of professional men and women. A common focus among these studies is the level of education attained and the effect that education has on a professional's salary. Beginning in 1980, there was a documented gap between the salaries of men and women. However, the level of education did not play a big role in the differentiation of salaries. Men's salaries tended to remain the same, regardless of the level of education, indicating that higher education had little impact on the salaries. On the other hand, women who had advanced degrees earned more than women who did not have advanced degrees.

Figure 1 Education and income

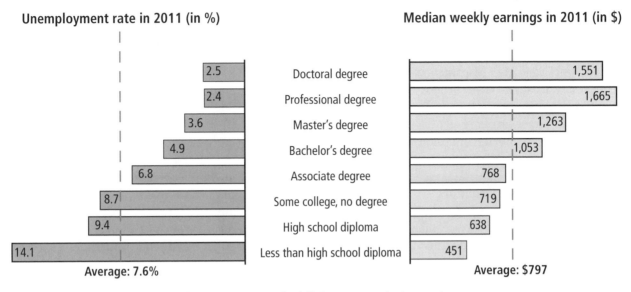

Unemployment rate in 2011 (in %)

2.5	Doctoral degree
2.4	Professional degree
3.6	Master's degree
4.9	Bachelor's degree
6.8	Associate degree
8.7	Some college, no degree
9.4	High school diploma
14.1	Less than high school diploma

Average: 7.6%

Median weekly earnings in 2011 (in $)

Doctoral degree	1,551
Professional degree	1,665
Master's degree	1,263
Bachelor's degree	1,053
Associate degree	768
Some college, no degree	719
High school diploma	638
Less than high school diploma	451

Average: $797

Note: Data are for persons age 25 and over. Earnings are for full-time wage and salary workers.

Source: Bureau of Labor Statistics, Current Population Survey.

Women with advanced degrees, in the 1980 scenario, might have an advanced degree and still earn less than a man with only a bachelor's degree. In 2000, the gap between men and women had narrowed, with younger women earning an amount closer to their male counterparts having similar degrees. The gap persisted, however, with the number of women earning advanced degrees, and older women tended to earn far less than their male counterparts, regardless of their level of education.

Younger women tend to begin their professional work lives earning amounts closer to their male counterparts. Despite this apparent gap, certain trends regarding overall growth potential were seen, regardless of the sex of a worker. Obtaining a certain degree or level of education had an effect on the amount a worker's salary would increase as they aged and acquired more experience.

Gap Among Different Racial Groups

Just as studies were conducted to measure the gap in earnings and earning potential between men and women, similar studies were done comparing different racial groups. Earnings of workers who were white, Hispanic, African American and of Asian descent were compared according to their levels of education. Salary amounts were measured over the course of an individual's work life. Of workers who were not high school graduates, whites earned about $1.1 million, African Americans and Hispanics earned $800,000, and Asian Americans earned $900,000. Of workers who obtained a high school diploma alone, whites earned $1.3 million, Asian Americans and Hispanics earned $1.1 million, and African Americans earned $1 million. A larger gap was seen among workers who completed some college courses. Of the workers in this group, whites earned $1.6 million, Asian Americans and Hispanics earned $1.3 million, and African Americans earned $1.2 million. Of workers who obtained an associate's degree, whites earned $1.6 million; Asian Americans earned $1.5 million, while African Americans and Hispanics earned $1.4 million.

The gap appeared to widen when considering workers who had obtained a bachelor's degree. Of these workers, whites earned $2.2 million, African Americans and Hispanics earned $1.7 million, and Asian Americans earned $1.8 million. Of those workers who had obtained an advanced degree (such as a master's or doctorate), whites and Asian Americans earned $3.1 million, African Americans earned $2.5 million, and Hispanics earned $2.6 million. Without question, an earnings gap exists among racial groups. On average, white Americans earned more than their counterparts in other racial groups, regardless of the level of education obtained. Asian Americans tended to be the closest, in earnings, to white Americans. African Americans and Hispanics were, on average, the lowest wage earners, regardless of the level of education obtained. Regardless of race, workers with degrees had a larger earning potential than those who either had a high school diploma alone or had not finished high school.

Career and Technical Schools

Studies involving career and technical schools showed that graduates earned, on average, salaries in the same neighborhood as those graduating from four-year schools with degrees in education. These technical certifications included tool making (average of $59,000), fire science (average of $59,388), apprentices (average of $53,232), and computer specialists (average of $51,616). While these figures were encouraging, the same studies found that they could be increased further when technical school graduates earned more degrees in their fields of expertise. The conclusion was that by combining a career or technical program, in addition to attaining further education, graduates maximized their overall salary potentials.

Kristen Brodie
Walden University

See Also: Gender Inequality: Returns on Educational Investments; Occupational Aspirations/Expectations; Racial Inequality: Returns to Educational Investments; School-to-Work Transitions.

Further Readings

Day, Jennifer Cheeseman and Eric C. Newburger. "The Big Payoff: Educational Attainment and Synthetic Estimates of Work-Life Earnings" (July 2002). U.S. Census Bureau. http://www.census.gov/prod/2002pubs/p23-210.pdf (Accessed August 2012).

Fitzgerald, Robert A. "College Quality and the Earnings of Recent College Graduates. Research and Development Report" (August 2000). National Center for Education Statistics. http://nces.ed.gov/pubs2000/2000043.pdf (Accessed August 2012).

Pencavel, John. "Higher Education, Productivity, and Earnings: A Review." *Journal of Economic Education*, v.22/4 (1991).

Ebonics (African American English) and Education

Ebonics is a popularized term coined by an African American social psychologist, Dr. Robert Williams, in 1973. The term blends the words *ebony* and *phonics* to describe "black sounds" and what was referred to as Black English. Most linguists tend to prefer the terms *African American vernacular English* (AAVE) or *African American English* (AAE) to describe the linguistic expression and speech practices of some North American slave descendents, while avoiding the highly stigmatized and sometimes pejorative term *Ebonics*.

The notoriety of Ebonics rose to national and international prominence in the mid-1990s, with Oakland (California) Unified School District's proclamation regarding Ebonics and changes in pedagogical practices for the instruction of 53 percent of the district's students who were African American. In the decades following the Ebonics controversy, scholars, researchers, and classroom teachers are still seeking effective ways to address the needs of language maintenance among bi-dialectical speakers of Ebonics by enabling them to gain access to higher education, social mobility, wealth, and power through mastering use of Mainstream American English (MAE).

In 1996, as one component of a broad plan to address widespread achievement disparities for its African American students, Oakland's School District declared that the primary language of the majority of its African American students was Ebonics. Further, this resolution asserted that students' home language was to be respected and maintained in an effort to address students' development and to improve their overall academic performance. The resolution provided for training for all teachers on methods to support students' home language, including use of knowledge of the linguistic features of AAE to design and implement appropriate instruction for their AAE-speaking students. Citing the Federal Bilingual Education Act of 1968, the board laid the groundwork to request funds earmarked for children of limited English proficiency with the argument that their African American students faced many of the same challenges to becoming proficient in MAE as did those of Asian, Native American, or Hispanic origins.

A number of conclusions arose in the aftermath of the district's proclamation, including the distorted mainstream view that Ebonics was street slang and that students would be taught Ebonics in Ebonics by their teachers. The media bred and propagated these ideas, and as a result, much of the national discussion was not based on linguistic knowledge about the rule-governed and systematic nature of AAE. The media coverage and resulting public discourse accompanying this controversy was the genesis of racist, derogatory, and demeaning jokes, cartoons, and parodies of speakers of AAE. At the same time, resolutions and policy briefs in support of Ebonics and the pedagogical decisions of the school district were issued by the Linguistics Society of America (LSA) and Teachers of English to Speakers of Other Languages (TESOL).

The tenets of multicultural education support affirming students' home environment and cultural capital as a means of promoting academic performance. In a similar way, national and international language acquisition research indicates that second and mainstream language varieties are more effectively learned when teachers acknowledge and take into account students' home languages (also known as vernaculars). In other words, educators should accept the linguistic integrity of AAE as the linguistic capital of its speakers. Further, teachers must understand that AAE is as systematic and rule-governed as any other variation of English. Some research has revealed that students respond positively in terms of their development of reading and writing skills when they use AAE as a bridge to mastery of MAE. These findings are supported by established approaches to second and bilingual education where English language learners (ELLs) receive support in their native languages while they are taught English.

Contrastive analysis has also been used successfully in the instruction of AAE speakers. This involves drawing learners' attention to similarities and differences between their language production and that of MAE. For example, because AAE has unique phonological features (the ways sounds are organized and used in language), teachers can use contrastive analysis to help AAE speakers learn to produce words using MAE pronunciations. In AAE, consonant sounds such as *t* may be omitted in final positions as in the words "past" or "first," such that they are pronounced as "pas" or "firs." Teachers can draw AAE students' attention to these differences in pronunciation, without labeling their production as wrong or deficient. Educators can then provide modeling, instruction, and opportunities to practice production of the MAE pronunciation, thus providing access to MAE in the classroom and beyond.

Erica K. Dotson
Clayton State University

See Also: At-Risk Students; Bilingual Education; Black Cultural Capital; California; Classroom Language; Cultural Capital; English as a Second Language; Multiculturalism/Multicultural Education.

Further Readings
Linguistic Society of America. http://www.lsadc.org (Accessed August 2012).
Taylor, O. L. "Ebonics and Educational Policy: Some Issues for the Next Millennium." *Journal of Negro Education*, v.67/1 (1998).

Ecuador

The Republic of Ecuador is located in western South America, adjacent to the Pacific Ocean. It measures 110,039 square miles (285,944 square kilometers). There are three primary geographic regions, the Oriente in the east, the Sierra, which is the Andes highland area, and the Costa, which is the coastal region. Ecuador has a wealth of resources, including considerable petroleum deposits in the Oriente region. The economy has benefitted from oil exports, but other resources include shrimp, timber, gold, and copper. In 2010, the gross domestic product (GDP) was $57.9 billion, with 14.2 percent from oil and mining, 11.4 percent from commercial trade, 10.6 percent from construction, and 9.2 percent from manufacturing.

The population was estimated at 15.2 million in July 2012, consisting of a majority of *mestizo* (mixed Amerindian and white), along with lesser groups of indigenous peoples, Spanish, and blacks. Originally part of the northern Inca Empire, Ecuador became a republic in 1830 and annexed the Galapagos Islands two years later. The acquisition of this territory was disputed by Ecuador's neighbors, Colombia and Peru. After decades of war and conflict, border agreements reduced Ecuador's area to less than half of its original boundaries. Ecuador has also suffered from misuse of its resources, as well as the volatile nature of world market oil prices. Beginning in 1980, a series of natural disasters and economic crises further challenged the country. Government and private-sector corruption has been an ongoing issue in Ecuador, as well as a lack of fiscal supervision and regulation, which weakened its overall economy. This lack of good governance led to a severe recession, low economic growth, indebtedness, bank failures, and many government interventions and reform efforts that often resulted in poor social development, increased poverty, and further unemployment.

In 2006, roughly 40 percent of Ecuadorans lived in poverty, and this number was further exacerbated in remote and rural regions of the country. There has been a traditionally disproportionate exclusion of access to education, health, and welfare opportunities, especially among the indigenous populations. Public spending on education as a percent of gross national product was 2.4 percent in 1991 and 6.4 percent during 2002–05. Ecuador's adult literacy rate increased from 83.6 percent in 1982 to 84.2 percent in 2009. Ecuador had 2.039 million students enrolled in primary school in 2007 with a gross enrollment ratio of 119 for males and 118 for females. Ecuador achieved gender parity in secondary education in 2008 and had 1.142 million secondary education students enrolled in 2007. In terms of higher education in 2008, the country maintained a gross enrollment ratio of 43 for females and 37 for males.

Education in Ecuador

Ecuador's education system is directed by the Ministry of Education. Ecuador maintains compulsory education for children aged 5 to 14. The education structure includes a preprimary level (for students 3–4 years old) and primary or basic level education (grades 1–6, beginning at age 5–6). Next, the system includes compulsory lower or basic secondary education (grades 7–9) and upper or specialized secondary education (lasts for one to three years; grades 10–12), which comprises learning vocational and technical training skills for individuals to fill mid-level professions. Another track in upper-secondary school also helps prepare students to attend higher education. The 2010 Higher Education Law increased government oversight of higher education nationwide in an effort that many critics argue further limits autonomy and academic freedoms gained in recent years. The law prevents private higher education institutions (HEIs) from setting tuition rates without prior government approval. With over 70 HEIs nationwide, there is a severe shortage of faculty members with doctorate degrees. The National Council of Assessment and Accreditation, established in 2000, is a government agency that serves to improve academic quality and management of HEIs through the processes of institutional self-evaluation, external evaluation, and accreditation.

Political instability continues to be an issue that challenges the education system in Ecuador. The high turnover rate for national education ministers has led to instability at top-level government leadership positions (there were 20 different ministers of education from 1985 to 2005). Access to equal education opportunities is a challenge for many Ecuadorans, especially in rural and remote areas of the country. The cost of specialized secondary education makes anything beyond compulsory schooling difficult, especially for those from low socioeconomic status backgrounds. Education is considered a human right by the government. Some of the current government education foci include ensuring the holistic development of children and youth in the framework of respect for human rights. Schooling is to be inclusive, intercultural, democratic, and should encourage diversity, quality learning, and safe schools. The government also actively promotes gender equity, social justice, and peace education. Critical thinking skills and the promotion of helping students learn to take individual initiative are also encouraged in the national curriculum.

Spanish is the official language, but the national constitution allows the right of individuals to learn in their native language, of which Quechua is the dominant non-Spanish language. In 1988, successful bottom-up efforts by indigenous peoples led to the creation of the Directorate of Bilingual Intercultural Education (within the Ministry of Education) that helped establish bilingual education programs in schools in order to help preserve indigenous languages and cultures. Today, bilingual intercultural education programs exist in many schools and are widely supported, especially among indigenous populations. Many efforts in recent years have been made to better enable students with disabilities to have access to education. Still, most students with physical or mental disabilities remain marginalized from participation in schooling, with only a small percent of those with disabilities completing secondary school.

Lynn Purvis-Yund
University of Pittsburgh

See Also: Bilingual Education; Colombia; Governmental Influences on Education; Peru.

Further Readings

López, Luis Enrique. *Reaching the Unreached: Indigenous Intercultural Bilingual Education in Latin America.* Paris: United Nations Educational, Scientific and Cultural Organization, 2009.

Nazmi, Nader. "Failed Reforms and Economic Collapse in Ecuador." *Quarterly Review of Economics and Finance,* v.41/5 (2001).

Torres, Rosa María. *Illiteracy and Literacy Education in Ecuador: Options for Policy and Practice.* Quito, Ecuador: Fronesis Institute, 2005.

United Nations Educational, Scientific and Cultural Organization (UNESCO) International Bureau of Education. *World Data on Education: Ecuador.* 7th ed. Geneva, Switzerland: UNESCO-IBE, 2010.

World Bank. *Ecuador Development Policy Review— Growth, Inclusion and Governance: The Road Ahead.* Report No. 27443. Washington, DC: World Bank, 2004.

Educational Aspirations/ Expectations

Educational expectations and aspirations are strongly correlated with educational outcomes, levels of educational attainment, and future careers of youth. Although the literature sometimes uses the terms *expectations* and *aspirations* interchangeably, it is possible to distinguish these two constructs, with educational aspirations representing hopes that individuals have for their future educational attainment, and expectations incorporating societal, school, and individual assessments of ability. A pervasive theme in research on educational aspirations/expectations is that of the role of race/ethnicity, gender, and socioeconomic status in limiting individuals' aspirations and expectations for educational attainment.

The most famous and influential work on educational expectations was published by R. Rosenthal and L. Jacobsen in 1966, when they shared the results of an experiment where teachers were told that certain students had exceptional potential to learn over the coming academic year, as indicated by scores on an intelligence test. In reality, the students had been randomly selected. At the end of the year, those students performed statistically significantly higher than their counterparts. To describe the phenomenon of individuals living up to peoples' expectations of them, the authors coined the term *Pygmalion Effect,* using the title of George Bernard Shaw's play *Pygmalion,* which was the basis for the popular 1964 movie *My Fair Lady.*

Although critiques of the study's research methods and occasional dismissals of the work on more ideological grounds have made their way into the literature, Pygmalion Effect findings have been replicated over and again, confirming that teachers' expectations of students' academic performance are important factors in students' academic success. Much of the literature refers to the phenomenon as teachers creating a self-fulfilling prophecy: Positive expectations foster positive outcomes; negative expectations foster negative outcomes. Additionally, the literature shows that students from privileged socioeconomic backgrounds are more likely to experience positive expectations from their teachers, and students from underprivileged socioeconomic backgrounds are more likely to experience negative expectations. Because of intersections between race and class, students of color are also unlikely to experience many learning environments where their teachers hold the kind of high expectations that their more privileged, white peers experience. Girls also experience low expectations in math and science, a finding often linked to the relatively lower outcomes of females in these subjects and their subsequent avoidance of careers in science, technology, engineering, and math (STEM) fields.

The effects of low academic expectations are not exclusively linked to individual teachers; schools can also send pervasive messages to youth about the academic expectations that educators in the building share, compounding the impact of individual teachers' low expectations. Conversely, schools' overall learning climate and level of academic challenge and support can mitigate socioeconomic challenges, improving students' academic achievement through a nurturing culture, interesting and rigorous curriculum, and strong supports. Since principals can directly improve climate and academics in a school, research increasingly has examined the role of the principal in setting high academic expectations in the building and in helping build the structures and norms that help students meet those expectations.

Societal Expectations and Assumptions

Although most educational expectations' research historically focused on direct connections between an individual and a personally experienced expectation, in 1995, Claude Steele introduced a radical new notion into the literature, establishing that even when expectations were not directed at individuals, stereotypes about groups could affect individuals' outcomes. In these experiments, where academically successful African American and white students were divided into two groups to take difficult verbal tests, African Americans were found to underperform compared to white counterparts when told that the purpose for the test was to diagnose their ability. However, when told the tests were not diagnostic of ability, African Americans did not under-perform compared to white students. These studies have been replicated across many groups, including white males and Asians on math achievement, and women and men in math, with the patterns the same across populations: When individuals are part of a group that has a negative stereotype, they are more likely to respond to that stereotype's expectation and underperform. This "stereotype threat" research has become one of the fastest growing research areas in social psychology.

Positive Self Esteem, High Expectations, and Nurturing Support for Challenging Work

As one way to counteract the negative impact of low expectations, many U.S. educators in the second half of the 20th century adopted curricula to promote students' self-esteem. These efforts often focused on helping students develop a positive sense of personal identity. Supporters of these approaches identified qualities of personal resilience that could be enhanced through explicit focus on positive identity development. With a stronger positive identity, students were expected to be able to better tap into their natural abilities and to navigate negative expectations that have been so pervasive in the educational system. Some critics, generally from more conservative camps, argued that this kind of work was not the purview of schools, but rather of families, and that education should focus on imparting content knowledge and the skills to apply that knowledge. Other critics, from more liberal or left-leaning perspectives, argued that the underlying assumptions of self-esteem improvement presumed that those most targeted for these efforts—usually children of color from low-income backgrounds—were somehow deficient in their sense

of self, placing the blame on the children, when it was the adults who needed to change.

In fact, for youth who are less academically prepared, these positive messages alone have not been able to change educational outcomes; affirming comments are necessary, but not sufficient aspects of high expectations. Youth need to be challenged in meaningful ways that reflect the kind of praise they are receiving, and they also need to be provided supports within a nurturing environment to meet those challenges. Study groups, nonpunitive additional work and tutoring, and real-life problem-solving projects all are among the ways that educators can provide the combination of supports and challenge that youth need to build their capacities to succeed academically at high levels.

Cultural Assumptions and Expectations

At the same time, some evidence exists that the focus on helping youth see themselves positively has improved students' self-image. On longitudinal surveys and tests that have asked students to assess their abilities, items related to self-esteem in the United States have risen. In comparison to other countries, youth in the United States report very high self-assessments of abilities compared to youth with similar achievement scores from other countries. This phenomenon has driven new research into cross-cultural differences in expectations and achievement. In the United States in particular (and in the West more generally), academic achievement is culturally associated with an assumption of innate ability. Thus, a high academic expectation is culturally linked to identifying a presumably fixed trait, such as "being smart." Low expectations, conversely, presumably identify those who are not smart—or, worse, "being dumb," language that struggling youth often use to describe themselves. In other countries, most prominently in Asia, academic achievement is associated with hard work and effort, more than with a presumed fixed intelligence level. This cultural orientation in ways neutralizes any potential Pygmalion Effect, since, unlike the identification of an innate trait, how hard someone works is within that individual's control.

Many fields of research, from psychiatry to medicine, sociology, and social psychology have increasingly challenged prior assumptions of fixed traits related to achievement, designing innovative experiments to explore how individuals develop and change their understandings of their own capacities. For instance,

Carol Dweck has identified two basic mindsets that mirror these cultural assumptions: the fixed and the growth mindsets. When individuals approach a situation with a fixed mindset, they are more likely to give up when they hit a challenge. When they approach situations as learning opportunities, or with a growth mindset, they are more likely to persist and ultimately succeed. Although there is no empirical research to date on the question, the linkages are strong between cultural assumptions of fixed traits and the impact of academic expectations in the United States.

Expectations and Education Reform

In the 1990s, a focus on high expectations began to become part of a national movement for education reform, with organizations like Teach For America (TFA), New Leaders for New Schools, and Knowledge Is Power Program (KIPP) creating national networks of influential individuals dedicated to changing education in the country. While these reformers often diverged politically on many issues, they shared an unwavering commitment: changing the rhetoric of academic achievement in order to shift the culture of schooling so that all students received educations imbued with high expectations. These commitments have played out differently across different groups, from charter management organizations that tightly control hiring and curriculum, to teacher and leader preparation groups creating alternative pathways into teaching but maintaining extremely selective entry processes ensuring individuals share their missions, to efforts to train a new breed of individual for district and state leadership positions. The leaders of these organizations have been successful in shifting public discourse and policy about academic achievement away from using students' socioeconomic status as an explanation for low performance. By establishing "proof points" that high outcomes for traditionally under-performing groups are possible, and at least marginally replicable, they have brought their reform efforts, sometimes called "no excuses" for low academic achievement, into the mainstream.

Although the impact of the high expectations movement in education reform is far-reaching, its most important effects have been in three areas. First, the reauthorization of the Elementary and Secondary Education Act in 2001 (known as No Child Left Behind) used the rhetoric of high expectations for all students as a cornerstone of the bill and a justification for the reliance on equal outcomes, rather than equal opportunities. The resulting changes in the world of K–12 education in the United States have been monumental, and are still only beginning to be understood. Second, teachers have become in many ways the villains of the system, since adults' expectations and efforts are defined in many public and policy realms as the only factors in student achievement. As a result, teacher evaluation systems are being overhauled dramatically. This fact in itself is not necessarily bad, given that historic evaluation processes were perfunctory at best. However, the demoralization of teachers throughout the first decade of the 20th century has been widely documented, and evaluation systems have often contributed largely to the unfriendly contexts that educators experience. Finally, teacher preparation programs are increasingly under attack, and in some states have been forced to make significant changes. Given the important fiscal role that schools of education play in higher education, and given how many students historically have become education majors, the press for deep changes in how higher education prepares teachers could have important ramifications for the overall higher education system.

Educational Aspirations, College Access, and Success

What level of educational attainment an individual aspires to is a strong predictor of actual educational attainment once socioeconomic status and achievement are taken into account. Thus, the construct is important for the understanding of how individuals progress through their educational trajectories. Generally, research on educational aspirations assumes a college-oriented frame, with studies tracking students' postsecondary aspirations and achievements. The empirical literature is framed largely with economic, instrumental, and rational lenses, presuming that individuals have college aspirations as a result of their desires for certain careers that will provide them with levels of security and economic benefit that meet their individual desires.

Over most of the last half of the 20th century, the proportion of individuals who aspired to go to college after high school remained relatively stable. In the past two decades, much has changed, with nearly twice as many individuals aspiring to attend college. One important factor associated with these increased aspirations is the cultural shift that began to see access to higher education as an inclusive right—for women, people of color, individuals with disabilities, and the economically disadvantaged. A second powerful factor is the dramatic decline of well-paying jobs available for the high school graduate. College attendance rates have shown corresponding increases, with some 70 percent of high school graduates enrolling in postsecondary education, compared to what had been a very stable 50 percent in prior decades. However, actual college graduation rates have not improved. The gap between these heightened aspirations and stagnant outcomes has been termed the "achievement paradox."

Most prominent in the explanations of the achievement paradox is the social reproduction theory. These analyses find that youth pursue and succeed at the educational levels that either their parents attained or their parents nearly attained and envision for their own children. For those whose parents did not attend college, explanations of educational aspirations and attainment often are linked to the lack of role models and career knowledge available in underprivileged neighborhoods, again invoking a social reproduction explanation. Some studies have tracked changes in students' aspirations over time, noting that aspirations lower when students receive low assessments of their achievement levels. Other work has tracked the impact of higher education costs and the negative effects of poor secondary preparation on changed aspirations. Some have used the achievement paradox to argue that students need to be guided toward "realistic" or "aligned" aspirations so they can pursue education and careers appropriate to their abilities, inciting critiques of neoliberal orientations to postsecondary access.

Recent developments in globalization are driving dramatic changes in the ways that researchers conceptualize college aspirations. Since 2000, there has been more than a 50 percent increase in postsecondary attendance, and between 2000 and 2005, the number of individuals aspiring to postsecondary education increased from under 100 million worldwide to over 260 million. These global developments will heighten the complexities of historic achievement gaps and promote significant developments in higher education, including more of the increased online and open-source learning opportunities currently part of many institutions, and new forms of postsecondary credentialing.

Karen DeMoss
The New School

See Also: Class Inequality: Achievement; Class Inequality: College Enrollment and Completion; Cognitive Skill/Intellectual Skill; Gender Inequality: Mathematics; No Child Left Behind; Racial Inequality: Achievement; Racial Inequality: College Enrollment and Completion; Self-Esteem; Teacher Expectations.

Further Readings

Brill, Stephen. *Class Warfare: Inside the Fight to Fix America's Schools.* New York: Simon & Schuster, 2010.

Bryk, Anthony, Penny Bender Sebring, Elaine Allensworth, Stuart Luppescu, and John Q. Easton. *Organizing Schools for Improvement: Lessons From Chicago.* Chicago: University of Chicago Press, 2010.

Csikszentmihalyi, Mihaly. *Flow: The Psychology of Optimal Experience.* New York: HarperCollins, 2008.

Pink, Daniel. *Drive: The Surprising Truth About What Motivates Us.* New York: Penguin, 2009.

Rosenthal, R. and Jacobson, L. "Teacher Expectations." Psychological Reports, v.19 (1966).

Steele, Claude. *Whistling Vivaldi and Other Clues to How Stereotypes Affect Us.* New York: W. W. Norton Co., 2010.

Tough, Paul. *Whatever It Takes: Geoffrey Canada's Quest to Change Harlem and America.* Boston: Houghton Mifflin, 2008.

Educational Policymakers

The term *educational policymakers* refers to those entities, both formal and informal, that create and implement policy decisions that impact schools and universities. Policies, in the context of education, may take the form of legislation, law, and policy. The policy process typically occurs in four phases: issue definition, agenda setting and proposal development, support mobilization, and decision enactment and implementation. Throughout this process, various policy actors become involved.

In education, policies are made at all three levels of government: local, state, and federal. Typically, members of the executive branch will be more involved in the beginning stages of the process, while the legislative branch becomes involved during the latter stages. Historically, schools were locally controlled. Those in positions of influence to the schools were the entities that controlled the policy decisions of schools. Policies varied by school district.

The federal role in education is limited by the Constitution, which leaves to the states all powers not specifically given to the federal government. Education is not enumerated as a federal power in the Constitution. Therefore, for much of history, education was a local function, deemed best coordinated by towns and states. The newly emerging federal government remained largely quiet with respect to education issues. From 1777 to 1937, Congress enacted only 23 laws pertaining to education. During the next 24 years, Congress enacted 33 laws, the majority of which provided money for construction of schools and compensated veterans for war service. Public education is not a right guaranteed under the U.S. Constitution. As such, the Tenth Amendment ("Those powers not delegated to the United States by the Constitution, nor prohibited by it to the States, are reserved to the States respectively, or to the people.") is often invoked to announce the authority over public education to the states. Some of the earliest roots of federal education policymaking are relatively recent in history. By the mid-20th century, the end of World War II signaled a return to the workforce of thousands of American soldiers. Baby boomer children were entering public schools in record numbers.

The Servicemen's Readjustment Act of 1944, commonly referred to as the G.I. Bill, provided college or vocational training to returning servicemen of World War II. The bill continues to provide support for servicemen today, even in times of peace, to further their formal education. The Office of Education, created in 1867, was largely authorized to collect and report statistical information about education in the United States. Although officials advocated for decades to increase the scope and authority of this federal office, the idea was defeated on the basis of the lack of constitutional authority. A century later, President Jimmy Carter signed into law the Department of Education Organization Act in 1979. The leader of the department, the U.S. secretary of education, became a member of the president's cabinet and subject to the appointment confirmation proceedings of Congress. As such, the secretary's presence established the federal government as a policymaker and player in the context of public education.

Scholars point to the mid-20th century as the beginning of federal interest in education policymaking. Specifically, with the launch of the Russian satellite *Sputnik*, the federal government began to focus funding and support for schools. U.S. governmental officials worried that military and technological advantages would be lost to the Russians, who were investing heavily in space and defense. Focus on education shifted to preserving and advancing America's superpower status through education of its citizenry. The congressional response, with the support of President Dwight Eisenhower, was passage of the National Defense Education Act (NDEA) and the Education Development Act of 1958, both aimed at strengthening mathematics, science, and foreign language education at the Pre-K–12 and university levels. In the years that followed, there was an increased focus on the compulsory nature of schooling and the curriculum necessary for the United States to remain competitive in a global society. Inequity in the schools was also seen as a problem for the federal government to intervene. Following the lack of state response to the mandates of desegregation, federal policy was created to encourage the progress of integration and to provide resources to the states for implementation.

Federal Level of Policy

Despite the emphasis on policymaking at the state level, policymaking in education does occur at the federal level. At the federal level, education policy is often created by the U.S. Department of Education (USDOE). Under the direction of the secretary of education, the USDOE issues regulations on a variety of educational policy issues. Before the regulations become law, the public has a chance to comment during a specifically prescribed period of time. Once done in a governmental reading room, the public comments may now be made online. As an appointee, the secretary of education has the ear of the president, and also becomes a policy vehicle for the executive branch. While the president may propose an education agenda, it must be enacted via another actor.

Presidents throughout time have influenced public perception of the role of the federal government in public education. They continue to be quite influential in setting agendas, refining debates, and recasting specific policy goals. Presidential interest in public education dates back to George Washington. Washington urged the promotion and diffusion of knowledge as the main vehicle for preserving the Constitution and democracy. Washington's message provided an impetus for states to establish public schools. Thomas Jefferson changed the focus of public education from the preservation of the democracy to concern with absorbing the millions of immigrants flocking to the country and working their way into the workforce and citizenship. Because education had come to be understood as the primary vehicle for assimilating and Americanizing immigrants, public schools during this period began, for the first time, to be examined as social as well as educational institutions.

With the advance of the Industrial Age, schools were charged with promoting the economic and technological prowess of the country. Franklin D. Roosevelt declared education to be a right, though the U.S. Supreme Court has consistently refused to endorse this view. As a result of the Great Depression of the 1930s, Roosevelt's New Deal offered educational policies aimed at constructing schools, addressing teacher pay, and addressing the pressing needs of black Americans. These policies set the stage for federal intervention in later years. Congress is constitutionally authorized to create laws. Despite the absence of education in the federal Constitution, Congress has used the commerce and general welfare clauses in Article 1 of the Constitution to expand their reach into the nation's classrooms. Perhaps the most powerful aspects of Congress, the House and Senate Education Committees, play a vital role in shaping and steering legislation through the process. If the committee fails to pass a bill, it is highly unlikely to be revived in the same legislative session.

Traditionally, the judicial branch of government is charged with interpreting laws. The U.S. Supreme Court has been active in promoting policies in education. Its decisions often spark changes in policies at the state and local level with respect to various educational issues. The landmark court case *Brown v Board of Education* (1954) forced states and school districts to adopt policies aimed at providing equal opportunity to students of color and to move toward the desegregation of its schools. Another highly influential case, *Tinker v. Des Moines* (1969), protected student speech rights under the First Amendment. Although the case stemmed from a silent protest of the Vietnam War, the case is still applied in today's context of Internet and other student-related speech. In 1973, the court rendered its decision in *San Antonio v. Rodriguez*, which famously declared education to not be a fundamentally protected right under the federal constitution. As such, some states have taken measures to constitutionally protect education at the state level.

State-Level Policymakers

As a state responsibility, education policy is made by those who have formal policymaking ability in the state. Primary policymakers include the governor, state legislators, the chief state school officer, and the state board of education. Each state has a formal governing structure for its K–12 education system, typically including a chief state school officer (often called a state superintendent) and a statewide governing board of education. Each state has a chief state school officer who typically heads an administrative state education agency. The process of selecting a chief state school officer varies by state. In 22 states, the position is appointed by its state board of education, while 11 states authorize the governor to make the appointment. Three states use a combination of the two, with the state board appointing the chief state school officer upon approval of the governor. A total of 14 states allow the public to elect the state officer directly. As agency head, the chief state school officer usually relies on senior staff members as policy advisors. Teachers, often through their union representatives, will also hold influence on the policy process at the state level.

States typically have a state board of education that has the authority to create policies relating to education. Two states, Minnesota and Wisconsin, do not have state boards. The remaining states have boards that vary in size, selection, and composition of members. Currently, 37 states have boards that contain between seven and 11 voting members, with the remaining 11 states having between 12 and 21 members. Historically, these boards consisted of ex officio positions of state officials (i.e., the governor and the chief state school officer). During the 20th century, many states adopted changes to the composition of state boards. Today, members may be appointed (typically by the governor) or elected by the populace. In some states, a combination of elected and appointed members comprises the board. In addition to general board members, several states include other stakeholders as representatives to the state board process. Although often as nonvoting members, several states include ex officio positions, members who hold spots on the board by virtue of the position or job held.

A total of seven states include state higher education commissioners as representatives, three states include the governor as a member, nine states include a student member on the board, one state includes a private school representative, and one includes a military representative. This allows various stakeholders to have a represented voice in state policymaking. Similar to the federal process of rulemaking, state boards typically enjoy administrative law authority. Policies are written and offered for a period of public comment before they are promulgated into law. Once promulgated, such policies typically have the force and effect of law.

State legislatures, primarily built of two houses (Nebraska is the exception with a unicameral system), are responsible for enacting or revising state laws pertaining to education, and often to allocating state funds to support schools. Similar to their federal counterparts, state legislatures have an education committee in each house. These committees serve a crucial role in the policy process, shepherding legislation to passage. It is often at these committee meetings where members of the public and other stakeholders can address legislators on specific provisions within bills. Despite not having direct authority over schools, state governors are influential in education policymaking. In each state, governors typically enjoy a level of appointment authority over policymakers. In many states, governors may have the authority to appoint multiple members of the state education board; the chief state school officer; and in three states (Montana, Oklahoma, and Washington), the governor enjoys a presence on the state board as a nonvoting member.

The governor, as the highest state executive, enjoys visibility and resources to influence the education issues facing an individual state. Public education, as perhaps the largest state expenditure, is reflected in the governor's annual budget. Governors may also include education issues as part of a campaign platform, placing specific policy issues at the forefront of public debate. Similar to the federal system, the governor also enjoys veto power over state legislation. Governors must sign a bill into law, or provide a formal veto. If the governor vetoes a bill, it typically must go back to the state legislature, and can pass with a greater percentage of agreement.

Local Level of School Policymakers

Traditionally, the entity with the most direct influence over school policy was the local school board. Local citizens, typically parents of children in the school system, have more direct means to influence and interact with local policies at the schools, either through direct participation at meetings or through the election process of its members. Despite the prevalence of the notion that the school board makes policy while the local school superintendent administers it, Frederick Wirt and Michael Kirst argued that they stimulate and affect each other. Although the school superintendent may hold additional policymaking ability, seeing as the position is usually one served at the behest of the school board, policies tend to reflect both entities' desires. School boards are organized to conduct the three roles of government. Legislatively, they initiate polices that help schools operate and adopt budgets to fund schools and projects. Judicially, school boards serve as an appellate body for issues of student suspension and expulsion, as well as employment conflicts. Executively, school boards approve expenditures and contracts, as well as principal and teacher assignments. Traditionally, mayors have had little influence over the policy process. Although some cities enable their mayors to make appointments to the local school boards, the executive branch of local government is typically silent in the operation of local schools. However, during the past three decades, sentiment has shifted in several of the nation's largest cities. Perceived bureaucratic dysfunction and inefficiency has led mayors in cities such as Chicago, Boston, New York, and Los Angeles to seize control of schools and exercise greater authority over the management of local school systems.

Interest Groups and the Influence on Policy

While once important in the education policy process, local actors such as parents, local school board members, and community groups have become less a force in the policy process than policy elites, those who wield great influence with state and federal legislatures. Corporate leaders, think tank advocates, and foundation officials have become influential actors in the policy process by utilizing financial resources in elections and influencing policy agendas. Special interest groups also influence the policy process in public education. Certain groups are academically oriented. For example, the National Council of Teachers of Mathematics (NCTM) offers a network for teachers of mathematics for professional development and advocacy. The organization also offered the first set of standards for the subject of mathematics in 1989. The organization remains an advocate for mathematics education. Some interest groups represent the policy actors. The National Governors' Association (NGA) and Council of Chief State School Officers (CCSSO) are extremely influential in the policy process. Both groups were vocal in criticism of No Child Left Behind provisions, and both groups were instrumental in creating the new Common Core Standards.

Teachers unions are also players in the policy process. Founded in 1857, the National Education Association (NEA) is the oldest and largest national union, representing over 3 million education professionals. The American Federation of Teachers (AFT), an affiliate of the AFL-CIO, was founded in 1916, and currently represents over 1.5 million members. The unions formed to present a united front for teachers, fighting against rules prohibiting teachers from being married or forced to take mandatory leave while pregnant. In the latter half of the 20th century, the unions focused on collective bargaining, promoting policies of teacher evaluation and salary enhancement. An anti-union movement occurred following the midterm congressional elections of 2010. States such as Wisconsin passed laws limiting the ability of unions, and worked through state legislatures to reform teacher tenure and evaluation programs. Such policies were often championed and lobbied by business interest groups in an effort to import policies and practices from the business sector into public education.

Belinda M. Cambre
University of New Orleans

See Also: Administration of Education; Governmental Influences on Education; *Nation at Risk, A*; No Child Left Behind; Schools as Bureaucracies.

Further Readings

Berube, Maurice. *American Presidents and Education.* Westport, CT: Greenwood Press, 1991.

Campbell, Roald "Federal Influences on Educational Policy." *Public Administration Review,* v.6/3 (1970).

Cross, Christopher. *Political Education: National Policy Comes of Age.* New York: Teachers College Press, 2004.

Fowler, Frances. *Policy Studies for Educational Leaders: An Introduction.* 3rd ed. Upper Saddle River, NJ: Prentice Hall, 2008.

Mitchell, Douglas, Robert Crowson, and Dorothy Shipps, eds. *Shaping Education Policy: Power and Process.* New York: Routledge, 2011.

Thompson, Kenneth, ed. *The Presidency and Education.* Vol. 1. Lanham, MD: University Press of America, 1990.

Wirt, Frederick and Michael Kirst. *The Political Dynamics of American Education.* 2nd ed. Richmond, CA: McCutchan Publishing, 2001.

Educationalization

For more than a century, virtually all societies throughout the world have undergone a schooling revolution. Beginning at primary grade levels, and then at secondary levels, and most recently at postsecondary levels, more and more people are spending larger portions of their lives enrolled in formal schooling of one type or another. In a world in which formal education is increasingly pervasive, the term *educationalization* describes the way in which practices, processes, and forms associated with schooling increasingly penetrate other social spheres, as well as the ways in which formal schooling is assigned more responsibility for social problems that originate in those spheres. In its most expansive definition, educationalization can also refer to the increasingly schooled society, in which schooling shapes whom one marries, where one lives, how one raises children, and even what sort of self is desirable. Three meanings of educationalization are as follows:

- As the importing of school forms to other social spheres
- As the assigning of responsibility to formal schooling for a range of noneducational problems
- As formal education powerfully shaping many other arenas of social life

Importing School Forms to Other Social Spheres

Sociologists such as John Meyer have documented the worldwide diffusion of formal school organizations over the 20th century, and their contemporary legitimacy. But the import of school forms to other societal fields has been understudied. School imports can assume a variety of guises: alternative sentencing programs and prison classrooms in the criminal justice system; hospital classes for expectant parents in health care; job search, anti-drug use, anti-racism, anger-management, and conflict-resolution in the welfare sector, and all sorts of training in corporations.

Each of these activities was once learned informally in other kinds of settings—in personal relationships or community organizations—but is now increasingly "schooled." Educationalization can be seen as one part of the broader rationalization of modern society, as the informal learning that characterized earlier epochs is giving way to increasing efforts to impose aspects of formal schooling onto learning of all types.

School imports combine elements of a school form with some prevailing practices in another institutional field. Importers can range from bird lovers to police officers to human resource managers. Each can utilize instructor–student roles and curricula to create a bird-watching leisure course, a "john school," or a corporate health and safety module. They may also jettison other elements of school forms such as grading systems, credentialing procedures, and instructor certification, instead of just record pass-fail status based on attendance. Likewise, since these imports lack the socialization mandate that is typically assigned to public schools, they generally drop disciplinary and extracurricular components of the school form.

In some respects, school importing is a social process with parallels to medicalization. Medicalization is the growing tendency for social problems to be defined, diagnosed, and treated as physical health problems, and thereby come under the authority of medical professionals. This process is driven by the power, prestige, and scientific legitimacy of the medical profession. For instance, whereas alcoholism, drug use, and unconventional sexual activity were long defined in moral terms and were therefore seen to require interventions from religious or justice authorities, their reframing as addictions has redefined them as health conditions that require medical remedies.

Likewise, many social problems are now redefined in cognitive terms, with school forms as their solution. For instance, criminal justice interventions redefine offenses like drinking and driving and soliciting prostitution as poor choices to be solved by offering more information and tools that can make for effective decision making, both to be learned in DWI and johns schools. But there are some important differences between medicalization and educationalization, namely, that teachers are rarely the driving force behind school imports, and lack the jurisdictional clout of the medical profession to require that licensed educational professionals be used in other spheres. As

a result, school forms are generally imported by professionals in these other spheres, who create hybrid organizational forms by mixing school-like practices with practices of their field.

Formal Schooling Tackling Nonschool Problems

Educationalization can also have two other meanings. Paul Smeyers, Marc Depaepe, David Bridges, and others have written about the way in which many social ills have been educationalized, by which they mean that formal school institutions are assigned responsibility for pervasive problems such as crime or joblessness. In this guise, school forms are not necessarily imported; rather, formal school institutions take on new roles that modify their original mandate and alter the role of the educator, making it more like that of a social worker. In the view of some writers in this tradition, this places an unreasonable burden on schools, and should be resisted.

Schooling Shaping Modern Life

The most powerful version of educationalization is the idea that schooling is increasingly shaping other spheres of modern social life, the "educationalization of society." Take four major realms: housing, marriage, childrearing, and notions of self and personhood. In systems where school assignment is determined by residence, real estate markets have becoming increasingly dependent on school markets. Real estate agents advertise the quality of local schools, and migration patterns within metropolitan areas are driven in part by the quality of the schools. At the same time, as social class becomes increasingly dependent on educational attainment, marriage markets are also increasingly structured by schooling. Research on childrearing suggests that an increasing number of parents are organizing significant portions of their leisure and child-parent time around preparing students to compete for positions in formal education, thus taking one of the most personal and private realms and orienting it toward the requirements of formal schooling. Finally, as the economy shifts away from providing solid middle-class jobs for those with a high school education or less, the very notions of what it means to be a successful member of society are increasingly defined by success in the formal educational system. Education is thus reshaping not only how people spend their time, but also their sense of what kinds of self are valued.

Underbelly of Educationalization

Educationalization affects everyone, though in ways that are highly uneven and stratified. At the same time that postsecondary enrollments are rising, there is stagnation of basic literacy levels and high school graduation rates, masked partly by rising numbers of General Education Development tests (GEDs). Moreover, much school expansion comes in arguably diluted forms. Most growth in postsecondary enrollments has been not in highly selective universities, but in nonselective, broadly accessible colleges that have considerable rates of attrition, where many courses are taught by adjunct faculty, and where many students are disengaged from their studies while receiving inflated grades. Schooling can spread and be imported, despite a lack of evidence that it is necessarily effective. None of the criminal justice alternatives, for instance, are shown to reduce recidivism. They are likely adopted because they are seen as more humane, inexpensive, and flexible than traditional criminal procedures. School forms can thus proliferate, whether or not they actually achieve stated goals.

Conclusion

Recognizing processes of educationalization can bring at least two broad benefits to sociologists of education. First, it significantly broadens perspectives on what it means to be schooled and opens up entire new vistas of potential study, including the many arenas in which school forms appear outside of formal education. Charting the continual spread of school forms throughout society also spotlights social change that would be otherwise ignored by limiting the conception of school to only its standard categories, such as K–12 schools and post secondary institutions. Second, it highlights the fuller role of schooling in contemporary stratification. Sociologists have extensively demonstrated the predictive power of schooling for labor market outcomes and for processes of status attainment. But educationalization points to something more: how education not only affects working lives, but also reshapes arenas as diverse as housing, marriage, child-rearing, and leisure. Moving ever further toward a knowledge economy, processes of educationalization will continue to grow.

Scott Davies
McMaster University
Jal Mehta
Harvard University

See Also: Career and Technical Education; Educational Policymakers; Labor Market Effects on Education; Schools as Bureaucracies; Technology Education.

Further Readings

Arum, Richard and Jospika Roska. *Academically Adrift.* New York: Oxford University Press, 2010.

Bridges, David. "Educationalization: On the Appropriateness of Asking Educational Institutions to Solve Social and Economic Problems." *Educational Theory*, v.58/4 (2008).

Conrad, Peter. "Medicalization and Social Control." *Annual Review of Sociology*, v.18 (1992).

Davies, Scott and Neil Guppy. *The Schooled Society.* 2nd ed. Toronto: Oxford University Press, 2010.

Davies, Scott and Jal Mehta. "The Deepening Interpenetration of Education in Modern Life." Working paper, 2011.

Schofer, Evan and John Meyer. "The World-Wide Expansion of Higher Education in the Twentieth Century." *American Sociological Review*, v.70 (2005).

Smeyers, Paul and Marc Depaepe, eds. *Educational Research: The Educationalization of Social Problems.* Dordrecht, Netherlands: Springer, 2008.

Egypt

Egypt is an ancient nation known for its advances in material culture, represented by the archeological findings of monumental architectures, artifacts, written documents, and institutions that were the basis of civilized continuity and change in the nation's 5,000-year existence. Underpinning Egypt's historic success has been the extraordinary role that knowledge and learning have had in the nation's management of its political institutions and social structures. The high value accorded to learning and skills is illustrated by the system of governance carried out by a large number of scribes who kept meticulous official records and facilitated the harmonious conduct of public affairs.

In 1952, Egypt's long history of domination by world powers and their surrogates came to an end with the successful overthrow of the monarchy by Gamal Abdel Nasser, who established himself as the first native leader in over 2,000 years. Vowing to rid the country of the vestiges of poverty and humiliation, he declared Arab socialism as the guiding principle of the nation, with the goals of independence and rapid economic progress charted as central tenets of the new political and educational philosophy. Education was adopted as a major public policy instrument for economic development, as well as narrowing wide social and regional inequalities. The two succeeding governments of Anwar Sadat and Hosni Mubarak inherited the structures of centralized rule, rhetoric, and practices of Nasser's educational policy. However, the defining doctrine of his governance, socialism, which emphasized state control and the redistribution of wealth, were largely abandoned.

Modern education in Egypt is traced to Mohammed Ali, considered the father of modernization. During his rule, the physical and educational infrastructures of modernity were laid by adopting a system of training while maintaining social structures of wide inequality and alienation. The reformed modernization project pioneered by Nasser and continued by his followers enshrined the policies and practices of expanding education through a centralized system of patronage, government control, and strict supervision. The enlargement of enrollment in primary schools, similar rises in secondary school enrollments, and significant increases in the number of university students came with the adoption of the constitution in Nasser's Egypt. He sought to redress the previous regime's inequitable system by providing opportunities to previously neglected social groups. Nasser placed justice at the center of his educational policy, promising guaranteed jobs for all graduates of the public school system. Rapid expansion of education as the foundation of the country's nation-building vision became the model for succeeding decades, even under administrative systems that officially embraced liberal models of modern education.

The continued expansion of education to the present era is indicated by the growth of primary enrollment, from 91 percent in 1991 to 98 percent in 2010, and secondary enrollment from 61 percent in 1991 to 69 percent in 2010. Approximately 30 percent of Egyptians go to university. The ratio of high school, post-high school educated youth achievement is ranked at 29 percent, even compared with higher income nations such as Turkey and Iran. Egypt's success in achieving the highest status in providing universal primary education in the Middle East is augmented by its strong record of similar opportunities at high school and college levels, with 33 universities and 51 professional schools and technical institutions opening their doors to female students.

Figures of success in expanding Egyptian education have, nonetheless, been attenuated by a host of deficiencies discussed by civic groups and scholarly evaluations. Observers, noting the wide gap between education and current realities, have labeled the predicament as education for unemployment. Major indicators of the problem are the proliferation of private schools and individual tutoring, which consume as much as 60 percent of surveyed families' income. Structural problems exposing gaps between social classes and urban and rural areas are also symptoms of the failures of the system in meeting regular standards with equitable public resources. While only 50 percent are estimated to graduate, unemployment rates for college graduates are estimated at between 30 percent and 50 percent. Concerns include the over-centralization of education systems, inadequate funding, and devaluation of teacher's roles.

Suggestions to address these challenges include reversing traditions of authoritative systems that emphasize elitism, rote learning, and expansion with little regard for training; and empowering teaching by providing adequate resources for institutions and personnel directly involved in the process at the grassroots level. Education's central place in the history and future of Egypt is underscored by the role that the nation's educated youth have played in leading the vision for change. Sustainable transition to democracy, represented by the nation's first popularly elected government in 2012, depends on fulfilling the large youth population's quest for curricula that provides marketable skills, critical thinking, and values of citizenship in an interconnected world.

Alem Hailu
Howard University, Graduate School

See Also: Labor Market Effects on Education; Poverty and Education; Worldwide Education Revolution.

Further Readings

Arab Republic of Egypt. *The National Plan for Education For All*. Cairo, Egypt: United Nations Educational, Scientific and Cultural Organization (UNESCO), 2003.

Sayed, Fatima, *Transforming Education in Egypt: Western Influence and Domestic Policy Reform*. Cairo, Egypt: American University in Cairo Press, 2006.

Tignor, Robert T. *Egypt: A Short History*, Princeton, NJ: Princeton University Press, 2010.

El Salvador

Located on the Pacific Coast, bordering Guatemala and Honduras, El Salvador is geographically the smallest Central American country, with a land area of 8,124 square miles (20,720 square kilometers) and a coastline of 191 miles (308 kilometers). The World Bank estimates the population at about 6.1 million. At the time of the Spanish conquest, Amerindians known as the Pipil inhabited the region now known as El Salvador. In 1525, they were defeated by the Spanish, who claimed the area as a colony. The country gained independence in 1821, and became a republic in 1859.

Civil unrest in El Salvador developed into a violent civil war from 1980 to 1992, with estimated casualties numbering nearly 80,000, and record levels of internal displacement and out-migration. The percentage of the Salvadoran population living in rural areas decreased from more than half (53 percent) in 1980 to less than two-fifths (39 percent) in 2010. The 2004 Central American Free Trade Act (CAFTA) created 15 free trade zones that have enabled the máquila industry to grow rapidly, providing nearly 100,000 jobs, primarily in textile mass production. Remittances from the Salvadorans living in the United States and other countries represent 17 percent of the gross domestic product (GDP) and over half of all export earnings, offsetting a trade deficit of nearly $3 billion.

El Salvador experienced steady growth averaging 7 percent in its GDP in the years immediately following the 1992 Chapultepec Peace Accords that put an end to the civil war. In 1996, a period of fluctuating economic growth began, hitting a low of minus 3.5 percent in 2009, when El Salvador's external debt was valued at $10 billion. The percentage of Salvadorans living below the poverty level dropped from 66 percent in 1991 to a current rate of 38 percent. The per capita GDP is estimated at $3,360. Major changes to the economy were introduced post–1992, including mass privatization of banks, telecommunications, electricity, and the civil service pension system. In 2001, El Salvador's economy was converted entirely to the U.S. dollar.

Education in El Salvador

Compulsory education in El Salvador is free and spans nine years. Baccalaureate (pre-college) studies are not compulsory, but are required for entrance into post-secondary education. El Salvador has three public and 12 private universities. School participation rates drop significantly between primary and upper-secondary studies, with enrollment rates of nearly 95 percent of eligible children in primary and 55 percent in secondary school. Although rates of enrollment and retention have increased in pre-primary, primary, and secondary school in El Salvador since the 1990s, retention of students across all educational levels is still less than 70 percent. Among the greatest challenges to education in El Salvador is the rural–urban divide in school access. School attendance and completion rates in rural areas are much lower than those in urban areas, resulting in high rates of illiteracy among youth and adults in rural areas and stagnated economic growth and human capital development. Illiteracy rates in El Salvador were extremely high during the first half of the 20th century, with limited access to schooling, low numbers of teachers in rural areas, and poverty as major factors. In addition, low numbers of teachers living in rural areas means that rural schools had limited access to trained teachers and often provided education only through the primary level. In the 1970s, fewer than 66 percent of children in rural areas attended primary schools, as compared with more than 90 percent of their urban counterparts.

About 8 percent of the country's total enrollments in middle-secondary education, grades 7 through 9, were rural children; at the upper secondary level, grades 10 through 12, about one percent was rural children. In addition, illiteracy was twice as prevalent among women as among men; only about 30 percent of higher education students were female. Contrasting conditions in El Salvador's urban areas provided more teachers per student, and more schools through grade 9, resulting in much higher levels of school attendance in urban areas. In rural areas, many students interrupted their formal schooling as early as age 14 or 15 to earn needed family income or assume domestic chores at home.

Because they had started school at age 8 or 9, this often meant that they had only completed primary school. Despite the small geographic size of the country, El Salvador's governmental campaigns to increase access to schooling have typically impacted only urban areas. Nonetheless, officially reported literacy rates increased from 26.2 percent of adults in 1930 to almost 60 percent in the early 1970s. At present, about one-third of the adult population is considered functionally illiterate. These figures, however, mask the complexities of who attends school in El Salvador and to what level: A study conducted in the mid-1970s indicated that only one-third of all Salvadoran students completed compulsory schooling, and only 15 percent completed high school. Government sponsored education reform with the goal of modernizing the education system and increasing access to education in rural areas was launched in 2000. Current literacy rates are reported at 83 percent, yet a rural–urban divide in attendance and completion persists.

Marguerite Lukes
City University of New York

See Also: Guatemala; Honduras; Rural Schooling; Urban Schooling.

Further Readings

Fariña, L. P., S. Miller, and J. L. Cavallero. *No Place to Hide: Gang, State, and Clandestine Violence in El Salvador.* Cambridge, MA: Harvard Law School Press, 2010.

Gould, J. L. and A. A. Lauria-Santiago. *To Rise in Darkness: Revoluntion, Repression and Memory in El Salvador, 1920–1932.* Durham, NC: Duke University Press, 2008.

Johnson, M. H. "National Policies and the Rise of Transnational Gangs." *Migration Information Source.* Washington, DC: Migration Policy Institute, 2006.

Elementary Education

Educating young minds is crucial for the future of humanity, and can often influence young people to consider the issues of poverty, the environment, and world peace. Education is seen as a necessary step to achieving a good quality of life. Elementary education for the young existed across cultures throughout history. In ancient Greece, Plato brought the concept of compulsory education to Western culture in his book *The Republic* around 380 B.C.E. Martin Luther advocated compulsory education in Europe and promoted the importance of reading and understanding the Bible. The Reformation in 1524 prompted the first national compulsory educational system in Scotland. In 1774, Empress Maria Theresa introduced compulsory primary education to Austria.

At the beginning of the 19th century, national elementary education was introduced to several Western countries as an alternative education option to the existing church-controlled schooling. In France,

Francois Guizot promoted national elementary schools during the reign of King Louis Philippe. In the United Kingdom, the Elementary Education Act of 1870 created the concept of compulsory education for children under 13.

Evolution of Elementary Education

In early African societies, education was based on artistic performances, ceremonies, dancing, and singing, as opposed to the pre-European colonial school system. The goal of education was to prepare the local children to take part in society, and every member of the community had a responsibility in contributing to the education of the child, as in the African proverb: "It takes a village to raise a child." The Aztecs in the 14th century formed compulsory educational systems in South America. Male children under the age of 16 are required to attend schools. Since 1991, Mexican children benefit from the Basic Education Development Project that provides additional funding for infrastructure, school materials, and incentives for teachers to the poorest elementary schools in isolated parts of the country. In the early Islamic era, in the 8th century, in the Middle East, boys were taught the basics of religion, to read and write, by tutors or slaves. By the end of 16th century, a *maktab*, or "elementary school," was built as part of a mosque, and the curriculum centered on the Qur'an, which was used to teach reading, writing, and grammar through recitation and memorization.

According to a World Bank report from 2007, from 2002 to 2005, the number of out-of-school children of primary school age declined from about 43 to 26 million in the south Asia region. Basic education became crucial to alleviating poverty, improving quality of life, and driving economic growth. In India, the Right of Children to Free and Compulsory Education Act passed in 2009 to provide free and compulsory elementary education for children 9 to 14 years old. Worldwide, around 89 percent of primary-age children are enrolled in primary education. Under the United Nations Educational, Scientific and Cultural Organization's (UNESCO) Education for All initiative, most countries have committed to increasing elementary education enrollment by 2015. American public education differs from many other nations in that the primary responsibility of education is given to states and local school districts. Education, especially elementary education, has been the center of public debate and discourse since the birth of the nation, over 340 years ago. From the Massachusetts Act of 1642 to the No Child Left Behind Act 2001, there is a quest for better pedagogy, educational resources, and content for children in order to improve test scores and compete successfully in the global economy.

In the United States, elementary education is called primary education, grade school, or grammar school. Elementary education is compulsory, and refers to a period of formal education prior to secondary school. In most schools, children are divided into grades by age group. Depending on the state or school district, most elementary schools start at age 5 or 6 with kindergarten, followed by first through fifth grade, and some elementary schools go up to eighth grade. Kindergarten is also part of elementary schools, but attendance is not mandatory. In 1837, Friedrich Fröbel coined the word *kindergarten* or "garden where children grow," emphasizing the importance of play, games, stories, music, and art in developing the social and motor skills of children prior to elementary school. In 1855, Margarethe Meyer-Schurz opened the first German-language kindergarten in Wisconsin.

Approximately 3.8 million students attended kindergarten in fall 2011. Magnet schools attract students from different school districts. Magnet and charter schools provide alternatives to public schools with specialized courses and curriculum. Just like magnet schools, charter schools are also publicly funded, innovative, and outcome-based public schools. Charter schools are independent from some of the rules and regulations that apply to other public schools. They offer models for autonomous school curriculum, promote school choice, and provide lottery-based enrollment to students who live in a different geographic area.

In addition to publicly funded public schools, compulsory education requirements can be fulfilled by a home school program or state-approved private school. This compulsory public education was clarified by the *Pierce v. Society of Sisters* U.S. Supreme Court decision in 1925. The Compulsory Education Act or Oregon School Law of 1922 required school age children to attend only public schools. The Supreme Court struck down the law as unconstitutional, ruling that it violated the Fourteenth Amendment due process guarantee of "personal liberty." Private schools also are known as independent schools. They are funded by the tuition fees charged to students, rather than relying on the local, state, or federal government. There are three different types of private elementary schools: Catholic, other religious schools, and nonsectarian. Catholic schools, also called parochial schools, provide religious education in addition to conventional elementary education. Nonsectarian schools are secular private educational institutions, such as Waldorf, Montessori, and Reggio Emilia, three progressive approaches to early childhood and elementary education that appear to be growing in influence in North America.

History of Elementary Education

The history of elementary education in the United States traces its roots to Puritan and Congregationalist religious schools in the Colonial era, and later to the common school movement in 1800s led by Horrace Mann and his efforts to convince the public to provide universally free schools that would be "the cheapest means of self-protection and insurance" and a "great equalizer of the conditions of men." Social, legal, and cultural factors have all influenced public education. In early American society, education had its roots in European culture, especially English, and it was primarily based on private schools. The European settlers tried to recreate the school systems based on their heritage language and culture in the 16th and 17th centuries. The goal of elementary education is to learn to read the Bible and religious catechism. Schools and curriculum were usually controlled by the church, and offered a basic curriculum of reading, writing, arithmetic, and religion.

Massachusetts originally passed the Old Deluder Satan Act, requiring every town to create and operate a grammar school in the American colonies in 1647. The other New England colonies adopted the town school model. The small one-room schools were founded in rural areas and in small towns. Although one-room schools existed in other countries, the ones in the United States were unique because they were locally governed by an elected board and served the needs of the local school district, as opposed to controlled by the government. Children enrolled in the local one-room schools in mixed aged groups ranged between 5 to 17 years old and studied basic reading, writing, spelling, grammar, arithmetic, history, and hygiene. Over 78 percent of children ages 5 to 17 years old attended public schools by the 1930s. All states passed compulsory education laws, first in Massachusetts in 1852, and the last state was Mississippi in 1917.

In the middle Atlantic colonies of New York, New Jersey, Pennsylvania, and Delaware, in addition to English, there were Scotch, Irish, Dutch, Swedes, and Germans. Because of the diverse ethnic and religious groups with different language backgrounds, elementary schools were parochial schools controlled by the different churches, as opposed to only Puritan values in New England. Formal education in the United States started to develop during the American Revolution by trying to lessen the European influence. Privately funded charity schools and district schools were established.

During the early national period, Thomas Jefferson introduced the Bill for the More General Diffusion of Knowledge, to promote public school system. Although not enacted, his ideas shaped the basis of formal education systems in the United States. In the early 19th century, monitorialism, also known as mutual instruction, was a popular teaching method in an elementary classroom. It was especially cost effective in large classrooms in big cities. Advanced students who were trained by a master teacher taught the younger and less advanced children.

New England's common school model was integrated into the new states as they joined the Union. In the south post–Civil War era, ex-slaves opened "native schools" to promote basic literacy. Before the war, southern slaves were prohibited from receiving education instruction, while a number of free African Americans attended elementary schools in the Northern states. In the southern colonies of Maryland, Virginia, the Carolinas, and Georgia, plantation owners preferred private tutors to educate their children, or sent their children to Europe. The southerners believed that education was a private matter, and not a concern for the state.

Modern Elementary Education

Throughout the 20th century, there have been long-standing trends in the United States: (1) Americanization, (2) democratization, and (3) professionalization that led to controversies about equal opportunity in a culturally pluralistic society, teaching philosophy, and the curriculum and pedagogy on how to be taught.

In response to the launch of *Sputnik* in 1957, the progressive education system was blamed for lacking rigor, and essentialist education philosophy flourished. Congress passed the National Defense Education Act (NDEA) in 1958 to compete with the Soviet Union in science and technology, as well as to improve science, mathematics, and foreign language education in elementary schools. This was the birth of science, technology, engineering, and math (STEM) education in the United States. By the end of the Civil War in 1865, slavery officially ended, but segregation in the schools continued until the 1960s in the United States. The U.S. Congress established the Freedmen's Bureau to provide former slave students a segregated elementary education. In 1954, *Brown v. Board of Education of Topeka* was a landmark decision of the U.S. Supreme Court that declared state laws establishing separate public schools for black and white students unconstitutional. The decision overturned the "equal but separate" phrase used in *Plessey v. Ferguson* decision of 1896, which allowed state-sponsored segregation.

Starting at the end of the 19th century, the federally assisted Bureau of Indian Affairs provided education stressing a basic curriculum of reading, writing, arithmetic, and vocational training to Native American children. Children were removed from their families and sent to boarding schools in order to assimilate into white society. Just like other multilingual nations, such as Canada and India, bilingual education in elementary schools has been highly controversial since the 19th century.

The children of non-English-speaking immigrants were assimilated into American culture by providing English-only education in the elementary school curriculum. Since the Bilingual Education Act (BEA), Title VII of the Elementary and Secondary Education Act of 1968, there has been a debate over how to implement bilingual education: provide a transition to help students get into regular English-speaking classrooms? Or design curriculum to maintain the non-English language and culture? The BEA was the first piece of U.S. federal legislation that recognized the needs of limited English speaking ability students. It provided federal aid to "develop and carry out innovative elementary school programs to meet the needs of non-English-speaking children. The Department of Education, established in 1867, originally focused on collecting information on schools and teaching. The department's mission broadened during the 1960s anti-poverty era and 1970s civil rights movement. Title VI of the Civil Rights Act of 1964, Title IX of the Education Amendments of 1972, and Section 504 of the Rehabilitation Act of 1973 prohibited discrimination based on race, sex, and disability, respectively. The Elementary and Secondary Education Act of 1965, including the Title I program of federal-provided aid to disadvantaged children to address the problems of poor urban and rural areas.

Curriculum and Organization

Elementary school curriculum prepares children in fundamental skills and academic knowledge areas in reading, writing, and mathematics, as well as introduces them to natural and social sciences, health, arts, music, library, and physical education. The American school year traditionally begins at the end of August or September, after the two to three months of summer recess, totaling approximately 180 days a year of schooling. By the end of May or June, children advance from one grade to the next. In the United States, the curriculum is more highly generalized at the elementary level, with a great emphasis on methods and styles of teaching and focus on the process of learning, inquiry skills, and social participation than in primary schools in other countries. Elementary curriculum is more differentiated and interdisciplinary than secondary levels. Creativity in elementary education is considered especially critical because educators design the lessons, according to Sir Ken Robinson.

Thematic units are designed, integrating mathematics, science, social studies, and language arts. The U.S. Constitution does not address public education, but under the Tenth Amendment "reserved powers" clause, states are given responsibility to control school systems. The curricula, funding, textbooks, employment, and other policies for schools are set up by locally elected school boards for the school district. For instance, methods of teaching vary in elementary schools. Some teachers and school districts prefer phonics; others use the whole language approach, or eclectic methods. Educational standards and standardized testing decisions are usually made by state governments. In order to receive Title I funds, the No Child Left Behind Act of 2001 requires that states and school districts must develop and conduct annual assessments in reading and mathematics in grades three through eight. Most of the states have established standards and require testing in these areas. Recently, there is a new initiative to nationalize the curriculum. The Common Core State Standards Initiative is a state-led effort to establish a shared set of clear educational standards for English language arts and mathematics. These standards are ready to be adopted by the states.

Standards-based school reform has become a predominant issue facing public schools. It gained momentum in the late 1990s, right after the publication of *A Nation at Risk* in 1983. More standardized testing is imposed on U.S. elementary education, even though the 1995 study *The Manufactured Crisis: Myths, Fraud, and the Attack on America's Public Schools* by David C. Berliner and Bruce J. Biddle refuted the 1983 report. They indicated no recent drop in student achievement. They found no evidence that private schools are superior to public schools. Over the past few decades, there are several alternative programs being tested instead of the one-teacher in one-class model. Multi-age programs, where children in different grades share the same classroom and teachers, are becoming a popular alternative to traditional elementary instruction. Another alternative is a two-teacher, two-class model, where students go to another teacher's room for one subject while the teacher for that subject stays in his/her main classroom. Another model is to give the children one set of classroom teachers in the first half of the year, and a different set of classroom teachers in the second half of the year. At the beginning of the 21st century, curriculum is being shaped by an emphasis on subject-matter competencies in language arts, mathematics, sciences, and 21st-century skills. Computer literacy, computer-assisted instruction, and other technologies in school programs reflect the nation's transition to an information society in a technologically advanced global world.

Teacher Education

There was no formal teacher training in Colonial America. Female tutors provided private elementary education, called "dame" or "petty" schools. In order to improve teacher training, normal schools were established in the United States at the beginning of the 19th century. The term *normal school* comes from France's *école normale* teaching institutions. The first American teacher education institution opened in Massachusetts in 1839. Today, there are certification standards for teachers that are determined by individual states, and are integrated into teacher education programs in the colleges and universities that are accredited by The National Council for Accreditation of Teacher Education (NCATE) or the Teacher Education Accreditation Council (TEAC). In addition to attending a teacher education program receiving either a bachelor's or master's degree in early childhood and elementary education, focusing the principles of curriculum design on human cognitive and psychological development, some states require standardized content area tests, as well as instructional skills tests for teacher certification. Public school systems in the United States employ about 1.7 million elementary school teachers, resulting in a pupil/teacher ratio of 15.5, whereas there are 216,328 teachers working in private elementary schools for a pupil/teacher ratio of 12.9. Professionalization of teaching started in 19th century, as national formal education was started and the demand for teachers was growing. The National Education Association (NEA) was founded in 1857, followed by the American Federation of Teachers (AFT) in 1916, to increase teachers' salaries and benefits.

Statistics

Over 33 million students, enrolled in schools from kindergarten through elementary schools, attended approximately 90,000 public and private elementary schools for the fall 2011 term. According to the recent National Center for Education Statistics (NCES), 2008 to 2009 school year, there were 67,148 public elementary schools, including 2,513 charter and 2,193 magnet schools that served 31,446,040 children in fall 2011. In 2009 to 2010, there were 21,425 private elementary schools serving 2,269,301 students in Catholic, other religions, and nonsectarian schools. Elementary education students in the United States constitute about 10 percent of the U.S. population. Among these 33 million, approximately 6.5 million students are in special education, corresponding to about 13 percent of all public school enrollments. Also, there were approximately 1.5 million students home schooled in 2007, a 36 percent increase since 2003. While the majority of home schooled students received all of their education at home, 5 percent attended school between nine and 25 hours per week. Since the 1970s, there has been a home education movement in the United States led by John Holt who coined the term *unschooling* in 1977. In addition to home-schooled students, there were an estimated one million students attending online K–12 schools in the United States, according to the Sloan Consortium Report: K-12 Online Learning Follow up Survey 2008. That report indicates that 14 percent of the students who attend online K–12 schools are in grades K–5.

Public school education systems receive funding from local, state, and federal levels. In 2009, the total funding was $590.9 billion. The highest portion came from state governments, contributing $276.2 billion

(46.7 percent), followed by local sources, $258.9 billion (43.8 percent), and the federal funding provided the remaining $55.9 billion (9.5 percent). The federal contribution to elementary and secondary education includes funds not only from the Department of Education (ED), but also from other federal agencies, such as the Department of Health and Human Services' Head Start program and the Department of Agriculture's School Lunch program. The U.S. census of 2009 also indicated that property taxes accounted for 65.2 percent of revenue for public school systems, from local sources. Where you reside makes a big impact on what type and quality of elementary education one will get. Public elementary and secondary schools were projected to spend about $525 billion for the 2011–12 school year. Expenditures for public elementary education per pupil were $10,499 in fiscal year 2009. Even though the United States spent more than Organisation for Economic Co-operation and Development (OECD) countries, which spent an average of $7,401 in 2007, American students ranked 17th in the world in 2010.

Jonathan Kozol argues that racial segregation is still alive in the American educational system because of the disparities in education spending per pupil between schools of different races and classes in his book called *Savage Inequalities: Children in America's Schools*. In 1991, for instance, the lowest per capita spending on students ranged from just over $3,000 in Camden, New Jersey, to a maximum expenditure of up to $15,000 in Great Neck, Long Island. According to the U.S. census in 2009, New York ($18,126) spent the most among states, and Utah ($6,356) spent the least per pupil. In order to prevent this disparity, alternative measures are being offered by different states. For example, Abbott school districts in New Jersey receive public education on the first ruling of *Abbott v. Burke*. The ruling declared that public elementary education in poor communities throughout the state was unconstitutional substandard. According to an NCES report, the percentage of Hispanic students doubled from 11 to 22 percent, while the percentage of white students decreased from 68 to 55 percent in U.S. public schools between 1980 and 2009; the number of English language learners increased from 4.7 to 11.2 million. The percentage of 5 to 9 year olds who spoke a non-English language at home and spoke English with difficulty was 7 percent, 4 percent higher than the percentages of 10 to 13 year olds and 14 to 17 year olds. According to the National Assessment of Educational Progress (NAEP), at fourth grade, the average mathematics score in 2011 was 1 point higher than in 2009, and 28 points higher than in 1990. Approximately 34 percent of students in fourth grade performed at or above the "*proficient*" level in the NAEP science assessment in 2009. Scores were also higher in 2011 than in 2009 for white, black, and Hispanic students, but did not change significantly for Asian/Pacific Islander or American Indian/Alaska Native students. The United States has a reading literacy rate at 99 percent of the population over age 15, while ranking below average in science and mathematics understanding compared to other developed countries. This poor performance has pushed public and private efforts, such as the Elementary and Secondary Education Act (ESEA) of 1965, the No Child Left Behind Act in 2001, and the American Recovery and Reinvestment Act of 2009.

Philosophical Orientations

In perennialism, the aim of education is to ensure that students acquire knowledge about the ideas of Western civilization. It is teacher-centered, and the focus of the curriculum is to get the highest level of knowledge in each subject field. To become "culturally literate," students should study the most significant works of humanity. Essentialism was a response to progressivism. It is a back-to-basics movement that emphasizes basic fact and reading, writing, speaking, and computing skills and advocates a conservative philosophical perspective that needs to be presented in a systematic, disciplined way. The emphasis is on intellectual and moral standards. Schooling should be practical, and have nothing to do with social policy. Influential essentialists include William C. Bagley, H. H. Rickover, and William Bennett. Progressivism focuses on the whole child, rather than the subject matter or the teacher. Students' interests are important. They are encouraged be active in their learning, solving problems, and reflecting on their experiences. Curriculum is derived from student interests and questions, and the role of the school is to help students develop personal and social values. John Dewey and Francis Parker are influential progressivists. Social reconstructionist theory goes beyond progressivism. Curriculum focuses on the social reform to transform and reconstruct a better society. Other influential resconstructionists are Theodore Brameld, Paulo Freire, and Henry Giroux. Freire argued the importance of literacy as the vehicle for social change. He challenged "banking education"

and instead advocated inquiry, dialogue, and multiple perspectives in his education model.

Teaching Material and Technology in Elementary Education

Educational textbooks and tools moved from slates to mobile technologies in the elementary classroom. While contemporary textbooks and teaching materials reflect a multicultural view on American society, historically, the textbook and teaching materials, such as the *hornbook,* reflected the dominant values. For instance, in colonial America, the New England Primer was first printed in Boston in 1690 by Benjamin Harris. The text focused on Puritanism and ethical values. Noah Webster's American spelling books emphasized American patriotism. The McGuffey readers written by Reverend W. H. McGuffey in 1836 became one of the first and most widely used textbooks, ranging in difficulty from the first to the sixth grade level. The stories encouraged children to be honest and hardworking. In the 1930s, *Dick and Jane,* written by William S. Gray and Zerna Sharp, portrayed the culture and lifestyle of the dominant middle class. In 1963, computer giant IBM partnered with Stanford's Institute for Mathematical Studies in the Social Sciences to develop programmed-learning software for elementary schools, jointly created by computer scientists and learning experts. In 1966, IBM introduced its Model 1500 computer, especially designed to run instructional programming. LOGO, a language created in 1967, extended the supposed benefits of programming to elementary school students. In 1974, the "Oregon Trail" computer game, designed to teach about pioneer life, was introduced. Apple's Macintosh computer was introduced and quickly gained popularity, especially in elementary schools, in 1984.

The Education for All Handicapped Children Act of 1975, modified as the Individuals with Disabilities Education Improvement Act (IDEA) in 2004, provided free public education to all children with disabilities and demanded technological innovations and assistive technologies, from speech to text to magnification of the textbook materials. Today's elementary students are interacting and collaborating with schools around the world with new telecommunication systems. In a 2008 NCES technology report, all elementary schools in the United States had an Internet connection, and the ratio of students to computers is 3.2. Starting in 2011, a new Florida law allows charter schools and individual school districts to offer online instruction, and permits elementary school students to study full time at Florida Virtual School. The Computer Science Education Act of 2011 was introduced in the House and Senate to bring more programming and computer problem solving to students. From equity in schools to bilingual education, from accountability to standardization, from voucher systems to privatization of education, elementary education and its controversies will stay in the focus of public debate as global competition increases.

Melda N. Yildiz
Kean University

See Also: *Brown v. Board of Education*; Catholic Schools; Charter Schools; Curriculum Standardization; Home Schooling; Magnet Schools; Montessori; Multiculturalism/ Multicultural Education; Reggio Emilia Approach; School Choice; Waldorf.

Further Readings
Altenbaugh, R. J. *The American People and Their Education: A Social History*. Upper Saddle River, NJ: Merrill/Prentice Hall, 2003.

Berliner, David C. and Bruce J. Biddle. *The Manufactured Crisis: Myths, Fraud, and the Attack on America's Public Schools*. Reading, MA: Addison-Wesley, 1995.

Hirsch, E. D., Joseph F. Kett, and James S. Trefil. *Cultural Literacy: What Every American Needs to Know*. Boston: Houghton Mifflin, 1987.

Parkay, F. W. and Beverly Hardcastle Stanford. *Becoming a Teacher*. Boston: Pearson, Allyn, and Bacon, 2005.

Renzulli, Linda A. and Lorraine Evans. "School Choice, Charter Schools, and White Flight." *Social Problems*, v.52 (2005).

English as a Second Language

English as a second language (ESL) instruction addresses the English language learning needs of non-native English speaking populations within English-dominant societies. Second language learning pertains to a minority language speaker learning the dominant language of the society of interest (e.g., learning Spanish in Mexico or English in the United States). ESL targets a specific subgroup of the language minority (non-native English speaking) population in the United States, those in the process of learning English. ESL services in schools grew in response to a Supreme Court decision that mandated language services to provide language minority students equality of educational opportunity. The services in schools have expanded in the United States, largely to address the needs of the growing immigrant, language minority population. Sociologists have questioned whether the provision of language services provides students better or worse opportunities to learn academic subjects.

Broadly, ESL instruction comprises one type of linguistic support services for immigrant and other language minority individuals in the process of learning English. The federal government has used the term *limited english proficient*, or LEP, to identify language minority individuals learning English. More recently, many K–12 educational agencies (states, districts, and schools) use the term *English learner*, or EL, to avoid the deficit connotation inherent in the federal definition. Language minority individuals are identified as non-native speakers of the dominant societal language; in the U.S. context, these are non-native English speakers. Language minority individuals who do not demonstrate proficiency in English are generally expected to take advantage of ESL instruction. Among the adult population, this is largely voluntary; among the school-age population, however, ESL is provided in the context of compulsory schooling. Upon a child's first entry into the school system, parents complete a home language survey indicating which language(s) are spoken at home and with whom. This initial identification of language minority status leads to the identification of language minority students who are not yet proficient in English, and the placement of these students into some sort of linguistic support services to ensure equitable access to academic content. As such, students in ESL coursework comprise a very specific segment of the language minority population, with distinct linguistic needs, and clustered in common linguistic support services.

Policy Backdrop
In 1968, following the Civil Rights Act of 1964, Congress passed the Bilingual Education Act (BEA) as part of President Johnson's overarching War on Poverty. The BEA provided financial support to state and local education agencies to develop innovative programs to facilitate the acquisition of English among

language minority students identified as LEP and needing ESL support. This legislation came on the heels of increased immigration following the passage of the Hart-Cellar Act of 1965, which prioritized family reunification in immigration and resulted in an influx of children of immigrant parents in the K–12 school systems. In 1974, the *Lau v. Nichols* Supreme Court decision addressed this issue of equity in academic access, deciding that equal was not equitable: Receiving the same instruction, by the same teachers, in the same classrooms as their native English speaking peers did not constitute equitable access to the content matter. The *Lau* decision required that schools ensure that English learners have access to math, history, and science, the core content while learning English; the court recommended that schools ensure such academic access via instructional modification and linguistic support services, although no particular program was mandated. Through *Lau*, the Supreme Court identified a new status group in schools, English learners (ELs, or LEP students), whose opportunity to learn would, in theory, be addressed through linguistic support services. For the most part, such support was provided through ESL instruction supplemental to the student's general academic program.

ESL Across the Life Course

The mode of delivery and target audience for ESL services and instruction varies across the life course. Just as native language development follows a given path relative to the cognitive development of the individual, so does second language development. Where preschool-age learners are tasked with labeling and identifying their world, for more cognitively advanced (i.e., generally older, more educated) learners, the second language can be developed as a tool for communication, negotiation, and establishment of identity. In the United States, ESL instructional support can begin as early as preschool; in fact, federally funded Head Start programs incorporate the learning of ESL as part of the standard curriculum for their target population. Although the youngest English learners appear to acquire English more quickly and efficiently than their adult counterparts, this is largely because of the malleability of their phonemic production and reception system prior to the onset of puberty. Despite the fact that young learners are easily able to mimic the tone, tenor, and accent of native English speech, they lack the academic foundation necessary to negotiate and comprehend difficult concepts in

the second language. Although the youngest ELs may sound the most native-like, it is critical to monitor their academic development, all of which will occur in the child's second language, as they receive ESL instruction.

Local education agencies are required to ensure equitable academic access for EL students. The most frequently occurring programs include: ESL pull-out, ESL push-in, content-based ESL, and ELD. ESL pull-out occurs when EL students are taken out of the classroom by an ESL teacher to receive a discrete period of ESL instruction, traditionally a targeted English language development lesson that may focus on vocabulary development, a grammatical construct in English, or review of academic content covered in class. ESL push-in differs from ESL pull-out in that the ESL teacher offers a targeted English language development lesson to the EL students within their classroom. In theory, ESL push-in teachers are able to collaborate with the classroom teachers to align their language development lessons with the general classroom curriculum. Last, the content-based ESL approach requires that the classroom teacher is ESL certified. A content-based ESL approach incorporates instructional modification and scaffolding to develop students' academic English proficiency through grade-level math, science, history, and language arts. Although less costly than the ESL push-in or pull-out models, which require an additional teacher, the content-based ESL approach is the rarest as it requires that all teachers receive professional development in order to facilitate EL students' simultaneous academic and linguistic development.

At the secondary level, middle and high school, students generally receive ESL instructional support in two distinct formats: separate language-based ESL classes and modified content area (math, science, and social studies) instruction. Many states require that secondary EL students are placed in structured ESL instruction to develop their English language proficiency until they exit from linguistic support services. The regimented structure of secondary schools in the United States also supports the provision of content-based ESL through "sheltered" math, science, and social studies. Sheltered coursework (e.g., sheltered algebra) is designed to cover the same academic content relative to its mainstream counterpart (e.g., algebra), the primary difference being the teacher's use of modified instructional strategies. In practice, however, critics have argued that the content of sheltered courses is often "watered-down" and less academically rigorous. Many states also mandate that secondary EL students be placed only with teachers who hold ESL certification, inadvertently limiting the range of classes to which the students have access.

Language minority individuals of all ages arrive in the United States requiring ESL services. The majority of adult language minority immigrants are active in the workforce, potentially limiting their access to ESL instruction to outside work hours. Adult ESL, thus, is offered in a variety of settings, from the most institutionally defined community college classes to classes offered through the schools in immigrant areas, to community-based church and outreach programs taught in migrant labor camps. Adult ESL instruction covers a range of needs, from the most basic survival English to workplace-specific vocabulary, and English for academic purposes for those immigrant language minority adults entering into higher education.

Placement in, Exit From ESL Services

Annually, and throughout every academic year, new immigrant language minority youth enter into the U.S. school system, and through some sort of language proficiency battery are (or are not) identified for placement in ESL. Identification for and length of tenure in ESL services reflect several important student and family characteristics beyond English proficiency; these include: primary language literacy, amount of schooling in the home country, and academic concept development.

For example, a secondary student who completed 10th grade in the home country and arrives in the United States with well-developed reading and writing skills in his or her native language may only need a short period of intense, academically focused vocabulary development in English before jumping into biology and algebra II in English. In contrast, an EL who entered in first grade with little academic background in the primary language may find himself or herself at a disadvantage as he struggles to simultaneously learn English and learn the fundamental math and science concepts in English—both the academic concepts and the language in which they are learned are new to him or her. Research generally advocates for five to seven years of ESL support in order for a student to demonstrate proficiency. Currently, U.S. high schools must educate a wide variety of students in their ESL programs: recent immigrants with high levels of prior schooling in the home country, and recent immigrants with limited or interrupted prior schooling.

Perhaps the most pedagogically challenging group for schools is long-term English learners who have been in ESL programs since the early elementary grades. These students may have limited proficiency in both their native language and English, and may have been subject to years of remedial classes. These students highlight possible problems in the system, of mismatch between ESL entry and exit criteria.

Identification of a student for ESL instruction is based largely on the student's level of proficiency in English. However, for exit from ESL programs, students most often must demonstrate not only proficiency in English, but also academic achievement at grade level. As most ESL programs are language-based, only recently has the pedagogical focus turned to ensuring students rigorous academic instruction while learning English. Across the majority of states, grade level academic achievement is most commonly measured through one or more of the following: course grades, teacher recommendations, and standardized test scores. Although the *Lau* decision mandated that schools provide students learning English with equitable access to the academic content, the effectiveness of current linguistic support services has been called into question.

ESL and Opportunity to Learn

In theory, ESL should be positive for English learners; ESL programs are designed to offer instructional, academic, and linguistic support, integrating the language learning process within the academic focus of the classroom. However, in practice, the actual implementation of ESL programs may demonstrate negative consequences for students. Traditionally, ESL programs have prioritized a linguistic, rather than academic focus; in addition, the bureaucratic requirements of identification for and placement into ESL programs has inadvertently led to the academic stratification of ELs, manifested in relatively low levels of academic course taking, grades, and test scores relative to native English speaking peers of similar social, demographic, and academic backgrounds. Essentially, for a host of possible reasons, from availability of ESL teachers and classes to other formal and social processes in schools, evidence suggests that some students do not benefit from the services. While ESL programs have been shown to benefit the most recent immigrants, relatively new to U.S. schools and the language of schooling, prolonged tenure in ESL programs appears to preclude access to the more rigorous coursework required for entry into higher education and the workforce.

Policy Support and Future Research

The need for ESL services is projected to increase as the children of immigrants population continues to expand. In addition, post-1996 immigration has resulted in the migration of the immigrant population from the traditional immigrant-receiving urban centers and states (California, Texas, New York, Florida, and Illinois) into rural and suburban America, and many new destination states and districts. This immigrant expansion has brought language-minority families into new receiving schools and districts at unprecedented rates. No longer is ESL education the domain of educators in immigrant enclaves; rather, teachers in rural, suburban contexts will require professional development to meet the needs of their growing student population. Understanding the effects of ESL and how to deliver the best services while maintaining equality of educational opportunity will continue to be a pressing priority in the years to come.

Rebecca M. Callahan
Chandra Muller
University of Texas at Austin

See Also: Bilingual Education; English Proficiency/ Fluent English Proficient Students; Immigrants, Children of; Migrant Students; Multiculturalism/Multicultural Education.

Further Readings

Callahan, Rebecca M., Lindsey Wilkinson, and Chandra Muller. "Academic Achievement and Course-Taking Among Language Minority Youth in U.S. Schools: Effects of ESL Placement." *Educational Evaluation and Policy Analysis*, v.32 (2010).

Capps, Randy, Julie Murray, Jason Ost, Jeffrey S. Passel, and Shinta Herwantoro. *The New Demography of America's Schools: Immigration and the No Child Left Behind Act*. Washington, DC: Urban Institute, 2005.

Gibbons, Pauline. *Scaffolding Language, Scaffolding Learning: Teaching Second Language Learners in the Mainstream Classroom*. Portsmouth, NH: Heinemann, 2002.

Hakuta, Kenji. "Educating Language Minority Students and Affirming Their Equal Rights." *Educational Researcher*, v.40 (2011).

Kanno, Yasko and Linda Harklau. *Linguistic Minority Students Go to College: Preparation, Access, and Persistence*. New York: Routledge, 2012.

Olsen, Laurie. *Made in America: Immigrant Students in Our Public Schools*. New York: New Press, 2008.

Valdes, Guadalupe. *Learning and Not Learning English: Latino Students in American Schools*. New York: Teachers College Press, 2001.

English Proficiency/ Fluent English Proficient Students

K–12 students whose first language is not English are identified upon enrollment in U.S. schools through a home language survey and are immediately assessed to determine whether English as a second language (ESL) services are required. Students who do not pass this initial screening assessment are classified as English language learners (ELLs), or as limited English proficiency (LEP) students, and are identified to receive school-provided English language development (ELD) and accommodations. Students who pass the initial screener or who demonstrate English proficiency two years in a row on state-mandated annual assessments are deemed fluent or fully English proficient (FEP) students and are exited from ESL services. Students who exit ESL services must be monitored for two years to ensure that they continue to be academically successful without ESL services.

The United States has always been a polyglot nation of immigrants. Early American immigrants spoke German, French, Dutch, and Spanish. Some of the earliest American schools were German/English bilingual schools. In fact, German was so predominant that Benjamin Franklin, in a famous speech, harshly condemned German immigrants and despaired of their sheer numbers, claiming that he feared that English would be subsumed by German as the national language. In spite of these fears, following the first Great Wave of immigration in the 19th century, immigrants created schools, churches, clubs, neighborhoods, and societies based on ethnicity and language preference.

In American history, immigration and English acquisition have tended to follow fairly predictable patterns: The first generation of adults maintain their home language, struggling to survive perilous economic conditions, and are forced to work in substandard, often dangerous, manual labor requiring little or no communication in English. Much of American infrastructure and industry stand as a testament to the work of these immigrants. The second generation is often native-born Americans, who are raised speaking the parents' language at home, but who acquire basic levels of transactional English and who serve the family as intermediaries in public. Second generation immigrants who are able to attend school develop greater fluency and literacy in English, but maintain the home language among the family or in the neighborhood. The third generation adopts English as its preferred language, often losing the ability to communicate in the home language as English fluency and high levels of English literacy are obtained through schooling. As the first generation grows older and dies, community organizations and neighborhoods begin to wane and whither as subsequent generations see no need for them and are absorbed into mainstream American culture.

However, current first generation immigrants are encountering more challenging conditions as progressively more and more jobs require unprecedented levels of English and English literacy skills, even for unskilled laborers (e.g., custodians are expected to read complex sets of directions to mix dangerous cleansers; and increasing technology demands in many jobs require the use of highly specialized English). Current economic tensions and high levels of unemployment following the economic crash of U.S. markets in 2008 spurred a political and legal backlash against undocumented workers, with increased surveillance and increasingly stringent laws prohibiting the employment of undocumented immigrants. A renewed nationwide political push for "English only" and the establishment of English as the official national language, although currently a failed venture, reflect increasing animosity toward immigrants in general and undocumented workers in particular.

From 1990 to 2005 there were huge waves of immigration, with large numbers of K–12 ELL students arriving in schools that had never before received ELLs. While states on the coasts have long enrolled newly arrived immigrants in their schools, states like Wisconsin, Indiana, North Carolina, and Tennessee saw sudden influxes of students arriving in their schools, often with little or no English, limited or no first language literacy, and interrupted formal schooling. Adolescent students with interrupted formal educations (SIFEs) face particular challenges in middle schools and high schools, where they are sometimes overwhelmed by the content and literacy demands and are compelled to make up years of gaps in their learning while acquiring English. Some districts experienced an explosive 400 percent growth of ELLs between 1990 and 2005. Many states scrambled to provide training for both mainstream and for specially licensed ESL teachers in the wake of this explosion.

English Language Learners in U.S. Schools

In U.S. schools, ELLs have historically been underserved, often denied access to the basic school curriculum, and even punished for speaking their native languages in school. Several landmark lawsuits paved the way for significant reforms for ELLs, beginning in 1965 with the passing of Title VII of the Elementary and Secondary Education Act, which was later called the Bilingual Educational Act when it was passed by Congress in 1968. The Bilingual Education Act created funding sources for bilingual education and ESL programs in K–12 schools. Schools inconsistently implemented these programs and sometimes created programs alongside the traditional curriculum while isolating ELLs from the mainstream. In the 1974 *Lau v. Nichols* case, the U.S. Supreme Court determined that "identical education does not constitute equal education under the Civil Rights Act," in acknowledgement that students who do not speak English cannot access the academic skills and content learning necessary to make progress in school.

The No Child Left Behind (NCLB) Act of 2011 replaced the Bilingual Education Act, providing Title III funding for specialized programs and staff, and simultaneously instituting the English Language Acquisition, Language Enhancement, and Academic Achievement Act, making schools responsible for the annual standardized assessment performance of all students, including ELLs. Previously, schools had generally declined to include ELLs (and other students deemed likely to fail) in annual standardized assessments; now, schools were mandated to demonstrate "adequate yearly progress" (AYP) for all subgroups of students (e.g., student categories broken down by race, gender, socioeconomic status, English language proficiency [ELP], and special education identifiers). These annual state assessments require ELLs to demonstrate grade-level core subject skills, knowledge, and abilities in English, with few accommodations or exclusions permitted. Ironically, NCLB has provided both increased support for ELLs and improved access to mainstream curriculum while placing immense pressure on ELLs and schools to demonstrate English literacy mastery more rapidly than is feasible. Research indicates that ELLs need between five to seven years to develop academic language proficiency, whereas ELLs are currently required to begin taking standardized assessments within the first year of U.S. school enrollment. In addition, while many educators applaud the expanded attention and support provided to ELLs, schools suddenly became aware of how unprepared most K–12 educators and administrators were to meet the needs of ELLs, and have struggled to design programs that meet the needs of ELLs.

Second Language Acquisition (SLA) Theory

Stephen Krashen has defined the difference between language learning and language acquisition: language learning is similar to what happens in foreign language classrooms (where the emphasis is on imitating and practicing language patterns and structures in a formal setting, coupled with conscious attention to these processes), whereas second (or third) language acquisition is unconscious and more closely mimics the process that babies experience when they are learning their native language (where one listens, experiments with new phrases, receives real-time feedback, experiences the pleasure of communication, and does not think of the activity as "studying"). Language learning produces results similar to the long-term effects of formalized foreign language study; there is some value in learning these patterns, but they are limited to what is practiced, restricted to what the patterns make available. Acquisition tends to produce deeper, longer-lasting, and more immediately useful language production and reception skills. Both are useful under the right conditions; learning is easier to replicate within school settings than acquisition, but opportunities for acquisition are what ELLs need most.

One popular misconception is that younger children acquire new languages more readily than adults or older students. While young children have some advantages (have more time available, are perhaps less inhibited, and face reduced language demands), adults bring many strengths to the SLA process, including sophisticated structural and grammatical understandings of their first language (L1), literacy skills from the L1 that can be applied to the second language (L2), and strong intrinsic motivation.

Researchers believe that those who learn new L2s after adolescence may never acquire an authentic, native-like accent, but otherwise there is no serious disadvantage for adults or older ELLs. ELL children who begin school in English before becoming literate in their L1 begin to struggle over time to keep up with grade mates on standardized assessments, often beginning to flounder after fourth grade. Paradoxically, it is older adolescents with no interrupted formal education and who demonstrate strong L1 literacy skills who transition more readily into English-speaking schools and graduate from high school at higher rates than ELLs who entered U.S. schools in primary grades. While it might seem that ELLs should be confined to specialized ESL classrooms until they can "catch up" and join the mainstream, this isolation does not speed up the SLA process and could actually prevent ELLs from gaining access to grade-level skills and knowledge, as well as prevent them from becoming productive, functioning members of the school community. Participating in mainstream classes for much of the school day gives ELLs access to *comprehensible input,* or language production surrounded by context, visual cues, body language, and builds on students' prior knowledge, which can be grasped more readily by ELLs than normal language production.

Instruction of ELLs in K–12 Schools

Schools provide a variety of instructional ELD support services, depending upon local needs, available resources, and existing trained school personnel. ESL classes may be taught in a pull-out (ELLs leave the mainstream classroom for specialized ELD sessions with an ESL teacher), push-in (a licensed, trained ESL teacher comes into the mainstream classroom to co-teach), or self-contained (ELLs are taught together in a separate classroom using specialized curriculum to teach both ELD and content knowledge) models. Schools may offer short-term newcomer programs to newly arrived ELLs to help them adjust to U.S. schooling, or may provide sheltered instruction in which ELLs learn both English literacy skills and grade-level content knowledge in specialized classes. Some states provide bilingual (L1 and L2) education or dual language instruction, in which the goal is for ELLs to develop strong bilingual and biliteracy skills through academic content taught in both languages.

ELD teachers are licensed and certified in several ways; each of these certifications requires a thorough understanding of SLA. K–12 teachers often add an ESL license to their existing teaching certificate by taking additional, specialized university courses. Some states offer a bilingual education license in which the applicant must demonstrate academic language proficiency in two target languages. Others become certified through completion of certificate programs through organizations such as Teachers of English to Speakers of Other Languages (TESOL).

Susan Adams
Indiana University and Butler University

See Also: Bilingual Education; English as a Second Language; Immersion; Immigrant Adaptation; No Child Left Behind.

Further Readings

Brooks, K. and K. Karathanos. "Building on the Cultural and Lingusitic Capital of English Learner (EL) Students." *Multicultural Education*, v.16/4 (2009).

Brooks, K., S. R. Adams, and T. Morita Mullaney. "Creating Inclusing Learning Communities for ELL Students: Transforming School Principals Perspectives." *Theory Into Practice*, v.44/4 (2010).

Cummins, J. "Rethinking Monolingual Instructional Strategies in Multilingual Classrooms." *Canadian Journal of Applied Linguistics*, v.10/2 (2010).

Krashen, S. and G. McField. "What Works? Reviewing the Latest Evidence on Biligual Education." *Language Learner*, v.34 (2005).

Menken, K. "How Have Laws Regarding English Language Learners Evolved in the United States?" In *English Language Learners at School: A Guide for Administrators*, E. Hamayan and R. Freeman, eds. Philadelphia: Caslon, 2006.

Epistemological Issues in Educational Research

Epistemology is a branch of philosophy concerned with the study of the nature of knowledge. A conflation of the Greek *episteme*, which refers to knowledge or science, and *logos*, which refers to thought or the principle of reasoning, epistemology seeks to explore fundamental philosophical issues regarding what knowledge is, how we acquire knowledge, and how we know what we think we know. In educational research, epistemology is also used in a wider sense to refer to the following:

- The philosophical stance of the researcher in relation to the research
- The philosophical basis of the methods used for producing knowledge through research
- The philosophical basis of the justification of knowledge claims made in research reports, articles, and outcomes

Epistemology is often twinned with ontology, which concerns questions about the nature of being, and axiology, which refers to the values and beliefs the researcher holds. These three philosophical precepts are considered fundamental to the whole process of research, including the initial idea of the research, the formulation of research questions, researcher role, methodological choices, selection of methods, data analysis procedures, and ways of writing about research findings. Epistemological assumptions are linked to choice of research paradigm.

Epistemological Issues Within the Two Dominant Research Paradigms

Until recently, educational research has been dominated by two paradigms, worldviews, or ways of thinking about research. These two paradigms are widely known as positivism and interpretivism. Each paradigm is underpinned by a different set of epistemological assumptions about what counts as knowledge, how to produce knowledge through research, and how to interpret and make meaning from knowledge. Each paradigm also articulates different concerns about truth and legitimacy in research.

The positivist paradigm has its historical roots in the European Enlightenment and the role that scientific knowledge was deemed to play in increasing human mastery over the natural world and in providing a basis for progress and improvement of human civilization. Positivism is based on the epistemological presumption that the social, cultural, economic, and educational world can be known and researched in much the same way as the natural and physical world. Two suppositions about knowledge underpin positivism. The first derives from empiricist philosophers such as John Locke, George Berkeley, and David Hume, who think that knowledge is derived from the evidence of the senses. The second arises from the rationalists, for example, Rene Descartes, Gottfried Leibniz, and Baruch Spinoza, for whom knowledge is a demonstration requiring the use of reason. The wide acceptance of empirical rationalism after Immanuel Kant—that knowledge is obtained from the operations of reason and the evidence of the senses—informed the development of positivism.

From the start, positivist thinking gave rise to a series of epistemological issues. The first issue concerns the assumption that the use and application of rational knowledge can guarantee the discovery of objective facts. The second issue relates to the assumption that scientific methods and procedures—observation, hypotheses, experiments, replicability and verifiability of results (or what became known as the hypothetico-deductive model)—will produce universal truths or laws. The third issue concerns the question of whether the researcher is a rational and neutral knowing subject. The fourth issue relates to whether knowledge produced by such methods will (even can) be objective, truthful, certain, and legitimate, as positivists assume.

Debate

In the early 20th century, sociologists such as Wilhelm Dilthey and Max Weber initiated debates on these epistemological issues, questioning whether the social sciences could, or even should, emulate knowledge production within the natural sciences; and disputing the possibility and desirability of value freedom within research. At the same time, questions about the rationalist epistemology of science were raised from within the philosophy of science. Karl Popper argued that science practice frequently diverges from empirical rationalism because knowledge often proceeds on the basis of falsification; while Thomas Khun's notion of paradigm shift drew attention to the way that scientific communities operated as social communities, highlighting that agreements about what constituted scientific progress involved social norms, values, and beliefs about current knowledge frameworks, rather than purely objective or neutral truth. These post-positivist critiques occurred at a time of other broad social, cultural, and theoretical shifts from the 1960s onward, at a time when feminism, critical race theory, poststructuralism, postmodernism, and other interpretivist approaches were raising other pertinent questions about positivist epistemology.

The interpretivist paradigm is often seen in binary opposition to the positivist paradigm. While the many schools of thought within this paradigm have different aims, value commitments, and theoretical stances, they share some key epistemological presumptions about knowledge and its production through educational research. First, interpretivists dispute that knowledge of the social world can be obtained by emulating scientific practice; second, they are skeptical of research practices that seek generalization or promote the idea that human behavior can be understood in relation to universal laws; and third, interpretivists emphasize the role played by subjective human understanding in constructing knowledge about social, cultural, and educational behavior. Unlike positivists, who think that an objective understanding is possible, interpretivists share an epistemological presumption that meaning can only be made through human interpretation of reality.

The epistemological basis of interpretivist educational research gives rise to research practices that seek to gain insight into, explain, and account for individuals' interpretations. There is an epistemological orientation toward knowledge based on "thick descriptions" of participants' realities, which expresses the complexity and variety of educational realties, experiences, and contexts, and which discloses the details of individuals' interpretations and enactments of broader educational processes and changes. Interpretivism assumes that people have social agency and that they act with deliberate and often creative intent, but that their ability to act autonomously is conditioned and sometimes determined by social relationships, networks, contexts, and structures. Interpretivists are interested in exploring relations between macro-, meso-, and micro-levels, for example through pedagogic classroom relations or how teachers' identity formation is influenced by professional workforce reform.

Interpretivist epistemology is said to produce forms of knowledge that analyze and explain educational processes, practices, and problems from the perspective of the participants; that provide rich and complex accounts of educational experiences; and that recognize that knowledge produced this way will include multiple and competing views, interpretations, and insights. Positivist and interpretivist paradigms clash over significant epistemological issues, including the possibility of objectivity in knowledge practices, the value-laden or normative nature of knowledge practices, the relation between knowledge and its social, cultural, and historical contexts, whether new knowledge enables social progress, the role of the researcher and whether that is cast as neutral (positivism) or inevitably involved and subjective (interpretivism), and how to assess the quality of research.

These two paradigms have been important for educational research on two scales. At the macro scale of the entire research field, early educational research from the beginning of the 20th century to the 1960s was firmly situated within the rational empiricist epistemology of positivism, when much of the research focused on using psychometric testing to study intelligence and ability. The 1970s saw the beginning of a shift toward research within the interpretivist paradigm, consolidated in the 1980s and 1990s with the rapid growth of qualitative studies. These were often in-depth case studies of relations between education and social factors, including: social class, gender, ethnicity, sexuality, and disability, and were underpinned by epistemologies that explored participants' meanings, values, and understandings of their scope for agency within constraining social structures. From the early 1990s onward, there has been a concerted shift back to positivist approaches, as national political contexts sought to use quantitative research to inform policy and more effectively drive practices of institutional change.

Contemporary forms of research, such as evidence-based research, outcomes-based measures of learning and assessment, evaluation studies, and practitioner action research are often underpinned by an epistemological focus on what works, and are aligned, whether explicitly or implicitly, with the objectivism, experimentalism, and rationalism of the positivist paradigm. At the same time, the diversification of interpretivist epistemologies has continued. These often small-scale, local- and micro-level studies have sought to develop innovative and creative means to apprehend participants' understandings of their changing social and educational contexts. These parallel research movements—sometimes referred to as "paradigm wars"—demonstrate the ongoing vitality of epistemological struggles within the contemporary field of educational research.

Postmodernism and Epistemological Proliferation

Many social theorists think that we now live in postmodern (or late-modern) times, in which scientific knowledge no longer guarantees social progress. More than that, the many dominant forms of knowledge, such as science, Christianity, patriarchy, and Marxism—those "big stories" that have so far sustained human societies—are no longer considered to command immediate allegiance or widespread belief. As Jean-Francois Lyotard says, postmodernism is characterized by "incredulity towards metanarratives." The epistemological relevance of this is that postmodernism is seen to open up a much larger cultural space for the proliferation of *petit recits*, that is, "little stories," which pay attention to the local, contextual, and specific, which offer otherwise marginalized groups and silenced voices the opportunity to bring their narratives to bear on mainstream accounts that have either denigrated or ignored them.

While it is difficult to assess the ongoing impact of postmodernism on educational research, current educational research shows the marks of some profound epistemological shifts and diversification. Epistemologies that inform contemporary educational research include: positivism, postpositivism, anti-positivism, feminist epistemologies (Marxist, liberal, socialist, radical, and standpoint), post-structuralism, deconstructionism, postmodernism, critical race theories, and rhizomic epistemologies. There are also hybrid epistemologies arising from interdisciplinary research, such as the participatory user-engagement research focus of disability-focused education studies; the literary-poetic epistemologies found in autoethnography, autobiography, and other forms of narrative educational research that can be seen as post- or trans-disciplinary; as well as politically informed modes of educational research that display epistemological commitment to student voices as a form of participatory democratic citizenship.

These different forms of educational research, together with other forms of social science research, have helped unpack both the epistemic codes of science and the social status of science as an elite, privileged mode of knowledge production. By including uncertainty and radical doubt, by accepting that there are now many truths, rather than one truth, and by opening epistemological space for many more diverse and often competing forms of knowledge, contemporary educational research has played a part in unsettling established knowledge hierarchies and boundaries, developing more democratic ways of including those who had previously been "othered" by mainstream forms of knowledge, and giving epistemological credibility to a greater number of ways of knowing, being, and thinking.

Some Key Epistemological Issues in Contemporary Educational Research

There is ongoing debate as to whether a researcher ought to decide, and make explicit, their epistemological, ontological, and axiological stance at the start of the research, and then use this as a basis to guide all aspects of the research that follows; or whether research questions ought to act as guides to the subsequent research process and, from these pragmatic decisions, the researcher's epistemological (and ontological and axiological) orientation emerges and is clarified. Such debates draw attention to the ways in which epistemological questions are a fundamental part of the actual practice or craft of doing empirical real world research. They also indicate that different epistemologies will offer different solutions to research dilemmas.

In addition, debates such as these have been influential in the shifts toward greater reflexivity in many contemporary educational research epistemologies. Reflexivity is recognition of the need for researchers to acknowledge the philosophical bases of their study, and to reflect on how they are part of the social world they are researching. Reflexivity encourages, even requires, researchers to exercise greater degrees of openness, for example, about their epistemological stance as researchers, their biographies, methods, interpretations, and political and emotional investments in their research. Reflexivity also has ethical dimensions, as transparency in research practice brings with it greater accountability to research constituencies and audiences, including research participants and scholarly research communities, as well as to notions of truth in and quality of research.

A second key issue concerns power relations in research. Feminist epistemologies, for example, have been instrumental in drawing attention to scientific research, not as a rationalist, neutral process of objective knowledge production, but as the largely exclusive domain of men, whose research interests were aligned to masculine norms, values, and experiences, and who presumed to generalize knowledge from their partial, powerful, and often patriarchal position. The feminist argument—that knowledge is neither neutral nor objective, and that all knowledge is a "view from somewhere"—is now widely accepted in educational research. As a consequence, greater attention is

required to epistemologies that have social origins in gender, social class, race, ethnicity, and sexuality. Postmodern, post-structuralist and feminist epistemologies also seek to pay greater attention to the micropolitical power dimensions of research, including how knowledge claims may speak for or with research participants, the use of methods to reduce, level, or mitigate power relations, and how knowledge may impact on social equality. Michel Foucault's analysis of the inseparability of knowledge and power relations, and the constitution of knowledge as a form of power, has been significant in explaining the detailed ways in which epistemology has a basis in history, culture, and social relations.

Epistemological diversity also raises some sharp issues about research quality and research evaluation criteria. Positivistic forms of educational inquiry have usually relied on the criteria of validity, reliability, and generalizability. However, the contestability of notions of legitimacy and truth that epistemological proliferation has brought about has meant that for many contemporary researchers, these traditional criteria are no longer sufficient; when the starting assumption and ultimate goal is to understand the specificity and concreteness of educational phenomena, along with their contexts and social relations, then other criteria have become necessary. Some researchers have devised entirely new evaluation criteria, such as coherency, confirmability, trustworthiness, dependability, and aesthetics; others have recast validity through a post-structuralist-feminist lens as, for example, transgressive, voluptuous, or rhizomatic; while many accord evaluative credence to research in which reflexivity on processes of knowledge production is given a high priority.

Epistemological issues are fundamental to the practice of educational research. How epistemological issues are framed and dealt with gives insight into a researcher's view of what matters in education, their values and commitments, and how they make meaning through the knowledge produced by research. The proliferation of epistemologies in contemporary research points to the contestability of knowledge, and the multiplicity of truths concerning education.

Carol Taylor
Sheffield Hallam University

See Also: Feminist Research Methodology; Positivism, Antipositivism, and Empiricism; Qualitative Research on

Education; Quantitative Research on Education; Research Paradigms in Educational Studies.

Further Readings

Cohen, L., L. Manion, and K. Morrison, eds. *Research Methods in Education*. 7th ed. London: Routledge, 2011.

Dunne, M., J. Pryor, and P. Yates. *Becoming a Researcher: A Research Companion for the Social Sciences*. Maidenhead, Berkshire, UK: Open University Press, 2005.

Foucault, M. *Power/Knowledge: Selected Interviews and Other Writings 1972–1977*. New York: Harvester Wheatsheaf, 1980.

Lather, P. *Getting Lost: Feminist Efforts Toward a Double(d) Science*. Albany: State University of New York Press, 2007.

Lyotard, J.-F. *The Postmodern Condition: A Report on Knowledge*. Minneapolis: University of Minnesota Press, 1984.

Scott, D. and R. Usher, eds. *Understanding Educational Research*. London: Routledge, 1986.

Stronach, I. and M. MacLure. *Educational Research Undone: The Postmodern Embrace*. Buckingham, UK: Open University Press, 1997.

Ethics in Education

The term *ethics* refers to a process of gaining knowledge about making life choices. Many educators believe that all students, even elementary students, can benefit from processes of ethical learning. By elementary school, children are able to look at life in a self-conscious manner and to ponder issues of right and wrong. Some believe that young children are highly interested in ethical issues and need to have that interest affirmed through discussions of written narratives, as well as through oral narratives. By high school and college, students learn ethics largely through civic education, including service-learning courses.

Ethical issues also occur within schools in the form of bullying and related forms of conflict. Strategies for dealing with ethical concerns within schools have come to place more emphasis on changing the school culture. More educators are advocating a communal approach to learning at all levels of schooling as a way to teach ethics and deal with a variety of ethical concerns within schools. In the 1960s and 1970s, there was a low point in the teaching of ethics in schools. The first attempts to bring ethical teaching back into schools in the late 1970s stressed process over content. One of these attempts was based on a theory of moral development that emphasized different stages of moral reasoning and the importance of moral debates based on hypothetical moral dilemmas. A more recent process-oriented approach—care ethics—includes an emotional component to moral growth, as well as an emphasis on caring. Open-ended dialogue is a fundamental aspect of care ethics. Advocates of a process approach believe that it is important that children learn to develop ethical thinking skills. They also believe that such an approach allows teachers to learn from children as children learn from them, making ethical teaching a two-way street. Other educators favor a focus on moral content, rather than ethical processes. They advocate a return to an earlier approach to American moral education based on the teaching of specific virtues. Sometimes referred to as "character education," this approach advocates a focus on moral values and good conduct. Teachers are encouraged to use a variety of techniques—stories, discussions, role playing, and case studies—aimed at having students practice the virtues that they have been taught. This approach relies upon instilling moral habits through repetition, rather than through self-reflection.

Ethical Learning Requires Both Dialogue and Introspection

Many developmental psychologists have stressed the need for dialogue as a means of developing moral thinking. Some believe that children can discuss with others forms of ethical reasoning that are not available to them individually. Others believe that while communication is not essential for reaching new levels of moral thinking, dialogue can be of value because ethical decisions often concern relationships with others. Because ethical concerns are often social concerns, discourse can often clarify a range of interpretations to the same ethical dilemma. Further, because the ability to understand ethical concerns depends on the ability to interpret social cues from other people and incorporate the interests of other people, communication is a useful vehicle for ethical learning. At the same time, because ethical concerns often represent a deeper level of understanding about life experiences, other researchers and educators have emphasized the value of introspection. Robert Coles has come to see that many children think deeply about moral and ethical issues. In his interviews with children, he saw how they tried to comprehend the universe by calling upon family, teachers, past experience, and their contemplative capacity. To encourage introspection, some educators advocate the use of journal writing after hearing a teaching story or as a supplement to ethical dialogue. This and other reflective exercises allow students to integrate what they have learned socially into their sense of who they are and how they view the world.

Drawing on Ethical Teaching From Many Cultures

As American schools seek to expand ethical teaching, there are many cultural traditions to draw upon. American schools have tended to focus on academic learning for individual success, rather than on advancing the needs of the entire community. In contrast, many cultures have long emphasized a stronger link between knowledge and community. As one example, the term for education in Spanish, *educación*, means to give children a sense of moral, social, and personal responsibility.

To most Mexicans, teaching cognitive skills alone is not enough. They believe that children also need to know how to live as caring, responsible, and respectful people. This includes a focus on how to be a good community member. This focus on ethics and community is also true of many indigenous cultures in North and South America. For example, knowledge of ethics is a central aspect of Navajo teaching, where children learn that respect is the foundation upon which all relationships are built—respect to the self, others, the animate world, and the inanimate world. Further, many Navajo children learn the importance of community-based planning, maintaining self-awareness, and responsibility to future generations. Gregory Cajete, a Tewa scholar, explains how many American Indians have kept affective elements at the center of education. These include communal relations, ecology, and psychological and spiritual orientations. Their nature-centered philosophies represent the oldest continuing expression of environmental education. He believes that a common stance in American schools of being detached and objective has led to a basic alienation of modern people from themselves, as well as from the natural world. Other scholars agree and believe that insights from indigenous

cultures could benefit the broader educational community, given the problems of today's society.

Role of Narratives in Ethical Teaching

The use of written narratives as a starting point for ethical dialogue has been found effective by many educators. Those advocating a process approach to ethical learning prefer using stories that problematize ethical decisions. The use of such stories leads to more open-ended dialogues that explore a range of ethical issues, without trying to fix or resolve dilemmas. In the past, fables such as Aesop's fables were often used in educational settings as a form of ethical teaching. Most editions of these fables end with a single moral attached to the end of the text. In one study, the researchers found that the use of fables with a single moral determined and limited the ethical lessons that children derived from the stories. In contrast, using the same fable without including the moral led to a broader dialogue from which many lessons surfaced, and children debated the importance of different ethical themes.

Dialogues about particular ethical issues such, as social justice, are often more effective when they are based on a growing body of multicultural literature. For example, one teacher used a book about Mexican immigrants, *Esperanza Rising*, to initiate dialogue among her sixth graders. These students, most of whom were Mexican American, raised some thought-provoking questions about race and social class based on this book. While some multicultural literature has been found to open up empowering dialogues among students, this is not always the case. In another classroom, the book *Maniac Magee*, about a well-meaning, but naive, white child and an older black male, resulted in polarized views of race among elementary students. In this case, some of the students were unable to identify with the characters because of their gender or race, while others dismissed the portrayals of racial dynamics as too simplistic.

This suggests that teachers need to better understand which narratives elicit children's perspectives, and which constrain children's ability to identify with or interpret ethical meanings. High school students also benefit from the use of narrative. In one high school, white and black students responded enthusiastically to a short story on race relations. Previously, the same students had responded to direct discussions of race with suspicion, frustration, and boredom. Guiding such dialogues presents certain challenges for both elementary and secondary teachers. In order to encourage students' capacity for ambiguity, some teachers find it is helpful to show their wonderings and hesitations by asking questions like, "I'm confused. What do you think is going on?" Teachers seek to find the right balance between leading and following, avoiding too much control as well as too little direction.

While American schools tend to focus on written narratives, oral narratives have been used by many cultures as a way to promote greater awareness of ethics and the value of community. These oral stories are often rich with multiple layers of meaning and multiple messages. Children learn many values, such as the importance of cooperation and respecting all people, regardless of their physical size or social status. Through storytelling, children also come to see a variety of solutions to moral issues, rather than coming to believe that there is a single "right" way. Increasingly, educators are realizing that even the most highly literate people still depend on oral stories. The value of oral stories lies in their ability to attach effective responses to the messages, making the messages more likely to be retained after the stories are told. The oral format also encourages children's use of imagination and role taking. Students reason through the process of reflecting on ethical situations by putting themselves in the place of the characters in the story. In addition, storytelling is often a communal event that brings together a variety of adults and children. Following the story, children are generally encouraged to give their responses. Because these stories tend to have multiple meanings, children are able to gain the messages they most need from a story, rather than be limited to the lesson that an adult might have in mind.

Children respond well to stories from other cultures, even if they have had limited contact with people from different cultures. When children hear stories of different cultures, they are exposed to a variety of ethical perspectives, as well as developing a greater understanding and respect for different cultures. They also come to identify with people, despite cultural differences, as they recognize common human values and dilemmas. One study found that teaching stories involving animals tend to elicit considerable identification with the characters since they are not limited by race or gender in many cases. The children who the teachers perceived to be most troublesome were some of the most active participants in dialogues following storytelling. This suggests that storytelling dialogues might be especially useful to children who confront

complex, ethical situations in their lives. Through these dialogues, they have a chance to begin to sort through complex ethical dilemmas and move toward greater understanding of the issues they face in their lives. Another use of storytelling is to have children tell their family or life stories. As students share their personal life situations, adults can gain greater awareness of their life circumstances, as well as their ethical development. It is difficult for teachers to respond thoughtfully to students unless they know what children's interests, beliefs, and values are. Storytelling is one avenue for adults to learn more about the children they work with. This has been especially valuable for immigrant students who were encouraged to share family narratives as a way to examine their lives and to take ethical stands.

Civic Education and Service Learning

Civic education is a broad term covering many distinct approaches such as civic skills, social justice, and teaching an ethic of caring and service. These approaches are more commonly taught at the secondary and college level as part of the social science curriculum, but also are used in some elementary classrooms. Civic learning typically includes discussions of current and historical events, simulations, role plays, experience with student governance, and increasingly, service-learning classes. Recently, there has been an increased interest in public service at the college level, as well as in civic education at all levels. One key goal is to increase civic involvement in the future by offering civic training and helping students develop an expanded view of power and politics. By teaching students new problem-solving skills, teachers hope that students will be better able to address problems in their future communities.

Postmodern thinking has posed some unique challenges for civic education. In the past, students were taught to think critically as they applied democratic ideals to ongoing civic life. When criticism becomes an end in itself, as it has for some postmodern writers, it is difficult to motivate students to care about ethical ideas. At the same time, to the extent that historical contexts and contingencies are privileged, it is difficult to strike a balance between the universal ideals of a culture and its specific historical moments. Eamonn Callan has suggested that we should teach students to be civically engaged and uplifted, while also genuinely critical. He suggests that this can avoid creating a sense of despair about the past by seeking out what is the best of a tradition, and then comparing it to what has been most dominant in certain periods. He also advocates use of literature when teaching civic issues since it allows students to better see and feel injustice in ways that social analysis alone might not. Some teachers and students are placing more emphasis on social justice and social change. One study found that elementary teachers who focus on social justice gave the most attention to themes of caring and fairness as they engaged students in dialogues about stereotypes and historical movements for social justice. At the secondary level, another study found that high school students' beliefs about civic engagement are changing. They now consider it less important to join a political party or participate in political discussions than adolescents in the past, while considering it more important to promote human rights and protect the environment.

At the college level, some sociology professors are placing more emphasis on teaching students how to act as advocates for those facing inequality by providing empowering experiences in the community, along with a critical understanding of processes of inequality. These professors tend to focus on small, community-level attempts at social change, believing that by showing the possibilities for change at the grass-roots level, they can shift students from a top-down view of power and politics. Recently, educators have promoted civic engagement as a particular way of doing teaching, service, and research in and with the community. This approach has led to a stronger focus on service-learning classes in which needed community services are provided, while also enhancing students' critical thinking skills. Through these classes, students develop civic skills as well as motives for sustaining community involvement. This is "learning to serve" as much as it is "serving to learn."

In service-learning classes, critical reflection exercises provide a way for students to integrate action and thought, as well as caring and intellect. The outcome is often a greater sense of wholeness, as well as greater flexibility and responsiveness to changing community needs. Students also gain greater tolerance for ambiguity as they come to see concepts learned in the classroom within the complexities of a real world context. Studies find that service learning in high school has more impact when student decision making is promoted. Adolescents are better prepared to be effective in adult civic life when they learn and experience civic engagement skills such as working in groups,

organizing others to accomplish tasks, and working through differences to reach common goals. To best promote students' active participation, they should be included in the design and organization of service activities, or at least be empowered to deal with problems as they arise.

Service-learning classes have their ethical dilemmas, however. For example, instructors must sometimes decide which comes first—student learning or community empowerment? Related to this question is the question of who decides which service projects are most crucial—instructors or community members? In an ideal situation, there are strong partnerships between community organizations and the school setting so that these issues are dealt with in a collaborative and egalitarian manner. At any rate, many service-learning instructors now emphasize the importance of egalitarian approaches to interaction, of intercultural competencies, or respecting local ways of knowing and of approaching service-learning activities so that all participants feel empowered.

Ethical Concerns Within Schools

One of the most pressing ethical concerns within schools is the problem of bullying. Bullying is generally defined as a negative and often aggressive act or series of acts. It typically includes physical abuse, verbal abuse, and indirect abuse (ignoring, excluding, and isolating). More recently, cyber bullying has created a new form of abuse that is often highly destructive. Studies show that children who are bullied, bullies, or both in elementary school often experience similar roles in later years of schooling. Bullying occurs at all levels of schooling. It increases throughout the grade school years, reaching a peak in middle school, before decreasing during high school. Research on middle school students indicates that some of those targeted for bullying engage in atypical gender behavior, have lower intelligence, or engage in unusual behaviors (often students with special needs), or are girls who are perceived to be unattractive (overweight or "poorly" dressed). At special risk for bullying are any students who are socially isolated and lack the protection of a friendship group.

There are many reasons why students bully other students. In middle school, adolescents tend to have social insecurities that they often cope with by scapegoating others. This practice can reduce their fears of being thought unpopular or abnormal by making other students appear even less popular or less normal. While there are emotional costs for all targets of bullying, the costs for homosexual students are especially high. Homosexual labels are often part of verbal abuse as students deal with their sexual insecurities by targeting others. This labeling tends to further associate homosexuality with social rejection and in extreme cases, has led to suicide attempts by homosexual students who are victims of bullying. A large study found that 70 percent of students believe that schools respond poorly to bullying. Teachers have been found to contribute to a bullying atmosphere when they use domineering behaviors to control students or when they dismiss student complaints without taking action. In schools lacking conflict intervention programs, peer bystanders tend to either support the bullying in some way or remain passive.

In recent years, more efforts have been aimed at reducing bullying in schools. Many of these efforts focus on elementary students where bullying first begins. Bystanders, as well as targets of bullying, are taught strategies to keep less serious teasing from escalating into serious bullying. These strategies include helping students learn how to interpret more playful forms of teasing, and also how to respond in playful ways to potentially more serious comments. Assertive behaviors and avoidance strategies are also taught. By learning effective responses to teasing and ridicule, targets and bystanders can often deescalate a potentially abusive episode. Some schools advocate a zero-tolerance approach, in which all offenses are punished, regardless of how minor they are. However, after 10 years of implementation, this approach has failed to reduce bullying.

Other schools advocate a school culture approach that seeks to create a positive school environment. This alternative approach typically involves creating a sense of community in which teachers, students, and administrators work together to address bullying and other school problems. This approach advocates cooperation, respect, and appreciation of diversity. It might also include collaborative teaching techniques that bring popular and less popular children together, working in ways that highlight everyone's strengths. In some schools, these changes in school culture have reduced bullying by 50 percent or more. Other strategies that have proven to be effective include the use of peer mediation, by which some students are trained to mediate conflicts as well as a "no-blame" approach. In the latter case, the focus is not on the attacker or the attacker's motivation, but instead on the feelings of the victims, bringing students, including the attacker, together in order to find ways to reduce the negative consequences that victims have experienced. Some schools also have programs that create "special buddies," by pairing students with special needs with other students in the school. By fostering these friendships, students with special needs experience less isolation, reducing the extent to which they become targets of bullying.

Ethics and Communities

Developing a sense of community is critical for dealing with a variety of ethical issues within schools, like stereotyping, labeling, and biased thinking, as well as bullying. Many believe that students can best learn to become more respectful of others by participating directly in learning communities. Parker Palmer has advocated community as an essential part of the teaching environment in order to have ideas tested, biases challenged, and knowledge expanded. He believes that strong educational communities have certain aspects such as creative conflict to correct biases, honesty, and expressions of diversity to reveal the complex nature of life. He also believes that learning within a community is important since a truly ethical education needs to deal with the most basic questions in life.

When dealing with these issues, a great deal of trust is required as students draw deeply upon each other's resources. While Parker Palmer aims his writing at college instructors, instructors at many levels have sought to develop stronger learning communities. In some elementary schools, "family meetings" are used to provide forums for students to develop their school rules and responses to disrespectful behavior. In high schools, "positive peer culture" groups are used as forums for students to talk about a variety of social concerns and ethical dilemmas. In one high school, these discussions followed a set of guidelines including the use of active listening; avoiding lecturing, moralizing, and name-calling; and a focus on problematic behavior, rather than problematic people. Even though ethics in education covers many aspects, one common theme has been the concept of community.

Most psychologists believe that students develop ethical skills through dialogues with others since ethical concerns are often social ones. Education in other cultures has privileged respect for others, communal relations, and becoming a good community member. Storytelling promotes these social lessons through both the content of stories and its communal nature.

Civic education now involves more direct contact with surrounding communities by promoting teaching and service in collaboration with community partners. Finally, changing school culture in a way that strengthens community has been found to be an effective way to reduce bullying and other types of disrespectful behavior. In all of these cases, by learning to deal with social and ethical issues in a communal manner, students gain the skills needed to be more effective community members as adults.

Donna Eder
Indiana University

See Also: Disabled Students; Morale in Schools; Service Learning; Social Role of the Teacher; Youth Friendship and Conflict in Schools.

Further Readings
Coles, Robert. *The Moral Intelligence of Children*. New York: Random House, 1997.
Eder, Donna and Regina Holyan. *Life Lessons Through Storytelling: Children's Exploration of Ethics*. Bloomington: Indiana University Press, 2010.
Noddings, N. *Educating Moral People: A Caring Alternative to Character Education*. New York: Teachers College Press, 2002.
Palmer, Parker. *The Courage to Teach: Exploring the Inner Landscape of a Teacher's Life*. San Francisco: Jossey-Bass, 2007.
Sprod, Timothy. *Philosophical Discussion in Moral Education*. New York: Routledge, 2001.
Sullivan, K., M. Cleary, and G. Sullivan. *Bullying in Secondary Schools: What It Looks Like and How to Manage It*. Thousand Oaks, CA: Sage, 2004.
Thompson, M., C. O'Neil Grace, and L. Cohen. *Best Friends, Worst Enemies: Understanding the Social Lives of Children*. New York: Ballantine, 2001.

Ethiopia

Ethiopia, located in the Horn of Africa, occupies approximately 0.7 million square miles (1.1 million square kilometers) of extremely varied terrain. The United Nations (UN) estimated the population in 2010 at 83 million. The economy is dominated by agriculture, and coffee is the most important cash crop. In 2008, more than one-third of government financing was provided by foreign aid, principally from the United States and Europe. Ethiopia experienced economic growth averaging 5.6 percent per year between 1990 and 2010, and paid a public debt of 13 percent of gross national income in 2010. Unlike other countries in sub-Saharan Africa, Ethiopia was colonized only briefly; however, a history of oppression of the peoples of southern Ethiopia by historically dominant highland groups of northern Ethiopia has influenced social arrangements, including access to formal education. A total of 82 languages are spoken in Ethiopia, those with the most speakers being Amharic, Oromo, Tigrinya, and Somali. Ethiopian Orthodox Christianity and Islam are the largest faiths, and count approximately equal numbers of followers. In 1993, Eritrea, formerly a province, seceded and became an independent nation-state.

Ethiopia has the longest history of formal education of any country in sub-Saharan Africa, with a tradition of ecclesiastical schools dating to the early 2nd millennium C.E. Until the 20th century, however, literacy was largely a preserve of clerics and the nobility. The origins of secular schooling in Ethiopia date to 1905, when Emperor Menelik (r. 1889–1913) opened a boys' school in the newly founded capital, Addis Ababa. Under Menelik, education was available only to male children of the Abyssinian nobility, who constituted the landowning class. The first girls' school opened in 1930. During the Italian occupation (1936–41), schools were closed to all Ethiopians, but following World War II, Emperor Haile Selassie (r. 1930–74) oversaw expansion of the school system. Secondary schools, however, were confined mainly to cities, and by the final years of Haile Selassie's reign, there were still fewer than a million students.

In 1974, a revolution led to the overthrow of Haile Selassie, and shortly afterwards a military council known as the Derg took over the government. With the Soviet Union as its most important ally, the Derg enacted sweeping land reforms, reorganized the administrative structure of the country into "peasants' associations," and carried out educational reforms. A series of adult literacy campaigns were launched (1976–85), with students from the cities serving as teachers in the countryside. As before, the primary language of instruction was Amharic, but literacy training materials were also produced in Oromo and other languages for the first time. Disparities in gender access to education decreased.

However, many educated Ethiopians were murdered in the "Red Terror" (1977–78) as the Derg sought to stamp out opposition.

After the fall of the Soviet Union, the Derg collapsed under attack from regional insurgencies, and in 1991, a transitional government was formed by former insurgents under the banner of the Ethiopian People's Revolutionary Democratic Front (EPRDF), with Meles Zenawi as prime minister. A new constitution established the right of each of the "nations and nationalities" of Ethiopia to use their languages, including in schools.

Growth of Formal Education

With economic liberalization, a private education sector emerged. After Ethiopia's first multiparty elections in 2000, there was an opening up of political space, but this trajectory was reversed after contested elections in 2005, when demonstrations against the ruling party were violently suppressed and opposition politicians were jailed. Under the EPRDF, enrollment increased dramatically at all levels of the education system, with gross enrollment in primary schools reaching close to 100 percent for both sexes in 2005, and net enrollment (children ages 7–10) in primary schools increasing to 71 percent for boys and 66 percent for girls. Adult literacy rates remain low by international standards, at approximately 50 percent for men and 33 percent for women.

Formal education under the EPRDF consists of primary (grades one to four and five to eight), and secondary (nine to 10), followed by technical/vocational or college preparatory schools and universities. In most of the country, mother tongues are used as the language of instruction in grades one through five, with English as medium of instruction thereafter. The Ministry of Education mandates multiple-choice examinations in eighth and 10th grades. Examination results determine whether students may pursue further education, and of what kind: The lower-scoring students are channeled to teacher training and technical schools, and higher-scoring students to university. Among university entrants, those with highest scores study medicine; those with somewhat lower scores study engineering, and so on.

Ethiopia is unlikely to meet the Millennium Development Goal of universal primary education by 2015, because net enrollment continues to lag behind gross enrollment. This discrepancy reflects competing priorities for rural parents between sending children to school and obtaining their help with household work—a tradeoff that often means delayed enrollment and high rates of attrition in teenage years. Despite English being the language of instruction after grade five, many teachers are not fluent, which creates incentives to employ a didactic pedagogical style. The rapid expansion of the education system since 1991—including the establishment of several new universities—has come at the cost of quality of instruction at all levels, including widening teacher-student ratios. High levels of unemployment among urban school graduates, high rates of emigration ("brain drain") among university educated professionals, and a political climate that stifles free speech serve as obstacles for Ethiopia in realizing its goals of socioeconomic development.

Edward Geoffrey Jedediah Stevenson
Emory University

See Also: Globalization; Poverty and Education; Worldwide Education Revolution.

Further Readings

Human Rights Watch. *Development Without Freedom: How Aid Underwrites Repression in Ethiopia.* New York: Human Rights Watch, 2010.

Negash, Tekeste. *Rethinking Education in Ethiopia.* Uppsala, Sweden: Nordiska Afrikainstitutet. 1996.

Serneels, P. "The Nature of Unemployment Among Young Men in Urban Ethiopia." *Review of Development Economics*, v.11/1 (2007).

Wagaw, Teshome. *Education in Ethiopia.* Ann Arbor: University of Michigan Press, 1979.

World Bank. *Education in Ethiopia: Strengthening the Foundation for Sustainable Progress.* Washington, DC: World Bank, 2005.

Ethnography

Etymologically the composite of two roots: *ethno-* (people) and *-graphy* (describing), ethnography is a research methodology that enables researchers to describe a particular human society as understood by the members of the society itself, especially in relation to collective behaviors such as the use of language and observation of customs and religion. Aiming to achieve deep understanding of the actions, motives, feelings, and beliefs of the members of a society under study, an ethnographer typically conducts the study by immersing himself or herself within the traditional cultural setting of the society. What makes ethnography stand out from many other research designs is that, as opposed to simply collecting data from the researcher's convenient location and interpreting the data solely by the values and standards of researcher's own worldview (often manifested as hypothesis), an ethnographer goes to where his data reside, spends extended period(s) of time with his subjects, carries out an in-depth investigation, and tries to interpret their activities in their frame of reference. In sum, an ethnographic researcher describes social phenomena, participants, and/or entire societies in terms of their local contexts and worldviews. The importance of ethnography is growing in social research and education apart from other areas including business and psychology.

Because ethnographic data collection processes are often unstructured (or semistructured) and sometimes chaotic, ethnographers use various techniques and tools to come up with a satisfactory picture of social phenomena and society. Qualitative research techniques such as observation, interviews, audiovisual recordings, and document analyses are more commonly used in ethnography. Therefore, ethnography is regarded primarily as a genre of qualitative research methods. However, some quantitative methods such as surveys and statistical procedures are also used in order to analyze patterns, to determine samples, and to compare findings and interpretations. These additional methods help triangulate research findings and are often coupled with ethnographic studies to strengthen findings collected from only one technique.

Going beyond the dichotomy of qualitative or quantitative methods, ethnographers characteristically share a common goal of describing and interpreting observable relationships between human practices and social systems of meaning in a particular human society or in regard to a social phenomenon. In accomplishing this goal, researchers' observations are extremely important because the members of society may not always be able to describe implicitly what they have been doing themselves. Hence it is up to the researcher to find out what participants do and why they behave in the way(s) that they do. Ethnography's strengths lie in researchers' ability to maintain a reflexive approach, which includes serving two sometimes conflicting roles—that of participant as well as observer—during the study period of exploring, experiencing, and giving accounts of social phenomena and societies

Historical Context

Research had been traditionally dominated by positivism, the belief that descriptions should be universal and lend themselves to be tested and verified with scientific rigor. In recent years, this dominance began to wane as many researchers tend to understand the importance of naturalism, the belief that social complexities are not the same everywhere, and these social complexities should be captured in their natural settings to understand the unique contextual significance of social practices for their performers. This view recognized that the more empathetic detail that goes into an ethnographic description, the richer our understanding will be and the more valuable that account will be to its readers. This recognition of naturalism gave birth to many exotic ethnographers who came up with lengthy accounts of remote cultures with theoretical explanations of their observations at the end of extended stays as participant observers.

Scholarly endeavors of studying events and social practices in the closest possible manner to understand the contextual meaning are found in ancient times in the works of scholars such as Thucydides in Greece, Manu and Kautilya in India, and Sima Qian in China. Western roots of ethnography can be traced back to European explorers' accounts of different social customs, religions, and unique behaviors of non-Europeans. However, such descriptions often lacked empathy, objectivity, and in-depth observations to be considered "true" ethnographies. Ethnography as a professional field began around the turn of the 20th century. Polish-born British anthropologist Bronislaw Malinowski's study in the Trobriand Islands of Melanesia and the American anthropologist Margaret Mead's fieldwork in Samoa are considered to be two of the more prominent pioneering ethnographical works.

Limitations and Challenges of Ethnography

Although ethnography is often considered an ideal research design for gaining understanding about a culture, it also has its weaknesses. There are two types of influences that often challenge the validity of the ethnographic research: researcher-induced challenges, and subject-induced challenges. Researcher-induced challenges are those where ethnographic researchers cannot maintain their own role as participant-observers in an objective manner due to at least two reasons: (1) the researchers inevitably bring some inherent biases from their own background and (2) since ethnographers often spend years in the field learning local languages and cultures and participating in day-to-day life of the people they are studying about, the practice of participant observation is challenged as they are often unintentionally influenced by members of the community.

The second type is induced by the community under study and again for at least two reasons: (1) the chance that ethnographers might be misguided by their informants (i.e., individuals who provide detailed and specific information on important aspects of cultural life such as rituals) often to keep the secrecy of or to maintain the solidarity with the community, and (2) the chance of cultural change created because of the presence of foreign ethnographic researchers being integrated into local group settings for extended periods of time. Such weaknesses often prevent ethnographers from obtaining a systematic and thorough understanding of the cultures, social phenomena, and societies they study.

Uttam Gaulee
University of Florida
W. James Jacob
University of Pittsburgh

See Also: Immersion; Qualitative Research on Education; Quantitative Research on Education; Research Paradigms in Educational Studies.

Further Readings

Blommaert, Jan and Dong Jie. *Ethnographic Fieldwork: A Beginner's Guide.* New York: Multilingual Matters, 2010.

DeMarrais, Kathleen and Stephen D. Lapan, eds. *Foundations for Research: Methods of Inquiry in Education and the Social Sciences.* Mahwah, NJ: Lawrence Erlbaum Associates, 2004.

Denzin, Norman K. and Yvonna S. Lincoln, eds. *The SAGE Handbook of Qualitative Research*, 3rd ed. Thousand Oaks, CA: Sage, 2005.

Geertz, C. "Thick Description: Toward an Interpretive Theory of Culture." In *The Interpretation of Cultures: Selected Essays.* New York: Basic Books, 1973.

May, S. and S. Aikman. "Indigenous Education: Addressing Current Issues and Developments." *Comparative Education* v.39/2 (2003).

O'Reilly, Karen. *Key Concepts in Ethnography.* Thousand Oaks, CA: Sage, 2010.

Singer, Jane B. "Ethnography." *Journalism & Mass Communication Quarterly* (March 1, 2009).

Taylor, Bryan C. and Thomas R. Lindlof. *Qualitative Communication Research Methods.* Thousand Oaks, CA: Sage, 2011.

European Union

The European Union (previously known as the European Community or European Economic Community) is a unique economic and political partnership among 27 European countries. The EU is headquartered in Brussels, Belgium, and has a mission to build peace, stability, equality, and prosperity to the European continent and the world. The EU is managed by the European Commission (EC), which has representation from each of the EU member states.

The EC is responsible for establishing EU legislation, policies, strategic planning, and providing the daily operational personnel for the EU. Beginning with six member countries in 1951—Belgium, Germany, France, Italy, Luxembourg, and the Netherlands—the EU has since grown to include Austria, Bulgaria, Cyprus, Czech Republic, Denmark, Estonia, Finland, Greece, Hungary, Ireland, Latvia, Lithuania, Malta, Poland, Portugal, Romania, Slovakia, Slovenia, Spain, Sweden, and the United Kingdom. Additional countries have applied to join, with several other countries considering membership. Collectively, the EU population was just over 500 million in January 2012. The land area is 1.6 million square miles (4.3 million square kilometers). In 2010, the gross domestic product (GDP) for the European Union was $21.2 trillion (16.4 trillion euros), or about 28 percent of the global GDP). German is the most spoken first language, and English is the most common second language spoken among EU members.

History and Social Structure

After World War II, Europeans had great optimism for lasting peace and the unity of Europe. The emergence of the Cold War quickly ended this hope, polarizing much of the continent between two dominating ideologies—capitalism as supported by the United States and its Western European allies, and communism as advocated by the Soviet Union and its Eastern European allies. During this post-war period in Europe, social progress and economics overshadowed education, and each European country operated its education system independently. The 1960s and 1970s brought more common ideals in education. In the 1970s, the European community began to outline education policies and program cooperation among members, marking significant progress in education. By 1974, intercultural education was valued and advanced collaboration and voluntary commitment to work together while making allowances for the diverse educational policies and traditions of each member state. The first six priorities of cooperation during this period included: education of migrant workers and their children, promoting closer relations between member state education systems, documentation and statistics, cooperation among higher education, foreign language instruction, and equal access to education opportunities.

Unifying Education Systems

The Cold War came to an end with the fall of the Berlin Wall in 1989, and Europe entered a phase of unification for Germany and division in other countries (e.g., the former Czechoslovakia and Yugoslavia). Balancing capitalist and socialist ideologies and practices created a significant challenge for newly admitted EU members from eastern Europe during the post–Cold War era. The opportunity allowed all nations to gain deeper understanding and acceptance of good economic and education practices from each of the EU members. During this transitional period, significant attempts were made to unify a diverse patchwork of education systems. This was especially evident at the higher education level, with the European Community Action Scheme for the Mobility of University Students (ERASMUS) in 1987, and the Bologna Process in 1999.

The Bologna Process established the European Higher Education Area (EHEA). Today, the EHEA unites 47 countries committed to higher education. The EC, Council of Europe, UNESCO-European Centre for Higher Education (CEPES), and representatives of higher education institutions, students, employers, and quality assurance organizations strive to forge international cooperation and academic exchange to facilitate broader access, mobility of students, graduates, and higher education staff, and prepare students for future employment. The three-cycle structure of higher education (e.g., bachelor's, master's, and doctorate) is the national framework followed by each country. ERASMUS and the Bologna Process have helped improve acceptability and the relevance of European higher education worldwide.

Resolutions agreed upon during the Lisbon European Council in 2000 included the recognition of the emergence of a knowledge-based society and the need to adapt education systems to better meet the needs of this knowledge society by providing relevant training that would ultimately lead to quality employment. This approach gained visibility, continuity, a new sense of common objectives, and a working method to facilitate greater convergence of the EU member countries. It became the guiding principle for political cooperation and the integrated education and training programs from 2007 to 2013. These EU structural policies began a new era of cooperation and tested the commitment of member states to implement common objectives at the national level to strengthen education. With 27 member countries, there are also 27 education structures within the EU. Some member education structures are similar, and others vary based on historical and local contexts. The EC compares its member education structures through the establishment of the International Standard Classification of Education (ISCED), although many exceptions exist. In 2012, education was compulsory for children in the EU starting around age 5 or 6, depending on the EU member state's age entrance policy (compulsory education is required for 8–12 years, depending on the country); primary education is compulsory for all EU member states. At the higher education level, EU members adhere to ERASMUS and the Bologna Process, which ensures greater mobility access and transferability of credits and degrees across member state education systems.

Current Issues

Education in the 21st century is a central part of the EU's growth strategy and it is pivotal for each member state to best build local capacity and maintain competencies in an increasingly global and knowledge-based economy. Information technology skills, multiple language fluencies, and intercultural and entrepreneurial competencies are essential ingredients for young people to succeed in the globalized economy and diverse societies. Youth education and lifelong learning programs are key investments for addressing the global competitiveness and social cohesion of the EU. The EC's goals to help prepare youth for the 21st century include (1) student competencies on literacy and numeracy, personalized approaches to learning, assessing learning outcomes, and vocational training; (2) efficiency and equity in education, including access to higher quality preschool education, measuring and improving the equity impact of schools, successful transitions between different schools, and providing more personalized learning approaches for students with special needs, and reducing early school leaving; and (3) strengthening of teachers and school staff by improving quality of teacher education programs. The Europe 2020 strategy recognizes that education, EUs most valuable asset, is the springboard for innovation, which is the key to future success in the complex society worldwide.

The EU's strategy emphasizes member countries working together and learning from each other. With each EU member state responsible for its education and training systems, EU-level policies support national actions and help address common challenges such as: aging societies, skills deficits among the workforce, and global competition through early childhood, school, higher, vocational, and adult education. The benchmarks in education through 2020 include: increasing participation in compulsory primary education at 4 years old; improving the number of 15 year olds with sufficient abilities in reading, mathematics, and science; reducing early leavers from education and training; improving job skills training in higher education institutions among 30–34 year olds; and increasing the number of adults (25–64 years old) participating in lifelong learning.

W. James Jacob
Lila De Klaver
University of Pittsburgh

See Also: College Transferring; International College Partnerships (Sister Colleges); International Data.

Further Readings

Directorate-General for Education and Culture. *Progress Towards the Common European Objectives in Education and Training: Indicators and Benchmarks, 2010/2011.* Brussels, Belgium: Directorate-General for Education and Culture, 2011.

European Commission. *The Structure of the European Education Systems 2011/12: Schematic Diagrams.* Brussels, Belgium: Eurydice Network, Education, Audiovisual and Culture Executive Agency, 2011.

Expansion of Education

Education has grown for several centuries in Western societies, and more recently in the rest of the world. While education, defined as enrollments in schools or other formal institutions of instruction, expanded slowly through much of history, the pace of change stepped up during the past 200 years. Consequently, most of the research on educational expansion, and related theorizing in sociology and other disciplines, has concerned that period. Because of potential links between education and economic development, it is also an important policy question. For much of history, education was a luxury that few could afford. Schooling requires that children be free from labor, along with resources to support teachers, facilities, and books and other materials, so it requires a rather advanced level of social wealth. While it was occasionally provided for children in ancient and medieval societies, it rarely extended beyond what later was described as elementary or primary instruction. More advanced forms of education were limited to those who could afford tutors or exclusive schools, principally in larger cities.

Religion was an early impetus to educational growth. The rise of universities during the Middle Ages in western Europe provided an impetus to educational expansion, although their direct contributions to overall growth were modest. Far more significant was the Protestant Reformation, beginning in the 16th century, which unleashed a prolonged era of growth in schooling. Protestant emphasis on reading and interpreting the Bible prompted a revolution in literacy rates, and the Catholic counter-reformation also added to literacy. The result was a significant increase in support for and interest in education.

Nation-States in the Industrial Era

Educational expansion gained force during the 19th century, when Western economies expanded rapidly because of industrialization, and schooling became an integral dimension of nation-building. The United States and Germany emerged as leaders in educational development, with expansion focused first on primary schools, and then on secondary institutions. The United States, however, quickly supplanted Germany and other European nations as the leader in educational expansion with the rise of high schools, which became mass institutions and the leading edge of educational growth in the 20th century. This phase of educational growth is sometimes labeled as the second transformation of American schooling. The third transformation occurred in the postwar era, with the expansion of postsecondary education. Much debate has revolved around factors accounting for educational expansion in both the 19th and 20th centuries. Some have suggested that industrialization and rapid economic growth contributed to educational growth, despite child labor in early factories, and others have emphasized the role of the state in fostering schooling for political socialization. In the United States, education first expanded most rapidly in the industrial north, but was also associated with the westward movement of Protestant settlers. It is likely that economic development, cultural/religious values, and state-sponsored political socialization goals all contributed to the process.

Twentieth Century Expansion

Explanations of more recent educational growth have proven controversial. In explaining enrollment trends across the 20th century, economists have linked the high school to demand for educated workers, especially in the growing white-collar sector of the labor force and industries affected by technological change. Most of this research, however, has focused on the years prior to 1940, when secondary schooling initially became widespread. Other analyses generally affirm these findings, pointing to the importance of labor market conditions in shaping attainment patterns. With regard to broad tendencies in school attendance, place did matter, largely because of the differing labor market conditions that shaped decisions about schooling. Other researchers introduce additional considerations.

With respect to the postwar era, the rise in attainment was also influenced by the improved educational and economic status of parents. A number of studies have also found improvements in school quality linked to enrollment growth: Better schools helped students to succeed or persist in pursuit of greater attainment. These explanations are consistent with the idea that investments in educational institutions reflected a larger public commitment to schooling, boosting attainment apart from the influence of the labor market. Another line of inquiry has examined the impact of ethnicity on school attendance, focusing on differences in the experiences of various immigrant and racial groups in U.S. history. Their findings can be considered ethno-cultural

explanations of variation in school enrollment. Most such research has focused on the 19th and early 20th centuries, periods of high immigration, rather than the postwar era, but there is considerable evidence that these factors continued to be important, especially race, up to the present.

Worldwide Expansion Since 1950

Yet another interpretive tradition in the study of enrollment growth has been represented by the neo-institutionalist perspective, focusing primarily on the international expansion of education in the postwar decades. Its proponents also argue that the primary determinants of growth, once enrollments reached a relatively high threshold, are the appeal and demands of the school system, and the size of relevant population cohorts to be educated. This viewpoint suggests that as formally organized and officially sanctioned forms of behavior (such as school enrollment) become a widespread social norm, participation can rise independently of particular contextual influences. Empirical work in this area has shown that social and economic factors tend to predict the spread of new forms of behaviors, norms, and policies during the early phases of diffusion. In later stages, the process of diffusion appears to advance of its own momentum, regardless of context.

Somewhat similarly, enrollment expansion also can be tied to the Weberian proposition that status competition historically fueled rising demand for credentials in modern settings, resulting in educational investment without immediate reference to employment advantages or other measureable social influences. Expansion can be seen as largely independent of such exogenous conditions as the economy, employment trends, political development, or cultural differences. Such explanations of enrollment growth have been demonstrated principally with international data, using longitudinal and cross-sectional analyses of educational expansion in scores of countries. Recent accounts of educational growth in the United States have also supported this interpretive frame. Educational expansion remains a contentious political issue, as politicians and researchers debate the importance of schooling to the economy and future social and political stability. For these reasons, it will likely remain a critical topic in the sociology of education.

John Rury
University of Kansas

See Also: Educational Aspirations/Expectations; Educational Policymakers; Educationalization; Labor Market Effects on Education.

Further Readings

Goldin, Claudia and Lawrence Katz. *The Race Between Education and Technology.* Cambridge, MA: Harvard University Press, 2008.

Labaree, David, *Someone Has to Fail; The Zero Sum Game of Public Schooling.* Cambridge, MA: Harvard University Press, 2010.

Meyer, John W., et al. "World Expansion of Mass Education, 1870–1980." *Sociology of Education*, v.65/2 (April 1992).

Rury, John, et al. "Exapnding Secondary Attainment in the United States: A Fixed Effects Panel Regression Model." *Historical Methods*, v.43/3 (July 2010).

Extended Kinship and Education

Extended kinship and significant others in education have been underinvestigated, despite their potentially powerful effects on schooling practices and outcomes. Researchers claim that there is a need to understand how social processes operate as intervening factors between social characteristics and performance variables. Some of the studies that have been conducted in this area have analyzed the influence of extended kinship and significant others' support on academic achievement, educational expectations, academic adjustment, social influences on undergraduates' decision to leave or remain in higher education, and the educational expectations and achievement of racial minority groups. The majority of these studies have used quantitative approaches.

Extended families comprise multigenerational and interdependent networks of social, emotional, and instrumental support; while significant others are those exercising a major influence over the attitudes of individuals, such as teachers, peers, and community members. Extended kin networks facilitate adaptive behavior, which translates into stronger school values and higher aspirations. These networks represent a potential source of socialization, and may even constitute an important form of social capital. Through exchanges of support and resources, social networks more generally can also impede potential familial problems, such as child abuse and neglect, and even encourage positive parent-child relations. Based on social support theory, the function of the support of extended kinship and significant others is to enhance recipients' well-being. However, research evidence demonstrates that the identity of the significant other makes a difference, based on their importance to the student. For example, faculty members are generally less influential than peers and other family members.

Research in industrialized countries has shown that educational aspirations held by extended kinship differ by race and social class. For example, African American children consider their extended kinship as important references for educational expectations. Kinship might include fictive kin and nonrelated adults. Research evidence demonstrates that racial differences in educational expectations of extended kinship are among the sources of racial inequalities in school performance. With respect to white students, some authors suggest that support from their extended kinship is less extensive than in African American families, although this type of involvement has been generally underinvestigated. The majority of studies have focused mainly on families from disadvantaged contexts, and more research is needed on white, middle-class, extended families.

Research in less industrialized countries, on the other hand, has revealed the buffering effect in education of larger kinship structures. For example, nuclear families in Africa are usually embedded in larger kinship networks that help children gain access to higher-quality schools. Consequently, the impact of extended kinship on students' educational trajectory is a cultural practice that varies across communities. In higher education, the involvement of extended kinship among working-class students consists of emotional engagement, either positive or negative, toward university enrolment. By contrast, for better-off students, the involvement goes beyond emotional support, and may be an active influence on decision making regarding which institutions to attend. This usually involves the mobilization of alternative kinds of support and resources taken from an extensive social network, such as careers advisers, work placements, and voluntary work.

Marta Cristina Azaola
University of Southampton

See Also: Family Structure and Education; Grandparents' Role in Education; Parental Involvement.

Further Readings

Graham, A. and K. Anderson. "'I Have to Be Three Steps Ahead': Academically Gifted African American Male Students in an Urban High School on the Tension Between an Ethnic and Academic Identity." *Urban Review*, v.40/5 (2008).

Román, S., P. J. Cuestas, and P. Fenollar. "An Examination of the Interrelationships Between Self-Esteem, Others' Expectations, Family Support, Learning Approaches and Academic Achievement." *Studies in Higher Education*, v.33/2 (2008).

Ryan, C. S., J. F. Casas, L. Kelly-Vance, B. O. Ryalls, and C. Nero. "Parent Involvement and Views of School Success: The Role of Parents' Latino and White American Cultural Orientations." *Psychology in the Schools*, v.47/4 (2010).

Samuel, O. S. "Roles of Personality, Vocational Interests, Academic Achievement and Socio-Cultural Factors in Educational Aspirations of Secondary School Adolescents in Southwestern Nigeria." *Career Development International*, v.13/7 (2008).

Extracurricular Activities

Extracurricular activities have been of interest to sociologists since James Coleman's *The Adolescent Society,* in which he posited that peer acceptance is central in adolescent culture, and academic success represents only one avenue to acceptance. Drawing on Coleman's insights, sociologists focus on extracurricular activities as a route to peer acceptance and causal influence on youth behavior. They find that participation in school and community-based extracurricular activities—sports, arts, student government, volunteering, academic clubs—promotes youth development, including positive emotional, behavioral, and academic outcomes, yet opportunities to participate are not equally distributed among adolescents.

Because extracurricular offerings are contingent upon funding, there is inequality in students' access to participation, which contributes to socioeconomic gaps in social and academic outcomes. Explanations for the positive (and sometimes negative) effects of extracurricular participation focus on learned skills and values, socialization toward future-orientation via peer influence, social support from and attachment to conventional adults, identity formation, time allocation, and selection bias.

Who Participates in Extracurricular Activities?

Most adolescents engage in at least one extracurricular activity, with athletic activities as the most popular type, yet most studies identify a sizable minority of nonparticipants. Researchers identify several demographic characteristics associated with individual involvement in extracurricular activities. With the exception of sports, girls engage in more, and a more diverse range of extracurricular activities than their male peers. Participation rates are similar or higher among African American adolescents compared to white youths, with the exception of vocational activities. Family environment also influences whether adolescents engage in activities. Youths in families characterized by high levels of parental engagement, parental involvement in adolescents' lives, and family connectedness, as well as low levels of family conflict, tend to be more engaged in extracurricular activities than those with less-ideal family contexts. Maternal depression also predicts lower levels of involvement, and this effect operates through weakened relationships between mothers and their adolescent children, as well as through adolescent cognition. Youths who report low self-worth and negative attributions about life events are less engaged in extracurricular activities than their more confident, optimistic peers.

Students with lower socioeconomic status are disproportionately underrepresented in extracurricular activities, as are students who perform poorly academically. School-based involvement in extracurricular activities is voluntary and open to all students. Therefore, individual-level characteristics, such as socioeconomic status, need not shape patterns of participation. Nonetheless, research demonstrates inequality in access to extracurricular activities, partially because of financial constraints experienced by low-income families. For example, participation in team sports requires the purchase of uniforms and equipment, and participation in band or orchestra requires ownership or rental of a musical instrument, as well as lessons for developing skills. Inequality in access on the basis of socioeconomic status and academic performance also arises from teachers and peers acting as gatekeepers, who recruit students into activities with a limited number of available spots. Minimum grade requirements further restrict participation to students who perform above a specified level, and talent/skill requirements bar some from joining, as in the case of cheerleading or marching band. Moreover, funding cuts for extracurricular activities have led to pay-to-participate programs, which further exclude disadvantaged students. Spending cuts to student transportation create even more barriers to participation.

School characteristics often determine the amount and types of extracurricular activities available to students. Larger schools and schools with an economically advantaged student body offer more, and more diverse, types of activities than smaller and less-advantaged schools. This can be seen in the effects of the percentage of students receiving free or reduced-price lunch: the higher the percentage, the fewer service, honors, and sports activities offered. Additionally, schools with lower per-student expenditures offer fewer recreational sports and ethnic clubs than schools with more money allocated for each pupil. In turn, schools with more extensive offerings have higher rates of participation.

Notably, the types of sports activities available at schools with high rates of economically disadvantaged and racial/ethnic minority students are those that tend to have either no effect or even negative effects on academic outcomes, including football and basketball. Unequal access to a wide range of extracurricular activities concerns scholars who note that involvement in many activities promotes youth development. Those who would benefit the most from participation—socioeconomically disadvantaged students and those who struggle academically—have the least access to extracurricular activities because of both individual-level and school-level factors. The activities to which they have the greatest access are those that are the least beneficial.

Extracurricular Activities and Youth Outcomes

In general, participation in extracurricular activities positively influences emotional, academic, and behavioral outcomes during adolescence. Extracurricular involvement—particularly sports participation—fosters identity formation, which confers prestige and produces higher levels of self-esteem. Activities provide adolescents with a domain outside of the academic context of school in which they make self-appraisals, and peer acceptance partially explains why sports involvement improves self-esteem. For

example, a youth who feels poorly about his struggles in science class has the opportunity to feel competent when on the basketball court and when he receives approval from peers who value athleticism. The positive effect of sports participation on feelings of self-worth is strongest for those who identify as scholar athletes, rather than as just athletes. Participants in extracurricular activities perform better academically during middle and high school, are more engaged in school, have higher aspirations and expectations for college, and are more likely to graduate from high school and to go on to college than noninvolved peers. Plus, the broader the range of activities in which adolescents are involved, the more likely they are to manifest these positive academic outcomes, although this effect levels out at very high rates of participation. The favorable effects of extracurricular activities are not shared equally by all: The academic benefits of extracurricular activities are strongest among low-achieving participants and those with low socioeconomic status, as well as for youths who fulfill a leadership role in their activity.

Extracurricular activities also influence nonacademic behavior. With the exception of boys involved in sports, adolescents who participate in extracurricular activities engage in less criminal behavior and substance use than their peers, and involved girls have lower rates of teenage childbearing. In addition, participation fosters friendships because of increased time spent with co-participants, an emphasis on teamwork that encourages emotional management, and exposure to similarly interested peers. This friendship-promoting effect is stronger among those in less-popular (i.e., lower-status) activities, such as arts clubs, and weaker among those in high-status activities like sports. In addition, extracurricular activities promote interracial and cross-age friendships by connecting like-minded youths who would not otherwise socialize together. The positive behavioral effects of involvement in extracurricular activities extend into adulthood, with adolescent participants achieving higher occupational status and income in adulthood, even when controlling for ability and social class. They also enjoy better mental health and former sports participants are more involved in physical fitness activities during adulthood than nonparticipants. In addition, some types of extracurricular involvement, such as student council, promote volunteering, political participation, and other types of civic engagement in adulthood.

Effects vary by the type of activity, and not all effects are positive. For instance, sports participation, although associated with heightened academic performance, is also linked to higher levels of alcohol use and truancy, whereas other types of participation, such as student government, volunteering, and faith-based activities, are only associated with positive outcomes. In addition, when a high proportion of activity participants engage in delinquent behavior, participation in that activity leads to increased delinquency for youths who join. Furthermore, some types of sports participation have a negative influence on academic achievement. For example, playing basketball or football decreases scores on standardized tests, and the negative effect of sports participation on grades is found particularly among African American students. Some argue that this is because sports operate as a drain on attention and energy, pulling students away from school, and that the racial difference is because of high expectations for a career in professional athletics among African American student athletes. Others contend that the racial difference arises from a complex selection process based on racial variation in resources for achieving academic success: Those with limited financial and cultural resources are more drawn to sports participation than other students.

Why Do Extracurricular Activities Influence Youth Outcomes?

Sociologists offer several potential avenues through which extracurricular activities contribute to youth development. First, adolescents who engage in debate team, student council, basketball, or any other activity learn social and intellectual skills, as well as develop conventional values that improve classroom performance when applied to educational settings, in part because these skills and values are favored by teachers who reward students who display them in the classroom. Such skills include the ability to work well in groups, goal-setting, and taking direction from adults. Learned values entail a strong work ethic and an appreciation of the importance of school for future success. For example, marching band participants learn that collective success requires concentration, endurance, and willingness to follow the bandleader's directions. In turn, concentration, endurance, and behavioral compliance are consistent with teachers' expectations and lead to higher achievement in the classroom. Addressing this causal process directly requires identifying specific features of extracurricular programs.

In doing so, sports psychologists identify several characteristics of effective sports programs, including practices that motivate students to develop mastery, strong behavioral norms, and leadership experience. Their findings support a skills/values perspective.

Second, youths who participate in extracurricular activities have more extensive pro-social networks and, as a result, are exposed to more peers and adults with whom they form beneficial interpersonal relationships. These networks help integrate disengaged students into school and facilitate the transfer of information that helps students to succeed, including information about college and careers. This explanation draws on social capital theory in sociology, which emphasizes the value of social ties: Extracurricular activities increase social capital for participants. Third, and along similar lines, extracurricular activities create a "hook" into school such that disinterested students develop a stake in remaining in school and performing well. Fourth, participants develop activity-based social identities that shape future behavior. Voluntary involvement in activities permits youths to craft a public persona such as "jock" or "brain." In turn, through their participation, youths become embedded in a culture that solidifies this identity and rewards behaviors that are consistent with the persona. For instance, some sociologists attribute negative behavioral consequences of sports participation to a "jock" identity, and affiliation with similarly oriented peers who support alcohol use. In contrast, risky behavior is inconsistent with intellect-based identities, like "brain." Fifth, extracurricular activities foster positive youth development by altering adolescents' out-of-school time allocation. In the United States, more than half of children's and adolescents' waking hours are spent in leisure activities, much of which are unstructured activities spent with peers or alone (e.g., watching television or playing video games). Extracurricular involvement structures youth leisure time, limiting exposure to delinquent peers and increasing exposure to pro-social others, such as coaches and other adult leaders. As such, structured leisure activities are particularly important for adolescents in disadvantaged communities who face high levels of neighborhood risks.

Extracurricular activities have a causal effect on youth outcomes. Evidence of reversed causal ordering and selection bias present challenges to these explanations. For example, early cross-sectional studies of sports involvement and delinquent behavior suggested that joining a sports team reduces adolescent law violation. Longitudinal studies that measured sports involvement and delinquency over time, rather than cross-sectionally, revealed that the direction of effects was reversed. Instead of sports suppressing delinquency, delinquents are simply more likely than conventional youths to quit the team.

Additionally, participation effects are partly because of selection bias, which means that the association between extracurricular participation and youth outcomes is because of some characteristic of adolescents that predisposes them to both extracurricular involvement and the outcome of interest. For example, college-oriented students are especially likely to engage in multiple extracurricular activities because they are embedded within the school culture and they want to appear desirable in the college admissions process. Because of this orientation, they are also likely to perform well in school, graduate from high school, and pursue higher education. Thus, what appears to be a causal effect of extracurricular activities on academic outcomes is, in fact, because of a preexisting feature of participants. These types of effects can be ruled out through experimental study or, in the absence of experimental design, by measuring change in the outcome before and after participation occurs, as well as with sophisticated statistical techniques that match involved and noninvolved students based on

their shared propensity to engage in extracurricular activities. Empirical evidence from studies like these indicates both selection and causal effects.

Rena Cornell Zito
Westminster College

See Also: Adolescence; After-School Programs; Gender and School Sports; Social Capital; Sports and Schools.

Further Readings

Broh, Beckett A. "Linking Extracurricular Programming to Academic Achievement: Who Benefits and Why?" *Sociology of Education*, v.75 (2002).

Coleman, James. *The Adolescent Society*. Oxford: Free Press of Glencoe, 1961.

Eccles, Jacquelynne S. and Janice Templeton. "Chapter 4: Extracurricular Activities and Other After-School Activities for Youth." *Review of Research in Education*, v.25 (2002).

Garey, Anita Ilta. "Social Domains and Concepts of Care: Protection, Instruction, and Containment in After-School Programs." *Journal of Family Issues*, v.23/6 (2002).

McNeal, Ralph B. "High School Extracurricular Activities: Closed Structures and Stratifying Patterns of Participation." *Journal of Educational Research*, v.91 (1998).

F

Failing Schools

When most critics of public education refer to "failing schools," they are referring primarily to urban schools where students fail to make sufficient or expected gains on standardized tests and schools that have low graduation rates and correspondingly high dropout rates. These so-called dropout factories are failing to educate a large proportion of students successfully who live in impoverished circumstances, especially in the nation's largest cities.

These students are primarily members of minority groups (e.g., African American or Latino/a) and may be members of linguistic and ethnic minorities such as Hmong and Vietnamese. Under the policies of the No Child Left Behind (NCLB) legislation, beginning in 2001 under the administration of U.S. President George W. Bush, schools that failed to meet academic performance targets for several years in a row became labeled as "failing schools." This label then triggered a set of policy interventions. The schools that failed to meet Adequate Yearly Progress (AYP) were identified as turnaround schools, in need of improvement or even closure, or restarting as charter schools. Such policy interventions often required dismissal of current administrators and teaching staff. Failing schools are those that failed to meet predetermined benchmarks or adequate performance targets set by states under the policy of NCLB. State departments of education set these targets or cutoff scores. Under NCLB policy,

however, the performance levels were mandated to increase each year, until by 2014 every student was expected to be proficient, or above average.

Educators reacted to the articulation of this 100 percent proficiency policy with dismay. How could every student be above average? This is a statistical impossibility, given current standardized assessment tools designed to sort students into groups. Some states reacted by lowering their target benchmark on their state mandated tests to arbitrary levels, and their students appeared to be meeting desired proficiency levels. By manipulating the cutoff level in this way, a state's schools could appear to be adequate or not failing. This is not what the original legislation had intended; however, without a common set of standards or widely accepted norms or standards for performance, states could control perceptions of the effectiveness of schools.

National Assessment of Educational Progress

The National Assessment of Educational Progress (NAEP) is a national sampling of students drawn from each state and is often used as another yardstick for the academic performance of U.S. students. This measure counteracts the influence of the states by providing a state-to-state comparison. Comparisons to the NAEP scores in those same states that manipulated their target scores showed large discrepancies between student performance on the NAEP sample from those states and student performance on the state assessment test. Beyond this narrow policy definition under NCLB, however, to understand both the phenomenon and the more general criticisms of failing schools, it is important to look at American schools in a much broader context. According to the federal repository for education data, the National Center for Education Statistics (NCES), the United States had an estimated 13,890 K–12 school districts and 98,706 individual schools, with an enrollment of 48,000,000 students from 2008 through 2009.

Is it possible that all, or nearly all, of these schools, school districts, and students were failing? Is it possible that this richly diverse system of public schools in the United States was a complete failure? If that is not the case, what else might be involved in this debate? These critics were particularly focusing on urban schools. According to NCES, among the 100 largest school districts in major cities, there are approximately 15,396 schools, educating more than one in every five students in the United States. Despite significant challenges, especially in the very largest districts (e.g., New York, Philadelphia, and Chicago), many urban school students are performing adequately and moving on to prestigious colleges and universities.

Still, according to the latest NCLB reports, the state of Florida had the highest failure rate in 2011, with 89 percent of all schools in that state failing to meet their AYP targets. A total of 24 states reported that more than 50 percent of their schools were failing. The contradiction at work here, and what this actually means, is that the NCLB policy was flawed, and the assessment tools were too crude to measure student growth appropriately. Educators have long demanded that instead of arbitrary state benchmarks, schools should track student growth in academic progress. Such a growth model would start where the students are performing, and show accountability when schools and teachers are able to move them forward in their learning.

Can public schools accomplish this goal of student gains? While conventional wisdom often suggests that private schools are better in all ways at achieving academic success for students, research by C. Lubienski, C. Crane, and S. T. Lubienski finds that public schools, holding constant for students' socioeconomic status (SES), actually do a better job in educating students. Thus, many K–12 educators look at the flawed policy of NCLB and the extreme criticisms of public education currently abounding in the media and conclude that there is a propaganda campaign intended to discredit public education, according to D. Berliner and B. Biddle.

The term *failing schools* then is seen to be part of an ideological movement and a political attempt to privatize schooling, much as other public services have devolved to the private sector. Education researchers who focus on more holistic or ecological causes of poor school performance cite an entire constellation of issues—lack of financial resources, fewer highly qualified teachers, high student/teacher ratios, and less than adequate physical facilities and technology—as reasons for the real academic problems of these schools and students. Others who view school failure from an even more radical social and economic perspective, such as Jean Anyon and Martin Haberman, suggest that this phenomenon of failing schools and students who are not reaching academic potential actually is intentional policy that supports the status quo by maintaining the existing social class stratification of American society.

Demographic Determinants

Schools reflect the societies that they serve. L. Fusarelli describes demographic changes in the U.S. population in which city residents became older, poorer, less white, and more linguistically diverse over the last 40 years. Increases in immigration and the rapid growth of minority groups mean that whites who have been a dominant population group are fast becoming become a minority group. Hispanics, in particular, represent the largest and fastest growing population group. Many of these ethnic and immigrant groups live in densely populated cities, causing these areas to have concentrations of poverty, as described by sociologist William Julius Wilson.

Such concentrations of poverty create intense problems for communities and schools, and have created a high demand for social services. Crime, unemployment, poverty, poor health and living conditions—all of these critical social problems are exacerbated in these dense urban neighborhoods. Because of the recent recession, more and more families are living in poverty, losing their homes, and facing unemployment. Stress from these various economic and social conditions contributes to marital discord, child abuse, alcoholism, and a variety of other social ills, all of which flow into the schools and classrooms, negatively affecting the ability of students to focus on academics and teachers to focus on teaching. High concentrations of poverty result in high-poverty schools,

Figure 1 Percentage of schools that did not make adequate yearly progress (AYP), 2006 to 2011

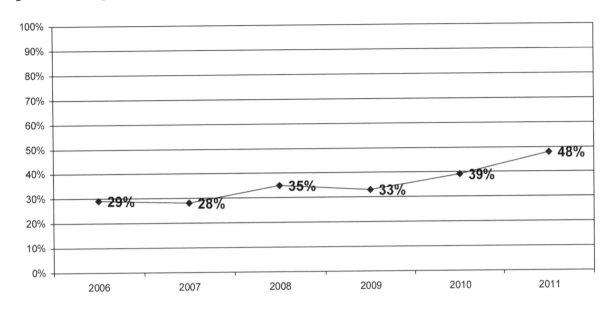

In 2006, 29 percent of U.S. schools did not make adequate yearly progress. By 2011, this percentage had increased to 48 percent.

Source: AYP Results for 2010 to 2011, Center on Education Policy, 2011.

which are defined as schools where 76 percent or more of the students are eligible for free and reduced-cost lunches. A majority of students in such schools are also students of color, attending highly segregated schools. Traditionally, definitions of poverty refer to income; but researchers are increasingly using additional social factors, such as access to health care, as additional concerns that can affect a student's ability to succeed in school. As one example, the prevalence of asthma among urban high-poverty students is rising and accounts for lost school days and opportunities to learn because of lack of appropriate, sustained, and timely medical treatment.

Changes in the composition of families have also occurred during this period, resulting in few children having the benefit of a two-parent household seen in past generations. Children brought up in single-parent households struggle more with academics and may suffer from a variety of other problems with physical and mental health care, nutrition, and psychological stressors. Schools as social institutions are slow to respond to such changes and may still operate as though each student had the same parent and community resources as in the past. Teachers in the Pre-K–12 system are primarily white, female, and middle class; they often need special preparation to deal with the types of social issues they encounter with urban students, including neighborhood violence, drug abuse, and parental incarceration. The recession of 2008 to 2011 resulted in dramatic expansion of foreclosures, leaving more families homeless, forcing additional relocation moves and affecting school attendance patterns. Homelessness also disproportionately affects students of color and results in loss of opportunity to learn and to progress from grade level to grade level. Students affected by these conditions often read below grade level expectations when they suffer loss of continuity in teaching as they move from school to school, despite attempts by school districts to respond by coordinating curriculum and standardizing instruction.

Fewer poor children and children of color experience high-quality early childhood education, and as a consequence may enter kindergarten not ready to learn at the same level as other children. While some students can progress rapidly, others fall further behind at each grade level, contributing to the achievement gap in reading and math. Students who face such early struggles mentally disengage from school and become disruptive until they eventually drop out. Youth who drop out of school are then more likely to encounter the correctional system, and thus enter the school-to-prison pipeline. Because most state education systems base their support on local property taxes, another issue that causes disparities in student academic performance is school funding. In recent years, school finance has moved away from the equality and equity models of earlier decades, and has focused on the notion of adequacy of funding for 21st century skills.

Numerous challenges to the constitutionality of state funding systems have resulted in these systems being found totally inadequate to the task. The *Abbott v. Burke* cases in New Jersey provide one of the best examples of the complex problems faced by the states in building adequate education funding mechanisms, particularly for urban schools. The courts have struggled with these multiple lawsuits for 31 years, weighing the responsibilities of the state for the most impoverished students. As these suits have shown, if adequate funding is not available for high-need students, schools will not be able to provide the resources that students need to learn and the states are not fulfilling their legal obligation to provide a functioning system of education.

No Child Left Behind

The philosophical underpinnings of the No Child Left Behind legislation stressed the notion of accountability of educators for supporting student academic performance, with no excuses for demographic changes and social problems. Relying on economic and tax theories about return on investment, these critics of public education sought sanctions against failing schools, even though schools could not reverse these trends, without support of a much more comprehensive social policy. Another development that has led to concerns about the performance of the U.S. student is the emergence of various international tests.

Comparisons with other industrialized countries (such as the members of the Organisation for Economic Co-operation and Development) frequently show American students falling behind their global peers in standardized test performance, despite comparatively high per pupil expenditures in the United States. These comparisons added to the calls for sanctions against failing schools in the United States. While these international tests are important, the U.S. education system and those of many other countries differ in curriculum, access, and participation, and U.S. educators and policymakers must study

these results to see what can be learned about how to improve instruction in U.S. schools.

Finally, it is critically important to note the aims of the American public education system. While the ability to compete in the global economy is of strategic national interest, education in a democracy has unique goals. Educators who are concerned about the success or failure of today's schools also are looking at their record in producing active and engaged citizens capable of sustaining democratic institutions. NAEP is a national sampling of students drawn from each state, and is often seen as another yardstick for the performance of U.S. students.

Kathleen Sullivan Brown
University of Missouri, St. Louis

See Also: Charter Schools; Funding of Schools; No Child Left Behind; Poverty and Education; Standardized Testing.

Further Readings

Anyon, Jean. *Ghetto Schooling: A Political Economy of Urban Educational Reform.* New York: Teachers College Press, 1997.

Anyon, Jean. *Radical Possibilities: Public Policy, Urban Education, and a New Social Movement.* New York: Routledge, 2005.

Berliner, David C. and Bruce J. Biddle. *The Manufactured Crisis: Myths, Fraud, and the Attack on America's Public Schools.* Reading, MA: Addison-Wesley, 1995.

Downey, Douglas B., Paul T. vonHippel, and Melanie Hughes. "Are Failing Schools Really Failing? Using Seasonal Comparison to Evaluate School Effectiveness." *Sociology of Education*, v.81 (2008).

Fusarelli, Lance. "School Reform in a Vacuum: Demographic Change, Social Policy and the Future of Children." *Peabody Journal of Education*, v.86/3 (2011).

Haberman, Martin. "Who Benefits From Failing Urban Schools: An Essay." *Theory Into Practice*, v.46/3 (2009).

Lubiensksi, Christopher, C. Crane, and S. T. Lubienski. "What Do We Know About School Effectiveness? Academic Gains in Public and Private Schools." *Phi Delta Kappan*, v.89/9 (2008).

Usher, Alexandra. *AYP Results for 2010–11.* Washington, DC: Center on Education Policy, 2011. http://www .cep-dc.org/displayDocument.cfm?DocumentID=386 (Accessed May 2012).

Wilson, William Julius. *When Work Disappears: The World of the New Urban Poor.* New York: Knopf/Random House, 1996.

Family Structure and Education

Traditionally, a family is a group of people living together with some shared kinship (such as common ancestors or descendents), marriage, or adoption. However, societies are increasingly accepting variations in which people care for one another, share resources (e.g., food) and divide responsibilities (e.g., household chores) without any kinship ties (e.g., childless and unmarried couples). Families with kinship ties across generations reproduce society via procreation and socialization of children, with the aid of legal, social, and/or religious recognition of family members' rights and obligations.

The predominant family structures in developed countries are nuclear families, couples without children, and single parents with children. Other important contributors to family structures include extended family members and siblings. Two-parent families constituted the majority of households in past decades in most countries, but their numbers are falling (below 50 percent in the United States in 2010). Nuclear families, consisting of two parents and their children, only comprise 23 percent of all U.S. households. Among two-parent households, half include at least one divorced parent who remarried (blended families), and a traditional nuclear family in which the father is the sole income earner is uncommon (30 percent). Three generation households with grandparents are rare (1 percent). Moreover, many two-parent households do not include children. Birth control, slow economic growth, and less interest in having children have sharply increased the proportion of married couples without children (26 percent). A substantial proportion does not plan to have children (23 percent). Furthermore, many couples cohabit before marriage, instead of marriage, or because same-sex marriage is not recognized (7 percent, of which 80 percent were heterosexual).

Many marriages end in divorce. The greater prevalence of working women, women's increasing years of schooling, and voluntary divorce ("no-fault" divorce laws) drove the divorce rate within the first 25 years of marriage to 45 percent in 2010. Younger couples, poorer couples, black couples, or same sex couples (especially lesbians) are more likely to divorce than other couples. After parents divorce, their children typically live with one parent (single-parent households comprised 8 percent of all households, of whom 80 percent were headed by single, female parents). Children living with single parents are also rising around the world (15 percent in Organisation of Economic Co-operation and Development [OECD] countries). Black children are especially likely to live with a single parent (72 percent). Single-parent households are typically poorer than two-parent households (27 versus 6 percent below poverty level, respectively). Of these single parents, 23 percent are separated (more than 70 percent of them eventually divorce), 38 percent are divorced, 34 percent never married, and less than 5 percent are widowed. Furthermore, divorced single parents are typically more educated and richer than never-married single parents (85 versus 67 percent high school graduates; 80 versus 65 percent above poverty level, respectively). Hence, extended family members such as grandparents often live with single parents, share resources, and help raise their children (in 11 percent of single-parent households), which reduces their likelihood of falling below the poverty level (20 percent, rather than 75 percent).

Other households have no parents and are headed by extended family members such as grandparents (8 percent). As some parents cannot care for their children, over 4 percent of children live with their grandparent(s), aunt, uncle, or older relative. Less than 1 percent of children live with no adult, though that number rises to 3 percent for 15-year-olds in OECD countries (most live with friends and only a few live alone). (The remaining 27 percent of U.S. households were single adults.) Many of these children do not have siblings, unlike families around the globe 100 years ago. The number of children per family has steadily fallen in the United States and worldwide. In the United States in 2010, families averaged 0.91 children under the age of 18. In short, the traditional, nuclear family is no longer the norm. Instead, it is being replaced by a variety of family structures, such as single parents, blended families, same-sex couples, and mixed households with extended family members.

Impact of Family Structure on Children

Family structure affects children through the degree to which family members provide resources or compete for them. Family members who provide additional resources for a child (e.g., most parents) tend to enhance his or her socialization (as a resource provider). In contrast, family members who primarily compete with a child for family resources (e.g., younger siblings) reduce their access to family resources and tend to hinder his or her socialization (resource dilution). Families with more adults (parents, aunts, uncles, and grandparents) often have more capital that they can share with their children to facilitate their socialization. For example, families with two parents typically have more time to share with their children, especially compared to single-parent families who often work longer hours to pay for basic necessities.

Among children who live with single mothers, sons are more likely than daughters to be visited by their fathers, and to benefit from their time and resources. In general, families that spend more time with their children tend to communicate with one another better, trust one another more, and feel greater solidarity. Two-parent families not only have a numerical advantage over other families with fewer parents, but also often have qualitative advantages. People who are more educated, earn higher incomes, or have higher social status (socioeconomic status, or SES) are more likely than others to attract mates and to be married (or remarried). Hence, each spouse in a two-parent family typically has higher SES than a single parent (especially never-married parents). Families with more adults (especially parents or guardians) tend to have more wealth (financial capital), education (human capital), social network resources (social capital) and knowledge of dominant culture and society (cultural capital). For example, families with more capital can support their children's academic achievement through greater quantity and higher quality of each type of capital.

Adult family members provide financial capital in the form of education resources (such as books, computers, and art supplies). Families with more parents typically have more financial capital to buy educational resources, create a richer learning environment, and give their children more learning opportunities, on which children can capitalize to learn more. Buying proportionately more resources that are educational also highlights stronger parental commitment to their children's learning, implicitly suggesting further social rewards and incentives for higher achievement. Furthermore, noneducational resources, such as expensive clothes, serve as status symbols that can enhance children's status among their peers. Children with higher peer status tend to have more friends and have positive attitudes about school. Families with

more adults also have more human capital to create conducive physical environments and engage in supportive conversations to help socialize children into society. In particular, families with highly educated parents tend to appreciate and buy (or make) higher quality physical resources, such as rooms for quiet study and age-appropriate books for children. By doing so, they create stimulating yet reflective learning environments. Parents with more human capital also create suitable reward and discipline structures to foster compassionate, social interactions; diligent, academic study; and joyful, creative expression. For example, these families are more likely to encourage children to consider how other people's preferences and perspectives differ. They are also more likely to discuss why some behaviors were unacceptable after age-appropriate time for reflection (time-outs).

Socializing Children

Families with more human capital can help socialize children through both education-specific activities and general activities. For example, a parent might talk with a child about homework, recent political events, and books. They can also chat during dinner, tell one another stories, play games, wash dishes together, or generally spend time together. Through these interactions, family members can serve as role models, ask provoking questions, or give detailed explanations, all of which can help children learn linguistic, cognitive, behavioral, and social skills. Highly educated family members, especially parents, can monitor and supervise children more actively and have more information and skills to teach them. Family members' conversations with children also affect their development of specific role-taking, problem solving, and organization skills (metacognitive skills).

During dinner conversations, for example, children can learn other family members' perspectives and engage in critical thinking about family members' concerns. Children can also learn to organize and shift among many dinner activities—asking for, serving, and eating food, planning family activities, and following societal norms of pleasant conversations. Much communication occurs in the form of individual or jointly constructed stories, precursors to reading literacy. These stories and other conversations help children develop language skills and enrich their vocabulary. By engaging in these activities, children develop enhanced cognitive capacities that can help them approach intellectual matters in a more reflective, open, considered, and sustained way, thereby improving their academic performance.

Family members can also create organizational structures and routines to help children develop self-regulation skills. For example, family members can help children develop productive routines and habits with carefully placed posters, such as a bathroom door poster of a toothbrush to remind children to brush their teeth before going to bed. Furthermore, standardized procedures for resolving disputes, such listening to each person's narrative of a contested incident and asking information questions, can help children develop self-regulation skills and discipline to behave properly with both family members and non-family members. Families with more parents typically have more opportunities to interact with children and to enhance their development of social capital.

Family communication helps children develop linguistic skills, including discourse skills that help children communicate with both their peers and teachers. Children with more effective communication skills are more liked and more accepted by their peer group, resulting in a larger network of friends and acquaintances (social capital). Families with more adults often have larger and richer social networks of family, friends, and acquaintances. Likewise, families with two parents tend to be more educated than families with one parent, and as a result, they tend to have social networks with highly skilled or educated people who can offer more and complementary material, human, social, and cultural capital for raising children. Furthermore, children can connect with their family members' networks to further add to their social capital.

Families with more parents typically have more cultural possessions, cultural experiences, and cultural knowledge (cultural capital). As a result, they can give their children more opportunities to learn cultural knowledge, skills, and values to help them fit into the culture of their family, school, and local community. Cultural possessions at home (such as paintings and poetry) can exemplify the importance of one's culture and facilitate family communication about cultural values and norms. During cultural conversations, family members can model appropriate cultural behaviors and explain cultural norms to help their children learn the cultural values of their family, school, and society. Specifically, these cultural conversations can help children better understand teachers' and classmates' expectations in school so

that they can behave appropriately and build better relationships with them. By doing so, families can help children understand and adapt to other people's expectations of them. Combined with their cognitive skills, metacognitive skills and social skills, children's adaptation to others' expectations helps them build friendships more easily, thereby facilitating their use of social and cultural capital. Supported by teachers and other children, these children with more cultural capital might receive more learning opportunities, be more motivated, learn more, and be more successful in school.

Family Members Competing for Resources

Siblings, separated parents, and extended family members can compete for family resources (resource dilution), thereby reducing children's access to family resources and hindering their socialization. As siblings share parent attention and resources, each sibling receives fewer resources, so children with more siblings have lower academic achievement. Birth order also affects sibling competition for family resources. A child competes with older siblings during his or her entire childhood, but a child competes with younger siblings only after they are born. As older siblings are typically stronger and have more knowledge than younger siblings, older siblings can capitalize on these advantages to obtain a larger share of parent attention and family resources. Even when siblings help one another, the sibling giving the help often elaborates and reorganizes his or her knowledge, and thereby learns more than the sibling receiving the help. As older siblings often help younger siblings, older siblings typically benefit more. Hence, children with younger siblings typically have higher academic achievement than children with older siblings.

Children living with a birthparent and a step-parent (blended family) can benefit from three parents' resources (two birthparents and a step-parent), but they often share family resources with step-siblings, half-siblings and the separated birthparent. As children in blended families typically have more siblings (specifically step-siblings and half-siblings) than children in other families, they must compete with more siblings for access to limited resources. Furthermore, parents share more genes and common experiences with their children than with their step-children, so they often give more attention and resources to their children than to their step-children. Thus, a child might receive the fewest resources from a step-parent, with a half-sibling receiving more and a step-sibling receiving the most. Child(ren) in blended families often compete with the separated birthparent for the other birthparent's resources. If divorces are contentious, parents often spend substantial time (e.g., court appearances) and financial resources (e.g., lawyers) on each other, rather than on their children. Furthermore, the stress from conflicts between biological parents and other adults often results in poorer psychological health for all family members and poorer quality time among family members. Hence, children in blended families often have fewer family resources than comparable children living with both birthparents. As a result, children in blended families often have more discipline problems in school, learn less, complete fewer years of schooling, are less likely to enroll in college, and have poorer psychological health than children living with two birthparents.

While extended family members (grandparents, aunts, and uncles) can provide resources for a child, those who are destitute, ill, or poorly educated might compete with a child for family resources. A child's parents might give or lend money to poor relatives, thereby reducing the immediate resources available to the child. Similarly, family members might pay for an ill relative's medical treatment and tend to his or her needs, rather than spending the time or resources on a child. Relatives who are too poor or too ill to live on their own and instead live with the child's family are especially likely to compete for family resources. Poorly educated relatives often lack the academic or cultural knowledge to help children succeed in school. Even worse, poorly educated relatives might have incorrect academic knowledge or out-dated cultural knowledge that competes with parents' or teachers' ideas for attention, which obstructs children's learning. Extended family members who live with their children are generally poorer, less healthy, and less educated. Thus, children who live with extended family members (especially grandparents) typically have lower academic achievement than those who do not live with extended family members.

Differences Across Countries

Family structure effects differ across countries. Family structure effects are generally weaker in countries with substantial family welfare policies or in countries with more collectivist cultural values. Also, family structure has some country-specific effects. Family structure effects were weaker in countries with family welfare policies. These policies can include parental leave, free school lunches for poor children, and universal health care. These policies reduce resource disparities between two-parent families and other families, which reduces family structure differences in student achievement and discipline. Family structure effects are also weaker in countries whose cultural values favor group interests over individual interests (collectivist). In collectivist cultures, extended family members typically live near one another and help with childrearing. Specifically, grandparents, aunts, uncles, and cousins in collectivist societies often attend to children's care and early education, in part because a child's success or failure in school affects the entire family's reputation. Hence, extended family members who live nearby a child typically have a greater impact (positive or negative) on their children's lives (e.g., academic achievement) in collectivist countries, compared to their counterparts in individualistic countries.

As extended family resources dilute the effects of the immediate family structure in collective societies, the link between immediate family structure and academic achievement is weaker (collectivist dilution). Studies in some developing countries show some major differences. In Malaysia, children of divorced mothers are less likely to attend school compared to other children, including those of widowed mothers. However, father absence can also benefit children's schooling, especially that of daughters. In sub-Saharan African countries, for example, a single mother can place her academically able daughters in high quality schools through the help of a relative in her extended family network.

Families can have different possible structures, and these structures can affect children's socialization. The traditional nuclear family with a single, male income earner is uncommon and is no longer common in the United States and many developed countries. A growing number of families consist of single parents, blended families, and households led by extended family members. Families with more adults typically provide more financial, human, social, and cultural capital to help socialize children to behave properly outside the family (especially school) and to achieve academically. However, siblings; separated birth parents; or underprivileged, resident, extended family members can compete for family resources and hinder a child's socialization. These family structure effects differ across countries, according to their family welfare policies and collectivist cultural values.

Ming Ming Chiu
State University of New York, University at Buffalo

See Also: Grandparent's Role in Education; Household Educational Resources; Intergenerational Closure; Sibling Effects in Education; Single-Parent Household Structure and Education.

Further Readings

Bengston, Vern. "Beyond the Nuclear Family." *Journal of Marriage and the Family*, v.63 (2001).

Chiu, Ming Ming. "Families, Economies, Cultures and Science Achievement in 41 Countries." *Journal of Family Psychology*, v.21 (2007).

DeLeire, Thomas and Ariel Kalil. "Single-Parent Multigenerational Family Structure and Adolescent Adjustment." *Demography*, v.39/2 (2002).

Hank, Karsten and Isabella Buber. "Grandparents Caring for Their Grandchildren." *Journal of Family Issues*, v.30/1 (2009).

Horvat, Erin, Elliot Weininger, and Annette Lareau. "From Social Ties to Social Capital." *American Educational Research Journal*, v.40 (2003).

Feeder Patterns/ Catchment Zones

The term *feeder patterns* refers to the processes of transition between levels of schooling—for example, from elementary school to middle school and from middle school to high school. Catchment zones are the bounded geographical areas used to determine the distribution of students among schools—in the United States, neighborhoods serve as the most common geographic unit. Where and with whom students go to school is largely determined by these related structural characteristics. Student assignment and school composition are related to academic outcomes, such as achievement and attainment. The schools that students attend and the processes that link levels of schooling pertain to issues of educational equity. Students are differentially affected by feeder patterns. Catchment zones figure centrally in the way

students are distributed among schools, but neighborhood-based student assignment has been challenged by judicial mandates for desegregation, and by the ascendancy of school choice policies. Researchers examining social networks and using geographical information systems (GIS) are developing promising intervention strategies.

Catchment Zones and Student Assignment
Public school students in the United States have typically been assigned to schools based upon the neighborhood in which they reside. Local school officials assign students to particular schools by creating formal zones that are designed to be convenient for students and parents while fostering connections between schools and communities. The goals of administrative efficiency and individual convenience are often in conflict. Determining student placement in schools is both a technical problem for administrators and a political problem for communities. Catchment zoning has often reflected and reproduced residential segregation by race and socioeconomic class. Parents with financial means frequently exercise educational choice by deciding where to live, in part based on perceptions of school quality.

Local district authorities may draw the boundaries, but federal courts have been engaged with student assignment for decades through the various court-supervised school desegregation plans that emerged in the wake of the *Brown* decisions. The new student assignment logic of racial integration interfered with the practice of neighborhood catchments and the principle of geographic contiguity. New stakeholders, including parents, courts, and community organizations emerged as key actors in political struggles to determine student assignment policies. With judicial oversight, intradistrict and some interdistrict desegregation programs sprouted across the country. In urban areas, busing programs and magnet schools were two examples of new technologies of student assignment designed to overcome segregation. But catchments remained the primary method to match students with schools.

In recent decades, many urban districts have been declared unitary by the courts, thereby ending court supervision of student assignment plans. The 2007 U.S. Supreme Court decision in *Parents Involved in Community Schools v. Seattle School District #1* further eroded the use of race for student assignment. Some districts have maintained desegregation programs or enacted plans aimed at socioeconomic integration. At the same time, school choice and its free-market logic of student assignment has become a major force in educational policy and research. School choice reform policies, which include open enrollment, magnets, charters, and vouchers, are intended to promote students' mobility across public, charter, and private schools. Many U.S. districts now maintain a portfolio of school options, including traditional neighborhood schools, citywide magnets, and charters. There is no research consensus on the effects of school choice, but significant research indicates that the absence of desegregation policies and the adoption of race-and class-neutral school choice policies contribute to school segregation by race and socioeconomic status, even when residential segregation declines. Further, research indicates that high-achieving students and students whose families have the social and financial resources to exercise choice in the educational market reap most of its benefits.

Public school choice policies still operate within the constraints of districts and catchments. For example, school choice options are sometimes exercised not within an entire metropolitan district, but within a few large catchments that divide a district. Technical advances of GIS modeling have led to sophisticated technical solutions to boundary drawing. While technical improvements do not remove the politics from designing catchments, GIS can produce district catchment maps that mix choice options with feeder patterns. Algorithms can optimize student assignment based on the objectives of a district and various geographic constraints. Contiguity can be embraced by designing catchments that place all students within walking distance of schools while accounting for actual school enrollments, differing grade levels, and placing siblings in the same school. At the same time, maps provide visual tools for decision makers and the public to weigh the possible tradeoffs between neighborhood contiguity and racial or socioeconomic balance.

Feeder Patterns and Transitions

The process of transitioning from one school organization, such as an elementary school, to another, such a middle school or junior high school, can create disruptions, regardless of the specific grade level during which the transition occurs. These transition years often coincide with puberty and other developmental benchmarks that make adolescents particularly

vulnerable to turbulence. Academic declines are evident during transition years and the negative effects can persist for years; the declines observed upon entering middle school can linger long enough to increase the likelihood of school dropout, for example. Declines in self-perception and self-esteem and decreased personal and interpersonal functioning also accompany such transitions. Individual students experience the effects differently. Research indicates, for example, that high-achieving middle-school students academically prosper by attending high school alongside the majority of their classmates, while switching schools benefits the students that did not perform as well. African American and Latino students experience heightened psychological and academic disruptions if the percentages of students from their ethnic groups significantly decrease from middle school to high school. Bridging programs that ease such transitions are a positive intervention for some students. Creating new school governance structures among schools in a feeder pattern that facilitate network building, stabilizing social relationships, and encouraging information sharing among the school staff has shown promise in some urban districts.

Christopher Hamilton
Washington University in St. Louis

See Also: Residential Mobility and Education; School Catchment Zones, Politically Defined School Boundaries; School Choice; School Mobility and Education; Tracking; Transitions, School.

Further Readings

Alspaugh, John W. "Achievement Loss Associated With the Transition to Middle School and High School." *Journal of Educational Research*, v.92/1 (1998).

Benner, A. D. and S. Graham. "The Transition to High School as a Developmental Process Among Multiethnic Urban Youth." *Child Development*, v.80/2 (2009).

Caro, F., T. Shirabe, M. Guignard, and A. Weintraub. "School Redistricting: Embedding GIS Tools with Integer Programming." *Journal of the Operational Research Society*, v.55/8 (2004).

Noreisch, Kathleen. "School Catchment Area Evasion: The Case of Berlin, Germany." *Journal of Education Policy*, v.22/1 (2007).

Parsons, Eddie, Brian Chalkley, and Allan Jones. "School Catchments and Pupil Movements: A Case Study in Parental Choice." *Educational Studies*, v.26/1 (2000).

Schiller, Kathryn S. "Effects of Feeder Patterns on Students' Transition to High School." *Sociology of Education*, v.72/4 (1999).

Sohoni, Deenesh and Salvatore Saporito. "Mapping School Segregation: Using GIS to Explore Racial Segregation Between Schools and Their Corresponding Attendance Areas." *American Journal of Education*, v.115/4 (2009).

Wohlstetter, P., C. L. Malloy, D. Chau, and J. L. Polhemus. "Improving Schools Through Networks: A New Approach to Urban School Reform." *Educational Policy*, v.17/4 (2003).

Feminist Critiques of Educational Practices

Feminists critique how patriarchy and sexism influence educational practices, such as the androcentric curriculum, segregated classrooms, and the historical exclusion of females. Schools socialize students into particular modes of gender and race, as well as promoting heterosexuality and sanctioning homosexuality. Critiques include gendered harassment and violence in educational settings, disparities in occupational status despite educational achievement, and the devaluation of teaching as a profession.

The curriculum of American education is androcentric, meaning that European and American white men provide the lens to understand the world through their limited viewpoint. In addition, men in positions of power present themselves as the source of noteworthy achievements, without acknowledging the significant contributions, labor, and collaboration of women and minorities; in addition, indirect labor, such as managing a household and childrearing, is ignored. Feminists note women's absence in stories or photos and lack of female inventors, artists, political actors, and authors. When women are shown, it is often in select roles, such as assistant; or particular spheres, such as the domestic. Acknowledgement of women's exclusion from the source and production of knowledge contribute to other marginalized groups' push for radical overhaul of the curriculum. Various groups participate in ongoing debates about multiculturalism, Ebonics, health education, and mainstreaming in special education. For example, postcolonialist feminist educators question the validity of

Eurocentric and androcentric grand narratives. The domination and oppression of marginalized groups stems, in part, from teaching and reinforcing these incomplete grand narratives. Another way in which curriculum and content are biased against women is through the use of offensive and derogatory language, such as the terms *spinster* or *school marm*, or that excludes women by using male pronouns and words, such as the terms *mankind* and *firemen*. Classic critiques also point to metaphors used to describe scientific processes and nature that represent females as passive and males as aggressive.

School Organization and Structure

Several classic ethnographies about school culture, interactions between teachers and students, and the organization of bodies and space in the classroom document concrete examples of inequalities and segregation. In *Gender Play*, Barrie Thorne finds that teachers routinely separate boys and girls during contests and classroom exercises, for seating or forming lines, and through language such as "boys and girls." On the playground, the complicated culture of boys' play and girls' play determine the kind and location of play, leading to minimal opportunities for mixed gender activities. Other studies reveal that the higher the proportion of males in the classroom, the less females participate in the conversation.

Traditionally, girls are expected to study subjects such as English literature, foreign languages, and art; while boys are tracked toward science, math, and engineering, which lead to clear cut paths to well-paid, high-status careers. Historically, for women who were supposed to be supported by their husbands, college and advanced degrees were optional or superfluous. Some propose single-sex education as a cure for these problems, while others argue that it abandons the goal of transforming social institutions, does not prepare students to work with the opposite sex, and implies that men cannot change and that women need special treatment. Tracking, the process of sorting students into various levels of schooling, does not only occur along gendered lines.

Many working-class youth, immigrants, and minorities are categorically tracked into low-level courses, leading to low status careers. Recent research highlights that boys, and especially minority boys, are likely to be tracked into special education or vocational training. Feminist critiques about gender parity are germane to other groups of students, who feel disempowered by low expectations and stereotypical assumptions about their interests, abilities, and goals. Issues of equity for all students, including differences in access to advanced level courses, resources between wealthy and poor schools, and the racial and ethnic achievement gap, are ongoing feminist concerns.

School as Socializing Agent: Gender, Class, Race/Ethnicity, and Sexuality

American schools both socialize students into gendered and racialized roles and sort and select students into careers; these socialization functions closely reproduce existing inequalities. Such critiques led to investigations of how complex socialization processes interact with multiple social locations and identities. Appropriate gender roles in society are taught and reinforced in classrooms, lunchrooms, and playgrounds, and through interactions with peers and teachers. Girls are rebuked for behaviors that are seen as masculine, such as being too loud, competitive, or aggressive, and boys are teased or corrected by peers or adults for feminine behaviors such as interests in the arts, being emotional, lacking an adequate display of tough, heterosexual masculinity. Racial and ethnic minority girls and white working-class girls' behaviors are judged using the stereotypical feminine traits attributed to white middle-class girls, who may in some ways benefit from the hidden curriculum that holds them as the standard, whereas all other girls may be viewed negatively by teachers, such as African American girls as too dominant and Latinas as too promiscuous. Male and female minorities, as well as working-class white students, struggle to overcome the cultural boundaries and to negotiate differences in expectations between home, peers, and school. For some, these boundaries are easily crossed, but for others, problems such as white middle-class teachers' lack of cultural fluency and trust, or pressures from friends, can impede educational success.

In the classroom, boys are seen as needing more attention to keep still, while girls' nurturing behaviors and games are easily accommodated. Girls are expected to be polite, raise hands, and take turns, whereas boys are allowed to shout out answers and dominate classroom discussions. In addition, when boys give the wrong answer, they are redirected and pushed until they work out the correct answer, unlike girls, who receive less explicit feedback. Girls are rewarded for good behavior, being quiet, neat, and pretty, helping others, and cleaning up, rather than their academic accomplishments. Eventually, these learned behaviors lead to assumptions about females' natural abilities that lead to underpaid helping careers. Although it varies by race/ethnicity, some girls' self-esteem plummets in middle school, depressing their aspirations, which in turn affects educational outcomes.

In the past, girls who broke boundaries, such as being pregnant and having a baby, could find themselves permanently prohibited from public education. Heterosexual behavior is heavily policed in schools through rejection or isolation of openly gay/lesbian teachers and students. In particular, girls who participate in unconventional female activities, such as science or sports, and boys who participate in activities categorized as feminine, such as theater, are subject to threats about their gender identity and sexuality. Around middle school, close attention to boys' presentation of masculinity results in fear of being labeled "weak," "girlie," or "gay," and can result in bullying and physical harassment about being gay.

Harassment and Violence

The women's movement brought attention to sexist comments by male administrators, teachers, and students, particularly in secondary and postsecondary educational fields where female teachers and students are underrepresented, such as science, engineering, math, and computer science. These may include jokes and insulting comments about women's intelligence, bodies, and sexuality that force women to participate in a state-run and enforced educational system that is a blatant site of discrimination, exclusion, and subordination for women and racial/ethnic minorities. The organizational and social structure of fraternities, other male-only groups, elite organizations, athletics, and sporting facilities are noted examples of male control and exclusion of women.

It is not only verbal abuses, but also the threat or existence of physical violence, harassment, sexual assault, and rape that threaten female endeavors for education and independence from patriarchal family and relationship structures that reinforce women's roles as dependents. Similar patterns of exclusion, segregation, harassment, violence, and reinforcement of heterosexist values are also experienced by lesbian, gay, bisexual, transgender, and queer (LGBTQ) teachers and students, often by peers with tacit approval or consent of adults in authority positions. Abuse and discrimination create hostile school climates and discomfort in the classroom that degrade girls and women, diminish close mentoring relationships with teachers, undermine self-confidence, and skew choices of disciplinary study and occupation.

Educational Outcomes and Opportunity Structure

Currently, boys from all racial and ethnic and racial categories have higher dropout rates than girls; however, African American and Latino males have the highest dropout rates. Male and female minority youth living in impoverished neighborhoods with extreme segregation are likely to have high dropout rates. Inequalities, including fewer opportunities for early learning, lack of high quality curriculum, less access to well-trained teachers, historical and contemporary unequal school funding, and increased standardized testing create a two-tiered American educational system predominantly based on race and class.

As such white, middle-class girls and boys benefit from an educational system that disadvantages minority, working class, and poor girls and boys. Despite girls' great progress catching up to boys' educational achievements, for example in math scores, and surpassing them, for example in GPA and graduation rates, women do not reap commensurate employment and pay returns on their educational investments. In vocational education, girls are tracked into cosmetology, child care, and health aid positions, while boys are pushed toward higher-paying occupations such as plumbing, electrician, and automotive worker. Females attend college at higher rates than males, partly because of males' higher high school dropout rate and because males from working-class families and some ethnic groups may experience more pressure to join the labor force. However, while women have better grades in college and a higher graduation rate than men, there is gender ghettoization into majors that tends to lead to less lucrative jobs for women and better jobs for men.

Teaching as Profession and Educational Hierarchy

Because of the small number of males in positions of administrative power, such as principals and superintendents, and the overwhelming number of females in the rank and file as teachers and aides, schools are referred to as "educational harems." This gendered hierarchy is also evident among teachers based on grade divisions, with more male teachers in secondary and postsecondary positions, and more females in less-prestigious and lower-paid levels, such as daycare, preschool, and elementary education. Gendered stratification is also seen in higher education, where male professors occupy more full-time tenure track jobs and receive tenure more quickly than female counterparts. Teaching is a critical means for upward mobility for women from immigrant, poor, and the working and lower-middle classes.

For some racial and ethnic groups, particularly African American women, it is also a form of social activism and racial uplift. In comparison to other Western industrialized countries, the profession of teaching in the United States, which generally requires a high level of education and continual training, is undervalued and underpaid. Reasons for this include the predominance of women in educational fields, the association with care work, and the belief that, much like childrearing, the rewards should be intrinsic, rather than through pay and status. The resistance to framing this historically female occupation as a profession is linked to rhetoric such as: "those who can't do, teach" and "anyone can teach."

Caitlin Killian
Susan Rakosi Rosenbloom
Drew University

See Also: Gender Inequality: College Enrollment and Completion; Gender Inequality: College Major; Gender Inequality: High School Dropout Rates; Gender Inequality: Mathematics; Gender Inequality: Occupational Segregation of Teachers; Gender Inequality: Returns to Educational Investments; Gender Theories in Education.

Further Readings

DiGeorgio-Lutz, JoAnn, ed. *Women in Higher Education: Empowering Change.* Westport, CT: Praeger, 2002.

Pascoe, C. J. *"Dude, You're a Fag": Masculinity and Sexuality in High School.* Berkeley: University of California Press, 2007.

Sadker, Myra and David Sadker. *Failing at Fairness: How America's Schools Cheat Girls.* New York: Simon & Schuster, 1994.

Thorne, Barrie. *Gender Play: Girls and Boys in School.* New Bunswick, NJ: Rutgers University Press, 1993.

Weis, Lois and Michelle Fine, eds. *Beyond Silenced Voices: Class, Race, and Gender in United States Schools.* Albany: State University of New York Press, 1993.

Feminist Critiques of Educational Research

In many ways, feminist critiques of educational research embody feminist critiques of social science research developed during the women's movement of the 1960s and 1970s. A central idea is that much of what passes as "objective" scientific research can be categorized as "subjective" in the sense that it is patriarchal, androcentric, and ignores the experiences of people of color and/or the working class. Research projects that primarily investigate middle-class, white males and use biased assumptions based on a limited and singular viewpoint of a predominantly male perspective of the world are problematized for legitimizing and maintaining existing gender inequalities, exploitation, and oppression. The "malestream" perspective is usually framed as objective and used as the standard to which females, racial and ethnic minorities, and immigrants are then compared. Feminist critiques of these questionable theoretical assumptions undergirding much research have led to new modes of relational, participatory, and action research methods in education that question sampling, generalizeability, purpose of research, and attainability of objective knowledge. Using historical and cross-cultural comparisons, feminist researchers question how and why negligible variations in biological makeup are used to legitimize inequalities that can be and have been significantly reduced when changes in institutional, structural, and cultural choices are implemented.

History of Feminist Critiques

Feminists critique deterministic biological assumptions about innate differences between the sexes, especially when they are used as evidence of women's inferior intellectual capacity in comparison to men's. In the late 19th and early 20th centuries, male authority figures made statements that women's bodies, and often specifically their reproductive organs, made them unfit for a range of higher order thinking and therefore incapable of learning, research, and higher education. These claims were not backed by rigorous research and demonstrated skewed interpretations that became key points of contention for researchers and the women's movement. By the latter part of the 20th century, biological statements that women's and men's intellectual strengths and weaknesses differed were largely made on the basis of brain and educational testing research conducted by biologists, neurologists, and psychologists. Research arguing that girls are better suited to languages and art and boys to math and science is disputed by feminists on several grounds. Girls' scores in math vary in different countries; for example, in countries as diverse as Singapore and Israel, girls outscore boys on math tests, and in the United States, girls' math scores have improved almost to the point of parity. The former president of Harvard's comments about natural gender differences in math and science aptitude caused outrage, and were also disputed on the grounds that women in academia are disadvantaged by social constraints, such as family care responsibilities, and must work harder than men to prove themselves before reaching tenure and being promoted. The majority of feminists posit that institutional, cultural, and social factors, rather than biology, lead to visible differences in female and male academic interests and achievements, and can therefore be ameliorated over time through improved learning opportunities for girls and women. The same opportunity gap argument is used to refute claims about the purported intellectual inferiority of historically colonized groups or people of color.

Feminists' critiques of androcentric research launched re-evaluation of extant research and theory that questioned the core foundations of the research process, such as the purpose and use of research, power inequalities between researcher and participant, research design, and the interpretation of data. At a basic level, this paradigm shift questions the gender and racial composition of research teams, as well as using all male, white, middle-class samples to then generalize to a larger population; this limited sample potentially produces weak and inaccurate results because it excludes many groups, such as racial/ethnic minorities and students from various class backgrounds. Educational research is now more self-consciously aware, and there is much agreement that sound qualitative and quantitative research requires diverse samples of students, and that without sample diversity, the goal of generalizeability is problematic. On a more theoretical level, some feminist educational researchers question the attainability or necessity of generalizeability. Instead, some utilize nongeneralizable research methods, such as case studies, commonly used for teaching purposes in schools of education. Ongoing debates question if particular research methods and designs are feminist or result in feminist research, and if studying boys and girls as separate categories reifies a hierarchy based on false dichotomies (also known as essentialism). Some argue that feminism is a perspective or viewpoint and does not imply a particular research methodology.

Educational Research Critiques

One of the first and most influential critiques of educational research was made by Carol Gilligan's *In a Different Voice*, which served as a catalyst for many future feminist critiques of research. In this groundbreaking work, Gilligan refuted Lawrence Kohlberg's well-established model of the development of children's moral reasoning because the male sample used to create the initial hierarchy of reasoning scale not only excluded girls, but also devalued girls' ways of knowing. When girls were tested for moral reasoning, they consistently scored lower than boys, appearing as if they had lower moral reasoning skills. According to Kohlberg's model, higher scores were given to the ways in which boys tended to make moral decisions using abstract reasoning, such as following the letter of the law. In contrast, Gilligan found that girls made moral decisions based on relationships and obligations to other people, thus relying on an ethic of care. Gilligan's critique launched a feminist rethinking of many core assumptions used to produce research that claimed scientific objectivity and that also functioned to support commonly held beliefs that women are less capable of intellectual pursuits.

Gilligan's research also proposed and popularized new ideas about a key component of the research process—the relationship between the researcher and the participant as they share their stories, thoughts, and experiences. The feminist "relational" model of research emphasized the passionate subjectivity of this interaction as opposed to the tone of detached objectivity prevalent in "malestream" research. Some feminist researchers argue that because women work more collaboratively and the research process is inherently unequal, research design should seek to equalize power and knowledge differentials between the researcher and the subject by rejecting traditional research roles. The concept of "giving voice" to the research participant means using several kinds of research techniques to hear the complexities, contradictions, emotions, and reality of the participant's world; this methodology is particularly geared toward exploring the worlds of oppressed groups or those with minimal access to power. In developing standpoint theory, Dorothy E. Smith asserted that research

questions should emanate from women's personal experiences, rather than from a lacuna in the existing body of research. As such, the research question leads to an investigation of the ways a personal experience is socially, politically, economically, and culturally organized. In educational research, the ideas of relational research, giving voice, and standpoint theory have produced in-depth qualitative, longitudinal studies that are particularly useful for developing new research questions and challenging widely shared theoretical assumptions about girls and students of color.

Feminist research, conceptualized as a shared endeavor that includes the participant in all or many aspects of research design and interpretation, resulted in particular methodologies, such as Youth Participant Action Research (YPAR). Participatory methods acknowledge youths' exclusion from the process that produces knowledge about them by teaching research skills such as designing and participating in the research process, investigating self-defined problems, and developing plans to ameliorate them. In educational research, this might include teaching students how to do research, asking students to define research questions, or using students to interpret data. Students might be taught how to do an oral history interview as a way of understanding history or a particular person's relationship to historical events. The student learns to not only do research, but also to contribute to the body of research knowledge.

Action research begins with the assumption that research and policy will not produce social change without an emphasis on political action or transformation of a sexist and racist social order. Instead of research that is narrowly disseminated in professional circles, feminist researchers use their power to raise the consciousness of those in positions to change the situation. Schools are key sites for challenging the artificial boundaries between research and action and/or basic and applied research by allowing researchers to become deeply involved in the use of data to influence education. A progressive trend is to train and conceptualize teachers as researchers who then perform research to improve the process of teaching and learning. Feminist action researchers in education build collaborative relationships with teachers, administrators, students, and parents to share their findings and become involved in the implementation of change. Action research in education has been used to build stronger parent and school connections, to investigate environmental problems in schools, and to create innovative schools whose missions are directly influenced by researcher input.

Susan Rakosi Rosenbloom
Caitlin Killian
Drew University

See Also: Feminist Critiques of Educational Practices; Gender Inequality: Mathematics; Gender Inequality: Returns to Educational Investments; Gender Theories in Education; Racism in Education.

Further Readings

Gilligan, Carol. *In a Different Voice*. Cambridge, MA: Harvard University Press, 1982.

Harding, Sandra. *Feminism and Methodology*. Bloomington: Indiana University Press, 1988.

Reinharz, Shulamit. *Feminist Methods in Social Research*, Oxford: Oxford University Press, 1992.

Feminist Research Methodology

Feminist research methodology seeks to challenge hegemonic and positivist paradigms toward thinking and research. Unlike typical scientific inquiry, feminist research methods incorporate participants' voices and lived experiences to illuminate the heterogeneity within social groups. Fieldwork, ethnography, case studies, interviews, and narratives are utilized to develop a cohesive story that is connected to larger social issues. This commitment to documenting within group differences, diversity, and the value of research to promoting social activism and change can highlight the complexities within the field of education. Within academia, traditional scientific inquiry has been defined by research that was objective and quantifiable. The researcher theorized, studied, analyzed, and described the phenomenon that was the focal point of the project. Little to no interaction occurred between the researcher and the subject(s) and the subject(s)'s opinions and voices are largely omitted from the study to maintain objectivity.

During this time, the majority of research conducted (and published) was largely focused on men, with little attention given to women and other subordinated social groups (i.e., people of color, the working class, or working-poor communities). The emergence of the feminist movement during the 1960s and 1970s was the impetus in rethinking the traditional research process. Feminist researchers believed that these boundaries often led to "one-sided" interpretations of data. They rejected traditional hegemonic thinking and practices that defined scientific research, in search of creating a paradigm where identity, difference, and power were central to the analysis.

Feminist Frameworks

Feminist research methodology incorporates three overall frameworks: feminist empiricism, feminist standpoint theory, and feminist postmodernism. Feminist empiricism examines the overall research design to diminish gender biases that might exist. For example, research questions are examined for sexist language, research samples are analyzed to prevent homogenized results, and conclusions are drawn largely from the methods used (i.e., the voices of the participants). In feminist standpoint theory, researchers acknowledge how different standpoints (i.e., social groups) structure a person's reality and actively engage those involved in the research to examine their standpoints and how these may impact the data. Feminist postmodernism centers on the use of qualitative methodology in conducting research as a way to capture data that is often omitted in statistical analyses. Combined, these frameworks led to the emergence of feminist research methodologies.

Moving away from the positivist thinking that dominated research, feminist researchers began to interrogate the dichotomies within their work. The work of Sandra Harding, Patti Lather, and Shulamit Reinharz was influential in calling attention to the notion of the object as subject, the emotional being rational, the abstract as concrete forms of knowledge, and the use of qualitative methods over quantitative design. In addition, feminist researchers recognized their subjectivity by acknowledging their different social group memberships, how these positions create opportunities of both power and privilege, and how these memberships (such as being the researcher) can create unequal power dynamics within the research process. Unlike traditional paradigms, doing feminist research meant an explicit commitment to the role of gender and eliminating the sexist bias that existed within research. Moreover, Harding, Lather, and Reinharz (as well as others) believed that it was important for researchers to write "ourselves into the analysis" to illuminate these differences to readers. Transparency in research, incorporating the lived experiences of the subject, and acknowledging one's positionality came to define feminist research methods within the academy.

Defining Feminist Research Methods

There are four major themes within a feminist methodological framework: challenging traditional scientific inquiry, interest in diversity, a consideration of power within the research design, and recognition of gender. Researchers who employ a feminist methodology seek to challenge traditional scientific inquiry, where the researcher and the participant are seen as separate entities. Rather, a feminist researcher often rejects this paradigm by developing strong interpersonal relationships with the subject. According to Patti Lather, these relationships are vital in transitioning the research process from a positivist to a feminist paradigm. In addition, the researcher utilizes mixed methods that include both quantitative and qualitative analyses because of the inherent biases that can be derived from quantitative measures. For example, feminist researchers often incorporate a variety of methods, such as listening to participants through interviews, observing behavior, and examining historical records to capture the overall phenomenon. The emphasis on developing fieldwork relationships between participant and researcher is critical in conducting feminist research.

Second, a feminist researcher is invested in integrating a diversity of experiences and voices within their study. They believe that it is essential to challenge specific categories (i.e., women) and explore the diversity within these social groups. Integrating a diversity of experiences means that the researcher must acknowledge how these group memberships shape individual experiences and how these experiences might manifest in the research. By utilizing personal testimonies and negotiating the tensions between interpretation and experience, it is the goal of the feminist researcher to foster an environment where participants feel that they are included, rather than simply studied. Moreover, the researcher finds value in focusing on issues faced by particular social groups (i.e., effects of poverty on single mothers) and seeks to affirm their experiences through research.

In the third theme, feminist researchers recognize the hierarchical power relationships that exist within the overall research paradigm. Specifically, the researcher is aware of the power inequities that exist between themselves and the participant and attempts to minimize these to facilitate trust and disclosure. For example, feminist researchers understand that they are neither neutral nor objective in their research, and are aware of how these can be reflected in their interpretation and analysis of data. Shulamit Reinharz refers to this as "reflexive." Reflexivity means that the researcher acknowledges how their lived experiences and social group memberships come to shape how they interpret the data, and how their positionality might affect their relationship with the subject. To resolve these issues, researchers often utilize reflexive techniques, where they assess themselves and ask their participants to evaluate the overall research process. These evaluations are then used to maintain open lines of communication between the researcher/participant and to empower the participants, so that they view themselves as not subjects, but actual members of the research process. Patti Lather also felt that researchers should disclose their histories, values, and assumptions in their writing to further decrease the notion that researchers are neutral observers.

Fourth, feminist researchers recognize the significance of gender (and other subordinate social groups) as a category that should be considered when conducting research. Employing a feminist research methodology means an awareness of how social categories are socially constructed and the importance of recognizing this throughout the research process to minimize essentialist conclusions. The work of Sandra Harding was paramount in redefining who was thought to be an "ideal" subject. Rather than focusing on the differences between men and women, Harding (as well as others) called attention to the need to acknowledge the heterogeneity that exists within these groups and discuss these differences when analyzing the data. Understanding that gender is socially constructed and that these multiple conceptions of gender can transform how the researcher interprets data are essential in feminist research.

Feminist research is committed to reducing the potential "harm" and "control" that exists within traditional scientific methodology. Unlike positivist methods, feminist research methodology promotes social activism and social change by centering the participants' experiences (in this case, women) within research and using their findings to illustrate the value that research can have on improving women's lives.

Feminist researchers seek to utilize methodologies that are participatory in nature, incorporate involvement in research, and can lead to potential action.

Critiques and Implications for Disciplines

Employing feminist research methods is not without faults. Critics of this methodology believe that the interpersonal relationships and qualitative analyses that are the cornerstone of feminist values can lead to multiple interpretations of data, where not one single truth can be proven statistically significant. However, this is not the goal of feminist researchers. Value is placed on the context in which the data are collected and how this context affects the experiences of its participants. Overall, a feminist research methodology is defined by its rejection of neutrality in favor of engaged research that uses a multiplicity of methods to capture the lived experiences of social groups that have been omitted from traditional research.

Janelle M. Silva
University of Washington, Bothell

See Also: Ethnography; Feminist Critiques of Educational Practices; Feminist Critiques of Educational Research; Qualitative Research on Education.

Further Readings

Harding, Sandra. *The Feminist Standpoint Theory Reader: Intellectual and Political Controversies.* New York: Routledge, 2004.

Lather, Patti. "Critical Frames in Educational Research: Feminist and Post-Structural Perspectives." *Theory Into Practice*, v.31 (1992).

Naples, Nancy. *Feminism and Method: Ethnography, Discourse Analysis, and Activist Research.* New York: Routledge, 2003.

Worell, Judith. "Opening Doors to Feminist Research." *Psychology of Women Quarterly*, v.20 (1996).

Field Trips

Field trips are quintessential educational experiences. Though there is no explicit conceptualization of field trips in the literature, they can be broadly defined as educational experiences that involve leaving the classroom to engage in activities related to learning. Also known as instructional trips, field trips include traditional visits to institutions like museums or parks away from school grounds, virtual trips that connect students to people and places through digital media, and nontraditional excursions to noninstitutional sites that may be close to or part of school grounds. The purposes of field trips most often include familiarization with and appreciation for students' communities, as well as the construction of new knowledge. Activities during these trips may be structured or unstructured, hands-on or experience-based. The theoretical foundations of field trips can be traced back to John Dewey's argument that education is derived from experiences. Because not all experiences are necessarily educative, a primary analytic focus of field trip research is to examine an experience in relation to its cognitive learning outcomes. The relationship of enjoyment to field trip learning and the connection to affective experiences with students' memories are also intertwined with attempts to articulate the nature of educative field trip experiences.

Current research also frames field trips as processes through which to probe constructivist theories of learning. How activities are understood, resisted, contested, and reconstructed by students in museums, for example, helps explain the process by which students make sense of the surroundings in which they are immersed. Constructivists have highlighted how field trips can change students' perspectives of topics and challenge previous learning; for example, tour guides may reveal the relationship of colonial powers and indigenous nations on a visit to a historic early American fort. Students also tend to be organized into small groups while on field trips in ways that highlight the dynamics of collaborative learning. Researchers grounding their work in critical theory point to the ways in which field trips may serve as a mechanism through which state standards and official knowledge are diffused and/or contested. Particularly in the United States, there is a strong trend for many traditional field trip sites to explicitly link their exhibits to and design activities around standardized curriculum and testing.

As schools become increasingly anachronistic in their preparation of students for high-stakes standardized exams, nonschool institutions like museums often have wider opportunities to engage students in hands-on and experiential learning. That the novelty of these visits is so different from everyday school life, however, can be both distracting and absorbing. Improved planning and communication of expectations between teachers and on-site staff are imperative ways to enhance traditional field trip site visits, yet is often inconsistent or incomplete. Funding cuts both to schools and to cultural institutions represent a significant challenge for educators.

Virtual field trips represent a wide variety of platforms, including video conference calls, online interactive learning modules, and live broadcasts from a site location. Frequently, institutions that offer real world field trips design and support these services. Virtual field trip formats can help alleviate financial concerns, allowing students to "visit" faraway places and people. These opportunities, however, depend on districts with the appropriate technologies and teachers who know how to use those resources. Some research finds these visits should not supplant traditional, real world field trips and work better as supplementary resources for students.

Local neighborhood visits or innovative use of the school's facilities take little time to reach and little money to visit. Greater accessibility permits multiple visits, which can allow students to better know a place and to mitigate any distractions instigated by traditional trips' novelty. Few prepared curriculum materials and no teacher support staff, however, may discourage some educators from using the local community as a field trip site. These types of trips are often classifiable as "place-based education," a growing movement that advocates learning experiences reconnecting students with nature. Place-based curriculum tends to be designed around engaging students in solving "real world" (or local) problems and utilizes field work to gather information in local settings.

While the corpus of empirical research focusing on the effects of field trips is slim, there are promising findings that field trip learning yields cognitive and effective benefits. Investigation of specific conditions that stimulate situational interest in particular contexts is almost absent. Studies investigating the impact of field trips are also fairly methodologically limited to pre- and post-assessments, though discourse analyses, participant interviews, and longitudinal studies are beginning to enrich the literature. There is very little work investigating the training of educators to facilitate meaningful field trips. And though these issues have been noticeably absent from past work, researchers are beginning to pay attention to the ways

in which culture, social class, race, and ability level affect students' experiences of field trips.

Sarah A. Robert
State University of New York, University at Buffalo
Katy Swalwell
George Mason University

See Also: Constructivism; Curriculum Standardization; Dewey, John; Informal Fundraising in Schools; Museums; Resource Allocation in Schools; Sociocultural Approaches to Learning and Development.

Further Readings
Cassady, J. C., A. Kozlowski, and M. A. Komman. "Electronic Field Trips as Interactive Learning Events: Promoting Student Learning at a Distance." *Journal of Interactive Learning Research*, v.19/3 (2008).
Davidson, S. K., C. Passmore, and D. Anderson. "Learning on Zoo Field Trips: The Interaction of the Agendas and Practices of Students, Teachers, and Zoo Educators." *Science Education*, v.94/1 (2009).
Eschach, H. "Bridging In-School and Out-of-School Learning: Formal, Non-Formal, and Informal Education." *Journal of Science Education and Technology*, v.16/2 (2007).
Munday, Penny. "Teacher Perceptions of the Role and Value of Excursions in Years 7–10 Geography Education in Victoria, Australia." *International Research in Geographical and Environmental Education*, v.17/2 (2008).
Power, S., C. Taylor, G. Rees, and K. Jones. "Out-of-School Learning: Variations in Provision and Participation in Secondary Schools." *Research Papers in Education*, v.24/4 (2009).
Trofanenko, B. "The Educational Promise of Public History Museum Exhibits." *Theory and Research in Social Education*, v.38/2 (Spring 2010).

Finland

The Republic of Finland is a Nordic country in northern Europe, with an area of 130,596 square miles (338,424 square kilometers), bordering Sweden, Norway, and Russia. Numbering 5.4 million, Finland's residents live mostly in the southwest portion of the country, near the capital city of Helsinki. The national languages of

Finland include both Finnish and Swedish. Approximately 83 percent of the population are Christians. Finland has been a member of the United Nations since 1955, the European Union since 1995, and the euro zone since its launch in 1999. With a 2010 gross domestic product (GDP) of $239.2 billion and growth rate of 3.1 percent, the Finnish economy is largely reliant on exports and manufacturing, specifically in the wood, metal, engineering, telecommunications, and electronics industries. A strong educational system is one of the most important hallmarks of Finnish society.

Finland was part of Sweden from the 12th to 19th centuries, first as a province, and then as a grand duchy. In 1809, Finland became an autonomous grand duchy of Russia, before winning independence on December 6, 1917. The current Finnish Constitution came into effect on March 1, 2000. Finland is a parliamentary republic with universal suffrage at 18 years of age. In addition to its central government, Finland is divided into 336 administrative divisions that are ruled by local municipal governments. These municipalities provide services for their residents through local income taxes and subsidies from the Finnish national government. Finland's workforce of 2.7 million is divided primarily among the following four professions:

1. Public services (33 percent)
2. Commerce (19 percent)
3. Finance and business (13 percent)
4. Industry (17 percent)

Unemployment is around 8 percent, and is addressed largely by vocational training programs designed to respond to labor market demands.

Basic education is a right afforded to Finnish citizens by their national constitution, ensuring that all people have equal opportunities independent of their geographic residence, socioeconomic position, and native language. Education is provided and administered by the Ministry of Education and Culture and financed in part by the national government and in part by municipalities. At all levels, education is heavily subsidized by the government to provide students with free or very low-cost tuition, textbooks, meals, and transportation. Free, voluntary pre-primary education is offered to children beginning at the age of 6, used by most families. Children begin comprehensive school at age 7, and continue for a compulsory nine years. Upon completion of their compulsory schooling, students have the option to pursue general upper

secondary education or vocational education and training (VET). Both options take three years and grant access to higher education at universities, polytechnics, and vocational institutions. The 16 Finnish universities offer higher education in academic and artistic subjects, conferring bachelor's, master's, licentiate, and doctoral degrees. Polytechnics, which were offered on a trial basis in 1991 and made permanent in 1996, are designed to train students in response to specific labor market needs. Universities and polytechnics both offer master's degrees.

Adult education is an important cornerstone of the Finnish educational system. Adults can study for all the same qualifications as youngsters, in institutions prepared to handle the needs of mature and often working learners. Competence-based qualifications allow adults who possess vocational skills, but who have not completed their schooling, to test for the relevant certifications. Liberal adult education to pursue new skills and interests is popular among Finnish adults, regardless of previous educational attainment. Education in Finland is co-financed by the central government (43.5 percent of costs) and municipal authorities (54.7 percent of costs). Special education is provided to children with learning disabilities, using an integrated model. Children from outside Finland can receive free schooling in their native language. All teachers in the Finnish school system have at least a master's degree and entry to the profession is highly competitive. Since 2000, Finnish students have excelled on the Programme for International Student Assessment (PISA), a literacy and numeracy survey created and administered by the Organisation for Economic Co-operation and Development (OECD). Researchers looking to explain this have posited teacher training, the availability of high-quality school experiences for all students, regardless of socioeconomic position, and Finnish cultural attitudes toward the importance of education as possible factors for Finland's success in PISA.

Lila McDowell
University of Oxford

See Also: Adult Education; Norway; Sweden.

Further Readings

Finnish Ministry of Education and Culture. "Education." http://www.minedu.fi/OPM/Koulutus/?lang=en (Accessed December 2011).

Statistics Finland. "Educational Structure of Population." http://www.stat.fi/til/vkour/2010/vkour_2010_2011 -12-02_tie_001_en.html (Accessed December 2011).

Valijarvi, Jouni, et al. *The Finnish Success in PISA – And Some Reasons Behind It: PISA 2000.* Jyvaskyla, Finland: University of Jyvaskyla Institute for Educational Research.

Florida

Florida is the 22nd-largest state in the nation, with a total area of 58,560 square miles. The state of Florida is a peninsula bordered by the Atlantic Ocean on the east and the Gulf of Mexico to the west. Approximately 54,136 square miles of Florida's total area is land, while water comprises 4,424 square miles.

The capital of Florida is located in Tallahassee. The executive branch of the government comprises the governor and cabinet consisting of the attorney general, chief financial officer, and commissioner of agriculture. While the state has a 6 percent sales tax, there is no state income tax in Florida. The state legislature consists of 120 House districts, and 40 Senate districts. Prior to the 2012 redistricting process, Florida had 25 congressional districts. The state is likely to gain two congressional districts because of reapportionment. According to the 2010 census, Florida's population is 18,801,310. A total of 4,002,091 of Florida's residents are under the age of 18, and 4,223,806 of Florida's residents identify as Hispanic or Latino. The demographic composition of Florida by race speaks to the relative diverse population of the state, with 14,109,162 identifying as white; 2,999,862 as African American; and 454,821 as Asian. Over 1 million of the remaining 1,237,465 residents identify as "other" or indicate that two or more census categories would best characterize their racial identity.

While Florida has been inhabited by humans for over 12,000 years, the first permanent European settlement was established by Spain in 1565, on the east coast of the state in what is now St. Augustine. The United States acquired Florida as a territory from Spain in 1821. Florida was admitted to the United States as the 27th state in 1845. In Florida, education reform efforts have historically outpaced national trends. Between 1976 and 1984, the Florida legislature initiated more educational reform than the legislative body of any other state. By 1984, Florida had enacted laws in 16 of the 20 categories recorded in *A Nation at Risk.* Additional legislation enacted during these years implemented performance-based provisions for certification and evaluation of teachers and principals, as well as an individual-level merit pay mandate and a school-level merit pay mandate. Since the 1980s, Florida has continued to lead the nation in several areas of education reform. In the area of school governance, Florida has implemented deregulatory strategies that allow some schools to become charter schools that, via a waiver process, can request exemption from some aspects of state control. In Florida, charter schools, along with the more controversial voucher system, form part of the larger school choice policy framework. While the state has implemented deregulatory strategies, it has also increased the emphasis on performance-based formulas for funding. Such programs as the 1999 Florida A+ Plan allowed Florida policymakers to link school choice and performance-based accountability within the same plan. Florida's A+ Plan, in this instance, predated the federal No Child Left Behind Act of 2001, which also combined choice and accountability.

Florida has 67 counties. Each county has one school district. In Florida, school superintendents may be

Table 1 Elementary and secondary education characteristics

	Florida	U.S. (average)
Total number of schools	4,289	1,988
Total students	2,643,347	970,278
Total teachers	175,609.29	60,766.56
Pupil/teacher ratio	15.05	15.97

Source: U.S. Department of Education, National Center for Education Statistics, Common Core of Data (CCD), 2010–11.

Table 2 Elementary and secondary education finance

	Florida	U.S. (average)
Total revenues	$29,321,189,042	$11,464,385,994
Total expenditures for education	$31,518,715,453	$11,712,033,839
Total current expenditures	$24,224,113,873	$9,938,906,259

Source: U.S. Department of Education, National Center for Education Statistics, Common Core of Data (CCD), "National Public Education Financial Survey," FY08 (2007–08).

elected or appointed. Development research schools operate outside of the county district structure while still within the governance of the state Department of Education. The charter school movement has flourished in Florida, subsequent to the success of the choice initiatives promoted in the 1990s. Students in Florida may also use vouchers to attend private schools. Florida has taken steps to increase virtual education options for K–12 students. Florida recently instituted a voluntary pre-kindergarten program in an effort to address school readiness and improve literacy across the state.

In Florida, voter referendums in the form of constitutional amendments have represented one recent strategy for implementing reforms in education policy. In 2002, for example, two education policy initiatives were presented to the Florida electorate as referendums. One referendum allowed Floridians to pass a constitutional amendment that would require the state to institute universal pre-kindergarten education. Revenue shortfalls in Florida have impacted education policy. For example, the legislative mandate to establish universal pre-kindergarten programs evolved into the implementation of the more fiscally conservative voluntary pre-kindergarten program. On the same ballot, in 2002, Florida voters approved a constitutional amendment to limit class size. To date, economic issues have plagued the implementation of the class size law. Floridians once again addressed class size via ballot referendum in 2010. The will of the people to uphold class size restrictions has created a legal and logistical bind for local school districts that are obligated to follow state law while struggling to balance limited budgets. Policy initiatives, such as the universal pre-kindergarten program and the class size amendment, have exacerbated the ongoing teacher shortage in the state. Florida, in response to the combined impetus of the growing teacher shortage and the federally mandated No Child Left Behind Act of 2001 (NCLB), began to allow school districts to offer a alternative professional preparation and certification programs to bring new teachers into the profession.

Rachel Sutz Pienta
Valdosta State University

See Also: Charter Schools; *Nation at Risk, A*; No Child Left Behind; On-Line Education; School Choice; School Size/Class Size; Teacher Recruitment, Induction, and Retention; Voucher Programs.

Further Readings
Brewer, T. M. "The 'Grand Paradox' in Teacher Preparation and Certification Policy." *Arts Education Policy Review*, v.104/6 (2003).
Chapman, L. H. "No Child Left Behind in Art?" *Art Education*, v.58/1 (2005).
Cohen-Vogel, L. "Integrating Accountability With Choice: Implications for School Governance." *Peabody Journal of Education*, v.78/4 (2003).
Herrington, C. D. and V. Weider. "Equity, Adequacy and Vouchers: Past and Present School Finance Litigation in Florida." *Journal of Education Finance*, v.27/1 (2001).
Watlington, E. J. "Variables Associated With Teacher Retention: A Multi-Year Study." *Teacher Educator*, v.40/1 (2004).

For-Profit Education

For-profit education is the fastest growing sector of U.S. postsecondary education today. The sector includes some smaller, privately owned colleges, as well as larger institutions owned by publicly traded corporations. For-profit institutions are similar to public and private nonprofit colleges and universities with respect to degree offerings, but in contrast to these traditional institutions of higher education, for-profit institutions provide an education while seeking to make a profit for their stockholders and investors. Enrollment in for-profit institutions has increased rapidly since the 1990s, and these colleges and universities award a substantial number of postsecondary certificates and degrees. At the same time, the sector has come under scrutiny for some of its marketing strategies, recruitment practices, and the high rate of loan default among its students.

For-profit education has been around for some time, but traditionally, for-profit institutions were small, local, independently owned colleges, focused mainly on vocational certificate programs in fields such as cosmetology, medical assistance, and truck driving. During the 1990s, the sector expanded rapidly, and publicly traded companies began operating institutions that enrolled large numbers of students. In 1990, there were 322 for-profit institutions that enrolled 213,693 students. By 2000, the sector had grown to 724 institutions, and enrollment had more than doubled, to 450,084 students. A decade later, in 2010, there were 1,310 for-profit colleges and universities that enrolled 2,018,397 students; and three of the five largest postsecondary institutions in the country were for-profit institutions—the University of Phoenix, Kaplan University, and Ashford University. The University of Phoenix was the largest degree-granting postsecondary institution in the country, with an enrollment of 307,965 students.

Of the more than 2 million students enrolled in for-profit institutions in 2010, the majority attended four-year institutions as undergraduates. For-profit institutions attract more nontraditional students, including many women, African American, and Hispanic students, lower-income students, and students over the age of 25. Women enroll in for-profit institutions to an even greater extent than other sectors of higher education—they were 64 percent of students at for-profit colleges and universities in 2010, but were 54 to 57 percent of students in other sectors. Many lower-income students attend for-profit institutions, although on average, for-profit colleges and universities charge relatively high tuition and fees compared to four-year public institutions and community colleges that also attract lower-income students. In 2010 to 2011, the average undergraduate tuition and fees were $13,935 at for-profit institutions, but $2,713 at a community colleges, and $7,605 for in-state students at four-year public institutions.

The overwhelming majority of for-profit students rely on financial aid, including student loans, to cover the cost of tuition. Students at for-profit institutions are more likely to have student loans and borrow more, on average, compared with students in other sectors. From 2009 to 2010, among full-time, first-time undergraduates in four-year institutions, 86 percent of for-profit students had school loans, compared to 50 percent of students at four-year public institutions, and 63 percent of students at four-year private nonprofit institutions. For-profit students borrowed $9,641 in student loans on average. In comparison, students at four-year private nonprofit institutions and public institutions borrowed $7,466 and $6,063, respectively.

On average, for-profit students have lower outcomes (retention and graduation rates) compared with students at public and private nonprofit colleges and universities. For example, the six-year graduation rate for bachelor's degree–seeking students who first enrolled in 2004 was 65 percent at private nonprofit

institutions, 56 percent at public institutions, but just 28 percent at private for-profit institutions. Men had a higher graduation rate than women (30 percent compared to 27 percent) at for-profit institutions. However, the graduation rate for certificate and associate's degree-seeking students enrolled at two-year institutions was highest at for-profit colleges. For students who first enrolled in 2007, the graduation rate (within 150 percent of normal time to certificate/degree) for for-profit students was 60 percent, 51 percent at private nonprofit institutions, and 20 percent at public institutions.

Overall, for-profit institutions have helped increase postsecondary educational attainment. from 2000 to 2010, the number of degrees conferred by for-profit institutions increased at a faster rate than the number of degrees conferred by private nonprofit and public institutions. From 2009 to 2010, for-profit institutions conferred 19 percent of associate's degrees, 5.9 percent of bachelor's degrees, 10.2 percent of master's degrees, and 2.9 percent of doctoral degrees (including first professional degrees). The majority of the degrees were conferred in business, computer, and information sciences, and health professions. Other popular fields were education, homeland security/law enforcement/firefighting, and psychology.

Critiques

The rapid growth and increasing prominence of for-profit colleges and universities is not without controversy, and the sector has come under increased scrutiny from the federal government. An undercover government investigation found evidence that staff at some for-profit institutions encouraged prospective applicants to make false statements on financial aid documents and misled applicants about the cost and duration of programs, as well as the employment and salary opportunities in different occupations.

In 2011, a ban was instituted on incentive compensation for recruiters at for-profit institutions in an attempt to reduce the prevalence of hard-sell recruitment practices. There is also concern about the high levels of student debt and the high default rate among for-profit students. The Department of Education proposed "gainful employment" regulations, which were designed to ensure that students were not borrowing large sums of money to pay for expensive programs that offered credentials with limited value in the labor market. The regulations applied to vocational programs in all sectors, but the for-profit sector lobbied strongly against the new regulations, which were supposed to go into effect July 2012, but were vacated.

Andresse St. Rose
American Association of University Women

See Also: Career and Technical Education; Community Colleges; Funding of Schools; Online Education.

Further Readings

Aud, S., et al. *The Condition of Education 2012.* Washington, DC: U.S. Department of Education, National Center for Education Statistics, 2012.

Berg, Gary A. *Lessons From the Edge: For-Profit and Nontraditional Higher Education in America.* Westport, CT: Praeger, 2005.

Snyder, T. D. and S. A. Dillow. *Digest of Education Statistics 2011.* Washington, DC: National Center for Education Statistics, Institute of Education Sciences, U.S. Department of Education, 2012.

France

France is a republic located in western Europe, with several overseas territories and islands in the Caribbean, Atlantic, Indian, and the Pacific oceans. With an area of 674,843 square kilometers and an estimated 64,876,618 inhabitants (in 2010), it is one of the largest countries in Europe. Service industries (79.5 percent), manufacturing (18.5 percent), and agriculture (2 percent) are the main contributors to its gross domestic product (GDP), which was $2.56 trillion in 2010. According to the World Bank, France's economy is ranked fifth worldwide. France is a founding member of the European Union, and a member of North Atlantic Treaty Organization (NATO). Since 1958, France has been structured according to the constitution of the Fifth Republic as a presidential-parliamentary democracy.

France's history of education has been shaped by several political battles: centralization, several attempts to abolish the monarchy, and the separation of church and state (*Laïcité*, law established in 1905). From the political and republican viewpoint, French public schools have always represented the ideals of democracy and secularism, with compulsory schooling introduced in 1882 during the era of French statesman Jules Ferry (*Loi Ferry*). French statesmen,

for example Cardinal de Richelieu, attempted to unify the country by centralizing its administrative system. France is still a centralized state, and major functions are governed by the Ministries in Paris, including the organization of schooling and education. The historical religious neutrality (*laïcité*) of public schools has led to a strong private school sector, with many Catholic schools accredited by the state.

The French educational system is centralized. The National Ministry of Education governs all major orientations, policies, and curricula across the nation. The French school system is organized in the primary school sector, with the noncompulsory *école maternelle* ("nursery school") for children ages 3 to 6, and the compulsory *école élémentaire* ("elementary school") for children from grades 1 to 5. The secondary school is divided into *collège* (grades 6–9) and *lycée* (grades 10–12). The *lycée* is divided up into different types: *lycée d'enseignement général*, *technologique*, and *professionnel*. The general *lycée* grants access to university. The other *lycées* lead toward occupational/technological and professional degrees. Graduation from *lycée* occurs after the completion of the *Baccalauréat*, a national, centralized exam at the end of grade 12 (*Terminale*). Schooling is compulsory until the age of 16.

France's commitment to the separation of religion and state has often been in the public eye, as its multiethnic population has grown since the end of World War II, with an increasing presence of immigrants of African and Arab descent. Thus, the question of whether girls and young women of Muslim faith should be allowed to wear the hijab ("headscarf") in schools has been an ongoing controversy, which culminated in legislation in 2004, outlawing the ostentatious wearing of religious signs in public schools (*Loi de 2004 sur les signes religieux dans les écoles publiques*). This law, while prohibiting any religious sign, targets the wearing of the hijab by Muslim girls and young women. If the student refuses to take off the hijab, the public school ultimately has the duty to exclude her from school. Lately, France's government has gone even further by banning the wearing of *burqa* and *niqab* from all public spaces. The ongoing controversy reflects France's challenge of recognizing its multicultural and multiethnic populations, as it fails to acknowledge that wearing the hijab cannot automatically be considered a sign of oppression of women. The French republican model follows an assimilationist model of integration of immigrant populations, which also applies to its public schools. Recognition of diversity inside this model is limited.

Concerning the education of children with disabilities, France also has a system of special institutions and classes, which are interwoven between the Ministries of Social Services, Health and of Justice, and Education. The new legislation of 2005, *pour l'égalité des droits et des chances, la participation et la citoyenneté des personnes handicapées* ("for equality of rights, equity, participation and citizenship of disabled persons"), requires that every child with a disability is administratively enrolled in a neighborhood school. Inclusion of children with disabilities into regular schools increased slowly before this legislation, especially after the 1990s, but the law has sparked many debates about where and how to best educate these children by constructing models of mixed schooling between mainstream schools, special classrooms, and special institutions. France's ratification of the UN Convention on the Rights of Persons with Disabilities (2006), which calls for the commitment to inclusion, will strengthen the pledge to develop a more inclusive educational system that recognizes and welcomes diversity.

Cornelia Schneider
Mount Saint-Vincent University

See Also: Elementary Education; Governmental Influences on Education; Secondary Education; Special Education.

Further Readings

Altglas, V. "Laïcité Is What Laïcité Does: Rethinking the French Cult Controversy." *Current Sociology*, v.58/3 (2010).

Lelièvre, C. *Histoire des institutions scolaires (depuis 1789).* Paris: Nathan, 1990.

Plaisance, E. "The Integration of 'Disabled' Children in Ordinary Schools in France: A New Challenge." In *Policy, Experience and Change: Cross-Cultural Reflections on Inclusive Education*, L. Barton and F. Armstrong, eds. Dordrecht, Netherlands: Springer, 2008.

Schneider, C. *Une Étude Comparative de L'éducation Inclusive des Enfants avec Besoins Particuliers en France et en Allemagne: Recherches dans Onze Salles de Classe.* ("A Comparative Study of the Inclusion of Children With Special Needs in Mainstream Schools in France and Germany: Case Studies of Eleven Classrooms.") Lewiston, NY: Edwin Mellen Press, 2011.

Weill, N. "What's in a Scarf? The Debate on Laïcité in France." *French Politics, Culture & Society*, v.24/1 (2006).

Freire, Paulo

Brazilian philosopher and educationalist Paulo Freire (1929–97) is regarded as one of critical pedagogy's most influential theorists. Freire is best known for his book *Pedagogy of the Oppressed*, in which he presents his educational outlook and the key concepts of his theory: *dialogic teaching*, *liberating education*, and *banking concepts in education*. His work still greatly influences educational discourse, research, and practice.

Freire was born in Recife, Pernambuco, in northeast Brazil. Following the Great Depression of 1929, his family was forced to leave Recife. His personal experience of great poverty affected young Paulo's world view. In 1943, he enrolled in the University of Recife, where he studied law, philosophy, and psychology. Freire never worked as a lawyer; instead, he chose to teach Portuguese in high school, and eventually became head of the Pernambuco Department of Education and Culture. In 1958, Freire completed his doctorate in philosophy at the University of Recife, where he also served as professor of philosophy and history of education. After the 1964 coup d'état in Brazil, Freire was arrested and exiled to Bolivia. He moved on to Chile, where he taught illiterate peasants and collaborated with the United Nations Educational, Scientific and Cultural Organization (UNESCO) in adult education programs. The publication of *Pedagogy of the Oppressed* in 1968 (English version, 1970) introduced Freire as a great critical thinker. The book immediately achieved fame, and even canonic status in pedagogical thought, resulting in appointments at the Harvard University School of Education, as well as lectures and consultancies worldwide. Freire returned to Brazil in 1980. In 1986, he was appointed to head the Department of Education in Sao Paulo, where he died in 1997.

Freire's intellectual point of view draws from both Marxist and anticolonialist traditions. His writings are based on his personal experience and with the local community's way of life in the developing world, which he was well acquainted with. According to Freire, living under the domination of economic, social, and political hegemonic power results in ignorance and lethargy.

Individuals from subjugated social groups are incapable of viewing their personal conditions reflectively and critically. Freire called this the "culture of silence" and identified the main role played by the education system to conserve and restore this situation. The main contribution of his work was at the core of his critical pedagogy, namely the connection he drew between the social actions of education and politics. Freire claimed that every educational act is political in nature; the product of ideological perceptions, including what is learned and how it is taught. Education may play two basic roles: it is either used to integrate the young generation into the social order and economic system, or it acts as a tool for human liberation. Freire suggested that the appropriate aim of education should be the liberation of the oppressed and the restoration of their humanity. He sought to adjust the necessity and methods of education to the way the local community lived, within its specific cultural and historical context. He also demanded a modern education, not a continuation of the hegemonic culture.

Freire attacked existing education as a suppressive and hierarchical continuation of the unequal socioeconomic order, comprising an asymmetrical relationship between the knowledgeable teacher and the pupils who lack this knowledge. The liberating education helps students to develop an awareness of the social contexts in which their lives are designed, to discrimination, inequality, and the vulnerable populations exposed to it. The students are to use the knowledge and understanding they have acquired through their life experience and, guided by the teacher, learn to ask questions about reality by inquiring about it and evaluating it accordingly. Some of the questions that can arise from this method deal with the distribution of power in society, the beneficiaries and losers of this socioeconomic structure, and what can be done in order to promote values such as justice and equality.

Freire aspired to eliminate the common dichotomy between teacher and student, creating a more equal situation where the teachers are willing learn and the students have the opportunity to teach. This happens while the teachers maintain their authority, without being authoritarian. Depending on these assumptions, a key concept in Freire's work is "dialogic teaching." The aim of the dialogue is to free oneself from the dominant social structures of thinking. Its essence is the equal discourse established between teacher and students, one based on mutual respect, love, cultural acquaintance,

and hope. This kind of education process assumes that the pupil's knowledge is as important and meaningful as the teacher's. They experience cooperation, decision making, and collaboration in relation to the content and methodology of the educational experience. Through dialog, the teacher learns what is important to his or her students, their standpoints, and opinions. This empowers and encourages both the individual and the group. Not only do individuals learn to recognize their abilities and the meaning of their knowledge, but they also discover that a group with a common awareness and goals has more power to change reality.

Freire strongly believed in people's capability to not only recognize an unjust and oppressive society, but also to learn how to look critically and creatively at the possible active positions that could be taken and the power to make changes for the best. Freire's pedagogy and theory are obliged to raise an awareness that will lead to that change. Though written under different political and historical circumstances, his work has profound implications and relevance for the different challenges confronting 21th century education around the globe.

Yaron Girsh
Hebrew University of Jerusalem

See Also: Adult Education; Banking Concept of Education; Critical Discourse Analysis; Critical Theory of Education.

Further Readings

Freire, Paulo. *Pedagogy of the Oppressed*. New York: Seabury Press, 1970.

McLaren, Peter and Peter Leonard, eds. *Paulo Freire: A Critical Encounter*. New York: Routledge, 1993.

Shor, Ira and Paulo Freire. *A Pedagogy for Liberation: Dialogues on Transforming Education*. South Hadley, MA: Bergin and Garvey, 1987.

Functionalist Theory of Education

Functionalism is a social theory that has been applied to education. Within the functionalist paradigm, society is understood as stable and the components of society in balance with one another. At the core of functionalism are two ideas. First, it is possible to study the social world through scientific methods used in the sciences. A functionalist would expect that objective examination of social phenomena would yield an understanding of the laws of social behavior. The second core belief of functionalism is that society is comprised of interrelated parts that can be understood in terms of the function they serve in the total system. This concept is closely related to the biological understanding of how organisms survive. Each organ serves a vital purpose in the overall health of the organism. Similarly, each system serves a vital purpose in the overall health of society.

Functionalists view individuals and institutions in terms of their contribution to the growth and stability of a society. Institutions are thought to be are constantly interacting and adjusting to maintain equilibrium in the system. According to functionalism, most members of a society share core beliefs and values. Functionalist thinking is rooted in the work of French sociologist Émile Durkheim (1858–1917). Durkheim was one of the first sociologists to use scientific methods to explore the social world. He saw the social sciences as an extension of the natural sciences and believed that the sociological method should be based on the same principals.

Role of Schools Under Functionalist Theory

The functionalist theory of education is a significant perspective in the sociology of education. Some scholars use functionalist theory to explain the role of education in society. The functionalist theory of education focuses on how education serves the needs of society through development of skills, encouraging social cohesion and sorting of students. According to functionalists, the role of schools is to prepare students for participation in the institutions of society. Schools socialize students to be a part of economic, political, and social institutions. They should shape individuals to fit into existing social practices. At the same time, schools teach students how to belong to mainstream society, thus creating a cohesive social structure. In this way, schools play an important role in system maintenance.

In American schools, this involves the transmission of ideas about individualism and competition, for example. In a different context, key values like cooperation and social esteem might be emphasized instead. For functionalists, schooling helps each individual to become a functioning part of the cohesive whole society. Education also provides skills for students to become productive contributors to society. Those who view society from a functionalist perspective believe that different members of society perform different tasks, and that schools should provide equal educational opportunity to develop students' skills and talents to perform these tasks. Given this equal opportunity, a meritocracy emerges, where individuals reap the rewards of their achievements. In this system, individuals are sorted based on merit, and schools offer a means to social mobility through effort. Education provides the basis for the division of labor in society. Schools help identify who will become a doctor and who will become a janitor.

Criticism of Functionalist Theory

A key criticism of functionalist theory is that it does not take into account what happens when a society changes. If there is always a state of equilibrium, then social change is not possible. Critics also point out that functionalist theory supports the status quo, seeing conflict and challenge as harmful to society. These criticisms are rooted in conflict theory, a perspective frequently contrasted with functionalism. Rather than equilibrium, conflict theorists see competition for limited resources in society. Conflict theories are focused on power relations in society. Conflict theorists contend that schools function in the interest of elite groups and produce ideologies that legitimate the status quo and the reproduction of cultural capital for dominant groups. Conflict theorists say that schools prepare students for the jobs corresponding to their social backgrounds, rather than positions matching their skills. Working-class students learn skills, such as following directions, which are related to working-class jobs. At the same time, their middle-class peers work on critical thinking skills and other areas associated with middle-class jobs. In this conflict view, educational attainment represents one's status, instead of skills. Individuals are sorted based on their social status. In both the conflict and functionalist views, education serves to sort students.

The disagreement is on the mechanism for sorting. A functionalist would see students as sorted by merit; conflict theorists believe that students are sorted by their backgrounds. Functionalism is a consensus theory, emphasizing social order and stability. The functionalist paradigm is one lens used to examine education and the role of schooling in societies. According to a functionalist view of education, schools contribute to the stability of societies. Schools provide skills that allow students to become productive members of society. They transmit social norms, strengthening cohesion, and they sort individuals for the labor market based on merit.

Cambria Dodd Russell
Teachers College, Columbia University

See Also: Durkheim, Émile; Human Capital Theory; Sociocultural Approaches to Learning and Development.

Further Readings

Brint, S. *Schools and Societies.* Thousand Oaks, CA: Pine Forge Press, 1998.

Feinberg, W. and J. Soltis. *School and Society.* New York: Teachers College Press, 2009.

Sandovik, A. "Introduction." In *Sociology of Education: A Critical Reader,* A. Sandovik, ed. New York: Routledge, 2007.

Funding of Schools

The primary sociological relevance of K–12 public school funding in the United States lies in its unequal distribution. Understanding the sources of unequal school funding is an issue of concern to the subfields of sociology of education, social stratification (inequality), and political sociology. In addition, school funding is one of the many factors that sociologists of education consider as potentially important social determinants of students' educational outcomes (i.e., achievement and attainment). Both of these matters—the unequal distribution of school funding and its consequences for students' outcomes—are complex, ever-changing, and surrounded by scholarly and political debates. According to the National Center for Education Statistics, public school districts in the United States spent an average of $10,297 per student from 2007 to 2008. Around the average, however, lies tremendous variation in the amount of money that states, school districts, and individual schools within districts receive.

It is this variation, or inequality, that is of primary sociological interest. When sociologists study social inequality, they aim to find out who gets what

and why. School funding is unequally distributed across space and across groups in society as a result of a complicated system involving federal, state, and local governments. Unlike other affluent societies, the United States obtains a sizeable portion of its revenues for public schools from property taxes levied on homes and businesses within each of the roughly 15,000 local school districts across the country. As a result, districts with more valuable homes and businesses tend to receive more locally based revenue than districts with less valuable homes and businesses. This disparity must be considered within the context of spatial locale, social class, and race.

Inequality in School Funding

The contemporary United States is highly segregated by social class and race. In suburban and small-town areas that are home to primarily upper- and middle-class white families and thriving businesses, property values are high and schools are well-funded because of the strong local tax base. In large cities, especially in the deindustrialized Rust Belt that are home to primarily working-class and poor minorities and a declining manufacturing sector, property values are lower and weak local tax bases generate less school funding.

Many remote small-town and rural areas that are home to working-class and poor residents from various racial and ethnic groups similarly struggle to fund schools because of a weak tax base. In his classic, scathing account that contrasted crumbling and underfunded urban and rural schools with modern and well-equipped suburban schools, former teacher-turned-activist Jonathan Kozol described the U.S. school funding system as one of "savage inequalities." Inequalities in locally generated revenues are only part of the school funding equation. School districts' revenues come from a combination of local, state, and federal sources, each of which has an impact on inequality in school funding. From 2007 to 2008, according to the National Center for Education Statistics, 44 percent of all public elementary and secondary education revenues came from local sources; 48 percent came from state sources, and 8 percent came from federal sources.

This breakdown varies from state to state and has changed over time. In some states, there is an equal balance between state and local sources of educational revenue; in some states local sources provide most of the revenue; and in some states most of the revenue comes from the state. In Iowa, 46.5 percent of the revenue comes from the state and 45.9 percent comes from local sources (7.6 percent from the federal government); in Illinois, just 31.2 percent of the revenue comes from the state, while 60.9 percent comes from local sources (7.9 percent federal); in Vermont, 85.9 percent of the revenue comes from the state, and only 7.9 percent comes from local sources (6.3 percent federal).

Between-state variations in the sources of funding stem from the fact that in the U.S. states are responsible for school funding. The U.S. Constitution says little about education, a point that was reiterated in the U.S. Supreme Court's 1973 decision in the case of *San Antonio Independent School District et al. v. Rodriguez et al.* In that case, a group of parents had sued a number of school districts in the San Antonio area, as well as the state of Texas, arguing that the state's school funding method violated the Fourteenth Amendment's Equal Protection Clause. While the parents won in a federal district court in San Antonio, the U.S. Supreme Court reversed the lower court's decision and ruled that relying on local property taxes to fund public schools is not a violation of the Equal Protection Clause. The *Rodriguez* decision essentially established that school funding is up to the states, and not the federal government. Following the *Rodriguez* ruling, many states have lost court battles in which their school funding policies have been ruled unconstitutional for failing to provide all students with an equitable or adequate education.

According to the National Education Access Network, in September 2011, school funding systems had been challenged in court in 44 out of 50 states; only 6 states had not yet seen any school funding litigation. Lawsuits initially tended to seek "equity" in school funding between districts during the 1970s and 1980s, pointing to equal protection clauses in state constitutions. This strategy began to fail during the 1980s, as courts became reluctant to outline solutions to unequal school funding. Beginning around 1990, plaintiffs shifted their aim to achieve "adequate" funding for poorer districts, pointing to sections of state constitutions that guarantee an adequate education. This strategy has been more successful because courts can avoid having to establish equal funding, and instead can focus on which resources are needed in order to provide an adequate education, and whether states are providing all students with those resources.

Partly because of the various court decisions, over time, the percentage of school funding revenue coming from local sources has declined as the percentage coming from state and federal sources have increased. The gradual shift away from local sources and toward state and federal sources reflects the idea that the latter two tend to be more equalizing than the former. Revenue from local property taxes primarily drives inequality in school funding. As states have been ordered to reduce inequality or increase the adequacy in school funding, they have done so by increasing their share of funding—which, by default, reduces the proportion that comes from local sources.

The Education Trust, an organization dedicated to improving the educational opportunities and outcomes of low-income and minority students, has conducted analyses showing how federal, state, and local distributional policies all contribute to inequality in school funding. At the federal level, the government allocates more funds to states that have more poor students and higher levels of per-student spending. By allocating more federal funds to states that already have higher per-student expenditures, the federal government helps widen the funding gaps between states. At the state level, more than half of the states spend less per student in low-income and heavily minority districts than they spend in high-income and predominantly white districts. The overall funding gap between high- and low-income and high- and low-minority districts is roughly $1,000 per student (based on 2004 data).

States' continued reliance on local property taxes for a portion of school funding is seen as a primary culprit for these inequalities. At the district level, evidence is mounting that the distribution of teachers and the allocation of unrestricted funds to schools lead to funding disparities between schools within the same district. Within a district, more affluent schools tend to be staffed by the more experienced, and thus more highly compensated, teachers. Conversely, high-poverty schools are staffed by less-experienced and lower-paid teachers. Since teacher salaries constitute a large portion of districts' expenditures, the unequal distribution of teachers across schools is a leading source of financial disparities within districts.

School Funding and Educational Outcomes

These issues pertain primarily to educational opportunities, but school funding is also relevant when it comes to understanding the social determinants of educational outcomes, such as achievement and attainment. Do well-funded districts or schools produce more academically successful students than poorly funded districts or schools? More simply put, does money matter? On the one hand, a number of studies and meta-analyses have concluded that school expenditures and related resources, such as teacher quality and class size, have little or no impact on students' academic achievement. This view, which traces back to the infamous 1966 Equality of Educational Opportunity report conducted by James Coleman and colleagues for the U.S. government, is part of larger paradigm that views attributes of schools as shaping students' learning to a much lesser degree than attributes of students, their families, and their neighborhoods.

On the other hand, a number of more recent studies and meta-analyses have concluded that school expenditures and related resources do have an impact on students' achievement. This body of work finds not only that more school funding boosts students' achievement, but also aims to delineate the mechanisms through which money matters.

For example, evidence suggests that additional funding boosts students' achievement by affording districts or schools more highly educated teachers, smaller class sizes, and better physical conditions. Speaking to the debate, Karl Alexander, a leading sociologist of education over the past four decades, took the position that money does matter in his 1997 Presidential Address to the Southern Sociological Society. Alexander stated that ". . . this is one area where common sense has it over the so-called experts." Similarly, the documentary film *Children in America's Schools*, based on Jonathan Kozol's book, poses the question of why affluent communities fund their schools at such high levels, if doing so does not help their children succeed academically.

School Funding and Achievement Gaps

Students' family and social class backgrounds shape their educational outcomes in important ways. Children from more advantaged backgrounds have more educational resources, such as books in the home, more highly educated parents communicating with them, helping them with their schoolwork, and organizing their extracurricular activities, and more learning opportunities provided to them during summer vacation. These advantages accrue and

contribute to affluent students' higher levels of educational achievement and attainment relative to their disadvantaged counterparts, regardless of the impact of schools. A number of studies have shown that the socioeconomic achievement gap grows mainly during the summer, when school is not even in session. In light of this evidence, it seems unlikely that unequal school funding is a primary source of socioeconomic learning disparities. The impact of nonschool factors on socioeconomic achievement gaps is important to consider in the context of school funding for at least two reasons.

First, even if school funding has little or no impact on students' educational outcomes (and the evidence is not clear on this point), inequality in school funding still shapes the degree to which the U.S. education system provides equal opportunity. Currently, economically advantaged students attend well-funded schools and economically disadvantaged students attend poorly funded schools. In order for school funding to promote equal opportunity, the opposite should be true: Greater resources should go to economically disadvantaged students in order to make up for the lack of resources in their out-of-school environments. In sum, school funding is fundamentally an issue of educational opportunity, regardless of whether more funding boosts students' achievement or whether equal funding closes socioeconomic achievement gaps. Second, the reality that nonschool factors contribute primarily to the achievement gap between affluent and poor students is important to consider when it comes to policy implications. To improve disadvantaged students' educational opportunities and outcomes, should additional scarce public resources be allocated to schools, or rather to improving the economic prospects of the families in which children spend far more of their time? Advocates of equal or even adequate school funding should not expect school funding reforms to fully close the achievement gap between affluent and poor students, because such gaps stem largely from out-of-school factors.

Conclusion

Despite the sociological relevance of school funding to educational opportunities and outcomes, it remains a relatively understudied topic in the sociology of education. It is often necessary to look beyond the sociology of education subfield to disciplines such as education finance, economics, law, and public policy, to find sociological and other information pertaining to the funding of schools.

Dennis Condron
Oakland University

See Also: Poverty and Education; Rural Schooling; Schools as Bureaucracies; Urban Schooling; Wealth and Education.

Further Readings

Alexander, Karl L. "Public Schools and the Public Good." *Social Forces*, v.76/1 (1997).

Condron, Dennis J. and Vincent J. Roscigno. "Disparities Within: Unequal Spending and Achievement in an Urban School District." *Sociology of Education*, v.76/1 (2003).

Elliott, Marta. "School Finance and Opportunities to Learn: Does Money Well Spent Enhance Students' Achievement?" *Sociology of Education*, v.71/3 (1998).

Kozol, Jonathan. *Savage Inequalities: Children in America's Schools.* New York: Crown Publishers, 1991.

Wenglinsky, Harold. "How Money Matters: The Effect of School District Spending on Academic Achievement." *Sociology of Education*, v.70/3 (1997).

G

Gender and School Sports

Sports have been a part of schools and colleges in the United States since the early 20th century. Even under a largely coeducational system of schooling and postsecondary education, schools and school-based sports are highly defined by gender. Girls and women participating in school-based sports and physical education have always created tensions between equality of opportunity and difference in athletic participation. Today, Title IX reinforces the strong ties between American sports and schooling and presents the challenge for schools to offer different but equal athletic opportunities. Girls and boys, or women and men, have a long history of participating in educational experiences together in the United States. Coeducation became the norm in postsecondary and higher education by the early 20th century. Despite the coeducational school structure, student life was characterized by separate but parallel experiences. As coeducation grew, extracurriculum also grew, ushering in concerns about women's participation in school-based sports. Would women become too masculine by participating in sports? Would men's sports or schools in general become too feminized? As women students participated in school-based athletic competition, mainly basketball, they highlighted a tension between masculine sport and feminine womanhood.

In the 1920s, women students made up almost half of the enrollment at coeducational institutions. Many schools, however, implemented tactics to curtail their impact. Women leaders in schools and colleges promoted separate programs for women students in extracurriculum by building strong, women-led professional associations within feminized fields. Women's physical educators in schools shifted the philosophy for women's athletics from competition to one that emphasized participation and recreation in interscholastic and intercollegiate programs. This new philosophy focused on moderation and curtailed threats to physical and moral health of girls and women that were characterized in many men's competitive sports. Competitive teams for women and girls were replaced with social and recreational activities. The women's physical education (PE) model for school-based sport protected the role of women's physical educators in schools and appeased fears of the feminization of sports, and even schools.

Outside the schools, women and girls participated in grass-roots competitive sports through the Amateur Athletic Union teams (AAU), community, and industrial leagues. Without school-based limitations, women competed in swimming, track and field, and basketball. Among black community groups and schools, women's competitive sports was promoted as having a positive connection between sports and womanhood. After World War II, the philosophy of women's physical educators came into conflict with the emergence of a new generation of women who sought competitive sports in their schools and colleges. Yet, the dissonance between masculine and feminine sports in education remained a significant and critical tension in many coeducational institutions.

Title IX: Gender Separate Equity

The passage of Title IX policy marks a shift from a "girl for every sport and a sport for every girl" gender-specific model, to one where women have the same access to school-based athletic opportunity as boys and men. On June 23, 1972, Title IX of the Education Amendments Act of 1972 was signed into law, stating:

No person in the United States shall on the basis of sex, be excluded from participation in, be denied the benefits of, or be subjected to discrimination under any educational program or activity receiving Federal financial assistance.

In the first few years after Title IX passed, attention was directed toward whether the law meant that athletic opportunity should be coeducational in elementary physical education classes, or if interscholastic and intercollegiate varsity athletics would remain gender separated. Title IX regulations, set forth in 1975, established equal opportunity based on gender separate varsity athletic teams. As a result, rather than having boys and girls compete on the same teams, participation is on gender-segregated interscholastic and intercollegiate teams. Under this gender-separated model, the number of girls and women participating in sports has grown, but women's participation overall is still behind boys and men. In 1972, 3.6 million boys and 294,000 girls played high school sports. By 2010–11 almost 5 million boys participated in high school sports, while girls' participation topped 3.2 million. In addition, Title IX has been largely ineffective for women of color in interscholastic sports and intercollegiate athletics, partly because of previous segregation practices in predominately white educational institutions during the emergence of coeducation. Title IX policy has been praised for its powerful impact in giving women greater access to all aspects of education. Yet, the effect of the policy under gender-separate teams raise questions about what equity is in school-based sport.

Gender, Schools, and Sports

Gender equality in school-sponsored sports has meant access for female students to participate in the same athletic opportunities as male students. Because gender equity in education-based sports conforms to

gender-separate teams, coed teams are much rarer. In some individual sports, such as track or swimming, coed or combined women and men's teams with a single head coach exist. Still, women compete with and against women peers. Only in very rare circumstances do boys and girls compete together, such as in high school wrestling, where competition is organized by weight class and fewer all-girls' teams are available. Therefore, because many team sports favor the physical advantages of boys and men, if women and men were to compete for opportunities on the same team, it is likely that only girls and women with those attributes would make the team. Outside of schools, however, coed teams are more common in intramural and community sports. Within school, athletic opportunities continue to emphasize gender-separate teams, in part to preserve opportunity for girls and women in existing sporting structures.

For many children, their earliest athletic experiences are cultivated on elementary school playgrounds or during PE classes in the school gymnasium. In middle school and high school, intramural, club, and varsity sports further reinforce the connection between schooling and athletic experiences. However, encouragement for girls and boys to be physically active on the playground or in elementary school PE shifts in later childhood. Although there are fewer concerns today over girls who are tough and rugged within the confines of the playfield, expectations remain for girls to emulate dominant cultural standards of femininity off the field. For boys, sports continue to provide a space to demonstrate traditional masculine dominance, through physical aggression and athletic accomplishments. Although school teams can play an important role in shaping athletic experiences for girls and women, many school- and college-based opportunities in sports remain highly differentiated by gender.

Jennifer Lee Hoffman
University of Washington

See Also: Cheerleading Equity Policy; Extracurricular Activities; Feminist Critiques of Educational Practices; Sexism in Education; Sports and Schools.

Further Readings

Brake, D. L. *Getting in the Game: Title IX and the Women's Sports Revolution*. New York: New York University Press, 2010.

Cahn, S., K. *Coming On Strong: Gender and Sexuality in Twentieth-Century Women's Sport*. Cambridge, MA: Harvard University Press, 1995.

Festle, M. J. *Playing Nice: Politics and Apologies in Women's Sports*. New York: Columbia University Press, 1996.

Grundy, P. *Learning to Win: Sports, Education, and Social Change in Twentieth-Century North Carolina*. Chapel Hill: University of North Carolina Press, 2001.

Ware, S. *Title IX: A Brief History With Documents*. Boston: Bedford/St. Martin's, 2007.

Gender Inequality: College Enrollment and Completion

Gender disparities in higher education have shifted significantly over time. While for much of the 20th century there was great concern over improving college access for women, in the past 30 years, women have come to outnumber men in both college enrollment and graduation. However, despite making huge gains in college enrollment and graduation, women still face obstacles in college admissions as schools struggle to maintain a gender balance on campus. There are significant variations by race and income level in the gender gap favoring women in college enrollment and completion, which furthers inequalities among some groups.

Before the Civil War, American women had few higher education options, and these were mostly limited to women's colleges or sister schools to elite universities such as Harvard/Radcliffe and Columbia/Barnard. Few schools were coeducational (Oberlin was the first, in 1937). Over time, however, more schools began testing coeducation, and women's enrollments grew almost on par with men during the early part of the 20th century. After World War II, many returning soldiers took advantage of the G.I. Bill, and male attendance at colleges and universities soared, surpassing that of women. Since then, women's enrollments have steadily increased, and by the early 1980s, undergraduate populations had reached gender parity. Since the 1980s, women's college enrollment has continued to increase at a faster rate than men's enrollment, though both have been growing. The most recent statistics from the U.S. Department of Education indicate that approximately 57 percent of those enrolled in college are women, while 43 percent are men. Since the early 1980s, the percentage of women who complete college has also increased, and women now exceed men in earning bachelor's degrees, with approximately 60 percent going to women. These statistics are mirrored in other industrialized nations, particularly in western Europe, where women also outnumber men in college attendance and completion.

Gender Gap: Possible Explanations

For many years, much of sociology was concerned with gender inequality that favored men over women in college enrollment and graduation; however, the focus has now shifted to investigating the current gender gap, where women outnumber men. One explanation for the current gender gap in college attendance focuses on the academic choices that students make in high school and the numbers of men and women who make certain life course transitions. Research has found that more females take a college preparatory curriculum and less females drop out of high school than males. More females also tend to make the transition to college right after high school. Attending college directly after high school not only increases the chance that a student will attend college, but also their chance of graduation. From this perspective, the gender gap is a result of students' high school choices and experiences.

Another explanation draws from the status attainment literature. This line of thought views each individual's social status trajectory as influenced by ascriptive characteristics such as gender, race, family size, and parents' education and incomes. These characteristics are thought to influence the future occupation, income, and social status of an individual, both directly and indirectly. Prior to the shift in college enrollment, this theory was used to explain why fewer females were enrolled in college, particularly among the working class: families with limited resources would choose to spend those resources on sons, rather than daughters, since educated sons were more likely to generate higher incomes. However, this perspective no longer explains college enrollments, since women now surpass men in college attendance. Recent evidence also suggests that the gender gap is larger among working-class and poor students, and that it closes moving up the socioeconomic ladder. Aspects of the status attainment model also support a gender socialization view of education: A mother's education level influences her daughter's and a father's education level influences his son's, which explained why fewer females were going on to college in the earlier part of the 20th century. However, this model is also called into question. Studies are conflicted as to whether a parent's educational level has a greater effect on the same-sex child or if the effect is the same regardless of gender.

Gender socialization processes may also be affecting women's enrollment in and graduation from college through cultural norms that encourage females to be "good girls," which consists of complying with parental and teacher expectations to do well in school and to act appropriately in class. In contrast, males face cultural expectations to be tough, do well in sports, and be "manly," which many times does not coincide with being a good student. These cultural expectations may explain why women do better in K–12 schooling than men, and therefore go on to higher education at higher rates. Yet another explanation draws from human capital theory. This perspective argues that individuals gain human capital, or education and professional experience, in order to reap an economic return. Individuals make calculated decisions based upon the economic return they anticipate receiving. Some sociologists who support this theory argue that the kinds of jobs that do not require a college degree and still pay a living wage are not traditionally available to women. Women tend to work in white or pink collar professions, not blue collar jobs. Therefore, women make the decision to invest in education at greater rates because they will reap greater financial reward than if they did not. On the other hand, some scholars question this theory because women do not seem to benefit as much from a college education as men. There is still a wage gap among similarly educated men and women.

Intersection of Race and Class

The current gender gap among men and women varies by both race and class, as does the pattern of change. According to U.S. Department of Education data, the gender gap favoring women in college completion is larger among African Americans, Hispanics, and Native Americans than among whites, while the gender gap among Asian Americans is similar to that of whites. Among African Americans, females have long held an advantage over men in both enrollment and completion; however, for other ethnicities, the shift in the gender gap is more recent. In addition, while there used to be a larger gap favoring males among working-class and poor Americans in college enrollment, and more gender parity among the middle class, this has also shifted in some ways. Now, more women than men from the working class enroll and graduate from college, while the gap is much smaller or nonexistent among middle-class Americans. These variations in the gendered patterns of enrollment and completion among students of different races and social origins has intrigued scholars, though there is little consensus on possible explanations. Some suggest that cultural attitudes regarding minority and working-class male masculinity run counter to the image of a successful student, leading males to reject school and academic success. Other explanations look to parenting, school, and neighborhood effects that may affect minority students and those of different socioeconomic statuses differentially by gender.

Continuing Disparities

Although women currently make up a larger portion of undergraduates and graduate at higher rates than men, there are still a number of inequalities that women face within higher education. The gender gap is more pronounced on less-selective college campuses, suggesting that while more women are going to college, they are not attending elite colleges at higher rates than men. There has also been a significant amount of attention paid to the issue of maintaining gender balance on college campuses, and there is evidence that colleges and universities are now favoring less-qualified men over highly qualified women in the college admissions process in order to keep campuses gender balanced. Once in college, women are also significantly underrepresented in science, technology, engineering, and math (STEM majors) and are overrepresented in the social sciences, humanities, and education. After graduation, women still earn less than men, even when they have the same educational level.

Megan Holland
Harvard University

See Also: Class Inequality: College Enrollment and Completion; Gender Inequality: College Major; Gender Inequality: Returns to Educational Investments; Gender Theories in Education.

Further Readings

Bobbitt-Zeher, Donna. "The Gender Income Gap and the Role of Education." *Sociology of Education*, v.80 (2007).

Buchmann, Claudia and Thomas A. DiPrete. "The Growing Female Advantage in College Completion: The Role of Family Background and Academic Achievement." *American Sociological Review*, v.71/4 (2006).

Jacobs, Jerry A. "Gender Inequality and Higher Education." *Annual Review of Sociology*, v.22/1 (1996).

King, Jacqueline. "Gender Equity in Higher Education: 2006." American Council on Education Center for Policy Analysis. http://www.acenet.edu/bookstore/pdf/ Gender_Equity_6_23.pdf (Accessed May 2010).

U.S. Department of Education. "Gender Differences in Participation and Completion of Undergraduate Education and How They Have Changed Over Time" (2005). http://www.nces.ed.gov/pubsearch/pubsinfo .asp?pubid=2005169 (Accessed May 2010).

Gender Inequality: College Major

Although women have surpassed men in earning bachelor's, master's, and doctoral degrees, the fields in which they earn these degrees tend to be different than their male counterparts. Women are more likely to major in social sciences, humanities, and education, while men major in science, technology, engineering, and math (STEM) fields. Although these differences are sometimes explained away by preference, STEM fields are associated with greater earnings potential, higher occupational prestige, and lower rates of enemployment. As such, the equal-but-different paradigm allows for the reconciliation of gender segregation by college major with principles of equal opportunity, but ignores the ways that socialization into gender roles shape these preferences and the long-term inequalities that result from such segregation.

The extent of gender inequality by college major has changed historically and diversity of institutions within the U.S. higher educational system has allowed a wide range of orientations toward women's education. While elite women's colleges and some early land-grant institutions intentionally provided male and female students with instruction in the same subjects, "coordinate colleges" for women at many established universities tended to provide fewer curricular offerings for women—focusing on preparing women to be wives and mothers. Decreased enrollment of male students during World War II increased opportunities for women to enroll in programs like science and medicine, but at the conclusion of the war, gender segregation by field returned to prewar levels. By the early 1960s, gender segregation by major reached its postwar peak, with over 70 percent of female graduates studying in six fields: education (including over half of undergraduate women), English, fine arts, nursing, history, and home economics.

Levels of gender equality by college major increased throughout the 1970s and early 1980s, with women earning over half of undergraduate degrees in the life sciences and 47 percent of mathematics degrees by 1990, and increasing their share of engineering degrees from 1 percent in 1970 to 20 percent in 2001. Despite these hopeful signs, progress slowed in the late 1980s, and remained relatively stagnant through the 1990s and into the 2000s. As a result, many college majors today remain predominantly male or predominantly female. During 2008 to 2009, the five fields with the highest percentage of female majors were family/consumer/human sciences (87 percent), health professions and related clinical sciences (85 percent), public administration and social services (82 percent), education (79 percent), and psychology (77 percent); females received the lowest percentage of undergraduate degrees in physical sciences and science technologies (41 percent), computer and information sciences and support services (18 percent), and engineering and engineering technologies (16 percent). This initial integration and subsequent stagnation may stem from the move of women into traditionally male fields like business (which was the most popular major among women in 2010), but subsequent failure of men to move into traditionally female fields at similar rates. At present, roughly one-third of women (or men) would have to change majors to completely eliminate gender segregation by college major.

Global Patterns

Similar patterns of gender inequality by college major exist globally, although the particular fields in which women are more or less prevalent varies by country and exceptions to the scientific/humanistic divide exist. In Europe, both patterns and overall levels of gender segregation are highly consisent across countries, following closely the scientific/humanistic divide prevalent in the United States. Globally, men earn the majority of science and engineering degrees in most countries, even when the majority of graduates are women. Rates between countries differ radically, however (women earn 51.6 percent of engineering degrees in Kuwait and only 3.3 percent in Japan). Likewise, in 90 percent of countries, women degree-earners outnumber men in the fields of education, humanities and arts, social science, business and law, and health/welfare. Women are a minority of education majors in some countries, including Morocco (35 percent), Cambodia (33 percent), Ethiopia (14 percent), and Aruba (11 percent). Comparative international research suggests that larger social structural factors may also predict higher or lower overall levels of gender inequality between fields of study. In particular, countries with more egalitarian gender norms and those with higher rates of female labor force participation tend toward higher levels of integration in most fields of study. In contrast, those with very diverse postsecondary systems (e.g., the U.S. system, which includes both public and private two-year, four-year, and other institutions offering a variety of degrees and certificates) show higher levels of gender segregation by field.

Pipeline Model

Most of the literature on women's under-representation in science employs a "pipeline model," whereby students follow a linear trajectory through college preparatory courses in math and science during high school, an undergraduate science concentration, and possible science graduate study, to employment in a science career. Thus, women's under-representation in science fields is attributed to women's exiting the pipeline. Although this model dominates the literature, it has been critiqued for ignoring the often complex and mutliple paths by which women, in particular, enter science careers, as it assumes that nonparticipation at any stage indicates dropping out and virtually ignores movement back into the pipeline. As such, the pipeline model disregards how family demands/expectations affect students' academic trajectories, factors shown to disproportionately impact women.

Leaks in the Pipeline

Individual preference and experience, familial influences, and social and organizational context are all called upon as intervention points to keep women in the science pipeline. Although all of the evidence suggests that there are no signficiant differences in scientific ability between men and women, men and women continue to be socialized into different academic trajectories and/or career aspirations. Following the pipeline model, many people assume that female students are simply less academically prepared to enter STEM majors. Yet, girls receive better grades than men in all major subjects (including science and mathematics), at all levels of instruction (kindergarten through college) and are taking as many and as equally difficult courses in mathematics and science as their male peers. Despite this apparent lack of difference between men and women in terms of academic preparation, they report different expectations regarding careers, and may be motivated by different occupational incentives. For example, women are more likely to select careers in which they can help people, although they may offer fewer financial rewards.

Familial influences also play an explanatory role. Orientation to cultural gender roles, portrayal of work and family demands as competing obligations, perceived demands of particular majors and professions, and expected timing of future familial responsibilities (including childcare and elder care, which remain disproportionately female responsibilities) have been shown to significantly influence women's choice of major. Finally, social and organizational contexts include students' experience beyond the home, in neighborhoods and schools. Neighborhood factors include the availability and accessibility of role models (such as male nurses or female engineers), the gendered organization of extracurricular and employment activities, and formal neighborhood resources (e.g., libraries) that may shape students' awareness and perceptions of career opportunities. At the elementary and secondary levels, school factors may include: teacher expectations and quality, availability and quality of guidance counselors, course availability, extracurricular activities, and peer groups. Organizational context at the postsecondary level includes recruitment techniques, staffing patterns, organizational mission, and support services (e.g., women are more likely to enter and successfully complete STEM majors in departments with higher percentages of female faculty).

Impact on the Gender Wage Gap

College major has been identified as the single biggest factor influencing the gender wage gap, explaining between 19 and 25 percent of the gender wage gap for college graduates. Some of this effect may be attributed to differential skills and human capital development among majors; studies have found that the gender income gap disappears among men and women at the highest professional ranks in fields of math and science. Yet, the effect of college major exists above and beyond the skills and responsibilities associated with a particular occupation. In the first year after graduation, workers (of both sexes) with female-dominated majors earned, on average, 20 percent less than their peers with male-dominated majors, even when they entered comparable occupations with comparable skills. As such, gender pay gaps are not simply a matter of individual women choosing poorly paid fields or preferencing nonfinancial returns to work; female-dominated majors have become socially and economically devalued. Thus, even as trends in higher education participation are advantaging women, college majors are playing an increasingly important role in perpetuating lingering income inequality.

Christina R. Steidl
Emory University

See Also: Gender Inequality: College Enrollment and Completion; Gender Inequality: Mathematics; Gender Theories in Education; Women in Math/Science.

Further Readings

Bobbitt-Zeher, Donna. "The Gender Income Gap and the Role of Education." *Sociology of Education*, v.80 (2007).

Charles, Maria and Karen Bradley. "Equal but Separate? A Cross-National Study of Sex Segregation in Higher Education." *American Sociological Review*, v.67 (2002).

UNESCO. *Global Education Digest.* UNESCO Institute for Statistics, 2009.

U.S. Department of Education. "Stats in Brief: Students Who Study Science, Technology, Engineering, and Mathematics (STEM) in Postsecondary Education." NCES 2009161 (2009).

Xie, Yu and Kimberlee A. Shauman. *Women in Science: Career Processes and Outcomes.* Cambridge, MA: Harvard University Press, 2005.

Gender Inequality: High School Dropout Rates

Research indicates that high school dropouts are more likely to experience unemployment, prison, divorce, and live in poverty. The consequences of dropping out not only affect the individual, but they have long-term effects that negatively impact their children when they cannot provide for them economically. Children of dropouts are also more likely to underperform in schools and drop out of high school. On a national scale, the high school dropout rate indicates that the issue is improving. Since 1960, the United States has decreased its number of high school dropouts by almost 20 percent, from 27 percent in 1960 to 8 percent in 2008. Despite this decrease, males who drop out of high school consistently exceed that of female students. Throughout the 1990s, the male dropout rate ranged between 11 and 13 percent, while the female dropout rate fluctuated between 10 and 11 percent. Moreover, female dropout rates have generally decreased since 1996, while the male dropout rate substantially increased in 1994, 1998, and 2000. By 2008, the female dropout rate had fallen to 7.5 percent, while the male dropout rate stood at 8.5 percent. The gap enlarged by 2009, where female dropout rates continued to decline to 7 percent, while the male dropout rate increased to 9 percent.

The data on high school dropouts demonstrate a pattern of male underachievement. Despite the information collected on dropout rates, policymakers and educators question the accuracy of this data. Oftentimes, schools have trouble verifying who has dropped out or transferred to other schools. In particular, it is difficult to account for all dropouts, given the lack of longitudinal studies and mechanisms to fully capture where students may go after they leave a high school. In response, researchers use high school graduation rates to understand how many students actually complete high school. Similar to high school dropout rates, the data on high school completion point to a pattern of male underachievement, but with worse outcomes. In 2001, 72 percent of females graduated from high school, where only 64 percent of males completed high school, indicating an 8 percent gap. In 2006, only 65 percent of males graduated from high school, compared to 72 percent of females. Nationally, 67 percent of male students graduated from high school and 74 percent of females graduated from high school in 2010, a consistent 7 percent gender gap.

Race and Ethnicity and Dropout Rates

Additionally, national education data demonstrate that graduation rates vary greatly among subgroups beyond gender. In 2001, 77 percent of white females graduated, whereas 71 percent of white males finished high school. Asian American females had the highest rates of high school graduation, at 80 percent, of any subgroup (gender or race/ethnicity), and when compared to the 73 percent of Asian males who completed high school. Generally, males graduate at lower rates than women, but upon closer analysis, males from historically underrepresented groups have even lower graduation rates than all other ethnic/racial groups, as well as their female counterparts. For American-Indian students, 51 percent of females earned a high school degree, and 47 percent of males in this subgroup completed high school. The gender disparity continues, but only worsens for African American and Latino students, who already have lower graduation rates in schools when compared to their white and Asian peers. For instance, 48 percent of Latino males graduate from high school, compared to 59 percent of Latina students. For African American students, only 43 percent of male students graduated, compared to 56 percent of African American female students.

State and district data also reveal how African American and Latino male youth are more likely to have worse graduation rates than their female and white or Asian peers. In particular, minority-majority and economically segregated California high schools graduate only 58 percent of African American and Latino students, but this rate decreases to 50 and 54 percent for African American and Latino males, respectively. State data from graduation classes of 2003 identify San Bernardino City Unified in California as having the lowest graduation rates for males, at 36 percent. New York City, Baltimore City, and Milwaukee public schools only graduate 39 percent of male students, while the female graduation rate was up to 18 percentage points higher in some of these districts. And when district graduation rates are studied closely, African American and Latino males suffer from the lowest graduations rates. For example, only 30 percent of Latino and 33 percent of African American male youth in New York City schools graduated in 2003, which was the lowest of any other subgroup. The low number of African American and Latino male youth who graduate from high school has a negative impact on the quality of life of these individuals. These youth are more likely to enter the juvenile detention and prison systems. In fact, one in three African American boys and one in six Latino boys are affected by the school-to-prison pipeline, which predicts that these male youth of color will be incarcerated at least once in their lives.

Theoretical Explanations

Research provides some analyses to explain the gender disparity in dropout and graduation rates. Selected cognitive studies contend that male and female brains develop differently, where females develop verbal skills earlier than males, thus giving them an advantage in schools. Males develop verbal skills later than females, but are also said to develop their visual-spatial skills more fully. Given that schools place such a high value on verbal skills, girls may then experience school differently than boys, whose behaviors and skills may not be fully appreciated in schools. Still, the research of physiological differences between male and females is limited, and has not been able to provide a causal relationship between the onset of these skills and performance on math, verbal, and visual-spatial tests.

Researchers posit that there are two forces at work that impact the gender disparity of high school dropouts, as well as the ways that boys and girls experience schools. The first framework highlights individual attributes of students, such as their values, attitudes, and behaviors that influence their decision to drop out of high school. These studies maintain that dropping out of high school is the culmination of a series of beliefs and behaviors that were already moving the student toward academic and social disengagement from school. Utilizing this framework, researchers correlate individual predictors, such as poor academic achievement, student engagement, absenteeism, student mobility, working more than 20 hours per week, and retention of students with higher dropout rates.

Social Forces

Another body of research illuminates the strong role of institutional forces and social contexts on students. These studies focus on the role of students' families, peers, schools, and communities and their relationship to students' decision to drop out of high school. In general, students in families, schools, and communities with less resources and capital are more susceptible to dropping out of high school. Additionally, this literature provides evidence of how minority students from historically underserved communities are more likely to drop out of high school given the lack of resources, low quality education, strict school policies, and high stakes testing that is so prevalent in poorer communities. More recently, research in this area has begun to investigate how race, class, and gender can be factored into the individual and institutional frameworks to better understand why minority male youth are most vulnerable to dropping out of high school. A small body of work indicates that cultural and social norms for young men of color, individual and institutionalized racism, and a lack of institutional resources serve to negatively impact the academic trajectories of African American and Latino male youth.

Ursula S. Aldana
University of California, Los Angeles

See Also: Class Inequality: High School Dropout Rates; Cognitive Skill/Intellectual Skill; Dropouts; Gender Theories in Education; Racial Inequality: High School Dropout Rates.

Further Readings
Edley, C. and Jorge Ruiz de Velasco. *Changing Places: How Communities Will Improve the Health of Boys of Color.* Berkeley: University of California Press, 2010.
Greene, Jay P. and Marcus Winters. *Leaving Boys Behind: Public High School Graduation Rates.* New York: Manhattan Institute for Policy Research, 2006.
Grossman, Herbert and Suzanne Grossman. *Gender Issues in Education.* London: Allyn and Bacon, 1994.
Lopez, Nancy, *Hopeful Girls, Troubled Boys: Race and Gender Disparity in Urban Education.* New York: Routledge, 2003.
Orfield, Gary, ed. *Dropouts in America: Confronting the Graduation Rate Crisis.* Cambridge, MA: Harvard Education Press, 2004.

Gender Inequality: Mathematics

Issues surrounding gender and mathematics participation and performance have been of growing interest internationally. During the mid-20th century, there was a considerable amount of research indicating that men and women differ in performance and abilities in mathematics. However, the findings during and after this period utilized historical facts and perspectives, along with empirical research, to develop theories and belief systems related to gender inequality in mathematics. In more developed countries, the debates related to gender inequality and mathematics are more pronounced and widely utilized than in developing countries, largely because of issues related to general educational access and equity. While there are many uses of the term *gender*, its use in regard to mathematics and any differences that exist between male and females has primarily been situated around a few primary themes and perspectives—characteristics relating to sex, social roles, and gender identity as they relate to mathematics. Gender inequality is a capacious concept that is better framed within the larger context of societal exclusion based on tenants related to sex and gender identity. Responses to gender inequality in education, and more specifically mathematics, are aligned with an increase in parity and equity in education and mathematics. Mathematics gender equality is situated around females and males holding equal conditions, opportunities, and rights in their ability to learn and participate in mathematics. Gender and mathematics have been approached from various aspects, although beliefs about women and mathematics have been largely negative.

During the 1960s and 1970s, there was a substantial amount of research on gender inequality in mathematics that served as a launch for future research and developmental work. For example, the U.S. Agency for International Development (USAID) published a gender equality framework and focused on historical perspectives of equality, in addition to the dimensions of equality in education—with a specific focus on Science, Technology, Engineering, and Mathematics, commonly referred to as the STEM fields. Previous research on gender equity in mathematics encompassed and produced a number of key theories and themes. While some focused on biological differences as a means to explain differences in mathematics by gender, this research was not widely adopted or utilized as a primary factor in explaining any present inequalities. Many maintain strong views that gender differences in mathematics are a result of a variety of factors. Some of these factors include: early-childhood and adolescent socialization related to sex roles, sexism, gender stereotyping, and more prominently, attitudes, beliefs, and perceptions about girls and women and mathematics. However, among certain sets of scholars, there is an agreement that these differences in mathematics participation and performance are solely related to individual-level factors. For example, that boys and girls are socialized differently by their parents, or children's individual expectations are based on gender perceptions.

Sex roles, sexism, and gender stereotyping of mathematics and mathematical ability is largely thought to occur within organizations and, in particular, families and schools. Thoughts surrounding sex roles are a response to traditional roles of women as homemakers and mothers. Beliefs about sexism and gender stereotyping help explain how perceptions of gender and equity combine to create the gender inequality problem; namely, stereotyping that maintains a cycle of inequality between men and women. Additionally, these stereotypes are related to an individual's attitudes and beliefs about the presence of women in mathematics and their performance. The research about attitudes and beliefs of mathematics, and women's participation and performance, are related to perception. Perception, particularly negative stereotypes about women in mathematics, is the largest predictor of women's participation and achievement in mathematics. Research on "stereotype threat" and other predictors of perception have shown that exposure to and reminders of gender stereotypes negatively impact women's performance in mathematics. These exposures have an overall negative effect on women's participation in mathematics beyond secondary school. Additionally, negative stereotypes about women in mathematics lower girls' and women's self-assessments of mathematics ability and judgment of harsher standards.

Studying Reasons for the Disparities

Gender disparities in mathematics outcomes do not show up until high school, and for some, until the later years of college. For primary school students, inequities between boys and girls are generally small and negligible. However, during the secondary years of schooling, primarily middle and high school years, girls' performance in mathematics begins to decline. Those beliefs surrounding gender inequality in mathematics, particular to the postsecondary education and instruction of women in mathematics and STEM related fields, are wide in range. Some concentrate on differences from mathematics no longer being a compulsory subject, while others revisit biological differences by sex, specifically, innate gender differences in mathematics ability. Larry Summers, for example, resigned as the president of Harvard University in 2006 in part because of a speech given a year earlier suggesting that the lack of participation and representation of women in STEM related fields was because of aptitude-related differences.

Some findings suggest that the differences that exist by gender in mathematics are not universal or constant. In the United States, access to formal and higher education for women was not common until the mid-19th century. Among third world and developing countries, access to education for women, in general, is still not a common practice today; therefore, the issues surrounding gender inequality in mathematics are a subset of a larger issue of education and access to formal instruction. While women's participation in mathematics is still low, progress has been made, and formal efforts have been adopted to respond to these differences. For example, in the United States and the United Kingdom, funding through private organizations and governmental programs has concentrated on increasing women's participation in mathematics. More recently, improvements in women's jobs and incomes relative to men concerned with mathematics stem from an increase in the number of women entering higher-paying occupations where mathematical backgrounds serve as an asset. However, improvements in women's earnings for both mathematical and non-mathematical related careers tend to lag behind men, despite these advances. Also, among women mathematicians, there has been research on their success in mathematics, but some stories align with these women feeling that they are outsiders within the mathematics community. In addition to the continuing gender disparities in mathematics related careers, the biases that exist are held unconsciously by members of society and are left unexamined.

Nathan N. Alexander
Columbia University

See Also: Gender Inequality: Occupational Segregation of Teachers; Gender Theories in Education; No Child Left Behind; Sexism in Education; Single-Sex Education; Women in Math/Science.

Further Readings
Burton, Leone, ed. *Gender and Mathematics: An International Perspective.* London: Cassell Educational, 1990
Gallagher, Ann M. and James C. Kaufman, eds. *Gender Differences in Mathematics: An Integrative Psychological Approach.* New York: Cambridge University Press, 2005.
Steele, Claude M. "A Threat in the Air: How Stereotypes Shape Intellectual Identity and Performance." *American Psychologist,* v.52 (1997).

Gender Inequality: Occupational Segregation of Teachers

Occupational segregation of men and women teachers is a persistent, though not static, phenomenon throughout history. Segregation varies within the occupation for different ages taught. Teacher segregation also varies in different places. Women and men's differing rates of entry into teaching are attributed to labor market factors such as pay, opportunities for advancement, autonomy, and prestige afforded the occupation in broader society. Teaching, for example, is devalued in the United States as a profession, and in the ways the language and discourse of "professionalism" is gendered. Workers' beliefs, behaviors, and preferences for occupations also impact whether or not individuals enter teaching. For example, underlying notions of elementary teaching work as feminine, or as women's work, influence both women's and men's entry to the occupation. Broader systems of gender inequality related to educational access, work expectations, and life trajectories also contribute to persistent occupational segregation of teachers.

The majority of research in the field of occupational segregation, including studies covering teaching, look at quantitative measures of sex. This means that investigations examine the proportion of females and males in positions related to a variety of causes and across nations and time. There are two sexes acknowledged in such studies. Gender, simply defined, refers to social and cultural values and practices of masculinities and femininities. Gender is produced by persons in their everyday lives and is structural or part of broader systems that differentiate women and men. Gender inequality in occupations arises as a result of differences enacted along a broad spectrum of feminine and masculine behaviors and beliefs and as part of a broader system that favors women over men, or vice versa. Discussions of the relationship of gender inequality to teachers' occupational segregation apply sex as an ascribed, biological characteristic and gender as a concept for understanding segregation of women and men teachers.

Historical Context

Men dominated the ranks of teaching throughout history. Drawn from elite sectors, boys were educated, and some became learned men who, in turn, taught in private homes or in institutions restricted to males. Male teachers and tutors also came from religious organizations and primarily served young males from privileged sectors. Gender inequality in educational access for women and girls, as well as restrictive social and cultural ideas about the abilities and life outcomes of women and girls, supported men's seemingly perfect segregation in teaching. With the rise of capitalist economies and mass education in the 19th century, girls and women around the world began to obtain higher levels of education and gain access to teaching, so much so that the iconic or symbolic teacher became associated with a woman.

The image of women as natural teachers grew out of the stereotyping of women as biologically programmed with nurturing and care giving attributes and affinities, considered to be teaching skills and qualities. The diffusion of ideologies of gender equality, beginning in the 1970s, has also been attributed to changing compositions of teacher corps. Throughout the 20th century, sex-based segregation within the profession shifted to women being overrepresented in elementary and secondary classrooms. Exceptions are in sub-Saharan Africa and south and west Asia, where men are in the majority, and in Arab States where there is relative parity among women and men. Men continue to be overrepresented in postsecondary or tertiary education.

Sex-Based Segregation Around the World

According to the United Nations Educational, Scientific and Cultural Organization (UNESCO), women are overrepresented in elementary education by 62 percent and have achieved relative parity with men in secondary classrooms at 52 percent, when percentages are averaged for nations around the world. This segregation seemingly favoring women may be explained in terms of the feminization of teaching work or lower wages, lower prestige, less autonomy, less opportunity for promotion, and poor or precarious work conditions.

In Arab states, however, women and men teach at close to parity, with women making up 55 percent of elementary teachers and 47 percent of secondary teachers. This may be the result of girls and boys being segregated for education, requiring women and men teachers for each group. Otherwise, the percentage of either women or men overrepresented in the profession is significant in all other regions.

Central Asian nations registered the highest over-representation of women at elementary and secondary levels, with 89 percent and 71 percent, respectively. North American, western, central, and eastern European nations all had similar percentages of disparity favoring women. Exceptions to women's overrepresentation in elementary and secondary education are the overrepresentation of men in sub-Saharan Africa (58 and 71 percent, respectively) and south and west Asian nations (55 and 66 percent, respectively). Teaching in rural, or isolated, schools where it is not considered safe or appropriate for women to travel to work or to live alone, as well as restrictions on women's movement and ability to obtain an education or seek work, may contribute to this composition. Broader gender inequality related to women's ability to and decisions to earn an education, work, and travel are potential causes for occupational segregation of teachers.

Vertical and Horizontal Segregation

The field of teaching is segregated not only horizontally, with more women in the field overall, but also vertically, with more men in positions of authority and prestige, such as headmasters. This fact reflects a trend in gender segregation across occupations: While women in male-dominated professions often face a "glass ceiling" preventing their promotion to higher-level positions, men in female-dominated professions often discover a "glass escalator," which increases their chances of promotion. Understanding the factors that lead to vertical segregation requires an understanding of the complex factors that influence promotion. The pattern of men holding higher-level positions is often seen as reflecting teachers' choices. Yet, several researchers have called for notions of choice to be problematized in recognition of the structural forces that can influence individual choice. For example, the construction of women's responsibilities to their families and of their caring work in the classroom as natural may make them less likely both to seek and to be considered for higher-level positions. Thus, even when equal opportunities for promotion exist, women do not have equal chances of being promoted, based on self-selection and structural discrimination.

Another form of vertical stratification is also evident in the teaching positions held by women and men, with women making up a strong majority of teachers at the elementary level, a smaller majority at the secondary level, and a minority at the postsecondary level. This stratification mirrors both the societal value and the reward attached to each type of teaching. Teaching young children often carries the least prestige and monetary reward, in part because of a devaluation of the caring work associated with such teaching.

Feminization of Teaching and Women's Work

The predominance of women teachers in Western educational systems is particularly notable at the elementary level. Research points to a number of factors that explain the dearth of male elementary teachers: these include comparatively low status and salaries; societal perceptions of this work as focused on nurturing and, thus, as women's work; and societal perceptions of male elementary teachers as either pedophiles or gay men. The gendered nature of school environments and societal conceptions of male elementary teachers affect the lived experiences of these teachers in complex ways. On one hand, some male teachers and teacher candidates describe such stereotypes as constraining their occupational choice. Few enter teaching. On the other hand, male elementary teachers experience certain privileges, including increased respect and faster promotion. Calls to reduce gender segregation at the elementary level by recruiting more male teachers are common, and draw upon several distinct discourses. Perhaps the most frequently offered rationale is that students—particularly boys, from single-parent households headed by women—need male role models. Calls for more male elementary teachers also have been connected to notions of a "boys' crisis" by linking achievement gaps between boys and girls, especially on language-based subjects, to the feminization of teaching. Such calls argue that the predominance of female teachers at the elementary level has created environments more suited to girls' interests and learning styles, and that male teachers will be better able to relate to boys and to engage them in learning.

These discourses have been critiqued on both theoretical and empirical grounds. Calls for male role models have been linked to the reproduction of hegemonic, stereotypical, and heteronormative conceptions of masculinity. Several studies have suggested that children do not perceive their teachers' gender as significant, and that matching students with teachers of the same gender does not impact student achievement. Other calls for more male teachers, however, have relied upon different discourses: for example, that a teaching force composed of more male elementary teachers will better reflect the composition of society.

Some researchers have also argued that male elementary teachers can challenge, rather than reinforce, gender norms and stereotypes. For example, rather than teaching boys how to act in ways that are traditionally masculine, male teachers could teach all children that men can play nonstereotypical roles (e.g., nurturing and caring roles). Furthermore, an increase in the number of male elementary teachers may reduce the bias and discrimination that these teachers face, thus helping weaken the stereotypes that construct the teaching of young children as "women's work" and that discourage men from entering the profession.

Sarah A. Robert
Heather Killelea McEntarfer
University at Buffalo

See Also: Deskilling of the Teaching Profession; Gender Theories in Education; Occupational Aspirations/Expectations; Social Role of the Teacher; Social Status of Teachers.

Further Readings

Anker, Richard. *Gender and Jobs: Sex Segregation of Occupations in the World.* Washington, DC: International Labor Organization, 1998.

Carter, Susan B. "Occupational Segregation, Teachers' Wages, and American Economic Growth." *Journal of Economic History*, v.46/2 (1986).

Paton, Graeme. "Young Boys 'Turned Off Books' by Lack of Male Teachers." *Telegraph* (June 29, 2012).

Reskin, Barbara F. and Heidi I. Hartmann, eds. *Women's Work, Men's Work: Sex Segregation on the Job.* Washington, DC: National Academies Press, 1986.

Watson, Lemuel W. and C. Sheldon Woods. *Go Where You Belong: Male Teachers as Cultural Workers in the Lives of Children, Families, and Communities.* Rotterdam, Netherlands: Sense Publishers, 2011.

Gender Inequality: Returns to Educational Investments

Women have made remarkable progress in education worldwide in the past few decades. In many countries, including the United States, women have constituted the majority of college students and graduates. However, women have not made parallel progress in returns to education. The gender pay gap is salient, albeit reduced. Factors pertaining to education and noneducation are relevant in understanding gender inequality in returns to education. Gender differences in college majors play a significant role in gender inequality of returns to education. Women are generally concentrated in fields such as humanities, social science, and education, while men are concentrated in natural science, engineering, and economics. While there is positive relationship between a country's development level and women's educational attainment, no such relationship exists between a country's development and women's representation in male-dominated fields. For example, the percentage of females in computer science is similar in Turkey as in Sweden. In the United States, although women have made significant inroads into previously male-dominated fields such as biology and business, gender integration in college majors is generally slow, if not stalled.

Major debates center on the explanation of the effects of college major choices on earnings. Human capital theory dominates the explanatory framework, which argues that returns to different majors depend on the scarcity of the type of human capital they are associated with, and that human capital formed on the basis of mathematical ability is scarcer than that formed on the basis of verbal ability. Fields that men dominate, such as natural science and engineering, are math-intensive, and women's lower achievement and/or confidence in math, coupled with their higher achievement and/or confidence in verbal abilities, are important to understand gender differences in college majors. An important complication of human capital interpretation involves selection bias. Specifically, the impact of college majors on earnings could be from the common factors that influence both college major choice and earnings. Such common factors could include prior abilities and preferences.

Female Devaluation Theory

Contrasting with human capital theory, female devaluation theory focuses on the aspect of gender composition of fields of study in explaining gender pay gap. Female devaluation theory is originally derived out of examining gender segregation in occupations, which has been supported by numerous studies, concluding that the high representation of females in an occupation would dampen the pay. Parallel to female-dominated occupations, female-dominated college majors such as education, nursing, and social work are of caring and nurturing nature, tasks and skills traditionally associated with women. The lower pay in these fields reflects the fundamental devaluation of skills traditionally associated with women. In addition to college majors, women are also less likely than men to go to selective institutions, more so in developing countries than in developed countries. Because of financial constraint and the general lower status of girls, parents invest less in girls than boys in developing countries. In developed countries, with more resources and established notions of gender egalitarian attitudes, women almost reach parity with men in attending selective institutions. However, women do not reap the same returns. Other than college major choice, which can partially account for the gender gap, some noneducation factors are relevant to understanding gender inequality in returns to education investments.

Occupational Aspirations

College majors are significant because they channel students to different occupations. Some work in the occupations closely linked with their college majors, such as engineering, education, and nursing. Others work in the occupations remotely linked or even those that have no relevance to their college major. Research shows that women are less likely than men to follow the normative major-occupation paths, which indicates two steps of segregation processes: one is that women are less likely to major in the fields that are closely linked with occupations; second is that in the same major, women are less likely to be employed in the occupation that is closely linked with their major. This major-occupation link contributes to gender pay gap. With similar education in terms of both quantity and quality, women still do not reap the same returns as men.

The most frequently invoked explanation from perspectives other than the terrain of education is the differential impact of family formation on earnings for men and women. While some evidence shows that married women earn less than unmarried women, the opposite turns out to be true for men. Having children also incurs cost for women, and the number of children is inversely related to women's earnings. However, the earning penalty of parenthood does not apply to men. The negative influence of family formation on women's earnings mainly works through women's decreased labor market participation. After marriage,

particularly after having children, women are more likely to work part time, reduce working hours, or quit employment altogether. That women have to compromise their career more than men in balancing work and family is driven by the workplace culture that is not family friendly, as well as the persisting family culture that prioritize men's careers over women's.

Gender differences in occupational aspirations are the key to understanding gender inequality in returns to education investments. Men attach more importance to money than women, and as such, men aspire to enter lucrative occupations more than women. This difference in occupational aspirations directly influences in the educational and occupational choices that men and women make, in that men are more likely than women to choose lucrative fields of study and enter lucrative occupations. Even with nonlucrative fields of study, men sometimes can still navigate their way toward lucrative occupations.

For example, a history or English major works in investment banks on Wall Street. In addition to the higher aspirations of entering lucrative professions, men have more social networks from schools to workplaces to convert their aspirations into realities. On the other hand, even with lucrative fields of study, women could still end up with nonlucrative occupations. For example, a law school graduate works in the public or nonprofit sector, rather than private law firms. Studies have found that women are disproportionately concentrated in the public and nonprofit sector, which pay less than the private sector. In sum, gender inequality in returns to education investments can be traced back to several distinct social processes, including college major choice, major-occupation linkage, gendered aspirations in occupations, and differential influence of family formation on men and women on employment outcomes. These social processes are integral parts of the gender structure that individuals inhabit.

Yingyi Ma
Gokhan Savas
Syracuse University

See Also: Gender Inequality: College Enrollment and Completion; Gender Inequality: High School Dropout Rates; Gender Theories in Education.

Further Readings
Bobbitt-Zeher, D. "The Gender Income Gap and the Role of Education." *Sociology of Education*, v.80 (2007).

Buchmann, C., T. A. DiPrete, and A. McDaniel. "Gender Inequalities in Education." *Annual Review of Sociology*, v.34 (2008).

Charles, Maria. "What Gender Is Science?" *Contexts* (2011).

England, Paula. "The Gender Revolution: Uneven and Stalled." *Gender and Society*, v.24 (2010).

Gender Theories in Education

Theories of gender in education have evolved from earlier feminist analyses of schooling to include more nuanced dimensions of gender, sexuality, and race. Contemporary theories of gender in education consider interactional and cultural facets of students' lives and how they interact with the institutional conditions of schools. Early feminist research on gender and education focused on the experiences of girls and women in schools. Scholars developed theories of gender and education that aimed to explain the widespread unequal access and differential treatment that girls and women face in educational institutions.

Two such theories, socialization theory and sexual/gender difference theory, emerged in the 1970s and early 1980s. Socialization theory's assertion was that parents and teachers treat boys and girls differently, socializing girls into believing that they are not capable of performing and succeeding in certain academic fields. A major outcome of socialization theory in educational settings was a push for gender-neutral curricula and teaching under the assumption that by ensuring equality in treatment, there would be equality in educational outcomes. Sexual/gender difference theory, on the other hand, argued that boys and girls are inherently different, and that womanhood and femininity need be recognized and valued to ensure the success of girls in schools. Instead of promoting a gender-neutral ethos in education, difference theorists argued that femininity needed to be promoted as an important characteristic of school culture, and in society more generally. This theoretical camp contested policies and practices in educational institutions that encourage restrictive behaviors celebrated by dominant masculine ideology, such as competition, domination, and traditional definitions of rationality.

In the 1980s and 1990s, theories of structure and deconstruction emerged that challenged earlier feminist perspectives and shaped the direction of educational research. Structural theories contend that hegemonic power practices impose and sustain unequal treatment for women and other minorities. Structural theory argues that if marginalized populations succeed, the dominant group, that is, men, will revise the very standards of success that grant systematic privileges to ensure that the dominant group maintains its position. Some research use structural arguments to encourage the development of programs in schools aimed at raising the status of women, such as the creation of women's studies or gender studies departments, providing safe spaces for women, and promoting counter-hegemonic contexts to learn and grow.

In ways often contrary to structural theory, deconstructionism views categorical definitions with skepticism, arguing that the very category of gender is constructed through social forces across time, history, and place. Deconstructionists problematize the assumptions of earlier theory, and in particular sexual/gender difference theory, which assumes that a natural category of male and female exists. This theoretical perspective argues that research should examine and exploit how we come to understand the meaning of categories like gender in order to subvert inequalities that result from everyday assumptions about difference. Contrary to differentiation theorists' assertion that femininity needs to be recognized and valued in schools, deconstructionists argue that such categorical benefits must be deconstructed in order to assess equality in educational practices and outcomes. Deconstructionism has also paved the way for broader studies of gender, such as how masculinity and femininity are constructed in schools and among youth.

Gender Crises in Education

Although feminist research made considerable inroads documenting how girls and women experience systematic disadvantage in education, claims about gender crises in education have emerged periodically throughout the 1900s, and quite recently again in the late 1990s/early 2000s. Gender crises, or more specifically the "boy crisis," describes research and public outcry that suggest that boys are falling behind girls in schools with regard to academic achievement and educational outcomes. Michael Kimmel argues that the debate about the educational well-being of boys is in fact a reaction to the loss of patriarchal power following industrialization and the expansion of political democracy. As men were forced out of self-employment because of urbanization, traditional masculinity was asserted in new ways. One outcome was the Boy Scouts of America, an institution designed, in part, to combat the feminization of young boys subjected to female-controlled homes and schools. The improper rearing of boys was identified as a major source of male failure into adulthood. Contrary to claims made by the emergence of third-wave feminism, Robert Bly argued that boys and men have a masculine nature that needs to be respected in schools, throughout adolescence, and into adulthood. Bly sparked a movement of masculinists, who were committed to reclaiming masculinity from feminized culture. Masculinists advocate schooling and childrearing based on the assumption that intrinsic differences between sexes exist.

Two main theoretical camps exist with regard to the debate about the gender crisis in education. Gender essentialists align with gender/sexual differentiation theory and believe that unitary, essential experiences exist for men and women, and these can be isolated separate from other social statuses, like race or class. Gender essentialists often tie boys' experience with claims about biological and chemical differences, such as the idea that boys are naturally more physical than girls. Gender essentialists' argue that schools should modify their classroom practices to be, in some cases, more competitive, and in some cases to feel more like a sports game. Gender constructionists, aligning with theories of deconstructionism, argue that these differences in educational achievement are because of the fact that boys are raised to embody certain constructions of masculinity that impede learning and school performance. Recent studies have shown that in some cases, women's educational achievement and outcomes surpass men—more women attend college and elite graduate programs than men. However, scholars argue that although educational attainment for women has increased dramatically in the last few decades, occupational outcomes still remain highly unequal; average salaries are still significantly higher for men than they are for women, and despite high educational attainments, women still are not well represented at the highest rungs of the corporate ladder.

Gender and the Hidden Curriculum

Research on the hidden curriculum argues that educational institutions, through tacit assumptions about rules and social order, reproduce dominant norms and stifle conflict. Although the hidden curriculum may operate across a number of social statuses, considerable work has examined how schools regulate gender norms through this mechanism. Through a hidden curriculum, schools subtly promote messages to students that teach youth standards of gender that not only affect their experiences in schools, but also imbue baseline understandings of difference that shape broader society. Hidden curricula foster gender inequality through a variety of means. Some of these hidden messages may include teachers' assumptions about boys' and girls' relative intelligence: Boys are good at math and science, and girls are better at reading and writing. Other research has argued that history textbooks' exclusion of women conveys that they are not a valuable part of history. And yet other studies have argued that the imposition of certain school uniforms implicitly regulate acceptable gender codes in schools. Scholars have also argued that teachers impose a hidden curriculum on students through everyday interactions in the classroom. Examples include when teachers reward boys' aggressive behavior, while girls are punished for showing assertiveness; boys are punished for displays that are coded by teachers as effeminate; and teachers' tolerate boys' sexual harassment of girls.

Scholars have argued that the messages conveyed by the hidden curriculum are transmitted not only by teachers through lessons, but also through regular events and traditions at the school. Major events, like school proms, have been argued to promote hidden curriculum of compulsory heterosexuality and gender-appropriateness. At these events, same-sex couples or gender nonconforming student attendees are harassed or prevented from attending, conveying that these identities are marginal and unwelcome in educational settings. Scholars have exploited many empirical contexts to analyze how the hidden curriculum operates in schools.

Gender and Sexuality in Schools

In recent decades, scholars have theorized that gender and sexual identities are often constructed and negotiated through social processes situated in schools. Barrie Thorne, in her study of elementary school youth culture, shows that children's play activities create and reproduce boundaries across lines of gender, as well as age, race-ethnicity, class, and sexuality. Although these interactions occur through everyday children's play, they construct consequential gender boundaries among youth in school environments. Thorne's research is representative of a turn in sociological studies of education and youth that consider how youth are not simply socialized by adults into their gender identities and roles, but are instead active participants in the construction of these identities. Other work has shown how school-sanctioned sports teams actively reproduce gender inequalities. Michael Messner found that although federal rules prohibit the exclusion of girls and women from sports, school sports teams reproduce standards of masculinity that compel violence and male dominance. He finds that gender norms operate at the heart of sports, and interaction in and around sports events create tacit conditions whereby women are differentiated and excluded from particular kinds of participation. Recent research on gender and sexuality in schools argue that educational institutions privilege heterosexuality on a day-to-day basis, both through its routine teaching practices and school events, as well as through the school youth culture it tacitly promotes. C. J. Pascoe found that high schools engage in interactive social practices that ward off threats of status loss by being called "gay" in order to stabilize normative constructions of gender and sexuality. School events often provided opportunities for youth to condemn or project satirized images of non-normative gender identities. Moreover, teachers regularly ignored, and sometimes encouraged, homophobic behavior in class.

Gender and Race-Ethnicity

Earlier feminist work on gender in schools does not well consider how race-ethnicity intersects with gender in ways that contribute to educational inequality. Contemporary education research argues that both gender and race-ethnicity matter to more fully explain inequalities in schools. Some scholars argue that schools, as institutions run by predominantly white, middle-class people, systematically disadvantage non-white youth by invoking oppressive evaluative standards in schools. In this view, teachers reward student behaviors deemed appropriate for students across dimensions of race and gender. Schools routinely punish black and Latino boys for bad behavior more than white boys, and the penalties are more severe. Moreover, racialized standards of masculinity and femininity shape students' ability to succeed in schools. Although black and Latino children do not differ from white children in their educational goals, black and

Latino youth meet resistance from schools and among their peers in ways that privilege white students. Theorists have argued that race-gender identities that youth of color internalize, such as tacit understandings that black and Latino boys are less educationally fit than girls, also shape their experience in schools. Prudence Carter's study of urban black and Latino students in a low-income community showed that black girls are supervised by parents more than black boys, structuring differential preparation for success in schools. Moreover, she finds that black and Latino boys are encouraged to become tough and hardened, however these behaviors are not welcomed in schools.

Matthew H. Rafalow
University of California, Irvine

See Also: Cultural Capital and Gender; Feminist Critiques of Educational Practices; Feminist Critiques of Educational Research; Gender and School Sports; Oppositional Culture; Race and Cultural Capital; Sexism in Education; Youth Cultures and Subcultures.

Further Readings
Apple, M. "The Hidden Curriculum and the Nature of Conflict." *Interchange*, v.2/4 (1971).
Carter, P. L. *Keepin' It Real: School Success Beyond Black and White*. Oxford: Oxford University Press, 2005
Messner, M. A. *Taking the Field: Women, Men, and Sports*. Minneapolis: University of Minnesota Press, 2002.
Noguera, P. *The Trouble With Black Boys: And Other Reflections on Race, Equity, and the Future of Public Education*. Hoboken, NJ: Jossey-Bass, 2008.
Pascoe, C. J. *Dude, You're a Fag: Masculinity and Sexuality in High School*. Berkeley: University of California Press, 2007.
Thompson, A. "Caring in Context: Four Feminist Theories on Gender and Education." *Curriculum Inquiry*, v.33/1 (2011).

General Educational Development

The General Educational Development certificate (GED) is a secondary school certificate that allows those who leave high school early to obtain a credential by passing a battery of tests that cover five subject areas: reading, writing, mathematics, social studies, and science. The tests are designed at a level of difficulty such that about 60 percent of graduating high school seniors are able to pass the entire battery. GED certification has grown dramatically in the United States, and is recognized by many institutions as a high school equivalency degree. The academic literature on the benefits of a GED, however, provides extensive evidence that a GED does not offer the same benefits as a regular diploma.

The tests are developed and administered by the American Council on Education (ACE) GED Testing Service. The GED was originally developed in the 1940s to help veterans gain access to college. Civilians were soon allowed to take the test as well, and the credential became widely recognized as an alternative to a high school diploma. By 2001, about 11 percent of people ages 15 to 34 with a secondary credential held a GED. ACE sets the minimum standards for eligibility for taking and passing the test, but states can require higher standards (e.g., a higher eligibility age or score for passing). As a baseline, people are eligible to take the GED if they are not enrolled in high school, are at least 16 years old, and meet local requirements for age, residency, and length of time since leaving high school. ACE requires a minimum score in each subject area, as well as an average standard score across the five tests. Testing fees vary locally, and range from no charge to $150.

Attending College

The GED serves an important role in the American education system. In a highly age-graded system with few re-entry options, the GED is the most common route for people who drop out of high school to resume their schooling. Many who leave high school early get a GED, and dropouts who earn GED certificates are much more likely to enter college than those with no certification. The GED is promoted and legitimated by institutions such as public welfare programs and prisons that offer it as a form of basic education, and by governmental and educational institutions that equate it with a high school diploma. The GED also serves an important social function. It gives people without a high school diploma a way to change their status as a dropout.

GED recipients generally fall between traditional graduates and those with no secondary credential in terms of family background and personal characteristics. Traditional graduates are more likely to have better educated parents, live with their biological father at age 14, live in a two-parent household at age 14, have parents with higher occupational status, and score higher on tests of cognitive ability. GED recipients fare better on nearly all these measures than adults with no secondary credential. Traditional graduates and GED recipients also differ in patterns of family formation. GED recipients are more likely to have a first birth before marriage, have lower average ages at first marriage and first birth, and are more likely to have had their first birth or marriage by age 20. In contrast, GED patterns of family formation are nearly indistinguishable from those with no secondary certification. GED recipients report that they chose the credential for personal and family reasons, to pursue additional schooling, and for job-related reasons. Many also report that they thought it would be easier to get a GED than complete high school, did not like school, were failing school, or had missed too many school days.

Average Age at Completion

Only 36 percent of GED recipients complete their credential before age 19. The average age of certification is 21 years. Recipients who go on to enter college complete their certificate earlier, on average at age 20. When they enter college, GED recipients enter college at later ages. The average age of college entry for traditional graduates is 19, versus 23 for GED recipients. Traditional graduates who go to college are also far more likely to enter college immediately after graduating from high school. About 70 percent of traditional graduates who go on to college do so in the same year as they graduate, versus 27 percent of GED recipients. Among college-goers, the average time elapsed between high school and college is one year for traditional graduates, and three years for GED recipients. GED recipients catch up in their 20s with low, but steady rates of first-time college entry. This means that their educational careers are spread over a longer period of life.

The costs and benefits of the GED and the role it plays in the American educational system is the subject of extensive academic debate. Traditional graduates are much more likely to enter and complete college than GED recipients, and are more likely to enter a four-year college, while GED recipients are more likely to enter two-year colleges. Studies also show that the GED does not offer the same economic opportunities as a diploma. Although getting a GED may benefit dropouts with the lowest cognitive skills, it is not associated with higher earnings for dropouts with stronger skills. Moreover, relative to traditional graduates, GED recipients have lower earnings later in life. Studies suggest that differences in labor market outcomes are explained by the fact that GED recipients accrue substantially fewer years in school than traditional graduates.

Vida Maralani
Yale University

See Also: Adult Education; At-Risk Students; Dropouts; Transitions, School.

Further Readings
Heckman, James J., John Eric Humphries, and Nicholas S. Mader. "The GED," In *Handbook of the Economics of Education,* Hanushek, Eric A., ed. Vol. 3. New York: North Holland (2010).

Maralani, Vida. "From GED to College: Age Trajectories of Nontraditional Educational Paths." *American Educational Research Journal,* v.48/5 (2011).

Tyler, John H. "Economic Benefits of the GED: Lessons From Recent Research." *Review of Educational Research,* v.73 (2003).

Georgia

The 1945 Georgia State Constitution established the current organizational structure of pre-K–12 public schools, which includes 186 school districts, mostly county-based, and 27 municipal or "independent" school districts, the majority of which are city-based. The Georgia Department of Education (GADOE) is in charge of these districts, and was created in 1870 to oversee all aspects of pre-K–12 public education in the state. Its purpose is to ensure that education-related laws are obeyed and that state and federal education funds are properly allocated. Oversight of the GADOE is determined by Georgia state law, specifically, the Official Code of Georgia (O.C.G.A.) Section 160. The head of the GADOE, the state superintendent of schools, reports directly to the governor. The superintendent also serves as the chief executive officer for the state's Board of Education, composed of 13

members, who each represent one of Georgia's federal congressional districts. Pre-K–12 private schools in Georgia are not under the jurisdiction of the GADOE, and are instead governed by separate entities.

There are an estimated 2,000 public schools within the state. A total of 24 of these serve students with severe disabilities. In 2005, the state began to operate a virtual school, which largely serves high school students. Additionally, the state operates three schools for students with special needs between the ages of 3 and 21. The Atlanta Area School for the Deaf serves students in metropolitan Atlanta, the Georgia School for the Deaf provides day and residential education for deaf students throughout the state, and the Georgia Academy for the Blind provides residential education for children who are blind and offers a program for students with multiple disabilities.

According to figures provided by the Governor's Office of Student Achievement (GAOSA), the race/ethnicity of children enrolled in Georgia pre-K–12 schools from 2010 to 2011 was 44 percent European American, 37 percent African American, 12 percent Latina/o, 3 percent Asian, and 3 percent multiracial. Statewide, over 20 percent of students are enrolled in special education programs (including gifted), and English for speakers of other languages (ESOL)

Table 1 Elementary and secondary education characteristics

	Georgia	U.S. (average)
Total number of schools	2,541	1,988
Total students	1,677,067	970,278
Total teachers	112,459.60	60,766.56
Pupil/teacher ratio	14.91	15.97

Source: U.S. Department of Education, National Center for Education Statistics, Common Core of Data (CCD), 2010–11.

Table 2 Elementary and secondary education finance

	Georgia	U.S. (average)
Total revenues	$18,671,345,027	$11,464,385,994
Total expenditures for education	$19,007,701,383	$11,712,033,839
Total current expenditures	$16,030,039,288	$9,938,906,259

Source: U.S. Department of Education, National Center for Education Statistics, Common Core of Data (CCD), "National Public Education Financial Survey," FY08 (2007–08).

programs, serve a steadily growing 4 percent of students. Three other manifestations of pre-K–12 schools in Georgia are charter, private, and home schools.

Charter schools in Georgia are public schools that operate according to the terms of a charter that has been approved by the state Board of Education. A charter school may be exempted from certain rules and policies of standard public schools. In exchange for this flexibility, the school is required to meet the performance-based objectives specified by its charter. As of 2011, 113 charter schools were active in the state. In 2011, the Georgia State Supreme Court struck down an existing state commission that had the power to approve charter schools and direct local funding to charter schools over the objection of local boards of education.

In 2011, there were a reported 581 private schools (parochial and independent) in the state, enrolling roughly 120,000 students. Private schools in Georgia are subject to specific state laws regarding length of school year as well as curricular, testing, and reporting standards. Georgia state law provides home schooling as an alternative option for parents who possess a high school diploma or GED. There has been an escalation of home schooling across the state of Georgia, largely fueled by parental dissatisfaction with the direction that public education has taken and/or by parental desire to provide a more structured or experiential environment. State law requires home study programs to include instruction in reading, language arts, mathematics, social studies, and science.

A governor-appointed Board of Regents, created in 1931 to unify public post-secondary education under a single governing authority, governs public colleges in Georgia. Currently, the Board of Regents has 18 members, five who are appointed from the state at large, and one from each of the 13 congressional districts. The board elects a chancellor, who serves as chief executive officer and chief administrative officer of the university system.

The board oversees all public colleges and universities that comprise the University System of Georgia. Private colleges and universities are under private systems of governance. In 2009–10, Georgia was home to a number of postsecondary institutions: 18 universities, six state colleges, nine two-year colleges, and 22 private universities/colleges. Georgia is home to three "research one" schools, as designated by the Carnegie system: Georgia State, the Georgia Institute of Technology, and the University of Georgia. There are also a number of postsecondary professional/trade schools located in the State of Georgia, where students have the option of selecting from trades such as business, seminary, law, medicine, nursing, chiropractic, dentistry, and art/design. The Atlanta region enjoys a concentration of colleges and universities matched by few U.S. metropolitan areas. Also unique to the city of Atlanta is a zone known as the Atlanta University Center (AUC). This area consists of five well-known, historically black institutions: Spelman College, Clark/Atlanta University, Morris Brown College, Morehouse College, and the Morehouse School of Medicine.

In 2011, Georgia placed 48th in student SAT scores, a ranking that has seen little deviation over time. Many top-down educational initiatives have been put forth, most with little or no clear influential effect on student achievement. Debates have ensued across the state about educational reform issues such as curriculum narrowing, class sizes, standardized testing, school closings, and teacher evaluations. The most recent controversial initiative is Race to the Top; a federal government grants-based program that includes problematic mandates, such as teacher merit pay based on students' standardized test scores. In response to these initiatives, many grassroots educational advocacy organizations, supported by students, teachers, and parents/caretakers, have emerged. Some of the most active organizations are Metro Atlantans for Public Schools (MAPS), a teacher- and parent-driven organization; Empower Education for Georgia (Empower Ed.), which is teacher driven; and the Georgia Chapter of the National Association for Multicultural Education (GA NAME), primarily supported by university professors.

Mari Ann Roberts
Clayton State University

See Also: Black Colleges and Universities, Historically; Charter Schools; Home Schooling; Race to the Top.

Further Readings

Georgia Department of Education. http://www.doe.k12 .ga.us (Accessed December 2011).

Georgia Home Education Association. http://www.ghea .org (Accessed December 2011).

Governor's Office of Student Achievement. http://www .gaosa.org (Accessed December 2011).

Germany

Germany has been a federal democratic–parliamentary country since 1949 in central Europe, consisting of 16 states. It is a founding member of the European Union, and a member of North Atlantic Treaty Organization (NATO). With an area of 137,838 square miles (357,104 square kilometers) and an estimated 81,702,329 inhabitants, it is one of the largest European countries. Service industries (72.6 percent), manufacturing (26.6 percent), agriculture, forestry and fishing (0.9 percent) contribute to Germany's economy. Germany's gross domestic product (GDP) in 2010 reached approximately $3.3 trillion. Germany is an exporting nation with goods such as cars, car parts, machines, and chemical products. According to the World Bank, in 2010, Germany's economy ranked fourth worldwide.

The history of the German educational system is connected with its history of federalism, as there is not one unified German school system, but diversity from the states' historical autonomy in educational matters. This diversity has only been disrupted during the two totalitarian regimes in German history (Nazi Germany, and communist Eastern Germany) where the educational system was more unified under a centralized state doctrine. Compulsory schooling began in 1592 in Pfalz-Zweibrücken, and was by 1835 introduced in all German states.

Historically, the tripartite system that still prevails in Germany was to educate children from different social standing in different schools. The tripartite system was abolished during the communist regime in East Germany and was replaced by a comprehensive school system, while it was maintained in West Germany. Debates about equity led to the establishment of comprehensive schools in states with a social democratic orientation. After the fall of the Berlin Wall in 1989 and reunification, the tripartite system continued to exist in all 16 German states, regardless of political orientation.

Germany's educational system is strongly imprinted by its federal structure. Educational policies, curricula, and structures are under the responsibility of each of the 16 states and therefore vary depending on the particular state. In general, Germany's mainstream educational system is organized into elementary school (*Grundschule*) that goes from grades 1 to 4, 5, or 6. At the secondary level, all German states have a tripartite streaming system with the matching curricula:

- *Hauptschule* (Main School), which leads up to grade 9 and offers access to certain trades, manufacturing, and service industries
- *Oberschule/Realschule* (Upper School), which leads to grade 10, and offers access to apprenticeships in service industries, secretarial, and some educational professions
- *Gymnasium,* which leads to graduation with the *Abitur* (Baccalaureate) after grade 12 and grants access to university

Discussions around school reform and education equity in the 1960s led to the creation of a fourth school type that intends to abolish streaming by schooling all children in the same secondary school until grade 10, the *Gesamtschule* (comprehensive school). Most German states also have an elaborate system of schools and curricula for children with special needs (e.g., those with learning, mental, and physical disabilities, behavioral challenges, the deaf and hard of hearing, the blind and visually impaired, and sick children). Inclusive education of children with disabilities exists at differing degrees in all German federal states.

Current issues are arising out of the very structure of the educational system. Germany has been repeatedly criticized for the streaming nature of its secondary school system, from national as well as international viewpoints. This became most apparent through the "PISA-shock" (Programme for International Student Assessment), which ranked Germany below the Organisation for Economic Co-operation and Development-average, and demonstrated how the tripartite school system impedes equity for children of lower social class backgrounds and with a migratory background, as they are systematically streamed into the lower school tracks. However, the call for a more comprehensive school system has been highly politicized in Germany. Similarly, the debate around inclusive education for children with special needs has been very controversial, but has received new fuel since Germany has signed and ratified the United Nations Convention on the Rights of People with Disabilities, which engages the country to generalize inclusive education. The implementation of this engagement has sparked new discussion around the question of where and how children with disabilities learn best.

Cornelia Schneider
Mount Saint-Vincent University

See Also: Class Inequality: Achievement; Cultural Capital; Elementary Education; Governmental Influences on Education; Secondary Education; Special Education.

Further Readings

Gruber, K. H. "The German 'PISA-Shock': Some Aspects of the Extraordinary Impact of the OECD's PISA Study on the German Education System." In *Cross-National Attraction in Education. Accounts From England and Germany*, H. Ertl, ed. Oxford: Symposium Books, 2006.

Hinz, A. "A World of Difference: Inclusive Education in Canada and Germany." *Education Canada*, v.46/1 (2006).

Szydlik, M. "PISA und die Folgen." ("PISA and Its Consequences.") *Soziologische Revue*, v.26/2 (2003).

Ghana

Ghana is located in west Africa and borders Burkina Faso, Côte d'Ivoire, Togo, and the Gulf of Guinea. It is a former British colony, known as the Gold Coast, and in 1957 it became the first sub-Saharan African country to gain independence. Ghana is culturally diverse, consisting of various ethnic groups, including the Akan, Mole-Dagomba, Ewe, Guan, and Ga-Adangbe. Although it has one of the strongest-performing economies in west Africa, Ghana is still a relatively poor country. Ghana and its contemporary education system are products of its colonial history, rich ethnic diversity, economic prosperity, and recurrent poverty. Ghana has a long history of formal schooling, dating more than 100 years prior to the establishment of the first British school. Charles Kwesi Graham notes that Portuguese merchants established the first school at Elmina Castle during the 16th century. Dutch, Danish, and British merchant companies followed suit. However, unlike the other merchants, the operation of schools by British merchant companies during the 17th and 18th centuries served primarily commercial interests. By the middle of the 19th century, the British Crown established the Gold Coast colony via the annexation of the castles and forts operated by British merchant companies and rival colonial powers.

School Structure

The missionary societies operated the majority of schools in the Gold Coast colony during the mid to late 19th century; however, their influence over formal schooling waned by independence and eventually disappeared with the implementation of Dr. Kwame Nkrumah's Education Act in 1961. Successive governments since independence adopted a series of education policies to address colonial inequities, create a stock of human capital to stimulate the economy, and tackle the growing poverty. These policies include the restructuring of secondary education; establishment of technical/vocational, pre-primary, and special education; and the promotion of Free Compulsory Universal Basic Education (FCUBE) as part of Ghana's commitment to Education for All (EFA) and the Millennium Development Goals (MGDs).

The Ministry of Education, Science, and Sports (MOESS) is responsible for the administration and provision of formal education in Ghana. The MOESS consists of several statutory bodies, such as the Ghana Education Service (GES), which implements educational policies and programs. The MOESS centrally manages specific elements of the education system, including the curriculum, textbooks, new school construction, and teacher deployment and salaries. Formal education in Ghana consists of compulsory kindergarten (two years), primary (six years), and junior secondary education (three years); senior secondary education (four years); and tertiary education (two to 10 years). The Ghanaian examination system consists of the Basic Education Certificate Examination (BECE) and the Senior School Certificate Examination (SSCE). The West African Examination Council (WAEC) administers both examinations.

The BECE certifies the completion of junior secondary education and is the selection mechanism for entry to senior secondary education. The SSCE certifies the completion of senior secondary education, while polytechnics, teacher training colleges, and universities use student performance on the SSCE to select prospective students for certificate, diploma, and degree programs. While there are a growing number of private schools in Ghana, the majority of pretertiary schools are government schools. This is not the case for tertiary education, where there are a relatively similar number of private and government tertiary institutions (although the majority of students attend government institutions).

Current Status

Ghana's education system experienced considerable enrollment growth and greater financial commitment during the last decade. Yet, even with increased access to compulsory education and added financial resources, the Ghanaian education system faces serious challenges. The benefits of these improvements did not equally reach all segments of Ghana. There are still ample gender, ethnic, socioeconomic, and geographic disparities in terms of access to quality teachers, adequate school infrastructure, and learning materials. The disparities produce sizeable student dropout and retention, poor student achievement, failure to pass the BECE or SSCE and transition to higher levels of schooling, and perpetuate occupational and income inequalities.

William Joshua Rew
Florida State University

See Also: International Data; Poverty and Education; Worldwide Education Revolution.

Further Readings
Akyeampong, Kwame. *50 Years of Educational Progress and Challenge in Ghana.* Brighton, UK: Consortium for Research on Educational Access, Transitions, and Equity, 2010.

Graham, Charles Kwesi. *The History of Education in Ghana: From the Earliest Times to the Declaration of Independence.* London: Frank Cass and Company Limited, 1971.

International Bureau of Education. "World Data on Education: Ghana." Geneva: International Bureau of Education/United Nations Educational, Scientific and Cultural Organization, 2011.

Republic of Ghana. "Report on the Development of Education in Ghana." Accra: Ghana Education Service/Republic of Ghana, 2008.

World Bank. *Education in Ghana.* Washington, DC: World Bank, 2011.

Gifted Education

The term *gifted* has been used in educational settings since the early 1920s when Lewis Terman conducted a study of students with high IQs. Giftedness was formally defined by the U.S. federal government in 1972 in a report by John Marland, which noted that gifted students showed evidence of or potential for advanced academic achievement. Approximately 3 million U.S. students have been identified as gifted and talented. It is generally used in education today to refer to students who learn at a faster pace than average students, or who show potential for outstanding artistic, athletic, or academic achievement. Students may be gifted in one or more areas. They may also be advanced in some areas and slower in others.

Not all gifted students are motivated or high-achieving students. Gifted students require modifications to typical curriculum to meet their advanced cognitive, social, and emotional needs. There is no federal law mandating services for gifted students. Although 31 states have laws mandating gifted education, they vary on the requirements of identification and provision of programs and services. Currently, 14 states do not collect information about gifted students, 20 states do not monitor programs for gifted and talented students, and only 10 states publish an annual report on gifted and talented education. The only federal funding that exists for gifted education is the Javits Gifted and Talented Students Act, which is renewed every year. Funding for this act has declined significantly since 2001, which fell from $11.25 million to the current $7.46 million. Current federal education spending for gifted education is 0.026 percent, compared to 64 percent for No Child Left Behind and 32 percent for children with disabilities.

Identification

Although the field of gifted education research does not have a uniform definition of giftedness, there are several characteristics that indicate possible giftedness. Some intellectual characteristics include high levels of curiosity, passion for learning, divergent thinking, and rapid rates of learning new material. Some personal characteristics that may be displayed are the need for mental stimulation, intensity, sensitivity, and insightfulness. Not all gifted people demonstrate all of the characteristics. Some traits of giftedness may increase difficulties for gifted children, such as divergent thinking and intensity. It is necessary that programming for gifted students include social/emotional as well as academic support. There are several methods of identifying gifted students. Common measures include standardized achievement tests, intelligence tests, and tests of nonverbal ability. Teacher recommendations are often the first gateway for students to be identified as eligible for gifted programming. Typically, scoring above the 90th percentile on a standardized achievement test allows students to be considered for more in-depth testing. Some tests that may be administered are the Cognitive Abilities Test (CogAT), which is a group-administered test that measures students' reasoning abilities in verbal, quantitative, and nonverbal areas; and the Naglieri Nonverbal Test, which measures students' ability to reason, using progressive matrices or individual intelligence tests such as the Wechsler Intelligence Scale for Children–Fourth Edition (WISC-IV). The use of testing has drawn criticism because students who do not typically perform well on tests (e.g., minority, low-income, and English language learners) may be gifted, but not able to demonstrate it through test performance, and are thus excluded from beneficial programming.

Using nonverbal testing as a means of identifying gifted students may be viewed as a means of increasing the diversity in gifted programming. However, nonverbal reasoning does not play as prominent a role in academic learning as verbal or quantitative skills, therefore students who do well on matrices testing may not show advanced abilities in the classroom and require modification. Recently, researchers have recommended that schools use local norms, comparing students of similar backgrounds in the school to determine appropriate performance levels. For example, students of similar limited English language exposure would be compared to one another, instead of comparing them with students for whom English is the native language. Another issue in using teacher recommendations and testing for identifying students that would benefit from gifted programming is that issues may prevent a student from expressing their gifts. A small percentage of students are identified as twice-exceptional, possessing characteristics of giftedness and one or more learning disabilities. Issues such as students with dyslexia or autism may mask high abilities in other areas. Teachers frequently focus on remediating student weaknesses and may neglect to foster areas of strength.

Programming

Gifted education, or programming for gifted students, can take on many forms. Pull-out programs are the most commonly used in elementary schools, also called the enrichment model. This model, created by Joseph Renzulli, proposes that exploratory supplemental activities be offered to all students. Following the schoolwide enrichment courses, teachers provide accommodations for advanced students to enable them to pursue areas of interest, instead of repeating coursework that they have already mastered. In secondary education, students are encouraged to take advanced placement and honors classes to meet their educational needs. Enrichment opportunities, such as apprenticeships and mentorships, may be provided to students who have demonstrated a commitment to working at advanced levels in areas not typically taught in school.

Differentiation is most commonly used in the regular classroom and occurs when teachers modify the process, content, or product to meet the needs of diverse learners. Curriculum compacting, individual learning contracts, and allowing students to choose more challenging assignments are common means of differentiation. Curriculum compacting occurs when teachers use a pre-assessment to determine the areas of the curriculum that the student has already mastered. The student is then allowed to skip the instruction in these mastery areas, and the time may be spent on other projects that appeal to the student. Individual learning contracts are extensions of curriculum compacting, where the teacher and student create a written contract that details several enrichment options for the student, and agreements regarding the conditions by which the student will be allowed to participate in enrichment activities. Providing students with choices regarding the assignments allows teachers to differentiate for the entire class. Creating activities with differing degrees of complexity and challenge encourages students to work at a level that is appropriate for their readiness.

Cluster grouping, where students are taught at different ability levels, is another way to accommodate students who learn at a faster pace. This practice may occur within a single classroom, or across classes and grade levels. One benefit is that the students are at similar levels of readiness, which makes teaching easier. It is also beneficial for students to be placed with others of common readiness because they are able to learn and progress at a similar place, and are not forced to wait for others who may be significantly behind them in their understanding. Cluster grouping is different from tracking because the groups are flexible and may vary from subject to subject. For example, a student may leave the classroom to be grouped with other advanced students for math instruction, but would return to the classroom for all other subjects. Acceleration is the means by which students who have already learned the subject matter currently being taught may move to a higher level of curriculum. Acceleration may be accomplished by allowing students to go to higher level classes for a specific subject, enter kindergarten or college early, or move to a higher grade level. It is not uncommon for gifted students to enter a new school year already knowing 40 to 50 percent of the curriculum that will be taught that year. Forcing students to remain with their age mates may retard their academic progress by failing to allow them to learn new material. Research has shown acceleration to be the most effective and least costly intervention to aid gifted students in receiving appropriate educational opportunities.

Current Educational Issues

Gifted education is controversial. Some view gifted students as already possessing an advantage, and feel that special programs and teaching accommodations are giving more privilege. An overwhelming percentage of students recommended for gifted education programs tend to be white, middle-class students. This fact may lead some to believe that gifted programs are elitist. Others incorrectly believe that because gifted students are academically advanced, they do not require teaching or special accommodations to be successful. In fact, the Marland report recognized that gifted students require curricular modifications because of their advanced abilities. A major contributor to misconceptions regarding the needs of gifted students and special accommodations that are necessary is the lack of teacher training. This lack of training compounds the problem of identification because teachers who are unfamiliar with the characteristics of gifted students may misinterpret student behavior. Untrained teachers are forced to use their conceptualization of giftedness, which may be inaccurate, to identify students who need curricular modification. Approximately 61 percent of teachers report that they did not receive any training on the needs of gifted students. There are no federal requirements regarding teachers to receive instruction in working with gifted children. Although teachers are working with classes of heterogeneous abilities, they do not receive instruction on differentiation to meet the needs of all of the learners. Gifted students spend the majority of their day in a general education classroom, even in schools that have programming for gifted students. If classroom teachers do not provide accommodations to meet the needs of gifted students on a daily basis, the students' educational experience may suffer.

Emphasis on standardized testing has increased teacher attention to students functioning below average. Recent studies have shown that teachers spend the majority of their time on struggling students, leaving gifted students lacking teacher attention and curricular modifications. It also showed that although the achievement gap has been closing for low-achieving students, it is widening for high-achieving students. Students who score at the upper distribution on standardized achievement tests have shown less growth year-to-year than students in the middle and lower distribution. This lack of attention to the progress of high-ability students raises issues regarding students displaying one year of educational progress for each year of instruction.

Antonia Szymanski
Kirkwood Community College

See Also: Ability Grouping; Early Graduates; No Child Left Behind; Skipping Grades; Standardized Testing.

Further Readings

Colangelo, N. and G. Davis. *Handbook of Gifted Education.* London: Pearson Education, 2003.

Lohman, D. F. "The Role of Nonverbal Ability Tests in Identifying Academically Gifted Students: An Aptitude Perspective." *Gifted Child Quarterly*, v.49/2 (2005).

Loveless, T. *An Analysis of NAEP Data. High-Achieving Students in the Era of NCLB.* Washington, DC: Thomas B. Fordham Institute, 2009.

National Association for Gifted Students. "Why We Should Advocate for Gifted Students." http://www.nagc.org/index.aspx?id=538 (Accessed November 2011).

Reis, S. M. and D. B. McCoach. "The Underachievement of Gifted Students." *Gifted Child Quarterly*, v.44/3 (2000).

Silverman, L. *Counseling the Gifted and Talented.* Denver, CO: Love Publishing, 2000.

Gintis, Herbert

See Bowles, Samuel and Herbert Gintis

Globalization

With globalization, the process of ongoing interconnection of markets, human mobility, communication, and social and political ideas, education has become a key element and how it has been shaped has adapted. In order to better understand the extent of education and its sociological process under the occurrence of globalization, one needs to allude to the historic idea propagated by the Stoics. Education became a key element in the idea of inclusion and the nation-building project. The political worldview of the Stoics used education to propagate a more inclusive economic, political, and educational form of world unification.

In 1795, Immanuel Kant used the terms *universality* and *global* in *Perpetual Peace* to explain the Law of Global Citizenship. Events such as print allowed in the 18th century for the expansion of literacy and an increment in education. Furthermore, during the Enlightenment, especially in Europe, the idea of a more inclusive education began to propagate. Literacy rates in England alone from 1640 grew from 30 percent for males to 60 percent by mid-1700s. In France, from 1686 to 1690, the numbers grew significantly. There was a rate of 14 percent of educated women, and it climbed to 27 percent. For men, it went from about 29 percent to 48 percent, according to James Van Horn Melton. Furthermore, The Industrial Revolution in the 18th century initiated an economic, political, and cultural influence that was to have a direct impact on education in this new or "modern" form of globalization. It is imperative to understand the historical process of economic, political, and cultural process that has taken place during recent history in order to better grasp the progression of sociology of education.

The historical framework behind globalization and education is closely tied to economic development. This is not to undermine the cultural, political, and social aspects that were also achieved through the globalization process of education. The formation of members of a larger society took many Western developed countries on the path of economic governance of less developed countries; the action of colonization implied economic dominance. However, it also brought political, cultural, and social influences, which permeated educational systems. Globalization can be seen as a palpable process that has been taking place for a long time. There have been different stages in this process, however; during the past century, globalization has had an underlying trend. Globalization has influenced not only politically and economically, it has also permeated educational systems worldwide. Several dilemmas can be placed under globalization. During the 20th century, new political and economical patterns took place. There were no public education systems in the world before the 19th century. Furthermore, these public educational systems came

into existence primarily to meet the needs of industrialism; it was the intention of educating people to get a job.

Globalization is understood as a process of international integration of ideas, products, and human interaction. Some scholars assert that the process of globalization has been occurring since before the Greco-Roman period. Alternative theories state that it began in 1492 when Christopher Columbus arrived in the Americas in search of spices. Furthermore, contemporary theorists claim that the modern beginning of a globalization project occurred in 1944, during the first three weeks of July, when World War II was still being fought. Representatives from 44 allied nations gathered in Bretton Woods, New Hampshire, and formed the International Monetary Fund (IMF) and the International Bank for Reconstruction and Development (IBRD), two world organizations that were part of a political and economic project that sought to preserve world peace and do away with economic discrimination among nations.

Sociology of Education

Education is a building structure of every society. Some argue that it is the main conductor for social change. Enlightenment thinkers like Jean-Jacques Rousseau believed that education, particularly science and art, should be utilized to improve the human condition. However, others have stated that education has allowed for a world division, which has permeated into economic domination of the developing world. Some global analysts have described this global educational process as a "McDonaldization" phenomenon where Western, mostly economic patterns are strongly promoted across the board. One is educated to work and consume. Furthermore, the promotion and increase of modern education has in many parts of the world produced large masses of unemployment in urban populations. They are overeducated for the types of jobs that are available in mostly developing countries. However, schooling in the era of globalization has in fact developed psychological dispositions that train the individual for work and citizenship. The development of educational policy has been focused on a functionalist effort, where schools serve individuals to adapt to a changing society.

In the context of sociology, globalization and education can be seen from the vernacular, where the process of global integration has become an irreversible trend. Multicultural education promotes polyglots and cosmopolitan citizens who are better able to grasp the global economic and political division worldwide. Sociological aspects have worked alongside educational systems to try and produce better individuals who are able to cope with change and seek progress. We can envision a more conscious global citizen who will promote an environmental responsibility and a better *modus vivendi* for every individual in the global village. On the other hand, globalization and education can be viewed as a division of core and periphery countries, where economic fragmentation has dominated the world scene since colonization up to present time. This is a utilitarian perspective of education, where the natural design of economic and educational policy generates winners and losers.

In order to understand sociology of education, we need to grasp the consensus that globalization has endorsed on educational policy. Western countries adopted a postwar idea of progress and economic development. One could question if economic prosperity and economic opportunities have in fact been a wrong path for the focus of education. Before the processes of global economic reform, educational systems were mostly restricted to the elite population. Many of these schooling systems were inefficient and bureaucratic. Transnational economic activities provided infrastructure on educational systems where no structure had existed. However, without many of these transnational economic structures, segments of the population, such as women, black people, and other minorities, would not have been educated.

Examples of Education and Globalization

In the United States, for example, in the 1600s, there were some private schools in the New England colonies of Massachusetts, New Hampshire, and Connecticut. However, during the Industrial Revolution in the 18th and 19th centuries, major social, economic, and cultural changes occurred. These were important events that created a great impact in educational systems, particularly in Europe and the United States. Even though educational opportunities for a greater part of the population, such as elementary education during the 1700s, were still uncommon because of child labor; it was the beginning of a more visible path for public education. Before the institution of a public educational system, education was exclusively for the elite class, which for the most part was carried out by private tutors. Since the signing of the

Declaration of Independence in the United States in 1776, seven of the 14 states of the Union had specific provisions for public education. In the United States, the economy created difficult and variant scenarios. The Roaring Twenties and then the Great Depression had a direct impact on the education system. From 1890 to 1996, the percentage of students who graduated from the public school system went from 6 to 85 percent. Compulsory education also came into law during this period. It was now a legal requirement for every young American to remain in school up to the age of 16. During the early 1900s in the United States, the term *progressive education* came to predominate the schooling environment of the time.

One must understand the process of industrialization as a key element in the globalization of education. The new global economy expansion gave way to a more globalized education. Economic structures like the the G-7 were formed, and the United States, Canada, Germany, and Japan experienced great economic success during the last part of the 20th century. New educational systems were designed to meet technical instructions that supported the division of labor and service economy models. During this period, globalization and even post-Fordism education focused on quite specific outcomes. For example, flexible education that worked hand-in-hand with industrial production was necessary, as was a primary education that developed skills and competencies required by future workers in a globalizing world. All of these new skills were sought out by educational systems around the world. Newer models, such as international education and global distance education, have been established as disciplines that are now part of higher education. In the beginning of the capitalist order, the primary goal of education was to form citizens for the nation-state.

In regards to education, even though it was not a direct negotiation on the part of the Bretton Woods agreement, important educational strategies and programs came about thanks to these political and economic affiliations. Proof of this endeavor is the current program of the World Bank, which still promotes two themes on global education: Education For All (EFA), focusing on the 1990 global commitment to give "every citizen in every society" the opportunity for a basic education, and Education for the Knowledge Economy (EKE), based on the need to develop a well-trained workforce "capable of generating knowledge-driven economic growth." The

World Bank, in its effort to promote a global education system, began lending money in the early 1960s. In 2005, The World Bank loaned about $2 billion for educational projects; this sum increased from $728 million given out in 2000. Elementary education gets the largest percentage of these loans. In 2005, 29 percent of the entire budget was destined for primary education worldwide.

The modern age is recognized as a process that took place during the 20th century. Neoliberalism challenged the welfare state and Keynesian economic policies. Trickledown economic systems backed up by world powers like the United States (Ronald Reagan) and Great Britain (Margaret Thatcher) defended liberal economic ideologies that forced state powers to modify educational systems worldwide. The fundamental creed behind the liberal economic ideology promoted at this time was that developing countries should provide themselves with what is needed to train skilled and capable human capital. Young people in particular are required to compete in a demanding global market. The teaching and learning of "new technologies" became a trademark for this New Age globalization process. Globalized education focused primarily on secondary, trade, and university education. Areas of study such as science, technology, innovation, business, information, and communications technology became the pattern across educational systems.

Influential economists of the 20th century influenced the role of governments on economic policies in relation to institutionalized education around the world. In *Capitalism and Freedom,* Milton Friedman stated that education should form free individuals with rational capabilities in order to endorse autonomous thought. However, he also believed that schooling should be free and that government should have little say in what is taught in schools. Governments, for example, might become interested in subsidizing vocational training of individuals because this type of education increases chances of economic productivity.

On the other hand, authors like Martha Nussbaum, Anthony Appiah, Charles Taylor, Amy Gutman, and Amartya Sen have used terms like: multiculturalism, cosmopolitanism, and universality to describe some of the current issues that education must now confront. The development of globalization and education has in fact pushed for a promotion of world unification toward the achievement of a perpetual peace, where individuals come to understand the world that all humans share. One of its utmost purposes is to promote humanity and a better consciousness in regards to the less fortunate in regard to political, social, economic, and educational conditions. The idea of global citizenship promoted by the Stoics sought to endorse a civic education that fostered a global responsibility. Key elements in this type of education are: humanity, shared responsibility in issues dealing with the environment, a world community of justice, and international alliances that allow for human alleviation in the case of man-made or natural disasters; human dignity is understood as an intrinsic element in this globalized education effort.

Changing View of the World

Educational research and educational policy have documented specific case studies in many different parts of the world, and the different effects that globalization has had. Important aspects that deal with issues like: internationalization, government decentralization, standardized testing, gender equity, and human rights. Educational reforms all across the board have had a direct impact on curriculum inquiry and the construction of different local and global realities that everyday students must encounter in relation to receiving a globalized education.

Globalization in education has had recurring effects and alternative responses in every part of the world. Sociology of education and globalization can be viewed as a natural process of adaptation for the humane cosmopolitan view or the constant re-adaptation for the ongoing transnational capitalistic class that must be built to satisfy a global economy. Globalization in education has changed the way we view the world, particularly social, political, economic, and human relations.

Isaias R. Rivera
Tecnologico de Monterrey (ITESM)

See Also: Educationalization; Ethics in Education; International Data; Labor Market Effects on Education; Worldwide Education Revolution.

Further Readings

Bretton Woods Project. http://www.brettonwoodsproject .org (Accessed January 2012).

Burbules, Nicholas and Alberto Torres Carlos. *Globalization and Education: Critical Perspectives.* New York: Routledge, 2000.

Friedman, Milton. *Capitalism and Freedom.* Chicago: University of Chicago Press, 1962.

Nussbaum, Martha. *For Love of Country.* Boston: Beacon Press, 2002.

Thattai, Deeptha. "A History of Public Education in the United States." http://www.servintfree.net/aidmn-ejournal/publications/2001-11/PublicEducationInTheUnitedStates.html (Accessed January 2012).

Governmental Influences on Education

The function or purpose of education systems has been an issue for debate throughout history, and in particular in modern times, when some forms of education have become compulsory and increasingly funded by public money. The increase in the use of taxation to pay for education naturally leads to a parallel increase in political involvement in not only how education should be resourced, but also how it should be constructed, and what purpose it should have. At the same time as such issues are debated, however, the influence of different political ideologies that are more-or-less publicly espoused or debated also needs to be taken into account.

The educational policies of governments of different political persuasions reflect the ideologies or philosophies that underpin the political parties that control the legislature at any particular point in time. It has been argued that governments are more likely to influence—or interfere—with educational policy and provision than with any other potential area of interest (e.g., public health care or financial policy). There are two reasons for this. First, governments are easily able to demonstrate to the public that they are actively involved in a policy area that is of concern to the majority of the population. Second, governments are more able to actually change educational policy and practice than they are able to change economic or health care policy more generally.

Although governmental influence on educational policy and practice is, if considered from a historical perspective, both complex and changeable, there are nonetheless a number of key themes that can be identified as characteristic of contemporary espoused governmental influence on education—that is, ambitions of influence that governments openly espouse. These tend to revolve around two key and interlinked themes: first, the role of education in preparing people for employment; and second, the role of education in promoting social equality or social justice. The extent to which these ambitions are impacted by different ideologies or philosophies is a matter of considerable academic debate in both political and educational cultures.

Education as a Vehicle for Preparation for Employment

Educational provision of different kinds has long been used as a way of preparing the students who pass through the system for employment. Historical forms of provision, such as apprenticeships (used to train young men, and occasionally women, who were taking up a craft or trade occupation) or universities (used to train future generations of clerks and civil servants) have equivalents in many contemporary settings. Then, as now, the espoused aim of such provision was functional, driven by a need to provide a new generation of workers with the skills, knowledge, or other abilities that they would need in employment. Government at both national and local levels took an interest in the nature, quality, and content of education and training, sometimes in response to petitions from concerned trade or commercial bodies. For example, several centuries ago in Europe, trade and craft guilds were responsible for the nature and quality of the work of their members, a role that included maintaining the quality of the training of apprentices. The earliest example of state legislation in England that sought to influence apprentice training was during the 16th century, and was not abolished until the beginning of the 19th century, over 300 years later, according to J. Simon.

However, in order to understand current governmental imperatives, it is necessary to contextualize recent and contemporary political, economic, and social themes. For example, the pace of industrial and technological change, and linked to this the globalization of economic activity, has had a profound impact on the kinds of work that are carried out in societies in different parts of the world. In some parts of the globe, manufacturing output has declined drastically, whereas in others it has expanded greatly. Newer economies, such as the high-growth economies of Brazil, Russia, India, and China (BRIC) now have to manage the expansion of the kinds of industrial education and training that Europe has now left behind, but at a greatly increased speed in order to cope with an increased demand, which is growing at an exponential rate. Older economies in Europe, in contrast, have to shift their education and training policies in order to prepare people for work in an increasingly uncertain climate, where workers frequently have to reskill or upskill in order to change occupations. It is against the backdrop of "new capitalism" that current government policies and agendas have to be understood, as noted by J. Gee et al. There is now a requirement for education and training systems to produce individuals who are trained in generic employability skills such as problem-solving and creative thinking, concepts that are highly contested. The "new vocationalism" argues that a worker's identity is no longer defined by what he or she knows, or what specific technical skills or abilities he or she may possess. Rather, a worker is identified as possessing particular kinds of attitudes and attributes: being a self-starter; being a good communicator; being a team-player; and being committed to their lifelong learning so that they can maintain employment in changing times, as claimed by scholars.

Governments, therefore, have in recent times been obliged to pursue two distinct avenues of educational policy. First, they have been obliged to sustain those central controls over compulsory schooling that have been characteristic of educational systems over recent decades. Second, they have been increasingly obliged to intervene either directly (through national curricula) or indirectly (through promoting the role of organizations that represent the interests of employers and industries) in curriculum design and implementation in order to not only provide specific courses to meet the needs of specific sectors of the jobs market, but also to provide students with the transferable and generic employability skills that current discourses of workplace competence require workers to possess. This has involved not only changes in the ways that governments influence compulsory educational provision in schools and colleges, but also an increased focus on employability skills within university curricula. This has also involved greater governmental involvement in workplace learning. Historically, learning at work has been an informal and unregulated arena of education and training provision. However, the requirements of new capitalism to equip workers with the transferable skills that they require has led to significant increases in educational forms, such as the accreditation of workplace learning, mentoring

and coaching, and the accreditation of experiential learning. These models of learning, which are characteristic of human capital theory, rest on ways by which informal learning can be accredited and made accountable: processes that necessarily require governmental intervention.

Promoting Social Justice Through Education

A second theme is the ways in which governments intervene at different times and in different parts of the educational structures that fall within their remit, in order to pursue a specific avenue of social policy, or to in some way improve or ameliorate the social and/or economic position of the individual who is within the education system. At this time, there is no meaningful equivalent dominant discourse of educational policy that borrows from the classical liberal tradition and argues for the purpose of education for the benefit of the cultural, intellectual, and spiritual growth of the individual and, by extension, the society within which she or he lives.

Governmental policies that regard education as a vehicle for promoting social justice also position social justice as an outcome of greater economic prosperity. At the same time, they position economic and social amelioration as an individual achievement. Characteristic of neoliberal discourse, governments argue that it is through the efforts of the individual person—engaging in continuous lifelong learning, in order to obtain a better standard of paid employment, enter a more lucrative profession, or even simply maintain employment—that the social goals of education can be met. Putting the individual at the center of this process of social change at best marginalizes and at worst removes completely structural or overarching theoretical arguments regarding links between educational achievement, social inequality, and economic prosperity from public discussion and debate.

Social inequality is assumed to be a consequence of individual fecklessness or unwillingness to engage in learning for the purpose of securing work and thereby also securing economic independence. This analysis rests on a discourse of individualism and of deficit: If an individual lacks the skills that he or she needs to gain employment, then the socially responsible course of action is to undertake new training in order to gain employment. Analyses of educational, and by extension social, inequality that focus on structural or cultural factors as impacting on the life chances of the individual (e.g., the social and economic profile of a particular geographical area, or family histories of educational engagement and employment) are therefore automatically discarded. Education becomes a tool for economic growth to be picked up by the individual learner, as related by G. Biesta.

Governmental Influences on Educators

If governments are going to take their ambitions to influence educational practices and structures seriously, then it follows that this influence will also need to extend to educators. Like any other workforce, educators—or a meaningful proportion of them—will need to be convinced, perhaps more or less willingly, to align themselves to the agendas of any particular government at any point in time. This need for alignment need not preclude the continued existence of independent professional bodies, pressure groups, and trades unions. But if governments can find ways to work either with or around such groups, then their agendas can be enacted. As educators have become more highly professionalized (where professionalism is defined as being educated to university degree level and holding a license to practice that is granted and audited by a professional body), one key element of professional autonomy—control over curriculum content—has been gradually eroded.

One of the more profound recent political debates can be dated back to 1976, to a speech given by James Callaghan, the British prime minister, at Ruskin College in Oxford. To supporters, Callaghan's speech was a timely critique of an educational system that was under the excessive control of unaccountable teachers who failed to prepare students adequately for employment. To his critics, Callaghan's speech was a direct attack on the professionalism and independence of educators, and gave the first hint of a national curriculum that would reduce teacher autonomy and increase the influence that central government had over educational structures more generally. The speech was not simply an attack on teacher autonomy, nor was it a flawless blueprint for a national curriculum that would allow education systems to meet perfectly the needs of business and industry. At the heart of this debate lies not the extent to which government should or should not influence the curriculum, but the extent to which educational systems need to serve the political or economic needs of the country, as distinct from doing something quite different: producing a well-educated society, simply because that is how a society should be.

The diverse themes that have been explored thus far—the impact of the new capitalism, new vocationalism, human capital theory, and the extension of direct governmental control over curriculum—all converge when discussing the ways in which educators have been rendered powerless by successive governments. The emergence of managerialist cultures as a consequence of the proliferation of neoliberal market models within public sector organizations has led to a significant increase in bureaucratic work that has in turn expanded as a consequence of greater central control and audit of educational provision across all sectors (i.e., from early years through to higher education, adult education, and workplace learning). The concomitant growth of surveillance technologies, such as inspection and audit, enforced by legislation, combined with increased demands on teachers, serve to deskill, rather than upskill or reskill the education workforce. In this sense, educators, as a profession, are prone to the same pressures as are any other sector of the workforce. Just as upskilling and maintaining employability are devolved to the individual, the management and associated bureaucracy of increasingly complex centralized educational systems are devolved to teachers—practitioners—who in turn have to have these elements of their work supervised by a hugely increased class of education management professionals. At the same time, teachers are told that these management and bureaucratic roles are empowering because they imbue the teaching workforce with greater degrees of autonomy.

Critical Perspectives on Governmental Influences on Education

These arguments assume that governments are active and purposeful agents within contemporary cultures. Proponents of the "third way," an intellectual and political attempt to reconcile now-discredited forms of state-controlled economics with unfettered free-marketism, argue for a different role for governments that in turn impacts on the way that government influence over educational structures can be theorized and understood, as described by A. Giddens. According to third way politics, the role of government becomes one of brokerage between the demands of capitalist structures and the responsibilities of the individual, tempered by a commitment to social justice and equity. The role of governments in helping individuals mitigate the potentially deleterious effects of the *risk society*, as termed by U. Beck, which is understood as a society within which neoliberal marketization, globalization, and technological innovation have combined to create uncertain futures for everyone, can therefore be seen as applying to education as much as to other areas of public policy concern, such as public health care. According to this perspective, therefore, any governmental influences on educational provision need to be understood as informed and possibly led by the market, rather than by government policy or ideology, let alone through a mutually reflexive dialogue with education professionals and professional bodies. As such, structural inequalities within societies remain unchallenged and the place of education remains primarily as serving the needs of a globalized capitalist economy, rather than any other aspect of the human condition.

Debates about government influences on education, therefore, perhaps need to be reframed, and the limitations that governments operate under need to be foregrounded. In contrast to the position that governments spend disproportionate amounts of time interfering with educational systems because they provide conspicuous ways of demonstrating policy engagement, an alternative perspective might be to consider the ways in which the fundamental purposes of education and curriculum have in fact been either partially or entirely removed from the direct control of governments of all political colors.

Jonathan Tummons
Teesside University

See Also: Administration of Education; Curriculum Standardization; Deskilling of the Teaching Profession; Educational Policymakers; Schools as Bureaucracies.

Further Readings

Beck, U. *The Risk Society: Towards a New Modernity*. London: Sage, 1992.

Biesta, G. "The Learning Democracy? Adult Learning and the Condition of Democratic Citizenship." *British Journal of Educational Psychology*, v.26/5 (2005).

Gee, J., G. Hull, and C. Lankshear. *The New Work Order: Beyond the Language of the New Capitalism*. St. Leonard's, Australia: Allen and Unwin, 1996.

Giddens, A. *The Third Way and It's Critics*. Cambridge, UK: Policy Press, 2000.

Knight, P. T. and M. Yorke. *Assessment, Learning and Employability*. Maidenhead, UK: Open University Press/Society for Research into Higher Education, 2003.

Osborne, M., M. Houston, and N. Toman, eds. *The Pedagogy of Lifelong Learning*. London: Routledge, 2007.

Shore, C. and S. Wright. "Audit Culture and Anthropology: New-Liberalism in British Higher Education." *Journal of the Royal Anthropological Institute*, v.5/4 (1999).

Simon, J. *Education and Society in Tudor England*. Cambridge: Cambridge University Press, 1979.

Grade Inflation

Grade inflation happens when higher grades are assigned for work that would have received lower grades earlier, and is usually attributed to lax academic standards and low instruction quality. It can also lead to credential inflation, and makes it difficult to identify truly excellent students. Grade inflation is also not uniform across schools and disciplines. National and international standardized tests are often considered as counterbalancing forces, equalizers, and warning signals of grade inflation.

For instance, in the United States in the 1980s, while *A Nation at Risk* (1983) reported an overall mediocre or poor performance and falling achievement on standardized national and international tests of American students, grade point averages (GPAs) received both at secondary and postsecondary levels started to increase dramatically. This discrepancy is often considered one of the significant factors to have triggered the discussions on grade inflation, academic quality, and student performance both in the United States and around the world, and has made a number of countries reconsider standards of assessment criteria.

On average, private universities grade 0.3 point higher than public universities. Grading in public and private universities was more or less similar during the 1940s and the 1950s. The process began to diverge in the 1960s, and became vivid in the 1980s. In the United States in the 1930s, the average GPA was about 2.35. By the 1950s, the average GPA increased to 2.52. Grades started to rise faster in the 1960s, and the inflation process became most vivid in the 1980s, and is continuing to present. The average GPA of a school appears to be strongly related to its selectivity. For instance, in Dartmouth, mean GPA rose from 3.06 to 3.23 from 1968 to 1994. At schools with average selectivity, the GPAs were lower, 3.11 and 2.98

at private and public institutions respectively. At a number of community colleges, the reverse tendency, grade deflation, has been observed.

Qualitatively, much of the increase in average GPA has been accounted for by the improvement in student quality since the mid-1980s. Quantitatively, a coefficient of 0.14 was found to prove the relationship between SAT and GPA for a 100 point increase. A 0.1 relationship between a 100 point increase in SAT and GPA was found using data from over 160 institutions with over 2 million students. Therefore, quantitative studies have proven that grade inflation is not strongly related to student improvement. A number of researchers have expressed opinions that other factors causing grade inflation might be at work. For instance, some faculty regard nonuniform grading systems as the primary cause for grade inflation. Moreover, in many countries, the privatization of higher education is also considered to have triggered grade inflation. Retaining students by assigning higher grades is a common practice, especially in transition countries that are just opening up private universities and are trying to retain students, although the information on their Web sites and in booklets usually emphasizes academic rigor and quality to present themselves as competitive to wider society.

In a number of transition countries, grade inflation has been connected with corruption and bribery, both in secondary and higher education. Awarding higher grades to students who offer bribes to teaching staff is widespread in many postsocialist countries. Throughout the world, the spread of consumer-based culture of higher education has been regarded as one of the primary causes of grade inflation, particularly since the 1980s. This fact, in turn, is believed to have weakened both grading standards and intellectual rigor in higher education.

Trying to get positive feedback from students in the end-of-term evaluation sheets is yet another incentive for faculty to inflate grades in the hope of a return favor. Many academics believe that students focus on learning and concentrate better on issues covered during classes when they do not worry about grades. Therefore, professors try to diminish the grading stress factor to the minimum and direct students' attention and energy toward a deeper understanding of academic issues. Over the past decades, attempts have been made to look into the problem of grade inflation and decrease it. For this reason, making grades and data publicly accessible has been one

solution; for instance, Princeton University made its data publicly available, requiring from staff to clarify grading criteria in 2004.

Mariam Orkodashvili
Vanderbilt University

See Also: Community Colleges; Curriculum Standardization; Grading; International Data; *Nation at Risk, A*; Standardized Testing.

Further Readings

Johnson, V. E. *Grade Inflation: A Crisis in College Education.* New York: Springer, 2003.

Rojstaczer, S. and C. Healey. "Grading in American Colleges and Universities." *Teachers College Record* (March 4, 2010).

U.S. Department of Education. *A Nation Accountable: Twenty-Five Years After* A Nation at Risk. Washington, DC: U.S. Department of Education, 2008.

Grading

Grading refers to the act or process of assessing the performance of an individual. In schools, percentages, raw scores out of a possible total (e.g., eight out of 10), descriptive adjectives (e.g., "excellent" or "proficient") and other quantifiable symbols (e.g., a letter grade of "A") are common means of representing the achievement level or competence of a student on a given assignment or course. Grading is a vital practice in the structure of traditional educational institutions because it is believed to quantify the proficiency and quality of a student's ability. Social, educational, and economic institutions and systems often rely on the grading process as a means of comparing the quality of individuals for selection, promotion, and employment. Most countries use individual grading scales that are deemed appropriate for their education systems and communities. Several internationally recognized standards (e.g., the international baccalaureate) are used in various jurisdictions. In the United States, grading standards and processes are influenced by national, regional, state, district, and school level policies.

From their inception, schools have found methods to gauge individual performance and differentiate among students, even when grading was not a standardized system of measurement. The development of grading systems occurred within the context of larger schoolhouse developments, such as entrance requirements, curricular modifications, and the conferment of degrees and awards.

Social class has also served as a means of marking or differentiating among students. Yale University was the first college to use grading to evaluate students' academic standing. Historical records indicate that grading practices in the form of descriptive adjectives (e.g., *optimi* and *inferiores*) were used as early as 1785 at Yale. By 1813, a 4.0 scale was utilized at Yale, and Harvard had begun to use various numerical scales to measure student achievement by the 1830s. The mid- to late 1800s would see many schools and universities experiment with various grading practices. By 1883, letter grades were used at Harvard; and in 1897, Mount Holyoke merged descriptive labels, percentages, and letter grades to create a grading system that would serve as the model for the most common grading systems used today.

Grading is typically used as a means of comparison. Grading produces data that are used to compare students with other students, which is a common practice in standardized testing and when students are graded on a curve. Grading on a curve is a mathematical adjustment to allow the highest individual score to become the top mark possible, without regard to total points possible. Grading is also used to compare students with established standards (e.g., the use of letter grades, percentages, and grade point averages to determine admission criterion). Grading also serves as a method to compare students with themselves. For example, grading can help determine student aptitude—the difference between a student's potential and his/her actual performance. Similarly, grading is used to compare student performance with effort, to compare student performance with a student's improvement, and to determine the most appropriate teaching practices to improve student performance.

There are many ways that instructors award grades. One of the most common ways is to assign a score for performance in either the numerical or alphabetical format. This performance score is applied to assignments, quizzes, tests, reports, projects, and papers produced by the student. Grades can be assigned in letters (e.g., A, B, C, D, or F), as a range of numbers (e.g., 4.0–1.0), as a number out of a possible total (e.g.,

out of 20 or 100), as commendations (excellent, great, satisfactory, needs improvement), or in percentages. It is not uncommon for a teacher to simply offer a pass/fail grade or general comments about the student's performance. The instructor uses grades to show varying levels of student mastery. A high letter (A), number (4.0), or percentage (100 percent) attained leads the teacher to feel that the student is more likely to have completely mastered a concept. Similarly, the middle and bottom of those scales offer details about mastery to the opposite effect.

Some contend that grading benefits the student by serving as tangible feedback that reinforces the expectations of the teacher with regard to standards of learning. Grading also provides parents with necessary information to closely monitor their child's development and progression in a particular class or level of schooling. Grading can offer necessary measures to determine how to promote students, and grades are a typical approach for determining eligibility for promotion. Some believe that grades cause students to focus on merely getting the correct answer or earning sufficient points, instead of focusing on learning and developing. Grading is emotionally taxing on students because of the pressure to make a good grade. Students may enroll in less challenging classes in order to secure a good grade, rather than maximizing their potential in more advanced courses. This is the most detrimental effect that grading has on overall learning.

Ty-Ron M. O. Douglas
University of North Carolina at Greensboro
Jahni M. A. Smith
Teachers College, Columbia University

See Also: Grade Inflation; Standardized Testing; Tracking.

Further Readings
Durm, Mark. "An A is Not an A is Not an A: A History of Grading." *The Educational Forum*, v.7/3 (1993).
Guskey, Thomas. "Making the Grade: What Benefits Students?" *Educational Leadership*, v.52 (1994).
Kohn, Alfie. *Punished by Rewards: The Trouble With Gold Stars, Incentive Plans, A's, Praise, and Other Bribes.* Boston: Houghton Mifflin, 1999.
Smallwood, Mary. *An Historical Study of Examinations and Grading Systems in Early American Universities.* Cambridge, MA: Harvard University Press, 1935.

Grandparents' Role in Education

According to recent U.S. censuses, more grandparents are living with school-age children, so the impact of grandparents on their grandchildren's education is becoming increasingly important. Grandparents can give grandchildren extra resources to aid their education, or they can compete with them for scarce family resources, which can hinder the grandchildren's learning. Furthermore, these effects differ across societies with different cultural values. As more families face economic or relationship difficulties, they increasingly turn to grandparents to help raise their children. Because of low marriage rates and high divorce rates, over 47 percent of children do not live with both biological parents, and extended family members such as grandparents help care for them. Likewise, inflation-adjusted, median individual income has fallen over the last two decades. As a result, often both parents in a household work, and grandparents care for their children during working hours.

Grandparents can give their grandchildren extra capital (material, human, cultural, or social) and more learning opportunities, on which they can capitalize to achieve more (as a resource provider). Grandparents can provide material capital in the form of education resources (such as a quiet study room, books, or a computer) to create a rich learning environment for their grandchildren. By giving grandchildren these educational resources, grandparents reinforce the importance of education.

Grandparents' knowledge and skills (human capital) can enhance grandchildren's learning both indirectly and directly. Grandparents can aid a grandchild's learning indirectly by creating a vibrant, high-quality learning environment and by rewarding grandchildren's academic success psychologically, socially, or materially. Grandparents can also directly help grandchildren learn through both education-specific activities and general activities. A grandparent might talk with a grandchild about their arithmetic, or their creative writing. They can also discuss their hobbies, share stories about relatives, or just spend time together. Through these interactions, grandparents can serve as role models, ask provoking questions, or give explicit instructions, all of which can help children learn cognitive and social skills. Highly educated grandparents also monitor and supervise grandchildren more actively and have more information and skills to teach them.

Cultural Values and Norms

Grandparents also typically have more experience within a culture than parents have, and can help their grandchildren learn cultural knowledge, skills, and values (cultural capital). Cultural possessions at home (such as paintings and poetry) can exemplify the importance of one's culture and facilitate family communication about cultural values and norms. During cultural conversations, grandparents can model appropriate societal behaviors and explain cultural norms to help their grandchildren learn the cultural values of their family, school, and society. Specifically, these conversations can help grandchildren to better understand teachers' and classmates' expectations in school so that they can behave appropriately and build better relationships. Supported by teachers and students, these children might receive more learning opportunities, be more motivated, learn more, and be more successful in school. Last, grandparents often have large social networks of family, friends, and acquaintances (social capital). This social capital can provide further resources for a grandchild's education, complementing the resources of family members. Students with higher socioeconomic status grandparents often have higher academic achievement. This effect is especially strong for children living with single mothers, who rely more on grandparents and other extended family members.

On the other hand, grandparents can also compete with grandchildren for scarce family resources, thereby reducing available family resources for grandchildren (resource dilution). Grandparents who are too poor or ill to live by themselves often live in a household with three generations of family members. Furthermore, these grandparents may consume limited family resources that might otherwise support a child's education. As a result, grandchildren who live with their grandparents typically have fewer learning resources and learn less than those who do not live with their grandparents. In countries that have recently implemented universal education, uneducated or poorly educated grandparents might be less helpful than other grandparents to their grandchildren. Such grandparents often lack the academic or cultural knowledge to help their grandchildren in school. Even worse, these grandparents might have incorrect academic knowledge or outdated cultural knowledge that competes with parents' or teachers' ideas and thereby obstructs their grandchildren's learning. Grandparents who live with their grandchildren are generally poorer, less healthy, and less educated. Thus, grandchildren who live with their grandparents typically have lower academic achievement than those who do not live with their grandparents.

Grandparents' roles also differ across individualistic versus collectivist cultures. In individualistic cultures, people favor individual interests over group interests, and grandparents tend to live farther away from their grandchildren. As a result, these grandparents are less likely to engage with their grandchildren. In collectivist cultures, extended family members typically live near one another and help with childrearing. Grandparents in collectivist societies often attend to their grandchildren's care and early education, including reminding them that their success or failure in school affects their entire family's reputation. Hence, grandparents in collectivist countries typically have a greater impact (whether positive or negative) than those in individualistic countries on their grandchildren's lives.

Ming Ming Chiu
State University of New York, University at Buffalo

See Also: Family Structure and Education; Household Educational Resources; Intergenerational Closure.

Further Readings

Bengston, Vern. "Beyond the Nuclear Family." *Journal of Marriage and the Family*, v.63 (2001).

Chiu, Ming Ming. "Families, Economies, Cultures and Science Achievement in 41 Countries." *Journal of Family Psychology*, v.21 (2007).

Hank, Karsten and Isabella Buber. "Grandparents Caring for Their Grandchildren." *Journal of Family Issues*, v.30/1 (2009).

Greece

With nearly 1,600 surrounding islands, Greece covers about 51,000 square miles (132,000 square kilometers), and is located at the southeastern edge of the European continental mainland. It neighbors Albania, Macedonia, and Bulgaria in the north, and Turkey in the east. However, the majority of its land is bordered by seas, the Ionian Sea on the west, and the Aegean Sea on the east, giving it the 11th-longest coastline in the world. It had an estimated population of 10.7 million in July 2012, the majority living in urban areas, primarily the capital of Athens and in Thessaloniki. The Greek economy accounts for approximately $318 billion in gross domestic product (GDP). The Greek state employs over 40 percent of the labor force, represented by union leadership, while the service industry produces 78.8 percent of the GDP. The European Union (EU) gives Greece about 3.3 percent of its GDP in aid, but because of a growing budget deficit, in 2011, the GDP real growth rate was estimated to be negative 6 percent. Greece has had to borrow more than its GDP to service its debts, and is presently struggling because of the unpopularity of government spending cuts imposed by its lenders, with measures especially unpopular among unions. Greece has lost much consumer confidence in the current global financial crisis.

Greece has inherited elements of European, Balkan, Mediterranean, and Near Eastern cultures. However, because of the vestiges of celebrated classical contributions, it is more frequently renowned for being the cradle of democracy. Greek recorded history began around 2000 b.c.e., with the Minoan and Mycenaean cultures. The Dorian period, 1200 b.c.e., included the Trojan wars, about which Homer wrote his epics. Education espoused a warrior morality, where subservience to the gods and their laws was paramount. Subsequently, the rise of Greek city-states enabled the defeat of Persia in 490 b.c.e., and the golden age of Greece began, where education in literature, philosophy, art, medicine, and even athletics excelled, as in the Olympic Games. Sparta and Athens had education for free males; Athenian education centered on the mind as well as the body, including Homer's moral poetry. Higher education became open to all free men by the time Socrates and Plato (Socrates's student) started the Academy, a school to help youth search for the ultimate "good." A Platonic student, Aristotle started a school, the Lyceum, and his writings became influential in philosophy and education.

Aristotle taught Alexander, who conquered the known world, Hellenizing it. Because Rome conquered Greece, the Hellenic culture affected their empire, as well as the ensuing Christian Church, which influences education today. The Christianized eastern part of the Roman Empire, Greek Byzantium, survived the collapse of Rome for over a thousand years, and continues to influence education. Despite four centuries of subsequent Ottoman Turkish rule, nearly 97 percent of the population remains Greek Orthodox. The Church influenced the desire for independence, helping establish the current republic in 1821. Before becoming a member in the EU in 1981, the republic overcame World War II occupation by fascist Italy and Germany, as well as communism during the subsequent civil war in 1949. The Greek civilian republic was established in 1974, has been part of the EU since 1981, and part of the Eurozone since 2001.

Educational Organization

The Greek education system is organized to accommodate students from ages 2.5–26, where compulsory education extends from ages 5 to 15. The system is classified into five levels: pre-primary (ages 2.5–7), primary (ages 6–12), lower secondary (ages 12–15), upper secondary (ages 15–18), and higher education (ages 18–26). To cater to students with special needs, vocational education is provided, starting from the upper secondary level. After completing lower secondary education, students have the option to attend either educational lyceum or vocational training schools. A similar alternative is also presented at the higher education level, where students can attend vocational training institutes or technological education institutes. In 2009, enrollment rates for primary, lower secondary, upper secondary, and higher education were 31.7, 17.1, 19.5, and 31.7 percent, respectively. As of 2008, the number of students in tertiary education was 637,623, 49.9 percent of whom are male and 50.1 percent female.

Greek people have acknowledged the value of formal education since the Hellenistic period, thus they strive for the highest quality. The country is also known for incorporating very difficult entrance exams for its elite higher education institutions (HEIs). Unfortunately, because of the severe economic crisis crippling the country, the strain on the higher education system has increased in the midst of recurrent budget cuts and hiring restrictions. Consequently, as the number of high school students pursuing a higher education degree increased to 40 percent in 2008 (from 15 percent in 1974), so did the competition. Other than governmental HEIs, there has been little competition at the higher education level, and poor academics are driving an exodus of serious higher education students, to the extent of 40,000 in 2011, to study abroad. Hence, the passage of a new bill that would permit

some privatization of a governmental monopolistic hold on higher education.

Recent protests are quite vocal, claiming that stakeholders' voices are not taken seriously. Spending on secondary education, additional higher education preparatory schools, and private tutoring services expenditures can reach a point where parents are spending almost 1.5 times as much as that of the state on secondary education. The severe economic crisis and cuts on the national education budget have translated into an extra financial burden on parents, who are forced to spend more than 5 percent of their income on higher education preparatory services.

Nancy Wehrheim
Selim Selvi
University of Pittsburgh

See Also: Bulgaria; European Union; Turkey.

Further Readings

Cribiore, Raffaella. *Gymnastics of the Mind: Greek Education in Hellenistic and Roman Egypt.* Princeton, NJ: Princeton University Press, 2001.

Damanakis, Michael. "European and Intercultural Dimension in Greek Education." *Greece European Educational Research Journal*, v.4/1 (2005).

Hope, Kerin. "Students March Over Greek University Reform." *Financial Times* (August 25, 2011).

Katsimi, Margarita and Thomas Moutos. "EMU and the Greek Crisis: The Political-Economy Perspective." *European Journal of Political Economy*, v.26/4 (2010).

Ministry of Greek Education, Lifelong Learning and Religious Affairs (MGELLRA). "Greek Education System." http://archive.minedu.gov.gr/en_ec_page1531 .htm. (Accessed February 2013).

Guam, U.S. Virgin Islands

Situated on opposite sides of the globe, Guam and the U.S. Virgin Islands are connected by their dependency status as organized, unincorporated territories of the United States. Guam is the largest and southernmost of the Mariana Islands, an arc of volcanic islands located in the northwestern Pacific Ocean, with Japan to the north and New Guinea to the south. The U.S. Virgin Islands include Saint Croix, Saint John, Saint Thomas, and their surrounding minor islands, which are located east of Puerto Rico in the Caribbean Sea. The U.S. federal government maintains policy relations with the territorial governments through the Office of Insular Affairs under the U.S. Department of the Interior.

Archaeologists believe that the Mariana Islands were inhabited for several thousand years prior to the arrival of Europeans. The indigenous culture and language of the islands is known as Chamorro. Guam and the other Mariana Islands were claimed by Spain in 1565, but colonization did not begin in earnest until a century later, at which time the native population was decimated by disease and violence. After more than three centuries under Spanish control, Guam was ceded to the United States in 1898. The island was briefly occupied by Japanese forces during World War II, and has since remained an important strategic site for the U.S. military. In the most recent U.S. census (2010), the population of Guam numbered 159,358. A demographic profile is not yet available for 2010. The previous census (2000) identified the three largest subgroups as Chamorro (37.1 percent), Filipino (26.3 percent), and other Pacific Islanders (11.3 percent). In the same year, 23 percent of the population were living below the poverty line. The island's economy is supported by military spending and tourism, with roughly two-thirds of the labor force employed in the service sector (2004 est.). In 2009, the gross domestic product (GDP) per capita was $28,232.

The islands of Saint Thomas and Saint John were colonized by Denmark in the latter half of the 17th century, and in 1733, Saint Croix was added to the Danish West Indies by purchase from France. Under Danish rule, the islands were part of the sugar, rum, and tobacco economy, which depended largely on slave labor. Economic decline and racial conflicts followed the abolition of slavery in 1848, eventually leading to the U.S. purchase of the three islands from Denmark in 1917. In the most recent U.S. census (2010), the population of the U.S. Virgin Islands numbered 106,405. In the previous census (2000), 76.2 percent of respondents identified as black, 13.1 percent identified as white, and the remaining 10.7 percent identified as other or mixed ancestry. In the same year, 32.5 percent of the population were living below the poverty line. Tourism is by far the largest share of the economy, with roughly 80 percent of the labor force employed in the service sector. Petroleum refining, rum distillation, and other manufacturing activities also contribute to the islands' economy. In 2009, GDP per capita was $39,876.

Structure of Education

In both Guam and the U.S. Virgin Islands, the public education system is administered by the respective territorial government. The territories receive funding from the U.S. Department of Education and must comply with federal regulations, including portions of the No Child Left Behind Act of 2001. As in the 50 United States, education is compulsory up to age 16. Both territories also have private schools with religious and cultural affiliations. The Guam Department of Education administers 27 elementary schools (grades K–5), eight middle schools (grades 6–8), and five high schools (grades 9–12), with a total enrollment of 31,095 in 2011. The graduation rate for the four-year cohort of students entering high school in 2007 was 68.9 percent.

Since 1997, the U.S. Department of Defense (DOD) has operated separate schools for military dependents in Guam. The University of Guam, established in 1952 as a teacher-training college, is now a public comprehensive university, with 3,639 students enrolled in undergraduate and master's degree programs in 2011. The U.S. Virgin Islands Department of Education administers 22 elementary schools (grades K–5/6), six middle/junior high schools (grades 6/7–8), and four high schools (grades 9–12), with a total enrollment of 13,123 in 2010. The graduation rate for the four-year cohort of students entering high school in 2005 was 63 percent. Established in 1962, the University of the Virgin Islands is a public liberal arts university with 2,642 students enrolled in undergraduate and master's degree programs in 2010.

Guam and the U.S. Virgin Islands experience many of the same educational challenges as other areas of the United States with high poverty rates and sharp inequalities. Both school systems are struggling to improve reading and math proficiency and to increase graduation rates. Additionally, Guam is anticipating a significant population increase in the coming years. With the closing of U.S. military bases in Okinawa, DOD plans to transfer 8,600 marines and their dependents to Guam. Although military dependent children will attend DOD schools, the expected influx of civilian workers may lead to an increase in the school-age population, thus putting a strain on the resources of the public education system.

Daniel C. Narey
University of Pittsburgh

See Also: No Child Left Behind; Puerto Rico; Race to the Top.

Further Readings

Guam Department of Education. "Annual State of Public Education Report, SY 2010–2011." Agana, Guam: Department of Education, 2011.

U.S. Census Bureau. "Chapter 7: Puerto Rico and the Outlying Areas." In "Geographical Areas Reference Manual." Washington, DC: U.S. Census Bureau.

U.S. Department of the Interior, Office of Insular Affairs. http://www.doi.gov/oia (Accessed February 2012).

U.S. Virgin Islands Department of Education. "2009–2010 NCLB Report Card." St. Thomas, U.S. Virgin Islands: Department of Education, 2011.

Guatemala

Guatemala is the most populous country in Central America. A former Spanish colony, Guatemala obtained its independence in 1821. Guatemala is between Mexico and El Salvador and Honduras; it borders the Gulf of Honduras and Belize to the east. As of July 2011, its population was approximately 14.38 million. Guatemala has a high percentage of indigenous people, around 50 percent. Poverty and income inequality are still some of the most important problems in Guatemala. Its economy is based on agricultural products, such as coffee and bananas, but recently there has been an increase in exports of ethanol and investments in general. Remittances from the United States to Guatemala represented 10 percent of its gross domestic product (GDP).

Guatemala was part of the great Mayan empire. However, when the Spanish arrived in 1524, the great Mayan cities were already in ruins. There were some small tribes and kingdoms of indigenous people that were classified into two families, the Mayans and Nahuatl, according to the language they spoke. Guatemala was a Spanish colony until 1821, and it was briefly part of Mexico until 1823. The current Republic of Guatemala was officially established in 1838, when General Rafael Carrera ousted Mariano Gálvez, the governor of Guatemala. From 1838 until 1871, Guatemala was governed by the Conservative Party. In 1871, the Liberal Party gained control of the government through a revolution. During the 20th century, Guatemala had a mix of civilian and military governments, dictators, and revolutions. The past century was also characterized by governmental corruption, social unrest, and repression. Its 36-year civil war ended in 1996 with the signing of the Peace Accords.

The education system in Guatemala is divided into four levels: preschool, elementary, secondary (with two modalities, basic and diversified), and higher education. Elementary education is compulsory and is divided into two three-year cycles known as fundamental and complementary education. Secondary education is divided in two cycles, basic and diversified (or professional). The basic cycle lasts for three years; after completion, students receive a diploma. The diversified or professional cycle is either two or three years, according to one's choice of specialization. At the end of this cycle, students receive a degree, which enables them to get into college or practice their elected profession. The curriculum for the basic cycle is standard throughout the country; there are no electives.

Educational Reforms

As with most Latin American countries, Guatemala has embarked on a series of recent education reform initiatives. After signing the Peace Accord of 1996, a series of education goals were established, such as providing more access to education and equal opportunities to its population, increasing government investment in education, alleviating poverty and discrimination, and increasing the rate of literacy. There were specific goals, such as reducing the illiteracy rate to 30 percent (the Guatemalan illiteracy rate was 38 percent in 1994, and 24 percent in 2004). Even though there have been improvements in this area, a deeper analysis shows that the illiteracy rate is still high among indigenous peoples, especially among indigenous women. For instance, the illiteracy rate among indigenous people who are older than 15 years is 48 percent. Access to education has improved in recent decades. For instance, in 1995, only 72 percent of children eligible for primary education were enrolled, but that percentage rose to roughly 96 percent in 2006. However, the same cannot be said about preschool and secondary education, where enrollment rates for 2006 stood at 53 percent and 35 percent, respectively.

Bilingual education programs have expanded throughout the country in order to attend to the needs of the different ethnic groups, especially among indigenous peoples. However, access to bilingual education is not universal, and existing bilingual programs are generally of poor quality. Higher education is offered by one public and nine private universities. The gross enrollment ratio in 2007 for tertiary education was 18 percent, which was up from 9 percent in 2002. At the University of San Carlos, which is the oldest (established in 1676) and only public university, enrollment increased from 82,384 students in 1996 to 109,679 in 2002.

There are frequent fluctuations guiding education policies, primarily because of regular changes in the government. There are still great inequalities in terms of ethnic groups and rural versus urban populations. The rates of repetition, illiteracy, and dropouts are higher among indigenous than *ladinos* (people of mixed Amerindian and Spanish ancestry). There was an effort to expand coverage to rural populations through PRONADE, a community-managed program for educational development. However, it was cancelled in 2008, despite its success in reaching out to many populations in rural settings. Preschool is still an area in which the government could invest more, and as a result, preschool education is only available to a small percent of the population.

Liza Valle
University of Pittsburgh

See Also: El Salvador; Honduras; Mexico.

Further Readings
Alvarado, Felix. *AED and Education in Contexts of Fragility*. Washington, DC: Academy for Educational Development, 2010.
Menéndez, Luis. *La Educación en Guatemala 1954–2004* ("Education in Guatemala 1954–2004"). Guatemala City: Editorial Universitaria, 2006.
Rivas, Felipe. *El Estado de la Educación en América Central, 2000–2008* ("The State of Education in Central America, 2000–2008"). San Salvador, El Salvador: Imprenta Criterio, 2008.

Guidance Counselors, Role of

Most high schools employ guidance counselors to assist students in transitioning after graduation to postsecondary education or work. They also help students select and schedule the appropriate coursework for their chosen career path, and support the college search and selection process. Guidance counselors help students identify their strengths and weaknesses and choose the appropriate post-graduation path. Students from low-income and minority backgrounds, as well as those who would be the first in their family to attend college (first-generation college students), benefit greatly from the support of guidance counselors. But there has long been some controversy surrounding the differential access to counselors that students are granted according to their socioeconomic status (SES), as well as the extent to which counselors should focus on college preparation, given that not all students plan to attend college. However, in today's college-for-all climate, counselors play an important role in helping more students transition successfully to postsecondary education, despite the concern that many students are not adequately prepared for college-level work.

Counselors as Gatekeepers
Guidance counselors are gatekeepers; students often rely on them for support and information regarding colleges and careers. Early literature suggested that guidance counselors were overly influenced by a student's SES when providing advice, and they spent more time with students of higher-SES backgrounds. In this way, early scholars accused guidance counselors of helping reproduce social stratification through their work. There is a large body of literature related to the role of curriculum placement and tracking and how this practice reflects and reinforces social class. Some studies have found that verbal ability, highly correlated with SES, is more of a factor than class background in predicting the time spent with a counselor and the content of their advice. Verbal ability strongly influences initial curriculum placement, which affects students' course-taking trajectory, a key component of college preparation. Other factors include the students' early educational aspirations, and those which their parents have for them. Some researchers have found that when intelligence and parental and student educational aspirations are controlled, there is no SES effect on the content and time spent with a counselor. However, scholars maintain that counselors spend more time with higher-SES students. The literature also suggests that counselors on the whole do little to stretch or expand upon students'

aspirations, but merely reinforce them. This has direct implications for students who might be prepared for college, but because of familial or SES background, do not expect to go.

Changing Role of the Guidance Counselor

While guidance counselors have always been charged with supporting students as they make transitions to life beyond high school, in recent years, counselors' roles have expanded to include many other responsibilities. Inadequate research on the effectiveness of counselors, as well as a lack of professional organization of the field, has meant that counselors have been vulnerable to budget cuts, and guidance offices in many public high schools have shrunk. Today's counselors are frequently tasked with scheduling, testing, discipline and behavioral issues, and supervision, as well as guidance.

According to L. Perna and colleagues, in 2006, only 21 percent of public high schools in the country had a dedicated college counselor. This is coupled with very large caseloads. While the American School Counselor Association now recommends a student to counselor ratio of 250:1, the national average in 2008–09 was 457:1, and states such as California, Minnesota, Arizona, and Utah all exceed 700:1. These represent the ratios in public high schools throughout the country; private and parochial schools traditionally place greater emphasis on college guidance. Though many believe that counselors should spend more time on college guidance and preparation, this has not been a focus of their professional education historically. Particular topics, such as financial aid and completing the Free Application for Federal Student Aid (FAFSA), are highly complex, and many counselors report that they are not adequately prepared to support students.

Influence of Habitus and the Local Context

Patricia McDonough uses the term *habitus* to describe the social norms, expectations, and contexts surrounding the college culture of the high school. School size and location, course offerings and tracks, and racial and socioeconomic status of students impact the habitus, or college-going culture of the school, which is reinforced by counselors and teachers. Other factors include district expectations and policies regarding college-going behavior, relationships that counselors have with postsecondary institutions, and counselors dedicated solely to college preparation, rather than scheduling, discipline, or other administrative tasks.

A school's habitus, in turn, impacts the focus for postsecondary preparation in the rest of the school, such as curricular offerings and extracurricular activities. While guidance counselors play a key role in creating the college-going culture of the school, they do so in the context of the local habitus. Some districts endeavor to make college-going a priority, and allocate additional resources in support of this aim. These resources include providing support for counselors to attend conferences, helping them build relationships with postsecondary institutions, and addressing gaps in their college knowledge. These schools are also more likely to offer college preparatory courses, including Advanced Placement and International Baccalaureate programs, to support this goal. However, these districts tend to be in high-SES areas, thus exacerbating the gap between the richest and poorest students in college preparation.

Implications for First-Generation and Low-Income Students

Meanwhile, poorer schools in both urban and rural areas are forced to make difficult choices with limited funds. School counselors are tasked with many responsibilities beyond postsecondary guidance, and the focus of that guidance is constrained. Lower-SES schools direct more resources toward insuring that students stay in school and graduate on time, rather than boosting college enrollment of their graduates. Hence, the habitus of these schools tends to be such that only a handful of students are expected to go to college, or are directed to less-selective four-year schools and community colleges, and the rest are prepared for work, trade school, or the military. Counselors at low-SES schools are more likely to be managing many other responsibilities, and have little time for one-on-one attention with students. The responsibility is therefore placed on the students and families to make contact with the counselors and get the necessary support for the college-going process. This becomes an additional barrier for students who require extra help because of a lack of college knowledge at home. Students who need help the most, including lower-achieving students, as well as higher-achieving students who might be eligible for more selective postsecondary institutions, are therefore not receiving the support that they need to make these transitions.

Kri Burkander
Michigan State University

See Also: Educational Aspirations/Expectations; Parental Educational Expectations; Poverty and Education; Tracking.

Further Readings

McDonough, P. M. *Choosing Colleges: How Social Class and Schools Structure Opportunity.* Albany: State University of New York Press, 1997.

Perna, L. W., H. T. Rowan-Kenyon, S. L. Thomas, and A. Bell. "The Role of College Counseling in Shaping College Opportunity: Variations Across High Schools." *Review of Higher Education*, v.31/2 (2008).

Plank, S. B. and W. J. Jordan. "Effects of Information, Guidance, and Actions on Postsecondary Destinations: A Study of Talent Loss." *American Educational Research Journal*, v.38/4 (2001).

Guyana

Guyana became the first cooperative republic in the world after gaining independence from the British in 1966. In the 1980s, under Linden Forbes Burnham, Guyana changed its constitution to install Burnham as president for life (a post he held until his death in 1985), as well as making Guyana a Socialist Republic. Guyana was a founding member of the Caribbean Free Trade Association (CARIFTA) in 1968, its postcursors the Caribbean Community (CARICOM) in 1973 and the Caribbean Single Market in 2006. Its main exports are bauxite, alumina, sugar, gold, rice, shrimp, molasses, rum, and timber. Guyana is the only English-speaking country in South America, and consists of some 83,000 square miles (214,969 square kilometers)—bordered to the west by Venezuela, east to Suriname, and Brazil at the southwest and south—and continues to have long-running contiguous and maritime border disputes with its neighbors. The people of Guyana are mainly of African or East Indian descent, a direct result of slavery and the importation of east Indians as indentured servants. In 2011, the World Bank estimated its population to be 744,768, and the 2011 Human Development Index ranked Guyana 117 out of 187 countries surveyed, giving it a medium developed country rating.

History of Education

Formal education in Guyana dates back to 1807. In 1835, the Negro Education Grant was administered to subsidize the work of religious institutions, and the 1876 Educational Ordinance made educational attendance for residents of urban cities possible. Postcolonial education was based upon the spirit of cooperation in the form of cooperative socialism from 1971 to 1985 under Prime Minister Forbes Burnham and the People's National Congress (PNC), with the dual objectives of: engendering the Guyanese people a greater role in the economy, and ridding its economy of the effects of dependent capitalist development. The goals of cooperative socialism included feeding, clothing, and housing the nation by 1976, and expanding the welfare sector, particularly education. In education, cooperative socialism reforms focused on de-privatizing (e.g., privately owned church schools were nationalized) and expanding mass schooling to make education free, building new teachers' training colleges, making schools coeducational, and introducing a new secondary school of excellence, the President's College.

In 1972, Guyana joined the Caribbean Examination Council (CXC), which provides secondary school exit examinations in the form of the Caribbean Secondary School Certification Examination (CSEC) and the Caribbean Advanced Proficiency Examinations (CAPE). By 1985, Regional Democratic Councils dotted the reform landscape as a decentralization mechanism. Cooperative socialist education reform ended with Burnham's death, and after democratic elections were held in 1992, education reform focused on deregulation, decentralization, and privatization with the aid of loans from the World Bank and the International Monetary Fund (IMF). Under austerity measures, in 1994, the University of Guyana (UG), established in 1963 as a free public university, was forced to implement cost recovery measures in the form of tuition fees. Despite this history, education in Guyana developed most robustly in the mid- to late-20th century in four distinct phases: (1) from 1966 to 1976, an indigenous curriculum was developed; (2) by 1990, education was made free; (3) equity of access was reached by 1995; and (4) quality basic education was enacted by 2000. Currently, Guyana has a literacy rate of 98 percent.

Formal nursery schooling (kindergarten) began in 1976, and education is free and compulsory for ages 5 to 14. Starting at age 3, children have two years of pre-primary education, followed by six years of primary education (grades 1–6). Community high school (grades 7–10) or junior secondary and high school slots (grades 7–12) are awarded based on assessments in grades two, four, and six that began in 2007. In secondary school, students write the CSEC, and if they wish to pursue further studies, some students spend two additional years (grades 13–14) in secondary school and write the CAPE, to be awarded the CXC Associate Degree, or go directly to university or work. However, students in community high school write the Secondary Schools Proficiency Examination (SSPE), and if they are successful, they can transfer into junior secondary school or high school and write the CSEC. Students need a minimum of five passes (of either grades A, B, or C) at CXC, including passes in both mathematics and English, for admission to the University of the West Indies (UWI) and UG.

Funding

In 1999, Guyana qualified as a Heavily Indebted Poor Country (HIPC) through the Paris Club Lyons terms and received $256 million in debt forgiveness. By 2001, Guyana's debt dropped to $150 million. Educational improvements include the Primary Education Improvement Project (PEIP), funded by the IDB for $51 million in 2000, the Secondary School Reform Project (SSRP), funded from 1996 to 2004 by the World Bank, and the Guyana Education Access Project (GEAP), funded by the United Kingdom Department for International Development (DFID) with $20 million from 1998 to 2008. Guyana is also a Fast Track Initiative (FTI) country, with funding of $45 million for 2003 through 2015. Since the late-1990s, privately owned schools, as well as church- and faith-based schools, have been established. Low teacher salaries, shortfalls in financing education, and the impact of HIV/AIDS are all current challenges that the Guyanese education system faces.

Tavis Jules
Loyola University Chicago

See Also: Bahamas; Barbados; Cuba; Trinidad and Tobago.

Further Readings

CARICOM. *The Future of Education in the Caribbean.* Georgetown, Guyana: CARICOM, 1993.

International Monetary Fund and International Development Association. "Final Document on the Initiative for Heavily Indebted Poor Countries" (1997). http://www.imf.org/external/NP/hipc/pdf/guyana.pdf (Accessed August 2012).

Lee, Franz. *The Evolution-Involution of "Co-Operative Socialism" in Guyana, 1930–1984.* Pandemonium Electronic Publication (2000). http://www.franzlee.org.ve/coopguy.html (Accessed August 2012).

Rose, Euclid A. *Dependency and Socialism in the Modern Caribbean: Superpower Intervention in Guyana, Jamaica and Grenada, 1970–1985.* Oxford: Lexington Books, 2002.

H

Haiti

Haiti shares the island of Hispaniola with the Dominican Republic, located approximately 48 miles (77 kilometers) east of Cuba. Haiti occupies one-third of Hispaniola, and had a population of 9,719,932 in July 2011, maintaining half of the island's total population. Its official languages are French and Haitian Creole. According to the Central Intelligence Agency, Haiti ranks among the poorest of the world's countries: approximately 80 percent of the population is below the poverty line.

Haiti's history of rebellion and subsequent economic and governmental struggle has affected life on the island, including education. While Haitians rebuild their nation, education becomes a priority. Christopher Columbus landed on the island of Hispaniola in 1492. The Spanish ruled the island until 1692, when they yielded a third of the island to the French, who were beginning to colonize in significant numbers. For over 100 years, forestry and sugar cane were the primary industries, maintained by African slaves. Slavery continued in the country until January 1, 1804, when Haitian slaves, led by Toussaint L'Ouverture, won their freedom and gained independence from French colonization. Jean-Jacques Dessalines, a leader in the revolution, declared the nation independent from France and named the country Haiti. In response to the new country's violent revolution, France demanded that Haiti pay 150 million francs in order to have Haiti's independence recognized, as well as to compensate for the revenue that slave labor would no longer provide. Since its independence, Haiti has experienced more periods of unrest than peace. Jean-Jacques Dessalines became the first president of Haiti, and was assassinated by his countrymen. For decades afterward, corrupt leaders have taken control of Haiti, and self-serving foreign policies have contributed to the economic disenfranchisement of the small country. Most presidents have been ineffective at best, and destructive at worst.

The 1987 Constitution of Haiti mandated that education be required and free for all children, however, this has not been feasible. Schools are typically funded by the national government, religious organizations, and nonprofit organizations. The Haitian school system comprises the equivalent of 13 grades. Primary school begins at preschool age, after which students enter *Enseignement fundamental* (fundamental education). After nine years in fundamental education and the attainment of a diploma, students proceed to *enseignement secondaire* (secondary education.) At approximately 18 years of age, students enter the final year of secondary school, *terminale,* at the end of which students must take a final exam to be conferred the *Baccalauréat* diploma. At early cycles of education, students can begin to make decisions about which track they would like to follow: a professional and vocational path, or the formal one to the *Baccalauréat.* After graduating with the *Baccalauréat,* top students have the option of entering one of Haiti's universities. However, because of cost and strict admissions, students seek postsecondary education in the United States, France, and Latin American and Caribbean countries. Because of limited job opportunities, and brain drain, the gradual departure of intellectual leaders, is a concern for Haiti.

In January 2010, a 7.0 magnitude earthquake hit Haiti and devastated Port-au-Prince. The earthquake affected nearly 2 million people who lived and work in the capital city and the surrounding areas. In October 2010, the U.S. Centers for Disease Control and Prevention confirmed an outbreak of cholera in the country. Since then, the nation has been in a period of delayed reconstruction. Since the earthquake, Haiti's political infrastructure has also seen some change.

In 2011, after a controversial and lengthy election process, Michel ("Sweet Mickey") Martelly became the 56th president of Haiti, succeeding Rene Preval. A former popular musician, President Martelly campaigned with an eye toward educational reform, including free education for all children. Although critics have been skeptical of his ability to put his plan into action, there has been some progress during his short tenure in the presidency. After naming George Mérisier the Minister of Education, President Martelly opened a number of schools across the country. At the beginning of the 2011 academic year, Martelly partnered with the United Nations Children's Fund (UNICEF) and the World Food Programme to provide meals for students in school. Issues of well-educated teachers and rebuilding school buildings remain, but the president's highest priority is education. Much work remains re-establishing primary, secondary, and postsecondary education in the wake of the earthquake.

Barbara Thelamour
Michigan State University

See Also: Cuba; Dominican Republic; Jamaica; Poverty and Education.

Further Readings

Centers for Disease Control and Prevention. "Haiti Cholera Outbreak." http://www.cdc.gov/haiticholera (Accessed December 2011).

Central Intelligence Agency. "The World Factbook: Haiti." https://www.cia.gov/library/publications/the-world-factbook/geos/ha.html (Accessed November 2011).

Dayan, Joan. *Haiti, History, and the Gods.* Berkeley: University of California Press, 1998.

Embassy of Haiti. "Education." http://www.haiti.org/index.php?option=com_content&view=article&id=181 (Accessed December 2011).

White, Ashli. *Encountering Revolution: Haiti and the Making of the Early Republic.* Baltimore, MD: Johns Hopkins University Press, 2010.

World Food Programme. "Haiti." http://www.wfp.org/countries/Haiti/News/President-Michel-Martelly-on-School-Meals---It-s-good--very-good- (Accessed December 2011).

Hallinan, Maureen

Maureen T. Hallinan, past president of the American Sociological Association, past editor of *Sociology of Education,* member of the National Academy of Education, and prolific scholar, has helped shape the field of sociology of education through her research on student learning and school organization. Her research addresses organizational characteristics, both within (ability grouping) and between schools (Catholic school effects), which helps explain inequality in student outcomes. Hallinan's early work with Aage B. Sorensen addresses three necessary components of student learning: ability, effort, and opportunity to learn. While ability and effort are student characteristics, schools control the opportunities for student learning. Opportunities to learn are situations that provide students with the potential for learning and set the upper limit for the amount of learning that can take place. Throughout her career, Hallinan's research focuses on two aspects of school organization related to opportunities to learn: ability grouping and school sector, particularly Catholic schools. Hallinan's research contributes to the field of sociology of education by furthering the understanding of student learning through the relationship between school organizational structure and differential access to opportunities to learn.

Ability grouping is the practice of placing students into separate groups for the purpose of tailoring instruction to their needs and abilities. Hallinan distinguishes between two types of ability grouping: curricular tracking, where students are assigned to particular classrooms for differential instruction;

and within-class ability grouping, where students are in various ability groups within the same classroom. Much of Hallinan's research in this area focuses on the former, curricular tracking, which impacts student learning because of the variation in quantity and quality of opportunities to learn across track placements. Rather than schools adjusting their tracking structure to the student population, Hallinan finds that schools place students into the pre-existing tracking structure of the school. Ideally, curricular track placement should be determined by student ability. While higher ability students tend to be in advanced curricular tracks with more academically challenging content, there are overlapping ability distributions across curricular tracks. Hallinan finds student placement is not based solely on student ability.

Other student background characteristics, such as student socioeconomic status, influence track placement. Students from families with higher socioeconomic status are more likely to be in academically challenging curricular tracks. While students in lower levels of curricular tracks tend to have fewer opportunities to learn, students are able to move between curricular tracks in order to improve opportunities to learn. Hallinan finds that students are more likely to move up into a higher curricular track than move down into lower curricular tracks. This finding indicates that students are sometimes able to increase their opportunities to learn through track mobility. Hallinan's research on curricular tracking helps show how the organizational structures of schools are related to student opportunities to learn. Unequal access and quality of opportunities to learn often lead to unequal learning outcomes.

Current Work

More recently, Hallinan's research focuses on Catholic schools. Much Catholic school research, which is studied under school and sector effects perspectives, focuses on differences in student learning by the type of school that students attend. In her edited volume, *School Sector and Student Outcomes,* Hallinan and others systematically examine school characteristics in relation to student learning outcomes. In her chapter with Brandy J. Ellison, Hallinan focuses on sector differences in student placement in ability groups. They find that students in Catholic schools are exposed to more opportunities to learn than public school students, no matter what the students' ability group levels are. This helps explain the higher academic achievement of

Catholic school students as compared to public school students. Through support from the U.S. Department of Education, Hallinan was principal investigator for the Comparative Analysis of Best Practices in Public and Catholic Elementary and Secondary Schools. This study focused on examining the practices that teachers use to provide students with opportunities to learn academic skills and to improve social development. Research that has resulted from this study did not find a Catholic school advantage in middle school, an often neglected grade range for Catholic school research. Hallinan's continuing research on the relationship between school characteristics, opportunities to learn, and student outcomes provides researchers with a framework for understanding how organizational characteristics both between and within schools influences student learning.

Elizabeth Covay
Michigan State University

See Also: Ability Grouping; Catholic Schools; School Effects; School Organization; Tracking.

Further Readings

Hallinan, Maureen T. *School Sector and Student Achievement.* Notre Dame, IN: University of Notre Dame Press (2006).

Hallinan, Maureen T. "Tracking Mobility in Secondary School." *Social Forces,* v.74/3 (1996).

Hallinan, Maureen T. and Warren N. Kubitschek. "School Sector, School Poverty, and the Catholic School Advantage." *Catholic Education: A Journal of Inquiry and Practice,* v.14/2 (2010).

Hauser, Robert

Robert Mason Hauser is a Vilas research professor, emeritus and Samuel A. Stouffer professor of sociology at the University of Wisconsin, Madison. After retiring in 2010, Hauser was appointed executive director, Division of Behavioral and Social Sciences and Education at the National Research Council (National Academy of Sciences). Hauser received his Ph.D. in sociology at the University of Michigan in 1968 under the tutelage of Otis Dudley Duncan. He joined the faculty at Brown University in 1967 and the

University of Wisconsin, Madison, in 1969—where he helped establish a world-renowned sociology department and mentored generations of leading scholars in the field. While at the University of Wisconsin, he directed the Center for Demography of Health and Aging, the Institute for Research on Poverty, and the Center for Demography and Ecology. Hauser's work has influenced social stratification, social demography, and statistical methodology. However, his seminal insights into the roles of families, individuals, schools, and schooling in educational and occupational attainment have established him as a titan in the field of sociology of education. He is a member of the National Academy of Sciences, American Academy of Arts and Sciences, the National Academy of Education, and the American Philosophical Society.

Occupational Origins to Occupational Destinations

The model of "status attainment" (SA) that Peter Blau and Otis Dudley Duncan elucidated in *The American Occupational Structure* examined the mechanisms that linked father's occupational origins and son's occupational destinations through the educational and social experiences of the son across childhood and adolescence. Hauser made key contributions to this literature by refining the measurement of key components of the attainment process, as well as by adapting data from Wisconsin siblings to understand how shared unobserved family factors might explain previous estimates of the SA model. These contributions significantly improved scholars' understanding of the importance of schooling relative to family origins in the process of status attainment. Scholars in the related field of comparative social mobility research examined the extent to which fathers and sons in nations like the United States tended to share similar occupations across generations. Hauser's work established that associations between father's and sons' occupational statuses were largely the same across the industrialized world and across time. Hauser's work in the status attainment and comparative social mobility literatures greatly improved both the understanding of the role of education in the placement of individuals in the status hierarchy, as well as the understanding of the limitations that educational expansion has had on loosening the bonds of family origin on individuals' attainment over time in industrialized nations.

Hauser has been an investigator at the Wisconsin Longitudinal Study (WLS) since his arrival in Madison in 1969 and has been the director of the project since 1980. The WLS has followed the lives of 10,317 men and women who graduated from Wisconsin high schools in 1957, and those of their randomly selected brothers and sisters, for more than half a century. The WLS demonstrated that continuously collecting data from the same individuals allows for researchers to track growth and apply methodological techniques that enhance the consistency of results from investigations.

In this respect, the WLS was highly influential in the subsequent adoption of this data collection technique by various agencies of the federal government and other universities. Hauser's application of these data to the status attainment literature led to key methodological and substantive contributions. For example, using data from siblings and cousins, Hauser's work demonstrated that the effects of individuals' educational attainment on subsequent labor market attainment are independent of genetic or cognitive traits that are similar across family members. His work with the WLS also provided insights into the effect of birth order on education, the effects of educational expectations on educational attainment, and the effect of poverty on educational outcomes. These and many other insights into grade retention, educational expectations, obesity, cognitive functioning, end-of-life planning, and mortality have been hallmarks of Hauser's involvement in the WLS.

Current Endeavors

Hauser has been involved in many federal panels and committees throughout his career that have advised on issues related to research on educational progress and inequality. These efforts have produced insights into high school completion and adult literacy, among many others. Through his current position within the National Academy of Sciences, Hauser continues to pursue questions about measurement that promise to enhance the quality of the data that will drive future generations of social scientific inquiry. Some of Hauser's recent efforts have focused on refining the measurement of family socioeconomic status within the National Assessment of Educational Progress, as well as the proper use of accountability measures in the era of high-stakes testing for the National Academy of Sciences.

Steven Alvarado
University of Notre Dame

See Also: Sewell, William; Sibling Effects in Education; Status Attainment.

Further Readings

Blau, P. and O. D. Duncan. *The American Occupational Structure.* New York: John Wiley & Sons, 1967.

Featherman, D. L. and R. M. Hauser. *Opportunity and Change.* New York: Academic Press, 1978.

Featherman, D. L., F. L. Jones, and R. M. Hauser. "Assumptions of Social Mobility Research in the U.S.: The Case of Occupational Status." *Social Science Research*, v.4/4 (1975).

Hauser, R. and P. Mossel. "Fraternal Resemblance in Educational-Attainment and Occupational-Status." *American Journal of Sociology*, v.91/3 (1985).

Hauser, R., S. Tsai and W. H. Sewell. "A Model of Stratification With Response Error in Social and Psychological Variables." *Sociology of Education*, v.56 (1983).

Sewell, W. H. and R. M. Hauser. *Education, Occupation, and Earnings: Achievement in the Early Career.* New York: Academic Press, 1975.

Hawai'i

Hawai'i was granted statehood in 1959, and is the youngest American state. It consists of a group of islands located in the Pacific Ocean, about 2,400 miles (3,900 kilometers) west of San Francisco, and has a total area of 6,470 square miles (16,758 square kilometers). Hawai'i consists of eight major islands (Maui, Oahu, Hawai'i, Kauai, Molokai, Lanai, Niihau, and Kahoolawe) and 124 smaller islands. The 2010 U.S. census estimates the population of Hawai'i at 1,360,301. Tourism is Hawai'i's leading business, although agriculture, aquaculture, mining, and film production have also begun to increase state revenue. Hawai'i has been shaped significantly by its experience as a sovereign kingdom, republic, U.S. territory, and U.S. state.

Hawai'i's earliest inhabitants were Polynesians, who came to the islands 1,500 years ago. Hawai'i was discovered by Captain Cook in 1778. At the time of Western discovery, each island was ruled by a hereditary chief, but in 1810, King Kamehameha I unified the islands and established the Kingdom of Hawai'i. Schooling occurred in the community *halau* (work house), where the family and community took responsibility for teaching youth the traditional values of the culture, as well as occupational skills like canoe making and fishing. Kamehameha died in 1819, one year before Protestant missionaries arrived in Hawai'i. These missionaries established the first formal schools in Hawai'i. In 1824, Kamehameha III took the throne and created the first public school system in 1840, after Protestant missionaries convinced him of the importance of a formal education institution. Most of these early schools were missionary schools geared toward teaching Christianity. Hawai'i's education system is the oldest school system west of the Mississippi River.

The mid-1800s saw the Kingdom of Hawai'i recognized by the United States, Britain, and France, but also saw increasing American presence on the islands and increased pressure for U.S. annexation as a way to protect American business interests. In 1893, Queen Liliuokalani was deposed by a group of American businessmen, who established a provisional government until the United States officially annexed Hawai'i in 1900. The annexation was vehemently opposed by native Hawai'ians, who sent a delegation to Washington, D.C., with a protest petition signed by 21,000 people. In 1896, public and private schools that were taught in Hawai'ian were outlawed, and English

Table 1 Elementary and secondary education characteristics

	Hawai'i	U.S. (average)
Total number of schools	290	1,988
Total students	179,601	970,278
Total teachers	11,395.95	60,766.56
Pupil/teacher ratio	15.76	15.97

Source: U.S. Department of Education, National Center for Education Statistics, Common Core of Data (CCD), 2010–11.

Table 2 Elementary and secondary education finance

	Hawai'i	U.S. (average)
Total revenues	$2,498,083,255	$11,464,385,994
Total expenditures for education	$2,342,493,477	$11,712,033,839
Total current expenditures	$2,122,779,119	$9,938,906,259

Source: U.S. Department of Education, National Center for Education Statistics, Common Core of Data (CCD), "National Public Education Financial Survey," FY08 (2007–08).

was made the official language. While some individual families continued to teach their children the Hawai'ian language and culture at home, the lack of formal schooling and formal recognition meant that a great deal of Hawai'ian culture was lost or displaced by Western practices, a phenomena that continues today. Hawai'i was a U.S. territory until 1959, when it became the 50th state. In 1993, President Clinton issued an official apology from the United States to the Hawai'ian people for the illegal overthrow of the Kingdom of Hawai'i. This apology, coupled with the UN Declaration on the Rights of Indigenous Peoples and the Coolongatta Statement of Indigenous Peoples Rights in Education, has supported greater Hawai'ian sovereignty in governance and schooling.

Hawai'i has 288 public schools, serving approximately 180,000 students. There are 256 regular schools, two special schools, and 30 public charter schools. Several of these charter schools are working to reclaim native Hawai'ian education through emphasis on Hawai'ian culture, language, and ways of learning. In addition to public schools, Hawai'i has 123 private schools, which serve an additional 38,000 students. Hawai'i is the only state with a centralized education system that controls public schooling across the entire state. The statewide Department of Education is governed by a 10-member elected school board. There has been significant debate in recent years over whether Hawai'i's system should remain centralized, or be split into smaller local boards. Proponents of centralization argue that this helps make the system more equitable because funding decisions happen at the state level. Unlike other states, Hawai'i's public education system is funded primarily through state and federal sources, rather than local property taxes. Those favoring decentralization want to see greater control in local communities. Hawai'i's public schools are grouped into *complexes* consisting of a high school and its associated feeder middle and elementary schools. For administrative and support purposes, multiple complexes are grouped together into complex areas.

An ongoing issue in Hawai'i is the disparity between native Hawai'ian students and non-Hawai'ians. According to a recent study, 79 percent of schools with a predominantly Hawai'ian student body are undergoing corrective action, compared to 17 percent of predominantly non-Hawai'ian schools. Additionally, native Hawai'ians have average test scores in reading and math that are almost 10 percentage points lower than their peers. Graduation rates of native Hawai'ian students are among the lowest of all students in the state, and grade retention rates are among the highest. In addition, native Hawai'ian students have the highest rates of school absenteeism of all students.

Many educators reason that the lack of cultural sensitivity within schools and the lack of incorporation of Hawai'ian epistemologies play a significant role in this underperformance. It is therefore important that educators examine the ways in which current standards, curricula, and teaching/classroom practices include or devalue the knowledge and experiences of native Hawai'ian youth and establish education practices that meet the needs of all students.

Jamie N. Burke
University of New Hampshire

See Also: Charter Schools; Multiculturalism/Multicultural Education; Native American Students.

Further Readings

Hunt, J. R. and Hawai'i Department of Education. *Education in the States: Historical Development and Outlook*. Washington, DC: National Education Association, 1969.

Native Hawai'ian Education Council. http://www.nhec.org (Accessed August 2012).

Sing, D. K., A. Hunter, and M. A. Meyer. "Native Hawai'ian Education: Talking Story With Three Hawai'ian Educators." *Journal of American Indian Education*, v.39/1 (1999).

Head Start

Project Head Start is a national compensatory education program serving economically disadvantaged children from ages 3 to 5. The mission of Head Start is to promote school readiness through education, health, nutrition, and social services. Parental and community involvement are considered key aspects in a comprehensive approach. Students attend preschool at Head Start centers throughout the United States and its territories. Launched in 1965 as an eight-week summer program, Head Start now includes year-round, full-day services.

Newly sworn in President Lyndon B. Johnson launched the War on Poverty. Although many educational and anti-poverty initiatives were discussed under the Kennedy administration, President Johnson began the large-scale effort to leverage government in the fight against poverty. Poverty was considered a generational disease, and the Johnson administration devised programs that it hoped would alleviate its symptoms, cure it, and, prevent it from reappearing. To that end, the Economic Opportunity Act of 1964 was passed and signed into law. The Office of Economic Opportunity (OEO) was hence created, and R. Sargent Shriver, husband of Eunice Kennedy Shriver, was chosen to head it. New initiatives included job programs, as well as education and training for those with low literacy and/or low job skills. Partly because of evolving understandings about childhood development, President Johnson also called for a preschool initiative: Head Start. Of 30 million Americans living in poverty, half were children. Cultural gaps and impoverished environments accounted for discrepancies in IQ, and were thought to handicap children from future success. Child development theorists argued that early intervention, before age 5, could reduce negative affects and create opportunity for positive change.

Robert E. Cooke, a professor of pediatrics at Johns Hopkins School of Medicine, headed the OEO's interdisciplinary Head Start Planning Committee. Other members specialized in pediatrics, child development, retardation, and early childhood education. From the president's announcement in January 1965, the Cooke Committee had a few months to devise, advertise, and launch Head Start that summer. There were internal debates about the size and scope of the program. Academics and social scientists on the committee suggested that the launch should include 25,000 students in a pilot program. It was more prudent, they argued, to start small, evaluate, make improvements, and scale up. Shriver disagreed with this tact, believing that a small program was easy to dismiss and cut, and that political expediency dictated a massive and immediate launch.

Initial decisions sometimes sacrificed quality, and made later changes difficult. For one, rushed calculations suggested that the summer program could be run for $180 per child; experts thought that a reasonable allocation was $1,000 per child. That low number guaranteed low salaries for Head Start teachers. Later critiques of the program included the lack of qualified teachers, who were hard to recruit with little pay. Centers employed low-paid workers and volunteers—some who were low literate. Experts later noted that this was not the high-quality early intervention that could help ameliorate the effects of poverty, although it was beneficial to employ parents and enlist community support. Additionally, the goals for the program were vague. Social competence and school readiness were not clear and measureable objectives. Was the program an educational one or not? What did it really mean to be ready for school? Furthermore, the lack of a national curriculum allowed local centers to develop the programs that most suited their populations, but this made it difficult to evaluate the effectiveness of the program as a whole. Eventually, a longitudinal study, the Family and Child Experiences Survey (FACES), was implemented.

Immediate Success

Project Head Start was immediately declared a success, especially with respect to noncognitive domains. Moreover, early findings revealed that students also experienced cognitive gains. Unfortunately, cognitive gains were not sustained over time. Defenders said that the results were caused by the brevity of the summer program, and that more lasting gains would occur once students enrolled in the year-round program, to be launched in 1966. Insiders complained that evaluations defaulted to cognitive gains, yet the program was never envisioned as a purely, or even mostly, educational one. School readiness, they felt, encompassed much more than IQ.

Almost immediately after the launch of the first summer program, a year-round program was announced. The Head Start program has been funded continuously, although not without controversy, since 1965. Head Start funding surpassed the $1 billion mark for the first time in 1985. By 2009, the appropriation had grown to over $7 billion. A portion of the Head Start budget is designated for American Indian–Alaska Natives, and migrant and seasonal programs. In the 1990s, Head Start was funded for expansion and quality improvements. Reauthorization packages also included revised program standards, with a more specific focus on school readiness and literacy. Head Start has also added provisions for children with disabilities, as well as bilingual and bicultural programs. Recent statistics highlight the diversity of enrollment: 40 percent of enrollees are white, 30 percent are black, and 35 percent are Latino. A large majority of students are ages 3 and 4. The current average cost per child is $7,600. Over 27 million children have been served since the Head Start program began in 1965.

Nicole D. Collier
University of South Florida, St. Petersburg

See Also: Class Inequality: Achievement; Early Childhood; Poverty and Education; Preschool Programs.

Further Readings
Vinovskis, Maris. *The Birth of Head Start: Preschool Education Policies in the Kennedy and Johnson Administrations.* Chicago, IL: University of Chicago Press, 2005.

Washington, Valora and Ura J. O. Bailey. *Project Head Start: Models and Strategies for the Twenty-First Century.* New York: Garland, 1995.

Zigler, Edward and Sally J. Styfco. *Head Start and Beyond: A National Plan for Extended Childhood Intervention.* New Haven, CT: Yale University Press, 1993.

Zigler, Edward and Sally J. Styfco. *The Head Start Debates.* Baltimore, MD: P. H. Brookes, 2004.

Hermeneutics

The term *hermeneutics* refers to the science or art of interpretation and is rooted in ancient traditions of theological and juridical understanding. Within the field of education, hermeneutics primarily deals with the theoretical and philosophical principles associated with the interpretation of texts and individuals. Although often associated with ideas of early hermeneutic philosophers such as Friedrich Schleiermacher, Wilhelm Dilthey, and Edmund Husserl, the work of Martin Heidegger and Hans-Georg Gadamer also plays a definitive role in the way hermeneutics is conceptualized in philosophy and the human sciences. As a result, different traditions within the field of hermeneutics distinguish between these specific perspectives.

For example, conservative or objectivist hermeneutics involves bracketing out fore-conceptions as an essential part of finding meaning. In contrast, critical hermeneutics, based on the work of Jürgen Habermas, seeks to elaborate on theories in order to interpret and make sense of human action. Often associated with the work of critical theorists, its aims are to empower through meaning. In contrast, John Caputo and Derrida use radical hermeneutics to point out gaps in understanding and disrupt traditional interpretations of texts in order to ultimately raise questions that concern the human condition and further dialogue. Although the work of Heidegger represents the beginning of the field of philosophical hermeneutics, this tradition is most often associated with the ideas of Gadamer and Paul Ricoeur. Philosophical hermeneutic traditions focus specifically on understanding and interpreting the other. However, this other is not limited to written texts; rather, it includes other people, traditions, beliefs, or cultures that the interpreter seeks to understand. In each case, meaning hinges on interpretation.

Basic Philosophies
Although the concepts and ideas associated with hermeneutic philosophy are extensive, a few remain central to comprehending basic hermeneutic philosophies. Dialogue exists as one of the central tenants of hermeneutic thought. Gadamer positioned the reader as in conversation with the text, and meaning-making as occurring through a dialectical relationship of questioning and answering. When encountering a text, the reader enters into a conversation already occurring. As readers interpret texts, they consider their understandings against the backdrop of their experiences and within their positions in the world. These fore-conceptions cannot be isolated and extracted from the way that readers make sense of the texts; rather, readers must acknowledge these fore-conceptions and the way they may influence their interpretations. In other words, what readers understand from the text depends, in part, on what they bring to it.

As an element of this dialogue, the reader moves between past and present, previous and new understandings, abstract and concrete, and smaller parts and the larger whole. This back and forth movement results in a cyclical process of learning, referred to as "dialoging" within the hermeneutic circle. The ongoing movement between positions means that the reader never reaches a final understanding. However, although no ultimate meaning results, through this back and forth process, multiple meanings are constructed. Engaging in these dialogues shapes individual understandings, as what was once part of the other becomes part of the individuals' ideas. While this shift doesn't always change the individual's understandings, this new perspective is essential to dialogue. To

Gadamer, true dialogue only occurs when both partners enter the exchange with the intent to truly consider the position of the other. In such encounters, a "fusion of horizons" occurs when one individual's frame of reference meets that of the other. Although the two positions don't necessarily come into agreement, the participants have the opportunity to develop new understandings by realizing the perspective of the other. The very nature of the hermeneutic circle positions the individual as entering dialogues already occurring. Although the reader or interpreter comes to the text at a certain point in time, the dialogue existed before this encounter, and continues after the reader leaves the text. By contributing his or her perspectives and then stepping out of the circle, the individual leaves with new understandings, but the dialogue continues.

Influences in Educational Research

The influence of hermeneutic ideas in the field of education may be seen in approaches to literary criticism and textual analysis, but is most evident in terms of educational research. Hermeneutic philosophies inform the way that qualitative research is conducted, and influence the methods used. Although hermeneutics does not offer a precise method to employ when conducting research, it posits research as a dialogue that opens up alternative interpretations, rather than a prescriptive study of facts to be discovered. Within qualitative research, hermeneutic approaches are most often applied to examinations of texts, ideas, and images representative of education, as well as ethnographic and narrative work that offer interpretations of lived experience. Rather than seeking out a singular meaning or answer, hermeneutics seeks out multiple meanings in the data. In doing so, the researcher troubles solitary discourses and brings out perspectives previously overlooked.

Dawan Coombs
University of Georgia

See Also: Critical Theory of Education; Phenomenology, Existentialism and Education; Qualitative Research on Education.

Further Readings

Dahlberg, K., H. Dahlberg, and M. Nystrom. *Reflective Lifeworld Research.* 2nd ed. Lund, Sweden: Studentlitteratur, 2008.

Freeman, M. "Hermeneutics." In *The Sage Encyclopedia of Qualitative Research Methods,* Vol. 1. L. Given, ed. Thousand Oaks, CA: Sage, 2008.

Gadamer, H. G. *Truth and Method,* 2nd ed. J. Weinsheimer and D. G. Marshall, trans. New York: Continuum, 1989.

Grondin, J. *Introduction to Philosophical Hermeneutics.* New Haven, CT: Yale University Press, 1994.

Schwandt, T. A. "Three Epistemological Stances for Qualitative Inquiry: Interpretivism, Hermeneutics, and Social Constructionism." In *Handbook of Qualitative Research,* 2nd ed. N. Denzin and Y. Lincoln, eds. Thousand Oaks, CA: Sage, 2000.

Hidden Curriculum

According to various sociologic studies, the hidden curriculum is that which is not explicitly taught in a classroom setting. In other words, social norms and behaviors are taught through the experience of school and classroom organization. Elements of the hidden curriculum serve to prepare students for the hurdles that they will face in life as a whole, and in their work lives. There are several key areas that are often considered part of the hidden, social curriculum for most public and private schools. Testing and other assessments are necessary because they paint a picture of what a student knows and understands. Assessments are not limited to the school experience, as certain evaluations should be expected in the course of a student's career. For these reasons, students must learn how to tackle tests and other types of assessments. These test-taking skills are an essential part of the hidden curriculum, and their benefits continue even beyond the completion of schooling.

The inclusion of grading scales in schools allows teachers to aid in fostering effort and productivity on the part of students. For example, a student who receives a grade of 75 on a spelling test learns that more effort must be expended if he expects that grade to improve. Further, students rely upon grades and grading scales for feedback on their overall level of performance. These grading scales are, therefore, an essential part of the school experience because of their ability to boost productivity and enhance the amount of effort expended by students. In addition to learning through the use of grades and grading scales, collegial and collaborative behaviors may also be developed through the school experience. Working in pairs or small groups, for example, allows students to practice aspects of teamwork that will be helpful later in their professional work life. These group experiences also teach students how to deal with uncooperative workers while maintaining focus on the ultimate objective or task. These skills are essential for understanding how to work well with others, and also tend to enhance overall problem solving and mediation skill.

Improving Performance

Similar to fostering effort and productivity, students learn how to set goals and make successful changes in their academic and interpersonal lives. First, students who struggle with a particular content area are taught to improve their performance by learning to set goals. They also learn to set reasonable goals, differentiating them from goals that are less attainable. Learning to set and reach goals is important for workplace scenarios because it enables workers to function at levels expected by employers. Learning to set personal goals and work to attain them helps a worker make the kind of changes and adjustments needed to be successful in the workplace. Similarly, by interacting with others, students learn which behaviors are appropriate and which are not. Through a process of trial and error, students are able to discern which behaviors will tend to make collaboration easier, and which will complicate those relationships. This information will allow students to foster and maintain healthy workplace relationships, enhancing their overall workplace performance.

Success in school requires that students become committed to their personal academic growth. A part of the school experience is devoted to teaching students how to make commitments without becoming overcommitted. Part of the hidden curriculum includes learning the difference by way of practical experience. Further, students learn how to stay on course academically by maintaining their focus on completing tasks. By learning to be committed to completing assignments and projects, students are preparing for similar workplace tasks they will encounter in the future. Success in school and in life requires that individuals expend energy and have the proper amount of motivation to put in the necessary effort. Through the school experience, students are given the opportunity to learn how to summon a boost of energy when they are tired or bored. Understanding that fatigue is a normal part of life is something that students must

learn through experience. Additionally, students must learn how to respond when they feel fatigued or ill so that they are able to function. Similarly, students learn how to develop the amount of motivation needed to complete tasks that are required for them to be successful. Motivation is produced by students; it cannot be manufactured artificially. Learning to stay motivated to complete tasks and assignments is part of the hidden social curriculum.

Learning Life Skills

Learning to pay attention to what is important with regard to success in both school and in life is a skill that is learned through participation in the school experience. Classroom procedures require that students complete certain tasks that are repeated at certain intervals. For example, students are taught to stand in line before moving from the classroom to another part of the school. Additionally, students are assigned homework and other projects that are due at a certain time. These activities and behaviors teach students how to organize and complete tasks, preparing them for duties they would assume once their working life begins. Each of these areas offers something to the overall social learning of students. Additionally, they contribute to the type of positive culture within schools that serve to benefit overall growth and learning. Elements of the hidden curriculum serve to create learning environments that are safe and orderly, while teaching those skills and promoting healthy, positive behaviors that will ensure more successful careers throughout students' work lives.

Kristen Brodie
Walden University

See Also: Curriculum Standardization; Homework; School-to-Work Transitions.

Further Readings

Hartlep, Nicholas. "Reflection on Theory: Whose Knowledge, and the Hidden Curriculum" (2000). http://www.eric.ed.gov/ERICWebPortal/search/detailmini.jsp?_nfpb=true&_&ERICExtSearch_Search Value_0=ED504296&ERICExtSearch_SearchType _0=no&accno=ED504296 (Accessed February 2012).

Jerald, Craig D. "School Culture: 'The Hidden Curriculum.' Issue Brief" (December 1, 2006). Center for Comprehensive School Reform and Improvement. ERIC. http://www.eric.ed.gov/ERICWebPortal/search/

detailmini.jsp?_nfpb=true&_&ERICExtSearch_Search
Value_0=ED495013&ERICExtSearch_SearchType
_0=no&accno=ED495013 (Accessed February 2012).

Joughin, Gordon. "The Hidden Curriculum Revisited:
A Critical Review of Research Into the Influence of
Summative Assessment on Learning." *Assessment &
Evaluation in Higher Education*, v.35/3 (May 1, 2010).

High School Exit Exams

High school exit exams are part of a broader educational agenda that seeks to increase standards in public education. Requiring graduating students to take an exam to demonstrate mastery of content upon finishing high school reflects the academic achievement of the individual and provides an accountability measure for schools by indicating the proportion of their students that meet graduation standards. Some argue that requiring students to take exit exams to graduate improves equality in education by setting the same high bar for all students; others argue that there may be negative consequences of exit exams, and that the most at-risk student populations may be affected the most. There is no consensus in the research on the effectiveness of exit exams policies to improve the quality of education for individuals, or how the overall quality of education in the United States has changed. By the 1970s, most students were enrolled in secondary schools, completed high school, and earned a diploma. However, there was growing concern over the quality of education that students received and the value of a high school diploma. It was uncertain what graduating students knew, and how well schools were preparing students for future educational and occupational opportunities.

States responded to this concern by starting to design a system of standardized tests to assess students' learning of basic skills and their mastery of curriculum. For some states, part of this first wave of standardized assessments in the late 1970s and early 1980s included requiring students to pass an exit exam in order to graduate from high school. When the groundbreaking educational report *A Nation at Risk* was released in 1983, one of its many recommendations was for states to adopt exit exams as a part of graduation requirements. With the passing of No Child Left Behind (NCLB) in 2001, more explicit expectations were required for student assessment mechanisms in which states could demonstrate adequate yearly progress toward education goals. With this heightened accountability climate over the past 10 years since NCLB, and the increased pressure to hold students and schools to higher standards, several more states adopted policies that raised graduation requirements, including the addition of high school exit exam requirements.

In 2011, there were 31 states that had some variation of an exit exam policy. A total of 25 states had policies that required students to pass a comprehensive exit exam to graduate; five states had policies that expected students to take an exit exam, but did not require passing it to graduate; and one state was still developing its policy. However, with the development and implementation of the national Common Core of State Standards (CCSS), many states are moving away from comprehensive assessment and are shifting toward having "end of course assessments." The end of course assessments are aligned to the CCSS and are administered at the completion of each course (e.g., Algebra I or American History). Students must often demonstrate mastery to move to more advanced coursework and as part of their graduation requirements. The upward trend in states adopting exit exam policy has shifted, partly because of states responding to the CCSS. From 2009 to 2010, 74 percent of public school students nationwide were required to pass an exit exam, compared to 65 percent in 2010 and 2011, as more states transition to requiring students to pass end of course assessments that are aligned to the CCSS. Although exit exams were originally motivated with the intention of assessing what a student learned in high school, more states are using this policy as an opportunity to look forward and assess a student's college and career readiness upon leaving high school. Some states have also linked their exit exams with college entrance exams (e.g., the ACT or SAT) because of the increased focus on college readiness.

Higher Standards and Equality

There is a debate in the research over how exit exam policies contribute to racial and socioeconomic achievement gaps. There are a disproportionate number of low-income students and students of color who are required to take exit exams. Of the 76 percent of public school students who are impacted by this policy, 84 percent are students of color and 78 percent are low income. As the stakes for graduation increase, the likelihood of students not graduating, being retained, or dropping out of high school also increases. Many states have recognized the potential barrier that exit exams pose for students and provide multiple opportunities to pass, with some states beginning their exit exams in the eighth or ninth grade to allow several years and opportunities for a student to pass. Some research has found that exit exams have increased the number of students that are being retained or dropping out of high school, and have lowered graduation rates, while other research has found no negative effect of these policies on different student populations. Several studies have found that students who drop out are more likely to be black, Hispanic, or from low-income families. Researchers argue that because exit exams assess basic skills, the average student is largely unaffected by exit exams, while the struggling student faces another obstacle to graduation and another factor that contributes to his or her decision to stay in school. While the ideal that all high school graduates should meet high academic expectations is universal, there is concern that raising standards through exit exams may exacerbate inequalities in education.

Exit exams can also be used to hold teachers and schools accountable. The percentage of students passing exit exams and graduating can provide an additional measure of accountability of the quality of a school. These exams can provide achievement targets for students and teachers to work toward, with clear learning objectives that are aligned from kindergarten through high school. However, exit exams may also provide incentives for teachers to narrow their instruction on what is tested. Skills taught to improve college and career readiness, such as writing or conducting a lab, are not easily assessed and teachers may not have the incentive to spend instructional time on them, which may not be testable on exit exams.

Implications of Exit Exams

As with other forms of standardized assessment, exit exams reduce the evaluation of students' learning to a numeric score, which may not capture all of the attributes of what society values in a high school graduate. The labor market in states with exit exams may also be affected because of the increased requirements to attain a high school diploma. Thus, the value of a high school diploma may increase because of the higher expectations and mastery of those graduating. Conversely, labor market outcomes of those who drop out may also be improved, because under weaker standards, these

individuals would hold diplomas, but do not under the higher standards. With the adoption of the CCSS and the national movement toward high school students being college and career ready upon completing high school, states are adapting their exit exam policies and graduation requirements. Georgia is currently the only state where students report their exit exam scores when applying for employment and in the college application process, however, several other states are in the process of developing similar policies that link secondary education with postsecondary options. Research on the effects of high school exit exam policies is difficult because of the varying state expectations and complex data collection issues. Several states are building or expanding state data systems to track students from elementary school through high school and beyond (K–16), to assess the impact of policies such as high school exit exams that target students who are transitioning out of the K–12 system into the labor market or postsecondary institutions.

Justina Judy
Michigan State University

See Also: Curriculum Standardization; Dropouts; Prior Learning Assessment; Racial Inequality: High School Dropout Rates; Standardized Testing.

Further Readings
Center on Education Policy. "State High School Tests: Changes in State Policies and the Impact of the College and Career Readiness Movement." Washington, DC: Center on Education Policy, 2011.

Dee, T. S. and B. A. Jacob. "Do High School Exit Exams Influence Educational Attainment or Labor Market Performance?" Cambridge, MA: National Bureau of Economic Research Working Paper, 2006.

Grodsky, E., J. R. Warren, and D. Kalogrides. "State High School Exit Examinations and NAEP Long-Term Trends in Reading and Mathematics, 1971–2004." *Education Policy*, v.24 (2009).

Papay, J. P., R. J. Murnane, and J. B. Willett. "The Consequences of High School Exit Examinations for Low-Performing Urban Students: Evidence From Massachusetts." *Educational Evaluation and Policy Analysis*, v.32/5 (2010).

Warren, J. R. and M. R. Edwards. "High School Exit Examinations and High School Completion: Evidence From the Early 1990s." *Educational Evaluation and Policy Analysis*, v.27 (2005).

Higher Education

The term *higher education* is defined as the top-level education opportunity available in society. This definition has changed over time, however. In ancient times, because higher education opportunities were limited to relatively few individuals, the focus of this training tended to prepare individuals for employment in government positions and as leaders in religions. In contemporary times, there are different names associated with higher education, including tertiary education, postsecondary education, college, vocational education, and university education. It is the terminal education experience that equips individuals with the needed skills to function in the workplace and society.

Higher education prepares students for life beyond college by socializing them into responsible employees, functional society members, problem solvers, and critical thinkers. There are two main categories of Higher Education Institutions (HEIs), private and public. Private higher education includes HEIs funded by nongovernmental organizations or individuals. Religious organizations, humanitarian organizations, and for-profit organizations are some examples of private HEIs. Private HEIs have consistently ranked among the top universities in the world; the top-ranked private HEIs are predominantly located in the United States, United Kingdom, and Canada.

Nonprofit private HEIs founded by religious organizations raise their income from tuition fees and donations, and are subsidized by the founding organization. In recent years, private higher education provision has expanded globally, comprising more than 50 percent of all HEIs and enrollments in countries like Brazil, Japan, Philippines, South Korea, and Uganda. Public higher education is funded either in part or in whole by governments. There are several examples of different types of public HEIs, including community colleges funded by local communities, state and provincial colleges and universities, and national universities.

Public HEIs have traditionally been entirely funded by the government. In recent years, this single-funding source has become increasingly diversified, where nongovernmental entities provide a substantial percentage of financial support. These sources of funding may come from various organizations (e.g., corporations, NGOs, and other businesses) and/or individuals, and may include joint-venture opportunities for training and employment. The top public HEIs in the United States look and operate more like private HEIs than public ones. For example, the University of California (U.C.) system was primarily funded by the state of California. U.C. funding has changed over the past century, however, and during the 2011–12 academic year, U.C. received only 11 percent of its total budget from the state of California general funds. This privatization trend of public HEIs is not unique to U.C., but is reflected across the United States and in other countries. Both private and public HEIs increasingly rely on tuition from students, grants received from government and nongovernmental donor agencies, services provided through such areas as medical schools (e.g., hospitals), registered patents, and from local and international businesses.

History of Higher Education

Higher learning and higher education is not a new concept. Evidence of higher learning existed in many of the great ancient societies. The ancestors of American Indians had superior understanding and training in disciplines like astronomy, medicine, and agriculture. Advanced writing, military technology, and numeracy skills were taught in ancient Egypt. The ancient peoples of the Pacific Islands and the Malay Archipelago had advanced seafaring knowledge, including in trade and navigation. Much of contemporary philosophical roots can be traced back to ancient Europe (Socrates, Plato, and Aristotle) and Asia (Buddha, Confucius, and Mencius). Based on limited records that remain from ancient times, higher education institutions (HEIs) were established in ancient Africa, the Americas, Asia, and Europe. Among the most famous of these ancient HEIs include the library of Alexandria in Egypt, the Imperial Nanking University in China, and the University of Bologna of Italy. Many other HEIs started later on, between the 11th and 17th centuries. Most Western HEIs were established by religious denominations to train their clergy. For instance, church missionaries established Harvard University in the United States in 1636 to professionalize their clergy and to equip them with skills they needed to deal with more advanced administrative roles in society. During the past two centuries, most HEIs taught general knowledge, law, civic education, liberal arts and sciences, philosophy, medicine, theology, social sciences, and technology.

Role of Higher Education in Society

The role of higher education has evolved during different eras and in different geographic regions.

Generally, higher education has played a central role in historic and contemporary times. Higher education has traditionally offered specialized training and skills for specific employment of the day. In contemporary society, graduates fill jobs throughout communities worldwide at all levels, but especially in senior administration positions of governments, local businesses, and multinational corporations. HEIs usually orient and socialize their students into university life through lectures, public debates, extracurricular activities such as sports and games, music, and drama, theatre, and other social activities. This socialization process helps establish and perpetuate societal norms, traditions, and cultures. Traditional HEIs included residences for students and faculty members, which served as venue to give them more opportunities to participate in all higher education curriculum and activities. Students who successfully complete their higher education training gain much-needed self-esteem, self-identity, and self-confidence—skills fundamental in the world of work and in contributing to society. The trend toward mass higher education, which is the norm for many advanced societies at the onset of the 21st century, has enabled learners to access higher education in traditional classroom settings, by correspondence, or via an online medium. HEIs are much more porous and fluid today, than ever before. HEIs have also been the center of political change in many countries, including in Africa, Asia, Europe, Latin America, and North America. This political nexus is reflected in regular student and staff strikes and demonstrations.

Access to Higher Education

In ancient times, higher education opportunities were significantly more restrictive in terms of access, equity, and equality. Higher education access and equity has changed over time, however, and some countries like Singapore, South Korea, and Taiwan have achieved universal higher education. From the 17th to the 20th centuries, the nature of European colonialism— where colonies were established to provide natural and human resources for meeting the requirements of colonial power—had a stifling impact on the establishment and continuity of higher education development in the respective colonies. In Africa, access to elite schools and HEIs was generally restricted to chiefs, kings, and royal family members. Many European colonial powers established government-curtailed education strategies that limited secondary- and higher-education opportunities to approximately five

percent of the population. This provided higher education access for a minimal number of local expertise, training in primarily low-level leadership positions, such as office clerks, teachers, transportation workers, and police officers. In all cases, the top higher education opportunities required individuals to be trained in the respective colonial powers' HEIs (e.g., Oxford and Cambridge in the United Kingdom, École Normale Supérieure in France, University of Coimbra in Portugal, and the University of Madrid in Spain). Where HEIs were established in European colonies, they tended to be restricted in terms of the curriculum offerings. Rather than designing a curriculum based on local existing knowledge, technologies, and expertise, a colonial power-imposed curriculum was mandated. This had a significant and lasting negative influence on the preservation and nurturing of local languages, cultures, and identities.

The fall of European colonialism led to a general increase in global higher education access. Most governments of former colonies took on the burden of funding public higher education for a limited number of students. This allowed a few, low-income, but academically and exceptionally gifted students to access higher education. However, with the increasing costs associated with providing higher education opportunities in the 1970s and 1980s, many nation-states experienced budget cuts, and these cuts were reflected in reduced amount of government funding available for higher education. The introduction of neoliberal structural adjustment programs during this time forced many countries to reduce government spending on public services such as health and higher education. Part of the rationale behind these structural adjustment programs was the notion that higher education was generally viewed as an individual investment, rather than a public good, like investment in basic education at the primary- and secondary-education levels. The neoliberal perspective has had a substantial influence over the past 30 years in guiding government policies and overseas development assistance in support of lower-level education subsectors over an investment in higher education systems.

Gender Imbalance

Historically, higher education opportunities were predominantly available to men. This gender imbalance has changed over time in many countries, especially within the past 50 years. While there remain some notable exceptions, the number of females attending higher education has increased steadily. For instance, in the United States in 1980, 51.4 percent of higher education students were female; in 2009, roughly 57.1 percent of higher education students were female. Some disciplines remain for the most part gender biased in the United States and elsewhere. Many natural science disciplines have been, and for the most part remain, male-dominated areas of higher education; social science disciplines like education, foreign languages, and the humanities have become increasingly popular for females. Worldwide, nursing remains a predominantly female field; engineering remains heavily male dominated. There are changes in these traditional norms, however, where increasingly women are gaining access and excelling in senior medical, engineering, and business fields.

HIEs are challenged to become more cost effective and cost efficient in utilizing ever-shrinking resources. The cost of providing a quality higher education has consistently increased. This global higher education financial dialectic has only increased the inequalities in higher education access, especially among the most disadvantaged and poor students. Cost-sharing policies have become common practice in most HEIs worldwide to help offset some of these increasing costs. Consequently, children from the most well-to-do families have greater opportunities in receiving excellent higher education preparation, including having access to the best secondary schools and money to pay for private tutoring. These factors give the wealthy a substantial advantage in accessing the top HEIs in each country. These same affluent students are also generally in a better position to establish and maintain more sophisticated social networks, usually become important agents of social influences, and obtain top leadership positions in government and private sectors. This persistent lack of equity in higher education has exacerbated social inequalities in many countries of the world.

Academic Freedom and the Autonomy of Higher Education

Higher education is widely regarded as a seedbed for learning, creativity, and innovation. At the center of this knowledge creation is the notion of academic freedom and autonomy. Higher education academic freedom exists in an environment where people are able to research, speak, and publish freely without government and/or scientific community interference. Higher education autonomy is the ability for a HEI to operate

without restrictions and encumbrances in determining what curriculum to offer and how to deliver the curriculum, in establishing partnerships with local and international businesses, in choosing their leadership, and in managing their budget. HEIs are hubs for discussing and generating political ideas. Too often, however, government restrictions prevent a conducive or autonomous environment that facilities academic freedom in sharing scientific and political ideas. Many governments continue to maintain control over public higher education to the extent that, in some countries, they even nominate the senior administrative officers for these institutions. Consequently, this deprives HEIs of the autonomy and academic freedom required to operate in the most efficient and effective way. These two issues have always been important in the reproduction of existing knowledge and in setting the stage for discovery and innovation. Governments that provide greater higher education autonomy and academic freedom are better equipped to enable students and scholars to generate new ideas related to science, politics, environmental protection, and disease control.

Future of Higher Education

The future of higher education will depend upon the way that HEIs deal with numerous challenging issues, including financing, autonomy and academic freedom, access, quality of instruction, and the negative perceptions of higher education by the some of the general public. HEIs need to be able to identify and capitalize on current opportunities, such as advancing ICT initiatives, growing internalization and cutting-edge collaborative research, and sharing and optimizing rare human resources. The recurrent challenge of financing higher education remains a huge burden in virtually all country contexts. There are more efforts toward accessing alternative and diversified funding sources of higher education, which range from tuition fees, government and donor grants, and partnerships with industry. Consequently, HEIs are forced to reduce their spending through provisions such as outsourcing of services to the private sector and engaging more non-tenure-stream faculty members to carry teaching and advising loads. There is also an increase in the use of non-traditional mediums of instruction and a shift toward ICT as the standard for reducing stationery, communication, and data management. This volatile financial climate has required higher education administrators to do more with less financial and human resources.

Higher education autonomy and academic freedom continue to be highly contested and debated issues. Given that autonomy and academic freedom are fundamental for knowledge creation and innovation, this is a challenge that must be continually overcome if higher education is to reach its full potential and maintain its central role in society. There is a growing negative public perception of higher education in some contexts on issues dealing with increasing costs of higher education, the desire to achieve greater student enrollments, and the challenge to maintain the quality of instruction expected from HEIs. The major concern here is that there are more students accessing higher education incommensurate to the available facilities and resources in HEIs (i.e., infrastructure and human resources). With increased use of part-time staff/faculty members, larger class sizes, and higher student-to-faculty ratios, it is difficult to establish and maintain the quality standard of instruction. It is also difficult to ensure that higher education curricula is and maintains relevance to practice.

The dramatic changes in technology in recent decades have opened countless possibilities to advance higher education that weren't imaginable in previous generations. In the wake of the Internet revolution, higher education has been able to capitalize on new modes of instruction, learning, research, and day-to-day managerial operations. Mobile technologies are also becoming more valuable tools for everyday higher education use. Many HEIs rely on such provisions as email, Facebook, Twitter, VoIP phones, and a host of Web 2.0 applications to better connect with their students and faculty members. Innovations such as Skype, Google Apps, Internet course management platforms (e.g., Blackboard, Moodle), blogs, wikis, and YouTube serve as important tools for research and teaching.

Currently, instructors can instantaneously disseminate and share information with their students and colleagues. Likewise, students can now better share their work with their peers and instructors and receive timely feedback. Many HEIs are enrolling more international students, as well as offering online courses and services to broader clientele. These tools and improved connectivity have also leveraged possibilities for collaborative research in HEIs and enhanced social networks between colleagues across the globe. Within the knowledge economy, there is an ever-important need for individuals to receive a higher education degree. A basic or high school education that was sufficient to obtain employment in past generations is no longer the case in most countries. In the 21st century, higher education training is generally viewed as the minimum standard for most careers.

W. James Jacob
University of Pittsburgh
Christopher B. Mugimu
Makerere University

See Also: College Advising; College Proximity; College Transferring; Community Colleges; International College Partnerships (Sister Colleges).

Further Readings

Barnett, Ronald and Robert Di Napoli, eds. *Changing Identities in Higher Education: Voicing Perspectives.* London: Routledge Taylor & Francis Group, 2008.

University of California Office of the President (UCOP). "Budget for Current Operations: Summary and Details, 2012–2013." Oakland, CA: UCOP, 2012.

U.S. Census Bureau. "Statistical Abstract of the United States: 2012." Washington, DC: U.S. Census Bureau, 2012.

Välimaa, Jussi and Oili-Helena Ylijoki, eds. *Cultural Perspectives on Higher Education.* Dordrecht, Netherlands: Springer, 2008.

Weidman, John C., Darla J. Twale, and Elizabeth L. Stein. "Socialization of Graduate and Professional Students in Higher Education: A Perilous Passage?" *ASHE-ERIC Higher Education Report*, v.28/3 (2001).

Home Schooling

This is an era of discontent over the quality and efficacy of compulsory public schooling. Concerned about the education and safety of their children, an increasing number of parents are seeking educational alternatives. The options include private schools, charter schools, and school vouchers. A small, but growing number of parents are forgoing institutionalized schools altogether in favor of home schooling. Estimates of the number of children currently home schooled in the United States range from 1.5 million to 2 million. Though parents vary in their justifications for teaching their children at home, they share a common family structure: most are white, middle-class, with at least two children, a breadwinning father, and a stay-at-home mother. In virtually all cases, the mother is responsible for the daily operation of the home school. Home schooling, defined as educating children primarily at home, rather than in schools, has been practiced in the United States as long as public schools have existed. The contemporary American home school movement has emerged out of two historical strands, both beginning roughly four decades ago: one counter-cultural and leftist, the other conservative and religious. Education researcher Jane Van Galen refers to these groups as "pedagogues" and "ideologues," respectively. In general, pedagogues promote home schooling because they view public schools as incapable of catering to the specific needs of each child. Ideologues, on the other hand, fault schools for not teaching the conservative social values and fundamentalist religious beliefs that their families espouse at home. Understanding the varied origins and ideologies of these two movements within a movement provides some insight into the characteristics and beliefs of the current generation of home schoolers.

Pedagogues and Radical School Reform

Early proponents of the modern home school movement were initially more interested in keeping children in public schools than taking them out. During the 1960s and early 1970s, countercultural scholars and social critics focused their energies on reforming public schools. Radical scholars such as Herbert Kohl, Jonathan Kozol, and Ivin Illich criticized public schools for their one-size-fits-all curricula and their hierarchical structure. They opposed the unequal power dynamics between the teachers and administrators who ran schools, and the students and families they served. These critics saw schools as factories that reproduced unequal social relations. Their first impulse, however, was not to abandon schools altogether, but to work to change them.

Radical school reformers sought to wrest control of educating American children from the state, and give it to parents and local communities. They envisioned schools that would provide high-quality education for all children. In their view, schools could, if properly reformed, promote democratic principles and ameliorate race and social class inequalities. For many, this optimism quickly faded, as efforts to change school were thwarted by conservative politicians and

nonsympathetic parents and educators. A number of these reformers gave up on schools and began to promote a new way of educating young children: home schooling.

The most prominent and influential radical school reformer, turned home schooling advocate, was the late John Holt. Holt, a former teacher in private schools, wrote extensively about the inadequacies of public schooling and, at the end of his career, the promise of teaching children at home. In *Why Children Fail* (1964) and *How Children Learn* (1967), Holt synthesized his theories on the failure of compulsory public education. His main criticism was that schools squash children's natural curiosity with standardized testing and inflexible curricula. Holt opposed formal instruction of any kind, and thought that children best learned when left to their own devices. In *Teach Your Own* (1981), his only book on home schooling, Holt advocated a pedagogy of "unschooling," which is a child-centered, self-directed, informal approach to education. By the late 1970s and early 1980s, most home schoolers in the United States identified with Holt's counter-cultural philosophy.

Ideologues: Religion and Authority

What John Holt was to the pedagogues, Raymond and Dorothy Moore were to the ideologues. During the 1970s, the Moores were well-known across the United States for their controversial views on early childhood education. Trained educational researchers and Seventh Day Adventists, the Moores challenged the assumption that schooling was good for young children. Working with a team of like-minded colleagues, the Moores surveyed thousands of studies and consulted with over 100 family and child development specialists. They concluded that placing young children in institutionalized schools before the age of 10 could negatively affect their normal development.

Though they initially supported school reform, the Moores eventually shifted their focus. Like Holt, they became advocates of taking children out of public schools and teaching them at home. While they shared Holt's commitment to home education, they developed a different pedagogy of home schooling. Whereas Holt and his followers rejected hierarchical, authoritative relationships of any kind, the Moores presumed the God-given authority of parents over their children. In their widely read books *Home Grown Kids* (1981) and *Home-Spun Schools* (1982), the Moores advocated a model of home schooling that was based on parental authority, formalized curricula, and Christian values. The unabashed religious conviction of the Moores' message appealed to scores of conservative Christian families, who were becoming increasingly disenchanted with the secular social institutions of the state. A new wave of home schooling had begun.

By the mid-1980s the countercultural pedagogues, the first home schoolers of the modern movement, were eclipsed in size and visibility by the fundamentalist ideologues. At 20 years later, religiously oriented home schoolers are arguably the best organized and largest segment of the movement. However, some observers suggest, this initial distinction between counter-culturalists and conservative Christians is no longer completely accurate. A broader range of families is choosing to home school than was true two decades ago, and their motivations sometimes blend both pedagogical and ideological concerns.

Inside Home Schooling: What We Know

There is currently no mechanism for locating and identifying all home schooling families in the nation. Though currently legal in all 50 states, the extent of state oversight of home schooling varies. In some states, parents are required to register their children with the local school board and to keep meticulous records of their children's educational goals and achievements. Other states have no such requirements, and some parents choose not to register their children. Hence, statistical accuracy varies by state. There is also an ideological dimension to the difficulty in studying homeschoolers. Many hold alternative world views and are reluctant to participate in studies conducted by unfamiliar researchers. This makes it less likely for them to voluntarily offer information about their activities.

Home school advocacy groups, such as the National Home Education Research Institute, have estimated the current population of home-schooled students to be 1.5 million to 2 million in the United States. Meanwhile, the federal government's estimates are slightly more conservative, ranging from 1 million to 1.1 million. The home schooling population has grown significantly over the past 30 years, and it continues to grow. The U.S. Department of Education estimates that there were between 10,000 and 15,000 home schoolers in the early 1970s, as many as 244,000 by 1985, and up to 300,000 in 1988. According to some researchers and home schooling advocacy groups, the number of home

schoolers grows annually by 15 to 25 percent. Second, home schooling may be the largest of the current educational movements, yet receives less public attention than other school options. Charter schools, for example, receive far more scrutiny by both scholars and mass media, despite attracting fewer students.

Why Home School?

There are four sets of overlapping frames that parents use to justify home schooling. First, there are religious motivations. Between 30 and 39 percent of home schooling parents teach their children at home in order to provide religious instruction and to shield their children from public schools' alleged anti-religious bias. Second, there are families who are primarily motivated by academic and pedagogical concerns. Nationwide, about a third of home schooling parents feel that the academic quality of schools is lacking, and about one-half feel they can do a better job of teaching their children than schools. A third category includes general concern about the school environment. For these parents, concerns about the safety of their children and negative peer influences are paramount. Finally, there are some families who cite "family lifestyle" reasons. This includes families who home school because it provides a source of family cohesion and unity.

Who Is Home Schooling?

Despite the methodological challenges of studying home schoolers, researchers have produced a demographic picture of home schooling families. Based on socioeconomic variables, most are middle class. Home schooling parents have higher than average incomes and levels of education, and the fathers tend to be employed in professional positions or are self-employed. In most cases, the father provides the family's main source of income and the mother does not work outside of the home. When mothers work, it tends to be part time. The vast majority of home schooling families comprise married couples with two or three children. Research also suggests that although increasing numbers of people of color are choosing to home school, this remains largely a white phenomenon. Between 75 and 90 percent of home schooled children in the United States are white. Home schooling families tend to be more religious and politically conservative than the general population and the largest segment of religious home schoolers is fundamentalist. Researchers have also shown that the overwhelming majority of the daily work of home schooling is done by mothers. Some estimate that mothers are the primary teachers in 90 percent of families. Most of these women are financially dependent on their husbands. In one large scale study of home schooling families, 78 percent of women listed "homemaker/home educator" as their primary occupation, while most of their husbands worked in professional, technical, and managerial positions. Furthermore, women are also responsible for most of the local and national organizing on behalf of the movement.

Sociology of Home Schooling

There is a small, but growing literature that explores home schooling from a sociological perspective. For example, some scholars have applied a social movement perspective to examine the role of resources, cultural beliefs, and politics in this burgeoning movement. Other research has explored the gender dynamics of home schooling. This research tends to focus on the experience of mothers as the primary home educators, within a broader context of feminist critiques of social institutions such as family, education, and the workplace. In general, this literature needs to be further developed to understand the social significance of this growing alternative education movement.

Brian Kapitulik
Greenfield Community College

See Also: Charter Schools: Family Structure and Education; Feminist Critiques of Educational Practices; Religious Education; School Choice.

Further Readings

Collom, Ed and Douglas E. Mitchell. "Home Schooling as a Social Movement: Identifying the Determinants of Homeschoolers' Perceptions." *Sociological Spectrum*, v.25 (2005).

Lois, Jennifer. "The Temporal Emotion Work of Motherhood." *Gender & Society*, v.24/4 (2010).

Miller, Ron. *Free Schools, Free People: Education and Democracy After the 1960s.* Albany: State University of New York Press, 2002.

Ray, Brian D. *Research Facts on Homeschooling.* Salem, OR: National Home Education Research Institute, 2006.

Stevens, Mitchell. *Kingdom of Children: Culture and Controversy in the Homeschooling Movement.* Princeton, NJ: Princeton University Press, 2001.

Homeless Children

A homeless child is any child under the age of 18 who lacks consistent or adequate housing. This includes children who are living alone or with their guardians in shelters, hotels, motels, vehicles, parks, campgrounds, or doubled up in single-family dwellings with other families or other children. Children experiencing homelessness are a diverse population, though they often experience greater emotional, social, and educational instability. Some of the causes can be linked to poverty, joblessness, domestic and family violence, and unstable home environments. Homeless children and youth, unaccompanied by a parent or guardian, may be escaping volatile home environments, or may be struggling with mental illness, drug addiction, issues related to gender or sexual identity, or other social or emotional problems.

Because of their marginalized status as children, unaccompanied youth are more likely to engage in illicit activities in order to ensure their survival on the streets, including theft, selling and/or using drugs, and prostitution. They also have high rates of infection from diseases, like HIV/AIDS and tuberculosis, internationally. Children experiencing homelessness frequently struggle with additional developmental, health, and/or social problems as a result of the instability faced during this time. These children may suffer from malnutrition, developmental and learning disabilities, and may experience abuse and violence in temporary housing facilities, on the street, or in foster homes. Children and youth experiencing homelessness alone in the United States lack parental, foster, or other institutional care and are often an invisible population. These children are frequently visibly indistinguishable from other children and youth with more stable housing, as they may receive clothing and access to bathing facilities through outreach groups, and keep hidden during times of the day when they are expected to be in school.

Ensuring the education of children who experience frequent and consistent periods of homelessness can be a particular challenge because these children tend to have higher rates of truancy, change schools with greater frequency, and lack adequate academic and immunization records. The McKinney-Vento Homeless Assistance Act: Education for Homeless Children and Youths was passed in 1987 and reauthorized in 2002 as a part of the No Child Left Behind legislation. The purpose of this act is to safeguard equal access to education for children experiencing homelessness. The act was set up to ensure that homelessness not be a factor in any child's ability to access the same free and appropriate education afforded to other children in the state where they currently reside. This act also places regulations on schools and districts to ensure that the residency requirements in place do not prevent a child from accessing education because they are unable to provide proof of residency. Despite intentions, barriers to education still exist, including immunization requirements, transportation, and fees associated with schooling. Throughout the United States, several schools cater specifically to homeless children. These schools, in addition to the traditional and compulsory curriculum, provide a variety of social services to children and their families, including clothing, toiletries, and the coordination of dental and health care visits/checkups.

Homeless children in most developing nations are known as "street children." Children who make their ways on the streets may do so for short or long periods of time. While there are some children and adolescents who make the street a more permanent resting place, others may return to their families, find work in an attempt to transition out of street life, go to prison, fall victim to communicable diseases like tuberculosis or AIDS, or disappear. Discourse about street children often places the population into one of two categories: "children of the street" and "children on the street."

Children of the street are children whose main source of subsistence is the street, while children on the street are those who spend the majority of their time on the street, but return home frequently. This dualistic conception of street children and the term *street child* may be limited, because many street children live somewhere between these two extremes. While the reasons that children come to the streets are similar to the causes of homelessness in the United States, children living on the street in developing nations are often more visible than homeless children in the United States. These children frequently participate in the informal economy, engaging in various income-generating acts such as shining shoes, guarding cars, washing car windows, carrying water and packages, and selling items such as candies, flowers, bags of fruit, newspapers, or cigarettes.

Jamie Patrice Joanou
Arizona State University

See Also: Adolescence; At-Risk Students; Childhood; Diseases and Education; Dropouts.

Further Readings
Barret Wiik, K. "Justice for America's Homeless Children: Cultivating a Child's Right to Shelter in the United States." *William Mitchell Law Review*, v.35/3 (2009).
Scheper-Hughes, N. and D. Hoffman. "Kids Out of Place." *NACLA Report on the Americas* (May/June 1994).
Vissing, Y. *Out of Sight, Out of Mind: Homeless Children and Families in Small-Town America*. Lexington: University Press of Kentucky, 1996.

Homework

Homework generally contributes to positive academic outcomes. However, there are conditions in which children will get more out of homework, such as when parents and teachers help children see the value in homework, as opposed to pressuring them to get it done merely because it is required. Homework is an important part of educational development. As students approach middle and high school, they receive more homework. When teachers provide homework assignments, they intend for them to deepen and extend students' classroom learning. Conversely, some educators view homework as ineffective and refrain from assigning it, and many students complain when teachers assign homework. Many parents get frustrated with homework because of the power struggles they have with their children about doing it. Because of the controversy over homework and the fact that many students dislike it, it is important to ascertain whether homework is positively associated with academic achievement.

Multiple studies indicate that completing homework predicts higher achievement for students of various ethnicities and from various countries, especially for students in middle and high school. Based on analyses of many studies on homework and achievement, Harris Cooper recommends that children receive very little homework in grades one through three and progress to approximately two hours a day in high school, but Ulrich Trautwein and colleagues have found that homework effort and completion are more important for promoting student achievement than a specific amount of time. Furthermore, when children perceive that the homework assignment is of high quality (i.e., helpful and interesting), students achieve more. Simply assigning homework does not guarantee that it will be completed or completed well. Teachers have relatively little control over whether students invest sufficient effort in their homework because it is not conducted under the teacher's supervision; it is conducted after school, usually at home. Therefore, it is important for students to be motivated to complete their homework, either on their own or with some support from parents. Teachers can promote students' intrinsic motivation for homework completion by explaining the purpose of the assignment and the real-life applicability of the topic. Unfortunately, many teachers solely emphasize that the homework must be done by a deadline in order to avoid a lowered grade, which promotes minimal compliance, rather than a desire to master the material.

Gender Differences

Girls complete more homework than boys, in part because girls are better at managing their motivation and emotions toward homework. For instance, Jianzhong Xu found that high school girls are more likely to use optimistic self-talk when facing homework challenges. Whereas gender differences are rather robust, in tightly controlled studies, a student's socioeconomic status (SES) does not predict more motivation and effort in the realm of homework among older students. However, SES predicts better achievement when more homework is assigned in elementary school, indicating that higher SES children benefit more from homework, partly because of greater support from parents.

Parental Involvement

Parents have an important role to play in supporting their children's homework. Research indicates that elementary school students benefit more from homework when their parents have higher education levels, which is partly because of the greater confidence that highly educated parents have in supporting their children during homework. On the other hand, controlling parental communication surrounding homework backfires by decreasing student's intrinsic motivation to study. Controlling communication entails providing unsolicited help, pressuring children, and not listening to their feelings about homework, which leads to academic anxiety. The risk of parental involvement in homework being ineffective is heightened in middle school, where it is somewhat negatively related to achievement.

Children struggle for autonomy more than ever during adolescence and perceive many adults as controlling. As children get older, parents can best support children in their homework by conveying that they expect that their children will succeed academically and providing help when requested in an autonomy supportive way (e.g., acknowledging their children's feelings, pointing out the value in the homework topic, and encouraging their children to believe that their homework-related effort will prepare them to meaningfully contribute to society). Homework provides children with the opportunity to further their understanding and skills. It is important for teachers to make the value of specific homework assignments clear, and for parents to use autonomy supportive communication when discussing homework with their children. Homework is effective and should be utilized strategically by educators to promote the further growth of students.

John Mark Froiland
University of Northern Colorado

See Also: Parent Education; Parental Educational Expectations; Parental Involvement.

Further Readings

Dettmers, S., U. Trautwein, O. Lüdtke, M. Kunter, and J. Baumert. "Homework Works if Homework Quality Is High: Using Multilevel Modeling to Predict the Development of Achievement in Mathematics." *Journal of Educational Psychology*, v.102/2 (2010).

Froiland, J. M. "The Long-Term Effects of Early Parent Involvement and Parent Expectation in the U.S." *School Psychology International* (in press).

Froiland, J. M. "Parental Autonomy Support and Student Learning Goals: A Preliminary Examination of an Intrinsic Motivation Intervention." *Child and Youth Care Forum*, v.40 (2011).

Martinez, S. "An Examination of Latino Students' Homework Routines." *Journal of Latinos and Education*, v.10/4 (2011).

Ronning, M. "Who Benefits From Homework Assignments?" *Economics of Education Review*, v.30 (2011).

Xu, J. "Homework Emotion Management at the Secondary School Level: Antecedents and Homework Completion." *Teachers College Record*, v.113/3 (2011).

Honduras

Honduras was a Spanish colony until 1821, when it gained independence from Spain. It is located in Central America and has borders with Guatemala and El Salvador to the west and Nicaragua to the south. Honduras is approximately the size of Tennessee, with an area of 43,243 square miles (112,090 square kilometers). According to the Central Intelligence Agency (CIA), its estimated population is 8.1 million. Its population is mainly *mestizos* around 90 percent, a mix of Spanish and Amerindian, the rest is composed of native Indians, blacks, and whites. The economy of Honduras is "diversified" and includes not only agricultural products, but also manufacturing. According to the World Bank, more than 59 percent of Honduras is poor and 36 percent is very poor. Unemployment and poverty has aggravated the problems of drug trafficking and gang violence. In 1998, the country was devastated by Hurricane Mitch, which worsened the problem of poverty.

The Mayans inhabited the western part of Honduras for many centuries and founded the great city of Copán. When the Spanish conquered and colonized Honduras in the 1500s, the Mayan empire had already collapsed. However, there were other important indigenous groups, such as the Lencas and the Xicaques. There was mass Indian resistance to Spanish colonization, which ended with the assassination of the Indian leader, Lempira. Honduras was a Spanish colony for over 300 years, until it gained independence in 1821. After independence, Honduras was characterized by political instability, and during the 20th century, had a dictatorship and several military governments. Honduras returned to democracy in 1982, by electing Roberto Suazo. Unlike its Central American neighbors, Honduras did not have civil wars in the 20th century. However, anti-Sandinistas Contras from Nicaragua and Salvadorian soldiers operated from Honduras to fight leftist guerrillas. Honduras enjoyed a democratic transition between governments, except for the ousting of President-elect Manuel Zelaya in June 2009. This event became an international crisis that was resolved by the election of the current president, Porfirio Lobo, in November 2009.

Establishment of Educational System

Its educational system was established around 1820 and it has two subsystems: the formal and non-formal. The Secretary of Education (SEC) is in charge of preschool, elementary, secondary, and adult education, while the National University of Honduras (UNAH) is in charge of professional and higher education. According to the organic law in Honduras of 1966, the state has the function of providing education, and all Hondurans have the right to an education. Primary education is compulsory, and public education is free at all levels. In 1996, basic education was expanded to include nine grades, instead of six. Basic education is organized in three cycles of three years each, and secondary education is three years. Within secondary education, there are two modalities, academic and professional. After three years of secondary schooling, pupils can enter higher education.

Like most Latin American countries, the Honduran government embarked on modernizing education by improving enrollment and quality. There were projects to improve elementary education, such as the Primary Education Efficiency Program, funded by the USAID. In 1999, the Honduran Project of Community Education (PROHECO) was established, in which communities are in charge of running schools in rural areas. In 2010, 11 percent of students enrolled in basic education attended one of these schools. The reforms initiated in the 1990s helped Honduras decrease illiteracy and increase coverage. For instance, when comparing enrollments for 2000 and 2009, there was an increase in all levels. It went from 86 to 90 percent in basic, 25 to 26 percent in secondary, and 12 to 17 percent in higher education. However, there are high rates of dropouts and repetition, despite the fact that Honduras invests 7 percent of its gross domestic product (GDP) in education, one of the highest rates in Central America. Most of its educational budget, according to the 2010 "Report on the Educational Progress in Honduras," is for teachers' salaries.

Honduras still has problems with the quality of education, and even though gender inequalities are almost nonexistent, socioeconomic disparities are still present. Furthermore, teacher education is still done at the secondary level. There has been a deconcentration of education, not a real decentralization. A new law, approved in 2011, would decentralize education at the departmental level; departments would be in charge of the administration of human resources and finances. Under the new law, English would be taught, beginning in preschool. Moreover, the state must provide at least one year of preschool until secondary education. This new law will derogate the organic education law established in 1966. Public education will still be free and compulsory from preschool to secondary education. It also establishes that teachers should hold college degrees in order to teach.

Liza Valle
University of Pittsburgh

See Also: El Salvador; Guatemala; Mexico; Nicaragua.

Further Readings

"Programa de Promoción de la Reforma Educativa de América Latina y el Caribe (PREAL). ("Report on the Educational Progress in Honduras"). Washington, DC: PREAL, 2010.

United Nations Educational, Scientific and Cultural Organization (UNESCO) International Bureau of Education. *World Data on Education: Honduras.* 7th ed. Geneva, Switzerland: UNESCO-IBE, 2010.

Villatoro, Rivas and Felipe Alexander. *The State of Education in Central America, 2000–2008.* San Salvador, El Salvador: Fundación Innovaciones Educativas Centroamericanas, 2008.

Hong Kong

While Hong Kong's society, economy, culture, and parents all value education, its government spends little on education, and few students attend college, when compared to most developed countries. Parents choose from a variety of schools for their children and increasingly participate in school as school reforms reduce its hierarchical nature. During two decades of school reforms, student performance on international tests on mathematics, reading, and science have gradually risen to the top 10 percent of participating countries and regions. Grounded in government exams, collectivist beliefs, and economic rewards, Chinese people have traditionally supported children's education. The *Keju* civil service exam system from 606 to 1905 not only selected mainland China's government officials, but also gave financial rewards, prestige, power, and fame to their extended family, thereby encouraging collectivist beliefs, values, and norms. Hong Kong's economy further rewards education; a high school teacher earns a manual worker's lifetime wages in 15 years, while a professor earns the equivalent within five years.

Hong Kong parents value their children's education and high exam scores, and invest in their education accordingly. As most of these parents view their children's effort as more important than their ability, they invest in their education (e.g., tutoring) regardless of past achievement. As many Hong Kong families only have one child, parents support their child's education, regardless of gender. Girls outperform boys in all school subjects on average, and women are visibly successful at all levels of Hong Kong society. Despite education's cultural importance, the Hong Kong government's educational spending is small, even after the United Kingdom returned governance to mainland China in 1997.

Public education comprised only 3 percent of Hong Kong's gross domestic product (GDP) in 2010. For example, over 90 percent of children attend kindergarten (none managed by the government), but Hong Kong only began subsidizing about 25 percent of the cost of full-day, nonprofit kindergartens in 2007. Hong Kong has had 12 years of free and compulsory education since 2008, nine years since 1979, and six years since 1971. The British colonial view of using universities to train only government officials is slowly changing; still, admission to Hong Kong's nine public universities was limited to 2 percent, 8 percent, 18 percent, and 22 percent of the relevant age groups in 1980, 1990, 2000, and 2010, respectively.

Hong Kong's school system is also notable for its degree of parent choice. Each kindergarten and university has a selection process, while public primary and secondary school admission occurs through a two-stage system. In the discretionary stage, parents can apply to one primary school (or two secondary schools) for each child. Half of these primary school students are selected according to a government formula based on geography and whether a sibling attends that school. Meanwhile, secondary schools select 30 percent of their students based on their publicly announced criteria, which often include primary school grades. Then, the government centrally allocates the remaining students to a primary or secondary school in their district, based on parent rankings of schools, a student's allocation band, and a random number. A student's allocation band (low, medium, or high) is based on primary school grades and sampled students' scores on a city-wide test. Each allocation band consists of one-third of all students. Hence, these schools are largely stratified by past student achievement.

Primary and Secondary Schools

Hong Kong has four types of primary and secondary schools: government, aided, direct subsidy scheme, and private. The government funds government schools and aided schools ($4,033 per primary school student; $4,954 per secondary school student; 2009) and dictates their curricula. Over 80 percent of students attend aided schools, which are managed by nonprofit sponsor organizations that hire their own staff, unlike government schools. Meanwhile, direct subsidy scheme schools receive per student government funding inversely proportional to their tuition, and have greater freedom in hiring staff, selecting students, and designing curricula. Last, private schools receive no government funding and have full autonomy.

Hong Kong has a hierarchical culture, in which decision-making power and status inequities are more openly accepted than in most Western societies. However, school-wide reforms during the last two decades are slowly changing school governance. Hong Kong schools are increasingly empowering teachers to participate in department and school decisions. Likewise, more schools are encouraging meaningful parent participation through consultations on major changes. Hong Kong's curricula, textbooks, and classroom lessons emphasize breadth over depth. As school reputations depend in part on their graduates' exam scores and acceptances to the best schools at the next level of study, teachers typically use exam-based textbooks and design class lessons to cover all content that might be on city-wide or university multiple choice exams.

Ming Ming Chiu
State University of New York, University at Buffal

See Also: China; Governmental Influences on Education; Standardized Testing.

Further Readings

Bray, Mark and Ramsey Koo. *Education and Society in Hong Kong and Macao.* Hong Kong: Springer, 2005.

Lee, Clarie. "Hong Kong Frets Over 'China Model' Patriotic Education." Reuters (July 11, 2012). http://www.reuters.com/article/2012/07/11/us-hongkong-patriotism-idUSBRE86A09L20120711 (Accessed August 2012).

Solloway, Anthony J. *Does It Have to Be Like This? Education and Socialisation in Hong Kong.* Charleston, SC: CreateSpace Independent Publishing Platform, 2010.

Household Educational Resources

Children's educational environments are affected by the social class of their parents. Parents are their children's first teachers and the resources they use at home have important implications for child cognition, child social adjustment, and children's success in formal schooling. Children's educational environments begin at birth with the interactions they experience in their families.

Scholars have become increasingly attuned to the inequality of family resources as they impact young children's development, and have argued that by the time children reach school age, their educational environments have already prepared them either well or poorly for formal schooling. If children experience weak household learning environments during formal schooling, such lack of resources will further hinder school performance. Conversely, children who experience enriched home learning environments over time will find their chances of success in school enhanced. Compounding these inequalities is the reality that, all too often, children who are advantaged at home will also be advantaged at school, with other children being disadvantaged in both environments. Thus, children who at birth are initially disadvantaged at home may, over time, find that these initial disadvantages are compounded, not ameliorated, by unequal school environments.

An important educational resource for infants and young children is the sheer quantity of verbal interaction they experience with adults. There is considerable variation by social class in the quantity of words and types of sentences that very young children experience. Children in households receiving welfare experience less verbal interaction with adults than children in working-class households; children who have parents in professional occupations experience even more verbal interaction than working-class children. There also are differences by socioeconomic status in terms of the richness of language. Children in professional households are exposed to more complex sentences and questions that encourage their verbal responsiveness. Children in households that receive welfare experience simpler sentences and more frequent direct commands. These differences are associated with predictable differences in children's verbal capabilities by age 3.

Children's Home Environments

Researchers have also demonstrated that other dimensions of children's home environments are consequential for their future well-being. Children are advantaged when their home environments are reasonably clean, uncluttered, and free of hazards, and when they experience affectionately warm home environments. In such homes, over and above safety, parents express verbal affection, introduce children to visitors, speak pleasantly to them, and typically avoid physical punishment and harsh verbal rebukes. Children are also advantaged when their homes contain age-appropriate intellectual resources that can encourage cognitive development. For the youngest children, resources would include age-appropriate books and toys; someone who will teach the child their numbers, colors, and letters; and the frequency with which the child is read stories.

For older children, key resources would include being encouraged to pursue hobbies or create collections; having access to musical instruments; and the expectation of their providing help at home. For children 10 years of age and older, additional relevant resources include whether children manage their own time. A combination of a safe home, a warm affectionate environment, and a stimulating cognitive environment constitutes a better home environment, which is a strong predictor of both child academic success and strong child social behavior. Weaker home environments place children at risk for increased behavior problems and for weaker academic outcomes.

Children with more-educated and higher-income parents will also experience stronger home environments. Although better home environments may not be strongly associated with parental education and financial resources, some of the markers of cognitive enrichment, such as music lessons or visiting museums, require household funds. Researchers have discovered that households of varying financial means are now reading to their young children frequently, while earlier such enrichment was associated with higher levels of social class. Even more contemporary perspectives stress the importance of technology in the home, such as access to computers. Children who have access to computers at home may experience an educational advantage over those who do not.

Social Class and Socialization

In addition, middle-class children are advantaged because their parents engage in "concerted cultivation." Specifically, middle-class parents determine what their children's special talents and abilities are and encourage their children to develop them. They provide extensive opportunities for extracurricular activity in sports, the arts, and/or other age-appropriate venues that are led by adults. Through these activities, middle-class children become comfortable negotiating with adults, and see themselves as worthy of attention and adult investment. In turn, children use these resources in a variety of other contexts, including with teachers at school.

Lower-income parents provide fewer of these adult-led extracurricular opportunities, and instead encourage free play and relationships with extended family members. These children have less exposure to adults outside the family, and develop fewer skills in dealing with them. This limits their ability to negotiate adult-led environments at school, which may result in reduced learning and less identification with middle-class educational goals. Middle-class parents also view the schools as their partners, while working-class parents view the schools as authorities that may threaten or censure family arrangements. In turn, these attitudes are communicated to children. Finally, middle-class parents may also transmit advantage by having higher expectations for their children's future educational and occupational achievements compared to the expectations of lower-income parents.

Family Structure, Resource Diffusion, and Parental Work Schedules

Household educational resources are a function both of the absolute level of parental resources they can use in child rearing, as well as the demands that parents face in using them. For example, households that are headed by single parents have, on average, fewer monetary resources to invest in children, as well as fewer adults to supervise them and take them to activities. In addition, those households with greater numbers of children may find that the personal and financial resources that adults have, even if ample, are more finely divided across children, leaving fewer resources for each child. Finally, if parents work multiple jobs, and/or nonstandard schedules, they may also find that using household resources to benefit children's learning will be more challenging.

Toby L. Parcel
North Carolina State University

See Also: Class Inequality: Achievement; Concerted Cultivation/Natural Growth; Social Capital.

Further Readings

Hart, B. and T. R. Risely. *Meaningful Differences in the Everyday Experience of Young American Children.* Baltimore, MD: Paul H. Brookes, 1995.

Lareau, A. *Unequal Childhoods: Class, Race, and Family Life. Second Edition with an Update a Decade Later.* Berkeley: University of California Press, 2011.

Parcel, T. L. and E. G. Menaghan. *Parents' Jobs and Children's Lives.* New York: Aldine de Gruyter, 1994.

Teachman, Jay. "Family Background, Educational Resources and Educational Attainment." *American Sociological Review,* v.52 (1987).

Human Capital Theory

Human capital theory is important to scholars in sociology and economics of education. Human capital adherents argue for investment in people through education and health care, risking a short-term loss of resources for long-term gains. According to human capital theory, economic growth depends not only on the nation's physical capital (such as roads), but also on the education and health of the labor pool. Human capital theorists suggest that schooling promotes economic and social development because the benefits to the individual spill over to help society. Theodore W. Schultz introduced his theory of human capital in the early 1960s. He asserted that the transition from traditional to modern society requires investment in people. This investment in people through education and health care creates human capital. Schultz asserted that the rates of return on such human capital investment are greater than those for nonhuman capital investments, especially in developing countries. People with poor health or few skills are not able to contribute to society, while healthy, educated individuals can. In this view, education is not consumption, but an investment that develops skills in individuals, and increases their productivity and earnings.

Direct and Indirect Expenses

Investments in human capital are comparable to investments in other resources. Effective use of resources yields profits for individuals and society.

There are a two types of costs to consider, direct and indirect. Textbooks and tuition are direct costs. The lost wages from not being in the labor market (or not full time) while in school are opportunity costs. It is also important to distinguish social and private costs (and benefits) of human capital investment. Private costs and benefits are those incurred by individuals. Lost wages and higher salaries are private outcomes of human capital investment. Social costs and benefits are those accrued by society. Salaries for public school teachers are a social cost; economic growth is a social benefit. It is difficult to measure the social returns on education. Cross-national studies of the connection between educational attainment and economic growth have yielded inconsistent results. At the same time, numerous studies have found correlations between an individual's level of education and earnings.

One example of human capital investment is participation in higher education. An individual expects lifetime earnings to exceed the short-term loss of time and money required for attending college. These individual benefits should then have a positive impact on society through improved contribution to the labor force, political participation, and economic contributions. Human capital theory has provided the rationale for widespread investment in education. An increase in school participation and increased incomes of developed countries gave legitimacy to human capital theory. It is widely assumed that increased schooling will lead to increased productivity and development of societies. Human capital theory is, therefore, the basis for much development work. Human capital investments, such as literacy campaigns in developing countries, are intended to create a more productive labor force, bolster the economy, and increase standard of living.

Key Criticisms

Human capital theory assumes that education develops skills, that these skills increase a worker's capacity to be productive, and that increased productivity leads to higher wages. These assumptions pave the way for some of the key criticisms of human capital theory. A major critique of human capital theory is that it places responsibility on the individual to access education, find employment, and contribute to society. This creates the implication that if an individual does not succeed, it is their fault. This logic negates any bias in the system. Human capital theory also fails to offer an explanation for the underemployment of educated individuals and for recent stagnation of economic growth in the face of increased participation in education.

Cambria Russell
Columbia University

See Also: Critical Theory of Education; Functionalist Theory of Education; Longitudinal Studies of Education.

Further Readings

Becker, Gary S. *Human Capital: A Theoretical and Empirical Analysis.* New York: Columbia University Press for NBER, 1975.

Hartog, Joop and Henriétte Maassen van den Brink, eds. *Human Capital: Theory and Evidence.* Cambridge: Cambridge University Press, 2007.

Schultz, Theodore W. "Investment in Human Capital." *American Economic Review,* v.1/2 (1961).

Hungary

Hungary is situated in central Europe, with an area of 35,910 square miles (93,030 square kilometers). The terrain, mostly flat, includes low mountains in the north, a temperate climate, and is bordered by Slovakia to the north, Romania and Ukraine to the east, Serbia and Croatia to the south, Slovenia to the southwest, and Austria to the west. The Central Intelligence Agency's *World Factbook* estimates the population of Budapest, the capital city, at 2 million people (2012). Other principal cities are Debrecen, Miskolc, Szeged, and Pecs. Hungary joined the European Union (EU) in 2004, the North Atlantic Treaty Organization (NATO) in 1999, and the Organisation for Economic Co-operation and Development (OECD) in 1996. Hungarian, also known as Magyar, is the official language. The economy depends on bauxite, natural gas, coal, and the manufacturing of textiles, pharmaceuticals, and machinery. It has a gross domestic product (GDP) of $115.96 billion. The United Nations estimates that 17.3 percent of the population lives below the poverty line.

Hungary was settled by western Siberian tribes in the 9th century. The Reform Age, at the beginning of the 19th century, produced the Hungarian Academy of Science, the National Museum, and modern railways. Kaiser Franz-Joseph of Austria-Hungary invaded Serbia, beginning World War I. World War II, communism, and Soviet rule produced a bitter period of crises, poverty, and food shortages. Free and democratic elections ended communism in 1990. Hungary suffered from the global economic crisis, and is currently under restriction by the Economic and Financial Affairs Council of the European Union (ECOFIN). The government is a parliamentary democratic republic. The National Assembly adopted a new constitution on April 18, 2011; it entered into effect on January 1, 2012. Laszlo Solyom is president and head of state. The prime minister is Viktor Orban, head of government. The Council of Ministers, the executive body, oversees domestic and foreign policy. Hungary is predominantly Christian, predominantly Roman Catholic (51.9 percent), Calvinist (15.9 percent), Lutheran (3 percent), and Greek Catholic (2.6 percent). The Law on the Right to Freedom of Conscience and Religion and on Churches, Religions and Religious Communities was enacted July 12, 2011, and recognizes only 14 religions. Muslims must apply for official status.

Educational Structure

Education has been part of Hungarian life since early medieval times, when teaching was a fundamental part of monastic life. School is mandatory until age 16, with low student-teacher ratios. The Public Education Act guarantees a free eight-year elementary education and upper secondary level general or vocational education. Students can obtain their first degree without cost at public-funded state universities and colleges. The Ministry of Education controls public education. In 1999, public expenditure on education was estimated at 4.6 percent of GDP. Hungarians have a 99.4 percent literacy rate. Basic education in Hungary is provided by the general (primary) school. Secondary education includes technical, vocational, and general secondary schools, or gymnasiums.

Approximately 15 percent of Roma children attend school. The Law on Public Education ensures the right to minority education and the right to be educated in the mother tongue. The National Core Curriculum recognizes instruction in the minority language (mother tongue program) and bilingual education. Hungarian is the language of instruction, with minority language taught as a foreign language.

The Law on Freedom of Religion and Belief allows students to choose a denominational or other private school. A total of 90 percent of children attend public-sector institutions. The 1995 National Core Curriculum, in union with the EU, set standards for methodology and content of public education at the primary and secondary levels.

Career Choice

Choice of career is determined by the need for social mobility and family background. Achievement in primary and secondary school is still the determining factor in career choice. Pressure from the EU and global markets is at the forefront of educational reform. Globalization of the world economy requires educational restructuring in the areas of critical thinking, morality, ethics, and the environment. A push away from the state-controlled school systems, where neutral thinking predominated, has been in evidence since the 1990s. Both local and national educational systems strive to bridge the gap between reform, innovation, and traditionalism. Cultural factors and discrimination continue to plague Roma students, with only 13 percent completing secondary education. Many educated students move abroad to work for multinational companies.

Kay Castaneda
Ivy Tech Community College

See Also: Austria; Career and Technical Education; European Union.

Further Readings

Hungarian Culture, Language and Relocation Resources. http://www.filolog.com (Accessed February 2012).

Maroy, Christian. "Convergences and Hybridization of Educational Policies Around 'Post-Bureaucratic' Models of Regulation." *Compare: A Journal of Comparative and International Education*, v.39/1 (2009).

Susskind, Jack. "Hungary: A Nation in Transition." *Social Education*, v.57/6 (1993).

I

Idaho

Idaho is a western state, admitted to U.S. statehood in 1890. Idaho has traditionally had a largely rural population, served by one-room common schools. Growth and development led to the emergence of a modern educational system and facilities. It had a 2010 population of 1,567,582. Idaho maintains state public education standards by grade level for a variety of core content areas. Idaho has adopted the national Common Core State Standards for mathematics and English language arts, and will introduce them into the classroom during the 2013 to 2014 school year.

The recent economic crisis and legislative budget cuts to education funding are among the most daunting challenges facing Idaho education. Congress established the Idaho Territory in 1863, and Idaho became the 43rd state in 1890. Idaho's size and the difficulty of travel meant that its early population lived a largely rural and isolated existence, resulting in difficulties in establishing and populating schools. Key early industries included agriculture, ranching, mining, and lumber. Industries such as railroads played a role in early education through the organization of subscription schools. Early schools were often located in buildings that served other purposes, such as saloons, fire stations, or churches. Most dedicated school buildings were one-room common schools in which children of varying cultural and socioeconomic backgrounds and grade levels were taught together by one teacher. Historical preservationists and educators have sought to preserve the old wooden one-room schoolhouses as both historical landmarks and educational opportunities for current and future students. Native American children were educated on reservation schools built by religious denominations or the federal government, or in off-reservation boarding schools where they were forced to abandon their families and traditional cultures.

Idaho's growing population led to the need for an expanded school system. Early challenges included weather, transportation, rural isolation, the need to leave school for agricultural work, teacher shortages, funding, and inadequate teacher training and administrative oversight. "Normal schools," or teacher training schools, were developed to instruct early teachers. Curriculum and teacher certification became more standardized, and teachers began organizing professionally. The Idaho State Teachers' Association (now the Idaho Education Association) was founded in 1892 to promote the interests of educators, such as pay and benefits, and educational funding levels. The Idaho School Trustees Association was founded in 1943. Rural county school consolidation began in the 1930s, with rural children often bussed to distant central schools located in the closest towns or cities. Modernization also included the construction of larger school buildings of more substantial building materials, such as brick or stone, to replace the earlier one-room schoolhouses. Schools also benefited from improvements in texts and

Table 1 Elementary and secondary education characteristics

	Idaho	U.S. (average)
Total number of schools	755	1,988
Total students	275,859	970,278
Total teachers	15,672.54	60,766.56
Pupil/teacher ratio	17.60	15.97

Source: U.S. Department of Education, National Center for Education Statistics, Common Core of Data (CCD), 2010–11.

Table 2 Elementary and secondary education finance

	Idaho	U.S. (average)
Total revenues	$2,167,454,727	$11,464,385,994
Total expenditures for education	$2,324,360,442	$11,712,033,839
Total current expenditures	$1,891,504,817	$9,938,906,259

Source: U.S. Department of Education, National Center for Education Statistics, Common Core of Data (CCD), "National Public Education Financial Survey," FY08 (2007–08).

equipment. Other notable milestones included the 1965 Exceptional Child Education Act. Kindergartens were introduced by 1975, but their presence within individual school districts was not mandatory.

Idaho contains public, private, and charter elementary and secondary schools. The Idaho State Department of Education enforces state and federal education policies and oversees the state's modern educational system. State legislation currently caps the formation of new charter schools at six annually. Idaho houses five state colleges, three state universities, seven private colleges, and five private universities. The state universities are Boise State University, Idaho State University, and the University of Idaho. Idaho maintains state public education standards by grade level for health, humanities, language arts, science, mathematics, physical education, and social studies for kindergarten through the 12th grade. Idaho has also adopted the national Common Core State Standards for mathematics and English language arts, designed to increase standardization and academic rigor among the states. Professional development training in the new standards for educators is underway, with a planned start date of the 2013 to 2014 school year. Idaho is also among the states participating in the development of national assessment measures for the standards.

Idaho ranked 22nd among all states and the District of Columbia on the National Assessment of Educational Progress (NAEP), covering fourth through eighth grade students from 2003 to 2009. Estimates for 2006 to 2010 show that 11.8 percent of Idaho students did not complete high school, while 28.8 percent did. Approximately 24.3 percent of Idaho students went on to graduate college. Current issues facing Idaho education include disputes over the superintendent's 2011 Students Come First Plan. Contentions include educator collective bargaining rights and the issue of basing teacher pay on classroom performance, and of how such performance will be measured. Ongoing issues include class size reduction and funding. One of the key issues facing Idaho's public school system during the recent economic crisis is inadequate educational funding. Idaho ranks second to last of all 50 states and the District of Columbia in terms of funding per student, according to 2007 to 2008 U.S. Census Bureau figures. Idaho's average was $6,931 per student, compared to the national average of $10,259. Education funding cuts only deepened in the following years, with the state legislature budgeting less money than the previous year for the first time in 2009 to 2010. Federal funding has temporarily offset some of the state funding loss, and individual school districts are granted some flexibility when faced with financial crises.

Marcella Bush Trevino
Barry University

See Also: Curriculum Standardization; Funding of Schools; Native American Students.

Further Readings
Idaho State Board of Education. http://www.boardofed .idaho.gov (Accessed February 2012).

Idaho State Department of Education. http://www.sde .idaho.gov (Accessed February 2012).

Mondale, Sarah and Sarah B. Patton. *School: The Story of American Public Education.* Boston: Beacon, 2001.

Illinois

Illinois is located in the midwestern region of the United States. According to the 2010 census, the state population is approximately 13 million, and is approximately two-thirds Caucasian, 15 percent Hispanic, and 15 percent African American. This is in sharp contrast to the demographic makeup of Illinois' largest city, Chicago, which has a population of about 2.7 million people and has roughly equal numbers of European Americans, African Americans, and Latinos. Similarly, while the percent of persons below the poverty level in the entire state is 12.6 percent, the percent living below the poverty level in Chicago is just over one-fifth of the population. Between Chicago, its wealthier suburbs, and the rest of rural Illinois, there are large differences in educational needs across the state. Illinois' diverse population characteristics, unique politics, and strong educators union have shaped its history, educational structure, and the issues the state faces today.

When Illinois was founded in 1818, with a population of primarily farmers and a few wealthy businessmen, there was no free public education in the state. In 1853, leaders in Illinois established the state's first educators union, the Illinois State Teachers Association (ISTA). In 1855, the Free School Bill was passed in Illinois, requiring all towns with more than 15 families to provide a free school for at least three months out of the year. Soon after, normal schools (e.g., now Illinois State University and Northern Illinois University) were founded as some of the first institutions for educating teachers, making Illinois a leader in education for the nation. In 1871, the ISTA granted voting and membership rights to women, well before the time when women were granted the right to vote in governmental elections. This was an early display of regard for teachers' rights by the union. In the early 1900s, Chicago was burgeoning, and job opportunities outside of the teaching profession grew. In an effort to keep teaching a desirable profession, the ISTA lobbied to make a minimum salary for teachers, as well as to grant tenure after five years of teaching.

Thanks to their early efforts to maintain teacher loyalty, the union in Illinois is a strong force, both in politics and public education. The Illinois Education Association (IEA), formerly the ISTA, contributes significantly to political parties, in particular to the Democratic Party. Furthermore, according to IEA's Web site, more than 80 percent of teachers in Illinois are members of a teachers union. For this reason, it is extraordinarily difficult for any change in education legislature to occur if it does not align with the desires of the teachers unions. Despite the difficulty presented by the unions and politicians in initiating educational change, Chicago, because of its social justice oriented

universities, large minority population, and proportion of citizens living in poverty, has been one of the most widely researched cities in the United States on the topic of educational reform.

Chicago is a large and diverse city, famous for the bustling downtown area on Lake Michigan. However, many tourists never see the highly impoverished parts of the city. In contrast, many of the suburbs are affluent, although the first ring suburbs often have a large proportion of low socioeconomic status (SES) residents. In the rest of the state, sometimes referred to as downstate, there are a few medium-sized cities (e.g., Springfield, the capital; and Peoria), but it is largely rural. There has been tension at times between the needs of Chicago, its suburbs, and the rest of the state; this may be because of vastly different lifestyles and demographics.

Before the age of 5, there is no free preschool system in place. Families that can afford a private preschool may choose from parochial or alternative private schools; and families who qualify as "at risk" (generally those living in poverty) can enroll for free in the Head Start program. Currently, the only place where families who are not "at risk" but cannot afford private preschool can enroll their child in state-funded preschool is in Chicago, where the Early Childhood

Table 1 Elementary and secondary education characteristics

	Illinois	U.S. (average)
Total number of schools	4,439	1,988
Total students	2,091,654	970,278
Total teachers	132,982.73	60,766.56
Pupil/teacher ratio	15.73	15.97

Source: U.S. Department of Education, National Center for Education Statistics, Common Core of Data (CCD), 2010–11.

Table 2 Elementary and secondary education finance

	Illinois	U.S. (average)
Total revenues	$25,426,958,611	$11,464,385,994
Total expenditures for education	$25,246,942,487	$11,712,033,839
Total current expenditures	$21,874,484,088	$9,938,906,259

Source: U.S. Department of Education, National Center for Education Statistics, Common Core of Data (CCD), "National Public Education Financial Survey," FY08 (2007–08).

Education Program was founded. In most of Illinois, parents of kindergarten through 12th grade children have the choice to either pay for private schooling, or send their child to the public school that they are residentially zoned to attend. In Chicago, however, there are elite public schools, as well as charter schools. In the rest of the state, the concept of "school choice" (whereby students can attend public schools that are not their neighborhood school) does not yet exist as it does in other states. Illinois is home to many colleges and universities, some of which, like the University of Illinois (in Urbana-Champaign), University of Chicago, and Northwestern University (in Evanston), are regarded as among the best in the nation.

Illinois faces many of the same issues in education as other states, including budget cuts and being forced to raise taxes in order to pay for education costs. The state is also working to increase its accountability for educational outcomes with the "Race to the Top" program implemented by President Obama's administration. This is important because neighboring Iowa often has the best academic outcomes in the nation with much lower teacher salaries. In 2012, the governor of Illinois was supporting a bill to raise the age where it is legally acceptable to drop out of school, from 16 to 18, and Chicago public schools are increasing the length of their school days and school year. This is in order to implement more intervention programs for low-performing students and to give more challenging instruction to high-achieving students.

Emily Oros
John Mark Froiland
University of Northern Colorado

See Also: At-Risk Students; Early Childhood; Iowa; Unions of Teachers; Urban Schooling.

Further Readings

Bone, Robert Gelhmann. "Education in Illinois Before 1857." *Journal of the Illinois State Historical Society*, v.50/2 (1957).

Diamond, John B. "Accountability Policy, School Organization, and Classroom Practice: Partial Recoupling and Educational Opportunity." *Education and Urban Society*, v.44/2 (2012).

Illinois Education Association. "Mission and History." http://www.ieanea.org/inside-iea/history (Accessed February 2012).

Immersion

Though the term *immersion* is associated with Canadian French *immersion*—a program viewed as the best vehicle for developing proficiency in a second (L2) or foreign language (FL) while maintaining fluency in the mother tongue, and developing literacy in both—immersion programs have expanded to other countries and have responded to local conditions and needs. The term has also been inappropriately applied to other programs. The popularity of immersion programs shows no signs of abating.

On the contrary, it is likely to expand as bi-/multilingualism is increasingly viewed as a necessary condition for participation in today's interconnected global economy. Immersion education is one model of bilingual education: an "enrichment" model. Bilingual education entails content-based instruction through the medium of two languages. It differs from learning an L2 or FL as a subject (e.g., Italian class) where the focus has traditionally been on learning grammatical concepts and vocabulary lists. Immersion entails language use and learning content matter (e.g., history or mathematics) through the medium of an L2/FL. For instance, English-speaking children can learn history and other subjects through a FL like Italian.

The difference between immersion and other forms of bilingual education is that the home language (e.g., English, the L1) and the L2 or FL (Italian) is still used as media of instruction, even at the end of the program. As a result, students experience "additive" bilingualism; they maintain their L1, become literate in it, and add on a second language at no cost to the first. One is seen as enriching the other. In other forms of bilingual education, the goal is for children to develop literacy in the language of schooling (their L2), not in their L1. That is, biliteracy is not a programmatic goal. For children to become literate in the language of schooling (their L2), not their L1, often results in a language shift away from the home language with a subsequent loss of fluency in it; hence, that form of bilingualism is referred to as "subtractive" (i.e., with children progressively losing their L1 proficiency as they progress through school).

Immersion Versus Submersion

Immersion is often contrasted with submersion. The two differ in the amount of pedagogical, linguistic, and paralinguistic supports offered to L2/FL learners. In the case of English-speaking children in Canada learning French in a French immersion program, teachers only speak French in class—even to rank beginners; however, the teachers understand English and respond appropriately when the children speak to them. The teachers speak French back to the children, but provide linguistic (simplified language, slower speech rate) and paralinguistic support (gestures). Their focus is on producing comprehensible language. As such, instruction is orchestrated around predictable routines, so that even rank beginners can "read" the situation and piece together the language presented through contextual cues, key phrases, and visual supports (e.g., pictures and graphs). While teachers may employ these same instructional techniques in submersion settings, they will not understand all immigrant children's L1s; nor will teachers' instructional language or efforts be geared to meeting the needs of L2 learners because native-speakers are also in class. English-learners in submersion settings must read texts produced for native speakers—again, putting them in a "sink or swim" situation as the teacher cannot focus solely on their needs. French immersion teachers, on the other hand, are always cognizant of the fact that the entire cohort is made up of L2 learners, and put L2 learning needs at the forefront of lesson planning and delivery.

In the early years of French immersion (in the 1960s and 1970s), English-speaking parents feared that their children would not master complex content such as math taught through the medium of French. Extensive testing was done to verify whether the children learned as much as their peers in English programs. This concern led to French immersion becoming the most widely researched L2 education program in history. Though the percentage of L1 and L2 instructional time varies in different immersion programs, generally: All of the instruction takes place in French in early French immersion (beginning in kindergarten or first grade), middle immersion (beginning in fourth grade), and late immersion (beginning in seventh grade); half of the instruction takes place in French and half in English in secondary school in early, middle, and late immersion; and half of the instruction takes place in French and half in English from beginning to end in partial immersion programs (from kindergarten to 12th grade). The key tenet of all immersion programs is that students continue studying some proportion of their content subjects through the medium of both languages, straight through to the end of secondary school, as the goal is for students to become bilingual and biliterate.

Once Canadian parents and policymakers were assured that immersion was viable, and that students in the program learned as much and as well as their peers receiving English-medium instruction, the research focus shifted to find out why. A new generation of process studies investigated why immersion worked. For over a decade, more than 10 percent of the school-age population of Canada has been enrolled in French immersion programs, and not only children are enrolling in immersion. Indigenous languages are highly endangered in North America. Children are growing up without speaking their ancestral language in the home. To remedy this situation, adults are calling for indigenous language immersion courses. In this variant, adults learn their ancestral language as a second language in an immersion instructional setting. International interest in immersion is also growing.

Future of Immersion

English–Welsh immersion is well rooted and highly successful in Wales; there are English–Vietnamese immersion programs in Australia; and English–Japanese programs are sprouting up across the United States. In Asia, there is growing interest in novel approaches to immersion. For instance, "English Villages" in Korea feature mock villages with post offices, stores, and other institutions operated by "villagers" who are actually teachers from English-speaking countries, hired to play the role of shopkeepers, doctors, and so on. Not all innovations can be classified as immersion, though. In the United States, an approach to teaching English as a second language (ESL) instruction is called "structured English immersion." Though it purports to be modeled after French immersion in Canada, its purpose is to develop children's English skills well enough to transition them to English-medium instruction. The goal is not to develop biliteracy in the students' L1 and English; as such, it does not constitute immersion. Neither does it fall under the category of enrichment bilingual education. Rather, it is a form of ESL programming intended to develop children's English skills. As recognition of the value of multilingualism in today's increasingly global economy and globalized world grows, forays into immersion education will continue to expand and diversity.

While immersion initiatives may redefine how immersion looks to meet local needs, conditions, and constraints, key tenets need to be respected to qualify as immersion (e.g., additive bilingualism, biliteracy, and an enrichment model of bilingual education).

Shelley Kathleen Taylor
University of Western Ontario

See Also: Bilingual Education; Canada; Classroom Language; English as a Second Language; Globalization; School Effects.

Further Readings

Parrouty, Josiane. *Burnout Among French Immersion Teachers in British Columbia, Canada.* Saarbrucken, Germany: VDM Verlag, 2010.

Swain, M. and S. Lapkin. *Evaluating Bilingual Education: A Canadian Case Study.* Clevedon, UK: Multilingual Matters. 1981.

Tedick, D. J., D. Christian, and T. W. Fortune, eds. *Immersion Education: Practices, Policies, Possibilities.* Buffalo, NY: Multilingual Matters, 2011.

Immigrant Adaptation

The United States has a rich immigrant history. Prior to 1965, most immigrants were of European descent. Contemporary immigration, however, is more racially and ethnically diverse and is transforming American society. Understanding immigrant adaptation is important to the sociology of education because outside of the family, schools are one of the most influential social institutions for immigrant children. In recent decades, there have been significant shifts in the experiences of immigrant children, primarily because of their country of origin, parental human capital, and structural influences. The study of immigrant adaptation suggests that both individual and contextual factors influence adaptation outcomes. Immigration scholars typically distinguish between two waves of immigration.

The "old" wave of immigration is characterized by migration from European countries and peaked before 1965. These immigrants migrated from Germany, Russia, Sweden, Italy, and Ireland. Their experiences initially informed scholarly understandings of immigrant adaptation. However, the 1965 Immigration Act, which lifted restrictions on migration from

certain countries, ushered in a new era of immigration, often referred to as contemporary immigration. Contemporary immigrants migrate primarily from Latin America and Asian countries, including Mexico, the Philippines, China/Taiwan, South Korea, Vietnam, El Salvador, and Jamaica. These immigrants are not only racially and ethnically diverse, but also vary by how they arrive in the United States, the human capital they bring with them, and where they settle. Scholars find that each of these factors significantly influences the process of immigrant adaptation.

Over time, two dominant perspectives have emerged to understand the process of immigrant adaptation. Classical or straight-line assimilation theory assumes that there is a natural process by which immigrant groups adopt the culture, language, and behaviors of the host country. This assimilation process is inevitable and irreversible, such that each subsequent generation will be less distinguishable from the dominant group. In the straight line assimilation perspective, old cultural ways, native language, and ethnic enclaves are sources of disadvantage. Straight-line assimilation theory was the dominant perspective in the immigrant adaptation literature for quite some time. But with the advent of contemporary immigration, immigration scholars questioned the usefulness of straight-line assimilation theory for explaining the experiences of migrants who were very different from previous European immigrant groups. The other major perspective to emerge to explain immigrant adaptation is segmented assimilation theory. Segmented assimilation's unique contribution to explanations of immigrant adaptation is the concept of "modes of incorporation." Segmented assimilation theory explains that immigrants will experience assimilation, but because of their migration processes, structural opportunities in the host country, and different experiences with discrimination, immigrants will assimilate into different segments of the host society. Unlike straight-line assimilation, which assumes a trajectory of upward mobility, segmented assimilation theory argues that immigrants can experience either upward or downward social mobility.

For immigrant children, schools are an introduction to and primary point of contact with the host country, and attending school is an important first step on the pathway to successful adaptation. For these children, levels of adaptation are measured by educational attainment, including academic orientation, academic aspirations and expectations, and academic performance. In the United States, the ready availability of public schooling and a social mobility structure dependent upon educational success makes performance in school an important predictor of later occupational and economic attainment, as well as social adaptation. Previous research suggests that the educational adaptation experiences of immigrant children are shaped by both individual and contextual factors. Parental socioeconomic status plays a significant role in the educational adaptation experiences of immigrant youth because this determines the kind of neighborhood and school that immigrant children attend. Immigrant children whose parents migrate to work as professionals or in managerial positions benefit from access to better schools and safer neighborhoods, while immigrant children with parents who migrate to work in the unskilled labor force face increased exposure to poverty, neighborhood violence, and poorer schools. Additionally, how immigrants arrive in the host country is another determinant of successful educational adaptation; this is referred to as the "context of reception." Some scholars argue that a favorable societal welcome leads to a better integration process, and this can specifically impact the educational experiences of immigrant children.

Immigrant children have the most contact with American culture in school, and how immigrant children negotiate two cultures is integral to successful adaptation. Immigrant children who view the acculturation process as additive, instead of replacing their language and cultural values, are the most likely to experience educational success. This process is referred to as "selective acculturation." Immigrant children who feel pressure to Americanize before their parents and cannot draw on a strong ethnic community or ethnic ties are more at risk of experiencing poor school performance, a process referred to as "dissonant acculturation." Schools facilitate the successful adaptation of immigrant students by recognizing their unique cultural and educational histories. Research suggests that newcomer programs that emphasize the academic as well as social, and cultural adjustment of immigrant students can facilitate positive adaptation outcomes. Finally, immigrant children and their parents may benefit from educational experiences in their home country, where schooling may have been less readily available. Immigrant children may view their initial adjustment difficulties as temporary. This, coupled with their parents' expectations for upward mobility, can facilitate positive adaptation outcomes for immigrant youth. Experts refer to this as immigrant optimism, and research suggests that this helps explain why immigrant youth outperform their later generation counterparts, despite significant language and cultural barriers.

Edelina Burciaga
University of California, Irvine

See Also: Assimilation Without Acculturation; English as a Second Language; Human Capital Theory; Social Capital.

Further Readings
Kao, Grace and Marta Tienda. "Optimism and Achievement: The Educational Performance of Immigrant Youth." *Social Science Quarterly*, v.76/1 (1995).
Portes, Alejandro and Rubén G. Rumbaut. *Immigrant America*. Berekely: University of California Press, 2006.
Zhou, Min. "Growing Up American: The Challenge Confronting Immigrant Children and the Children of Immigrants." *Annual Review of Sociology*, v.23 (1997).

Immigrants, Children of

Children of immigrants are one of the fastest growing populations under the age of 18 in the United States. Most children of immigrants have a tenuous connection to their home countries and are not likely to consider a return home. In recent decades, the educational achievement of children of immigrants has captured the interest of sociologists because this population has grown rapidly, but also because this group provides a unique opportunity to examine theoretical constructs for immigrant adaptation and the sociology of education.

True second-generation immigrants are the native-born children of at least one foreign-born parent. The term *second generation* is also sometimes used to refer to children who immigrated to the United States before reaching adulthood. Experts agree that a more appropriate term for this group is the "1.5-generation." However, usage of these terms is inconsistent. Designation to a particular generation is normally defined by age at arrival. For example, a child who arrives between the ages of 0 and 4 is much more likely to have social and educational experiences very similar to those of the true second generation, whereas children who arrive after the age of 13 may have experiences more like those of the first generation. An important area of study about the experiences of children of immigrants is the impact of age at arrival on educational outcomes. The new second generation refers to the children whose immigrant parents arrived after the 1965 Immigration Act, which repealed quotas on immigration from certain countries. The experiences of this second generation are significantly different than those of immigrants who arrived at the turn of the century. Most of the research about the children of immigrants has focused on the social, cultural, and educational experiences of the new second generation. Racial and ethnic diversity is a hallmark of the new second generation, with most immigrants migrating from Latin American and Asian countries.

Theoretical Perspectives About Children of Immigrants

Straight-line assimilation theory predicts that, over time, immigrants will follow a path to upward social mobility. Straight-line assimilation theory assumes that with each subsequent generation, immigrants will naturally become more integrated into the host society culture, eventually adopting the English language and American culture. For the children of immigrants, straight-line assimilation theory assumes that the home culture and language will be initially disadvantageous to successful educational outcomes, but as they are able to assimilate, children of immigrants will experience more successful educational outcomes.

Straight-line assimilation theory was developed through the study of the assimilation experiences of the children of European immigrants, and in recent years has been called into question by scholars who study the children of immigrants. Segmented assimilation theory assumes that the children of immigrants will assimilate, but the modes of incorporation, or how their immigrant parents are welcomed to the host country, significantly impact both the educational opportunities and life chances of the children of immigrants. The mode of incorporation is measured by the availability of assistance programs for recent immigrants, the legal context of reception, and the amount of racial or ethnic discrimination the immigrant group faces in the host country. Segmented assimilation theories argue that the children

of immigrants can experience either upward or downward mobility. In addition to modes of incorporation, the children of immigrants are impacted by their ability to maintain and foster strong ties with their families and ethnic communities, which can safeguard against second-generation decline.

One major challenge facing children of immigrants is balancing American culture and the culture and traditions of their parents, referred to as biculturalism. The children of immigrants have the most contact with American culture through school, and acculturation gaps can develop when the children of immigrants acculturate faster than their immigrant parents, leading to conflict, a process referred to as dissonant acculturation. Research suggests that intergenerational conflict is less likely to occur in families with both parents, and when siblings or other community members are available to help children negotiate responsibilities like homework. Children who are able to selectively acculturate, that is, adopt the English language and the customs of schools while still maintaining ties to their ethnic culture, are the best poised to experience successful educational outcomes.

Adaptation of Second Generation Immigrants

The successful adaptation of the children of immigrants is defined by their academic achievement outcomes as measured by grades, test scores, school completion, as well as aspirations and expectations. Traditional theoretical frameworks that explain academic achievement among students are also relevant for understanding the educational outcomes of the children of immigrants. Studies of the academic outcomes of the children of immigrants conclude that parental socioeconomic status has a significant influence on their educational success. The children of immigrant parents with high human capital, as measured by education and job skill, tend to achieve well throughout the schooling process. Female children of immigrants are more likely to experience positive educational outcomes. Scholars suggest that this is partly because of females retaining their home language and having higher educational expectations. Additionally, children of immigrants in intact families are also more likely to complete school. The type of school that children of immigrants attend also has an enduring impact on educational experiences.

During the late adolescent years, educational aspirations and expectations, as well as self-esteem, begin to play a more significant role in the academic outcomes of the children of immigrants. These psychosocial factors are important measures of the adaptation of the children of immigrants that have important long-term effects. In high school, both educational expectations and self-esteem strongly and positively influence academic outcomes. Children of immigrants who are able to maintain their home language and connections to their families are more likely to experience successful academic outcomes. The hopes that immigrant parents bring with them to the host country, referred to as immigrant optimism, can positively influence the academic outcomes of their children. One longitudinal study found that the children of immigrants had lower dropout rates among both males and females in every racial and ethnic category.

The most recent development in the study of the children of immigrants is about their transition to adulthood. Using data collected through longitudinal studies of the new second generation, scholars understand the impact of the educational experiences of the children of immigrants on their occupational opportunities and life chances. These studies have found that some adult members of the new second generation are experiencing a process of downward assimilation, while others are experiencing upward mobility. But neither pattern predominates, suggesting that the lived experiences of the children of immigrants are complex and nuanced, and therefore merit continued scholarly exploration and attention.

Edelina Burciaga
University of California, Irvine

See Also: Asian Americans; Bilingual Education; Family Structure and Education; Mexican American Students; Migrant Students; Oppositional Culture; Parental Educational Expectations.

Further Readings

Feliciano, Cynthia. *Unequal Origins: Immigrant Selection and the Education of the Second Generation.* El Paso, TX: LFB Scholarly Publishing, 2005.

Kasinitz, Philip, John Mollenknopf, Mary C. Waters, and Jennifer Holdaway. *Inheriting the City: The Children of Immigrants Come of Age.* New York: Russell Sage Foundation, 2008.

Portes, Alejandro and Rubén G. Rumbaut. *Legacies: The Story of the Immigrant Second Generation.* Berkeley: University of California Press, 2001.

Incarcerated Students

Globally, there are an estimated 8.5 million adults in prison today and approximately 1 million children held in secure detention in young offender units. Only a small proportion of these prisoners and detainees will be provided with any sort of education, and even then, the quality will vary depending on the country or state where they are incarcerated. Prisoners are often confined to their cells for long periods of time, with few opportunities for purposeful activity such as education or training, even though most authorities acknowledge that education would improve prisoners' life chances and promote their reintegration into society. Historically, prisons have been allocated meager resources for education; the emphasis of funding prioritized on health, safety, and security issues, with education viewed as a marginal and sometimes optional activity.

A large body of literature demonstrates the need for remedial education in prisons. The provision of such remediation for all prisoners recognized as illiterate has now become an international priority. Human rights legislation gives all prisoners the right to be provided with educational activities directed toward developing their social, cultural, and economic potential, and that all young offenders, particularly juveniles of compulsory school age, should be given an education appropriate to their age and needs. Enabling prisoners to gain relevant vocational or academic qualifications will help them become useful citizens when released, make them more employable, and will reduce reoffending and recidivism rates. Education can also decrease violent and noncompliant behaviors among inmates, thus improving the overall working environment within prisons for everyone. Therefore, prison education is beneficial to individual prisoners, the prison-staff, and wider society. However, the reality is that many prisons have difficulty delivering these education-related rights.

Over two-thirds of all adult prisoners need basic (elementary) education, particularly in literacy, numeracy, and life skills. Therefore, the emphasis for many prisons is to educate the majority of their inmates, at least to this basic level, thus using their limited resources as efficiently as possible. Most prisons also have mandatory correctional courses, specifically to help prisoners address their offending behaviors. Other courses, such as drug and alcohol awareness, anger management, and assertiveness training often form part of an offender's prerelease program, aimed at helping him or her negotiate socially appropriate interactions when released back into the community. However, the literature suggests that prison education should not just be focused on preventing reoffending and gaining vocational qualifications to improve employability, but should also offer a broad-based curriculum that helps individuals improve their life skills. This should include critical thinking, problem solving, creativity, and emotional literacy. Where this has been tried, the results demonstrate a reduction in violence inside the prison, as well as helping inmates establish better social relationships when released.

Young offenders (under 25 years of age), are particularly vulnerable while incarcerated, and therefore need high-quality, intensive education to prevent any significant interruption to their learning. Unfortunately, for many young offenders, particularly those who only spend a short time in secure units, meaningful education is not offered at all. The majority of people in prison serve very short sentences, of less than one year's duration. When resources are limited, it becomes difficult for an institution to invest in a prisoner who will only stay for a few weeks. Diagnosis and assessment of prior knowledge and skills on admission into prison can take several weeks, by which time a prisoner may be ready for release or transfer to another institution. However, meaningful early intervention, particularly if it remediates an educational deficit, would begin to meet the most pressing learning needs of prisoners. The best educational interventions begin in prison and continue after release, particularly if an employer is actively involved with the prisoner's aftercare. These continuous or overlapping programs have been proven to significantly reduce recidivism and reoffending behaviors, but are costly to implement. For prisoners given longer sentences, including a whole life tariff, educational provision needs to be tailored both to the individual's needs and the length of time they will serve. This provides the opportunity for some prisoners, who may have begun their sentence with very little formal schooling behind them, to engage in scholarship. They may be given the opportunity to gain academic accreditation, a first degree, and even post-graduate qualifications. However, the funding of such program remains controversial.

One of the biggest barriers that incarcerated students have to overcome is the prevailing, negative culture that dominates prison life. Prison ethos echoes the views of wider society, which often sees criminals as unworthy of investment and people who have forfeited their right to an education. The cost/benefit calculation is not simple, particularly when set against human rights legislation and the deeply held convictions of many people who resent society's investment in the rehabilitation and reform of offenders. Today, many authorities recognize the positive relationship between prisoners' access to high quality, relevant, personal, social and vocational education and a reduction in reoffending rates, and thus recognize its cost effectiveness. Public funding of prison education services will continue to be a controversial topic, fueled by a discourse centered on prisons as places of retribution, rather than rehabilitation: punishment, rather than reintegration.

Mich Page
Independent Scholar

See Also: Adult Literacy; Labor Market Effects on Education; Oppositional Culture; Prior Learning Assessment.

Further Readings

Borges, T. "Studying in Prison Now Reduces Jail Time in Brazil." *Globe and Mail* (July 3, 2012).

Page, M. "Bringing a Lemon to a Lifer: Tutoring in Prison." *Research in Post-Compulsory Education*, v.14/2 (June 2009).

United Nations. *Human Rights and Prisons. A Pocketbook of International Human Rights Standards for Prison Officials.* New York: United Nations, 2005.

Vacca, J. "Educated Prisoners Are Less Likely to Return to Prison." *Journal of Correctional Education*, v.55/4 (December 2004).

Williford, M., ed. *Higher Education in Prison: A Contradiction in Terms?* Phoenix, AZ: Oryx Press, 1994.

India

The Republic of India, in southeast Asia, is the seventh-largest country geographically, and the second-largest demographically, with a population of over 1.2 billion people. India has a large and rapidly growing economy—the ninth-largest, according to nominal gross domestic product (GDP); however, approximately 25 percent of the population lives below the international poverty line. India is a pluralistic and highly differentiated society, in terms of religion, ethnicity, caste, and economic status. India offers universal, free, and compulsory education for children aged 6 to 14, and produces globally competitive graduates. However, there are a number of serious issues within the education system, including poor school infrastructure, high dropout rates, inequality in educational opportunity, and limited funds. There are wide discrepancies in educational access and attainment in terms of gender, caste, economic status, and state. India has the largest illiterate population in the world.

An indigenous formal education system existed in India for over a thousand years before the British colonial rulers established a European system of education—intentionally promoted and funded at the expense of the indigenous system. The explicit aim of the British education policy was to educate a class of "natives," fluent in English and willing to support the ideals and aims of their colonial rulers. India gained independence from Britain in 1947, after a long struggle. Free and compulsory education for children ages 6 to 14 was written into the national constitution of 1950. The initial deadline for universal provision was 1960, but it was not until the 1980s that there were enough schools for children of primary school age.

Post-independence education was viewed by the government as central to nation-building, economic progress, and national stability and unity following the "divide and rule" policy of the British colonial administration. Initially, two contrasting systems were considered for the national model. Mahatma Gandhi, leader of the Indian independence movement, advocated the system of *Nai Talim* ("basic education"). Children would produce handicrafts as central to pedagogy and learning in school; this, he argued, would ensure that school was relevant to children's lives, integrated in the wider community, and self-sustaining. In contrast, Jawaharlal Nehru, the first prime minister of independent India, and his Congress party advocated a broad liberal curriculum and expansion of facilities for technical education. This, they argued, would be instrumental for national progress through modernization and industrialization. Gandhi's scheme was implemented on a significant scale in many parts of India after independence, but did not survive the drive for industrial development of the 1960s. The Nehru government adapted the bureaucratic and centrally controlled education system established by the British. According to some

scholars, this colonial legacy of hierarchy and bureaucracy remains a major impediment in attempts to improve educational standards.

Progress in Education

Since the 1980s, good progress has been made in terms of initial school enrollment. Approximately 93 percent of children now enroll in primary school, however 43 percent of children drop out within five years, and only 47 percent of children enroll in secondary school. Access to secondary education varies widely in relation to gender, caste, and economic status, and in different states. For example in Bihar, one of the poorest states, 50 percent fewer girls enroll in school then boys; in Kerala, one of the richest states, there is equal enrollment among girls and boys. The 1997 Public Report on Basic Education (PROBE) report, the first national survey of primary facilities, found that school infrastructure was poor, particularly in rural areas. For example, 59 percent of schools had no drinking water, and 89 percent had no toilet facilities. The 2005 Annual State of Education report found some improvements; 34 percent of schools were without water, and 58 percent were without toilets. Both reports found that many schools had low attendance rates and high levels of teacher absenteeism; on average, 25 percent of teachers in government primary schools were absent from school on a given day. Even among teachers who were present, only about half were found to be engaged in teaching. Poor school infrastructure and high dropout rates are identified as major factors in the continuing high rates of illiteracy in India. In 2011, literacy rates were 82.14 percent for men and 65.46 percent for women.

Since the 1990s, government structural readjustments have resulted in reduced government funding for school. In this context, nongovernment schools have proliferated. These include well-funded "English-medium" schools teaching primarily urban, middle-class pupils in English, Islamic *Madrasahs,* and low-cost schools in areas with scarce government provisions that are often attended by children living below the poverty line. A household survey in 2006 found that approximately 30 percent of children attended private schools. Scholars have noted that the growth of fee-charging schools represents a growing inequality of educational opportunity. They have also noted a gulf between a minority of well-funded elite government schools and higher education institutions, and the majority of poorly funded and resourced government schools. These elite institutions produce globally competitive professionals, particularly in technology and engineering, but at the expense of quality education for the majority.

Academically, education in India has been primarily studied in terms of the production of human capital, a skilled workforce able to contribute to economic growth. These studies predict that this will result in a downward filtration of prosperity. However, more recently, some scholars have questioned the assumption that education automatically leads to increased equality and social transformation. They argue that formal education is a "contradictory resource" that may both reinforce existing inequalities and create new forms of inequality. Furthermore, in the context of government contraction and widespread unemployment in many areas of India, educational qualifications often do not lead to the secure, white-collar employment expected by young people and their families.

Sarah Winkler Reid
Brunel University

See Also: For-Profit Education; Governmental Influences on Education; Poverty and Education.

Further Readings

Drèze, J. and A. Sen. *India: Development and Participation.* New Delhi: Oxford University Press, 2002.

Jeffrey, Craig, Patricia Jeffery, and Roger Jeffery. *Degrees Without Freedom? Education, Masculinities, and Unemployment in North India.* Palo Alto, CA: Stanford University Press, 2008.

PROBE team. *Public Report on Basic Education in India.* New Delhi: Oxford University Press, 1999.

Indiana

Indiana was admitted to the Union as the 19th state on December 11, 1816. Corydon, Indiana, located in southern Indiana, was the first state capitol until 1825, when the capital was moved to a more central location in Indianapolis. Indiana, located in the midwest, was formerly part of the Indiana Territory, dissolved in 1798. The first governor of the territory was William Henry Harrison, who served from 1800 until 1813. Harrison later became the ninth president of the

United States, in 1840. Two constitutions have been ratified in Indiana: the first in 1816, and the current constitution in 1851. Indiana is only the 38th-largest of the 50 states geographically, but ranks 15th in the nation in population; the 2010 U.S. census indicates that 6,483,802 Hoosiers inhabit an area of 36,420 square miles. Historically, the primary economic engines have been agriculture, automobile production, and pharmaceutical production, although much of the past prosperity is also from the presence of natural resources, such as natural gas fields discovered in the 1880s. A former manufacturing hub because of its central location, abundant water, and the crisscrossing of hundreds of miles of railroads, Indiana is still renowned for its corn and soybean and limestone production, as the site of the Indianapolis Motor Speedway, and as the home campus of the Eli Lilly world corporate headquarters.

Forced removal of Indiana's Native Americans in the 1840s resulted in a large influx of Europeans, many of whom are still represented in the current Indiana population; 1980 census data indicated that 42 percent of respondents identified their ancestral origins as German, 32 percent English, and 24 percent Irish. U.S. Census data from 2010 indicates that Hoosiers were 84.3 percent white, 9.1 percent African American, 1.6 percent Asian, 2.0 percent from a biracial or multiracial background, and 0.3 percent Native American. Hispanic or Latino of any race, the fastest growing demographic, made up 6 percent of the population. Since 2000, Indiana has shown the fourth-largest growth of English language learners (ELLs) in the nation, with 2010 U.S. census data indicating that 7.6 percent of respondents speak a language other than English at home. The second-largest language group is Spanish-speakers, representing 4.3 percent of the Hoosier population; 2.0 percent of Hoosiers reported that they speak an Indo-European language, with German or Pennsylvania Dutch German spoken by many Amish families in Indiana's northern regions.

K–12 Education in Indiana

Formal education in Indiana is not mandated until the age of 7 because Indiana does not fund public kindergarten or preschool. Indiana's first state constitution in 1816 provided for a state-funded public school system, the first state in the nation to do so. Currently, approximately half of Indiana's college students attend state-funded universities, with the largest being the Indiana University system, its flagship

Table 1 Elementary and secondary education characteristics

	Indiana	U.S. (average)
Total number of schools	1,992	1,988
Total students	1,047,232	970,278
Total teachers	58,121	60,766.56
Pupil/teacher ratio	18.02	15.97

Source: U.S. Department of Education, National Center for Education Statistics, Common Core of Data (CCD), 2010–11.

Table 2 Elementary and secondary education finance

	Indiana	U.S. (average)
Total revenues	$12,295,900,750	$11,464,385,994
Total expenditures for education	$10,638,809,852	$11,712,033,839
Total current expenditures	$9,281,708,550	$9,938,906,259

Source: U.S. Department of Education, National Center for Education Statistics, Common Core of Data (CCD), "National Public Education Financial Survey," FY08 (2007–08).

campus established in 1820 in Bloomington. In 1865, Indiana State was created as the state's Normal College for teacher preparation. In 1869, Purdue University was developed as a land-grant college for agricultural research. In addition, Vincennes University, Ball State University, and the University of Southern Indiana were established in 1802, 1918, and 1965, respectively. Indiana also boasts a large number of private colleges and universities, most of which historically were established as religious institutions. These include: Notre Dame, Saint Francis, Marian, and Saint Mary of the Woods (Roman Catholic), and Anderson College, Butler University, Taylor, DePauw, Earlham, Valparaiso, Manchester, Hanover, and University of Evansville, which were founded by Protestant and evangelical churches.

The Indiana Department of Education (IDOE) indicates that there are currently 2024 public schools with a combined enrollment of 1,010,811 K–12 students. Of those enrolled, more than 820,000 are white, 125,000 are African American, and 48,000 are Hispanic or Latino. Less than 3,000 are Native American, while nearly 11,000 are Asian or Pacific Islander. By comparison, there are 742 private schools enrolling 115,866 pre-K–12 students, 84,000 of whom are white, less than 6,000 are African American, 3,600

are Hispanic or Latino, 111 are Native American, and 1,500 are Asian or Pacific Islander. It is estimated by the IDOE that more than 23,000 Hoosier children are home schooled; in 2005, this was an increase of more than 400 percent over previous years, and is likely an underestimate because of under-reporting.

Current Issues

Indiana Public Law 105-2005 created a new pathway toward high school graduation through completion of a Core 40 diploma (with increased credit requirements in math, English/language arts, science, and social studies). State data from 2010 indicates that 84.1 percent of public school students graduated in four years. When broken down by racial and socio-economic profiles, the 2010 data demonstrates that only 66 percent of African American students graduated in four years, while 68.9 percent of Hispanic or Latino students graduated with their age-mate cohort. Approximately 68 percent of those who receive free or reduced-cost lunch graduated, and only 58.6 percent of special education students graduated within four years. Females outperformed males, with 85.3 percent of females graduating in four years, versus only 77.7 percent of males graduating on time.

A 21-year longitudinal study by Victor A. Smith indicates steady improvement in Indiana's public education on such measures as attendance (95.9 percent), graduation (84.1 percent), SAT scores, ACT composite scores, NAEP assessments (at historic highs, except for fourth and eighth grade science), ISTEP (the state's standardized assessment) pass rates, numbers of graduates admitted to college, and the numbers of honors and Core 40 diplomas granted. Despite overwhelming quantitative data showing consistent improvement, Governor Mitch Daniels and State Superintendent of Public Instruction Tony Bennett claim that dismal school performance necessitates swift intervention by the state. Indiana has experienced an unprecedented wave of school reform measures passed in the Indiana General Assembly, and an explosion of charter schools, with the vast majority of charter schools opening in Indianapolis. Changes in school funding formulas resulted in school districts being forced to eliminate many basic services (e.g., bus service, and sports, music, and arts programs) and reductions in teaching forces (RIF) to balance declining school budgets. In 2010, the Indiana General Assembly passed a bill permitting qualifying students to enroll in private schools through a state-funded voucher program.

As the long-term consequences of the No Child Left Behind Act begin to take effect, IDOE has targeted six schools for state takeover, and an additional 104 schools in 76 school corporations will become eligible for state takeover in 2012.

Susan Adams
Butler University

See Also: English as a Second Language; No Child Left Behind; School Organization.

Further Readings

Indiana Department of Education. http://www.doe.in.gov (Accessed November 2011).

Smith, V. A. "A 21-Year Review: Improvement in Indiana's Public Schools." Indiana Coalition for Public Education (June 13, 2012) http://www.icpe2011.com/uploads/Decade_12.Summary_10.6.13.pdf (Accessed November 2011).

Streightoff, F. D. *Indiana: A Social and Economic Survey.* Indianapolis, IN: Stewart, 1916.

Taylor, R. M., E. W. Stevens, and M. A. Ponder. *Indiana: A New Historical Guide.* Indianapolis: Indiana Historical Society, 1990.

WPA Indiana Writer's Project. *Indiana: A Guide to the Hoosier State: American Guide Series.* New York: Oxford University Press, 1941.

Indonesia

Indonesia is a large and complex country that has achieved great success in extending basic education to its citizens. The challenges now are to improve the quality of that education, to enhance access to education and educational attainment for disadvantaged citizens, and to better match students' educational achievements with employment outcomes. Indonesia is an archipelagic country of 13,000 inhabited islands, straddling the equator.

It is the fourth-largest country in the world in terms of population, with about 245 million people. It is the largest Muslim-majority nation in the world, with 86 percent of the population Islamic; there are significant religious minorities. It is one of the most ethnically and linguistically diverse countries in the world; however the national language, Indonesian, dominates as the language of education, government, the media, and public life. Since 1998, Indonesia has enjoyed a strengthening democracy, integral to which has been a national process of economic and political decentralization.

Indonesia is a developing country with the largest economy in southeast Asia. It had a per capita gross domestic product (GDP) of $4,200 in 2010; about 13 percent of the population is under the poverty line. President Suharto (1966–98) instituted a massive program of economic development, which brought significant improvements in education, health, and infrastructure, a "green revolution," particularly in rice production, industrialization, and significant exploitation of oil and gas reserves, timber, and other natural resources. Indonesia has a relatively young and increasingly urbanized population: Less than half of the population now lives in rural areas. While Indonesia is seen as one of the Asian success stories, major challenges still exist, including: poverty and unemployment, corruption, unequal resource distribution among regions, and irresponsible exploitation of natural resources.

Educational Structure and Achievements

The education system consists of six years of compulsory primary education, three years of compulsory junior secondary, and three years of senior secondary education, followed by a variety of types of tertiary institutions. There is now a burgeoning system of kindergartens. Usually, students start school at 6 years of age, attend junior high from 13 to 15 years old, then senior high when 16 to 18 years of age. There are two parallel educational streams: one is the "secular" system that is run by the Ministry of Education and Culture; the other is the Islamic school system run by the Department of Religion.

There are two basic types of junior high schools in Indonesia: general (sometimes called academic, Sekolah Menengah Pertama, SMP) and Islamic day schools (Madrasah Tsanawiyah). At senior high school level there are three basic types: general (Sekolah Menengah Atas, SMA), vocational (Sekolah Menengah Kejuruan, SMK), and Islamic day schools (Madrasah Aliyah), with private and state schools in each of these categories. Over 90 percent of primary schooling takes place in the public system; at senior high school level, the absolute number of students in private schools is greater than the number in state schools; and over 90 percent of tertiary education takes place in the private sector of universities, colleges, and institutes.

Indonesia declared independence from the Netherlands in 1945. The formal educational inheritance from colonial times was a tiny elite of educated civil servants, teachers and the like, who led the nationalist movement, and then established the modern, Western-style education system. In the 1970s, great efforts were made to extend primary education to the masses, through the Sekolah Dasar Inpres program. This program supplied at least one primary school to each village. Now, virtually all children attend primary school. In 2007, 84 percent of those ages 13 to 15 years were enrolled in junior high school, while 55 percent of those aged 16 to 18 years were enrolled in senior high school. Approximately 17 percent of the eligible age group of youth were enrolled in tertiary education. The expansion of education has been one of the main achievements of independent Indonesia. The Islamic boarding schools (*pesantren*) are largely outside the state system. Some pesantren now include an Islamic religious school (*madrasah*) in their institution; many others are outside government control. Approximately 7 percent of students between the ages of 7 and 18 are educated in pesantren. Almost one-quarter of the 15,000 pesantren in Indonesia can be classified as *salafiyah* ("traditional"), in that they only teach the traditional Islamic texts known as *kitab kuning*; about 31 percent provide an education in general subjects, and 47 percent offer a mixed education.

Current Issues

Indonesia has had significant success in supplying the right quantity of education. It has also managed to reduce the gender gap in educational attainment: At all three levels of schooling, female enrollment rates are now the same as or exceed those of males. However, there remain some issues of access and equality. There are disparities in educational access and attainment between different provinces, within provinces (i.e., by socioeconomic class and degree of isolation), and between rural and urban areas of Indonesia. For instance, the provinces of Papua and Nusa Tenggara consistently underachieve in statistics on enrollment and promotion from primary to junior high school, and from junior high to senior high. However, the government has succeeded in narrowing the significant enrollment disparities between urban and rural areas. In 1993, 83 percent of children ages 13 to 15 and 61 percent of young people ages 16 to 18 years

in urban areas were enrolled in school; the figures for children in rural areas were only 60 percent and 28 percent. By 2007, the figures for urban children were 90 percent and 66 percent, and for rural children 80 percent and 45 percent.

It is the quality of schooling that is the focus of concern now. After the downfall of Suharto's authoritarian regime, the highly centralized and top-down education system was broadly renovated: Funding arrangements were decentralized, new curricula were devised, and there was to be a new focus on student-centered learning, local participation, and school-based management. More recently, there has been much attention paid to improving teacher qualifications. There was much inertia and some aspects of the overhaul were more successful than others. New curricula, gender mainstreaming, student-centered pedagogy, greater latitude for teachers, and enhanced local content are some features of the new system. The quality of schooling is highly variable, and it is difficult to generalize about the quality of the different types of schools: For example, the private school category includes some of the best schools and many of the worst schools in the country. State general schools are usually regarded as academically respectable, though the range in quality can be great. State junior high schools (SMP) dominate the junior high school level (SMA), providing schools for 63 percent of junior high school students; but at senior high level, private schools have mushroomed to take advantage of strong demand and a shortfall in government provision of SMA. SMP and SMA are the province and the source of the middle classes.

Students from lower socioeconomic groups typically attend vocational schools, which aim to equip their students to get work immediately after school. Parents and students usually choose vocational schools on the basis of hopes for future occupations that are strongly gendered: technical high schools are for boys who want to learn about automotive mechanics, design, and technology; business schools are dominated by girls who want to learn office procedures and computer skills; tourism schools are more gender-equal. In the vocational schools, the disadvantages of class and gender inequalities are freely reproduced. Islamic schools are traditionally the province of poor rural people, and have long been considered poor quality and poorly resourced. An interesting feature of Indonesian Islamic schools is that they have often educated girls. From the 1970s, the government has tried to integrate the madrasah into the national education system. The articulation of the state madrasah with the state Islamic universities (UIN), improved teacher education, the regulation that stipulates that madrasah must devote 70 percent of the curriculum to the secular subjects organized by the Ministry of Education and Culture, and the regulation that allows madrasah graduates to enter non-Islamic state universities have meant an improvement in their academic reputation and appeal. However, debate over responsibility for Islamic schools continues. Significant issues now are youth unemployment and the mismatch between educational attainments and employment opportunities. The upward credentialing of the labor market means that university graduates often find themselves in casual or inappropriate jobs. The rewards of investment in higher education are not often apparent to parents.

Lyn Parker
University of Western Australia

See Also: Career and Technical Education; Malaysia; Poverty and Education.

Further Readings

Bjork C. *Indonesian Education: Teachers, Schools, and Central Bureaucracy*. London: Routledge, 2005.

Jackson, Elisabeth and Lyn Parker. "'Enriched With Knowledge': Modernisation, Islamisation and the Future of Islamic Education in Indonesia." *Review of Indonesian and Malaysian Affairs*, v.42/1 (2008).

Parker, Lyn, et al. "Democratizing Indonesia Through Education? Community Participation in Islamic Schooling," *Educational Management, Administration and Leadership*, v. 39/6 (2011).

Raihani. "Reforms in Indonesia in the Twenty-First Century," *International Education Journal*, v.8/1 (2007).

World Bank. "Investing in Indonesia's Education: Allocation, Equity, and Efficiency of Public Expenditures" (2007). http://www.worldbank.or.id (Accessed March 2009).

Informal Fundraising in Schools

The four sources of revenue reported in school budgets are local, state, federal, and alternative (sometimes referred to as "other" or "private" by the school finance literature). The first three funding sources encompass all public funds spent on public education. Public funds constitute more than 90 percent of all public school expenditures. John Pijanowski and David Monk disaggregated alternative revenue sources, which make up less than 10 percent of public school revenues, into seven different categories: user fees, investment returns, education foundations, non-student user fees, business partnerships, fundraising and/or donations of money, supplies and equipment, and volunteering. Informal school funds are private pecuniary or monetizable resources that are allocated to schools via informal, unofficial mechanisms. The lack of involvement by the Local Education Authority (LEA) further distinguishes informal school funds from other alternative revenue sources.

While some alternative revenue sources follow a formal process in which they are first allocated to the LEA and then allocated by the LEA to the schools, informal school funds do not pass through the LEA, and are instead allocated directly by the funder to the school. Bypassing the LEA makes the funding process less formal, but it also makes measuring and tracking informal school funds more difficult. Of the seven alternative revenue sources listed above, only four can be defined as informal school funds. User fees, investment returns, and education foundations are formal arrangements that typically operate at the district-level. The remaining four alternative fund source categories: nonstudent user fees, business partnerships, fundraising, and volunteerism result from either enterprising activities or community-driven donor activities.

Examples of informal funds that result from school-directed or enterprise activities include nonstudent user fees and business partnerships. Nonstudent user fees are typically based on quid pro quo relationships in which schools generate additional revenue or assets in exchange for providing an organization with access to the facility, staff, or students. Nonstudent user fees generate resources for the school through the selling or leasing of services and facilities, including property or transportation rentals, advertising on school property or other marketing and licensing privileges, concession sales, and food or transportation service rentals. A study by Drew Tiene found that Channel One exchanged programming and equipment for 10 minutes of news and two minutes of commercials that, according to one estimate, reached one-third of the nation's teenagers. Business partnerships are often used to facilitate student experiences in the workplace. Certain partnerships may allow students to participate in career training or job placement programs. In large urban school districts, reformers have sought to increase business partnerships in a concerted effort to expose at-risk students to a broader range of career options.

Examples of informal school funds that result from community-driven activities include fundraising efforts and volunteerism. Unlike district-level fundraising conducted through education foundations, informal donor support is drawn from parent-teacher groups, booster clubs, local education or scholarship funds, and alumni associations. A study of private money in New York City's public schools by Amy Ellen Schwartz and colleagues found that 87 percent of the district's 1,100 schools received donations of cash, equipment, or services. Activities like fundraising provide opportunities for parents and community members to become involved with neighborhood schools. These activities rely heavily on voluntary support that may involve enterprise efforts that engage local businesses or parental participation in larger fundraising efforts. For example, while some parent-teacher associations will solicit community sponsorships for specific athletic or enrichment programs, others raise funds through national programs like Box Tops for Education or book fair sales with Scholastic or Barnes and Noble. Resources from fundraising activities provide a wide spectrum of support for public schools, ranging from extra teachers and teacher aides to classroom materials, technological upgrades, curriculum development, building donations, and construction projects.

Parental and community involvement in schools is not a source of revenue for schools. However, volunteers often provide needed labor and support for public schools, and such support is monetizable. Parental participation is also associated with better school outcomes, so many schools have policies to encourage their involvement. Parents and community members participate in a variety of ways, from serving on planning committees and parent-teacher associations to helping with after school events and activities. Volunteers act as tutors, supervise lunchrooms, and keep walking routes safe for school children. Volunteer staffing allows schools to use paid staff more efficiently. Some studies indicate that school volunteer rates have declined in schools as mothers increasingly

work outside the home. Retirees are being tapped to fill this growing void.

Lawrence Miller
Laura Chinchilla
Rutgers University

See Also: Extracurricular Activities; Funding of Schools; Leadership in Schools; Parent-Teacher Associations.

Further Readings
Addonizio, Michael F. "Private Funds for Public Schools." *Clearing House* (November/December 2000).

de Leon, Erwin, Katie L. Roeger, Carol J. De Vita, and Elizabeth T. Boris. "Who Helps Public Schools? Public Education Support Organizations in 2010." Urban Institute Center on Nonprofits and Philanthropy (June 9, 2010). http://www.urban.org/publications/412105.html (Accessed August 2012).

Hansen, S. Janet. "The Role of Nongovernmental Organizations in Financing Public Schools." in *Handbook of Research in Education*. Helen F. Ladd and Edward B. Fiske, eds. New York: Routledge, 2007.

Oyserman, Daphna, Daniel Brickman, and Marjorie Rhodes. "School Success, Possible Selves, and Parent School Involvement." *Family Relations*, v.56/5 (December 2007).

Pijanowski, J. C. and D. H. Monk. "Alternative School Revenue Sources: There Are Many Fish in the Sea." *School Business Affairs*, (July 1996).

Schwartz, Amy Ellen, Hella Bel Hadj Amor, and Norm Fruchter. "Private Money/Public Schools: Early Evidence on Private and Non-Traditional Support for New York City Public Schools." In *Fiscal Policy in Urban Education*, Christopher Roellke and Jennifer King Rice, eds. Ithaca, NY: ILR Press, 2002.

Tiene, D. "Channel One: Good or Bad News for Our Schools?" *Educational Leadership*, v.50 (1993).

Intergenerational Closure

Intergenerational closure is a type of social structure believed to benefit children. Most commonly, it refers to a social network in which a child's parent knows the parents of the child's friends. James S. Coleman argued that this enhances child outcomes by facilitating information exchange, social support, and social control. Others question whether it is inherently good and debate how it impacts children. There is some empirical evidence that links intergenerational closure to academic success, but questions remain about how to best measure and test its effects. Intergenerational closure describes a kind of social network containing people of different generations. In this network, some people have both intergenerational ties (e.g., between a parent and a child) and intra-generational ties (e.g., between a parent and another parent). The prototypical case of intergenerational closure is a network of a parent, a child, the child's friend, and the child's friend's parent.

Children are linked to their parents, and children who are friends are linked to one another, but intergenerational closure only occurs when parents from different families become socially tied to one another. This structure can be generalized to other intergenerational networks, such as ties among a parent, child, and teacher. Intergenerational closure is generally understood as a community resource that facilitates children's success. Knowing other children's parents means that parents can observe their children in new contexts by talking about them with other adults. Adults can work together to establish and enforce norms, more efficiently and effectively transmitting values and expectations to children. Intergenerational closure is also believed to increase access to beneficial information and social support. Through these functions, parents can impact child outcomes. There are two major theories about the role of intergenerational closure in children's academic achievement.

The dominant theory asserts that norms are a primary mechanism for children's educational success, and intergenerational closure is a key resource for parents to reinforce norms. Certain norms motivate children to behave in ways conducive to academic achievement, like attending class or studying for exams, and the coordinated monitoring of children's activities by multiple adults helps parents to direct their children toward pro-academic behaviors. A limitation of this theory is that it assumes that intergenerational closure will create the right kind of norms, but Coleman recognized that it may also reinforce unfavorable reputations or other norms with potentially negative outcomes. Stephen Morgan and Aage Sorensen offer an alternative theory, built around the notion that more diverse networks facilitate access to more expansive information sources and opportunities. While intergenerational closure may support norms, it also may

homogenize information and opportunities. They don't reject the idea that intergenerational closure may support academic achievement by facilitating norm enforcement, but they argue that it may not be the most important type of social structure to support educational success. Instead, the relative importance of norm-enforcing versus horizon-expanding networks is an open question.

Measuring Intergenerational Closure

Most empirical tests of intergenerational closure have relied on national datasets of U.S. children. Access to intergenerational closure has been linked to higher educational aspirations, more homework effort, and less frequent unexcused absences. There is also some evidence suggesting that such students have higher achievement in terms of test scores (at least for math) and grades, though this may vary by school sector, student race, and immigration status. Finally, adolescents with more access to intergenerational closure appear less likely to use alcohol, less likely to drop out of high school, more likely to graduate from high school, and more likely enroll in college. Still, the effects of intergenerational closure are debated, in large part because it is a difficult concept to measure empirically. Early tests relied on indirect measures. For example, it was argued that school mobility reflects lower intergenerational closure, since moving schools disrupts relationships between children and their friends. Similarly, intergenerational closure may be higher in religious schools because families are connected in multiple contexts. These measures don't uniquely identify the effects of intergenerational closure, but rather they represent a host of relative (dis)advantages. For instance, children who change schools often might come from families with less work stability and lower earnings.

For these reasons, it is more common to measure intergenerational closure more directly. Two common ways are: the degrees to which parents know their child's friends and the degree to which parents know their child's friends' parents. Yet, these measures aren't inherently meaningful, because knowing another parent does not necessarily lead to coordinated norm enforcement. As a potential pathway to academic achievement, intergenerational closure has a number of implications for education policy, two of which focus on the organization of schools. First, schools can support children's success by creating intergenerational closure within the school network. This can be done by providing opportunities for regular contact among parents, such as in Parent-Teacher Association meetings. Second, children can benefit from organizing schools around parents' existing social networks. This might involve organizing schools around where parents work, live, or go to church.

Megan Shoji
University of Wisconsin, Madison

See Also: Catholic Schools; Coleman, James S.; School Mobility and Education; Social Capital.

Further Readings

Carbonaro, William J. "A Little Help From My Friend's Parents: Intergenerational Closure and Educational Outcomes." *Sociology of Education*, v.71/4 (1998).

Coleman, James S. *Foundations of Social Theory*. Cambridge, MA: Belknap Press of Harvard University Press, 1990.

Dika, Sandra L. and Kusum Singh. "Applications of Social Capital in Educational Literature: A Critical Synthesis." *Review of Educational Research*, v.72/1 (2002).

Kao, Grace and Lindsay Taggart Rutherford. "Does Social Capital Still Matter? Immigrant Minority Disadvantage in School-Specific Social Capital and its Effects on Academic Achievement." *Sociological Perspectives*, v.50/1 (2007).

Morgan, Stephen L. and Aage B. Sorensen. "Parental Networks, Social Closure, and Mathematics Learning: A Test of Coleman's Social Capital Explanation of School Effects." *American Sociological Review*, v.64/5 (1999).

Morgan, Stephen L. and Jennifer J. Todd. "Intergenerational Closure and Academic Achievement in High School: A New Evaluation of Coleman's Conjecture." *Sociology of Education*, v.82/3 (2009).

International Baccalaureate Education

Founded by the International Schools Association (ISA), the International Baccalaureate (IB) diploma is a rigorous college-preparatory program of study created for academically advanced students. The program first began in 1964 in Switzerland, and is designed for students to critically examine six major areas of knowledge in depth, as well as how the subjects relate: mathematics and computer science, arts, individuals and societies, language, experimental sciences, and a second language. Writing is emphasized across the curriculum, and IB students complete written assignments and research papers in all classes, including math and science. Beyond knowledge of content, the program aims to develop globally conscious, socially aware, and service-oriented students. The IB curriculum is taught uniformly throughout the world, with end-of-course examinations that may be accepted for university credit. In recent years, there has been an increase in attention on IB coursework, given the growing popularity of college-readiness curriculum in the United States, as well as continued research on inequality in track placement by racial/ethnic group membership and socioeconomic status (SES).

Approximately 975,000 students in 3,300 schools in over 140 countries are currently enrolled in an IB program (primary, middle, or diploma). Entry requirements vary by school site and include grade point average, prior achievement on standardized tests, essays, and/or letters of recommendation. The capstone (IB diploma program) is typically a two-year coursework sequence that begins in the 11th grade and consists of the six subject areas and three additional activities. Students must pass exams in all six content areas, which are reviewed by external IB examiners. The diploma is awarded to students who show a certain level of performance across the entire program, as well as participation in the creativity, action, and service requirements. Schools offering the IB diploma, or an early and middle year program, must go through an authorization process and ongoing review that applies to all IB World Schools.

Historically, IB's close association with international schools, whose students come from privileged backgrounds, gave the program an elitist image. But as of 2010, more than half of IB World Schools were state-funded public schools. As the IB expands into public education, funding and teacher quality continues to limit access to a wider socioeconomic group of students. Sociologists have examined how course-based placement, also known as tracking, has become the principal form of sorting for American students. Like the literature on track placement, contemporary research investigates the degree to which IB course-taking is stratified or unequal by race and class. Research remains mixed with regard to the effects of race on IB course-taking, but an abundance of literature suggests that minority (specifically African

American and Latino) and lower-SES students are less likely to be placed in high-level courses, where the opportunity to be exposed to the most challenging curriculum is minimal. Additionally, studies show that the greater the racial diversity within the school, the greater is the competition for college-preparatory course taking.

As the competition for college admission increases, placement in college-preparatory courses has gained greater importance. Particularly for IB diploma courses, students are exposed to college-level material that is academically more rigorous than most general education coursework, and college admissions officers look favorably on students who have taken IB courses when making admissions decisions. Successful completion of the IB diploma signals that students are prepared for the college workload, but in many cases, also gives students a head start once in college because most universities and colleges offer credit for IB courses.

In fact, IB and Advanced Placement courses are implicit requirements for admission into America's most selective universities. Research finds IB students have more positive perceptions of school climate, better school attendance, fewer in-school behavior problems, higher levels of life satisfaction, and more scholastic self-efficacy. IB participation is also associated with a variety of academic outcomes, including higher university acceptance rates, higher American College Testing (ACT) and Scholastic Aptitude Test (SAT) scores, and success during postsecondary education. However, research also suggests that IB students' requirements for high school graduation far exceed the typical course load. The added pressure and demands on time, skills, and intellect translate into higher stress levels for IB students when compared to their peers who participate in a general education program.

Beth Tarasawa
Washington State University, Vancouver

See Also: Ability Grouping; Advanced and Honors Classes; Class Inequality: Achievement; Racial Inequality: Achievement; Tracking.

Further Readings
Conley, David T. *College Knowledge: What It Really Takes for Students to Succeed and What We Can Do to Get Them Ready.* San Francisco: Jossey-Bass, 2005.
International Baccalaureate Organization. http://www.ibo .org/who (Accessed August 2012).
Lucas, Samuel and Mark Berends. "Race and Track Location in U.S. Public Schools." *Research in Stratification and Mobility*, v.25 (2007).
Mathews, Jay and Ian Hill. *Supertest: How the International Baccalaureate Can Strengthen Our Schools.* Chicago: Open Court, 2005.
Shaunessy, Elizabeth, et al. "School Functioning and Psychological Well-Being of International Baccalaureate and General Education Students: A Preliminary Examination." *Journal of Secondary Gifted Education*, v.17 (2006).
Suldo, Shannon M., et al. "Coping Strategies of High School Students in an International Baccalaureate Program." *Psychology in the Schools*, v.45/10 (2008).

International College Partnerships (Sister Colleges)

The recent two decades have witnessed a boom of international college partnerships, or "sister colleges." As a type of exchange and collaboration of educational resources between different countries, and in many cases between diverse cultures, international college partnerships thrive along with the increasing mobility of international higher education stimulated by globalization. The implementation of international college partnerships might vary from region to region, yet in most cases, an international college partnership implies a long-term, collaborative relationship between higher education institutions based in different countries, which usually involves not only constant exchanges of students, faculty members, and college staffs carrying diverse knowledge of learning, teaching, and college administrating, but also a free trade of educational resources for monetary profit.

More often than not, international college partnerships are sealed in the form of written agreements between universities, reflecting a mutual respect and shared interests. In common practice, international college partnerships require no exclusive loyalty; a college can have partnerships simultaneously with more than one international educational institution. These days, international college partnerships can reach far beyond the traditional notion of study abroad programs and/or student exchange initiatives. On top of sending students overseas both for short-term and joint-degree programs, many colleges also dispatch their faculty members and research staff to sister colleges to teach and learn different methods, some of whom even establish a branch campus in collaboration with their sister colleges to secure and facilitate this exchange. Moreover, thanks to the rapid development of communication technologies, virtual exchanges via the Internet and multimedia have become efficient supplements to traditional physical exchanges.

Traditional international college partnerships usually involve a close focus on the exchange of language and culture resources. Many distinguished colleges in the United States and UK have developed mature exchange programs and initiatives with their oversea partners, to provide students with local experience in diverse cultures and language environments, and to accommodate international students on their home campuses. This form of trans-cultural exchange mostly benefits the development of a specific area study in participating colleges, and rarely intends to generate profits. Another form of international college partnerships emphasizes the exchange of academic and/or technical resources, which often happens within the same geographical region or cultural sphere. For example, for two decades, the EU has promoted intraregional college partnerships to strengthen collaborations among higher-education institutions in Europe, as part of the regional integration scheme of the EU. International college partnerships have also been thriving in developing countries, especially in the Asia-Pacific region, most of which are with developed countries. On one hand, colleges in developing countries seek to attract students from the West, not only to boost their global fame, but also to generate considerable revenues by charging international tuition, which is usually much higher than the tuition that local students pay. On the other hand, their overseas counterparts in developed countries are also eager to strengthen their links with Asian countries, to take part in the booming educational market in the Asia-Pacific area. This form of international college partnership overlaps more with an international business partnership between two institutions, emphasizing monetary profits.

Today's international college partnerships are quite different from early attempts to share educational resources in a limited range of activities. Along with the process of globalization and regional integration, cross-national collaborations between higher-educational institutions have been strengthened, diversified, and institutionalized. While traditional forms of language and cultural exchange remain an important component of today's international college partnerships, many colleges have explored possibilities in establishing multifacet, all-round, and in most cases profitable partnerships with their overseas counterparts. These horizontal arrangements usually involve multiple disciplines and projects, instead of a single exchange agreement on language and/or area studies. Hence, a higher level of administrative involvement, and a greater demand of financial feasibility, is not unusual in today's international college cooperation, which has been increasingly considered an integrated part of a college's overall strategic plan.

Conclusion

As international college partnerships naturally involve more than one country and/or region, it is hard to find a universal standard to regulate or evaluate the activities in this field. Hence, the education quality and accountability of international college partnerships remains questionable. Recent studies in China and Japan indicate that a number of exchange programs under the umbrella of international college partnerships do not meet a high standard because of a lack of strict criteria acknowledged by countries. Colleges may encounter the question as to how they should assure the quality of their education in a foreign cultural and regulatory environment.

Haiyan Wang
Cornell University

See Also: College Advising; College Proximity; College Transferring; Study Abroad.

Further Readings
Altbach, Philip G. and Jane Knight. "The Internationalization of Higher Education: Motivations and Realities." *Journal of Studies in International Education*, v.11/3–4 (Fall/Winter 2007).
British Council. "A Review and Taxonomy: International College Partnership Models" (2006). http://www.britishcouncil.org/intl_partnerships.pdf (Accessed August 2012).
McCarty, Steve. "Examining International Sister School Relations." *On Cue*, v.6/2 (1998).

International Data

International data on education are available through a variety of sources. This data can be used for research and to inform policy reform. International data allows sociologists to better understand education and its relation to societies around the world. Policymakers also use international data. Examination of international data can indentify processes and attributes of high-performing education systems, allowing one education system to learn from another. International data enable countries to gauge their system's performance over time or in comparison to other countries. Many international organizations collect data related to education. The International Association for the Evaluation of Educational Achievement (IEA) is a group of research institutions. IEA coordinates international comparative studies of education, such as TIMMS and PIRLS. IEA produces reports on each cycle of their assessments.

The Organisation for Economic Co-operation and Development (OECD) is an intergovernmental organization composed of 32 member countries. OECD sponsors several international studies, such as PISA. OECD provides access to a variety of demographic and education related statistics and data. The OECD indicators provide information on who participates in education, financing of education, and educational outcomes (such as tertiary entry and graduation rates). OECD's Education at a Glance series explores the state of education internationally. United Nations Educational, Scientific and Cultural Organization (UNESCO), an agency of the UN system, has a database of crossnational statistics on education. UNESCO also provides access to country reports with international data. UNESCO's Institute for Statistics (UIS) collects data for more than 200 countries and territories.

The UIS database covers all education levels and addresses a variety of policy issues (such as gender parity). The U.S. National Center for Education Statistics provides access to datasets collected by other organizations through their International Activities Program (IAP). The Eurydice network, managed by the European Union, has a focus on education systems and policies in Europe. On their Web site, information on education in 33 countries is available. The database also includes thematic studies (such as mathematics education or adult education in Europe) and data reports. The World Banks' World Development Indicators and the U.S. Agency for International Development's (USAID's) Global Education Database also have data related to education. The United Nations Development Programme's (UNDP) Human Development Report includes education relevant data, as does the United Nations Children's Fund's (UNICEF) *State of the World's Children*.

Country Reports

Country reports provide valuable basic information about a country and its education system. Country reports are primarily descriptive, and are sometimes referred to as education sector reviews. They are used to develop national plans for education. International donors frequently require a country to develop such a report or education sector strategy. Data included in these reports generally include information on access to education, quality indicators, and education finance figures. UNESCO's International Bureau of Education (IBE) provides access to many country reports on their Web site and on CD-ROM. The IBE reports comprise a variety of information about education in a country, including: general objectives of education, educational priorities, laws regarding education, educational administration and organization, the financing of education, higher education, special education, private education, means of instruction, infrastructure, adult and nonformal education, teaching staff, and educational research. Another UNESCO program, Education for All (EFA), also compiles country reports. Almost 200 countries have participated in evaluations of basic education as part of EFA. Country and regional reports are available through the UNESCO Web site (in the language of submission). The reports include description of education in the country, an analysis of progress toward EFA goals, and prospects for the future.

Cross-National Comparison

In the United States, the uneven performance of students on international assessments and a desire to remain globally competitive have fueled interest in cross-national comparisons. The data is collected in the same manner in each location. This allows for understanding results as they relate to an individual country, globally, or in terms of a particular attribute of an education system (such as class size or level of centralization). Unfortunately, the end users of this data are often ill equipped to interpret the data, and sometimes report simplified or misleading conclusions. In popular media, results from these assessments are regularly displayed as rankings, with only the average values by country included. While important information can be gained from these data, the statistics cannot provide a complete picture of a country's education system. More than 100 countries have participated in international education studies. These datasets with variables that are comparable across countries are available for analysis by scholars and policymakers. Some of the most significant data sets are: TIMMS, PIRLS, PISA, CivEd, SITES, ICILS, IALS, ALL, PIAAC, and TEDS-M.

TIMMS is the acronym for IEA's Trends in International Mathematics and Science Study. It is a comparative study that was first conducted in 1995. TIMMS reports on the math and science achievement of fourth and eighth graders every four years. The intent of the test is to determine mastery of school curriculum. In 2011, 64 countries and 14 communities participated in the study. TIMMS includes questionnaires for students, teachers, and principals to provide contextual information. Data on science and mathematics curricula are also included. In 1995 and 2008, TIMMS Advanced was conducted. TIMMS Advanced measures physics and advanced mathematics achievement of students in their final year of secondary education. It was conducted in 1995 and 2008. The National Center for Education Statistics provides a data explorer for individuals to access and work with TIMMS data.

PIRLS, the Progress in International Reading Literacy study, is another IEA study that was first conducted in 2001. PIRLS reports the reading achievement of fourth-grade students every five years. In 2011, 48 countries and nine communities participated. Like the TIMMS studies, PIRLS includes information on national policies and practices. Students, parents/caregivers, teachers, and principals also complete questionnaires. PIRLS data is available for secondary analysis on the PIRLS Web site.

PISA is OECD's Programme for International Student Assessment. The two-hour assessment is given to 15 year olds every three years. PISA measures application of knowledge and skills assumed necessary for participation in society. Unlike TIMMS and PIRLS, PISA does not include questions related to school curriculum. Reading, mathematics, and science skills are evaluated in each cycle, and one subject is assessed in depth during each round of testing. In 2003, problem solving was also assessed. OECD provides access to the PISA data through online education databases. Researchers can analyze the raw data.

The Civic Education Study (CivEd) was conducted in 1999. Ninth-grade students from 28 countries participated. Their attitudes toward democracy, international relations, national identity, and other topics were explored.

IEA has conducted several studies of information technology and education. The Second Information Technology in Education Study (SITES-M1) was conducted in 1998. SITES-M2 (in 2001) and SITES 2006 followed. The International Computer and Information Literacy Study (ICILS) is the next step in IEA's exploration of technology and education, and it will be conducted in 2013. The study will examine 8th-grade students' computer skills, specifically their ability to use computers to investigate, create, and communicate. More than 20 countries plan to participate in ICILS. Like other IEA studies, contextual data collected from teachers, students, and schools will be included.

Studies Focused on Adults

Unlike the previously discussed studies, the International Adult Literacy Survey (IALS), Adult Literacy and Lifeskills (ALL) Survey, PIAAC, and TEDS-M are focused on adults. IALS was conducted in 1994, 1996, and 1998 in 20 countries. The test measured prose literacy, document literacy, and quantitative literacy. A summary of results is available through the U.S. National Center for Education Statistics IAP. ALL measured the numeracy and literacy skills of a nationally representative sample from each of 6 participating countries. Highlights of the results are available through the U.S. National Center for Education Statistics IAP. The Program for the International Assessment of Adult Competencies (PIAAC) is another OECD project. It is a direct household assessment that was first administered in 2011 in 27 countries. Approximately 5,000 adults participated in each country. The study focuses on skills deemed necessary for participation in a global economy. PIAAC measures cognitive skills in the areas of literacy, numeracy, and problem solving. A background questionnaire investigates what skills participants regularly use in their jobs and at home, and how participants acquire those skills.

The Teacher Education and Development Study in Mathematics (TEDS-M) is a comparative study of mathematics teacher education. Conducted by IEA in 2008, TEDS-M examined how various countries prepare their teachers to teach mathematics. A total of

17 countries and communities participated. TEDS-M conducted surveys of teacher preparation institutions, a survey of educators of future teachers, and surveys of future teachers.

Publications

Research based on international data is regularly reported in academic journals. These articles are based on secondary analysis of datasets, in addition to international data collected by individual scholars. Journals that frequently print studies relevant to sociology of education in a global context are: *Compare, Comparative Education, Current Issues in Comparative Education, Comparative Education Review, International Studies in Sociology of Education, International Journal of Educational Development,* and the *International Review of Education.*

Cambria Dodd Russell
Columbia University

See Also: Policy-Oriented Research; Qualitative Research on Education; Quantitative Research on Education; Research Paradigms in Educational Studies; Worldwide Education Revolution.

Further Readings

International Association for the Evaluation of Educational Achievement (IEA). http://www.iea.nl (Accessed December 2011).

Meyer, John and David Baker. "Forming American Educational Policy With International Data." *Sociology of Education,* v.69 (1996).

National Center for Education Statistics. http://nces.ed .gov (Accessed December 2011).

Organisation for Economic Co-operation and Development (OECD). http://www.oecd.org (Accessed December 2011).

Iowa

Iowa is known for having one of the highest-quality public education systems in the nation; however, socioeconomic development in the state is limited significantly by the rural brain drain phenomenon, in which many of Iowa's students leave the state once they obtain their college degree. Iowa has been on the

Table 1 Elementary and secondary education characteristics

	Iowa	U.S. (average)
Total number of schools	1,487	1,988
Total students	495,775	970,278
Total teachers	34,642.08	60,766.56
Pupil/teacher ratio	14.31	15.97

Source: U.S. Department of Education, National Center for Education Statistics, Common Core of Data (CCD), 2010–11.

Table 2 Elementary and secondary education finance

	Iowa	U.S. (average)
Total revenues	$5,297,526,903	$11,464,385,994
Total expenditures for education	$5,286,896,181	$11,712,033,839
Total current expenditures	$4,499,236,132	$9,938,906,259

Source: U.S. Department of Education, National Center for Education Statistics, Common Core of Data (CCD), "National Public Education Financial Survey," FY08 (2007–08).

cutting edge of providing high-quality preventive services to children who are at risk for educational and behavioral problems. Iowa has a rich Native American history, and was cherished land for various tribes such as the Ioway, Sioux, and Sauk. Iowa has memorials attesting to its Native American history in various parts of the state, such as the Effigy Mounds National Monument in the northeast, along the Mississippi River. When settlers came to Iowa in mass numbers, the Native Americans were largely forced west (e.g., to Kansas and Oklahoma). Iowa has a relatively large rural and European-American population. Although Iowa has been famous for farming (especially producing corn) since shortly after its inception, the economy in Iowa has diversified significantly in recent decades. Nonetheless, signs of bucolic life and agriculture abound, such as corn fields, tractors, soybean fields, hog farms, and dairy farms. In certain parts of the state, Amish families still drive horse-drawn wagons and voluntarily live without the technological amenities of modern society.

Iowa has nationally acclaimed K–12 schools, distinguished by a strong high school graduation rate and a teacher-student ratio that is lower than the national average. The Iowa state average for student achievement scores on standardized tests is perennially one of the highest in the nation. Although most students in Iowa schools are European American, the student population is slightly more diverse than the broader population in Iowa. Iowa's delivery of specialized services to students via their nine Area Education Agencies (AEAs) is unique. School psychologists, social workers, special education consultants, speech-language pathologists, occupational therapists, audiologists, and physical therapists deliver services to individual districts via AEAs. Pedagogical experts (e.g., in science) also work for AEAs and provide professional development to teachers. This makes it possible for the Iowa Department of Education to promote broad educational innovation and research-based initiatives across the state via AEAs.

For instance, Iowa was the first state to mandate a problem-solving model of services for all children struggling academically or behaviorally. School psychologists and school social workers working within the problem-solving framework have helped many at-risk students and students with clinically significant difficulties thrive in general education without labels (e.g., learning disability or emotional disturbance), medication, or special education. The relative success of the problem-solving and response to intervention model in Iowa has positively influenced other districts and states across the nation. Iowa's AEAs also provide a wide range of services to private schools, which is uncommon nationwide.

Despite its high quality education system, Iowa struggles greatly with rural brain drain. A large proportion of Iowa's best students leave the state after obtaining their college degree. Furthermore, many college-educated adults who work in Iowa leave at some point to obtain significantly higher pay in midwestern cities such as Minneapolis, Chicago, and Kansas City. The state of Iowa has at times held meetings in those cities, hoping to entice former residents back with tax breaks and reminders of the peaceful life available in many parts of Iowa. Rural brain drain makes it harder to attract cutting-edge companies that require many knowledge workers.

Thus, Iowa's top quality schools do not benefit the state's economy as much as they would if more college graduates desired to stay in Iowa. Iowa not only has less college graduates living in the state than the national average, they also have trouble attracting and retaining those with graduate degrees. Iowa's teachers are paid significantly less than the national average, yet the public schools are among the best in the nation. In neighboring Illinois, teachers receive significantly higher compensation (among the best in the midwest), yet Illinois schools produce achievement scores in the average range. This challenges the idea that more spending leads to better outcomes. The teachers' union in Iowa is not nearly as influential as it is in neighboring Illinois because union membership is completely optional in Iowa and the state identifies with the philosophy of "right to work." Although the ecological demographics in Iowa and Illinois are considerably different (Illinois has more urban poverty), Iowa successfully applies certain principles that other states could consider adopting: a low student-teacher ratio is scientifically linked to better educational outcomes; rich, research-based professional development opportunities stimulate the growth of teachers, administrators, and support professionals; and a preventive problem-solving orientation helps more children thrive in general education.

John Mark Froiland
Nadia Benyamin
University of Northern Colorado

See Also: Illinois; Nebraska; Rural Schooling; Urban Schooling; Wisconsin.

Further Readings

Carr, P. J. and M. J. Kefalas. *Hollowing Out the Middle: The Rural Brain Drain and What It Means for America.* Boston: Beacon Press, 2010.

Froiland, J. M. "Response to Intervention as a Vehicle for Powerful Mental Health Interventions in the Schools." *Contemporary School Psychology*, v.15 (2011).

Hull, Christopher. *Grassroots Rules: How the Iowa Caucus Helps Elect American Presidents.* Palo Alto, CA: Stanford Law and Politics, 2007.

Iowa Department of Education. http://educateiowa.gov (Accessed August 2012).

Schwieder, D. *Iowa: The Middle Land.* Ames: Iowa State University Press, 1996.

IQ

IQ stands for intelligence quotient, which is a psychometric test (psychological measurement) for measuring a person's intelligence when compared to other people of the same age. The most popular IQ test was developed by a French psychologist Alfred Binet in early 19th century. The IQ score, or the quotient, reflects one's placement on a range in which the average score is 100 and the standard deviation is 15. For instance, a test taker who scores 130 on an IQ test is two standard deviations above the mean, or approximately the 95th percentile. The mental ability or intelligence was measured in the form of verbal, math, and logic deduction questions. The score for a test taker with normal intelligence level is 100. According to the Binet scale, test takers with an IQ score around 120 are considered very superior; test takers with an IQ score below 70 are considered mentally deficient. The test has been administered for screening out applicants for both academic and vocational purposes worldwide.

The most popular form of the test was developed in France in 1904, with an aim to distinguish children with special needs, for example mentally challenged students, from normal ones. The test was known as the Binet-Simon scale. As the original purpose of the test was to identify children with special educational needs, one of the most prominent caveats was that children with a low test score would be labeled and condemned by the general public, who might not have the knowledge to properly interpret the test scores. In 1916 a new version of the test, the Stanford revision of the Binet-Simon scale, replaced the old version and became the most popular standard IQ test in the United States. The test designers, Henry Goddard and Lewis Terman, believed that intelligence is inherent and could be quantified and measured. They developed a set of norm scores for children, stipulating a norm score for a particular chronological age. The norm scores were derived from American children who were white, mainly of European descent, and middle class. As such, critics challenged the generalizability of the test, especially when children of multiracial background and low socioeconomic status were taken into account.

During the 1960s, the major debate among psychologists and behavioral scientists was "nature versus nurture," that is, whether intelligence was inherently genetically coded or influenced by environments. Many of the studies supported the school of thought that IQ is inherited and genetically coded. These studies typically involved identical twins who were separated at birth and reared in different cultural environments. The researchers then compared the test scores of these identical twins and concluded that their similar IQ scores indicated that intelligence was inherited, rather than learned. However, some of the studies were later discovered to be fraudulent, raising more doubts to the original debate of nature versus nurture. In the 1970s, some psychologists followed the same group of test takers longitudinally, and found that IQ scores changed over the course of life, so that the test takers' educational progress, family and cultural background, and other social factors influenced their IQ scores. To date, there is no definite answer as to how much influence is from nature and how much from nurture.

However, because of the paradigm shift from positivism to social constructionism, more social scientists started to work on social factors when considering a student's performance at school. These social scientists criticized that the IQ test is an unfair assessment for children who are not middle class and white. Educational researchers of the most recent decade worked on a social emancipation framework, which emphasized the value of family traditions and cultural practices in the minority groups. The social emancipation framework aims at empowering social groups who are oppressed, disenfranchised, and underprivileged because of their cultural background, socioeconomic status, and skin color. As such, standardized tests that are norm-referenced and based on the performance and expectations of the mainstream social group are criticized as discriminatory. Though the spirit of measuring test takers' mental ability of aptitude persists in other forms of measurement, such as the American College Testing (ACT), Scholastic Aptitude Test (SAT), Graduate Record Examinations (GRE), Graduate Management Admission Test (GMAT), and Law School Admission Test (LSAT), the Binet-Simon scale has become obsolete because of its various limitations, that it is mainly for test takers below the age of 16, the scope of the test is too general, and it is mainstream biased in terms of its design.

Conclusion

The various forms of standardized tests for academic purposes serve the purpose of academic placement. For vocational placement, the focus has shifted toward a person's social competence, including the ability to control anger and fear, be empathetic, and adapt to changes in the environment. Any job requires social competence, which depends on a person's ability to adjust to a particular situation. The IQ test does not address these skill sets and therefore has been replaced by other psychometric tests developed by social psychologists. One of the most popular tests addresses individual differences in problem solving and decision making. It is called the Myers-Briggs Type Indicator (MBTI) and has been widely adopted in various vocational settings. To conclude, there is not a psychometric test that has been proven perfect for predicting success in academia or the job market. Any psychometric test has its strengths, weaknesses, and limitations. It is critical for the test takers and the institutions asking for test scores to have sufficient understanding of the test design and its limitations when making inferences from test scores.

Yin Lam Lee
St John's University, New York

See Also: *Bell Curve, The*; Cognitive Skill/Intellectual Skill; Critical Theory of Education; Racial Inequality: Achievement.

Further Readings

Hurn, Christopher. "IQ." In *Education and Sociology*. David L. Levinson, Peter. W. Cookson, Jr., and Alan R. Sadovnik, eds. New York: Routledge, 2002.

Kaufman, Alan. *IQ Testing 101*. New York: Springer Publishing, 2009.

Scarr, Sandra and Richard Weinberg. "IQ Test Performance of Black Children Adopted by White Families." *American Sociological Review*, v.31/10 (1976).

Iran

The Islamic Republic of Iran is the second-most populated country in the Middle East, with a population just over 76 million in 2012. Iran had a gross domestic product of $400 billion in 2011, with an economy reliant on the hydrocarbon sector. Not only is Iran the second-largest producer of oil among the Organization of the Petroleum Exporting Countries (OPEC), it controls the third-largest oil reserve in the world. Iran also stores the second-largest natural gas reserve in the world. The economy is transforming into a predominantly market-based economy.

The ancient historical and cultural roots of Iran can be traced back many centuries through empires including the Elamites, Medes, Persian, and Parthian.

A more current history of Iran is best understood in three phases, predominantly defined by the evolving role of Islam in the country. For five centuries, the Pahlavi dynasty enforced Shiism as the state ideology. During this monarchy, the Shiite clergy transmitted tradition, rules, and norms orally and held ultimate authority over religious affairs. The strength of the monarchy determined the level of adherence to religious doctrines. The influence the Shiite clergy holds on education institutions has continued to evolve, especially following the development of the Ministry of Education after an influx of universities in the 1950s and 1960s.

The Islamic Revolution of 1979 resulted in a written constitution that gave absolute authority to the supreme leader, Ayatollah Ruhollah Khomeini, over all political, religious, and defense matters. While the constitution calls for a democratically elected parliament, these members serve alongside an estimated 350,000 appointed Shiite clerics. Through the principle of expediency, the supreme leader may overrule any national law that is deemed contradictory to the regime. Around the time of the revolution, there was significant inequity in education. Only 10 percent of 20–24-year-old women from rural areas were identified as literate in 1976. Consequently, the literacy movement was established in 1979 to ameliorate gender and geographic literacy disparities. Ayatollah Khomeini's death in 1989 ushered in what many consider the modern Iran. The Assembly of Experts, a body of 86 Shiite clerics, selected Ayatollah Ali Khamenei as Supreme Leader. Theocracy continues to determine what is labeled Islamic or non-Islamic, especially with regard to education policy. In addition, the Special Court for the Clergy, which operates independently of the judicial system, is tasked with expediting the judicial process of any clergy accused of criminal acts.

In 2008, 43 percent of Iranian children enrolled in optional preprimary or kindergarten education. The state provides free and compulsory primary education for eight years, starting at the age of 6 (grades 1–8). The first five years are spent in *dabestan,* or primary school. The following three years are in *rahnamayi,* or "guidance schools." In 1992, the *dabirestan,* or secondary education, was reformed. In 2008, 97 percent of students progressed to the three options available at the secondary level. The most expensive branch, *kar-danesh,* offers the most challenging study in order to prepare students for university.

The other two branches prepare graduates for more technical or vocational careers. During the first three years of kar-danesh, students are able to select and focus on a particular field of study. In the final year of kar-danesh, students prepare for the *konkoor*, the "university entrance exam." In 2008, approximately 37 percent of age appropriate students were enrolled in some form of higher education study (45.7 percent of those students attended Islamic Azad University). In addition, 65 percent of admitted university students were female in 2007. The most popular fields of study of higher education graduates in 2007 were the humanities (38 percent) and engineering (32.7 percent). Only 22 percent of the labor force had a secondary education as of 2005, and only 15.4 percent had obtained a tertiary-level education.

Iran is continuing to address the Millennial Development Goals issued by the United Nations. In 2005, 98.3 percent of all eligible children were enrolled in primary education (and 93.4 percent completed primary education). With respect to literacy and gender equity, the 2007 overall literate population was approximately 84.6 percent, which represents more than twice the literate population 20 years before. Literacy movement courses enrolled 1.347 million adult learners in 2007. However, in 2007, literacy disparities persisted between rural (67.5 percent) and urban (81 percent) areas. In 2008, the gender disparity among Iranians over 15 years of age was less pronounced (89.3 percent of males and 80.7 percent of females are literate). Despite a 2011 Iranian study presenting evidence that females tend to be portrayed in textbooks in traditional roles, scholars attribute increases in gender equity with Islamic leadership encouraging family planning education shortly following the Iran–Iraq War.

Between the 1980s and 2006, fertility rates per woman decreased from seven children to below two. A final challenge comes from current President Mahmoud Ahmadinejad returning to stronger Islamic policies while resisting globalization and Western influence. A recent study analyzing elementary and secondary textbooks in Iran found lessons based heavily in supporting duty-based citizenship values, which more likely creates citizens supportive of the government.

However, studies demonstrate that increases in education levels lead to higher levels of interest in politics and can be linked to recent Middle Eastern revolutions. It remains to be seen if further exhibition of exemplary improvement in education equity will lead to civil unrest in Iran.

Everett Herman
University of Pittsburgh

See Also: Afghanistan; Iraq; Israel; Pakistan; Turkey.

Further Readings

Chanzanagh, Hamid Ebadollahi, et al. "Citizenship Values in School Subjects: A Case-Study on Iran's Elementary and Secondary Education School Subjects." *Procedia Social and Behavioral Sciences*, v.15 (2011).

Chanzanagh, Hamid Ebadollahi, et al. "Gender in School Subject: A Case-Study on Iran's Primary Levels—School Subjects." *Procedia Social and Behavioral Sciences*, v.15 (2011).

Farasatkhah, Maghsood, et al. "Quality Challenge in Iran's Higher Education: A Historical Review." *Iranian Studies*, v.41/2 (2008).

Halim, Ab Adlina and Daryoush Piri. "Diplomacy of Iran Towards Globalization: The Tension Between Globalization and Islamization in Iran." *Cross-Cultural Communication*, v.7/1 (2011).

Khalaji, Mehdi. "Iran's Regime of Religion." *Journal of International Affairs*, v. 65/1 (2011).

Lutz, Wolfgang, Cuaresma Jesús Crespo, and Mohammad Jalal Abbasi-Shavazi. "Demography, Education, and Democracy: Global Trends and the Case of Iran." *Population and Development Review*, v.36/2 (2010).

Iraq

One of the Arabic Middle Eastern countries, Iraq occupies an area of 169,234 square miles (437,707 square kilometers) and is bordered by Iran, Jordan, Kuwait, Saudi Arabia, Syria, and Turkey. Baghdad is the nation's largest city and is a center of unique historical prominence. Other major urban centers include Basrah, Mosul, and Kirkuk. The oil industry constitutes the majority of Iraq's economy. Iraq's population was over 32 million in July 2011, with Arabs comprising about three-fourths and Kurds about one-fifth of the population. The remaining Iraqis are divided into several ethnic groups, including Assyrian, Turkoman, Chaldean, Armenian, Yazidi, Sabean, and Jews.

The spoken language is Iraqi Arabic in most provinces, and Kurdish is the official language in Kurdistan. Saddam Hussein, of the Sunni Islam minority, rose to power in 1979, and remained until he was removed at the onset of the U.S.-led Iraq War in 2003. Iraq's contemporary history is marred by a series of wars with its neighbors, including with Iran (1980–88) and Kuwait (1990–91). Two additional wars with the United States (the First Gulf War from 1990 to 1991 and the Iraq War or Second Gulf War from 2003 to 2011) left the country bereft of infrastructure and social stability.

Established in 1921, the education system includes both private and public schooling opportunities. The government required all eligible-age children to attend primary school, and this helped lay the foundation for one of the most developed and literate populations in the region. From 1970 to 1984, a period some identify as the nation's "golden years," Iraq's education system gained significant leadership recognition in the Middle East. By 1984, some of the education milestones included gross enrollment ratios (GER) exceeding 100 percent, gender parity in student enrollments, and a drop to less than 10 percent in the nation's illiteracy rate among those ages 15 to 45.

Government spending also reached 20 percent of the country's total budget. The war years over the past three decades had a lasting negative impact on the education sector. Government spending was reduced to a fraction of that spent during the golden years. Gender imbalances and dropout rates increased. Teacher salaries were reduced to such a nominal amount that many of the best teachers left their work or traveled abroad. The wars also placed severe constraints on pre- and in-service teacher training programs and curriculum development.

Today, the Ministry of Education and Ministry of Higher Education, Science, and Research (MOHESR) manage the Iraqi education system. The formal education of Iraqi children begins with preschool at age 4, and generally lasts for two years. Primary education includes grades one through six, and is compulsory for children ages 6 to 11; secondary education is divided into two levels—intermediate (grades 7–9 for students ages 12–14) and preparatory secondary education (grades 10–12+, for students ages 16–21). Preparatory education can be further divided into an academic or vocational track.

The academic track lasts for three years, and students can choose either a science or humanities option. The vocational track lasts from three to six years, and helps prepare students for employment or for higher education study. Higher education in Iraq includes the following types of higher education institutions (HEIs): vocational, postsecondary institutes, colleges, and universities. Students are admitted into higher education institutions to complete diplomas, bachelor's, master's, and doctoral programs. Bachelor's degrees include four-year (e.g., education and science), five-year (e.g., engineering or pharmacy), and six-year programs (in medicine and surgery). In 2007, the tertiary education GER was 12 percent for females and 20 percent for males (an increase for both genders from 1999, with a GER of 15 and 8 percent, respectively). Of the 425,000 students attending HEIs in 2007, 36 percent were female.

Education in Postwar Iraq

Postwar Iraq faces a number of challenges to help regain the prominence that its education system once held in the Middle East. Many Iraqis give a higher priority to basic survival, rather than on pursuing education opportunities. The economic embargo imposed on Iraq during the 1990s and the sectarian violence after the 2003 war have had a lasting impact on the education system. Antigovernment activists and rebels often persecuted education administrators, teachers, and staff members by killing or kidnapping them or attacking the schools in which they worked. Enrollment rates have dropped and are lowest among young women in rural areas. Women are often forced to leave school to help their families, and security concerns make parents hesitant to send their children, especially daughters, to school. School infrastructure challenges remain in this postwar context, where over 80 percent of schools were damaged as a result of the most recent war.

There is also a need to build many more schools to keep up with an increase in the nation's population. Most schools are deprived of adequate water and toilets, and are in dire need of repair and maintenance. Other noticeable challenges facing the current and future education in Iraq include the need to build the infrastructure capacity of school libraries, laboratories, and information technology equipment. There is also a need to focus on improving teacher training programs at all levels. Recruitment and retention strategies are needed to help attract quality teachers into the education workforce. Population displacement was also one of the factors that affected Iraqi society. These issues have negatively impacted educational standards, which are now below average for the region.

Higher education in Iraq had a similar evolution over the past 30 years, as did the other education subsectors. The succession of long war periods and economic sanctions has hindered many areas of higher education progress. Infrastructure remains severely damaged and in need of maintenance. Higher education faculty members, administrators, and staff members who were either killed or fled during the war has left a human capacity gap that will take years to rebuild.

W. James Jacob
Razak Abedalla
University of Pittsburgh

See Also: Iran; Jordan; Saudi Arabia; Syria; Teacher Recruitment, Induction, and Retention; Turkey.

Further Readings
Baram, Amatzia, Achim Rohde, and Ronen Zeidel, eds. *Iraq Between Occupations: Perspectives From 1920 to the Present.* New York: Palgrave Macmillan, 2010.
Inter-Agency Information and Analysis Unit (IAU). *United Nations Supplementary Country Analysis for Iraq Thematic Working Group on Essential Services.* New York: United Nations IAU, 2009.
Issa, Jinan Hatem and Jamil Hazri. "Overview of the Education System in Contemporary Iraq." *European Journal of Social Sciences*, v.14/3 (2010).
United Nations Educational, Scientific and Cultural Organization (UNESCO) Institute for Statistics. *Global Education Digest 2009.* Montreal, Canada: UNESCO, 2009.

Ireland

The Republic of Ireland is located on an island with the same name in the northwest periphery of Europe. Ireland occupies more than 80 percent of the island, while the remaining part is occupied by Northern Ireland. Ireland has an extension of 27,000 square miles and a population of 4.5 million. Ireland was a British colony until 1922, when it gained independence and became a parliamentary republic. It has been a member of the European Economic Community (now EU) since 1973.

The modern Irish educational system can be traced back to British rule, when in 1831, Lord Stanley, chief secretary for Ireland, introduced the national educational system. The system was meant to be multidenominational; however, soon Catholics, Presbyterians, and Church of Ireland played a key role in the school system. School attendance, however, was poor until the Irish Education Act in 1892, when schools were established as free and compulsory. Ireland has been a country of emigration for centuries, and this was accentuated during and after the Great Famine of 1845 to 1849, when 25 percent of the population perished. During the economic boom of the Celtic Tiger (1995–2007), the country underwent rapid economic development, and for the first time, income migration outnumbered emigration. Since 2007, Ireland has experienced a deep economic crisis with high levels of unemployment.

The schooling system in Ireland is regulated by the Department of Education and Skills (DES), under the Minister for Education and Skills. According to the Programme for International Student Assessment (PISA), Ireland is ranked within the 20th best countries in science, with students having the second-highest levels of reading literacy in the EU. Education in the country is compulsory between the ages of 6 and 16, but most children start school between ages 4 and 5. The primary language of instruction is English, although primary and secondary level *Gaelscoileanna* (Gaelic Schools) are gaining much popularity, especially within the middle classes. In these schools, mostly located in the urban areas, Irish is the first language of teaching. Preschool in Ireland is privately run and must be paid for by parents, except one free year before starting school. The school system in Ireland is divided into three levels: primary (grades 1–8); secondary, divided into a junior cycle of three years: a noncompulsory transition year, and senior cycle (two years); and university or college. Further education (extra-university education) has gained much prestige in the last few years. Primary, secondary, and third level education are all free for EU citizens.

One of the major challenges of Irish school today is that the post–Celtic Tiger Ireland suddenly discovered itself as a multicultural society. A recent survey conducted by D. Byrne stresses that, although in Ireland there are no segregated schools like in many other EU countries, migrants tend to attend larger urban, disadvantaged schools, and that these schools tend to give fewer chances of entering third level education.

In 2010, the Fundamental Rights Agency of the EU annual report claimed that school admission criteria must be revised because they disadvantage newcomers. Another big debate today concerns the ownership of schools, in particular at the primary level. The majority of primary schools in Ireland are state-aided, but privately owned by different churches. In substance, most of these schools are Catholic in ethos and single-sex. In recent years, there has been a call for a more secular primary school in Ireland, given that today about 10 percent of students attending Irish schools are not Irish born, and many do not have a Catholic background. One of the most successful answers to this call came from the Educate Together (ET) movement. Since 1978, ET schools are a new kind of multidenominational, mixed-sex schools that reflect this call for a more secular education in the country. Today, there are 60 primary ET schools in the country with a number of campaigns asking for the opening of secondary level schools. Ireland is facing a moment of economic crises, and the educational system is facing hard financial cutbacks, with teachers facing relevant cuts on their stipends.

Maura Rosa Parazzoli
National University of Ireland, Maynooth

See Also: Catholic Schools; European Union; United Kingdom.

Further Readings

Byrne, D., et al. "Immigration and School Composition in Ireland." *Irish Educational Studies*, v.29/3 (2010).

Drudy, S., ed. *Education in Ireland: Challenges and Changes*. Dublin, Ireland: Gill and Macmillan, 2009.

Kirby, P., L. Gibbons, and M. Cronin. *Reinventing Ireland: Culture, Society and the Global Economy*. London: Pluto Press, 2002.

Israel

The state of Israel is located at the crossroads of Africa, Asia, and Europe, on the Levant coast of the Mediterranean. There, a growing population from diverse societies converges in a slice of land the size of New Jersey. Territorial acquisitions and disengagements as a result of wars and treaties have altered the size of the

Jewish state since its formal inception in 1948: Sinai (1952–59, 1973–79), Judea and Samariah (1967–present), Golan Heights (1973–present), southern Lebanon (1978, 1982–2000), Gaza Strip (1973–2005), and east Jerusalem (1967–present). Despite its tumultuous history, Israel has steadily developed to become the 41st-largest global economy in 2010, with a gross domestic product (GDP) of $217 billion. Approximately 7 percent of its GDP ($15 billion) was spent on education.

Prior to Israel's independence, the area was ruled by numerous empires, including the: British, Ottomans, Mamluks, Crusaders, Ummayads, Byzantines, Romans, Israelites and Judeans. Ancient Israel was a cradle of global religions (Judaism, Christianity, and Islam). Modern Israel remains a focal point for these religions, as well as the Druze, Bahai, and Samaritan religions. The influence of prior empires remains in aspects of the population and social structure today, particularly since the remigration of Jews to their ancestral homeland. Between 1881 and 1929, four waves of Aliyah (Jewish migration to Israel) occurred under the auspices of the World Zionist Organization (WZO). Under the Balfour Declaration (1917), the British accepted Jews' right to establish a homeland in Palestine.

During the colonial period, the Jewish population grew dramatically, but local Arabs remained the majority, until many were exiled after the independence war (1948–49), an event known in Arabic as the Nakba (disaster). Diverse waves of Aliyah have persisted to the present; Holocaust survivors, Yemenites, Moroccans, Iraqis, Iranians, Romanians, and Ethiopians have arrived in mass migrations. With the arrival of 976,988 immigrants from the former Soviet Union (1990–2008), Israel surpassed the United States as the largest Jewish population in the world. In 2009, Israel's population stood at 7,552,000 (5,703,700 Jews, 1,286,500 Muslim Arabs, 312,800 non-Jewish non-Arabs, and 249,100 non-Muslim Arabs). This statistic does not include the current 2,448,433 Arabs in the West Bank, 1,486,816 Arabs in Gaza, and 220,000 foreign workers and refugees in Israel proper.

Educational History

Israel's first prime minister, David Ben-Gurion, enacted the compulsory education law in 1949, providing free education for all children between the ages of 5 and 13. Arab schools faced difficulties, resulting from an influx of students required to attend school, a lack of qualified teachers (as many had fled), and confusion from Jewish administrators. Jewish schools faced difficulties integrating the new immigrant populations. Pre- and post-independence Jewish schools became increasingly split along secular, religious, and other tracks. Each track set up different curricula and standards. Mizrahim (Oriental Jews) gravitated toward religious-Zionist schools, Ashkenazim (European Jews) toward secular-Zionist schools, and Haredim (Ultra-Orthodox Jews) toward non-Zionist religious schools. Schools became a breeding ground for party politics. This led to a phenomenon called soul-stalking, where schools actively campaigned for students. The Frumkin Commission (1950) was established to investigate soul-stalking after religious families complained that their children were being secularized. Although the government signed the State Education Law (1953), in practice, the law didn't impact the religious and independent schools dependent on religious parties. The Mizrahi immigrants were frequently placed in peripheral areas of the country in Ma'abarot, makeshift tent villages, which later became Development Towns. These towns often offered subpar schools, making it difficult for students to pass the Bagrut (matriculation exam). The government began an affirmative action policy, lowering the high school admission standards for specific ethnicities. Later, the Free Compulsory Education Law (1979) mandated public education for all children between the ages of 5 and 18. The Israeli Pupil's Rights Law (2000) allowed minorities to attend the school closest to their residence.

Educational Structure

The Israeli school system is divided into state-secular, state-religious, state-Arab, and Haredi sectors. Approximately 1,530,237 students were enrolled in primary and secondary schools in 2010 (43 percent secular, 27 percent Arab, 17 percent Haredi, and 13 percent religious). Typically, a student will attend four levels of school: pre-primary (ages 2–5), primary (grades 1–6), lower secondary (grades 7–9), and upper secondary (grades 10–12), with a few local variations. The Ministry of Education and Culture administers all public schools, although Haredi schools maintain greater autonomy. All state schools are free and run from Sunday to Friday. Mandatory high school subjects include Bible, math, English, literature, history, Hebrew, and citizenship, with differing amounts of credit, depending on the school's track. Eight national universities are

competitive at a global level, and a growing number of private colleges offer postsecondary education. University admission is dependent on performance on the Bagrut. Students who do not receive sufficient matriculation scores for their selected course of studies often elect to take Mechina (a one-year college preparatory track) and/or a psychometric examination. A Matnas (center for culture, youth and sport), usually run by local government with support from the Ministry of Education, offers supplemental educational programs for children and adults. In addition, Ulpans (Hebrew language programs) serve a crucial role in educating new immigrants.

Current Issues

Achieving educational equity between the different Jewish ethnicities and Arabs remains a major issue. Gaps have decreased between Jewish ethnicities, but still persist. Besides the traditional Mizrahi-Ashkenazi comparison, recent research looks at Russian, Ethiopian, and other recent immigrants. Discrepancies in achievement between Jews and Muslims are more apparent. Only 49 percent of Muslims passed the 2010 matriculation exam, compared to 70 percent of Jews. Muslim students drop out of school more frequently and at a younger age, meaning that fewer will take the exam. In 2010, 10 percent of Muslims dropped out at grade 9, compared to 3 percent of Jews. Lack of educational resources has been cited as a cause of the educational gap. Many Arab students are relegated to poor, overcrowded schools. In 1959, average class size in Arab schools was 63.1, compared to 32.3 in Jewish schools. By 2010, the situation had improved to 28.3 students per class in Arab schools and 26.0 in Jewish schools, with both groups still claiming overcrowding. Although Arabs make up 20 percent of the population, only 12 percent of undergraduate students were Arab in 2010. There are signs that the situation is improving, as only 8 percent of undergraduate students were Arab in 2005.

The persistence of educational inequalities is often associated with cultural bias in the curricula and teaching standards. Arabic textbooks contain numerous grammatical errors and cultural biases favoring the Zionist narrative, such as excluding the word "Nakba" from textbooks. Likewise, Hebrew textbooks commonly present Arabs as instigators of conflict. In 1999, new history textbooks were introduced to promote multiculturalism between Jews and Arabs, but are still criticized for their Zionist bias. Additional subjects for media and academic research include the curriculum and rules of Haredi schools, religious education in public schools, youth groups (e.g., scouts), teacher quality, teacher strikes, academic boycotts, Israeli–Arab educational projects, and education in the occupied territories. For a country so small, Israel presents a large potential for studies on the sociology of education.

Keith Goldstein
Hebrew University of Jerusalem

See Also: Class Inequality: Achievement; Jordan; Racial Inequality: Achievement; Racism in Education; Religious Education; Textbooks.

Further Readings

Ayalon, Hanna and Y. Shavit. "Educational Reforms and Inequalities in Israel: The MMI Hypothesis Revisited." *Sociology of Education*, v.77/2 (2004).

Friedlander, Dov, et al. *Changes in Educational Attainments in Israel Since the 1950s: The Effects of Religion, Ethnicity and Family Characteristics.* Jerusalem, Israel: Central Bureau of Statistics, 2002.

Okun, Barbara S. and Dov Friedlander. "Educational Stratification Among Arabs and Jews in Israel." *Population Studies*, v.59/2 (2005).

Smooha, Sammy. "Minority Status in an Ethnic Democracy: The Status of the Arab Minority in Israel." *Ethnic and Racial Studies*, v.13/3 (1990).

Italy

Italy is located in a strategic position between central Europe and the Mediterranean Sea. The country has a population of 60.6 million inhabitants (the fifth-most populous nation in Europe) and the territory covers 116,347 square miles (301,338 square kilometers). The tenth-largest economy in the word, Italy has been a parliamentary republic since 1946, and was one of the founding members of the European Economic Community (now EU) in 1957. It is also a current member of G8 and NATO. Italy has been a national state since 1861, and the educational system before 2012 was regulated by the different kingdoms and states ruling each region.

Throughout the Middle Ages, education in Italy was provided solely by the Catholic Church, to very restricted portions of the population. With the Renaissance, public schools were opened, but education remained predominantly reserved for urban, upper-class males. In the 19th century, under the influence of the Enlightenment, a number of state schools opened. In 1859, the Casati Low established a four-year primary school, which was free and compulsory for all, while the Gentile Reform (1923), approved under the first Mussolini government, established the compulsory age of education at 14. From the 1960s, the education system underwent deep reforms, including the liberalization of access to university in 1969, and the rise of the compulsory age of education to 16 in 2007.

The current educational structure in Italy reflects the last two reforms of the school and university systems operated in 2003 and 2008 by Ministers of Education Moratti and Gelmini. A preschool level (*Scuola dell'Infanzia*) from 2.5 to 5 or 6 years of age, which is free and not compulsory, is followed by *Scuola Primaria* (primary school, five years). Secondary education is divided into a lower level, running for three years (*Scuola Secondaria di primo grado*), which is the same for everybody; and a higher level (*Scuola Secondaria di secondo grado*), which is divided into three curricula, each giving access to university. The *Liceo* (five years) gives students an academic preparation with a specialization in ancient classics, science, languages, arts, or human sciences; the *Istituto Tecnico* (five years) gives preparation to enter in the job market, with curricula in accountancy, economics, and foreign languages; and the *Istituto Professionale* (three or five years) gives a preparation to enter in the job market, with curricula in industry and handicraft. Public schools in Italy are free. A system of private schools, often led by Catholic institutions is also available. The university system in Italy is organized around a first level degree (*Laurea Triennale*, three years) and a second level (*Laurea Magistrale*, two years), plus a Ph.D. (*Dottorato di Ricerca*, three to five years). The majority of universities in Italy are state funded (with fees paid by students, according to their income). A number of private universities are also available, some of which hold a very high international reputation, such as Bocconi and Cattolica universities.

Italy is currently experiencing a moment of deep economic crisis, and education is one of the sectors facing major cutbacks. Teachers' unions have deeply criticized the recent reforms of the educational system for having the only purpose of decreasing the budget of the Minister of Education, without any attention to individual schools, and this is reflected in the inadequate number of teachers, the lack of resources to buy basics items (with many schools asking parents for "voluntary contributions" at the beginning of each year), and school principals assigned to more than one school (some with five or six schools).

In addition, compared to other Organization for Security and Co-operation in Europe (OSCE) countries, Italy has one of the lowest research budgets (1.1 percent), and this percentage has been unchanged since 2001. As a consequence, the brain drain (*fuga dei cervelli*), in particular toward other EU countries and the United States, is common. It is estimated that this brain drain generates a loss of $1.2 billion (1 billion euros) each year. Another major challenge is represented by migration. In the past 20 years, Italy has experienced an unprecedented flow of migrants, and the educational system is still struggling with the increasing number of international students. According to the Ministry of Education, the number of non-national students attending Italian schools (excluding universities) in 2009 was 629,000 (9.6 percent of the student population), and

while this presence is a structural reality, it is also problematic. N. Barban and M. J. White, for instance stress how students with a migrant background tend to have inferior grades in the middle school exam, and choose vocational secondary schools instead of university-oriented secondary schools.

Maura Rosa Parazzoli
National University of Ireland, Maynooth

See Also: European Union; France; Migrant Students; Switzerland.

Further Readings
Barban, N. and M. J. White. "Immigrants' Children's Transition to Secondary School in Italy." *International Migration Review*, v.45/3 (2011).
Enders, J., H. F. de Boer, and D. F. Westerheijden. *Reform of Higher Education in Europe*. Rotterdam, the Netherlands: Sense Publishers, 2011.
Genovesi, G. *Storia della scuola italiana dal Settento a oggi* (History of Schools in Italy From the Eighteenth Century to Today). Rome: Edizioni Laterza, 2010.
Hörner, W., et al., eds. *The Education Systems of Europe*. Dordrecht, Netherlands: Springer, 2007.

J

Jamaica

Jamaica is among the largest of the Caribbean Islands, with an area of 11,420 square kilometers, located 145 kilometers south of Cuba and 600 kilometers south of Florida. The World Bank estimates the population at 2,847,232. Its economy is dependent on tourism, manufacturing, bauxite, and remittances. Jamaica experienced a marginal growth rate of 1 percent between 1990 and 2009, and paid a public debt of 134 percent of its total gross domestic product (GDP) in 2010. As of 2010, Jamaica was approved for a $1.27 billion International Monetary Fund loan (IMF) for economic reforms. Currently, a fifth of the population lives below the poverty line. Jamaica's legacy as a former British colony until 1962 shaped its demographics, economics, and educational structure.

In the 18th century, Jamaica was a profitable plantation society with a social structure that pervaded all economic and social relationships. African slaves, whose descendants comprise the majority of the present population (91.6 percent, according to the 2000 census), provided the bulk of the plantation labor. Their descendants comprise the majority of the lower class, although significant numbers can be found in the middle and upper middle classes. Occupying the top of the rigid plantation system were the owners of plantations, the white elite. In modern Jamaica, whites consist of British expatriates and the former small merchant class—Syrians, Lebanese, Jews, and other lighter-skinned immigrants. They constitute 0.18 percent of the total population. This population retains the social privileges that were extended to whites in the plantation era—including access to higher-quality education than the masses. The descendants of unions between slave women and planters, the brown or mixed segment (who account for 6.21 percent of the current population), occupied a middle position in the plantation society. For this sector, access to educational opportunities, wealth, and political power grew as their numbers increased by the late 19th century. Finally, the east Indians and Chinese, who were brought to Jamaica as indentured laborers to work on plantations during the emancipation era, comprise 0.89 and 0.2 percent of the current population, respectively.

Colonial Era

During slavery, access to education reflected and reproduced social and racial inequities. After emancipation in 1834, large-scale educational reform was directed at the former slave population. These educational policies laid the foundation for future reforms that would continue to shape the nation's educational trajectory well into the postindependence era. Policies were aimed at establishing primary and secondary schools, such as the Negro Education Grant (1835–45) and curriculum development, and emphasized the cultivation of European values and Christian moral uplift. Despite an increase in primary

405

education attendance, secondary education was beyond the reach of the majority of ex-slaves because of prohibitive fees, the exclusivity of schools, and racist discourses about blacks and intelligence. A dual system of education was created, whereby the majority of the population (poor and black) was excluded from accessing quality education, certain employment, and university opportunities.

By the 1920s, recommendations to improve primary education shifted to curriculum reform, ensuring that materials reflected the local environment. As Jamaica moved toward self-government in the 1940s, the education system was faced with overcrowding, lack of teacher training, limited access to secondary education, increasing high school dropout rates, and inequities in the quality of education among various schools. For instance in 1948, among persons 7 years and older, 25.6 percent were illiterate. Roughly 20 percent of the population was not enrolled in school, and 90 percent dropped out before enrolling in sixth grade. Furthermore, in 1943 only, 9 percent of the brown population and less than 1 percent of the black population attended secondary school. The lack of reform of secondary education especially reflected the dominant ideology. Errol Miller suggests that for the elite, education was a tool to maintain the status quo; while for the masses, it was a means for upward mobility. In 1948, the University College of the West Indies, Mona Campus (UCWI), was established to meet the demand for higher education in the nation.

Post-Independence Era

In the post-independence era, the educational goals of the People's National Party (PNP) and Jamaica Labor Party (JLP) were aimed at widening access to education and promoting economic growth through educational reform. Under the government of the JLP, The New Deal for Education in Independent Jamaica (1966) provided compulsory education up to age 14. Loans from international organizations helped construct 50 junior secondary schools (JSS), which made provisions for 37,530 students. Funding was also allocated toward expanding teacher colleges. In the 1970s, the democratic socialist government of the PNP concerned with curriculum development in primary schools emphasized pride in local history and language, rather than British culture. Access to education was expanded and free primary and secondary education was offered, along with the development of adult educational programs. Because of the rising

price of oil globally and record unemployment locally, on the advice of the IMF, the PNP implemented several structural adjustment measures that cut funding from several social programs, including free education and cuts in teacher's salaries. These policies had long-term implications for education development. In the 1980s and 1990s, because of economic cuts in education, educational development was mainly achieved through loans from international organizations. Major educational initiatives included a focus on functional literacy in primary education through improvements in the primary curriculum and teacher training, career training for unemployed school leavers, and the creation of standardized curriculum for primary and lower secondary school to improve the quality of education among nontraditional (such as new secondary schools) and traditional elite schools. The National Assessment Program was charged with assessing learning and developing tests for the Grade Six Achievement Test (GSAT), which replaced the Common Entrance Exam as the main secondary school entrance exam in 1999.

Educational Structure

Formal education in Jamaica includes early childhood (basic school age); primary (grades 1–6) and all-age schools (grades 1–9); and secondary, including new secondary, technical high schools, and vocational schools. Traditional secondary also includes two cycles: lower secondary (grades 7–9), and the upper secondary or sixth form (grades 10–13), and tertiary. The Ministry of Education Youth and Culture (MOEYC) is responsible for running all public schools, along with various religious organizations and trusts. Equity and access to quality education to support economic development are still the main objectives of educational policy, according to MOEYC. Currently, there is universal access to primary education up to grade six for all public schools, and textbooks are provided free of cost in primary schools. Technological proficiency at the primary level and curbing functional illiteracy at the secondary level has also been included in the current government's initiatives.

Key Developments

In 2005 and 2006, primary school enrollment was at 97.9 percent. Improvements in primary education focus on curriculum reform for grades one through six. The Primary Education Improvement Program, an initiative funded by the Inter-American

Development Bank (IADB), has helped create a generalized curriculum for all public schools. Recommended textbooks are written by local authors and are published by local publishing houses or local subsidiaries of international publishing houses. Additionally, according to the IADB 2009 Report, $1 million has gone into refurbishing schools and adding new computers to rural schools. Curriculum reform is also the focus in secondary education. The World Bank and the Ministry of Education Reform of Secondary Education Project (ROSE) (1993–98) has implemented a common core curriculum for grades seven through nine. A project goal is to address inequalities in the quality of education at different schools, especially in nontraditional schools. ROSE plans to address grades 10 to 11 in the future. Criticisms of the reform suggest that the focus on quality should concentrate on the continued lack of basic resources for rural schools and alleviating the stigma attached to nontraditional secondary schools.

Current Issues

Male academic underperformance at primary and secondary levels, especially among low-income youth, and the marked decrease in male enrollment at the tertiary level are worrying educational developments. According to a Jamaica Millennium Development Goals Report, in 2007, 90.7 percent of females were literate, compared to 80 percent of males. Results from the University of the West Indies Mona Campus suggest that in higher education, female enrollment exceed males by 67.3 percent. Social scientist Barry Chevannes reasons that male privilege and unequal gender socialization are related to growing male underperformance.

Despite their high educational attainment, females face high rates of unemployed and a sex-segregated job market. When examining GSAT performance rates in government-run primary schools compared to private primary schools, it reflects a two-tier education system that still persists despite curriculum reforms. According to the 2009 Jamaica Millennium Development Goals Report, the mean score for government schools in language arts was 48 percent, compared with 72 percent for private primary schools. Math scores were similar, with mean scores at 46 percent for government schools, and 70 percent for private schools. Results indicate that social inequality still persists when competing for competitive high school places. Additionally, high rates of

nonattendance and school dropouts are still a major problem in rural schools, while a steady increase in school violence plagues mainly corporate area schools. In addition to rationalizing the curriculum and textbook content, studies by Ruby King, Mike Morrissey, Barbara Bailey, and Lois Parker suggest that continuous efforts should be made to examine the hidden race, class, and gendered messages that stem from colonialism and are still reflected in curriculum and textbook content and contribute to the perpetuation and development of negative racial and gendered ideologies and roles.

Jennifer Simon
Georgia State University

See Also: Bahamas; Barbados; Cuba; Dominican Republic; Haiti.

Further Readings

Bailey, Barbara and Lois Parkes. "Gender: The Not So Hidden Issue in Language Arts Materials Used in Jamaica." *Journal of Caribbean Studies*, v.17/2 (1995).

Chevannes, Barry. *What We Sow and What We Reap: Problems in the Cultivation of Male Identity in Jamaica*. Grace Kennedy Foundation Lecture Series, 1999.

King, Ruby and Mike Morrissey. *Images in Print: Bias and Prejudice in Caribbean Textbooks*. Mona, Jamaica: Institute of Social and Economic Research, University of the West Indies, 1998.

Miller, Errol. *Education Reform in Independent Jamaica: Themes in Education Reform in the Populist Era*. Mona, Jamaica: Institute of Social and Economic Research, University of the West Indies, 1991.

Statistical Institute of Jamaica. *Population Census 2001, Jamaica: Vol. 1, Country Report*. Kingston, Jamaica: Statistical Institute of Jamaica, 2003.

Japan

Japan is an island nation in east Asia, extending along the Pacific Coast of Asia. It has four main islands and more than 6,800 smaller ones. Japan is a major economic power and has one of the most advanced technological industrial structures in the world. In 2011, the population stood at about 127.7 million. Japan has a long history as a country and has a long tradition of education. Today, various aspects of Japanese culture affect many other parts of the world. Japan has historically had numerous disasters, such as earthquakes, and is the only country to have been devastated by atomic bombs.

The Early Kingdom Period began in the 4th century. Successive emperors created the foundation of the country through contact with cultures in China and Korea. Buddhism, Confucianism, Chinese social systems, and various cultures of civilizations on the Silk Road were introduced to Japan. The oldest national school system for fostering bureaucrats was established in 701, and the first school for all people, even commoners, was founded in 828 by a Buddhist monk named Kukai. Buddhism became increasingly important, and the sophisticated imperial court culture of classical Japan bloomed in Kyoto from the 8th to the 12th centuries.

Between 1192 and 1603, the Federal Era, the warrior samurai expanded their political and military power. Samurai values and moral codes based on homage reflect the origins of the "code of the warrior" (*bushido*). Buddhist temples provided high-level education as boarding schools, not only for samurai children, but also for those aspiring to become monks, and even commoners' children not aiming to become monks. During the Edo Period (1603–1867), the Tokugawa shogun and his government (*bakufu*) created a central bureaucracy and established complete dominance by the warrior samurai class (*bushi*). Stratification of society was intensified and elaborated. The government solidified its self-imposed isolation policy (1639–1854), prohibiting people from traveling abroad and banning Christianity. A long peace continued, and Edo culture flourished.

Schools for children of the samurai class, called *hanko*, were established in every domain (*han*). Further, there were more than 20,000 private elementary schools (*terako-ya*), all over the country. Each terako-ya was founded by popular demand and provided basic education in reading, writing, and arithmetic, mainly for the children of commoners, such as farmers and merchants, and even for samurai children. Therefore, by 1860, the literacy rate in Japan was quite high compared to other developed countries. Before the modernization process started in 1868, the Japanese people already had respect for learning and education. In 1868, the shogun returned his political power to the Emperor Meiji (Meiji Restoration), and the Meiji period (1868–1912) was a time

of rapid modernization in Japan. Based on Western models, the new Meiji government reformed various social systems. The samurai class lost its privileges, the old class system was abandoned, and an integrated modern public educational system was established in order to promote industrial development.

From the late 19th century onward, the military increasingly gained political power; Japan created colonies and engaged in the Sino–Japanese War (1894–95) and the Russo–Japanese War (1904–05). In 1907, as the concept of nationalism gained ground, the Ministry of Education increased the duration of compulsory education from four to six years, and adopted a curriculum that stressed the importance of the emperor and nationalism. After Japan was defeated and devastated by the United States in World War II, the nation's government, social, and educational systems were remodeled, and Japan emerged as a peaceful and democratic nation. During the postwar period (1945–present), rapid economic growth continued. The collapse of the bubble economy in 1991, however, brought about the current recession. Still, the Japanese worker is known to be well-educated and diligent. Gender inequality in income, however, still exists across all educational levels and age cohorts.

In today's Japan, obtaining a job depends mainly on one's personal capabilities and academic background. Further, the Japanese educational system is rooted in ideas of hierarchy and ranking, despite egalitarian primary education. In particular, each university is rated by a linear school ranking scale (*hensachi*). High educational credentials, such as enrollment at prestigious universities, promise good jobs and high social status. Parents invest a great deal of money in the education industry for their children, such as sending them to cram schools (*juku*), to get high test scores and pass the entrance exams. Severe educational competition is called "exam war" or "exam hell." Another characteristic of Japanese education is to respect group behavior and group conformity, rather than independence and individuality. Educational reform for primary and secondary education, called *yutori* educational reform, was implemented in 1992 to improve education, foster individuality, and alleviate stress on students by easing the curriculum and reducing school hours.

Educational Structure

The modern educational system was instituted in 1872 and changed after World War II. The Japanese academic year starts in April. The Japanese educational system is composed primarily of kindergarten, six years of elementary school from age 6, three years of junior high school, and three years of senior high school. An additional four years of university or two years of junior college are popular as higher education. Professional training colleges (*senmon-gakko*) have been classified as higher education since 1998. A majority of children ages 3 to 5 (90.5 percent) attended kindergarten or daycare centers in 2010. Elementary and junior high school are compulsory, and the enrollment rate at that level is 100 percent. According to a 2010 Ministry of Education, Culture, Sports, Science and Technology (MEXT) survey, senior high school enrollment is 98.3 percent, 59.2 percent of 18 year olds go on to university or junior college, and total enrollment including other types of higher education is 81.3 percent.

The rate of Japanese adults with higher education is within the top three among Organisation for Economic Co-operation and Development (OECD) countries. As of 2010, more than 90 percent of institutes of higher education were private. The number of graduate students has increased in the past 20 years, but the percentage is not so high compared with other developed countries. Primary and secondary education is standardized. MEXT supervises the school curriculum (curriculum guidelines) and examines the contents of textbooks (*kyokasho-kentei*) throughout the country for both public and private schools. Higher education is also supervised by MEXT. The sorting and tracking of students mainly begins in senior high school. Different senior high schools have specialized curricula.

Current Issues

Japanese society is changing in response to issues such as a declining population, falling birth rate, and rapid aging. A protracted economic recession after 1991 changed the economic structure, and dualism in the labor market grew. In 2010, 30.4 percent of young workers ages 15–24 was in nonregular work, temporary, or part-time jobs with low income and no insurance coverage. Income distribution for young generations became more unequal in recent years. Also, the Tohoku-Kanto Earthquake and Fukushima radiation devastated the large eastern part of Japan in 2011. Japanese education depends heavily on family household expenditure, especially at the higher educational level. Compulsory education is free: however, there are many additional costs such as school supplies, school meals, and school trips, in addition to family payments for juku to prepare for

the entrance exams. According to the MEXT survey in 2008, the average cost of education for a child paid by each household from public kindergarten to graduation from public university is approximately ¥10 million. In the case of students in private schools, this figure increases to approximately ¥23 million. One reason for the low fertility in Japan is believed to be the high cost of private education. Therefore, starting in 2010, free tuition at public senior high schools and a tuition support fund for students at private senior high schools were established.

Violent behavior in school became a big problem in the 1970s. Since then, school bullying (*ijime*) has become common in school since the 1980s. Also, despite the high quality of the Japanese teachers, the collapse of classrooms (*gakkyu hokai*) has become an increasingly serious problem. Yutori educational reform policy began in 1992, and ended in 2011. For instance, 30 percent of the curriculum was cut by the 1998 revision of curriculum guidelines. This reform raised public controversy and was an extremely contentious issue. Since this reform, academic achievement in Japan has declined, as shown in Programme for International Student Assessment (PISA) 2006. A 2009 white paper reports that the achievement gap from family income has increased, and equal educational opportunities have diminished.

Emi Kataoka
Komazawa University

See Also: China; Globalization; Standardized Testing; Technology Education; Working Parents.

Further Readings

Education in Japan. "Education in Japan: Resources & Networking for Parents & Educators" (October 2007). http://www.education-in-japan.info (Accessed December 2011).

Ministry of Education, Culture, Sports, Science & Technology in Japan (MEXT). "White Paper." http://www.mext.go.jp/english/a02.htm (Accessed December 2011).

Ministry of Internal Affairs and Communications. Statistics Bureau, Director-General for Policy Planning & Statistical Research and Training Institute. "Statistical Handbook of Japan." http://www.stat.go.jp/english/data/handbook/index.htm (Accessed December 2011).

Rohlen, Thomas P. *Japan's High Schools*. Berkeley: University of California Press, 1983.

Jencks, Christopher

Christopher Jencks's (1936–) work focuses on education, social policy, and inequality. Much of his research has explored the degree to which education, family background, genetics, and environmental characteristics influence achievement, labor market outcomes and socioeconomic outcomes. Jencks earned a bachelors and masters of education from Harvard, before enrolling in the sociology department of the London School of Economics. He held faculty positions in the department of sociology at both Harvard (1973–79) and Northwestern University (1979–96), and is currently the Malcolm Wiener Professor of Social Policy at the Harvard Kennedy School of Government. Throughout much of Jencks's career, his work has focused on the role of educational institutions in social stratification. Early work investigated stratification in the organization of American higher education and mechanisms of inequality in the distribution of tertiary education. The rise of American universities was accompanied by professionalization and bureaucratization of the academy. At the core of this system are university colleges, the most elite institutions that attract top students and serve as a training ground for graduate education. Special-interest colleges were founded to serve a niche, but stakeholders at these institutions now identify with broader roles than the institution's niche, modeling themselves after university colleges.

This academic revolution did little to change social stratification in America. Efforts to reduce cost or revise curricula did not result in a large enrollment increase of students from the lower strata of society. Instead, Jencks found, the less gifted children of the privileged benefitted most from the expansion of higher education. Jencks's work has also investigated how inequality in early education contributes to stratification in postsecondary education and in the labor market.

Jencks's Theories

Jencks views inequality as a function of many processes, such as: access to and use of educational resources; genotypic, phenotypic, and hereditary characteristics; and family background, socioeconomic status (SES), and environmental factors. Jencks's research found that middle-class students benefit from greater relative access to and utilization of educational resources, noting that these students consume more than their share. Many of the disparities in available resources can be addressed by allowing families the option of enrolling their students in any school in a given district, so that less economically privileged students can access institutions that offer more comprehensive facilities, teachers with higher qualifications, and higher achieving peers. While this would address disparities in access, Jencks notes that it does not address disparities in demand for education.

In his early work, Jencks found little support for the idea that inequalities observed in adulthood could be ameliorated by equalizing educational opportunities. While education was related to occupational destination, it was not found to affect how much individuals earn within a given occupation. Later research by Jencks, though, indicated that increased education can, in fact, reduce income inequality. Jencks's policy suggestions have evolved to reflect this change. Early on, he proposed reform efforts to view education as its own end, rather than a means to another end. More recent suggestions, though, have included cutting class size and eliminating low-skill teachers. Jencks has written on the controversial topic of the relationship between genetics and inequality in society. Interactions between the environment and genes are crucial considerations in the relationship between genes and other outcomes.

These interactions can include how surroundings react to an individual (e.g., differences in how societies treat the sexes) or the way that an individual's reactions to the environment are shaped by genetic characteristics (e.g., those who sunburn easily may tend to avoid prolonged exposure to the sun). Jencks emphasizes the interplay between the environment and genetic inheritance while pushing back on research that assumes a limit to the amount of test score variation that can be explained by environmental factors. It is important to not overemphasize the importance of genetics or assume that genetic inheritance in intelligence might be related to other phenotypic indicators—in more recent studies, Jencks has found that the role of genes in the black–white test score gap is either nonexistent, or very small.

Family background is another important consideration for Jencks. He broadly defines this as any environmental features to which similarities between siblings can be attributed. While the same set of background characteristics would not necessarily be equally applicable across a variety of dependent variables, for educational outcomes, pertinent background characteristics that are shared among siblings might include: household economic indicators; parental education, values, and priorities; neighborhood characteristics; and local institutions, such as schools and churches. Jencks has also made improvements to the abstractions that scholars use to study social stratification.

With Lauri Perman and Lee Rainwater, Jencks developed an index of job desirability—a more comprehensive metric for evaluating labor market position than previous measures of occupational status or income. With Susan Mayer, he proposed a holistic approach to understanding poverty—rather than simply looking at the ratio of income to needs, they set a framework for evaluating material hardship by considering access to food, housing, and medical care.

Jonathan Schwarz
University of Notre Dame

See Also: Class Inequality: Achievement; Concerted Cultivation/Natural Growth; IQ.

Further Readings

Jencks, Christopher. *The Homeless.* Cambridge, MA: Harvard University Press, 1994.

Jencks, Christopher. *Rethinking Social Policy: Race, Poverty, and the Underclass.* Cambridge, MA: Harvard University Press, 1992.

Jencks, Christopher, Lauri Perman, and Lee Rainwater. "What Is a Good Job? A New Measure of Labor-Market Success." *American Journal of Sociology*, v.93/1322–57 (1988).

Jencks, Christopher and Meredith Phillips. *The Black-White Test Score Gap.* Washington, DC: Brookings Institution, 1998.

Jordan

The Hashemite Kingdom of Jordan shares borders with Iraq, the West Bank and Israel, Saudi Arabia, and Syria. Measuring approximately 34,363 square miles (89,213 square kilometers), Jordan has a population of about 6.5 million people. According to the World Bank, the 2011 gross national income (GNI) per capita was $4,380, and the 2010 primary school enrollment was 92 percent. Secondary school participation

from 2007 to 2010, according to the United Nations Children's Fund (UNICEF), was 80 percent for males and 83 percent for females. Youth literacy rates measured from 2005 to 2010 were 99 percent for both males and females, according to UNICEF.

The official language of Jordan is Arabic, and English is widely spoken among the educated classes. Geographically, Jordan sits at the crossroads between Africa, Asia, and Europe. As such, it has historically been integral to trade and commerce across the region. Archeological artifacts from the Paleolithic period to the modern era give testament to Jordan's diverse history and social structures. In ancient times, Jordanian society saw significant evolutionary markers. For example, according to the Embassy of Jordan Web site, the Epipaleolithic period (17,500–8500 B.C.E.) saw the first ancient civilizations of Jordan begin to transform from a nomadic to sedentary society with the domestication of animals and cultivation of crops.

The Neolithic period saw significant growth rates of ancient Jordanian settlements because of new technological innovations such as pottery, new methods for animal husbandry, and new cultivation methods for growing beans and cereals. After World War I, the Ottoman Empire was dissolved, and by mandate, Great Britain ruled over much of the Middle East. By 1950, Great Britain had divided Transjordan from Palestine. Jordan had gained its independence, and had adopted the name of the Hashemite Kingdom of Jordan. In the modern era, scientific and technological research and development are at the forefront of both private and public initiatives.

Jordan's main educational goals are to provide its citizens with lifelong learning skills and to produce an educated population and skilled workforce able to compete in a global knowledge-based economy. Jordan's educational structure is composed of kindergarten (ages 4–5); basic education, including grades one through 10 (ages 6–16); general secondary education, including grades 11 and 12 (ages 17–18); and university education (ages 18–21). The general secondary education includes the choice of: academic secondary education, vocational secondary education, and applied secondary education. At the university level, students may attend universities or community colleges. Preschools and kindergartens are optional in Jordan, and are run by both public and private institutions. By age 6, education is compulsory until the end of 10th grade, when students are tested and classified into academic, vocational, or applied secondary education tracks. While secondary education is free, it is not compulsory. Academic and vocational education curricula include studies in science, literature, and Islamic law. Vocational studies include studies in areas such as nursing, hotel and home economics, and commercial, agricultural, or industrial studies. At the successful completion of 12th grade, students receive a certificate, and may have the choice to apply to universities or community colleges. University-level degrees vary depending on field of study.

Currently, the Jordan Education Initiative is among the leading educational development programs in Jordan. Established in 2003 by World Economic Forum partners, the Jordan Education Initiative program strives to aid teachers to improve learning and teaching. For example, the pilot program offers public school teachers the opportunity to download teaching lessons and tools that will enable them to teach students the educational skills they need to compete with students in developed countries. With successful implementation and results of the Jordan Education Initiative, Jordan strives to become a model to other countries for reforming their educational programs. The Jordan Educational Initiative focuses on areas of research and innovation, and international outreach and collaboration. Some of their current projects include helping members develop skills in: professional development, project management, technical evaluation of technology products, consulting, research and piloting programs, as well as internship programs where members can learn how to bridge theory and practice in educational development.

Bethsaida Nieves
University of Wisconsin, Madison

See Also: Expansion of Education; General Educational Development; Globalization.

Further Readings
Gubser, Peter. *Historical Dictionary of the Hashemite Kingdom of Jordan*. Metuchen, NJ: Scarecrow Press, 1991.
Jordan Education Initiative. http://www.jei.org.jo (Accessed September 2012).
Robins, Philip. *A History of Jordan*. Cambridge, UK: Cambridge University Press, 2004.

K

Kansas

While it is officially known as the Sunflower State, Kansas is also called the Midway State because of its central location within the United States. Kansas shares a northern border with Nebraska and a southern border with Oklahoma. Missouri lies to the east, and Colorado is located to the west. Because Kansas grows more wheat than any other state in the United States, it is often referred to as the "breadbasket of America." The fertile lands of the plains are also used to grow corn and soybean, and to raise cattle. Topeka, the fourth largest city, is the state capital. The largest cities are Wichita, Overland Park, and Kansas City. According to the 2010 census, the population of Kansas is 2,853,118. Like many other states, Kansas began experiencing a budget crisis in the early years of the 21st century. As a result, state legislators slashed $303 million from school funding. Parents and educational advocacy groups responded with rage and filed suit against the state. In 2005, an initial suit was withdrawn when legislators promised to channel $1 billion into the state's schools. When they failed to deliver on that promise, Schools for Fair Funding filed a second suit that is still making its way through the courts.

The area that became Kansas was originally inhabited by the Paleo-Indians between 11,000 and 7000 B.C.E. It was not until the 16th century that the first Europeans arrived. In 1541, Francisco de Coronado, a Spanish explorer, arrived in search of the Seven Golden Cities of Cibola. Coronado had been accompanied by Father Juan de Padilla, who returned the following year in hopes of spreading Christianity to the Native Americans who lived there. However, he was killed by the people whom he had come to help. In 1724, French explorers arrived and began establishing trading relations with the natives. Two decades later, Spain wrested control of the area from the French. In 1803, President Thomas Jefferson purchased the area as part of the Louisiana Purchase, and Kansas became part of the route for the Lewis and Clark Expedition. In 1830, Native Americans were relocated westward under the Indian Removal Bill as the white population grew. By the middle of the 19th century, there was an ongoing debate over whether Kansas should become slave or free. Ultimately, Kansas became a state in 1861, the year that the Civil War began, and entered the war on the side of the Union, losing more men to the war than any other state.

The first school established in Kansas was the Shawnee Methodist School in 1829, on land that is now part of greater Kansas City. In 1844, the first free school was built by the Wyandot tribe. Five years later, the Kaw Mission School was established by the Methodist Episcopal Church. In 1851, the mission became the first school in Kansas for the children of settlers. In the late 19th century, the state began to move toward standardizing education, establishing a statewide curriculum plan for elementary schools, and later for high schools. At the time, each of the 9,284 schools made

Table 1 Elementary and secondary education characteristics

	Kansas	U.S. (average)
Total number of schools	1,470	1,988
Total students	483,701	970,278
Total teachers	34,643.80	60,766.56
Pupil/teacher ratio	13.96	15.97

Source: U.S. Department of Education, National Center for Education Statistics, Common Core of Data (CCD), 2010–11.

Table 2 Elementary and secondary education finance

	Kansas	U.S. (average)
Total revenues	$5,528,071,490	$11,464,385,994
Total expenditures for education	$5,168,120,006	$11,712,033,839
Total current expenditures	$4,633,517,321	$9,938,906,259

Source: U.S. Department of Education, National Center for Education Statistics, Common Core of Data (CCD), "National Public Education Financial Survey," FY08 (2007–08).

up their school districts. A State Board of Education was installed in 1915. In the mid-20th century, Kansas became the center of one of the most famous court cases in American history when the father of Linda Brown, an African American, sued Topeka, challenging the separate-but-equal doctrine that allowed states to set up separate schools for white and black children. In 1954, in *Brown v. Board of Education of Topeka*, the Supreme Court held that the doctrine was unconstitutional, setting the stage for integration of public schools throughout the United States. In 1989, as an adult, Linda Brown sued Topeka on the grounds that schools in Kansas were still not fully integrated.

There are 474,489 students enrolled in schools in Kansas, 76.6 percent Title I schools. The student population is predominately white (68.8 percent), with smaller groups of African Americans (7.7 percent), Hispanics (15.7 percent), and Asian/Pacific Islanders (2.5 percent). Native Americans make up only 1.2 percent of students in Kansas. There are 1,458 schools in 316 school districts. Kansas has 35 charter schools. There are 3,700 teachers, and the student-teacher ratio is 13.7. Students consistently rank higher than the national average on achievement tests in mathematics, reading, and writing. In 2008, Kansas had a high school dropout rate of 75 percent. There were major

racial and ethnic differences in those who finished high school and those who did not. Asian students (84 percent) were more likely to obtain a diploma, followed by whites (81 percent), Native Americans (61 percent), and African Americans (59 percent). The lowest rate was found among Hispanic students, with only 55 percent completing high school. Estimated lost lifetime income of those who did not obtain a high school diploma was $2.6 billion.

When Congress funded President Barack Obama's Race to the Top program in 2009, states were invited to vie for education grants. Kansas was eligible for $166 million in funding. Placing 29th among the 40 states that applied, Kansas failed to make the first cut because of the lack of a statewide system for evaluating teachers and principals, and the failure to tie teacher compensation to student performance. In April 2010, officials announced that Kansas was dropping out of the second round of competitions because the state was unwilling make the changes dictated by the Obama administration.

Elizabeth Rholetter Purdy
Independent Scholar

See Also: Race to the Top; Racial Inequality: High-School Dropout Rates; Student/Teacher Ratio.

Further Readings

Aarons, Dakarai I. "63 Kansas School Districts Sue Over Millions in Funding Cuts." *Education Week*, v.30/11 (November 10, 2010).

Martinez, S. and L. Snider. "History of Kansas Education." Kansas State Department of Education (September 2001). http://www.ksde.org (Accessed August 2012).

National Center for Education Statistics. "State Profiles: Kansas." http://nces.ed.gov/nationsreportcard/states (Accessed February 2012).

Ryan, James E. *Five Miles Away, a World Apart: One City, Two Schools, and the Story of Educational Opportunity in Modern America.* New York: Oxford University Press, 2010.

Kentucky

The Commonwealth of Kentucky is a southern state in the United States, bordered on the north by Illinois,

Indiana, and Ohio; on the east by West Virginia and Virginia; on the west by Missouri; and to the south by Tennessee. The area now known as Kentucky was largely inhabited by various Native American tribes until approximately 1650, particularly in the waterway and game areas. Kentucky became the 15th state admitted to the union on June 1, 1792. The state is known for bluegrass music, a subgenre of country music, which takes its roots from Scottish and Welsh immigrants to Appalachian areas and African American influences from jazz music.

The state is famous for hosting the Kentucky Derby horse race for 3-year-old horses the first Saturday in May in Louisville. The rich soil in Kentucky aids in the growth of bluegrass, the state's nickname, and supports a strong agricultural economy, including horse breeding, goat farming, and beef cattle production. The state has recently diversified its economy by expanding opportunities in manufacturing and automobile assembly. Kentucky was one of the border states during the American Civil War. Although there was movement to secede from the Union, the state remained neutral and sympathetic to Union causes.

Kentucky has 174 school districts, containing 1,233 public schools, servicing 675,298 students. Home schooling is an option for Kentucky families, and 16,493 students were home schooled in 2010 to 2011. The chief state school officer is the commissioner of education, appointed by the 11-member Kentucky Board of Education. Board members are appointed by the governor and the board also includes the executive director of Higher Education as a nonvoting member. Geographically, Kentucky's Appalachian region in the eastern part of the state remained somewhat isolated from the rest of the state. Limited roads restricted development of the region, delaying the progress made to the education of children in the region. Dropout rates in Kentucky were persistently high, and as was common in other southern states, state funding for schools was well below the national average. In 1985, a consortium of school districts, boards of education, and public school students joined in a class-action lawsuit, challenging the discriminatory and inefficient nature of Kentucky's schools.

The Kentucky Supreme Court declared education to be a fundamental right under state law, and the court mandated the state legislature to authorize and monitor a system that was equitable for all children in Kentucky. Following the landmark finance case

Rose v. Council for a Better Education, Kentucky was forced to overhaul its educational and finance system. The result was the Kentucky Education Reform Act (KERA). KERA caused an overhaul of the entire educational system in the state, and required control of local education to shift to the state level. KERA required five major structural changes in the way that public education was organized in the state: move from an "inputs" system to an "outputs" system, looking at achievement, rather than specific resources put into schools; development of school sanctions and rewards; move to school-based performance assessment program based on new state curriculum standards; a shift to school-based decision making; and provisions for professional development. Elements of KERA were examined and adopted in other states.

In 2009, Kentucky passed Senate Bill 1, the Unbridled Learning accountability bill, which focuses on college and career-ready expectations, support for effective instruction, accountability for schools and districts, and reducing duplication in reporting requirements. The state has put great emphasis in providing advanced study opportunities to prepare students for postsecondary study. The Kentucky Virtual High School has offered online courses for students, on a per-course fee basis, since 2000. All Kentucky stu-

Table 1 Elementary and secondary education characteristics

	Kentucky	U.S. (average)
Total number of schools	1,577	1,988
Total students	673,128	970,278
Total teachers	42,041.84	60,766.56
Pupil/teacher ratio	16.01	15.97

Source: U.S. Department of Education, National Center for Education Statistics, Common Core of Data (CCD), 2010–11.

Table 2 Elementary and secondary education finance

	Kentucky	U.S. (average)
Total revenues	$6,561,268,205	$11,464,385,994
Total expenditures for education	$6,803,419,970	$11,712,033,839
Total current expenditures	$5,822,550,446	$9,938,906,259

Source: U.S. Department of Education, National Center for Education Statistics, Common Core of Data (CCD), "National Public Education Financial Survey," FY08 (2007–08).

dents are eligible to take courses. Public school districts may pay fees if the course is required for graduation, but students who are participating for credit recovery or advanced placement options may be responsible for their fees. Students at private or parochial schools, or who are home schooled, are also eligible to participate, but are responsible for paying course fees. Kentucky also offers a commonwealth diploma to students who take a precollege curriculum and successfully pass several Advanced Placement (AP) or International Baccalaureate (IB) courses and pass at least three of the associated examinations. In addition, the state offers higher education tuition scholarships for students to obtain advanced education in Kentucky, based upon their high school grades. Home schooled students and those who earn a GED are also eligible, based upon college entrance examination scores. Kentucky is home to eight public universities, two research universities (University of Kentucky and University of Louisville), and six regional universities.

As a southern state, Kentucky has struggled to erase the negative stereotypes associated with decades of inequitable and inadequate funding for its public schools. The state has placed great emphasis on advanced study in high schools, and higher education tuition support for students who successfully complete advanced coursework in high school. Following implementation of KERA, progress was made in improving educational outcomes for students. Kentucky was one of the first states to be granted a waiver from the federal mandates of No Child Left Behind. The waiver allows Kentucky to focus on one accountability system, its Unbridled Learning system, enacted in 2009. Rural education continues to be a struggle for Kentucky. Keeping children from the most remote parts of the state connected through technology, and equipping rural school with the proper resources for student success, continue to be challenges for the state. High school dropouts and adult literacy continue to be challenges for the state.

Belinda M. Cambre
University of New Orleans

See Also: At-Risk Students; No Child Left Behind; Schools as Bureaucracies.

Further Readings
Ellis, William. *A History of Education in Kentucky.* Lexington: University Press of Kentucky, 2011.

Klotter, James and Freda Klotter. *A Concise History of Kentucky*, Lexington: University Press of Kentucky, 2008.

Steffy, Betty. *The Kentucky Education Reform: Lessons for America.* Lanham, MD: R&L Education Publishing, 1993.

Kenya

Kenya is a former British colony, with an educational history marked by the continuous struggle for Free Primary Education (FPE). This is impacted by its many ethnic groups and languages and the physical environment of the region. The ongoing HIV/AIDS epidemic and other public health issues weigh heavily on this country. FPE has been a major focus of Kenyan politics since independence. The most recent reforms, of 2003, have had significant success, and the new constitution of 2010 includes reforms in terms of gender equality, ethnic and religious minorities, and children with disabilities.

Currently, the government provides eight years of free primary education, and promotes four years of secondary and four years of tertiary education. There are still many barriers to education in Kenya. It is traditional for children to wear uniforms, and many children remain home if they cannot afford a uniform. Other costs include books, supplies, and work hours lost by sending a child away from the farm or from caring for younger children or sick parents. Dropout and repetition rates have remained high, and only about half proceed from primary to secondary school. Children work toward two main examinations to receive the Kenya Certificate of Primary Examination (KCPE), and subsequently the Kenya Certificate of Secondary Education (KCSE). Classes taught in school are meant to prepare for these exams, and most schools are reluctant to provide any extraneous courses.

Only about 10 to 15 percent of children with disabilities attend school in Kenya, and the most recent constitutional reforms have attempted to increase this number. Schools are given small stipends to make them more "disability friendly," and there have been increasing educational and assessment campaigns to reach rural parents. Kenya boasts some of the only secondary schools for the deaf in eastern Africa, and when compared to its neighbors, it provides more resources for children with disabilities. Kenya has a generalized HIV/AIDS epidemic. While the average prevalence is about 6 percent and shows a decline in recent years, in the Nyanza province, as many as one in four women have HIV. There are over one million children orphaned by HIV/AIDS, and teachers are also a higher-risk group for infection. Educational efforts to reduce new infections and increase antiretroviral use are integrated into public school curriculum, and even into university-level courses.

The current borders of Kenya enclose the lands and peoples of over 42 distinct ethnic groups, each with distinct languages, religious customs, and histories. Major tribes include Kikuyu, Luo, Kalenjin, Luhya, Kamba, Kisii, Mijikenda, Somali, and Meru. While English is the official language, Kiswahili is considered the national language, and each Kenyan refers to the language of their village and ethnic group as their "mother tongue." Children grow up speaking a combination of all three, and more, to different extents, and both English and Kiswahili are taught as subjects in school. The main religions are Christianity and Islam, though these and other minority religions are also influenced by traditional religious beliefs of each tribe. Christian and religious education is a major subject taught daily in public schools, though its content includes topics such as science and civics. The postelection violence of 2007 and 2008 has its roots in the traditional tensions between different ethnic groups. Though traditionally tribes have been ethnically separate, in recent years many young Kenyans have intermarried and given their children ethnically neutral names, reflecting a change in Kenyan culture.

Over 80 percent of Kenya is described as arid and semiarid lands (ASALs), host to tribes who are traditionally nomadic and at constant risk of famine from drought, making traditional schooling a challenge. ASALs also stretch along the northern border of Kenya, adjacent to Somalia, making them extremely volatile and dangerous regions for travel, as well as common sites of refugee camps from the neighboring politically unstable countries. Most Kenyans live in the coastal or lake basin lowlands, some of which lie directly on the Equator. The Nyanza and Western provinces are lush, hilly lands, with heavy rainy seasons from March to May and October to December. Travel is difficult during these times, and while most schools have access to some power and clean water, during these rainy seasons, such resources are prob-

lematic. Malaria is endemic and water-borne illnesses are a major problem during rainy seasons when the normally clean water sources become contaminated with sewage runoff.

Nalini Asha Biggs
University of Oxford

See Also: Rwanda; South Africa; Sudan; Tanzania; Uganda.

Further Readings

Abagi, O. "The Impact of Politicised Educational Reforms on Quality of Primary Education: Experience From Kenya." In *Educational Dilemmas: Debate and Diversity, Quality in Education*. Vol. 4. K. Watson, C. Modgil, and S. Modgil, eds. London: Cassell, 1997.

Ackers, J. and F. Hardman. "Classroom Interaction in Kenyan Primary Schools." *Compare: A Journal of Comparative and International Education*, v.31/2 (2001).

Pontefract, Caroline and Frank Hardman. "The Discourse of Classroom Interaction in Kenyan Primary Schools." *Comparative Education*, v.41/1 (2005).

Kerckhoff, Alan C.

Alan Kerckhoff (1924–2001) was an American sociologist noted for his contributions to sociology of education through his work on the status attainment model, examining how structural conditions affect education and labor force outcomes. He applied these models cross-culturally, comparing intergenerational and career mobility rates and patterns across Western industrial societies, namely the United States and Great Britain, and later, with France and Germany.

Kerckhoff's work comes out of the status attainment literature of the 1960s, taking Peter Blau's and Otis Duncan's model of status attainment as a starting point for many of his analyses. In the original model, socioeconomic status was linked to educational attainment, and then both were linked to first and subsequent occupational attainments. Early elaborations of this, namely the Wisconsin model, included social-psychological variables to help explain educational and occupational outcomes. However, Kerckhoff recognized the absence and importance of including structural conditions in the models to account for variation in opportunity, achievement, and outcomes. To this end, he proposed an alternative to the status attainment model. The allocation model, as he called it, took into account structural factors, such as school type and ability group placement, that may sort students into differing paths of opportunity and achievement. Up until this point, many of the additions to the status attainment literature involved socialization factors, such as motives, skills, and ability, and structural conditions had been largely overlooked in empirical research.

Not only did his work focus on the link between education and labor force in terms of achievements and placements, it also explored how a child progresses through the educational system. In *Diverging Pathways*, Kerckhoff explored the existence, magnitude, and path of cumulative advantages and disadvantages in education, and the later impacts of educational placement and achievement on labor force outcomes. He longitudinally studied a cohort of British males from age 7 to 23, examining their pathways at five separate points in time. Here, he found that schools served as sorting mechanisms, affecting opportunities for students. He observed a cyclical process, whereby a student's location in school affected his/her achievement, which then later affected his/her placement. Current and past structural locations and achievement affected later outcomes. Kerckhoff also found that as students progressed through schools, because of the cumulative effects that structure had on opportunity and achievement, their pathways tended to diverge more and more, creating a wide distribution of attainment.

Much of the work on status attainment had focused heavily on the early education stages. Although the influence of social origin and ability are important for understanding educational attainment, Kerckhoff called for more research and theoretical developments to understand the link between education and occupational outcomes, particularly as there may be different structural factors and processes at play in each context. In this vein, he compared status attainment and mobility cross-culturally, focusing on the organization of educational systems to help understand differences in mobility across societies. Since occupational levels followed similar hierarchies across Western industrial societies, the educational system provided a better explanation for observed differences between nations.

Kerckhoff's additions to the status attainment model, focusing on the education–labor force link, along with his work with a cohort of British men for *Diverging Pathways*, influenced and contributed to life-course research. His inclusion and focus on structural factors also helped explain and set the context for larger issues of racial and gender inequality in educational and occupational attainments. With this theoretical approach, researchers can examine where students start in the educational hierarchy, and link that to where they have the opportunity to end up, both in education and the labor force. His empirical contributions provided a continual link between early childhood and adulthood, and also helped set the stage for larger stratification discussions, such as the reproduction of inequality and the accumulation of advantages and disadvantages over the life course. His ability grouping findings stimulated and added to the discussion of their role in schools. Specifically, Kerckhoff found that student achievement gains were affected by ability group placement. Students in high groups gained more, and students in low groups gained less than they would have if they were in mixed ability classes.

This finding questions the use of ability grouping in schools in terms of equal opportunities for students. Although he did not call to completely remove ability grouping from schools, he questioned how its use could be retooled to better serve all students, not just the high achievers. This call to action influenced future work in ability grouping, looking at curriculum differences and the organization of schools.

Kristi Lynn Donaldson
University of Notre Dame

See Also: Ability Grouping; Life Course Perspective and Education; Status Attainment.

Further Readings

Blau, Peter M. and Otis D. Duncan. *The American Occupational Structure.* New York: Wiley and Sons, 1967.

Kerckhoff, Alan C. *Diverging Pathways: Social Structure and Career Deflections.* New York: Cambridge University Press, 1993.

Kerckhoff, Alan C. "Education and Social Stratification Processes in Comparative Perspective." *Sociology of Education,* v.74 (2001).

Kerckhoff, Alan C. "Institutional Arrangements and Stratification Processes in Industrial Societies." *Annual Review of Sociology*, v.21 (1995).

Kerckhoff, Alan C., Stephen W. Raudenbush, and Elizabeth Glennie. "Education, Cognitive Skill, and Labor Force Outcomes." *Sociology of Education*, v.74/1 (2001).

Myles, John F. and Aage B. Sørensen. "Elite and Status Attainment Models of Inequality of Opportunity." *Canadian Journal of Sociology*, v.1/1 (Spring 1975).

Schoon, Ingrid. "A Transgenerational Model of Status Attainment: the Potential Mediating Role of School Motivation and Education." *National Institute Economic Review*, v.205/72–82 (July 2008).

L

Labor Education

Labor education is an applied, multidisciplinary field providing classes and programs for and about working people and the labor movement. Labor education takes place in both trade unions and colleges and universities. Increasingly, education about workers' rights also takes place in community-based organizations and workers' centers. Historically, labor education came from workers education programs that emerged during the Industrial Revolution.

Fundamental to their purpose was improving the lives of workers, both culturally and economically, and increasing the power of working people in society. After World War II, labor education programs were established at land-grant universities in the United States to produce graduates who could function effectively in the new legal environment of the New Deal, under which labor unions were given legal standing and protection. In 1976, there were over 42 programs in the United States and Canada. In 2010, there were about 36, reflecting the decline in union membership as jobs moved overseas, changes in technology, and the increasing conservatism of the political environment, including academia. Within colleges and universities in the United States, two traditions of labor education exist. One flows from the workers education programs, advocates for workers, and draws on the theoretical approach of the Brazilian Paulo Freire and Myles Horton, both popular educators. The other,

known as the industrial relations (IR) model, takes a more neutral perspective, emphasizing labor peace through dispute resolution and the minimization of conflict between employers and employees through the collective bargaining process. The IR approach derives from Sidney and Beatrice Webb in Britain, John Commons at the University of Wisconsin, and the institutional economists.

Staffing and Program Delivery

Education departments in unions (sometimes called "training departments") are typically small, with one or two staff. Often, the actual teaching of labor education is carried out within organizing departments or by union representatives who are not primarily educators. Delivery of programs may be occasioned by an upcoming campaign or response to a change in the legal or economic environment. Unions often contract with college and university labor education programs to develop and deliver curriculum. Labor education programs at colleges and universities range in size from one to nine positions, some tenure-track with significant research and publication requirements, but many outside the tenure system. They may be situated in schools of social work, economics, business schools, and schools of labor and employment relations, while some are free-standing programs. They are often linked to associate's and bachelor's programs in labor studies, the closely related academic (as compared to applied) sister discipline to labor education. Extension courses are typically noncredit certificate classes on a semester calendar, day-long workshops or conferences, and multi-day or weeklong schools, offered both on campus and throughout the state or community where the institution is located in local union halls or community centers. They do not lead to a degree. Once free or low cost as part of the land grant mission (like agricultural extension), they are now paid.

Curriculum

Core classes common to both trade union and college and university programs focus on skills that are immediately applicable to the workplace: shop floor representation, grievance handling, contract negotiation, health and safety, labor law, changes in technology and their impact on workers, organizing, and labor history. In the trade union setting, the curriculum is likely to be tailored to that particular workforce, or to address a particular challenge facing the union. In the academy, where workers from different sectors are likely to gather in the same class, the curriculum may be more general.

Also common in the academy are classes that draw from related fields, following the workers' education model, to provide a broad foundation for understanding the experience of work, such as international relations, communications and the media, ethnic and gender studies, economics, and political science. Like the early workers' education programs, they may also weave basic skills or the humanities, including music, art, drama, and especially history into the curriculum. Because labor education focuses on the relationships among workers and between workers and employers, which are regulated by national and state bodies and the courts, the specific content and delivery of labor education varies by location and the historical moment. For example, the passage of the Occupational Safety and Health Act in 1970 led to the creation of a large network of Committee on Occupational Safety and Health (COSH) groups dedicated to teaching the implementation of that law, which in turn worked with unions and college and university programs. The passage of the Family and Medical Leave Act (FMLA) in 1994 created the need for yet another curriculum.

History

Workers' education as an adult education movement was often shaped and led by workers. Organized workers' education associations emerged in the United States in parallel with those in Europe. In the late 1800s, the flow of European immigrants to the U.S. labor force helped spread socialist and sometimes anarchist ideas. The workers' education movement in Britain was split when more radical Marxist elements left Ruskin College at Oxford and relocated to London, leaving the others to affiliate with Oxford University to earn diplomas in applied economics and politics. The tensions that this split reflected are alive in labor education today. In the United States, labor education programs appeared sponsored by individual unions or organizations, such as the International Ladies Garment Workers Union (ILGWU), the Industrial Department of the Young Women's Christian Association (YWCA), the Trade Union Educational League (TUEL), settlement houses, and independently, notably Brookwood Labor College in Katonah, New York (1921–37), the Bryn Mawr Summer School for Women Workers (est. 1921), the Highlander Research and Education Center in Tennessee (1932), and the Labor Schools related to the Communist Party in the 1930s and 1940s. The big increase in the number of university and college-based labor education programs at land grant institutions came after World War II to train people to work in the new collective bargaining environment.

Professional Associations

There are two main professional associations for labor educators. One is the Labor and Employment Relations Association (LERA). LERA brings together labor side, management side, academic, and "neutral" (e.g., arbitrators, mediators, and government agency staff) actors in the employment relations context, with a focus on research. The other is the United Association for Labor Education (UALE), which focuses on education and research as it supports labor educators and their programs. UALE is the organizational descendent of the faculty union at Brookwood Labor College. It is also a member of the International Federation of Worker Education Associations (IFWEA).

Helena Worthen
University of Illinois, Champaign

See Also: Adult Education; Freire, Paulo; Unions of Teachers.

Further Readings

Burke, Bev, Jojo Geronimo, D'Arcy Martin, Barb Thomas, and Carol Wall. *Education for Changing Unions.* Toronto: Between the Lines, 2002.

Dwyer, Richard E. *Labor Education in the U.S.* Lanham, MD: Scarecrow Press, 1977.

Freire, Paulo. *Pedagogy of the Oppressed.* New York: Continuum, 1992.

Horton, Myles, Herbert Kohl, and Judith Kohl. *The Long Haul, an Autobiography.* New York: Teachers College Press, 1997.

Newman, Michael. *The Third Contract: Theory and Practice in Trade Union Training.* Sydney, Australia: Victor Publishing, 1993.

Werthheimer, Barbara, ed. *Labor Education for Women Workers.* Philadelphia: Temple University Press, 1981.

Labor Market Effects on Education

Schools and labor markets have a variety of mutual influences. While there is more research on the effects of the educational characteristics of individuals on their subsequent labor market outcomes, the effects of labor markets on education are equally sociologically significant. The various effects of labor markets on education operate at individual, organizational, and institutional levels. Labor markets influence the behavior of high school and postsecondary students primarily by providing the sort of information and motivation that inculcates educational and occupational aspirations and expectations. Students at all levels orient their educational behavior and cognition toward their anticipated or desired occupational futures. To varying degrees students perceive their educational experiences as preparation for the workplace and select coursework and programs of study commensurate with their anticipated career trajectories. Economic and financial success are among the most important goals held by young people, as shown by A. W. Astin.

But while high school and college students are highly motivated by their perceptions of the labor market, these perceptions are often inaccurate and ill-formed. This disjuncture between perceptions and reality is probably greater than it was for earlier generations, according to F. Carp. Recent research shows that student aspirations and the behaviors that they base on these aspirations are often not a well-considered and rational response to the realities of the labor market. Many students misread labor market signals. B. Schneider and D. Stevenson report that contemporary students are less likely than students of past generations to properly "align" their aspirations with labor market demands. Many of the students in their study had ambitious aspirations for labor market success, but had failed to take the coursework required to attain these positions.

J. Warren and C. Hamrock, counter to the predictions of human capital theory, found no evidence that increases in the minimum wage lowered the rate of high school completion. They observed that few students base their dropout decisions on rational assessments of labor market conditions. I. Beattie found that racial, class, and gender groups responded differently to labor market conditions when making educational investment decisions. White men from lower socioeconomic origins and with lower cognitive skills behaved most in accord with human capital theory of rational cost-benefit analysis, while women and minorities more often seemed to rely on calculi reflecting less rational norms.

Labor Market Effects on Organizational Behavior

The effects of labor markets on educational institutions are strong and persistent, and have probably grown stronger over the past several decades. Both secondary and postsecondary educational institutions have become more vocationalized over time, in that educators have become increasingly attuned and responsive to the stated needs of the business community and the reputed skill demands of a globalized and competitive economy, as noted by H. Kliebard. While course taking in traditional vocational education classes has recently declined in American high schools, contemporary college preparatory curricula typically have the stated purpose of providing access to postsecondary credentials, which are directly tied to remunerative employment opportunities.

Calls for schooling for the purposes of personal growth or citizenship are heard much less often in such a vocationalized environment. Higher education has also become increasingly oriented toward the labor market. In virtually all societies, a large edifice of credentials, certification, licensing, and professionalization link school experiences with labor market expectations and outcomes. Enrollments in professional and preprofessional university programs have steadily displaced traditional liberal arts offerings that lack a specific occupational clientele. The rapid growth in community colleges since World War II further signals the response of educators and educational policymakers to the perceived needs of the labor market.

Corporate Influence on Schools

Many analysts have lamented the corporate influence on schools. In his classic *Education and the Cult of Efficiency: A Study of the Social Forces That Have Shaped the Administration of the Public Schools* (1962), R. Callahan argues that schools long ago fell under the influence of a business model at the expense of an educational model. More recent observers, such as D. Labaree, maintain that schools have compromised their mission of producing informed democratic citizens in favor of a focus on providing the requisite credentials for social mobility and the development of a nationally competitive stock of human capital. Evidence for this effect of labor markets on education can be found in efforts by employers to influence school curricula, promote collaborations or partnerships between the educational and business communities, and corporate lobbying efforts to influence the educational sector. Others see these corporate initiatives to influence schools as more benign, and have even expressed concern that schools are insufficiently attuned to the needs of the workplace. Some observers, such as T. Bailey, see both secondary and postsecondary schools as too detached from the needs of the labor market, and advocate a greater focus on workplace skills. This impulse has been expressed in such policy initiatives as the 1994 School to Work Opportunities Act.

Labor markets have come to affect education on a broader institutional level. As J. Meyer and his colleagues have argued, schooling and labor markets attain their social legitimacy and cultural meaning largely because of their reciprocity. Under this understanding, the institutionalization of education and labor markets provides societies with legitimate ways to staff complex work organizations with people defined in terms of their broadly recognized credentials and certification.

David Bills
Christopher Swanson
University of Iowa

See Also: Career and Technical Education; Community Colleges; School-to-Work Transitions.

Further Readings

Astin, A. W. *What Matters in College: Four Critical Years Revisited.* San Francisco: Jossey-Bass, 1997.

Bailey, T. "The Integration of Work and School: Education and the Changing Workplace." In *Education Through Occupations in American High Schools,* W. N. Grubb, ed. New York: Teachers College Press, 1995.

Beattie, Irene R. "Are All 'Adolescent Econometricians' Created Equal? Racial, Class, and Gender Differences in College Enrollment." *Sociology of Education,* v.75/1 (2002).

Callahan, R. E. *Education and the Cult of Efficiency: A Study of the Social Forces That Have Shaped the Administration of the Public Schools.* Chicago: University of Chicago Press, 1962.

Carp, F. M. "High School Boys Are Realistic About Occupations." *Occupations,* v.28 (1949).

Kliebard, H. M. *Schooled to Work: Vocationalism and the American Curriculum, 1876–1946.* New York: Teachers College Press, 1999.

Labaree, D. F. *How to Succeed in School Without Really Learning: The Credentials Race in American Education.* New Haven, CT: Yale University Press, 1997.

Meyer, J. W. "The Effects of Education as an Institution." *American Journal of Sociology,* v.83 (1977).

Schneider, B. and D. Stevenson. *The Ambitious Generation: America's Teenagers, Motivated but Directionless.* New Haven, CT: Yale University Press, 1999.

Warren, John Robert and Caitlin Hamrock. "The Effect of Minimum Wage Rates on High School Completion." *Social Forces,* v.88 (2010).

Laos

Laos (Lao People's Democratic Republic) was part of the kingdom of Lan Xang, established under King Fa Ngum in the 14th century, which also included parts of Thailand and Cambodia. It was dominated by Thailand from the late 18th to the late 19th century, when it was colonized by France and became, along with Vietnam and Cambodia, part of French Indochina until the decisive military victory by the Viet Minh at the battle of Dien Bien Phu in 1954. In 1975, the Lao monarchy was ended by the Pathet Lao, who were closely aligned with the Indochinese Communist Party founded by Ho Chi Min in Vietnam. The communist state that was established continues to the present. Laos is a landlocked, mountainous country in southeast Asia, nestled between Thailand and Vietnam in the east and west, respectively, bordered by China and Myanmar in the north, and Cambodia in the south. The 6.5 million population includes 49 ethnic groups, with the largest Lao (55 percent), Khmou (11 percent), and Hmong (8 percent). Two-thirds of the people are Buddhist. Among people age 15 and over, 83 percent of males and just 63 percent of females are literate. Life expectancy for males is 62 years, for females it is 64 years. With a per capita gross national index of $1,050, Laos is among the least developed countries in the world, ranking in the bottom quartile. Even though only 4 percent of the land is arable, 75 percent of the workforce is engaged in agriculture. Rural areas are hard to reach because of a lack of paved roads. Telecommunications infrastructure is also limited. In 2010, international donors provided 43 percent of government expenditures.

The education system established during the French colonial period was replaced by a Russian-style system during the 1980s. Combined primary and secondary education totaled just 11 years, and the only available postsecondary education was for teachers. There was no comprehensive university that included research and graduate programs. After the collapse of the Soviet Union in 1990, however, Laos was forced to look to other international donors to support reform of the education system.

In the early 1990s, the Lao government began receiving support from the Asian Development Bank to formulate a systematic approach to improving its education system in ways that would increase attendance rates of females and the poor, serve the diverse ethnic populations living in remote areas, improve quality, and make graduates more competitive for jobs in the emerging, increasingly market-oriented economy, both inside the country and in the southeastern Asia region. This effort culminated in the document, Education Sector Development Framework 2009–2015 (ESDF), the basic plan for education reform in the country.

Basic education had increased to 12 years (five years of primary school, four years of lower secondary, and three years of upper secondary). This will require building more classrooms nationwide, recruiting and training additional teachers, as well as improving the skills of school administrators. ESDF puts particular emphasis on increasing the numbers of females in administrative roles (currently less than 10 percent)

and making improvements in the poorest districts in the country. The ESDF incorporates the concept of inclusive education, recognizing its importance for reducing barriers to formal school attainment. It "involves pro-poor approaches to social development," including targeting girls, children with disabilities, ethnic minorities, and children living in isolated areas. It includes increasing adult literacy through nonformal education, as well as ensuring greater and more effective participation of girls and women in civil society. The national strategy is to expand upper secondary education gradually, especially in vocational education. Postsecondary technical education will also be expanded.

Overall, there is a greater emphasis on responding to the demands of the labor market, including emerging manpower needs. Finally, ESDF calls for expanding higher education enrollments, not only to meet the increasing demand for teachers, but also to meet labor market demands for highly educated workers. Across all levels of education, there is an emphasis on improving quality through curriculum reform and improving facilities. Funding is to come from a variety of sources, including government allocations, donors, and the introduction of student, fees with scholarship and loan schemes established to support low-income students.

John Weidman
University of Pittsburgh
Keiichi Ogawa
Kobe University

See Also: Alternative and Second Chance Education; Cambodia; Thailand; Vietnam.

Further Readings
Hirosato, Yasushi and Yuto Kitamura, eds. *The Political Economy of Educational Reform and Capacity Development in Southeast Asia: Cases of Cambodia, Laos and Vietnam.* New York: Springer-Verlag, 2008.
Noonan, Richard. "Education in the Lao People's Democratic Republic: Confluence of History and Vision." In *Education in South-East Asia*, Colin Brock and Lorraine Pe Symaco, eds. Oxford: Symposium Books, 2011.
Weidman, John C. "Restructuring the University Pedagogical Institute of Laos: An Outsider's View." In *Higher Education in the Post-Communist World*, Paula Sabloff, ed. New York: Taylor & Francis, 1999.

Lareau, Annette

Annette Lareau is a qualitative sociologist who studies the relationships among parents, children, and schools. Her work examines both social class and racial differences among parents. She is currently the Stanley I. Sheerr Professor of Sociology at the University of Pennsylvania. She previously taught at Southern Illinois University (Carbondale), Temple University, and the University of Maryland, College Park.

In addition to many articles, book chapters, and edited books, she has authored two influential books in the sociology of education: *Home Advantage* and *Unequal Childhoods*. Her ethnographic work has helped sociologists to understand how social class plays a role in the ways that parents interact with their children and schools. The book *Home Advantage* is based on Annette Lareau's doctoral dissertation, completed at the University of California, Berkeley. She spent six months conducting participant observation in two first grade classrooms—one working class (Colton), and one middle class (Prescott). Additionally, she conducted interviews with teachers, principals, other school personnel, and 12 of the children's mothers. Her focus was on white children. In her studies, she examined teachers' expectations of parents, middle- and working-class parents' relationships with their children's schools and teachers, and the consequences of social class differences in parent-school relationships.

Home-School Interconnectedness

In the schools she studied, she found that all teachers wanted parents to read to their children, reinforce the lessons taught in school, respond to teachers' requests, and show respect to the teacher. This was the case at both Colton and Prescott. Although teachers' expectations were similar across schools, parents at each school approached the school and teachers differently. For middle-class families, school and home were interconnected, while for working-class families, home and school were treated as separate spheres. Colton had low rates of attendance at open houses, very few parent volunteers, and nearly no special requests from parents. Mothers from Colton saw school as equivalent to a job, with set hours and defined boundaries. They saw their responsibility as providing basic necessities for their children at home, and they saw teachers as professionals who were responsible for their children's education. At Prescott, mothers frequently visited their children's classrooms, and attendance rates were extremely high at parent-teacher conferences and open houses. In contrast to the Colton mothers, mothers at Prescott were very aware of what was happening in their children's classrooms. The mothers at Prescott saw their children's schooling as their responsibility and took a very active role in their education. Despite these social class differences, the two groups of mothers were similar in their gendered division of labor. Both Prescott and Colton mothers were the primary individuals involved with the schools, while fathers took on a more peripheral role.

For middle-class children, the biggest benefit from home-school interconnectedness was the ability for parents to customize their children's education. On the other hand, many teachers in the middle class school complained about parents' questioning of their approaches or decisions. For working-class children, the result of parents' lack of involvement was a generic educational experience. Annette Lareau proposed three possible explanations for why middle-class and working-class parents approached their children's schools differently. One explanation was that working-class parents did not value education. Interviews with parents, however, showed that both Colton and Prescott parents valued education very highly and wanted their children to succeed in school. A second explanation was that the schools discriminated against working-class parents and made them feel less welcome.

Based on interviews with school personnel and her observations of parent-teacher interactions, she did not find this to be the case. The final explanation—and the one supported by the ethnographic data—was that different social classes had different cultural resources (cultural capital) that could cause them to act in different ways when interacting with schools. Middle-class parents had relatively high education levels, professional occupations comparable to teachers, friends or relatives who were teachers, and social networks that could provide them with information about different schools and teachers. These resources made middle-class parents much more comfortable in interacting with their children's schools and making efforts to customize their children's educations. Working class families lacked these resources, and thus were in a different position when interacting with schools.

More recently, Annette Lareau completed *Unequal Childhoods*, another study examining social class differences in parenting. Although parent-school relationships were discussed to some extent, more focus was placed on the dynamics within the family, particularly the parenting strategies employed by different social classes. Based on extensive fieldwork, observations, and interviews, she concluded that working-class and poor parents engaged in the accomplishment of natural growth, where parents provided love, shelter, and other basic necessities, but expected the children to develop on their own, through play with other children. In contrast, middle-class parents practiced concerted cultivation, where they fostered their children's growth by involving them in multiple activities, acted on their behalf with authority figures, taught their children to advocate for themselves, and built their children's vocabulary.

Susan A. Dumais
Louisiana State University

See Also: Concerted Cultivation/Natural Growth; Cultural Capital; Ethnography; Parental Involvement; School-Parent Relationships.

Further Readings

Lareau, Annette. *Home Advantage: Social Class and Parental Intervention in Elementary Education.* 2nd ed. Lanham, MD: Rowman & Littlefield, 2000.

Lareau, Annette. *Unequal Childhoods: Race, Class, and Family Life.* 2nd ed. Berkeley: University of California Press, 2011.

Lareau, Annette. "Using the Terms 'Hypothesis' and 'Variable' in Qualitative Work: A Critical Reflection." *Journal of Marriage and the Family*, v.74/4 (2012).

Leadership in Schools

As important as it is in corporations and public organizations, leadership is integral to effectively managing teachers, staff members, and providing quality education to students. Schools with strong leadership tend to be more resource-efficient, have more robust human networks, and are more adept at responding to extreme conditions. Leadership in schools takes on a different shape than in other settings. It is also more diverse from an international perspective. This article will introduce readers to the central discourse of school leadership in the United States as well as its many variants in international contexts.

School Leadership Theories

Much of the existing literature relies on school leaders to reflect on what school leadership is and how it can be effectively practiced. These scholarly approaches, though plausible in their separate efforts, generally failed to recognize that school leadership has much more outliers than many school leaders themselves are aware of. School leadership theories have a non-educational origin thanks largely to James M. Burns who first proposed the notion of "transformational leadership" in 1978. Twenty years later, a few other scholars such as Kenneth Leithwood and Thomas J. Sergiovanni first applied this theory to the field of education. According to this theory, there are six dimensions of transformational leadership including building school visions and goals, intellectual simulation, individualized support, symbolizing professional practices and values, demonstrating high performance expectations, and developing structures to foster participation in school decisions. Despite the repeated efforts of other scholars to strengthen these six dimensions, transformational leadership suffers repeated criticism of not always taking into account the context in which leadership is exercised as well as the continuous attempts of scholars to add other dimensions to account for the weaknesses of the original six dimensions.

A recent theory which is gaining scholarly attention is the notion of "distributive leadership," which advocates a collective form of leadership in which teachers develop expertise and tackle challenges with a collaborative effort. It vetoes the claim that significant decision making comes always from the top administrative hierarchy. It encourages grassroots and individual teacher initiatives as well as decision making from middle- and lower-level administrators. Ultimately the whole school community is able to provide critical feedback and suggestions on how to best align with important issues related to school visions, mission statements, and institutional cultures. Two important things about distributive leadership are worth mentioning. On the one hand, distributive leadership is not a denunciation of leadership charisma; rather it focuses on delegation, inclusion, and leaders working with subordinate colleagues in synergistic networks. On the other hand, distributive leadership is not a passive, top-down delegation of troubling tasks; it is more of an appreciative recognition of required expertise suitable for leading certain tasks. Distributed leadership requires good interpersonal relationships between teachers and administrators as well as the necessity to assign the most qualified person to address specific needs than a de facto reliance on senior leadership in all cases.

Other theories suggest that effective school leadership requires an emphasis on understanding school culture in addition to traditional hierarchical leadership models. William H. Bergquist and Kenneth Pawlak introduced to university leaders six academic cultures including collegial culture, managerial culture, developmental culture, tangible culture, virtual culture, and advocacy culture. A descriptive approach is harnessed to help reveal how the academic culture school leaders keep wrestling so hard with what is actually very fluid in nature based on the realistic school settings. This structural view of school cultures suggests a strong linkage with the distributive leadership theory in the way that leaders at the top now have an approach to meaningful delegation of leadership roles to lower school divisions, based on the compatibility of those divisions with a certain academic culture (e.g., human resource managers often reflect a businesslike managerial culture that one would find in business settings).

School Leadership in a Changing World

School leadership is not exercised in a vacuum. External, national, or international trends and influences must be examined in order to make use of the theories related to school leadership styles, approaches, and methods. Global and regional economic conditions provide strong external influences on school leadership structures. Due to the economic financial crisis that has plagued higher education in many countries in recent years, the authority of managing key university affairs, including curriculum, financing, and human resources is often delegated to mid- and lower-level management (deans and department heads rather than more senior administrators within the university).

One of the reasons that has led to this form of distributive leadership is the eventual paradigmatic shift in thinking of many top-level higher education administrators. In order to fill the financial gap due to large state appropriation cuts in the United States, chancellors and presidents are often forced to assume a bigger role in fundraising and establishing closer networks with local industries and partner higher education institutions. In the meantime, tuition increases in higher education as an approach to ameliorate financial stagnation in some cases has lowered the admissions threshold into American higher education institutions, allowing a growing number of international students to arrive in the United States as long as they are able to pay. The increased level of student (and faculty) diversity calls for a closer scrutiny to the religious, cultural, and linguistic nuances in order to better accommodate those students (and faculty). Mid- and lower- level management and faculty members often have a unique advantage over their more senior administrator counterparts in best addressing the individual and collective leadership needs to accommodate this growing diversity at the higher education level.

School leadership at all levels—primary, secondary, and higher education levels—is under increased pressure to be held more accountable. Public school leaders are accountable for the prudent oversight of limited, and in many cases, reduced public financial resources. Quality assurance practices, including the four principles of good governance—information flow, coordination, transparency, and accountability—are essential skills each school leader must acquire and adapt in his or her respective setting in order to meet the increasing demands forced upon them by their stakeholders at all levels.

International development education agendas also play a significant role in shaping the outcomes of school leadership on a global level. Many countries rely on overseas development assistance and financial aid to help build local leadership capacity. Unfortunately, the brain drain phenomena is the reality of many of the capacity building initiatives, where many of the well-educated leaders who are trained in advanced degrees overseas, never return home to help strengthen the leadership gap that exists. Too often this perpetuates a vicious cycle of leadership deficiency at all school levels. Perhaps the best model for training current and future cadres of school leaders resides in having each country meet its individual leadership training needs. This will prevent overseas training requirements and enable countries to retain their costly investments in local capacity building of school leaders at all levels.

Internationalization is another strong external influence to higher education leadership norms and structure formations. Despite different education systems, internationalization provides increased opportunities to learn from each other in a reciprocal and synergistic manner. The higher education student inpour from developing countries often motivates administrators from countries like the United States, Western Europe, and Australia to revisit traditional leadership models. Conversely, upon graduation, many international students return to their home countries as next-generation leaders, bringing with them advanced skills and revolutionary thinking that will eventually influence the future of education and social structures.

Huiyuan Ye
W. James Jacob
University of Pittsburgh

See Also: Educational Policymakers; Globalization; Higher Education; Policy-Oriented Research; Schools as Bureaucracies.

Further Readings

Bergquist, W. H. and K. Pawlak. *Engaging the Six Cultures of the Academy: Revised and Expanded Edition of the Four Cultures of the Academy*. Hoboken, NJ: John Wiley & Sons, 2007.

Bodla, M. A. and M. M. Nawaz. "Transformational Leadership Style and its Relationship with Satisfaction." *Interdisciplinary Journal of Contemporary Research in Business*, v.2/1 (2010).

Leithwood, K. and D. Jantzi. "The Effects of Transformational Leadership on Organizational Conditions and Student Engagement With School." *Journal of Educational Administration*, v.38/2 (2000).

Shakir, F. J., et al. "Perceptions Towards Distributed Leadership in School Improvement." *International Journal of Business and Management*, v.6/10 (2011).

Zener, K. R. *Understanding Principals' and Lead Teachers' Perceptions of Distributed Leadership in Three High-Performing Public High Schools: An Exploratory Multiple Case Study*. Ann Arbor, MI: ProQuest, 2011.

Lebanon

Located on the Mediterranean coastline, the Republic of Lebanon is often referred to as the "gateway to the Middle East." It is one of the smallest countries in the region, with a total area of 3,861 square miles (10,452 square kilometers). In 2010, Lebanon's population was approximately 4,228,000, and its gross national income per capita was $8,800. Throughout its history, Lebanon has experienced many internal and external political conflicts that have had a lasting influence on the country. However, the economic status of Lebanon is relatively high in comparison with many of its neighboring countries. The average gross domestic product growth is about 9 percent since 2008, one of the highest in the Middle East region. This growth is primarily a result of the construction (and reconstruction) industry, tourism, trade, and financial services. In 2011, the literacy rate was at 90 percent, and total unemployment in the country was estimated at 9 percent.

Because of its location along the Mediterranean, Lebanon was a part of many great empires, including the Egyptian, Roman, and Persian empires. It was part of the Ottoman Empire for hundreds of years, until the end of World War I, when it became part of the French Mandate, until independence in 1946.

The modern history of Lebanon includes a unique social-political structure characterized by religious-political tensions. It comprises as many as 15 different ethnic groups, including the Maronites, Shias, Sunnis, Alawis, Druze, Armenians, and Copts. The governmental system of Lebanon is based on a permanent ratio between Christians and Muslims, according to the country's 1932 census, where members of parliament are divided according to the proportional size of the ethnic groups in 1932. Because of the Muslims' natural growth and the emigration of many Lebanese Christians, the government refrains from collecting current religious affiliation data, which might affect representation in parliament today. Following independence, Lebanon had a relatively stable postcolonial political transition until 1975, when a civil war erupted between militant Maronites and the Palestine Liberation Organization (PLO). Attempting to put an end to the war, Syria and Israel both invaded Lebanon, with Syria taking sides with the PLO, and Israel attempting to block the PLO from advancing to the Lebanese southern border. The civil war continued until 1990, when Israel withdrew to the security zone and the PLO leadership relocated to Tunis. In 2006, another period of conflict left much of the nation's infrastructure in disarray.

The education system in Lebanon is influenced by the pluralistic nature of the country; colonial influences also persist to some degree, and the current curriculum remains influenced by France and the United States. In 2009, the Lebanese government spent 7.2 percent of public expenditure on education, resulting in 85 percent of children completing primary education. The Lebanese education system is supervised by the Ministry of Education and Higher Education (MOEHE). Lebanon has nine years of compulsory education, and follows a national curriculum. The formal education system is structured with different levels, beginning at pre-primary education (for children ages 3–5). Primary education is organized into two cycles of three years each, starting at age 6. Complementary or intermediate education lasts for three years for students 13 to 15 years old.

Secondary education comprises two parallel paths: general education and technical education (ages 15–18). Higher education is regulated by MOEHE, and includes postsecondary technical and vocational education, college, and university. Student admission into higher education institutions hinges upon performance on entrance exams. The academic year in Lebanon is from October to June, and the languages of instruction include Arabic, English, and French. Universities generally offer a three- to five-year study program to obtain a bachelor's degree; for the award of doctorate, the thesis lasts for three years to attain the equivalency of a Ph.D. in the U.S. higher education system. Teachers' training lasts three years, after which they receive a bachelor's degree in elementary and primary school education. The training of secondary school teachers, however, lasts for a five-year period, which also includes the training of higher education teachers.

In 2012, Lebanon was still recovering from years of conflict. The Lebanese are forced to overcome religious disputes, build new infrastructure, and find ways to better incorporate social justice and citizenship into their national curriculum. Since its inception at independence, the Lebanese education system has experienced both successes and challenges, mainly around its unique political structure and sense of national identity compared to a complex religious context. With the help of such organizations as the International Medical Corps and United Nations Educational, Scientific and Cultural Organization (UNESCO), education is strengthened in such venerable areas as South Lebanon, which is control by Hezbollah. New schools and water networks have also been rebuilt or newly established. In addition, teachers are trained to help students and adults improve academic achievements. The literacy rate in the country is one of the highest in the Middle East, however, gender imbalances remain. There are fewer females than males enrolled at all levels, and school textbooks do not have equal representation of men and women. In many cases, women are portrayed in textbooks in their traditional roles in society, thus further perpetuating gender imbalances. Additionally, there is a dearth of sufficient literature in school and university libraries, which hinders education research and dissemination of research findings. Furthermore, the government is currently establishing a national quality assurance agency to oversee quality assurance services at the national level. Recent economic struggles have hindered the Lebanese education system, and the government has had to adapt to these downturns, which often parallel political turmoil experienced in Lebanon and in the volatile Middle Eastern region.

Efrat Avramovich
Joel Dumba
University of Pittsburgh

See Also: Gender Inequality: College Enrollment and Completion; Israel; Syria.

Further Readings
Akar, Bassel. "Citizenship Education in Lebanon: An Introduction into Students' Concepts and Learning Experiences." *Educate*, v.7/2 (2007).
Bahous, Rima and Nabhani, Mona. "Improving Schools for Social Justice in Lebanon." *Improving Schools*, v.11/2 (2008).
International Monetary Fund (IMF). "Lebanon: Staff Report for the 2010 Article IV Consultation." IMF Country Report No.10/306. Washington, DC: IMF, 2010.
Karam, Gebran. "Vocational and Technical Education in Lebanon: Strategic Issues and Challenges." *International Education Journal*, v.7/3 (2006).
Ministry of Education and Higher Education (MOEHE). Lebanon: Education System. Beirut, Lebanon: MOEHE, 2012.

Lesbian, Gay, Bisexual, and Transgender Issues and Schooling

The term *LGBT*, which refers to lesbian, gay, bisexual, and transgender people, was developed during the 1980s and 1990s as an evolving label by those who advocated for a more inclusive description of "gay" issues/rights/communities. Critics of the term *LGBT* assert that collapsing so many groups with disparate experiences and issues problematically homogenizes them. Nonetheless, the term *LGBT* is commonly used as an umbrella term for gender nonconforming people and/or people who engage in same-sex relationships and sexual practices. Although there have always been LGBT people in K–12 schools, targeted advocacy programs aimed to address related obstacles did not begin in the United States until the last decade of the 20th century. Action to improve educational experiences for LGBT students has taken place largely in geographic regions where the larger community is more accepting of LGBT individuals and communities. Though efforts to recognize that schools need to address gender and sexualities in different ways have been under way for over two decades, most public schools in the United States are still unsafe places for students who are perceived to be LGBT. Systemic obstacles for LGBT people in schools include omission from the curriculum, rampant and unchecked bullying, and lack of employment protection for LGBT faculty and staff in schools. Resistance to these and other obstacles, however, is multifaceted and growing.

In the vast majority of school districts in the United States, LGBT issues are systematically omitted from the curriculum. This curricular silence means that most students do not learn about the history of LGBT oppression and resistance in social studies classes, do not read literature with LGBT characters, and do not participate in a wide range of contemporary scientific conversations about human sexuality and/or gender identity. Abstinence-only and other narrow sex-education programs also do not provide important information about the wide range of adolescent sexual experiences. In January 2012, California became the first state in the nation to mandate that LGBT history be included in state-approved social studies textbooks.

School climate refers to the milieu of the institution. For many LGBT students—and for those who are perceived to be LGBT—schools are hostile places. Most students report hearing homophobic remarks in school, and in some instances, teachers are perpetrators of those taunts. Bullying based on perceived sexual orientation and gender nonconformity has a documented negative effect on students' academic, social, and psychological progress. As such, LGBT students have higher truancy and dropout rates than non-LGBT students, and fewer LGBT students have postsecondary educational plans. Negative school experiences are also a major factor in higher suicide rates for LGBT youth than for non-LGBT youth. Fewer than half of the states in the United States have statewide employment laws that ban discrimination on the basis of sexual orientation and/or gender expression. In the places where these are not enumerated categories, it is legal for sexual orientation and/or gender expression to be factors in nonhire and/or employment termination. In anti-union schools, districts, and states, LGBT employees are particularly vulnerable.

Initiatives and Legislation

The safe schools movement, which is a mobilization to improve school climate for LGBT and all students, is occurring at various intensity levels in different locales across the United States. Research consistently demonstrates that there are certain student, faculty, and/or staff-led initiatives that improve school climate. An example of student-led initiatives is the creation of Gay-Straight Alliances (GSAs). Open to all students, GSAs are student clubs that address issues pertinent to LGBT students. Common GSA missions include providing social support for LGBT students and their allies, educating others about LGBT individuals and issues, and advocating for safer schools. Schools that have a GSA are more welcoming than schools without a GSA, as members of the school community are more likely to be educated about the detriments of homophobic language and behavior, which is an important step in improving the climate. The presence of a GSA also allows LGBT students to identify peer and adult allies in the school, which has positive effects on isolated students' development.

Some are opposed to the creation of GSAs, claiming that there is no place for sexuality in schools, and that schools should not be condoning same-sex relationships. The Equal Access Act of 1984, however, provides legal precedence for existence of GSAs. This legislation mandates that if a school allows any extracurricular clubs, the school must allow all extracurricular clubs. Proponents of creating safer schools for LGBT and all students assert that schools are in no way sexuality-free spaces; normative heterosexuality is deeply engrained in schools. In the late 20th and early 21st centuries, LGBT-themed schools have emerged as a response to the verbal and physical violence that LGBT students continue to experience in many other schools. The Harvey Milk High School in New York City and the Alliance School for middle and high school students in Milwaukee, Wisconsin, are examples of such schools.

Jillian C. Ford
Kennesaw State University

See Also: Feminist Critiques of Educational Practices; Sex Education; Single-Sex Education; Youth Cultures and Subcultures.

Further Readings

Campos, David. *Understanding Gay and Lesbian Youth: Lessons for Straight School Teachers, Counselors, and Administrators.* Lanham, MD: Rowman & Littlefield Education, 2005.

Kosciw, Joseph, Emily Greytak, Elizabeth Diaz, and Mark Bartkiewicz. *The 2009 National School Climate Survey: The Experiences of Lesbian, Gay, Bisexual and Transgender Youth in Our Nation's Schools.* New York: GLSEN, 2010.

Quinn, Therese and Erica Meiners. *Flaunt It! Queers Organizing for Public Education and Justice.* New York: Peter Lang, 2009.

Liberal Arts Education

Liberal arts education is an approach to education that focuses on providing a broad educational experience, as well as the opportunity to conduct in-depth study on specific, student-generated topics of interest. Although the goals of liberal arts education vary, they generally revolve around students fostering and developing a strong sense of social responsibility, as well as critical thinking, and analytical and social skills that can be applied to real-world settings. Liberal arts education has a history of placing particular emphasis on knowledge as a process, rather than a product. Liberal arts education continues to ponder and redefine its academic identity to meet the needs of modern-day contexts.

Liberal arts education has its roots in the classical period, which consisted of the trivium of deductive reasoning and the quadrivium of quantitative reasoning. The original seven liberal arts included: music, geometry, astronomy, arithmetic, grammar, rhetoric, and logic. Medieval European universities added three philosophies to these original seven liberal arts, including: natural philosophy (empirical science), moral philosophy (human thought and behavior), and metaphysics (ontology). There are various definitions of what constitutes a liberal arts education, and this mere fact has caused discussion and controversy. Today, the primary commitments of liberal arts education seem to coalesce around an efficacious education, which is founded on an institutional ethos of coherence and integrity, strong student-student and faculty-student relationships, and an emphasis on a well-rounded education, rather than the acquisition of professional or vocational skills. In this way, advocates of liberal arts education suggest that it is the most appropriate and meaningful approach to learning for an ever-changing world. However, there is a surprising range of differences among liberal arts colleges.

Beginning in the 19th century, liberal arts colleges had a dual mission of disseminating culture and preparing for professional work. In 1828, Yale College developed the rationale for the importance of the liberal arts college. The goal of the college was to produce well-rounded intellectuals who were independent thinkers and self-starters with a clear life purpose. During this time, youth could learn occupations in noncollege environments. In fact, the earlier one began this training, the better. Until the end of the 19th century, the proportion of young people seeking a college education in the United States remained at about 2 percent. However, as the 20th century approached, so did the growth of industrial activity, and with that, a growing urban and cosmopolitan middle class. This marked a turn in the purpose and utility of a college education—the university became a location for training in a way that had not previously been the case. The university drew on German approaches, incorporating aspects such as seminars, lectures, experimentation, and research—with a particular emphasis and value on the doctoral degree as the ultimate production of knowledge. As newer professional fields arose, so did the need for credentials. The university also became a site for accessing social and cultural capital by way of personal connections and academic/intellectual assets.

Holistic Approach

Alongside the rise of the traditional university, liberal arts colleges also began to take hold of their missions by asserting that, while traditional universities prepared students for a profession, liberal arts colleges prepared students for life. Liberal arts colleges embraced the notion of a close student-teacher relationship and the importance of small size with regard to the campus and individual classrooms as sites for engaging discussions, assignments, and assessment in meaningful ways. Their holistic emphasis on the student gave liberal arts college a unique niche, valuing the intersection of academic, cocurricular, fellowship, and leadership experiences. Liberal arts in the 21rst century also mirrors the 20th century focus on intellectual and personal development, however, it has become increasingly inclusive and arguably necessary for all students to succeed in the global marketplace and as active, participatory citizens in the United States. The hope is that liberal arts is taught, engaged in, and practiced throughout all levels of education and across all fields.

In 1981, David Winter, David McClelland, and Abigail Stewart, three psychologists interest in understanding the impact of liberal arts education, listed the goals of liberal arts education: thinking critically or possessing broad analytical skill including differentiation and discrimination within a broad range of particular phenomena (especially within the history of Western culture), formation of abstract concepts, integration of abstract concepts with particular phenomena or concrete instances and making relevant judgments, evaluation of evidence and revision of abstract concepts and hypotheses, articulation and communication of abstract concepts, differentiation and discrimination of abstractions and identification of abstract concepts, and comprehension of the logics governing the relationships among abstract concepts. Other goals are learning how to learn; thinking independently; empathizing, recognizing one's own assumptions, and seeing all sides of an issue; exercising self-control for the sake of broader loyalties; showing self-assurance in leadership ability; demonstrating mature social and emotional judgment, and personal integration; holding equalitarian, liberal, pro-science, and antiauthoritarian values and beliefs; and participating in and enjoying cultural experience.

Curricular and environmental structures are supposed to facilitate the development, fostering, honing, and implementation of these goals. Generally, these structures include: a focus on intellectual arts, meaningful and frequent interaction with students and faculty, and curricular coherence that culminate in a final capstone project/experience. In sum, liberal arts education promotes conditions that are optimal for the kind of intellectual and psychosocial outcomes that are recognized as critical for a successful post-university life. The attributes that lead to these conditions are influenced by factors such as: high expectations and standards, emphasis on high academic engaged time, frequent assessment and prompt feedback, active student engagement, frequency of faculty contact in and out of class, collaborative learning, residential learning, individualized learning, and emphasis on active learning and connection to the institution during the first two years of college. These attributes are considered among the best of educational practices in undergraduate education. While many American universities claim to have liberal arts programs, colleges, or foci, the first thing that comes to mind when one refers to liberal arts in the United States is liberal arts colleges. It is important to highlight the distinction between liberal arts education and liberal arts colleges. Liberal arts education, in theory, can be implemented and practiced in any educational institution. Liberal arts colleges, however, refer to a particular kind of institution of higher education, primarily colleges, which focus on undergraduate education and liberal arts fields.

Liberal Arts Colleges

Liberal arts colleges possess distinguishing features that set them apart from other types of higher education institutions. These features include: effective practices in student efficacy, full-time residential living, small institutional size, innovative and effective teaching, learning communities, living learning centers, first year seminars, a focus on first-year impact, and an integrated commitment to academic and personal development. Highly selective liberal arts colleges pride themselves on having a particularly high impact on students' openness to diversity and challenge, reflexive and writing skills, and growth in reading comprehension and critical thinking. Liberal arts colleges are found all over the world; however, Harvard was the first American university to hold the liberal arts college title. For the most part, these institutions were relatively small and religiously affiliated. Others have abandoned their religious tenets. Liberal arts colleges are distinctly different from research institutions because of size, curricula, and mission. Oftentimes, liberal arts colleges are residential, with a strong focus on close interaction between faculty and students, coupled with a strong focus on liberal arts disciplines. The Yale Report of 1828 called for a breadth of curriculum that would lay the foundation for good citizenry, rather than prepare students for a particular vocation or profession. Centered on Latin and Greek literature, the report endorsed a prescribed classical curriculum that purported to lay a foundation for all livelihoods, as opposed to preparing undergraduates for specific professional work. While the report's conclusions left minimal room for curricular flexibility, it steadfastly made the case for preparing well-rounded and well-educated students through a rigorous training of the mind, rather than a discreet set of skills to prepare for labor. This report has become a central document in support of liberal arts education. Since then, liberal arts colleges have adopted much more versatile curricula, however, with a similar goal of laying a general academic foundation for all students.

Among the better known, highly competitive liberal arts colleges are: Williams College, Amherst College, Swarthmore College, Pomona College, Middlebury College, Bowdoin College, Carleton College, Wellesley College, Claremont McKenna College, Haverford College, Davidson College, Washington and Lee College, Wesleyan University, Vassar College, Hamilton College, Harvey Mudd College, Grinnell College, Smith College, Bates College, Colby College, Colgate University, Oberlin College, and Bryn Mawr College.

Future of Liberal Arts Colleges

Liberal arts colleges continue to decrease in numbers. In 1990, there were a total of 212 liberal arts colleges; by 2009, that number had dropped to 137. Many former liberal arts colleges have reshaped their mission to meet the seeming needs of the time, evolving into more complex institutions that have retreated from a sole liberal arts focus to one that also incorporates vocational/professional training across disciplines and, more specifically, in the physical sciences. Scholars and liberal arts college presidents alike agree that this trend is likely to continue. Liberal arts colleges are simply responding to the demands of society, including a pragmatic education that results in a steady, well-paid job within a pluralistic, global marketplace. Additionally, demographic shifts show that the growth of Hispanic and black students will grow considerably, and that this growing population of students will come largely from families in which neither parent has gone to college. As first generation, low-income students continue to grow, liberal arts colleges will face the challenge of finding students that can

both be drawn to a liberal arts college and its offerings and pay the full price of attendance. The relevance of a liberal arts college curriculum is often a difficult sell for students and families that simply seek a college education to get a job. This had led many liberal arts colleges to invest in and focus on the professional relevance of the liberal arts college experience.

Liberal arts colleges have been shown to produce scholars at a higher rate than other types of postsecondary institutions. Additionally, liberal arts colleges are innovative spaces which, theoretically, more freely examine alternative teaching practices, creative student programming, and academic projects. Among these are honors programs, experiential learning, unique study abroad opportunities, civic engagement projects, senior theses, internships, first- and second-year seminars, and cocurricular cultural events. Scholars such as Frederick Rudolph, Ernest Pascarela, Alexander Astin, Shouping Hu, George Kuh, and Patrick Terenzini point to the absolute dedication that liberal arts colleges exemplify and the ways in which this dedication equate to a powerful learning environment. Students report higher satisfaction with liberal arts colleges than other types of educational institutions.

There is controversy, however, regarding liberal arts colleges. Specifically, liberal arts colleges are increasingly experiencing an identity and financial crisis. Liberal arts colleges, while founded on the idea of the love of learning, are facing a climate of limited job opportunities. So, potential consumers of liberal arts education have grown leery of the practicality of a liberal arts education. The criticism of liberal arts colleges often revolves around the applicability of breadth versus depth in technical training that might better translate to a high-paying, meaningful career. The question that arises regarding liberal arts colleges is, "What are liberal arts colleges exactly?" The decline in the number of liberal arts degrees during the past century has given liberal arts college pause, as this phenomenon has raised questions about the financial sustainability of liberal arts colleges, as well as the value of their missions. The liberal arts purport to prepare students to be better people in the world; the uncertainty in this assertion lies in demonstrating that this is actually the case. Defining what higher education should be, specifically for liberal arts colleges, is paramount to their survival.

Aurora Chang
University of Wyoming

See Also: College Advising; College Proximity; College Transferring; Higher Education; School-to-Work Transitions.

Further Readings

Ferrall, Victor E. *Liberal Arts at the Brink*. Cambridge, MA: Harvard University Press, 2011.

Gleason, Abbott. *A Liberal Education*. Cambridge, MA: TidePool Press, 2010.

Koblik, Steven and Stephen Richards Graubard. *Distinctively American: The Residential Liberal Arts College*. New Brunswick, NJ: Transaction Publishers, 2000.

Pascarella, Ernest T. *Liberal Arts Colleges and Liberal Arts Education: New Evidence on Impacts*. San Francisco: Jossey-Bass, 2005.

Winter, David G., David C. McClelland, and Abigail J. Stewart. *A New Case for the Liberal Arts: Assessing Institutional Goals and Student Development*. San Francisco: Jossey-Bass, 1981.

Libraries, School

School libraries have a unique role in American schools today. Once thought of as complements to classroom content, school libraries are currently considered an important point of application and extension for classroom learning. As such, school libraries remain an important aspect of education. In addition, school libraries are a crucial point of study because of their location as one site of the development for new literacy practices. Given advances in technology, school libraries today occupy a role that is evolving from a depository one, where a single student might borrow books for research, to that of a gateway, where students might use library resources to produce informational media for wider distribution. School libraries today are a resource for research projects, as well as learning about the Web and technologies, including social media. School libraries also offer programming in the form of courses and workshops on specific software, such as Microsoft Office or Photoshop, to help students create educational products that teachers often require to support specific curricular activities.

Historically, school libraries have been responsible for maintaining collections that support and extend the school curriculum. Libraries must also supply students with varying interests with a wide range of reading material for extracurricular and personal reasons. The most important factors in school libraries are space, library materials, programming, and staff, including librarians, technology assistants, and archivists. While librarians have traditionally been encouraged to remain on the cutting edge of advances in information sciences, it has become increasingly important. As information technology has evolved, school libraries have become training grounds for students and faculty to learn how to conduct research within the library, but also offsite, including online databases.

Technological Advances

Advances in technology have led to shifting definitions of text, which have facilitated changing definitions of literacy, literacies, and literacy practices. While school libraries in the early 20th century were focused on print-based periodicals, newspapers, magazines, and books to maintain collections, modern school libraries often focus on introductions to the Internet, safe browsing practices, conducting research online, and media creation.

The shift from print-based text to digital media has affected the publishing world, and by extension, the world of school libraries. Whereas school libraries have historically focused on collecting and lending physical books, and other forms of print-based media, they increasingly circulate e-texts. School libraries are also increasingly acquiring e-readers, such as the Kindle and Nook, for students' use in the library. E-readers are thought to draw in tech-savvy student populations, who might enjoy the illustrations of a graphic novel, or reluctant readers who might find reading in a new format inviting. In addition, like public libraries, school libraries may also offer classes on using e-readers and downloading e-books for students.

Funding and Resources

School libraries are subject to the same funding disparities as public schools. Consequently, school libraries in well-resourced schools may offer more print-based media, such as books and periodicals, as well as more technology, such as computers and audiovisual equipment. School funding differences may also create literacy environments for students in economically advantaged districts that may be complex, in that they offer students more opportunities to connect print-based text with the real world through creating products such as videos or presentations in school library media labs. In some ways, school libraries are places where social markers such as class and socioeconomic status become apparent in school resources.

Outside of school funding, factors such as the content of the curriculum and composition of the student population influence school libraries. In many cases, the mission and curricular foci of the host school are important considerations for the school library. For example, schools that focus on math and science would need resources in these subject areas to support the work of teachers and students. In addition, school libraries serving student populations with increasing numbers of emergent bilinguals would need resources in more than one language to extend the learning experience beyond the classroom.

School libraries are often thought of as an important part of the extended school day movement, where the space and resources they offer can be used to increase opportunities to learn, and potentially increase academic outcomes for students. Studies that focus on the academic achievement of students have found that school-based library media centers can positively affect the attendance and standardized test scores of students, when specific instructional strategies are used to promote student use of the media programming that school libraries offer. In fact, researchers have found significant relationships between library features such as equipment, larger book collections, and endorsed staff and student achievement, as measured on reading tests.

Carleen S. Carey
Michigan State University

See Also: After-School Programs; Reading to Children; Technology Education.

Further Readings

Lance, K., M. Rodney, and C. Hamilton-Pennell. *How School Librarians Help Kids Achieve Stardards: The Second Colorado Case Study.* Denver: Colorado State Library, 2000.

MacBean, D. and B. Smith. "The Functional School Library." *American Library Association Bulletin*, v.47/2 (1953).

School Library Journal. http://www.schoollibraryjournal.com (Accessed August 2012).

Libya

Libya is a large, oil-rich country, with a relatively small population. While it is the fourth-largest country in Africa, with an area of almost 700,000 miles (1.8 million square kilometers), Libya had an estimated 6.7 million people as of July 2012. This makes the country one of the 10 least-densely populated countries in the world, and the country with the 10th-largest proven oil reserves. The recent political turmoil has impacted development, as well as obscured it. In 2010, Libya's gross domestic product was an estimated $92.62 billion, with a real annual growth rate of 4.2 percent.

In 2011, the United Nations (UN) ranked Libya 64 out of 187 countries on the Human Development Index. Libya was colonized by many invaders, including Romans, Arabs, and Turks. It was an Italian colony from 1911 to 1941, before being granted independence by the UN in 1951. Following a bloodless military coup in 1969, Colonel Muammar Gaddafi took control of the nation and ruled by espousing his eccentric ideology of third universal theory. He aggressively attempted to spread his theory internationally as an alternative to communist or capitalist models of government. However, Gaddafi remained controversial for supporting terrorism, and after the Lockerbie bombing, the country endured UN sanctions from 1992 to 2003. Libya is currently in a transitional period following the civil war that toppled the Gaddafi-led government. The Transitional National Council (TNC), formed in Benghazi in March 2011 with widespread international support, successfully overthrew the authoritarian Gaddafi regime in August 2011. After Gaddafi was killed, the TNC declared the country liberated on October 23, 2011. The TNC was recognized by the UN as the legitimate interim governing body of Libya, and pledged to guide the country to a pluralistic democratic state by conducting elections, forming a new democratic government, and drafting the country's first constitution. In August 2012, the TNC handed over power to the General National Congress, Libya's first elected assembly.

During the Italian colonial period, Libya had a dual education system. Although Libyan children could enroll in formal education, most children only completed the primary level (grades 1–6). There were also Kuttabs and Quranic schools for children, which concentrated on teaching Arabic and religious studies. In 2009, 88.9 percent of adults and 99.9 percent of youth were literate. Nine years of basic education is compulsory and free to everyone, completion of which opens two trajectories at the secondary education level. Students can either obtain three years of vocational training for employment, or four years of specialized secondary education as a ticket to attend higher education. The Libya government spent 2.7 percent of its 1999 public expenditures on education; in 2009, 86 percent of government funds toward education went to primary and secondary education.

Meanwhile, the gross enrollment ratios regional average for Libya was 97 and 68, respectively, for the basic and secondary education. Higher education in Libya has been growing rapidly after independence, as the establishment of many public higher education institutions followed to accommodate steadily increasing enrollments. There were 18 public universities, 264 government-funded higher education institutes, and more than 30 private universities in Libya in 2010. Higher education in Libya provides specialized technical and general liberal arts education (lasting four to six years), and advanced studies (three to six years) that grant master's and doctoral degrees. Libya also has compulsory military training incorporated into the curriculum, and requires all eligible males (17–35 years old) to undergo three years of military service in the army or four years in the air force or navy. Higher education is free in Libya, except in private institutions.

Libya's education system is in need of significant reform and improvement, mainly in leadership, capacity building, and research promotion. During the first decade of the 21st century, Libya attempted to introduce information and communication technology (ICT) into the education system at all levels. This introduction effort is still in its early stages, and cultural, linguistic, and socioeconomic background diversity make the implementation process particularly challenging. Other education challenges facing the country include the shortage of supporting resources for program development, the need to better link formal education as a relevant preparation experience for graduates entering the labor market, and outdated instructional and learning techniques.

Pre-service and in-service teacher training programs need improvement, with special focus on improving the quality of student learning. The Arab Spring civil war of 2011 had long-lasting impacts on Libya's education system. Almost all primary and secondary schools were forced to close during the war. Many schools were damaged and are in need of significant repair and maintenance. On January 7, 2012, the Ministry of Education reopened classes nationwide. The curriculum has been revised to reflect the transitional government's priorities for education, which include rebuilding schools and strengthening the quality of the overall education system.

Uttam Gaulee
University of Florida
Yi Zhou
University of Pittsburgh

See Also: Algeria; Egypt; Sudan.

Further Readings
Amal, Rhema and Iwona Miliszewska. "Towards E-Learning in Higher Education in Libya." *Informing Science and Information Technology*, v.7 (2010).
Clark, Nick. *World Education News and Reviews: Education in Libya*. New York: World Education Services, 2004.
Tamtam, Abdalmonem, et al. "Higher Education in Libya, System Under Stress." *Procedia—Social and Behavioral Sciences*, v.29 (2011).

Life Course Perspective and Education

The life course perspective in sociological research combines a theory of the institutionalized construction of people's "normal" ages, identities, and gendered lives with biographical studies of how individuals subjectively tell stories about their experiences. Where the lifecycle approach traces a linear biological path from birth to death, sociologists highlight the roles that history, social structure, and cultural context play in influencing people's trajectories through certain episodes of their lives. From a life course perspective, researchers pay particular attention to the contextual specifics of, for instance, being a college student during the 2010s, investigating how assemblages of experiences shape the demographic events of individuals and their age-cohort peers. Such a constellation may include, for example, the influence of new information technologies on university teaching, or crises in the economy leading to uncertainties in the graduate employment market. The challenge confronting researchers is to disentangle how these factors interplay on the one hand with the sociobiographical events shared by an age-cohort—such as graduation or a general election—and on the other with the life-as-lived biographies of each individual participating in the research project. In the face of these difficulties, a key aim of life course research is to produce findings about the common aspects of shared experiences, thereby highlighting how general social trends can be illustrated at the individual level and their network of relationships. As such, the life course perspective shares C. Wright Mills's aim to make the vital sociological link between personal troubles and public issues.

The institutionalization of the life course in modern nation-states was connected to the development of mass education and welfare systems. Through the 19th century until the mid-20th century, this institutionalization meant that most people experienced life course transitions and trajectories common among their peers, as defined by gender, ethnicity, and social class. However, in the current context of globalization and widespread social change, life course pathways and experiences have increased in variety with the breakdown of more traditional social structures—signified by the disappearance of jobs for life, or the rise in divorce rates, for example—leading some social theorists to call the current society "late modern." Consequently, life course research must increasingly consider both stability and change in people's lives as they unfold through historical and social time and across increasingly blurred cultural generations, where meanings of age and identity are frequently renegotiated. Empirical research may either follow a cohort over a period of time, perhaps through high school, or gather the extended story of life experience through interviews.

Lifelong Educational Trajectories

Within this framework, educational trajectories are considered across the whole span of an individual's life, so that developmental growth is seen as not only being in childhood and youth, but also continuing throughout adulthood. An educational trajectory refers to a set of transitions between educational institutions and levels, through which a person gains varying amounts of educational capital, in the shape of qualifications, practical skills, and different forms of knowledge. Each transition on an educational trajectory is affected by the choices that an individual makes and the context in which they must make their decisions: particularly the conditions of social inequality and the prevailing institutional

organization of the education system available to them, alongside the values and material circumstances of their community. Some conditions may lead to social mobility, where an individual gains employment with a higher income and social status than is common among those who share their background. Research demonstrates, however, that in the majority of cases, the status quo tends to be preserved, with young people gaining qualifications and subsequent employment that maintains their position in the social class hierarchy.

In these terms, the life course perspective toward education has become especially relevant for understanding the experiences of young people under the conditions of the "knowledge society" of the 21st century. As a further aspect of late modernity, the knowledge society reflects the move away from manual skills and the production of goods to an economy where knowledge has become the key commodity that people gain through education and bring to the employment market. Moreover, with the economy based on bodies of knowledge subject to rapid change, the employment market has become increasingly unstable, so that demands are placed on individuals to participate in lifelong learning in order to reinvent themselves as workers fit for a flexible economy. Yet, sociologists do not tend to treat the knowledge society as a neutral concept, with many interpreting it as a tool for the instrumentalization of education for the systemic benefit of the existing economy. In other words, this is not seen as an inevitable or welcome consequence of capitalist markets, but as a mechanism for sustaining the existing power relationships between individuals and vested corporate and state interests. Such a critique has become a central frame for researchers working with a life course perspective because it provides an understanding of the forces characteristic of the institutionalization of the life course today, and it combines grounded and observable societal trends with a critical perspective on how such trends serve the interests of dominant social groups.

Under these conditions, everyone is expected to become responsible for his or her learning career: a lifelong project to acquire skills and knowledge that will enable them to be the flexi-workers the economy requires. The biographical experiences of constructing and undertaking such a learning career can be understood through the life-as-lived accounts of research participants. These allow sociologists to gage how people deal with the pressures of "biographicity," meaning the ways in which children, young people, and other learners of all ages endow their educational trajectories with meaning, and continually reinterpret their lives as they experience and transfer through the different levels of education. It is through competent biographicity that individuals can assemble some kind of biographical coherence and stability in a period where the expectations, requirements, and processes for knowledge and learning are often subject to unpredictable change.

David Mellor
University of Bristol

See Also: Adolescence; Childhood; Class Inequality: High School Dropout Rates; Longitudinal Studies of Education; School Mobility and Education; Transitions, School.

Further Readings

Clark, M. Carolyn and Rosemary S. Caffarella. *An Update on Adult Development Theory: New Ways of Thinking About the Life Course.* Hoboken, NJ: Jossey-Bass, 2000.

Henderson, S., J. Holland, S. McGrellis, S. Sharpe, and R. Thomson. *Inventing Adulthoods: A Biographical Approach to Youth Transitions.* Thousand Oaks, CA: Sage, 2007.

Plummer, K. *Documents of Life 2: An Invitation to a Critical Humanism.* Thousand Oaks, CA: Sage, 2001.

Longitudinal Studies of Education

Longitudinal research follows individuals over time, often at regular intervals, over long periods. Longitudinal data are collected primarily via survey research methods. In contrast, cross-sectional studies collect information at one point in time, hence providing a snapshot of individuals within a specific time period and context. Longitudinal research on education is invaluable in that it can trace the behaviors, attitudes, and educational, labor market, and other life course experiences and outcomes, such as family formation and fertility patterns of individuals, in relation to their experiences within the educational system. Some longitudinal studies, such as the U.S.

High School Longitudinal Study of 2009 (HSLS:09) have education as their core organizing principle, whereas others, such as the 1970 British Cohort Study (BCS70), include questions about education as one of many life sphere experiences. Data may be collected from students, teachers, parents, and administrators, all of which will contribute to the longitudinal database. Data can be collected via questionnaires and interviews, and hence can be either quantitative or qualitative in nature, or both. Also, institutional records, such as students' grades and assessment scores, may be added to enrich the dataset.

Longitudinal studies on education may take many forms. Some studies focus on one particular life phase, such as early childhood. Others, such as those that follow individuals from school into the workforce, are transition specific. Other studies follow individuals over decades, and hence span multiple educational phases and transitions and focus on life trajectories. Some studies take a life course approach by focusing individuals' lives within social structures, with attention to the timing and sequencing of events across time. Educational longitudinal studies with a life course focus are informed primarily by the discipline of sociology. Other studies embrace a life span approach that focuses on individual traits, such as cognitive development. These studies are informed by the discipline of psychology. In theoretical perspectives from other disciplines, such as economics, medicine, and other health care fields, demography may inform both life course and life span research.

Samples

Samples of individuals in longitudinal studies in education can be constructed in a variety of ways. Cohort samples are composed of individuals who share a common characteristic or experience, for example, having been born on the same day in a given year, or who commenced the first year of school in the same month and year. Panel samples are less homogeneous in that they do not share a narrowly defined common characteristic. In panel studies, an initial panel of participants is identified, and they are followed over at least two points in time. Because both cohort and panel studies follow the same group of individuals over time, analyses are able to reveal the relationships between earlier conditions, experiences, events, and demographic characteristics and subsequent outcomes, experiences, and attitudes. Of particular interest in educational research are the relationships between background characteristics such as socio-economic status, exposure to certain curricula, academic achievement and competency development, and eventual educational attainment and labor market outcomes. Research questions can be framed to capture multiple life-sphere domains over time, including formal, informal, and nonformal education, the labor force and related workplace training, relationships and family formation, and health and well-being. In addition, studies can gauge the impact of educational policies and practices, such as year-round schooling, school lunch programs, or differential grading practices on the educational outcomes of students over time. Multiple cohort or panel studies can be constructed to compare younger cohorts or panels with older ones. Also, cross-sectional studies can be extended to include a longitudinal component. Ideally, longitudinal research on education seeks to establish cause and effect relationships that can be used to develop effective educational policies.

Examples

The U.S. High School Longitudinal Study of 2009 (HSLS:09) began in 2009. It is a nationally representative study of over 21,000 grade 9 students in 944 schools. In addition, parents, teachers, school counselors, and school administrators were surveyed in 2009. Also, the study contains a student assessment dimension. The planned data collection phase spans secondary and postsecondary careers of the baseline sample of students. The 1970 British Cohort Study (BCS70) began as a study of approximately 17,000 babies who were born in England, Scotland, Wales, and Northern Ireland during one week in April 1970, together with their respective families. The initial focus on medical issues was broadened over time to include physical, educational, social, and economic development.

Over time, a variety of data collection strategies have been employed, including initial questionnaires from attending midwives, medical and school records, and surveys of the children, parents, and teachers. This study is ongoing. The Swedish Evaluation Through Follow-up (ETF; Utvärdering Genom Uppföljning, UGU) has followed eight cohorts of children born between 1948 and 1992 from school through to adulthood. Data have been collected from students, parents, and teachers. In addition, the datasets include measures of academic ability. Because all Swedish citizens are assigned a unique personal identification number at birth, survey data collected can be linked easily to other existing registers, such as employment records.

The German National Educational Panel Study (NEPS) began in 2010 by collecting baseline data on four parallel cohorts in kindergarten, grade five, grade nine, and higher education. In addition, a cohort of newborns and mothers was established in 2009, and data collection from a cohort of adults will commence in 2012. A central focus of the study is the measurement of competencies across the life course.

Challenges

As with all longitudinal research studies, longitudinal studies on education face several challenges. Longitudinal research is both labor intensive and expensive to collect; hence, long-term funding commitments are necessary for a project's survival. Sample attrition or loss of individuals from the study over time may result in bias in the sample. Names and contact information of sample members must be kept up-to-date. If samples are school based, it may be difficult to maintain accurate contact information for children who change schools over the course of the study. Data collection instruments must be well constructed and extensively tested. Changes to the wording of questions across time must be considered carefully to ensure that data can be compared. Researchers employing longitudinal data on education must have strong backgrounds in data analysis. Analyses can range from simple descriptive statistics to advanced methods particularly conducive to longitudinal datasets, such as event history or survival analysis, sequence analysis, and structural equation modeling. Finally, freedom of information and right to privacy issues raise serious challenges to longitudinal research in education.

Lesley Andres
University of British Columbia

See Also: Epistemological Issues in Educational Research; Life Course Perspective and Education; Research Paradigms in Educational Studies.

Further Readings

Guarino, C. M., et al. "Teacher Qualifications, Instructional Practices, and Reading and Mathematics Gains of Kindergartners." Washington, DC: U.S. Department of Education. National Center for Education Statistics, 2006.

Kristen, C., A. Römmer, W. Müller, and F. Kalter. "Longitudinal Studies for Education Reports: European and North American Examples." Bonn, Germany: Federal Ministry of Education and Research, 2005.

Nash, R. "Controlling for 'Ability': A Conceptual and Empirical Study of Primary and Secondary Effects." *British Journal of Sociology of Education*, v. 27/2 (2006).

Louisiana

Louisiana is a southeastern state, geographically bordered on the north by Arkansas, west by Texas, east by Mississippi, and south by the Gulf of Mexico. The Mississippi River flows through Baton Rouge and New Orleans, creating port cities important for international trade. In 2005, Louisiana was devastated by two hurricanes. Hurricane Katrina made landfall in the southeastern part of the state on August 29, while Hurricane Rita struck the southwestern part of the state on September 24. The storms severely impacted 24 percent of the state's school population, as thousands of students fled their home parishes or left the state altogether, and many schools remained closed for six months or longer. While the economy is heavily dependent upon tourism, primarily in New Orleans, the seafood industry and oil and gas are the largest aspects of the state's economy. On April 10, 2010, the British Petroleum (BP) operated Deepwater Horizon oil platform exploded, killing 11 men and injuring 17 others, and releasing approximately 4.9 million barrels of crude oil into the Gulf of Mexico, ultimately causing great damage to the coastal ecology. Louisiana's economy suffered as the spill caused great damage to the local seafood industry.

History and Statistics

The first permanent settlement in Louisiana was established in 1697, initially as a French colony, and later following Spanish rule. The land was of great value since it housed the mouth of the Mississippi River. The state was transferred to the United States in 1803, as part of the Louisiana Purchase, becoming the 18th state in 1812. While Louisiana still enjoys a rich history and culture associated with French rule, the once widespread use of the language is slowly dying. The first school established in the state was by the Ursuline nuns. Catholic education was, and continues to be, a strong presence in the educational structure of Louisiana. Today, approximately 16 percent of the student body attends private or parochial schools. Louisiana allows parents to home school their children upon registration with the Department of Education. Students who are home schooled must participate in state testing. Approximately 15,000 students are home schooled in the state, approximately 2 percent of the student population. There were 696,558 students enrolled in Louisiana's elementary and secondary schools during 2010 and 2011, slowly rebounding from the pre-Katrina population of 724,002.

A large percentage of the population lives in poverty; approximately 52 percent of the student population is classified as minority and 66.2 percent receives free or reduced-price lunch. As a southern state, Louisiana experienced its share of segregation and exclusion of African American students. In the early 1960s, the state quietly passed laws giving authority to the governor to close schools if he felt rioting would occur. Today, several school districts are still under desegregation orders, while others have sought unitary status, a declaration that the district has complied with judicial orders and no longer operates a segregated system.

Compulsory education spans the ages of 7 to 17. Kindergarten is required to be provided by school

Table 1 Elementary and secondary education characteristics

	Louisiana	U.S. (average)
Total number of schools	1,509	1,988
Total students	696,558	970,278
Total teachers	48,655.03	60,766.56
Pupil/teacher ratio	14.32	15.97

Source: U.S. Department of Education, National Center for Education Statistics, Common Core of Data (CCD), 2010–11.

Table 2 Elementary and secondary education finance

	Louisiana	U.S. (average)
Total revenues	$7,861,129,528	$11,464,385,994
Total expenditures for education	$7,771,248,017	$11,712,033,839
Total current expenditures	$6,814,454,623	$9,938,906,259

Source: U.S. Department of Education, National Center for Education Statistics, Common Core of Data (CCD), "National Public Education Financial Survey," FY08 (2007–08).

districts, but it is not mandatory for students. With few exceptions, Louisiana school districts mirror the geographic county (known as "parishes" in Louisiana) boundaries. There are currently 69 public school districts, excluding independently operated charter schools. State education is governed by the state Board of Elementary and Secondary Education (BESE) and a State Superintendent of Education appointed by BESE. The board consists of 11 members, eight from statewide districts and three appointed by the governor. BESE enjoys policymaking ability as an administrative agency within the state government. The state currently has 36 public and private institutions of higher education, managed under the Board of Regents and subdivided under four systems. In addition, there are 130 proprietary schools throughout the state. Fewer than half of high school graduates enter postsecondary institutions, despite the availability.

In 1997, Louisiana implemented an accountability system containing the requirements that would later appear in the federal No Child Left Behind law: challenging curriculum and content standards; a comprehensive assessment program, which includes high-stakes testing at certain grade levels; school performance monitoring and reporting; corrective actions and assistance; and recognition and rewards for high-performing schools. State voters adopted a constitutional amendment in 2003, allowing the state to take control of failing schools through a state-run entity, the Recovery School District (RSD), for reconstitution as charter schools. Following Hurricane Katrina in 2005, the state legislature amended the law to allow for all schools within a failing school district to be transferred to the RSD. At the time, only the Orleans Parish School System received such a label, and following the storm, the majority of schools were opened as charter schools, with a few remaining under direct operation of the RSD. Today, there are a greater percentage of students attending charter schools in New Orleans than any other city in the nation. As the state continues to rebuild after the devastating 2005 hurricanes and 2010 oil spill, school reform continues to dominate policymaking. Despite the highly acclaimed accountability system, student achievement continues to be disappointing. Although improvement has occurred for schools in New Orleans, the pace of achievement has been slow.

Belinda M. Cambre
University of New Orleans

See Also: Charter Schools; No Child Left Behind; Poverty and Education.

Further Readings

Cline, Rodney. *Education in Louisiana: History and Development.* Baton Rouge, LA: Claitor's Publishing Division, 1974.

Louisiana Department of Education. http://www .louisianaschools.net (Accessed August 2012).

Manning, Curtis A. *The History of Higher Education in Louisiana.* Bloomington, IN: Xlibris, 2006.

M

MacLeod, Jay

Jay MacLeod is best known for his book *Ain't No Makin' It*, in which he interviews and observes two groups of adolescent boys: the Hallway Hangers and the Brothers of Clarendon Heights. MacLeod not only provides readers with traditional ethnographic analysis, but he offers additional insight into the lives of these boys by conducting longitudinal assessments. He follows up with them eight years after graduating from high school and again in their midlife. He was prompted to study these two groups of students because of his previous experience as a youth counselor, during which he recognized a tremendous amount of desperation and hopelessness in working-class youth's perceptions of their future prospects. His background as a youth counselor and a pastor makes for an informative glance at these two groups. They differed in their beliefs about their future achievements; the Brothers, mainly black males, were much more optimistic about their futures whereas the Hallway Hangers, consisting predominantly of white males, were pessimistic about their futures. In the end, he finds that both groups had different lifelong outcomes.

In characterizing both groups, he elaborates on how the Hallway Hangers behave stereotypically by engaging in drinking, violence, aggressive behaviors, and drugs. The Brothers participate in socially approved roles and behaviors, such as playing basketball and studying. There are tensions between these two groups because the Hangers are often perpetrators of overt racism against the Brothers. It is because of his comparison of these two groups that some suggest that his study is best viewed as two distinctive studies: one analyzes and evaluates the actions of the white youth, who are often neglected in research, while the second concerns the same approach but outlines the myth of black youth who are not opposed to educational ideals and accept them but whose choices are still constrained by other structures. Eight years later he finds that the Hangers are in despair while the Brothers have experienced some success and difficulties in attaining jobs.

MacLeod uses various theoretical perspectives to understand the situation and outcomes of these two groups; he draws on social reproduction theories and integrates ideas of linguistic capital and resistance. He draws on Pierre Bourdieu's ideas of capital and habitus, Paul Willis's resistance theory, concepts of structure from Samuel Bowles and Herbert Gintis, and linguistic capital from Basil Bernstein. Although his overall goal was to reconcile ideas of structure and agency, some have called his attempt theoretically confusing but intriguing. In applying the concept of habitus, MacLeod focuses on various aspects: family, culture, work, and school. By concentrating on these aspects he manages to account for how these boys use a number of resources to make their choices and navigate their social reality, which some argue makes for a well-rounded ethnography. As he analyzes these two groups and their interactions with each other and with the education system, he concludes that there is no one contemporary theory or concept that is able to capture and explain how aspirations are regulated and expectations are altered for both the Hangers and the Brothers.

Evident by his writing, the third follow-up study was an emotional return for him, as interviews with all the boys were not possible; some had passed away or were not locatable. In his analysis, he finds the Hangers to be in despair even further, engaging with drugs, alcohol, and violence; one even passed away after contracting AIDS. However, the Brothers were all doing well, mostly employed in managerial positions and with families of their own. MacLeod published an article as a response to his first edition, and in his second edition of the book discusses this third set of interviews.

Family Life and Authority
The most interesting contribution that MacLeod provides is his analysis of two racially distinct groups and how, contrary to popular belief, black youth were not opposed to educational ideals. Some have argued that MacLeod's analysis of family life was lacking and could be one reason for their long-term outcomes. He describes family life to be much different for each group; that is, the Hangers respected their parents but not their authority while the Brothers respected parental authority but lived farther away from Clarendon Heights than the Hangers.

MacLeod argues that the achievement ideology cannot explain everything in these youth outcomes and that social and cultural capital interacts with structure to create choice. Reproduction theories, for MacLeod, could not adequately explain all that was found in his study but he concludes that social structures set up choices for these youth that ultimately shape their habitus. Habitus, then, for MacLeod, is dynamic and relational, reflecting current and past experiences of these boys. His work has prompted further research into the intersection of race/ethnicity, youth culture, family, and school dynamics. It has also has prompted research on the achievement ideology for black and white youth culture. It has furthered the debate on structure versus agency and provided a basic reference in ethnographic methods.

Christina DeRoche
McMaster University

See Also: Bernstein, Basil; Bowles, Samuel and Herbert Gintis; Cultural Capital; Resistance Theory; Social Capital.

Further Readings
Hoschild, Jennifer L. "Ain't No Makin' It: Leveled Aspirations in a Low-Income Neighborhood by Jay MacLeod." *Journal of Sociology*, v.94/1 (1988).
MacLeod, Jay. *Ain't No Makin' It: Aspirations and Attainment in a Low-Income Neighborhood*. Boulder, CO: Westview Press, 1995.
MacLeod, Jay. "Bridging Street and School." *Journal of Negro Education*, v.60/3 (1991).
Royster, Deirdre. "Ain't No Makin' It: Aspirations and Attainment in a Low-Income Neighborhood by Jay MacLeod." *Contemporary Sociology*, v.25/2 (1996).

Madagascar

The Republic of Madagascar is an island country situated 250 miles off the eastern coast of southern Africa across the Mozambique Channel, south of the equator. Over 1,000 miles (1,580 kilometers) long and 350 miles (570 kilometers) wide, it is the world's fourth-largest island. The country has an area of 226,657 square miles and a population of 20.6 million. The official language of Madagascar is Standard Malagasy, although French, English, Comorian, Hindi, Chinese, and other dialects are spoken. This island possesses a unique blend of Asian and African culture and is well known as the home of some of the world's most unusual and most endangered flora and fauna, from lemurs to giant tortoises.

History, Social, and Political Structure
Despite its proximity to Africa, Madagascar was not inhabited until 2,000 years ago. Around that time, it became populated by seafaring peoples from present-day Indonesia. This was followed by early contacts with Europeans attempting to establish trading settlements. A struggle for dominance between the British and the French resulted in a colonial period starting in the late 19th century. Madagascar became an independent country in 1960. Due to the continuing bond with France, resulting from the former colonial rule, the republic has developed political, economic, and cultural links with the French-speaking countries of western Africa. The country has moved from postcolonial

democracy to a transitional military government to a socialist regime to a parliamentary democracy. The president is elected by universal suffrage to a five-year term with a two-term limit. The prime minister is nominated by parliament and approved by the president. In January 2009, political tensions erupted and led to a military-backed, extraconstitutional transfer of power and the consequent establishment of an interim de facto government (*Haute Autorité pour la Transition*). This transitional government is not recognized by the international community (United Nations, European Union, African Union, and Southern African Development Community).

Educational Structure

The educational system consists of primary and secondary schools, technical institutes, teacher-training colleges, and a university system. Education is free and compulsory for five years, followed by four years of lower secondary education. Students may then attend a three-year program in either general upper secondary studies or technical school studies. Historically, the system has been characterized by an unequal distribution of education resources among the different regions of the country. Adding to these geographical inequities is the continued lack of educational opportunities for the poorest sectors of society. A final challenge revolves around the growing gap between a declining government-sponsored public school system and an increasingly vibrant and growing private school system. However, the gradual expansion of educational opportunities has had an impressive impact on Malagasy society, most notably in raising the literacy level of the general population.

Current Issues

Madagascar is a poor country with over 70 percent of the population falling below the poverty level of $50 a year. This high level of poverty has created vast inequities in the health and educational sectors. Due to the burdens of caste, gender, and class, women and children are particularly vulnerable to exploitation. Health, nutrition, and the fight against communicable diseases and human immunodeficiency virus and acquired immune deficiency syndrome (HIV/AIDS) are key goals of Madagascar's poverty reduction strategy, the Madagascar Action Plan (MAP). Agriculture, including fishing and forestry, is a mainstay of the economy, accounting for more than one-fourth of gross domestic product (GDP) and employing 80

percent of the population. Exports of apparel have boomed in recent years primarily due to duty-free access to the United States.

However, the current political crisis has dealt serious blows to the economy. Tourism dropped more than 50 percent in 2009, compared to the previous year, and many investors are wary of entering the uncertain investment environment. Deforestation and erosion, aggravated by the use of firewood as the primary source of fuel, are serious concerns. Other environmental areas of concern include surface water contaminated with raw sewage and other organic wastes and the fact that several species of flora and fauna unique to the island are in danger of extinction.

Karen Ragoonaden
University of British Columbia, Okanagan

See Also: France; Poverty and Education; Sexism in Education; South Africa.

Further Readings

Allen, P. M. and M. Covell. *Historical Dictionary of Madagascar*. Lanham, MD: Scarecrow Press, 2005.

Brown, M. *A History of Madagascar*. Princeton, NJ: Markus Weinus Publishers, 2002.

Brown, M. *Madagascar Rediscovered*. London: Damien Turnnacliffe, 1978.

Central Intelligence Agency. *World Factbook*. "Madagascar." http://www.cia.gov/library/publications/the-world -factbook/geos/ma.html (Accessed December 2011).

Worldmark Encyclopedia of the Nations. "Madagascar." http://www.encyclopedia.com/doc/1G2-2586700108 .html (Accessed December 2011).

Magnet Schools

Magnet schools are elementary and secondary public schools that enroll students on a voluntary basis from anywhere within the school district in which they are eligible and that employ innovative instructional methods or offer specialized curricula typically not found in other public schools.

Magnet schools come in a variety of forms. Some are described as "dedicated magnets" because all students who attend were selected from a districtwide pool of applicants and all participate in the magnet program. Magnet schools can also be created in a way such that they partially resemble traditional neighborhood schools while offering all the curricular and pedagogical features of magnet schools. Such schools offer magnet programs in which all students participate, but students are selected from both surrounding neighborhoods and a districtwide applicant pool. Magnet programs can exist within schools, such that only a portion of enrolled students participate in the specialized program of study or are exposed to the innovative teaching methods used. Magnet schools, thus, represent innovations at both the level of pedagogy and the admission of students. Their curricular offerings make them a subject of educational innovations, while the ways in which they enroll students make them a tool of school desegregation.

History

The first magnet school was created in 1968 in Tacoma, Washington. The Tacoma school board, having sought a solution to the segregation of its small black student population, reorganized its virtually all-black McCarver Junior High School into a magnet elementary school. Junior high students who had previously attended McCarver were assigned to other schools in a race-conscious manner designed to decrease school segregation. Elementary-grade students at McCarver were granted automatic admission to the new McCarver Elementary School. Other students were then admitted without consideration of where they lived. This approach to admissions reduced the amount of isolation experienced by African American students in the city. Prior to the reorganization of McCarver, African American students comprised 86 percent of its student body. That percentage fell to 53 percent one year after the new magnet elementary school opened.

As McCarver's own history illustrates, magnet schools have their origins in the struggle to racially integrate schools after the *Brown v. Board of Education of Topeka, Kansas* (1954) Supreme Court decision. That unanimous decision ruled formally racially segregated school systems unconstitutional. After *Brown*, a variety of measures were used to desegregate schools and achieve racial balance—the state at which a school's student body reflects the racial composition of the district. Some measures sought racial balance through "push" processes, whereby students are sent to particular schools via mandatory school assignments. In contrast, magnet schools were designed, as the name implies, to "pull" in students who otherwise

would not attend them. Key to attracting students are incentives designed to entice parents and students to forgo their neighborhood schools. This is particularly true in regard to attracting white students to previously majority-black schools—schools that are often viewed unfavorably by white families. Incentives include opportunities to pursue students' substantive interests with tailor-made curricula (e.g., in science and technology, language, the arts) or opportunities to experience innovative teaching methods not widely adopted in other public schools (e.g., Montessori). Given historically and continuing high levels of residential segregation between blacks and whites, the privileging of educational interests over nonacademic considerations in enrollment decisions, such as location of residence, is the primary feature of magnet schools that facilitates racial diversity. As such, magnet schools have been and continue to be a key tool used by segregated school districts to undo vestiges of their once *de jure* segregated school systems.

White Flight

Judicial, federal, and social support for magnet schools as a tool for desegregation grew because of their potential to increase integration without exacerbating "white flight." White flight is the phenomenon of white families withdrawing from a particular public school system, either by enrolling in private schools or in public schools in different districts, in response to mandatory desegregation efforts. In the wake of delayed school desegregation, courts ordered mandatory desegregation plans, some of which required busing students outside the neighborhoods in which they lived. In large measure, white parents resisted mandatory school assignments by sending their children to private schools or by moving to school districts that were not subject to mandatory desegregation orders.

The ability to avoid mandatory desegregation plans was greatly facilitated by the 1974 *Milliken v. Bradley* Supreme Court decision, which held that the suburbs of Detroit could not be forced to participate in Detroit's desegregation plans when those suburbs had no formal role in creating segregated schools in the city. By freeing suburbs from the responsibility to participate in city desegregation programs, the *Milliken* decision created places in which white families could relocate to avoid the threat of mandatory school assignments and associated busing. Because magnet schools operate on the premise of parental choice, they provide school districts a mechanism for integration free of coercion that may result in white flight.

The federal government has financially supported magnet schools and their use as desegregation tools, first through the Emergency School Aid Act from 1972 to 1981, then via the Magnet School Assistance Program (MSAP). However, the federal government's educational objectives have broadened in light of recent Supreme Court decisions, such as the 2007 *Parents Involved in Community Schools v. Seattle School District No. 1*, which restrict the use of race as a primary concern in school placements. In 2010, the most recent accounting period, MSAP awarded $100 million in grants to 36 school districts in 15 states stretching across every region of the country. Another $99.8 million was appropriated for 2011. The program reports substantial growth in magnet schools, which is consistent with changes in the number of magnet schools across the 1981 to 2001 period that show a growth of almost 2,100 magnet schools.

Controversies

Controversies surrounding magnet schools relate to their use as tools for desegregation in relation to how such schools are organized. In particular, concerns arise as to the racial and ethnic composition of magnet programs compared to the racial and ethnic composition of the schools in which they exist. Although the magnet program may meet its integration goals, the nonmagnet component of a school may not.

Under such circumstances, questions emerge as to the extent to which magnet programs achieve desegregation at the school level but reconstitute segregation at the level of classrooms for students who are not part of the magnet program. Magnet programs designed to attract whites to majority-black schools are typically the conditions under which internal resegregation can occur. Alternatively, magnet programs themselves may not be integrated, though their presence in schools moves participating schools toward greater integration. In this case, white students are concentrated in magnet programs, while minority students are concentrated in the nonmagnet components of schools. Under these conditions, the concern is that such arrangements may undermine the fundamental interest in the integration of learning contexts that magnet schools were designed to achieve; they may also strain race relations between white students in magnet programs and minority students outside them if minority students are stigmatized by their underrepresentation in magnet programs.

Debates also emerge regarding the cost of magnet schools. Given their mission to offer innovative content and methods, the extra costs associated with publicizing their options to parents, as well as (in some cases) additional transportation costs, magnet schools often require greater financial investments by school districts than do traditional schools. Questions then arise as to what constitutes equitable access to magnet schools when more students seek to enroll than there are slots to accommodate them.

Effects of Magnet Schools

Magnet schools have been evaluated primarily with respect to two outcomes: the amount of desegregation they produce and the amount of academic achievement experienced by their students. Research on the academic consequences of attending magnet schools is mixed, perhaps due to the challenging selectivity issues with which researchers must contend in order to draw conclusions about the causal effects of magnet schools on achievement. Studies of the effects of magnet schools on levels of desegregation are often investigations of the amount of in-school interracial contact between whites and blacks (or whites and other minorities). Recent research indicates that magnet schools achieve modest increases in school desegregation, though other research identifies the limits to which they do. Adding an increasing number of magnet schools to a school district that already employs a voluntary desegregation plan appears to yield relatively little additional return in terms of interracial exposure.

Pamela R. Bennett
Johns Hopkins University

See Also: *Brown v. Board of Education*; Busing; Private Schools; School Choice; School Effects.

Further Readings

Berends, Mark, et al. *Handbook of Research on School Choice*. New York: Routledge, 2009.

Flemming, Arthur S., Stephen Horn, Frankie M. Freeman, Manuel Ruiz, Jr., and Murray Saltzman. "School Desegregation in Tacoma, Washington." Washington, DC: U.S. Commission on Civil Rights, 1979.

Rossell, Christine H. *The Carrot or the Stick for School Desegregation Policy: Magnet Schools or Forced Busing*. Philadelphia: Temple University Press, 1990.

Rossell, Christine H. "The Desegregation Efficiency of Magnet Schools." *Urban Affairs Review*, v.38 (2003).

Rossell, Christine H. "No Longer Famous but Still Intact." *Education Next* (Spring 2005).

Saporito, Salvatore. "Private Choice, Public Consequences: Magnet Schools and Segregation by Race and Poverty." *Social Problems*, v.50/2 (2003).

Maine

Located in the far northeastern corner of the United States, Maine is bordered on the north by Canada and by New Hampshire on the south and west. The 35,387 square miles of Maine is heavily forested, and the state's official nickname is the Pine Tree State. It is also sometimes called the Lumber State. The first sawmill in the United States was built in Maine in 1623. According to the 2010 census, Maine has a population of 1,328,361. Although Augusta is the capital, it is the ninth-largest city in the state. The largest cities are Portland, Lewiston, and Bangor. Maine's manufacturing sector has been hit hard by the economic downturn of the early 21st century, and efforts are being made to expand the scope of adult education so that workers have greater opportunities for finding jobs. Other initiatives are dealing with reaching children and youth to prepare them for the technological advances of the new century.

In 2008, through the Harold Alfond Foundation, all children born in general hospitals in Augusta and Waterville were given a $500 grant to be used for college expenses. The following year, the program was expanded statewide. Maine is the only state in the United States to offer such a program to all babies born in the state and to those who move there before their first birthday, regardless of income. The hope is that parents will deposit regular installments to the college funds so that the total will be large enough to pay for college expenses by the time those babies grow to college age. Maine is also working with middle school and high school students through a laptop computer initiative that provides each student with a laptop with Wi-Fi capabilities.

History

Maine has a long history that began even before Europeans arrived on the North American continent, and the area was originally settled by PaleoIndians. According to legend, Norse explorer Leif Eriksson visited the area that became Maine while sailing around Canada in 1000 C.E. Even though English explorer John Cabot claimed the land for the British Crown in 1497, the first settlement was not built until 1604 along the St. Croix River. In 1652, Massachusetts Bay Colony laid claim to the Province of Maine and formally purchased the area in 1677. The first school was erected in 1647, but the land was sparsely settled and the risk of sending children away from their homes to attend school was generally considered too great.

Bedouin College, the first postsecondary school, was established in 1794 at the first legislative session. During the second session, legislators passed the first elementary school act. The responsibility for financing such schools was left in the hands of local communities. In 1800, there were only seven public grammar schools to be found in the entire state. By 1828, the state had begun providing financial support for public elementary schools. In 1820, Maine granted universal rights to both suffrage and education. Thus, it was fitting that author Harriet Beecher Stowe wrote *Uncle Tom's Cabin* while living in Brunswick. The novel was instrumental in rousing the ire of many

Table 1 Elementary and secondary education characteristics

	Maine	U.S. (average)
Total number of schools	657	1,988
Total students	189,077	970,278
Total teachers	15,384.30	60,766.56
Pupil/teacher ratio	12.29	15.97

Source: U.S. Department of Education, National Center for Education Statistics, Common Core of Data (CCD), 2010–11.

Table 2 Elementary and secondary education finance

	Maine	U.S. (average)
Total revenues	$2,601,562,891	$11,464,385,994
Total expenditures for education	$2,516,597,127	$11,712,033,839
Total current expenditures	$2,308,070,836	$9,938,906,259

Source: U.S. Department of Education, National Center for Education Statistics, Common Core of Data (CCD), "National Public Education Financial Survey," FY08 (2007–08).

Americans against the cruelties of slavery by making it a personal rather than an ideological issue. After petitioning Massachusetts for the right to become a separate state, Maine was granted statehood in 1820 as part of the Missouri Compromise, which sought to ensure a balance of slave and free states. The first school systems were established in Maine in 1846, and the following year, teacher institutes were established to provide training for educators. In the 1860s, Maine began setting up normal schools at selected academies for such purposes. It was not until 1968 that Maine established the University of Maine system that developed public postsecondary schools throughout the state.

Current Situation

In the 21st century, the manufacturing sector has been suffering, with more than 28,500 jobs lost between 2000 and 2010. Only a fourth of Maine's workforce has a college degree, and this leaves a large segment of the population with limited opportunities for finding employment. In order to expand opportunities for such workers, the state legislature now fully funds Maine College Transitions, a program that teaches adult learners academic and college readiness skills at little or no cost.

There are 189,225 students enrolled in Maine's schools, and 81.9 percent of them are in Title I schools. The school population is predominantly white (93.4 percent), but there are also African Americans (2.9 percent), Hispanics (1.2 percent), Asian/Pacific Islanders (1.7 percent), and American Indian/Alaska Natives (0.7 percent) among the students. There are 16,331 teachers, and the student/teacher ratio is 11.6. There are 662 schools in 246 school districts. There are no charter schools in the state. Maine spends $11,977 annually on each student, providing a third of all costs for public education in the state. Students consistently score higher than the national average on achievement tests in mathematics, science, reading, and writing.

Students in Maine are also learning about technology, and the state has the longest ongoing program to get laptop computers into the hands of teachers and students in the United States. Through the Maine Learning Technology Initiative, the 1-to-1 program, which was the brainchild of then governor Angus King, the state placed Apple iBooks in the hands of all seventh grade teachers and students in 2002. The following year, the program was expanded to eighth grade teachers and students, bringing the number of laptops to 37,000. By 2009, there were 60,000 laptops in use. The goal of the plan is to extend computer use to all grade seven to 12 teachers and students.

Elizabeth Rholetter Purdy
Independent Scholar

See Also: Adult Education; Student/Teacher Ratio; Technology Education.

Further Readings

National Center for Education Statistics. http://www.nces.ed.gov/nationsreportcard/states (Accessed February 2012).

Nickerson, Kermit S. "150 Years of Education in Maine." http://www.maine.gov/education/150yrs/150years.html (Accessed February 2012).

Waters, John. "Maine Ingredients." *T H E Journal*, v.36 (September 2009).

Malaysia

The Federation of Malaysia is a rapidly advancing southeast Asian nation. It consists of two parts: Peninsular Malaysia, which is also known as West Malaysia and has 11 states and two federal territories, and East Malaysia, which has two states and one federal territory. These two wings are separated by the South China Sea, and East Malaysia is located 400 miles (640 kilometers) away on the Borneo island.

Malaysia shares its borders with Thailand in the north, Indonesia in the south, and the Philippines in the east. It shares common maritime boundaries with Brunei, Singapore, and Vietnam, in addition to Indonesia, the Philippines, and Thailand. It has an area of 127,320 square miles (329,847 square kilometers). According to the World Bank, the estimated population of Malaysia was 28,401,017 in 2010, with an annual growth rate of 1.7 percent. The 2010 census shows that 34 percent of the population comes from the 15 years and under age group.

The estimated gross domestic product (GDP) for 2010 was $247.781 billion, ranking 30th in the world, with an annual growth rate of 7.2 percent. Agriculture accounts for 13 percent, industry for 36 percent, and the services sector for 51 percent of the nation's

GDP. Main export revenue totaled $210.3 billion in 2010 and came from the sale of electronic equipment, petroleum, liquefied natural gas, wood and agricultural products, rubber, textiles, and chemicals. Malaysia imported electronics, machinery, petroleum products, plastics, vehicles, iron and steel, and chemicals worth $156.6 billion in 2010. Main trading partners are China, Japan, Singapore, United States, Thailand, and Indonesia.

Malaysia has been ruled by almost all major colonial powers, including Portuguese, Spanish, Dutch, and British, at different times since 1511. It was also occupied by Japanese forces from 1941 to 1945; it became independent as the Malayan Union in 1946. Finally, it emerged as the Federation of Malaysia in 1963. Although over 75 percent of the population remained below the poverty line during 1963 to 1970, through significant reform in the agricultural sector, industrial institution building, and services sector development, among others, and because of its comparatively stable political system, the country's poverty level was reduced to 3.6 percent in 2007. Rapid growth in economic conditions and innovative inclusion of well-being-related ventures helped the country build modern education systems and modern social structures.

History and Social Structure

Historians found evidences that human settlements started in some parts of Malaysia over 10,000 years ago. Some distinct groups such as Negrito people, comprising several ethnic factions, were living in the country, and many of them expanded to other far regions including Taiwan, migrating from the Malay Archipelago during 6000 to 1000 B.C.E.

In the 9th century the Buddhist Malay kingdom of Srivijaya was founded. which controlled much of the peninsula until the 13th century. In the 14th century the Hindu Kingdom of Majapahit was founded. Conversion of the Malays to Islam started in the early 14th century, and in the 15th century the state of Malacca came under the rule of a Muslim prince. Malacca was the Malaysian hub for Malay trading with Arab, Chinese, and Indian counterparts at the time. International trade, religious conversion, and, later, European colonial legacies contributed significantly to shaping the sociocultural structure of the country. Malaysia has a stable intercultural mix. There are four major ethnic groups: about 50.4 percent of the total population are Malays, 23.7 percent are Chinese, 11 percent are indigenous, 7.1 percent are Indians, and 7.8 percent are of other origins.

According to the 2010 census about 61.3 percent of the total population are Muslim, 19.8 percent are Buddhist, 9.2 percent are Christian, 6.3 percent are Hindu, 1.3 percent are believers of Confucianism, Taoism, and other traditional Chinese religions, 0.7 percent are atheist, and the remaining 1.4 percent represent other religions including Jewish and Sikh. All the religious groups practice their respective faiths freely and peacefully. The country's administration and leadership have been successful in maintaining a nonviolent open society for mutually respectful coexistence of all ethnic and religious groups. Basic literacy rate among those 15 years and older was about 95 percent in 2009. Primary education is compulsory, with an estimated enrollment rate of 99 percent, of whom about 69 percent complete secondary schools, and about 200,000 complete postsecondary and university education annually.

Educational Structure

Formal education in Malaysia includes preschool playgroup (ages 3–4) and kindergarten (ages 4–6). Primary school education is offered following kindergarten under Darjah 1 (age 7), through Darjah 6 (age 12). After completion of Darjah 6 students are required to sit for the statewide Primary School Achievement Test in the areas of Malay comprehension, written Malay, English, science, and mathematics. Community-based school, including state-funded Chinese and Tamil school, students are required to take additional language tests in the areas of comprehension and written languages. In addition, if there are more than 15 students with other Indigenous languages attending a class, students are allowed to take special language tests in their native language. Malay and English are compulsory for all primary and secondary students.

Secondary school education is offered under Tingkatan 1 (age 13) through Tingkatan 5 (ages 17). After completion of the secondary school classes, students are required to take the Malaysian Certificate of Education examination to be able to continue their education or training through colleges, universities, and professional programs. Higher School Certificate examination, similar to the General Certificate of Education "A" Level examination, is also centrally conducted to identify students who plan to attend postsecondary education at the 18 public universities and 51 private universities and university colleges in Malaysia and take undergraduate courses. There are also 21 polytechnic institutes that offer skills-related technical and engineering courses.

A large number of community colleges in addition to secondary schools offer an 18-month preparation course as the prerequisite for taking the Malaysian Higher School Certification exam. A race-based quota system is applied in the admission process to reach out to underserved communities, in total, 90 percent of the seats being reserved for the Bumiputeras (son of the soil) and the remaining 10 percent are filled by others.

Current Trends

Restructuring and strengthening of education and training has started in Malaysia, with a large educational allocation of about $13 billion, of which about $2.09 billion was allocated for upgrading schools and related facilities in 2011. A new innovative approach was taken by allocating about $70 million dollars to reward good teaching practices with increased remuneration to effective teachers, high-performance-school principals, and head teachers. Over 1,700 new classes and 800 new teachers were added. About $190 million was added in scholarship funds to provide in-service training and education opportunities to the continuing educators, and another $190 million was added to improve school curriculum with an objective to enhance students' proficiencies in Malay and English languages. About $6.5 million was added to recruit university faculty with doctoral degrees. With a promise to continue educational reform, the educational sector allocation has been increased to $16.2 billion.

Existing tuition and examination fees of $8 to $11 are in the process of being abolished, with a fresh allocation of about $50 million for the school program. Further, income tax exemption of 70 percent or investment tax allowance of 100 percent is to be put in place to encourage continuing higher education in all areas. Tuition fee assistance will be provided to civil servants to further their studies on a part-time basis, as well as 5,000 master's-level scholarships and 500 doctoral-level scholarships will be given under the new $39 million scholarship plan. Over $26 million will be used to offer undergraduate-level degrees to 20,000 schoolteachers with certification.

Despite all the investments in education sectors, very soon the language of instruction will be Malay instead of English, which has been the language of science education at higher levels for the last 300 years. This new policy of rejecting English, an international business language, may impact Malaysia's capacity-building efforts in some areas, including globalized knowledge economy, technology integration, modern cost-effective community building, and global scholarly competitiveness. Sole use of the Malay language in the higher-level curriculum may limit creative participation and contribution of indigenous, Tamil, and Chinese, as well as diverse students from international communities. Further, curriculum and course content may suffer greatly due to a lack of scholarly resources in the field of study.

Malaysia is heading toward reaching its 2020 goal to become one of the world's developed nations, and such a vision requires a globally competitive futuristic but most inclusive education system. Although only a negligible percentage of people in Malaysia live below the poverty line, economic disparity among different ethnic communities, genders, rural, and urban settings remains a big challenge. The condition of economically poor working class Malay and Indigenous communities needs more innovative educational and social business-oriented stimulus packages in light of participants' social, economic, and cultural realities.

Matiul Alam
University of British Columbia

See Also: Community Colleges; Funding of Schools; Governmental Influences on Education; Worldwide Education Revolution.

Further Readings

Gooch, Liz. "In Malaysia, English Ban Raises Fears for Future." *New York Times* (July 9, 2009).

Musa, M. Bakri. "Towards a Competitive Malaysia." Petaling Jaya: Strategic Information and Research Development Centre, 2007.

Mustafa, Shazwa. "Malay Groups Want Vernacular Schools Abolished." *The Malaysian Insider* (2009).

Nusajaya, Johor State. "Education in Malaysia: A Reverse Brain Drain." *The Economist* (May 5, 2011). http://www.economist.com/node/18652195 (Accessed June 2012).

"Pressure on Multi-Faith Malaysia." BBC (May 16, 2011).

Snow, Philip. *The Star Raft: China's Encounter With Africa.* Ithaca, NY: Cornell University Press,1989.

World Bank. "Population, Total." http://data.worldbank.org/indicator/SP.POP.TOTL (Accessed June 2012).

World Bank. "Population Growth (Annual %)." http://data.worldbank.org/indicator/SP.POP.GROW/countries (Accessed June 2012).

Marx, Karl (Marxism and Education)

Karl Marx (1818–83) was the most influential of the socialist thinkers and a philosopher who radically altered how society and history could be viewed. Throughout his life Marx's writing centered on a critique of political economy, in which he developed an analysis of how different social classes evolved in circumstances where the people who produced goods were not the same as those who benefited from them. In terms of the capitalist societies of the 19th century, Marx referred to these classes as the proletariat, who comprised the workforce, and the bourgeoisie, who controlled the means of production and therefore exploited the labor of the proletariat. Many social theorists argue that his ideas remain critical for analyzing society today. In Marx's view of society, education is part of a "superstructure" that also includes the family structure, religion, cultural values, and legal and political systems. Education, along with the other various aspects of the superstructure, is in a complex, dynamic, and mutually influential relationship with the economic "base" of society, which in capitalism equates to the fundamental class relations of labor, production, and exploitation. All critiques of capitalist societies and their education systems make central reference to his work.

Capitalism and Social Inequality

Broadly, the Marxist view of education systems in developed Western societies is that they reproduce social inequalities through coercing people to accept their roles in an unequal capitalist system. Schools are not seen as neutral institutions but are considered as being instrumental in the reproduction of social classes and therefore the conditions required for sustaining the wider capitalist economy. Through their delivery of the official curriculum, teachers are seen as helping perpetuate the exploitative relations of capitalism, as their work involves categorizing young people into a hierarchy of different types of pupil or student and, therefore, helping determine where individuals enter the labor market. Moreover, behind the official curriculum there is a "hidden curriculum" of values that encourage children and young people to passively accept the established organization of work, inequality, and social hierarchy.

For Marxists, both forms of curriculum can be seen as working together through the process of schooling in class-divided societies. So while the roots of class can be found in the way that a society produces, education helps entrench a particular set of productive relations by granting them an apparent ethical, moral, and even natural legitimacy. Antonio Gramsci used the term *ideological hegemony* to refer to the influence that the dominant class has over what counts as knowledge in an education system, while Louis Althusser defined schools as being part of what he termed the Ideological State Apparatus. This is not to suggest a conspiracy on the part of the dominant class; in Marxist terms, it is a natural effect of the way that what counts as knowledge is constructed from the very division of social relations that defines a society.

Consequences of Dominance

The Marxist view of beliefs that underpin Western systems of education—such as liberty, freedom of the individual, and competition—is that these are historically generated as a consequence of the dominance of a particular social class within capitalism. Ideas like these are not neutral or for the benefit of everyone but rather are ideas that serve the dominant class that are accepted by most people as if they are actually for the common good. While Marx and his frequent collaborator Friedrich Engels wrote very little directly about education, their use of the theory of "praxis" provides the basis for a concept of education that has become deeply influential. Praxis essentially means all the symbolic and practical physical relationships we have as individuals with the people and things around us, which provide the basis for our knowledge and social development. So for Marx, an ideal or proper education system is one that enables the production of fully developed and free human beings; that is to say, people who are genuinely conscious of and invested in their own creative actions in the world rather than alienated from their learning and labor. From a Marxist position it is not sufficient to simply reflect on knowledge and experience. A proper education system must also enable people to see how their actions can and do change the world.

Yet Marx also understood an inherent paradox about education and society: a fundamental change of social circumstances was necessary for the establishment of a proper education system, but a proper education system was essential for bringing about a fundamental change in society. In this way, education has been positioned by Marx and those who draw on his theories as key to both the reproduction and revolution of social relations between the classes divided within capitalism. Marxism has developed in numerous ways and there have been many different schools of theoretical thought, although due to this emphasis on inequality and the potential for conflict between social groups, all approaches share a joint commitment to sociological analysis and political reform. In terms of education, Marx realized that the starting point for reform must be the actual circumstances that we face rather than an idealized situation.

This is most clearly borne out in the field of critical pedagogy, where Marxist ideas about praxis, political reform, and social analysis are brought together by educators in order to develop approaches to teaching and learning that attempt to overcome the ideological hegemony of the dominant class. This is achieved through showing the value-laden nature of knowledge, where teachers work together with learners to alter their perceptions of the established order of social inequalities and encourage them to engage in practical action to solve the problems of their everyday lives. Marx emphasized that everyday life is not determined by consciousness, but consciousness by everyday life. The core idea informing Marxist-influenced critical pedagogies then is that a radical change in the way that education is organized will be reflected in the way that educators and students think and therefore the kind of world they are able to create.

David Mellor
University of Bristol

See Also: Banking Concept of Education; Bowles, Samuel and Herbert Gintis; Conflict Theory of Education; Critical Theory of Education; Freire, Paulo.

Further Readings

Anyon, J. *Marx and Education.* New York: Routledge, 2011.

Small, R. *Marx and Education.* Aldershot, UK: Ashgate, 2005.

Wheen, Francis. *Karl Marx: A Life.* New York: W. W. Norton & Co., 2001.

Maryland

Maryland is a moderate state, diverse in people and geography, with a strong investment in education. It is located in the midatlantic region, bordering

Table 1 Elementary and secondary education characteristics

	Maryland	U.S. (average)
Total number of schools	1,457	1,988
Total students	852,211	970,278
Total teachers	58,428.47	60,766.56
Pupil/teacher ratio	14.59	15.97

Source: U.S. Department of Education, National Center for Education Statistics, Common Core of Data (CCD), 2010–11.

Table 2 Elementary and secondary education finance

	Maryland	U.S. (average)
Total revenues	$13,084,018,085	$11,464,385,994
Total expenditures for education	$12,758,707,718	$11,712,033,839
Total current expenditures	$11,211,175,523	$9,938,906,259

Source: U.S. Department of Education, National Center for Education Statistics, Common Core of Data (CCD), "National Public Education Financial Survey," FY08 (2007–08).

Washington, D.C., Virginia, West Virginia, and Pennsylvania. The state stretches from the Atlantic Ocean to the Allegheny Mountains. The capital is Annapolis.

According to the U.S. Census, Maryland's population was 5.8 million in 2010. Close to 60 percent of state residents are white and 30 percent are African American. Eight percent are of Hispanic descent. The non-Hispanic white population is declining as all other groups are increasing. Approximately 12 percent of residents are foreign born and 15 percent speak a language other than English in the home. Educational attainment is high, with 87.5 percent of residents 25 years and older holding a high school diploma and 35 percent holding at least a bachelor's degree.

The median household income was $69,000 in 2009. Nine percent of residents lived below the poverty level. Approximately 80 percent of workers are employed in the private sector, with the remaining 20 percent in federal, state, and local governments. In 2010, Maryland had 7.5 percent unemployment.

Maryland's leading industries are information technology, telecommunications, aerospace, and defense. One-third of the land is used for farming. Agricultural products include corn, soybeans, dairy, poultry, and seafood from the Chesapeake Bay.

History and Social Structure

Native American tribes lived in the region when Europeans arrived in the early 17th century. In 1632, British King Charles I granted a charter to Cecil Calvert, a Catholic. His descendants established Maryland as a colony where all Christians could worship, conduct business, and hold public office. The colonists tried several crops before settling on tobacco, a labor-intensive crop that fueled the expansion of slavery.

The first state constitution was adopted in 1776. During the War of 1812, Francis Scott Key wrote what would become the national anthem while watching the British attack in Baltimore Harbor. As a border state, events leading up to and during the Civil War occurred within the state or nearby. Maryland remained in the Union but many citizens sided and fought with the Confederacy. The state constitution emancipated slaves in 1864.

Efforts to broaden access to and funding for education were under way by the mid-1700s. However, it was not until 1864 that a public education system was established. Maryland schools were segregated from 1865 until 1955, following the federal *Brown v. Board of Education* decision banning segregation. Thurgood Marshall, the Baltimore-born lawyer and first African American to later serve on the U.S. Supreme Court, argued that case.

Educational Structure

Maryland has a state and county governance structure. The governor is the chief executive of the state government. The General Assembly is a bicameral legislature that convenes each January for a 90-day session. The state has 23 county governments and one municipality, Baltimore City.

Public education is the shared responsibility of state and local governments. A governor-appointed Board of Education oversees the state Department of Education and appoints the state superintendent of schools. There are 24 county-based school districts, including Baltimore City. Local school boards are elected, appointed by the governor, or appointed jointly by the governor and the local leader. Maryland's charter school law gives districts primary authority to grant charters. In 2011, state and local funds in roughly equal proportions accounted for 94 percent of the $12 billion for public schools.

Education is compulsory for children between ages 5 and 16. The school year is a minimum of 180 days. The Maryland School Assessment (MSA) is administered annually to measure student progress in grades three through eight in reading/language arts, math, and science. Maryland is the only state to require service learning for high school graduation. Over half of public school teachers hold a master's degree or higher, and over half possess 10 or less years teaching experience. Maryland ranked sixth in the nation in teacher salaries.

State oversight of early childhood, postsecondary, and adult education is the responsibility of diverse agencies. The Department of Education oversees early childhood education efforts. The Maryland Higher Education Commission (MHEC), an independent agency of governor-appointed/senate-approved members, coordinates and supervises higher education institutions and administers state financial aid programs. The Department of Labor, Licensing, and Regulation oversees federally funded adult education and administers the state's General Educational Development (GED) testing program.

Approximately 850,000 students were enrolled in 3,000 Pre-K–12 schools in the state, half of which are public. Montgomery, Prince Georges, and Baltimore City are among the 25 largest school systems in the United States. Maryland has 57 colleges and universities and over 175 private career schools.

Current Issues

In 2011, Maryland led the nation in the number of students passing Advanced Placement exams. Education Week's "Quality Counts" report ranked the state's Pre-K–12 education first overall for three consecutive years. While Maryland has fared better than many states, the economic recession is creating significant budget challenges for state and local education systems. The education department is in transition following the retirement of Nancy Grasmick, the longest-serving state superintendent of schools in the country.

State priorities include revising the Pre-K–12 curriculum, assessment, and accountability system based on the Common Core Standards; building a technology infrastructure; preparing, retaining, and evaluating educators; and improving low-performing schools. Maryland received a $250 million federal Race to the Top (RTTT) grant in 2010 to support these efforts. School readiness and narrowing the achievement gap is a major focus. From 2010 to 2011, 81 percent of kindergartners were fully ready for school and the readiness gap among kindergartners appeared to be narrowing. In 2011, Maryland won another RTTT grant to strengthen support of early childhood efforts.

Catherine Dunn Shiffman
Shenandoah University

See Also: Adult Education; Advanced and Honors Classes; Career and Technical Education; General Educational Development; Higher Education; Race to the Top.

Further Readings

Brugger, R. J. *Maryland: A Middle Temperament: 1684–1980*. Baltimore, MD: Johns Hopkins University Press, 1988.

Maryland Higher Education Commission. http://www.mhec.state.md.us (Accessed June 2012).

Maryland State Archives. "Maryland at a Glance." http://www.msa.md.gov/msa/mdmanual/01glance/html/mdglance.html (Accessed June 2012).

Maryland State Department of Education. "The Factbook 2009–2010: A Statistical Handbook" (2011). http://www.marylandpublicschools.org/MSDE/newsroom/publications (Accessed June 2012).

Maryland State Department of Education. "Getting Ready: The 2010–2011 Maryland School Readiness Report" (2011). http://www.marylandpublicschools.org/msde/newsroom/publications/school_readiness (Accessed June 2012).

"Quality Counts" *Education Week*. (2011). http://www.edweek.org/ew/toc/2011/01/13/index.html (Accessed June 2012).

U.S. Census. "State and County QuickFacts" (2011). http://www.quickfacts.census.gov/qfd/states/24000.html (Accessed June 2012).

Massachusetts

Massachusetts is the seventh-smallest state in the United States with an area of 10,555 square miles (27,340 square kilometers). Located in New England, Massachusetts is one of the oldest states in the nation.

Massachusetts was originally inhabited by Algonquian tribes such as the Pocomtuc and Massachusett, for which the British colony was later named. In the early 1600s, the native people came in contact with Europeans. Many indigenous people were killed by disease. In 1617–19, smallpox killed 90 percent of the Massachusetts Bay Native Americans. The first European permanent settlement had been established at Jamestown, Virginia, in 1607, followed by the colony at Plymouth, Massachusetts, in 1620, and in 1630 by the Massachusetts Bay Colony, which is now present-day Boston. When the colonies sought independence from Great Britain, Massachusetts was at the center of it. Protests against the British taxes began after the French and Indian War and led to the Boston Massacre (1770) and the Boston Tea Party (1773). The battles of Lexington and Concord, both in Massachusetts, launched the American Revolutionary War. After independence and the formation of the new United States of America, Massachusetts became the sixth state to ratify the Constitution.

As of 2011, Massachusetts had a population of 6,587,536. The population is 76 percent white, 9 percent Latino (4 percent Puerto Rican), 6 percent African American, and 5 percent Asian, with a very small portion of the population being of American Indian descent.

Governance

Massachusetts' governance reflects that of the United States and is divided into three branches: executive, legislative, and judicial. The state constitution was drafted by John Adams in 1780. The governor heads the executive branch and has the power to veto legislation, fill judicial appointments, grant pardons, and prepare the state annual budget. The legislative branch has two houses, the 160-member House and 40-member Senate. The judicial branch has as its highest court the Supreme Judicial Court of Massachusetts, consisting of a chief justice and six associate justices. The Supreme Judicial Court serves over several lower courts.

Educational Structure

Education has been a priority in Massachusetts for most of its long history. Massachusetts in 1647 was the first state to require cities to appoint a teacher or establish a grammar school. Horace Mann pushed further education reforms in the 19th century, setting the base for universal public education. The oldest elementary school, Mather School founded in 1639, and oldest high school, Boston Latin School founded in 1635, were both established in Massachusetts. In 1852 Massachusetts became the first state to pass mandatory school attendance laws. Today Massachusetts

Table 1 Elementary and secondary education characteristics

	Massachusetts	U.S. (average)
Total number of schools	1,849	1,988
Total students	955,563	970,278
Total teachers	68,754.39	60,766.56
Pupil/teacher ratio	13.90	15.97

Source: U.S. Department of Education, National Center for Education Statistics, Common Core of Data (CCD), 2010–11.

Table 2 Elementary and secondary education finance

	Massachusetts	U.S. (average)
Total revenues	$14,602,937,454	$11,464,385,994
Total expenditures for education	$14,444,055,769	$11,712,033,839
Total current expenditures	$13,182,986,762	$9,938,906,259

Source: U.S. Department of Education, National Center for Education Statistics, Common Core of Data (CCD), "National Public Education Financial Survey," FY08 (2007–08).

has an excellent reputation for supporting education. In 2004 Massachusetts ranked fifth in the nation for per-student expenditures in elementary and secondary schools. In 2007 Massachusetts scored highest of all the states on the National Assessment of Educational Progress.

Despite its small size, Massachusetts houses 121 institutions of higher education. The state also has the oldest college (Harvard University, established in 1636) and oldest women's college (Mount Holyoke College, established in 1837). The state system of higher education consists of the five campuses of the University of Massachusetts. The flagship campus is in Amherst. Recently, the University of Massachusetts created an honors university at the Amherst campus.

Current Issues

While on average Massachusetts performs well on standardized achievement tests, the achievement gap between low-income, minority students and their high-income, nonminority peers persists. In 2008 only 65 African American students in Massachusetts public high schools had qualifying scores on Advanced Placement (AP) science exams. In struggling high schools from 2008 to 2009, fewer than 20 percent of students scored proficient on the state exam. The

state launched the Excellence Agenda and Massachusetts Math and Science Initiative (MMSI) to bring up achievement levels. Among the goals of these programs is to use AP math, science, and English as the focus to reduce the gap for high-poverty and minority students. Further, the Excellence Agenda has pledged to turn around 100 of Massachusetts' failing schools. The outcomes of these two reforms on the achievement gap in the state are unclear as of this writing.

M. Felicity Rogers-Chapman
Claremont Graduate University

See Also: Higher Education; Maine; New Hampshire; New York; Truancy; Wealth and Education.

Further Readings

"Annual Estimates of the Resident Population for the United States, Regions, States, and Puerto Rico: April 1, 2010 to July 1, 2011." In "2011 Population Estimates." Washington, DC: U.S. Census Bureau, Population Division, December 2011.

Brown, R. D. and J. Tager. *Massachusetts: A Concise History.* Cambridge: University of Massachusetts Press, 2001.

Lockridge, Kenneth A. *A New England Town: The First Hundred Years.* New York: W. W. Norton & Co., 1985.

Maternal Education

The idea that education should help women to become better mothers first gained wide acceptance in 19th-century Europe and America. As schooling expanded worldwide during the late 20th century, international demographic surveillance programs were launched, permitting assessment of the intergenerational effects of education.

Survey data show that higher levels of mothers' schooling are associated with delayed onset of childbearing, fewer lifetime births, decreased child mortality risks, and improvements in children's educational attainment. In most settings, these associations are stronger for mothers' than for fathers' schooling. There is continuing debate, however, as to whether these relationships are causal. Proponents of causal mechanisms draw upon theories of human capital, women's empowerment, and bureaucratization; opponents view schooling as a dimension of socioeconomic status and emphasize the influence of selectivity. The literature on maternal education in the developing world focuses mostly on mortality and fertility rates as outcomes, while studies in developed countries focus more on educational outcomes in the next generation.

The Developing World

In the late 1970s, demographers demonstrated strong associations between mothers' schooling and child survival in Africa and Latin America. These findings precipitated analyses of data from the World Fertility Survey and its successor, the Demographic and Health Surveys. In most countries of the developing world, these studies show, one or two years of mothers' schooling is associated with reduced risks of child death; protective effects of mothers' schooling are stronger in childhood (ages 1–4) than in infancy (birth–1 year); and household socioeconomic status accounts for only about half of the effect.

Maternal education is also associated with more frequent use of clinics in cases of child illness, and with more optimal child nutritional status. Relationships between maternal education and birthrates are more variable across regions. In most countries in south Asia and Latin America the relationship is inverse, with increasing years of schooling associated with progressively lower numbers of lifetime births; in other countries (mainly in sub-Saharan Africa) women with low levels of schooling have higher fertility than those with no schooling, and very low fertility occurs only among women with high school education or above.

The Developed World

In the developed world, mothers' education is consistently associated with improvements in children's educational attainment and decreases in behavioral problems. Effects of mothers' schooling on lowering fertility or mortality are evident between those who do and those who do not complete high school, and between high school- and college-educated women.

Theories and Mechanisms

Hypothetical pathways linking maternal schooling to child outcomes can be divided into two categories: one focused on income and place of residence and the other focused on schooling as a form of socialization that imparts values and skills conducive to lower fertility and more optimal child development.

Socioeconomic Correlates of Schooling

Women with education are more likely to live in cities, with easier access to medical care and wage-earning occupations. These structural features of school access raise the possibility of selection bias. Assortative marriage, with more educated women marrying husbands with higher socioeconomic status, is also a factor that could confound the relationship between mothers' schooling and child outcomes.

Causal Pathways

According to human capital theory, education provides knowledge and skills that help individuals to raise earnings and to make decisions conducive to health. Similarly, women's empowerment theories posit that women with schooling are more able to make reproductive decisions and to allocate household resources in a manner favorable to their children. Both of these positions have been subject to critique on the grounds that sociocultural context modulates the effects of women's empowerment on child outcomes and constrains the scope of health decisions that women can make. An explanation relevant to children's educational attainment focuses on home environments and contends that effects of mothers' schooling on children's education may be explained in part by variation in linguistic socialization in the home. As shown by S. B. Heath, in the United States mothers who have attended a university use an Initiation-Reply-Evaluation pattern of speech typical of teacher-student interaction with their children, thereby preparing their children for the communicative environment of the school. Mothers with lower levels of education are less likely to use this speech pattern at home, and their children are consequently less prepared to engage constructively in classroom discourse when they reach school.

R. A. LeVine and colleagues have applied these insights from language socialization to explain health impacts of maternal schooling. The bureaucratic environment of the school, they suggest, prepares women for interactions with health bureaucracies such as clinics and makes them more effective in obtaining treatment for children in times of illness. These hypotheses are supported by data on the literacy abilities and communicative practices of mothers with varying levels of schooling in four countries.

Conclusion

Mechanisms connecting maternal schooling to child outcomes remain a subject of contention. Currently, most data come from cross-sectional studies designed for other purposes; targeted longitudinal designs are needed to unravel mechanisms and to better inform education policies.

Edward Geoffrey Jedediah Stevenson
Emory University

See Also: Adult Literacy; Classroom Language; Human Capital Theory; Life Course Perspective and Education; Parent Education; School Effects; Schools as Bureaucracies.

Further Readings

Caldwell, J. C. *Demographic Transition Theory*. Dordrecht, Netherlands: Springer, 2006.

Carneiro, P., C. Meghir, and M. Parey. "Maternal Education, Home Environments, and the Development of Children and Adolescents." Working Paper 15/07. London: Institute of Fiscal Studies, 2007.

Cleland, J. and J. van Ginneken. "Maternal Education and Child Survival in Developing Countries: The Search for Pathways of Influence." *Social Science and Medicine*, v.27/12 (1988).

Heath, S. B. "What No Bedtime Story Means: Narrative Skills at Home and School." In *Language Socialization Across Cultures*, B. B. Schieffelin and E. Ochs, eds. Cambridge: Cambridge University Press, 1986.

Jejeebhoy, S. *Women's Education, Autonomy, and Reproductive Behavior*. Oxford: Oxford University Press, 1992.

Maximally Maintained Inequality

The maximally maintained inequality (MMI) hypothesis claims that education expansion causes the decline in quantitative inequalities in enrollment rates once the enrollment rate for the most advantaged socioeconomic (SES) group approaches the saturation point. MMI predicts the decrease of family background effect on educational attainment after the saturation point for the high SES groups has been reached.

Originating from Mare's model of educational transitions and developed further by A. E. Raftery and M. Hout, maximally maintained inequality is often referred to as the persistence of intergenerational educational inequality.

A commonly held belief maintains that educational expansion reduces socioeconomic inequalities of access to education by increasing equality of educational opportunity. The counterarguments of MMI maintain that educational inequalities persist despite expansion. This is because those from more advantaged socioeconomic backgrounds use new educational opportunities created by expansion and access qualitatively better kinds of education at that level (i.e., effectively maintained inequality, EMI).

Empirical Evidence

Raftery and Hout's empirical work, which focused on Ireland, proved the MMI hypothesis. Despite expansion throughout the mid-20th century, class inequality in rates of enrollment in secondary education remained, and declined toward the mid-1970s after the enrollment rate for the most advantaged socioeconomic group had reached saturation point.

Empirical results obtained so far show that, despite a tenfold expansion of higher education in Britain between 1950 and 1995, quantitative inequalities between socioeconomic groups in the opportunities of higher education attendance remain persistent. In other words, despite expansion, socioeconomic inequalities of access to higher education in Britain have been both maximally and effectively maintained. The research was conducted in Ireland, the Philippines, France, Japan, Russia, Scotland, Spain, China, Hungary, Britain, Germany, Poland, and so forth. In 10 out of 13 national studies, MMI showed variations. The educational structures of the nations that conformed to the MMI model varied considerably. Britain, West Germany, Switzerland, Italy, Poland, Hungary, Czechoslovakia, Israel, Australia, and Taiwan possessed patterns consistent with MMI. The MMI shows a general but not universal pattern. It has been difficult to measure the strength of intergenerational associations because most studies look into the patterns of one country. Comparative studies that compare similar data across countries have been relatively scarce. The International Social Survey Program (ISSP) is an exception and compares cross-country data.

One additional point that should be made is that a number of studies have been conducted on influences on education attainment showing that sampling decisions play an important role in drawing conclusions. For instance, in wealthy countries with high social stratifications SES has revealed stronger influences on academic achievement than in poor countries with more uniform social structures. The studies have gone through several revisions, accounting for social changes across regions; however, social stratification of a society versus social uniformity remains an important factor in SES influence on education attainment. Furthermore, the MMI hypothesis offered by M. Hout and A. Raftery is maintained in market economies but not in socialist ones (where social structures are more uniform).

MMI Issues

MMI claims that the effect of family background does not have the same strength everywhere and depends on the existence of specific class barriers to educational opportunity. When a particular level of education reaches near-universal completion stage, the effect of social background on that transition decreases. If there is no growth in educational systems, there is no redistribution of educational opportunity among social classes. Inequality is maintained as upper-class students attain higher levels of education. Besides, the strength of the association between family background and educational attainment is proportional to the spread of postsecondary education. The expansion of postsecondary education weakens the association between family background and educational attainment.

Class affects earlier educational transitions more than it affects later ones, as it has, for instance, in Ireland. Greater class barriers are associated with completion of secondary education than with the entry into postsecondary education. In some nations, the successful completion of a university degree does not depend on family background. For example, a secondary education was optional in many nations 60 or 70 years ago. However, when secondary education became universal the high class barrier between primary and secondary education became irrelevant.

Parents' educational status and occupation affect most the transition to secondary school, but these factors decline for subsequent transitions, including the move to higher education.

Raftery and Hout offer certain recommendations, namely, they suggest that first, expansion must proceed faster than the rise in demand for education that is caused by population growth. Otherwise, the absolute number of enrolled students will increase but the overall enrollment rate will not. Second, expansion must also continue faster than the rise in demand for education caused by the upgrading of social origins over time. If this does not happen, the absolute number of enrolled students and the overall rate of enrollment will increase, but class differences in the chances of enrollment will remain.

Mariam Orkodashvili
Vanderbilt University

See Also: Class Inequality: Achievement; Class Inequality: College Enrollment and Completion; Coleman, James S.; *Coleman Report, The*; Expansion of Education; Family Structure and Education.

Further Readings

Coleman, J. S., et al. "The Equality of Educational Opportunity Report." Washington, DC: U.S. Government Printing Office, 1968.

Heyneman, S. P. "Student Background and Student Achievement: What Is the Right Question?" *American Journal of Education*, v.112 (November 2005).

Hout, M. "Maximally Maintained Inequality Revisited: Irish Educational Mobility in Comparative Perspective." In *Changing Ireland, 1989–2003*, Maire NicGhiolla Phadraig and Elizabeth Hilliard, eds. Berkeley: Survey Research Center, University of California, Berkeley. 2004.

Lucas, S. R. "Effectively Maintained Inequality: Educational Transitions and Social Background." *American Journal of Sociology*, v.106 (2001).

Mare, R. D. "Educational Stratification on Observed and Unobserved Components of Family Background." In *Persistent Inequality: Changing Educational Attainment in Thirteen Countries*, Y. Shavit and H. P. Blossfeld, eds. Boulder, CO: Westview Press, 1993.

Raftery, A. E. and M. Hout. "Maximally Maintained Inequality: Expansion, Reform, and Opportunity in Irish Education, 1921–75." *Sociology of Education*, v.66 (1993).

Mentoring

For many underachieving youth, school is not a place where they experience empathy, praise, and attention; nor where adults model clear, consistent, and supportive behaviors. Mentoring programs provide opportunities for students to develop relationships with older students or adults. Providing mentoring in the school context affords youth the opportunity to develop relationships with caring adults while creating a positive association with school. Successful school-based mentoring programs have the potential to benefit not only the individual but also the school as a whole by establishing social support networks that integrate caring adults from the school and surrounding community, serving as a protective factor for a number of adverse behaviors.

Providing mentoring opportunities in the school setting also allows for greater access by minority youth and others who may not otherwise participate. Research suggests that school climate factors are key to supporting the transition to college for urban and low-income youth, for whom college-going rates still lag. Therefore school-based mentoring at the high school level may be an effective strategy for improving students' sense of connectedness with school, improving academic outcomes, and easing the transition to postsecondary education for those students most at-risk in our schools.

Transition to College

Negotiating the many steps of the college search and application process as well as finding a way to pay for college is a challenge for many students. But this process is much harder to navigate for students from low-income and minority backgrounds and those who would be the first in their family to attend college. Additionally, minority students may face difficulty in developing relationships with college professors in their early years because of large class sizes, which can lead to dropping out. Mentoring programs may ease this transition by boosting participants' academic self-concept, helping them develop coping strategies, and providing critical college knowledge and support.

Social capital, conceptualized by James Coleman, is present in relationships between two people, in which trust builds, resources flow, and norms for behavior are reinforced. Mentoring is an opportunity for students to build trust with a caring adult and to gain resources and knowledge through their relationships with those adults. In addition, these adults can help establish and reinforce norms about college-going. For low-income and minority students, as well as first-generation college students,

relationships with mentors may be their only access to the college knowledge and support vital for successful transition.

Special Populations

Mentoring programs must be responsive to the particular needs of special populations. In a mentoring program for Latino/Latina students, researchers found that students were motivated by both negative role modeling ("do what I did not/could not, so that your life can be better") and affiliative achievement (i.e., achieving to give back to those who helped you). Research on mentoring programs for African American boys emphasizes the need for any intervention focused on African American boys to consider proactive steps that connect the young men's self-identification with academic success, as well as opportunities for African American young men to mentor and support each other in their academic pursuits.

Outcomes of Mentoring

There is a significant body of research looking at the outcomes of various modalities of mentoring, including community-based, school-based, group, and informal mentoring. Mentoring is credited with positive outcomes in many adolescent life domains. Mentoring outcomes appear to be strongest when relationships are long term and characterized by strong emotional connections, for duration maximizes trust and social capital. While some early studies suggested that mentor-mentee matching on race and socioeconomic status (SES) was beneficial to the mentoring relationship, later studies have refuted this. Most studies report improvements in youths' perception of scholastic competence, and many have observed decreases in problematic behavior such as delinquency, truancy, and discipline issues.

It is unclear whether this is a direct result of the mentoring activities or whether it is a natural consequence of an improved sense of generalized competence and better relationships with parents and other responsible adults (i.e., teachers). It has been suggested that by conveying messages about the value of school and role-modeling success, mentors may stimulate adolescents' improved attitudes toward school achievement, perceived academic competence, and school performance. While some researchers have expressed concerns about the impact of school-based mentoring, given the short duration of the intervention, others have found that this can be an effective model, particularly when programs find a way to continue relationships through the summer months.

Program Considerations

Mentoring programs designed for high school students must be sensitive to the particular developmental needs of adolescents. From a developmental perspective, programs should nurture youths' cognitive skills, help them form positive realistic views of themselves to make informed decisions and plans; stress future plans and support high educational goals; and bolster connectedness to self and others. Successful programs support students' academic experiences through cognitive guidance, emotional support, informational and experiential support, modeling, and tangible support.

The literature is unequivocal in its emphasis on the importance of initial and ongoing training and support for mentors, particularly for cross-race matches. Training should include information about the developmental needs of the mentees, as well as issues related to the population being served (at-risk youth, the working poor, white privilege, immigration). Successful mentors are consistent, recognize that the relationship might be a little one-sided, respect the youth's viewpoint, involve the youth in shared decision making, and ask for help from staff; whereas unsuccessful mentors tend to be inconsistent, try to instill a set of values that is inconsistent with those of the youth, act like a parent and ask for too much change, and emphasize behavioral change over the development of mutual trust and respect.

Kri Burkander
Michigan State University

See Also: At-Risk Students; Social Capital; Student Attachment to School; Urban Schooling.

Further Readings

Portwood, S. G. and P. M. Ayers. "Schools." In *Handbook of Youth Mentoring*, D. L. DuBois and M. J. Karcher, eds. Thousand Oaks, CA: Sage, 2005.

Sipe, Cynthia. "Mentoring Programs for Adolescents: A Research Summary." *Journal of Adolescent Health*, v.31 (2002).

Wheeler, M. E., T. E. Keller, and D. L. DuBois. "Review of Three Recent Randomized Trials of School-Based Mentoring: Making Sense of Mixed Findings." *Social Policy Report*, v.24/3 (2010).

Meritocracy

A meritocracy is a social system in which people are rewarded on the basis of their own merit (i.e., ability and skills) rather than characteristics like race, sex, and social class. In addition to being a fundamental interest of sociological studies, meritocratic ideas are closely linked to the American dream, or the notion that any hard-working person in America has an equal opportunity of experiencing upward social mobility. Upward social mobility refers to an adult achieving a higher social class than that of his/her parents. Research in sociology of education is particularly informed by meritocratic notions, because Americans perceive their public school system as providing equal opportunity to all citizens, building merit, and certifying who has merit (with diplomas and degrees). This article describes the role of meritocratic ideas in both research and our national ideology.

Meritocracy as a Myth

Although the term *meritocracy* is credited to a British sociologist, Michael Young, meritocratic notions date back to the works of the Chinese philosopher Confucius. Ancient China implemented the world's first civil service exams sometime between the 6th and 2nd centuries B.C.E., which enabled people to advance on the basis of merit rather than blood lineage. China's ideas spread to British India during the 17th century and then to Europe and the United States. Young's 1959 work introducing the term *meritocracy* was actually satirical. He portrayed elites as using meritocratic ideals to appear to be interested in a fairer society while still perpetuating the status quo. Similarly, sociologists expose America as less meritocratic than popularly perceived by comparing adults' educational or occupational attainment to that of their parents. In a perfect meritocracy, a person's social class at birth would be unrelated to their social class as an adult. Peter Blau and Otis Duncan used 1962 census data to show that boys with fathers in high-status occupations were much more likely to have high-status occupations themselves than boys with fathers in lower-status occupations. Research from the 2000s finds that the United States has less upward social mobility than many other industrialized countries.

College admission would be based entirely on a person's merit in a true meritocracy, but sociologists also debunk meritocratic ideals by showing how the definition of "merit" changes, depending on the interests of the dominant class. In the 1900s, men with merit, or men admitted to selective colleges, were knowledgeable in the traditional curriculum (Latin and Greek). In the 1920s, merit described the "all-around man" of sturdy character, sound body, and proper social background, which enabled colleges to restrict access to immigrants and people of a lower class who were strong academically. Finally, the civil rights movement led to diversity being defined as meritorious. Although student bodies at colleges have diversified in many ways, few of the white students at very selective colleges come from a lower-class background. The persisting lack of transparency in college admissions systems suggests that characteristics besides "merit" are deciding factors in college admissions decisions and that the definition of merit continues to evolve.

Equality of Educational Opportunity

Other sociologists undermine perceptions of America as a meritocracy by demonstrating America's lack of equal educational opportunity. For one, free public schooling does not result in equal outcomes, or equal levels of academic achievement, for all students. Students from middle- and upper-class families, who experience the culture of the school at home, are better able to reap the benefits of schooling than students from lower-class families. Moreover, research demonstrates how IQ and test scores are a product of family background rather than being pure indicators of merit or ability. Public schools are not a remedy for all of the differences in material, cultural, and social capital across families that enable or prevent upward social mobility.

In 1975, James Coleman asked if "equality of educational opportunity" meant equality of results of schooling, or equality of input school resources. The spirit of "equality of educational opportunity" is that reasonably intelligent kids would not have poorer adulthoods because of their family background, but many researchers have found that a person's family background impacts academic achievement more than experiences at school. If this is so, how do we achieve equal educational opportunity? Coleman concluded that disadvantaged students need more from schools than advantaged students if they are expected to achieve at comparable levels, and that it was more honest to describe public education as "reducing inequality." In other words, the idea central to meritocracy and the American dream—that

schools level the playing field—is more myth than fact at this point.

Meritocracy as Ideology

Meritocratic ideas are central in our national ideology. Robert Turner's 1960 piece, contrasting the American and British systems of mobility, highlights how our meritocratic values perform a function within our society even if they are not based in fact. First, the individualism of meritocratic ideals (that we determine our own fate rather than social forces or structure) convinces Americans to believe they deserve their social status. For instance, high-status people credit their status to their own merit, and low-status people believe they weren't smart enough or didn't try hard enough. The pervasiveness of meritocratic ideas in America is illustrated by sociologists' finding that disadvantaged youth recognize structural barriers but still blame themselves for their failure to advance. Turner argues that even if these ideals are more ideology than fact, the individualism of meritocratic ideas quells unrest among the lower classes, while the hope and optimism inherent in meritocratic ideas preserves national allegiance. Despite sociologists' efforts to dispel meritocratic notions, research in the sociology of education continues to be motivated by meritocratic ideals.

Dara Shifrer
University of Texas at Austin

See Also: Class Inequality: College Enrollment and Completion; Earning Potential and Education; Mobility, Contest Versus Sponsored; Occupational Aspirations/ Expectations; Status Attainment.

Further Readings

Alon, Sigal and Marta Tienda. "Diversity, Opportunity, and the Shifting Meritocracy in Higher Education." *American Sociological Review*, v.72/1 (2007).

Blanden, Jo, Paul Gregg, and Stephen Machin. *Intergenerational Mobility in Europe and North America: A Report Supported by the Sutton Trust.* London: Centre for Economic Performance, 2005.

Breen, Richard and Jan O. Jonsson. "Inequality of Opportunity in Comparative Perspective: Recent Research on Educational Attainment and Social Mobility." *Annual Review of Sociology*, v.31 (2005).

Coleman, James S. "What Is Meant by 'an Equal Educational Opportunity'?" *Oxford Review of Education*, v.1/1 (1975).

Collins, Randall. *The Credential Society: A Historical Sociology of Education and Stratification.* New York: Academic Press, 1979.

"Economic Policy Reforms: Going for Growth." *Family Affair: Intergenerational Social Mobility Across OECD Countries.* Paris: Organisation for Economic Co-operation and Development (OECD), 2010.

Karabel, Jerome. *The Chosen: The Hidden History of Admission and Exclusion at Harvard, Yale, and Princeton.* Boston: Houghton Mifflin, 2005.

Reisel, Liza. "Two Paths to Inequality in Educational Outcomes: Family Background and Educational Selection in the United States and Norway." *Sociology of Education*, v.84/4 (2011).

Turner, Ralph H. "Sponsored and Contest Mobility and the School System." *American Sociological Review*, v.25/6 (1960).

Young, Michael. *The Rise of the Meritocracy, 1870–2033: An Essay on Education and Inequality.* London: Thames & Hudson, 1958.

Mexican American Students

Mexican American students have a long and important presence in the educational system of the United States, particularly in the Southwest. The first large wave of Mexican migration to the United States began in the 1890s and has since steadily contributed to the American landscape, making them the largest immigrant group both historically and presently. As a result, Mexican American students across generations have influenced major sociopolitical events in education and continue to spark interest given their increasing percentages throughout the United States.

Segregation

During the first half of the 20th century, Mexican American students experienced racial segregation in the public school system. "Mexican schools" were common throughout California and Texas and forced children of Latino and Mexican American descent to attend these schools. Government officials called for separate Mexican schools and in 1923, the University of Texas issued the "Report on Illiteracy," which denigrated Mexican children on the grounds

of cleanliness and encouraged local municipalities throughout Texas to segregate Mexican students. By 1946, the historic *Mendez v. Westminster* case ruled that the segregation of Mexican and Latino students was unconstitutional in California, as did the subsequent *Delgado v. Bastrop ISD* case in Texas. These cases later influenced the monumental *Brown v. Board of Education* case that ended racial segregation. However, given the residential segregation patterns embedded in cities throughout the United States, today two-thirds of Latino students in major urban centers attend segregated schools where 10 percent or fewer of their fellow students are white.

Bilingual Education

Mexican American students have also been at the middle of the native language use or the bilingual education debate in the United States. Throughout the 1900s, Spanish-speaking students, who were most often of Mexican descent, experienced "No Spanish" rules in schools. An investigation of these rules described Mexican American students being victims of verbal, physical, psychological, and academic abuse when they spoke Spanish in classrooms, playgrounds, and even the cafeteria. By 1968, the federal government enacted the Bilingual Education Act (Title VII of the Elementary and Secondary Education Act), which provided funds and attention to improve educational programming for immigrant students. In the later part of the 20th century, as the population of Mexicans increased, so did resentment toward immigrant students, and three states—California, Arizona, and Massachusetts—passed restrictive language policies that severely restricted bilingual education in schools.

Student Activism

During the 1960s, Mexican American youth organized into various groups in an effort to protest the subpar educational opportunities as well as other pertinent issues that often plagued their communities. The United Mexican American Students (UMAS) organization formed to help increase Mexican American enrollment in college. They also mentored and organized Mexican high school youth in Los Angeles (L.A.), which later influenced the 1968 L.A. Blowouts. This historic walkout called attention to the dire school conditions as well as racist school policies. The students protested "no Spanish rules," a curriculum that largely ignored or denied Mexican American history and the placement of Mexican students in vocational classes rather than college preparatory classes. Most recently, in 2011, Mexican American students protested the Tucson Unified School District's attempt to dismantle the Mexican American studies program in Arizona public schools and successfully saved it from being eliminated.

Achievement

In general, Latinos are the nation's most undereducated group in the United States; Mexican Americans comprise two-thirds of this population. Results from the National Assessment of Educational Data continue to reveal a persistent achievement gap of a little over 30 points between Mexican American students and their white counterparts for students ages 9, 13, and 17 tested in reading, math, and science. A consistent finding in educational research exposes that Mexican Americans are not only low academic performers but also have low college graduation rates compared to their Asian and white counterparts. And these low educational outcomes are not limited by generation. An empirical study found that Mexicans in the first through fourth generations score at the lowest educational attainment levels compared to other groups in the United States.

Theoretical Frameworks

Research indicates that achievement in education is usually a function of socioeconomic status and mother's education level. Additionally, assimilation theorists posit that immigrant student achievement can be explained by the social and cultural practices of the group. Using these aforementioned frameworks, a litany of literature explains Mexican American underachievement as a function of the low socioeconomic status, immigrant status, and cultural traditions of the group.

In response to these studies, research has begun to interrogate the role of socioeconomic status and investigate the factors that ameliorate the low-income status and low parent education levels of Mexican American students to better understand the disparity in educational achievement of this group. Generally, Mexican American students are more likely to be from low-income homes (52 percent) and come from homes with parents who did not graduate from high school, but their educational outcomes are not completely a function of social class. More than one in four high-achieving Mexican American students come from a low-income background, which is much

higher compared to the one in 20 white low-income students who successfully perform in school. These studies cite the importance of parental involvement and student engagement and highlight the need for more qualified teachers who connect with Mexican American students to improve the educational experiences of Mexican American students.

A wave of research has also enumerated the detrimental effects of structural inequality and discrimination in schools and links these to low student performance. The literature demonstrates how subpar schooling conditions (e.g., less access to certified teachers or advanced placement classes) and teachers holding Mexican American students to lower standards serve to impede the success of Mexican American students.

Ursula S. Aldana
University of California, Los Angeles

See Also: Bilingual Education; Immigrants, Children of; Mexico; Racial Inequality: Achievement.

Further Readings

Gándara, Patricia and Frances Contreras. *The Latino Education Crisis: The Consequences of Failed Social Policies.* Cambridge, MA: Harvard University Press, 2009.

Gibson, Margaret, et al. *School Connections: US Mexican Youth, Peers and School Achievement.* New York: Teachers College Press, 2004.

Pycior, Julie L. *LBJ and Mexican Americans: The Paradox of Power.* Austin: University of Texas Press, 1997.

Sanchez, George. *Becoming Mexican American: Ethnicity, Culture, and Identity in Chicano Los Angeles, 1900–1945.* New York: Oxford University Press, 1995.

Telles, Edward and Vilma Ortiz. *Generations of Exclusion: Mexican Americans, Assimilation and Race.* New York: Russell Sage Foundation, 2008.

Valencia, Richard. *Chicano School Failure and Success.* New York: Routledge, 2002.

Mexico

Mexico is a developing and mostly urbanized country, with few remaining agricultural regions. The country has a free market economy, the second-largest in Latin

America, and has evolved from a state-dominated and protectionist economy to one of the most open in the region. In 2010, its population was 112.3 million. Mexico experienced average annual growth of 2.43 percent between 2004 and 2011. In 2010, unemployment was reported at 5.4 percent with an estimated underemployment of 25 percent. According to the World Bank, 47.4 percent of the total population lives below the poverty line. The unequal development between urban and rural areas is significant. As of 2005, 54 percent of rural households reported asset-based poverty compared to 32 percent of urban households, and this prompts strong migration to cities and abroad. In 2010, 78 percent of the total population lived in urban areas.

History and Social Structure

A multicultural country with an inheritance of millennial Mesoamerican civilizations, Mexico was colonized by Spain for over three centuries and recovered its independence in 1810. However, this left a legacy of social inequality that still persists in modern Mexico. There are three main ethnic groups in the country: 60 percent mestizo (mix of Amerindian and Spanish), 30 percent Amerindian (or indigenous), and 9 percent white, with the indigenous and to a lesser extent the mestizos comprising the subordinate groups within the stratified society.

The modern phase of Mexico may be traced from the Mexican Revolution (1910–17), which overall sought better living conditions for the country's vast population. With the foundation of the Public Ministry of Education (SEP) in 1921, a national education system aiming to bring schooling to historically neglected communities was for the first time established. This allowed the federal government to freely extend its educative enterprise throughout the national territory.

Educational Structure

The education system is large and heterogeneous. The basic education system consists of a year of reception, six years of primary schooling, and three years of secondary schooling (at age 5 to 14). Official estimates for 2006 indicated that 94 percent of children attended basic education (although net enrollments for primary and secondary levels differ at 98 percent and 70 percent, respectively). By law, all children have the right to access basic education and since 1992 it has been considered compulsory. In that same year, the basic education system was decentralized to transfer the administration and operation to the states, although the federation maintains control of the curriculum, school-provided textbooks, and the evaluation of the system; 87.5 percent of the national education system is public, although there is increasing participation by the private sector in all levels of education. According to the World Bank, 8.1 percent and 15.5 percent of the population attend private primary and secondary schools, respectively.

The high school system consists of a further three years schooling (at age 15 to 18); it is not compulsory and offers two different pathways: university or vocational training. In 2006, 58.6 percent of students attended high school. As the Organisation for Economic Co-operation and Development (OECD) suggests, alternative and remote learning schemes are offered in both the basic and the high school systems in order to guarantee access to a culturally diverse and geographically dispersed population. The higher education system consists mainly of universities and technical institutions (both public and private) that offer graduate and postgraduate diplomas. In 2006, 24 percent of students attended higher education, whereas only 6.5 percent of students were enrolled in postgraduate studies as of 2005.

Current Challenges

Overall participation in education has increased for both genders, although disparities still persist in rural and indigenous communities. As of 2005, the proportion of the total population age 15 and over that could read and write was 86.1 percent (86.9 percent of males and 85.3 percent of females). The national average of school life expectancy from primary to higher education is 14 years and is equal across genders, although disparities persist across geographical locations. For example, 21.4 percent of the population in Chiapas is illiterate, compared to just 2.6 percent in Mexico City. In 2005, 55 percent of the urban population reported at least nine years of schooling, whereas the rural population reported only 5.6 years. In other words, 72 percent of the rural population reported gaining just a primary education or even less.

Education expenditure in 2007 was 4.8 percent of gross domestic product (GDP), and spending per student remains below the OECD average. Issues of quality persist because, for decades past, the focus of educational policies was on providing basic education for an increasing young population. Programme for International Student Assessment (PISA) results for 2009 showed that Mexico performed significantly below the OECD average in reading, mathematics, and science. In 2010, 29 percent of youths ages 15 to 29 were not in education or employment. Research has found that the key factors behind this phenomenon are a low socioeconomic background and lack of child care for women within this age group.

Marta Cristina Azaola
University of Southampton

See Also: Argentina; Brazil; Chile; Class Inequality: Achievement; Educational Policymakers; Rural Schooling.

Further Readings

Arceo, E. and R. Campos. *¿Quiénes son los Ninis en México?* Mexico City: Colmex, 2011.

Bonfil, G. *México Profundo. Una civilización negada.* Mexico City: DeBolsillo, 1987.

Economic Commission for Latin America and the Caribbean (ECLAC). *México: impacto de la educación en la pobreza rural.* http://www.eclac.cl/cgi-bin/get Prod.asp?xml=/publicaciones/xml/4/35044/P35044 .xml&xsl=/mexico/tpl/p9f.xsl&base=/tpl/imprimir.xslt (Accessed December 2011).

Public Ministry of Education (SEP). *Plan Nacional de Educación 2001–2006.* Mexico City: SEP, 2001.

Public Ministry of Education (SEP). *Programa Sectorial de Educación 2007–2012.* Mexico City: SEP, 2007.

World Bank. "Mexico." http://www.data.worldbank.org/ country/mexico (Accessed December 2011).

Meyer, John

American sociologist John Meyer has been a central figure in the development of neoinstitutional or sociological institutional theory. Along with a large number of collaborators, he has contributed important ideas about education's institutional effects on society, the expansion of mass schooling, and the nature of world society. Meyer's institutional theory counters the assumption that there is a natural, realist account of education premised on the rational choices of interested actors. He argues instead that institutions construct conceptual models of the world, affecting individuals at the cognitive level. As a social institution, education does not simply socialize individuals. It creates new social roles, identities, and forms of knowledge. Meyer's work further depicts the emergence of education as a global institution, a central component of a pervasive world culture.

In the landmark article "The Effects of Education as an Institution" (1977), Meyer addressed the question of why a large variation in school quality seems to have little effect on students' outcomes, one of the puzzles that emerged from the *Coleman Report* (1968). According to the functional theory of education, schooling expands individuals' knowledge and skills, but this theory fails to explain how schools of the same sort have similar effects, regardless of internal socializing processes.

Allocation theory, also termed conflict theory, describes how schools allocate individuals to certain social positions on the basis of education's institutional authority. Meyer acknowledged this chartering function of education but argued that education has even more direct and profound effects on the social universe. Rather than just allocating individuals to a fixed set of social positions, education expands the social structure, creating new classes of knowledge and personnel. The effects of education are so powerful because they are seen as highly legitimate. The importance of education for individual development and social progress becomes taken for granted, and compliance becomes ritualized.

Meyer's subsequent work continued his critique of functional perspectives at the global scale. The central educational event of the 20th century has been the rapid spread of mass schooling. Nation-states adopted similar models of formal schooling, despite their particular needs and resources. From the functionalist perspective, nations are distinctive, bounded social systems and education systems are closely integrated with their economic and political systems. However, in Meyer's institutionalist account, the organization of school systems is largely determined by common models circulated in the wider global environment, or world culture. Mass schooling expanded because it was a central component of the legitimate modern nation-state. In order to meet standards of rationality, states had to follow certain global rules and build certain institutions. To Meyer, nation-states are embedded in a world society that provides abstract models or scripts, and modern systems of education are more powerfully shaped by world cultural norms than by national needs and interests. World culture provides core beliefs in human equality, the rights of children to education, and the injustice of using ascriptive statuses like race, gender, and religion to limit access to education.

Meyer's work also describes the way national systems of education have become increasingly homogenous as a consequence of isomorphism. For example, the curriculum of school systems around the world has become more similar, conforming to a world curricular frame. Particularistic subjects like the study of sacred texts give way to standardized subjects like mathematics and science. Vocational education, typically closely tied to the economic needs of particular nations, has declined around the world in favor of schooling that is less differentiated and more focused on cognitive skills. World cultural associations are important engines of isomorphism. Nongovernmental organizations have proliferated, almost uniformly espousing world cultural principles of human rights and the development of citizens. Higher education enrollment continues to expand rapidly, particularly in those countries with the strongest world society links.

Institutional theories have been challenged by culturalist scholars who argue that global models of education are subject to local interpretation and adaptation. Meyer describes the gap between the policies that nations adopt and actual practice as "decoupling," arguing that world cultural scripts are enacted in widely different settings and isomorphism is never complete. Despite pervasive decoupling, the influence of dominant world cultural models is ubiquitous. Meyer's work illuminates the striking degree to which everyone knows how to do school and believes that individual and national well-being depend on being schooled.

Meyer is, at this writing, a professor of sociology emeritus at Stanford University, where he began teaching in 1966. He received his Ph.D. in sociology from Columbia University, studying with Paul Lazarsfeld, who influenced Meyer's subsequent focus on quantitative methodology and longitudinal processes. His most recent work has concerned the global diffusion of environmentalism, science, and human rights.

Victor J. Sensenig
Pennsylvania State University

See Also: *Coleman Report, The*; Conflict Theory of Education; Functionalist Theory of Education; Worldwide Education Revolution.

Further Readings
Baker, David P. *The Schooled Society: The Educational Transformation of the Postindustrial Society*. Palo Alto, CA: Stanford University Press (in press).
Baker, David P. and Gerald K. LeTendre. *National Differences, Global Similarities: World Culture and the Future of Schooling*. Palo Alto, CA: Stanford University Press, 2005.
Meyer, John W. "The Effects of Education as an Institution." *American Journal of Sociology*, v.83/1 (1977).

Michigan

Michigan is located in the northern portion of the U.S. Midwest. It is bordered by four of the five Great Lakes (Huron, Superior, Michigan, and Erie). Michigan has 10,083 inland lakes and over 3,000 miles of shoreline on the Great Lakes. It shares lakes with Canada on the north and east and with Illinois and Wisconsin on the west. Michigan is composed of two peninsulas, which are connected by the Mackinac Bridge, one of the largest suspension bridges in the United States.

The Upper Peninsula (UP) comprises 16,452 square miles. It is mostly pine forest and rural towns. The major industries of the UP are mining, wood products, and tourism. The cool temperatures and access to nature make this location a popular summer tourist attraction. However, its remote location makes the UP isolated during the winter months.

The Lower Peninsula is shaped like a mitten and is bordered by Ohio and Indiana on the south. It is 42,075 square miles excluding the lakes. The land of the Lower Peninsula is varied from rich farmland in the north and west to swampy areas in the southeast. Access to Canada and the eastern states through Lake Erie and the Detroit River have made the southeast portion of the state very industrialized.

The state of Michigan has 9,883,640 inhabitants according to the 2010 U.S. Census, making it the eighth most populous state. The population comprised 79 percent white, 14 percent black, 2 percent Asian, 4.4 percent Hispanic, and 3 percent of people reporting more than one race. The population of the UP was 299,184. The Lower Peninsula reported 9,584,456 residents. Twenty-four percent of Michigan residents are under the age of 18 and 14 percent are over age 65.

Table 1 Elementary and secondary education characteristics

	Michigan	U.S. (average)
Total number of schools	4,115	1,988
Total students	1,587,067	970,278
Total teachers	88,614.71	60,766.56
Pupil/teacher ratio	17.91	15.97

Source: U.S. Department of Education, National Center for Education Statistics, Common Core of Data (CCD), 2010–11.

Table 2 Elementary and secondary education finance

	Michigan	U.S. (average)
Total revenues	$19,620,054,956	$11,464,385,994
Total expenditures for education	$19,729,953,224	$11,712,033,839
Total current expenditures	$17,053,521,094	$9,938,906,259

Source: U.S. Department of Education, National Center for Education Statistics, Common Core of Data (CCD), "National Public Education Financial Survey," FY08 (2007–08).

Major cities in the Lower Peninsula are Lansing (state capital), Detroit, Flint, Grand Rapids, and Ann Arbor. While the major cities were the population centers in the state, during 1950–60, subdivisions were created and people began leaving cities in search of less expensive housing and less crowded living spaces. The shift in population from the cities to the subdivisions has continued unabated. In the past decade, the population of Detroit has decreased by 25 percent. This loss of inhabitants and businesses has affected several aspects of the city, including public safety and education.

History/Social Structure

Michigan was significantly impacted by the industrial revolution. Ransom Olds began the first automobile assembly line in Lansing, Michigan, and the birth of the automotive industry earned Michigan the title "Automotive Capital of the World." Detroit is commonly referred to as Motown or the Motor City in reference to the large number of automobile factories that were built in the city. However, the automotive influence is felt throughout the state, with numerous factories located in Flint, Lansing, and Dearborn. Ford Motor Company, General Motors, and Chrysler all have their company headquarters in Michigan. The

creation of factories provided jobs for the influx of immigrants in the early 1900s. People came to Michigan from all over the world to build a future for their families by working in the factories. A large number of African Americans came from the south to Michigan to work in the factories.

Public schools were established and the compulsory education law passed in 1871. Michigan has 15 state colleges and universities as well as 549 public school districts. The public schools were created to train future factory workers and provide them with basic literacy and mathematical skills. Henry Ford established one of the country's first trade schools in 1916.

Educational Structure

Michigan students begin kindergarten in public schools if they are age 5 before December 1 of the current enrollment year. Students attend primary school until eighth grade and secondary school from ninth through 12th grade. Secondary schools may include magnet schools, which specialize in certain areas of education (math and science, vocational, drama and the arts). Although most students are taught through the public school system, charter schools, private schools, and home schooling are beginning to show increased enrollment as frustration with public school performance increases among some families. In compliance with the federal No Child Left Behind Act, students are required to take the Michigan Educational Assessment Program (MEAP) standardized achievement tests in various grades. As an incentive to increase participation and high performance on these statewide assessments, the state offered college scholarships to high school students who scored in the top two levels of the exam and maintained a 2.5 grade point average. However, that program was cancelled in 2009 due to budget constraints.

Current Educational Issues

As in many states, the most pressing current educational issue is the lack of funding available to schools. Michigan was one of the states hardest hit by the recession period of 2005–present. The state and local debt as a percentage of gross state production is 18.31 percent; the national average is 17.39 percent. Unemployment in Michigan is significant at 10.6 percent, making it the fourth-highest state in unemployment. As people are unable to find work and the number of foreclosed homes increases, tax revenue for schools is reduced.

State and local education spending as a percentage of gross state production is 6.89 percent. The average of all states combined is 5.61 percent. However, the amount of spending per pupil varies widely from city to city within the state. Among some of the wealthier districts, 2009 spending per pupil averaged $11,017, though the poorer districts averaged just $7,382 per pupil. Such a large variance in spending calls into question whether the students are receiving equal educations.

Another alarming issue is the low graduation rate of students from poor, urban districts. Although the overall state graduation rate is 88 percent, in Detroit the percentage of students who complete high school in four years is only 33 percent, making it the lowest-ranked large school district in the nation. Michigan has been ranked as the seventh-highest state for the number of students who will not graduate in 2011.

Antonia Szymanski
Kirkwood Community College

See Also: Funding of Schools; Poverty and Education; Urban Schooling.

Further Readings

Chantrill, Christopher. "US Government Spending: Spending by State." http://www.usgovernmentspending.com/compare_state_spending_2011pZ0D (Accessed October 2011).

Poremba, D. *Michigan.* Northampton, MA: Interlink Books, 2006.

Swanson, C. "Nation Turns a Corner." *Education Week*, v.30/34 (2011).

U.S. Census Bureau. "Guide to State and Local Census Geography 2010." http://www.census.gov/geo/www/guidestloc/st26_mi.html (Accessed November 2011).

Migrant Students

Migrant students are the children of U.S. laborers who migrate with their families from location to location in order to secure work. Migrant agricultural workers and fishers tend to migrate along three principal streams: the eastern stream, which includes the southern states and the eastern seaboard; the midcontinent stream, beginning in Texas and extending north through the Grain Belt; and the western stream, primarily within California and the Pacific Northwest. Approximately 80 percent of migrant students are Hispanic, and approximately 90 percent of migrant students come from homes where English is their second language.

Migrant students and their families contribute greatly to the American economy through their rigorous manual labor while also upholding their native traditions and customs. Migrant students are equipped with unique skills, such as cultural brokering (person who facilitates the border crossing of another person or group of people from one culture to another culture), bilingualism, and biculturalism. They also face various risk factors associated with low educational achievement in U.S. schools.

Among these challenges are disruption of education because of frequent moving, cultural shock, language learning, and social isolation. Additionally, migrant students tackle poverty and poor health, often due to the poor working and living conditions to which they are relegated. Migrant children are confronted with critical family responsibilities—a role in which they take great pride—despite the sacrifice it entails for them in the long term. Primarily, migrant students need to work alongside their parents in order to survive financially and therefore may be unable to attend school temporarily or permanently. The research reveals that migrant children report frequently missing school for reasons that include illness, having to assist parents by translating, accompanying family members to appointments, as well as other tasks associated with negotiating a new cultural system. These responsibilities both add to migrant students' set of nuanced life skills and can restrict their participation in school-related activities.

Mobility

Decisions about when and where to move are based primarily on economic need and availability of work. Additional factors in choosing migration patterns include the length of seasons, wages, housing availability, and crop seasons. These migration patterns do not align with the traditional school year and therefore present a disruption in educational attainment. This misalignment interferes, delays, and suspends migrant students' academic paths. Migrant students often do not receive enough academic credit to keep pace with their nonmigrant peers and therefore rarely remain at appropriate grade levels. Additionally, migrant students' ability to experience new stable personal relationships within their new community, consistent quality curricula, and/or social groups can be affected by their frequent mobility. Migrant summer programs enable many students to make up missed instructional time; however, they generally cannot compensate for the time lost.

Work and Family Responsibilities

Migrant students are often expected to work in the fields or to care for younger siblings as part of their familial contribution. This presents a significant help to their family's income. Consequently, this arrangement results in an increased level of absenteeism and exacerbates the low graduation rate of older migrant students. Working in the fields and other labor exposes migrant students and their families to a variety of health risks from accidental injury and/or exposure to pesticides. Additionally, poor working conditions, including below-minimum wages, lack of adequate work breaks, substandard housing conditions, and maltreatment from bosses illegally employing them, add to the mental and physical hardships that migrant families undergo.

Poverty

The majority of migrant students come from families whose earnings are below the poverty level. The cost of migration adds to the financial burden of migrant families, often resulting in dire economic circumstances. Migrant children are at greater risk than nonmigrant children of living in poverty. Research on immigration and inequality suggests that this socioeconomic disadvantage remains throughout migrants' working lives and is likely to carry forward to their children.

Academic Success

The U.S. Department of Education's Migrant Education Program has worked with states and local districts to improve high school graduation rates of migrant students. As a result, graduation rates have risen from 10 percent to more than 40 percent. Data regarding migrant college entrance and completion rates are limited because few programs track students beyond high school graduation.

When migrant students are able to complete their high school education and go on to college, research shows that their success on an undergraduate level depends on the following factors: (1) taking rigorous, college-preparatory coursework in high school, (2) guidance in application to and acceptance into

college, (3) securing funding to attend, and (4) taking advantage of undergraduate student support services through college to graduation. While these steps may appear basic, migrant students' frequent moves, poverty, gaps in previous schooling, and language barriers complicate this process.

It is essential to assess what each student knows both from schooling in the home country and schooling in the United States. In this way, both educators and students can contribute in a meaningful way to maintaining the educational and cultural continuity that is vital for migrant students to succeed.

Aurora Chang
University of Wyoming

See Also: Class Inequality: Achievement; Poverty and Education; Prior Learning Assessment; Student Work and Educational Effects.

Further Readings
Melecio, Ray and Thomas J. Hanley. *Identification and Recruitment of Migrant Students: Strategies and Resources.* Charleston, WV: ERIC Clearinghouse on Rural Education and Small Schools, 2002.

Orozco, Carola, Marcelo M. Orozco, and Irina Todorova. *Learning a New Land: Immigrant Students in American Society.* Cambridge, MA: Belknap Press of Harvard University Press, 2008.

Rong, Xue Lan and Judith Preissle. *Educating Immigrant Students in the 21st Century: What Educators Need to Know,* 2nd ed. Thousand Oaks, CA: Corwin Press, 2009.

Sadowski, Michael. *Teaching Immigrant and Second-Language Students: Strategies for Success.* Cambridge, MA: Harvard Education Press, 2004.

Military Involvement/ Military Service

Military service can range from a short-term commitment (e.g., two years) to a long-term career (e.g., 20 years). Individuals join the military either through enlistment or commission as an officer. Enlistment involves qualifying for and committing to military service. One becomes a commissioned officer by earning a college degree in combination with Reserve

Officer Training Corps (ROTC), Officer Candidate School, Officer Training School, or military academy. Before the military became an all-volunteer force in 1973, persons also entered the armed services via the draft during times of military conflict. Currently, the military seeks to attract recruits by offering entry-level salaries and benefits that exceed those that can be secured in the civilian labor market, particularly by those who do not possess a college degree. Although the military offers base earnings that are comparable to those high school graduates obtain in the civilian labor market, the addition of medical, housing, dependent, and other benefits afford enlisted persons a higher standard of living than that offered by many jobs in the civilian sector.

A willingness to serve, however, is insufficient qualification to join the military given enlistment standards set by the Department of Justice and individual branches of the military. For example, a felony conviction or repeated minor criminal offenses can disqualify someone for military service. Citizenship and legal status comprise another important enlistment requirement. Based on 2000 census data, about 15.9 percent of all noncitizens are of military "recruitable age" (18–24 years old). Of all noncitizens in this age group, approximately half are without legal status; thus, they are, for the most part, ineligible to join the military. Noncitizens who are legal permanent residents, however, are permitted to serve, and have done so since the Revolutionary War. It is estimated that approximately 47,000 noncitizens serve in the military, National Guard, and Reserves, with about 8,000 enlisting each year. Legal residents from Mexico represent the largest number of noncitizen military service members.

There are also educational requirements that must be met in order to join the military. Although a high school diploma is not required to serve, the military accepts few people who do not possess this credential. Moreover, potential enlistees must demonstrate a level of math and verbal proficiency by achieving a minimum score on the Armed Forces Qualification Test (AFQT). Myriad military occupations are available to enlisted persons, with access to them determined by the level of education and AFQT score.

A career in the military is not a given, however, even for those who meet enlistment standards. Although barriers to entry are relatively low, remaining in the military until retirement (after a minimum of 20 years of service) requires continuous upgrading of

knowledge and skill. Failure to do so, as evidenced by the achievement of particular milestones (e.g., completion of courses, passage of tests, promotion) can lead to separation from the military.

Effects of Military Service in the Civilian Labor Market

Research on the economic consequences of military service has produced mixed results due, perhaps, to the challenging selectivity issues with which researchers must contend in order to draw conclusions about the causal effects of military service. Early expectations were that veterans would be disadvantaged in the civilian labor market compared to those who never served because of less time working in the civilian labor market and, perhaps, because the skills they acquired in the military would not be directly applicable to civilian jobs. However, others argued that veterans would command higher wages than comparable nonvets because of the training, skills, and socialization they received in the military, along with employers' use of military service as a screening tool by which to select among applicants.

Although the question is not settled, research suggests that veterans from disadvantaged socioeconomic backgrounds enjoy an economic premium relative to similarly situated nonveterans, and may even benefit from military service more so than members of advantaged groups in terms of the magnitude of earnings differences between themselves and civilians. Consistent with the idea that military service distances service members from problematic pasts are findings that even veterans with episodes of delinquency in their youth have benefitted socioeconomically from military service. However, some studies find no net benefit for disadvantaged groups, while other studies find that positive benefits fade over time. It is unclear how veterans who served during the 1990s and 2000s have fared in the labor market, as well as those who saw combat in the Iraq and Afghanistan wars.

Educational Benefits of Military Service

A major benefit of military service is its provisions for postsecondary education, a benefit that dates back to Title II of the Servicemen's Readjustment Act of 1944, which became known as the "G.I. Bill of Rights." The act facilitated the acquisition of additional educational and training by returning World War II veterans. It entitled veterans to four years of tuition and fees at the college or university of their choice.

Alternatively, benefits could be used to complete high school, attend vocational school, or obtain job training. Almost eight million veterans increased their levels of education and skill through the original G.I. Bill, which helped pave their way back into the civilian labor market. Currently, two G.I. bills provide educational benefits to veterans—the Montgomery G.I. Bill and the Post-9/11 G.I. Bill. The Montgomery G.I. Bill, created in 1984, provides benefits to veterans who completed their service prior to September 11, 2001. The Post-9/11 G.I. Bill, created in 2008, is available to those who served after September 11, 2001, including those who began service prior to and remained in the military after that date.

There is general consensus that the G.I. Bill increased the educational attainment of veterans of World War II, the Korean War, and the Vietnam War. However, there is less agreement about whether it has done so for veterans of the all-volunteer force era. Moreover, the educational effects of the G.I. Bill have varied across sociodemographic groups. Research shows that substantial benefits flowed to those from higher socioeconomic backgrounds, those who used their benefits in colleges versus vocational-technical schools, whites nationally, and African Americans outside the south.

The financial and educational benefits of military service do not come without costs. Although military conflicts have, historically, represented grave threats to the well-being and lives of military personnel, more recent conflicts like those in Grenada (1983) and Bosnia-Herzegovina (1995–2004) had few casualties. The wars in Iraq and Afghanistan are exceptions to that trend. The Department of Defense reports that as of February 3, 2012, 4,487 persons died in Iraq (i.e., Operation Iraqi Freedom and Operation New Dawn), while 1,879 persons have died in Afghanistan and other locations (i.e., Operation Enduring Freedom).

Pamela R. Bennett
Johns Hopkins University

See Also: Career and Technical Education; Higher Education; Reserve Officers' Training Corps (ROTC).

Further Readings

Asch, Beth, et al. *Military Enlistment of Hispanic Youth: Obstacles and Opportunities.* Santa Monica, CA: RAND, 2009.

Browning, Harley L., Sally C. Lopreato, and Dudley L. Poston, Jr. "Income and Veteran Status: Variations Among Mexican Americans, Blacks, and Anglos." *American Sociological Review*, v.38 (1973).

MacLean, Alair and Glen Elder. "Military Service in the Life Course." *Annual Review of Sociology*, v.33 (2007).

Sampson, Robert J. and John H. Laub. "Socioeconomic Achievement in the Life Course of Disadvantaged Men: Military Service as a Turning Point, Circa 1940–1965." *American Sociological Review*, v.61 (1996).

Veterans Administration. "VA History in Brief." Washington, DC: U.S. Government Printing Office. 1977.

Minnesota

The state of Minnesota is located in the upper midwest region of the United States of America and covers an area of 79,627 square miles (204,609 square kilometers). It is bordered on the north by Canada, on the west by North Dakota and South Dakota, on the south by Iowa, and on the east by Wisconsin and Lake Superior. According to the U.S. Census Bureau, Minnesota's population in 2010 was 5,303,925 people. Minnesota's early economy was characterized by raw material acquisition, including forestry, agriculture, and mining. However, its contemporary economy rests on corporations, financial institutions, and the health care industry. Minnesota is home to UnitedHealth Group, Target, Best Buy, and 3M. All of these are among the top 100 largest U.S. companies. However, Minnesota's top employers include the state of Minnesota, the Mayo Foundation, the U.S. federal government, Target Corporation, and Allina Health System.

History and Social Structure

Originally populated by Native Americans, including the Anishinaabe and the Dakota, Minnesota joined U.S. territories in two stages. The land east of the Mississippi River, initially part of the Wisconsin Territory, became U.S. land in 1783. The land west of the Mississippi River joined the United States as part of the Louisiana Purchase in 1803. Minnesota became the 32nd state in the Union in 1858. The first European settlers were French fur traders, who came into conflict with Native Americans in the area, who were eventually relocated to reservations. Later European settlers included mostly Germans and Scandinavians, as well as Irish, English, and Polish. Today, most Minnesotans trace their heritage to these groups, with small but significant numbers of Minnesotans who have African, Mexican, and Asian American heritage. According to the census, just over 85 percent of Minnesotans claim European ancestry. The largest population density surrounds the Minneapolis-St. Paul metropolitan area, which is often referred to as the Twin Cities.

In 1847, before Minnesota established statehood, the first public school was established in St. Paul, the city that would become Minnesota's capital. This would set the stage for Minnesota's eventually establishing free public schools. In the state constitution, Minnesota placed the duty of creating a public school system on the state legislature and allowed the state to secure funding for those schools through taxation. Alongside the system of free public schools, Minnesota established a school for the deaf in 1863. In 1885, the state legislature passed a mandatory school attendance law, which required children ages 8 to 16 to attend 12 weeks of school per year.

Minnesota's first public university was founded in 1851. During the Civil War, however, the University of Minnesota experienced financial hardship and was forced to close. Entrepreneur and statesman John Sargent Pillsbury helped the university win support from the Morrill Land Grant College Act. The University of Minnesota, located in Minneapolis and St. Paul,

became the state's land-grant university. Over the next 150 years, campuses in Duluth, Morris, Crookston, and Rochester joined the university.

In 1858, the same year that Minnesota became a state, the new Minnesota legislature created a normal school (a teacher training institution) for the education of teachers in the city of Winona. Normal schools in Bemidji, Mankato, Moorhead, and St. Cloud were created in subsequent years. This group of teacher training colleges eventually became standard four-year universities. Years later, they joined two other four-year state universities and 24 two-year colleges to form the Minnesota State Colleges and Universities System. A 1991 law created the Minnesota State system. When the law went into effect in 1995, Minnesota's public community colleges, technical colleges, and state universities merged. All 24 two-year colleges and seven state universities are now governed by a single chancellor and board of directors. While both the Minnesota State Colleges and Universities System and the University of Minnesota are publicly funded institutions, they remain separate.

Educational Structure

Minnesota's K–12 public education system, like many others, ran into problems with school funding. Until 1971, schools had been funded through property taxes. Different municipalities competed for industry and development in order to buoy their tax base. Enormous disparities between rich and poor districts emerged, leading to widening gulfs in school funding. A Republican-led legislature worked together with a Democratic governor to pass new laws solving these funding disparities. The new laws became known as the Minnesota Miracle of 1971 and made funds available more equitably across rich and poor school districts. Those laws persisted for 30 years, and today the state provides funding aid to public K–12 education.

The Minnesota Department of Education works with schools and districts through a variety of advisory boards, councils, and task forces. From an Advisory Committee on Financial Management to a Principal Evaluation Work Group to a State Assessments Technology Work Group, these organizations pursue specific goals across Minnesota schools. The Minnesota Department of Education oversees traditional school districts and schools, which are structured around location. However, an increasing number of charter schools have appeared across the state, most frequently in the Twin Cities. Under Minnesota law, a

Table 1 Elementary and secondary education characteristics

	Minnesota	U.S. (average)
Total number of schools	2,461	1,988
Total students	838,037	970,278
Total teachers	52,671.71	60,766.56
Pupil/teacher ratio	15.91	15.97

Source: U.S. Department of Education, National Center for Education Statistics, Common Core of Data (CCD), 2010–11.

Table 2 Elementary and secondary education finance

	Minnesota	U.S. (average)
Total revenues	$10,293,654,640	$11,464,385,994
Total expenditures for education	$10,412,448,487	$11,712,033,839
Total current expenditures	$8,426,263,566	$9,938,906,259

Source: U.S. Department of Education, National Center for Education Statistics, Common Core of Data (CCD), "National Public Education Financial Survey," FY08 (2007–08).

charter school is defined as a publicly funded school that is operated by a nonprofit organization.

Minnesotans continue to debate the mechanisms for funding their public schools as well as the advisability of increasing numbers of charter schools. Both of these debates surround issues of student achievement. Minnesota's student achievement, according to the National Assessment of Educational Progress (NAEP), is above the U.S. average. However, when NAEP scores are separated by racial background, the state averages closely align with national averages. The achievement gap separates students from different backgrounds in Minnesota, even though the state's combined scores beat the national average.

Beth Wright
Tavis D. Jules
Loyola University Chicago

See Also: Charter Schools; Funding of Schools; Racial Inequality: Achievement; South Dakota; Wisconsin.

Further Readings

Guy, M. J. "Financing Education in Minnesota: A Tradition of Progress, 1971–1998." *Educational Administration Abstracts*, v.34/4 (1999).

Orfield, M. and N. Wallace. "The Minnesota Fiscal Disparities Act of 1971: The Twin Cities' Struggle and Blueprint for Regional Cooperation." *William Mitchell Law Review*, v.33/2 (2007).

Wallace, S. "In Search of Vision and Values: The Minnesota Higher Education Merger." *New Directions for Community Colleges*, no.102 (1998).

Mississippi

Mississippi is a southeastern state geographically bordered on the north by Tennessee, on the west by Arkansas and Louisiana, on the east by Alabama, and on the south by the Gulf of Mexico. The capital city and largest by population is Jackson.

In 2005, Hurricane Katrina hit due west of Mississippi, causing major damage to the Gulf Coast areas. State officials calculated approximately 90 percent of structures within one-half mile of the coast were completely destroyed due to storm surge. Half of the 13 casinos, floating on barges along the coast, were washed hundreds of yards inland. Two bridges along the coast were completely destroyed, impacting travel along U.S. Highway 90. In all, 238 people died in Mississippi, another 67 were missing, and billions of dollars in damage resulted from the storm surge and resulting high winds and tornadoes. Mississippi's economy has primarily been agricultural, with cotton the primary crop. Mississippi is the second-largest producer of cotton in the nation and is the largest producer of pond-raised catfish.

History and Social Structure

Mississippi was first explored by the Spanish, followed by the French, and owned by the British following the French and Indian War. The land was seized by the United States following the Revolutionary War and annexed as part of West Florida. Mississippi became the 20th state in the Union on December 10, 1817.

Prior to statehood, education in Mississippi was left to private schools and academies. The first free school was established in 1821, yet it was largely reserved for the education of the wealthy. Like in other southern states, education for black children was unavailable. When it was, the inequity between facilities for white students and those for black students was evident.

By the early 1900s, the one-room schoolhouses that dominated the state were organized around the schedule of cotton farming. Students attended school while the fields were not being planted, harvested, or cultivated. Agricultural high schools were created to provide skills to the many students in rural and agricultural parts of the state. In the midst of the Supreme Court desegregation cases *Brown v. Board of Education* and the subsequent *Brown II*, Mississippi lawmakers passed laws ordering the immediate closing of public schools to resist compliance with the Supreme Court decisions. Following the decisions the state continued to maintain a segregated society. In 1956, Governor James Coleman created the State Sovereignty Commission, which received a $250,000 budget to develop a network of spies and detectives to investigate and inform the government of those who threatened the segregated society in the state.

Into the 1960s, in an effort to resist full desegregation, the state continued putting state tax dollars into private schools and organizations. The next step was to institute a school choice option that integrated one school grade each year. Successful challenges through the court system forced the state to create a plan that would fully integrate all schools by the 1967 to 1968

Table 1 Elementary and secondary education characteristics

	Mississippi	U.S. (average)
Total number of schools	1,115	1,988
Total students	490,526	970,278
Total teachers	32,254.83	60,766.56
Pupil/teacher ratio	15.21	15.97

Source: U.S. Department of Education, National Center for Education Statistics, Common Core of Data (CCD), 2010–11.

Table 2 Elementary and secondary education finance

	Mississippi	U.S. (average)
Total revenues	$4,388,016,156	$11,464,385,994
Total expenditures for education	$4,273,450,567	$11,712,033,839
Total current expenditures	$3,898,401,177	$9,938,906,259

Source: U.S. Department of Education, National Center for Education Statistics, Common Core of Data (CCD), "National Public Education Financial Survey," FY08 (2007–08).

school year. Although school districts were essentially desegregated in the years following, and black students were incorporated into much better facilities than those predesegregation, many black teachers and administrators were deemed less qualified than their white counterparts and were often fired or demoted to lower positions. An additional outcome of the desegregated school system included the concept of "white flight," a time when white students left the public school system to attend the numerous private schools that appeared during the same time frame. During this same period, the Mississippi Private School Association was formed and successfully lobbied for state funds for support.

Mississippi followed other states in the latter decades of the 20th century by adopting a uniform state curriculum and a testing program to measure student performance. To comply with mandates of No Child Left Behind, the state calculates an accountability score for schools and districts that counts student proficiency data in language, reading, and math and also includes graduation and attendance rate information. Failing schools are subject to takeover.

Educational Structure

The current structure of educational governance in Mississippi includes a nine-member Board of Education that appoints a State Superintendent of Education. The Mississippi governor appoints five of the members, including one representative from the state's Northern Supreme Court District, one from the Central Supreme Court District, one from the Southern Supreme Court District, one public school teacher, and one school administrator. The lieutenant governor and the speaker of the state House of Representatives each appoint two at-large members.

There are currently 152 school districts in Mississippi, 68 drawn by county lines, 81 separate school districts, and three agricultural high schools. There are approximately 1,058 public schools serving approximately 500,000 students. Compulsory attendance laws require children between the ages of 6 and 17 to attend school.

Mississippi is one of three states to elect superintendents for each of its county-drawn school districts. There are 23 public two- and four-year universities plus various branch campuses, along with 12 private colleges and universities, to service the needs of higher education in the state.

Current Issues

Resegregation appears to be an issue Mississippi still faces. It is not uncommon to find majority black schools, majority white schools, and private schools in majority black districts today. Although all schools are arguably better than they were at the time of the *Brown* decision, the integration sought does not appear to be achieved. The state continues to work toward the goals established following the *Brown* decision.

Student achievement continues to lag at the bottom nationally. Although education officials boast a high percentage of successful schools on the state's accountability testing system, student performance on the National Assessment of Educational Progress (NAEP) exam reveals a different picture and routinely places the state at the bottom of national performance.

Belinda M Cambre
University of New Orleans

See Also: *Brown v. Board of Education*; Funding of Schools; No Child Left Behind; Racial Inequality: Achievement.

Further Readings

Bond, Bradley. *Mississippi: A Documentary History.* Jackson: University Press of Mississippi, 2005.

Moody, Anne. *Coming of Age in Mississippi.* St. Louis, MO: Turtleback Books, 1992.

Nash, Jere, John Grisham, and Andy Taggart. *Mississippi Politics.* Jackson: University Press of Mississippi, 2009.

Missouri

The state of Missouri the 21st-largest U.S. state in land area, with 69,704 square miles (180,533 square kilometers). Located in the heart of the continental United States and near the country's population center point, Missouri has 5,988,277 citizens, ranking the state 18th in population.

Missouri's population is predominantly white (4,958,770, or 82.8 percent). African Americans make up the next-largest group at 693,391 (11.6 percent). Hispanic or Latinos represent the fastest-growing group, currently at 212,470 (3.5 percent). Asians number 98,083 and represent 1.6 percent. The remainder is made up of American Indians, Pacific Islanders, and others. In educational attainment, 86.8 percent of all Missourians have completed a high school education or higher. College degrees are held by more than 25 percent of the population, and 9.5 percent hold advanced degrees. Approximately 13.4 percent of individuals in the state fall below the poverty level, which ranks Missouri 19th among all states.

The economy of the state is dominated by the agricultural, manufacturing, and service sectors, with a gross domestic product (GDP) of $238 billion in 2008, ranking the state 22nd in GDP. St. Louis is the economic engine of the state, with strong manufacturing, financial, legal, and health care services. Missouri benefits from an extremely low cost of living, with housing, for example, well below the national median. The median household income is $48,867 in 2008, ranking the state 35th.

Missouri has two large metropolitan areas, on the opposite boundaries of the state. St. Louis, on the eastern edge, is a metro region of nearly three million people, including those who reside in the Illinois portion of the Greater St. Louis area. St. Louis sits on the banks of the Mississippi River, the longest river in the United States. St. Louis is near the confluence of the Mississippi, Missouri, and Illinois Rivers, and its history is closely tied to the river as a transportation corridor and source of economic activity. Kansas City,

on the western edge, is located on the Missouri River. Two other major urban areas, Springfield and Columbia, are both located in central Missouri.

The region is rich in history and geological interest, with evidence of early occupations of indigenous people dating back to 1000 B.C.E. The Cahokia people were early mound-builders and archaeologists are still uncovering sites and documenting their advanced civilization. The river bluffs show the effects of centuries of flooding of the great rivers, and the plains reveal evidence of ancient glaciers.

French fur trappers began to settle the area in the 1700s. As part of the Louisiana Territory, Missouri was part of the frontier that attracted pioneers searching for freedom and prosperity. Following the exploration of the Louisiana Purchase in 1804 directed by President Thomas Jefferson, settlement of Missouri rapidly grew because of its strategic location on the rivers, which provided transportation, commerce, and brought new settlers.

Missouri was admitted to the Union in 1821 as the 24th state, under what became known as the Missouri Compromise. The compromise resulted from the need to balance the number of pro-slavery and antislavery states. As a large border state with both urban and rural areas, Missouri was often the center

Table 1 Elementary and secondary education characteristics

	Missouri	U.S. (average)
Total number of schools	2,451	1,988
Total students	918,710	970,278
Total teachers	66,734.84	60,766.56
Pupil/teacher ratio	13.77	15.97

Source: U.S. Department of Education, National Center for Education Statistics, Common Core of Data (CCD), 2010–11.

Table 2 Elementary and secondary education finance

	Missouri	U.S. (average)
Total revenues	$9,876,930,097	$11,464,385,994
Total expenditures for education	$10,093,669,024	$11,712,033,839
Total current expenditures	$8,526,640,711	$9,938,906,259

Source: U.S. Department of Education, National Center for Education Statistics, Common Core of Data (CCD), "National Public Education Financial Survey," FY08 (2007–08).

of controversies between factions of the north and south, east and west, slavery and abolition, industry and agriculture.

The coming of the transcontinental railroad was another major historical event that caused rapid population growth in Missouri. St. Louis became known as the "Gateway to the West" as settlers came on their journey to settle the West. St. Louis and Kansas City were main routes for these pioneers. The Gateway Arch in St. Louis stands as a monument to this great westward migration.

Education System

Formal education systems began early in Missouri. French nuns established the first academy for girls at St. Charles in 1804. The Religious of the Sacred Heart, an order of French sisters, came to St. Louis by way of New Orleans to educate the daughters of the affluent French families. They also chose to provide schooling for the Potawatomie Indians they discovered to be in the area. The Jesuits founded St. Louis University, the first university west of the Mississippi, in 1812. Private institutions still remain a large part of the broader education landscape, with strong Catholic, Lutheran, and other religious systems flourishing today.

The Missouri rural countryside was dotted with one-room schoolhouses during the 19th century. Following the Civil War, participation in education grew rapidly, with major urban school systems being developed in St. Louis and Kansas City.

Many educational innovations followed quickly in the rapidly expanding region, and the region produced several well-known educators. William Torrey Harris was the first superintendent of the St. Louis public schools, one of the first and largest comprehensive urban school systems in the nation. With Harris's support, Susan Blow founded the first public kindergarten in 1873.

The University of Missouri (UM) was created in 1839, the first public university west of the Mississippi. Under the first Morrill Act of 1857, which established the American land-grant colleges, the university received land grant status in 1870. The four-campus system began in 1962 and now serves approximately 64,000 students.

In addition to the UM system, Missouri has nine public and 22 baccalaureate-granting higher education institutions and supports a total of 132 postsecondary institutions, public and private, in the state.

These institutions enroll about 400,000 students annually.

Current Issues

Similar to most states, Missouri struggles with current issues of school funding and accountability in the elementary and secondary system for its nearly one million students. Structurally, the state education leader is the commissioner of education appointed by the governor. The commissioner reports to the State Board of Education, also appointed by the governor. Missouri is a low-tax state. Missouri ranks low in average per-pupil spending at $9,318, ranking the state 41st. At an average salary level of $41,751, the state ranks 44th in teacher salaries, among the lowest in the nation.

Long an innovator in educational practice, Missouri was one of the first states in the 1980s to adopt standards for students and teachers under the Missouri Outstanding Schools Act (1985). The state Department of Education has been a leader in school administrator preparation, as one of the first 12 states to adopt the Interstate School Leader Licensure Consortium (ISLLC) standards for school principals and superintendents in 2008. These innovations predated the No Child Left Behind law, which incorporated many of those policies, such as promoting research-based practice and standards-based assessment.

Missouri high school graduating seniors have consistently performed above the national average on the ACT college entrance exam; for 2010, the national average was a score of 21, and Missouri students generally scored at 21.6. In the K–12 arena, Missouri's 2009 National Assessment of Educational Progress (NAEP) performance was also consistently higher than national averages.

Missouri, again like other states, has struggled in recent years with funding for higher education. The governor appoints the State Higher Education Commission, and the Curators of the state university system. Missouri ranks low in funding for its higher education institutions, relying heavily on student tuition. State operating appropriations have fallen to below 2006 levels. Enrollment remains strong, however, as Missouri enrolls 72 percent of its college freshmen in-state and imports many college students from other states especially in the Midwest.

Kathleen Sullivan Brown
University of Missouri-St. Louis

See Also: Administration of Education; Rural Schooling; Urban Schooling.

Further Readings

McLachlan, Sean. *Missouri: An Illustrated History*. New York: Hippocrene Books, 2008.

Parrish, William E. *A History of Missouri*. Columbia: University of Missouri Press, 2000.

Phillips, Charles and Betty Burnett. *Missouri: Crossroads of the Nation*. Sun Valley, CA: American Historical Press, 2003.

Thomas, Sue. *A Second Home: Missouri's Early Schools*. Columbia: University of Missouri Press, 2006.

Mobility, Contest Versus Sponsored

The conceptual framework of "sponsored" versus "contest" mobility was introduced in 1960 by American sociologist Ralph H. Turner to analyze normative patterns of upward mobility in different societies. He sought to illuminate how a society allocates elite status to its ambitious members and to specify the role of the school system in this process. Turner suggested that recruits are either selected by the established elite, in which case status is given to them by their sponsors, or the aspirants take part in an open contest, in which case status is earned by their own efforts. Turner used the conceptual dichotomy to explain the differences between American and British secondary systems, the latter of which was at that time not yet a comprehensive system. This theory was highly influential in the social sciences and has proven to be useful for comparative and historical analysis of educational practices and career patterns.

The two normative patterns are designed as ideal types in the tradition of Max Weber. Sponsored and contest mobility differ from each other in various dimensions:

- With respect to the assumed desirability to expand education and to offer opportunities to as many individuals as possible
- Regarding the procedures and criteria by which individuals are selected and assigned to elite

- They have different assumptions about the stability of social hierarchies, the homogeneity of each social stratum, and the distance between them

Sponsored Mobility

Within the norm of sponsored mobility the established elite acts as a gatekeeper controlling selection and training of its successors. This pattern is based on the belief that demand for highly educated and trained people is limited and that society would not benefit by providing education in excess of that demand. Indeed, such "overeducation" might be harmful because it could create a group of individuals who would be unable to achieve the social status that fits their aspirations and expectations. Instead of wasting efforts educating less able people, society should concentrate its resources on the few individuals who are highly talented and have the potential to be promoted to elite positions. According to this perspective, it is crucial to identify this small group of promising individuals as early as possible.

The sponsorship norm is based on the belief that high achievement is the result of natural talent and that neither education nor efforts can change the rank of innate abilities. Accordingly, it is in the best interest of society to sort out the promising few from the less talented masses as soon as possible. For that purpose, different tracks in the school system separate the future elite from the rest of their age cohort and limit the time in which the whole peer group shares a common educational experience in a comprehensive setting. It is the established elite who determine the criteria for selection into the elite track. Under the sponsorship system it is assumed that special skills, possessed only by the elite, are required to identify those abilities that qualify for elite education.

Within a sponsored mobility framework, early selection in different tracks of the school system will not only provide a beneficial educational environment for the promising few who deserve special promotion in the best interest of society, but it will also help sort the rest of the age cohort into their proper social niche and convince them to accept their inferiority. The sooner they are separated from their talented peers, the more likely it is that they will limit themselves to "realistic" career paths and not waste their time with overly ambitious plans that they will never achieve.

Hence, early selection at school is a mechanism that stabilizes the social order. The sponsorship norm is based on the assumption of a stable and sharp division between a small elite and the vast masses. The elite is separated from the less talented masses by a huge cultural distance without gradual intersections. According to this conviction, any attempts to raise the education of the masses in order to converge their cultural standards with those of the elite are useless and potentially damaging. From the perspective of the sponsorship norm, expansion of higher education bears the risk of compromising the "gold standard" of elite culture and higher education.

Contest Mobility

Within the norm of contest mobility, elite positions in society are the outcome of a tournament in which as many aspirants as possible should take part. This pattern is based on the conviction that there are no given limits to the demand for highly trained people and that it is in the best interest of society when a maximum of young people aspire to achieve higher levels of education. The ambition to get ahead is not only considered legitimate but a mechanism to raise the levels of intangible human capital of the whole society.

Instead of focusing on "natural talent," the contest norm emphasizes the role of efforts for achievements that lead to elevated social positions. This has important consequences for the school structure. As the motivation to work hard may change over time, it is crucial to avoid premature judgments. Instead of sorting promising children into separate tracks, learning takes place in a comprehensive setting that allows an open contest of the age cohort for the whole period of compulsory schooling—and, in some cases, longer. Second, the school culture under the contest norm tends to be "forgiving"; underperformers will get second chances and be encouraged to remain in the contest. The contest norm avoids absolute points of selection, unlike sponsored mobility, in the career structure. Eventually, there will be winners and losers, but, as Burton Clark points out, this is a result of an extended tournament in which the ambitions of the less successful gradually "cooled out."

The contest norm corresponds to a social structure in which no singly elite enjoys a monopoly but multiple elites compete among each other. Hence, social hierarchies are less stable and the cultural distance between the elite and the masses is less accentuated as in the sponsorship pattern. Social stability is less based on a sense of inferiority by the "ordinary" people but on a sense of fellowship with the elite that results from the feeling that they had a fair chance. Instead of sharp and categorical divisions between the elite and the masses, this norm rather emphasizes gradual intersections between the different social positions. Accordingly, the cultural gap is less accentuated. Elite culture is not separated by a "gold standard" that is unattainable for the masses. The contest norm assumes that "more is better than less"—an assumption that sharply differs from the preoccupation of the sponsorship norm with the watering down of quality by semieducated individuals from uncultured backgrounds. Hence the contest norm is conducive to mass higher education without compromising rigorous selection at the top end.

Within the pattern of contest mobility, education systems differ with respect to the age at which students are exposed to competitive pressure. In many Western countries this is delayed to age 14 and older. There is, of course, competition within one's peer group, predominantly driven by values and status symbols of youth culture, but school culture is not competitive. In some countries students in elementary school are not graded.

At the high school level, streaming is soft in North America, although students anticipate the competitive pressure of admission to higher education at higher grades. In sharp contrast to that pattern are countries that Simon Marginson describes as "Confucian education regimes." These regimes emphasize competition at a very early age and are characterized by a combination of strong group solidarity and conformity on the one hand and high expectations of individual performance on the other hand.

Hans Pechar
University of Klagenfurt and Higher Education Research

See Also: Cultural Capital; Hidden Curriculum; Meritocracy; Overeducation; Tracking.

Further Readings

Clark, B. R. "The 'Cooling-Out' Function in Higher Education." *American Journal of Sociology*, v.65 (1960).

Marginson, S. "Higher Education in East Asia and Singapore: Rise of the Confucian Model." *Higher Education*, v.61 (2011).

Morgan, H. P. "Sponsored and Contest Mobility Revisited: An Examination of Britain and the USA Today." *Oxford Review of Education*, v.16 (1990).

Turner, R. H. "Sponsored and Contest Mobility and the School System." *American Sociological Review*, v.25 (1960).

Montana

Known as "Big Sky Country" since the 1960s, Montana is a land of scenic beauty with the majestic Rocky Mountains to the west and rolling plains to the east. With its great wealth of minerals, Montana has historically been nicknamed the "Treasure State." Tourists come from all over the world to visit Yellowstone and Glacier National Parks. With a land area of 14,556 square miles, some 20,000 acres have been set aside as a wildlife refuge. The fourth-largest state and the seventh–least populated state in the United States, Montana has a population of only 989,415 according to the 2010 census. Montana shares a northern border with Canada and an eastern border with North and South Dakota. Idaho stretches to the south and west, and Wyoming forms the remaining section of the western border.

The state capital is Helena, which is the sixth-largest city in the state. The largest cities are Billings, Missoula, and Great Falls. Montana has a large Native American population that raises special concerns, and a new law requiring that the history and culture of Native Americans be taught as part of the regular K–12 curriculum took effect during the 2010 to 2011 school year. Isolation and poverty take their toll in rural areas, particularly among the Native American population. Montana is using technology to expand opportunities for students. In 2010, the state opened Montana Virtual Academy, which offers 40 high school classes online at no cost to students. All classes are taught by certified teachers.

History

It is believed that the first humans arrived in Montana from Asia in 15,000 to 13,000 B.C.E. Except for Native Americans, much of the land remained unsettled until 1803, when the United States acquired most of the land that now makes up Montana as part of President Thomas Jefferson's Louisiana Purchase. The first official exploration occurred during the Lewis and Clark Expedition that soon followed. The first fort in the state was built on the Yellowstone River to be used in fur trading. Lawlessness reigned during the following decades, but the land was slowly settled. In 1872, Congress created a national park at Yellowstone. Montana became the 41st state in 1889. In 1910, homesteading began in earnest, and by 1930, Montana had become a popular destination for tourists.

In 1972, delegates met to draft a new state constitution, resulting in a commitment to recognizing the contributions of Native Americans to the culture and history of the state. Although it took several decades to bring the idea to fruition, it finally resulted in passage of the Indian Education for All Act. The state legislature provided full funding in 2010, and all parts of the curriculum are now required to integrate Native American history and culture.

Current Situation

There are 141,807 students enrolled in Montana schools, and 78.7 percent of those are Title I schools. Nearly 40 percent of those students are eligible for free lunches. The student population is predominately white (83.1 percent), and the largest minority group is American Indian/Alaskan Natives (11.8 percent). There are smaller groups of African Americans (1.1 percent), Hispanics (2.8 percent), and Asian/Pacific Islands (1.2 percent). There are 828 schools in 422

Table 1 Elementary and secondary education characteristics

	Montana	U.S. (average)
Total number of schools	829	1,988
Total students	141,693	970,278
Total teachers	10,360.99	60,766.56
Pupil/teacher ratio	13.68	15.97

Source: U.S. Department of Education, National Center for Education Statistics, Common Core of Data (CCD), 2010–11.

Table 2 Elementary and secondary education finance

	Montana	U.S. (average)
Total revenues	$1,559,091,112	$11,464,385,994
Total expenditures for education	$1,564,569,076	$11,712,033,839
Total current expenditures	$1,392,449,155	$9,938,906,259

Source: U.S. Department of Education, National Center for Education Statistics, Common Core of Data (CCD), "National Public Education Financial Survey," FY08 (2007–08).

districts. Montana has no charter schools. The state expends $10,092 per pupil annually. There are 10,521 teachers, and the student/teacher ratio is 13.5. Students consistently rank higher than the national average on achievement tests in mathematics, science, reading, and writing. In a 2011 study conducted by the Thomas Fordham Foundation, Montana ranked last of 49 states on teacher quality. Similarly, *Education Week's State Report Cards* gave Montana a D plus on teacher proficiency and an F on teacher accountability for quality. The state fared better in other others, receiving a B minus on chance for success and a B on early foundations, resulting in an overall grade of C minus.

In 2010, Montana unsuccessfully applied for a Race to the Top grant that would have brought $74 million in educational funding into the state. However, Montana did receive an $11.5 million grant through the School Improvement Grant program, which was part of President Barack Obama's American Recovery and Reinvestment program. The funds are being used to turn around the lowest-performing schools in the states.

Even in the 21st century, Montana still has large sparsely settled areas. In the little town of Spring Creek near the Wyoming border where the 1876 Battle of Rosebud pitting General George Crook against Crazy Horse took place, there is one of only 200 one-room schoolhouses still in existence in the United States. The 2010 census recorded the town's population at 119, and the nearest elementary school is some 72 miles away. Spring Creek School has only one teacher, who is responsible for 45 lesson plans at a time. There are also two full-time aides who assist in teaching a classroom that contains anywhere between three and 12 children at a time.

Poverty and Suicide

Montana educators face a unique set of problems in isolated rural areas of the state where there is widespread poverty and inadequate access to mental health care. This situation received national attention in 2009 when five students in grades five through seven at Poplar Middle School committed suicide and another 20 members of the student body attempted suicide. Two high school students in the same area killed themselves the same year. Poplar Middle School is located in the Fort Peck Reservation. It is designated as a frontier because less than three people inhabit each mile of the area. Some 90 percent of the population of 1,000 are Native American, mostly of the Sioux

and Assiniboine tribes. The unemployment rate is 85 percent. Some parents blamed the principal of Poplar Middle School for the tragedy, insisting that she had shamed the students by announcing their failing grades in front of a schoolwide assembly. The situation served to draw national attention to the extreme poverty and isolation of the area, and federal funds were channeled into the area to help the community recover from the loss. The Senate held hearings at Fort Peck in 2011, and a filmmaker documented the tragedy in a short film designed to help other students who might be suffering from depression.

Elizabeth Rholetter Purdy
Independent Scholar

See Also: Native American Students; Poverty and Education; Race to the Top; Student/Teacher Ratio; Wealth and Education.

Further Readings
Carjuzaa, Jionna, et al. "Montana's Indian Education for All Applying Multicultural Education Theory." *Multicultural Perspectives*, v.12/4 (October–December 2010).
Deam, Jenny. "A One-Room School Fit for 21st Century." *Los Angeles Times* (June 12, 2011).
National Center for Education Statistics. http://www.nces.ed.gov/nationsreportcard/states (Accessed February 2012).
"Senate Hearing in Montana Examines Indian Suicides." ABC News. http://www.abcnews.go.com/US/wireStory?id=14267397 (Accessed February 2012).
"State Report Cards: Montana." *Education Week*, v.31/16 (2012).
U.S. Department of Education. *Mapping Montana's Educational Progress, 2008.* Washington, DC: U.S. Department of Education, 2008.

Montessori

Over a century ago, a pioneer named Maria Montessori envisioned an educational approach based on children's innate power and curiosity to learn. The Montessori educational approach, often called "an education for life," has evolved over time and is one of the broadest-reaching educational systems in the world. There are over 22,000 Montessori schools in 117 countries serving children of all economic strata and diverse ethnic backgrounds in both public and private sectors.

The Life of Maria Montessori

Maria Montessori was born in Italy in 1870 and became one of the first women to practice medicine in Italy. She became profoundly interested in children's development, and in 1907 she opened her first Casa dei Bambini ("Children's House") for children ages 2 to 9 in one of the poorest areas of Rome. She encouraged children to move around the room and to choose activities that interested them. These young childen became incredibly focused, self-motivated, and independent. Six months after it opened, people from around the world began visiting to observe these "miracle" children.

Maria Montessori observed children and realized that they possess potentials above and beyond what is traditionally attributed to them, and they can educate themselves by interacting with their environment. She saw that children naturally chose activities that stimulated their minds. In 1929 she founded Association Montessori Internationale (AMI) to protect the integrity of her life's work throughout the world. She was nominated three times for the Nobel Peace Prize. After her death in 1952, her son and major collaborator, Mario Montessori, ran AMI and advanced his mother's life's work. In 1960 an organization unaffiliated with AMI, the American Montessori Society (AMS), was founded in the United States. Today both AMI and AMS train teachers and certify Montessori schools in the United States.

Maria Montessori's Observations Regarding Child Psychology

Maria Montessori spent her lifetime objectively observing children. She realized that movement is connected with learning and that children prefer independence to dependence. She watched young children engage in long periods of concentration, after which they were calm, cooperative, and happy. When children were allowed to make independent choices, they naturally gravitated toward activities needed for their own development. Children sought challenging and purposeful work. They learned rapidly using hands-on materials and gained intense satisfaction through work. Rewards, punishments, and praise were not necessary and actually inhibited learning. Children

formed a classroom society and cared about the people and materials around them.

Maria Montessori described four Planes of Human Development: ages 0 to 6, 6 to 12, 12 to 18, and 18 to 24. She observed that children in the First Plane (age 0–6) have what she called "Absorbent Minds." This is a child's innate power to absorb and internalize the world around him. She believed this information contributes to the child's social, emotional, and intellectual skills. She also witnessed "Sensitive Periods" when a child is passionately involved with a particular aspect of the environment.

In the Second Plane (6–12) the Absorbent Mind transitions to a mind that is characterized by heightened reasoning and imaginative abilities. Elementary-aged children want to know how and why the world works the way it does. They begin to think logically, make educated judgments, become more social, complete sizable and meaningful projects, desire justice, worship heroes, and crave adventure. In the Third and Fourth Planes, children become more introspective as they ponder their place in the world and obtain specific skills as they prepare for and enter adulthood.

Montessori Schools: A Child-Centered Educational Approach

Montessori learning environments are based on the psychological characteristics observed by Maria Montessori. Each is uniquely suited to meet the characteristics of children at a particular stage of development. Children move freely around Montessori classrooms. They choose the material they want to work with, where to work, and with whom to work. There are three-hour uninterrupted work cycles so children can attain periods of intense concentration. Classrooms have three-year age spans so they learn from each other and benefit from the enriched social and intellectual environment.

There are generally 28 to 35 students accompanied by one trained teacher and one assistant. High student-teacher ratios are preferred so children develop independence. Teachers move around the room and teach lessons individually or to small groups of children. They use engaging hands-on materials to get children excited about history, mathematics, biology, and many other topics. Maria Montessori wrote, "The secret of good teaching is to regard the child's intelligence as a fertile field in which many seeds may be sown, to grow under the heat of flaming imagination. Our aim therefore, is not merely to make the child understand and still less to force him to memorize, but so to touch his imagination so as to enthuse him to his inmost core."

Maria Montessori stressed the importance of a "Prepared Environment." Montessori classrooms are ordered, uncluttered, clean, and filled with beautiful materials that pique the children's interest. Furniture is child-sized and materials are kept on low shelves so children can reach them independently.

Montessori teachers are the link between the Prepared Environment and the child. They move around the classroom and make presentations to individuals or small groups of children. They establish a work ethic and nurture a culture of respect within the classroom. They have self-control and allow children to make their own discoveries rather than providing the information.

Maria Montessori observed that children who received the proper mental and physical support at each Plane of Development became "Normalized" learners. Normalized children are independent, self-motivated, peaceful, happy, and can work well alone or with others. They love learning and can achieve periods of deep concentration. Normalized children exhibit few psychological deviations such as laziness, selfishness, submissiveness, lying, aggression, dependence, inferiority, possessiveness, and fear. Maria Montessori thought Normalized children would grow into self-confident adults.

Montessori schools serve children as young as 6 weeks old. "Nido" ("nest") communities nurture loving bonds between babies and caregivers. Aspects of human development such as movement, language, sleep, and exploration are allowed to occur naturally. Toddler communities continue supporting the child's natural development and independence until they enter the Children's House. There are more Children's House environments than any other within Montessori. Children ages 2.5 to 6 work together and receive lessons individually. They are taught to be independent and choose their own activities. The environment has four areas: practical life, sensorial, language, and mathematics. Many schools extend the prepared environment to include outside gardens and nature areas.

Montessori Elementary classrooms serve children in 6 to 9, 9 to 12, and sometimes 6 to 12 age spans. Children receive lessons in small groups. Maria Montessori's plan for the elementary years is called "Cosmic Education." Students receive a sweeping view of the universe, our planet, life on earth, the history

of humans, and an appreciation for their interrelationships. Students receive presentations in biology, geography, history, mathematics, geometry, language, music, and art in an integrated manner that demonstrates how these topics are inextricably linked. Small groups of children routinely "Go Out" of the classroom to pursue further research on a chosen topic and to interact in a meaningful way with the broader community.

Montessori programs for adolescents and high school students are less developed and less prevalent than those for younger children. Her "Erdkinder" ("land children") programs included land-based physical work and business activities to prepare teenagers for the adult world. Maria Montessori outlined her plan for adolescents in the appendix of her book *From Childhood to Adolescence*.

Research on Montessori

There are few studies to date that track the overall outcomes of Montessori programs. K. R. Doherman's 2003 study of the Milwaukee public schools studied high school students who had Montessori schooling (from ages 3–11) and compared them to children of similar age, gender, ethnicity, and socioeconomic status who were not in Montessori. Those with Montessori schooling scored significantly higher on standardized tests in math and science (ACT and WKCE) than the comparison group.

Though there are few comprehensive studies of Montessori over time, the book *Montessori: The Science Behind the Genius* (2005) describes numerous studies that support facets of how Montessori classrooms function, including the impact of movement on learning, how choice and interest affects learning, negative impacts of extrinsic rewards, importance of learning from peers, learning within meaningful contexts, order in the environment, and how adult interactions affect outcomes.

Conclusion: An Education for Peace

Maria Montessori rejected the traditional educational system of her time that viewed children as empty receptacles who should passively receive information from an adult. Rather, she observed the innate power within children to educate themselves. Her educational environments nurture the psychological characteristics she observed in children with the goal of helping them become happy and independent adults. Maria Montessori traveled the world as a tireless advocate for forms of education that nurtured the human spirit rather than repressed it.

Maria Montessori believed that children who grew up with freedom, self-confidence, social skills, an innate love of learning, and a respect for living creatures were our best hope for peace on earth and the future of mankind.

Leanna Ampola
Loyola University Maryland

See Also: Adolescense; Childhood; Early Childhood; Student/Teacher Ratio.

Further Readings

Doherman, K. R. *Outcomes for Students in a Montessori Program*. Rochester, NY: Association Montessori Internationale/USA, 2003.

Lillard, Angeline Stoll. *Montessori The Science Behind the Genius*. New York: Oxford University Press, 2005.

Montessori, Maria. *The Absorbent Mind*. Adyar, India: Theosophical Publishing House, 1949.

Montessori, Maria. *The Discovery of the Child*. New York: Random House, 1962.

Montessori, Maria. *Education and Peace*. Amsterdam: Montessori-Pierson, 1949.

Montessori, Maria. *The Formation of Man*. Amsterdam: Montessori-Pierson, 1955.

Montessori, Maria. *From Childhood to Adolescence*. Amsterdam: Montessori-Pierson, 1948.

Montessori, Maria. *To Educate the Human Potential*. Amsterdam: Montessori-Pierson, 1948.

Standing, E. M. *Maria Montessori: Her Life and Work*. New York: Penguin, 1984.

Morale in Schools

Morale in schools is not simply a matter of keeping all members of the staff happy. The morale of staff, students, and parents all have to be considered and there are many different facets that can impact each of them: satisfaction with work, a clear understanding of their role and what is expected of them, praise and recognition for doing good work, opportunities for continuing growth and development, and a sense of safety and security are among the many issues that can play a role in determining the overall level of morale in schools. Because there are so many different people and components involved, constant attention must be paid to building strong morale among stakeholders as well as ensuring that it is maintained in the long term.

Evaluating Morale

A high level of morale among those involved in a school is essential for all aspects of the educational process to work effectively. The level of morale impacts student learning, parental involvement, staff's professional development, and parents' willingness to work closely with the school's staff. Accepting that morale plays a key role in these essential aspects of schools, the first step in getting a handle on it is to figure out how to measure it effectively. This is not as simple as handing out a survey asking how happy people are, however: as noted earlier, there is a wide range of impacts on morale and these are different for each group and for each person.

Evaluating morale involves collecting a range of information from many different people on a regular basis. It also demands a deep and nuanced understanding of people and their work so that the information gathered taps into the most important areas for each person and each aspect of the school. Gathering and analyzing data is best done following a planning process, from multiple perspectives, of what are the key realities and goals for the school. As discussed below, these will be connected to both internal and external factors. When these types of inputs and their likely impacts are understood, it allows more refined questions to be asked of people. It also means the information gathered can be analyzed within these known contextual factors, enabling more insightful and useful conclusions to be drawn. It is this incisive analysis of data that allows effective decisions to be made about teaching and learning, communication, training, and other key areas of schools.

Internal and External Impacts on Morale

As discussed above, a wide range of factors can impact the morale within a school. These factors can be internal—staff turnover, teacher quality, student engagement, or test results—or external to the school—the state's and district's financial situation, legislation such as No Child Left Behind (NCLB), or rezoning of the school district. There is often greater control over those inputs that are internal to the school; this control means that the internal factors can be leveraged most easily to either build up morale or maintain high levels of morale if it already exists. Some of these internal factors are "formal," which can make them easier to identify: types of staff meetings, timetabling of classes, criteria for internal promotion, and the hiring and firing process can all be changed, sending a strong signal to all stakeholders regarding the intent to change to improve morale. Other, more "informal" aspects, such as camaraderie among staff or how welcome parents feel in the school, are just as important but often more difficult to pinpoint. Though there are constraints on what individual schools can do, particularly in the public sector, looking at how internal factors can be adjusted to improve morale should almost always be the first place to look because these are more easily adjusted to meet changing needs.

Factors external to the school are just as impactful on the morale within a school, though often more difficult to control. In the same way that internal aspects can range from large to small, external issues can range from economic recessions to the loss of a few prominent members of the school's Parent-Teacher Association (PTA). While it is natural to worry most about the larger-scale external issues, the smaller components are often most open to being influenced by school stakeholders to make positive changes. So while "huge" events generate more attention, morale is more likely to be effectively managed by tackling a large number of smaller issues. This is especially true in relation to external forces because the largest of them are often almost entirely beyond the control of a school's stakeholders.

Unintended Consequences and Perverse Incentives

It is prudent to insert a word of caution here that even the best intentions regarding improvements to morale can backfire. Sometimes making changes for one group can have negative impacts on others, so any improved morale in one area can have an inverse impact on the morale of others in the school. For example, efforts to recognize good teaching by rewarding teachers when their students achieve high scores on standardized tests could improve morale for teachers whose students perform well but could also bring down the morale of teachers with students who started the year well below grade level and were never going to score high on the test. This type of nuanced understanding is essential when making changes to both formal processes and more informal moments,

such as how people talk to each other in the hallways. While some of these choices may seem small on their own, they can add up to a profound impact on morale, ideally in a positive way; again, it is important to consider the potential positives and negatives when making choices that may impact morale.

Managing Morale in a School

The administrators of most schools will need to take responsibility for the level of morale among the school's stakeholders. This means that they need to be adept at monitoring morale, interpreting any information they get on needs related to this, and then creatively devising processes to improve low morale and/or maintain high levels of morale. While administrators with formal titles, such as principals and assistant principals, remain at the top of most schools, it is nearly impossible for them to carefully monitor morale across all relevant people on a regular basis. Therefore these positional leaders need to depend on others in the school to be able to evaluate issues related to morale.

This dovetails well with many current pushes for more distributed and collaborative organizational dynamics in schools as a way to move away from the "superhero" principal knowing everything and solving all problems. This article has hopefully illustrated just how complex and dynamic morale can be in schools; schools that have people in a variety of roles able to monitor and adapt creatively to issues impacting morale will be more likely to buoy morale and then keep it high.

Tim London
Queen's University, Belfast

See Also: Classroom Dynamics; Classroom Interactions: Teachers and Students; Deskilling of the Teaching Profession; Leadership in Schools; School-Parent Relationships.

Further Readings

Jackson, Philip, Robert Boostrom, and David Hansen. *The Moral Life of Schools*. San Francisco: Jossey-Bass, 1993.

Schein, Edgar. *Organizational Culture and Leadership*. San Francisco: Jossey-Bass, 1985.

Shafritz, Jay, J. Steven Ott, and Yong Suk Jang. *Classics of Organization Theory*. 6th ed. Belmont, CA: Wadsworth/Thomson, 2005.

Morocco

Situated in north Africa, the Kingdom of Morocco is 172,413 square miles (446,550 square kilometers) with a population of approximately 35 million inhabitants. The government structure is a constitutional monarchy, with legislative, judicial, and executive branches. In 2002, Morocco's primary trading partner was the European Union, which accounted for 67 percent of its imports and 55 percent of its exports. The international use of the English language in business and diplomacy has increased English language use for the European Union and, in turn, for Morocco. In 2004, the United States and Morocco signed the Morocco-U.S. Free Trade Agreement, thereby reducing most customs duties of consumer and manufactured goods. In addition, the United States granted Morocco non-North Atlantic Treaty Organization (NATO) ally status in 2004, which gives the United States access to Morocco's airfields and coasts and provides Morocco with U.S. military training and technology. In January 2006, this bilateral free trade agreement went into effect. The agreement reduces tariffs on 95 percent of consumer and industrial products traded between the two partners. The agreement increases market access and intellectual property rights protection.

Educational Structure

Education policy reforms of the past 15 to 25 years have focused primarily on the revitalization and modernization of Standard Arabic. The education policy goals of the Maghreb have been to replace French and English with Arabic in all school subjects, including the sciences. This process of the Arabization of the sciences has been in place since the 1970s, but general Arabization policies have been in place in Morocco since its independence from France in 1956. Although the Arabization policies have sought to Arabize education and government administration, there was a need for a bilingual system of education because by the time of independence in 1956, French had become a major influencing force in Moroccan government and society. Complicating modern Arabization policies, Standard Arabic, French, Spanish, and English are making their linguistic marks on Moroccan society. For example, Standard Arabic is a variety of Arabic that has emerged in Morocco because of the blending of Classical Arabic (Qur'anic Arabic) and Moroccan Arabic (a dialectical form of Arabic). Standard Arabic is now common in education, administration, and the mass media. However, French is still used in the media, finance, government, science, and technology, and Spanish is used extensively in northern Morocco. Moreover, since the 1960s, American humanitarian programs such as the U.S. Agency for International Development (USAID) and the Peace Corps have worked toward building amicable alliances with the Moroccan government and its peoples. The interest in learning and teaching English has grown further in Morocco with the rapid spread of the English language in the era of globalization.

Current Issues

The African Development Bank Report of 2005 cites Morocco's 2000–09 National Charter for Education and Training reform of the education system as a period aimed at expanding education and making it relevant to the economic environment, reforming curriculum content, learning languages, integrating new education technologies, and promoting decentralization and deconcentration of education and training. In 2000, Morocco began a comprehensive program of educational reform using information and communication technologies (ICTs) to "...help improve quality, equalize disparities, decentralize administration, and build a 21st century workforce," according to USAID. The United States has contributed to Morocco's efforts to build a 21st century workforce by hosting educators from Morocco's Ministry of Education to learn about computer-mediated teacher-training tools. Morocco's efforts to educate a citizenry that is competitive, adaptable, and marketable is perceived to be in its best economic interest. Notions of what constitutes "high quality" and "qualified workforce" are defined by the discourse of the new global economy, which is currently focused on innovative technology and adaptability.

Bethsaida Nieves
University of Wisconsin, Madison

See Also: Globalization; Saudi Arabia; Technology Education.

Further Readings

African Development Bank. *Morocco: Evaluation Of Bank Assistance to the Education Sector* (2005). http://www.afdb.org/fileadmin/uploads/afdb/Documents/Evaluation-Reports/09398231-EN-OPEV-SHARING-2006.PDF (Accessed February 2012).

Cooper, William H. "Free Trade Agreements Impact on U.S. Trade and Implications for U.S. Trade Policy. CRS Report for Congress, RL31356." Washington, DC: Congressional Research Service, Library of Congress, 2004.

Ennaji, Moha. *Multilingualism, Cultural Identity, and Education in Morocco.* New York: Springer, 2005.

Hart, David M. *Tribe and Society in Rural Morocco.* Portland, OR: Frank Cass, 2000.

Sadiqi, Fatima. *Women, Gender, and Language in Morocco.* Leiden, Netherlands: Brill, 2003.

U.S. Agency for International Development (USAID). "LearnLink, Digital Tools for Development: Modernizing Teacher Training" (2003). http://www .pdf.usaid.gov/pdf_docs/PNACK879.pdf (Accessed February 2012).

U.S. Department of State. "Diplomacy in Action. Bureau of Near Eastern Affairs: Kingdom of Morocco." http:// www.state.gov/r/pa/ei/bgn/5431.htm (Accessed February 2012).

Multicultural Navigators

Drawing on the canon of literature on the critical values of social capital, sociologist Prudence Carter has coined a term for a specific type of informational and social resource for low-income and racial and ethnic minority students: *multicultural navigators*. In response to the confluence of factors—such as poverty, racism, and social marginalization—that cripple the educational mobility and attainment of low-income or disadvantaged racial and ethnic minority students, Carter discusses in her book, *Keepin' It Real: School Success Beyond Black and White*, the critical need for persons who can assist these youth on their trajectories for better lives. Multicultural navigators are critical social ties for disadvantaged students who are limited in their fluency for navigating mainstream cultural practices requisite for educational and economic mobility.

In another highly influential book, *The Truly Disadvantaged*, sociologist William Julius Wilson argued for the presence of persons in neighborhoods and communities who help keep alive the perception that education is meaningful, that steady employment is a viable alternative to welfare, and that family stability is the norm, not the exception. With the multicultural navigator concept, Carter pushes the idea of social models even further, since, as she argues, the assumptions about their value rarely explore the interplay among effective social ties, culture, and identity. Carter argues that given what we know about the resources of diverse social ties, we can assume that students' exposure to persons possessing dominant cultural capital helps them climb the proverbial social ladder. Still, in a society characterized by fraught racial, ethnic, class, and sociocultural dynamics, many low-income African American and Latino youth seek exposure to those who understand their own social realities and the value of their nondominant cultural capital. *Nondominant cultural capital* is the term defined by Carter to contrast with the ways that social scientists utilize Pierre Bourdieu's notion of "cultural capital" to define the set of dispositions, ways of being, and cultural resources that dominant social groups utilize to reproduce their economic and social status. By contrast, nondominant cultural capital is the set of cultural practices, resources, and tools that socially marginalized groups utilize to garner social prestige and esteem within their respective families and communities.

Multicultural navigators are individuals who harvest the cultural resources both from their own ethnic or racial or class heritages and from sociocultural environments in wider, mainstream society. They possess the insight and an understanding of the functions and values of both dominant and nondominant capital and cultures. As social resources and connections, multicultural navigators provide, for example, advice about how to write a college essay or how to interview for a job or even how to recommend a student for a summer internship that can assist his or her social mobility. At the same time they demonstrate for youth how to discern different cultural rules and expectations within myriad environments and how to strategically negotiate norms and practices that range anywhere from self-presentation in terms of dress, tone, and language to interactional styles with various authorities to knowledge about universities and colleges, careers, politics, art, food, or sports. Multicultural navigators demonstrate how to possess both dominant and nondominant cultural capital and how to be adept at movement through various sociocultural settings, where cultural codes and rules differ. They are sensitive to the backgrounds of students from marginalized and disadvantaged communities and have a critical understanding of how society operates to create a status hierarchy. For Carter, a deep familiarity with and comprehension of the experiences of "minority" or disadvantaged individuals and groups in any social context encourage a richer type of cross-cultural enlightenment. Although they may understand what it takes for individuals to navigate the codes of success in mainstream society, multicultural navigators also empower youth to locate and appreciate the riches embedded within their own respective cultures. Essentially, multicultural navigators, according to Carter, facilitate the ability of youth to be culturally flexible and to move more fluidly across different sociocultural settings.

Becoming Multiculturally Fluent

Being upwardly mobile and achievement oriented is a necessary but insufficient condition for becoming a multicultural navigator. Although, according to Carter, no particular race, gender, class, or other social factor prevents any of us from becoming multicultural navigators, there is reason to believe that many educators and other adults critical of low-income minority youths' lives do not themselves possess the requisite cultural competences to help students become multiculturally fluent. Multicultural navigators exist both inside and outside schools, and they work in the various professional sectors, from academia to creative writing to entertainment to law to software development to veterinary medicine, to name a few professions. The need and demand for more multicultural navigators have implications for diversely populated schools, communities, and workplaces, especially since they are more likely to facilitate multiple cross-cultural interactions and exchanges. With the assistance of multicultural navigators, youth, especially those who are at risk for school failure, will learn to effectively move through the worlds of school, work, and community.

Prudence L. Carter
Stanford University

See Also: Black Cultural Capital; Burden of Acting White; Noncompliant Believers, Cultural Mainstreamers, and Cultural Straddlers; Oppositional Culture.

Further Readings

Bourdieu, Pierre. "The Forms of Capital." In *Handbook of Theory and Research for the Sociology of Education,* J. G. Richardson, ed. Westport, CT: Greenwood Press, 1986.

Carter, Prudence. *Keepin' It Real: School Success Beyond Black and White.* New York: Oxford University Press, 2005.

Carter, Prudence. *Stubborn Roots: Cultivating Cultural Flexibility and Equity in U.S. and South African Schools.* New York: Oxford University Press, 2012.

Wilson, William J. *The Truly Disadvantaged: The Inner City, the Underclass, and Public Policy.* Chicago: University of Chicago Press, 1987.

Multiculturalism/ Multicultural Education

Multiculturalism/multicultural education is a set of ideological and pedagogical commitments to providing education for and about diverse groups. Though most often associated with education for students of underrepresented races, multiculturalism more accurately refers to students of all races, ethnicities, genders, religions, sexualities, abilities, ages, socioeconomic backgrounds, national or geographic origins, and languages. This approach to teaching and learning is rooted in the belief that all students can achieve at high levels, especially when supported by pedagogy that affirms their cultural identities. The broadest goal of multiculturalism/multicultural education is for students to become empowered, caring citizens who critically engage in self- and social transformation.

Multiculturalism/multicultural education has evolved over time to include more oppressed identity groups and to evaluate the interrelatedness of multiple strands; for example, how do ethnicity, gender, and sexuality intersect in unique ways that can be addressed in a diverse classroom? It is not meant to be solely for the benefit of marginalized groups and, indeed, some argue that multicultural education is more important for students of dominant groups because they have the least experience and most misunderstandings about diversity.

Historical Context

Multiculturalism/multicultural education's roots date back to the early ethnic studies movement of the late 1800s and 1900s. The first African American historian, George Washington Williams, and other leading scholars like Carter G. Woodson and W. E. B. Du Bois developed a body of knowledge about African American history that could be used in school curriculum and could challenge prevailing stereotypes. In particular, Carter G. Woodson claimed that educating students about European history without simultaneously teaching African American students about their African heritage was miseducation and tantamount to genocide.

During the early to mid-1900s, schools, like all other public spheres, were segregated by race. Though a landmark Supreme Court case, *Plessy v. Ferguson*, maintained the legitimacy of separate facilities as long as they were equal, all-black schools remained unequal. For example, these segregated schools had fewer teachers, older textbooks, and less money to spend on salaries and per pupil. Despite the fact that they had fewer resources with which to teach and learn, black teachers in segregated schools, research has shown, were talented, knowledgeable, caring, and supportive of their students. Part of what made these teachers so successful was their commitment to teaching black children about their historical roots and to instilling a positive self-worth.

Later, civil rights activists pursued desegregation of public schools as a primary goal. Though *Brown v. Board of Education* overturned *Plessy*, no specific desegregation time line was mandated, and many states, particularly in the south, did not immediately desegregate. During this time, the advocacy of education *for* all began shifting, as it had during the early ethnic studies movement, to education about all. In the 1960s and 1970s, other minority groups that advocated for women's rights and gay rights joined in the struggle to have their histories included in the curriculum and their children educated equitably in schools.

Multiculturalism/multicultural education, then, gained prominence in the 1980s as former ethnic studies scholars developed innovative ways to teach pre-K–12 students and future educators about the history of various groups. These scholars, such as James Banks, Geneva Gay, Carl Grant, and Sonia Nieto, began advocating for multiethnic education that transformed the whole school environment into an equity-focused, student-centered space. Simultaneously, policymakers became more aware of the gap in educational attainment between white students and students of color. This came on the heels of "A Nation at Risk," a federal report in which U.S. citizens were warned that the country's future was in jeopardy as children's international assessment scores were rapidly falling behind the scores of their international peers. Thus, at the same time that multiculturalism advocates were championing the need for a more comprehensive and inclusive curriculum, policymakers were promoting a "back to the basics" curriculum and intensive instruction in the Western canon.

The push for standardized curriculum, assessment, and accountability continued through the 1990s and 2000s. Schools began spending more time on reading and mathematics. Concurrently, school demographics began an intense shift toward the majority of pre-K–12 students—as well as the broader population of the United States—being people of color. Teachers, however, continued to be predominantly white females. Throughout its history, multiculturalism has garnered many proponents and equally as many critics, whose arguments will be discussed in subsequent sections.

Arguments for Multiculturalism/ Multicultural Education in Schools

With the election of Barack Obama, the first black president of the United States, some have argued that the United States is now a post-racial society, in which the lingering effects of slavery, Jim Crow laws, and desegregation have evaporated because there is a nonwhite family in the White House. However, proponents of multicultural education counter that policies and practices in many K–12 schools demonstrate that issues of power, privilege, and oppression are still existent and relevant.

Advocates of multicultural/multiethnic education cite various examples of how oppression is replicated in school settings. Students of color are disproportionately punished with administrative referrals, suspensions, expulsions, and sentences to alternative schools than are their white peers, even when guilty of similar infractions. They are also overrepresented in special and vocational education. Additionally, tracking policies result in racially, economically, or linguistically oppressed students being placed in low-level or remedial courses more often than white students are assigned to similar courses. These courses have been shown to emphasize rote memorization, test preparation, and low-level thinking skills, whereas higher-level courses or gifted classes emphasize critical thinking and hands-on learning.

Oppression through bullying is also rampant in K–12 schools. Students who are perceived to be different are targeted through verbal or physical harassment, isolation and exclusion, or cyberbullying. In particular, the increase in suicides of lesbian, gay, bisexual, and transgender (LGBT) children or those perceived to be LGBT in the 2000s has spurred safe space advocacy efforts and continued the push for education that teaches tolerance and acceptance.

Empirical evidence also suggests that teachers often have lower expectations for certain groups of diverse students. For example, teachers may believe that black students are unable to read as well as white students, that girls are not as mathematically or scientifically able as boys, or that second-language learners or those who speak nonmainstream dialects are intellectually inferior to native, standard English speakers. Multiculturalism/multicultural education seeks to dismantle these policies, practices, and attitudes by providing a space for students and teachers to challenge them through ideological and pedagogical commitments.

Arguments Against Multiculturalism/Multicultural Education in Schools

Critics of multicultural education argue that it distracts from more important scholastic ventures, fosters intercultural conflict where none exists, and is biased toward liberal ideology. Some of the most vocal critics are neoconservative policy makers who believe that multiculturalism/multicultural education diverts students' and teachers' attention away from more essential pursuits. In education reform, neoconservatives contend that returning schools to a curriculum of Western tradition, along with standardization and assessment, will lead to increased achievement. They believe that students should possess a core body of knowledge to participate in society and that keeping students from possessing that knowledge further inhibits their democratic participation.

Critics also contend that multiculturalism breeds divisiveness between and among identity groups. While advocating that dominant cultural traditions need to be restored, neoconservatives argue that diversity and identity politics are threatening to national unity. Some educators, especially white teachers, may accept as true that talking about cultural diversity is counterproductive and that they do not "see" race. For advocates of this colorblind ideology, acknowledging race is seen as unimportant or as engendering conflict. Further, critiques of multiculturalism frequently cite its liberal bias. While multiculturalists contend they are advocating for human rights regardless of political affiliation, critics assert that talking about gay rights or calling

for bilingual education policies, for instance, are more aligned with liberal values than other political agendas.

Ideological Commitments

According to renowned multicultural education scholar James Banks, there are five dimensions of multiculturalism in schools. These dimensions emphasize moving beyond curricular change toward seeing multiculturalism as an ideological commitment to democratic values and cultural pluralism.

Multicultural educators must first be committed to changing curriculum to reflect students' identities and to share the histories and experiences of oppressed groups. Next, they must help students construct and interrogate the curriculum, allowing students to critique the information they are commonly taught. Discussing who creates knowledge and whose knowledge is of most worth requires that multicultural educators not teach their subjects as bias free but instead asks them to consider the sociohistoric contexts in which their disciplines developed.

Additionally, multicultural educators must be committed to equitable pedagogy. This requires teachers to diversify their teaching methods in ways that enable all students to feel successful. Cooperative groups, hands-on experiments and discovery, and inquiry-based teaching, for example, may allow children to experience learning in ways that are meaningful for them. Further, educators of all grades and subjects can demonstrate commitment to multiculturalism by helping students to reduce prejudice toward groups different from their own. Finally, multicultural teachers must extend their ideological commitments beyond the classroom and into the wider school and social communities. This empowers teachers, students, administrators, and parents to be active citizens and to engage in fighting against marginalizing and disempowering school policies.

Pedagogical Commitments

Just as multiculturalism/multicultural education includes salient ideological commitments, it also includes common pedagogical commitments. According to well-known social justice scholar Sonia Nieto, a curriculum that emphasizes multiculturalism should have several overarching goals: to develop multiple historical perspectives, to nurture cultural consciousness and intercultural competence, to combat discrimination in multiple forms, to raise awareness of the state of the planet, and to develop social action skills.

In practice, there are a variety of ways that multiculturalism/multicultural education might look. According to James Banks, there are four approaches to implementation, each with varying degrees of effectiveness. Teachers may take the Contributions Approach in which they discuss prominent multicultural figures and related contributions to the nation. They may also include mentions of cultural holidays, food, or customs in a superficial manner, especially during cultural heritage months or celebrations. The most common type of multiculturalism/multicultural education that this approach resembles is studying civil rights during Black History Month or learning about Chinese New Year by eating Chinese food.

Teachers may also use the Additive Approach as they plan individual units or activities focused on a unique faction of society. This approach sees multiculturalism as an add-on whereby teachers isolate specific topics without assimilating them into the class's other curricula. For example, a teacher practicing this approach may propose a reading unit on African American authors or a math unit on famous female mathematicians.

The third approach is the Transformation Approach. This requires more work for teachers, as it asks them to fundamentally alter the curriculum. The transformed course focuses on ideas or concepts versus individual groups and asks students to evaluate multiple perspectives on the concept. A transformative multicultural teacher might present the history of de/colonialism and ask students to imagine the movement from the points of view of both the colonizers and the colonized. Or a science teacher might transform a unit on DNA and genes to include the ways that race is socially, not genetically, constructed.

Finally, a teacher can adopt the Social Action Approach to multiculturalism/multicultural education, in which teachers model for students the ways the education and knowledge can be used for civic engagement and democratic citizenship. Teachers allow students the opportunity to reflect on what they have learned and become engaged participants in their communities in order to benefit themselves, school, and society. A socially active teacher may help students write letters to campaign for healthier options in the cafeteria. Thus, even young students can participate in multicultural education. The Social Action approach requires students to make meaning of their learning and think critically about their world, thus combating the banking concept of education.

Related Theories

Multiculturalism/multicultural education is closely related to two other theories. The theory of culturally relevant pedagogy details the way that curriculum can and should relate to students' lives with a wider transformative purpose. The theory of white privilege details the ways that whites in the United States receive systematic advantages based on their skin color and a history of dominance rather than through merit.

Culturally Relevant Pedagogy

Like multiculturalism/multicultural education, culturally relevant (or responsive) pedagogy breaks with the cultural deficit model that claims students of color are inherently inferior because of innate deficiencies. Culturally relevant pedagogy also considers the teacher-student interpersonal context, institutional context, and societal context, and practitioners address the need for and how to attain student achievement. Further, it helps students accept and affirm their cultural identity and the identities of others and allows students to develop critical perspectives. Well-known scholars of culturally relevant pedagogy include Gloria Ladson-Billings, Geneva Gay, and Jacqueline Jordan Irvine. Their research and others' findings have indicated that there are several tenets of culturally relevant pedagogy that are related to multiculturalism/multiethnic education.

In culturally relevant classrooms, a teacher's identity matters. It is important for teachers to address who they are with their students. Just as culturally relevant teachers need not come from the same ethnic minority group as the students they teach, merely because a teacher is from the same minority group as her students does not mean she is automatically culturally relevant. Further, teachers must understand the realities—social, historical, political, cultural—that their students face, even if and especially if those realities are different from the teachers' realities. This often involves challenging the myth of meritocracy, or denying the notion that all people can achieve the same level if they only exert enough effort. Culturally relevant teachers exhibit warmth, care, and high expectations for all students. They do not lower their expectations out of pity for students who may have difficulties outside school but instead understand that maintaining high standards is a sign of value and respect.

In addition to teacher behavior, content can also be transformed. Academic content that is culturally relevant will connect to students' prior knowledge and past lived experiences. It will foster their cultural identities and teach them ways to levy their own identities to be successful in mainstream society. It will make explicit the ways that school is a site of power that, like other parts of society, privileges certain cultural assumptions over others. Students are encouraged to question the school's hidden curriculum. If students are English language learners, culturally relevant pedagogues also believe it is desirable to make use of students' first languages. Finally, culturally relevant pedagogy extends beyond teachers and content to the school itself. The theory advocates the inclusion and active, equitable engagement of parents and families. School policies would also reflect culturally relevant classroom management in which teachers are encouraged to respond indirectly rather than confrontationally if a difficulty arises, use an unhurried pace to allow time for all students to learn the material, and avoid embarrassing individual students by reprimanding them in front of the entire class.

White Privilege

White privilege is the dominance bestowed upon white individuals based on skin color and other unearned advantages. Privilege is a corollary of racism whereby as one group is systematically advantaged, other groups are consequently oppressed because of their skin color. White privilege is often invisible to those who have it because they have been taught not to see it. Though the dominant cultural rhetoric advances the notion that whites succeed because of merit alone, this theory contends that a history of dominance rooted in Eurocentric traditions has, over time, provided whites with a cache of understandings and skills to which oppressed groups do not have access.

The most reputed scholar of white privilege is Peggy McIntosh, who asserts that white privilege is akin to an invisible knapsack filled with tools and codes that enable white dominance to persist. For example, white privilege means that white adolescents can walk around a shopping mall without being profiled and followed. It means that white children can turn on the television and see the majority of shows featuring people who look like them. It means white professionals can achieve financial success and not garner surprise and awe, or file bankruptcy and not have it be seen as a testament to their racial inferiority.

White privilege is an important component of multiculturalism/multicultural education. Often, whites do not think of themselves as racial or ethnic beings; rather, they are "normal" and everyone else is "the other." Part of multicultural education involves talking about white privilege with students and making explicit the ways the privilege—historically and contemporarily—influences school curricula, policies, and relationships. Because white privilege and color-blindness have been shown to influence teachers' perceptions of students' abilities, multiculturalism/multicultural education can also provide preservice and inservice teachers with methods for thinking about their own cultural identities and providing tools to analyze and challenge systemic racism in schools.

Alyssa H. (Hadley) Dunn
Georgia State University

See Also: *Brown v. Board of Education*; Ebonics (African American English) and Education; English as a Second Language; Lesbian, Gay, Bisexual, and Transgender Issues and Schooling.

Further Readings

Banks, James A., ed. *Encyclopedia of Diversity in Education* (4 vols.). Thousand Oaks, CA: Sage, 2012.

Banks, James A., ed. *Handbook of Research on Multicultural Education*. 2nd ed. San Francisco: Jossey-Bass, 2004.

Banks, James A., ed. *Multicultural Education, Transformative Knowledge, and Action*. New York: Teachers College Press, 1996.

Gay, Geneva. *Culturally Responsive Teaching*. New York: Teachers College Press, 2000.

Ladson-Billings, Gloria. *The Dreamkeepers: Successful Teachers of African American Children*. San Francisco: Jossey-Bass, 1997.

Nieto, Sonia and Patty Bode. *Affirming Diversity: The Sociopolitical Context of Multicultural Education*. London: Allyn & Bacon, 2008.

Stairs, Andrea J., et al. *Urban Teaching in America: Theory, Research, and Practice in K–12 Classrooms*. Thousand Oaks, CA: Sage, 2011.

Multiracial Students

The racial and ethnic fabric of the United States is changing. Those changes are reflected in the U.S. Census and demonstrate the fluidity of racial classification over time. The option to identify oneself as belonging to one or more racial groups was included in the U.S. census for the first time in 2000. Approximately 6.8 million people identified with more than one racial category in the 2000 Census. The most commonly selected multiple racial categories were white and Native American. Of this multiracial group, over 2.8 million were children and youth under the age of 18. This school-age population of youth will join a growing demographic group that is expected to be a majority-minority of students in schools and postsecondary institutions in the United States by 2020. A majority-minority population is composed of members of minority groups that are demographically a majority, even though they occupy a minority-like status in society.

Students whose parents self-identify with two or more federally defined racial or ethnic groups are considered multiracial. Informal terms like *mixed-race* or *biracial* also exist for multiracial. People who self-identify as multiracial do so for a variety of reasons. They are either viewed by others as mixed-race or biracial or they possess characteristics or phenotypes that are stereotypically thought to apply to certain races in the United States. The multiracial category of children and youth in the United States is a rapidly expanding demographic group. The increase of multiracial students is expected to place certain demands on the education system in addressing the needs of a population that simultaneously claim several different races and ethnicities in their ancestry. Multiracial youth tend to identify with multiple heritages and shared destinies and may have immigrant lineages. The U.S. Census indicates that the multiracial population is not only growing, but the willingness to self-identify as multiracial is becoming more common. By the year 2050 it is expected that one in five Americans will check more than one box in the racial categorization question on the U.S. Census.

Multiracial Beginnings

Historically, America has always been a multicultural society with multiracial people. The importation of African slaves and the infusion of immigrants from throughout the world increased contact between different groups, including the indigenous populations of America, the Native Americans. Stigma as well as laws against miscegenation have lessened over time, increasing contact. Miscegenation is the intermixing of various ethnic and racial groups through interracial coupling, marriage, and procreation. Historically,

people produced from a black and white union were referred to as "mulatto." This term is no longer used and has been replaced by multiracial, mixed-race, and biracial.

The interest in more precisely defining race-based categories has increased over time. Between 1810 and 1860 a number of more refined classifications were added to the race question on the census: Asians, colored persons, Indians, and foreigners. Due to the tradition of hypo-descent—known as the one-drop rule, anyone with racial mixture of the subordinate group, no matter how minuscule, is automatically classified in the subordinate group and not the dominant group. President Barack Obama, the 44th president of the United States, has a white mother from Kansas and an African father from Kenya. Despite his well-publicized multiracial background, he is more often perceived as the first African American president of the United States than the first multiracial president. Obama also discusses in his autobiography that he self-identifies as an African American.

The tradition of hypo-descent is based upon a system of racial hierarchy and caste that placed blacks and other minorities at the bottom of the ladder. Laws against miscegenation, or race mixing, as it is commonly called, existed in the United States as far back as 1619 in Virginia and persisted until 1967 as a way to maintain caste. The Supreme Court in 1967 struck down Virginia's 1924 Racial Integrity Act that prohibited marriage between whites and nonwhites. The Supreme Court ruled in *Loving v. Virginia* that Virginia's antimiscegenation statute violated the constitutional rights of Richard Loving, a white man married to Mildred Loving, a black woman.

Implications for K–12 Education

Over time, ethnic and racial boundaries have become more crossable. Diverse groups have become more assimilated, visible, and free to date, procreate, and marry across racial and ethnic lines. Yet, almost from inception, the U.S. government had an interest in collecting and classifying data based on race and ethnicity. The first federal census was carried out in 1790 and continues until today. Data derived from the census is important as it informs social and economic policy decision making. Demographic classification of race continues to be a very serious undertaking precisely because of the social and legal implications tied to racial classifications, despite their arbitrariness. Race is arbitrary in that it is not a firm or fixed biological category. Race is a socially constructed category based on the value that society places on superficial characteristics like skin color and hair texture.

In primary and secondary schools, the implications are vast for multiracial students. Schools are encouraged by the federal government to collect the appropriate ethnic and racial classification data so that they are able to meet the accountability requirements of the No Child Left Behind (NCLB) legislation. Under NCLB schools must provide evidence of satisfactory performance of all students on academic achievement tests. These data must be disaggregated along ethnic and racial lines to assess the progress of groups of students. These data inform instructional decision making and help target funds in the neediest areas. The NCLB legislation is intentional in its focus on low-performing schools, disadvantaged youth, special education students, and immigrant children by utilizing yearly improvement data to monitor their progress. The NCLB law has been criticized by segments of the education community as an unfunded mandate that is too focused on accountability and standardized testing to be effective. They argue that the standardized tests assess a narrowly defined curriculum that limits student learning. Collecting data on the new category of multiracial students will require schools systems and NCLB policy makers to rethink what these data may mean in reference to the arbitrariness of another broadly defined racial classification and what associated school services may be needed to adequately support multiracial students' needs.

Implications for Higher Education

As schools and universities are asked to collect data on multiracial students, educators and psychologists are interested in their psychological well-being, academic achievement, and social engagement. In reference to psychological well-being and social engagement, researchers are interested in the perceptions that multiracial students have of themselves and the perceptions that teachers, faculty, staff, and their peers have of them. Though important questions, especially as more students identify as multiracial, they are not new. The tragic mulatto figure was a common theme in 19th- and 20th-century American literature. The tragic mulatto figure symbolized America's racialized fears of race-mixing and unprecedented levels of immigration in the early 20th century. Critics of the tragic mulatto stereotype argue

that the tragedy lies outside the person, not inside. In other words, how accepting or nonaccepting society is of the multiracial person is what makes the difference. Author Heidi Durrow, whose mother is white and father is black, makes the same claim in her award-winning novel *The Girl Who Fell From The Sky*, which won the Bellwether Prize for fiction that focuses on social equality.

Researchers are examining the question in both directions. What school and environmental contexts enable multiracial students to thrive, and what are the inhibiting factors? However, false assumptions can be made about multiracial identity when using the multiracial–monoracial dichotomy to make comparisons and explain differences. When multiracial students are assumed to be a homogenous group—which they are not—that can be studied and compared to students who identify with only one race or ethnicity, the results can be misleading. This is a concern for the interpretation of NCLB and other assessment data. This approach mirrors the lumping together of the widely diverse Hispanic population and studying them as if they were one unified group of Spanish speakers. Researchers suggest that examining within the multiracial category will better explain how something as complex as multiracial identify is constructed and performed. This is more productive than examining across nonuniform categories.

Multiracial identify is complex. When examining within categories, some studies suggest that identifying as multiracial may have potential benefits for students that better prepare them for more diverse environments like college and living and working abroad. Being multiracial requires students to navigate multiple cultures, multiple perspectives, and potentially multiple languages, making them more adept for diverse environments in the 21st century. In some situations multiple identities may even be competing ones, which requires even greater levels of resilience and self-reflection, if managed properly. However, it might be that students who choose to identify as multiracial are already better adept at managing multiracialness and use their skills in navigating the complexity of multiracial life. Other multiracial youth may simply respond to the one-drop rule by identifying with the category that their appearance is most associated with. Colleges and universities are already under pressure to collect admissions data on the multiracial population and to find ways to better serve this population. As the multiracial population continues to grow, more studies are needed that delve deeply inside the category.

Helen Bond
Howard University

See Also: Class Inequality: Achievement; Ebonics (African American English) and Education; Immigrants, Children of.

Further Readings
Bolgatz, J. *Talking Race in the Classroom*. New York: Teachers College Press, 2005.
Davis, B. M. *The Biracial and Multiracial Student Experience*. Thousand Oaks, CA: Corwin Press, 2009.
Singleton, G. and C. Linton. *Courageous Conversations About Race: A Field Guide for Achieving Equity in Schools*. Thousand Oaks, CA: Corwin Press, 2005.

Museums

Similar to schools, museums are spaces of knowledge production. This production of knowledge reflects and depends upon the complex social relationships that exist within museums between people, objects, and personal experiences. More recent understandings of museums have posited that these relationships are dynamic and fluid, resulting in multiple ways of producing meaning.

The Historical Context
The American Association of Museums currently recognizes all institutions that collect, preserve, and interpret objects as museums, including art and history museums, aquariums, science and nature centers, and zoos. Most of the scholarship and historiography of American museums has focused on art and history museums. The painter Charles Wilson Peale opened one of the first American museums in 1794 in Philadelphia, when he displayed his personal collections of anthropological and art objects. Peale intended his museum to provide a national model for preserving collections and educating the public. This idea of a museum's potential to educate a nation's citizenry based on its displays and interpretations followed the European museum model and influenced the development of American museums.

Many well-known American museums, including the Metropolitan Museum of Art, the Art Institute of Chicago, and the Field Museum of Natural History, were built during the "Museum Age" of the late 19th and early 20th centuries. Often a city's civic leaders and philanthropists were instrumental in a museum's development by donating their own collections or facilitating the acquisition of objects. The ways in which general audiences created meaning for objects within the museum's public spaces was often guided by the ways in which a limited number of museum workers researched and designed displays in the museum's private spaces. Museums were places where the public could view objects and derive visual pleasure, but they did so within spaces that negated a complete contextual relationship with the objects. Such a divide suggested for many later researchers the ways in which museums maintained or reproduced social and class inequalities, as museums could legitimize meaning by controlling how knowledge could be accessed by visitors.

Theoretical Perspectives
The critical theories of Michel Foucault and Pierre Bourdieu have influenced recent museum scholarship. Foucault asserted that knowledge is in fact relative and shaped by specific cultural contexts. What thus counts as understanding and meaning within a certain place or set of relationships will often appear irrational within others. Rather than focus on a singular fixed understanding, Foucault suggested we can better understand history by searching for the disruptions and breaks in knowledge, or the places and times where we can discern the relative differences between cultural contexts.

Bourdieu suggested that access to understanding and awareness contributes to structural inequality. Shared knowledge and interests distinguish cultural groups, and often this knowledge is accessible through the common experiences of group members. The tastes and interests of the dominant group thus often distance other groups but also tend to be repeated and embedded within institutions and structures. Bourdieu believed this inequality was manifested in museums as nondominant groups either felt distanced from or pressured to conform to the meanings created in museums.

The theories of Foucault and Bourdieu speak to the potential of museums to create agency. Rather than understand museums as institutions that limit individual choice through fixed access to meaning, museums can be understood as sites that in fact embody several narratives within the possible relationships and contexts of objects and viewers. Thus the museum today is recognized as a space created through complex and layered relationships between people, objects, and experiences.

Museums Today

The current interest in museum research on the role of agency within knowledge production mirrors the focus on multiplicity within educational research. Developing awareness of how museums can best accommodate this potential for multiplicity informs current debates about the role and functions of museums. Some suggest that opening the production of knowledge within museums creates spaces where displaying objects becomes just one of many roles a museum may fulfill. Providing venues and opportunities for people to incorporate personal experience into meaning making through interactive galleries, reading rooms, digital collections databases, and narrative-based collections research changes the possible relationships between viewer, object, and personal experience. Viewers exercise agency through the relationships they choose to develop and explore.

Christine Baker Mitton
Cleveland State University

See Also: Cultural Capital; Field Trips; Multiculturalism/ Multicultural Education; Social Capital.

Further Readings

Fyfe, G. "Sociology and the Social Aspects of Museums." In *Companion to Museum Studies*, S. Macdonald, ed. Chichester, UK: Wiley, 2008.

Hooper-Greenhill, E. *Museums and the Shaping of Knowledge.* New York: Routledge, 1992.

Starn, R. "A Historian's Brief Guide to New Museum Studies." *American Historical Review*, v.110/1 (2005).

Music Education

Music education is a field of study primarily associated with experiences related to the teaching and learning of music. Predominant opportunities in the study of music education include public and private school programs continuing to the postgraduate level and private instruction. Music education is a multidisciplinary subject encompassing not only the study of music but also art, history, foreign languages, philosophy, and sociology.

Historical Framework

In the United States, there has been a long tradition of the inclusion of music within the school curricula. In 1832, Lowell Mason formed the Boston Academy of Music, where students could experience methods of teaching music, music theory, and vocal studies. However, not until 1838 when the Boston Schools approved adding music to the curriculum was music education recognized as a course of study. Its inclusion was due to the moral nature of singing psalms, improving church singing for congregations, and the exercise of the lungs.

By 1900, music had become integrated into the school curricula in most public schools. Music supervisors who were trained in teacher education schools taught music classes to the students. During the early 1900s, the development of instrumental music education in the United States coincided with the popularity of concert bands. The influx of immigrants from Europe brought their interest in instruments and music with them to the United States. Because of poverty, many of these immigrants were not offered the opportunity to learn a musical instrument in their former countries. These people sought to learn musical instruments in American schools where the opportunity was accessible to most. To meet this demand, instrumental music became more prominent within the school curricula. Additionally, music appreciation became increasingly popular in the early 1900s due to the availability of phonograph records, radio programs, and symphony concerts catering to young people.

During the 20th century, music education expanded to include singing, rhythms, critical listening, playing, and creating music on an instrument of choice. The music educator also had the option to receive an undergraduate degree in music from various universities in the United States. Music pedagogy became readily available, and band and choral organizations continued to expand.

Value of Music Education

Research shows an increase of involvement in musical activities during a student's school career seemingly has a positive effect on cognitive, social, and emotional growth of students. School systems often embrace it within their curriculum. Yet, due to increased accountability in core subjects placed on school districts, music education often faces cuts in funding and staffing. Administrators in school systems often see music education as a legitimate area of study, yet desire to see more interdisciplinary learning occurring in the music classroom.

National Standards

Completed in 1994, the National Standards for Music Education characterize a set of educational values designed to guide music teachers and their curricular decisions. The Music Educators National Conference (MENC), now known as the National Association for Music Education (NAfME), collaborated to develop nine standards that describe musical knowledge and skills that are essential to a comprehensive music education. Many states have adopted their own standards for music education based on the national standards.

The national standards developed by MENC do not exist without debate. The national standards are often addressed in the classroom unequally, depending on the teacher's abilities, values, or comfort with the curricular content. Music education philosopher Bennett Reimer suggests a reconceptualization of the standards. Reimer proposes that often the emphasis on music education in the United States is on a few standards rather than all. In contrast, others in the field have given accolades to how the profession is moving in the right direction in regard to instructional goals.

Criticisms of Music Education

Soon after music education was integrated into public schools, there began challenges to the inclusion of musical education in the curriculum and they persist today. The rationale for music education began with the correlation of formal vocal training and its capacity to increase the performance abilities of singers in churches. In the contemporary American school system, "music advocacy" is a key component in the rationalization of the subject within the curricula. Music advocacy is often generated from scholarly studies on the subject of music, learning theories, and brain-based education.

The reform efforts generated by the Elementary and Secondary Education Reauthorization Act, or No Child Left Behind, established the need for content standards in public schools designed to focus on standards-based education. An unfortunate consequence of contemporary education legislation is that curriculum is often narrowed to focus primarily on state-tested subjects at the expense of subjects not tested, such as music education.

Eric John Plum
Shenandoah University

See Also: Adult Education; Curriculum Standardization; Elementary Education; Extracurricular Activities; Higher Education; No Child Left Behind; Secondary Education.

Further Readings
Au, W. "High-Stakes Testing and Curricular Control: A Qualitative Metasynthesis." *Educational Researcher*, v.36/5 (2007).
Keene, James A. *A History of Music Education in the United States.* Lebanon, NH: University Press of New England, 1982.
Mark, M. L. and C. L. Gary. *A History of American Music Education.* 2nd ed. Reston, VA: The National Association for Music Education, 1999.
National Association for Music Education. "National Standards for Arts Education." http://www.menc.org/resources (Accessed January 2012).
Reimer, B. *A Philosophy of Music Education: Advancing the Vision.* Upper Saddle River, NJ: Prentice Hall, 2003.

Myanmar (Burma)

Myanmar, formerly known as Burma, is the second-largest southeast Asian mainland country with an area of 261,970 square miles (678,500 square kilometers). It is surrounded by the Bay of Bengal, Andaman Sea, and the Gulf of Thailand with a coastline totaling 1,100 miles (1,930 kilometers) and the countries of Bangladesh, China, India, Laos, and Thailand. Myanmar is a multiethnic country. It is divided into seven states and seven administrative divisions.

The estimated population for 2011 was 56 million, of whom 66 percent live in rural areas and 34 percent live in urban areas. Of the total population, 27.5 percent are children under 15 years of age, 67.5 percent belong to the 15 to 64 age group, and only 5 percent are 65 and over. Once Myanmar was the world's largest rice-exporting country, yet it still remained economically impoverished due to poor trade relations with the global economy and lack of modernization. Estimated gross domestic product (GDP) for 2010 was $53 billion, with an annual growth rate of 5.5 percent. Agriculture alone accounts for half of the nation's GDP. Its main export revenue comes from the sale of natural gas, agricultural products, stones, timber, and marine products.

Myanmar in 1948 became independent from British colonial rule, but since then the country has been under domination by either communist and socialist factions or undemocratic dictatorial leaderships supported by the army. Democratic voices have been silenced systematically by military iron man General Ne Win, who took over power to form a socialist one-party governance system on March 2, 1962. The worst attack was directed at a peaceful student demonstration on the Rangoon University campus on July 7, 1962, with the military killing over 100 students. In 1988 universities were forced to close for three years to deter student and citizen uprisings demanding democratic reform of the country.

The nation faced significant international pressure and isolation due to such dictatorial and oppressive behavior, and finally the government allowed a form of multiparty elections in May 1990. The National League for Democracy (NLD) formed an opposition and won the election with a landslide victory. However, the democratically elected leaders, including Aung San Suu Kyi, the 1991 Nobel Peace Prize winner, were not allowed to form the government; instead, they were placed under house arrest. International pressure kept mounting against the dictatorial government. However, some promising developments took place during late 2011 and early 2012, when both the United States and the United Kingdom leaderships took serious intergovernmental initiatives to facilitate the democratization process of the country.

Despite a long history of colonial and dictatorial rule, the country's distinct educational tradition, ethnic diversity, and social structures remain unchanged.

Educational Structure

Formal education in Myanmar includes preschool playgroup (ages 2–3), pre-kindergarten (ages 4–5), and kindergarten (ages 5–6). Elementary school education is offered following kindergarten under Standard 1 (ages 6–7), through Standard 4 (ages 9–10). Middle school education is offered under Standard 5

(ages 10–11) through Standard 8 (ages 12–14), and high school education is offered under Standards 9 (ages 14–15) and 10 (ages 15–16). After completion of the high school standard 10, students are required to take the final state-run examination (matriculation exam) to be able to receive Diploma A to enter the job market or Diploma B to continue their education or training through colleges, universities, and professional programs. Students, depending on their grades, social background, and/or economic abilities, are enrolled in university-level programs, vocational schools, or polytechnic institutes.

Members of military families have priority status in securing placements to better schools and programs. Bachelor of sciences, arts, and commerce degrees are granted in four years time (ideal ages 16–20), medical and engineering professional degrees take six years (ideal ages 16–22) after completion of the secondary school final. Master's degrees are two-year programs (ideal ages 20–22), and Ph.D. degrees require a three-year (ages vary) program. In 2008, there were 8,092,510 students attending schools, colleges, and universities. Of these, about 4,948,198 attended primary schools, 2,589,312 attended secondary schools, and 550,000 attended the nation's 150 colleges, polytechnic institutions, and universities.

Although basic literacy skills among those 15 years and older was about 92 percent in 2008, this literacy rate in Myanmar has been much higher compared to its neighboring countries, including Thailand, India, and Bangladesh. Primary education is compulsory with an estimated enrollment rate of 98 percent and estimated average school attendance between primary to tertiary levels is nine years.

Current Trends

Myanmar is still a closed society. Its traditional education programs served well in preparing leaders and human resources for the socialist republic. Now the country is preparing for a democratic transformation and, accordingly, its education system will have to be reformed to meet the need for a modern, free, open, and democratic society. Many innovative measures are needed to incorporate student-centered flexible approaches to instructional and curriculum design with more routes to learning the content, integrating technology, restructuring school environments, involving parents, and training educators. Teacher training programs have to be remodeled and reinforced with more emphasis on local needs, as well as meeting the challenges of global competitiveness. Parental and community involvement, creativity and critical thinking aspects, and futuristic technological innovations need to be given importance in shaping curriculum and related learning activities. There are some promising developments taking place. Electronic library systems are developing, and a few nongovernmental organizations are exchanging ideas with Myanmar institutions based on experience gained in Thailand and other neighboring countries.

Internet cafés and many other social media are being used by youngsters in growing numbers. An educational network (www.myanmar-network.net) initiated in 2010 by British Council Myanmar has drawn 19,000 members already. It is evident that Myanmar leadership is now opening up and seriously considering a new knowledge economy–based

pluralistic society. Education will have to be reformed to facilitate such changes.

Matiul Alam
University of British Columbia

See Also: Bangladesh; India; Thailand.

Further Readings

Booth, Jenny. "Military Junta Threatens Monks in Burma." *The Times* (London) (September 24, 2007).

Boudreau, Vincent. *Resisting Dictatorship: Repression and Protest in Southeast Asia.* Cambridge: Cambridge University Press, 2009.

Charney, Michael W. *A History of Modern Burma.* Cambridge, UK: Cambridge University Press, 2009.

Smith, Martin John. *Burma: Insurgency and the Politics of Ethnicity*, Illustrated ed. London: Zed Books, 1999.